1 MONTH OF
FREE
READING

at

www.ForgottenBooks.com

By purchasing this book you are eligible for one month membership to ForgottenBooks.com, giving you unlimited access to our entire collection of over 1,000,000 titles via our web site and mobile apps.

To claim your free month visit:

www.forgottenbooks.com/free165316

ISBN 978-0-428-96605-8
PIBN 10165316

J.Partridge delt & sculpt

JOSHUA TOULMIN, D.D.

THE

MONTHLY REPOSITORY

OF

THEOLOGY

AND

GENERAL LITERATURE.

——————— POPULUMQUE 'FALSIS
DEDOCET UTI
VOCIBUS. *Hor.*

"To do something to instruct, but more to undeceive, the timid and admiring student;—to excite him to place more confidence in his own strength, and less in the infallibility of great names;—to help him to emancipate his judgment from the shackles of authority;—to teach him to distinguish between shewy language and sound sense;—to warn him not to pay himself with words;—to shew him, that what may tickle the ear or dazzle the imagination, will not always inform the judgment;—to dispose him rather to fast on ignorance than to feed himself with error."

Fragment on Government.

JANUARY TO DECEMBER INCLUSIVE.

1816.

VOLUME XI.

HACKNEY:

Printed for the Editor, by Ann Stower,

PUBLISHED BY SHERWOOD, NEELY AND JONES,
PATERNOSTER ROW.

1816.

French Protestants.

Proceedings of the Committee of Ministers of the Three Denominations, resident in and about London.

In accomplishing the important objects confided to them by the General Body, the *Committee of Dissenting Ministers of London,* have had to encounter unexpected opposition from various quarters, and especially from certain Journalists, who have attempted to invalidate the statements that have been published, and to misrepresent the motives by which the Committee have been actuated in the whole of their proceedings.

With undiminished zeal, and undaunted by the clamour of their opponents, they have, however, persevered in the plain path of duty; and they now record with pleasure and gratitude, the support and approbation they have received from a very large portion of their enlightened countrymen, and particularly from those with whom they are more immediately connected,—the Dissenters of various denominations.

In addition to the Congregational Collections which have already been contributed, the Committee have information of many others which are in progress, to a considerable amount; while public meetings have been held and subscriptions commenced in several of the largest cities and towns of the Kingdom.

The eloquent, liberal, and Christian appeals, which have been addressed to assembled multitudes, and reported by the press, cannot but intimidate persecutors abroad, and excite benevolence at home: nor will they be less beneficial in diffusing those sentiments, which the ignorant ought to learn,—the instructed should never forget,—and all should frequently hear.

At Hull, the Rev. Messrs. Bromley and Dykes, Clergymen, and the Rev. Mr. Birt, and Dr. Alderson, Mr. Sykes, and others of the dissenting body, took a distinguished part in the discussions of the day.

At Newcastle, the proceedings were conducted by the Rev. Messrs. Turner, Pringle, Melndoe, Clarke, Syme, and Pengilly; and also by Mr. Alderman Reed, James Losh, and Joseph Clark, Esqrs.

At Glasgow, the Rev. Drs. Dick and Mitchell, and the Rev. Messrs. G. Ewing, R. Brodie, and J. Carment, were the principal speakers.

At Gosport, the Rev. James Collins, of the Established Church, and Messrs. Minchin, B. Goodeve, Cruickshank, J. Beasley, and J. Hoskins, displayed equal zeal and ability.

At Plymouth, the Rev. Messrs. Worsley and H. Mends, with Messrs. Prance, Collier, &c. submitted Resolutions, and

addressed the assembly. At Berwick and Sheerness, Meetings have been likewise held; and at Edinburgh and other places, they have been summoned.

The propriety of these continued and extended exertions, is confirmed by the information which the Committee are constantly receiving, and which convinces them that the disposition to persecute is more general and systematic than many persons have supposed.

While the storm has raged with signal, but unexhausted violence in the Department of the Gard, containing 322,000 inhabitants, a portentous gloom has overspread the Reformed Churches in general; and in towns far distant from the south, the sound of vengeance has been heard, and the most offensive treatment has been experienced, by the Professors and Ministers of the Protestant Religion.

'On the 12th of November last, on the assurance given to the pastors of the Reformed Church, that they might reopen their Temples, which had been shut about five months, that they had nothing to fear, and that all necessary measures were taken for their security, they determined to open the smallest of their Temples; but scarcely were they assembled, when a great multitude of men and women, armed with stones and sticks, and other weapons, began to menace them, and to pour forth against them the most horrible imprecations. The faithful assembly dispersed, and even as they retired they were so overwhelmed with insults and blows, that many are since dead. The assassins entered in a crowd into the sanctuary, turned out every thing they could find, tore in pieces the Bibles and prayer-books,&c. They went with full intention to massacre the pastors, who were expecting certain death, when eight officers surrounded them with drawn sabres, to repel the attacks of the murderers:— they escorted them into their houses, but not without having heard a thousand times, these barbarous words, " *Kill, kill, these chiefs of Brigands!*" During this tumult, General le Gard arrived with some troops; he began to employ his force to disperse the traitors, when a soldier of the *national guard* fired immediately at him. The assassin escaped, and has not yet been discovered.'

, After the attack on the Royal General Le Garde, a Royal Proclamation was issued against the assassin and his abettors, and soldiers were quartered upon the inhabitants till he should be surrendered to justice. That the intentions of the head of the Government must have been per-

A

verted is however evident; for the assassin has not yet been arrested, and the soldiers who, by a Royal Ordonnance of the 10th inst. were removed from Nismes, were quartered during their stay in that city, principally, if not solely, on the Protestant inhabitants. The weight of the extraordinary contributions, by the most partial and arbitary exactions, has been also made to fall on the Protestants, though equally protected and assessed by the Charter promulgated by the King. Thus out of 940 thousand francs, the contingent of the Gard, 600 thousand were laid on the Protestants, 200 thousand on the Jews, 140 thousand only on the Catholics; though these last form nearly the two-thirds of the population of the department. The Marquis de Calvieres, a Catholic gentleman, enjoying a landed estate of 60,000 livres a year, is assessed at 600 livres; while N. Brosse de Pierdon, a Protestant, whose income amounts to about 10,000 livres, has paid within this last year the sum of 15,000 livres towards those contributions.

The following facts, on which full reliance may be placed, will prove that in the order of time, up to the date of our latest accounts, the Protestants have been the victims of bigotry and persecution.

' In consequence of the King's Ordonnance of the 21st November, which was promulgated at Nismes on the 29th, several of the murderers of the Protestants and depredators of their property, were taken into custody; but on the 6th of December they were all set at liberty. On the 7th they spread over the neighbouring country. A party of them repaired to the house of a Monsieur Peyron, a rich farmer at Brossan, who, from the beginning of the persecutions, had been greatly exposed to the fury of the fanatics: not finding him, they commanded his three sons either to give up the father, or pay a sum of 50,000 livres. As the young men could not comply with either demand, they were dreadfully beaten by these villains (one of them being left for dead) and both house and farm were pillaged.

' On the same day, another party, of the same description, went to a country house inhabited by three respectable old men, brothers. After having offered them every indignity that fanaticism could suggest, they proceeded to acts of violence. Upon these unfortunate men attempting to resist, they were instantly charged with rebellion to the King; and, upon this pretence, seized, and carried by these fanatics before the King's Attorney General; who, indignant at the outrage, refused to commit them. They were then dragged before the Prefect, who ordered them to prison, *par mesure de sureté*, which was immediately executed, amid shouts of *Vive le Roi!*'

The following is an Extract of a Letter from Uzes, near Nismes, of the 1 December :—

' The chief persons of the Prot families have fled from their habit: which had considerably suffered. church is now in the most deplorabl dition: no public worship is celeb Ministers of our persuasion at Pari: are so near Government, forget no brethren of the South!—We have M. Ricourt, President of the Consi The late events have *hastened* his end had been obliged to desert first' his in town, and then that in the cou the latter has been pillaged.'

From Uzes, same date :—

' B—— informs us, that his so fled at Arpaillargues, near Uzes, having fled, and wandered in the for two months, has been arrestec conducted into the prison of Uzes, he still remains. A great many Protestants continue in the same pr ment.'

The efforts of the people, and the of this country, aided by the addit energy of the French Government, c the temples at Nismes to be opene order of the anthorities of that cit the 21st December; but it was nece to the possession of this boon, tha Protestants should comply with directly contrary to the spirit o Constitutional Charter. The follov is the Notice of the Mayor, so remark that it is worthy of a careful perusal acknowledges that *Europe accuses* Catholics of great crimes, it endeav to charge them on a *few women children*, and it acknowledges that worship of the Protestants is to be re ed, less as a consequence of the Roya thority, than the *result of a negocia* pacifying to the Catholics :—

NOTICE

To the Inhabitants of the City of Nis

' *Nismes, December* 19, 181

' The laws of the realm and the of the King, secure the exercise of Protestant worship. I tell you so. who am your Magistrate, your May 1, who have surely some claims to confidence. The Protestant Chu will be opened on Thursday next, that day will prove to the King France, and to Europe, who are ou cusers, that the blindness of *a few w and children* is not the crime of the of Nismes, which has distinguished on so many occasions, and even rece by its fidelity and devotion to the Ki

' *Women*, who are blinded y zeal, and perhaps, excited by your mies, you will not once more ruin city, and gratify by your errors the mies of the royal cause.

' I am assured, and for that reas have a pleasure in informing you, *conferences* are opened, and nearly

minated, with the Consistory of the Protestant worship. Their object is to restore, by common consent, to the worship *of the State*, the churches which have been conceded to the Protestant worship. Two churches will be built, and that very shortly, in lieu of that concession. During that short interval, the Protestants may enjoy undisturbed the churches thus conceded. The people of Nismes need only know the will of the King, and hear the voice of the Royal Authorities, to do their duty.   (Signed)
' Marquis de VALLONGUES, Mayor.'

The Temples which the Protestants relinquished, were not parochial churches, but conventual; and as all the property of Abbeys and Convents had been confiscated at the Revolution, one of these was *purchased* by the Protestants twenty years since, and the other was given to them eleven years back, by the Head of the then existing Government.

At the very time that apparent security was given to the Protestants, they were actually exposed to fresh injuries.—' The Royal troops which infested the environs of Nismes, exercised continual vexations on the Protestants. On the 2d of December, a detachment of about fifty men broke into the house of M. Mourier, a gentleman of property at St. Blancard, lately returned from emigration, who had just time to effect his escape. Failing in their main object, these brigands completely pillaged the premises, and daily continue their depredations in the neighbourhood.

' At Sommieres, the Protestants have attempted to *celebrate their worship* on the 24th of December, the power of which they had been deprived of since the month of July. They met with the most barbarous treatment on that account.'

The persecution at Sommieres is mentioned by two more Correspondents.

A letter from a distinguished Protestant of the Department of the Gard, dated so late as the 28th of December, states, that tranquillity was not established. He says,

' I have seen the Letter and the Resolutions of the Nonconformist ministers, who have had the true Christian charity to interest themselves in the disasters of the poor unfortunate people, devastated by the popular persecutions at Nismes and elsewhere.

' I have received, with singular consolation, your letter. This town is at present quiet; but we cannot say that furious persons have returned to charitable and Christian sentiments towards the Protestants. The troops only restrain them; but if they should be removed to other places, no one would be safe from the return of disorders.

Sunday again, the 24th of this month, there were fresh troubles at Sommieres, four leagues from Nismes. I must *suppress details* for the reasons I have mentioned. Many persons, pillaged and injured at Nismes and other places, have *great need* of the succours which you have offered in so Christian a manner.

' Blessed be God, who has put our ingratitude to shame by the love of our respectable brethren of England. The comfort we derive from it is as indescribable as our gratitude. I embrace with affection all our dear benefactors.'

One of the most fearful symptoms in the more recent events, is the public notification, in the papers of Le Gard and Paris, of the abjuration of the Protestant faith, by many families in the south. The *Journal des Debats* of the 10th instant, contained the following article, extracted from the *Journal du Gard*, published at Nismes:—

' An interesting ceremony took place on the 26th ult. in the church of St. Paul, at Nismes. Two *Protestant families*, forming altogether about 20 persons, made a public abjuration between the hands of the curé of the parish, and returned to the *bosom* of the Romish church. Some families had *already* given an example of this in the parish of St. Baudille; and others are, it is said, *preparing* to follow.'

Paris papers of the 18th inst. contain also additional notice on this subject. They say, ' Many Protestant families of the south embrace the Catholic religion.'

On this subject we have authentic accounts, which must demonstrate to the most incredulous and prejudiced the prevalence of a religious persecution.

One letter has the following passage: ' Several families at Nismes have abjured their religion, the motive of which is evident. They are families of mechanics and workmen, who are without bread in consequence of the persecutions they have undergone. The Protestant manufacturers have for the most part fled, and the Catholics will not employ Protestant workmen;— besides which, the looms and frames of the latter have been destroyed, and they are reduced to the alternative of recanting or starving.

This system of persecution has extended to Bourdeaux and its neighbourhood. Its effects have also been felt at Nantz, the President of the Consistory of that city having been sent into exile.'

The following Extract of a Letter from Nismes, received from a most respectable Protestant Lady, and on which the utmost confidence may be placed, will further illustrate the above cited articles : —

'*Nismes, January 3.*

' One's mind is weighed down at seeing the oppression and misery to which the Protestants are subjected, and from which they cannot relieve themselves. We are, however, allowed to pray to God with some tranquillity. The first time the Mayor, appointed by the King, expressly ordered us to ring the bell, I said to my husband, ' This is done to furnish an article for the journals.' I was not mistaken, and it has gone forth to France and to foreign countries that we are as happy as we can be. The police, on the other hand, will not suffer what has happened at Sommières to *be spoken of.* There the vilest of the mob, instigated by our persecutors, attacked the assembly of the faithful at the moment of their performance of Divine Worship. The Officers of the Regiment of Maria Theresa endeavoured to re establish order ;—one of the fanatics in the crowd snapped a musket three times at one of the officers ; but it missed fire, and the officer's life was saved. The man who attempted this assassination is known, but he has not been arrested ; on the contrary, two peaceable individuals, known to be respectable, have been arrested, one of whom is accused of having cried *Vive l'Empereur,* as if it were probable that persons capable of crying *Vive l'Empereur!* would declare against the Protestants. You will readily believe, that a department which abounds in assassins and robbers, will not be found wanting in false witnesses. Persons are always to be found who are ready to affirm any thing, no matter what ; and these people call themselves Christians, *par excellence !* Every thing done against a Protestant is regarded as a *pious* act by those who are in office.'

' The Protestants have been very unfortunate in having taken from them what they had enjoyed for 25 years. — Twenty Protestants were employed in the receipt of the imposts ; these have all been dismissed. The old and venerable Laune had the posts ; his place has been taken from him. He demanded of the Mayor a certificate, that he had always acted with honour in that situation, and it was refused him. When the wives and children of those detained in custody supplicate for their liberty, they are told that they *must turn Catholics !* You have no idea of the thousand petty vexations that are heaped in every shape upon our poor brethren. When will our miseries be at an end ? God only knows ! Our oppressors are supported by the fanatics, and by persons who live by disorder. Gen. la Garde has been for some days worse.'

Since this paper was put to press, a mass of important documents has been transmitted to the Committee, by private hands, from eye-witnesses, and persons of unblemished reputation, not only confirming the facts they have already published, but detailing enormities which surpass former accounts, and such as the nineteenth century could not expect to have witnessed !

To oppose the prevalence of such evils, to endeavour to annihilate them, or at least to alleviate their effects ; is so evidently the duty of all Christians, and especially of all Christian Ministers, that the *Dissenting Ministers* have not ceased to prosecute it since their preparatory meeting, held on the Second of November last, nor can the Committee but persevere, ' approving themselves the Ministers of God, by evil report and good report, by honour and dishonour, as deceivers, and yet true !'

This determination the Committee have solemnly proclaimed to their connections, and to the world, by the circular letter, and the Resolutions which immediately follow.

Library, Red Cross Street,
Sir, *Jan.* 15, 1816.

The events which have taken place since our last communication, have rendered expedient the adoption of the annexed Resolutions ; and in transmitting them to you, we avail ourselves of the opportunity of conveying to you information, which will abundantly demonstrate the utility of our past exertions, and the demand which exists for vigorous and liberal efforts on the part of all who are interested for the security of the Protestant faith. Attempts, as disgraceful as unexpected, have occasioned us additional labour and expence ; but happily they have led to results directly contrary to the designs of our opponents, who have stood forward as the calumniators of the Dissenters of England, and the apologists of the persecutors of France.—A letter from the Duke of Wellington, written in acknowledgment of a communication from the Secretaries of another Body, has been published in the Times Newspaper, as a document of importance, improperly suppressed. Without entering at all into the policy of withholding from the Public the entire contents of that document, we cannot but inform you, that the only part which in the least contradicts our previous statements, was printed in paragraphs in all the Journals, by the persons who received it. It stated, ' That the salaries of the Protestant Ministers had not been discontinued by the King.' If, by this was intended, that the payment had not been forbidden by a Royal Ordonnance, the statement is true : but if it was designed to convey an assurance that the salaries had been regularly paid, it is a false and unworthy effort to stifle the sympathy and benevolence of the British Public, while the ministers are at this moment at least nine months in arrears. By us it was never mentioned as a proof of persecution from the government : but as an aggravating circumstance in the calamity which has befallen the Reformed Churches, that while their flocks have been scattered—their merchants and manufacturers exiled—and their resources drained by foreign troops and heavy imposts, their ministers should have been destitute of that stipend on which for so many years they had regularly depended for their ministerial support ;—and though this defalcation has been common to the ministers of all religions, it must be considered, that the Protestant ministers have not those means of obtaining money, which the Catholic priests, by their various ceremonies, always possess.

Another Letter has been published in the same Journal, which had been sent to us by M. Marron, President of the Consistory of Paris, declining our aid and censuring our interference ; but you will. doubtless, have seen by other Journals, that another letter was received by the same conveyance, from the same person, stating, that our exertions had made a strong sensation in Paris, and were likely to produce the most beneficial results : in addition to which, it is now evident, that the letter in question was written by M. Marron, after an examination by the Police, and under the 'fear of individual persecution.' The effect of the Public Meetings which have been held, has been highly important, and the arrival of the report of the Proceedings of the Common Council of London in Paris, was the commencement of exertions by the French authorities, which had not been previously made. While some persons have deprecated these Meetings and Discussions, it will always be a subject of satisfaction to us, that they originated with the Dissenting Ministers of London ; and the paper which we had the honour to address to you, and which was produced in Court by all the speakers, was the document on which the public proceedings of that day were founded, which have been succeeded by similar proceedings in Hull, Edinburgh, Glasgow, Gosport, Newcastle, Plymouth, and other places.

No doubt, we presume, can now rest on your minds, as to the fact of he

Persecution being religious, and not political,—at least only political as far as the intolerants have endeavoured to deprive the Protestants of those political rights and advantages which since the Revolution they have enjoyed. The intervention of the Catholic Priests, where they have been well-disposed, at the same time proves, that the Protestants could not have conducted themselves improperly towards the professors of the Catholic religion ; and that their authority as priests was important in preventing or lessening evils which religious fury had inspired.

The additional Accounts which we now furnish, will prove that your Contributions (our intention to solicit which, was, in the first instance, submitted to the Prime Minister of his Royal Highness the Prince Regent) are even more necessary than we could have anticipated, from the authentic letters we had received, but which suppressed, thro' fear, many important details ; and as the efforts of our enemies have occasioned a serious increase in our expenditure, we must re-urge on you the propriety of making those Contributions as early, and as liberally as your convenience will allow.

As it will not be possible for us to provide an antidote to the poison daily diffused, we shall be content to assure you, that whenever any Intelligence arrives which alters our opinion, or renders your exertions unnecessary, you shall have immediate information.

By Order of the Committee,
THOMAS MORGAN, Sec.

RESOLUTIONS.

William's Library, Red Cross Street,
January 12, 1816.

'At a Meeting of the Committee, appointed by the General Body of Protestant Dissenting Ministers of the Three Denominations, ' for the Purpose of Inquiry, Superintendance, and Distribution of the Funds which may be contributed for the Relief of the French Protestants, suffering for Conscience-sake,'

It was unanimously Resolved,

1. That this Committee have observed, with astonishment and regret, that attempts are making, through the medium of the Press, to defeat their object, by misrepresenting their motives ; and altho' the Committee know too well what is due to that respectable body by which they are deputed, to engage in useless warfare with those who are labouring to stifle that public sympathy, which it is the wish of the body to excite, they yet owe it to their own character, and to the cause they have undertaken, to state candidly, once for all, the motives by which they have been guided and the end they have in view.

2. That this Committee, therefore, utterly disclaim for themselves and their Constituents all party feelings on a question which they conceive to be purely and exclusively Religious; but that if they must be ranked with a Party, they are happy in ranking, on this occasion, with that of the Government which listened so candidly to their representations,—entered so warmly into their feelings,—and pledged itself so readily to employ its good offices for the same humane purpose to which their interference has been directed.

3. That if any man, calling himself a Protestant, can impute to Dissenting Ministers, as a crime, that they have shewn themselves peculiarly forward, on this occasion, he should remember that they are the descendants of those who, for conscience-sake, suffered the spoiling of their goods, and the loss of their lives; and to whose constancy, under persecution, it is chiefly owing that religious liberty is now firmly established in this favoured land.

4. That, feeling the value of this inestimable blessing, they could not but be deeply interested by any occurrence which might threaten its loss to those especially, with whom they are united by the tie of a common faith, and a common worship; nor could they refuse their sympathy or their relief to men bleeding in the same cause which rendered the memory of their fathers immortal.

5. That though letters have been received from Ministers in France, expressing objections to the interference of their Protestant brethren in England, the Committee have ascertained, from *unquestionable evidence,* that some of those letters have been written under *constraint,* and that others have been dictated by an apprehension (it is hoped erroneous) lest such an interference should injure them in the estimation of their own Government, or rather, lest it should expose them to the fury of a faction, which sets the Government itself at defiance; and the Committee are of opinion, that if complaints are cautiously uttered, they deserve, the more, the consideration and sympathy of those who are aware of the cause in which this caution originates.

6. That while they have been acting consistently with their own principles, in expressing their abhorrence of all religious persecution, by whomsoever practised or countenanced, they cannot but suppose that in contributing to alleviate the distresses of the French Protestants, they are coinciding with the intentions of the French Government, which has been taking measures to suppress those outrages, which, if not suppressed, must occasion its own disgrace, and compromise its own safety.

7. That, in the subscriptions and collections already made,—in the spirit which is spreading throughout the kingdom,—and in the prospect that this spirit will ultimately enable them to grant important Relief to their suffering brethren, and to the widows and orphans of the victims of Persecution, the Committee have the most flattering encouragement to persevere. They do, therefore, earnestly request the unremitting co-operation of Protestants of every denomination, but especially of Protestant Dissenters, in this labour of love; and they express their confident assurance that in contributing to this object, without suffering their zeal to be damped by any insinuations or assertions whatever, they are promoting the spread and establishment of that Christian Liberty which is the greatest earthly boon that Heaven can bestow on man.

Signed (by order of the Committee)

THOMAS MORGAN,

Secretary.

Collections and Donations.

	£.	s.	d.		£.	s.	d.
R.H. Daw. Count. of Albemarle	5	0	0	Rev. Mr.Marsh's Cong. Hythe	2	0	0
Rev. Dr. Disney, Hyde	5	0	0	Farmer's do Leeds	6	2	1
Mr. Bickerdike's Con.Woolwich	7	7	0	Gooding's do. Lenham	2	10	0
				Independent Cong. Marden	2	12	7½
Browne's do.Gloucester	24	0	0	Rev.Mr. Moon's do. Deptford	25	0	0
Treleavan's do.Dorchester	7	0	0	March's do. Froome	7	0	0
Browne's do. N. Walsham	7	0	0	Whitehead's do. Creaton	10	0	0
Morris's do. Amersham	15	0	0	Mr. Nethersole, Clop-hill	1	1	0
Glover's do. Tring	11	1	6	Palmer's Cong. Romsey	14	6	7
Weybridge's do. Cheshunt	7	11	1	Belsham, London	5	0	0
Dr. Smith's do. Hackney	30	2	7	Mr. G. Lloyd, by the Rev. Dr.			
Deane's do. Chalford	1	0	0	Honeywell's Con. Melksh.	13	0	0
Rootе's do. Soham	2	2	0	Morris's do. Woodbridge	10	0	0
Walker's do. Preston	16	2	6	Williams's do. Stone	10	11	0
Mountford's do. Wincanton	5	0	0	Mark Wilks's do. London	50	5	6
Paul's do. Castle Cary	7	14	6½	Bains's do. Potter's Str.	8	12	0

	£	s	d
Rev. Mr. Kays's Con. Kendal -	9	13	0
Kemp's do. Tarling	10	0	0
Smith's do. Selby -	4	0	0
Williams's do. Edmonton	8	4	0
Marshall's do. St. Alban's	6	0	
Brown's do. Buntingford	4	14	2
Yockney's do. Stains -	6	0	0
Harsant's do. Beaconsfield	12	0	0
Allcock's do. Berkhampst.	8	0	0
Chapman's do Daman's-land	9	0	0
Giles's do. Eythorne -	5	6	6
Wright's do. Wisbeach and Lutton - - -	10	7	9
Mr. Jas. Manning - - -	1	1	0
Rev. Mr. Bollwel's Cong. Worthing - -	12	12	0
R. Spear, Esq. Millbank, Manc.	20	0	0
Rev. Mr. Mack's Con. Clipstone	5	5	10
Clark's do. Worstead -	6	3	2
Thodey's do. Ryde - -	6	0	0
Surman's, Sexton's, and Tomlin's do. Chesham	25	16	0
Chamberlain's do. Summers near Billinghurst -	2	14	6
Hunwicke's do. Kelvedon	7	0	0
Newman's do. Gainsbro'	8	2	8
Wilkinson's do. Howden	2	0	0
Cloutt's do. Staplehurst	1	0	0
Holden's do. Tenterden	12	0	0
Seymour's do. Beckington	10	0	0
Tozer's do. Taunton -	11	0	0
Golding's do. Pounsford	8	0	0
Winton's do. Bishop's Hull	8	0	0
Wallace's do. Chesterfield	13	4	6
Jerrard's do. Coventry -	21	0	0
Newton's do. Witham -	12	15	0
Mess. Wedd and Nash, Royston	3	3	0
Rev. Mr. Taylor's Con. Yeovil	6	2	0
Culver's do. Woolwich -	6	0	0
Cloutt's do. London	8	0	0
Mr. Gillaspie, by Mr. Cloutt	5	5	0
Independent Con. Westbury, by Mr. F. Evans - - -	9	11	1
Rev. Mr. Heinekin's do. Gainsborough - -	4	10	0
Towne's do. Royston -	8	8	8
Young Ladies in Mrs. Towne's Seminary - - - -	1	7	6
Rev. Mr. Smellie's Cong. Great Grimsby -	2	0	0
Higgs's do. Witney - -	5	1	4
Townsend's do. London	24	5	6
Hartley's do. Lutterworth	20	0	0
Finch's do. Lynn - - -	6	0	0
Brooks's do. Tutbury -	5	0	0
Craig's do. Bocking - -	34	6	2
Bishop's do. Gloucester -	9	0	0
Parker's do. Ashburton -	11	13	1
Mr. Miles's and Miell's do. Wimborne - - - -	3	0	0
Geary's do. Brentford -	6	6	0
Geary's do. Beaconsfield	5	3	6
Rees's do. St. Thomas's, London - -	22	8	2
Langdon's do. Leeds -	14	0	0
Bowden's do. Leeds -	30	0	0
Richards's do S. Petherton	4	1	0
Davis's do. Collumpton -	7	0	0
Rev. Mr. Sharp's Con. Bradnin.	2	0	8
Humphry's do Collumpton	1	12	6
Pickers's do. Ingham - -	7	4	3
Burnett's do. Woolwich	6	1	6
Giles's do. Lymington - -	12	3	0
Field and Keynes's do. Blandford - - -	17	0	0
Liddon's do. Hemel Hempstead - - - - - - -	10	8	8
Scott's do. Cleckheaton -	5	6	6
Holmes's do. Wantage -	3	5	0
Manning's do. Exeter -	33	8	0
Thomas's do. Enfield -	14	5	2
Trevor's do. and Friends, Liskeard - -	9	10	6
Millar's do. Oakham -	2	0	0
Fox's do. Chichester -	30	10	0
Heare's do. Mansfield -	5	5	0
Donoghue's do. Lydiate	5	0	0
Yates's do. Liverpool -	20	11	0
Adkins's do. Southampton	26	6	0
Johnston's do. Lewes -	6	12	6
Roger Lee, Esq. Clapham -	5	0	0
R. Wainwright, Esq. London	10	10	0
Rev. Mr. Harms's Con. Horsham	7	19	6
Holland's do. Preston -	6	0	0
Chadwick's do. Preston -	5	3	0
Mr. Luke Gilbert, W. Bromwich	1	0	0
Rev. Mr. Knight's Con. Staughton	4	9	0
Jones's do. Chalford -	11	11	0
Parker's do. Stockport -	8	0	0
White's do. Lymington -	12	5	0
Cobbin, London -	1	0	0
Clare's Cong. Downton -	2	7	0
Harris's do. Fordham - -	3	2	0
A Lady, anonymous - -	2	0	0
A Gentleman, ditto -	1	0	0
Mr. Barnes, Whitchurch -	2	0	0
A Gentleman, anonymous -	1	0	0
Rev. Mr. Hawkes's Con. Lincoln	4	7	2
Berry's do. Leicester -	30	0	0
Hoppus's do. Yardly, Hast.	6	8	3
Hinmere's do. Whitchurch	2	0	0
Rogers's do. Eynford -	10	0	0
Carver's do. Milbourne	10	0	0
Blomfield's do. Canterbury	7	7	0
Burgess's do. Chesterfield	7	4	5
Priestley's do. Fordingbr.	7	0	0
Mr. Worsley, London - - -	3	0	0
Mr. J. H. Merivale, London	1	1	0
Rev. Mr. Yarnold's Con. Romsey	3	5	0
Trickell's do. Bramley -	4	0	0
W. Fansey, Esq. London	1	0	0
J. Pearson, Esq. London	2	0	0
Rev. Mr. Williams's Con. Mansfield - -	19	5	0
Adamson's do. Patricroft	4	0	0
Jones's do. Whitchurch	8	12	0
Littlewood's do. Rochdale	8	5	0
Howes's do. Bridport .	40	0	0
Robertson's do. Stratton-under-Fosse -	15	12	0
Robinson's do. Hallford	2	2	0
Stuart's do. Sawbridgeworth - -	3	13	6
Hawksley's do. London	31	5	6
Franklin's do Coventry	10	0	0
Independant do. Leicester	17	7	7½

	£.	s.	d.
A. School Meet. Hayes, Sussex	6	0	0
Rev. Mr. Ree's Con. Rodboro'	17	0	0
Flower's do. Titchfield	3	0	0
Hopkins's do Christ Church	5	14	8
Varder's do. Cawsand	14 16 0 } 16	0	0
Children at ditto	1 4 0 }		
R. Langton, Esq.	1	1	0
Rev. Mr. Parson's Con. Chorley	8	7	8
Bakewell's do. Chester	24	0	9
Yates's do. Glasgow	14	3	0
Rotham's do. Willingham	2	0	0
Slatterie's do. Chatham	33	0	0
Hope's do. do.	8	10	0
Drew's do. Strond	9	1	0
Chester's do. Uttoxeter	5	0	0
Barnes's Con. Westbury	4	9	6
Wilks's do. Norwich	10	4	0
Wilks, Norwich	2	2	0
Mess. Davey and Son, do.	5	5	0
Miss Davey, do.	5	0	0
Mess. Cozens and Copeman, do	5	5	0
Mr. Spurgeon & Fr. Neatishead	4	13	6
Mrs. Calwell, by the Rev. Mr. Hughes	100	0	0
Rev. Mr. Corbishley's Con. Abbott Rooting	7	0	9
Sprague's do. B. Tracey	6	15	0
Green's do. East Budleigh	5	0	0
Scarlett's do. Gildersome	14	3	1
Steill's do. Wigan	12	0	0
Garthwaite's do, Cratfield	4	5	0
Hincliffe's do. Stockton	3	0	4
Sharpe's do. Skipton	4	0	0
Pendered's do. Royston	22	0	0
Dr. Phillip's do. Sheffield	19	9	8
Mr. Churchill and Fr. T. Ditton	3	3	0
B. T.	1	0	0
Rev. Mr. Norman's Con. Soham	2	2	0
Bonnsall's do. St. Columb	2	5	6
W. Russell, Esq. Upton	5	5	0
J. Gillemarde, Esq. London	5	0	0
Rev. Mr. Lewin's Con. Liverp.	19	5	2
Overbury's do Westbury L.	12	13	0
Fuller's do. Hand-Cross	4	0	0
Dr. Lindsay's do. London	80	0	0
Merryett's do. Ripley	5	0	0
Deer's do. Clutton	2	0	0
Reynal's do. Wellingboro'	5	7	6
Stuart's do. Sawbridgeworth, in addition	0	6	6
Ewing's do. Glasgow	57	13	10
Davidson's do. Newcastle-upon-Tyne	15	9	0
Middleditch's do Battlexden	3	3	0
Matthow's do. South Shields	9	2	6
Hinmer's do. Guisboro'	4	0	0
Hollis's do. Shiffnal	5	7	9
Harris's do. Whitchurch	7	0	0
Bidlake & Wells's do. South Petherton	8	0	0
Harris's do. Wallingford	10	0	0
Blackburn and Friends at Finchinfield	8	12	0
Rev. Mr. Hicks's do. Doncaster	5	8	0
Shepherd's do. Gataker	15	0	0
Morley Old Chapel	5	0	0
Rev. Dr. Collyer's Con. Peckham	40	15	0
Dr. Styles & Fr. Brighton	20	0	0
Crisp's do. Brighouse	5	5	0
Sykes's do. Guastwick	5	0	0
Hubbard's do. Banbury	6	6	0
Hatch's do. do.	4	4	0
Wood's do Jewin St. Lond.	15	0	0
Mather's do. Beverley	5	0	0
Palmer's do. Shrewsbury	8	6	0
Mr. Morrell & Friends, Baldow	5	7	6
Rev. Mr. Price's Con. Yeovil	1	3	1½
Morrison's do. Stebbing	7	10	6
Edward Swaines, Esq.	10	0	0
Baptist Con. Horsforth	3	11	7
Rev. Mr. Dean's do. Stand	10	0	0
Reynold's do. Chester	30	0	0
Rev. Mr. Burkitt's Con. Kennelworth	10	0	0
Gleed's do. Teignmouth	7	2	6
Mantell's do. Swindon	7	2	4
Bennett's do. Brighton	9	14	3
Do. do. Ditchling	5	3	6
Jarvis's do. Leeds	51	7	0
Anderson's do. Chalfont	11	0	0
Kerby's do. Lewes	4	7	2
Hudson's do. Rotherham	1	12	0
Edwards's do. Northiam	2	0	0
Welsh Cong. Wilderness Row, Deptford, & Woolwich	12	0	0
Anonymous, by Rev. Mr. Tracy	5	0	0
Rev. Mr. Ely's Con. Rochdale	5	10	0
Knight's do. Yelvertoft	5	0	0
Mr. Ludford, Newton	1	0	0
Rev. Mr. Ford's Con. Bridlingt.	4	0	0
Greathatch's do. N. Meols	2	0	0
Grendy's do. Ullesthorpe	12	0	0
Mr. Field and Fri. Warwick	10	0	0
Rev. Mr. Dymott's Con. Hillperton	3	0	0
Hawthorne's do. Dartford	6	4	0
Mr. Joyce, Highgate	1	1	0
Rev. Mr. Morrison's Con. Chelsea, London	5	0	0
Right Hon. Earl Crawford and Lindsay	10	0	0
Rev. Mr. I. Browne, Tiverton	2	0	0
Scott, Portsmouth	5	0	0
Independent Cong. Wareham	4	4	0
Rev. Mr. Bull's do. Bassinbourne	6	8	3½
Rogers's do. Fleet	5	0	0
Dr. Rees's Con. London	60	0	0
Campbell's do. Laurieston, Glasgow	20	0	0
Brown's do. Enfield	16	0	0
Groser's do. Watford	12	0	0
Williams's do. Uffculm	1	10	0
Jos. Hill, Esq. Uffculm	3	0	0
Rev. Mr. Fall's Cong. Rugby	6	13	3
John Hollis, Esq. Wycombe	5	5	0
Rev. Mr. Barrett's Con. London	30	1	6
Charrier, Liverpool	5	5	0
Kershaw's Con. Abingdon	9	14	0
Perrott's do. Guernsey	150	0	0
Evans's do. London	10	10	0
Chapman's do. Greenwich	20	12	6
Durant's do. Poole	19	12	0

THE

𝕸𝖔𝖓𝖙𝖍𝖑𝖞 𝕽𝖊𝖕𝖔𝖘𝖎𝖙𝖔𝖗𝖞,
&c.

| No. CXXI.] | JANUARY, 1815. | [Vol. XI. |

HISTORY AND BIOGRAPHY.

Account of the Mutineers in the Boun-
ty, 1789.
(From the Quarterly Review.)

IT is well known that in the year
1789 his Majesty's armed vessel
the Bounty, while employed in conveying the bread fruit tree from Otaheite to the British colonies in the
West Indies, was taken from her commander, Lieutenant William Bligh,
by a part of the crew, who, headed
by Fletcher Christian, a master's
mate, mutinied off the island of To-
foa, put the lieutenant, with the remainder of the crew, consisting of
eighteen persons, into the launch,
which after a passage of 1200 leagues,
providentially arrived at a Dutch settlement on the Island of Timor. The
mutineers, twenty-five in number,
were supposed, from some expressions which escaped them, when the
launch was turned a-drift, to have
made sail towards Otaheite. As soon
as this circumstance was known to
the Admiralty, Captain Edwards was
ordered to proceed in the Pandora to
that Island, and endeavour to discover
and bring to England the Bounty,
with such of the crew as he might
be able to secure. On his arrival in
March, 1791, at Matavai Bay, in
Otaheite, four of the mutineers came
voluntarily on board the Pandora to
surrender themselves ; and from information given by them, ten others
(the whole number alive upon the
island) were, in the course of a few
days taken ; and with the exception
of four, who perished in the wreck of
the Pandora, near Endeavour Strait,
conveyed to England for trial before
a court martial, which adjudged six
of them to suffer death, and acquitted
the other four.

From the accounts given by these
men, as well as from some documents
that were preserved, it appeared that
as soon as Lieutenant Bligh had been

driven from the ship, the twenty-five
mutineers proceeded with her to Too-
bodai, where they proposed to settle ;
but the place being found to hold out
little encouragement, they returned
to Otaheite, and having there laid
in a large supply of stock, they once
more took their departure for Too-
houai, carrying with them eight men,
nine women and seven boys, natives
of Otaheite. They commenced, on
their second arrival, the building of
a fort, but by divisions among themselves and quarrels with the natives,
the design was abandoned. Christian, the leader, also very soon discovered that his authority over his
accomplices was at an end ; he therefore proposed that they should return
to Otaheite ; that as many as chose
it should be put on shore at that
island, and that the rest should proceed in the ship to any other place
they might think proper. Accordingly they once more put to sea, and
reached Matavai on the 20th of September, 1789.

Here sixteen of the five and twenty
desired to be landed, fourteen of
whom, as already mentioned, were
taken on board the Pandora ; of the
other two, as reported by Coleman,
(the first who surrendered himself to
Captain Edwards) one had been made
a chief, killed his companion, and
was shortly afterwards murdered himself by the natives.

Christian, with the remaining eight
of the mutineers, having taken on
board several of the natives of Otaheite, the greater part women, put
to sea on the night between 21st and
22d September, 1789 ; in the morning the ship was discovered from
Point Venus, steering in a north-wes-
terly direction ; and here terminate
the accounts given by the mutineers
who were either taken or surrendered
themselves at Matavai Bay. They

stated, however, that Christian, on the night of his departure, was heard to declare that he should seek for some uninhabited island, and having established his party, break up the ship; but all endeavours of Captain Edwards to gain intelligence either of the ship or her crew at any of the numerous islands visited by the Pandora, failed.

From this period, no information respecting Christian or his companions reached England for twenty years; when, about the beginning of the year 1809, Sir Sidney Smith, then commander in chief on the Brazil station, transmitted to the Admiralty a paper which he had received from Lieutenant Fitzmaurice, purporting to be an " extract from the log-book of Captain Folger of the American ship Topaz," and dated " Valparaiso, 10th October, 1808." This we partly verified in our Review of Dentrecasteaux's Voyage, by ascertaining that the Bounty had on board a chronometer, made by Kendal, and that there was on board her a man of the name of Alexander Smith, a native of London.

About the commencement of the present year, Rear Admiral Hotham, when cruising off New London, received a letter addressed to the lords of the Admiralty, of which the following is a copy, together with the azimuth compass to which it refers:

" *Nantucket,* 1*st March,* 1813.

" MY LORDS,

" The remarkable circumstance which took place on my last voyage to the Pacific Ocean, will, I trust, plead my apology for addressing your lordships at this time. In February, 1808, I touched at Pitcairn's Island, in latitude 25° 02′ S. longitude 130° W. from Greenwich. My principal object was to procure seal-skins for the China market; and from the account given of the island, in Captain Carteret's voyage, I supposed it was uninhabited; but, on approaching the shore in my boat, I was met by three young men in a double canoe, with a present, consisting of some fruit and a hog: they spoke to me in the English language, and informed me that they were born on the island, and their father was an Englishman, who had sailed with Captain Bligh.

" After discoursing with them a short time, I landed with them and found an Englishman of the name of Alexander Smith, who informed me that he was one of the Bounty's crew, and that after putting Captain Bligh in the boat, with h[is] the ship's company, they returned to O[ta]heite, where part of their crew chose [to] tarry; but Mr. Christian, with eight othe[rs] including himself, preferred going to [a] more remote place; and, after making [a] short stay at Otaheite, where they to[ok] wives, and six men servants, they p[ro]ceeded to Pitcairn's Island, where th[ey] destroyed the ship, after taking ev[ery] thing out of her which they thought wo[uld] be useful to them. About six years a[fter] they landed at this place, their serva[nts] attacked and killed all the English, [ex]cepting the informant, and he was sever[ly] wounded. The same night the Otahei[tan] widows arose and murdered all their cou[n]trymen, leaving Smith with their wid[ows] and children, where he had resided e[ver] since without being resisted. I remai[ned] but a short time on the island, and [on] leaving it, Smith presented me a ti[me] piece, and an azimuth compass, whic[h he] told me belonged to the Bounty. [The] time-keeper was taken from me by [the] Governor of the Island Juan Fernan[dez] after I had had it in my possession ab[out] six weeks. The compass I put in re[pair] on board my ship, and made use of it [on] my homeward passage, since which a [new] card has been put to it by an instrum[ent] maker in Boston. I now forward it to y[our] lordships, thinking there will be a kin[d of] satisfaction in receiving it, merely f[rom] the extraordinary circumstances attend[ing] it.

(Signed)   MATHEW FOLGE[R]

Nearly about the same time a[no]ther account of these interesting p[eo]ple was received from Vice-Adm[iral] Dixon, in a letter addressed to [him] by Sir Thomas Staines, of his Ma[jes]ty's ship Briton, of which the foll[ow]ing is a copy:

" *Briton, Valparaiso,* 18*th Oct.* 1[8..]
" SIR,

" I have the honour to inform you [that] on my passage from the Marquesas [Is]lands to this port, on the morning of [the] 17th of September, I fell in with an is[land] where none is laid down in the Admir[alty] or other charts, according to the se[veral] chronometers of the Briton and Tagus[:] therefore hove to, until day-light, and closed to ascertain whether it was inhab[ited,] which I soon discovered it to be; an[d to] my great astonishment, found that e[ach] individual on the island (forty in num[ber]) spoke very good English. They prov[ed to] be the descendants of the deluded cre[w of] the Bounty, which from Otaheite, [pro]ceeded to the above mentioned is[land] where the ship was burnt.

" Christian appeared to have bee[n

leader and sole cause of the mutiny in that ship. A venerable old man, named John Adams,* is the only surviving Englishman of those who last quitted Otaheite in her, and whose exemplary conduct and fatherly care of the whole of the little colony, could not but command admiration. The pious manner in which all those born on the island have been reared ; the correct sense of religion which has been instilled into their young minds by this old man, has given him the pre-eminence over the whole of them, to whom they look up as the father of the whole of one family.

. " A son of Christian's was the first born on the island, now about twenty-five years of age, (named Thursday October Christian ;) the elder Christian fell a sacrifice to the jealousy of an Otaheitan man, within three or four years after their arrival on the island. They were accompanied thither by six Otaheitan men and twelve women ; the former were all swept away by desperate contentions between them and the Englishmen, and five of the latter have died at different periods, leaving at present only one man and seven women of the original settlers.

" The island must undoubtedly be that called Pitcairn's, although erroneously laid down in the charts. We had the meridian sun, close to it, which gave us 25° 4'S. latitude, and 130° 25' W. longitude, by chronometers of the Briton and Tagus.

" It is abundant in yams, plantains, hogs, goats and fowls, but affords no shelter for a ship, or vessel of any description ; neither could a ship water there without great difficulty.

" I cannot, however, refrain from offering my opinion that it is well worthy the attention of our laudable religious societies, particularly that for propagating the Christian religion, the whole of the inhabitants speaking the Otaheitan tongue as well as English.

" During the whole of the time they have been on the island, only one ship has ever communicated with them, which took place about six years since by an American ship called the Topaz, of Boston, Mayhew Folger, Master.

" The island is completely iron bound, with rocky shores, and landing in boats, at all times difficult, although safe to approach within a short distance in a ship.
　(Signed)　　　　T. STAINES."

We have been favoured with some further particulars on this singular

society, which, we doubt not, will interest our readers as much as they have ourselves. As the real position of the island was ascertained to be so far distant from that in which it is usually laid down in the charts, and as the captains of the Briton and Tagus, seem to have still considered it as uninhabited they were not a little surprised, on approaching its shores, to behold plantations regularly laid out, and huts or houses more neatly contructed than those on the Marquesas Islands. When about two miles from the shore, some natives were observed bringing down their canoes on their shoulders, dashing through a heavy surf, and paddling off to the ships ; but their astonishment was unbounded on hearing one of them, on approaching the ship, call out in the English language, " Won't you heave us a rope, now ?"

The first man who got on board the Briton soon proved who they were. His name, he said, was Thursday October Christian, the first born on the island. He was then about five and twenty years of age, and is described as a fine young man, about six feet high; his hair deep black ; his countenance open and interesting ; of a brownish cast, but free from that mixture of a reddish tint which prevails on the Pacific Islands ; his only dress was a piece of cloth round his loins, and a straw hat ornamented with the black feathers of the domestic fowl. " With a great share of good humour," says Captain Pipon, " we were glad to trace in his benevolent countenance all the features of an honest English face."—" I must confess," he continues, " I could not survey this interesting person without feelings of tenderness and compassion." His companion was named George Young, a fine youth of seventeen or eighteen years of age. If the astonishment of the captains was great on hearing their first salutation in English, their surprise and interest were not a little increased on Sir Thomas Staine's taking the youths below and setting before them something to eat, when one of them rose up, and placing his hands together in a posture of devotion, distinctly repeated, and in a pleasing tone and manner, " For what we are going to receive, the Lord make us truly thankful."

---

* There was no such name in the Bounty's crew ; he must have assumed it in lieu of his real name, Alexander Smith.

'hey expressed great surprise on see-
ng a cow on board the Briton, and
vere in doubt whether she was a
great goat or a horned sow.

The two captains of his Majesty's
ships accompanied these young men
on shore : with some difficulty and
a good wetting, and with the assistance of their conductors, they accomplished a landing through the
surf, and were soon after met by John
Adams, a man between fifty and sixty
years of age, who conducted them to
his house. His wife accompanied
him, a very old lady, blind with age.
He was at first alarmed lest the visit
was to apprehend him ; but on being
told that they were perfectly ignorant
of his existence, he was relieved from
his anxiety. Being once assured that
this visit was of a peaceable nature,
it is impossible to describe the joy
these poor people manifested on seeing those whom they were pleased to
consider as their countrymen. Yams,
cocoa-nuts, and other fruits, with fine
fresh eggs, were laid before them ;
and the old man would have killed
and dressed a hog for his visitors, but
time would not allow them to partake of his intended feast.

This interesting new colony, it
seemed, now consisted of about forty-
six persons, mostly grown up young
people, besides a number of infants.
The young men all born on the island
were very athletic and of the finest
forms, their countenances open and
pleasing, indicating much benevolence and goodness of heart : but the
young women were objects of particular admiration, tall, robust, and
beautifully formed, their faces beaming with smiles and unruffled good
humour, but wearing a degree of modesty and bashfulness that would do
honour to the most virtuous nation
on earth ; their teeth like ivory, were
regular and beautiful, without a single exception ; and all of them, both
male and female, had the most marked English features. The clothing of
the young females consisted of a piece
of linen reaching from the waist to
the knees, and generally a sort of
mantle thrown loosely over the shoulders, and hanging as low as the an-
cles ; but this covering appeared to
be intended chiefly as a protection
against the sun and the weather, as
it was frequently laid aside, and then

the upper part of the body was entirely exposed ; and it is not possible
to conceive more beautiful forms than
they exhibited. They sometimes
wreath caps or bonnets for the head
in the most tasty manner, to protect
the face from the rays of the sun ;
and though as Captain Pipon observes,
they have only had the instruction of
their Otaheitan mothers, " our dress-
makers in London would be delighted
with the simplicity, and yet elegant
taste, of these untaught females."

Their native modesty, assisted by a
proper sense of religion and morality,
instilled into their youthful minds
by John Adams, has hitherto preserved these interesting people perfectly chaste and free from all kinds
of debauchery. Adams assured the visitors, that since Christian's death there
had not been a single instance of any
young woman proving unchaste ;
nor any attempt at seduction on the
part of the men. They all labour
while young in the cultivation of the
ground ; and when possessed of a
sufficient quantity of cleared land and
of stock to maintain a family, they
are allowed to marry, but always
with the consent of Adams, who
unites them by a sort of marriage ceremony of his own.

The greatest harmony prevailed in
this little society ; their only quarrels, and these rarely happened, being,
according to their own expression,
quarrels of the mouth : they are honest in their dealings, which consist
of bartering different articles for mutual accommodation.

Their habitations are extremely
neat : the little village of Pitcairn
forms a pretty square, the houses at
the upper end of which are occupied
by the patriarch John Adams, and
his family, consisting of his old blind
wife and three daughters, from fifteen
to eighteen years of age, and a boy
of eleven ; a daughter of his wife by
a former husband, and a son-in-law.
On the opposite side is the dwelling
of Thursday October Christian ; and
in the centre is a smooth verdant
lawn on which the poultry are let
loose, fenced in so as to prevent the
intrusion of the domestic quadrupeds.
All that was done was obviously undertaken on a settled plan, unlike
to any thing to be met with on the
other islands. In their houses too,

they had a good deal of decent furniture, consisting of beds laid upon bedsteads, with neat coverings; they had also tables, and large chests to contain their valuables and clothing, which is made from the bark of a certain tree, prepared chiefly by the elder Otaheitan females. Adams's house consisted of two rooms, and the windows had shutters to pull to at night. The younger part of the sex are, as before mentioned, employed with their brothers, under the direction of their common father Adams, in the culture of the ground, which produced cocoa-nuts, bananas, the bread fruit-tree,¹ yams, sweet potatoes and turnips. They have also plenty of hogs and goats; the woods abound with a species of wild hog, and the coasts of the island with several kinds of good fish. Their agricultural implements are made by themselves from the iron supplied by the Bounty, which with great labour they beat out into spades, hatchets, crows, &c. This was not all: the good old man kept a regular journal, in which was entered the nature and quantity of work performed by each family, what each had received, and what was due on account. There was, it seems, besides private property, a sort of general stock out of which articles were issued on account to the several members of the community; and for mutual accommodation exchanges of one kind of provision for another were very frequent; as salt, for fresh provisions, vegetables and fruit, for poultry, fish, &c. Also when the stores of one family were low, or wholly expended, a fresh supply was raised from another, or out of the general stock, to be repaid when circumstances were more favourable;—all of which was carefully noted down in John Adams's Journal,

But what was most gratifying of all to the visitors was, the simple and unaffected manner in which they returned thanks to the Almighty for the many blessings they enjoyed. They never failed to say grace before and after meals; to pray every morning at sunrise; and they frequently repeated the Lord's Prayer and the Creed. " It was truly pleasing," says Captain Pipon, " to see these poor people so well disposed, to listen so attentively to moral instruction, to believe in the

attributes of God, and to place their reliance on divine goodness." The day on which the two captains landed was Saturday, the 17th September; but by John Adams's account it was Sunday, the 18th, and they were keeping the sabbath by making it a day of rest and of prayer. This was occasioned by the Bounty having proceeded thither by the Eastern route, and our frigates having gone to the Westward; and the Topaz found them right according to his own reckoning, she having also approached the island from the Eastward. Every ship from Europe proceeding to Pitcairn's Island round the Cape of Good Hope will find them a day later—as those who approach them round Cape Horn, a day in advance, as was the case with Captain Folger and the Captains Sir T. Staines and Pipon.

The visit of the Topaz is of course, as a notable circumstance, marked down in John Adams's Journal. The first ship that appeared off the island was on the 27th December, 1795; but as she did not approach the land, they could not make out to what nation she belonged. A second appeared some time after, but did not attempt to communicate with them. A third came sufficiently near to see the natives and their habitations, but did not attempt to send a boat on shore; which is the less surprising, considering the uniform raggedness of the coast, the total want of shelter, and the almost constant and violent breaking of the sea against the cliffs. The good old man was anxious to know what was going on in the old world, and they had the means of gratifying his curiosity by supplying him with some magazines and modern publications. His library consisted of the books that belonged to Admiral Bligh, but the visitors had not time to inspect them.

They inquired particularly after Fletcher Christian: this ill-fated young man, it seems, was never happy after the rash and inconsiderate step which he had taken; he became sullen and morose, and practised the very same kind of conduct towards his companions in guilt which he and they so loudly complained against in their late commander. Disappointed in his expectations at Otaheite, and the Friendly Islands, and

most probably dreading a discovery,
this deluded youth committed himself
and his remaining confederates to the
mere chance of being cast upon some
desert island, and chance threw them
on that of Pitcairn. Finding no an-
chorage near it he ran the ship upon
the rocks, cleared her of the live
stock and other articles which they
had been supplied with at Otaheite,
when he set her on fire, that no trace
of inhabitants might be visible; and
all hopes of escape cut off from himself and his wretched followers. He
soon however disgusted both his own
countrymen and the Otaheitans, by
his oppressive and tyrannical conduct;
they divided into parties, and disputes and affrays and murders were
the consequence. His Otaheitan wife
died within a twelvemonth from their
landing; after which he carried off
one that belonged to an Otaheitan
man, who watched for an opportunity of taking his revenge, and shot
him dead while digging in his own
field. Thus terminated the miserable
existence of this deluded young man,
who was neither deficient in talent
nor energy, nor in connexions; and
who might have risen in the service
and become an ornament to his profession.

John Adams declared, as it was natural enough he should do, his abhorrence of the crime in which he was im-
plicated, and said that he was sick at
the time in his hammock; this, we
understand, is not true, though he
was not particularly active in the
mutiny : he expressed the utmost willingness to surrender himself and be
taken to England; indeed he rather
seemed to have an inclination to re-visit
his native country, but the young men
and women flocked round him, and
with tears and intreaties-begged that
their father and protector might not
be taken from them, for without him
they must all perish. It would have
been an act of the greatest inhumanity
to have removed him from the island;
and it is hardly necessary to add, that
Sir Thomas Staines lent a willing ear
to their intreaties; thinking, no doubt,
as we feel strongly disposed to think,
that if he were even among the most
guilty, his care and success in instilling
religious and moral principles into the
minds of this young and interesting
society, have, in a great degree, re-

deemed his former crimes.

This island is about six miles long
by three broad, covered with wood,
and the soil of course very rich : situated under the parallel of 25°S. latitude, and in the midst of such a
wide expanse of ocean, the climate
must be fine, and admirably adapted
for the reception of all the vegetable
productions of every part of the habitable globe. Small, therefore, as
Pitcairn's Island may appear, there
can be little doubt that it is capable
of supporting many inhabitants; and
the present stock being of so good a
description, we trust they will not be
neglected. In the course of time the
patriarch must go hence; and we
think it would be exceedingly desirable that the British nation should
provide for such an event by sending
out, not an ignorant and idle evangelical missionary, but some zealous
and intelligent instructor, together
with a few persons capable of teaching the useful trades or professions.
On Pitcairn's Island there are better
materials to work upon than missionaries have yet been so fortunate as to
meet with, and the best results may
reasonably be expected. Something
we are bound to do for these blameless and interesting people. The articles recommended by Captain Pipon appear to be highly proper;—
cooking utensils, implements of agriculture, maize or the Indian corn,
the orange tree from Valparaiso, a
most grateful fruit in a warm climate,
and not known in the Pacific Islands;
and that root of plenty, (not of poverty, as a wretched scribbler has called
it) the potatoe; Bibles, Prayer Books,
and a proper selection of other books,
with paper, and other implements of
writing. The visitors supplied them
with some tools, kettles, and other articles, such as the high surf would permit
them to land, but to no great extent;
many things are still wanting for their
ease and comfort. The descendants
of these people, by keeping up the
Otaheitan language, which the present race speak fluently, might be the
means of civilizing the multitudes of
fine people scattered over the innumerable islands of the Great Pacific.
We have only to add, that Pitcairn's
Island seems to be so fortified by nature as to oppose an invincible barrier
to an invading enemy; there is no

spot apparently where a boat can land with safety, and perhaps not more than one where it can land at all; an everlasting swell of the ocean rolls in on every side, and breaks into foam against its rocky and iron bound shores.

O happy people! happy in your sequestered state! May no civilized barbarian lay waste your peaceful abodes; no hoary proficient in swinish sensuality rob you of that innocence and simplicity which it is peculiarly your present lot to enjoy!

MISCELLANEOUS COMMUNICATIONS.

Dr. Morell on Church Authority.
Kent Road, Nov. 30th, 1815.
SIR,

IT is impossible that a thinking Christian, of whatever class, should read the history of the Christian Church without melancholy and disgust; for in almost every page he is compelled to remark how ill it has hitherto performed the promise of its commencement. The religion of Christ rose upon the world with an illumination, that proclaimed its author to be the fountain of light. Before it pagan superstition melted away; and the grosser vices that had grown rank in that foul atmosphere began to shrink and wither in the light of heaven. Those " gay religions full of pomp and gold," though in full alliance with the temporal authorities, were unable to maintain their ground against the force of truth. The arm of power was raised in vain on the side of the priests of idolatry: they and their gods were deserted by the people, who acknowledged in the simplicity of Christian faith and worship, a deep and moral interest, which the pageantry of pagan temples could not inspire. This was the proper triumph of Christianity; from such a rising, what divine splendors were not to be expected in the perfect day? But it was decreed by God, and foretold in his revelation, that this day, so glorious in promise, should soon be overcast. The prediction was, however, accomplished by natural means, and by human agency; and it concerns every Christian to trace the process and detect the principles of the degeneracy of the Church. Most Protestants agree in ascribing it to the inordinate ambition of the Bishop of Rome, and this is as far as it is generally safe, for them to push the inquiry; but it is easy to see,

that the cause lies deeper, and that the ambition of the pastor of the church at Rome would have done as little harm to the great body of Christians as the pretensions of the most obscure enthusiast, had he attempted spiritual conquest, armed only with spiritual authority. Whether his succession to the Apostle Peter were real, or pretended, he could never have persuaded the Christian world to bend beneath his supremacy, had he not found more efficient support in temporal authorities, than in his boasted apostolic succession. It was the coalition of civil, and ecclesiastical powers that first broke down the freedom of the Christian Church, and made it pass under the yoke,—that most degrading yoke, which bows down the soul itself in voluntary slavery. It is lawful, and may not be useless to imagine what might have been the history of Christianity, had its ministers never been admitted into civil alliance. Intolerant spirits would have existed, for positive and severe men will be bigots; but wanting the instrumentality of the secular arm, their intolerance would only have wasted the heart that cherished it. Errors would have sprung up; but as they could not have twined their parisitical fibres round the pillars of the state, they would not long have sustained themselves where the growth of truth was unchecked by power. Sophistry would have been combated by argument, assertion by fact, ignorance by knowledge, and error by truth; and he must think meanly of the power of truth, who can doubt what would be the issue of an open conflict in a duration of many centuries. If uniformity of opinion had not been produced, it is probable that discussion unbiassed and unawed would have gained a much nearer approach to it, than authority has been able to compel. At all events, that sickening uniformity of darkness, which was extended like a pall over the middle ages, could never have covered the people, to whom the scriptures gave their light. The curfew of prelatical tyranny could never have rung out the signal that was to shut them in a long night of ignorance and terror. The sword of the magistrate, placed out of the grasp of the ecclesiastic, might have protected the rights of Christians, and of men, from the violation of misguided zeal and church-policy ; and law, regarding as it ought with indifference all opinions, that neither weaken the obligation nor impede the practice of justice, would have interfered between contending sects for no other purpose but to chain down violence and keep the peace. Hence if the cry of heresy were raised,—the magistrate not being coupled with the priest,—for the sake of good order the chase must have been made a bloodless one. Had the Church never been incorporated with the State, her sentences of excommunication would not have become as destructive to the estates and bodies of men, as they were terrible to their imagination and fears : but that association being once established the civil power was soon brought to think, that he who was rejected by the Church had forfeited the protection, and even incurred the heaviest penalties of the State.

The Christian has often triumphantly contrasted the early propagation of his religion with the ferocious conquests of Mahomet and his successors ; and he has reason in his triumph. The gospel made its way unaided by arts or arms : it had established itself in the conviction and hearts of men long before the stratagems and weapons of this world were employed in the service of the cross ; and none more than the enlightened Christian condemns, and deplores the officious and fatal interference of civil policy and power, after the time of Constantine, in the conversion of pagan nations to Christianity. The soldier usurped the office of the missionary ; the diplomatist became evangelist ; and the kingdom of Christ was forced into an alliance and abused into a resemblance to the kingdoms

of this world. The hand of blood was laid upon the sacred ark : its purity was fled, and a dark and debasing superstition succeeded to the pure, and undefiled religion of Christ. The Gothic tribes that broke into the south of Europe, brought with them better morals than they found. Rude they were, and fierce, rapacious often and cruel ; but the vices in the train of luxury had not wasted the powers of the soul, and destroyed the elements of future good.

Intrepid, and clear-sighted, and remote from the country of Odin, they were not fitted to move long in the fetters of the northern superstition. Had this race of men fallen among Christians, such as Christians were in the first ages of the church, and such as might have succeeded to them but for the pollution of secular connexion and worldly ambition, to accomplish their conversion to genuine Christianity had required no refinements of policy, no exertion of force. The sword of Charlemagne could only compel a feigned assent, where a band of zealous, faithful and truly evangelical missionaries would have planted Christianity in the mind, and in the heart. In those countries of Germany which were first roused from their long stupor by the voice of the Reformer, what noble materials existed for carrying up the Christian edifice ! At the time when the rude but manly inhabitants were vanquished into a spurious religion, and driven at the point of the spear to the baptismal fonts of the Roman Church ! And had England been brought into culture by such men as first preached the gospel in Britain, and happily escaped the pestilential blight from the Tyber, what a vineyard had she stood, thus planted and trained by labourers, who resembled the lord of the vineyard !

It may be said, that although, had the Church never been incorporated with civil governments its history would no doubt be different from what it is ; yet it does not follow that it would be better. On the contrary the abandonment of the religion of Christ to the guardianship of the people would have issued in greater evils, than any that have resulted from placing it under the patronage and advancing it into a participation of secular authority:—Heresies innumerable would have choaked the orthodox faith ; absurd opinions, which so easily establish themselves in the ordinary and uneducated mind, would have ejected Christian doctrine : some base plebeian superstition would have triumphed over Christian worship ; or that most overwhelming curse that can fall upon the earth, universal scepticism would have quenched the light of truth, and involved the world in worse than Stygian darkness. But who that has looked at all into Church history does not know, that the heresy of one century or climate has been the orthodox faith of another, and that the Christian world has continually divided and subdivided on every article of popular belief ? And as to absurd tenets, could the dullness of vulgar and unlettered men have fabricated any of grosser quality than have been spun by subtile schoolmen, woven into creeds by learned dignitaries, and stamped with the great seal of Church-authority in ecclesiastical councils, though held by princes and composed of prelates ? They consulted their Urim and Thummim, and gave out oracles that confound the reason of the believer, or baffle the ingenuity of the interpreter to the present day. To suppose that the faith of Christians would have been wrecked and lost, had not political men kindled the beacons that warn them from infidelity, carries in it an implication, not the most respectful to the evidences of the Christian revelation. Besides, scepticism is not natural to man. Few and cold are the hearts to which it can be dear. A being who is conscious of powers which assure him of an invisible power, who feels that he has but a dependent existence, and whose regrets, while they surround the tomb of affection, throw their shadows across the way that leads to their own, such a creature is not naturally irreligious. The sentiment of piety is latent in all the social feelings of his heart, and the affinity is too strong to be generally destroyed even in the dissolution of civil society. This law of God written in the heart does not require to be registered by human jurisprudence in her courts of record. To preserve this sacred fire from extinction there needs no college of priests, no order of vigilants, no decree of the

state. Man is prone to superstition, but he is rarely, and with difficulty perverted into scepticism. If the state could render any service to religion by taking her ministers, as such into a communion of power, the most likely service appears to be, that of restraining both priest and people in that descent to superstition, or those starts into fanaticism, which seem to be so easy to them. But the fact is, that princes and men in power have been for the most part either as unenlightened as the mass of society in matters of religion ; or anxious only to perpetuate the dominion of truth or error, superstition or religion, indifferently, from the dread of innovation. It is not difficult to find in their codes of law penal statutes, condemning to fines, confiscation, imprisonment and death, men, who could not believe without evidence, and would not subscribe what they did not believe, who refused to worship they knew not what, in ways more Pagan than Christian : And it were easy to shew that articles of faith too absurd to be believed, and rites of superstition, too childish to be performed honestly by any but the most uninformed members of the state, have continued to be the law of the land for a considerable time after they have been abandoned by the body of the people. When the multitude of Christians have suffered themselves to be surprised or seduced into spiritual chains, the civil power has not refused to rivet them on ; but the force which has burst the bonds asunder has proceeded from themselves. The reformation of opinion has, as was to be expected, dictated the reformation of law ; and governments have rarely become tolerant, till the spirit of the times has ceased to be intolerant. At this moment the lily, which has been so often steeped in the blood of the reformed, though it has been long preserved on a Protestant soil, and lately re-planted by Protestant hands, is become the inauspicious signal for a religious persecution in the south of France.

It may be said that the association of civil and ecclesiastical powers sets a limit to spiritual authority ; and that in fact the first step to the reformation from popery in this country was, the union of these powers in the sovereign when Henry VIIIth. caused himself to be constituted head of the church. If Christianity cannot flourish without a hierarchy it is no doubt necessary both to civil and religious liberty, that it be allowed to exercise no authority independently of the will of the State; still the association is not without danger. To what cause was it owing, that, before the reformation all Christendom was trodden under foot by ecclesiastics? And how did they contrive to raise themselves above the civil jurisdiction, till they were able to set prince and people at defiance? The priest was first placed on the same bench with the temporal judge: thence he soon found means to step over the head of his lay-colleague, and the magistrate, who planted him at his side, had his own folly to blame for the consequence. Thus the fable of the horse and his rider was naturally enough exemplified in his experience; he meant to be the ruler, but his more dextrous coadjutor made him the slave. One step more will take us to the grand source of the usurpation, intolerance and corruption, that darken the retrospect of the Christian church. The opinion to which I allude is well expressed in the following extract from a Consecration Sermon, preached by Dr. Graves, in St. Patrick's Cathedral, Dublin, July, 1806. "To suppose," says he, "that when the apostles were removed from their ministry, all authority to *govern* and *direct* the church of Christ was to expire along with them, and that the regulation of that society so extended, so important, so sacred, was to be abandoned to the caprice of individuals, the *unruliness* of multitudes, the mere casual exertions of transitory feelings, and undirected efforts, is as contrary to the dictates of reason, the analogy of nature, and the general economy of Providence, as to the direct declarations of scripture, and the clearest records of ecclesiastical history." If the Church has governors, who derive their authority either by succession or ordination from the apostles, two things are necessary; first, that the authority shall have been well defined by the apostles themselves, for the apostolic authority could not survive the office and the men: 2dly, That the governors of the church possess together with the authority the means to make it respected and obeyed.

As to the first; it would be c to produce the passages, or p in the New Testament, in whi authority of the rulers of the C whether bishops, or councils, byteries, is defined either ex or by implication. Let the i tious and credentials be fairl out and established, and the au shall be acknowledged; till th right to question it. Suppose ever, established; what mean the successors to the episcopal rity of the apostles (for more th is not pretended out of the Ch Rome) to make their governn ficient? Inspiration has ceas racles are no more; and thou sonal qualities may be respect for enforcing obedience in larg munities, the homage which to them can never supply th of that submission which is enforced by power and won and splendour. Divested of authority is but a name; it mu them either absolute or de The Catholic Church had t first in dependence on the trate; but it soon found m convert them into a freeho that, into an impious tyran restore the dependence was bour of the reformation; and testant countries this was a happily effected. If church-a must exist, the safety of the v quires that it be ingrafted up vil stock, which may miti sourness, and impart to it the of humanity. The compoun churchman and the man of tl is less dangerous, both to and religious interests of r than the mere ecclesiastic; participation of secular dist and civil powers may introd ciples of liberality into church ment, which are not indig any hierarchy: hence, less oppression is to be apprehen an Episcopal or Presbyteriar incorporated with the Sta from either of them, inves independent powers. The mistake in all these matters to be, the assumption of a authority, which is divine, timate Christian hierarchy, founded upon the Christian Grant that such a right of ru and it cannot be denied, tl a much good sense and knowledge of mankind in such remarks as the following: they occur in a Consecration Sermon, which was preached in the Chapel of Lambeth, 1807, by the Rev. Charles Barker, and published by command of his Grace the Archbishop of Canterbury. "They who talk of apostolical simplicity and lowliness, and contend that even now the same simplicity would best become the ministers of Christianisty, forget, or conceal from view, the real state of the apostolical character. They conceal from view the high and unattainable superiority over other men with which at all times, and in all places the apostle was personally gifted; his inspiration, his power of working miracles, and the immediate and irresistible operation of such endowments whether for the formation of a Christian church, or for its rule and governance when formed. In their day and for their purpose these were no defects; or if they were (while the choice of such men for such an office was designedly made to confound the pride of human wisdom) they were amply compensated by the constant and demonstrable interposition of God himself. With whatever rank and influence the incorporation of religion with the State, and with the order of society, has since invested the ministers of the gospel, the greatest and wealthiest, nay the best and wisest of those ministers possesses no substitution for the decisive and commanding authority of the humble fisherman who could heal the sick and raise the dead."

I shall add one more extract, which is in strong contrast with the spirit and doctrine of the last; but which, while it breathes more of the spirit of primitive simplicity, betrays a want of that practical knowledge, which is not so well acquired within the inclosure of a sect: it is taken from a charge delivered to the clergy of the Episcopal Communion of Edinburgh, 1807, by the Right Reverend Daniel Sandford, D. D. their bishop; and consequently a Dissenter on that side of the Tweed.

"It has often afforded 'me," says he, "great satisfaction to contemplate the resemblance, that the Christian society of which we are members bears, in its external condition, to the church of Christ, as it existed every where, before the conversion of the Emperor Constantine. During that period, indeed, the Church was frequently exposed to secular persecution, from which, blessed be God, we, enjoying as we do, a free and perfect toleration from the state, are mercifully exempted. But, as far as can be intended by the comparison our case is the same with that of our forefathers in the Christian faith, in ages which we are accustomed to consider with peculiar veneration. At that time the Church, unconnected with the State, subsisted by her own internal and inherent powers. Irenæus, Cyprian, Cornelius, and indeed all who held the office of a Bishop for the three first centuries, were possessed of no other authority, and probably encompassed with no more outward dignity than he who now addresses you; and this authority was preserved by the filial affection of the clergy, over whom they respectively presided. God forbid that I should ever have the presumption to compare my own talents, or my own zeal, to the talents or the zeal of those burning and shining lights, to which every succeeding age of the Church has looked back with reverence, inferior only to that which is due to the immediate apostles of our Lord. I mention them only because their history furnishes an incontrovertible proof that episcopacy can subsist, and bishops who are deserving of respect be highly respected, though destitute of the splendid but adventitious panoply of a legal establishment."

It appears from this passage, that the Bishop derived great pleasure from contemplating the episcopal communion over which he presided, as unconnected with the state; though he might not, perhaps, think secular connexion a sufficient ground of dissent from an Episcopal Church. Indeed with the Protestant Dissenters of England the incorporation of the Church with the State is neither the sole nor the ultimate ground of dissent. I suppose the greater part of them consider church-authority under every form as a usurpation: many of them are persuaded that it is the only enemy from which Christianity ever had or ever will have any thing to fear; that it has acted like a poison, and not a very slow poison, wasting and corrupting, as it has circulated through the body of Christians. If it were necessary to submit to a spiritual rule, many of them would choose the Episcopal as soon, and some sooner than any other; but they maintain that all ecclesiastical authority is unsupported by the New Testament, and rests only on human policy, ambition or mistake. Disconnect the authority of the Church from that of the State, and they would regard it with more apprehensive vigilance, and dissent from it with yet stronger disapprobation. They are better pleased that its powers, if such as can reach temporal condition, should emanate from the chief magistrate, and be subject to temporal controul, than that they should be established on the assertion of divine right, and exercised independently of civil regulation. It is probably on some such ground as this that several of them are of opinion that the *veto* upon the constitution of a Catholic episcopacy should not be conceded by the civil authority in any country, that wishes to remain free. · If any portion of Christian professors, say they, will be subject to an absolute ecclesiastical rule, or if they believe that the Christian religion binds them in this subjection, they are entitled to their opinions; no man can wrest from them, and the attempt would be injustice and violence. At the same time, they who think with the English Dissenters that all spiritual authority is usurped, and they who think with the laity and many of the clergy of the Church of England, that Christianity does not sanction, and sound policy will not allow the exercise of any authority, (and ecclesiastical least of all) independent of civil jurisdiction, are also entitled to their opinions, and should not be called upon to surrender them to the assertors of a spiritual authority, subject to no civil controul. The principle of such a claim is bad, and the experience of mankind has not taught us that the practice can be safe. Spiritual authorities might not indeed shoot up into active tyrannies, unless fostered in their infancy by political men; but powerful laymen have generally been found, who thought it might be worth their while to foster them; and it would be an experiment full of hazard to civil and religious liberty to set them above civil

inspection, (placing at the same time their vassals of the laity on the same political level with other men,) now that antiquity has made those authorities venerable, and the suspension of power has not made the possession of it less an object of desire. If any principle is incompatible with good government, and, when put into action, fatal to the civil rights of mankind, it is the divine right of a hierarchy : and if it can ever be right to guard a civil constitution, by disqualification to legislate, annexed to opinions, that doctrine deserves to stand first upon the list. He whose faith enslaves him to a hierarch, irresponsible on earth, is ill-fitted to assist in the legislative assembly of a free state. Such a faith is essentially intolerant, requires her to arm intolerance against her own life.

JOHN MORELL.

Sir,

THE following instances of the existence of Unitarian sentiments came within my notice during a late tour in Norway.

A Captain S——, master of a merchant vessel, a man both of family and education, he being connected with people of the first consequence, happened to be a fellow lodger with myself in the same room, at an inn at Christiania. We were much together during a period of three weeks, and living in the same room, it naturally occurred (as he spoke English remarkably well) that we often communicated our ideas upon various subjects to one another. Amongst others was also religion, and in the course of a conversation on this head, I took occasion to inform him that I did not myself belong to the Established Church of my country, for that I could not believe many things which were asserted to be true by its advocates. I instanced the doctrine of the Trinity in Unity, the Godhead of our Saviour, original sin, and I think some other points which I do not now recollect. I also declared my belief that Christ was simply a human being, extraordinarily gifted for wise purposes. Captain S—— who had hitherto studiously avoided religious topics, and once before checked me when I accidentally touched upon them, was greatly surprised to find my sentiments accord so entirely with his own, but remarked, that he generally endeavoured to avoid talking upon these points in his country, as those who were of a contrary opinion would never suffer themselves to be convinced against their will, and disputing on religion was often worse than useless.

A second instance of the existence of Unitarianism occurred to me likewise during my stay at Christiania. A Mr. C——, a merchant of the first eminence and a man of consequence in a political point of view, took a good deal of notice of me, by constantly inviting me to his house and other civilities of the like nature. He had been several years in England, where his uncle was formerly established; and it very naturally occurred, that as we saw one another often, subjects of various kinds would be started in conversation. I one day took occasion to remark, that the attendance at Church in Norway was mostly confined to high days, such as Christmas, Easter, Pentecost, St. John's, &c. on which occasions only is there much of a congregation to be seen. Sundays are for the most part neglected, particularly by the higher classes who but seldom visit a place of worship except on the days above stated. Mr. C— owned the remark was just; his opinion was, that this neglect partly arose from the miserable jargon that was usually delivered from the pulpit. I then told him that in England the practice of attending upon divine worship was extremely prevalent. We afterwards got upon the subject of the great variety of existing sects in my country, the leading tenets of some of which I explained to him. Amongst others I touched upon Unitarianism, without hinting that I was at all connected with this description of Christians, till after he had acknowledged to me, that their ideas were exactly those he had formed for some years. He further added, that it was well known that many of the clergy were of the same opinions as himself, but that the restraint of the law prevented them from openly professing their sentiments, as it is a fundamental part of the constitution just established, that no other but the Lutheran religion shall be openly professed and inculcated. The identical law upon this

head is singularly worded to avoid the reproach of bigotry and intolerance; it declares, "That all parents who profess the established religion shall educate their children in the same, no other mode of public worship being permitted." It may not perhaps be amiss to add here that Jews are not allowed to reside or settle in Norway. This harsh regulation opens a door for the commission of perjury; as it is well known that two opulent families at Christiania are merely professing Christians, in order to avoid being troubled.

T.

_____

SIR,

THE notion of translating the scripture *word for word* was not peculiar to John Canne, whose Bible is described, x. 548. I have before me a small pamphlet thus entitled:

"Essay towards a literal English Version of the New Testament in the Epistle of the Apostle Paul directed to the Ephesians; by John Callender, Esquire, Glasgow. London; reprinted for Alexander Grant," who thus begins his Preface:

"Mr. John Callender was a gentleman of undeniable character, and according to all accounts that ever I could learn of him he understood the originals well. 'Tis much to be regretted that he in his life-time, had not translated the whole of the New Testament from the original Greek, in the same manner as he has done the Epistle of the Apostle Paul to the Ephesians. With what literal ancient simplicity does this little translation appear, compared with the English idiom. Mr. Callender's words are as follows: ' Those who love to search the scriptures, and to read them divested of every human gloss, will not, perhaps, be displeased to see a version so entirely literal, as to abandon the English idiom altogether; that the genius of the Greek language may be every where preserved, and even the unlearned reader made to feel the energy of the divine original.' The above words are very expressive to a common understanding."

That your readers may judge whether with his editur they can regret that Mr. Callender's labours in *literal* translation were so limited, I will transcribe a few passages, beginning with the first sixteen verses of the epistle.

" Paul, an Apostle of Jesus Christ, by the will of God to the saints, being in Ephesus, and faithful in Christ Jesus : Grace to you, and peace, from God the Father of us, and of the Lord Jesus Christ. Blessed the God and Father of the Lord of us, Jesus Christ, who is blessing us by every blessing spiritual, in the places above the heavens, in Christ ; Like as he out-chose us in him, before the founding of the world, for us to be holy and blameless before him in love : Having selected us into sonship by Jesus Christ unto himself, according to the good pleasure of the will of himself, to the praise of the glory of the grace of himself, by which he graced us in the beloved. In whom we have redemption by the blood of him, the remission of sins, according to the richness of the grace of him. Of which he was abundant to us in all wisdom, and prudence, having revealed to us the mystery of the will of himself, according to the good pleasure of himself, which he before purposed in himself. For the dispensation of the fulness of the times, to bring under one head all things in the Christ, those both in the heavens, and those upon the earth in him. In whom also we are made heirs, selected according to the fore-purpose of Him who to all things giveth energy, according to the council of the will of himself ; that we might be to the praise of the glory of him, who first hoped in the Christ. In whom also ye having heard the word of the truth, the gospel of the salvation of you : in which also having believed ye were sealed by the spirit of promise, the holy : who is the earnest of the inheritance of us, in the redemption of the possession bought, to the praise of the glory of him. Wherefore also I, hearing the faith, among you, in the Lord Jesus, and the love to all the saints, do not cease giving thanks for you, mention of you making in the prayers of me."

Ch. iv. 25, &c. " Wherefore laying aside lies, speak truth, every one with the neighbour of him ; because we are of each other members. Be angry and do not sin : the sun let not set upon the wrath of you : neither give place to the accuser. The stealer no more let steal ; but rather let

him labour, working the r hands, that he may have to him that needeth." In vers " *in* Christ," instead of the rendering of the common ve

Ch. vi. 1, &c. " Child the voice of the parents of Lord. For this is just. H father of thee, and the mothe is command the first in a that well to thee may be be long-lived upon the eartl

There is no date to Mr pamphlet. By its appearan have been printed nearly one years. Mr. Callender was a contemporary of John Ca. seems to have been satisfied v shorter experiment on t " word for word."

BIBL

SIR,   *Oct.* 24,

READING in your Repo June last (x. 382, 3 the Report of the Protestan for the Protection of Religio ty, I observe that two ca been decided in favour of claiming exemption from pa pike tolls on the ground of th to places of divine worship.

This induces me to stat the following case, and to I one of your numerous corre will point out how I am t redress. Doubtless there persons who are in nearly si cumstances with myself ; co ly I shall not only be oblig but the dissenting interest will feel a like obligation for the removal of the grievan sure you, Mr. Editor, that any pecuniary advantages am seeking after, no :—my purely to support my priv Dissenter in particular, an vileges of the Dissenters in

In the Report above allu mention is made of the na parties whose case was dec Suffolk assizes, nor on wl parliament the Judge's expo decision was founded ; and case is equally destitute of of information which is ne me to lay before a magistr purpose of procuring redre

The Case :—I live in a vi three miles from a post-to West of England, and an

rian. (That is, *one who acknowledges the one only true God, and Jesus Christ as his messenger and servant.*) In general a chaise is ordered on Sundays to take myself and family to a place of divine worship in this town, and to take us back after the afternoon service. One shilling is demanded as toll at the turnpike gate, and of course paid. This has been the practice for many years.

J. P.

Bridport, Dec. 19, 1815.

SIR,

ON receiving the two circular letters from the Committee of the Protestant Dissenting Ministers of the three Denominations in London, on the merciless persecution which has for some months raged against the Protestants in the South of France, I took an early opportunity of laying their distressing case before my people, persuaded that this would be sufficient to excite their tender sympathy and prompt their ready relief. If you think the conclusion of my sermon on this occasion, in the least degree calculated to aid this benevolent cause, and at the same time, to check any unreasonable prejudice, jealousy and dislike towards the Catholics in the united kingdom, which the atrocities of those who bear their name in a neighbouring country, tend to produce, it is at your service for insertion in your liberal Repository. I mention the latter circumstance, because I perceive *danger* of it arising from the sympathetic feelings which are generally excited in favour of the persecuted, and indignation against the fanatical persecutors. Let the maxim, however, of the heathen moralist be observed, *fiat justitia.* Let not the innocent suffer for the guilty. As we are professing Christians, it becomes us to act towards others, at all times, on the comprehensive rule of our common master, " Whatsoever ye would that men should do to you, do ye even so to them." As a friend to the just rights of all classes of the community, I would suggest, that if the Catholics in this country, were as a *body* to express their abhorrence of this sanguinary persecution of the Protestants in France, and contribute to the relief of the sufferers, it would have a powerful tendency to restrain the outrages of those persons, who

are deluded by blind bigotry and in furiate religious zeal, and redound to the credit of their own humane feelings, liberality and Christian spirit.

THOMAS HOWE.

The preacher having read some of the interesting and affecting details of the sufferings of our persecuted brethren in the South of France, thus proceeded: " I am persuaded that there is not one among you come to years of understanding, whose tender feelings are not greatly excited by the details which have been now read, of a persecution originating in the most shocking religious bigotry and fanaticism, and conducted with peculiar savage cruelty ; a persecution carried on in despite of the Edicts of the King on the throne; supported by armed bands, raised and organized without his authority, and under a constitutional charter which guarantees to all the people the freedom of religious sentiment and public worship. I cannot doubt of your readiness, my friends, to contribute to the alleviation of distress, which cannot be contemplated without a mixture of horror and the tenderest emotions. ' Blessed,' said our divine Master, ' are they which are persecuted for righteousness' sake, for theirs is the kingdom of heaven.' And surely a blessing from the God of mercy may be expected to descend on him, who espouses the cause of the persecuted ; who does his utmost to alleviate their sufferings; who if he cannot restore to them their parents, their children, their brothers or sisters that have been inhumanly butchered, contributes to supply the destitute survivors with bread to eat, with raiment to clothe them, with habitations in which to reside, with Christian temples wherein to worship the God of love and grace, and with ministers to preach to them the words of consolation, hope and eternal life. As nothing can be more becoming a disciple of the tender-hearted Jesus, than thus to relieve his persecuted brethren, so such acts of piety and compassion tend to afford the purest satisfaction to his own mind, and we may be assured will be peculiarly acceptable to that gracious being who is declared to be ' the refuge of the oppressed,' and ' merciful to those who shew mercy.'

" Before I conclude, that candour

and liberality which I so often recommend to others, prompt me to speak a word in favour of a class of professing Christians in this country, whose peculiar religious system is as opposite to my own as the west is to east. I cannot doubt, that the inhuman treatment which the Protestants in the South of France receive from infuriate fanatics, is viewed with *abhorrence* by the *great body of Catholics* in the united kingdom. *Justice* therefore requires that *they* ought not to be deprived of any civil or religious privileges which would otherwise be granted to them on account of the intolerant outrages and cruelties of those in another country, who are called by the same name. Would not this be a violation of the first principle of *equity?* Would not this be worse than ' returning evil for evil,' which Christianity forbids, even visiting the iniquities and injuries of the *guilty* on the heads of the *innocent?* Such conduct would do honour to Britons, to professing Christians and Protestants. By the religious and moral instruction indeed of the poor in general, and by granting to all classes of the community the rights to which they are entitled, is in my opinion the best mode of making good subjects, kindly disposed neighbours, and of diffusing among *all* of them a spirit of mutual concord and Christian love.

" Had these principles been adopted and acted on by the governors of the nations of Europe, the British and Foreign Bible Societies, and the British and Foreign Schools, and similar institutions been generally established and supported in christendom *thirty* years ago, the sanguinary wars which have since devastated the Continent ; the shocking scenes exhibited in Ireland, and the present fanatical persecution of the Protestants in France, would according to human probability have been prevented. Let us then, as we regard the divine glory, the interest of Christianity, and the peace and happiness of our fellow-creatures, do our part towards removing the *cause* of the evils we deplore, by contributing to enlighten the minds of men with useful knowledge, and lead them into the paths of Christian truth, liberality and virtue. Let us also, as far as we are

able, alleviate the distresses of those who are suffering the direful effects of lamentable ignorance, blind bigotry and outrageous zeal. Parent of good! regard them with an eye of mercy; enable them ' to hold fast their integrity ;' to exercise fortitude, and to manifest towards their persecutors the disposition becoming the disciples of Christ, praying, ' Father forgive them,' and turn their hearts. Pour into their wounded souls the balm of divine consolations ; and may their fellow-christians readily afford them relief, as they themselves would wish for the sympathy and aid of others, were they deprived of their earthly comforts ; of their near relatives and beloved friends ; of their places of worship ; of their habitations, and driven destitute into the mountains and dens of the earth, by the rage of persecution and the violence of cruel men. May such atrocious deeds among professing Christians, so shocking to humanity, so disgraceful to religion, be never more repeated, but that happy period soon arrive, predicted in the page of inspired prophecy, when ' knowledge, truth, liberty, peace and righteousness shall cover the earth as the waters overspread the channels of the sea.' "

Nottingham, Nov. 17, 1815.

Sir,

ON the recommendation of your last Review [x. 654.] I procured a copy of Mr. Gilchrist's Sermon, delivered at Southampton, curious to read what was described as " an acute, able and eloquent" composition, and willing to determine the extent of my claims to that comprehension of mind of which your reviewer speaks. With disappointment, however, I find that I can neither admire nor be amused. Perhaps it will console some of my weak brethren in the Unitarian church to know that they have a companion in infirmity; and perhaps some of my fellow-christians who are without the pale of Unitarian orthodoxy, may be pleased to hear that there is *one* of their opponents at least who does not deem it necessary, or even right to lay aside the spirit of Christian moderation when he approaches them, or to address them in other language than that of Christian courtesy. *I am,* I confess, one of those " intellectual petit-maitres" who shrink with disgust from madness or " any thing like madness" in religious controversy; so ignorant indeed as never to have heard what *Christian madness* is; so confined in my reading as never to have met with any mention of it in the writings of Shakespear, Bacon, Taylor, or Barrow, to say nothing of the New Testament, which, however, I do recollect, says something of Christian meekness; and lastly, so mean-spirited as to rejoice that I live in an age, " finical and dwarfish," though it be, in which candour and courtesy are not *universally* deemed inconsistent with honesty and zeal; in which the odium theologicum is beginning to subside, in which the philosopher is no longer known by his tub, nor the Christian controversialist by his coarseness. But to come to the point, whatever may be thought of the argument of Mr. G.'s sermon (which though clear and simple does not I confess strike me as *peculiarly* ingenious or novel), of the manner and spirit of it I think there can be but one opinion amongst sober and serious Christians,—an opinion decidedly unfavourable. Where, I would ask the author, is the wisdom or the decency of those affected exclamations of disgust and repugnance to his subject, with which his discourse is so copiously interlarded, such as these: " I feel at every step as if condemned to a degrading task.—I feel as if brought upon the stage to fight with wild beasts or to contend with madmen."—" I am weary of such solemn trifling."—" It is a most irksome task to handle subjects to which one can neither apply argument nor ridicule," &c. Such exclamations if affected are disgusting, and if serious, are ridiculous. He who undertakes a task voluntarily (and a man need not print against his will, *even though* he should be asked) has no right to torment you with complaints of its irksomeness. He who voluntarily descends from his elevation, whether real or fancied, has no right to complain of being degraded. If Mr. Gilchrist really deemed his subject of serious importance he should have treated it with *serious* earnestness, if he did not deem it important, he was not obliged to treat it at all. An intolerant and contemptuous spirit seems to me to pervade almost the whole

composition,—a spirit which I do not hesitate to say, (even at the risk of being " trampled in the dust for a dwarfish tyrant") is unbecoming a Christian minister. Such fiery discourses seem to me likely to answer no one good end, neither of pleasure nor improvement, conciliation nor conviction. They may feed the vanity and illiberality of the red hot convert who is already too much disposed to merge his Christianity, I mean his charity, in his Unitarianism,—but they will grieve the serious and Catholic Unitarian whose comprehension of mind is not narrowed by party spirit,—and they will excite the determined hostility and aversion of the adversary when it ought to be the object first to conciliate, and then to convict. " Though speaking honourable things of God," says Bishop Taylor, an author in Mr. G.'s admiration of whom I warmly agree, " be an employment that does honour to our tongues and voices; yet we must tune and compose *even those notes so*, as may best profit our neighbour." It should not be forgotten that the same spirit of uncharitableness, which we condemn in the anathema of the Calvinist, may exist in no less lively vigour in the contemptuous sneer of the Unitarian. Coarse language and opprobious terms are a disgrace to any cause, and no real friend of Unitarianism will, I hope, be ashamed or afraid to avow that " his ears are shocked by them." In conclusion, Mr. Editor, I shall make an extract from Mr. Gilchrist's sermon, which might have served, I think, both for a favourable specimen, and for a review, and the candour of which ought perhaps to mitigate the severity of censure. " If any illiberal remark, if any unseemly expression escape from us, place it to the account of human imperfection,—place it to the account of the individual addressing you; on him be all the blame : let it not be charged to his opinions, nor to other men who profess them. A good cause may come into the hands of . . . . injudicious advocates : and if one man should give offence by his *manner* of treating a subject, you ought not on that account. to be offended with the subject itself, nor with a whole class of Christians." What a pity that the excellent feeling displayed in this, and the eloquent passage immediately preceding, did not prevail with the author to commit this abortion of his genius to the flames! I remain, a sincere friend to Unitarianism, not so much for its own sake, as for the sake of that Christianity of which I deem it the purest form.

A. A.

Sir,

THE following circumstance I know will give you great pleasure: A few weeks ago my brother-in-law, Mr. ——, of Dublin, was with me: he is an anxious promoter of the education of the poor; and it appears the Catholic Priests oppose generally, every thing in their power, what is done by the Protestants associated for that purpose, and too generally succeed; though, as it will appear, the people are not adverse to it and connive at its introduction. A person in humble life, but of strong mind, and an enthusiast to promote this great work, travels through the country in disguise, taking with him the Bible, translated into the language of the lower classes, and has succeeded in forming what he calls *Hedge Schools,* where sometimes twenty boys will attend, and generally great progress has been made in the cultivation of their minds. He gives prizes to those who learn by heart most of the parts of the scriptures that he points out. He subjects himself to every privation and on his last visit to the society in Dublin, his dress being so dirty and tattered, it was recommended that he should have a new suit: "No," said he, "that will never do, if I go back with a good coat, my scholars and friends will say, *You have been to Dublin and got bribed by the great, and we will have no more to do with you.*" His plans are carried on unknown to the priests, and no public notice is ever taken of it by the society, feeling that publicity would defeat the object. He has won numbers over from the Catholic faith, and sets about the task of conversion in a manner never suspected at first, by his opponents; sleeps in their wretched cabins and partakes of their coarsest fare. It appears he had from time to time various controversies with a priest; and at last not only succeeded in detaching him from his opinions, but also in leading him into his views;

and since, the priest has turned tinker and joined heart and hand in promoting the Protestant faith and instructing the poor. To meet in any house or cabin would draw the attention of the priests and perhaps excommunication on the person who permitted it would follow; this is the reason of his drawing the boys off to a distance in a manner beforestated; —the name of this great man is Thady ——.

J. W.

P. S. I add an anecdote of the singular but praiseworthy integrity of a Quaker tradesman:—a clerk at the general post office told me the other day, that one of the above society called every quarter to repay those letters that by mistake were *underrated.*

Natural Theology.   No. XII.

Of the Brain and Nerves.

THE brain is a soft pulpy mass of a whitish grey colour, which occupies all that cavity which is formed by the bones of the skull, and is surrounded by two membranes, the outermost called the *dura mater*, the second is denominated *pia mater*. The former lines the inside of the skull and prevents its eminences from giving injury to the delicate structure of the brain; it serves also to prevent concussions of the organ: it separates the whole mass into portions, which by its partitions it supports and protects from pressure. This membrane is strong and of a tendinous nature, like the other membranes of the body, which are only intended to perform subservient offices for the living parts; it is insensible, and may be torn without giving any pain. It adheres closely to the inside of the skull by a great number of filaments and small vessels which enter the bone every where.

The *pia mater* is a soft, thin, transparent substance, full of vessels, connected with the former by the veins which pass between them, and lies in contact with the surface of the brain, not only covering this organ, but insinuating itself into all its windings and fissures for the conveyance of vessels, and of nourishment, to supply the waste of this active machine. Between these two membranes there is spread a third, which is extremely delicate, resembling a cob-web; but does not dip into the convolutions of the brain.

There are three great divisions of the brain. 1. The *cerebrum* is the uppermost and by much the largest portion: it is separated into two hemispheres, each of which is divided into three parts, called lobes. 2. The *cerebellum* which lies at the under, and back part of the skull, and is divided into two portions by the descending fold of the dura mater. 3. The third division is called the *medulla oblongata*: it lies at the base of the skull, and is a continuation of the substances of the other two divisions. The *spinal marrow* proceeds without interruption from this third division of the brain; it passes out of the head by the great opening of the skull, and running down the canal of the backbone, where it is safely lodged, giving off nerves till it reaches the pelvis, where it splits into numerous thread-like nerves, resembling a horse's tail: the spinal marrow, like the brain, consists of the same sort of substance, and is protected by a continuation of the membranes belonging to that organ.

The nerves arise from the brain and spinal marrow: they come out in pairs and are distributed over the whole body. 1. To bestow an acute sensation in the instruments of sense. 2. To give the utmost facility of motion to the instruments of motion: and 3. To confer in all other parts a nice perception of whatever gives pain. "If any person," says Galen, "shall attend to dissections and consider attentively how nature has not distributed the nerves in equal measure to all the different parts of the body, but to some more abundantly, and to others more sparingly, he will find himself compelled to acknowledge that nature is eminently wise, just, skilful and provident in her arrangement of the animal economy. There are forty pairs of nerves: of these nine pair arise from the base of the brain within the skull; a tenth from the brain, as it passes through the great hole of the skull into the spine, and the remaining thirty take their rise from the spinal marrow. Those arising from the brain are chiefly distributed to the organs situated in the head, and to those contained in the chest and belly, while those that proceed from the spinal marrow go partly

among the internal organs of the trunk, to be distributed chiefly to the exterior parts of the body and to the limbs. Though the nerves run out in pairs, from their origin, they soon separate to go to different parts of the body, by splitting in innumerable ramifications.

To describe these nerves, and point out their several ramifications would take us much beyond the bounds assigned to these papers, but a single instance will illustrate the nature and uses of the whole, and this shall be taken from the fifth pair of nerves, which is branched to the ball, the muscles, and glands of the eye;—to the ear—to the jaws, the gums and teeth:—to the muscles of the lips:— to the tonsils, the palate, the tongue, and other parts of the mouth:—to the *præcordia* also, or parts situated about the heart and stomach, by coming in contact with one of its nerves, and finally to the muscles of the face, particularly the cheeks. Hence there is a great consent and sympathy between the parts, so that certain things seen or smelt excite the appetite, affect the glands and parts of the mouth, and in some instances excite what is known by the phrase of water in the mouth: some things seen or heard affect the cheeks with modest blushes;—on the contrary, if a thing pleases or tickles the fancy, it affects the præcordia, and the muscles of the mouth and face with laughter: others causing sadness and melancholy exert themselves upon the præcordia, and shew themselves by causing the glands of the eyes to emit tears, which by a most wise provision of nature are intended not only to brighten the cornea, and to express grief, but to alleviate sorrow: " *Fletus ærumnas levat*," and the muscles of the face put on the gloomy aspect of crying. Hence also the passions of anger, of hatred, of malice and envy, of love, of joy and hope are all produced, and exhibited by the countenance, so that, in fact, it is by means of this communication of the nerves, that whatever affects the mind is demonstrated spontaneously by a consentaneous disposition of the præcordia within, and a suitable configuration of the muscles and other parts of the face without. It is, says Pliny, an admirable contrivance of the great God of nature, that the face should be given to man, of all his creatures, to be the index of sorrow and cheerfulness, of compassion, of severity, &c. With this we consent and with it we deny. With this we manifest pride and contempt, and other passions that have their sources elsewhere.

Of the structure of the brain and nerves, and of the nature of their powers little is known. We read of the operation of the mind, and frequently measure its powers in the extent of genius and science : but though we can view the astonishing properties of the brain in their results, we are at a loss to explain how these results are produced. We know, however, first, That the brain and nerves constitute the organs of feeling and sensation : for upon touching the brain with a knife or other instrument, the animal is seized with convulsions : and if a probe be thrust into the spinal marrow all the muscles of the limbs will be violently convulsed. By irritating or tying a nerve, the muscles to which the branches are distributed will be violently convulsed, and the animal thrown into the most acute pain.

Secondly. All the other parts of the body derive their power of feeling and sensation from the brain, the spinal marrow and the nerves, being in themselves wholly insensible, and made capable of feeling only in proportion as they have the nervous branches distributed over them : this fact is made evident by tying up a nerve that leads to any part of the body, that part becomes immediately paralytic below the ligature; but will recover its powers on freeing the nerve. And it is further proved by the degrees of sensibility of the different parts of the body, bearing proportion to the quantity of nervous branches which can be discovered to belong to that part.

Thirdly. The excitement to all voluntary motion, or to those actions which are produced by the will, flows from the brain or spinal marrow, through the medium of the nerves, or to those parts of the body which we wish to move. For if the brain be compressed by any cause, the body becomes paralysed, and the power of motion is suspended, but on removing the pressure, the paralysis will cease, and the whole frame, unless it has been permanently injured, will reco-

ver its sense and action. Again, if a particular nerve, which conveys the immediate cause of motion from the brain, or spinal marrow, to a part to be moved, be injured or compressed, the part to which this nerve is distributed will become senseless, and lose its power of motion ; hence injuries of particular nerves produce palsies of the parts to which these are sent, as loss of voice, of hearing, of speech, &c.

Fourthly. The nerves are the organs, and the brain the receptacle of our sensations, and the source of our ideas. That sensation arises from impression made on a nerve and conveyed to it by the brain is evident from this, that if a nerve be irritated pain is produced, and the mind becomes instantly informed of the suffering : but if that nerve be compressed above the seat of its irritation, so as to cut off the channel of communication between it and the brain, the mind is then no longer conscious of any irritation that is made below the point of compression, and the affected parts are reduced to a state of insensibility similar to that of parts which are destitute of nerves, and may be injured or even destroyed without exciting pain.

Pain is occasioned by disagreeable sensations produced by the forcible contact of bodies with the organs of our senses, and it is wisely planted in the system to guard it against injury, for without pain, as the result of excessive sensations, the delicate structure of our frames would be almost constantly liable to destruction from various bodies in nature around. But as pain is the salutary consequence of excessive sensations, so sensations without pain are the results of a due impression on our sensitive organs, from the objects that are calculated to influence us : and as long as the body remains in health in all its parts, these impressions will continue to cause sensations in the nerves which will forward them to the brain, where ideas of the nature and properties of the impressing objects will be instantly formed for the instruction of the mind. Hence the skin and other parts possessed of what we call feeling is susceptible to the touch, and communicate to the brain and the mind the sensations of hardness, softness, &c. of such bodies as may be brought in contact with it ; while the eye, the ear, the nose and palate being differently organized, but still deriving their sensitive powers from the nerves, yet by their regular structure they are enabled to receive different kinds of impressions, each according to its properties and conformation : thus the eye is impressed by rays of light, the ear by sound, the nose by 'smell, the palate by taste. Hence the varied and extensive knowledge acquired by the human mind from impressions made on the brain by external objects.

From what has been said it is evident that the brain, spinal marrow and nerves, constitute the sentient or feeling part of the human system, and that all other parts are capable of feeling only in proportion as they receive the branches of nerves: and hence it has been inferred that there is a kind of gradation of feeling throughout the whole body, each of its organs and parts being endowed with that particular degree of sense, which is just sufficient for the performance of its function in the living machine.

The cellular membrane, for instance, whose use is to connect and unite into one whole all the moving parts of the system is without feeling : so also are the coverings of the brain, the coats of the nerves, the sheaths of muscles, tendons, and ligaments, and the apparatus of joints, with the substance of the tendons and ligaments themselves; for these parts performing only subservient offices to living organs would derange the whole system by being possessed of sensibility, which would leave them no longer capable of bearing the friction, blows, &c. which they now endure without injury in the different movements of the frame.

The feeling of the bones is doubtful, but the muscles are all endowed with this sense by a distribution of the nervous fibres every where throughout their substance ; this is necessary to their office: as agents of voluntary motion they must be capable of receiving and obeying the commands of the will : hence the mind no sooner wills an act, than the nerve is ready to obey the implied command, and the action is instantly performed: this dispatch is well illustrated in the rapid movements of an

opera dancer, every one of which are received in the mind, before they can be executed by the hands and feet : and also in the organs of speech, by which it is said 2000 letters can be distinctly pronounced in a minute every one of which requires a distinct and successive contraction of many muscles.

"The skin," says Mr. Burke, in his popular *Compendium of Anatomy*," possesses a finer degree of sense than the flesh, being fuller of nervous branches, and rising in the scale of sensibility, may be said to form the lowest of the organs of the senses. Feeling is the property and use of the skin of the human body, which enjoys it over its whole surface, but more exquisitely in some parts than in others : thus while the greater part of the skin possesses it in a degree sufficient only to guard the body from danger, by warning it of the contact of substances, which being too hot, too cold, too sharp or rough, might be injurious ; there are other parts, as the palm of the hands, and the sole of the foot, which are endowed with a greater sensibility, so as on a slight friction, to create a tickling kind of pleasure, and in some persons, involuntary laughter. But it is most perfect in the points of the fingers, which from their convexity, are particularly adapted to be the organs of touch, and from the nice discrimination with which our fingers enable us to examine the surfaces, and exterior properties of bodies, this sense has got the denomination of feeling. The tongue, the organ of taste, possesses this sensibility in a higher degree still ; for though it judges of the substances which constitute our food, by the same process as that used by the fingers, namely, contact; yet the latter with their finest feeling would be inadequate to discover bodies by their flavour. A step higher may be ranked the organ of smelling ; the nose is so acute in its sense, as to be impressed by the light and volatile effluvia rising from bodies, and floating in the air, and consequently distinguishes substances at a considerable distance. Higher again stands the sensitive faculty of the ear ; this organ is qualified to be acted upon by the mere vibrations of the air, which striking against this delicate part of our mechanism, produces sounds, and affords us information of things occurring at a great distance. But the most perfect of all the senses, and, perhaps, next to the more simple operations of the mind, is that of sight. The eye, the beautiful organ of this power, is a type of its functions ; in transparency, delicacy, and brilliancy, it surpasses all the other parts of the body, appearing to lose the grosser characteristics of animal matter, and to approach the nature of the mind, to which it serves as the most useful, rapid and extensive messenger, for procuring knowledge of the various objects in creation around us."

Such is the varied distribution of sense which the brain and nerves bestow upon the other parts of the frame. We are familiar with its uses; we know the kinds of bodies which are calculated to impress the different organs, and the manner in which those bodies effect their impressions, but of the nature of the brain and its operations we know nothing but by the effects produced.

To estimate the capacity of this organ we must trace the history of the human race from the beginning, and the systems which man has contrived and executed during this long period, for the accomplishment of his happiness: all his establishments, political, civil and military, are but developements of the mental faculty : by it have been framed all his regulations, social and moral. In short, every improvement has its origin from this source.

By his superior intellect the philosopher surveys the creation around him, and in a certain degree transfuses into the affairs of men, the wisdom, and the beneficence which he discovers in the system of the universe —the astronomer penetrates the heavens, discovers new worlds, and thus expands our admiration of the Supreme Being in his works——by the same means the chemist and experimentalist are enabled to analyse the various substances about him, and over which he has any power, and tracing nature to her recesses, draws forth valuable instructions for the application of bodies to our wants and enjoyments. While the bulk of mankind led by the knowledge of others are directed in their proceedings by the same intellectual faculty, though

acting in a more humble degree. What the powers of the brain may hereafter be capable of, under new circumstances and combinations in life, remains for futurity to ascertain.

———

Sir,

I AGREE with some writers in your valuable work, that the marriage service is a subject of great and just complaint to Dissenters in general, but particularly so to Unitarian Dissenters, who if they even consider it as a mere ceremony, their feelings must be hurt, and their minds revolt at, what is so opposite to their sentiments, the Trinitarian form of worship contained in it. And as no good reason can be given why the feelings and consciences of so large and respectable a class of society should be thus wounded and oppressed, and in a matter too the most serious of their lives ; let the evil be stated, the wrong be expressed, and if possible a remedy be procured. It may be asked, why not perform the marriage union before the civil magistrate, as it is now virtually a civil matter, and the breach of it an offence at common law. When a husband, or a wife so grossly fails in coujugal duty, that a remedy is sought for, recourse is generally had not to the Church, but to a civil court. The marriage service then ought to be performed in that court, where the parties can alone be made responsible for a breach of the contract. But if the marriage of two persons ought to be purely a religious contract and service, then let any one consider, whether in reason, such contract ought not to be performed agreeably to the religious sentiments of the parties immediately concerned, and whether such a mode would not be likely to be more binding, and have a more lasting influence upon their minds, than when performed according to the creeds and ceremonies of a church deemed by them erroneous. This is clearly a question of policy and of revenue on the part of the Established Church, as no good ground from scripture or reason can be made out for such monopoly. If the Quakers can properly marry amongst themselves, so might equally all other sects ; and Dissenters ought as men of honour and conscience, to protest against such partiality and oppression, and as knowing themselves to be loyal men and true, ought never to cease their efforts till every civil disability, imposed on the ground of differences of religious opinion, be removed. But even should this be attained, and all penal statutes against Dissenters as such, were removed, that might not alter the present mode of celebrating the marriage service in the Church ; and to this point I am desirous of calling the attention of your numerous readers ; I am the more induced to do this, as a member of parliament gave notice last session that he would early the next session bring the marriage act before the House for amendment. Would not this afford a proper opportunity for the Dissenters, who all complain of the grievance in question, to come forward as a body, and lay their complaint in a respectful but manly tone before parliament. If they were to act with zeal and union, their numbers and influence are of too much importance to be lightly disregarded ; Lord Sidmouth's bill is a case in point : If they are not wanting to themselves, similar exertions may produce similar results. Having thus briefly introduced the subject I trust some of your learned and able correspondents will enforce it in a more practical shape, and stimulate our Dissenting brethren to measures at once prompt and efficacious.

D. E.

On the Use of the Word BUT.

SIR,

IT is possible I may be mistaken : if I am I should be obliged to a better grammarian to set me right. The use of words is a matter of great importance, inasmuch as they are designed to give the clear and precise explanation of the thoughts of the mind ; I apprehend, however, that several of your correspondents, as well as other good writers, have erred in the use of the word *but*. This is a conjunction, which, when we meet with it, is a kind of stop to the sense, and prepares the mind to expect a change of subject, or an opposition to what went before. You shall have this, *but*—you shall not have that. In the passages I shall quote below, has not this word then been misused ?

" It cannot be doubted *but* the scribe, when he spoke these words,

meant the One Supreme."—*Gifford's Illucidation.*

" Four miles from this stands the Castle ; I have no doubt *but* the Romans occupied it, and possibly the Saxons and Danes."—*Hist. of Eng.*

" I take up the pen, not doubting *but* the remarks I offer will be received with candour and affection." —*Mr. Wright.*

The conjunction *that* would have distinctly conveyed the author's meaning.

Dr. Priestley appears to have been fond of the old fashioned way of uniting the two conjunctions in one place, by which means he certainly might convey an idea the direct contrary of what he intended. Thus

" It will not be denied *but that* any man has a right to employ one of his hands." He meant that he has the right.

" We have no occasion to enforce our principles by penal laws, having no doubt *but that* the clergy will be able to support them by reason and argument." Would not this seem to imply that we have a doubt ?

" But notwithstanding this, I have no doubt *but that* I shall make it appear perfectly intelligible to you." If the word *but* had been left out in these sentences his meaning would have been distinct. The following, in the same page with the last, clearly shews that this criticism is just.

" Indeed, if he had, many doubts could not *but* have arisen in his mind with respect to it." Here the *but* is proper.—See *Familiar Letters.*

Compare these two sentences ; the one conveying an idea contrary to the other, yet both formed alike.

" I trembling wak'd, and for a season after
Could not believe *but that* I was in hell."

He thought he was in hell.

" Having no doubt *but that* the clergy," &c. He had not a doubt of the matter, although the expression seems to convey it.

In the following sentence from Dr. Paley, appears a similar redundancy : " An agency so general *as* that we cannot discover its absence or assign its place."

Dr. Priestley is with great propriety regarded as an authority in the English language ; and I should have been fearful of remarking upon the use he makes of words were it not that it is well known Dr. Blair was himself guilty in his writings of the violation of all the rules he had laid down for the study and use of our language.

J. W.

Octavius Cæsar—William Pitt.

Aug. 18, 1815.

OCTAVIUS CÆSAR entering early into public life, was recommended no less by the celebrity of his uncle, *Julius Cæsar*, than by his own insinuating manners and address. *William Pitt*, also, on his first appearance, at an early age, was as much indebted to the high reputation of his father, *William Earl of Chatham*, as to a commanding and persuasive eloquence peculiarly his own. *Octavius Cæsar* at first, pretending great zeal for the republic, strenuously supported Cicero against the designs of Anthony, and raised an army for its preservation and defence. *William Pitt*, espousing with the same apparent warmth the great cause of his country, joined with Horne Tooke and other popular leaders, against the prevailing abuses of the representative system, and three times moved the House of Commons for their reform. *Octavius Cæsar*, afterwards coalescing with Anthony, turned his arms against the steady friends of the republic, and gave up Cicero to the vengeance of an enemy, by whom he was unjustly put to death. *William Pitt*, also, having with equal readiness, accepted office in alliance with the supporters of the old system, not only opposed successive motions for a reform in the representation of the people, but acquiesced in the prosecution of Horne Tooke, a more consistent reformer, on an unprecedented charge of High Treason. When, however, *Octavius Cæsar* abandoned the cause of the republic, he united with the adherents of his own family against the very men by whom his uncle had been publicly assassinated. But *William Pitt* on his apostacy, by a more flagrant dereliction of principle, entered into the closest union with the political enemies of his father, against his own early and most disinterested friends. *Octavius Cæsar*, also, when he had attained the object of his ambition, became the patron of literature and the arts ; and, after a long and prosperous administration, left his country in the enjoyment of external peace, and sole arbiter the destinies of the world. But W liam Pitt, in the plenitude of his po er, regardless of all liberal patrona involved his country in a most dis trous war: and, having contribu largely to the subjugation of Euro like another Phaeton, unable to gu the chariot of his father, peris amidst the conflagration which he so rashly caused. *Octavius Cæ.* therefore, having been, by the ge ral voice of his countrymen, procla ed *Augustus*, has been honoured the eulogy of eminent writers, in own and each succeeding age. Wh *William Pitt*, having no correspo ing claims to the applause of the torian or the poet, however flatte by his infatuated or interested ad rents, as the *saviour of his country* the *heaven-born minister*, will be n justly appreciated by posterity as bane of Europe, and the chief p moter of his country's fall. Wh therefore, in the comparison of th two men, the parallel at times pears so striking, the equally mar contrast is by no means favourabl the character of *William Pitt*.

SIR,

THE following extract from a bc seller's catalogue in Paris tend to shew in some degree the s of religion in France, which is happily confirmed by the report travellers into that unhappy coun

THEOLOGY.

" Selecti a sacris scripturis v culi ad usum stüdiosæ juventatis. partes in 12.

" On ne peut disconvenir que livres saints ne soient mainten presque aussi inconnus à nos je etudians que le Coran au les li mystiques de pretres' Indiens. Cet trait de toute lecriture sainte est posé de telle maniere que deux sets seulement appris chaque jour dant les cours des humanites peu en donner au moins cette connaiss generale de laquelle tant soit per instruit devroit se faire une oblig; rigoreuse."

TRANSLATION.

Verses selected from the Holy S tures for the use of young student

We cannot deny that our scriptures are at present almost as known to our young students as Coran or the mysterious book

Hindoo priests. This extract from them is formed in such a manner that two verses only learned every day during a course of classical studies will afford at least that general knowledge which every man, however slightly educated, should think himself bound to acquire. W. F.

Sir, *Oct* 6, 1815.

I WAS much gratified by remarking in your last number (x. 569.) a revival of the interesting inquiry already discussed in some former volumes of the Monthly Repository (the sixth in particular) relative to "the state of the human being after death."

After a serious and dispassionate perusal of much that has been stated in support of the various hypotheses to which the subject has given birth, I could wish to learn from any candid advocate of the opinion which supposes the human being wholly dissolved at death, in what sense we are to understand our Saviour's awful caution in Matt. x. 28, if man possess no principle that survives his dissolution ; or, what object we can in such a case conceive he could have in making any distinction between a mortal destructible being, and an immortal imperishable one co-existing in the human organization ?

The late Dr. Doddridge considered this passage as affording a *"certain* argument in proof of the existence of a soul in a separate state, and of its perception of that existence ; else (he added) the soul would be as properly killed as the body." *Family Expos.* V. i. S. 75. N. *h.* How far such a separate principle of the human organization may *exist* in a state of *perception* after death appears to me a very distinct question. Nor am I in the number of those who consider *that* question as of any material importance to the Christian's hope and comfort. To him, surely, it is the same *when* he enters into a state of happiness : whether directly on his dissolution, or after a long interval of suspended consciousness. In either case the prospect itself of future joy remains the same ; the promises of the gospel remain unaltered in each view of the subject ; and are in the one case as much as in the other, I trust, equally the object of his hope, his affection and pursuit.

V. M. H.

P. S. It may be observed that our Saviour does not speak of the soul as the *successive* principle of man ; or as the man in his second state, but seems to refer to both soul and body as *co-existing.*

Sir,

I WAS much pleased with seeing a physiological correspondence begun in the year 1813, in the Monthly Repository (viii. 443), by a writer who signs his name Cantabrigiensis, and which letter was answered at p. 734, under the signature of T. P. In hopes of reviving a controversy which may make more clear the doctrine of the resurrection, I have taken the liberty to lay before you the substance of the letter and reply, and my reasons for being dissatisfied with both.

Cantabrigiensis laments that scripture evidence is in favour of that system which holds man to be one and indivisible, and wholly mortal, an hypothesis with which natural appearances agree, because, owing to this, should there be a resurrection, not only will a large portion of time and consciousness be lost in the grave, but also

1. If man wholly dies, a resurrection does not appear to be within the bounds of probability.

2. A new creation cannot rightly be called a resurrection ; if it is allowed that there may be a new creation of an individual *myself* from the former being, it must also be allowed that there may be created from the same being an indefinite number of beings, all of them *myself,* if it is the will and power of the Creator which alone constitutes individuality and identity.

3. That the resurrection of Jesus is not a case in point. Never was his body corrupted, broken up and dissipated ; miraculous power was not required to re-create it, but only to enable it to re-act. If a total dissolution and separation takes place, it is not then a resurrection which was the apostolic doctrine, but a re-creation.

4. The hypothesis of Dr. Watts (Logic, P. 1. c. 6. § 6.) is but a supposition to avoid a difficulty. "Our *own bodies* must rise at the last day *for us to receive rewards and punishments in them ;* there may be, perhaps, *some original fibres* of each hu-

man body, some *stamina vitæ* or *pri-maeval seeds of life*, which may remain through all the stages of life, death and the grave; these may become the springs and principles of a resurrection, and sufficient to denominate it the same body. But, *if there be any such constant and vital atoms they are known to God only.*" To this principle, Dr. Priestley and some of his disciples appear willing to refer for *the principle of individuation.*

In consequence of these difficulties this writer asks, "If the immortality of the soul wants support from scripture, and the restoration of the same body involve in it a physical contradiction, how is the preservation of individual consciousness and the resurrection of the same man to be explained, understood or believed?

To this letter T. P. replied.

1. That the resurrection of the same body, if there be but one absolute and eternal cause, is within the bounds of probability. For the existence of every being, being only the result of the will and peculiar operation of this cause, the restoration of any being, and all its parts, however long its existence has been suspended, has not in it any thing impossible or improbable: the same creative cause still possessing the same power. If the originally created being be renewed in the same manner, the same created effect must be the result of the operation; and not any reason appears why the same exact operation cannot be renewed, as well as it was originally excited, continued and suspended by the Infinite Operator.

That this reasoning is confirmed by the historic evidence of the human mind. By night, the perception for useful and practical purposes is suspended; but this, instead of destroying, strengthens and restores perception and consciousness. In trances and suspended animation, the existence of life is only known by its preserving the body from putrefaction. Why then cannot Deity by immediate intervention suspend existence, disorganise the mechanism, and again with such alterations as new relations and circumstances may require to re-organise it?

2. The mind is a representation of external things, therefore a unity of person must be essentially connected with conscious identity. By a mul-

tiplication of persons exactly similar confusion would ensue, and such an idea arises from supposing matter and mind to have such an independent existence, that certain portions of each may constitute the same being. Such a view arises from mistaken notions o the Creator and the created. He is one and independent; all existence must be either Deity himself or the result of his operations; our future existence therefore must be the exercise of his power, and not from the ordinary operation of what is called a second cause.

The scripture compares death with sleep; *he slept with his fathers* is their language for death. Jesus *awakened* Lazarus out of sleep after he had been dead four days, and his body become putrid; and this he did by the intervention alone of that power which first formed man from the dust, the same power which increased the widow's cruse of oil, and at another time fed five thousand from five loaves and a few small fishes.

3. The resurrection of Jesus is in point to prove our resurrection, for though it was the same body raised, yet that body was raised changed to a spiritual body, as was evidenced by its becoming at will invisible, and by its ascending the heavens. Yet though spiritual its capability of being handled, its ability to eat and drink as also to converse, prove its identity, and were to his apostles sufficient evidence that he who could produce this varied effect of visibility and invisibility, materiality and apparent immateriality with conscious identity could in like manner raise their dead bodies and can do the same also by all who are in their graves.

If I have correctly stated the arguments of both these gentlemen, and I have so done to the best of my power, I am free to confess, Mr. Editor, that T. P. has not done justice to the objections of Cantabrigiensis; he appears to me instead of giving a philosophical answer as expected so as to have the subject intelligibly explained that it might be believed with the understanding, to have rather begged the question, resting the whole of his answer on the mighty power of God.

1. C. asserts that if a man wholly dies the resurrection of that man is not within the bounds of probability. T. P. instead of shewing that it is pro-

bable because it is rational, consistent with the nature of man, and therefore credible, contents himself by closing a long-metaphysical argument,
with asking why the same God who
first created and has now intervened
to suspend existence, cannot alter
and re-organize? But the question
put by C. remains unanswered. It
was not what Almighty power could
do, but as a reason for his after question he asserts the resurrection of the
same man to be improbable, and
wants it to be so explained that it
may be understood and believed.

2. The next difficulty of C. is, that
if the Deity creates him anew from
any part of himself, and that part
partakes of the conscious identity of
his present state of existence, he might
also equally well create from the large
remainder of himself, many other individual beings, all of whom would
have the same consciousness of identity; and that, after all, such *new creation would not be a resurrection.* I
have too good an opinion of the understanding of C., though known to
me only by his letter, to suppose
that he can be satisfied with the
vague and laboured answer of T. P.
He had sufficient evidence in nature
to have shewn that the future life
must be a resurrection of the one man
that died, and if that one man was
divided it was no longer a resurection;
instead of which, as in the former difficulty, he cuts the knot by a reference to the creative power of God;
that creative power which increased
the widow's oil and multiplied the
bread and fish in the hands of Jesus.
His argument and illustration go to
shew that because God has the power to multiply individuality with conscious identity to each part, therefore
he will not exercise it.

3. C. next asserts, that the resurrection of Jesus, his body never having been by corruption broken up
and separated, is not a case in point,
ours being a re-creation, but his a resurrection. To this T. P. replies by
endeavouring to prove that they are
in all points alike; but as his argument contradicts the scriptures which
bring only the resurrection of Jesus
as an evidence of the divine capability
and a manifestation of the divine intention to raise and judge mankind,
T. P. appears to me in this also to
have failed, and that his scriptural

quotations are foreign to the subject,
and some of them demand evidence
of his having justly applied them, particularly the spirituality and invisibility of Jesus prior to his ascension.

4. Lastly, C. asserts that the hypothesis of Dr. Watts, "That each
human being may have *some stamina
vitæ* or *primæval seeds of life*," is but
an hypothesis to get rid of a difficulty:
whether it be so or not, I will endeavour to examine in my next, should this
letter meet with your approbation. I
shall then endeavour to shew that the
difficulties Cantabrigiensis has brought
forward are not insurmountable, and
that though the resurrection of the
same body does involve in it many
absurdities as well as contradictions,
yet the resurrection of the man and
the preservation of his individual consciousness accords with nature as well
as scripture, and though it cannot be
demonstrated it may be so explained
as to be undertood and believed.

CREDO.

Tenterden, Dec. 7, 1815.

SIR,

OPENING the last number of your
valuable Repository, accidentally
at the 902d page, the name of Mr.
Soame Jenyns met my eye. With
your respectable correspondent, Mr.
Rutt, I also am old enough to have
in perfect recollection the interest excited by the above-mentioned gentleman's view of the internal evidence of
the Christian religion. The different
opinions entertained of the writer are
also in my recollection; not a few
considering it as a covert attack on
Christianity itself. I confess myself
to have been strongly tempted, at
the time, to entertain this latter opinion. But that patriotism is not a
Christian virtue, is one of those positive assertions which appears to me
to be totally destitute of proof.

It is with pleasure admitted, that
there is an almost irresistible charm
in a spirit of universal benevolence.
Actuated by it we resemble our Creator in his most glorious attribute; in
his disinterested, inexhaustible and
everlasting goodness: nor do I conceive there to be any thing inconsistent with this, in a pure and generous love to our country.

If ever there was a true patriot,
Jesus Christ was that person. His
public ministry was principally con-

fined to Jerusalem and Judea. To Jews were his instructions delivered; and for the benefit of his countrymen were his miracles wrought. When they returned all with ingratitude and hatred, he wept over them ; nor do we meet with two more pathetic passages in the course of his history, than those which applied to the devoted city he had at the time in view : passages, which the reader cannot but have in recollection. Even after his crucifixion, upon his again meeting his disciples, when he directed them to go into all the world and preach the gospel to every creature, he added those memorable words, *beginning at Jerusalem.* Yet in perfect consistency with this true patriotism, was also his love to the whole world.

The Apostle Paul's patriotism was such that he even wished himself accursed from, or rather in Christ ; i. e. that he might, like his Master, die the accursed death of the cross, for his brethren, his kinsmen according to the flesh, could he but effect their conversion. Yet no one will for a moment call in question his unconfined benevolence and charity.

Mr. Soame Jenyns's definition of patriotism possibly deluded him. " *That patriotism is to oppress all other countries, to advance the imaginary prosperity of our own.*" But this is a false and wholly unfounded definition. It might be a convenient argument in favour of the slave-trade ; but a true patriot would be ashamed to use it.

Assuredly, neither Jesus Christ, nor his apostles, ever interfered in the political regulations of their own, or any other countries. Their commissions did not apply to them. The kingdom of Christ was not of this world. Yet I cannot but consider them as *the noblest and most disinterested band of patriots the world ever knew;* and that they were equally, in the most important sense of the term, *true philanthropists.*

If a person is an affectionate father of a family, may he not also be a good neighbour ? Does neighbourly kindness prevent love to our country ? or love to our country, benevolence to all mankind ? *The first circle may be of very confined diameter : the last, embrace the universe.* If in error, in the above statement, I shall be happy in receiving the correction of any of

your correspondents. Leaving fore the discussion of this subj[e] abler pens, and expressing the cordial good wishes for the incr[e] success of your highly useful sitory,

I am, &c.
                                    L.

Sir,   *Nov.* 16, 1

AS you occasionally devote pages to general literat[ure] am induced to offer you, from book, a short extract concerni[ng] island, of which we had sc[arcely] heard, till it became connected the fortunes of that extraor[dinary] man, who, whether an Empe[ror] a captive, will be regarded as indeed, at least, in the world' mate, compared with any who mere accidents of birth have royal or imperial ; for, accord a plebeian sentiment which o[nce es] caped a courtly poet,

Pigmies are pigmies still, though p
        on Alps,
And pyramids are pyramids in vale[s]

or, as was said of Grotius, a man is like a famous statue, to mired, whether on or off the pe[destal]

The passage which I propose fer you is the following, fron *moires of the affairs of France* the reign of the present king, the XIVth. Done out of I 18mo. 1675.

" 1646. *Portolongona,* a pl[ace si]tuated in the isle of *Elb,* lying Tuscan Sea, between the Co[ast] of Italy and Corsica, which wa tofore usurped from its own Lord by a Captain of the E[mperor] Charles the Vth, in the year after that delivered into the sion of his son Philip the II[d] whose successors held it ever was now besieged and taken French army. In the midst island rises a spring, on this a the more admirable, that its are observed to hold proportio[n] the length of the days of the y[ear] such manner, that when they the longest, the stream is drive a mill, but when at the s 'tis almost dry."—Mem. p. 38.

After making due allowance propensities of a credulous ag[e] will remain, to have occasion[ed] statement, some very unusual

ances respecting this spring, of which perhaps one of your readers, versed in Natural History, can communicate a further account.

HYDROPHILUS.

Sir,

SOMETIME ago I copied the following paragraph from Ware's Cumberland Pacquet, dated 21st Feb. 1815, a choice thing for the 19th century.

"The Archbishop of Cashel has refused to consecrate (at the instance of Lady Caher) the new Church erected at Caher, in Ireland, on account of its not being built due East and West as the Canon requires; it is a well finished piece of Grecian architecture."

I have been puzzled to find out what can be done with the church; but having lately observed that a strong disposition has manifested itself among the natives to resist the tithes, it has occurred to me that it may serve as barracks, that the privileges of the Clergy may be protected by the soldiery.

W. D.

Mrs. Cappe, on the Adaptation of Divine Revelation to the Human Mind.
York, Dec. 6th, 1815.

Sir,

I REJOICE to see the subject of the British and Foreign School Society warmly advocated by a much respected writer in your liberal Magazine [x. 614.] for I cannot but consider that excellent institution, and its no less illustrious sister, the British and Foreign Bible Society, as the brightest luminaries of the European firmament, at this time in many other respects sufficiently dark and gloomy. This darkness, however, is not to be ascribed to the want of many excellent writers, who have given the most clear, comprehensive and consolatory views of the government and providence of God, and especially of his goodness and parental care as from time to time developed in the writings of the Old and New Testament, and more particularly in their striking adaptation to the mental progress and the peculiar situation and circumstances of the long series of generations to whom they were successively vouchsafed.

In this view I have lately perused with the greatest interest the elaborate work of the excellent Dr. Cogan, and I am induced to send you a few reflections suggested by that work, and by some other recent publications which if not further illustrative of some of the subjects on which they treat, may not perhaps be deemed wholly irrelevant.* What at this hour Mr. Editor, is the state of those countries in respect of religion who do not possess the scriptures? What is the still more deplorable state of those where they are set at nought, or ridiculed, or despised, or miserably obscured and debased by the most bigoted, abject, superstition? Let a great neighbouring nation give the answer. But we will not exact it of them. Alas! it may be read in that total demoralization which has infected all ranks of men among them. We may read it in the frivolous amusements, the ferocious vindictive passions, the never-ceasing round of trifling, seductive dissipation which makes shipwreck of all sober reflection, of every virtuous sentiment and of every patriotic, benevolent or useful pursuit.

C. C.

On the striking adaptation of the leading objects of divine revelation to the known phenomena of the human mind, as contradistinguished to that of the inferior animals, demonstrating the strong presumptive evidence arising from thence, that both have the same great and good Being for their Author.

It appears that the following are the great primary outlines of distinction between the human race and the various tribes of inferior animals placed below them.

1. The power of discriminating between virtue and vice, and of making their election accordingly; from whence arises human responsibility.

2nd. In that comprehension of mind which is capable of looking forward beyond the present to the future, and of regulating their actions according to certain, or even highly probable remote consequences.

3rd. In the power of deliberating

* See an excellent Sermon on the Religious and Moral Improvement of Mankind, preached at Leeds, in June last, by the Rev. Charles Wellbeloved. Longman and Co. London.

upon and choosing in respect of two modes of action, which is the wisest the safest or the best, whether in its present or its future consequences; or, in other words, of the freedom of the will.

4th. In the power of speech, and of inventing or adopting various methods of giving stability and permanence to numerous classes of ideas and discoveries, which would otherwise have been merely fugitive, or which at least must have perished with the inventors or their immediate successors; such as the discovery of letters, and of various ingenious machinery, which enable the people of one age to possess as it were by inheritance the moral and mental acquirements of past generations, and thus to begin their career at nearly the same point where that of their predecessors closed.

5thly, and preeminently. The power of discovering and of looking up to the great. Source of all these endowments, "in whom we live and move and have our being," whether as discoverable through the medium of his works, or by express revelation from himself; of earnestly deprecating his displeasure; of humbly and devoutly adoring his goodness; of thanking him for all his mercies; and of putting our whole trust and confidence in his parental care.

These primary qualities distinctly mark the species, and are equally found to discriminate between the brute creation and man, who is permitted to rule over them, whether in his most highly cultivated and civilized state, or in that of the wild hunter of the forest; for it is abundantly evident that the magnificent structure of virtue and knowledge raised by divine revelation, and by the successful cultivation of the arts and sciences, and which places the one at such an immeasurable distance from the other, rests equally for its basis on these original superior endowments.

In respect of the first of these, namely, the power of discriminating between virtue and vice, and thus of determining our choice, provision is made for its cultivation and improvement in the very frame of nature, by the opposite effects visibly consequent on the two modes of conduct wherever other previous circumstances are at all similar; the one, producing

health, peace and tranquillity; other, disease, inquietude, discon and remorse; together with the train of malignant tormenting sions, which render the wicked the troubled sea that cannot r But as these most important c quences, however demonstrable, not produce conviction in the unless calmly weighed and duly sidered, it would appear highly bable, antecedent to all inquiry the fact, that some additional would be vouchsafed by the great ther of mercies during the early of the world, and when such a tal process would be impractica for the guide and direction of his ble, erring children; and as we that in the Jewish and Christian pensations, this most desirable has actually been afforded, the str est presumption hence arises that are what they assume to be, di revelations.

But it is not from the mere pr bility that our great and mer Creator, considering the goodness nifested in all the works of his tion, would in some other way su the unavoidable defects of wan knowledge and experience, the dom and fitness of the manne which this is done, by prohib and command, is a still stronger sumptive evidence in favour of reality of such a revelation. an infant, allured by the brillianc a lighted taper, stretches out his to grasp the flame, a prudent p would not merely prevent his it at the moment, but would against similar attempts in futur indeed by endeavouring to con him of the fatal consequences o experiment deduced from the n of the destructive element, but express prohibition on pain o highest displeasure; and it is a ing fact, that on this very prin the positive commands of the logue are founded.

Again, it is remarkable tha Jewish and Christian dispens pay particular attention to th provement and expansion of th culty of the human mind which the second line of demarcation upon which so much of the res bility, virtue and happiness character depends; namely, t power of looking forward beyon sent enjoyments or privations to future consequences and of acting accordingly.

The young man it is true, sees, or may see, that if he is not sober, provident and industrious whilst he is able to labour, that poverty and wretchedness will be his portion when he is helpless and old: the husbandman knows assuredly that if he does not cultivate his land and sow his seed, he can have no harvest. These things are so plain and obvious that they need not the additional light of revelation to demonstrate them more clearly.

But there are a great variety of other obligations and duties dependent upon the higher advancement and perfection of this faculty in all its various relations and bearings, which although equally important in their final results are not equally obvious ; and it might therefore be expected from a divine revelation, that especial attention would be paid to its progressive extension and improvement, and we find accordingly that this has actually been done throughout the whole series of the Jewish and Christian dispensations. The promise of a son to Abraham, the medium of his future eminent distinction, was not fulfilled until great old age : the inheritance of the promised land was not obtained by his descendants until many successive generations had passed away. Now it is evident that the slow fulfilment of these interesting promises would have a powerful tendency to widen the distinction between man and the inferior animals, who act merely from the present impulse : to gain him the constant habit of looking up to God as the spring of all his hopes, the great source of all his blessings, whether past, present, or to come ; and to enable him to form more just and exalted sentiments of that great Being, with whom " one day is as a thousand years, and a thousand years as but one day."

It is true that after the {Israelites were put in possession of the promised land, national and sometimes individual rewards and punishments, generally followed immediately as the fruits of obedience or rebellion ; but this was absolutely necessary as an example to the neighbouring nations, as well as a repeated proof to themselves, of the moral government of God which was the leading object of their selection ; it merely formed an exception for a very important purpose, and does not invalidate the general argument. On the same merciful and benevolent principle, that of teaching and inuring a rude, ignorant people to look beyond the present to the future, were the solemn denunciations all along delivered by holy men and prophets ; and for the further cultivation of this important intellectual process, were the promises, at first very obscure, and afterwards more explicitly given through a long series of ages, of the future advent of that illustrious personage, who was destined in the counsels of divine wisdom, when the world should be sufficiently prepared for his reception, " to put away sin, and to bring in everlasting righteousness." And when at length this new dispensation did actually take place, a similar gracious and wise plan of distant remuneration or punishment was not only strictly adhered to, but is carried much farther, the sanction being principally placed in a future unseen world, the great interests of which may require, and not unfrequently do actually require, a partial, or even a complete sacrifice of the interests of the present.

But as in this dispensation, unlike the former, complete conviction of the fulfilment of the promises could not be obtained by experience, the everlasting barriers that separate this world from the future were mercifully thrown open. A brother of the human race, of the most consummate wisdom, of perfect virtue, wholly devoted to the will of his heavenly father, is called to enter upon his public career of unceasing beneficence under circumstances which would not merely subject him to all the various evils of extreme poverty, but to the contumely, the contempt and reproach of his deluded, infatuated countrymen. He was to be despised and rejected of men, a man of sorrows and acquainted with grief ;" and after having endured every species of ignominy, suffering and contempt, that malice could invent, or cruelty inflict, the whole was to terminate in a lingering, and excruciatingly painful death. Of this fatal termination he was himself fully apprized from the very first of his public ministry, which to a mind like his, of the keenest mental and moral sensibility, could not fail to encircle the scourge and the cross with tenfold horrors. But did he shrink from the dreadful ordeal ? "God called, and did the Son of God refuse to answer ?"* He well knew that nothing short of all this would decisively prove that those things which are so highly esteemed among men, a life of ease, of sensual enjoyment, great riches, high station, worldly honours and distinction, are of no estimation in the sight of God ; that the truest humility may be united with the greatest dignity of character, and the acutest sensibility with the most unshaken fortitude. He knew that his public death in this dreadful manner, in which there could not be any deception, was requisite to demonstrate its reality :—That on this wholly depended the proof from fact, first, by his triumphant resurrection, that death is not the end of man ; and secondly, by his ascension to the right hand of God, and from thence dispensing the gifts of the spirit, to prove also from fact, the reality of a future retribution ;—to convince his faithful followers that those " who by patient continuance in well doing, seek for glory, honour and immortality," should finally attain everlasting life.

Can we wonder then, when we seriously reflect upon all these things, that the apostles, who were the living witnesses of such transcendant virtue, filled with the highest admiration, and impelled by holy ardour, should speak of their ascended Lord in the highly figurative, hyperbolic eastern phraseology, as having been made "sin for us"—of having been made a willing sacrifice—as giving himself for our sins ; not indeed to make God propitious, but to render his erring imperfect creature, so liable to transgression, so incapable of knowing his true interest, more worthy of the divine favour ; of raising him higher in the scale of intellectual being, and of rendering him meet, when all sublunary things shall have lost their influence, for that eternal felicity which

" eye hath not seen, nor ear heard, neither hath it entered into the heart of man to conceive."

Thirdly, the power of deliberating upon and of choosing between two different modes of action in respect of all their various and complicated results, is not only taken for granted, but more strongly, more promptly, and with greater authority called into action by revelation, than by the slow deductions of reason, although eventually it perfectly harmonizes with them. " Thou shalt not steal," "Thou shalt not commit adultery," are prohibitions, which the most ignorant, if acquainted with the meaning of the terms, cannot fail to comprehend ; whereas, on the contrary, to see the foundation on which they rest, to feel the importance whether to the individual or to society at large, of holding the right of private property sacred, fully to appreciate the misery, the wretchedness, the jealousies, the endless mistrusts, together with the whole train of baneful, malignant passions engendered and excited by a breach of the nuptial tie, requires a very considerable degree of previous mental and moral progress; and hence the unspeakable importance of a positive divine command to the great bulk of mankind, at all times and in all ages.

It is readily admitted, that there have occasionally arisen sages and philosophers who have been capable of making some of these important deductions without the aid of divine revelation, and of thence becoming the guides and instructors of others ; but notwithstanding the praise so justly due to their virtuous exertions, it is very obvious to anticipate how very small would be the fruit of their labours without consulting the page of history, not bearing the stamp of divine authority.†

Again. A written history of the series of extraordinary interpositions of divine providence for the guidance and improvement of the human race, presupposes and requires the possession of those faculties which form the fourth line of demarcation between man and the inferior animals, and is therefore exclusively suited to them.

---

* See, on the Great Importance of the Public Ministry of Christ, Discourse XX. page 388, of a volume of Sermons by the late Rev. Newcome Cappe ; edited by Cath. Cappe. 1815.

† See Vol. iv. p. 71, of Dr. Cogan's admirable treatise.

Could not an account of these extra-ordinary events have been first publicly preached, and afterwards committed to writing, the knowledge of them if it had reached us at all, could only have been conveyed on the frail, uncertain authority of oral tradition, casually floating down the stream of time from generation to generation.

In respect even of that great event, momentous · in its consequences · beyond all others, the resurrection of Christ, although the very same care had been taken in the arrangements of divine providence which is now so apparent, and although the people of that day might therefore have been equally convinced of its reality, yet had not the relation been circumstantially committed to writing by eye-witnesses, we of this distant age should not only have received the account, loaded with and obscured by many human inventions, but we should have wanted all those various proofs, arising from minute circumstances incidentally noticed, with which it now abounds, and on which the firm conviction of its truth, in respect of us, so essentially depends.

In respect of the fifth and last mentioned line of demarcation, namely the unspeakable privilege of being capable of forming some small conception of the adorable and ever-blessed God; of confiding in his goodness, and of rendering him, however imperfectly, the humble ascription of adoration and praise, there is no need to prove that without an especial revelation these most desirable privileges, important beyond all others, would not have been obtained.

Exeter, Jan. 8, 1816.

SIR,

IN your number for July last, (x. 459,) it was proposed to raise a fund in order to defray the expense of republishing some important works, which though not perhaps directly Unitarian, might have great efficacy in weakening the influence of religious bigotry, and preparing for the diffusion of our principles: and reference was particularly made to Bishop Taylor's Liberty of Prophesying, and Whitby's Last Thoughts, with his four Sermons, published with them. These, and particularly the latter, are almost inaccessible to the public:

and the Last Thoughts ought, in justice to the learned Commentator, to be in the hands of every one who possesses his commentary on the New Testament, because they furnish his own corrections of his work. It was also stated that a gentleman, who seemed impressed with the importance of the object, offered a *loan* of 100*l.* towards the accomplishment of it, if others could be found to unite with him.

Your correspondent A. Z. in the number for September, (x. 549,) inquires for particulars respecting my plan, and my opinion as to the necessary funds. The subject has often been in my thoughts, but I have seldom had time to commit my ideas to paper.

I think the simplest way would be for a few individuals to raise among them, *by way of loan*, from 200*l.* to 300*l.*, and be joint proprietors of the editions republished, which (if the selection of books were made with due caution,) would always be a good security for the money advanced. The books should be printed neatly, but as cheap as possible; and the price should be regulated by the probable time of sale, the cost of advertising, &c. For instance, if the expenses of *reprinting* any book be 75*l.* for 1000 copies, in 8vo.; allow 25*l.* for advertising at different periods of the sale, and consider it as employed at once for the purpose. Then suppose the impression to sell completely in eight years; and allow interest for five, (as small sums on their return could not easily be made profitable:) the whole return, to remunerate the proprietors, should be 125*l.* Now for booksellers' profit and the publisher's commission on the selling price, we must allow 48 per cent on this *cost* price. The price to the public would therefore be about 3*s.* 8*d.* in quires, or say 4*s.* 6*d.* in extra boards. I should think it probable that for Whitby's Last Thoughts encouragement might be expected from the societies.

The experiment might be made, in the first instance, with the Last Thoughts, where I should suppose there can be but little risk, and which, if I had any capital to spare, I would myself immediately reprint, upon the above mentioned system of estimating the price. If any friend to free inquiry feel disposed to do it, any advice or assistance I can give in the execution of the object will be at his service.

Shall I request from the able reviewer of Townsend's Armageddon, to furnish us with a few more *horrors*, particularly such as have their service in the popular ideas of atonement. I am persuaded that the exposure of such representations is of great service : they shew us how careful we should be to keep close to the doctrines of revelation; and the contemplation of them must make us thankful that we have not so learned Christ.

In this connexion, allow me to beg Mr. Frend (if his views respecting the death of Christ really differ, in essence, from those commonly entertained by Unitarians,) to state them, and the grounds of them. Why, if he possess important truth, and believe us to be in error, does he withhold the communication of it from the readers of the Repository ?

In reference to Dr. Lloyd's proposal for a pamphlet on the Greek article, I wish to observe, that if he have any decisive facts and principles *in addition* to those which Winstanley,[*] Gregory Blunt and Middleton himself, have advanced, (which, however, to my mind are satisfactory,) I should conceive that a subscription might easily be raised to defray the expense, and should readily take a share in it. Dr. Lloyd does not refer at all to what has been done by Blunt and Winstanley; and as their tracts are not now easily accessible, he will perhaps excuse my referring him to the Appendix, No. III. in the *second* edition of Unitarianism the Doctrine of the Gospel. If on perusing this outline of the proof which has *already* been given, that Mr. Sharp's renderings of the controverted passage are not required by the Greek idiom, Dr. L.

----

can give ground for his present confidence that he can offer a fresh demonstration against them, let him announce his intention of preparing it for publication, as soon as a subscription is raised to defray the expense of printing it : and I cannot doubt that he will meet with sufficient encouragement to proceed.

I will avail myself of this opportunity to say that I have a youth with me preparing for York, where he will be ready to go next session, and I suppose may gain admittance without any great difficulty. He is, however, so circumstanced, that he cannot defray those expenses which are not included in the Foundation. I shall, therefore, feel myself particularly obliged to any of your readers, who can obtain for him, (or shew me how to obtain) such assistance from funds, exhibitions, &c. as will enable him to go on in the object to which he desires to devote himself. If any one having this power, will favour me with a line on the subject, I think I can give him satisfactory proof that the assistance would be well directed.

I am, Sir.

Yours very truly,

L. CARPENTER.

Mansfield, Jan. 19, 1816.

SIR,

HAVING been favoured, by the Rev. Joseph Hunter of Bath, with a list of Dr. Doddridge's pupils (accompanied by many valuable remarks), and by the Rev. Wm. Tullideph Procter, of Prescot, with a list of those who were educated by Mr. Horsey, after the resignation of Mr. Belsham ; I have been employed in collecting information from every quarter accessible to me, that I might be enabled to execute my purpose of drawing up as complete an account as possible of the seminaries established at Northampton and Daventry. But, my hope of receiving the necessary intelligence concerning the Academy at Daventry having been so long disappointed, I find myself compelled (on the supposition that the work is not undertaken by some other hand,) again to request the grant of that information without which I cannot proceed. I shall be happy to receive it, not only from the gentle-

----

* Winstanley's excellent little pamphlet has lately been attacked by Bishop Burgess, who seems determined that he will, *pedibus et unguibus*, exterminate Unitarianism, if not Unitarians themselves. I have not had an opportunity yet of seeing the Bishop's tract ; but I am not apprehensive as to the result.

men who have already been particularly mentioned, (M. Rep, x. 391,) but from any other who may be able and willing to afford it. Communications (post paid), addressed to me at Mansfield, Nottinghamshire (which is now the place of my fixed residence) are once more earnestly solicited, and will be thankfully received, by, Sir,

Yours sincerely,
JOSIAH TOWNSEND.

GLEANINGS; OR, SELECTIONS AND REFLECTIONS MADE IN A COURSE OF GENERAL READING.

No. CCXLI.

Tahtar (or Tartar) *Hospitality.*

When the French Resident to the Khan of the Tahtars was travelling through Tartary, on his route to Constantinople, on arriving towards dusk, at a village in Bessarabia, under the conduct of an officer, appointed by the Khan, they found every inhabitant standing at his door; and on inquiring the cause of this of a venerable old man whose interesting appearance had determined the travellers to make choice of him as their host), he answered—" Our eagerness to come to our doors is only to prove that our houses are inhabited ; their uniformity preserves an equality, and my good star alone has procured me the happiness of having you for my guest. We consider the exercise of hospitality as a privilege."

Frenchman. " Pray tell me, would you treat the first with the same humanity ?"

Old Man. " The only distinction we make, is to go and meet the wretched, whom misery always renders timid; in this case the pleasure of assisting him is the right of the person who first approaches."

Frenchman. " The law of *Mohammed* cannot be followed with greater exactitude."

Old Man. " Nor do we believe that, in exercising our hospitality, we obey this divine law. *We are* MEN *before we are Mahometans : humanity*

has dictated our customs, and they are more ancient than the law."
De Tott's Memoires. Vol. I. Pt. i. p. 212.

No. CXLI.
Popish Renderings.

The Papists, in their versions of the scriptures into the modern tongues, have contrived by various falsifications, to make them speak the language of their *Missals* and *Breviaries,* in order to sanctify their novel rites by the authority of the apostles, and make the people believe that they had been practised from the times even of the gospel. Thus to countenance the practice of *beatifying* or *making saints* in the Church, they have rendered a passage of St. James, v. 11, not as it ought to be, *Behold how we account those blessed*, but *Behold how we* BE-ATIFY *those who have suffered with constancy :* and in favour also of their *processions,* where it is said, Heb. xi 30, *that the walls of Jericho fell down, after they compassed it about seven days,* their versions render it, *after a* PRO-CESSION *of seven days around it.* And to give the better colour to their trade of *pilgrimages,* St. Paul, according to their versions, requires it, as the qualification of *a good widow, that she have lodged* PILGRIMS. 1 Tim. v. 10. And St. *John* praises *Gaius,* for having dealt *faithfully with* PILGRIMS iii John 5.

See Serces' *Popery an Enemy to Scripture,* quoted in *Middleton's Letter from Rome,* Works, v. 49. Note *f.*

No. CXLII.
King by the Grace of God.

In the French *National Assembly,* in 1789, Petion de Villeneuve proposed giving to the King the title of " King of the French by the Consent of the Nation," and suppressing the form of " by the Grace of God."—" It is calumniating God," cried he; " was Charles the IXth, too, King by the Grace of God?"

Biographie Moderne, iii. 93.

REVIEW.

" Still pleased to praise, yet not afraid to blame."——Pope.

Art I.—*Evangelical Christianity considered, and shewn to be synonimous with Unitarianism, in a Course of Lectures on some of the most controverted Points of Christian Doctrine, addressed to Trinitarians.* By John Grundy, one of the Ministers of the Congregation assembling in the Chapel in Cross Street, Manchester. In Two Volumes. 8vo. Pp. 538 and 552. Eaton. 1813, 1814.

IN the winter of 1813, Mr. Grundy began a course of Unitarian Lectures at Manchester, on the alternate Sunday evenings. Public attention was immediately aroused. The Chapel in which the Lectures were delivered was crowded to excess; in four or five other places of worship opposition-lectures were regularly delivered; pamphlets also appeared against the Lecturer; the strangest reports were put in circulation; and some of the more timid Unitarians were alarmed. Under these circumstances, Mr. Grundy published the Lectures singly soon after their delivery. Illness interrupted him in his course; and he devoted his hours of involuntary retirement to the collection of the Lectures already published into volumes, adding a few others which he would have delivered if at the time his health had been sufficiently recovered. This is the history of the present publication; which independently of its merits recommends it strongly to the notice of the advocates of free inquiry and the friends of truth.

The following are the Contents of the volumes:—Vol. I. The Unity of God. Explanation of the Trinity. The Existence of a Devil. The distinct Existence and Personality of the Holy Spirit. The Impersonality of the Holy Spirit. The Deity of Jesus Christ. Nine Hundred Passages of Scripture proving the Unity of God. The Pre-existence and Divinity of Jesus Christ. Extracts from various Authors on the Trinity. The Humanity of Jesus Christ. Appendix addressed to the Members of the New Jerusalem Church.——Vol. II. The Opinions of Christians in the First Century on the Person of Christ.

Opinions in the Second and Third Centuries. Opinions after the Third Century. The Atonement. Ditto. The Eternity of Future Torments. Ditto. Ditto. The Plenary Inspiration of the Scriptures. The Miraculous Conception and Nativity. Ditto. Original Sin. Practical Summary.

From these tables it will appear that the volumes contain a body of Unitarian Divinity. The author agrees in opinion for the most part with the well-known writers of his denomination, of whom he makes a free but judicious, and *acknowledged** use. At the same time, he is no servile follower or blind partizan; he dares to differ from those whom he most honours; and in justification of himself, he presents his readers with his reasons, which are never captious, impertinent or weak.

Although the subjects of the Lectures are not novel, the mode in which they are discussed gives them an appearance of originality. The liveliness of a personal address relieves the heaviness of a continued argument, and the dullness of verbal criticism; and Mr. Grundy's manner of writing (and this is said to be more particularly the case with his manner of speaking) keeps the attention awake from first to last, and allows neither listlessness nor lassitude.

On the Athanasian Creed no argument would have been so striking as the following anecdote, which the experience of every one that has been much in the world will shew to be by no means incredible.

" I know a clergyman of some celebrity, who previously to going to Church on one of the Saint's Days, specified, said, ' I am going to read the Athanasian Creed; may God forgive me, for I utterly disbelieve it." I. 34.

The following is the conclusion of the address to the members of the New

---

* We employ this word in order to hint to some of our polemical brethren that it is scarcely candid to avail themselves of the researches of others without acknowledgment or reference; *ne gloriari libeat alienis bonis. Bonas in partes, Lector, accipias velim.*

Jerusalem Church (the Swedenborgians),—

"I think that you and we are engaged only in a war of words. I believe that if we could divest ourselves of prejudice and passion, and calmly explain, so as thoroughly to *understand* each other, we should very nearly accord. I believe that as far as you allow reason, coolly and deliberately to influence your decisions, you go hand in hand with us; but that when you separate from us, you then give up reason, you use mystical, unintelligible arguments; that many of you do not yourselves thoroughly understand what you mean, and of course, that you can never give a lucid explanation to others.

"I am inclined to think that many of us accord with you in your idea of the New Jerusalem; of a time fast approaching when there shall be a family of Christians in practice as well as in theory, Jesus Christ being the *head* or chief cornerstone,—when all shall be happy in themselves, happy with each other. But I also believe that you are making many Unitarians; and that ere this arrive, you will yourselves become Unitarians; that whilst you acknowledge that there is but *one* Jehovah, and that his name is ONE, you will also receive Jesus, the anointed, as his messenger, welcome him as an elder brother, hail him as the great Messiah, the father of the long enduring age, till all things shall be subdued unto him, and he shall deliver up his kingdom to his Father, that God Jehovah may be all in all." I. 513, 514.

There is considerable force in the following observations at the close of the Lectures on the Miraculous Conception; they were penned in the true spirit of a reformer; they immediately follow a clear recapitulation of the evidence against the genuineness and authenticity of the introductory chapters of Matthew and Luke:

"The spuriousness of these chapters does not at all affect the genuineness or authenticity of the remainder of the gospel history. I know that a doubt has arisen in some well-disposed minds, whether it would not be better to let the question alone, lest if we once begin to pull down we should not know where to stop. My friends, it is this objection which prevents any reformation from taking place in the established religion of this country. There are many well-disposed minds in the church, who, like Archbishop Tillotson, would be glad to be well rid of the Athanasian Creed, and parts of the liturgy; who yet earnestly say, "Let us not begin to amend; because it is impossible to say,

where we may stop!" Indeed this objection is not at all consistent with our profession as Protestants. It is not the principle upon which the *Reformers* acted, not the principle upon which the *Apostles* acted, not the principle upon which our *Saviour* acted. And to the objection allow me to answer briefly, that every sound and discriminating mind *will* know where to stop. It will stop where *good evidence* ceases. It is the part of judgment to discriminate. And I conceive it to be an equal proof of a weak mind, to *believe* all, or to *doubt* of all; especially when the degrees of evidence are so disproportionate. And in the case before us, the difference is great and obvious. The gospel histories in general are founded on a rock. Their genuineness and authenticity both collectively and individually are unshaken and incapable of being shaken. But I am not therefore bound to believe that there is not a particle of dross mixed with the gold. Nor am I to believe, that by removing this dross, I must infallibly destroy the metal. On the contrary I contend that I render it more pure and valuable." II. 496—498.

In his view of the practical effects of the opposite religious systems of Unitarianism and Calvinism, Mr. Grundy relates an anecdote which serves to shew the dangerous use to which the latter scheme of doctrine may be applied; scarcely a year passes that does not furnish equally strong proofs of the same alarming fact:—

"I have formerly mentioned an occurrence which chilled me with horror, more, I think, than any other circumstance connected with religion, which has come within my own knowledge. It was the sight of a letter from a person of a most depraved and abandoned character, whose life had consisted of a series of frauds and vices, and who, at length, by the laws of his country had been condemned to die. The letter was written the day before his execution—written in exultation and triumph—in exultation at the all-atoning blood and merits of Jesus—in triumph, that on the morrow, he was going to fly into his arms!! Funeral Sermons for those who have lived in profligacy but died in faith, may probably have been heard by most. I have shuddered when I have heard the praises pronounced upon such characters, and assertions made that they were then *angels in heaven*." II. 539, 540. *Note.*

The peculiar excellence of the Lectures is that they are scriptural. The author has brought forward, examined, compared and explained every text relating to the most important subjects; this may be seen particularly in the Lectures on the Unity of God, the Miraculous Conception and Eternal Torments. Whether his exposition of these be satisfactory or not, all must allow that this is the true way of deciding a theological question.

If any subjects of moment, in controversy between Unitarians and Calvinists, be passed over by Mr. Grundy, they are the special influences of the Holy Spirit, Imputed Righteousness, and perhaps Election and Reprobation : the first, the source of all the enthusiasm in the Christian world; the second, the fascinating tenet, which in its strongest operation, lulls all Christian inquisitiveness concerning truth and all anxiety concerning virtue ; the third, the astounding, fearful doctrine *(horrible decretum,* says Calvin himself) of which the most rigidly orthodox in the present day are somewhat suspicious, and of which they never willingly exhibit one side, the dark and portentous side of reprobation, to the world. We suggest this, not as a defect in the present work, but as an addition which the author may possibly hereafter make.

We cannot drop our imperfect notice of these volumes without recommending them strongly to our readers and thanking Mr. Grundy for the valuable addition which he has made to the defences of Unitarian, or in another word, *Evangelical* truth.

Art. II.—*A Sermon on Universal Benevolence : containing some Reflections on Religious Persecution, and the alleged Proceedings at Nismes,* By the Rev. James Archer. 8vo. Booker. 1816.

MR. ARCHER is a Catholic Priest, and we understand one of the most popular preachers in his communion. This sermon is stated on the title-page to be " Printed at the Particular Request of the Nobility, Gentry, and others, before whom it was delivered, in the Roman Catholic Chapel at Bath, on Sunday, the 10th, and at Warwick Street, Golden Square, on Sunday, the 17th of December, 1815." We note this circumstance, because it is creditable to the feelings of the Roman Catholic body, and may tend to counteract the unfavourable impression which may

have been made on the minds of some of the friends of liberty by the late outrageous proceedings of the Roman Catholics in the South of France and elsewhere.

The sermon is not remarkable for its argument or eloquence, but it contains passages which are entitled on a moral and Christian account to the highest praise.

On the subject of *heresy,* Mr. Archer says,

" Never be so uncharitable and so gross as indiscriminately to give the harsh and odious appellation of of *heretics* to all those who belong not to our communion. That word implies *guilt* as well as *error.* You have been taught in your catechisms, that heresy is an *obstinate* error in matters of faith. He only is a *heretic,* who, when he has discovered truth, wilfully and perversely, from human respects, for worldly interests, or some such unworthy object, shuts his mind against it : or who obstinately or negligently refuses · to be at the pains necessary for discovering it ; and how can you presume to pronounce of any individual man, that this is his case, unless he acknowledges it ? Can you assert, that the doctrines which you know to be true, have been proposed to him in such a light of evidence, as to give conviction to his mind : or that he is not so satisfied with his own creed, as to preclude every idea of an obligation to make farther inquiry ? Those who carefully seek the truth, and sincerely follow the best light they can obtain in their respective circumstances, are innocent in the sight of God, and secure of his acceptance, whatever may be the errors into which they involuntarily fall. *Who art thou, then, that judgest another man's servant ? To his own master he standeth or falleth."*—— Pp. 11, 12.

Having asserted these Christian and charitable sentiments, the worthy preacher proceeds to remark upon the persecution of the Protestants in the South of France, as follows :

" This is the doctrine of the Catholic Church—a doctrine, which I have often inculcated to you, but to which I feel it particularly incumbent on me to call your attention at this time, when we are daily receiving afflicting accounts from the continent, of atrocities committed by Catholics against Protestants, in the southern provinces of a neighbouring country, and when great endeavours are made in this country to have these atrocities be considered as the consequences of our religious system. Of the facts I know nothing, but from the public journals, and I sincerely hope they will be found to have been much exaggerated; and from recent information have more and more reason to believe, that all has proceeded, at least, as much from political, as from religious animosity. But, be that as it may, if truly stated, they are a violation of every moral, religious and civil duty : in the sight of God they are an abomination, and in the view of every well regulated state must be ranked among the worst of crimes. Too often, alas! among Christians of every denomination has fanaticism usurped the place of religion ; abused the multitude, and led them to every excess : but *the truth of God remaineth for ever.* Certain, however, it is, that religious persecution, whatever its mode, whatever its measure, is directly opposite to the spirit of Christianity, and must be reprobated by every virtuous man. Hence St. Martin, in the fifth century, refused to communicate with those who had persecuted the Priscillianists : and, in the seventeenth century, Fenelon would not enter on the mission to convert the Protestants of Poitou, till the soldiery was withdrawn, that every idea of coercion might

be done away. To the spirit of these great and good men, may the Catholics of Nismes if really guilty of what is imputed to them, be regenerated in Jesus Christ. May his celestial graces change their hearts. May they, by their subsequent conduct, atone for the scandal they have given to the universal church, and to no portion of it more than to their Catholic brethren in this kingdom." Pp. 13, 14.

It is natural for a Roman Catholic to ascribe the atrocities at Nismes to political causes, but we have no doubt that they are the immediate effect of religious bigotry. If it be so, however, the Roman Catholics in general ought not to suffer for this reason in public opinion, whilst, as in the present instance, they disavow the principle of persecution. Let all the preachers of the different sects imitate Mr. Archer in his real *Catholicism* and our religious differences will be no longer political evils.

POETRY.

To-morrow.—An American Poem.

HOW sweet to the heart is the thought
of to-morrow
When hope's fairy pictures bright colours
display ;
How sweet when we can from futurity borrow
A balm for the griefs that afflict us to-day !

When wearisome sickness has taught me
to languish
For health and the comforts it bears on its
wing,
Let me hope (oh ! how soon it would lessen my anguish,)
That to-morrow will ease and security
bring.

When travelling alone, quite forlorn, unbefriended
Sweet to hope that to-morrow my wand'rings will cease,
That at home then with care sympathetic
attended
I shall rest unmolested, and slumber in
peace.

Or when from those friends of my heart
long divided,
The fond expectation, with joy how replete !
That from far distant regions by providence
guided,
To-morrow will see us most happily meet.

When six days of labour each other succeeding
With hurry and toil have my spirits opprest,
What pleasure to think as the last is receeding
To-morrow will be a sweet sabbath of rest !

And when the vain shadows of life are retiring,
When life is fast fleeting and death is in
sight,
The Christian believing, exulting, expiring,
Beholds a to-morrow of endless delight.

But the infidel then, surely sees no to-morrow,
Yet he knows that his moments are hasting
away ;
Poor wretch ! can he feel without heart-rending sorrow
That his joy and his life will expire with
to-day ?

To Ignota,
On reading her Verses (x. 752.)

My youth's rude lyre's unstrung by time,
Be thine, dear Girl, a poet's praise,
And chant, in many a lasting rhyme,
The minstrel's themes of other days.

The Chiefs, in armour richly dight
The wrongs ambition's victims knew,

Virtues, the prize of lawless might,
Or love by fortune " link'd to woe."

Yet live there those, I feel it true,
Whose fates a happier love has join'd ;
Whose age, delighted, can review
The days that time has cast behind.

And, should it prove, dear Girl, thy lot
Connubial joys and cares to blend,
In city, vil, or lonely cot,
Still meet content, a constant friend·

And still engage thy sprightly powers
To charm the dear, domestic board,
What time some rare, unbending hours,
May *Themis* to the Muse afford.

Or should intruding sorrows come,
Probations of thy mortal hour,
Be thine to greet, like me, a home,
Where love can smile at fortune's pow'r.

And, long as age computes thy years,
Bright scenes may Christian hope display,
Where earth's quick-varying smiles and
    tears
Shall usher heav'n's unchanging day.
                                    IGNOTUS.

Lines written on the first page of an An-
    nual Pocket·Book.

    Deo duce omnia bona.

" All is best though we oft doubt,
What th' unsearchable dispose,
Of highest wisdom brings about,
And ever best found in the close."
                                    MILTON.

Suspense, alternate hope and fear
Await, with me, the rising year ;
And where's the mortal can divine
He shall await the year's decline ?
Hence, should the tide of fortune flow
A course I long have ceas'd to know,
Nor disappointment still be near,
To smile, as oft, at hope's career ;
My grateful praise may heav'n receive,
Worthless, though all that man can give.
Or, while the promis'd good delays,
If few and evil be my days,
Still trusting, howsoe'er they close,
That *all is best* in Heav'n's dispose.
*Jan.*7, 1816.   SENILIUS.

    The Virgin's Cradle Hymn.
    (From an old Newspaper.)
[Found inscribed under a print of the Vir-
    gin Mary and her Child, at a small pub-

lic house of a Catholic village in Germany.

Dormi Jesu ! Mater ridet,
Quæ tam dulcem somnum videt,
    Dormi, Jesu ! blandule !
Si non dormis, Mater plorat,
Inter fila cautans orat,
    Blande, veni, somnule !

    Translation.

Sleep, sweet babe, my cares beguiling,
Mother sits beside thee smiling ;
    Sleep, my darling ! tenderly :
If thou sleep not, mother mourneth,
Singing, as her wheel she turneth,
    Come, soft slumber ! balmily.

Latin Epigrams, by Mons. Marron, Pre-
    sident of the Protestant Consistory, at
    Paris, communicated by him to the
    Editor.

    Ad Theologos Montalbanenses.

Dipthongus Christi quondam diviserat una,
    Et nunc dipthongus dividit una gregem.
O nimium indignos Magni præcepta Ma-
        gistri
    Discipulos diro qui pede sancta terunt !
Hoc spectat te, GASCE ; hoc adversam tibi
        turbam ;
    Dissidiis promptus ni medeatur amor.

    Orthodoxia et Hæresis.

    Orthodoxia.

Mens humana novos incassum tendit in
        ausus :
    Quam trivere atavi, sola terenda via.
Metior Immensum, cancellis claudar ut
        arctis,
    Nec falli mecum, nec dubitare licet.

    Hæresis.

Diversis diversa locis ego temporibusque,
    Ex Acherontæo gurgite nata feror.
Vndique probrosa lacerant me verbera lin-
        guæ ;
    Quoque magis nescis, sum mage tetra
        tibi.
Virtuti et meritis jungar licet, optima
        quæque
    Viperea credor sola necare lue.
Nec miseranda tamen, dum sim mihi con-
        scia recti :
    Hoc sperno hostiles tegmine tuta minas.
                    IRENOPHILVS LVTETIANVS.
Ipsis Kal. Febr. CIƆIƆCCCXIII.

OBITUARY.

*Character of the late Rev. Dr. Toulmin,
by Mr. Howe.*

(See X. 462, 523; 661, 665.)

Bridport, January 6, 1815.

MR. EDITOR,

"**B**E not slothful, but followers of them who through faith and patience inherit the promises," is the admonition of the writer to the Hebrews. The death of our late venerable friend, Dr. Toulmin, led me to direct the attention of my people, to whom he was well known, and by whom he was highly respected, to the excellences which adorned his character, and to exhibit him as an example to his fellow-christians, of the pious, amiable and attractive virtues of pure religion. I have since read, with much satisfaction, the judicious account given of him by his worthy colleague. If you think the following extract from the Discourse which, agreeably to public notice, I delivered at Bridport on this occasion, about three weeks after this eminent servant of God was called " to rest from his labours," tends to strengthen the salutary impressions which Mr. Kentish's Sermon is calculated to make upon the mind of the reader, it is at your service for insertion in your valuable Repository.

THOMAS HOWE.

1 Cor. xv. 58. After illustrating the several parts of the text, the preacher thus proceeded. " I have chosen this subject with a view to the recent death of my reverend and beloved brother, and your highly esteemed and amiable friend Dr. Toulmin. Acquainted with him in my early youth, my veneration for his character, and my affection for him, produced by the sweetness of his disposition, and the goodness of his heart, increasing in proportion to my intimacy with him, I feel myself peculiarly called on, by a sense of duty to departed worth, to pay a tribute of respect to his memory. In describing the excellences of his character, as an exemplary Christian, a useful member of society, an ardent friend to the best interests of mankind, a judicious, faithful, serious minister of the gospel, I shall take for my guide the several particulars of the apostolic exhortation in the text; and shew in what respects he became, what Paul exhorted the Corinthian Christians to be ' steadfast, unmoveable, progressive and persevering in the work of the Lord.'

" Our deceased friend was steadfast. Persuaded that the New Testament contains the revealed will of God, communicated to mankind by his well-beloved son Jesus Christ, he considered it incumbent on him, as a professing Christian, to deduce his articles of faith and rules of conduct from this pure source, and not from creeds and formularies of human device. He gave every possible proof which one in his circumstances could exhibit, of his searching the sacred records of divine truth, with a pious, humble and candid mind. This led him in the progress of his inquiries, to somewhat different views of the Christian doctrine, from those he entertained in the *early* part of his ministry. ' The truth as it is in Jesus,' was his noble aim, the object worthy of his diligent pursuit, and when he thought he had attained it, he openly and conscientiously avowed his convictions. These he steadfastly maintained. Persuaded that Unitarianism is the pure doctrine of the gospel, he was its zealous but liberal advocate. From the current language of the sacred scriptures, our judicious friend deduced the supremacy, unity and overruling providence of God. He plainly perceived that our blessed master Jesus Christ did not assume the glory of the wonderful powers he possessed to himself, independently of any other being, but often ascribed them to his heavenly Father as their source, that he was in the language of an apostle, ' a man approved of God, by miracles and wonders and signs which God did by him.' Whatever were our friend's views of the doctrines of religion, it must be admitted by those who differ the most widely from him in sentiment, that he did not vindicate them in the spirit of arrogance and illiberality. He pronounced no anathemas on those who rejected them. Though steadfast in maintaining what appeared to his mind to be Christian truth, always respecting the rights of private judgment, he treated other denominations of religious professors with the most amiable candour, and generous liberality. For the justness of this remark, let the appeal be made to his controversial writings, in which I believe there is not a *single sentence*, that Christian candour would blush to read and wish to erase.

" The Rev. Dr. Toulmin was also ' unmoveable,' nobly preserving his integrity, ' amidst good report and evil report,' amidst allurements and oppositions. There was a period in the recollection of many of us, when the open avowal of the sentiments he maintained, and a fervent zeal in the cause of civil and religious liberty exposed its advocates, in some places, even to popular vengeance, as well as to the misrepresentations and harsh censures of those from whom better things might have been expected. When, however, a violent party spirit, either in religion or politics, is excited, it is apt to blind the judgment and to rouse the irritable passions of persons who are *generally* mild, candid and amiable. This which drove that eminently pious philosopher and undaunted theologian Dr. Priestley, from Birmingham, his place of abode, and eventually from his native country, endangered in some degree the personal safety of his esteemed friend Dr. Toulmin, then residing at Taunton. They had, however, abundant sources of consolation in the testimony of an approving conscience, and were disposed to adopt the petition of their divine Master respecting their persecutors, on which the former published a sermon suited to the occasion, breathing the most truly Christian spirit, ' Father, forgive them, for they know not what they do.' Let us, however, turn aside our views, my friends, from these melancholy scenes, so disgraceful to this age and country, with a fervent wish and ardent hope, that they may never more be repeated, and with sincere congratulation on the prevalence at present of a milder spirit, among both religious and political parties. Though to be zealous in what we deem a good cause is commendable, it should never be forgotten by us, that ' the wrath of man worketh not the righteousness of God.'

" By a mysterious, but no doubt wise and benevolent, dispensation of providence, Dr. Toulmin was visited with great relative afflictions. He was, however, supported under them by the animating principles of religion. These, notwithstanding the tenderness of his feelings, and an *occasional* depression of the animal spirits to which he was subject, enabled him to preserve a general composure, an *habitual cheerfulness* of mind, the offspring of true rational piety devoid of superstition, and of Christian hope with its eye fixed on heaven.

" Our deceased friend was not only ' steadfast and unmoveable, but he also always abounded in the work of the Lord.' On this point, it is very difficult to do justice to his character. He was unwearied in his labours to promote the noble cause in which as a Christian minister he was engaged, and to advance the knowledge, holiness and happiness of his fellow-creatures. Besides his stated ministrations to his own congregation, he was often called on by other societies of protestant dissenters, sometimes to advocate the cause of Christian truth, and at others to plead for the relief of human distress, and few ministers were better qualified for either of these purposes. As he has occasionally officiated in this place, you cannot but recollect, my friends, the seriousness and decorum of his deportment in the pulpit, and the strain of rational, fervent, practical piety, scriptural argument, and Christian affection for the

best interest of his hearers, by which his discourses were distinguished. He was, in the genuine sense of the term, an *evangelical gospel* preacher. His sermons were neither philosophical essays, unsuitable to the capacities and circumstances of men in general, nor wild incoherent rhapsodies, in which the hearers are treated as having *passions* only, and *no understanding.* When he entered the pulpit, he never forgot that he was a professed minister of the glorious gospel of Christ, and that the service required of Christians, is declared to be ' a *reasonable* service.'

" His many publications on a great variety of subjects, chiefly religious, or connected with the history of religion, bear witness to his unwearied ' labours in the Lord.' They bespeak an active mind, a sound judgment, a candid disposition, and a benevolent heart; all which were engaged in the daily investigation of some of the most important points of human inquiry. His acquisitions in theology and general literature, in ecclesiastical history, and biography, more especially, were very extensive, and few persons have applied the talents God has given them, and the learning, human and divine, they have acquired to a nobler and more useful purpose. Many a just tribute of respect and veneration will,

ble correspondent * of mine who well knew his worth, thus characterizes him. ' Our excellent friend was' *an Israelite indeed ;* ' a man of great simplicity and singleness of heart, of inflexible integrity, and one of the most active, zealous, able, useful and valuable men among us, whose memory is entitled to the highest esteem and regard of all the friends of truth, liberty and virtue.'

" We were favoured with an opportunity of hearing the instructions of Dr. Toulmin in this place, about the middle of the preceding year. From his age, and the distance of his residence from us, we had reason to apprehend it would be the *last,* and thus it has proved. It seems indeed as if he then came among us to bid his final adieu, and to pronounce the blessing of an aged minister and friend on this society, (for which he always professed great respect and fervent wishes for its prosperity,) before his eyes were closed and his tongue rendered silent, by the icy hand of death. We shall now see him no more in this world. No more shall we converse with this intelligent and cheerful companion, this humble and affectionate friend. No more shall we hear the words of heavenly wisdom drop from his lips; but ' though dead, he yet speaketh.' He speaketh by the exemplary character he has left behind him. He speaketh by the many useful

---

* The Rev. Thomas Jervis, of Leeds.

writings which were dictated by his pious and enlightened mind. Though his revered head now lies low in the dust, we may still have him for our instructor in useful knowledge, and what is of most importance, in the way of Christian truth and holiness which leads to immortal bliss. Neither are we to entertain the gloomy idea of an *eternal* separation. If the junction of virtuous friends hereafter be not a pleasing delusion, but sanctioned by reason and confirmed by the Christian revelation, (as I think it is,) we may hope, if we are diligent and faithful in our master's service, to renew our delightful intercourse with this eminent servant of God, at the illustrious period ' when Christ, who is our life, shall appear, and all his true followers shall appear with him in glory.' "

On Sunday the 24th of December, 1815, died at St. Ives, Cornwall, in the 65th year of her age, Mrs. MARY GIBBS, wife of Mr. Silvanus Gibbs of that town, to whom she was united nearly forty years, and by him had five children, two only of whom survive to lament her loss.

Her illness was of short duration: and though her health had been rather indifferent for the last eleven or twelve years, she encountered a journey, forwards and backwards, of 148 miles, about four months since, with little difficulty, in order to visit (and, as the event has proved, take her final adieu of,) the writer of this article. The Monday evening preceding her dissolution, she was seized with a violent pain in her stomach, and shortly afterwards brought up a quantity of blood. Five years before she was attacked in a similar manner; and has been frequently subject to pain in the stomach, though she had experienced nothing of the kind in the course of the last two months. Tuesday and Wednesday she became worse, and, at different times, emitted six or seven quarts of blood; but towards the close of Wednesday the medicine prescribed, for the time, prevented any farther evacuation; and, notwithstanding her feeble and low state, she seemed to be getting better. Most unfortunately, however, a fire happened in the town that night, and the alarm excited by it so overpowered her spirits, that, from this moment, she grew progressively worse, but suffering little pain; and about 7 o'clock on the ensuing Sunday morning, she yielded up her life, with perfect resignation, into the

hands of her Creator, without a struggle or a groan! Happy are those who die in the Lord; they rest from their labours—and their works follow them.

> " So fades a summer cloud away ;
> So sinks the gale when storms are o'er ;
> So gently shuts the eye of day ;
> So dies a wave along the shore."

How mysterious to us are the dispensations of Providence: let us learn submission to its will! When our kindred and friends are separated from us by the awful hand of death, it surely ought to stimulate us to closely examine our own hearts, and thoroughly prepare them for that solemn period to which we are all rapidly hastening; for " the Son of man cometh at an hour when we think not—and happy will be those whom, when he cometh, he shall find watching. The venerated person who has just left us, never affected any *singularity* on the score of religion; nor was she particularly attached to any *system*. She believed that holiness of heart and life are, in the estimation of the Almighty, of far superior importance to those disputed points of doctrine which have severed the Christian world into so many sects and parties. It was her opinion that " whatsoever a man soweth, that he will also reap; that he who soweth to his flesh, from the flesh will reap destruction; but he who soweth to the spirit, from the spirit will reap everlasting life:" and that " the hour cometh, in which all that are in their graves shall come forth; they that have done good, to the resurrection of life; and they that have done evil, to the resurrection of condemnation." From her youth, she regularly attended divine worship in the chapel belonging to the Weslean Methodists; though, I believe, she never enrolled herself as a *member* of that community. Her attachment to this people was doubtlessly much strengthened in consequence of her father, and some of her other relations, having been among the first of the inhabitants of St. Ives who joined the cause of Mr. Wesley; and who always continued his warmest admirers and most steady friends. In times of *persecution*, that gentleman and his colleagues uniformly found an asylum among her relatives: a minister, at one time, lay concealed for several weeks in her father's house, when closely sought after by an infamous *press-gang!* The early Methodists underwent considerable persecution in that place; and once had their little chapel demolished by an ignorant, infatuated mob, headed by some of the Corporation, who ought to have known and respected the sacred rights and liberties of Englishmen! But, poor deluded souls, they considered themselves staunch members and champions of the Established Church, and thought, by such a procedure, they were rendering her an important service!!! At present, the major part of the inhabitants are either Methodists or favourably disposed towards them: so great is the change wrought there, as well as in other parts of the kingdom, in favour of the liberties of conscience. Though the writer is obliged, after much reading and reflection on the subject, to dissent from some doctrines which are held by the Methodists as essential to salvation, (and which he himself once believed to be so,) yet he cannot withhold his tribute of praise justly due to their labours and indefatigable exertions in Cornwall, in civilizing and christianizing the rude parts of the county, and in exciting a taste for reading and obtaining usesul knowledge; which has, of late years, produced a considerable spirit of religious inquiry among the inhabitants in general, and will, no doubt, eventually lead to their embracing and openly professing purer and more dignified sentiments of the gospel.

In the excellent subject of this article, society has lost one of its most amiable and most worthy members; and her family their steady counsellor and most affection friend. As a wife, she was truly industrious, economical, neat, discreet and prudent; as a parent, she bore a tender regard to her offspring, and was ever solicitous to inculcate in them habits of usefulness, decency, sobriety and virtuous dispositions; and as a member of society, she was mild and affable in her demeanour, and universally esteemed by all who knew her.—Peace be to her memory.

Perhaps the following tribute of real affection, which was composed shortly after the writer was made acquainted with the death of his beloved parent, may not be an unsuitable appendage to what precedes:

And must I think it! is she gone,
  My secret heart's exulting boast?

And does she heedless hear my groan?
  And is she ever, ever lost?
Eternity will not efface
  Those records dear of transports past;
Thy image at our last embrace;
  Ah! little thought we 'twas our last!
Burns.

Dearest of earthly comforts! art thou fled?
Alas! thou'rt number'd with the peaceful dead.
Thy radiant smile I shall no more behold,
Nor hear thy tongue its kind advice unfold:
With accents sweet thy lips no more shall move,
To sooth my woes in strains of tender love.
Affectionate and kind thou wert to me
From earliest youth; and from moroseness free.
Though troubles dire I many years have borne,
Thy sympathizing heart was ever warm
In my behalf, t' impart thy gen'rous care,
And raise my boding mind from dark despair.
But now, in silent gloom, I must deplore
My friend torn from me, ne'er to see her more!
O gracious Heav'n! thy consolation send,
And to my anguish put a speedy end:
Bid my sad spirit from the dust arise,
And fix my hope above the azure skies.
When frail our natures, and when prone to grief,
The glorious *Gospel* gives the best relief;
It bids us look beyond the mournful tomb,
And dry our tears,—for there's a *World to come!*
This world, with all its cares, will pass away,
And that succeed with bright and spotless day.
In that pure region, may those weeping eyes
Again behold (and there for ever prize)
My worthy parent who is gone before,
And safely landed on yon blissful shore;
Where pain and sorrow shall no more destroy
The holy calm which saints shall there enjoy.
O, sov'reign balm for my deep wounded heart,
To join *her* there, and never, never part!
To tread those fields of never-fading green,
And view with rapture the surrounding scene:
With all our friends Jehovah's name adore,
And praise his boundless *love* for evermore.
S. G.

Plymouth-Dock, Jan. 7, 1816.

At Turnham Green, aged 62, the Rev. Christopher Lake Moody, LL. D. greatly respected by all who knew him, for his estimable virtues, his social qualities, his native talents and his literary acquirements.

The late Dr. Zouch (whose death was recently announced) was a gentleman, of considerable literary attainments. He was of Trinity College, Cambridge—took his B. A. degree 1761, and was third Wrangler of the year—proceeded to M. A. 1764, and D. D. 1802. In 1765 he gained the Seatonian Prize, *The Crucifixion.*

About thirty years ago he published an enlarged edition of " *Walton's Lives of Donne, Wotton,*" &c. in 4to; and in 1808, " *The Life of Sir Philip Sidney.*"—It is said the Doctor refused a Bishopric some years ago, on account of his age and bodily infirmities. He was uncle to the Earl of Lonsdale.

INTELLIGENCE.

Persecution of the French Protestants.

Library, Redcross Street, Tuesday, Nov. 21, 1815.

At an Extraordinary Meeting of the General Body of Protestant Dissenting Ministers of the Three Denominations, summoned to take into consideration the propriety of applying to his Majesty's Government to interpose their good offices with the Government of France, for the Protection of the French Protestants, who appear to be suffering the most violent and inhuman persecution on account of their attachment to that Religion, in defence of which our Forefathers shed their blood,

Rev. D. TAYLOR, in the Chair,

It was unanimously resolved,

1. That we have learned from our holy religion, and from happy experience that liberty of conscience and of religious worship, is one of the best blessings of the Almighty Creator.

2. That enjoying this inestimable blessing ourselves through the signal mercy of Divine Providence, and the equity and liberality of the legislature and government of these realms, we cannot but desire its universal extension.

3. That we are prompted by the liveliest sympathy to take an interest in the condition of our Protestant brethren on the Continent of Europe, whose fathers, in concert with our own, at the period of the Reformation, recovered the precious rights of conscience at the expence of their property and lives.

4. That we had hoped from the experience of the inefficacy, impolicy and impiety of persecution, and from the spread of knowledge throughout Europe, that the time was at length

come when religious liberty was universally acknowledged to be the inalienable birth-right of every human being.

5. That we have learned with astonishment and grief the state of our Protestant brethren in the South of France, who are suffering under the horrors of persecution—their dwellings and property ravaged or consumed, numbers of them driven into exile, their pastors silenced, their temples shut up, their children dragged from the arms of their parents, in order to be re-baptized according to the Roman Catholic ritual, and whole families brutally massacred.

6. That our surprise and horror at these merciless deeds are aggravated by the recollection that the present government of France has been in a great measure restored and sustained by British treasure, British valour, and British blood, exertions and sacrifices, which his Majesty's government has avowedly made for the promotion and preservation of the peace, independence and happiness of all Europe, and which must be considered as made in vain, if our French Protestant brethren be not protected by the restored government of France, from the fury of savage persecutors, whether single or combined.

7. That we are not uninformed, that the events which we behold, with so much concern and alarm, are attempted to be accounted for and excused by the state of political parties in France—but that whilst, as ministers of religion, we hold it to be a sacred duty to stand aloof from all political factions, whether at home or abroad, we cannot suffer this pretext to deaden our sympathy with our suffering Protestant brethren—because the history of persecution in all ages shews, that

persecutors have done homage to liberty and charity, by disguising their cruelty under political pretences—and because, in the present instance, it appears that the Protestants of France, have been, and are, as much divided in their political opinions and predilections as any other body of Frenchmen—that the rage of the persecutors has been directed against Protestants without distinction, and that Protestants only appear to be the objects of their unchristian resentment and vengeance.

8. That the British government has often distinguished itself by using its power and influence with due respect to the independence of other nations, on behalf of the injured and oppressed for conscience sake,—and that the august House of Brunswick have been justly and honourably considered, from the era of their happy accession to the throne of these realms, as the Protectors of the Protestant interest of Europe.

9. That it appears to us that never was there a more urgent call for the interposition of the government of the United Kingdom, than in the present instance, when persecution is raging in France against such as hold the same religious faith which is professed by Britons, and that under the reign of a monarch, who owes his restoration—to the supreme power—to the energy—valour and perseverance of the arms of this Protestant Empire.

10. That on these grounds a deputation be appointed to represent our sentiments to his Majesty's government, and to express our confidence that the ministers of his royal highness the Prince Regent will employ their good offices with the Court of France, in obtaining for our suffering Protestant brethren immediate relief and permanent security.

11. That such deputation consist of the Rev. Robert Aspland, the Rev. Mark Wilks, the Rev. William Newman, and the Rev. Thomas Morgan, Librarian and Secretary.

DAN. TAYLOR, Chairman.

12. That the thanks of this body be given to the Chairman, for his conduct in the Chair.

T. MORGAN, Secretary.

Library, Redcross Street, Tuesday,
Nov. 28, 1815.

At an Extraordinary Meeting of the General Body of Protestant Dissenting Ministers of the Three Denominations, convened to receive the Report of their Deputation, appointed on the 21st instant to request an interview with his Majesty's Government on the subject of the Persecution of our Protestant Brethren in France,

Rev. A. REES, D. D. F. R. S. F. L. S. in the Chair.

It was unanimously Resolved,

1. That this meeting receives with the highest gratification the assurances of his Majesty's government, to the deputation from this body ; that they feel the deepest regret at the dreadful scenes lately witnessed in France, and that they are using, and will continue to use, their best efforts in their communications with the French government to secure to all classes of French subjects, whether Protestant or Catholic, the full enjoyment of the advantages which the Constitutional Charter provided for them.

2. That deeply compassionating the case of our French Protestant brethren, who have been despoiled of their goods, and deprived of their houses of prayer, we recommend it to our brethren, and our congregations throughout the United Kingdom, to raise pecuniary contributions for the relief of these sufferers for conscience sake.

3. That a Committee of inquiry, superintendance and distribution, consisting of six members of each denomination, be appointed to correspond with our brethren in the country on the subject of the foregoing resolution, and otherwise to carry the said resolution into effect.

4. That the following gentlemen constitute the said Committee :—

The Rev. R. Aspland, J. Barrett, T. Belsham, G. Burder, J. Coates, T. Cloutt, F. Cox, S. Evans, J. Hawkesley, J. Hughes, Dr. Lindsay, W. Newman, Dr. Rees, Dr. Rippon, G. Smallfield, Dr. Smith, J. Townsend, D. Taylor, Dr. Waugh, Mark Wilks, Dr. Winter.

5. That with the consent of the trustees of the late Dr. Williams, the Meetings of the Committee be held at the Library, Redcross Street, where all communications and contributions will be received by the Rev. Thomas Morgan, the Librarian and Secretary to the three denominations.

6. That publicity be given to these and the foregoing Resolutions under the direction of the Committee.

A. REES, Chairman.

That the Chairman be requested to accept the thanks of the Body, for his conduct at this Meeting.

THOS. MORGAN, Secretary.

Williams's Library, Red Cross Street, January 12, 1816.

At a Meeting of the Committee appointed by the General Body of Protestant Dissenting Ministers of the Three Denominations, "for the Purpose of Inquiry, Superintendance, and Distribution of the Funds which may be contributed for Relief of the French Protestants, suffering for Conscience sake,"

It was unanimously Resolved,

1. That this Committee have observed, with astonishment and regret, that attempts are making, through the medium of the press, to defeat their object, by misrepresenting their motives; and although the Committee know too well what is due to that respectable body by which they are deputed, to engage in useless warfare with those who are labouring to stifle that public sympathy which it is the wish of the body to excite, they yet owe it to their own character, and to the cause they have undertaken, to state candidly, once for all, the motives by which they have been guided and the end they have in view.

2. That this Committee, therefore, utterly disclaim for themselves and their constituents all party feelings on a question which they conceive to be purely and exclusively religious; but that if they must be ranked with a party, they are happy in ranking, on this occasion, with that of the government which listened so candidly to their representations,——entered so warmly into their feelings,—and pledged itself so readily to employ its good offices for the same humane purpose to which their interference has been directed.

3. That if any man, calling himself a Protestant, can impute to Dissenting ministers, as a crime, that they have shewn themselves peculiarly forward, on this occasion, he should remember that they are the descendants of those who, for conscience sake suffered the spoiling of their goods, and the loss of their lives; and to whose constancy, under persecution, it is chiefly owing that religious liberty is now firmly established in this favoured land.

4. That, feeling the value of this inestimable blessing, they could not but be deeply interested by any occurrence which might threaten its loss to those, especially with whom they are united by the tie of a common faith, and a common worship; nor could they refuse their sympathy or their relief to men bleeding in the same cause which rendered the memory of their fathers immortal.

5. That though letters have been received from ministers in France, expressing objections to the interference of their Protestant brethren in England, the Committee have ascertained, from *unquestionable evidence*, that some of those letters have been written under *constraint;* and that others have been dictated by an apprehension (it is hoped erroneous) lest such an interference should injure them in the estimation of their own government, or rather, lest it should expose them to the fury of a faction, which sets the government itself at defiance; and the Committee are of opinion, that if complaints are cautiously uttered, they deserve, the more, the consideration and sympathy of those who are aware of the cause in which this caution originates.

6. That while they have been acting consistently with their own principles, in expressing their abhorrence of all religious persecution, by whomsoever practised or countenanced, they cannot but suppose that in contributing to alleviate the distresses of the French Protestants, they are coinciding with the intentions of the French government, which has been taking measures to suppress those outrages, which, if not suppressed, must occasion its own disgrace, and compromise its own safety.

7. That, in the subscriptions and collections already made,—in the spirit which is spreading throughout the kingdom,—and in the prospect that this spirit will ultimately enable them to grant important relief to their suffering brethren, and to the widows and orphans of the victims of persecution, the Committee have the most flattering encouragement to persevere. They do, therefore, most earnestly

request the unremitting co-operation of Protestants of every Denomination, but especially of Protestant Dissenters, in this labour of love; and they express their confident assurance that in contributing to this object, without suffering their zeal to be damped by any insinuations or assertions whatever, they are promoting the spread and establishment of that Christian Liberty which is the greatest earthly boon that Heaven can bestow on man. Signed (by Order of the Committee),
THOMAS MORGAN, Secretary.

———

At a Special General Meeting of the Committee of the Protestant Society for the Protection of Religious Liberty, convened at the New London Tavern, Cheapside, London, on November 21, 1815, " To consider the Situation of the persecuted Protestants of France,"
SAMUEL MILLS, Esq. in the Chair,
 It was Resolved,

1. That *this* Committee, who include several Members of the National Church, and who represent many hundred Congregations of Protestant Dissenters—and of Friends to Religious Liberty of all denominations, throughout England and Wales— have been taught by their forefathers, and ever will continue, to regard the right of every man, in every age, and in every country, to worship God according to his conscience, as an inviolable—sacred—unalienable right— which no individuals—or governments —or legislatures can, without injustice and oppression, directly or indirectly, infringe.

2. That although this Committee be principally appointed to protect the Religious Freedom of their fellow-countrymen, in their native land—yet they should be undeserving of the name of Britons—of Protestants—of Christians—and even of men, if their philanthropy was not extensive as the world—if they did not sympathize with all who suffer for conscience sake—if they did not regard religious persecution, by any sect, with alarm and abhorrence—and if they did not endeavour to effect its extinction, by the exertion of every energy which they possess.

3. That at this period—when instruction is so extensively diffused— when liberal principles are so generally professed—when the most solemn

treaties and the most powerful Monarchs have recognized the rights of conscience—and when nations of every Christian denomination have united in resistance to oppression and for the restoration of permanent peace and prosperity to Europe and to the world —This Committee did hope that perfect Religious Liberty would have been regarded as an hallowed plant— and that all nations would have participated the beneficial fruits, which that liberty must produce.

4. That, even if this Committee could have apprehended that persecution would revive, they could not have expected that revival, and especially the revival of a persecution of Protestants, under princes—whose obvious interests demanded conciliation—whose predecessors had devastated their own countries by former persecutions— some of whose Charters had declared " that all religions should be protected by the law, and that all men of all religious professions should be eligible to the offices of state"—and whose restoration and continued authority had been chiefly effected and upheld by Protestant liberality, Protestant perseverance, Protestant valour, and Protestant support.

5. That the Committee have therefore learnt, with astonishment and deep regret, that at Nismes, and other places in the South of France, a systematic and cruel persecution of Protestants has excited, since the restoration of the present Monarch to the Throne of that Country; that their property has been seized or destroyed —that many persons interesting for their youth and sex, or respectable for their industry, their loyalty, their virtue and their piety, have been assassinated—that an aged, venerable and excellent Minister of Religion has been put to death—and that the enormities which superstition, interest and cruelty have effected in former ages have there been re-performed;—and that they have learnt, with augmented sorrow, that these barbarities yet continue to be perpetrated, as they have not been suppressed with that promptitude and firmness which wisdom, gratitude, benevolence and Christianity indispensably require.

6. That against deeds so full of horror, this Committee must publicly protest; and that they assure the unhappy, surviving sufferers, by such

conduct, that they commiserate their destiny—and that, if such assistance should be unfortunately necessary, they will endeavour, in this Country, to provide for them an Asylum—to mitigate their sorrows—and to supply relief.

7. That although the Committee are not insensible to the principles which, under ordinary circumstances, might restrain the Government of this Country from direct interference, on this subject, with the Government of France:—yet they cannot forget that in former and even in less enlightened times such interposition has repeatedly and usefully occurred, under our best Princes and ablest Statesmen—that such persecutions are inconsistent with general peace, and violate those universal rights which all nations are bound to protect—and that the Government of England now possess claims to attention and respect which no former period could present:—and that this Committee, who know the liberal principles of their own Government, and who have repeatedly experienced their attention and their aid, will humbly but earnestly entreat them to remonstrate against the evils which they announce—and to exert their influence to prevent the continuance of a system which they cannot but deprecate and abhor.

8. That these Resolutions be respectfully communicated, by the Secretaries, to the principal Members of Administration;—and that they be inserted in the Daily Papers and Periodical Publications—and be circulated throughout Europe, as future circumstances may require.

9. That this Committee cannot separate without expressing their thanks to their worthy Secretary JOHN WILKS, Esq. for the benevolence and zeal which he has continued to manifest in convening this Meeting—and for preparing and proposing the Resolutions, which they have unanimously adopted.

SAMUEL MILLS, CHAIRMAN.

10. That this Committee renew their acknowledgments to the Chairman for his attention and ability, and for that cordial attachment to the great cause of Religious Freedom which he has constantly displayed.

THOMAS PELLATT, } JOHN WILKS, } Secretaries.

To whom any Communications, or

VOL. XI.

any authentic Intelligence, on this subject, may be addressed, at the New London Tavern, Cheapside, London.

At a Meeting of the Committee of the Protestant Society for the Protection of Religious Liberty, held at the New London Tavern, Cheapside, London, on December 5, 1815, SAMUEL MILLS, Esq. in the Chair,
It was unanimously Resolved,

1. That having experienced from the Prince Regent's Government the most prompt and polite attention to their application respecting the Protestants of France—having received their assurances " that it has been the invariable object of the British Government, and of their allies, to support, and on every suitable occasion to assert, the principles of Religious Toleration and Liberty, and that in their recent communications with the Government of France, they have brought forward these principles as the foundation of their policy, and of their just expectations:—and that they are, therefore, using their best efforts to arrest the progress of evils which they most deeply deplore ;"—and having been convinced of the benefits which have already resulted from their avowal of this policy, and from the declaration of these truly British and honourable sentiments, this Committee cannot delay to record and to communicate their cordial gratitude to the Right Honourable the Earl of Liverpool, and to the other Members of the present Administration, for their past and useful efforts, and for their judicious and liberal disposition to maintain, on behalf of the Protestants of France, those great principles of Religious Freedom which this Committee most devoutly approve, and are appointed to protect.

2. That desirous to co-operate with the British Government in conduct so enlightened and beneficent, this Committee will continue to observe the measures which may occur in France, and will neither abate their vigilance, nor their humbler but utmost exertions, until the Protestants of that country shall be allowed practically, perfectly, and permanently, to exercise that Liberty of Worship, and those Rights of Conscience, which the Constitutional Charter of their own Monarch has justly recognized, which his recent Ordonnance has wisely re-

assured, and which the, and every man throughout the world are entitled to enjoy.

. Thomas Pellatt, ⎫ Secretaries.
. John Wilks,   ⎭

———

At a Meeting of the Friends of Civil and Religious Liberty, held in the Meeting-House of the Fourth Dissenting Congregation, in Belfast, the 11th of December, 1815, Rev. Robert Acheson, in the Chair,
Resolved unanimously,
That the exercise of private judgment in forming religious opinions, is the unalienable right of every individual, and that no Government ought to interfere between the mind of man and his God, nor ought any persons to taunt or revile their fellow-citizens or opinions deliberately and conscientiously formed.

Resolved unanimously—That having petitioned the two Houses of Parliament, during the two last years, without success, on the manifold evils arising from the system of Orangemen, which still continues with unabated violence in many parts of Ireland, it is inexpedient to present similar petitions at this time.

Resolved unanimously—That in coming to the foregoing resolution, we are not actuated by any dereliction of duty, nor do we less strongly feel disapprobation of the system, nor less dread its hurtful consequences, being thoroughly persuaded that this Protestant combination against Catholics is illegal, and keeps up a spirit of irritation and animosity on both sides, and is an attempt to persecute for religious opinions.

Resolved unanimously—That we earnestly entreat the Earl of Donoughmore and Sir Henry Parnell to bring forward motions on this subject during the ensuing Session, as we are convinced that the permanent tranquility of Ireland depends on the suppression of the grievances sustained from the Orange party.

Resolved—(With several dissentients to an amendment substituted as the last paragraph, in place of one expunged)*—That actuated by a spirit

consistent with our first resolution, we behold with abhorrence the restoration of the Inquisition in Spain, as an abridgment of the legitimate rights of the people, which are essentially of more importance than the so much talked of legitimacy of Princes. We likewise view with the strongest emotions of disapprobation the persecution of the Protestants in the south of France, commenced apparently under the countenance of some of the branches of the Bourbons. And while we lament that this persecution should only have commenced under a Government established in France by the power of the allies, in the erecting of which they professed to have in view the establishment of social order, we hail with pleasure the pledge which the British Government have given, in their answer to the English Protestant Dissenters, of their disposition on this subject.

Resolved unanimously—That the United States of North America hold out an object worthy of imitation, where all sects live peaceably together, and are equally protected in the right of forming their religious opinions.

Resolved unanimously—That the Thanks of this Meeting be returned to Daniel O'Connel, Esq. as being the first in Ireland to call public attention to the persecution of the Protestants in France, at a meeting of the Catholic Association in Dublin, thus evincing that in the honourable pursuit of Catholic Emancipation, and protection from the hostility of Orange outrages, he only sought for himself, and his fellow Catholics, that liberty which he was equally ready to grant to others.

Resolved—(With several dissentients on an amendment carried for insertion in the Belfast News-Letter) —That these resolutions be published in the Belfast Commercial Chronicle, the Belfast News-Letter, the Dublin Chronicle, the Dublin Evening Post, and in the Morning Chronicle and

———

* The paragraph expunged in the 5th resolution, was in the following words :— " We the more lament these outrages as being perpetrated by men supported by the British Government, at the termination of

a contest, which affected to be for the restoration of social order, more especially as in the various revolutionary Governments of France, however great were their excesses, or their transgressions against the principles of general liberty, they generally preserved the sacred rights of conscience inviolable."

Statesman, and also that 250 copies be printed, and sent by John Hancock, who continues a tender of his services to conduct the correspondence, to Members of Parliament, and others, by whom it may be hoped the cause of Universal Liberty of conscience will be aided.

Resolved unanimously—That our aim in adopting the foregoing resolutions is, as well to turn public attention to the disturbed state of Ireland, from the persecutions of the Orange Societies, as to excite to sympathy on the part of the people, and an interference of the British Government with the outrages committed on Protestants in France. It is far from our intention to throw blame on Protestant or Catholic Communities generally, but only on such individuals as either in Ireland or France, violate the principles of Civil and Religious Liberty, and in this feeling we earnestly call upon the liberal of all sects to join, that by a general expression of public sentiment the evils complained of may be remedied.

Robert Acheson, Chairman.

Meeting at the Mansion House, Hull,
18th December, 1815.

At a Meeting of the inhabitants of this Town, held at the Guild-Hall, this day, to take into consideration the Persecution which our Protestant Brethren are now suffering in the South of France,

Christopher Bolton, Esq. Mayor, in the Chair,

Resolved,

1. That this Meeting has heard with feelings of the most poignant grief, that well-authenticated accounts have been received in this country, of a violent and sanguinary persecution now prevailing against our Brethren of the Protestant Faith, in the South of France; of which persecution the dreadful effects are stated to be, the sacrifice of multitudes of innocent and valuable lives, the pillage and destruction to an incalculable amount of private property, the utter demolition of many of their religious edifices, and the total deprivation of the means and advantages of assembling themselves together for the Public Worship of God.

2. That we have sufficient reason to believe this persecution to be purely of a religious nature, and directed against the faith and worship of the sufferers: and that the object of it is to suppress and extinguish, as far as possible, the inalienable right of private judgment in matters of religion.

3. That, happy in witnessing and enjoying religious liberty ourselves, under the mild and equitable government established in this United Kingdom, we should think it a dereliction of duty not to use our best endeavours to extend and secure the same inestimable blessing to our fellow-creatures in every part of the world; and that consequently we will earnestly and without delay, intercede with his Majesty's government to make every effort, consistent with the political relations of this country and France, to restore to our Protestant Brethren that security and freedom in religious profession and worship, of which they are unjustly and inhumanly deprived.

4. That we reflect with grateful satisfaction on the kind and flattering reception, given to the deputation from the general body of Protestant Dissenting Ministers of the Three Denominations in London, which on the 25th of November last waited on his Majesty's Ministers; who liberally and humanely expressed the deepest regret at the horrid scenes lately exhibited, and a disposition to use their best efforts for the support of the freedom of religious faith and worship.

5. That the thanks of this meeting be given to the General Body of Protestant Dissenting Ministers of the three denominations in London, for taking the lead in this labour of love; and that a copy of these Resolutions be transmitted to their Secretary.

6. That commiserating the state of extreme penury, to which numbers of the French Protestants, both clergy and laity, are reduced by the devastations of their oppressors, we will immediately institute in this place a subscription for their relief.

7. That a copy of these Resolutions be transmitted by the Chairman to the Earl of Liverpool, his Majesty's First Lord of the Treasury, with a request that he will promote the wishes of this Meeting, to the utmost of his power.

8. That a copy of the same be transmitted to his Grace the Lord Archbishop of York, in the hope that they will receive his Grace's approbation and concurrence.

9. That a copy of these Resolutions be sent to the Lord Lieutenants of the Ridings of the County of York. .

10. That a copy be also sent to the Members for the County of York, and to the Members for this Borough, with a request that they will use their influence with his Majesty's Ministers, and their efforts in Parliament, in furtherance of the object desired.

11. That a copy of these Resolutions be inserted in the Courier and Morning Chronicle, London Newspapers; in the York Herald and Leeds Mercury, and in each of the Hull Papers.

12. That the Bankers in this Town be requested to receive Subscriptions.

13. That the Gentlemen who signed the Requisition be appointed a Committee, to carry these Resolutions into effect.

14. That the Thanks be given to the Right Worshipful the Mayor, for his promptitude in calling this Meeting, and for his conduct in the chair.

Gosport, Dec. 19, 1815.

At a numerous and respectable Meeting of the inhabitants of this Town, held at the Star Inn, and convened by public advertisement,

The Rev. JAMES COLLINS, A. M. in the Chair,

Resolved unanimously,

That this Meeting cannot but express its horror and concern at the existence of Religious Persecution in France, and that the Protestants in any part of that country, should be the victims of dreadful massacre, pillage and desolations, and have their places of worship destroyed or shut up.

That sympathizing as men and as Christians with the Protestants thus suffering, and observing that a Fund is already opened in London for their succour and relief, we are also willing to contribute our aid, and that a Subscription be immediately opened for such benevolent purpose, at the Banks in this Town.

That deriving the liveliest gratification from learning that the ministers of his Royal Highness the Prince Regent, have supported and asserted the principles of Religious Toleration and Liberty, in their recent communications with the government of France, and are using their best efforts to arrest the progress of evils

they most deeply deplore; this meeting cannot, therefore, but cherish the most sanguine hope, that the noble exertions of his Majesty's government on behalf of the suffering and persecuted Protestants of France, will at length meet with complete success.

That a dutiful and loyal address be presented to his Royal Highness the Prince Regent from this town and neighbourhood, expressing our horror at these persecutions, and humbly praying his Royal Highness to continue his influence, and the adoption of such measures as may effectually remove and prevent the recurrence of such enormous evils.

That the petition now proposed is approved, and remain for the signature of the inhabitants, at the Star Inn, during the present week.

That Wm. Clute, Esq. and T. F. Heathcote, Esq. our county representatives, be requested to present the same to his Royal Highness.

That these Resolutions and the Address be inserted in the Courier, the Morning Chronicle, and the County Newspapers.

That the subscriptions be paid to the Chairman, and after defraying the expenses of the advertisements, that he remit the balance to one of the Banks in London, appointed to receive the Fund for the relief of the suffering Protestants.

JAMES COLLINS, Chairman.

That the thanks of this Meeting be given to the Chairman for his very able, liberal and impartial conduct in the chair.

To his Royal Highness the Prince Regent.

The Dutiful and Loyal Petition and Address of his Majesty's Subjects, Inhabitants of the town of Gosport and its neighbourhood,

Most humbly sheweth to your Royal Highness,

That your petitioners having learnt with horror the cruel and inhuman persecutions which the Protestants in France have been doomed of late to suffer, by the merciless rage of infuriated bigotry and superstition, do most humbly pray your Royal Highness to continue your gracious influence with his Majesty the King of France, and to adopt such other measures as will most effectually repress and utterly prevent the repetition of such outrages, and in the end secure to our Protestant brethren there the undisturbed enjoyment of the unalienable rights of conscience and religious worship.

.. And as in duty bound, your petitioners will ever pray.

Meeting of Roman Catholics of the Counties of Northumberland, Durham, and the North Riding of Yorkshire.

At a most numerous and highly respectable Meeting of Roman Catholics as above, holden at Newcastle-upon-Tyne, on the 27th of December, for the purpose of taking into consideration the Persecution of the Protestants in the South of France, and their own condition as Roman Catholics and Subjects of Great Britain,

G. SILVERTOP, Esq. in the Chair, The following Resolutions were unanimously adopted:

Resolved—That attached as we are to the faith of the Catholic Church, we do maintain the right of every individual, in every age, and in every country, to judge of the reasonableness of his belief; and we do moreover maintain, that no man can be deprived of this sacred, inalienable right, without injustice or oppression.

2. That attached as we are to the sacred cause of religious freedom, we should be undeserving the name of Christians or of Britons, if our philanthropy and the feelings of our sympathy did not extend to all who suffer for conscience' sake; and if we did not regard religious persecution, by any sect, or by any power, or by any people, as a horrid and detestable crime.

3. That maintaining, as we do, these principles, we have beheld with the deepest sorrow the misfortunes and persecutions of our fellow-christians, the Protestants in the South of France, and whilst we regret that religious rancour has had its share in instigating these atrocities, we are willing to believe and hope, from the best information we can obtain, that they are less to be attributed to religious than to political hatred; arising as it has done, from animosities between citizen and citizen, and proceeding from the varying and protracted scenes of the French Revolution.

4. That we anxiously look forward to a speedy termination of these atrocities; but if our hopes shall be disappointed, (an event which we should most sincerely deplore,) we shall consider ourselves called upon by every principle of Christian charity and benevolence, to co-operate with our Protestant countrymen in extending to the Protestants of France the same relief and assistance, which, under similar circumstances, we should be ready to afford to persons of our own persuasion.

5. That these, together with the subsequent Resolutions, be made known, signed by our chairman, to his Majesty's Principal Secretary of State for Foreign Affairs, requesting the Noble Viscount to accept and to convey to the other ministers of the Prince Regent's government, our most unfeigned thanks for the assurances made by them to the deputation of the Protestant Society for the protection of Religious Liberty, stating, "That it has been the invariable object of the British government and of their allies, to support, and on every occasion to assert the principles of Religious Toleration and Liberty; and that, in their recent communications with the government of France, they have brought forward these principles as the foundation of their policy and of their just expectations; and that they are, therefore, using their best efforts to arrest the progress of evils, which they most deeply deplore."

6. That we have seen with singular satisfaction, not only the declaration of the Congress of Vienna, relative to Religious Freedom, in the different States of Germany; but we have likewise beheld with real pleasure the Declaration of the Constitutional Charter of France, by which every Frenchman, whatever may be the principles of his faith, is equally entitled to the liberties and privileges of his country.

7. That contemplating as we have been the misfortunes of our fellowmen, nature forces upon us the melancholy idea of our own degradation. Britons and Englishmen as we are, and we glory in the name and in the happy Constitution of our country, although we are by law, for conscience' sake, shut out from every one of its political privileges; taxed without the power of choosing our repre-

sentatives; willing and anxious to risk our lives and shed our blood in defence of our Protestant King, we are, by law, precluded from holding a commission in his service; every civil office and situation is by law denied us; all means of attracting the notice of our country, or the favour of our Sovereign, are placed beyond our reach; and we are thus permitted to drag on our existence, as aliens, on this our native soil.

8. That assembled as we are this day together, for the first time in our lives, we feel it a duty we owe to ourselves, to our fellow-citizens, and to our posterity, to state candidly, and openly, and honestly, our objects and our wsihes. They are these:—That every inhabitant of this United Empire, who will swear allegiance to his King and to his Country, who is equally taxed with his fellow-citizens, and who is willing to risk his life and to shed his blood in defence of his king and his country, should be equally entitled to the enjoyment of the rights and privileges of the British Constitution.

9. That in looking forward to the happy moment of our entrance into the temple of the British Constitution, we do most solemnly assert, that we entertain not a wish or a view to interfere with the Protestant establishments of these realms. That if the legislature of our country require any further security than that of our oath, the greatest and the strongest, we consider, that can be given by man —such legislative provisions will be made, we are persuaded, in a spirit of non-interference with the faith and security of our Church—and thus formed, will be accepted by us, in a spirit of conciliation, calculated, we sincerely hope and trust, to meet the fears, to satisfy the scruples, and to remove the prejudices of every individual of the British Empire.

10. That an Address to his Royal Highness the Prince Regent, together with a humble Petition to the Legislature, be prepared—that Edward Jerningham, Esq. of Lincoln's Inn, be requested to prepare the same— and that a copy of these Resolutions, signed by our chairman, be sent to him; and that our thanks are hereby given to him for his great and various exertions in our behalf.

Geo. Silvertop, Chairman.

The Chairman having left the Chair, resolved, that the cordial thanks of the Meeting be given to him for his able conduct in the Chair.

———

At a Meeting of the Inhabitants of Newcastle-upon-Tyne, convened by public Advertisement, to take into consideration the state of the Persecuted Protestants in the South of France, held in the Town Hall, on Thursday, December 28,

The Right Worshipful the **Mayor** in the Chair,

It was unanimously Resolved,

1. That, having learned from our holy religion, and from happy experience, that liberty of conscience and of religious worship is one of the best blessings of the Almighty Creator, this meeting had hoped, from the known inefficacy, impolicy, and impiety of persecution, and from the spread of knowledge throughout Europe, that the time was at length arrived, when religious liberty was universally admitted to be the inalienable birth-right of every human being.

2. That this meeting, deeply impressed with the afflicting details which have now been laid before it, respecting the persecuted state of the Protestants in the South of France, desires to express its cordial sympathy with them, in the sufferings which they have now for many months experienced.

3. That this meeting desires to express the liveliest sentiments of satisfaction and gratitude, for the prompt and explicit assurances of his Majesty's government, " that they feel the deepest regret at the dreadful scenes lately witnessed in France, and that they are using, and will continue to use, their best efforts in their communications with the French government, to secure to all classes of French subjects, whether Protestants or Catholics, the full enjoyment of the advantages which the Constitutional Charter provided for them."

4. That this meeting desires also to express its ardent hope, that the Ordonnance lately published by the French King, will prove the commencement of vigorous measures for the punishment of those who have so long harassed and murdered the Protestants with impunity.

5. That, in the mean time, it. ap-

pears to this meeting highly necessary, that some effectual measures
should be taken for relieving our
brethren in France from the losses
which they have experienced in the
destruction of their churches, and the
spoliation of their property.

6. That a subscription be entered
into for this purpose, and that the
following gentlemen be appointed a
Committee for the management of
this benevolent business, in such way
as they shall see most expedient,
viz :—

The Chairman, Archibald Reed,
Esq., James Losh, Esq.; William
Batson, Esq., Thos. Henderson, Esq.,
S. W. Parker, Esq., Stephen De
Mole, Esq., James Potts, Esq., Mr.
Hugh Spencer, Mr. Joseph Clark,
Mr. John Fenwick, Mr. Benj. Brun-
ton, Mr. W. H. Angas, Rev. John
Parkin, Rev. William Turner, Rev.
David M'Indoe, Rev. James Pringle,
Rev. R. Pengilly, Rev. George Mann.

That William Batson, Esq. be requested to act as Treasurer ; and the
Rev. William Turner, as Secretary ;
and that the several banks be requested to receive subscriptions.

7. That copies of these Resolutions,
signed by the Chairman, be transmitted to the Right Hon. the Earl of
Liverpool, the Lord Lieutenant of
the county, the Hon. and Right Rev.
the Bishop of Durham, and the Members for Northumberland and Newcastle-upon-Tyne.

HENRY CRAMLINGTON, Mayor,
Chairman.

8. It was moved by Mr. Alderman
Reed, and seconded by Mr. Losh,
that the thanks of this meeting be
given to Mr. Mayor, for his readiness
in calling the Meeting, and for his
able conduct in the Chair.

Glasgow, Jan. 3, 1816.

At a Public Meeting of the Inhabitants of Glasgow, called by Advertisement to express disapprobation
of the Persecution of the Protestants in France,

WILLIAM MUIR, Esq. one of the Magistrates of Glasgow, in the Chair;

It was Resolved unanimously,

1. That, as Protestants, we cannot
but feel a brotherly sympathy with
Protestants, and a profound interest
in that great and common cause on
account of which they have been
made so often to suffer.

2. That we have heard with deep
concern of some late movements, on
the part of the Court and Church of
Rome, indicating a design to suppress, wherever their power may extend, the right of private judgment,
and the religious liberties of mankind,
particularly the expulsion of the Protestants from the Papal dominions and
adjacent territories of Italy, the revival of the abhorred Inquisition, and
the restoration of the Order of the Jesuits which had been abolished by the
common consent of all Europe.

3. That our sorrow and surprise
have been heightened by the intelligence of the sufferings of our Protestant brethren in the South of France,
intelligence, the truth of which has
been admitted by the highest authorities, both in France and in this
country, and confirmed by the most
authentic private information.

4. That while we reflect on all
circumstances, we cannot but be convinced, notwithstanding the attempts
which have been made to disguise or
deny the facts, that these sufferings
have arisen, in a great degree at least,
from religious prejudices, and partake
of the nature of *persecution* for conscience' sake.

5. That the inhabitants of this
country will, we have reason to believe, be greatly disappointed and afflicted, if the result of that struggle
in which the nation has been so long
engaged, and in which so much treasure and blood have been expended,
shall have been to place the Protestants in France, with whom we are
united by the ties of a common profession, and to whom we owe so much
in a religious view, in a worse situation as to liberty of conscience than
they held under the preceding government.

6. That, recollecting the many effectual interferences of the government of this country on behalf of persecuted Protestants on the Continent
of Europe in former times, and, contemplating the peculiar relative situation of Great Britain and France at
present, we conceive ourselves authorized and called upon to remonstrate
thus publicly against the violation of
what we deem the most sacred of all
rights—the right which every man
has to worship God according to the
dictates of his own conscience—and
we feel entitled to expect that the go-

vernment of France, which owes so much to this country, and is upheld at present in part by the British arms, will speedily adopt the most energetic and efficient measures to repress this spirit of outrage, and to secure to its Protestant subjects that full freedom of worship, and of the public and peaceable profession of religion, in every respect, which is guaranteed to them by the Constitutional Charter.

7. That we regard with the liveliest satisfaction the assurances early and promptly given by his Majesty's government to the first application made to them, on behalf of our Protestant brethren in that country— " That they feel the deepest regret at the dreadful scenes lately witnessed in France, and that they are using, and will continue to use their best efforts in their communications with the French government to secure to all classes of French subjects, whether Protestant or Catholic, the full enjoyment of the advantages which the Constitutional Charter provided for them," and contained also in a letter from Lord Liverpool, in reply to another interposition in their favour from a most respectable quarter, " That the Prince Regent's government are using their best efforts to arrest the progress of the evils, which no persons can deplore more deeply than themselves ;"—and we trust that the British ministry will redeem this sacred pledge, and will continue to exert themselves for the Protestants of France, with that propriety and energy which become their character, as well as the cause, and which may be so justly expected from the government of one of the first Protestant States in Europe; and one which has been so signally instrumental in accomplishing the recent Revolution in that kingdom.

8. That our warmest thanks are due, and be given to the Dissenting Ministers of London, and to " The Protestant Society for the Protection of Religious Liberty," who so promptly took up this subject, obtained from the British ministry the communications quoted above, and besides have been at such pains in exciting the attention of the public, by their Address and Resolutions, as well as by the circulation of other important and authentic documents relating to matters of fact.

9. That the thanks of the meeting be also given to the Corporation of the City of London, and to such other public bodies and individuals as have manifested their sympathy with the Protestants of France, and their present afflictions.

10. That, desirous of keeping the interesting object of this meeting in view, till it shall have been brought to a favourable issue, we appoint a Committee to watch over it, to follow out such measures as may appear to be necessary to give effect to these our Resolutions, and (if it shall seem to them expedient) to call us together again at any future period, to express our sentiments regarding circumstances which may occur in the progress of an interposition, the success of which must be near the heart of every affecting and zealous Protestant.

11. That the Chairman be instructed to transmit a copy of these our Resolutions to his Majesty's government.

(Signed)   WM. MUIR, Chairman.

The Chairman having quitted the chair, and Mr. Mathew Urie being called to it, the unanimous and warm thanks of the Meeting were given to Baillie Muir for his conduct in the Chair.

(Signed)   MATHEW URIE.

———

Borough of Plymouth.

At a numerous and respectable Meeting of the inhabitants of this Borough, convened by the Worshipful the Mayor, and held at the Guildhall thereof, this 9th day of January, 1816, in pursuance of a requisition from several respectable inhabitants, to take into consideration the present state of the Protestants in the South of France, and the best means of alleviating their distresses,

The Worshipful the MAYOR, in the Chair,

Resolved,

That we are deeply impressed with the high value of that Religious Liberty, which the subjects of the United Kingdom of Great Britain and Ireland enjoy under the auspicious reign of the House of Hanover; and we are grateful to Almighty God for the possession of so inestimable a privilege.

Resolved, That it is our persuasion, founded on the very principles of the

Gospel, and arising out of the spirit which it breathes, that all men possess an equal right to worship God according to the dictates of their conscience.

Resolved, That influenced by these convictions, we have learned with deep heartfelt concern, that persecutions have arisen against the Protestants residing in the South of France ; where the persons of many hundreds of innocent and useful members of society have been ill-treated and murdered, their property pillaged and destroyed, their families deprived of the means of support, their houses of worship shut up or demolished; and that under the influence of fear, thousands have fled from the pursuit of the persecutors, and are now suffering wretchedness and want amongst the mountains of the Cevennes and in other parts of the French territory.

Resolved, That we should ill deserve the advantages by which we are distinguished, if we did not make a public avowal of our abhorrence of the spirit which has actuated the Catholics in the South of France, and the violence to which that spirit has led them, and our determination to employ whatever influence we may possess to remove the miseries of the persecuted Protestants, and restore to them peace and security.

Resolved, That it affords us much pleasure to learn that his Majesty's ministers have declared their disapprobation and regret, of measures, which must fill every benevolent heart with sorrow, and we do express our hope that they will continue to use all their influence with the Court of France, to stop the present cruel proceedings, and prevent the recurrence of similar violence and misery.

Resolved, That with these views, copies of these Resolutions be respectfully transmitted to the Earl of Liverpool, his Majesty's first Lord of the Treasury, to the Lord Bishop of Exeter, to the Lord Lieutenant and Members for the County of Devon, and to the Members for this Borough, entreating them to embrace every opportunity which may present itself to them, both in and out of Parliament, to promote in France and in all other countries, as far as they consistently can, the full enjoyment of liberty of conscience, and a free exercise of religious worship.

Resolved, That a subscription be immediately set on foot, and books to receive the names of subscribers opened at the Banks in this town, and at the Guild-hall, for the purpose of affording relief to the unhappy sufferers; that Mr John Tingcombe be requested to be Treasurer for the same, and that the Mayor, together with the Gentlemen who signed the requisition, form a Committee, to see that the money which is raised, be properly applied.

Resolved, That these Resolutions be signed by the Chairman, and published in the Plymouth Chronicle, the Plymouth and Dock Telegraph, and in the Courier and Morning Chronicle Newspapers.

Resolved, That the Thanks of this Meeting be given to Mr. William Prance for bringing forward these Resolutions, and for the able manner in which he has supported them.

WILLIAM LOCKYER, Mayor.

The Mayor having quitted the Chair,

Resolved, That the Thanks of this Meeting be given to him for his readiness in conveying it, and for his great attention to the business thereof.

The Prefect of the Department of L'Isere to the Mayors of Communes.
Grenoble, Dec. 21.
(Circular.)

M. LE MAYOR,

Attempts have been made to establish, in some of the departments of the South, a pretended secret royal association, and in order to draw to it a greater number of proselytes, the chiefs have dared to abuse the august name of the king, by stating that their instructions emanated from his Majesty himself.

I doubt not that if insinuations of this kind have reached you, you have pointed out their falsehood, knowing as you do that the king never transmits orders or makes known his will except through the medium of his ministers and magistrates charged with assisting in the administration of the state. If in unfortunate times the true friends of the king have been sometimes obliged to envelope their proceedings in secrecy, those times are at length past, and every individual who without an express mission recognized by the government seeks to intermeddle in its operations, is no other than a factious person who wishes to deceive and seduce you. Every secret association, although even its members should be actuated by good sentiments, is dangerous on account of the facilities which it affords for disturbing the public tranquillity.

Upon these grounds the king orders that every secret association, whatever may be its apparent or presumed object, shall be immediately dissolved, and his Majesty prohibits the organization of any of that description.

I enjoin you specially, M. le Mayor, and on your personal responsibility, to look to the execution of this formal order. If the persons already initiated in associations of this description, or disposed to be so, are truly attached and faithful to the king, they will be eager to obey; but if, notwithstanding your injunctions, they should be contumacious, they will become factious persons, whom you will immediately denounce to me, that I may proceed against them with the just severity of the law.

I rely, M. le Mayor, on all your zeal to conform exactly to these instructions, and to render me precise account of what you shall have done in this respect. It is indispensably necessary that I should receive this Report before the 30th of the present month. I have the honour to be, &c.

The Prefect of l'Isere,
    Count de Montlivault.

The following has been handed to us as an extract of a letter from France relative to the Protestants of the South. We hope the highly laudable exertions of the friends of humanity in this country have at length had their intended effect in compelling the French government to adopt effectual measures for restoring the persecuted Protestants to all their former privileges.

"The Prefect of the Department of Gard having invited to his house two ministers of the Protestant communion, and two members of the Consistory, with the Mayor of the city of Nismes and his adjunct, informed them that the French government took the greatest interest in the opening of the temples, and seemed even to accuse him, the Prefect, of

negligence in this respect; he therefore invited and even enjoined them to re-open their temples, assuring them of every protection, but added, that the Roman Catholics, seeing with dissatisfaction that these temples were before the Revolution, Catholic Churches, it was agreed, in order that there might be no pretext for disturbance, that there should be new temples. The city would give the land for building them on: one to be situated to the North and to the South, and to cost 110,000 francs, towards which, he informed them, the Duke d'Angouleme would give 15,000 francs. The proposition has been accepted, and the work is about to be commenced. The temples will be without the city, and until they are finished the Protestants will have peaceable possession of the present temples."—*M. Chron. Jan. 3.*

The Lancasterian System of Education had commenced in France under the happiest auspices; but its great end, universal education, is defeated. The Directors, the mouthpieces of superior power, *have refused to admit* Protestant Children. The affairs at Nismes was not an isolated act, but essentially connected with the religious policy of that horde of bigots who dictate to the crown. My next will convey further particulars.—*M. Chron. Dec. 26.*

Duke of Wellington's Letter.
Paris, Nov. 28, 1815.

Gentlemen,

I have had the honour of receiving your letter of the 24th inst. and I take the earliest opportunity of replying to it. I have every reason to believe that the public, and the society, of which you are the secretaries, have been misinformed regarding what is passing in the South of France. It is natural that there should be violent contests in a country in which the people are divided, not only by a difference of religion, but likewise by a difference of political opinion, and that the religion of every individual is in general the sign of the political party to which he belongs, and at a moment of peculiar political interest, and of weakness in the government on account of the mutiny of the army, that the weaker party should suffer, and that much injustice and violence should be committed by individuals of the more numerous preponderating party. But as far as I have any knowledge acquired during my residence at this court last year, and since the entry of the allies into Paris, the government have done every thing in their power to put an end to the disturbances which have prevailed in the South of France, and to protect all his Majesty's subjects, in conformity with his Majesty's promise in his Royal Charter, in the exercise of their religious duties according to their several persuasions, and in the enjoyment of their several privileges, whatever may be their religious persuasions. In a recent instance, an officer, General La Garde, was sent down to Nismes, specially by government, to inquire into the state of affairs in that country, and upon his first report he had orders to open the Protestant Churches, which, in the course of the contest between the parties, had been closed. He was severely wounded when in the execution of these orders ; and I have been informed by good authority, that his Royal Highness the Duc d'Angouleme has since marched at the head of a body of troops against those who had opposed themselves to the execution, by General La Garde, of the orders of the government. I enclose the copy of the King's Ordonnance, issued in consequence of this event which sufficiently shews the views and intentions of government. I have further to inform you, that it is not true that the salaries of the Protestant ministers have been discontinued by the King of France. I trust that what I have above stated will convince the society of which you are the Secretaries, that the King of France's government, at least, are not to blame on account of the unfortunate circumstances which have occurred in the South of France.

I have the honour to be, &c.
(Signed) WELLINGTON.
Mr. J. Wilks and Mr. T. Pellatt, Secretaries to the Protestant Society for the Protection of Religious Liberty.

———

Copy of a Letter written by M. Marron, President of the Protestant Consis- tory at Paris, and addressed to M. M. of the Committee for the Affairs of the French Protestants.

Paris, Dec. 7.

GENTLEMEN,

I have made it a duty to oppose every proposition tending to foreign interference in the affairs of the French Protestants. I cannot, therefore, see with satisfaction what passes in England on this subject, and I cannot concur in it. If the zeal of your fraternal love edifies and affects me, it appears to me, nevertheless, to go beyond the line of true prudence, and even the spirit of true charity. It is not thus that the latter virtue proclaims its assistance, especially when it may have reason to dread, that by such a conduct it may compromise the very interests of the cause which it undertakes to support and defend. I am far from admitting that there can be, as you imagine, any thing hostile in the conduct or in the intentions of the French government, with regard to the Protestants. The sufferings at Nismes are great, doubtless, but they are local ; and local causes, however unfounded, may have contributed to provoke them and to prolong their duration. The French government laments them as much as you or I. The king has pronounced, in the most unequivocal manner, his displeasure, his horror at the late events. His wishes and his efforts to remedy the evil, to calm the lamentable exasperation of public feeling are attested by the Royal Ordonnance, by what the Duc d'Anguouleme said to the deputation of the Consistory, and by the flattering distinction with which one of the pastors of the Cevennes (M. Maliues) was lately honoured, in receiving the decoration of the Legion of Honour.

I do not know, gentlemen, who could take it upon him to excite your commiseration for the delay which the ministers of the reformed religion experience in the payment of their stipends. What we experience in this respect, we only participate with all other public functionaries. They do not impute it, any more than ourselves, to any other cause than to the deplorable situation into which we have been thrown. We ought rather to bless the government for what it has done, than blame it for what it has not done; and I must again solemnly disavow here, every appeal to foreign commiseration. I beseech you, therefore, to write to me no more in the style in which you have now done. I respect, I honour the signatures of your letter; I render justice to the motives of all; and I dare hope that you will not be offended on your part with my frank disapprobation. None can subscribe themselves with more fraternal regards,

Yours, &c.

Southampton, 15th Jan. 1816.

Mr. Editor,

By desire of our Committee, I send you the annexed copy of a letter containing the resignation of the Pastoral Office of our much esteemed friend, the Rev. Mr. Travers, earnestly requesting the early insertion of it in your valuable Repository, as it may be the means, under Providence, of procuring for us that relief and assistance, which we so greatly stand in need of.   JOHN TAWKINS.

Shirley Common, 13th Jan. 1816.

My Worthy Friends,

I am greatly concerned to inform you, that in consequence of a severe fit of sickness, with which it has pleased Almighty God to visit me; I see no prospect of being able to resume the honourable and important office of your Minister. But great as my regret is, upon the present occasion, it would be infinitely increased if I thought that this event would put a stop to the pure and rational worship of God in Southampton, which I have much at heart, for which we have exerted ourselves so zealously, and upon which we have abundant reason earnestly to implore and expect the divine blessing. Let us not, therefore, be discouraged on account of this calamity, but let us redouble our efforts, for " greater is He who is with us, than he who is against us." And be assured my Christian friends, that " in due season we shall reap, if we faint not." Let me recommend you boldly to look your situation in the face, and not suffer yourselves to be needlessly cast down; only consider what it was a twelvemonth ago, and what it now is! Our debts then were about 500*l.*, at present they don't much exceed 100*l.*, such have been our exertions and success; and the little loan of 85*l.*

which is against us, I am well persuaded will be kindly continued, until we are able to pay it off. If it had pleased God to have preserved me in health, but a few months longer, it was my intention to have solicited the assistance of our zealous and liberal-minded brethren, in those parts of the country which I have not yet visited, to enable us to liquidate this remaining incumbrance; and from what I have already experienced of the zeal and fellow-feeling of a large proportion of our Society, I am confident I must have been successful—but the divine Being has ordered it otherwise, and it becomes us to be resigned to his supremely wise and kind disposals. I consider this spot to be an important part of the Christian vineyard in England, which we have in some measure cleared of what I conceive to be the corruptions of Christianity; and it never can be imagined for a moment, that the respectable and wealthy body of Unitarians, throughout the kingdom, would be backward in strengthening our hands as our necessities might require. To *them,* therefore, we may confidently look for co-operation and support. Mr. Coates, one of the trustees of the *Regium donum,* upon whom I called when I was in London, very properly considered us entitled to relief, and assisted us accordingly, and I am warranted to believe, from what passed between us, that this assistance would be annually continued. It would give me great pleasure to add an annual subscription on my own account, but the expenses attendant upon my present infirm state of health, forbid my making any positive engagements. I will, however, do what lies in my power, to enable you to make good your necessary annual out-goings. And in particular, I will write to Mr. Christie, (with whom I am intimately acquainted,) who is the Treasurer of the Unitarian Fund, stating to him our situation, and requesting him to lay it before the Committee, that they may immediately take such steps, as may be necessary, to prevent the extinction of our interest in these parts, by affording us, from time to time, all necessary assistance and supplies. It may not be improper also to mention in this place, for the information of the Society, that an Association of

Unitarian Christians, has been formed within the last six months, in this department, one of whose objects is, the support of those congregations which may require its assistance, of which the Rev. Mr. Fox, of Chichester is Secretary, and to whom I shall make a point of writing an early letter for our succour and relief, and I have no doubt it will be cheerfully granted. Under these circumstances, let me conjure you not to think of parting with the chapel, until we have strained every nerve to retain it, and find from experience, that it is utterly out of our power so to do. It would be a calamity which could never sufficiently be regretted, to see our pretty chapel trodden under foot by those who have departed from the simplicity of the gospel. May we not hope that in a little time it may please God, provided we are patient and united among ourselves, to raise up for us a gentleman of popular and respectable talents, and irreproachable character, whose circumstances are independent, and who may be fired with equal zeal and ardour with myself, in the diffusion of Christian truth and liberty. I shall take care to make such a call through the channel of the Monthly Repository, and should we be so fortunate, as to meet with such a person, it may tend greatly to enlarge and strengthen our interest. In the mean time, I should strongly recommend your meeting together, once every Sabbath-day, and by means of religious exercises, such as reading, prayer, conversation and singing the praises of God, to comfort, edify and strengthen each other.

If my life should be spared, it is my intention in the course of three months, to quit my present situation, and sit down within ten or twenty miles of the metropolis, for the sake of being nearer to my immediate relatives and friends, who have kindly expressed their wishes to this effect; but wherever I am, I shall be rejoiced to hear of your increasing prosperity, shall be happy to promote it in every way that lies in my power, and shall never cease to pray, that the divine blessing may ever accompany you and yours.   I am, my dear friends, -

Yours very sincerely,
B. TRAVERS.

MONTHLY RETROSPECT OF PUBLIC AFFAIRS

OR,

The Christian's Survey of the Political World.

THE persecution of the Protestants in France has since our last given rise to very important discussions. The question, originally taken up by the Dissenting Ministers of London, and the Protestant Society, has been investigated in various parts of England, and made such an impression, that its effects have been felt through France, and even their cabinet has been compelled to take various steps to remove the odium, that has been excited against the principal agents in the nefarious transactions at Nismes. The attempts to stifle the inquiries into these wicked transactions have been of a very extraordinary nature; and that paper, which, if Buonaparte had committed the hundredth part of the atrocities, that have taken place in the South of France, would have made all Europe resound with the bitterness of its invective, has launched forth into the vilest calumnies against those, who have nobly stood forward to assist the oppressed and the persecuted. The Morning Chronicle, however, remained firm in the cause which it undertook; and has produced such proofs of the existence of the evils complained of, that none but the wilfully blind can doubt that there has been much suffering at Nismes and its neighbourhood solely on account of religion.

But what need have we of many proofs. The facts allowed by all parties speak for themselves. No one can deny, that the Protestant places of worship have been shut up: for they have been re-opened by authority. No one can deny that a bitter spirit of persecution has been excited at Nismes, for otherwise the idea would not have been started of banishing Protestant worship out of the city. By whom this spirit was excited, to whom the long existence of the evil is to be attributed, may be a matter of doubt. They who would make it a merely civil question will have to account for the singularity of the circumstance, that during the Revolution and throughout the whole despotism of Buonaparte the Protestants enjoyed equal liberty of worship with the Catholics. Many have been the civil dissensions, but they never took this turn, till the Bourbons were re-established, and not till the Duke of Anguouleme had made his appearance in the South of France.

It is now asserted, and no one can feel a pleasure in its being otherwise, that the cabinet of France are entirely disposed to grant religious liberty to the Protestants. Happy shall we be to learn that this is the case: but the exertions in England will be found to have been very useful. The strong and decisive manner in which London, Exeter, Glasgow, Hull, Newcastle, Plymouth and other places have declared their sentiments, do honour to this country. Even if they had merely met to express their abhorrence of persecution in general their meetings would have been beneficial : for even in a country, Protestant like our own, this sentiment is not, we fear, as yet, universal. It cannot be too often impressed upon Christians, that persecution is alien to their religion : they are under the law of love; and no one, who taketh upon himself the name of Christ, must dare to condemn his neighbour or insult and revile him for a difference of religious opinion. To his own master he standeth or falleth, and in religion no one upon earth has a right to call himself lord or master. This says the Saviour, is the case in other communities; but it shall not be so in mine.

The name of the Duke of Wellington has been brought forward upon this occasion, in consequence of a letter written by his Grace to the Protestant Society. In this much is attributed to the state of parties in the South of France, and the disposition of the French government to religious liberty is strongly maintained. But

as to the facts themselves they are not attempted to be denied, and it does not by any means appear, that the Duke of Wellington had better means of information than might be had in London. In the circles, in which his Grace moves, it cannot be expected that the situation of Protestants would be the subject of much attention ; and the state of France is such, that their complaints would be very much stifled, before they reached the capital.

The Protestant ministers have also lately appeared with addresses to the court, from different places, and letters to the societies in England. But besides that the representation of the quiet state of Protestants in one place is no argument against persecution in another, these addresses seem to have been got together as in England sometimes, when compliments agreeable to the court are procured from various places, and the little dependence to be placed upon them is proverbial. It was not to be expected, that an attack upon the Protestants would begin in Paris. The attempt to excite such a measure might be attended with dangerous consequences: for, if the Protestants are few in number, the Catholics themselves are far from being a considerable body; and they, who have no religion at all, might involve in common ruin both the parties.

The horrors that have taken place are to be traced up to a remote source, to the revocation of the edict of Nantz, by the infamous Louis the XIV.; whose name we are glad to see not quoted, when an attempt is made to cast a lustre upon that of Bourbon, Henry the IV., Louis the XII., and St. Louis are spoken of, but the great hero is Henry the IV., who was a Protestant, and for political purposes having changed his religion, his name is tarnished in one of his descendants, who became a faithless persecutor. The conduct of Louis the XIV. has been beyond measure ruinous to France. In the first instance it banished from the country a very great proportion of its arts, sciences and literature. At the time of the revocation of the edicts, the Protestants possessed a very learned clergy, and several schools and universities. There was great emulation between the learned of the two sects, and the Catholic clergy were kept in order by the respectability and talents of their opponents. The effect of the persecution of the Protestants was not at first seen, but it appeared in the following reign, when the clergy had different opponents to deal with, and found themselves unable to cope with the rising body of infidels. If it were allowable to speak positively on the judgments of God, we might almost say, that the Bourbon family, the emigrant nobility, and the Catholic clergy, received in the revolution the just retribution for the atrocious acts of their ancestors in the reign of Louis the XIV. Assuredly the rise and progress of infidelity may be attributed to this cause. The morality of France was undermined by the expulsion of the Protestants, and we will venture to prognosticate, that the restoration of that body will be the great means of restoring better principles to the kingdom of France.

Policy might have taught the French the folly even of their persecution. Where there is a great established sect, the Dissenters from it are generally to be found in the middle walks of life, and in them chiefly among the most industrious and economical. If any of this class rises to opulence, his wealth soon finds its way into the establishment. It is a proverbial saying, that it is not easy to find three generations of Dissenters, who rode in coaches. The reason is obvious; increasing wealth brings the occupier more in contact with the higher classes. His sons and daughters, by this association, gradually indulging in a little relaxation from the severe principles of the father; or perhaps the father himself, when settled on his country estate, may have led the way by occupying occasionally the squire's seat in the parish church. The nearest meeting may be too vulgar. An advantageous match may occur for sons and daughters, and to abstain from church or customary visits, exposes to the imputation of singularity. A variety of similar circumstances, will be suggested to the mind of the reader, and lead him to reflect on our Saviour's words: " hard is it for a rich man to enter into the kingdom of heaven:" and perhaps it is one of the hardest trials of a parent to reflect upon the changes that may take place in his posterity. This,

however, should stimulate us to impress most strongly on the minds of our children the importance of scriptural truth, not teaching them to gabble over like parrots catechisms, and creeds, and confessions of faith, but to exercise their understandings daily in the divine word, that they may esteem the gospel as the precious jewel, to purchase which a man will part with all his substance.

The amnesty bill has passed in France, modified from that which was presented by one of the hot-headed royalists, but containing greater severity than that which had the sanction of the court. A considerable degree of discussion took place in the Commons' house, but when it was brought to the House of Peers, it was passed by acclamation, and in a manner, which in England would be deemed most unfitting and indecent. The king's consent soon ratified the deed, which drives away from France a number of the regicides, and exposes to pains and penalties a number of persons involved in the administration, under the three months' reign of Buonaparte.

The anniversary of the execution of Louis the XVI. has been kept with great solemnity, and by a very judicious regulation, instead of a sermon, by which the passions might have been inflamed, the will of the deceased sovereign, calculated to sooth them down, was read in all the churches. It is to be wished, that this may produce the desired effect; but in opposition, as it were to it, a plan has been struck out, which can but be of a very dangerous tendency. This is to have manifestos in different places, expressing detestation of the crime of regicide, and to these people are invited to subscribe their signatures. It was not considered by the framers of this measure, that more than one half of the present population of France had nothing to do with the sentence on the late king: they were at the time of its passing, too young to enter into the merits or demerits of the case, and it cannot answer a good purpose to compel them now to examine the question. Whether kings may be justly dethroned by their subjects or not, is not a question for the multitude to decide upon. The history of the world proves that, whether right or wrong, the case has frequently occurred, and will frequently occur again, and in the most despotical kingdoms the occurrences are most frequent. Revolutions cannot always be prevented, even where discretion sits at the helm: the storm may be too great for the most prudent pilot: but, where the laws are good, and are executed with fidelity, the sovereign has little to fear. Papers and protestations will not support a throne. Its base must be fixed on more solid ground; and the king, who reigns in the hearts of his people, is the most secure.

Among the strange events of these troubled times, may be ranked the seizure, by the French government, of three English officers, on the alleged crime of aiding the escape of Lavalette. One of these gentlemen is a highly distinguished character, and what is more remarkable, one against whom Buonaparte is supposed to have entertained the most decided enmity. Sir R. Wilson, without doubt, gave him just cause, for no one has by pen and sword proved himself a greater foe to his tyranny. It would be improper in the present state of the case to make any comments on this event. These officers, it is said, will be brought to a trial, but Sir Robert, with great propriety, has refused to answer those interrogatories, which it is the custom, and a base custom it is, to put to an accused. We shall see in what manner the French courts conduct themselves upon this occasion, for

without doubt care will be taken that they may have a fair trial.

The affairs of France occupy at present so large a space in the contemplation of Europe, that little room is left for observations on what is taking place in other parts of the Continent. Prussia's new constitution is not yet fixed. The independence of the two kingdoms of Sweden and Norway under one sovereign is settled. Spain goes on its usual course, and its best men are in prisons and gallies. This does not, however, advance its cause with the colonies. Carthagena is not taken. The independents in Mexico are increasing in power, and Buenos Ayres has fitted out a fleet under the command of an Englishman, which will clear the Pacific of every ship wearing Spanish colours.

At home all eyes are directed to the approaching sessions of parliament. The great business of the Continental peace is to come under early discussion, and the state of the landed interest will make a prominent feature in its debates. The corn bill has not answered any of the intentions for which it was designed by its framers. A temporary distress has been occasioned, and in the attempt to remedy it great care must be taken, lest the evil should be increased. This country's prosperity is owing to its trade, commerce and manufactures; and if the landed interest should injure them, it must participate in their sufferings.

l₂

CORRESPONDENCE.

Our Subscribers will receive with this number, to face the Eleventh Volume, a Portrait of our late venerable friend and correspondent, Dr. Toulmin. A few Proof Impressions have been pulled in Quarto, on fine Paper, price 5s., which may be had of the Publishers, as also the Proof Prints, in the same size and at the same price, of Dr. Priestley and Servetus. It is particularly recommended to such as wish to preserve a complete set of the *Monthly Repository Engravings* to supply themselves early; for in a little time the early prints, like the early numbers of the work, will be unobtainable.

Owing to the Editor's unavoidable absence from home, various articles intended for the present number, must lie over; particularly some promised articles of Review and some communications of Intelligence.

It is intended to make the present Volume a complete Register of the Proceedings on behalf of the French Protestants, and our country Correspondents are requested to supply us with copies of Resolutions, &c., which they may observe to be omitted.

We have received Subscriptions from *Mr. Jevans* and others for the *Unitarian Fund;* from *Mr. Scott,* &c. for the *Greenock Chapel;* and from *Dr. Carpenter* for *Rossendale,* all which will be more particularly acknowledged in the next number.

The Obituary of the Rev. *Francis Blackburne,* of Richmond, in Yorkshire, (who we lament to say died on Sunday, the 21st inst.) did not reach us till that department of our work was closed.

We intended to press upon the notice of our readers the proposed Edition of *Dr. Priestley's Works,* by our much-esteemed friend and highly valued correspondent, *Mr. Rutt;* but we must content ourselves at present with expressing an earnest hope that so useful a purpose will be warmly supported by the Unitarian body.

THE

Monthly Repository,
&c.

| No. CXXII.] | FEBRUARY, 1816. | [Vol. XI. |

HISTORY AND BIOGRAPHY.

Bromley, Jan. 28, 1816.

SIR,

THE following early account of the *Moravian Brethren*, by Dr. Doddridge, so far as I can learn, has never been printed. It came into my possession among some old family papers, and must have been copied at least sixty years ago, probably much nearer the date of Dr. Doddridge's letters. These dates are omitted in the *extracts*, but from internal circumstances may be safely fixed at 1736 or 1737. It appears from Mr. La Trobe's English edition of Crantz's *History of the Brethren*, in German, (p. 213,) that Count Zinzendorf arrived in London, Jan. 20, 1737, and there received in August following a congratulatory letter from Potter, Archbishop of Canterbury, on his having become a Bishop of the Moravian Church. The Latin original and translation are preserved by Mr. La Trobe, in his preface, where he adds, that " Dr. Isaac Watts also gave a testimony to this church, *under the patronage of that noble and excellent person, Count Zinzendorf*, in a letter, dated Dec. 21, 1738." By a note (p. 240) it appears that this letter is preserved in the *Acta Fratrum*, App. 56, p. 42, and that Dr. Doddridge corresponded with the *Brethren* the same year.

It would be unjust to the memories of such men as Watts and Doddridge, and indeed of the persons mentioned in these extracts, to introduce them in connexion with such an equivocal character, to say the least, as Zinzendorf, without recollecting that the Count, at the date of these extracts, and, as I apprehend, for some years afterwards, was known in England, only as a very zealous and indefatigable Christian *Propagandist*. Watts and Doddridge were both deceased before Mr. Rimius, the historian of *the House of Brunswick*, published in 1753, his *Candid Narrative*

of the Rise and Progress of the Herrnhuters. Mr. Rimius was a German who had frequented their public religious meetings. In his Narrative he has given the German originals and translations of numerous passages from the Count's published Sermons and Hymns, which shew what shocking indecencies, at least in phraseology, he had connected with his theological system. Of these Dr. Maclaine has preserved quite sufficient, to surprise and disgust any reader, in his Translation of Mosheim, Ed. 2nd. (p. 85. Note s.) A larger account is in the Gen. Biog. Dict. 1784 (ix. 327).

In 1754, Mr. Rimius added *A Solemn Call on Count Zinzendorf*, and in 1755, *A Supplement to the Candid Narrative*. Count Zinzendorf, who lived till 1760, *died and made no sign*. He could not venture to examine the *Candid Narrative*. Nor has *Crantz*, who wrote in 1771, nor *Mr. La Trobe* his editor, in 1780, and whose sobermindedness, like that of Mr. Gambold, tended to redeem the character of his sect, ever mentioned the name of Rimius or referred to his Charges against Zinzendorf; a sufficient proof of their inability to refute them, though no evidence of their candour, or even integrity as historians.

I have added a few notes to explain or confirm some passages in the *extracts*, and remain, Sir,

Yours,

J. T. RUTT.

Extracts of two Letters from the Rev. Mr. [Dr.] Doddridge, at Northampton, to the Rev. Mr. [Dr.] Isaac Watts.

Letter I.

SIR,

I am ashamed to think how long I have neglected to fulfil my promise of sending to you some account of those remarkable particulars, relating to the Moravian Brethren, which I promised you several months ago. I had just then received an account from my reverend and worthy friend, Mr. Ingham, a Clergyman of the Church of England,* who having spent almost a twelvemonth at Savanna, in company with several of them, received the greatest part of his information from them, and especially, from the Rev. Mr. Spangenberg, Pastor, or as they call it, Bishop of the Moravian Church at Philadelphia.†

I need not tell you, Sir, how well the names of the Moravian and Bohemian Brethren were known, long before Luther's time, for I doubt not but you are much better acquainted than I with those singular footsteps of Divine Providence by which the beginning of a reformation was raised among them, as it had been long before among the Waldenses, from whom, nevertheless, I cannot find that doctrine or discipline was derived; though there was a great resemblance between them. Those churches, throughout all the succeeding ages, have remained, in part at least, a distinct body, neither incorporated with the Lutherans, nor Calvinists, nor any other sect in Germany; and in consequence of that, together with the remarkable strictness of their discipline, though in doctrine they have indulged to a great latitude; they have been continually exposed to persecution not only from Papists but from Protestants too.

I think it now about fifteen years since five of them, flying from the violence to which they were exposed at home, took refuge in a wood at Herrnhut, which was a part of the celebrated Count Zinzendorf's estate. That pious nobleman, returning from the Court of Dresden, weary of their impieties and immoralities, and fearful of hazarding his salvation by a longer continuance there, happened to pass through that wood, and saw a little hut lately raised, and perceiving a smoke in it, had the curiosity to alight and go into it, where he found these five refugees who, in a very respectful manner, owned themselves trespassers on his ground, and discovering their religion and circumstances implored his protection. This he readily granted, and entering into some religious discourse with them, was so much impressed that he invited, and encouraged their frequent visits, and soon set up, first weekly, then daily preaching, exposition and prayer, in his family, to which any one that pleased to come was admitted.‡

The number of the congregation soon grew considerable, and one of the Moravians was dispatched to carry the agreeable news into his native country: but, either in his journey or return, he was seized by the Roman Catholics, whipt from town to town like a felon, frequently threatened with immediate death, all the intimations of which he received with the most heroic resolution, and at last died of their repeated ill usage.‖ Nevertheless

* Benjamin Ingham, in the same ship with John and Charles Wesley, accompanied to Georgia in the spring of 1735, the *third* colony sent out by the Moravians. "Ingham, in conjunction with the Bohemian brother *Rose* and his wife set up a school for the Indians, not far from an Indian village." In 1738, Mr. Ingham, with John Wesley, accompanied from England a "Moravian brother," into Germany, which Mr. I. appears soon to have left, and become a very popular preacher in Yorkshire. See La Trobe's History, pp. 194, 226, 228.

† Augustus Gottlieb Spangenberg, A.M. of the University of Halle. He united himself to Count Zinzendorf at Herrnhut in 1733, was in Georgia, and afterwards at Philadelphia in 1736, but not consecrated Bishop till 1744. He finally returned to Europe in 1762, and was commissioned in 1764 to write the Life of Zinzendorf. Id. pp. 182, 258, 310, 531, 664.

‡ The five refugees from Moravia were brothers, named *Neisser*, who had joined *Christian David*, a carpenter. He began the settlement at *des Herrn Hut* or *the Watch of the Lord*, by striking his axe into a tree, and exclaiming, *Here hath the sparrow found an house, and the swallow a nest for herself; even thine altars O Lord of Hosts.* Count Zinzendorf "even in the 10th year of his age, had formed the resolution of being a preacher of the gospel," though in 1721, "in obedience to his grandmother he had accepted a post in the administration at Dresden." That year, however, he became acquainted with Christian David. Yet he does not appear to have been apprized of the settlement at Herrnhut till 1722, when he was returning from *Ebersdorf*, where he had married the Countess *Reuss*. "On the 21st of December, he was conducting his Lady to Hennersdorf; and having descried from the road a house in the wood, he signified his surprise, but also his satisfaction; went in to these Moravians, and, bidding them welcome, fell with them upon his knees and prayed. Soon after, he moved into his newly-erected mansion at Berthelsdorf." Id. p. 94—101.

‖ No account agreeing to this appears in *Crantz's* History or *La Trobe's* Notes. It appears that in 1723, "Christian David set out again for Moravia," where "his conversations occasioned a great emotion," and roused the zeal of *Melchior Nitschmann*, who was confined "a long time in prison, and was there treated most unmercifully; but was at length set free with derision." Another of the same name

wheresoever he was carried, and even while they were lashing him, he preached the gospel with great success ; and in consequence of his witness and sufferings crowds flocked into the Church at Herrnhut, in which there are, if I recollect right, about six hundred adult communicants, four hundred of whom, being under religious convictions, they call illuminated, and two hundred catechumens. They sent out missionaries to propagate the gospel in various parts, and particularly in Lapland, where I am told they met with considerable success.*

Though the Count, who, it seems, has taken orders, has devoted his whole estate, which is very considerable, to charitable uses ; yet the number of exiles, flowing in upon them, has been greater than his liberality could support,† which joined with their zeal of propagating their religion has induced many of them to go over to Georgia as others have done to Pennsylvania. Friend Ingham had the pleasure of the pious company of fifteen in the ship which conveyed him and Mr. Wesley to Georgia, and I cannot forbear mentioning a little circumstance which I find in the journal now, by the favour of that fraternity, in my hands, which is, that a violent storm arising, in which the whole company expected to perish, immediately when the

English sailors were in the utmost consternation, the Moravians stood upon deck singing psalms, with all the marks of joy and composure in their countenances, imagining they were come to the period of all their trials and just entering upon glory. On which Mr. Wesley observes that he could not forbear representing to the sailors, in a short discourse, the singular happiness of the servants of God above all others.

I may, perhaps, communicate to you from their original papers the substance of a conference which these Englishmen had with Mr. Spangenberg. It will be sufficient to add that they soon entered into measures for a mission to the Indians of Georgia, with some remarkable success. Those poor creatures run seven or eight miles, after their day's work, and spend great part of the night in receiving religious instructions, though they are sure, at their return, in the morning, to be most severely scourged by their Christian masters, if their journey has been discovered.‡ I will, in my next, which you may very quickly expect, give you a particular account of some very remarkable providences with respect to these Moravians which, if they may be believed, on the credit of the gentleman mentioned, are worthy of notice, to which I shall add something further of Mr. Ingham.

Letter II.

I resume the subject of my last, and mention two or three more remarkable circumstances, relating to the Moravians, which I had from my good friend, Mr. Ingham.

He tells me there is a most remarkable spirit of prayer amongst them, and especially for the propagating of religion in the world ; to which end, that prayers may be made continually, there are a certain number of them formed into two little societies, one of men and the other of women, who do in their turns keep up prayers through all the hours both night and day.‖ The

---

is said to have "ended his race on Maunday Thursday, 1729, in prison, after three years' confinement for the sake of the gospel, which he attempted to bring to his country people in Moravia." Id. pp. 103 and 107.

* In 1734 three of the *Brethren* offered to undertake a mission to Lapland. They traversed Swedish Lapland, but attempting a mission to Russian Lapland, they were arrested at Archangel, in 1738, as *Swedish Spies*, and after suffering great hardships, brought to Petersburg, where "their simplicity and uprightness helped them through. A certain great minister furnished them with a passport to Lubec, with these words: *Ye may go your way, good people ; your service is not wanted here.*" Id. pp. 188, 189.

† The *Brethren* early "established a fund, called by them the *Lamb's*, or the *Saviour's Chest*, which became very considerable by the contributions of the proselytes of *Herrnhutism*. From the beginning two brethren were trusted with it, of whom one kept the chest and the other the key." The Countess is said to have "so well husbanded the scanty funds of the society that nothing was ever wanting, either in her family, or among the brotherhood, though there had been a necessity of furnishing from thence above one million of crowns for sundry undertakings." Rimius's Cand. Nar. p. 28.

‡ This is an exact description of the treatment negroes have often endured, but it appears from *Morse* that Negroes were not at this time employed in Georgia. It is difficult to understand who were these *Indians, Slaves* to Christian Masters, as the school mentioned in Note *, p. 66, was for the children of free Indians, the *Creeks*, and encouraged by their King *Tomo*. See Morse. Georg. 8vo. p. 453, &c. and La Trobe, *Hist.* pp. 194 and 230.

‖ "At all hours, whether day or night, some persons of both sexes are appointed by rotation, to pray for the society: These people, without call, clock or watch, are acquainted by an inward feeling when their hour comes, in which they are to perform

i

children of those who are members of the church are, as they were amongst the Lacedemonians, looked upon as the property, rather of the public, than their own parents, from whom they are taken when a year old, and put to a school, where the first lesson taught them is simple obedience and quietness.* They have several elders whose business is to give the Bishop, or Pastor, who, by the way, is a mechanic, the most exact information they can relating to the religious state of the whole community.† They suspend each other from communion, or withdraw themselves from it, not only from any scandalous offence, which seldom happens among them, but on account of any little misdemeanor, which seems contrary to the honour of the gospel. Count Zinzendorf was once suspended for being in a passion with one of his servants, and was obliged to acknowledge his fault, and to ask pardon publicly before he was restored.

They tell one remarkable story concerning a person who was a member with them, but something offended at the strictness of their discipline. He did not submit to fraternal correction, as they call it. They therefore proceeded to admonish him, at which he was greatly exasperated. Being a person of eminent rank, he then set them at open defiance, and insulted them in a very audacious manner. Upon which they excommunicated him, very solemnly. He was then seized with violent agonies, both of body and mind ; and when he had for several weeks tried most noted physicians, and every method of amusement and comfort he could think of, to no purpose, he at last sent for the elders, and desired them to pray for him. But they insisted on his being brought, I think, on his couch, to their public assembly, where he made an open confession of his sin. It is a very melancholy incident they tell of another of their number who having made a very florid profession, not without some

mixture of ostentation, one day, receiving the sacrament amongst them, was taken with convulsive pains and died in the assembly, crying with his last breath, and with the greatest horror, *Spiritual Pride !* *Spiritual Pride !*

These people were misrepresented to the late King of Poland, so that he sent an order against them, which would probably have ended in extirpation; but it was very remarkable that a few days before it was to be executed he got that accidental hurt in his toe, which mortified and proved the occasion of his death. The present King sent a commission to inquire after them, but received a report so much in their favour that he secretly protected them.

Mr. Ingham assures me that he has seen amongst them such extraordinary answers of prayer as has thrown him into great amazement.‡ Persons have been recovered from dangerous and desperate illness, as it seems, by this means ; and he added a little story, for the truth of which he undertakes to answer, upon his own knowledge. One of the brethren, who is an Elder, was bathing in a river, a little above Savanna, when an alligator darted directly at him. The Moravian did not attempt to fly, but finding himself inwardly supported, as he afterwards declared, with a full assurance of being delivered, he swam directly towards the alligator, and laid his hands on the head of that voracious creature, without the least degree of fear upon him. Upon which the alligator sunk down like a stone, to the bottom of the river, and made no other attempt upon him. He says that several of the inhabitants were at that time within sight, and it was as a sort of a standing saying among some sort of the English, that the little man had beat the alligator.

I might have added, that in dubious cases their Church has often recourse to the determination of lots,‖ and Mr. In-

---

their duty." *Le Long*, a Moravian Author, in *Rimius*, p. 10.

* " They pay an uncommon attention to the instruction of youth. There are assemblies held of little children that are not yet in a condition to walk. They are carried thither. Hymns are sung in these meetings and prayers made ; even sermons are preached to them, suitable to the capacities of these infant hearers." *Rimius*, p. 9.

† " Every member is daily visited by one of his class, who gives him exhortations, and takes notice of the actual state of his soul, whereof he makes a report to the Elders. The Elders have the sole right of making matches. No promise of marriage is of any validity, without their consent." *Rimius*, pp. 8 and 11.

‡ Dr. Doddridge himself, as Dr. Kippis, his biographer, who knew him well, has observed, carried his notions on this subject " somewhat farther than reason and truth will warrant," so as to ascribe to prayer " such an immediate influence upon the Supreme Mind, and to expect from it such interpositions as are scarcely consistent with the regular order of Providence, and the stated course of events in the world." Dr. K. considers Dr. Price and Dr. Ogden as having also exceeded, on this point. B. Britt., v. 305.

‖ This mode of determination was adopted on a remarkable occasion by the *Congregation-Church.* In 1731, " The Count having endeavoured to evince the utility of a total conformity with the Lutheran Church, it was resolved that we

gham passed his last voyage upon that issue. The Moravian Church was called
together upon the occasion, at least, the
elders of it, and after several hours spent
in prayer, one of them threw a lot which
determined him to return to England. Nevertheless the good man, in whom, I must
say, there is as much of the Christian
apostolic spirit as I ever saw on so little
acquaintance in any person living; is

fully determined to return, as soon as Providence gives him an opportunity. He
speaks of the four months he spent amongst
the Indians, as the most delightful part
of his life, though he was but beginning
to understand their language, and had no
accommodations of life about him but such
as they use, his English dress being excepted.

MISCELLANEOUS COMMUNICATIONS.

Sir,   *Jan. 12, 1816.*

THE following character of Mr.
Fox, as a parliamentary orator,
at the age of twenty-eight, may suitably follow the interesting extracts
from his speeches, which have appeared in your last volume.

"Mr. Fox is certainly one of the first native orators in the House, but he is extremely negligent. His discourses are frequently finished pieces of argumentation,
abounding in the best pointed observations,
and the justest conclusions; and supported
by a weight of reasoning, a manly boldness
and energy of expression, almost unequal-
led; and never, within the course of our
knowledge or experience, surpassed. His
extemporary speeches on facts, arguments
and details, not immediately arising from
nor connected with the proper subject of
debate, at least not foreseen, are truly admirable. They bear every appearance of
the most studied and laboured harangues,
in every thing but the delivery, which,
however rapid, is not able to keep pace
with the crowded conceptions of the speaker. His ideas are inexhaustible, and are
ever ready at his command; but even if

should resign ourselves to the entire will
of our Saviour. Therefore the two following lots [texts] were written, and with
fervent prayer, one of them was drawn by
a child of four years old:

1. *To them that are without law, &c.*
1 Cor. ix. 21.

2. *Therefore brethren, stand fast, &c.*
2 Thess. ii. 15.

The *last* was drawn. We entered from
that day, into a covenant with each other,
to remain upon this footing, and in *this*
constitution to carry on the work of the
Lord, and to preach his gospel in all the
world and among all nations, whithersoever
he should be pleased to send and scatter
us abroad, and sang,

Guard thou us, in thy affair,
With the holy watcher's care."

La Trobe Hist. p. 137.

this were all, we could account for it easily; but we must listen in silent astonishment, when we observe him rise upon some
sudden unexpected incident, and discuss
perhaps a deep intricate subject for an
hour, with an ability, perspicuity and
precision, that would induce such as are
unacquainted with his habits, or are ignorant of his talents, to be persuaded that
he came to the House previously prepared
and informed, in order to deliver his opinion. With these almost unrivalled gifts
which nature has bestowed, Mr. Fox is
far from being a pleasing or persuasive
orator. His utterance is rapid, disagreeable, and sometimes scarcely intelligible.
He speaks always as if he was in a passion,
and the arguments of passionate people do
not come well recommended. He sometimes descends to personal attacks, to anecdotes and puerilities, much beneath the
dignity of a British Senator, particularly
a man of his consummate talents."

I copy this passage from P. iii. of
"Characters: containing an Impartial
Review of the Public Conduct and Abilities of the most Eminent Personages
in the Parliament of Great Britain;"
published at *Dublin* in 1777. Those
Prime Actors in the political Drama
of their day, have all quitted the stage;
*their love and their hatred and their
envy is now perished.* They were nineteen in number, of whom the Duke
of Grafton was, I believe, the last
survivor.

. N. L. T.

Bath, January 3, 1816.

Sir,

YOU will give me leave to introduce to the notice of your readers one uncommon sentiment of Dr.
Chauncey, which was, that the righteous, in successive ages, would pass
through many deaths, or states of
oblivion. As they must die in this
present world before they can enter

into·heaven, and as they to ·endless ages, are to be exalted from one state of glory to a greater, he presumed that they were destined to die again, for some short interval, on every promotion to still greater degrees of felicity.

But my present design is to give you his paraphrase upon Romans v. 12, to the end of the chapter. This .will .exercise .your..ingenious correspondents, from whose united labours we may .hope,to learn the true,meaning of the original.

" For this cause or reason, we have received reconciliation by Jesus Christ, namely, as sin entered into the world by the one man, Adam, and death by his sin in eating the forbidden fruit, and thus by this sin of his, death hath come upon all men, whereupon, in consequence of which, they have all sinned ; and yet that death passed upon all by means of ·the sin of the one man, Adam, as I observed .in the foregoing verse, and would briefly prove before I proceed to finish the comparison I there began, is exceeding evident : for all along from the time of Adam's lapse to the giving the law by Moses, sin was in the world. But whatever sin may, in its own .nature, be supposed to deserve, it is not reasonable to suppose, that it should be universally .reckoned to both, when no law is in being that makes death the special penalty of transgression : and yet death reigned thus universally through the whole period of time between Adam and Moses, and over those too who did not violate, as they might have done, a positive command of God, " after the similitude of Adam's transgression;" between whom and him that was to come, namely, the Messiah, there is a likeness as to the damage occasioned by the one, and the gift bestowed through the other : not that .the damage occasioned by the lapse of the one man, Adam, and the advantage arising from the free gift through the one man, Jesus Christ, exactly correspond to each other ; for if the many, that is, all men, are subjected to death, through the lapse of the one man, Adam, the grace of God, and the gift by this grace of his, which grace is bestowed through the one man, Jesus Christ, hath more abounded, unto the same many, or all men. And, not as the damage, to repeat

what I observed in the beginning of the former verse, that I may be more explicit in opening myself upon a matter of such importance ; I say, not as the damage through the one man that sinned, that is, in the one instance in which he was .tried, so is the gift through the one man, Jesus Christ : for the judicial sentence .took rise from the lapse of the one man, Adam, and proceeded to condemnation, condemnation subjecting mankind to mortality, and thereupon to sin also ; but the gift takes rise from the many sins which men commit in the course of their lives, and proceeds in opposition to the power and demerit of them all, so as finally to terminate in justification, justification including in it their deliverance from sin as well as death, their being made righteous as well as reigning in life : and it is quite reasonable to think thus of the matter ; for if by the lapse of the one man death in all its consequences reigned through this one man over all .men ; much more shall these all men, who are the recipients of the abounding of the grace of God, and of the ·gift that shall make them righteous, finally reign in life through the one man Jesus Christ. I say, therefore, to return now and pursue the comparison, I began in the twelfth verse, as it was by the lapse of the one man, Adam, that the judicial act, " dust thou art and unto dust shalt thou return," came upon all men, subjecting them to ·death ; even so, by the righteousness of the one man, Jesus Christ, the opposite advantageous gift is come upon the same all men, which delivers them from death to reign in life for ever ; and this may be admitted without difficulty : for to proceed in the comparison, as by the disobedience of the one man, Adam, the many, or all men, by a divine constitution, subjecting them to a frail mortal state, occasioned by this disobedience of his, became sinners ; even so, by the disobedience of the one man, Jesus Christ, the same many, or all men, in consequence of an opposite constitution, grounded on this obedience of his, shall become righteous persons, and as such be subjectively qualified for the justification of life, or what means the same thing, an eternal reign in happy life. Now the introduction of the law among the Jews is so far from being an ob·

jection, as some persons may be ready
to think, against what I have been
saying, in the above verses, that it
perfectly coincides with the design of
it: to which purpose let it be observed, the law was introduced among
the Jews, a small part of mankind,
that sin, upon supposition of its being
committed, might abound, be increased, heightened in its malignity
or guilt, by means of the law:
insomuch that it may be concluded
and fairly said, as sin has universally
reigned by death, so shall ' grace
reign as universally and triumphantly
through righteousness unto eternal
life, by Jesus Christ, our Lord.'"

W. H.

Sir,

THE sentiment of your readers coinciding with your own wishes,
they are very sorry that you cannot
favour them with an exact portrait of
the late Mr. Francis Webb. If his
cousin, Dr. Jefferies, had been living,
he could have particularly described
him from his cradle to his grave.
Others are still existing in our world,
who can do much to this purpose.
But, I can do little more than say,
that he was uniformly a strenuous
advocate for pure liberty, and that
according to his favourite maxim,
"The love of money is the root of all
evil," he was never influenced by a
regard to pelf. Above fifty years ago
he married an amiable lady, a Miss
Milner. At this time he took a house,
the rent of which exceeded his income.
Some years after, he accepted the
place of deputy searcher at Graves-
end, which was accompanied with
500*l.* a year. Whether the occupation was injurious to his feelings or
not, I cannot positively say, but he
resigned this lucrative situation, after
holding it seven or eight years. Being at a distance from him after this,
I cannot be his historian any further.
But, I presume, that he never lost
sight of liberty. In conversation he
was peculiarly eloquent and entertaining. He published two volumes
of sermons, when he was a young
man, which made all who read them
wish for more. I conclude with hoping that you will be able soon to furnish us with many more particulars.

Y. Z.

*Analysis of a Work by a Jewish Au-
thor, Mr. Bennet, on Sacrifices.*

Sir,

A PRUSSIAN Jew, of respectable character, who is, I am informed, a portrait painter in London, moved with indignation against
what he calls the Christian Doctors, and
especially against Dr. Adam Clarke,
who has had the effrontery to declare
that there is not a Jew in the present
day that knows the Hebrew language
and the literature of that people, has
published a small pamphlet on the
subject of the Sacrifices of the Levitical Law; and as this subject has much
engaged your readers of late, you may
not be unwilling to lay an analysis of
his little work before them. I confess
there seems to me an antecedent probability that the Jewish people are
acquainted with the laws of their forefathers: but even if they were not,
since Mr. Bennett does not affect to
establish his proof upon any other
ground than the Scriptures, it is in
our power to ascertain whether his
argument is conclusive.

I am, Sir, yours,
J. W.

" The great body of Christians
maintain that all the laws which regard sacrifices were *absolute laws,* that
no remission could be expected but
by the shedding of *animal blood;* and
then they conclude that, to cleanse
the spiritual leper, the *Lamb of God*
must be slain, the sprinkling of his
blood must be applied: and 'without
the shedding of his blood there can be
no remission; and, if this hypothesis
be well founded, that the House of
Israel in their present state of dispersion, being without animal sacrifices,
and without the salvation of the great
sacrifice, i. e. the Lamb of God, must
remain without any salvation whatever, and no quarter can be given to
the ancient house of Israel." He then
proceeds:—

1. " If we adhere to the instructions
of the Mosaic code, we shall find that
the primitive sacrifices, either animal,
vegetable, or libations, were not in-
stinted for trespasses and remission
of sins. In the history of the Patriarchs we meet with quite different
notions on this subject; for in all the
accounts of the patriarchal sacrifices,
those of Cain, Abel, Noah, Abraham,
&c. they were neither absolute nor

for the remission of sin. They were all voluntary gifts and free donations, as tokens of gratitude and obedience to the Universal Benefactor: but in process of time, when mankind became more numerous, the practice deviated from its primitive simplicity; it became an inheritance to the priests, and the servants of the temple: and in consequence they were varied and multiplied; they became moreover absolute, and were insisted upon as of indispensable obligation. *

"Profane history informs us that the heathen sacrifices did not only extend to thanksgivings and sin-offerings, but that they were also augurial and soothsaying—employed for inquiries respecting events to come, and discoveries either of political and public concerns or of private interest. These were regulated according to the fancies of the augurial priests; and a most productive system it certainly was to them.

"At the exit from Egypt, when the Commonwealth of Israel was formed, this practice of sacrifices was so generally spread that it could not altogether be dispensed with. The divine wisdom, which wrought miracles in the firmament and the elements of nature, never wrought a miracle on the human character. Any super-natural change in the human mind would militate against the emphatical charge in Deut. xxx. 19, " I testify unto you this day, I have set before you life and death, a blessing and a curse—*Choose life.*" To change the manners and customs from one extreme to another would have been a violence done to the choice of the mind: therefore the divine Legislator thought proper not to abolish the general practice of sacrifices, but only to reduce them to a more limited system. Generally speaking they were reduced to two classes; the one free-will offerings, thank and peace-offerings; the other, duty-offerings, for sin and guilt. The sacrifices of both classes were also ordained according

to the fortune of the donor or the transgressor, and were either animal or vegetable according to ability: they were to be offered to the Supreme Power alone, in Jerusalem only, and by the hands of the tribe of Levi." We are lead to believe upon reading the history of Moses, that it was the original design of the Lawgiver not to burden the Israelites with many ceremonies; the first institution was extremely simple, and it would probably have continued so, had not the Jews discovered such an absolute determination to attach themselves to rites and ceremonies which all the other nations were fond of, that it was found necessary to load them with burdens, in order to keep down their rebellious spirits—truly does it appear, upon tracing onwards their history, that the prophet spoke truth when he said, ' My people will have it so.'

" 2. When we examine the order of sacrifices as it is described in Leviticus, we find that the shedding of blood was not at all necessary for the remission of sins. Thus Leviticus, 1st and 2nd chapters, there is an order for meat-offerings of flour with oil and incense. But, still more to the purpose, in xi. xiv. ' But if he be not able to bring two turtle doves, then he that sinned shall bring a tenth part of an ephod of fine flour for a sin-offering. He shall put no oil therein.' Nothing can be more distinctly intended here, than that the shedding of animal blood, according to the Mosaic dispensation, was not *essential* for trespasses, and sin-offerings at large; but was purely ceremonial and circumstantial.

" 3. If we examine the prophetical books at large, we shall find that they all confirm what I have advanced—that the whole system of sacrifices was neither essential to salvation nor of absolute commandment. Thus in Samuel, ' Hath God as great delight in burnt-offering and sacrifice as in obeying the word of God? Behold to obey is preferable to offering sacrifice, and to hearken is more acceptable than the fat of lambs." King David said, ' Sacrifice and offering thou didst not require; ears hast thou opened in me.' (Meaning that men ought to listen to absolute rational commandments applicable to human welfare). See also xvth Psalm at large,

---

* Does not this account of the tricks of Priests in the most ancient times correspond with what may clearly be traced out in the history of the Christian Church, of the revenues, obtained by priests, and the various means they gradually brought about of obtaining money from the believers?

in which, amongst the grounds of human salvation, the psalmist does not mention one word about sacrifices. King Solomon declared, that "To do justice'and judgment is more acceptable to God than sacrifice." Isaiah, " To what purpose is the multitude of your sacrifices unto me, saith the Lord, &c.; Am I to be served with burnt-offerings of rams and the fat of fed beasts, or with the blood of bullocks, of lambs and of he-goats—things of which I have no desire?" See also Isaiah viii. at large, where moral and philosophical principles are laid down, and no mention whatever is made of sacrifices. He also quotes Jer. vii. 22, Hosea vi. 6, Micah vi. 6, and alludes to many other prophetic passages pointing to the same object.

From these prophetical declarations, he adds, " we obtain in the plainest language the validity of my third assertion, that the whole of the commandments of sacrifices were neither absolute ones, nor essential to human salvation ; for how could the prophets be in unison in exclaiming against absolute laws, enacted by a divine legislator as essential to salvation, and in declaring them null and void ? Either the declaration of the first prophets or of the latter ones must then be absolutely false. But it appears from what has been proved, that the primitive institution of sacrifices was not established as essential to the remission of sin, and that the shedding of animal blood was not in any wise indispensable to salvation—that the institution of them was not absolute, but merely ceremonial and temporal ; and therefore the prophets did, with a truly philosophic air, justly exclaim against the infatuation of the vulgar practices and forms of false devotion, which sought to appease an offended Deity by a fat ram, a roasted bullock or a vessel of good wine, while the heart was corrupted and depraved, and destitute of all divine and moral principles.* Throughout the Penta-

teuch we observe, that in the trespasses between man and man the first and chief thing required was retribution ; the sacrifice was but an inferior matter—and so with a transgression of a civil or moral nature, which was an offence against God."

Mr. Bennett then proceeds to produce some authorities from the most ancient rabbies, whom he calls the Links of Tradition ; from whom he makes it appear that all commandments which relate to the productions of the land were applicable only to the land of Israel; that tithes, agricultural donations, sacrifices, &c. being land productions, were not obligatory nor ever esteemed so, without the boundaries of Palestine. And he quotes a case, in which many of the dispersed Jews of Babylon, Mesopotamia, Syria, &c. countries adjoining Palestine, brought sacrifices to Jerusalem ; and that the Doctors of the Temple would not accept them on this very ground that, *They might not encourage the belief that the law of sacrifices was an absolute law;* from which we obtain the assurance that they were *local, temporary* and *ceremonial,* by no means *absolute* and *not essential to human salvation.*

Another argument he adduces appears to be conclusive, that while all the other commandments of the Pentateuch, both of jurisprudence, criminal, conjugal, inheritant, &c. as well as the rites of the sabbath, public festivals, impure animals, circumcision, &c. were general and universal, given to the nation at large for all times and all places, of abode, the laws relative to sacrifices have these peculiar exceptions,—they were limited to a class, the tribe of Levi; to place, the temple of Jerusalem ; to time, while the commonwealth of Israel was in possession of their patriarchal inheritance (Palestine). Is it consistent with reason, and still more with divine justice, that sacrifices should be essential to human salvation, and yet that their observance should be conditional and confined to three things—class, place and time ?†.

---

* It is surprising that our Calvinistic friends do not see the striking analogy between the effect produced by the Jewish system of sacrifices, and their system of salvation through the atoning blood of Christ. With many of them, as we are persuaded with many ancient Jews, their " Better Nature" opposes the influence of their system, and leads them to virtue.

Not so, alas ! the mobile vulgus that follow their faith !

† One cannot help being struck with the uncommon resemblance between the corruptions of Judaism and those of Christianity ; nor are we surprised to find that

It also deserves our notice, that all the prophets who censure the misconduct of their nation held the subject of sacrifices as the point in question, and never referred to the abuse of any other rite.

He concludes with summing up his argument thus :

I. The institution of sacrifices was not invented for the remission of sins.

II. Neither was the shedding of blood essential as an atonement ; for pancakes served also as a pacification to cleanse the sinner.

III· That, generally speaking, sacrifices were not at all essential to human salvation, and accordingly they were ceremonial, local and temporary by law, but by no means absolute.

On the Divine Government.

THERE are only two schemes of the divine government, either consistent in themselves, that I know of, or which have any pretensions to reason or the common apprehensions of mankind. The first is, that at the creation, the Divine Being, subjected all that he had made to fixed and invariable laws, that both matter and mind, whatever they be, are governed by such laws, that consequently every thing happens, as he has appointed it, every thing was to him foreseen and determined, all is an universal settled scheme of Providence ; prophecies are possible, because nothing is contingent ; and miracles are also possible, as they might be included in the first and general plan of the divine economy. Every being performs his part, and the final dispensations of Deity will follow his pleasure concerning all creatures.

The second scheme is, that God at the creation subjected matter to fixed laws, but gave a power to mind, of self-determination, so that man, the previous circumstances being the same, can perform the action A. and its contrary B. This scheme supposes, that whatever depends upon the determination of the human mind, was left loose, and could not be foreseen by the Creator, yet that pleasure and pain were fixed within

certain limits, and that the divine Being will so regulate his final dispensations, that rewards and punishments shall be adapted to the actions done, and man's final state be determined according to his merit. Prophecies foretelling events dependent on the determinations of the mind of man, are impossible under this scheme as they involve a contradiction. And it is dangerous to say, that human reason is so weak, that that may yet be possible which implies a contradiction ; because according to this mode of reasoning, all our conclusions concerning religion would be equally uncertain, nor could we deduce the being of a God from any apparent contradiction that the supposition that there is no such being involves. Miracles according to this scheme are possible, as well as in the former scheme.

That God has given to the human mind such a power as this second scheme supposes, appears to be agreeable to the common apprehensions of mankind, who seem generally to imagine that at any given time of action, they had it in their power to do this or its contrary. Both schemes seem to provide for the divine government ; for although the latter admits, that when God created man he knew nothing what, in this world, would be the result of his conduct ; yet having by the fixed laws of matter, limited the power of mischief, his ultimate dispensations can adjudicate all things according to perfect equity.

I know of no other scheme of the divine government consistent with itself ; and if any of your correspondents choose to advert to them, it will gratify your humble servant.

AN INQUIRER.

Leigh Street, Red Lion Square,
Jan. 16, 1816.

SIR,

YOUR correspondent, Mr. Prout, in a letter to you, which you have put into my hand, after referring to my papers in reply to Mr. Belsham, on the pre-existence of Jesus Christ, published in the third volume of the Monthly Repository, pp. 379—382, 470—475, 551—558, 653—659, and 718—723, says, " I confess that I am rather surprised at his (Mr. Marsom's) *almost instantaneous conversion to the Unitarian faith so late in*

the advocates of the latter are eagerly catching at every twig which falls from the decayed tree of the former to support their equally corrupt, and, we trust, devoted cause.

life. I hope," he adds, " I shall not give offence by requesting your highly respected friend to point out the path in which he has *recently* trodden in order to attain his present view of things." And further, he requests that he would favour the readers of your interesting Miscellany with an illustration of certain passages of scripture which he particularly mentions. The circumstances of the case, I admit, sufficiently warrant such a request. I have appeared in the above mentioned volume as the advocate of the doctrine alluded to by your correspondent, and it was natural for one who " candidly acknowledges that he felt the force of my reasoning," to wish to be informed of the means by which I was led to renounce a sentiment which I had so strenuously laboured to defend ; and it is but right that I should endeavour to shew, that I have not adopted my present views without such reasons as were fully sufficient to carry conviction to my mind. I cannot, however, admit that I have been either *recently* or *instantaneously* converted to the *Unitarian faith* ; because I have been an Unitarian, (in the proper sense of that term, as much so as I am at present) more than fifty years, nor have my views undergone any material alteration either respecting the unity of God, or the nature of the person of Christ during that period. My recent change of sentiment has no relation to the nature of Jesus Christ, but simply to the time when he began to exist : whether that existence commenced when he came in the flesh, or whether he existed from the foundation of the world.

As to the "almost instantaneous" nature of my conversion, your correspondent should recollect that it is now seven years since my replies to Mr. Belsham appeared in the Repository. There is a certain process which takes place in the mind in order to a conviction of the truth or falsehood of any doctrine ; that process may be long or short ; it may be attended with many difficulties and struggles arising from a variety of causes; but a change of sentiment, the result of that process by which the mind is made up upon the subject, is probably almost always instantaneous. But what adds to the surprise of your correspondent is, that such a change

should have taken place " so late in life." I reply that I never made any pretensions to infallibility ; I have often changed my opinions, and I dare not say that I am now in possession of all truth, or that I shall not undergo some future change of mind with respect to religious truth : I hope I shall never be too old to learn, or unwilling to attend to any evidence that shall be presented to me.

Before I proceed to give an account of the steps that led to my recent change of sentiment it may be proper to state what were my former views. In defending the pre-existence of Jesus Christ I never supposed that in his pre-existent state, or in any stage of his existence he was any more than a man. That he was a divine person truly and properly God, and became man; that he was a super-angelic being and took upon him human nature; or that he pre-existed as a human soul or spirit which in the fulness of time assumed a human body in the womb of the virgin, and so became a proper man ; neither of these ideas formed any part of my creed ; I considered them all as unscriptural and indefensible. In my letters in reply to Mr. Belsham I have not, in any instance, adverted to the nature of Christ's pre-existence, to what he was in that state, or to the nature of the change which took place in him in his humiliation ; but have confined myself to the plain matter of fact, whether or not the pre-existence of Jesus Christ is a doctrine contained in the scriptures. Those who wish to see what my views were on those subjects may see them fully stated in the third volume of the Protestant Dissenters' Magazine for 1796, pp. 130—135, and 172—177. With respect to the steps that have led to my present views, I observe,

First, that Mr. Belsham's arguments, in his Letters to Mr. Carpenter, on my first perusal, appeared to me to possess considerable weight, and for some time made a deep impression on my mind, which led me to re-consider them with close attention; upon doing so, I discovered (at least I thought I discovered) that in some instances he had made use of declamation instead of argument ; that in other instances his arguments were inconclusive; that he had laid himself open to considerable animadversion, and that much of his declamation and argument derived their whole force from the supposition that the doctrine of the pre-existence of Jesus Christ necessarily included in it that of his possessing a super-human or super-angelic nature; that he was a being of extraordinary powers, a subordinate Jehovah, a delegated Creator, under God the maker and upholder of all things. Upon the discovery of such " amazing facts," " Would not the mind of a Jew," exclaims Mr. Belsham, "who had never heard of *delegated Creators* and *subordinate Jehovahs,* have been overwhelmed with astonishment when this new and strange doctrine was first discovered to him?" These ideas opened to him a wide field for declamation, but to me, believing they had no foundation in scripture or any connexion with the pre-existence of Jesus Christ, they furnished strong objections to his hypothesis, and laid him open to much animadversion, and this gave rise to the following interrogations in my first letter, M. Rep. Vol. iii. p. 381:—" Is not Mr. B. guilty of the same fault which he would be ready enough to charge on the opposers of Christianity, that they attack its corruptions and not Christianity itself as left in the New Testament ? Will he say in reply, that he finds this new and strange doctrine maintained as a doctrine of scripture by his learned friend to whom he is writing ?" So may they say, that these corruptions, as we call them, are maintained as Christianity by its advocates."

These considerations determined me, by a reply to Mr. Belsham, to bring the subject before the public in order to obtain some further light upon it, and to settle my own mind which had been in a measure unsettled by Mr. B.'s Letters.

Mr. Belsham, however, for reasons best known to himself, did not think proper to take any notice of my arguments in reply to him, leaving me in possession of the field. He probably thought my arguments too contemptible to merit any notice, and his own so perfectly clear, conclusive and convincing as to stand in no need of correction, explanation or defence.

Secondly. I considered the doctrine of Christ's pre-existence as necessarily involving in it that of his

miraculous conception, although his miraculous conception does not necessarily imply his pre-existence ; because had he pre-existed his conception must have been preternatural ; but it might have been preternatural if he had not existed before ; as was the case respecting Isaac and Samuel. If then it should appear that his conception was not miraculous, I was fully convinced that the doctrine of his pre-existence must necessarily be given up. Under these impressions a work published in 1813,[*] fell into my hands, in which, I think, the author has proved that the accounts of the miraculous conception, as they now stand in the beginning of Matthew and Luke, are spurious ; and he has stated some facts as taking place, not at Bethlehem, but at Rome, from which the stories, recorded in the two first chapters of Matthew and Luke, probably originated. These circumstances, together with the improbability of their truth which appears upon the face of the accounts themselves, led me to conclude that they were not the genuine productions of those Evangelists to whom they are ascribed.

Thirdly. The inconsistency of those accounts with each other—with historical fact—and with the current language of the New Testament, furnish additional evidence that those accounts were not written by Matthew and Luke. With respect to their inconsistency I shall mention but one circumstance. The flight into Egypt recorded by Matthew, is not only unnoticed by Luke, but his account evidently, as I conceive, contradicts it. He tells us, ch. ii. 22, that, " When the days of her (i. e. Mary's) purification according to the law of Moses, were accomplished (that is when Jesus was forty days old) they brought him to Jerusalem, to present him to the Lord." And after relating what passed in the temple, he says, 39th and following verses, "And when they had performed all things according to the law of the Lord, *they returned into Galilee to their own city,*" not Bethlehem, but *"Nazareth.* And the child grew and waxed strong in spirit, filled with wisdom and the grace of God, was upon him. Now

* Jones's Sequel to his Ecclesiastical Researches.

his parents *went to Jerusalem every year* at the feast of the passover ; and when he was twelve years old they went up to Jerusalem, after the custom of the feast." The writer here represents Jesus when he was forty days old as being carried by his parents from *Nazareth, their own city,* up to Jerusalem, and returning to *Nazareth,* and from thence, annually, for twelve successive years, going up to Jerusalem to the passover ; and in chap. iv. 14, 16, Luke tells us that Jesus returned from the wilderness into Galilee, " and he came to *Nazareth, where he had been brought up.*" We have *here* therefore, the whole of the life of Jesus, for the first twelve years, accounted for as spent with his parents at Nazareth, leaving no possible period for the flight into Egypt; whereas the writer of the story in Matthew states, that he was *born at Bethlehem,* that *from thence* they went into Egypt, and continued there till after the death of Herod, who sought his life. Now two stories, so inconsistent with each other, cannot possibly be, both of them, true.

I might add, that if the massacre of the children of Bethlehem by the direction of Herod had been a fact, it is extremely improbable that neither Josephus, who wrote the Life of Herod, nor any other contemporary writer should mention so remarkable a circumstance.

With respect to historic fact. If it be sufficiently ascertained, as I think it is, by incontrovertible testimony, that Jesus was not born till after the death of Herod, then the whole of the stories related in the two first chapters of Matthew must be false and spurious.

Again, the birth of Jesus with the circumstances attending it, as recorded in the beginning of Matthew's Gospel, are inconsistent with the language of the New Testament, which represents Jesus as being *of Nazareth,* but never *of Bethlehem.* He is called *Jesus of Nazareth* about twenty times in the New Testament. Peter on the day of Pentecost, speaking as the Holy Spirit gave him utterance, calls him *Jesus of Nazareth.* The angels at his sepulchre call him *Jesus of Nazareth.* He calls himself so when he appeared to Paul as he was going to Damascus ; and his apostles wrought their miracles in the name of *Jesus of*

Nazareth. Had Jesus been indeed born at Bethlehem is it possible that the sacred writers should so invariably speak of him as being of Nazareth ? From any thing recorded in the New Testament it does not appear that Jesus himself, his apostles, or his historians knew any thing of his miraculous conception and birth at Bethlehem ; there is not any where in the preaching or letters of the apostles the most distant allusion to them ; and this is the more extraordinary if they were attended with such singular circumstances, and were the fulfilment of prophecies respecting him, as they are said to be by the writer of the two first chapters of Matthew's Gospel.

It is true, the Jews seem to have had a tradition amongst them, that the Christ was to come out of Bethlehem, and his enemies, who disputed his claims, are represented as saying, John vii. 41, 42, " Shall Christ come out of Galilee ? Hath not the scripture said, ' That Christ cometh of the seed of David, and out of the town of Bethlehem where David was ?' " And in another place, " Out of Galilee ariseth no prophet— Can any good thing come out of Nazareth ?" Is it not strange, if Jesus and his historians knew that he was born at Bethlehem, that they should in no instance have corrected this mistaken idea, that he was a Galilean, and refuted the argument founded on it to prove that he could not be the Christ, by stating, that in fact he was not of Nazareth in Galilee ; but that he did indeed *come out of Bethlehem ?* On the contrary, they every where assert, that *he was of Nazareth.*

The above passage, I believe, is the only one in the New Testament in which Bethlehem is so much as mentioned, excepting those in the beginning of Matthew and Luke where it repeatedly occurs. But

Fourthly. This matter is put beyond all possible doubt, if Mr. Jones is right (as I think he is), in his translation of Luke iii. 23,—" And Jesus himself began to be about thirty years of age, being (really) as he was thought to be, the son of Joseph." I shall not transcribe his criticisms on the construction of the Greek of this passage, but only the conclusion he draws from them. " It is therefore a

thus by one single unequivocal expression, he has set aside the story of his miraculous birth as false, and the two disputed chapters as a forgery of a subsequent period." See Sequel, p. 241. Note.

Thus, Sir, I have laid before you the steps by which I have arrived at my present views, and hope they will be as satisfactory to your correspondent as they are to myself.

I am, Sir,
Yours, &c.
JOHN MARSOM.

St. Ardleon, Oct. 30, 1815.

SIR,

THE following lines, in Prior's *Solomon*, (B. iii.) have, I believe, been much oftener admired than examined, as to the justness of the sentiments they express :—

Happy the mortal man, who now at last
Has through this doleful vale of mis'ry
     past,
Who to his destin'd stage has carried on
The tedious load, and laid his burden
     down ;
Whom the cut brass and wounded marble
     shows
Victor o'er life and all her train of woes.
He happier yet who privileg'd by fate
To shorter labour and a lighter weight,
Receiv'd but yesterday the gift of breath,
Order'd to-morrow to return to death.
But O ! beyond description happiest he,
Who ne'er must roll on life's tempestuous
     sea ;
Who with blest freedom from the gene-
     ral doom
Exempt, must never force the teeming
     womb,
Nor see the sun, nor sink into the tomb.
Who breathes must suffer, and who thinks
     must mourn :
And he alone is blest who ne'er was born.

I am not aware that the Pagan origin of these lines has ever been conjectured. Prior appears to have had in his recollection not so much the passage in *Ecclesiastes* (iv. 2, 3) as the following verse of Sophocles in his *Œdipus Coloneus* :—

Μὴ φῦναι τον ἅπαντα νι-
κᾶ λόγον· τὸ δ', ἐπεὶ φανῇ,
Βῆναι κεῖθεν ὅθεν περ ἥκει,
Πολὺ δεύτερον, ὡς τάχιϛα.

free,
Shall whence he came with speediest foot
     return.

With which may be compared Potter's version :—

Not to be born is Heav'n's first grace,
If born, extinguish'd soon the vital flame ;
Back to return from whence it came,
Is heav'n's next blessing to man's wretch-
     ed race.

I am here reminded of a note in Wakefield's Matthew, 4to. p. 367, on the Case of Judas (xxv. 24). That scriptural critic, who brought his various learning, as a glad offering to the Sanctuary of Religion, remarks on the expression *had not been born*, that it is " a proverbial sentence, meaning in general that this action would be attended by very calamitous consequences to the criminal." He adds, citing a couplet from the Greek Epigrams, that " it is common for unhappy people to wish that they had never been born;" and subjoins from Maimonides (Mor. 'Nev. i. 32, *Buxtorf*) this *Jewish sentence*, "Whoever does not spare the glory of his Creator, it were better for him not to have come into the world."

It is remarkable that Mr. Wakefield, who has here qualified the force of the phrase, *had not been born*, appears to have forgotten that at p. 361, of the same work, (on Matt. xxv. 46) he had taken it strictly as an argument against the *hypothesis* of the *final happiness* of the wicked," which he, with evident reluctance, concludes to be " *unscriptural*, because then, in no instance, can it be better for a man *never to have been born :* a case, which the N. T. not only supposes, but exemplifies"—*aliquando bonus dormitat.* Gilbert Wakefield (of whom I had some knowledge) had considered the divine attributes and the perfectability of man with too much attention to have easily become a consistent advocate for the dreary doctrine of human destruction.

R. B.

———

American Proclamation of a Fast-Day.

[It is perhaps to be regretted that in any country, Religion should be associated with War, which is seldom on any side justifiable. The different manner, however, in which governments appeal, in their quarrels, to the Lord of Hosts, is characteristic of the spirit of their institutions. In this view, we have been considerably impressed with the following Proclamation of a Day of Humiliation by the President of the United States, during the late unhappy contest with this country; and venture to insert it in our Repository, wishing it to be read, as it surely may, now that the two countries are at peace, not as a political manifesto, but as a *State Curiosity.* Ed.]

WHEREAS the Congress of the United States, by a joint resolution of the two houses, have signified a request that a day may be recommended, to be observed by the people of the United States with religious solemnity, as a day of *Public Humiliation and Prayer;* and whereas in times of public calamity, such as that of the war, brought on the United States by the injustice of a foreign government, it is especially becoming, that the hearts of all should be touched with the same, and the eyes of all be turned to that Almighty Power, in whose hand are the welfare and destiny of nations: I do, therefore, issue this my proclamation, recommending to all who shall be piously disposed, to unite their hearts and voices in addressing, at one and the same time, their vows and adorations to the great Parent and Sovereign of the Universe, that they assemble on the second Thursday of September next, in their respective religious congregations, to render him thanks for the many blessings he has bestowed on the people of the United States; that he has blessed them with a land capable of yielding all the necessaries and requisites of human life, with ample means for convenient exchanges with foreign countries; that he has blessed the labours employed in its cultivation and improvement; that he is now blessing the exertions to extend and establish the arts and manufactures, which will secure within ourselves supplies too important to remain dependent on the precarious policy, or the peaceable dispositions of other nations; and particularly that he has blessed the United States with a political constitution, founded on

the will and authority of the whole people, and guaranteeing to each individual security, not only of his person and his property, but of those sacred rights of conscience, so essential to his present happiness and so dear to his future hopes:—that with those expressions of devout thankfulness be joined supplications to the same Almighty Power, that he would look down with compassion on our infirmities, that he would pardon our manifold transgressions, and awaken and strengthen in all the wholesome purposes of repentance and amendment; that in this season of trial and calamity, he would preside in a particular manner over our public councils, and inspire all citizens with a love of their country, and with those fraternal affections, and that mutual confidence, which have so happy a tendency to make us safe at home and respected abroad; and that, as he was graciously pleased, heretofore, to smile on our struggles against the attempts of the government of the empire of which these states then made a part, to wrest from them the rights and privileges to which they were entitled in common with every other part, and to raise them to the station of an independent and sovereign people; so he would now be pleased, in like manner, to bestow his blessing on our arms in resisting the hostile and persevering efforts of the same power to degrade us on the ocean, the common inheritance of all, from rights and immunities, belonging and essential to the American people, as a co-equal member of the great community of independent nations; and that, inspiring our enemies with moderation, with justice, and with that spirit of reasonable accommodation, which our country has continued to manifest, we may be enabled to beat our swords into ploughshares, and to enjoy in peace, every man, the fruits of his honest industry and the rewards of his lawful enterprise. If the public homage of a people can ever be worthy the favourable regard of the holy and omniscient Being to whom it is addressed, it must be that in which those who join in it are guided only by their free choice, by the impulse of their hearts and the dictates of their consciences, and such a spectacle must be interesting to all Christian nations;

mity with the resolution aforesaid, to dedicate the day above-named to the religious solemnities therein recommended.

Given at Washington this twenty-third day of July, in the year of our Lord 1813.

J. MADISON.

York, Jan. 4th, 1816.

Sir,

IN a former paper I endeavoured to state to you some thoughts which had occurred to me with increased emphasis, after reading the enlightened and consolatary treatise of Dr. Cogan, in farther illustration of the strong presumptive evidence which arises from a careful examination of the known phenomena of the human mind, compared with the leading objects of divine revelation, that both have the same great Being for their Author: and I now beg leave to occupy a few of your pages by the insertion of some additional reflections tending to corroborate the still more important truth, closely connected indeed with the former, that the great and benevolent object of both, is the ultimate perfection and happiness of the whole human race. We would even presume to go further, and add, if creatures so ignorant and liable to error might indulge in a speculation so vast and magnificent, that all things not only in this world but throughout the boundless Universe, "are working together for good," for the production of the greatest general perfection and happiness, so that every rational being, from the highest to the lowest

part of habitable space : and if this be the fact, there must have been in the intermediate gradation between the creatures governed by mere instinct and those next above them, to whom the power of reason is superadded, a creature such as man ;*—a creature at first, impotent, and wholly governed by present objects, subject during a series of years, if not through the whole of his probationary state to innumerable errors and follies, but capable, if he gain the victory over them, of attaining to very high de-

---

* The writer is tempted to subjoin the following passage on this subject from a volume of Discourses chiefly on practical subjects, recently published. P. 8, " When we reflect," says the author, " that the springing-grass, the opening flower, the spreading tree, are each of them the habitation of innumerable living things, all of them enjoying the utmost perfection of their natures, rejoicing in the liberality of an unknown God ; when, from these minute and invisible objects of his bounty, we raise our eyes and indulge our memory and imagination, and extend our view more widely through all the regions of the earth, the waters and the air ; of the stagnant lake, the flowing river and the restless ocean, on every climate, under every sky ; on the lonely forest, the barren hills and uncultivated vales ; when we find them all inhabited by their proper people ; every element replete with life ; not a corner of the world, scarce an atom of his creation but where some happy being is rejoicing in his goodness ; our souls are elevated with diviner transports, we seem to sympathize with the whole creation of God, and in some measure to enjoy the happiness of the world !"

grees of mental and moral excellence, and eventually of being fitted for a very exalted place, when this life shall be over, in those celestial abodes, where dwelleth everlasting uprightness.

Now it is clear, that in addition to the faculty of reason, he who forms this link in the immeasurable chain, must possess the power of deliberating and choosing between two contrary modes of action, (call it freewill, or being influenced by motives, or by whatever other name you please) for otherwise he could not be deemed an accountable creature, or gain those permanent habits by a long series of conscientious self-government and virtuous exertion, which are requisite for the formation of a finished character, and essential to his being fitted for heavenly happiness.

If it should be inquired, why man was not originally endowed with such superior faculties as should have effectually preserved him from every sinful deviation ;—with views so just and extended of his duty to God and his own happiness, as should have led him unerringly forward in the plain tranquil paths of piety and virtue ? it is obvious to reply, that this in fact would be to inquire why such a creature as man should ever have been formed. Besides, had he been created impeccable, without the possibility of transgressing, or even had he been placed in a situation where the temptations to transgress were less frequent and less powerful, he might indeed have remained innocent, but could hardly have been called virtuous ; and although his existence might still have been a blessing, yet surely not a blessing compared with his, who " by patient continuance in well doing," has at length formed a character which may in some measure be deemed his own ; and who has thereby become fitted, through the infinite mercy of God, for " honour, glory and immortality." How do we know that the previous discipline arising from great imperfection within, and multiplied temptations from without, may not have been indispensable to the attainment of that firmness and stability of virtue, which the future exalted stations to which such happy persons will be promoted, may absolutely require ? We know who it was that was made perfect

through suffering. And it may be true, for any thing we know to the contrary, that every order of created being from feeble man to the glorious Archangel that stands before the throne of the Most High ; may all of them have previously passed through a scene of probation ; or, in other words, may from very small beginnings have made continual advances from one degree of perfection to another.

But be this as it may, in respect to ourselves at least, that this is actually the fact, is suggested by reason, and amply confirmed by revelation. If the amiable, diligent child will eventually become the intelligent, virtuous man, is it probable, is it at all analogous to what we certainly do or may know of the power, the wisdom, and the goodness of God, that when the man thus disciplined and prepared, shall have fully attained to all the wisdom and all the knowledge of which in this mortal state he is capable ; when the great object of his life, it may be for a series of succeeding years, shall have been to devote himself faithfully to the service of God and the good of his fellow-creatures; that, at the very moment when these rare endowments, obtained with so much labour, and fostered with so much care, appear to have formed a complete habit, that they should then in an instant be for ever extinguished; lost and eternally buried in the silence of the tomb ?—Most happily, however, for the sincere believer in the gospel of Christ, what reason intimates and piety most fervently desires, revelation demonstratively confirms. There we are fully apprized that the present life is but the seed-time of human being, that "whatever a man sows, that shall he also reap," and that those who overcome the temptations to sin, shall finally attain " the prize of the high calling in Christ Jesus our Lord."

But the interesting, important question will be asked, If those only who are Christians in deed, as well as in name, shall attain to this blessedness, what must be the portion, not alone of the incorrigibly wicked, but of the myriads on myriads in every age and in every country who unhappily fall far below this Christian standard; and this, through all the various stages of imperfection from mere harmlessness, of character to the sad extremes of profligacy and vice? Alas, shall they all perish for ever? Or where and how must the line of demarcation be drawn? On this subject, reason has but little to depose, and the page of revelation is not explicit. Of this, however, we may rest assured, though it is not for us to know the times and the seasons, that the judge of all the earth will do right. But if we have no data from which to reason accurately, and no explicit declaration from scripture, perhaps from analogy some little information may be derived on this perplexing subject, remembering, however, that in the region of conjecture, even when aided by this borrowed light, we ought always to proceed, if not with timid, yet with wary, cautious steps.

If then it is highly probable, as we have seen, that in the various orders of beings superior to man, the ascent above him should be regular and gradual, in like manner as we see the descent below him, and especially if it be requisite that all must equally pass through a state of probation before they are fitted for durable, complete happiness; may it not be, that those who have not duly improved the opportunities of the present state, may be destined to occupy some of those intermediate stages in a future life in which greater and more severe discipline may be employed to remove the deep stains of guilt; contracted, not merely by ignorance and folly, but by pride, sensuality, ambition, cruelty and revenge?

In corroboration of this suggestion it may be observed, that every thing we see or witness around us, whether in the material, the vegetable, the animal, or the intellectual creation, are parts of one great whole, evidently subservient to each other, and working together (as we continually more clearly perceive in proportion to our advancement in knowledge) for the greater good of all. In this world nothing is of itself complete; and from analogy may we not conclude that, as the whole universe is equally dependent upon the great Creator and Sovereign Lord of all, the same general law extends to other systems and other worlds, and that all have a mutual relation to, and act and react upon each other? In fact, we are certain, that in respect of the general

laws of which we have any knowledge, this mutual subserviency does actually take place. We know that the same sun which gives light and heat and animates the principle of vegetation in our little planet, dispenses in like manner similar advantages and blessings to other planetary worlds, which like our own, move around him; that the ebbing and flowing tides of the ever-changing ocean are regulated by the immediate influence of the friendly satellite, which monthly completes her revolution around its shores, and which may probably in her turn be curiously connected with and dependent upon our globe for multiplied phenomena essential to her welfare, of which we have no knowledge. We perceive likewise that even the fixed stars which illuminate immeasurable space, and are probably so many suns that like our own dispense light and heat to systems of revolving worlds, do not refuse their friendly assistance, notwithstanding their inconceivable distance, to the bewildered mariner, who, without their aid, would infallibly perish.

What then is God? How transcendantly glorious is the small glimpse we thus transiently obtain of Him, " in whom, and through whom and to whom are all things!" Well might the pious psalmist of antiquity exclaim, " Whither shall I go from thy spirit, or whither shall I flee from thy presence? If I ascend up to heaven thou art there, if I make my bed in hades behold thou art there! If I take the wings of the morning and remain in the uttermost parts of the sea, even there shall thine hand lead me, and thy right hand shall hold me!" Of what infinite importance it is that we should desire above all things to impress this great truth upon our minds, and should make it our most ardent endeavour to live always as in his sight!

If it be indeed true, that God is every where, at all times present, what a subject of alarm to the impenitently wicked! What a source of trust and confidence and consolation, and triumph, to the godly and upright! Surely, Mr. Editor, Unitarians beyond all others, they who profess a purer Christianity, should especially labour to cultivate this devotional spirit; they, whose belief is so simple and sublime; so perfectly consonant to all the grand and striking phenomena they see around them; so wholly unmixed with metaphysical subtleties and scholastic contradictions, should be anxiously solicitous, in humble obedience to the solemn injunctions of their divine Master, " to let their light so shine before men," that others seeing their incorruptible integrity, their exemplary piety, their courage in refusing to be conformed to this world, its delusive maxims and its unhallowed, dissipated pursuits,—their unbounded Christian benevolence, ever ready to join in every good work and labour of love, should thence be more powerfully stimulated " to glorify their father who is in heaven!"

May we indeed hope to see the happy day when the superior excellence of Unitarian practice shall perfectly harmonize with the superior purity of Unitarian faith? And that the Monthly Repository may have the distinguished honour of contributing towards this glorious result, is the ardent wish of a sincere friend, and constant reader,

C. C.

Sir,   *Oct.* 22, 1815.

IT appears suitable to your design of connecting Theology and Literature, to notice in works, where they might not have been expected, any hints of a theological complexion. With this view I offer you the following passages :

Mr. Rymer, Historiographer to King William, who appears to have been well versed in polite literature, but is now chiefly known by his great Collection of the *Fœdera*, wrote on " the Antiquity, Power and Decay of Parliaments," in the form of a Letter, published in 1714, a few months after the author's decease. Having described an " artificial mixed sort of government that always has obtained in *Europe*, and that which all, in some manner or other, with more or less success and perfection, have tended to as the centre and only place of rest," he says, p. 9,

" The first writers among us had their imaginations so overborne with the excellency of kingly government, that they fancied in heaven Jupiter to be the King of the Gods. And yet they thought the Common Council so necessary and essential, that

Homer represents even Jupiter, upon a great occasion, calling his θεῶν ἀγορὴν, his *Parliament of the Gods.*" The author then adds the passage for which I have quoted him:

" I have heard Divines observe something of this kind, as figured of God Almighty from those words, *Let us make man.* Those words, in the plural number, to them seemed to import, *as if God summoned a Parliament of the Trinity,* to consult upon that arduous affair. Our Christian Poets have taken the same liberty, and fancied this, as an image of greatness, where could be no accession to the Wisdom and Omnipotence."

Mr. Rymer has at least insinuated his doubts of the popular Theology, on a very important point, by this manner of referring to it. He might, I apprehend, have quoted several *Christian Poets,* who had thus indulged in *theological* as well as poetical licence. I conjectured at first, that *Milton* was in his thoughts. Yet on refreshing my recollection, by a reference to Paradise Lost, I find the author, to be no Trinitarian, but what, for distinction, has been denominated a *high Arian.*

I am not aware that throughout that Poem there is any acknowledgement of what has been called the distinct personality of a Holy Spirit, or any thing beyond a subordinate Deity attributed to the Son, *the filial Godhead,* who goes forth to the work of creation (B. vii.) *in paternal glory.* On the creation of man the poet, instead of introducing a Trinity, sings how

—————th' Omnipotent
Eternal Father (for where is not he
Present?) thus to his Son audibly spake,
Let us now make Man in our own image, man
In our similitude.

It is a later poet, *Young,* who, somewhere in his prose works, infers the dignity of man from the whole Trinity having been employed in his creation. Young's theological ideas were indeed so gross, that in the *Night Thoughts* he describes the *Crucifixion* as

Expended Deity, on human weal;

and ranks this as principal among

——the *great truths,* which burst the tenfold night
Of *Heathen* error, with a golden flood
Of endless day.

As if a dying God or, as he quaint-
ly sings, an *expended Deity* had been
a novelty to *Heathens*, who could
have referred the *Christian* poet to
their *Jupiter's* tomb.

Well might a theologian of such a
wide swallow complain, as Young
does at the commencement of the
Centaur, that " Socinus, like our infidels, was one of a narrow throat ;"
thus also discovering the ignorance
or injustice too common with the
reputed Orthodox, on such subjects.
Yet could Young be really ignorant
that a Bishop of St. David's, not a
Burgess, had recommended, in a
Charge to his Clergy, the work of
Socinus, *de auctoritate sacræ scrip-
turæ*, as *a valuable performance*, and
that a Clerrgyman had published a
translation of the work, dedicated to
Queen Caroline, under the title of *a
Demonstration of the Truth of the
Christian Religion.* I have now before me the 2nd edition, 1732.

IGNOTUS.

Sir,   *Jan.* 27, 1816,

AMONG the *Say Papers*, in your
Vol. iv. p. 483, is an account
in one of Mrs. Shepherd's letters, of
a *Jubilee* celebrated at Stockholm in
1717, on the 2nd Centenary of the
Reformation, which was considered
as commenced by Luther, when "on
the eve of *All Saints*, in 1517, he affixed on the Church adjoining the
Castle of Wittemberg his Thesis containing thirty-five Propositions against
Indulgencies, challenging any one to
oppose them either by writing or
public disputation." That this Jubilee was, at least partially, observed
in England, appears from a published
Sermon, entitled,

" *The Duty of Reformation.* Set
forth in a Sermon, preached at St.
James's, in the Chapel of his late
Royal Highness Prince George of
Denmark, on the nineteenth Sunday
after Trinity, 1717. On occasion of
the *Jubilee*, kept about this time, by
some Protestant Churches, in remembrance of the Reformation begun two
hundred years ago. By Anthony
William Boehm, Chaplain to his late
Royal Highness. London. 1718."

The name *Jubilee* has been rendered almost contemptible, in this country, by the servile purposes of courtly
adulation, to which, not many years
ago, it was applied. Otherwise a re-

ligious Jubilee may be not unworthi-
ly celebrated by those who shall survive to the now approaching third
Centenary of the *Reformation*, an
event, to be valued not so much for
the state of things it immediately produced, as for that which it has occasioned.

The door, opened by Luther, to
free inquiry in religion, can now no
more be shut than the gates of the
poet which barred the passage out of
Chaos. Notwithstanding a transient
obscurity the light will surely shine
unto the perfect day. Nor can I for-

gnative cloud,
Rais'd by thy breath, has quench'd the
orb of day?
To-morrow he repairs the golden flood
And warms the nations with redoubled ray.

It will probably be the admiration
of posterity that modern statesmen
should have given themselves credit
for having secured the repose of Europe while they have united *Tros
Rutulusve*—Papist, Protestant, and
Greek, to restore that spiritual domination which had sunk into insignificance under the genius of Napoleon,
but which for ages before had continually embroiled the world. *Dagon*
is indeed again set on his pedestal,
yet, I trust, his mutilations can never
be repaired.

OTIOSUS.

Sir,

AMONG the many laudable efforts now making to decrease
what I must take the liberty of calling
idolatry, and to increase the number
of Unitarian Christians, I have sometimes been a little surprised, that it
has not hitherto been thought of sufficient importance to make the road
more generally easy for the members
of the Established Church. It is well
known that great numbers of them
are highly dissatisfied with much of
what they there meet with—with the
Trinity—with their creeds—with the
length of their services—and with
the frequent repetitions in the same
service. Notwithstanding all these
solid objections, however, it is equally well known, that but few of them
can be prevailed upon to quit " the
Church" for " the Meeting-house,"
where the minister prays, not in a

form agreed upon by his congregation, but according to his own good pleasure, which sometimes introduces a little politics into his religion.

Most sincerely therefore do I wish that Unitarians would adopt the liturgic form of prayer, as a mean the most probable of inducing the members of the establishment to join them. In a Liturgy, consisting of as many services as you please, the Trinitarian would see—that you had kept clear of all his objections—all the world would have the clearest evidence that Unitarians are not the atheistical or deistical persons they are too generally supposed to be—and, to name no further advantage, in the event of the minister's absence or illness the devotional part of the service need never be omitted. This I am sorry to see, by the last number of the Christian Reformer, has been the case lately at such a place at Norwich; and, in the present dearth of ministers, is too frequently the case elsewhere.

In fine, Mr. Editor, I beg leave very respectfully to propose, that the term Meeting-house be entirely discarded, and that of Unitarian Church be substituted throughout the country —that a Liturgy of two or more services be universally adopted—that the churches every where be kept in the best possible condition, and comfortably warmed in cold weather—and, the road being thus made both straight and pleasant, I am satisfied we should much more frequently see the serious and respectable members of the establishment in our churches than we have hitherto done, or are at all likely to do under the present system; the gulph between the Church and the Meeting-house being so great, that few there be who attempt to pass it.

L.

P. S. Although we have lately heard nothing of the plan for forming Unitarians into a more compact body, so important an object is, I trust, in progress.

Royston, Dec. 10, 1815.

SIR,

I SHOULD not have sent this letter to your Repository if I had not known, that your readers are generally reckoned among the *thinking* part of the religious world. The subject is the Lord's Supper. My at-

tention was excited to this subject, by a remark in Hall's publication on "Terms of Communion," page 129, where it is said that, "the Lord's Supper is a *positive* and *arbitrary* institution, in consequence of which the right to it, is not to be judged of by moral considerations and general reasoning, but by *express prescription* and command." Now then, I wish to know from honest men and Christians, how it happens, that the *modern* disciples of Christ, eat *leavened* bread, contrary to express prescription and the example of their Master? Who can claim a right to *alter* a tittle of a *positive* and *arbitrary* institution? This is Antichrist in the only true sense of that word; and he who can claim a right to alter *one* part of a positive institution, has the same right to alter any other part, or to alter the whole. A *few* words are sufficient for the wise, and the thinking part of mankind.

Yours, &c.

F.

Birmingham, Jan. 2, 1816.

SIR,

I CONGRATULATE you and the friends of uncorrupted Christianity on the proposal for publishing a uniform and complete edition of *Dr. Priestley's Theological Works.* The editor (our much-respected friend, Mr. Rutt) is richly entitled to the thanks of the Unitarian public. It is evident, from the proposed mode of publication,[*] that the only objects he can have in view in entering upon so laborious an undertaking are the promotion of the great cause of rational Christianity, and of erecting an honourable and lasting monument to the memory of one of the best Christians and greatest philosophers of the age.

Looking forward to this publication with much pleasure (though, I confess, not altogether unmixed with anxiety, lest the expense of the undertaking should prevent many warm friends to the cause from giving it their support) I beg leave particularly

---

[*] A friend of mine, conversant with the expenses of publishing, tells me that a volume of the same bulk with that proposed for the *Works* (which will cost the subscribers about 13s. 6d.) could not be sold to the public by a bookseller for less than 18s.

to recommend it to the managers of our different *Congregational Libraries,* which are now pretty generally scattered throughout the kingdom; and as three or four hundred subscribers will, I conceive, be sufficient to ensure the appearance of the *Works,* these Libraries would certainly go a great way in making up that number.

It would be too much to expect that, in addition to the gratuitous labour of such an undertaking, the worthy Editor should also be subject to loss; it is therefore highly desirable that those friends, who are able and willing to countenance the publication should do so *without delay,* as the carrying so large a work through the press must necessarily occupy a considerable portion of time.

I am, Sir,
Yours, &c.
A SUBSCRIBER.

Bromley, Feb. 12, 1816.

Sir,

I SHALL thank you to give a place in the Repository to my Proposals for publishing Dr. Priestley's Theological Works. I am, of course, unable to ascertain, at present, whether the projected edition will be sufficiently encouraged by subscriptions. I wish, however, whatever may be the result, to leave recorded among your pages an account of the nature and extent of the design. I remain, Sir,
Yours, &c.
J. T. R.

Proposals for publishing by Subscription, in Medium, 8vo., Dr. Priestley's Theological Works. To be edited by J. T. Rutt.

It may be fairly presumed that many persons, disposed to religious inquiry, especially amongst the now increasing number of Unitarians, will be inclined to encourage an edition of Dr. Priestley's Theological Works, on an economical plan.

To accommodate such persons, it is proposed, (under the general title of Theological Works,) to reprint such of Dr. Priestley's publications as are classed, in the Catalogue annexed to his Memoirs, under the following heads :—*Metaphysics — Religious Liberty — Ecclesiastical History — Evidences of the Christian Revelation — Defences of Unitarianism* and *Miscellaneous Theology;* including his Papers in the Theological Repository, and the Prefaces to his Scientific and

Miscellaneous Works, or any incidental passages in them, where he has declared or defended his theological opinions. This enumeration cannot fail to comprehend several repetitions of subjects, first hastily sketched, and afterwards more elaborately detailed. The proposed Editor is, however, desirous of ascertaining whether persons may not be found, to encourage the projected edition, who may wish to possess all these Works of Dr. Priestley, to observe, for themselves, the progress of such a mind, and to discover the first hints of those opinions which subjected their author to so much evil as well as good report.

It is designed to accompany the edition with Notes, some of which appear to be required from the lapse of years since Dr. Priestley became known as a theological writer. These notes to be as concise, as the purpose of conveying useful information will permit; and generally employed to notice such inconsistencies or variations of opinion as could scarcely have been avoided in publications which extended through nearly forty years —to correct any errors which may be discovered in dates or references, such as the considerate will readily excuse in a writer who was so often urged by the ardour of his mind and an impulse of incumbent duty to a rapid employment of his ready pen—to supply additional authorities, where such can be discovered, and especially to quote the passages from authors whose works have become less accessible than when Dr. Priestley alluded to their opinions. By these notes it is also intended to form a connexion between the author's works, to remark what strictures they at first excited, or the more extended controversies to which they gave occasion.

In the arrangement of such an edition, it is proposed to make the contents of each volume succeed in the order of time as nearly as a proper connexion of subjects will allow. The first volume is intended to include the *Institutes,* which will be preceded by a Life of the Author, compiled, with a particular reference to the projected edition, chiefly on the authorities of his own Memoirs, incidental notices in his Works, the Continuation by Mr. Priestley, and the Memoirs of Mr. Lindsey by the Rev. *T. Belsham,* on whose approbation and concurrence the proposed Editor is happy to be allowed to rely. Should any friends to the memory of Dr. Priestley, and to this design, be in possession of unpublished letters or papers, which they would commit to the Editor's discretion, he would be much obliged by such communications. He begs leave, also, generally to solicit the readers of Dr. Priestley's works, to give him any information, through the medium of the Monthly Repository, or otherwise, which may assist him in rendering the projected edition a tribute, not altogether unworthy of the well-earned reputation of the author, whose memory will be always cherished by the friends of civil and religious liberty, of free inquiry and of evangelical simplicity and truth.

In the edition now proposed the types of the text and notes are intended to be the same as those of Lardner's Works, in the late Mr. Johnson's octavo edition, with an equally full page, which will contain more than two of the usual octavo pages. The typographical execution, especially as to correctness, will be, deservedly, an object of peculiar attention.

It is expected that sixteen volumes, each containing from 500 to 600 pages, will complete the intended publication, or at most eighteen such volumes, should the proposed notes extend further than at present apprehended. These volumes will include, under the general title of Dr. Priestley's Theological Works, what are now extended into nearly forty octavo volumes, and more than fifty pamphlets of various sizes.

To accomplish this design, a subscription of *Two Guineas* is proposed to be paid on subscribers giving their names, and *Half a Guinea* on the delivery of each volume. Only a small number of copies, beyond those subscribed for, to be printed.

The following friends to the proposed undertaking have obligingly offered to promote its success by receiving subscriptions :

London—Rev. *R. Aspland,* Durham House, Hackney Road ; Mr. *R. Hunter,* Bookseller, St. Paul's Church Yard; Mr. *D. Eaton,* Bookseller, No. 187, High Holborn ; and Messrs. *Stower* and *Smallfield,* Printers, Hackney.
Bath—Rev. *Joseph Hunter.*
Bilston—Mr. *S. Bassford,* Bookseller.

Birmingham—Rev. *J. Kentish;* Mr. *J. B. Toulmin.*
Bristol—Rev. *Dr. Estlin.*
Chichester—Rev. *W. J. Fox.*
Cranbrook—Mr. *S. Dobell.*
Crewkerne—Rev. *W. Blake.*
Derby Row—Rev. — *Higginson.*
Dorchester—Rev. *B. Treleaven.*
Exeter—Rev. *Dr. Carpenter.*
Glasgow—Rev. *James Yates;* Mr. *George Harris,* College.
Kidderminster—Rev. *R. Fry.*
Leeds—Rev. *T. Jervis.*
Lewes—Mr. *Ebenezer Johnston.*
Lincoln—Rev. — *Hawkes.*
Liverpool—Rev. *John Yates;* Mr. *F. B. Wright,* Printer.
Manchester—Rev. *J. Grundy.*
Newcastle—Rev. *W. Turner.*
Norwich—Rev. *T. Madge.*
Nottingham — Rev. *James Tayler;* Mr. *E. B. Robinson,* Bookseller.
Portsmouth—Rev. *R. Scott.*
Southampton—Mr. *B. Travers.*
Stockport—Rev. *Samuel Parker.*
Warrington—Rev. *W. Broadbent.*
Wisbeach—Rev. *R. Wright.*
Wolverhampton—Mr. *Joseph Pearson.*
Yarmouth—Mr. *W. Alexander,* Bookseller.
York—Rev. *C. Wellbeloved.*

The friends to this undertaking who design to encourage it by their subscriptions are requested to give their names immediately, as the first volume will be prepared for the press, as soon as the number of subscribers appears sufficient to defray the mere expenses of publication. One volume will be delivered, if possible, every three months.

Should it unexpectedly appear, after a fair experiment, that this design has failed for want of even a moderate encouragement, the sums subscribed shall be punctually returned to the subscribers.

Bromley, Middlesex, Dec. 27, 1815.

———

SIR, *Nov. 27, 1815.*
ONE of the four Poets whom Johnson specially recommended for insertion in his Collection, was Dr. Yalden. I lately discovered a powerful reason for the choice of Yalden, who, in the following lines, anticipated the malignity of the Biographer towards the principles and character of Milton.

On the re-printing Milton's Prose Works,
  1698. *Written in his Paradise Lost.*
These sacred lines with wonder we peruse,
And praise the flights of a seraphic Muse;

Till thy seditious prose provokes our rage,
And soils the beauties of thy brightest
page.
Thus here we see transporting scenes arise,
Heav'n's radiant host, and opening para-
dise ;
Then trembling view the dread abyss be-
neath,
Hell's horrid mansions, and the realms of
death.
Whilst here thy bold majestic numbers
rise,
And range th' embattled legions of the
skies,
With armies fill the azure plains of light,
And paint the lively terrors of the fight,
We own the poet worthy to rehearse
Heav'n's lasting triumphs in immortal
verse :
But when thy impious mercenary pen
Insults the best of princes, best of men,
Our admiration turns to just disdain,
And we revoke the fond applause again.
Like the fall'n angels in their happy
state,
Thou shar'dst their nature, insolence and
fate :
To harps divine, immortal hymns they
sung,
As sweet thy voice, as sweet thy lyre was
strung.
As they did rebels to th' Almighty grow,
So thou prophan'st his image here below.
Apostate bard ! may not thy guilty ghost,
Discover to its own eternal cost,
That as they heaven, thou paradise hast
lost !

The "impious and mercenary pen"
of Milton, and Charles, "the best of
princes, best of men," are poetic fancies, equally amusing. Yalden, who
died in 1736, aged 65, had been a
contemporary, at Magdalen College,
Oxford, with Addison and Sachever-
ell, adhering to the political principles of the latter. In the heaven of
Court-Divines and Poets, Kings, or
Protectors, when Kings could not be
found, have always shone as stars of
the first magnitude. Thus Sprat,
who, as a young collegian, in 1658,
while hopeless of the return of royalty,
chaunted the praises of the deceased
Cromwell, "the subject of the noblest pens and most divine phansies,"
was ready, as a grateful Bishop, to
celebrate, in a mournful Pastoral, the
Apotheosis of Charles II. How different a place was discovered by the
uncourtly Quevedo, in one of his Visions, for "all the Kings that ever
reigned." Grotius too, in his *Votum
pro pace*, as translated in 1652, quotes
for a "true saying," that "all good

Princes may have their names easily
inscribed within the compass of one
ring." He, however, advises the people " to desire the best, and give God
thanks for the middle sort, and bear
with the worst, for the doctrine and
example of Christ."

PLEBEIUS.

Bromley, Feb. 4, 1816.
SIR,

IN the number for Feb. 1813, Vol.
viii. p. 110, a curious " Quaker
Creed" is given with some judicious
remarks on it by " N. C.," in order
to shew your readers " what sort of
a Trinity it is, which at least some
highly accredited members of this
Society profess to believe." He was
furnished with it " by a Friend," who
had, it seems, questioned his right to
consider himself a Christian, " because
he was understood not to believe in
the Divinity of Christ."
Your correspondent replied, " that
if by divinity was meant, divine commission and authority, he believed it
as firmly as any person"—but that if
this term meant, " essential Deity,
equality with the Father," he did not
conceive " that any person could
prove such a doctrine from the scriptures." The friend " declined entering into any explanations," observing,
" that it was not the practice of their
Society to engage in theological controversy." But in return for Dr.
Priestley's Appeal, and Elwall's Trial,
he furnished " N. C." with the said
" Quaker Creed," which the latter
sent for insertion in your Journal. It
does not, as he remarked, even hold
the doctrine of " a mere *modal* Trinity," explicitly disavowing the idea
of " three *persons*, or essences," in the
Deity. That in short, like other modifications of the Sabellian scheme it
only supplies " a pretence for the
[partial] use of orthodox language,
while the real doctrine is strictly Unitarian."
Yet has this Creed been lately re-
published, verbatim, by an accredited
Elder in the Society of Friends, William Alexander, of York, in his "Annual Monitor, for the year 1816," with
this commentary preface : THE following *explanation* of *the Unity* of the
Divine Being was found in MS. a few
years ago, bearing the marks of not
being a very modern production ; but
without any clue by which to disco-

ver the author. Its coincidence with the sentiments of the Editor induced him to request a copy of the individual among whose papers it was found, and he trusts it will not be less pleasing to many of his readers.

" The words, in the general, are placed in brackets, being an addition which he has ventured to insert; as he does not conceive by the *tenure* [tenor] of the whole piece, that the author intended so unqualified a restriction of the several appellations as his words may otherwise possibly imply."

To enable your readers to judge of this singular piece of conjectural criticism, I will subjoin the paragraph to which it relates, with the intended amendment, viz. " The different appellations of Father, Son, and Holy Spirit are, nevertheless, not to be used indifferently or indiscriminately one for another, because [in the general] they are properly and consistently used *only,* as this one Supreme, Self-existing Essence is considered in different points of view."

I have put the above word *only* in italics, as Wm. Alexander seems to have overlooked its import, and because the passage is absolutely incompatible with the construction he would put upon it. His criticism reminds me of the groundless and fanciful notion of a worthy man, and a reputedly orthodox divine, who being closely pressed with scriptural proofs, that prayer should only be offered *to God the Father,* admitted that *in the general,* such was the duty, and had always been the practice of Christians; but nevertheless contended for the propriety of *sometimes* addressing prayer *to Christ* in cases of *peculiar emergency !*

The above and every other modification of the Sabellian hypothesis, that I have seen, asserts that there is " but one true God," as all Christians agree, and also that this Supreme Being does not consist, as all Trinitarians affirm, of " three distinct persons," and is so far sound and scriptural. As it is also, in representing this one true God, as the " first Cause of all things, from whence the whole universe derives its origin and existence," the proper Author of all temporal and spiritual blessings.

When, however, it declares that " the different appellations of Father,

Son, and Holy Spirit," are essentially and identically *one* and *the same,* each signifying *the true God,* my reverence for the authentic records of the Christian Revelation induces me to withhold my assent. I cannot find that they contain any such doctrine.

And although the author of this Creed, like other Sabellians, uses such very incorrect language, it is obvious he felt the necessity of distinguishing those " different appellations" from each other, and that he exclusively ascribed the creation and existence of all things both animate and inanimate " to God the Father."

The first part of this Creed is purely Sabellian. If the second part concerning the Son is pure Quakerism, N. C.'s correct observation that not a word is used under this head " that can be supposed to have the remotest reference to the history, doctrine, death or resurrection of the Lord Jesus Christ," is well worthy the serious attention of its members, and especially of Wm. Alexander, the publisher and patron of this Creed. Recommending it to their notice,

I am, sincerely yours,
    THOMAS FOSTER.

Newington Green, Feb. 6, 1816.
Sir,

YOUR last number (p. 16,) contains animadversions on a Sermon of mine, to which I deem some reply necessary. Such animadversions may not be unprecedented, but they are rather unusual, and I conceive hardly justifiable. Is it not enough that authors be subjected to the judgments and decisions of anonymous reviewers without the privilege of appeal or reply ? Must they also be exposed to the attacks of anonymous letter-writers ?

There are several circumstances connected with the indictment in question not very creditable to him who drew it up. He is an officious accuser. For the same reason that he writes reprehensively of me or of my publications a thousand others might do so; but I do not suppose that he has an ex-officio commission to put himself forward as accuser-general. He says that " there can be but one opinion" respecting my Sermon; but for that very reason the publishing of his opinion was uncalled for and unnecessary. I would not hastily suspect or impute bad motives ; but I must be permitted to say that there is some appearance of envy about his strictures. He indirectly confesses it was the character given of the sermon as " acute, able and eloquent," that provoked his reproaches ; and without considering the abatement made in the concluding remarks of the Review, he reluctantly, and grudgingly admits of any excellence by saying, " whatever may be thought of the argument which, though clear and simple, does not strike me as peculiarly ingenious or novel." If this be not the language of envy it is so very like it as to be in danger of misleading common understandings. I have a higher opinion of the talents of the writer than to suppose he cannot rise to honourable distinction by the native buoyancy of his own genius ; or that he must attempt to pull down the reputation of surrounding talents lest his own should be overshadowed and concealed. But why does he not abstain from the very appearance of ignoble motives ? He complains loudly and bitterly of uncourteousness and uncharitableness; yet he can be very uncourteous and uncharitable in his turn ; which is something like (to use an old vulgar saying) Satan reproving sin. In the small space of a short letter the reader will find a great many hard words (though the arguments be soft and slippery) well barbed with personal reflections. In this respect, at least, the accuser has outdone the accused ; and I hope to convince him that however hot and violent I may be when I have no one human being in view, I can use the gentlest words in the English vocabulary when repelling a personal attack. I do not object to the words applied to me or to my sermon : they are as truly respectable as the hypocritical misnomers and slavish inuendos rendered to the arbitrary laws and despotic fashions of modern etiquette are mean and contemptible. But I have a right to meet people on the ground which themselves have chosen, and to demand consistency between their professions and their practice. I am sorry to speak unhandsomely of one, who gives himself the airs of a gentleman ; assailant in question, that he does not come forward as an honourable challenger, but rather attacks in the manner of one whom I shall not name, lest I should be be uncharitable enough to shock his ears and hurt his delicacy ; for he need not be told what class of men wear a mask and shoot from ambush. There is a sort of wild justice and generosity to be met with at times even among them ; but was it just or fair in your correspondent to pretend he was criticising my sermon when he was only quoting from the *notes* appended to it ?

I am unwilling to consider his ingenious, original and classical allusion of the philosopher's *tub* in the light of splendid poverty. It is always easier to repeat than to invent; but he is surely not necessitated after such a wide range of reading to bedeck his compositions with the worn-out finery of fabulous traditions. Does he really believe in the Tale of a Tub ? Did it never occcr to him that Diogenes was calumniated like our own Hobbes ; and that merely because he had sagacity to discern and courage to ridicule the nonsense of such popular philosophers as Socrates, Plato and Aristotle, the holy trinity of classical idolatry ?

But these are only circumstances— let us come to the matter of the indictment. It may be resolved into uncourteousness, uncharitableness and contemptuousness. The ears of your correspondent have been long accustomed to the language of scripture, else they would be shocked with the specimens of Christian courtesy which might be selected from the speeches of Christ and his apostles. I intend no reproach to his understanding by remarking that, it is of great importance to reflect carefully on the nature of things and meaning of words ; especially on such words as are ever sounding in our ears ; for. without much attention, our roting begets a silly habit of repeating after repeaters as the a chattereth English. Charity (as I understand the term) means benevolence ; and therefore to the charge of uncharitableness I plead not guilty; for I sincerely wish those whose opinions differ from mine all the blessings of the life that now is, and of that which is to come. But, if, as I suspect, your correspondent means by charity, what the French (from whom we borrowed it) call the *art of pleasing* and *the art of liv-*

ing, I glory in being uncharitable; and in setting all the petty ordinances of the modern idol at defiance. If your correspondent wishes to go into the merits of *bienséance* and *courtesy* (of the same origin with *courtesan*) I am prepared to give my reasons for verging towards the opposite extreme from that of the fashion; and 'what will probably have more weight with his judgment, I am prepared to back those reasons with high authorities; for though I do not borrow my opinions they are not quite so singular as some readers may suppose.

Your correspondent ought to have sagacity enough to discern that the objectionable matter in the *notes* added to my sermon, is a literary rather than a theological question. Whether he perceived this and did not think proper to notice it, but chose rather to speak of the *odium theologicum,* is not for me to determine. As, however, he glories in belonging to the dwarfish age of smooth, courtly *petits maitres,* he might have been expected to repel the violent attack made upon its tender delicacy and accomplished refinement. But I am contemptuous. Towards whom am I contemptuous? The only living author named by me is Robert Hall; but so far from contempt, I have the highest admiration of his splendid talents and pre-eminent genius; and would rather read a volume of his writings than a page of the dull censors' of faults which they have not talent enough to commit. Your correspondent will not assert that I have expressed any contempt for the other names introduced; and to these I could add, if not a multitude, at least a goodly number of authors for whom I have the greate⸱t esteem and affection. I am not conscious of expressing contempt towards that numerous and respectable body of the people who are of the orthodox faith. I am persuaded that there is as much intellectual dignity and moral worth among them as in the *Catholic church of Orthodox Unitarians.*

The question then returns—towards whom am I contemptuous? I will tell your correspondent——sciolists, witlings and pretenders of all descriptions, who have the vanity and presumption to write on subjects while they know not what they say nor whereof they affirm. Whatever sub-ject I may have to treat of, I shall certainly not spare the insect generation of scribblers; for I would rather bear the marks of their displeasure than have the hum of their approbation. There are many Trinitarian believers for whose understanding as well as character I have the greatest respect; but none who know how to argue would attempt to support the doctrine of the Trinity by argument. Bacon was of opinion that reason ought not to be employed about the *mysteries* of the church; and one of the ablest reasoners and most eloquent writers among the orthodox in the present time has been frequently heard to say, that the doctrine of the Trinity cannot be supported by argument. It is highly improbable that ever I shall write or publish on that subject again; and whatever your correspondent may say about disgusting affectation, or ridiculous vanity, I can once more declare that I do think it a degrading task to have to reason with third-rate mystical declaimers. I have already wasted more time than the occasion called for; and shall conclude with a remark or two on the *object* of your correspondent's letter.

He must have intended to correct the offender—or simply to punish him—or thirdly, to proclaim to the Catholic church of orthodox Trinitarians, that though the Catholic church of orthodox Unitarians, might through the laxness of her discipline harbour such a daring heretic, yet that he was rather tolerated than approved. As to the first purpose, your correspondent has written very unhappily and unsuccessfully; and though he says something about *conciliating* and *pleasing,* I fear he will be an unsuccessful candidate for the reward promised by his supreme holiness in the Vatican to the best prize-essay on that important subject. But perhaps he did not wish to conciliate but to irritate; and despairing of correcting, hoped simply to punish. Being a gentleman of exquisite delicacy and courtly accomplishments he thought, perhaps, that dull admonition and pointless satire are the most effectual means of refined torture; for the blunter the instrument the longer it is of dispatching the victim. I confess my pride is deeply wounded to think that your correspondent should suppose me unworthy of acute pains and costly ceremonies; or that such musty, murdered metaphors as *abortions of genius*, *red-hot* ashes, and old *philosophers' tubs* were good enough for me. I thought I had written better than to deserve such scornful treatment; and though I have not seen the Sermon in question since the last proof-sheet passed through my hands, I begin to think it deserves to be committed to the flames. But finally—if it was the holy, catholic purpose of your worthy correspondent to inform the church of orthodox Trinitarians that the church of orthodox Unitarians does not approve of my sermon—he might have surely saved himself the trouble of writing a letter. I was conscious of peculiarity and singularity in my style; and took care to inform the public that I was not the organ of the Unitarian *Church*, and that all the faults of manner and spirit in my composition, were ascribable and chargeable to me alone. Your correspondent is no doubt a most charitable Christian and refined gentleman; but perhaps some of your readers will think his sense of honour is not very high-mettled which suffered him to make an attack upon the manner and spirit of a sermon after the above declaration from the author.

JAMES GILCHRIST.

Moreton Hampstead, Feb. 8, 1816.

SIR,

IT seems to me, that it was not necessary for your correspondent J. P., p. 14, of your number for January last, to make a profession of his faith, however correct it may be, in seeking information on the subject of *Sunday Tolls.* Our highway acts have nothing to do with the *faith*, but only the passing of travellers: and to know who is to pay, and who is exempted, on Sundays, he must consult the local Act under which the gate has been erected, at which toll is demanded of him, or the table, which is, or ought to be, hung at the gate, containing the tolls and exemptions. The Act, under which the road which passes by my door has been made says, in the clause of exemptions,—" No toll shall be demanded, of or from any person or persons going to or returning from his, her or their proper parochial

church or chapel, or other place of religious worship on Sundays, or any other day on which divine service is ordered by authority to be celebrated, or going to or returning from attending the funeral of any person who shall die and be buried in any of the parishes in which the said road lies, &c."

But all other persons, travelling on the said road on Sundays, are obliged to pay double toll, even though they attend public worship in the church of the parish where the gate stands, if it be not their proper and usual place of attending the said worship. So that a person in a chaise and pair, passing to attend in our church, or any Dissenting place of worship in this or any other town (for we make no invidious distinctions of denominations) from or into a parish in which our road does not lie, must pay a toll of *two* shillings, though on other days he passes for *one* shilling. This double toll has been provided because it was thought that such as travel for amusement on the Lord's Day can afford such payment for the benefit of the road. The regulations of other local Acts may be different, and therefore reference should be had, as before observed, to the Act under which the gate alluded to by J. P. was erected.

Were all Acts worded as the clause above extracted, I should hope no person would think of demanding from a Dissenter a toll to which a Churchman is not liable. And if there be any Act which exempts the latter and not the former, it must be owing, I should think, to the neglect of Dissenters at the time of passing it; and they must bear it with patience until the next time of renewal, which cannot be obtained without their knowledge, unless it be again their own fault. At the meeting of the trustees which is called to prepare for such renewal, they should appear, and make their claim to the same exemption as others, and without doubt they will prevail: but if they should not, they should by their counsel in parliament, petition for it, or against the renewal of the act,—and surely they cannot fail of full redress.

J. J.

No. CCXLIII.

Death of Truth in order to a Revival.

The *Great* Mr. Howe, in his Funeral Sermon for the *silver-tongued* Dr. Bates, has the singular supposition of Truth being destined to die and then to experience a resurrection. His text, which he judiciously explains and happily applies, is John xi. 16, " Let us also go that we may die with him :" referring to Dr. Bates, he says, in conclusion,

" But be it far from us to say, "Let us die with him," as despairing of our cause. If our cause be not that of any self-distinguished party, but truly that common Christian cause, of which you have heard. While it is the divine pleasure to continue us here, let us be content and submit, to live and own it, to live and serve it to our uttermost. If ever God design good days to the Christian church on earth, this is the cause that must prevail, and triumph in a glorious conquest over death.

"But I must freely tell you my apprehensions, which I have often hinted, that I fear it must die first ; I mean a temporary death; I fear it, for it hath been long gradually dying already: and spiritual diseases which have this tendency are both sinful and penal. Lazarus's death and resurrection, I think to have been meant, not only for a sort of prolusion to the death and resurrection of Christ, both personal, but mystical. I only say this for illustration, not for proof.

" That sickness and death of his was not in order to a permanent death but *for the glory of God*, that when the case was deplorate and hopeless, and he four days buried, he might surprisingly spring up again alive.

" I know not but the sickness and death of this our incomparably worthy friend and (for ought I know of many more of us) may be appointed the same way to be for the *glory of God;* that is, as tending to introduce that death which is to pass upon our common cause; which such men help to keep alive, by their earnest strugglings, though in a languishing, fainting condition every hour.

" Think me not so vain as to reckon exclusively the cause of Dissenters, the cause I now speak of: No, no; I speak of the common cause of all serious, sober-minded Christians, within the common rule or without it. I neither think any one party to include all sobriety of mind or to exclude all insobriety.

" But though it should seem generally to have expired, let us believe it shall revive. When our confidences and vain boasts cease, *The Temple of the Lord ! The Temple of the Lord ! Lo, here is Christ, and there is Christ!* And one sort ceases to magnify this Church, and another that, and an universal death is come upon us, then (and I am afraid, not till then) is to be expected a glorious resurrection, not of this or that party ; for living, powerful religion, when it recovers, will disdain the limits of a party. Nor is it to be thought that religion, modified by the devised distinctions of this or that party, will ever be the religion of the world. But the same power that makes us return into a state of life, will bring us into a state of unity, in divine light and love. Then will all the scandalous marks and means of division among Christians vanish; and nothing remain as a test or boundary of Christian communion, but what hath its foundation as such, in plain reason or express revelation.

" Then as there is *one body* and *one Spirit*, will that *Almighty Spirit* so animate and form this body, as to make it every where amiable, self-recommending and capable of spreading and propagating itself, and to ' increase with the increase of God.' ' Then shall the Lord be One, and his name One, in all the earth.' "

Howe's Works. (2 Vols. Fo. 1724.) II. 458, 9.

No. CCXLIV.

Demoralizing effect of War.

Ten or twelve generations of the world must go to the making up of one wise man or one excellent art : and in the succession of those ages there happen so many changes and interruptions, so many wars and violences, that *seven years' fighting sets a whole kingdom back in learning and virtue, to which they were creeping; it may be a whole age.*

Jere. Taylor. H. Dying.

REVIEW.

ART. I.—*Almanach Imperial, pour l'Année M.D CCC.XIII.* Présenté à S. M. L'Empereur, et Roi, par Testu. A Paris chez Testu et Co. De L'Imprimerie de Testu, Imprimeur De L'Empereur. The Imperial Almanack for the year 1813, presented to his Majesty, the Emperor and King, by Testu. Paris. Sold by Testu and Co. From the Press of Testu, Printer to the Emperor. Pp. 978.

ART. II.——*Almanach Royal pour les Années M.DCCC.XIV. et M.DCCC.XV.* Présenté à Sa Majesté, par Testu. A Paris. Chez Testu et Co. Testu, Imprimeur de LL. AA. SS. Mgr. Le Duc D'Orleans et Mgr. Le Prince De Condé. The Royal Almanack for the Years 1814 and 1815. Presented to his Majesty, by Testu. Paris. Sold by Testu and Co. Testu, Printer to their Most Serené Highnesses, the Duke of Orleans and the Prince of Conde. Pp. 830.

WE have here presented, in a striking contrast, the Imperial Eagle and the Royal Lily, each forming a vignette to its appropriate title-page.

In our Sixth volume (p. 615,) some account was given of "the Imperial Almanack for the year 1811," chiefly with a view of noticing the Chapter entitled, "Organization des Cultes," as a part most likely to interest our readers. This chapter is the seventh in the Imperial Almanack for 1813. The Catholic Religion, *Culte Catholique,* occupies the first section, with no other màrk of distinction, than priority, or as *primus inter pares. Cultes Protestans,* fill the second section, while the third is devoted to the disciples of Moses, under the title of *Culte des Juifs.* This is probably the last time that *Culte Catholique* will be constrained to associate with Protestants or Jews, unless France should unexpectedly again possess a government, enlightened to understand the benefits of impartial toleration, and courageous enough to pursue them.

Under these circumstances we cannot be satisfied to lay aside this last Imperial Almanack without further describing the ecclesiastical state of France and its dependencies, as modelled by the tolerating policy of the Emperor and King.

The first Section of Chapter 7th (p. 256,) is devoted to the Archbishops and Bishops of the Church of *Imperial* France. Fifteen Archbishoprics, including their Suffragan Sees, are thus arranged: Paris, Malines, Besançon, Lyon, Aix, Toulouse, Bordeaux, Bourges, Tours, Rouen, Turin, Genoa, Florence, Pisa, Sienna. The Bishoprics appear to be ninety-eight. The list is closed (p. 266,) with Osnaburgh, a name familiar to an English ear, as having been once under the ghostly care of our Duke of York, who, from his infancy till the French irruption was Prince Bishop of that See! It is remarkable that, excepting two or three Italian Prelates, none of the bishops in this list were appointed before 1802.

The Second Section, appropriated to *Cultes Protestans* commences with the Protestants of the Confession of Augsburgh, or Lutherans. Their order and connexion with the government are thus described:

The churches of the Confession of Augsburgh have Pastors, Consistories, Inspections and General Consistories.

The Consistories superintend the discipline, and the management of the property of the church, and of the interest accruing from charitable contributions.

The Inspections are composed of a pastor and one elder of each of the five Consistorial Churches. Every Inspection elects from its own body, two laymen and one ecclesiastic, who are called inspectors. The inspector superintends the ministers or pastors, and maintains order in the Consistorial Churches. The Inspection cannot hold its sittings, without the authority of the government.

The General Consistories form the superior administration of all the Consistorial Churches and the Inspections.

Besides the General Consistory, and in the interval of their sittings, there is a Directory composed of a president who is eldest of the ecclesiastical inspectors and of three laymen, one nominated by the

Emperor; the other two chosen by the General Consistory. (P. 267.)

Excepting two ministers at Paris, (p. 854,) a General Consistory at Mentz, and one for the departments of the Rhine and Moselle, in which no churches are named, the Lutherans appear to be all included in the General Consistory of the Departments of the Upper and Lower Rhine, established at Strasburgh. There they have two churches, and one at each of the following places: Petite-Pierre, Wissembourg, Bouxviller, Colmar, Montbeliard.

The Protestants of the Confession of Augsburg have an academy or seminary, at Strasburg, for the instruction of ministers.

They *profess* there theology, philosophy, belles-lettres, and the ancient, modern, and oriental languages.

A *Gymnasium*, or College, forming a school of primary instruction, is attached and subordinate to the academy. (P. 268.)

The next division is occupied by the Reformed Protestants or Calvinists.

The Reformed Protestants have pastors, consistories and synods.

The consistories of every reformed church are composed of one of the pastors attached to each church, and of elders or eminent laymen, *(notables)* chosen from the citizens who are rated the highest in direct contributions.

· The consistories maintain discipline, and take charge of the property of the church and of the interest accruing from charitable donations.

One half of the elders are replaced by new elections, once in two years.

The elections of the pastors are made by the consistories and confirmed by the Emperor.

The synods have the charge of superintending all that concerns the celebration of worship, the doctrine taught *(l'enseignement de la doctrine)* and the conduct of ecclesiastical affairs.

Their decisions are submitted to the Emperor's approbation.

Five consistorial churches form the circuit of a synod. Each synod is composed of one pastor and one elder, or. eminent person, *(notable)* of each consistorial church, and cannot assemble without permission of the government, nor continue its sitting more than six days. (P. 269.)

It thus appears that the French Protestant Churches as to the controul of government, over their internal regulations, and the absence or limitation of a popular voice, assimi-

lated to the Established Church of Scotland, and even of England, rather than to the Churches of the English Nonconformists, who, however denominate d, are all, in practice, Independents. Thus their late commendable zeal against persecution could not be excited by sectarian similarity. They felt, we trust, that far nobler motive, with which Tillotson would have inspired a rigid doctor in his day, even the commanding influence of *Charity*, which is *above Rubrics.*

Excepting Paris, there appear to have been 140 Churches of the Calvinists in *Imperial* France, divided among 46 departments, here arranged alphabetically. As an historical document not easily procured from any other quarter, we subjoin the catalogue of names.

Aisne, Seine and Marne, Moineaux near Château-Thierry. *Higher Alps,* Gap. *Ardèche,* Lamastre, Privas, Vernoux, Lavoute, Saint Pierre Ville. *Ardennes,* Sedan. *Ariege,* Maz-d'Azil. *Aveiron,* Saint Afrique. *Calvados,* Caen. *Charente,* Jarnac. *Lower Charente,* Saintes, Rochelle, la Tremblade. *Cher,* Sancerre. *Dordogne,* Bergerac, Montcarret. *Doubs,* Besançon. *Drôme,* Crest, Dic, Lamotte, Dieu-le-Fit, Valence. *Dyle,* Brussels. *Scheld,* Sluys, Isendike, Axel. *Gard,* Alais, Saint-Ambroise, Vezenobre, Saint-Jean-du-Gard, Anduze, Uzés, Ste-Chaptes, Nismes, Vauvert, Aigues-Vives, Calvisson, Sommieres, Vallerauque, Vigan, St. Hyppolyte, la Salle, Sauve. *Upper Garonne,* Calmont, for Toulouse. *Gers,* Mauvesin. *Gironde* Chartrons, F. B. de Bordeaux, Sainte-Foy, Gensac. *Herault,* Latt, F. B. de Montpellier, Montagnac, Massilargues, Ganges. *Isere,* Mens. *Leman,* Geneva, Carouge and Ferney. *Upper Loire,* Saint-Voy. *Lower Loire et Vendée,* Nantes. *Loiret* Orleans, Chatillon. *Lot et Garonne,* Tonneins, Clairac, Castelmoron, Lafite, Nérac. *Lozere,* Florac, Meyrueis, laBarre, St. Germain-de-Colberthe, Vialas. *Meurthe,* Oberstenzel, Nancy, Lixheim. *Lower Meuse,* Maëstricht. *Mont-Tonnere,* Obeingelheim, Sprendlingen, Alzey, Oppenheim, Osthosén, Hippenheim, or the vicinity *(auprés),* Freinsheim, Frankenthal, Spire, Edenkauben, Neustadt, Kaiserslautern, Rokenhausen, Obermoschel, Hombourg, Menbach, Deux-Ponts, Annweiler. *Moselle,* Metz. *Nord,* Lille, Quesnoy, Pô, la Tour, Prarostino, Ville-Sèche. *Lower Pyrennees,* Orthés. *Lower Rhine,* Strasbourg, Bischweiller, Bergzabern, Billigheim, Landau. *Upper Rhine,* Bienne, Saint-Imier, Corgemont, Bevillard, Mulhausen. *Rhine et Moselle,* Creutznach,

Sobernheim, Stromberg, Simmern, Kirch-
berg. *Roer*, Stolberg, Crevelt, Odenkir-
chen, Meurs, Cleves. *Rhome*, la Croix-
Rousse, Suburb of Lyons. *Mouths of
the Rhone*, Sainte-Margueritte, Suburb of
Marseilles. *Sarre*, Sarrebruch, Coussel,
Meisenheim. Lower-Seine, Bolbec for
Havre, Bonsecours for Rouan. *Two Sevres*,
S. Gelais, Suburb of Niort, Chalons, Suburb of S. Maixent, la Barriere, Suburb
de la Motte S. Heraie, Bretagne, Suburb
of Melle, Lezay. *Tarn*, Castres, Maza-
met, Vabre, la Caune. *Tarn et Garonne*,
Montauban, Negrepelisse. *Vaucluse*, Lour-
marin. *Vienne*, Rouillé.

To each of these churches is annexed the name of the minister, whether *Pasteur* or *President*. At Paris
the proportion of Protestants must be
very inconsiderable. Besides two
Lutheran ministers, before mentioned,
there are only three ministers of the
Calvinists, M. Marron, President,
and Messieurs Rabaut Pomier and
Monod (p. 854). There is no account
of any collegiate institution belonging
to the Calvinists, except that the minister of Montauban, M. Froissard
is described as " President and Dean
of the Faculty of Theology" in that
city.

From the third Section, which
places Jews on the same level of toleration with Christians, we learn
that

A central Consistory is established at
Paris, and twenty-two Synagogues in the
Empire. (P. 271.)

The places where these synagogues
are formed then follow, with the
names of the Grand Rabbins and Lay-
Members.

Such was the example of religious
forbearance proposed to *Imperial*
France in this seventh Chapter, which
brought together, equally controuled
indeed, yet equally protected by the
government,

Men of all climes that never met before
And all persuasions too :

a chapter, as little likely to be
imitated as that France should become
again *Imperial*.

Before we finally quit this last Almanack, presented to the Emperor
and King, we cannot help noticing a
short passage which now only serves
to display the vanity of human expectation. At p. 852, we are informed that " Par Décret du 20 Fév-
rier 1806, l'église de Saint Denis est
consacrées à la sépulture des Empe-
reurs." By a decree of the 20th Feb.

1806, the Church of St. Denis is reserved for the burial-place of the Emperors. Alas! the Imperial burial-
place will now, to all human appearance, be found on that remote rock
which British magnanimity has assigned for Napoleon's prison, where
he who gave law to Kings and Emperors, in their capitals, must be content to receive the accommodations of
existence, as a *princely* boon

Till all Atrides *be* an empty shade!

We never offered the homage of
unqualified applause to the late Emperor while he was seen to " ride on
the high places of the earth," nor will
we join the vulgar herd, in court or
city, who " watch the sign to hate,"
and would insult over his fall. Those
who have been accustomed to

——drop the man in their account
And vote the mantle into majesty,

cannot fail to maintain an unappeasa-
ble quarrel with an *upstart*, " ennobled by himself," *un homme de rien*,
as Father Orleans styled *Buchanan*,
though obliged to confess *qu'il étoit
homme d'esprit*.

" There is no person more odious
than the man who makes himself greatly eminent. It is a sort of tacit reproach
on the rest of the species: and every
one feels his own meanness the more
sensibly, when he looks towards those
exalted geniuses, who have gained a
superiority over the rest of mankind."
(Spense on Od. Pref.) The future historian of these eventful times, free
from the passions of a contemporary,
and possessed of documents now inaccessible, will best decide how far
that *odium*, so justly felt by *regular* governments, contributed to
form and cement a confederacy, the
result of which has closed the public
life of Napoleon, probably for ever.
That extraordinary man such an historian will scarcely fail to represent
as an instance, not more remarkable,
of unstable fortune, than of human
inconsistency ;

a Genius bright and base,
Of tow'ring talents and terrestrial aims..

Yet, amidst the inexpressible miseries, felt or feared, during the last
twenty years, under the pitiless dominion of the sword, it became the
friends *of virtue and of human bliss* to
rejoice that the ambition of a military
Chieftain had, on some very important
points, a reforming tendency. Espe-

cially that the *spiritual wickedness in high places*, against which our fathers prayed and argued, and the far distant prospect of whose fall they hailed with grateful rapture—that this *man of sin* was suddenly brought to desolation, or at least despoiled of his baneful influence wherever the genius of Napoleon prevailed.

He is no sooner fallen than the Pope re-ascends the throne of St. Peter and calls around him his Jesuits. The *beloved* Ferdinand again invigorates the Holy office, while the Restoration of the Bourbous is speedily followed by a persecution of French Protestants. This persecution Louis appears, publicly, to disavow. Whether the king or his family took any measures to prevent such a catastrophe, or whether the orders or neglects of his government were calculated to encourage the persecution are questions of a serious import. But we must return to M. Testu and notice his Royal Almanack.

M. Testu is one of *the children of this world, wise in his generation*, and equally prepared to become an *Imperial*, or a *Royal* Editor, a *Vicar of Bray—whatever King shall reign*. This Almanack for 1813, like the former, had been specially recommended and patronized by the Emperor, but M. Testu had no inclination

To fall uncourtly with a falling Court.

He thus worships the rising sun in an *Avis des Editeurs*:

"The Almanack for the year 1814 was ready for publication when an ever-memorable Revolution restored to France her lawful sovereign. All our labour became useless, and the expense incurred a total loss. We sustained a considerable injury but we were consoled by the hope of happiness to come. That hope indulged by all good Frenchmen, is every day realizing under the paternal government of Louis XVIIIth. Let us be permitted here to render the homage of our fidelity, our affection and our profound gratitude towards the August Monarch who has granted to us a signal proof of his justice and benevolence by securing to us, for twenty years, the exclusive right to the publication and sale of the Royal Almanack." P. 2.

After some details respecting the arrangement of the work, the *Avis* closes with the following significant declaration: "Nous nous sommes conformés, pour sa rédaction, aux ordres supérieurs que nous avons reçus." We

have been regulated, in forming this compilation by the commands we have received.

Under such well-understood *ordres supérieurs* these editors introduce indeed the Protestants in the Section of *Administration Générale des Cultes*, under the head of a public office for the affairs of *Cultes non Catholiques ;* but appear, in a very marked manner to separate them from the Catholic Clergy, to whom they assign a station immediately after the Foreign Ambassadors and before the Royal Household, under the head of "Clerge de France." This *Deuxieme Partie* occupies only one page, and that contains nothing but the following Note : "'Le travail relatif à la nouvelle organization du Clergé n'étant pas terminé, nous n'avons pas cru devoir donner de détails sur cette partie." The arrangements for a new Organization of the Clergy not being completed, we have thought it our duty to omit any details on this Part. (P. 38.) Thus the editors, by securing a new and more dignified station, for *Clergé de France* provide easily for the entire omission of that Chapter in the Imperial Almanack, entitled, *Organization des Cultes*, in which the Protestants ranked in company with the Catholics, as *equally* recognized and respected by the government. What must France understand by this omission but that the *eldest son of the Church* forbad the further profanation of *Culte Catholique* by such an association ; and at the same time refused to sanction *heresy* by describing the Clergy and Colleges of the Protestants in a *Royal* Almanack ?

It is well known that many of the Protestants in France, whatever might be their political attachments, became alarmed for their *toleration* soon after the first return of Louis. They considered themselves as secured by the success of Napoleon's enterprise from Elba, and again exposed to danger by his defeat at Waterloo. Had Louis, indeed, returned in 1814 with sentiments of toleration, like those of his Imperial predecessor, would he have directed, or even suffered, the names of the Protestant Ministers and an account of their churches and institutions to have been excluded from a Royal Almanack, published at such a critical juncture; while the admission of them could not possibly injure the Catho-

than such a *paternal* government?

R.

ART. III.—*A Candid and Impartial Inquiry into the Present State of the Methodist Societies in Ireland:* wherein several important points relative to their doctrines and discipline are discussed. By a Member of the Society, 8vo. pp. 512. Belfast, printed; sold by Commins, Lincoln's Inn, London, 1814.

THIS work contains much important information respecting the state of opinions on some of the most leading points in theology among the Methodists in Ireland. The author regards as an evil, the want of uniformity in religious doctrine, which his statements prove to exist, and to shew itself publicly, among the ministers of his denomination, as well as among the people. The object of his book appears to be, to stir up his brethren to provide a remedy for this imagined evil, by forming " an official compendium" of the doctrines of the Methodists, " compiled from the voluminous writings wherein they now lie scattered, and bearing the stamp of legitimate authority." P. 348.

That among so numerous a body of Christians as the Methodists now are, a diversity of opinion on a variety of subjects should exist, might naturally be expected; but we were not aware that inquiry had extended itself so far, or that what is called *heterodoxy* existed to such a degree, as this writer shews to be the case among the societies in Ireland: not a few of his pages are filled with the proofs of this supposed departure from the truth, and the discussion of the controverted points. A statement of the subjects on which the Methodists in Ireland are divided in their opinions will not be uninteresting to our readers, and it

ward association with the powers of darkness, if not an actual participation in a diabolical nature " is contended for as a first principle by the Methodists, he adds

" But although this doctrine is generally received in the Methodist connexion, yet it is important to know that this is not universally the case. There are, both among preachers and people, those who cannot reconcile the popular opinions respecting this point, to their notions, either of the wisdom, the goodness, the justice, or the truth of God. For denying the necessity of the continuance of a corrupt nature, transmitted through the ordinary course of generation, as a foundation of redemption, they contend that this redemption should operate to the extirpation of the principle of evil from our nature in its initial state, and thereby prove its claim to the glorious title it sustains, and exhibit in infants the full accomplishment of the important objects it is intended to attain. And under these impressions, the opposers of the doctrine as above delineated say, it is incompatible with the divine wisdom, to permit the actual propagation of sin ; for, say they; if God really wills the salvation of all men, and if holiness be essential to that salvation, can the propagation of a nature positively and actually unholy in the extreme, have any tendency to promote that glorious end ? Certainly not. On the contrary, it would be a radical, and in most cases, an effectual opponent to the hopes of salvation." P. 70.

The author states in the following pages, the reasoning of his brethren who reject the doctrine of Original Sin, assert its inconsistency with the goodness and truth of God, and maintain that neither sin nor holiness are susceptible of propagation. But though the arguments, many of which are strong and pointed, are given as the language of others, he himself seems to take the *heterodox* side on this subject. He says,

" As our object is not to foster prejudice, but to ascertain and vindicate truth, it is highly necessary in the investigation of any point of doctrine, to turn it on every side, to look at it in all its bearings, and with patience and candour to appreciate its real merit by the acknowledged criterions of orthodoxy. With this view let us put to ourselves the questions which follow.—If, as is generally supposed, Original Sin, propagated as an active principle in the soul, be the efficient cause of the universal prevalence of evil, will not this exonerate mankind from much of the responsibility which would otherwise attach to their dispositions and actions, as moral agents in a state of probation? For really if our nature be radically evil, or if evil be so closely interwoven with its fabric as is generally believed, it would appear unreasonable to expect any good fruit from so corrupt a tree. Yet we find God both expects and demands it." (See Jer. ii. 2.—Isa. v. 4.) P. 185. *Note.*

Imputed Righteousness. "Upon this interesting subject also," says the author, " there is a considerable diversity of opinion in the Methodist connexion." P. 95. He acknowledges " the popular feeling appears to be rather against it;" and though he labours to prove it by quotations from the writings of Mr. Wesley, he is compelled to admit that the founder of the Methodist connexion, if in the early part of his ministry he maintained, afterwards rejected, and openly opposed the views of the subject for which he contends. He quotes a passage from Mr. Wesley, which it is impossible to reconcile with the notion that Christ's righteousness and merits are imputed to the sinner.

" Again; Mr. Wesley proceeds, least of all does justification imply that God is deceived in those whom he justifies; that he thinks them to be in fact what they are not, that he accounts them to be otherwise than they are. It does by no means imply, that God judges concerning us, contrary to the real nature of things; that he esteems us better than we are, or believes us righteous when we are unrighteous. Surely no. The judgment of the all-wise God is always according to truth; neither can it ever consist with his unerring wisdom to think that I am innocent, to judge that I am righteous or holy, because another is so. He can no more in this manner confound me with Christ, than with David or Abraham." P. 168.

The author lays the greatest stress on the doctrine of Imputed Righteousness, and laments the opposition it meets with amongst the Methodists.

Sentiments respecting the death of Christ, which alarm him, are entertained by some of the preachers.

" The author has heard from a Methodist pulpit, the doctrine inculcated that the death of Christ was not essential to the salvation of mankind, but that God made choice of that as the most eligible and advantageous mode of reconciling the world to himself. And he has been told by another preacher, and one of very distinguished rank and eminence in the connexion, that the death of Christ was not a meritorious sacrifice for the sins of the world, which was a Calvinistic notion; that God chose indeed to manifest his grace and extend his mercy to men through that medium; but that if it had so pleased him, he might have done the same through the death of a bullock or any similar medium." P. 355. *Note.*

We are informed, p. 138. " The most general sentiment in the Methodist connexion concerning" Justification " is, that it is perfectly synonymous with the forgiveness of sins; the removal of guilt, and of the liability to punishment which we incur thereby; a mere exoneration from the penalties to which a breach of the divine law subjects every transgressor." To this the author objects, though it appears from his own account, that it was the sentiment of the founder of the Methodist societies, and has been from the first the sentiment most generally maintained in those societies.

He makes great complaint of the increase of legality among the Methodists, because they do not insist on some popular doctrines which are generally termed *evangelical*, but continually enforce reformation and good works, without directing their hearers to depend on the personal righteousness of Christ imputed to them for their justification, pp. 130—134; and with all his veneration for Mr. Wesley he hardly acquits him of being too legal. He says, p. 278, " Mr. Wesley's zeal for God, and for the honour of the divine law, carried him with a full tide into the bosom of the strongest Arminianism." And adds, in a note, " We may here notice an instance of Mr. Wesley's having about that time lost all dread of danger from the introduction of *legality* into his system of divinity. In a letter to Miss Bishop, of Bath, dated November 5, 1770, he observes :—" I cannot find in my Bible any such sin as legality. Truly, we have been often afraid where no fear was. I am not half legal enough, not enough under the law of love." And again, in a subsequent letter to the same lady, February 16, 1771, he says; "Legality, with most who use that term, really means tenderness of conscience.'" The Methodists have already done much good, and we have no fear of their usefulness being diminished by their preaching becoming more practical.

We are glad to find that rational ideas respecting the nature of faith, are making progress among the Methodists in Ireland; for which they are censured by this writer. Complaining of the pharisaism of some of the preachers, he says, p. 130, "faith according to them, being only a *rational conviction* of the great truths of revelation, and its only use to act as a spur to our endeavours to fulfil the righteousness of the law, which is to be our chief passport to heaven." Again,

"The advocates for this doctrine (and they are numerous in the Methodist connexion,) contend that the faith which is ordained of God to be the instrument of our salvation, is essentially the same with that reliance which we repose upon the testimony of a man, in whose integrity we can place implicit confidence; the distinction between these consisting only in the diversity of the objects which they embrace. And accommodating their language to their principles, they divide faith into human and divine: human faith is, according to them, the assent which we give to human testimony; and divine faith the assent which we give to divine testimony.' And they insinuate, that the one is as much the spontaneous act of the natural powers of the human mind as the other.

"The evidence upon which this 'divine faith' is required and supposed to rest, is that which is' contained in the oracles of inspiration. But little or nothing is either said or admitted respecting the particular influence of the spirit of God, in applying the truths of scripture to the conscience, or inspiring a conviction of their reality and importance." P. 224.

The following is the view of Regeneration, which this author states as entertained by some of his brethren the Methodists, and to be rapidly gaining ground among them. "They appear to believe that every man possesses what may properly be termed a *natural power* to obey the divine commandments, to repent of his sins, and believe the gospel at his pleasure;

the spirit of God being always ready (so far as his influence may be necessary,) to co-operate with the sinner, and *assist him* in the work of conversion. But it would appear, from this system of doctrine, that by far the greater part of the work rests with the sinner himself, who, it seems, has it completely in his power to become a saint whenever he pleases; only in consideration of the foolish and sinful habits he has long indulged, it will necessarily be a work of some time and labour to get his heart thoroughly converted to the ways of truth and holiness. No extraordinary degree of divine influence, however, is to be expected, or is indeed supposed to be requisite to effect the great work of conversion; and accordingly it is a principle held by the favourers of this doctrine, 'That God, prompted by his own goodness, hath already done all that he possibly can do, consistently with his own glory, for the present happiness and final salvation of every human creature upon earth; and that consequently no farther interference of divine power or influence need be expected to effect the conversion of any individual; although, as the divine spirit is omnipresent, and is in fact the *primum mobile* of all physical, intellectual, and moral power in the universe, his aid in a general way cannot be excluded, particularly as it is admitted, that 'God is loving to every man, and his tender mercy is over all his works.'" Pp. 177—178.

Though this writer asserts, p. 287, that "the Methodist societies are well grounded in the fundamental and important doctrine of a trinity of persons in the Godhead;" it appears from his account at large that a dissonance of language is found among them respecting the divinity of Christ, and that a complete uniformity of opinion on the subject does not exist in their societies. He says, p. 288. "The generality both of preachers and people seem content with a general, but often very confused idea of the divinity of Christ." In a note, he adds, "A preacher, who certainly has no mean opinion of his own talents and orthodoxy, was delivering a discourse from Col. i. 12—18. He admitted that the terms Jesus Christ applied only to the manhood of our Lord, and were descriptive of his vicarious character, as the Saviour of the world, and the only mediator between God and man. And he contended strenuously that his person and character had no kind of existence until the formation of the former in the womb of the virgin mother, and the subsequent developement of the latter in the life and death of Christ." Even some of the writer's own expressions will be found difficult to reconcile with the proper doctrine of the trinity, of which he declares " Athanasius the great oracle." P. 295. He represents the notion that God died, as the greatest of absurdities.

" But is any one among us weak enough to conclude from this figurative expression, (Acts 20—28.) that the eternal God literally shed his blood for us? This preposterous notion would be incomparably more grossly absurd than the Popish doctrine of transubstantiation. The idea of a suffering and expiring Deity is so repugnant to our enlightened reason, so degrading to the divine character, so much at variance with the principles of all theology, and so subversive of every attribute of the Godhead, that it is beyond measure astonishing how such a notion could ever find its way into the doctrines of Christianity; or that any figurative expression of scripture could, by men of sense, be ever tortured into the support of a doctrine so full of absurdity and contradiction. It is deifying the material body of the blessed Jesus, and laying the foundation of the grossest idolatry, in the very person of the immaculate Son of God. Doubtless the idolatry of the mass originally sprang out of this absurd notion of a corporeal Deity: whereas we know that ' God is a spirit, whom no man hath seen nor can see:' and they that worship him acceptably must do it in spirit and in truth." P. 297.

Again, he says,

" It is very commonly supposed that the vengeance of God, which was satiated by the blood of Christ, was infinite in its extent, and boundless in its demands; and hence it has been concluded that the Deity himself must have participated in the suffering, and have given merit to the atonement, which otherwise could not have been adequate to the purposes of reconciliation upon legal principles. The accuracy of these sentiments may be justly questioned; they appear to be the offspring of a fallacious mode of reasoning, unsupported by divine authority, and instituted for the purpose of accommodating a pre-conceived opinion of an excessive rigour in the divine economy, which even transcends the boundaries of strict justice, and which induced God to require an infinite satisfaction for a finite offence. We call it a finite offence,

because although committed against a being infinite in his perfections, yet it was the transgression of a finite creature who was incapable of performing an infinite act, and it was also the violation of a law instituted for the regulation of the conduct of that finite creature; consequently its terms were suited to the limited capacity of that being, or those beings who were to be its subjects. Now we argue, that if the fulfilment of that law did not demand the exertion of infinite powers, so neither could its violation require an infinite atonement." P. 299.

He justly censures the following lines in the Methodist hymns, which he says, " carry their own condemnation on their face."

" The immortal God for me hath died!"

And—

" I thirst for a life-giving God,
" A God that on Calvary died!"

It will be difficult for the author to reconcile the above passages with his ascribing to the Son of God all the essential attributes of Deity, p. 287, for if, as he justly asserts, God could neither suffer nor die, it follows that he who actually suffered and died was not God: but Paul declared, " It is Christ that died," and that he was " declared to be the Son of God with power, according to the spirit of holiness, by the resurrection from the dead." Could the author induce the Methodists to form a creed, under the name of " An Official Compendium " of Doctrines, it is not at all likely it would produce uniformity, though it might dissimulation and hypocrisy. If creeds when enforced by the civil power, and fenced by all the terrors of persecution, never produced uniformity of opinion, how can it be thought that one unsupported by the state and not so fenced would do it? The most probable effect of such a measure would be, that no longer permitted to exercise freedom of opinion in the methodist connexion multitudes would leave it, and form separate societies where they could freely think for themselves, and openly declare their views of divine truth. We trust the Methodists are too sensible of the value of religious liberty, ever to submit to the yoke of bondage this writer wishes to see imposed upon them. Is it not enough that the societies are denied the liberty of choosing their own ministers; must the preachers also be put in fetters by their " perfect coincidence in their public capacities, with the essential doctrines therein contained:" that is, in the proposed compendium? The adoption of the author's plan would be a direct violation of the rights of conscience, and a gross departure from the principles of liberty, which he states as asserted and acted upon by the founder of the Methodist connexion. The following note deserves the attention of every person in that connexion, and should the plan recommended by this writer, ever be proposed at Conference, it is hoped some of its members will move that this note be read.

"It is both interesting and important here to refer to the minutes of the First Conference, held in June 1744, where we find the ground of private judgment distinctly laid down as the unalienable privilege of every Christian; and, at the same time, the boundaries are ascertained at which a surrender of that judgment is required of a Methodist preacher. These fundamental principles being coeval with the preacher's character as a Christian, and his admission as a minister of the gospel in the Methodist connexion, are in full force at the present day, and must continue so to the end of time. These therefore must form the basis of all future regulations, respecting the belief and propagation of doctrines in the Methodist societies. They run thus:—
"Question. How far does each of us agree to submit to the judgment of the majority?—Answer. In speculative things each can only submit so far as his judgment shall be convinced. In every practical point, each will submit so far as he can without wounding his conscience.
"Question. Can a Christian submit any farther than this to any man, or number of men upon earth?—Answer. It is undeniably certain he cannot, either to Bishop, Convocation, or General Council. And this is that grand principle of private judgment on which all the reformers proceeded, 'Every man must judge for himself, because every man must give an account of himself to God.' It is impossible to read this without admiring it; let it never be forgotten that these principles formed the basis of the Methodist Conference." P. 236.

After reading the above, we were ready to ask, can this writer be in earnest in wishing to have the religious opinions of the whole body of the Methodists fixed by " An Official Compendium?" Most inconsistently with the plan he recommends, speaking of John and Charles Wesley, he says,

"But neither of these eminent men, no, nor all the conferences at which they assisted or presided, had any power to enact laws, to establish principles, or institute regulations, binding upon their successors or their posterity. Our acquiescence in these is a matter of choice, and not compulsion; and we possess the unquestionable power of revising, altering, or abolishing any part of our religious establishment." P. 340.

The length to which this article is already extended, compels us to pass over several things we had intended noticing; we conclude our extracts with the following note, p. 231. It is quoted by the author from the *Belfast Monthly Magazine*, for March, 1813.*

"AN EXAMPLE TO MODERN METHODISTS.—The Rev John Wesley himself has asserted in his writings, not only that an Anti-trinitarian may manifest a desire of escaping future misery, but that he may be a truly good man. In one of the numbers of the Arminian Magazine, published a few years before his death, he inserted an extract of the memoir of the life of that eminent Unitarian, Thomas Firmin. In introducing this extract, he observed, that 'he had been formerly inclined to think, that a person who was unsound with respect to the doctrine of the Trinity, could not be a converted or good man. But that now he thought differently, since the subject of the memoir was undoubtedly a pious man, though erroneous in the doctrine of the Trinity, and that there was no *arguing against facts.*'"

ART. IV.—*Discourses chiefly on practical Subjects,* by the late Rev. Newcome Cappe. Edited by Catharine Cappe, 8vo. pp. 492. York printed, sold by Longman & Co. 12s. 1815.

TO such of our readers, and we believe they are many, who are ac-

* The extract which follows was taken by the editor of the *Belfast Magazine,* from our number for January, 1813, Vol. VIII. From the Belfast Magazine it has been copied into the "Inquiry," and copied back by our reviewer into the Monthly Repository. A striking proof, that when facts and truths are put into print, it is impossible to guess how widely, and by what means they may be made known to the public. The statement concerning John Wesley, which was the original of these several publications, was made in a letter to us "On the Methodist Excommunication at Flushing," under the signature of *Sabrinus,* adopted in the former volumes of this work, by the late much-respected *Rev. W. Severn,* of Hull. ED.

quainted with the former volume of sermons, [M. Repos. I. 31 & 93.] by this truly Christian preacher, we should think it unnecessary to do more than announce the present publication. They know what to expect, and they will not be disappointed.—Simplicity and godly sincerity, unaffected earnestness in the cause of religion and virtue, benignity and zeal in happy union, speak in their proper language through the whole volume. The name of Baxter has often occurred to us in the perusal of it; for like the works of that very impressive preacher, it abounds in affectionate, practical appeals, ardent expostulations, and that persuasiveness of address which is suggested, and therefore recognised by the heart. We no where detect an endeavour to win admiration or extort applause by ornament or artifice or labour. The author appears to have lost sight of himself, his thoughts and feelings wholly occupied by the grandeur and importance of his subjects; and the serious reader can scarcely fail to lose sight of him too, attending solely to the matter and objects of his address.

For the sake of such of our readers as may not be acquainted with the preacher's manner, we insert the following specimens of his devout oratory. In one of the sermons on the final Consequence of our present Conduct, he thus pours forth his convictions:

"Could I make you privy to the good man's thoughts, to the best man's feelings in his happiest hours, when, musing on the works and providence of God, or meditating on the glorious discoveries of his gospel, his soul, dilated into the noblest sentiments of charity, and elevated into the sublimest transports of devotion, triumphs in the government of God, and with all the ardour of gratitude for what is past, unites all the prospects of the liveliest and most exalted hope in respect of what is yet to come; when, finding all things right within, he forgets whatever is amiss without, overlooks the sufferings that are present with him, overlooks the sufferings he has yet to undergo, overlooks the death he has to die, and anticipates his union with the innumerable company of angels, with his departed friends, with the spirits of just men made perfect, with Jesus, whom not having seen he loves, and with God the standard of excellence and the fountain of all good; could I make you privy to his feelings in these happy hours, when, encouraged by the testimony of his conscience, he is not afraid to indulge his hope and confidence in God, you might think that these wanted

nothing but stability and immortality, to convert this earthly happiness into Heaven." Pp. 262, 263.

The following passages are extracted from the series of sermons on Christian Perfection.

"We must propose to ourselves an exalted standard if we mean no more than to make a moderate progress.

"Every man's experience may be appealed to, how much in all affairs, and particularly in those of religion, our designs ordinarily surpass our execution. We propose great things; it is but little ones we perform. In the most enlarged views, with the most intense desires, with the most elevated purposes, with all the ardour and ambition of our souls stretching forward towards perfection, if we make no speedier progress in the Christian character, and our progress is liable to so many interruptions, disgraced by so many failures, what would be done, how much less could be expected from narrow views, from grovelling purposes, from cold desires, and faint endeavours? To rest content with the attainments we have already made, bespeaks such a degree of self-complacency and self-confidence as bodes very ill to our patient continuance in well-doing; it bespeaks much of that pride which goeth before destruction, and of that haughty spirit which precedes a fall." Pp. 115, 116.

"Departed hours, and neglected talents, are like departed and neglected friends. When they come to stand upon the margin of the grave, when from the bed of death, they look back upon their forepast life, and on their former talents, then it is that men wish most earnestly to call back the years that are gone by; then it is that they lament their insensibility and negligence. They might have made better preparation for the tribunal of their Judge; they might have raised a better harvest from this only seed-time of their existence: but, alas! the season is gone, and they too must go, with what they have done, and what they have neglected to do, to the bar of an all-knowing and all-righteous God." Pp. 121, 122.

The following animated appeal to Christian professors is in the last series of discourses, on the great Importance of the public Ministry of Christ.

"Among all your schemes and purposes of improvement, does it never enter into your thoughts, that your capacities of usefulness may and ought, not only to be employed, but to be enlarged? Are the riches of beneficence, the only riches you have no solicitude to increase? Are these the only pleasures of which you are contented with a little sphere? Are these the only honours in which you are willing to be undistinguished? Can you pass from week to week, and from year to year, so-

licitous in every thing that regards yourselves and your sublunary interests, to be
making progress; without labour, with-.
out care, without desire to become more
capable of serving those who are within
the sphere of your beneficence? Can your
capacities of usefulness be actually though
not intentionally enlarged, and yet your
good works become neither more numerous, nor more perfect; neither more, nor
greater? Can you content yourselves to
have more of the sources of human happiness within your power, and not a soul
of the human race be the more happy for
it?" P. 435.

　" What a difference between Christ and
Christians; between his life and their
lives; between his sentiments and theirs!
What a contrast, between the constancy,
the ardour, the perfection of his beneficence; and the interruptions, the lan-
guors, and the blemishes of theirs! How
deplorable is the dissimilitude that appears
between the exemplar that is proposed unto the sons of men, and many who avow
the obligation, and even make profession
of conforming to it! How glaring is the
opposition between his activity, and their
indolence in doing good; between his usefulness, and their self-indulgence; between his disinterested zeal in works of
charity and kindness, and their undiverted
application to the gains and profits of the
world! P. 437.

　These sermons are presented to the
public by the pious hand of affection,
and we join most cordially in the earnest prayer of the Editor Mrs. Cappe,

　"——that by a wider circulation; sentiments like these, so serious and awful,
yet at the same time so just and important,
may eventually contribute to form in many
others those habits of diligence, of resignation, and piety, which were a source of
continual satisfaction to himself, and of
consolation, hope, and joy, when all other
consolations failed." P. 130. Note.

　This volume of practical sermons
consists principally of four series of
discourses: the first on Christian Perfection; the second on the Final Consequences of our present Conduct; the
third on the Imperfection of our Knowledge concerning God; and the fourth
on the great Importance of the public
Ministry of Christ. They are all very
properly styled practical sermons, but
with some difference of character notwithstanding. Into the third series
on the imperfection of our knowledge
concerning God, the nature of the
subject has thrown a mixture of speculation; but the speculation is chastised and reverential, neither presumptuous nor timid, always pious and

sometimes original. In the last series
on the importance of the public Ministry of Christ, the reader, who is
acquainted with the "Critical Remarks
on many important Passages of Scripture," by the same author, will recog-
nise with pleasure the same ingenious
and satisfactory mode of illustrating
the language of the New Testament.
On the whole, we cannot better explain the leading objects of these discourses, than as the editor has explained
them in her preface,

　"——simply to demonstrate the unspeakable importance of holiness of heart and
life; of piety, humility and benevolence;
of attaining to that truly Christian comprehension of mind, which habitually looks
forward, beyond the present to the future."
Pref. p. 10.

　And after the specimens which we
have laid before our readers, it is superfluous to add our recommendation
of what must so well recommend itself
to the pious and intelligent of every
Christian denomination.

　The volume is dedicated in a very
sensible and affectionate address to the
Divinity and Lay-students, educated
in the Dissenting College, York; and
in addition to the reasons alleged by
the editor, her dedication of it has this
propriety, that it offers to their perusal the discourses of an eminent Christian Minister, written in the pure and
ardent spirit of his religion, and in a
style which has nothing in common
with the false eloquence that often seduces the young and sometimes daz-
zles the old, that incumbers truth with
ornament which it does not require,
and invests in a gaudy rhetoric subjects too lofty to be raised by a metaphor, and interests too grave and
momentous to be decked in flowers.
　　　　　　　　　　　　　　M.

――――――

Art. V.—*A Sermon on Free Inquiry
in Matters of Religion.* By W. J.
Fox, 12mo. Pp. 24.
Art. VI.—*A Reply to Popular Objections against Unitarianism:* A Sermon preached at Bristol, on Wednesday, June 21, 1815, before the
Western Unitarian Society. By
W. J. Fox, 12mo. Pp. 48. Hunter
and Eaton.

IT is difficult to speak of these sermons as they deserve, without
running into the style of extravagant
panegyric. Mr. Fox is always master
of his subject, master of his temper

and master of the English language. He treats the most common topics with originality. If we were to single out one excellence amongst so many, we should name the skill with which he detects and the ability with which he exposes the fallacies by which Calvinists cheat themselves in matters of religious feeling.

Art. VII.—*A Second Letter to the Rev. Dr. Goddard.* By A Layman. 12mo. pp. 90. Chichester printed : Sold by Longman and Co. London. 3s. bds. 1815.

THE character which we gave of the Layman's first Letter [M. Repos. vii. 642, 643,] belongs to this Second : 'it is decorous, elegant and spirited.

Dr. Goddard appears to have judged the Layman's Letter worthy of consideration, and accordingly he attempted a reply in " a Sermon lately delivered at the Consecration of the Bishop of London." The Layman could not have flattered himself with the hope of such a distinction. The arguments delivered *ex cathedrâ* on this notable occasion have not, however, either satisfied or silenced our author ; he boldly investigates the learned dignitary's well-written passages ; and has, we think, put in an effectual claim to a more detailed answer than can be given in the florid periods of an oration before the clergy.

The Layman had endeavoured to shew that no *alliance* subsists between the Church of England and the State; Dr. Goddard considers the expediency of such an alliance so ably proved [by Bp. Warburton] that it is unnecessary to enter into the argument : but the Layman maintains that the alliance is impossible.

"The meaning of the term forbids it. An *alliance* supposes a *treaty*, and a *treaty* supposes the *mutual independence* of the parties who treat. To contend therefore for an *alliance* between Church and State, is to contend for a principle which would introduce *imperium in imperio*, and thus incur the offence called *præmunire*." * Pp. 39, 40.

Of Bp. Warburton's book, the *Alliance*, the Layman says, (p. 41,) that it " has in the course of the last fifty

---

* " See Blackstone's Comment. Vol. iv. p. 115."

years been so successfully assailed both with reasoning and ridicule as to render hopeless any attempt to build an argument on its exploded foundations."

Whilst the Layman objects to an *alliance* between Church and State, he says very smartly and very truly,—

" —— but there is one species or mode of this alliance which I admit to be extremely convenient to the individuals concerned, and to have been exemplified in history. I mean that close and intimate connexion which has occasionally subsisted between infidel statesmen and bigoted ecclesiastics. Had a bishopric been at the disposal of Lord Bolingbroke, he would (independently of personal friendship) have much sooner given it to Dr. Swift than to Dr. Clarke." *Note.* P. 67.

Dr. Goddard had quoted Mr. Hume's eulogium upon the English Church, as " mitigating the genius of the ancient superstition" and " preserving itself in a happy medium." The Layman lays open the unmeaning verbosity of the passage, and says, in the language that becomes the unfettered Christian advocate,

" —— a consistent Protestant will not waste a thought on any *medium* between error and truth, and between integrity and imposture, and an honest and enlightened reformer will feel that he has something else to do than merely to *mitigate superstition.*" P. 65.

In a Postscript the Layman inserts some reflections on the Council of Nice, from the pen of Dr. Lardner, whom he justly characterizes as " one whom divines of every sect, party and denomination regard with great and increasing deference :

Crescit, occulto velut arbor ævo, Fama."

Would our *laymen* of learning and leisure copy the example of this respectable writer, and embrace every opportunity of asserting truth and liberty, the cause of Protestantism and liberal and rational Dissent would be a certain and great gainer.

Art. VII.—*An Essay on the Principles of Dissent :* in which the True Ground of Separation from the Established Church is stated and proved. By Richard Wright, 12mo. Pp. 24. 6d.

" WE cannot," says Mr. Wright, " give too much for a good conscience." Hence he argues the question of Dissent morally as well as theologically. His arguments are worthy of the attention particularly of unthinking Conformists and inconsistent Non-conformists.

Mr. Wright is well known as an Unitarian Dissenter, (the terms should be tautological,) but he treats the subject of Dissent so generally, that any Dissenter may read his Essay with satisfaction, and so candidly, that any churchman may read it without offence.

Art. IX.—*Zeal in a good Cause Recommended and Enforced.* A Sermon preached, Tuesday, May 16, 1815, at Worship Street, before the General Baptists' Annual

Assembly. By Jc 8vo. pp. 32. Eaton

THIS is evidently t of a thinking an It is particularly adapt neral Baptists, but wi to the taste of no Chr a value upon plainness simplicity of manner judgment. Since 'the printed Mr. Couplan moved from the prese tion : this gives a pecu the publication, espec lieve that the sale of i vice to a widow and less children, who ha besides the interest w of a Dissenting minist ate amongst his surviv

POETRY.

Sir,   *Feb.* 13, 1816.
The following lines, though not original, may be worthy of your insertion, as peculiarly seasonable, for there can be no better employment of an interval of peace than to inculcate and apprehend the true character of war

—a game which, were their subjects wise, Kings would not play at.

The Great Victory was an offspring of Mr. Southey's Muse in her juvenile days, and then published in one of the Anthologies, yet now apparently deserted, though not disowned, by the *Poet Laureat.* He has lately collected his smaller pieces into three volumes, among which I was rather sorry than surprised not to find the uncourtly dialogue of Old Kaspar and Peterkin.

PACIFICUS.

The Great Victory.

Ode on the Battle of Blenheim, by Mr. Southey.

IT was a summer evening,
    Old Kaspar's work was done,
And he before his cottage door
    Was sitting in the sun !
And by him sported on the green
His little grandchild Wilhelmine.

She saw her brother Peterkin
    Roll something large and round,
That he beside the rivulet,
    Whilst playing there, had found ;
He came to ask what he had found
That was so large, and smooth, and round.

Old Kaspar took it from the boy,
    Who stood expectant by;

And first the old man sho
    Then heav'd a deep-
" Tis some poor fellow's
" Who fell in the great v

" Now tell us what 'twas
    Young Peterkin, he
And little Wilhelmine lo
    With wonder-waiting
" Now tell us all about t
And what they kill'd ea

" It was the English," '
    " That put the Fren
And what they kill'd ea
    I ne'er could well m
But every body said," '
" That 'twas a famous v

" My father liv'd at Bl
    Yon little stream ha
They burnt his dwelling
    And he was forc'd t
So with his wife and cl
Nor had he where to re

" With fire and sword t
    Was wasted far and
And many a childing-m
    And new-born infa
But things like these ye
At every famous victor

" And every body prais
    Who such a fight di
" But what good came
    Quoth little Peterki
" Why that I cannot te
" But 'twas a famous v

Rabboni!
John xx. 16.

The Tomb is ope. Ah then, some felon band
(Heav'n!) has stol'n its mysterious pris'ner.
Spirit accurst. ... . . . But hush! some nimble foot
Flits through the murky air. And still its step
Wakes the faint echoes of the ling'ring night.
'Twas light as hurrying. Then welcome Dawn!
Bore it th' unhallow'd tidings? Haply so:
For on thy confine grey two forms appear,
Hasting this way, the foremost surely he
That on the bosom of the Master lay,
As if an inmate there; the other, who but he,
The good old man, whose bitter tears
Still chase each other down his manly cheek,
For that in evil hour an honest heart
(The very thought, else, of disloyalty
Had well nigh burst in twain,) gave way to zeal
Too confident to go unvisited.
  Oh! lov'd disciples.—Yet ah! not to joy,
Ye speed: rather at sorrow's ice-clad font
To drink the last chill dregs of numb despair.
And see, the first has reach'd the grave. Alas!
Too true the tale. He bends towards its brink
In breathless agony—but goes not in.
Not so the distanc'd partner of his woe:
See how he springs into its womb—surveys
Each grave-cloth—now with eager hand
Grasps his companion's, while he gently wins
E'en to his side yon nerveless, tott'ring frame!
Friendship, 'tis well. Nobly hast thou atchier'd
Thy duty. Stay not then—away, away,
Death presses on thy lingerings. They leave
The sepulchre, and with reflected eye,
*But hopeless heart, again each hies him home.
Ah then, what now usurps their place? In form
So much resembling hers. . . . In sooth 'tis she,
(I know her by that sigh, poor Penitent!)
The same who lav'd in tears his feet, and lov'd
So well that she had been so much forgiv'n:

---

* For surely the word "not" must have been originally subjoined to "believed" in the 8th verse.

Our fond heart-broken Magdalene. Yet say
What only thou stay'd here, sole, left to brave
Substantial noon-day woes, nor horrid less
To wake 'mid this dim light crepuscular
In fancy's eye to more than midnight fears! -
(O woman! faithful soul! In peril's hour
Though not the autumn leaf reft by the blast
So fluttering, when urgent duty bids
Or warm affection prompts, e'en at her post
Aye constant found, th' antediluvian rock
That mocks the idle dashing of the surge,
Less callous, rooted, and immovable.)
Yes! 'tis her streaming eye—her braidless hair,
Her livid lip, that " fain would meet again
Though but the impress of those hallow'd feet,
Which ah! not vainly so she late bedew'd,
When through her inmost soul one marv'lous look
Diffus'd unutterable extacy.
How marr'd that visage now!" That love-fraught eye,
" That beam'd no mortal tenderness, fast clos'd,
And mingling swiftly with its kindred clod!
That front on which erst Heav'n's own Shech'nah shone,
Cheerless and cold for ever!—O kind Sir,
Say hast thou borne the wond'rous relic hence?
Then tell me where it rests, and never more"—
Her eye look'd upward at the word, dreading
To meet the stranger's sterner glance, when hark!
A voice, no stranger voice, that " Mary!" spake,
And at his feet the mourner falls, answ'ring
" Rabboni!"—Tell me now ye pow'rs of sense
If from that hour when first ye wak'd to life
Upon this earth, such magic spirit e'er
Through mortal members trill'd?
                              TE TACE.
. *Feb.* 12, 1816.

Extempore on the late War.
(Morn. Chron.)

Whene'er contending Princes fight,
For private pique, or public right;
Armies are rais'd, the fleets are mann'd,
They combat both by sea and land.
When after many battles past,
Both tir'd with blows, make peace at last;
What is it, after all, the people get?
Why! Widows, Taxes, Wooden Legs and Debt!
                              W. H. H.

OBITUARY.

1815, Dec. 30, at Coseley, Staffordshire, Mr. JOSEPH MAULLIN, aged 85. In his early days he was one of the catechumens of the Rev. Samuel Bourne, then one of the ministers of Coseley, in conjunction with Birmingham, the memoirs of whose life have, not long since, been given to the public by the late truly excellent Dr. Toulmin. Under the pious and well-adapted instructions of that able and assiduous pastor, Mr. Maullin had in his youth a serious sense of the importance and value of religion impressed upon his mind, which was afterwards greatly beneficial to him in the regulation of his conduct. So strongly did he feel himself indebted to his useful admonitions and good counsels, as to retain a lively and grateful recollection of him to the latest period of remembrance; and he never spoke of his labours, or mentioned the name of Mr. Bourne but with high applause, evidently prompted by the feelings of grateful respect. Being thus disposed in early life he formed good habits before he attained to manhood, which led him to sobriety, industry, practical integrity, a regular attention to divine worship, and an exemplary concern for the promotion and prosperity of religion. From his youth to the decline of life he was industrious and active in his worldly occupation, and it pleased God in his providence to crown his assiduity with considerable success. His zeal for the interest of the place of worship which he constantly attended as long as he was able, and for the welfare of the schools belonging to it, was no less conspicuous; for it was enlightened by a good understanding, and animated by warm benevolence. Indeed he was ardently desirous of seeing the cause of sacred truth in a flourishing state, and of having education and religious instruction extensively diffused among the numerous poor children of his neighbourhood, which was testified by his liberal contributions towards the support of religion, and the school institutions established by charity, and by his unwearied endeavours to render himself useful to them.

It is not pretended that the deceas-ed was thoroughly perfect and without blemish, this is not the lot of frail humanity; but, though his unusual energy of mind and warm feelings might sometimes betray an over-hastiness of temper, yet he certainly bore the general traits of a valuable and excellent character. He was upon principle a Protestant Nonconformist, and well understood the rational grounds of dissent from the hierarchy set up and endowed by human authority. In his religious opinions he was completely Unitarian, having a clear view of the doctrinal sentiments which are usually so denominated, and a strong attachment to them, as the genuine truths of divine revelation. He frequently avowed his firm persuasion of the entire unity of God, and of the instrumentality of his Son the Mediator, of the perfect freeness of divine grace, and of eternal life's being the gift of God the Father through Jesus Christ our Lord. These most important truths of the glorious gospel formed the foundation of his Christian hope, were his satisfaction in active life, and the support and consolation of his mind in the various vicissitudes he experienced.

In his declining years, and when the infirmities of age were making rapid advances, his life was embitter-ed by some sore afflictions both in his person and family. While suffering the frequent and violent attacks of an asthma, and the increasing symtoms of losing his sight, the ravages of mortality among his near relatives, some of whom might have been expected from their comparatively youthful age, long to survive him, were painfully felt. But he was far from considering these mournful events as occurrences of chance, or repining at them as the effects of an undue severity. He devoutly acknowledged the providence of God in these afflictive strokes, regarded them as the fatherly chastisements of an all-wise and merciful Being, as means to be improved for weakening his love of this life, promoting his preparation for leaving the present world, and advancing his meetness to inherit a better state. He accordingly expressed it to be his desire, prayer and endeavour, to exercise the most humble and patient submission to the will of God under all the adversities with which he was tried.

When low sunk in the vale of years, reduced by infirmities to helpless decrepitude and total blindness, and enduring acute bodily pains, he still retained a considerable portion of his former mental faculties and vigour; and his piety shone with a mild lustre through the decay of nature. Just views of the gracious sovereignty of the Divine Being, and the resigned spirit of his holy Master, were often present to his mind, for to this effect he frequently exclaimed, " I wish to bear all my afflictions in such a manner as becomes a rational creature of the great God, and a faithful disciple of the Lord Jesus Christ, who, when enduring the heaviest afflictions and sufferings, said, ' Not my will but thine be done,' and ' The cup which my Father hath given me to drink shall I not drink it ?' " Under the influence of this great example he was solicitous that his heavenly Father would afford him strength equal to his day, and not permit his faith or patience to fail to the last moment of his mortal existence. His surviving relatives may with satisfaction indulge the hope that his pious wishes were accomplished, that he calmly fell into the sleep of death as a subject of the Divine favour, and as a sincere disciple of Jesus; and that he will be numbered among them who will hereafter joyfully awake to a blissful immortality.

F.

1816, Jan. 13, aged 70, Mrs. Lewin, the wife of the Rev. R. Lewin, of Liverpool. The greatest part of her life was spent in the domestic circle, though she possessed mental acquirements that would have adorned the most polished society: her suavity of manners appeared in all her actions, her conversation was energetic, but mild, never giving way to ill-natured remarks; her performance of the duties of a wife and parent have stamped upon her afflicted family the most lasting impression of her excellent heart; nor was the character of the Christian ever more brightly exemplified; her heart was always open to the keenest sensibility for those in distress, and her hand ready to re-

lieve. Her sorrowing friends will draw consolation from her firm faith in the Christian religion, which fortified her mind on all occasions; her truly religious character which led her never to pass over a single day without devoting a considerable part of it to her Maker; and her rare and excellent virtues, while they deeply regret her loss.

D. N.

Sunday, the 21st of January, at Richmond, in Yorkshire, the Reverend **Francis Blackburne**, Vicar of Brignall, which living he held thirty-five years, residing upon it and performing in the most exemplary manner all the duties of a parish priest, till increasing infirmities compelled him to retire to Richmond, whence, however, he in every year paid frequent visits to his parishioners, by whom he was universally beloved. He was buried, at his express desire, on the 24th, at Brignall. Mr. Blackburne was the eldest son of the late venerable Archdeacon Blackburne, whose sentiments on religious and civil liberty he asserted on all proper occasions, with that calmness and dignity which was peculiar to his character. He was the intimate friend of Mr. Wyvill, and co-operated with him in all those measures, whose object was the amelioration of the representation in parliament, and extension of religious liberty to all classes of his Majesty's subjects, being firmly convinced that wherever the truth lay it was to be maintained in the spirit of brotherly love, and not by pains or penalties, or restrictions of any kind. The peculiar feature in his character is delineated by a term we believe peculiar to and most expressive in our own language, Good Temper. By this, and a charity extensive as his means, he was endeared to all around him, and particularly to the poor, whose blessings will accompany him to his grave. As a father, husband, neighbour, friend and parish priest, his memory will be long cherished by those who stood in these relations to him. He left behind him a widow and three children, two sons and a daughter; the latter married to Mr. Frend, whose name frequently occurs in this Repository.

Feb. 9, greatly respected, and in the full enjoyment of her faculties, at Cheshunt, Herts, in the 90th year of her age, Mrs. HANNAH JOYCE, relict of Mr. Jeremiah Joyce, who died in the same place, Sept. 17, 1778. Mrs. Joyce was granddaughter by her mother's side to the Rev. John Benson, a dissenting minister residing at Hoddesdon, in Hertfordshire, at the period of the Revolution; but who, in 1690 or 1691, removed to Sandwich, in Kent. This gentleman had nine children, of whom the eldest, John, was educated for the ministry, among the Dissenters, and was afterwards settled at Chertsey, in Surrey. His sixth child, Martha, was married to Mr. John Somersett, of St. Mildred's Court, London, by whom he had six children. Of these, Hannah was born Sept. 5, 1726, O. S. and was baptized the following day, by the Rev. Mr. Grosvenor, of Crosby Square. The fact is noticed in the Register kept by Mr. Benson, who adds, " And she is now, June 8th, 1727, visiting (with her mother) her grandfather John and grandmother Hannah Benson, at Sandwich, in Kent, whom God long preserve as a blessing to herself and parents." Hannah remained in London only till she was about twelve years of age, when she was taken into the family of Mrs. Harding, of Cheshunt, who kept a very respectable and flourishing boarding school in that village, but who afterwards married Mr. Lewis Jones, at that time of Reading, in Berkshire, who removed to Hackney, where he and Mrs. Jones died and were buried.

While with Mrs. Harding, the subject of this article married Mr. Joyce, by whom he had eight children. She was from a very early period seriously and deeply impressed with the importance of religion, and it appears from a sort of diary, in her own handwriting, but which was never seen, by her children even, till after her decease, that though she had been extremely assiduous in her attendance upon public worship, and exhibited the most decisive proofs of undissembled piety, yet when she was in her 19th year, she made what she denominates a solemn re-dedication of herself to God and his service, by joining the church under the pastoral care

of the Rev. John Oakes.[*] This was in the year 1745, and she continued a member of that church so long as it remained in the same connexion. The successor to Mr. Oakes was the Rev. John Mason, author of numerous excellent works, of which the most celebrated is, a " Treatise on Self-Knowledge;" an edition of this with some alterations, and a biographical account of the author was in 1803 published by Mrs. Joyce's youngest son, who dedicated it to his mother as the last surviving member of Mr. Mason's church. She has left four children, who cannot cease to remember with emotions of filial piety and gratitude, the constant care and attention which she ever manifested in forming their minds to habits of usefulness, integrity and virtue.

J. J.

Highgate, Feb. 24, 1816.

[*] After the death of Mr. Oakes, a volume of his Sermons to young persons was published by his successor, Mr. Mason. The following Questions in Mr. Oakes's hand-writing, will shew on what terms persons were admitted to church communion with him at that time, who was pastor of a presbyterian congregation.

QUESTIONS *publicly proposed to such as offer themselves to the communion with us.*

1. Do you believe that Jesus Christ is the Son of God and the Saviour of the world ?

2. Do you believe that Jesus Christ died for our sins according to the scriptures, and that he rose again from the dead for our justification ?

3. And do you *so* believe these things, as that you do hereupon sincerely and heartily devote yourself to him, and to God by him ; as it becomes those to do who are bought with the price of his precious blood ?

4. And is it your fixed resolution and the solemn purpose of your soul (in dependance on divine grace) to lead the life you live in the flesh by the faith of the Son of God, and in a course of dutiful obedience to his commandments ?

MINISTER. If this be the sincere belief of your heart, and these your settled resolutions, then in the name of Jesus Christ, and in the name of this Christian Society, I bid you welcome to this feast of the gospel.

Tuesday, Jan. 30, at his house, in St. Thomas's Square, Hackney, Mr. JAMES HENNELL, aged 33. By a most mysterious visitation of Divine Providence, this interesting young man is taken away from a numerous family and a wide circle of friends in the midst of activity and usefulness. A Sermon on occasion of his death was preached by Mr. Aspland to the Gravel-Pit Congregation, Hackney, of which he had been a member, for several years, on Sunday morning, Feb. 18th, when a numerous audience testified by their deep sympathy their sense of the loss sustained by society in this melancholy event. At the request of the family of the deceased, the Sermon is put into the press; we shall extract the conclusion of it, containing some account of his character and happy death, in our next.

On Saturday, Feb. 3, at Wicken, in the county of Cambridge, at the age of 64, Mrs. HANNAH ASPLAND, relict of the late Mr. Robert Aspland, of the same place. Her sufferings were severe and long-continued, but a deep sense of religion which she had cultivated from earliest youth bore up her mind with exemplary fortitude and patience. Her faculties were clear to the moment of her dissolution, and her last breath was spent in prayer to her heavenly Father. By her express desire, her funeral sermon was preached at Wicken, on the Sunday following her interment, Feb. 11th, by her son, the only survivor of several children, Mr. Aspland, of Hackney, from 1 Peter iii. 3, 4, 5, words of her own choice, which had been her comfort in the failure of heart and flesh. A very crowded auditory was deeply affected throughout the whole of this trying service.

Lately, at Park House, Hayes, the Hon. Mr. JUSTICE HEATH, one of the Judges of the Court of Common Pleas. He was in point of service, the father of the Bench, all his brethren having taken their seats subsequent to him. He was esteemed the best *black-letter* man of these times, deeply learned and of the most solid and fixed principles. He was justly ranked among those few men, whom no power nor persuasion could divert into a relaxation from what he thought right; yet this virtue had degenerated into the vice of obstinacy in his old age, and thus begat sternness and severity.—*Monthly Mag.*

Lately, at the age of 77, *the very Rev.* WILLIAM VINCENT, Doctor of Divinity. He had been preferred, in the year 1808, to the deanery of Westminster, and resided, at his death, in the cloisters be-

longing to that cathedral. This elevation was considered as a most appropriate reward of his long and skilful discharge of the functions of master of Westminster School.

It was brought as a reproachful charge against Milton, that he had once employed his superlative talents in the instruction of youth. Abilities not inferior to his own would be required to attach disgrace to an employment not to be compared in absolute utility with any other. The duties of it may be ill performed, and it then becomes dishonourable and injurious. Yet few instances of its abuse would probably occur were due judgment exercised in the selection of proper persons, and due honour paid to the qualified and meritorious. Milton has been defended, with almost superfluous ability, by Dr. Johnson; and nothing further needs to be urged in vindication of the respectability of Dr. Vincent, and of the ample remuneration bestowed upon him. The example of John Milton is enough to give dignity to any avocation.

Dr. Vincent was educated at the celebrated school which he afterwards directed with such success. On that foundation he was elected to Trinity College, Cambridge. At the end of four years he returned, and never quitted the walls of that seminary, till it was judged right to terminate his conscientious diligence by an ample provision for his old age. Hundreds of the nobility and gentry of the land acquired under him that taste and that erudition which so much distinguish the higher orders of society in Great Britain. Without injustice to his name, it cannot be separated from the praises merited by British learning during one half of a century.

In other respects, Dr. Vincent acquired no extraordinary literary reputation. What, indeed, could have been done more than he has done? Leisure and opportunity were denied him in the midst of a most arduous engagement, which, instead of admitting the intrusion of other pursuits, stood itself in need of aid and division. Yet, he managed to steal from the school sufficient time to compose his admirable work on the Navigation and Commerce of the ancients. This proof of his learning and industry is well known at home, and perhaps more highly appreciated by the learned abroad, who may be pronounced equally discerning with his own countrymen, and perhaps less subject to hostility or partiality. This was enough for fame.

Dr. Vincent was not less intent and assiduous for heaven. He had talents; he had learning; he had a rare felicity in communicating the store of his mind to others. However, he had higher qualifications. His heart was simple, his manners were, pure. Those whom his station or closer affinity placed under his guidance and protection experienced in him every kindness which could be prompted by true philanthropy. Religion had in Dr. Vincent an enlightened friend of its cause, and a bright example of its excellence and consolation.—*Weekly Mag.* No. VI. ·

INTELLIGENCE.

FOREIGN.
Persecution of the Vaudois.

We request the attention of our liberal and feeling readers to the subject of a new persecution of our Protestant brethren, commenced in another quarter, a persecution which, though in appearance not so glaring as that already noticed in France, is in reality more atrocious. It has not, we believe, as yet been brought before the public eye in this country, and should any reader not be aware of the circumstances which render this persecution an act of peculiar meanness as well as of atrocity, we beg leave to state a few historical facts which will serve to represent the matter in its proper colours, and also enable every candid mind to judge how far our ministers have been anxious for the honour of this country, and the interests of the Protestant religion abroad, for which at home they profess so much devotion. The dreadful persecution commenced by the King of Savoy, in 1654, against his unoffending Protestant subjects, a persecution during which several hundred of innocent victims perished by the sword, and many others amongst Alpine snows, is unfortunately too well known to require any detail of its atrocities. When the account of that persecution reached England, Cromwell, who was at the head of the government, immediately wrote on the subject to the different powers in Europe, and to the King of Savoy in particular: so strongly did he express his abhorrence of the barbarous outrage, that the persecutions were not only put an end to by his interference, but even a treaty was made, by which the Protestant inhabitants of Piedmont, known under the name of *Vaudois*, were specially placed under the protection of Great Britain. This treaty was ratified at different times, and the worship of these Protestants was, in fact, supported by English contribution down to the time in which the present Sardinian King was expelled from Piedmont. Regardless as the French Revolutionary government was in many instances of church property, yet so great was the respect paid at all times to the virtues and poverty of the Vaudois, that even that government not only endowed the Protestant church of the Vaudois with a provision arising out of the revenues of the country, larger than the sum they had been in the habit of receiving from England, but they made that perpetual which

was before precarious, and they also gave them perfect and complete civil equality.

When at length the French were obliged to give up Italy, and the King of Sardinia was restored among the other legitimates, he issued a proclamation, declaring as *null* every act which had taken place during his absence. By this general declaration, the Vaudois have been actually deprived of the revenues for the support of their religion, and as our minister has neglected to insert, in the new treaties, the old covenant in their favour, they are thus subject to the fury of a bigotry which may again break out with the same rage as it did formerly, and in the mean time their teachers are deprived of all subsistence. A single word from our minister might have prevented the possibility of such an event.

The following genuine letter, which we have received from Piedmont, will give our readers a fuller description of the calamity which this persecution has brought upon that inoffensive people. Here, at least, there cannot be alleged against them the crime of *Buonapartism* :—

" *La Tour de Pelis*, 12*th Dec*, 1815.
"Consternation is in our valleys—we are threatened by the Agents of our King with being robbed of the little which had been granted to us by the preceding governments, for the support of our religious worship. The Court of Turin pretends not to be bound by any convention on this subject, and professes to do in this case as in every other, whatever pleases itself, or rather whatever pleases the cabal of Monks which rules under its name. In reality, neither the treaty of Paris in 1814, nor that lately concluded, makes any mention of the *special protection* granted by preceding treaties, particularly by that of Aix-la-Chapelle, to the Protestants of the valleys of Piedmont, known under the name of *Vaudois*. Can England, who formerly acted so generously towards them, have now changed her system with regard to these eldest sons of the evangelical religion, whose aversion to the Roman Church is anterior even to the Reformation of Luther? Can this population of 30,000 souls have appeared to the English minister an object too unimportant to employ his attention amidst the political dismemberment of so many nations? We cannot believe it; for nothing is trifling which involves a great moral principle. However, if at a

period when England was far from that preponderance on the Continent which the follies of Napoleon have put into her hands; if at a period in which religious freedom had not yet become a common maxim with all enlightened governments, the British Administration in former days could obtain so great a triumph on this subject over the prejudices of time and place, can any person doubt but that a single word from your ministers (whom the House of Savoy must regard as its restorers) would have been sufficient to assure, not only to the Vaudois, but to all the inhabitants of Piedmont, the free exercise of their religion? Since then, negociators, supported by so great an influence, did not think proper to insert in the new treaties the ancient guarantee to the Protestants of Piedmont, we must suppose that they could not foresee that the Court of Sardinia, by declaring every thing null which happened during its absence,. (that is to say, during sixteen years and more) would, under this general proclamation, rob the Vaudois of all the benefits with which a paternal administration had endowed their church, and of which the French fiscality had not the hardihood to despoil them. Deprived of this resource, the Protestants of the Alps will be obliged again to call upon the liberality of the English to contribute to the support of their religion ; but supposing that they should not be disappointed in their expectations from them, can any one compare this humiliating and precarious situation with that public and independent support of their worship, and that perfect civil equality which they enjoyed for so many years before the restoration of the Sardinian King? How much anguish and uncertainty through Europe might have been put an end to by a few words from your ministers, supported as they are on this subject by claims so strong and resources so immense ! Will they who have done so much for kings, do nothing for the people, especially for that portion of the European people whom the sacred ties of a common religion, and the recollection of similar sufferings, bind in so close a manner with the nation whom they profess to represent ? We hope, and dare believe, that these great personages partake themselves of the indignation with which we are penetrated, and that they who have headed the coalition of kings against their people, will not disdain to add to that glory, assuring their natural and legitimate rights to those nations whom they have forced to return under the *domination* of their ancient masters."—*Mora. Chron. Dec. 26.*

Holy Alliance.

" By the Grace of God, We, Alexander the First, Emperor and Autocrat of all the Russians, &c. hereby make known—
VOL. XI.

". As we have seen from experience, and from the unhappy consequences that have resulted for the whole world, that the course of the political relations in Europe between the Powers has not been founded on those true principles upon which the wisdom of God in his revelations has founded the peace and prosperity of nations,

" We have consequently, in conjunction with their Majesties the Emperor of Austria, Francis the First, and the King of Prussia, Frederick William, proceeded to form an alliance between us, (to which the other Christian Powers are invited to accede), in which we reciprocally engage, both between ourselves and in respect of our subjects, to adopt, as the sole means to attain this end, the principle drawn from the words and doctrine of our Saviour Jesus Christ, who preaches not to live in enmity and hatred, but in peace and love. We hope and implore the blessing of the Most High ; may this sacred union be confirmed between all the powers for their general good, and (deterred by the union of all the rest), may no one dare to fall off from it. We accordingly subjoin a copy of this union, ordering it to be made generally known, and read in all the churches.

" St. Petersburgh, on the day of the birth of our Saviour, 25th Dec., 1815.
" The original is signed by his Imperial Majesty's own hand,

" ALEXANDER."

" In the name of the Most Holy and Indivisible Trinity,

" Their Majesties, the Emperor of Austria, the King of Prussia, and the Emperor of Russia, having in consequence of the great events which have marked the course of the three last years in Europe, and especially of the blessings which it has pleased Divine Providence to shower down upon those states, which place their confidence and their hope on it alone, acquired the intimate conviction of the necessity of founding the conduct to be observed by the powers in their reciprocal relations upon the sublime truths which the holy religion of our Saviour teaches.

" They solemnly declare, that the present Act has no other object than to publish in the face of the whole world their fixed resolution, both in the administration of their respective states, and in their political relations with every other government, to take for their sole guide the precepts of that holy religion, namely, the precepts of Justice, Christian Charity, and Peace, which far from being applicable only to private concerns, must have an immediate influence on the councils of princes, and guide all their steps, as being the only means of consolidating human institutions, and remedying their imperfections.

" In consequence, their Majesties have agreed on the following articles :—

Art. 1. Conformable to the words of the Holy Scriptures, which command all men to consider each other as brethren, the three contracting monarchs will remain united by the bonds of a true and indissoluble fraternity, and considering each other as fellow countrymen, they will on all occasions, and in all places, lend each other aid and assistance, and regarding themselves towards their subjects and armies as fathers of families, they will lead them in the same spirit of fraternity with which they are animated to protect religion, peace and justice.

" Art. 2. In consequence the sole principle in force, whether between the said governments, or between their subjects, shall be that of doing each other reciprocal service, and of testifying by unalterable good-will the mutual affection with which they ought to be animated, to consider themselves all as members of one and the same Christian nation. The three Allied Princes looking on themselves as merely delegated by Providence to govern three branches of the one family, namely, Austria, Prussia and Russia, thus confessing that the Christian nation of which they and their people form a part, has in reality no other Sovereign than him to whom alone power really belongs, because in him alone are found all the treasures of love, science, and infinite wisdom, that is to say, God, our Divine Saviour, the Word of the Most High, the Word of Life. Their Majesties consequently recommend to their people, with the most tender solicitude, as the sole means of enjoying that peace which arises from a good conscience, and which alone is durable, to strengthen themselves every day more and more in the principles and exercise of the duties which the Divine Saviour has taught to mankind.

" Art. 3. All the powers who shall choose solemnly to avow the sacred principles which have dictated the present act, and shall acknowledge how important it is for the happiness of nations too long agitated, that those truths should henceforth exercise over the destinies of mankind all the influence which belongs to them, will be received with equal ardour and affection into this Holy alliance.

" Done in triplicate, and signed at Paris, in the year of grace, 1815, (14, O. S.) 26th Sept.

(L.S.)   " FRANCIS.
(L.S.)   " FREDERICK WILLIAM.
(L.S.)   " ALEXANDER.

" Conformable to the original,
(Signed)   " ALEXANDER.
" Done at St. Petersburg, the day of the birth of our Saviour, the 25th of Dec. 1815."

St. Petersburgh, Dec. 21, O. S.
Jan. 2, 1816.

Ukase of his Majesty the Emperor to the Senate.

(OFFICIAL TRANSLATION.)

Being returned after a happy conclusion of the external affairs of Europe, to the empire which God has entrusted to us, we have been informed by several nations [probably notices] complaints and reports of the following circumstances :—

The religious order of the Jesuits of the Roman Catholic Church had been abolished by a bull of the Pope; in consequence of this measure, the Jesuits were expelled, not only from the states of the Church, but from all other countries,—they were not permitted to remain any where. Russia alone, constantly guided by sentiments of humanity and toleration, retained them in her territory, gave them an asylum, and insured their tranquillity under her powerful protection. She did not oppose any obstacle to the free exercise of their worship; she did not deter them from it, either by force, persuasion or seduction; but in return, she thought she might expect from them fidelity, attachment and utility. In this hope they were permitted to devote themselves to the education and instruction of youth. Fathers and mothers entrusted to them their children without fear, to teach them the sciences and to form their manners. It is now proved that they have not fulfilled the duties which gratitude imposed on them; that they have not kept themselves in that humility which the Christian religion commands; and that instead of remaining peaceable inhabitants in a foreign country, they have endeavoured to trouble the Greek religion, which, from the remotest times, has been the predominant religion of our empire. and on which, as on an immoveable rock, repose the tranquillity and the happiness of the nations subject to our sceptre. They have begun first, by abusing the confidence which they had gained. They have turned aside from our worship young people who had been entrusted to them, and some women of weak and inconsiderate minds, and have drawn them to their church. To induce a man to abjure his faith, the faith of his ancestors, to extinguish in him the love of those who profess the same worship, to render him a stranger to his country, to sow discord and animosity in families, to detach the brother from the brother, the son from the father, and the daughter from the mother, to excite divisions among the children of the same church; is that the voice and the will of God, and his divine Son, Jesus Christ, our Saviour, who shed for us his most pure blood, " that we might live a peaceful and tranquil life, in all sort of piety and honesty?" After such actions, we are no longer surprised that the Order of these

Monks has been removed from all countries, and no where tolerated. In fact, what state can suffer in its bosom those who spread in it hate and disorder? Constantly occupied in watching over the welfare of our faithful subjects, and considering it as a wise and sacred duty to stop the evil in its origin, that it may not grow to maturity and produce bitter fruits,

We have, in consequence, resolved to ordain—

1. That the Catholic Church which is here, be again re-established upon the footing in which it was during the reign of our grandmother, of glorious memory, the Empress Catherine II. and till the year 1800.

2. To make all the Monks of the order of the Jesuits immediately to quit St. Petersburg.

3. To forbid them to enter our two capitals.

We have given particular orders to our Ministers of Police and Public Instruction for the prompt execution of this determination, and for all that concerns the house and institution hitherto occupied by the Jesuits. At the same time, and that there may be no interruption in the divine service, we have ordered the Metropolitan of the Roman Catholic Church to cause the Jesuits to be replaced by Priests of the same religion, who are now here, till the arrival of Monks of another Catholic Order, whom we have sent for, for that purpose.

Dec. 20, 1815.

The original is signed,

ALEXANDER.

(A true copy).—The Director of the Department, TOURGUKNOFF.

FRENCH PROTESTANTS.

At a Special General Meeting of the Deputies appointed for the Protection of the Civil Rights of the Three Denominations of Protestant Dissenters, held at the King's Head Tavern, in the Poultry, London, the 1st of December, 1815, WILLIAM SMITH, Esq. M. P. in the Chair;

The following Resolutions were unanimously agreed to:—

That this Deputation consider it a duty as absolutely incumbent upon them openly and forcibly to express their abhorrence of the persecutions under which the Protestants of France are now suffering, and of the spirit which has given them birth.

That a humble Address from this Body be presented to his Royal Highness the Prince Regent, respectfully, but most earnestly beseeching his gracious interposition with the French Government to put an immediate termination to the insults and injuries inflicted on the Protestants in that country, and to protect them in the peaceable enjoyment of their constitutional rights and liberties.

That this Meeting, deeply sympathizing with those of their fellow-christians who have already suffered, or who may yet suffer in their persons and properties from these lawless outrages, do most cordially concur in the recommendation of the Protestant Dissenting Ministers in this city to the several congregations of Dissenters throughout the kingdom, to make collections for the relief of the sufferers.

That the above Resolutions, signed by the Chairman, be inserted in the several public papers.

WILLIAM SMITH, Chairman.

That the thanks of this Deputation be given to Wm. Smith, Esq. M. P. for his attendance, and able conduct in the Chair this day.

At Edinburgh, Dec. 5, 1815,

The Ministers and Elders of the Edinburgh Associate Presbytery, this day assembled, having taken into consideration a letter, addressed to one of their number, by the Secretary to the Board of the Protestant Dissenting Ministers in London, and which letter contains certain Resolutions passed by that Body at an Extraordinary General Meeting, held on the 28th day of November last, respecting the persecution raised against the Professors of the Reformed Religion in the South of France, unanimously approve of the principles expressed in said resolutions; concur with these ministers in deep and most tender sympathy with the persecuted Protestants in France; and earnestly recommend it to all the congregations under their inspection, to make contributions in aid of the general fund, which is collecting in London and other places of the United Kingdom, towards the temporal relief of their suffering brethren.

They farther recommend that these contributions, when made, shall be paid into the hands of the Treasurer of the Presbytery, and be by him remitted to the Committee of Superintendance and Distribution at Williams's Library, Redcross Street, London, " some of the members of which Committee," as stated by themselves, " will, if necessary, examine on the spot the miseries they deplore, and distribute with impartiality the fruits of their Christian benevolence."

Meantime, the Presbytery embraces, with zeal, the present opportunity to express the liveliest feelings of satisfaction and gratitude at the assurances of his Majesty's Government to the Deputation from the said General Meeting, " that they feel the deepest regret at the dreadful scenes lately witnessed in France, and that they are using and will continue to use their best efforts in their communications with the French Government, to secure to all classes of French subjects, whether Protestant or Catholic, the full enjoyment of the advantages which the Constitutional Charter has provided for them."

The Presbytery, in fine, express their ardent hopes that, in the language of the said General Meeting, " the Ordonnance lately issued by the French King, occasioned by an assault on a Catholic officer at Nismes, will be obeyed, and prove the commencement of vigorous measures on the part of the French government, for the punishment of those who have so long massacred the Protestants with impunity.

ANDREW LOTHIAN, Moderator.
PATRICK COMRIE, Clerk.

Woon, *Mayor.*

A Common Council, holden in the Chamber of the Guildhall of the City of London, on Thursday, the 14th day of December, 1815,

Resolved unanimously,

That a dutiful and loyal Address be presented to his Royal Highness the Prince Regent, representing the feelings of this Court at the information we have received of the cruel and inhuman persecution and suffering of our Protestant Brethren in France, whereby their places of worship have been closed, their property pillaged and destroyed, and the lives of innocent and unoffending individuals have been sacrificed to the merciless rage of infuriated bigotry and superstition ; humbly praying his Royal Highness to adopt such prompt and efficacious measures as may best tend to suppress these enormous evils.

WOODTHORPE.

At a Special Meeting of the Committee of The Protestant Society, for the Protection of Religious Liberty, held at the New London Tavern, Cheapside, London, on January 23d, 1816,

SAMUEL MILLS, Esq. in the Chair;

The Committee, having considered the necessity and expedience of further immediate interference with the affairs of the FRENCH PROTESTANTS,

Resolved,

1. That this Society, including members of the Established Church, as well as numerous congregations of Protestant Dissenters, throughout England and Wales, has not been formed for the special purpose of affording relief to the Protestants in France, —is unconnected with any political party, —has invariably been disposed to afford to government all just support ;—and, although especially designed to protect the enjoyment of Religious Freedom according to the existing laws in the British Empire, could not, without selfishness and degradation, disregard the numerous statements long circulated in the daily journals and other publications, of the existence of

persecutions towards the Protestants in the South of France.

2. That the Committee, therefore, assembled on Nov. 21, 1815, and adopted Resolutions respectful to the French and British governments ; but declaratory of the great principles of Religious Liberty, of their hatred to intolerance,—of their determination to investigate the accuracy of the existing complaints, and of their inclination to afford to the persecuted all needful protection and relief.

3. That, adhering to the constitution of their Society, this Committee hastened first to communicate their Resolutions to their own government, and to request from them accurate intelligence, and that interposition which acquaintance with their principles and conduct induced them to expect :—and that they received from the Earl of Liverpool, and from other members of the Administration, admissions of the evils and assurances of their due exertions to prevent their continuance,— which they did not delay most publicly to announce.

4. That, gratified by this declaration, by an Ordonnance published on Nov. 23d, by the Court of France, and by the information of the Duke of Wellington of the disposition of that Court to repress the outrages, which he did not attempt to deny, the Committee, by public Resolutions adopted on Dec 5th, and by other statements, communicated the substance of the information they received, and expressed their intention not to augment public anxiety by active labours, but rather vigilantly to observe the measures which might occur in France.

5. That to these Resolutions they have firmly adhered—that they have sought for information by honourable means—that they have avoided all proceedings which might increase solicitude and discontent— that they have not invited public contributions which might not be required, which the sufferers might decline to accept, and which they might be unable to dispense—that they have addressed to the French Protestants a letter which calumny has not ventured to denounce—and that they have sought rather to conciliate than to offend, and to hush the elements of existing discord into permanent tranquillity.

6. That, able to discriminate between exaggerated complaints, and equally exaggerated exculpations : between details which gave universality to local oppressions, and assertions which denied that local cruelties had been displayed :—and that, regardless equally of inflated panegyric, and of unmerited obliquy, the Committee have pursued the path they originally designed, and have now arrived at the goal they intended to attain.

7. That, from the intelligence they have received, they learn that there are 89 consistories, 230 churches, and 251 ministers,

belonging to the Protestants in *forty* departments of France, and one college for their literary and theological instruction, established at Montauban; and that in the department du Gard a persecution, partly political but rendered most acrimonious by religious animosity, had continued during several months,—that many persons had been murdered,—that public worship was prevented,—that churches were despoiled, —that trade and manufactures were suspended, — that hundreds, appalled and alarmed, had quitted their occupations—their property and their homes, and become fugitives;—and that all the evils had locally existed, which mobs, unrestrained by adequate authority, and stimulated by party spirit, ignorance, desire of pillage and superstition, could inflict.

8. That although the Committee do not rely on letters influenced by fear,—on publications induced by interest,—and on assurances inserted in the subservient Journals which circulate in France;—and although they regret that perfect compensation has not been made to the sufferers, and more decisive measures earlier adopted against their aggressors,—they are convinced that, even in that department where the evils did exist, those evils are now much decreased: that the rights of the Protestants have been officially recognized, in reiterated publications:—another Royal Ordonance, for their advantage, has been announced;—civil and military authorities have united for their protection; — their ministers have been placed on an equality with the Catholic Clergy in the Electoral Assemblies, and flattered by titular and honourary distinctions;—their churches have been re-opened;—many fugitives have returned;—manufactures have revived;—some of their persecutors have been committed for trial; —and repose and security re-appear.

9. That this Committee cannot but attribute these results to the declarations of the Allied Powers, to the special efforts of the British Cabinet, and to those expressions of public opinion in England and throughout Europe, which have abashed the violent and unconstitutional Catholics in France—and, penetrating to the Thuilleries, have induced that Court to display an interest, a decision, and an energy, which had been too long deferred:—and that the Committee therefore rejoice in all the exertions which have not only contributed to this immediate effect, but which have formed an example for future labours—have announced the rights of conscience—have declared to the existing generation and to future ages, that Religious Freedom is esteemed and revered,—that Intolerance will no longer be endured, and that all persecutors must expect contemporaneous abhorrence, and a contempt permanent as the remembrance of their crimes.

10. That aware that imperious necessity can alone justify a foreign interference, and that such interference, especially when needlessly protracted, may increase jealousy, perpetuate suspicion, and inflame resentment, in foreign countries;—relying on the auspicious change which has obviously and actually occurred,—confiding in the promises of future and equal protection, now repeatedly promulgated by the Court of France,—encouraged by the recent assurances which have been given by Lords Liverpool and Castlereagh to the inhabitants of Glasgow, and the Catholics of the north, —and informed of the wishes and situation of the Protestants of France,—this Committee will not solicit Subscriptions on their behalf, and will now withdraw from active interposition with their affairs;—but that they will continue feelingly alive to their future destiny, and ready to afford them all that assistance,—cordial, prompt and abundant, which authentic applications may invite, or unexpected exigencies shall demand.

11. That the Committee cannot announce this determination without renewing their acknowledgements to the British Government for their wise and liberal conduct,—nor without expressing their thanks to the Corporate and other Bodies,—to the public spirited inhabitants of Glasgow, Hull, Newcastle, Gosport and Plymouth, and to the Catholics of Dublin and of the North of England, who have afforded them manly and Christian co-operation and support. And,

12. That convinced of the resistless power of public opinion in a free country, and of the inestimable value of the independence of the press, the Committee cannot but offer their unfeigned and grateful applause to the spontaneous perseverance and zeal with which the great majority of the Editors of the public Journals have, with judgment and eloquence, advocated the cause of humanity and freedom, have counteracted the efforts of opponents, and have promoted an important and memorable triumph for Religious Liberty and Truth.

T. PELLATT,
J. WILKS, } Secretaries.

At a Meeting of the Committee of the Protestant Dissenting Ministers of the Three Denominations, held at Williams's Library, Red-Cross Street, on Monday, January 29, 1816,

It was unanimously Resolved,

That the Committee, at length, feel it an imperious duty to declare publicly, that they have never had any connexion with the Association denominated, "The Protestant Society;"—that, from sufficient evidence, the Committee can assure the public of the correctness of their published statements; and that the contributions which have been, or still may be, entrusted to their care, continue to be highly neeesary, and will be appropriated to the efficient relief of the Protestants in the South of France, whose sufferings have not only equalled, but exceeded, the representations given by this Committee.

THOS. MORGAN, Secretary.

DOMESTIC.

RELIGIOUS.

Address of the Catholic Bishops to his Royal Highness the Prince Regent.

To his Royal Highness George Augustus Frederick, Prince of Wales, Regent of the United Kingdom of Great Britain and Ireland,

The humble and dutiful Address of the Roman Catholic Prelates of Ireland.

MAY IT PLEASE YOUR ROYAL HIGHNESS, We, his Majesty's most dutiful and loyal subjects, the Roman. Catholic Prelates of Ireland, beg leave to approach your Royal Highness, with the tribute of our humble and sincere congratulation on the late signal success, with which it has pleased Almighty God to bless his Majesty's arms; whereby the peace of the civilized world is likely to be established on a solid and permanent foundation.

We presume to avail ourselves of this first opportunity of expressing our gratitude, for the relaxation which has taken place during his present Majesty's reign, of many of those penal laws which oppressed the Roman Catholics of Ireland; and we humbly hope that the total abrogation of our remaining grievances is reserved for the auspicious Adminstration of your Royal Highness. To your Royal Highness it belongs to consummate the work of goodness, which was commenced by your august Father; and, great as the other achievements undoubtly are, which have distinguished and will signalize your Government, we presume to affirm, that the total emancipation of his Majesty's Roman Catholic Subjects will be recorded as a deed of grandeur, not inferior to any other of your memorable Administration.

While thus we venture to disclose our sentiments most respectably to your Royal Highness, may we be permitted to represent that which most nearly concerns us as Ministers of Religion? We beg leave most humbly to submit to your Royal Highness, that no portion of his Majesty's subjects is, or has, at any time, been more eminently distinguished for pure, conscientious, and disinterested loyalty, than the Roman Catholic Prelates of Ireland. With this impression of our minds, we cannot but be surprised and alarmed, that under the pretence of securing the loyalty of our body, an intention has been manifested of compelling us, in *direct opposition to the dictates of our consciences,* to submit, in the event of Catholic Emancipation, to the interference of persons of a different religious persuasion, in the appointment of

the principal Ministers of our church. Such a measure, may it please your Royal Highness, would only substitute, for one mode of servitude, another still more galling and oppressive.—The political freedom of Irish Roman Catholics might be enlarged; but their religious freedom, which they hold incomparably more dear, would be, materially diminished. Under such a restriction, the most extensive concession of temporal advantages would be followed by continual heartburnings and discontent.

Relying, therefore, on the wisdom and equity of your Royal Highness, we most humbly implore your gracious interposition, that our long hoped-for emancipation may be free from a condition so degrading to our characters as loyal subjects, and so alarming to our feelings as Ministers of Religion. So will your Royal Highness live in the hearts of a grateful and affectionate people; and we will endeavour to acknowledge this most signal favour of your Royal Highness, by our daily prayers for your prosperity and happiness, and by every demonstration of duty, gratitude and zeal.

The receipt of this Address is acknowledged in the following letter:—

Dublin Castle, Sept. 20, 1815.

SIR,

The Lord Lieutenant having transmitted the Address from the Roman Catholic Prelates of Ireland to his Royal Highness the Prince Regent, I am to acquaint you that his Excellency has received a letter from Viscount Sidmouth, one of his Majesty's principal Secretaries of State, signifying that his Royal Highness was graciously pleased to receive the same.

I am, Sir,
Your most obedient humble servant,
The Rev. Dr. Troy.   W. GREGORY.

The Report of Manchester College, York, (Founded at Manchester, February 22, 1786.—*Removed to York, September* 1, 1803.) *At the Twenty-ninth Annual Meeting, August* 4, 1815.

The Trustees of Manchester College have the satisfaction of presenting to its numerous Friends a favourable state of its Funds. The amount of Annual Subscriptions has this year been increased. The number of Congregational Collections, however, they are concerned to state, has been only six; and the supply derived from this source would have been very small, if it had not been for the very handsome contributions from the Members of the Old Meeting at Birmingham, from whom any similar assistance cannot reasonably be expected to be more than occasional.

The Trustees are particularly desirous to urge upon the Friends of the Institution this mode of assisting its Funds, both as it is the one best calculated to render its existence and objects generally known, and to obtain for it a supply, not only of Funds, but of

Students; and also became the custom of preaching annual, or at least occasional, Sermons for its support, may be made subservient to the interest of religious liberty, by supplying Ministers with a fair opportunity of addressing their hearers on those great principles which are the foundation of a Protestant Dissent, and on the expediency of providing for them a regular supply of enlightened and able advocates.

But while this is an object which the Trustees would particularly keep in view, they feel it, at the same time, very desirable, that the Friends of the College should be aware of the importance of keeping up the list of individual Subscribers to at least its present standard. This is probably the way in which the more opulent Dissenters will always choose to give their principal assistance: but to this purpose it is necessary that the subject should be frequently called up to their attention: for a considerable annual reduction may naturally be expected in any list of Annual Subscribers, in consequence of deaths and other contingencies, which it is therefore desirable to have supplied by new names.

The institution of Deputy-Treasurers in forwarding the interests of the College in this respect, has already been of such great importance. that the Trustees cannot but feel desirous of seeing their number increase, till at least one active and enlightened person be found in every neighbourhood where there are any considerable number of friends to free inquiry, who, by circulating among them the Annual Reports, promoting Sermons and Congregational Collections, and collecting and transmitting the Subscriptions of individuals, may render the most essential service to the College, and to the cause which it was instituted to promote.

An additional Benefaction of 100*l.* has been received from the Rev. John Yates, and has been appropriated, according to his kind intention, to the further reduction of the Debt upon the York Buildings; which it is hoped the continued liberality of the public will enable the Trustees shortly to discharge.

An anonymous Benefaction of 100*l.* has likewise been received through the hands of the Rev. Thomas Belsham; which has been laid out in books, and Philosophical Apparatus, in consequence of an intimation that this would be most agreeable to the generous intentions of the Donor.

An opportunity having occurred of redeeming the annual chief rent of 58*l.* 12*s.* charged on the Manchester Buildings, it has been purchased for 1172*l.*; to reduce the burden arising from which to the Funds, a chief rent of 14*l.* 11*s.* 10*d.* per annum, due from the Trustees of Cross-street Chapel, has been sold for 291*l.* 16*s.* 8*d.* There still remains, however, a balance of 336*l.* 0*s.* 9*d.* due to the Treasurer, which

the Committee hope the exertion of their Friends will furnish them with the means of discharging, before the publication of their next Report.

The Deeds relative to the York Buildings are now completed, and are enrolled in the Court of Chancery.

The Trustees beg leave to announce, that Benjamin Gaskell, Esq. M.P. of Thornes House, has accepted the office of President of the College, on the resignation of their present most worthy President, Samuel Shore, Esq.

Mr. Thomas Rankin succeeds Mr. Morgan (who resigns from ill health) as Deputy-Treasurer at Bristol; and the Rev. John Kentish succeeds his lamented colleague, Dr. Toulmin, in the same office at Birmingham; Mr. Robert Kay, of Bolton, and Mr. J. D. Strutt, of Derby, are also added to the List of Deputy-Treasurers, these being the first appointments for the above towns.

At the last Annual Examination on the 27th and 29th of June, the first Prize for Diligence, Regularity, and Proficiency, was adjudged to Mr. John James Tayler, of Nottingham; the second to Mr. Patrick Cannon, of Sheffield; the third to Mr. James Taylor, of Manchester: the Prize for Elocution, to Mr. William Bakewell.— Next year there will be only two Prizes of the former class; but the best Oration or Essay, delivered at the Annual Examination, is to be considered as a Prize Composition: and the Rev. William Shepherd, of Gateacre, has announced his intention of giving a Prize of Books, value Five Guineas, to the best Classical Scholar in the College.—Also, to encourage a perseverance in Theological Study, after the expiration of their Academical Course, a Prize of Five Guineas in Books will be annually given to the best Essay which shall be written by any of the Gentlemen who have been Divinity-Students in the College within the last three years, and have completed their course. The subject will be prescribed by the Tutors; and the Essays must be delivered in, on or before the first of May each year.

Of the Divinity-Students who left the College at the close of the last Session, Mr. Wallace is settled at Chesterfield, in the room of Mr. G. Kenrick, removed to Hull, and Mr. Bakewell, at Chester. The number of Students for the Ministry during the ensuing Session will be nine; Mr. Marden and Mr. Morris in the last year of their course; Mr. Cannon in the fourth; Messrs. Haslam and Wood (of Liverpool, from the University of Glasgow) in the third; Messrs. John Tayler and James Taylor, in the second; and Messrs. John Wellbeloved and Charles Thompson, of Norwich, in the first. There will also be ten Lay-Students.

The Trustees beg leave once more to call the attention of the public to the advantages which the Institution offers for the completion of a course of liberal Education.

Between the ordinary close of a school education, and the commencement of studies strictly professional, or of the occupations of civil and active life, an interval occurs during which it is of the utmost importance to the future character that the mind be cultivated with more enlarged and varied knowledge than is attainable at school, and be guarded by a superintending discipline, from the danger of having its moral principles corrupted.

With this view the Trustees, in pursuing their primary object, the education of Dissenting Ministers, have endeavoured to render their Institution at the same time subservient to the liberal education of youth in general, without distinction of party or religious denomination, and exempt from every political test, and doctrinal subscription. The course of instruction for the Christian Ministry comprehends Five Years; but it is so arranged, that, with the single exception of the study of Hebrew, the whole course during the first Three Years is equally applicable to Lay-Students.

In the *first* year the Students are instructed in the Greek and Latin Classics, in Ancient History, and in Latin and English Composition; in the Elements of Plane Geometry, Algebra and Trigonometry.

In the *second* year they proceed in the Greek and Latin Classics, and in the practice of Composition, and read a course of Modern History, in pursuing which their attention is particularly directed to the History and Principles of the English Constitution. They are instructed in the Geometry of Solids; in the Conic Sections; the Doctrine of the Sphere, and the higher parts of Algebra. Lectures are also given on the Philosophy of the Mind, and on Logic.

In the *third* year they are further instructed in the Greek and Latin Classics, and in the Belles Lettres; in some of the higher departments of Mathematical Science, particularly the method of Fluxions, and the Newtonian System of Physical Astronomy. They are also introduced to an extensive course of reading in Ethics, Jurisprudence, and Political Economy; and Lectures are delivered on the Evidences of Natural and Revealed Religion. An extensive course of Natural and Experimental Philosophy and Chemistry forms a part of the business both of the second and third Sessions.

The Students are lodged and boarded in a set of buildings near the dwelling-house of the Rev. Charles Wellbeloved, the Theological Tutor, and Director of the Institution. The other two Tutors, the Rev. W. Turner, jun. M. A., and the Rev. John Kenrick, M. A., reside in the buildings with the Students.

The terms for Lay-Students are 100 Guineas per annum, which sum defrays the board and lodging, and every other expense connected with a residence in the College.

Divinity-Students on the foundation have every expense of board and education defrayed.

In order to secure, as far as is possible, the respectability of the Students who shall be educated for the Ministry, in this Seminary, with regard both to character and literary attainments, the Trustees have resolved, "That, in future, no Candidate shall be admitted on its Foundation, but on the recommendation of three Protestant Dissenting Ministers, residing in the neighbourhood where he lives, who shall certify, that at the commencement of his Course, he will have attained the full age of sixteen; that on their personal examination, his moral character, natural endowments, and classical proficiency, are such as to qualify him for becoming a Student for the Ministry; and that the profession is the object of his own voluntary choice. His ability to read Homer and Horace, will be considered as essential to his admission."†—All applications must be addressed to "The Rev. Charles Wellbeloved, York," who will lay them before the Annual Meeting of Trustees, at York, on the last Wednesday in June; at which Meeting they will be taken into consideration, and those Candidates preferred, who appear, from the testimonials produced, to be most eligible.

Letters on the subject of this Institution, may also be addressed to George William Wood, Esq. Treasurer, Manchester, or the Rev. William Turner, Visitor, Newcastle-upon-Tyne, by whom, or by any of the Deputy-Treasurers, Subscriptions and Donations are received.

SAMUEL SHORE, President.
Manchester, August 2, 1815.

Case of the Unitarian Society at Thorne, Yorkshire.

Among other circumstances which serve to shew the rapid progress of Unitarianism, may be reckoned the formation of many new societies and the increased demand for places adopted to the purposes of public worship. To the cases of this kind which have of late occupied the public attention, that of an Unitarian congregation at Thorne, in Yorkshire, may be considered as an interesting addition. There have been several Unitarian Christians in this neighbourhood for about ten years. Their practice from the beginning has been to assemble together at the house of one of their friends on the Lord's day, and other convenient opportunities, to perform religious worship, as well as more fully to investigate the truth and importance of their religious sentiments. By these meetings, by the occasional services of Mr. Wright on his Missionary journeys, and the assistance of books which they have obtained, the society consisting of persons within a few miles of Thorne, may now be fairly considered in a flourishing condition. It is not the object of the present sketch, to take an elaborate survey of those circumstances which have had a remote or more immediate influence on their progress towards correct views of religion, but simply to make known to the world their present state and circumstances, as well as their prospect of future increase and prosperity. In justice to themselves, therefore, they state that their number is so materially increased, and the present place of meeting so inconvenient as to render it exceedingly desirable to erect a chapel. The expense, however, of such an undertaking, would far exceed their ability of supporting: and they are not without a hope, that by giving their case publicity through the medium of the Monthly Repository, their wants may excite the generous sympathy and benevolent feelings of their more opulent brethren. They have conceived it necessary, previous to their making this public appeal, to form an estimate of the expense which would be incurred by such an undertaking, and the result of their inquiries justifies them in stating, that a sum of not less than three hundred and fifty pounds will be required, in order to meet the expense of purchasing a suitable situation, and erecting a chapel sufficiently large for their purpose.

A situation has already been procured, and about one hundred and twenty pounds have been subscribed by persons in the immediate neighbourhood, and it is thought that more cannot at present be raised there. This would leave a deficiency of two hundred and thirty pounds to be supplied from some other source.

After having made this statement of their own case, they cannot conclude without earnestly appealing to the feelings of all who are interested in so good a cause, and soliciting the cordial co-operation of those who may be friendly to the plan proposed.

Subscriptions will be received by the following gentlemen :—

Rev. Robert Aspland, Durham House, Hackney-road; Rev. Richard Wright, Wisbeach, Cambridgeshire; Reverend P. Wright, Division-street, Sheffield; Mr. W. Darley, Thorne.

Subscriptions already received.

	l.	s.	d.
Congregation at Elland	14	3	0
J. P. Heywood, Esq. Wakefield	5	0	0
Mrs. Milnes, Freystone	5	0	0
Rev. P. Wright, Sheffield	1	1	0
A Friend, by ditto	0	10	6
Mr. S. J. Wood, Bury, Lancashire	1	0	0

Account of the Opening of the New Unitarian Chapel at Oldham, Lancashire.

On Thursday, January 4th, the New Unitarian chapel at Oldham was opened, and solemnly dedicated to the public worship of Almighty God. At an early hour of the day, it was filled by a serious and attentive audience, many of whom, regardless of the inclemencies of the season, had come fifteen or twenty miles, and some still further. Every individual seemed to participate in the joy of the Oldham Society, at the accomplishment of their arduous undertaking; and at the commencement of the religious services, when a hymn, suitable to the occasion, was read from the pulpit, the whole assembly joined to sing it, with such earnestness and spirit, as evidently to shew that the heart was engaged. The Rev. W. Johns conducted the devotional exercises, and the Rev. J. Grundy preached, from Joshua xxiv. 15,— *Choose you this day whom ye will serve,* &c. The deep and fixed attention with which this discourse was heard, was an involuntary tribute to the force of its arguments, and to the manly eloquence which characterised almost every part of it, as well as to the ability with which it was delivered.

After the conclusion of the service, the ministers present and their friends adjourned to a neighbouring inn, and a large party, composed of sixty-three gentlemen and twelve ladies, partook of a cheap and economical dinner. The union of ladies with gentlemen at our religious associations, we have twice witnessed with great pleasure in the midland counties, but this was the first instance of it in the north. Here the cold formalities of fashion have forbidden it, and it has hitherto been thought inconsistent with decorum. Those, however, who have been in the habit of attending these associations, will need few arguments to convince them, not merely of the strict propriety, but also of the great utility of such an union. On these occasions, a rich mental feast is generally furnished by the speeches of the ministers and gentlemen present; why should females be deprived of it? These addresses are exceedingly useful in stirring up the company to zealous exertions in support of religious truth; will the zeal of females do nothing in the good cause? Let their influence upon society in general, and especially upon the infant and youthful mind, be considered, and every thing will be hailed as an auxiliary to human improvement and happiness which tends to engage them in the cause of religion.

Mr. Grundy was called upon to take the chair, and by his able manner of discharging its duties, he effectually kept up the interest of the meeting. He proposed a succession of appropriate sentiments and toasts, which gave rise to several spirited addresses. Amongst these we recollect the following :—"Our Unitarian friends at Oldham; may their future conduct be consistent with their present professions."

" Our friend Dr. Thomson, who, though he has laid aside the robe of a minister, still retains the spirit of the profession." " Our persecuted brethren in the South of France." " York College; together with its worthy Treasurer, G. W. Wood, and the students present, who have been educated within its walls." " Mr. Aspland and the other tutor of the Unitarian Academy; may their labours in the education of ministers be crowned with success."

In the course of the afternoon the following gentlemen addressed the company: —Messrs. Allard, Browe, Donoughue, Freme, Goodier, E. Grundy, Harrison, Johns, Parker, J. Smethurst, Thomson, Wood and Wright (of Stannington). Several of the speakers insisted upon the establishment of an Unitarian congregation at Oldham, and the liberality which has been shewn in enabling them to build their chapel, as affording a demonstration of the fitness of Unitarianism for the poor, and of the increasing zeal of the Unitarian body.

Dr. Thomson, in adverting to a plan for uniting the Unitarian congregations of the Northern counties, which is now preparing by the Rev. C. Wellbeloved, the Rev. W. Turner, of Newcastle-upon-Tyne, and himself, observed, that he could not expect much good to result from the intended measure, unless the members of individual congregations were more closely connected. Each congregation must move around its own axis, before it can revolve around a common centre. He went on to remark, that the necessity of such an union is every day becoming more and more apparent, and is clearly shewn by the increasing calls that are now made on the liberality of the Unitarian public, from Oldham, Rossendale, Greenock, Thorne and Neath. Without something like a general co-operation, it is impossible that these calls should be properly answered. Individuals may, and do, subscribe liberally, but insulated and unsupported exertions can never furnish an adequate supply to the repeated demands now made. He therefore proposed that in every congregation there should be formed what he would call a *fellowship-society,* for the purpose of raising a fund, to which the poorer members should be weekly or monthly contributors, and which should be intended to assist infant societies (now happily becoming numerous), in erecting chapels and carrying on public worship. It remains to be seen, whether the company will content themselves with merely receiving this proposal with marks of approbation.

At half-past six o'clock, the chapel was again filled with a respectable audience, and an evening service was conducted by the Rev. W. Harrison and the Rev. R.

Parker. From the words, *Why even of yourselves judge ye not what is right?* the preacher delivered a spirited defence of the use of reason in matters of religion. Thus closed the services of the day, which will be long remembered by the society at Oldham, and which were peculiarly gratifying to all present. In connexion with the speeches delivered after dinner, these services kindled a zeal, an enthusiasm in some breasts which will not soon be extinguished.

Before we close this account, we are requested by our friends at Oldham, to express their grateful acknowledgments to those ministers, who so kindly undertook, and so ably performed, the religious services of this day. They wish also publicly to thank the ministers who have interested themselves in their welfare since the formation of their society, and who, for upwards of two years, have gratuitously supplied them, almost regularly, with preaching.

Their acknowledgments are also due to those congregations who, by subscriptions, have afforded them the most effectual assistance, in a time of need. The Christian affection and Christian zeal with which a lasting impression upon their minds.

They are desirous, also, of solemnly expressing their gratitude to Almighty God, the author of all good, who has granted his blessing to their labours, and has put it into the hearts of their Christian brethren to assist them in the accomplishment of an object, which has long called forth their ardent wishes and fervent prayers. They rejoice in the thought, that in a town, containing, with the neighbourhood, sixteen or seventeen thousand souls, they have been enabled to erect a temple, sacred to the worship of the One God and Father of all. They exult in the prospect thus opened of dispensing the Word of Life, uncorrupted by human additions; and of exposing the weakness of those doctrines which take away almost all gladness from the tidings of the gospel, and, to the greater part of mankind, render them tidings of misery and death. They trust that by this means many sinners will be converted from the evil of their ways, and directed heavenward; and that hundreds will be delivered from a system, which prevents many of the finest feelings of devotion and love towards God, by robbing him of his most glorious attributes; which destroys many of the kindly charities and benevolent sympathies of the heart, by libelling the human character; and which cramps the faculties of the mind, by setting reason and revelation at variance, as well as by presenting to the humble inquirer after truth, the most glaring contradictions, clothed in the awful garb of divinity. May these hopes never be disappointed! May peace and love dwell within the walls of the house they have built! May the ministers who shall there officiate be clothed with salvation!

" And in the great decisive day,
When God the nations shall survey,
May it before the world appear,
That crowds were born to glory there."
B. G.

P. S.—The following is a statement of the Treasurer's (Rev. W. Harrison's) accounts; by the insertion of which you will greatly oblige the congregation at Oldham, as, in consequence of several bills not having been brought in, it could not be prepared previously to the day of opening.

I. To congregational collections for the new chapel, Oldham, viz.

	£.	s.	d.
At Altringham and Hale	22	1	0
Blackley	8	10	6
Bolton	18	9	0
Bury	10	3	0
Chewbent	39	0	4
Chester	10	0	6
Cockey-Moor	12	17	9
Doblane	10	11	6
Gatacre, *near Liverpool*	18	0	0
Hindley and Wigan	5	0	0
Hyde	10	0	0
Liverpool { Paradise Street	37	6	6
{ Renshaw Street	36	1	0
Lydgate, near Huddersfield	5	1	0
Manchester { Cross Street	75	7	0
{ Moseley Street	35	0	0
Monton Green	19	0	0
Oldham	39	3	0
Prescot	8	11	6
Rochdale	10	6	0
Stand	17	1	6
Stockport	15	1	0
Warrington	12	18	6

II. To individual subscriptions, viz.

	£.	s.	d.
Mr. E. Grundy, Pilsworth, near Bury	5	0	0
Mr. C. Armitage, Dukenfield	5	0	0
Mr. Shore, Meersbrook	5	0	0
Mrs. Mary Hughes, Hanwood	2	0	0
Rev. R. Astley, Halifax	1	1	0
Dr. Thomson, do.	1	1	0
Mr. Dawson, do.	1	1	0
Rev. W. Whitelegg, Platt	1	0	0
Mr. P. Lyon, do.	1	0	0
Rev. W. Turner, York	1	0	0
Rev. W. Johns, Manchester	1	0	0
To waste wood, &c. sold	4	5	3
To Collection at the Opening	26	7	0½
	£530	5	10½
Deficit	119	0	7½
	£649	6	6

Expenses of the Building, &c.

	£.	s.	d.
By amount of bills already paid	505	3	6

Amount of bills received but not paid — 94 3 0
Estimated amount of bills yet to come in — 50 0 0

£649 6 6

Signed { B. GOODIER, } Auditors.
{ JOHN GEE, }

The chapel is a neat and commodious building, handsomely fitted up, capable of holding near three hundred people, and so built as to admit a gallery hereafter if necessary. It need not be added, that any donations towards the liquidation of the above debt, will be thankfully received by the Rev. W. Harrison, Treasurer, No. 20, Brazen-Nose Street, Manchester.

*** To the above account we have great pleasure in adding that the Committee of the UNITARIAN FUND have voted £20 towards the liquidation of the debt on the Oldham Chapel.

South-Wales Unitarian Society.

The Quarterly Meeting of this Society was held at Llanelly, Carmarthenshire, on Wednesday, the 3rd of January. Twelve ministers were present. On the preceding evening the Rev. John Griffiths, of Llandebie, prayed, and the Rev. Thomas Evans, of Aberdâr, preached from Rom. xiv. 5, " Let every man be fully persuaded in his own mind." Wednesday morning Mr. Wm. Williams, of Llangendeirn, conducted the devotional part of the service, when two sermons were delivered; the first, by the Rev. R. Aubrey, of Swansea, in English, from Job. xiii. 7, " Will ye speak wickedly for God and talk deceitfully for him?" The other by the Rev. John James of Cardiganshire, in Welsh, from 2 Cor. v. 19, " God was in Christ reconciling the world unto himself, not imputing their trespasses unto them; and hath committed unto us the word of reconciliation." In the evening the Rev. W. Williams, of Blaengwrach prayed, and the Rev. Thomas Edwards, of Penyfai, preached from 1 Peter iv. 8, " And above all things have fervent charity among yourselves; for charity shall cover the multitude of sins." And the Rev. D. Davis, of Neath, from Ephes. iv. 2, 3, 4, chiefly the 3d verse, " Endeavouring to keep the unity of the spirit in the bond of peace." The Rev. Thomas Evans concluded with prayer.

The several discourses delivered on the occasion were attentively heard by respectable audiences. The holding of this meeting at Llanelly has been the means of exciting a spirit of free inquiry in the place, and of quelling in a great measure the prejudice, which was very great in this part, against Unitarianism. As Dr. Estlin, in his excellent sermon, says,—" The whole current of fashion is against us—calumniated," &c. " but I solicit only for them a patient hearing. Let their principles be known and we are satisfied. With Ajax we only pray for light."

The services were conducted in Mr. John Thomas's school-room, late of Carmarthen Academy. He had previously preached a few times there and in the neighbourhood: he intends to officiate in in future regularly once a fortnight, and to exchange, as often as circumstances will admit, with neighbouring and other ministers.

Mr. Lyons, I think, was the first Unitarian who preached in the town, though others had, now and then, in the vicinity.

The next quarterly meeting is to be held at Aberdâr on the Wednesday in Easter week.

SIR,

The preceding account was sent to me by Mr. T. B. C. of Llanelly, a steady and warm friend to the cause, accompanied with a request that I would forward it to you for insertion in your valuable Repository. I am, Sir,

Yours very respectfully,

D. D.

Neath, Jan. 23rd, 1816.

Subscriptions to the Chapel, Neath, Glamorganshire. (See M. Repos. x. 261, 458, 596.)

Rev. W. Evans, Tavistock	1	0	0
Mr. S. Hornbrook, Do.	1	0	0
Miss S. Prance, Neath	1	1	0
Mr. J. Redwood. Do.	1	1	0
Monsieur Jean Bippert, Do.	2	2	0
Rev. Timothy Davis, Coventry	5	5	0
Rev. — Brown, of Gloucester, and Friends	3	0	0

Subscriptions to the proposed Unitarian Chapel, Greenock. (See M. Repos. x. 528, 660, 722, 776.)

	l.	*s.*	*d.*
English Students at College, Glasgow	15	15	0
By Mr. Aspland.			
Rev. Mr. Owen's Congregation, Loughborough	4	12	6
Mrs. M. Hughes, Hanwood	2	2	0
Rev. Russell Scott, Portsmouth	1	0	0
Miss Carter, Do.	2	0	0
Mr. David Laing Do.	2	0	0
Edward Carter, Esq. Do.	2	0	0
A Friend, Leicester	1	0	0
James Crowe, Esq., Stockton	1	0	0

Unitarian Chapel, Newchurch, Rossendale. (See Mon. Repos. vol. x. pp. 313, 392, 458, 461, 527, 596, 660, 721.)

Donations in aid of liquidating the debt (£350) upon this chapel will be thankfully received by Rev. R. Aspland, Hackney Road; Rev. R. Astley, Halifax; Rev. William Johns, Manchester; Mr. W.

Walker, Rochdale; and Dr. Thomson, Halifax; to some one of whom all who have interested themselves in behalf of the Rossendale brethren are requested to report the subscriptions in their hands, without delay; as it is desirable to proceed to liquidate the debt of the chapel as soon as may be, and as far as the liberality of the public may enable the above-mentioned gentlemen to do so. An accurate account of the amount of the subscriptions and of its appropriation will be published in the Monthly Repository.

	£.	*s.*	*d.*
Amount advertised, x. 721	222	7	0
Thomas Saxton, Esq. Lea-wood, Derbyshire,	1	0	0
William Jones, Esq. Manchester	5	0	0
Mr. Richard Mason, Bolton	0	10	0
Mr. Edmund Ashworth, do.	0	10	0
Sheffield Christian Tract Society (with a parcel of Tracts)	3	11	6
Dr. Alexander, Leicester	1	1	0
By Mr. Aspland.			
A Friend, Leicester	1	0	0
John Mackintosh, Esq. Exeter	5	0	0
J. F. Barham, Esq. do.	1	0	0
Collection at Tavistock Chapel	4	0	6
Do. at the Dinner at Tavistock	4	4	6
	249	5	0

N. B. The four last subscriptions communicated by Dr. Carpenter.

Unitarian Fund.

Additions to and Corrections in the List of Subscribers.

Mrs. Healing, Shrewsbury, annual	1	0	0
Rev. E. Cogan, Walthamstow, annual	1	1	0
A Friend, Leicester	2	0	0
Mr. Coltman, Do., annual	1	0	0
Major-Gen. Gifford, Hill House, near Swansea, annual	1	1	0
Capt. G. Jones, R. N. Glanmor, near Swansea, annual	1	1	0
A Friend, by Rev. Jos. Jevans, Bloxham	2	0	0
Richard Mead, Esq., Taunton, annual	1	1	0
An Anonymous Benefaction	50	0	0
Mr. G. Talbot, Jun., Kidderminster, annual	1	1	0
Mr. Hopkins, Do. annual	0	10	6

N. B. These two by the Rev. R. Fry, of Kidderminster, whose name was by mistake omitted in the List of Receivers.

Mr. Gundry, Bridport	5	0	0
Mrs. Meyer, Enfield, a further donation	10	0	0
Mr. L. Marshall, Dalston, life	5	5	0
Mr. J. Barnes, Homerton, annual	1	1	0

A. M. - - 1 1 0
Mr. Staniland, Dalston, annual 1 1 0
Mr. C. Stower, Homerton, annual 1 1 0

₊ Further Additions and Corrections
will be made from time to time.

*Committee of Deputies, of the Three De-
nominations of Protestant Dissenters,
for the year* 1816.

Messrs. William Smith, M. P., Chairman, Park-street, Westminster; Joseph
Gutteridge, Deputy Chairman, Camber-
well; James Collins, Treasurer, Spital-
square; John Towill Rutt, Bromley, Middlesex; Samuel Favell, Grove Hill, Cam-
berwell; B. Boswell Beddome, Walworth;

William Hale, Homerton; William Burls,
Lothbury; James Esdaile, Bunhill-row;
William Esdaile, Clapham Common; Wil-
liam Alers Hankey, Fenchurch-street;
John Addington, Spital-square; Joseph
Bunnell, Southampton-row; Samuel
Jackson, Hackney; James Gibson, High-
bury-place, Islington; Joseph Wilson,
Milk-street; William Titford, Union-street,
Bishopsgate-street; Joseph Towle, Wal-
worth; William Dudds Clark, High-
street, Borough; Joseph Luck, Clapton;
William Freme, Catharine-court, Tower-
Hill; Edward Shrubsole, Bank; James
Black, York-street, Covent Garden; B.
P. Witts, Friday-street.

MONTHLY RETROSPECT OF PUBLIC AFFAIRS;

OR,

The Christian's Survey of the Political World.

AMONG the strange events which the
state of Europe has produced, a treaty
entered into by three sovereigns, and to
which the other states are invited to concur, now calls our attention. It was signed
at Paris during the time that the sovereigns
were there, and in this instance they may
be considered as the representatives of the
three great sects, whose religion is established by law. These are the Greek
Church, the Romish Church and the Protestant Church. The personages are the
Emperors of Russia, Austria, and the king
of Prussia. The object of the treaty differs materially from that of the voluminous
ones which have been laid before parliament. It is not to settle boundaries, to
annihilate republics, exchange provinces,
set up or dethrone kings; it is a solemn
appeal to the whole world, a testimony in
favour of the Christian religion, a determination to make it the rule of their actions both in their conduct to each other
and to their subjects, and what is, however, a suspicious covenant, to assist each
other in the promotion of their laudable
designs.

The signatures of princes have been so
often affixed to treaties, broken almost before the wax of their seals has had time to
cool, that their language ceases to carry
with it that confidence which ought to attach to persons of their exalted rank. In
this case, however, there seems not to have
been any call for this voluntary association
and voluntary declaration. We may easily
conceive, that the great events in which
these sovereigns have been engaged, may
have made a deep impression on their
minds, may have led them to prostrate
themselves before the throne of the Al-

mighty, and contemplating the vanity and
folly of human policy, they may have felt,
that the only way to govern wisely was, by
adhering to the precepts delivered to us by
him who is emphatically styled our Saviour,
the Prince of Peace. If this is really the
case, we cannot but congratulate the world
on so great an event. If in the extensive
regions of Russia, Austria and Prussia,
every thing contrary to the mild spirit of
the Christian laws is abolished; if a new
system is set up, in which mildness and
Christian love should be as much predominant as heretofore cruelty and intolerance;
we cannot doubt that the example will
spread itself, and that other nations, observing their order, propriety, love of justice,
and hatred of war, will gradually assimi-
late their laws to a purer standard.

As yet we can know nothing of the effects of this treaty. We must allow a sufficiency of time for the great potentates
to introduce the gradual reformation into
their respective dominions. The boors in
Poland and the slaves in Russia, cannot
immediately be placed in the rank of freemen, nor is it adviseable that such a change
should be instantaneously enforced. Austria may find some difficulties from Popish
superstition, Prussia from its military system. But we shall be glad to hear of a
beginning made in the respective countries, and of the manner in which it is received by the subjects. Some things may
evidently be done without great difficulty;
as, for example, the seizing of a person on
suspicion of crime, and treating him with
as much severity in a prison as if he had
been guilty of it, will be no more. All
tortures should be abolished. Persecution on account of religion should cease,

and the freedom of worship, provided it does not behave unseemly to the public, should be allowed. The knout and exile to Siberia will not be frequent sentences, the codes of law will be purified from the barbarities of an ignorant age and the technicalities of the profession. The undertaking of the three sovereigns is noble in itself, requires prudence in the execution, and will establish their fame, if they act agreeably to their promises, on a more durable basis than what is achieved by military prowess. In the latter they have for competitors all the heroes of ancient and modern times, the Big Bens and Mendozas of history. They have opened to themselves a new career, they have ventured on an untrodden path. May the world not be deceived; may the sovereigns persist in the line of conduct they have chalked out for themselves; and may prince and people acquire daily more and more of a true Christian spirit.

In the extensive dominions of Russia are to be found professors of every species of religion. The Greek is the established church, but no hindrance is given to other forms of worship. The temple of the idolater, the churches of the Christian, the mosques of the Mahometans, are all to be found in the same district. The circumstances of the country have led to a toleration of a very extensive nature, and Jew and Christian, Mahometan and Idolater are to be found exercising offices under the state. The narrow policy of this country is there unknown; and indeed despotism itself would not permit the contemptible folly that prevails among us, of prohibiting the sovereign from availing himself of the services of a subject, unless he belongs to a peculiar sect, and that sect inferior in numbers to those who differ from it. Yet, even in Russia are some bounds set to toleration. Every one is permitted to follow his own form of worship, but he must be careful not to infringe on the domains of the established sect. He may meet his brethren of the same persuasion unmolested, but he must beware of the spirit of proselytism: he must not enter into the Greek fold, nor attempt to seduce any of that flock from their established pastures.

An instance has lately been presented to the world, by which the views of the Russian government on this subject are plainly manifested. It had given an asylum to the Jesuits, who devoted themselves agreeably to their former practice in other countries, to the education of children. Their superiority in literature and the art of instruction, induced the higher ranks to put their children under their care, and it seems that in consequence of this preference, several of them have quitted the Greek for the Romish communion. Now

this may have arisen either from a comparison of the two sects together, independent of any instruction received on the subject, or it may have been from the teachers' instilling into the minds of their pupils notions unfavourable to the established church, and gradually conducting them to a different persuasion. A jealousy of the latter kind is very natural from the known character of the Jesuits, but of the proofs nothing is known. The Russian government has expelled the Jesuits from the country, and given, as the reason, their abuse of the education of the children entrusted to their care, and perverting them, as it would there be called, by insinuating, contrary to the laws of hospitality, into their minds the doctrines of the Romish church.

If the three confederated sovereigns have manifested such good intentions, respecting their future government, the same spirit seems by no means to prevail in the neighbouring country. The exertions here in favour of our persecuted brethren abroad, have excited, it is evident, no small dissatisfaction in France. To the denials of the fact no unprejudiced mind will give any credit, and every day confirms the opinion the more that the truth is suppressed as much as possible. It remained, however, for the spirit of calumny to set the last seal to its atrocities, and this has been fully done in the French papers with the signature of a prefect, who does not scruple to assert, that the persons here who have undertaken the cause of the Protestants are a set of Jacobins, deserving of no confidence abroad and despised at home. The word Jacobin is constantly resorted to by men who, in a different shape, perform the same actions as those which distinguished the celebrated society under that name. In fact, there are royal jacobins and democratical jacobins: the prevailing feature in both is, the disregard of solemn treaties, covenants, obligations, every thing which is sacred between man and man, and making every thing bend to their own will and the caprice of the moment. The royal jacobin calls others by that name, who appeal to laws, religion and charters, and the Frenchman who dared to attach the contemptuous epithet to those respectable bodies which undertook the cause of the Protestants, has little knowledge of our country. To him, to be respectable there must be titles and dignities: virtue, honour and independence, united with religion, carry no weight. His insults, however they may be received in France, and however calculated to serve a party there, will meet with contempt among us. The minister of England will, without doubt, if necessary, take care that our ambassador should inform the cabinet of France, that if this language is countenanced by it, it misunderstands entirely the nature of our constitution and our country.

But the insinuations thrown out in the French papers against our countrymen, will be circulated without the means of refutation. The press in that country is in the most slavish state, and the government has paid the greatest compliment to ours, by refusing admission into theirs of the English newspapers. Though written in a language, which very few Frenchmen can read, the truths contained in them are of such a nature, that the government dreads their being made known to any. The free discussion which prevails here, is a most horrible thing in the eyes of superstition and despotism: and we cannot but be astonished at the servile minds of the French, with whom a change of government makes no change of system. The same plan of espionnage and censorship continues, whatever party holds the wire by which the puppets are moved. Whether a Bourbon or a Bonaparte gains the ascendency, it is the lot of the French to be in terror, and the only difference is, that in the one case there was a degree of splendour to flatter their vanity, whilst in the other they are subjected to the caprice of a party, which they cannot but despise.

Their legislative bodies continue to deliberate. Their great object is to save as much for the clergy as they can, and their vengeance is now directed to those who are married Our countrymen in confinement have not been brought to a trial. The regicides have quitted France, and numbers of persons engaged in the active scenes of the last twenty-five years have emigrated to America and Russia. The latter country opens its arms to all classes, and will benefit greatly by the event. The national institute has been purged also by the King's authority and the celebrated Abbé Maury, the staunch advocate of the Bourbons in the early part of the revolution, ceases to be enrolled among its members.

Germany seems likely to be soon in motion, and the proceedings in Prussia will lead to eventful changes throughout the whole of the empire The great blow struck against Bonaparte, was occasioned chiefly by bringing into action against him the force of the people, and in this the Landwehre of Prussia was particularly effective. In this body men of all ranks enrolled themselves, with little inquiry whether they were to serve as officers or common soldiers. In exciting them to come forward, great use was made of secret societies, and the spirit which prevailed in them, has not subsided. This has led to the circulation of a variety of publications, in which the principles of liberty have been laid down in a manner by no means suited to the military despotism by which that country was governed. The return of the army

animated by their success, diffuses an energy over the whole kingdom, and it is by no means clear what will be the result of it. The same spirit in a degree pervades the other armies, which will carry into their respective kingdoms new principles of action, and in this general agitation one is naturally anxious for the fate of our own armies, lest in their combination with the others, they may have acquired more of a foreign military spirit, and lost somewhat of the sentiments peculiar to our constitution.

A new turn has taken place in Spanish America. Carthagena oppressed by famine, has surrendered to the Spanish troops, which on taking possession of the place displayed its usual cruelties. In Mexico also the royal cause has had some successes, the prolongation of the conflict is now certain, the event doubtful.

At home the meeting of the parliament has been attended with the communication of voluminous treaties on the settlement of Europe; which gave rise to animated discussions. The minister had a considerable majority in his favour, but the conduct of the Bourbons in France and Spain met with severe reprehension. The intended measures of finance, however, created a greater interest, and the country heard with horror and astonishment, that in spite of repeated promises the Income Tax was to be continued, and a standing army kept on foot, quite incompatible with all the maxims of our ancestors on this subject. It was warmly urged, that the confederacy of the European powers overthrew the greatest and most horrible military power that ever tormented mankind: but if every kingdom was to carry on the same military system, the danger to Europe and the distress to each country were rather increased than diminished. There can be no liberty, no security to a free constitution where there is a large standing army. The men successively enrolled in it will gradually imbibe sentiments agreeable to the esprit du corps and inimical to freedom.

The continuance of the Property Tax has excited also no small alarm, not merely on account of the evident inequality in its assessments, in making a man with a precarious income, derived from personal exertions, pay the same sum annually as another whose income is derived from permanent property, but also from the vexations attending the collecting of the tax, and the injury that morals will suffer from the spirit of espionnage, that will be gradually diffused throughout the country. In fact, when such a tax is established, the consequences will be the same in this kingdom with respect to property, as attended the inquisition in Spain with regard to religion. The class of inquisitors, familiars and others connected with the inquisition, will become numerous; every one will look

with a jealous eye on his neighbour. Nothing will escape the scrutinizing eye of
of the searcher, and no honesty, no integrity,
will preserve a man from vexation. The
latter part of the question, as it affects the
morals of a country, deserves a most serious consideration; and it may be asserted,

that if a Standing Army and an Income Tax
become perpetual, the English will in a
very few years be a very different people;
the spirit that has animated its agriculture,
its manufactures and its commerce, will
vanish, and its riches will make to themselves wings and flee away.

NEW PUBLICATIONS IN THEOLOGY AND GENERAL LITERATURE.

The Christian Reformer, or New Evangelical Miscellany. Vol. I. for 1815.
With a Vignette Title-Page, by Partridge.
12mo. 6s. 6d. boards. Continued monthly in Nos. 6d. each.

A Letter to the Unitarian Christians in
South Wales; occasioned by the Animadversions of the Right Rev. the Lord Bishop
of St. David's. With Appendices. By
Thomas Belsham. 8vo.

A Unitarian Christian's Statement and
Defence of his Principles, with reference
particularly to the Charges of the Right
Rev. the Lord Bishop of St. David's: A
Discourse before the Annual Meeting of
the Welsh Unitarian Society. With Notes.
By John Prior Estlin, LL.D. 8vo.

Two Essays; one on the Effects of
Christianity, the other on the Sabbath.
By the late Rev. John Simpson. 8vo.
4s. 6d. boards.

An Essay on the Principles of Dissent.
By Richard Wright, Unitarian Missionary.
12mo. 6d.

An Essay on the Universal Restoration,

intended to shew that the Final Happiness
of all Men is a Doctrine of Divine Revelation. By the Same. 12mo. 6d.

The Trinitarian Catechised, and allowed
to answer for Himself. 18mo. 3d.

A Letter from an Old Unitarian to a
Young Calvinist. 12mo.

An Account of a Bible-formed Society
of Unitarian Christians, without the aid
of either other Books or Missionaries, at
New-Church, Rossendale, Lancashire.
(Extracted from the Monthly Repository.)
12mo.

Remains of William Reed, late of
Thornbury; including Rambles in Ireland;
with other Compositions in Prose, his Correspondence and Poetical Productions. To
which is prefixed A Memoir of his Life;
by the Rev. John Evans, Author of the
Ponderer. 450 Copies on Demy 8vo.
10s. 6d. 50 Royal 8vo. 15s.

The Final Prevalence of Unitarianism,
a Rational Expectation. A Discourse delivered at Palgrave, Dec. 19, 1815. By
John Fullagar. 8vo.

CORRESPONDENCE.

The first part of the Review of *Wilson's Dissenting Churches* in our next.

The Proof Prints of SERVETUS are nearly all sold; such as wish to possess copies are
requested to apply immediately. Price of the Print, as also of each of those of Dr.
PRIESTLEY and Dr. TOULMIN, 5s.

ERRATA.

Page 16, col. i. l. 26, for "Such conduct would do honour to Britons," &c. reads
"Such conduct would do no honour to Britons," &c.
—— 38, col. i. l. 22, for "borrible" read *horribile.*
—— 45, col. ii. l. 1, for "thirty" read *twenty.*
—— 49, col. ii. l. 14, from bottom, for "S. Evans" read *J. Evans.*

THE

𝕸𝖔𝖓𝖙𝖍𝖑𝖞 𝕽𝖊𝖕𝖔𝖘𝖎𝖙𝖔𝖗𝖞,

&c.

| No. CXXIII.] | MARCH, 1816. | [Vol. XI. |

HISTORY AND BIOGRAPHY.

*Brief Memoir respecting the Walden-
ses, or Vaudois, Inhabitants of the
Valleys of Piedmont ; the result of
Observations made during a short
residence amongst that interesting
People in the Autumn of 1814. By
a Clergyman of the Church of England.*

THE sympathy of the Christian
has been often powerfully excited by a description of the sufferings of disciples of an earlier day in
the cause of their Lord and Saviour.
Among these persecuted disciples the
Waldenses, it is on all hands acknowledged, are entitled to very high respect, since they were eminently our
Redeemer's witnesses, and advocates
for the purity of Christian doctrine
and worship, during those emphatically termed the dark ages, when the
introduction of unscriptural tenets and
ostentatious ceremonies had so much
contributed to seduce people in general from the simplicity of the gospel.
They were, in short, if the expression may be allowed, Protestants before the Reformation took place; and
some have even supposed that the
morning-star of that bright day, Wickliffe himself, derived some portion of
the light of religious knowledge from
them.

The writer of these remarks had,
in common with others, long revered
the name, and often read with interest the history of the Waldenses,
when a tour on the Continent afforded
him an opportunity of becoming personally acquainted with them : and
he will esteem it a happy circumstance
if this brief Memoir, the fruit of observations made whilst in the valleys,
should induce benevolent persons in
England to make some efforts in their
behalf.

The *ancient* history of this people
being far more generally known to
British Christians than more *recent*

events and their *present* condition, it
shall be my object to present a series
of remarks under the following heads :
1. Modern History. 2. Description
of the Valleys. 3. Character and
Manners of the Waldenses. 4. State
of their Schools. 5. Number and
Condition of their Ministers and
Churches.

1. The pathetic details of their sufferings during the fifteenth, sixteenth,
and seventeenth centuries, when the
malice of the Court of Rome, the fury
of the Inquisition, the weakness at
one time, at another time the perfidy
of their Sovereigns the Dukes of Savoy, conspired to render them, if in
this life only they had hope, of all
men most miserable, have been already recorded by their historians.
The wolves that infest the neighbouring Alps were, in fact, less cruel to
their defenceless prey than the brutal
soldiery employed to lead these sheep
of Christ's pasture to the slaughter ;
they massacred those whom age and
infirmity compelled to remain in the
valleys, pursued others who had fled
for safety to the hills, plunged the
steel into their bosoms, threw them
down precipices ; in short, committed
outrages of various kinds, at which
humanity recoils.

Their more recent history may be
said to commence at the last dreadful
persecution of 1686. Louis XIV. not
content with destroying and banishing his own subjects, (at the well-
known revocation of the Edict of
Nantz) instigated the Court of Turin
to adopt the same cruel measures. A
minister of the valleys has been so
kind as to make me a present of an
affecting relation of the sufferings of
the Waldenses at that period. It is
a manuscript of about one hundred
years old ; like Ezekiel's roll, full of
lamentations and mourning ; and the
truth of its contents is attested by ten

ministers, assembled in synod, the 19th Oct. 1716. As it refers to a persecution subsequent to the age of some of the best historians of the Waldenses, I will here insert the substance of the manuscript, premising, however, that whilst every thing material is extracted, there are circumstances connected with the sufferings of some of the martyrs, refinements in the art of cruelty, of so horrid a description, that I forbear to relate them.

On the 3rd of January, 1686, appeared an edict forbidding religious worship, requiring their temples to be destroyed, their ministers banished and their children baptized and educated in the Roman Catholic Church. Shortly afterwards the troops of Savoy attacked the valley of Luzerne, and those of France the valleys of St. Martin and La Perouse. The Vaudois made at first considerable resistance, but, deceived by a false promise, that their persons and families should be safe, they threw themselves on the Duke of Savoy's clemency. This, however, proved no security. Their enemies still breathed threatenings and slaughter, and events continually occurred to remind them that they must take up their cross, nor love even life itself, if they meant to preserve an unshaken attachment to " the truth as it is in Jesus." The following cruelties, amongst others, were exercised ;—

J. and Marguerite Maraude, of St. Jean, were murdered while defending Marguerite Maraude, a child aged fourteen.

Susanne Olivet, of St. Jean, and Marguerite Belin, of Latour, each, in resisting brutal violence, lost her life.

Jos. David was first wounded, then conveyed to a house and burnt.

Four women and three children, of Prarustix, were murdered in a cave where they had concealed themselves.

Marie Roman, of Rocheplate, a young person promised in marriage to J. Griot, lost her life in defending her honour.

At Fumian were found numbers of little children cut in pieces, and women who had been massacred.

In the village of Perouse six men were killed in the presence of their wives.

Jean Ribbet, of Macel, refusing to change his religion, had his legs and arms burnt.

A poor infirm man was tied to a horse's tail, and dragged till he expired.

An aged blind woman was hanged before her own house.

Four women were violated and hewn in pieces, after first seeing their children massacred, at Fontaines ; where also a great number of sick children were murdered, because they could not follow others to prison.

Twenty-two persons, chiefly women and children, were thrown over precipices at Mount Pelvon.

David Grand, of Bobbi, was hanged, and sang praises to God whilst led to execution.

Daniel Negrin, aged eighteen, and Pierre Mentinat, aged fifty, (of Bobbi) were led to the Alp of Pra, but so ill-treated because they would not change their religion, that they died on the way. Their dead bodies were then hanged and burnt.

Anne and Madeline Victoria, and several others, were burnt.

Daniel Moudon, elder of the church of Rora, after seeing his two sons beheaded, the wife and child of the one, and the two children of the other, massacred, was compelled to carry the heads of his sons upon his shoulders, to walk two hours barefooted, and was afterwards hanged.

Mr. Leydet, Minister of Pral, hid himself in caves, but was at length taken, and conveyed to Luzerne, to the palace of the Marquis D'Angrogne, where the Duke of Savoy was also at the same time. He was imprisoned and fed on bread and water ; and, in addition to other hardships, was constantly assailed by the Monks, over whom he as constantly triumphed in argument. When threatened with death if he did not abjure his faith, he replied, that he could not be justly put to death, since he was not armed when taken prisoner ; besides, the Duke of Savoy had promised a pardon to all his subjects : " Still," said he, " I am ready to die for the name of Jesus Christ." His example and exhortations exceedingly fortified his fellow-prisoners. When the sentence of death was pronounced, he heard it with Christian resignation. Although he begged to be left alone, in order to pray with freedom, the

Monks still harassed him with disputes till the time of execution, which took place at Fort St. Michael, arrived. On quitting the prison, he said, " it was a day of double deliverance, that of his body from captivity, and that of his soul from imprisonment in the body; for he cherished the expectation of partaking shortly in full liberty of the joys of the blessed." At the foot of the scaffold he prayed in a manner that very much affected the bye-standers, and on the ladder said, " My God, into thy hands I commend my spirit."—A martyr worthy of the best ages of the church of Christ!—Even his enemies were compelled to admit that he died like a saint.

About fifteen thousand of the Waldenses, men, women and children, who threw themselves on the Duke's clemency, were confined in fourteen castles and prisons of Piedmont, with a scanty allowance of bread and water; and various means were used to render this bread and water unwholesome. They always lay upon bricks or rotten straw, and so many together that the very air was infected: seventy-five sick have been reckoned in a single room at one time. Eight thousand persons died in consequence of these barbarities. After suffering nine months, those who survived were permitted to retire into Switzerland; but not before threatenings and allurements had been artfully employed to induce them to forsake their religion—in general without effect: and those who did apostatize, instead of recovering their houses and property, according to a specious promise made to them, were conveyed to the distant province of Verceil. A great number of children, however, taken away and dispersed in Piedmont, were not allowed to accompany their relatives to Switzerland; and the nine pastors were removed to Verrue, Nice, and Montmeillan, deprived of the privilege of imparting religious consolation to their beloved people. Eighty of the men were forced to work in chains for three years in the citadel of Turin. Even those permitted to seek refuge in Switzerland endured great calamities. One company was required to set out late in the evening, and walk five leagues on the snow and ice: more than one hundred and fifty died in the way

without succour. Another company, foreseeing dreadful weather, entreated the officer who conducted them to stay till after the storm; but he obliged them to set out, and eighty-six persons perished in consequence on Mount Ceuis. Their friends were not suffered to remain and bury them. Others of the Waldenses, who followed, found their bodies amidst the snow; several women with their infants still in their arms. Many expired by the time they reached the gates of Geneva, and all exhibited marks of peculiar suffering. These poor destitute fugitives, while they remained in Switzerland, were supported by the charitable contributions of the English and Dutch, which were administered with so much fidelity by Isaac Behaghel, Minister of Frankfort, that he was afterwards presented with a gold medal by William III. Through the generous interference of M. Valkenier, they obtained grounds in the dominions of the Duke of Wirtemberg, on the estates of the Margrave of Dourlach, the Landgrave of Hesse Darmstadt, and the Count of Hanau, where they established fourteen churches, naming their villages after the beloved spots they once inhabited in the valleys. Seven ministers and schoolmasters were there supported by his Britannic Majesty. Others of the Vaudois went to the marquisate of Brandenburg; others settled in the county of Neufchatel, at Bienne, and at Schaffhausen. In 1669 a party of somewhere between six and nine hundred, joined, I believe, by three hundred French exiles, resolved to re-occupy the houses and lands of which they had been so unjustly deprived. For this purpose they met by agreement in a wood between Nyon and Rolle, towns situated on the lake of Geneva; and on the 17th of August, at ten o'clock at night, crossed the lake and landed in Savoy. They then directed their course through Cluse, Maglan, and Salenches; forced their way at the point of the sword; took hostages, in order to secure a free passage through the towns where they met with opposition (yet paid for the provisions they took on their journey); and in this manner passed through Entigne, Tegue, Mont Marienne, Bonneval, Bexas, Mont Cenis; marching over snow, climbing up rocks, sustaining the attacks of troops sent against them; and, in short, overcoming every obstacle that presented itself in their progress. Arrived, at length, at the church of Guigon (a hamlet annexed to Pral), they engaged in worship, sang the seventy-fourth Psalm, and their colonel and pastor, Arnaud, preached on the 129th Psalm. But even after their return, they had frequent and severe skirmishes with their enemies, displaying upon all occasions a degree of valour and fortitude that has been seldom surpassed. One cannot, however, but regret, that M. Arnaud's account of their return affords too many proofs that they possessed more of the martial than the evangelic spirit; the same which at an earlier period characterized Zisca and those of the Hussites who followed his standard. After several unsuccessful efforts to dispossess this warlike company of Waldenses, the Duke of Savoy at length concluded a peace with them, and permitted the return of their wives and children. Hence the origin of the present race of the inhabitants of the valleys, a population of seventeen thousand souls. Since their return, their residence as before, has been attended with numerous hardships. To mention but a few: they have been compelled to desist from work on the Roman Catholic festivals; forbidden to exercise the profession of physician or surgeon; or to purchase lands; and very often their children have been stolen in order to be educated in the Roman Catholic faith, in a large and not inelegant building at Pignerol, called the Hospice, established for the express purpose of converting the Vaudois.* This last instance of cruelty, added to many similar atrocities, so ingeniously adapted to embitter the fountain of domestic happiness, too forcibly recalls that affecting language of the prophet:—" In Ramah was there a voice heard, lamentation and weeping, and great mourning: Rachael weeping for her children, and would not be comforted, because they are not." Thoughts of this nature would naturally occur to the mind of a stran-

ger when finding himself actually in the valleys: the first evening especially, when I held in my arms the very lovely child of Mrs. P. of. St. Jean, I could not but picture to myself, again and again, the agony of those parents " who wandered in deserts and in mountains, in dens and in caves of the earth," in that very neighbourhood, equally unable to succour themselves and their tender offspring. To whom could this " noble army of martyrs" look for support but to " the Holy Ghost the Comforter"? And what hope could sustain their souls but that of " a better country, that is, a heavenly"?

It may be thought by some, that the enemies of the Vaudois were chiefly tempted to injure them by avarice, and that they wished to rob them of their lands; but, however this may have mingled, as it did, no doubt, with other motives, the main-spring of the opposition seems to have been a rooted antipathy, because they professed doctrines and engaged in worship that differed from the Roman Catholic.† For, as to their lands, contrasting their bleak air, narrow valleys and barren mountains, with the soft climate and the fertile plain of Piedmont, they might much more,

---

* The institution, however, has been attended with little success, the greater number of converts being persons who, for misconduct, were no longer respected in the valleys.

---

† It is through the necessity of preserving a due regard to historic truth, and of maintaining the cause of a much-injured people, that circumstances of cruelty have been related so dishonourable to the Roman Catholic Church. It is hoped, however, that the writer will not be supposed to foster that antipathy against its members which he has so strongly condemned when it has appeared on their part. The principles of their church are unquestionably such as promote a spirit of persecution; but, happily, many of its members dissent from its spirit, and cultivate that Christian love which is a transcript of the Divine Nature itself. Whilst bigots have agitated the church and the world, they have pursued their course of humble piety. The writer has been always delighted 'to see or hear of Catholics of this description, and he has had this happiness whilst on the Continent. Even with regard to the massacres mentioned in this memoir, some of the assassins, probably, through a blind zeal, thought they did God service. To excuse in such a case is impossible; but one would wish in some measure to extenuate, for so did our Saviour upon the cross: " Father, forgive them, for they know not what they do."

justly express their surprise than Caractacus his, when he saw Rome, that any should. envy them their humble cottages and hard-earned possessions.

As it is probably what most readers would wish, I will here attempt a brief description of their valleys.— There are three—Luzerne, La Perouse, and St. Martin. That of Luzerne is the principal, and comprises the following *communantes,* or parishes.

1. Rora, situate in the mountains, which produces chesnuts and wheat.

2. St. Jean, the entrance to the valley from Piedmont, and the finest spot belonging to the Vaudois. The eye is there pleased with a fine assemblage of meadows, gardens, orchards, and vineyards: mulberry trees are also cultivated for the use of the silkworms, which bring in a good profit. The neighbouring eminences command an extensive view of the plain of Piedmont.

3. Angrogne, in the mountains, produces forage, chesnuts and fruit, but little wine. Here there was, in ancient times, a college for the education of ministers.

4. Latour, a borough-town in the vale; its vicinity producing wine, wheat, fruits, forage and chesnuts.— Not far from this town there is a cave in the hills, capable of containing three or four hundred persons, where, providentially, the Vaudois found a place of refuge when persecuted by their enemies. In this cave they prepared provisions in an oven, and, it is understood, resided occasionally for some time, while the danger was imminent; and here, in such perilous circumstances, it is not to be doubted that in imitation of their Redeemer, they frequently " offered. up supplication with strong crying and tears unto Him that was able to save them from death."

5. Higher up the valley is Villard, producing wheat and chesnuts, but very little wine. In passing by, I noticed people with goitres,. so often seen in the Valais, and described by Mr. Coxe, in his Travels through Switzerland; but I think there are few if any idiots.—In the Valais they are numerous.

6. Bobbi, still farther in the valley, borders on Dauphine. In this parish the scenery is stamped with an awful grandeur. On the mountain opposite

the village you see snow even as late as September; and now and then you meet with a fine cascade in the neighbourhood. The Pelis, which, descends towards Bobbi, and then runs along the valley of Luzerne, is in some places a very impetuous torrent: it takes its source above the Alp of Pra, and loses itself in the Po. In this parish you find little produce; scarcely any thing except cattle and chesnuts.

La Perouse is an extremely narrow valley, watered by the Cluson. Several villages in it, formerly inhabited by the Vaudois, are now *exclusively* so by Roman Catholics. They have only three parishes:—

1. Pramol, situate on the mountains; its produce wheat and fruit.

2. Pomaret, in which the hill and vale produce wine.

3. St. Germain, which is more agreeable and productive than the two others.

Between the valleys of Luzerne and La Perouse is situate the parish of Prarustix (comprising Rocheplate and St. Barthelimi), which produces good wine, wheat and fruit.

The valley of St. Martin is watered by the Germanasque. It is extremely narrow; in fact, all the lands are on the sides of the mountains. This vale comprises:—

1. Pral, situate among the higher mountains, which are covered with snow about nine months in the year. There is little wheat or fruit; the chief resource is cattle.

2. Maneille: I was particularly struck with the sterility of this parish. In the neighbourhood there is a fine cascade.

3. Villeseche.

The Vaudois had formerly much more extensive grounds; but at various times, and under various pretexts, they have been dispossessed of them. These three valleys have been left them rather as places of exile than of enjoyment, and though described as producing wine, wheat, &c. yet, with the exception of a few spots, it is by mere dint of hard labour that the barren soil of the sides of the mountains yields the means of subsistence to the inhabitants, whose principal diet is black wheat, potatoes, cow's or goat's milk, and chesnuts. The roads are often serpentine over rocky ground; the noise of the rushing torrent is generally heard; and sometimes, especially at Pral, the dreadful avalanche overwhelms an individual on the road, or a family in their cottage.

I now proceed to some cursory remarks on the character and manners of the Waldenses, premising that it is not at all intended to go through the round of mortal virtues, and shew how far they are respected or exemplified by the people, but merely to state a few particulars of which I was informed, or which fell under personal observation.

They preserve from their forefathers a sincere respect for pure and undefiled religion. Public worship is very generally and conscientiously attended; and when I had an opportunity of witnessing a communionday, the church was quite full, and the behaviour of the communicants solemn and pleasing.* Nor is their religion wholly confined to their temples: on the Sunday evenings in winter several families assemble in a stable (partly induced by the intense cold), and unite in religious exercises, as reading the scriptures, and singing psalms and hymns.

The *social* duties they also exercise to a very considerable extent. For instance, though more frequently persecuted than protected by their sovereigns, the Waldenses are loyal subjects. When the King of Sardinia was lately restored to his crown, they sang "Te Deum" on the occasion, as well as presented an address of congratulation: and when, at a former period, Louis the Fourteenth's army invaded Turin, Victor Amadeus II. was advised to rely upon their loyalty, and take refuge in Rora: he did so, and remained secure sill Prince Eugene came to his relief.

They are also remarkably honest. Whilst the immediate vicinity (the plain) is infested with robbers and assassins, these valuable men devote themselves, with that industry and patience which the nature of the soil requires, to useful labour for their subsistence. A robbery seldom or never occurs in the valleys. Assured of this, I felt no anxiety, though once overtaken by night near the woods, and entirely at a loss which of the numerous intersecting by-ways to choose. My companion and myself walked fearlessly along till we perceived a light, and got an obliging Vaudois to attend us home.

We find, indeed, more than mere honesty among them; even a generous disinterestedness, though so poor. I could not prevail upon a man at one time, upon a child at another, to take any reward for a trifling service they had rendered; and I recollect seeing a soldier, who offered himself to the King of Sardinia instead of his brother or some other individual, unaccustomed to war, who might be required to serve.

Hospitality is another very pleasing trait, and exercised in such a manner, that when you quit their roof, the Vaudois seem as if they had received, and not conferred a favour. Their humanity is also, on many occasions, conspicuous. If any one is ill, the neighbours cheerfully and gratuitously sit up at night in the sick chamber; and there is even a sort of dispute who shall pay the first and the greatest attentions. In case of an accident that a poor person has met with, a sermon is sometimes preached, and a collection made. But this kindness is by no means confined to their own friends. Whilst the Catholics around usually relieve the necessitous of their own religion, the Vaudois give what they can spare to the destitute of either communion. There is one illustrious instance, in particular, of their humanity, which should not pass unnoticed. When the Austrians and Russians, under Marshal Suwarrow, compelled the French army to retreat, three hundred wounded French soldiers received all the assistance, with respect to medicines, &c. that could be given; and at the request of M. Rustan, their Minister, the inhabitants of Bobbi carried these poor men on their shoulders over the mountains to the French territory—a most painful task, as those can well attest who have taken the tedious and difficult road of the mountains from Piedmont to Dauphine. Their conduct appears to have been a pure act of humanity,

* Religious instruction is very carefully instilled before young persons become for the first time communicants. I was told that a young lady of Turin had been four months at a relation and minister's house, passing through a course of religious studies.

not the result of any partiality to the French; yet, but for the generous interposition of Prince Bagration with the Commander in Chief, it would have exposed them and their property to considerable danger. The Austrians could not withhold their admiration; and the French General (Suchet) published an order of the day for the very purpose of acknowledging such a singular instance of benevolence.

I will mention but one moral feature besides, and that is, their gratitude. They have been long indebted (as will be seen in the sequel) to our nation for its sympathy and protection, and especially to a British Princess (their guardian angel, if we may so speak), for her munificence. These benefits have never been forgotten: on the contrary, the pastors and people regard the English as their best friends—in seasons of difficulty, their chief resource;* and I remember I was very forcibly struck with the remark of the amiable wife of one of their ministers, who told me, that they made a point of instilling into their children respect and esteem for the English from the very dawn of reason in their minds.

Having said thus much of some valuable qualities of the mind, a few observations may be added respecting their manners. They are in general very correct, such as one might anticipate amongst a people well instructed, little used to intercourse with the world, and devoted to the laborious occupations of ploughmen, herdsmen, shepherds and vine-dressers. The late war, however, has in some degree injured them, as it obliged many of their youth to become soldiers in the French service. There was also a fortress established by the French of late years, not far from St. Jean. They have experienced, no doubt, like most others, the melancholy truth of the maxim, "Evil communications corrupt good manners." The principal amusement of the people has in itself something of the martial; it is their great ambition to be expert marksmen; a circumstance to be traced, probably as much to a motive

of self-defence as of pleasure. After Easter the inhabitants of the several parishes (each body with an elected king at its head) receive each other with peculiar respect, fire at a mark with a musket ball, and afterwards adjudge rewards to the most skilful. This tends to cement the union of the several parishes. Their marriages, baptisms, &c. usually take place in winter, and then they often indulge in their favourite amusement of dancing. In 1711, a synod prohibited dancing, but the prohibition does not seem to have been attended with success.

I will next describe what I am persuaded will interest, I wish I could gratify, benevolent persons in England—the state of their schools. They were once flourishing, and the sum of six thousand livres of Piedmont† was annually remitted from Holland for the purpose of supporting fifteen great, ninety little (or winter), and two Latin schools; part of the money being reserved however, for the widows of ministers, for disabled ministers, for the poor, and for an allowance to five deans.‡ The events of the late war have entirely changed this happy aspect of affairs. Since the year 1810, two thousand livres per annum only (100*l.* sterling) have been received from Holland; and as half the people had not the means of paying, the schools have exceedingly declined, and even run the risk of complete decay. With the exception of the Latin schools, however, they exist at present *(barely exist,* and but ill provided with teachers), as charitable persons in the valleys have hitherto paid for the poor.

They have been equally unfortunate with regard to the pensions which Queen Mary II. granted to thirteen schoolmasters; for this resource has also failed since 1797. It is highly important that Christian benevolence should avail itself of the occasion here presented of benefiting the rising generation, both in granting such an allowance as shall procure efficient teachers, and in suggesting the various improvements in system which have lately taken place in the

---

* It is to the British representative they have confided their Memorial and interests at the present Congress of Vienna.

† About 300*l.* sterling.

‡ The five senior ministers are always deans.

education of the poor in our own country.

The next subject that claims attention is the condition of their ministers and churches.

Each of the thirteen parishes has a settled minister; and to each parish several hamlets are annexed, in which there are also temples. Queen Mary established what they term the royal subsidy, a grant of 400 livres (20*l.*) annually to each pastor; but from this fund nothing has been received since the year 1797. What they call the national subsidy, is the product of a collection in England about forty years ago. Part of this is intended for the widows of ministers; and ministers themselves derive from it the annual sum of four hundred livres, which has been regularly received. It is obvious, from this statement, that those pastors who have not private property, must be in unhappy circumstances; and indeed the royal subsidy having failed, some have been reduced to the painful necessity of borrowing money of their respective flocks.

Few would imagine that persons of learning and taste are to be found among them, and yet there are: their education places them on the same, or nearly the same, level with the generality of ministers in this country. The Swiss Cantons, which have ever shewn a friendly regard to the interests of the Waldenses, assisted them in this respect; and in 1729 an English lady settled a pension upon a student, which was paid through the consistory of Amsterdam. Their candidates were educated at Geneva and Lausanne; but I think I am correct in stating that their pensions have failed (the events of the late war having introduced change and disorder into every department), and that they will experience difficulties in future, on account of the expense of an academical education. I am sorry to say the case of at least some of the widows of deceased pastors is also distressing. There are now six: one, who has a daughter, has only about 10*l.* a year —she had a son, a student at Lausanne, who was compelled to serve in the army: he afterwards died at home of his wounds. The late Mr. O. had a very laborious parish in the mountains; often a long and fatiguing walk; and then, after both the intense heat in summer, and the rain

and snow in winter, no place of shelter and rest (the church standing on an isolated spot), before the service. He fell, at length, a victim to his exertions, leaving a widow and seven daughters, the eldest only fourteen years old, to lament so severe a loss. The pecuniary resources for the support of so numerous a young family are very slender indeed. When I stood near the grave and read this simple inscription on a rude headstone: " 1814, J. D. O. Pasteur et Juge;" and when I entered his library and opened the books he had been used to read, and looked thoughtfully around the room which had so often witnessed the prayers of a father for his family, and a pastor for his flock; this consideration that their circumstances were so reduced, could not but awaken still deeper sympathy for this afflicted family.

It has been already stated that there are thirteen parishes; of these my short residence only permitted me to see nine. The old chapel of St. Jean had been destroyed by persons hostile to the principles of the Waldenses; but of late years they have, with the assistance of friends at Turin, built a new church. This seems to confirm what has been advanced of the serious view of the importance of religion which reigns in the valleys. But this is not all: they have likewise erected a new church, almost wholly at their own expense, at St. Germain,[*] an earthquake (which is no uncommon occurrence among them) having greatly injured the former one in 1808. With regard to church government, there is a moderator elected at every synod; each church has a deacon, who attends to objects of charity; and several elders; the discipline is less strict than formerly; the liturgy used in public worship is that of Neufchatel; the festivals observed are Christmas, Easter, Ascension Day, and Pentecost.[†]

Other particulars, with which either

---

[*] The United Brethren kindly advanced something.

[†] All the offices of their church are in French, which they often speak; but the patois of Piedmont is also prevalent among them. The ancient Waldenses were Episcopalians with respect to church government, and the sermons in Italian, or a language in some measure similar to it.

personal observation or the information of others has made me acquainted, I forbear to mention in so brief a Memoir, and therefore pass on to a hint or two as to the means of promoting the welfare of this valuable class of our fellow-christians. They are clearly in want of pecuniary aid ; and such is the benevolent disposition of British Christians, that to mention this fact is quite enough. Yet, however anxious that they should not be overlooked in this age of beneficence, I am fully aware, that, since there are magnificent institutions in the country which have a much higher claim upon Christian liberality, donations are chiefly to be hoped for from persons whose affluence enables them, after subscribing to larger societies, to spare something for others of an inferior description. Very many such persons are to be found ; and one cannot for a moment suppose that they will permit this interesting people, so eminently protected by the English in the eighteenth, to be neglected in the nineteenth century. There was a time when the Waldenses did not so much receive as impart benefits. Their college of Angrogne sent forth zealous missionaries to convey pure religious knowledge to several parts of Europe, then involved in ignorance and superstition. They were, indeed, according to the import of their armorial bearings, a light shining amidst thick darkness.* If, in these latter days, something of the ancient splendour of their piety should, through divine grace, re-appear, those Christians will have reason to esteem themselves very happy, who, by their generous efforts, may be in some degree honoured as instruments of the revival. It is unquestionably the duty of believers to endeavour to promote and to pray for such a revival of vital piety in churches once renowned, as well as the diffusion of divine truth among the heathen.

I am sensible that this appeal in behalf of the Waldenses is in no respect worthy of the cause it undertakes to advocate ; yet since, however unadorned, it has at least the simplicity of truth, and the importance of the subject to recommend it, I could willingly cherish the hope that it will secure for this excellent people a warm interest in the best affections of their fellow-christians. Of this I am very sure, that if, instead of seeing their condition through the medium of an imperfect memoir, they found themselves actually in the valleys, and, holding a history of the Vaudois in their hands, cast the eye around spots consecrated by the sufferings of so many disciples of the Lord Jesus, they would be filled with esteem for the people, and a desire to promote their happiness. The evening before I quitted them, a solitary walk afforded me full scope to indulge such a train of feelings :—a sacred luxury it may well be termed, since the sensations of delight were really such as neither the treasures of art deposited in the Louvre, nor the stupendous views of nature unfolded in the cantons of Switzerland, had possessed in an equal degree the magic to impart. All around seemed to have a tendency to foster the disposition ; a torrent rushed by on the left ; the evening was so mild that the leaves scarcely stirred ; and the summits of the mountains, behind which the sun had just set, appeared literally above the clouds. The emotions produced by the scenery and recollections associated with it, will not be soon effaced : it might be the last time I should see those mountains, which had been so often the refuge of the oppressed—those churches, where the doctrines of the gospel had been so long and so faithfully maintained—and those friends, from whom a stranger from a distant land had received so many proofs of affectionate regard ! Full of such thoughts as I walked along, I arrived at length at the house of one of the pastors, to pass the night. The next day he accompanied me to the limits of his parish, on the Col de Croix, which separates Piedmont from Dauphine. The walk being long and tedious, he had brought bread and a flagon of wine, and observed, as he gave me the refreshment, it was " une espèce de communion"—might be almost considered a sort of communion. We then parted with expressions of Christian esteem ; and, descending the other side of the mountain, I soon lost sight of the lands belonging to the Vaudois—descendants of a class of men who were, for a series of ages, " destitute, afflicted, tormented, " but " of whom the world was not worthy !"

* " Lux in tenebris ;" the arms of the town of Luzerne, which once belonged to them.

MISCELLANEOUS COMMUNICATIONS.

*Difficulties on the Subject of the
Resurrection.*

Maidstone, Feb. 12, 1815.

Sir,

THOUGH I by no means wish
to interrupt your correspondent
Credo [p. 25,] in his purpose of ob-
viating the difficulties alleged by your
Cambridge correspondent, in what
he conceives to be a more satisfactory
manner than I was enabled to do;
yet justice to myself, and the cause
I have espoused, requires that I should
correct a palpable mis-statement which
occurs at the commencement of his
letter, and which appears and influences his remarks throughout. He
sets out with the phrase " physiological correspondence" as descriptive
of the Letter of Cantabrigiensis, and
consequently of the subject for our
mutual consideration. He also states,
that the leading difficulty to be considered was, whether if a man dies
wholly, a resurrection is within the
bounds of *probability.* The difficulty
which he has not very judiciously
severed, is thus ingenuously and succinctly stated by Cantabrigiensis himself : " If I die wholly a resurrection
appears scarcely within the bounds
of possibility. There may be a new
creation, but can the regenerated being be myself? If there be nothing to
constitute my individuality but the
will and power of the Creator, I seem
reduced to the absurdity of thinking
that my consciousness may be conferred on any number of created forms."
Thus it clearly appears that he felt
doubts concerning the *possibility* of a
resurrection by the energy of the
Creator alone, independent of some
secondary means, such as the " preservation of consciousness" in the interval between death and the resurrection. He suspected that a complete resurrection or restoration of vital existence after it had wholly ceased
to be, involved some absurdity, and
consequently was not an object even
of infinite power. To this difficulty
I undertook to reply, by shewing that
it is equally in the power of the Creator to *restore* life and consciousness
as it was originally to *impart, preserve*
and *withdraw* those blessings : and
that it is sufficiently agreeable to the

analogy of his actual proceedings both
in the ordinary course of nature and
by miracle ; and further, that he can
receive no assistance whatever, from
secondary means, all created existence, whether material, mental or
otherwise, existing only as the pure
effect of his power ; and consequently
being entirely at his disposal either to
preserve, remove or restore at his
pleasure. This was the leading subject of our discussion, or at least
which I undertook to discuss ; as I
perfectly coincided with him in opinion, that the hypothesis of Dr. Watts,
concerning " an indestructible germ
of matter, being the nucleus of the
regenerated man, is altogether a gratuitous supposition."

The question between us, therefore,
instead of being of a *physiological* nature, and relating to the *probability*
of a resurrection, by any such secondary means as *Credo* appears to have
in contemplation, was wholly *theological,* or relative to what was *possible*
as the pure result of the divine energies.

Whatever *Credo* may be *about to
do* in his next letter by way of more
effectually clearing up the difficulties
of Cantabrigiensis, he has hitherto
done very little except misrepresenting and distorting his expressions,
and making heavy complaints against
me, for not answering him by such
arguments as *he* deems most cogent.
In No. 1, of his remarks, he twice repeats his misrepresentation of the leading difficulty ; and then complains of
me for replying directly to it, instead
of wandering into other topics. He is
displeased with the length of my argument, and that it is metaphysical.
The first of these inconveniences he
has himself sufficiently remedied,
though so much at the expense of
perspicuity and sense, particularly at
the closing sentence of his abridgment
(I), that I should much rather he had
left it to speak for itself in its original,
uninviting condition.* The reason
why it could not be *physical* has been
explained ; it necessarily relates whol-

---

* *Excited* in the second paragraph,
Vol. viii. p. 734, should have been *exerted.*

ly to the Creator and the human mind; yet I had hoped that the illustrations derived from the familiar phænomena of sleep and dormancy, would have rendered it sufficiently intelligible. The affirmative of the question with which it concludes is the point which was to be determined, being the answer to Cantabrigiensis's chief difficulty, and Credo, though with rather an ill grace, appears to admit that it is perfectly easy.

The second head of his remarks commences with a sad distortion of sense contained in the concluding sentence of the above quotation from Cantabrigiensis. It by no means follows, that because the whole creation is the entire *production* of Jehovah, the pure effect of his power, therefore it must be a part of his substance. His attributes are all resolvable into infinite power, wisdom and goodness; and creation is the *effect*, not *a part* of those attributes. *They* are the *cause, this* in all its parts and modifications, whether material or discernible by our senses or not, is the *effect*. *They* constitute the one indivisible Jehovah, or self-subsisting God, who is necessarily from everlasting to everlasting, without variableness, or shadow of a turning. *This* subsists only as the result of his energies, and may therefore be altered, withdrawn or renewed at his pleasure. Though Credo terms this the *next* difficulty of Cantabrigiensis, it is in reality only an illustration of the preceding affirmation; shewing his reasons for suspecting that a resurrection in case of total death " is scarcely within the bounds of possibility ;" viz. that the supposition appears to lead to absurd consequences. Here again I am complained of for referring to the creative power of God, instead of alleging proofs from nature. Now had I merely referred to creative power, without shewing that there was no absurdity in the doctrine of a complete resurrection of the same individuals in number, as in every other respect, by its sole energies, there would have been just ground for complaint. But though Credo has charged me with an argument *going to prove* an impossibility, and also with " cutting the knot," and yet " labouring," which two last accusations are not very compatible with each other ;—he has not himself advanced a single argument

even *going* to prove any one of his accusations. He complains that my answer is vague ; yet according to his own account, it constantly applies to the point in view; viz. a resurrection by the power and will of the Creator alone.

Credo makes various complaints of my observations in proof that the resurrection of Christ is adapted to confirm and establish the doctrine of the resurrection of our race to a state of immortality ; and particularly that some of my quotations are irrelevant, and others want evidence of my having justly applied them. Now the principal question here is, whether Christ, notwithstanding his various appearances in his former body, which surely was the most satisfactory, if not the only mode in which he could *manifest himself* to men remaining *in the flesh*, did not in reality come out of his sepulchre, and usually continue after his resurrection in a state of invisibility ; or in which he could not when present be discerned by our eyes or any of our senses. For if Jesus rose to a state of invisibility, it is evident that his body must suddenly have sustained a greater and more inexplicable change than any to which our bodies are subjected in the course of nature, by the circumstance of his sudden invisibility alone ; and if in this state he received life and consciousness in great perfection, the single event of his resurrection must have been more extraordinary, as being compounded of more miracles than will attend the similar resurrection of mankind after their bodies have been dissipated and rendered invisible by a process of nature.—I observe then 1st. That if he had come visibly out of the sepulchre his appearance would have been the chief object to attract the attention of the watchmen who were stationed at its entrance for the express purpose of securing his body. But though the appearance of an angel from heaven, a sight of which they could have no expectation, and his rolling away the stone from the sepulchre were distinctly observed by them, yet no intimation whatever is given of their seeing Jesus. He must therefore have been miraculously concealed from their view ; for had they seen him, the mention of this sight would have formed the prominent feature in their narrative. 2.

The next direct proof of his change into a state of invisibility was pre-sented to the two disciples, with whom he joined company in their way from Jerusalem to Emmaus ; from whose sight at supper, after an interesting intercourse for a considerable time, he disappeared. 3. The same even-ing "*the doors being shut*," he was found standing in the midst of the apostles, after such an inexplicable manner, that though they were pre-viously convinced that he was *alive*, they now imagined that they saw on-ly the spirit or apparition of a dead man. 4. He again appeared to them in precisely the same manner seven days afterwards, Thomas being present, and afforded him exactly those proofs of the reality of his per-son, which he had required in his apparent absence. 5. It is evident that he was not usually visible to his disciples during the interval between his resurrection and ascension, but that he occasionally resumed his for-mer corporeal state, for the purpose of *manifesting himself to them*. To these occasional appearances the apos-tles constantly appealed as the evi-dences that he was really risen, and their narratives uniformly imply that though he was occasionally, he was not|uniformly nor generally present in a visible form. Yet his appearing at the most suitable junctures, and dis-covering an acquaintance with what passed in his apparent absence, prov-ed that he must have been invisibly or mentally present. 6. His ascension may justly be considered as a *gradual* representation of the change from this mortal state to a state of immortality ; his body which had just been repre-sented to his disciples, in its usual state previous to his resurrection, di-minishing in specific gravity as it as-cended, till at length, probably both from its height and its tenuity, it dis-appeared from their view. 7. From this time forward he has remained in a state of invisibility, with only two recorded exceptions; viz. his appear-ance to Stephen to encourage this first Christian martyr in his dying moments, and to Saul in effecting his conversion to the Christian faith. 8. That there was a very great change effected in the body of Christ at his resurrection, from a corruptible to an incorruptible, from an animal to a spiritual state, as there will be of all

his disciples, is the express doctrine of the Apostle Paul. (See Cor. xv. 31—53, particularly verses 42, 44 and 50.) Now the change from a dead, animal, corruptible body, to a living, spiritual, incorruptible one, being far greater and more inconceivable than any changes which can happen to material bodies in the course of na-ture, it is evident that the sameness of the renewed being could not de-pend on any sameness of materials in the composition of his body. It must depend wholly on the restoration of life and consciousness by that power from which all created existence ori-ginates. If therefore from the dead body of Jesus, an invisible, immortal person was produced, possessing the essentials of the same intelligent being who had previously lived in the com-mon state of humanity ; we may safe-ly confide in his assurance that our race in general will be restored to life in like manner, by the same pow-er alone, after that the materials of which our present bodies are com-posed have been wholly dissipated and lost. The bodies of mankind in general are rendered invisible by the gradual dispersion of their particles ; and we may conceive of the possibi-lity of the same identical particles being collected together, so as to form a body composed of the very same materials. But how the material bo-dy could be suddenly rendered whol-ly invisible, and at the same time, the same life and consciousness imparted, which before were so intimately united with that body, are *two* most extraor-dinary facts of which we can find no analogy in nature. They are present-ed to us in evidence and illustration only of *one* of these events as applica-ble to our race in general ; viz. that after their material bodies have been lost by a process with which we are well acquainted, renewed life and consciousness shall be in like manner imparted. In proportion therefore as we are satisfied, that a man like our-selves is now existing in a state so entirely different from this in which we remain, as an earnest of our com-mon destination, we may regard it not only as a direct proof, but a case in point strikingly illustrative of that event.

It is true, indeed, that according to the received ideas, concerning mat-ter and spirit, these things must appear extremely mysterious ; and the phrase *spiritual body*, may seem to express a contradiction. The disquisitions of Dr. Priestley have, however, thrown great light upon this subject ; but as I conceive he has not carried his principles in their application to the doctrine of a resurrection to their full extent, I may on a future occasion be induced to trouble you with some additional remarks.

Yours very respectfully,
T. P.

P. S. In your copy of my former letter there is a typographical error (T. B. instead of T. P.) in the signature, which, however, I perceive, has not misled your correspondent Credo.

SIR,

HAVING before [p. 25,] stated my reasons for considering the letter of T. P. not to be an answer to the objections of Cantabrigiensis to the Christian's hope of a resurrection from the dead, according to my promise I now resume the subject with an intention of proving that the doctrine of the Resurrection can be so explained, as to be understood and believed.

Founded on his objections C. puts this question, " If the immortality of the soul wants support from scripture and the restoration of the same body involves in it a physical contradiction, how is the preservation of individual consciousness and the resurrection of the same man to be explained, understood or believed ?" Now the difficulty appears to me, not to be in the doctrine itself, but in the manner in which Cantabrigiensis considers the doctrine to be taught, for he " laments that the scripture evidence is in favour of a system which holds man to be one and indivisible and wholly mortal ;" and it is on this ground that is put his first objection, " That if man wholly dies a resurrection does not appear to be within the bounds of probability."

But scripture does not represent " Man to be one and indivisible :" for Jesus says, " Fear not them who kill the (*soma*, the fleshly, organized) body, but are not able to kill the (*psuxan*, the desire, sensual) mind, but rather fear him who is able to destroy both mind and body in the grave." Matt. x. 28. Peter speaks (2 Pet. i. 14,) of knowing that he must

shortly " *put off*" his tabernacle ; and Paul, that himself and all Christians knew that if their " earthly house of this tabernacle was dissolved," they had a building of God ; hence, on this principle of consciousness, that their mind was inhabiting a tabernacle of clay, Christians were anxiously " desiring to be clothed upon" with their spiritual covering ; for they well knew that whilst they were at home in the body, they were absent from the Lord. Corresponding with this view of the subject he writes, I Cor. xv. 37, " Thou sowest not that body that shall be;" 38, " But God giveth it a body as pleaseth him, and to every seed its own body." The scripture therefore does not hold man to be one and indivisible as regards the body and mind ; but holds the mind to be the man, and the body to be his house, his tabernacle, his clothing. If therefore the whole body die, till it can be shewn that the mind also dies, a resurrection cannot be said to be improbable, but to such as know not the power of God, and have not heard of his promises, nor exercise their minds to discern his wonders in creation, and the reviviscence of all nature.

2. The next objection made by Cantabrigiensis is, that a creation is not a resurrection ; and that if a new creation is made from myself, many such may be made. But if the mind is the man, the new clothing of that mind is only a new creation of the clothing, but a resurrection of the man. And should that mind be divided, then the man would not be raised.

3. C. next objects to the resurrection of Jesus, that it is not any evidence to us, because his body was not corrupted or destroyed, as ours will be ; but this, like his former objection, falls to the ground, as it regards the resurrection of the dead taught by the apostles ; for they no where teach the resurrection of the body as it now is, but expressly assert, " Flesh and blood cannot inherit the kingdom of God ;" that the living body at the coming of Christ shall be changed, that this " corruptible must put on incorruption, and this mortal must put on immortality." We know that Jesus that was raised from the dead was the same Jesus as was crucified ; not only he was con-

scious of it, but his disciples were also; but we also are assured that his flesh and blood could not inherit the kingdom of heaven. When he was changed, whether in the tomb or at the time of the ascension, is of no consequence; the objection of Cantabrigiensis ceases to have force, unless he can shew that the flesh and blood of the body of Jesus inherited the kingdom of God.

4. Though the hypothesis of Dr. Watts may be, in part, a supposition to avoid a difficulty, yet to me it does appear that part of that supposition has a very close analogy to the scriptures and what we know of nature. The language of the Doctor would certainly have been more correct had he said " *We* must ourselves rise at the last day for *us* to receive rewards and punishments," instead of saying "*our bodies must rise.*" If the Doctor errs in saying " there may be, perhaps, some *original fibres* of each human body," perhaps he does not err in the continuing sentence, " some *stamina vitæ* or *primæval seeds of life,* which may remain through all the stages of life, death and the grave." In the present state of things, as Dr. Watts says, " If there be any such constant and vital atoms, they are known to God only." Yet man may conjecture whilst he keeps within the bounds of natural and revealed evidence./

All nature makes known a distinction between body and life, whether it is in vegetable or animal union: as far as we know, and here man has extensive evidence, all life is a two-fold production; without the animating principle the ovum corrupts, with it life is the consequence: that whose origin is from two may be long combined together ; but as it was at first united, it must necessarily have connected with it a possibility of separation ; but in all living bodies we have something more, for we have a continual struggle between the energies of the vital principle and the tendency of matter to corruption ; corporeality being preserved alone in existence by the energies of vitality. Nature itself does therefore demonstrate that man is not a one indivisible being as it regards body and mind; but that mind is the man, and the body is the organic instrument by which the mind obtains information and power to act.

Too many of the followers of Dr. Priestley, in the doctrine of the Materialism of the Mind, reason as though organization and mind were the same; but nothing can be more distinct : mind from infancy increases in knowledge and maturity to extreme old age, always feeling through the whole period accumulating evidence by memory of personal identity; whereas the whole of corporeal organization is so constantly passing away that though the man recollects the occurrences that have happened to him for more than a century past, it is probable that not one particle of the matter that constitutes his organization is of more than ten years' standing, and probably has not been one year a part of him. It is the confounding together the actor and the instrument that has confused this plain subject.

Be not alarmed, Sir, I am not going to revive the now exploded system of the pre-existence of the human mind, nor of its necessary immortality: neither to bring forward the spectres nor hobgoblins of past ages to terrify the nervous and alarm the fearful. With you, Sir, I believe that the beginning of life is the commencement, and that its earthly termination of existence is a stop to all consciousness till the great Creator has new clothed it with its etherial dress or habitation. In the mean time, I trust sufficient has been said to prove the scripture resurrection is not improbable or incredible; and that it is a resurrection of that which alone can be called the man, and that the resurrection of Jesus is and ought to be sufficient evidence for us to act upon the expectation of our own future resurrection.

If any of your correspondents wish to carry on this physiological research in connexion with scripture evidence and it meets your approbation to permit its continuance, it will give much pleasure to

CREDO.

Hackney, Feb. 5, 1816.

SIR,

THE following anecdote of a condemned criminal, extracted from a late publication, entitled, " Letters from a Gentleman in the North of Scotland," may not be unacceptable to your readers.

" Then the ministers of the town

went into the jail to give him ghostly advice, and endeavoured to bring him to a confession of his other sins, without which they told him he could not hope for redemption—for besides this murder, he was strongly suspected, &c. &c. * * * But when the ministers had said all that was customary concerning the merit of confession, he abruptly asked them, if either or all of them could pardon him in case he made a confession : and when they had answered ' No ; not absolutely,' he said, ' You have told me, God can forgive me ?' They said it was true. Then said he, ' As you cannot pardon me I have nothing to do with you, but will confess to him that can.' "

There are other curious matters related in the author's account of this extraordinary Highlander, but not of sufficient interest for your pages.

I remain, Sir,
Yours respectfully,
S. C.

London, Feb. 28, 1816.
Sir,

IT is well known that Mr. George Baring has lately resigned the vicarage of Winterbourne Stoke, Wilts, and seceded from the Church of England, and that several other clergymen of the same neighbourhood have also left the Establishment. But the grounds of their secession have not, I believe, been made public. I beg leave therefore to request of some one of your correspondents in the West an explanation of this curious piece of news. Have the seceders been actuated by love of *orthodoxy* or love of *heresy?*

NONCON.

Sir,   *H——, Jan.* 18, 1816.
IN the second vol. of the " Annals of Philosophy," by Dr. Thomas Thomson, (p. 247,) the editor has reprinted from his " History of the Royal Society," a " Biographical Account of Sir Isaac Newton," and to that part of the Memoir which touches upon Sir Isaac's religious sentiments, has subjoined the following note (page 322).

" I have heard it affirmed by some of the self-constituted philosophers of the present day, that Sir Isaac Newton believed the Christian religion merely because he was born in a Christian country; that he never examined it ; and that he left behind him a cart-load of papers on religious subjects, which Dr. Horsley examined and declared unfit for publication. These gentlemen do not perceive that their declarations are inconsistent with each other. Nobody who has ever read a page of Newton's works could believe that he could write a cart-load of papers on a subject which he never examined. Newton's religious opinions were not orthodox ; for example, he did not believe in the Trinity. This gives us the reason why Horsley, the Champion of the Trinity, found Newton's papers unfit for publication. But it is much to be regretted that they have never seen the light."

In the regret expressed by the biographer, I presume all your readers will participate ; and my reason for copying the note is a hope that, by being republished in your Miscellany it may meet the eye of some of your numerous readers, who may be able, through the same channel, to communicate information as to the existence and present situation of the papers in question.   I am, Sir,
Your constant reader,
A. F.

Plymouth, Dec. 25, 1815.
Sir,

I HAVE lately had the pleasure of perusing a work which I suspect is not so much known as it deserves to be ; nor do I recollect to have seen the name of its author amongst those of the champions of the proper unity and supremacy of God the Father, although he well deserves to have been placed in the very first rank of them. The copy I have before me is stated to have been published in the year 1815, and to be the fifth edition enlarged ; from which circumstance, and from the rank of the author, and the style of the work, I presume it has moved chiefly in the very highest circles, where I cannot but hope and believe it has produced a strong effect, although at present we have seen no better proof of it than the facility with which the persecuting laws relative to Anti-Trinitarians were repealed in the last session of our parliament. Indeed the way in which Mr. Smith's bill was carried after the bishops had been assembled to consider the expediency of it, and the very liberal views which are now generally entertained by the Lords of the Upper and the Gentlemen of the Lower-House of Parliament, are convincing proofs that a very different manner of thinking prevails in the higher circles upon religious subjects than that which induced our wary ancestors to furnish religion with props and shores, which, while they are no support, are an enfeeblement and a disgrace to it.

The book to which I refer is called "An Illucidation of the Unity of God deduced from Scripture and Reason." It is dedicated to the Society of Unitarian Christians at Montrose, in North Britain, by James Gifford; who resided at Girton, in Cambridgeshire; and was, I am informed, a Lieutenant Colonel in the Line, and an intimate friend of Mr. Lindsey. The dedication is dated July 25, 1787. It is accompanied by a letter to the Archbishop of Canterbury; and the whole of the performance exhibits a deep research into the sacred volume, and serious inquiry into the meaning of its declarations, with an uncommon degree of firmness of manner, yet mildness of expression, a *fortiter in re* with a *suaviter in modo*, scarcely ever to be found united in a case of such incalculable importance. The work is published for Rowland Hunter, (late Johnson) St. Paul's Church Yard.

I am desirous of calling the attention of your readers to this very interesting work; and especially to an illustration of the Divine Unity, which I conceive, to many, will be new. After speaking of the grand unity of design which all nature exhibits, and which points our intellectual powers distinctly to a unity of the Divine Nature, he adds,

"God has taken care that we should have more reasons than one to believe that all things were formed by one Great Mind, that all are the effects of the same Great Cause; and I think he has interwoven the truth of his Unity in our very nature, if we would attend to its operations. I shall endeavour to give proof of this by a familiar instance; but I beg leave to introduce it rather as an accessory circumstance than as a fundamental argument.

"Whenever a multiplicity of objects are presented to the mind, we find it necessary, in order to contemplate with any accuracy, to confine ourselves to one and drop all the rest. A consequence ever unavoidable while the *thinking principle* is closely engaged. And hence it happens, that the *Unity of God* forces itself upon us in the act of devotion, from the *indivisibility of thought*. For we may observe that, when we address ourselves intently in prayer, we find it impossible to fix our meditation absolutely on more than *one object of worship* at the same moment. All others are neglected in the instant, and cannot enter the mind without confusing and dissipating the attention. This alone plainly shews, that the mental faculties are not calculated to attend fixedly to more than *one object.* We may indeed associate *three or more* different things or persons in idea, and then consider them in one *collective* view, but this does not destroy their *individuality*, and when we would contemplate any one of these objects with precision we must dismiss the combination. Or we may blend three or more distinct things or subjects together in idea, and then consider them in the aggregate as one; but, besides that this is the mere work of the imagination, it would be held both dissatisfactory and dangerous with respect to the Trinity: because we are expressly enjoined in our present received doctrines *to preserve the distinction of the three persons,* and acknowledge them to be, not only *separate* but also *equal* objects of prayer and thanksgiving. Notwithstanding this in the solemn

this preference, we find, is generally given to *God the Father Almighty* himself, and every other object is ex-

For *He* incessantly rises in the collected soul, and fills it. Thus the great truth of *the unity of the Deity* seems to have been implanted by him in our nature; and the mind of man, with which it is in perfect concord, in its most serious and attentive moments, is necessarily led to acknowledge it.* In praying to or glorifying

---

* Notwithstanding the polytheism of the Heathen, it is certain from their own writings and monuments, that the belief of a *Supreme God* naturally prevailed among

the *Trinity in their turns,* we still give the *precedence to the Father,* but by a positive distinction in their persons, and in our worship, we unavoidably destroy the very notion of *one only God,* and, as I apprehend, overthrow the great basis of revealed religion.

" What will naturally follow from these observations is this: that, as the indivisibility of thought will not permit us to pray fixedly to more than one object at the same time, *for the very attempt to divide the attention confuses it;* therefore we are compelled, if we hold to the Athanasian system, to invoke and worship the three persons in a separate manner, as we find is done in the Litany and in many of the Collects. Thus when we worship *the Father,* we adore a person *different from the Son and the Holy Ghost;* and when we worship THESE, we adore *two persons different from the Father and from each other.* For, howsoever they may be connected, their *persons* are to be preserved distinctly in the mind, and their worship of course to be distinct also.

" Now, under these circumstances, it appears impossible, from the very nature of thought, to free ourselves from the idea of their being *three distinct Gods.* For since we cannot divide our attention, which if we could would be the highest disrespect to the *person* meant to be adored, it must be always *changed with the object* of our worship; and then it inevitably follows, that every other must be neglected at the time; and these are exactly the consequences with all polytheism whatsover; from which therefore I humbly apprehend it is extremely difficult to distinguish the present system. But, on the other hand, if we *blend the three persons together,* and consider them *as one and the same intelligent being,* then the Athanasian hypothesis is destroyed, and any distinct or discriminating worship appears totally superfluous and contradictory." I am, Sir,

Yours,

J. W.

them, and was sometimes openly testified: See Acts xvii. 22, 23. Most of them, indeed, conceived that *he* was too great or too far removed to attend to men or their supplications. We are obliged to revelation for the complete cure of this most discouraging apprehension.

P. S. Since writing the above, I have little doubt that the former editions of this work were of the size of a pretty large pamphlet, and that the present edition was published after Mr. G's. death, by his son, a gentleman also in his Majesty's service, enlarged into an octavo volume by numerous valuable notes, and other additions. Mr. Gifford had three sons, two in the army, the other in the navy.

New Jury Court of Scotland.

ON Monday, the 22d instant, the New Jury Court met for the first time.

The Right Hon. William Adam, Lord Chief Commissioner; Allan Maconochie, Lord Meadowbank; and David Monypenny, Lord Pitmilly, the two other Commissioners, being assembled; and the names of the thirty-six Jurymen returned to try the issues, being called over, and having answered to their names, the Lord Chief Commisioner opened the business of the Court in a speech to the following effect :—

MY LORDS—Before we proceed to the cause appointed for trial this day, I wish to say a few words to the Court. I believe I am justified, according to immemorial precedent, as a newly appointed presiding Judge of a supreme tribunal in this country, in addressing the Court. This has been the uniform practice of all Presidents on their appointment.

I believe I am justified in this Court which is to administer justice by a jury, as in the Criminal Courts of this country, according to the practice of those courts on their circuits, in saying something to you, Gentlemen of the Jury, upon your being assembled here; and I think I should not be justified at the opening of this new court for the first time, if I did not state what has occurred to me on this occasion ; exhibiting a new and an important feature in the judicial system of Scotland.

It may not be unfit, recent as it is since the Act of Parliament passed creating this court, shortly to retrace the circumstances which have given rise to the institution of this tribunal.

In the year 1808, an Act of Parliament passed for improving the judicatures of this country. It empowered and required that his Majesty should appoint commissioners to examine into that grave and weighty subject, and to report to the King and the two Houses of Parliament. Among other things, the commissioners were to be called upon by the Act of Parliament to inquire into the fitness of introducing trial by jury in civil causes into the Scotch judicial establishment. In the month of May, 1810, the commissioners reported on that subject, stating, that if care was taken " that no alteration of our municipal law was made by such institution, the enabling the Court of Session to direct issues of fact to be tried by jury, might afford a safe foundation on which important experiments might be made."

This Report lay untouched for several years. But in the interval between making this Report in May, 1810, and the close of the session of Parliament, 1814, many cases had occurred in the House of Lords, moving entirely on matter of fact, accompanied with long printed proofs, calling upon the Supreme Court of Appeal, which should only be required to decide matters of law, to perform a duty not properly belonging to it, by deciding cases resting upon intricate, difficult, and ill-proved facts. This created observation in the House of Lords, out of which the statute grew, under which this Court sits, and from which it derives its authority and constitution.

It is to be observed then, that the great distinguishing feature of this tribunal is, that it is the first duty of its Judges so to act, as not to disturb in any respect that ancient and admirable system of the municipal law of Scotland, handed down to us by our ancestors, and secured to us by the Act of Union, constituting, as it were, a charter for the preservation of the jurisprudential system of Scotland.

It shall be my peculiar care, as it is my duty, to walk in this course ; and however I may distrust my own ability, I feel assured I shall be able to do it with the assistance of your Lordships.

The object then, of the law under which we sit, is to receive and try issues directed by the decisions of the Court of Session, wherein matters of fact are to be proved by the intervention of a jury.

This institution has been long used

for this purpose which speak the language we speak. It is of a tradition so high that nothing is known

abated vigour and purity from its commencement to the present time.

It is the character of all other institutions for the investigation of facts to have become inadequate to their end. It is the character of this mixed

facts under the direction of a court, to have preserved its original perfection unabated. These extraordinary and important features of durability and perfection seem to arise out of causes which it may not be unfit to state upon the occasion of introducing it into the administration of civil justice in Scotland. They are the natural results of its modes of acting.

It is to be observed, first, that it can only proceed by settling of a clear distinct issue to be tried. The advantage of this is manifest, it obliges the directing Court to compel the parties to precision, and relieves the causes at the commencement of litigation from all dispute as to what the questions are between the parties. It enables the proof to be made clearly as applicable to those questions.

It requires no more enlarged statement to enforce the advantages of this effect of the trial by jury.

Secondly. It adds a *casual* to a *permanent* tribunal ; and, by their acting and re-acting on each other, the natural qualifications of both are improved, and their defects amended.

The great feature of the casual part of the tribunal, *The Jury*, is its being constituted and assembled, in a manner (as far as human wisdom can accomplish any end) to secure impartiality and perfect indifference in the causes to be tried by it.

It is chosen from among the people at large, according to a certain qualification, insuring the education and understanding necessary for the duty. A certain number are returned, greater than the number required to try, as you thirty-six Gentlemen are now returned here, to try the appointed issues. The return is made by the sheriff, a magistrate of high rank, unacquainted with, and uninterested in the parties, having no connexion with them ; and when returned, the twelve

Jurors to try the cause are selected by ballot, their names being to be drawn by a sworn officer of the court, from the box into which they are put fairly, under the sanction of a solemn obligation.

This is doing all that human contrivance can accomplish towards the attaining a tribunal free from all prepossession.

But the grand and important feature of this tribunal for the examination of fact, is, 3dly, *Publicity*, or the public and open manner in which its business is conducted.

Every thing is transacted with open doors—every thing, from the commencement of the trial to its close, except when the Jury retire for deliberation, is done before an inquisitive and observing public, who, hearing the evidence, form their judgments of the correctness of the Court and Jury in drawing their conclusions—so that they are secured by the responsibility of character, thus openly exposed to criticism, to form a correct and honest opinion in every case. This is aided by the constant presence of an enlightened Bar, whose learning and talents and practice in judicial concerns, are thus made subservient to the ends of substantial justice. In this way, and before such an audience, the case is sifted to the very bottom, and every part of the tribunal is always subject to the most rigid observation, and so called to the most correct attention to do justice.

This important feature of jury trial is remarkable for its happy influence on all those who administer to justice through the medium of that institution.

First. As to its influence on the witnesses. By public examination they are open to the observation of the tribunal who is to judge of their testimony, and of the value to be ascribed to it—as it respects their demeanour, their capacity and intelligence and the manner of testifying. Every witness in an open court, risks his character with the public and with his neighbours, and is kept correct by that influence. The witnesses are fully examined by counsel in chief, then cross-examined by adverse counsel; and, lastly, subject to the examination of the Jury and the Bench. By being examined before a supreme tribunal, the influence of judicial authority has its effect in producing correctness of deportment, and his evidence being submitted to the judgment of his fellow-subjects, *the jury*, he must have that circumspect attention to truth which such a situation naturally creates. Besides, in case of prevarication, the authority of a court, with sufficient power to commit, is held over him, to have an instantaneous operation.

Secondly. The effect of *publicity* is equally important in regard to the jury.

Their exposure to public view and observation, secures, in that respectable body, the *casual tribunal*, that steady attention, which is not only essential to the appearance, but to the reality of justice; and it is not unimportant to remark, that this solemnity of conduct reflects again on the surrounding audience, and secures in those who compose it, the same attention and decorum when they come to be jurymen.

The justice which they do, as I have already observed, is the subject of consideration by as many as the court will admit; the report of those present at a trial goes forth to the public at large, and the verdicts of jurymen are secured to be just, by the certainty that they must undergo the scrutiny of the whole extended and watchful community.

The evidence of which they have to judge is, owing to this publicity, and to the formation of the court, governed by rules which are calculated to exclude falsehood, and to secure the testimony of truth.

The introduction of a well-regulated law of evidence is a most important result of trial by jury. In order to exclude all evidence from the hearing of the jury, which, from its nature, may be false, and make an undue impression, the judges are called upon publicly to decide upon the admissibility of witnesses, and of questions, upon all objects of competency, as contradistinguished from those of credibility. This they do publicly upon the argument of counsel; and, here again, the subject is secured in a due and certain administration of justice in matter of fact.

This is a result only attainable by this institution, where there is authority and learning to decide, and a cause for decision. It is this which leads to the exclusion of hearsay, and of all those circumstances in proof where the fact may be false and yet the witness be correctly honest, as well as to all the exclusions of, testimony arising out of the various modifications of interest or concern in the cause, or in the question or connexion with the parties.

Thirdly. As to the Bar, this institution will have its just and beneficial influence.

When I refer to that most respectable body, the Bar of Scotland, I may safely and justly enlarge upon their great learning, their integrity, their eloquence, and other high attainments; and above all, I can rely on the most rigid honour and pure correctness of their practice in their profession. Yet, great as the learning and eloquence is which they bring into the hitherto ordinary practice of their profession, the public and immediate efforts which they will have to make in this tribunal, cannot fail to afford a new scene for their eloquence.

In guiding the course of justice, the Judges will derive assistance from counsel, while the system of jury trial will give new occasions to the Bar of Scotland for acute and masterly discussion, by watching and seizing circumstances and emergencies as they arise, as well as by previously preparing themselves upon the important features of the case; and thus these new opportunities for the display of conduct and address, by training them to a mode of exertion to which they have not been accustomed, will give new scope and enlargement to their professional talents, and render them still more useful ministers of justice in all the branches of their practice.

Fourthly. But, above all, *this publicity* is imp Judges who preside—in regulating and preserving correct what I have called the *permanent* part of the tribunal. This happy composition in judicature, when the functions are publicly and openly discharged, invigorates all the good qualities of the judicial character of the permanent Judge, and corrects all the defects to which the judicial character is prone.

On the Bench we must call to aid, temper, forbearance, attention, circumspection, a firmness in forming opinions, a readiness in re-considering them, no pertinacious adherence to first thoughts, and yet a decision calculated to enforce well-considered views,—and above all, in this seat, where justice is to be distributed within a period to be measured by the strength of man, dispatch must combine with deliberation, readiness of thought with correctness of opinion.

Our duties as Judges are to be performed before a judicious public, deeply interested in the justice which is to be dispensed, and before a critical and enlightened bar, ready to disseminate with freedom, as they ought, their opinions of our errors, but equally ready to do justice to our motives, and to bestow the just reward of praise when we are right and correct.

The error to which a court, composed of a single judge, is liable, is perhaps an over-weening self-willedness: this is corrected by the discharge of the function publicly with the aid of a jury. The necessity of attending to every point for their information—a necessary compliance with those modes of conduct which such interchange of thought as this tribunal requires, and the necessity of the judge weighing well what he is publicly to impart to others, under the controuling effect of their having to decide on the spot on the correctness of his views, secures against such self-willedness.

The error into which the Judges of a Court composed of several is apt to fall is carelessness. Trusting to the efforts of his fellow Judges, the public effort and the duty to impart all that passes, and all his views of it to others on the spot, and at the moment, proves a sure antidote to this propensity in the judges of a tribunal of several.

Thus it may be said that the well-doing of the permanent tribunal is secured, and the administration of justice in matters of fact (that extensive and ever-varying source of litigation) is better regulated by this contrivance of trial by jury, than by any that the wit of man has ever yet devised.

Such are the leading features of this institution, which we are now to try in this country, as an experiment, and as I have said in the outset, always anxiously attending to this, that it is not to interfere with any fixed rule, or with any part of the system of the municipal law of Scotland, and that we are only to try such issues as the Divisions of the Court of Session shall think it right in their discretion to send here : these, it may be material to observe, will be of three sorts :—

1st. Cases where the issue may comprise both the injury and recompence or damages.

2nd. Cases in which the Court of Session, or Lord Ordinary, having decided as to the injury, refer the damages to be assessed by a jury.

3rd. Cases where the Court of Session, or Lord Ordinary, wishes for information by the verdict of a jury to inform its understanding. so as to enable it to pronounce a judgment upon the law.

The case about to be tried is of the description last mentioned.

But in that, and in all cases, it will be easy to clear away difficulties.

In the first place, allow me to observe, more particularly addressing myself to you, gentlemen, who are assembled to serve on this jury, that our inquiries here are not into hidden and occult acts of crime, where the discovery of truth may often be involved in intricacy and difficulty, and in doubtful testimony, by the very nature of the acts. But we shall have to do here with the open acts and transactions of men in the ordinary affairs of life and intercourses of the world. In such transactions, when examined into in open Court, seeing and judging of the witnesses, as I have described their examinations to be conducted, with all the fences against the admitting falsehood, and all the securities for obtaining truth, which a well-regulated law of evidence affords ; with a tribunal judging from their own just and honest impressions, uncontaminated by intercourse or extraneous impressions, and only influenced by the detailed, explained, and fully delivered opinion of the presiding Judge, he being alike removed from undue impressions ; there is nothing likely to happen but an easy solution by a general verdict. But when there does occur prevarication, or contradictory testimony, that worldly sense and intercourse with mankind which those composing Juries possess, and which affords, perhaps, a better power of extrication than the learning

of more retired men, will never fail to guide you : while the court has it in its power, according to the nature of the case, to relieve all difficulties, by directing a special verdict, or even a verdict specially, finding the evidence as given, and returning it to the Directing Tribunal ; so that that court from which the issue comes will always attain, what it wants, the best possible information of the fact on which to ground its judgment.

The case for trial will soon afford a practical instance of what I here state ; and I trust by its event it will shew, though, from the great number of witnesses, it must be long, that in less than twelve hours we shall accomplish, to satisfaction, that which would not have been attained, in the ordinary course, in twelve months— that we shall, by our labour of twelve hours, put an end to all litigation ; while the other course would, at the end of twelve months, only give a commencement to litigation, with a power to a litigious spirit to continue it for years to come.

If this experiment is successful, and I augur sanguinely of it, although, as in all experiments, failure may be expected at first, there will be attained for this country the great objects of justice, viz. certainty, satisfaction, dispatch, and cheapness ; and with this I might conclude, but I cannot refrain from observing, before I close my address to you, that I augur success to the experiment most peculiarly, and with most certain hope, when I consider that the casual tribunal, as I have denominated the Jury, is to be derived from the body of the people of Scotland, distinguished for good education, for a most correct morality, for a love of justice, for extended information, and for a pure religious persuasion.

I trust and hope with unfeigned anxiety, that I may be able in my person to bring to the aid of this most important experiment, the qualities requisite to its success. But when I reflect that though I have, during all my professional life, been accustomed to courts thus administering justice, that I have never yet dispensed it—that, from being a critic on the acts of others in that awful station, I am now myself to be the subject of observation and remark, I cannot but be full of anxiety and apprehension; in having the interests and property of my fellow-subjects submitted to my untried judicial faculties.

In this situation, new to me, and new in the judicial jurisprudence of Scotland, I derive comfort when I look to my learned brethren on each side of me, who add to learning and a knowledge of mankind, high faculties and practice sanctioned by the opinion of an approving public in the dispensation of justice.

When I look before me to the bar, I derive comfort from the certainty that I am to be enlightened in the seat of justice by their learning and their eloquence, and that I am sure to receive comfort from their urbanity, and from the mildness of their judgments on my first exertions.

When I look to the Jury now assembled, and the succession of such a class of men to discharge this duty, there again I derive comfort, and feel convinced that their anxiety to do justice, and their steady attention to every case, will secure against any bad effects from my want of experience or incapacity.

If I should prove at all a serviceable instrument in giving success to this important measure of justice, while I live I shall enjoy the comforting reflection that my early education in Scotland, and my habits, have preserved unabated through life my devoted attachments to its interests and its people, and made the high station to which I have been graciously advanced an object of my most ardent desire. I will conclude, therefore, with the anxious hope, that it may be inscribed with truth upon my tomb, that the experiment has proved successful, and that I have not been useless in the accomplishment of this mighty benefit to my native land.

Sir,   *Feb.* 21, 1816.

AS a truly honourable mind will not hastily impeach the integrity of another's motives, more especially in matters of opinion, I cannot help suspecting that those strenuous supporters of the Church of England, who have recently assailed Unitarians with so many *charges of disingenuousness* and *misrepresentation*, are conscious of that very *obliquity* in their own conduct, which they so earnestly labour to affix on their opponents.

tuate minds of a different compass, or expansion, it is scarcely justifiable in such persons to attribute to others those principles of action, which, in similar circumstances, they would not have hesitated to adopt. The selfish hypocrite is rarely able to comprehend the grasp of truly generous and enlightened minds. The man of honour should not be reduced to the same level with the sycophant. And such as conscientiously resign preferments or prospects in an opulent estate, integrity, cannot be fairly estimated by the aspiring pluralist, who defers implicitly to his superiors, both in Church and State.

I am led to these reflections, by the virulent and illiberal censures, which have been of late so often cast on the judicious and truly scriptural *revisions* of Watts's Hymns and Moral Songs for Children, and Melmoth's Great Importance of a Religious Life; as if such revisions had been actually " palmed upon the public," as the

without any notice of the alterations whatsoever. Yet nothing can be fairer than the conduct of the editors, in their respective prefaces, by which all idea of deception or concealment is removed. The revision of Dr. Watts's

tive, or rather erroneous, in some particular doctrines and phrases, judged it expedient to make many alterations in both respects, in adapting them to the instruction of her own children ; and afterwards for the better accommodation of others in the same sentiment, and for the further early advancement of religious truth committed her useful labours to the press." Nor was the Editor of the Great Importance less " studious to avoid involving the original author in any responsibility for the omissions of doctrines originally adopted by him, or clandestinely ingrafting his own alterations on the labours of another ; earnestly hoping that no just cause of offence could be taken, by the most tenacious theologian, for the simple omission of occasional language or sentiments, thought to be derogatory from the genuine sense of the gospel of Christ, and distant from its true and even tenor." In conformity, therefore, to these statements, and in compliance with a more correct interpretation of the Bible, all ascriptions of praise and thanksgiving are confined to the one only living and true God; and all expressions omitted which gave countenance to the common though erroneous notions of " the sacrifice of Christ as a satisfaction to divine justice ;" "the eternity of hell-fire as a place of future torment," and " the all-pervading influence of the devil."

Such, Sir, were the candid and honourable proceedings which have been so vehemently arraigned. Such are the alterations which, alarming the prejudices of a narrow and petulant high-churchman, conscious of his own disingenuousness, as accessory to a secret and altogether unwarranted suppression, in the garb of a British Critic, or under the disguise of a Plain-Dealer, has been so idly and slanderously assailed. But it is in vain that facts have been distorted, and conjecture substituted for proof. In vain has Mr. Nares or Mr. Norris impeached the integrity of the Revisers' motives, where all idea of deception or concealment has been so clearly and unequivocally disavowed. And, in the face of this undeniable fact, it required no common effrontery, in a Parochial Vicar, in his " Remarks on Mr. Belsham's Letters to the Bishop of London," (pp. 11—13,) resting on their authority for his statements, to renew the slanderous and unfounded charge.

The judicious conduct of the Revisers as advocates for the supreme authority of the scriptures, correctly interpreted, in all matters of religion, was not less worthy of their benevolent design, of rendering these deservedly admired works, as unexceptionable in doctrine and language, as for inculcating moral virtues and Christian piety, they have long been universally approved. For how, let me ask this *new assailant*, has " the beautiful composition or Christian piety of Dr. Watts's Hymns," evaporated, or " the utility of Mr. Melmoth's Tract, for calling the attention of young minds to the observance of Christian morals, or to the knowledge of doctrines peculiarly Christian," been affected by their revision? Whilst they pretend not " to inculcate ALL the principles of the original writers,"

what moral precept, what truly scriptural doctrine, has been, in either case, withdrawn ? That " they are cleared of all doctrines peculiarly Christian," is an assertion as false as it is foul; unless the Vicar is prepared to shew that Christianity comprises no peculiar doctrines, when the Deity and atonement of its founder, the eternity of hell-torments, and the devil, are withdrawn. In rejecting all such unwarranted interpretations of detached or highly figurative passages, and in recurring to the uniform and consistent testimony of scripture to the divine wisdom and benevolence, the editors have essentially contributed to " the advancement of religious truth." And their little works may be safely put into the hands of children or reflecting persons without the fear of exciting those erroneous views of the dispensations of providence, which are calculated only to terrify or disgust. How can they be deemed " mutilated and imperfect," where every deficiency is so well supplied ; where the genuine simplicity of the gospel is restored by the removal of excrescences which tend only to vitiate and deform ? So far from being " *marred*," they are *meliorated* both in sentiment and language ; so far from being " *despoiled*," they are adjusted to the *legitimate standard, scripture ;* and instead of being " *eviscerated*," are lawfully *cleansed* from the *gangrene* which assails the vitals of the Christian scheme.

When the " real purpose" is so explicitly avowed, and the design so judiciously executed, where does the Parochial Vicar find any traces of " that ingenious management, or that imposing artifice," which he so uncharitably ventures to impute ? How is this " method of conveying instruction and persuasion inconsistent with what is generally understood by the terms, fair and honourable ?" And with what propriety can this common and most useful practice of revising books of instruction, be so vehemently censured by the clergy of the Church of England, whose boasted scheme is nothing more than the religion of Rome " marred, despoiled and eviscerated ;" whose Liturgy is no better than a Mass Book altered and revised ?

But, Sir, as the whole merit of these improved works is strictly due to the editors, who alone were concerned in the publication; upon what principle are Unitarians, who, as a body, were never called upon to sanction them, involved in the imputed blame? Would it be right to involve the numerous adherents of the Church of England, in the censure which may justly be attached to these unfounded charges, or to any other instances of misrepresentation or suppression, which individuals have practised in its support? Indiscriminate censure is at once illiberal and unjust; it cannot advance the cause of public reformation, or deter from the most mischievous pursuits. But in the present instance the censure is unfounded, and the Revisers entitled to unqualified approbation for their truly benevolent design. With as little reason has the Improved Version of the New Testament been involved in this unwarranted attack, as it is certainly founded on the basis of Archbishop Newcome's Translation, without involving that prelate in any responsibility for the numerous variations from his text.

On the whole, Sir, these censures could only have proceeded from persons determined to find fault; from men, resembling a certain high-church dignitary, who having vented his wrath against the new edition of the Great Importance, on the mere perusal of the preface, arraigned the conduct of the editor, as if his purpose had been studiously concealed. Want of candour and ingenuousness has prevailed through the whole of these pitiful attacks: unqualified assertions, remote from truth and probability, have supplied the place of evidence, whilst the most pure and disinterested motives have been " scandalously and industriously maligned." Can such unwarranted proceedings have emanated from correct and honourable minds? Are they calculated to support the credit of the Church of England, or consistent with the diffusive benevolence of the gospel, which inculcates charity and good-will to all? Do they not rather savour of those narrow prejudices, which to the destruction of every liberal principle and feeling, have too often marked the conduct of established churches, in their hostility to the claims of private judgment, and the free investigation of religious truth?

DETECTOR.

The Holy Alliance.

(See pp. 113, 114.)

A curious circumstance relating to the *Holy Alliance* lately made between the Emperors of Russia and Austria, and the King of Prussia, has come to our knowledge through so respectable a channel, that we conceive it deserving of being communicated to our readers.

In 1815, a Madame la Gridner was at Paris, whither she arrived from Riga, her native country, invited there, as is generally understood, by the Emperor Alexander, who had previously known and consulted her.

The Prophetess Gridner, who, like all the inspired persons of this class, is not devoid of talent, and particularly possessed of the sublime and obscure jargon of mystical rites, trusting to feeble minds, reasons about every thing, discusses facts tolerably well, supports her opinions by religion, and frequently interrupting her conversation to implore, by a fervent prayer, the rays of a divine Spirit, terminates by an emphatic prophecy developing some confused but brilliant idea, together with certain consequences which she foretells, as an infallible and almost divine solution of the conversation that had been agitated.

La Gridner arrived and established herself in a large hotel in Paris, prepared for her, which was furnished after her own fashion; that is, when one had traversed a suit of five or six apartments, where nothing but the bare walls were to be seen, and even no lights in the evening, one arrived at a large inner room, the whole furniture of which consisted of a few rush-bottomed chairs and a pallett, on which she was always reclined. It was on this throne or tripod, from which she never descended, that she ushered forth her mystical reveries and pronounced her oracles.

The Emperor Alexander was known to go almost every evening to the rendezvous of that Sybil, and here it was that the three Sovereigns, authors of the *Sainte Alliance*, discussed their projects, &c. as well as their interests and line of political conduct; and it is well understood that, under the dictates of the said Sybil, the treaty in question was drawn up and signed, without the intervention of any one of their respective ministers.

Whatever the ulterior object of this Convention may be, certain it is, that it is intended as a strong league, made in the name of God, against *liberal opinions.* How truly does this remind us of the Sovereigns of the thirteenth century ! ! !—*M. Chron.*, *Feb.* 19.

Bromley, *Jan.* 2, 1816.

SIR,

PERHAPS few of your readers are aware that under the sanction of the Yearly Meeting of Friends, Committees are from time to time appointed, to inspect periodical works as they come out, that any remarks concerning their principles or practices which require it, may be promptly noticed, and *their testimonies be supported.* The late *Joseph Gurney Bevan*, of Newington, was one of those appointed to have the theological superintendance of your Journal, so far as it might relate to *the concerns of Friends.* In the latter part of his life he was much disabled from writing or reading by a complaint in his eyes: I believe the last article from his pen, sent to your Work, was signed Breviloquus : it is inserted Vol. V. p. 647. I do not know who has been nominated in his room, but suppose such Committees of the Meeting for Sufferings are still appointed, although several articles which seemed loudly to call for replies, not being noticed, I have thought whether the members of these Committees are not become more fastidious than their predecessors, and wave giving any replies to anonymous writers.

Should this have been the reason why a paper signed "An Inquirer," in your last Vol. p. 546, has been passed over in silence, I would obviate that objection by the inclosed letter, which was sent to the Meeting, by which I was excommunicated. If you think fit to insert it, some member of the Society, if not of that Meeting, may feel the propriety, *when thus publicly called upon*, to attempt an explanation of the "apparent inconsistencies and contradictions," which your correspondent has pointed out. As to my letter, it was not even allowed to be read in the Meeting, and has not procured me any information how it is thought the Epistle for 1810, and the ostensible grounds on which I was excommunicated, can be reconciled with the Epistle of the last Yearly Meeting. I am,
Very respectfully,
Your sincere friend,
THOMAS FOSTER.

To Ratcliff Monthly Meeting, to be held 10th Mo. 19th, 1815.

DEAR FRIENDS,

Having incurred your censure for "calling in question" certain doctrines " professed by the Yearly Meeting, in its Epistle for 1810," and being now able with much sincerity to avow my cordial approbation of those which its Epistle for the present year contains *upon the same subjects*, I hope expressing the same to you will not be deemed an improper exercise of my Christian liberty, or give you just cause for dissatisfaction. How this Epistle can be reconciled to the former, I know not, but *this* I beg leave to refer to you, as being well worthy your consideration.

On hearing the latter epistle read in the Quarterly Meeting, I was forcibly struck with the soundness, clearness, and scriptural simplicity of its language, compared with that of the former, upon every point of doctrine on which erroneous opinions are imputed to me by your records, and that without feeling conscious of any change in my sentiments.

My attention was again drawn to this Epistle, as the latest and most authentic exposition of the doctrines of the Society, by the delivery of a copy to me, by one of your members appointed to distribute those Epistles. Since this time I have carefully examined its contents, and in the respective situation in which we stand to each other, as *fellow-christians*, and children of the same benevolent Parent of the Universe, even " THE GOD *and* FATHER *of our Lord Jesus Christ*," I feel that I owe it to you, before I close this letter, briefly to call your serious attention to those parts of the last Yearly Meeting Epistle to which I have alluded. In doing this I shall annex a few words to mark more plainly how I understand the Epistle, always distinguishing them from the text. It begins thus :

" In offering you this salutation of our love, we believe it right to acknowledge our thankfulness to THE AUTHOR OF ALL GOOD, that we have been permitted to meet together. We have had again to rejoice in a sense of the goodness of Him [" the Author of all good"] who, by his presence, owned us in times past—we have felt the consoling assurance that the Divine Power [of Him who is omnipresent, and whose mercies are over all his works] is both ancient and new." That is, I presume more properly, *is unchangeable.* " It is from this holy source [" of all good"] that every enjoyment," says this Epistle, "both spiritual and temporal, flows; it is to THE LORD ALMIGHTY that *we are. indebted for the blessing of existence,* for *the means of redemption,* and for *that lively hope of immortality* which comes *by Jesus Christ.*

This is *much more* than merely "*calling in question* the omnipotence of Jesus Christ." It is expressly to attribute *omnipotent power* and *boundless goodness* to *another being,* even to " THE LORD AL- MIGHTY," the ever-living and unchange- able God ; and to describe Jesus Christ as the medium by whom the "lively hope" of the greatest of these blessings, was made known to mankind through the gos- pel.

If we are "*indebted* to THE LORD AL- MIGHTY"—the giver of *every* good, and of every perfect gift, " for the blessing of existence," as this Epistle asserts, surely He " endowed us by nature," with those "talents--however great," by which we are distinguished from every other order of beings in this sublunary world. " To his service, then dear friends," adds the Epistle, " in obedience to the manifesta- tion of his power [which is fresh every morning, for the earth is full of his good- ness] *let us offer our talents* ; to the glory of his great and excellent name, *let us devote our strength* and *the residue of our days.*"

As to "*the propriety,*" and *the duty* of " *secret supplication,*" and *to whom* it should *be addressed,* this Epistle is *equally explicit* and *scriptural.* After recom- mending the youth " to allot a portion of each day to read and *meditate* upon the sacred volume [the Scriptures] *in private,*" this exhortation is added : " In these sea- sons of retirement, seek for ability to en- ter into a close examination of your own hearts ; and as you may be enabled, *secret- ly* pray to THE ALMIGHTY for preservation from the temptations with which you are encompassed." Again. " Let their ex- ample," that of some friends lately de- ceased, " encourage you to *offer all your natural powers,* and *every intellectual at- tainment,* to the service of the *same Lord,* and patiently to persevere in a course of unremitting obedience to *the Divine Will.*" If we pray then " with the spi- rit, and with *the understanding also,*" whether openly or in secret, surely it should be offered *only* to *the same Lord—* THE ALMIGHTY," as this Epistle enjoins, and not ever to *Jesus* " whom he [God] hath made—both Lord and Christ." Acts ii. 36.

The Epistle concludes thus : " Let us ever remember, that if we obey the Divine commandments, we shall do all to *the glory of God* ; we shall *always* acknow- ledge, that it is of his mercy, if we ever become partakers of the unspeakable pri- vilege of the true disciples of Him [' tho

Lord Jesus'] who ' died for all, that they that live should not henceforth live unto themselves, but unto him *who died for them,* and *rose again.*' " 2 Cor. v. 15.

From this passage I understand, that in the judgment of the compilers of this Epistle, we cannot become " true *disci- ples*" of " *the Lord Jesus,*" whom God raised from the dead, without being " al- ways" ready to " acknowledge," that we owe " *the unspeakable privilege*" to "THE MERCY OF GOD," *the Original* Source and proper *Author* of all the blessings confer- red on mankind by Jesus Christ, and by the gospel which he preached. I con- gratulate you and the Society on so speedy a *return* to the common language of our ancestors, and to that "form of sound words" which is to be found in the scrip- tures of truth, and remain your sincere well-wishing friend,

THOMAS FOSTER.

London, Feb. 25, 1816.

SIR,

I OBSERVE that Unitarian places of worship are rising up in differ- ent parts of the kingdom, and that appeals are frequently made on behalf of them to the liberality of the public. It is difficult however for an indivi- dual like myself to ascertain the me- rits of the respective cases, and though it would be painful to refuse my quota of contribution, it is unpleasant to subscribe without a full conviction of the serviceableness of a subscrip- tion. I have heard of a recent case where monies were collected for fit- ting up an Unitarian Chapel, and a considerable sum expended upon a building held on a short lease and subject to a charge of ground-rent which no small congregation can long pay.

Permit me to suggest then the ex- pediency of every application of this kind being first submitted to a body of competent judges, say the *Com- mittee of the Unitarian Fund,* with- out whose sanction any case should be considered as without recommen- dation. Any permanent body would answer the purpsoe, but some such sanction is necessary to satisfy the private individuals to whom appli- cants appeal.

I perceive with great satisfaction that in the cases of *Neath,* &c. pro- vision is made in the Trust Deeds that the chapel erected by public contribution shall, in the event of the discontinuance of public worship on Unitarian principles, come into the hands and be the property of some permanent Unitarian body. The same provision should surely be made whenever a new place of worship is raised by the help of the Unitarian public, for every such building is in some sort an experiment. If the experiment fail, let not individuals or other sects reap an advantage.

Once more, I recommend most earnestly that every new chapel should be erected on *Freehold Ground,* and that sufficient ground should be purchased in the first instance to lay out a *burying-place.* There is an unseemliness in Unitarians being interred with Trinitarian forms of religion, which must be the case where they have no church-yard of their own: besides that it is sometimes in the power of clergymen to insult the ashes of supposed heretics when death brings them under their " little brief authority." The tombs of fathers have a hold upon the religious profession of children when better ties are weakened; and sepulchres give a solemnity to Houses of Prayer, and supply that sentiment of reverence which fails to be excited by the small and unimposing temples of Dissenters. For these reasons I always inquire of those who solicit my subscription to our new chapels, whether accomodation be contemplated for the dead as well as the living!

ZELOTES.

Islington. March 1, 1816.

SIR,

THE insertion in your valuable Miscellany of the following curious fact, respecting the Field of Waterloo, will be gratifying to the more intelligent class of your readers. It is taken from the Life of the Duke of Marlborough. in the seventh volume of the British Biography, a work chiefly written by the late Dr. Joseph Towers, and uniformly favourable to the interests of Civil and Religious Liberty.

" On the 15th of August, 1705, the Duke of Marlborough moved from Mildert to Corbais, and next day continued his march to Genappe, from whence he advanced to Fischermont. On the 17th General Averquerque took the Post of Waterloo, and next day the confederate army was drawn up in order of battle before the enemy, who extended from Overysche, near the wood of Soignes to Neerysche, with the little river Ysche in front, so as to cover Brussels and Louvain! The Duke of Marlborough proposed to attack them immediately, and Averquerque approved of the design. But it was opposed by General Schlangenburgh and other Dutch officers, who represented it in such a light to the Deputies of the States who attended the army that they refused to concur in the execution. The Duke being obliged to relinquish the scheme wrote an expostulatory letter to the States General, complaining of their having withdrawn that confidence which they had reposed in him while he acted in Germany."

Thus it appears that in the reign of Queen Anne the Post of Waterloo was fixed upon by the celebrated Duke of Marlborough, with the view of annihilating the power of Louis the XIVth. at that time (like Bonaparte), the great troubler of Europe ! And as his Grace is said " never to have fought a battle which was not won, nor to have besieged a town that was not taken," he seems deeply to regret that the perverseness of his military associates prevented his reaping the usual laurels on this occasion. It is, however, singular that the Duke of Wellington, in conjunction with similar allies, should a century after, in the reign of George the Third, (June 18, 1815) consecrate this same Post of Waterloo by a signal victory for the restoration of the descendants of Louis the XIVth., as the best means of securing the peace and happiness of the Continental Powers ! This is is a curious fact, and the more worthy of attention as a parallel between these two distinguished British Generals hath been drawn by writers of the present day. Such is the mutation of human affairs—such the revolution of empires. May the awful and decisive battle of Waterloo ensure the permanent tranquillity of the civilized world! Torrents of blood have been poured forth in the unrighteous career of ambition. It was time, as at the birth of our Saviour, that *the Temple of Janus* should be closed, and that PEACE, the legacy of the Redeemer to his disciples, should diffuse her blessings among the nations of the earth. I am, Sir,

Yours respectfully,

JOHN EVANS.

Mr. Wright on the Unitarian Society
at Thorne.
Wisbeach, March 7, 1816.

SIR,

THE Unitarians at Thorne, in
Yorkshire, having, through the
medium of the Monthly Repository [xi.
120.], made known their intention of
building a meeting-house, and solicited the aid of the friends of the Unitarian
cause in the undertaking, a short
account of the origin, progress, present state and prospects of the Unitarian Society in that town and its
vicinity, may not be unacceptable to
your readers.

In the summer of 1805, I first visited Thorne ; it was in consequence
of a letter received by my worthy
friend, Mr. Vidler, informing him
that some persons in that town and
neighbourhood, were favourable to
the doctrine of the universal restoration ; but had never heard any preacher who taught it, and having heard
that a preacher of that doctrine sometimes travelled in Lincolnshire, they
were anxious he should visit them. On
my arrival I found them all Trinitarians, and learned that most of them belonged to the new connexion of Methodists, and that they differed from their
brethren only on the subject of future
punishment, having adopted the sentiments of the late Mr. Winchester.

During my first visit I preached on
the love of God, on the doctrine of
reconciliation, and on future punishment. The place of meeting was a
barn ; a crowd of people attended;
and a considerable impression seemed
to be made. I spent two evenings in
conversation with a pretty large party,
and found, though many persons were
full of inquiry, they laboured under
strong prejudices; I had occasion to recal to mind a maxim which I have always found useful, i. e. to despair of
nothing which it is practicable to attempt. As a proof of what their
views and feelings then were, I will
mention two things. The good woman at the house where I lodged
asked, " Are you an Arian?" I replied, " No, I never was an Arian."
She then said, " If you were an
Arian I dare not let you sleep in my
house." Dr. Priestley's name being
mentioned, I perceived it excited
alarm. This led me to ask if any of
them had either known the Doctor
or read any of his writings? They

answered in the negative. I then
gave them some account of his character, and of the manner in which
ment he had received. This led some
to think they had received false impressions respecting him. Having
proceeded as far as seemed prudent at
that time, before I left them I said,
" I have told you as much as I think
will be useful at present, if I live to
see you again I shall have something
further to say to you," and exhorted
them to keep their minds open to
conviction, and not to be afraid of
examining any subject.

About six months after I visited
them again, and found their prejudices had been greatly alarmed by the
books which had been sent them.
They had even consulted together
whether it would not be best to return the books and desire me to visit
them no more; but good sense prevailed so far as to lead them to resolve
to read the books first ; a first, inclined them to a second, reading ; and
I had now the pleasure to find several of them become Unitarians.
I again preached several discourses
among them, and found, though the
multitude was fled, which was no
more than I expected, the number of
converts was sufficient to keep the
standard erect, and become the foundation of a society. About this time
a donation of books was sent them
from York, including some of Dr.
Priestley's works ; these were read
with much attention, and contributed
to their progress in knowledge and
establishment in the Unitarian Christian doctrine.

Till the year 1810 their number
increased but little : they, however,
persevered in their inquiries after
truth, openly avowed their religious
sentiments, held meetings among
themselves and did what they could
to edify one another, and instruct
their neighbours. I usually visited
them twice in a year, preached several times each visit ; sometimes in
                    ouring villages, and
assisted in settling any differences
which had arisen among them. Several of the first converts were removed by death ; a few new ones
were added. They had from the first
many difficulties to encounter. They
were poor, unlearned people. Their
religious neighbours, who thought the

doctrines they espoused damnable heresies, attacked them on every side; but they soon became equal to the contest with their opposers, by never attempting to dispute about words, nor to meddle with criticism, to which they were utterly inadequate; but always keeping close to the plain facts and positive declarations of scripture, which all Christians admit, and bringing every controverted point to the test of those universally admitted facts and declarations.

In the autumn of 1809, a person of respectable character, an avowed unbeliever, came from a neighbouring village to hear me preach at Thorne, and was much affected by what he heard. This led him to an examination of the true Christian doctrine, and issued in his avowing himself an Unitarian Christian. His conversion, and firm and candid exertions to promote what he believes to be divine truth, with the influence of his worth of character, brought many other persons to attend, and produced an important accession to the Unitarians at Thorne. During the last two years, several respectable persons in that town have received the Unitarian doctrine, and are zealous for its success. Thus after occasional labours and exertions for more than ten years, things are come to that promising state which renders it not only desirable, but highly necessary to have an Unitarian chapel at Thorne, and a minister placed there, who might act as a Missionary in the surrounding district, where much inquiry is excited, and many openings for public preaching are found. The prospect is highly promising, and the success of the cause in the country between Gainsborough, Doncaster and Selby, will materially depend on what is done at Thorne. I speak from personal knowledge, and feel very deeply concerned for the success of the plan now projected by the friends in that place.

The expense of erecting the proposed chapel, &c. is already before your readers. It must be admitted the plan proposed is economical, and the sum raised by the people among themselves as large as can be expected, considering they are most of them poor. The plan of building has not been resolved on without much deliberation, and a rational prospect of its answering the end designed. Meetings for the worship of the one God have been held, and well conducted, for several years, in a private house; but many persons who would attend in a chapel will not go regularly to a private house, even if it were large enough to contain them.

I trust it will not be thought improper, for one who has happily succeeded in forming the above society, and assisting in bringing it to its present promising state, to solicit, on behalf of the brethren at Thorne, the pecuniary assistance of the friends of Unitarianism in different parts of the kingdom, that they may be enabled to complete the building they are about to erect for the exclusive worship of the one and only God. Permit me to do this, with much deference and respect, through the medium of your valuable Repository; which will much oblige, dear Sir,

Yours, &c.
R. WRIGHT.

On Poetical Scepticism.

No. I.

" Sure he that made us with such large discourse,
Looking before and after, gave us not
This capability and GODLIKE REASON
To rust in us unus'd."

SHAKESPEARE.

" So charming is divine philosophy,
Not harsh nor crabbed as dull fools suppose,
But musical as is Apollo's lute."

MILTON.

SIR,

THERE exists, at the present day, a curious species of infidelity, which, although not often obtruded on the public, has recently made considerable progress among amiable and virtuous minds. It seems, therefore, to deserve a more regular exposure than it has yet received, since it deprives those of the holiest consolations of the gospel who are best able to feel and most worthy to enjoy them. Though somewhat difficult to be defined, it may be described as a substitution of poetical feeling for religious principle—an avowed dislike of truth—and a contempt for all belief in which any share is allowed to the reasoning faculties. The defenders of these singular paradoxes, which seem to have their origin in Germany, express great veneration for Calvinism, which they esteem as a beautiful creation of the fancy, and which they regard with peculiar favour as not built upon any *rational* foundation. Of Unitarianism they express the utmost dislike and scorn. They deem every interference of reason with system as arrogant and profane. Religion is thrown back by them into the regions of imagination and mystery, as something too sacred to be examined or mingled with the business of life, and too majestic to be submitted to our choice or approval. At the same time, their reverence refines it into a phantom—a gorgeous dream—which would vanish if too nearly inspected. They one moment declare the opinions they eulogize as above all scrutiny, and the next acknowledge they could not endure it. It is their principle, therefore, to oppose all serious inquiry; to inculcate love where there can be no respect; to set up a kind of sentimental admiration in the place of belief; and to inveigh against all attempts to discover theological truth as hardening the heart, clouding the fancy, and throwing a chillness over all the social affections.

In exposing the fallacy of this novel scepticism, I shall not enter into many of the important points suggested by the inquiry. It would lead to a discussion too extensive were I to aim at shadowing forth the necessary connexion between truth and virtue, at shewing that imagination has increased in lustre in proportion as knowledge has extended, or at proving that genius is independent of opinion and our feelings distinct from our creeds. My object will be first to maintain that the Deist has no source of enjoyment which rational Christianity would diminish; and secondly, to prove that, even as a matter of poetical association, the doctrines of Unitarianism are far superior to that system of popular theology which the sceptic fancies he admires.

While the adversaries of rational investigation deride the scantiness of the Unitarian creed, they boast that they feel all the magnificence of Calvinism, and enjoy what the more credulous believe; and this pleasure they assert to be infinitely superior to that which results from a conviction of less mysterious doctrines. But in what does it consist? On whatever prin-

apply them to their own condition. They cannot even fancy they regard them in the same light with those who look on them as inseparable from their existence; who repose on them as their solace under the cares of life, and rely on them as the support of their dying hours. But the assertions of orthodoxy must be either true or false; and if our opponents enjoy them not as true they must if they admire them at all, admire them as a fable. And this, in plain language, is the whole basis of the undefined emotion which constitutes their religion. They contemplate the orthodox system as a prodigious creation of human genius, and as a vision in which the terrible and sublime are strikingly contrasted. So that their reverence for the objects they designate as sacred places them on a level with the dreams of Mahomet, and the mythologies of Homer.

What is it then which is offered us in the room of Christian hope? Nothing surely but what we may possess in full perfection with it. The poetical delight to be received from the contemplation of beautiful fictions need not be placed in the stead of a conviction of divine realities. To the enjoyment of fable *as such* it is absurd to require a belief in its actual existence. Who ever supposed that to relish the " Midsummer's Night's Dream," or the " Tempest," it was necessary to believe in the sportive fairies that " creep into acorn cups and hide them there," or in the pure and delicate spirits that float in the air with strange music? And, on the same principle, why must we admit the devil into our creeds to enjoy the sublimities of Paradise Lost, any more than satyrs and witchcraft in order to be enchanted with Comus? Though rejected as a religion, all the wonders of Pagan superstition have charms for us still. In the grandest regions of imagination, beyond the limits of this material world, they stand as fresh and as glorious as ever. Time has passed over them without witnessing their decay. There Hercules still rests on his club and Apollo tunes his immortal lyre. There Proteus rises from the sea; there old Triton " blows his wreathed horn," and there the Fates in awful silence, regulate the variously-coloured thread of human existence. But will these imaginations diminish our anxiety for our own eternal condition? Will they be less " assoiled from the grossness of present time," because our reliance is fixed on the rock of ages and our hopes have their resting place in heaven?

But it is boldly asserted that a spirit of inquiry into religious truth is incompatible with all poetical feeling—that it tends to make those who indulge it hard-hearted—and degrade them from imaginative into mere reasoning beings. In answer to these assertions it is not necessary to contend for the superiority of truth over fancy, it is quite sufficient to shew that both may exist together without the least injury to either. Our opponents themselves would exercise their reason in all the concerns of life; and would esteem those madmen who should refuse to apply it to any thing but religion. It is strange then that it should be debarred from the noblest of its uses, from the objects which are most worthy of its powers, and most nearly allied to the divinity which is stamped upon it. And surely it would be strange if heaven had endowed us with both intelligent and creative faculties, one of which must necessarily be left inactive, in order to the perfection of the other. And what luxury of imagination is there, which a Christian, whose belief is founded on understanding is unfitted to enjoy? He would no more allow reason to interfere with the delights of his fancy, than he will suffer poetry to take the place of conviction. He can muse with as delicious a suspension of thought over the still fountain, and people every lovely scene with images as beautiful and unearthly as if he had never investigated the doctrines of scripture. As far as respects the contemplation of the superstitions and errors of mankind he will have an advantage over the most poetical sceptic. For his religion teaches him to see a " spirit of good" in them all—to look at the dim glimpses of heaven which have shone through pompous ceremonials with gratitude —to trace the sweet affections which have flourished beneath the shade of institutions in themselves unholy—

and to hail the dawnings of imperfect light as the welcome harbingers of an unclouded day. An Unitarian is the only sectary who makes charity an article of his creed. And yet he must be scornfully accused of scorn, abused for want of kind-heartedness, and reproached for believing too little, and having, therefore, no power of enjoyment, by those who believe nothing in order to enjoy every thing.

Poetical fancies might have a better claim to take the place of religious conviction if, like it, they could last for ever. But alas! life cannot be all a holiday dream. Death must separate our dearest companions from us, and compel us to weep over their tomb. Will it then be enough to strew the grave with flowers, and vent our sorrows in the melody of woe;—or will it not be some additional relief to be able to cherish a sure and certain hope of meeting them in happiness hereafter? And even if we could pass along wrapt in one delicious vision through this vale of tears, we must awake to die! Surely in that awful moment when heart and flesh fail us, it will be some consolation to think that we are safe in the arms of the Almighty—that our noblest faculties will revive to an immortal youth—that our loveliest visions will be more than realized—and that imagination will expatiate for ever in those glorious regions, to which, in its happiest moments, it delighted to aspire.

S. N. D.

P. S. With your permission, I propose in a few essays in your succeeding numbers, to expose the other dogma of modern sceptics—that Calvinism is a more poetical system than Unitarianism—by comparing the leading doctrines of both, not as it respects their *truth*, but the beautiful associations which may be thrown around them and the kind affections they cherish and mature.

GLEANINGS; OR, SELECTIONS AND REFLECTIONS MADE IN A COURSE OF GENERAL READING.

No. CCXLV.

Self-election and Heresy of Pope John XXII.

Mezeray, an exact writer, describes the election of this Pope very pleasantly, and says that the Cardinals being shut up in the conclave by Philip, could not any otherwise agree upon the election of a Pope than by their joint referring it to the single voice of James D'Ossat, Cardinal and Bishop of Port : he without any scruple at all named *himself*, to the great astonishment of all the Conclave, who nevertheless approved of him ; and so he took the name of John XXII. and reigned quietly eleven years or thereabouts, without ever having his election questioned or doubted.

This John the Two and Twentieth declared *that the souls of the dead were neither happy nor miserable till the day of judgment;* which opinion was generally held in the former age. But the university of Paris (says *Clarendon, Relig. and Pol.* i. 34.) having more exactly examined this point, corrected the Holy Father in it, as Mezeray says, and thereupon the king Philip of Valois, writ to the Pope in these terms : *Que s'il ne se retractoit*

il le feroit ardre. Whether he was converted by this threat, or convinced in his conscience; the Pope did not only change his opinion, but published an act of retractation. So far was the holy chair from being infallible when it rested in Avignon.

No. CCXLVI.
Eighty Thousand Jacobins.

In England and Scotland, I compute that those of adult age, not declining in life, of tolerable leisure for such discussions, and of some means of information, more or less, and who are above menial dependance, may amount to about four hundred thousand. Of these four hundred thousand political citizens, I look upon one-fifth, or about *eighty thousand*, to be pure Jacobins; utterly incapable of amendment; objects of eternal vigilance, and when they break out, of legal constraint.

Burke's Letters on a Regicide Peace.

No. CCXLVII.
John Bradshaw.

It is to this day problematical and can never be ascertained whether the bodies of *Cromwell* and *Bradshaw* were actually taken up and dishonoured at the Restoration. It is in secret tradition that *Bradshaw* was conveyed to *Jamaica*. His epitaph is descriptive of him and full of spirit. In a public print of 1775, it was said,

The following inscription was made out three years ago on the cannon, near which the ashes of President Bradshaw were lodged, on the top of a high hill, near *Martha Bay*, in *Jamaica*, to avoid the rage against the Regicides exhibited at the Restoration.

Stranger !
Ere thou pass, contemplate this Cannon,
Nor regardless be told
That near its base, lies deposited the Dust of
JOHN BRADSHAW,
Who nobly superior to all selfish regards,
Despising alike the pageantry of courtly splendour,
The blast of calumny and the terrors of royal vengeance,
Presided in the Illustrious Band of Heroes and Patriots,
Who fairly and openly adjudged
Charles Stuart,
Tyrant of England,
To a public and exemplary Death,
Thereby presenting to the amazed World,
And transmitting down through applauding Ages,
The most glorious Example,
Of Unshaken Virtue, Love of Freedom and Impartial Justice,
Ever exhibited on the blood-stained Theatre of human Action.
O ! Reader,
Pass not on till thou hast blessed his Memory :
And never, never forget,
THAT REBELLION TO TYRANTS IS OBEDIENCE TO GOD.

[From Dr. Ezra Styles's History of the Three Judges, Whalley, Goffe and Dixwell, who fled to America and concealed themselves to avoid the Fury of Kingly Violence. 12mo. Hartford, America. 1794.]

REVIEW.

" Still pleased to praise, yet not afraid to blame."—POPE.

ART. I.—*Poems, by William Cowper, of the Inner Temple, Esq. Vol. III. containing his Posthumous Poetry, and a Sketch of his Life.* By his kinsman, John Johnson, LL.D., Rector of Yaxham with Welborne, in Norfolk. London: Printed for Rivingtons, &c. &c. 1815. 8vo. pp. 434.

"WHAT is Poetry?" inquired Boswell[*] of his *guide, philosopher and friend.* "Why, Sir," answered Johnson, " it is much easier to say what it is not. We all *know* what light is; but it is not easy to tell what it is." To hazard a definition of Poetry,' after such a judgment, might be presumptuous: let us satisfy ourselves with the account given of it by this great writer. " Poetry," he observes,[†] " is the art of uniting pleasure with truth, by calling imagination to the help of reason." If, by this statement, he intended to define the exalted art of which he speaks, some critical objections might be taken to his language; which, nevertheless, is for all useful purposes sufficiently exact.

That poetry may communicate pleasure, two objects must be kept in view by the poet: he must raise his diction above mean and ordinary modes of speech; and, at the same time, he must address himself to the associations of ideas existing in the minds of those readers whose approbation is substantial praise. Many of our poets and critics have been extravagant in their respective efforts and decisions. Some of them have bestowed a disproportionate care on splendid images and a well-poized and agreeable versification. Others have become vulgar and insipid, through an affectation of *simplicity:* it is not that they are destitute of *genius,* but that they fail in *taste.* We may admit, though not without obvious exceptions and qualifications, that the " materials" of poetry " are to be found in every subject which can interest the human mind."[‡] Yet, surely, it will not follow that " the language of conversation in the middle and lower classes of society is adapted to the purposes of poetic pleasure." To afford pleasure, poetry must call *imagination* to the aid of reason: fancy must create, or at least combine, arrange and select the " materials." The votary of the muse may avoid " the gaudiness and inane phraseology of many modern writers," without deviating, however, into rusticity and childishness. Facts disprove the proposition that the customary style of conversation in the humbler ranks of life is calculated for poetic uses. We are silent concerning recent exemplifications of this doctrine. From instances more remote it certainly receives no support. In what estimation do we hold the pastorals of *Ambrose Philips*[||]? By whom will *Swift's* " humble petition of Frances Harris to the Lords Justices of Ireland" be dignified with the name of *Poetry?* We could refer to many metrical compositions which *as pictures of ancient manners* are highly attractive, but of which the dialogue would otherwise be disgusting. For the poet, like the painter, must copy *general,* not *individual,* nature. His employment supposes discrimination: he must elevate what is mean, he must soften what is harsh; and these objects he will not reach if his style is familiar and provincial. The poetry of a cultivated age, must itself be cultivated; since it can yield no delight unless it correspond with the habits of thought and feeling, of taste and reading, which distinguish the times and the people to whom its productions are submitted.[¶] Faithfulness in the " delineation of human passions, human characters and human incidents" may exist in combination with lofty and harmonious numbers, beautiful and

---

[*] Life of Johnson. 8vo. (ed. 3rd.) Vol. iii. 37.

[†] Works, (Murphy's Ed.) ix. 160.

[‡] Lyrical Ballads (1798): *Advertisement.*

[||] Guardian, No. XL.

[¶] Poetry should be something more than *true eloquence in metre.* See Mason's Gray, (1778) Vol. iv. 32. Note.

majestic images and a truly poetical skill: it is the union of these excellencies which causes *Homer* to be the poet of all countries and periods.

The most popular of his translators has been accused of " a monotonous and cloying versification :"* and ridicule is attempted to be thrown on

—his cuckoo-song verses, half up and half down."

No ridicule however can deprive him of his well-earned fame. It may be true that his pauses are not sufficiently varied. In this respect he is, no doubt, inferior to some of his predecessors. Still, he has redeemed the fault by various and characteristic charms: nor is it accurate to speak of " his rhyming facilities ;" it being perfectly ascertained that his lines were laboured into ease, and, by repeated efforts, polished into elegance. If it has been the fate of Pope to have injudicious imitators, it were, nevertheless, heartily to be wished that the care and diligence which he bestowed on his versification were copied by many of his censors.

Let not our readers consider these observations as misplaced in a critical notice of the poetry of *Cowper.* This amiable writer holds, we think, a middle rank between the race of poets who have formed their versification on that of Pope, and those who introduce the language of common life into compositions professing to be poetical. Besides, Cowper is a favourite and popular author. His pages interest readers of nearly all classes. And though it be readily admitted that " the magic of his song" is to be found in his virtues; yet, to have been so generally acceptable in this capricious age, he must have possessed intrinsic excellence as a poet.

In those of Cowper's poems to which he owes his high reputation, he is neither mean and infantine, on the one hand, nor fastidiously attentive to cadence and ornament, on the other.† Doubtless, some of his lines are harsh and unfinished : and there

are those of his productions which partake greatly of the nature of the *sermo pedestris.* Yet where he trifles it is at once with dignity and ease : his descriptions of natural objects exhibit a proof of his having looked through creation with a poet's eye ; and his choice of topics, his lively and faithful pictures of human manners, his keen and delicate and playful satire, his ardent sensibility, his quick and graceful transitions, his skill in painting those domestic scenes and retired employments which he loved —these are his appropriate recommendations. He who has once read Cowper, is desirous of reading him again, and even of becoming familiar with his strains. There are writers whom we can enjoy only in certain states of our minds : Cowper *always* gains admittance to us ; he is our companion and instructor, he can soothe and engage us, at every hour.

An additional volume of the poems of such an author was sure of raising expectation: if that expectation be not gratified, the cause of the disappointment appears in the declaration of the respectable editor, who says,

" It is incumbent on me to apprize the reader, that by far the greater part of the poems, to which I have now the honour to introduce him, have been already published by Mr. Hayley," *Preface.*

In the *Dedication,* too, he speaks of " the few additions inserted in this collection." Among these additions, which should have been distinctly marked, we perceive an " Address to Miss ——, on reading the Prayer for Indifference,"‡ some Latin translations from the Poems of *V. Bourne,* and some English ones of the Epigrams of *Owen ;* together with a few minor pieces. The translations of the Latin and Italian Poems of *Milton,* are here presented again to the world; notwithstanding they had been published in 1808, in a quarto volume. We confess therefore that we are doubtful of the necessity of this part of the undertaking of the Rector of Yaxham, as well as of the propriety of entitling the larger portion of the volume, the *Posthumous* Poetry of Cowper.‖ In selecting the produc-

---

* Feast of the Poets, ii. 27.

† —" simplicity, though frequently naked, is not consequently poor: for nakedness may be that of a Grace, and not of a beggar." Headley's Introd. to *Select Beauties,* &c. (2nd. ed.) Introd. p. xx.

‡ By Mr. Greville.

‖ Though, strictly speaking, it be *posthumous,* yet the word, so used, conveys

tions that were previously unpublished, some readers will regard the editor as sufficiently bountiful. But we feel so greatly indebted to him for his sketch of his kinsman's life, which we shall soon notice, that we are not disposed to make any complaints or pass any censures.

Cowper's admirable good sense qualified him for placing in a clear and striking light every subject in which the manners of men are concerned: nor would it be easy to mention any poem, of its class, at once so instructive and interesting as the verses on *Friendship*, preserved, though not for the first time printed, in the present volume. The following stanzas, in particular, are deserving of being impressed on the memory, and will indeed be very easily retained:

" As similarity of mind,
Or something not to be defin'd,
 First rivets our attention ;
So, manners decent and polite,
The same we practis'd at first sight,
 Must save it from declension.

The man who hails you Tom—or Jack,
And proves, by thumping on your back,
 His sense of your great merit,
Is such a friend, that one had need
Be very much his friend indeed,
 To pardon, or to bear it."

In these lines there are singular justness of thought, fidelity of description, poignancy of satire and sprightliness and terseness of expression. *Theophrastus* himself was never more successful.

The *Montes Glaciales*, a truly classical poem, was written by Cowper in 1799, at a time when his health, both of body and mind, was considerably impaired. But he appears to have been fond of composing Latin verses, which he framed with a readiness and felicity demonstrative of his having left Westminster school with " scholastic attainments of the first order."

His lines *on the loss of the Royal George* [Aug. 29, 1782], he translated into the language of ancient Rome: and he has well preserved the simplicity, pathos and force of the original; an elegiac ballad of uncommon merit. Let the rendering of the following stanzas be a specimen:

the idea of these poems not having been before published.

" Toll for the brave !
 Brave Kempenfelt is gone ;
His last sea-fight is fought ;
 His work of glory done.

It was not in the battle ;
 No tempest gave the shock ;
She sprang no fatal leak ;
 She ran upon no rock.

His sword was in its sheath ;
 His fingers held the pen,
When Kempenfelt went down,
 With twice four hundred men."

Magne, qui nomen, licèt incanorum,
Traditum ex multis atavis tulisti !
At tuos olim memorabit ævum
 Omne triumphos.

Non hyems illos furibunda mersit,
Non mari in clauso scopuli latentes,
Fissa non rimis abies nec atrox
 Abstulit ensis.

Navitæ sed tum nimium jocosi
Voce fallebant hilari laborem,
Et quiescebat, calamoque dextram Im-
 pleverat heros." (96.)

Some of our readers will here call to mind the frequent recurrence of the compellation *Magne* in the *Pharsalia* of *Lucan*, and the dignified and plaintive manner in which that poet applies it.

With the life of Cowper the public had already been made acquainted by Mr. Hayley. There was still wanting, however, the sketch of it which Dr. Johnson has exhibited in the present volume. He speaks of this composition with the greatest modesty. Yet, in truth, it possesses distinguished excellence as a biographical narrative, and is characterized not only by faithfulness of delineation, but also by that simple and artless, that lively and decorously minute relation of circumstances, which renders us, for the time, the companions of Cowper and his kinsman. In illustration of this remark we transcribe a passage descriptive of some incidents on the journey of the poet and of Mrs. Unwin from Weston into Norfolk ; whither they were attended by the editor: lii.

" As it was highly important to guard against the effect of noise and tumult on the shattered nerves of the desponding traveller, care was taken that a relay of horses should be ready on the skirts of the towns of Bedford and Cambridge, by which means he passed through those places without stopping. On the evening of the first day, the quiet village of St.

Neot's, near Eaton, afforded as convenient a resting place for the party as could have been devised; and the peaceful moon-light scenery of the spot, as Cowper walked with his kinsman up and down the church-yard, had so favourable an effect on his spirits, that he conversed with him, with much composure, on the subject of Thomson's Seasons, and the circumstances under which they were probably written."

In August, 1795, the two invalids, together with Dr. Johnson, went " to the village of Mundsley, on the Norfolk Coast; having previously resided, for a very short time, at North Tuddenham, in that county." However, " the effect of air and exercise on the dejected poet being by no means such as his friends had hoped, change of scene was resorted to as the next expedient:" lvii.

" About six miles to the south of Mundsley, and also on the coast, is a village called 'Happisburgh,' or Hasboro', which, in the days of his youth Cowper had visited from Catfield, the residence of his mother's brother. An excursion therefore to this place was projected, and happily accomplished, by sea; a mode of conveyance which had at least novelty to recommend it; but a gale of wind having sprung up soon after his arrival there, the return by water was unexpectedly precluded, and he was under the necessity of effecting it on foot through the neighbouring villages. To the agreeable surprise of his conductor, this very considerable walk was performed with scarcely any fatigue to the invalid."

The party afterwards took up their residence at Dunham Lodge, in the vicinity of Swaffham. Here (lix),

" As the season advanced, the amusement of walking being rendered impracticable, and his spirits being by no means sufficiently recovered to admit of his resuming either his pen or his books, the only resource which was left to the poet, was to listen incessantly to the reading of his companion. The kind of books that appeared most, and indeed solely to attract him, were works of fiction; and so happy was the influence of these in rivetting his attention, and abstracting him, of course, from the contemplation of his miseries, that he discovered a peculiar satisfaction when a production of fancy of more than ordinary length, was introduced by his kinsman. This was no sooner perceived, than he was furnished with the voluminous pages of Richardson, to which he listened with the greater interest, as he had been personally acquainted with that ingenious writer."

" At this time, the tender spirit of Cow-

per clung exceedingly to those about him, and seemed to be haunted with a continual dread that they would leave him alone in his solitary mansion. Sunday, therefore, was a day of more than ordinary apprehension to him; as the furthest of his kinsman's churches being fifteen miles from the Lodge, he was necessarily absent during the whole of the Sabbath. On these occasions, it was the constant practice of the dejected poet to listen frequently on the steps of the hall-door, for the barking of dogs at a farm house, which in the stillness of the night, though at nearly the distance of two miles, invariably announced the approach of his companion." lx.

We cannot resist the temptation of making a few more extracts :

" —in the month of April [1796] Mrs. Unwin received a visit from her daughter and son-in-law, Mr. and Mrs. Powley. The tender and even filial attention which the compassionate invalid had never ceased to exercise towards his aged and infirm companion, was now shared by her affectionate relatives; to whom it could not but be a gratifying spectacle to see their venerable parent so assiduously watched

emplary pers

tary custom of reading a chapter in the Bible to their mother, every morning before she rose, was continued by the writer of this Memoir, who, as the dejected poet always visited the chamber of his poor old friend, the moment he had finished his breakfast, took care to read the chapter at that time." lxi.

" —Being encouraged by the result of the above experiment, the conductor of the devotions of this retired family ventured in the course of a few days, to let the members of it meet for prayers in the room where Cowper was, instead of assembling in another apartment, as they hitherto had done, under the influence, as it proved, of a misconception, with regard to his ability to attend the service. On the first occurrence of this new arrangement, of which no intimation had been previously given him, he was preparing to leave the room, but was prevailed on to resume his seat, by a word of soothing and whispered entreaty." lxii.

We pass over the narrative of the occasion of Cowper's engaging in a revisal of his *Homer:* the account is deeply interesting, but has long been in possession of the public.*

------

* Preface to the 2nd ed. of Cowper's Translation of the Iliad.

Who can be unaffected in reading the following anecdote?

"—as a faithful servant of his dying friend [Mrs. Unwin] and himself was opening the window of his chamber on the morning of the day of her decease, he said to her, in a tone of voice at once plaintive, and full of anxiety as to what might be the situation of his aged companion, *Sally, is there life above stairs?*" lxv.

Of the last moments of Cowper his kinsman has left a record, from which we make a single extract: lxxvii.

"In the course of the night [of Thursday, April 24th, 1800], when he appeared to be exceedingly exhausted, some refreshment was presented to him by Miss Browne. From a persuasion, however, that nothing could ameliorate his feelings, though without any apparent impression that the hand of death was already upon him, he rejected the cordial with these words, the very last that he was heard to utter, *What can it signify?*"

"At five in the morning, of Friday the 25th, a deadly change in his features was observed to take place. He remained in an insensible state from that time till about five minutes before five in the afternoon, when he ceased to breathe."

The assiduity, the wisdom, the affection and the tenderness with which Dr. Johnson soothed the dejected spirits of his relative, do much honour to his principles and feelings, and claim the gratitude of the numerous admirers of Cowper, as a poet and a man. Though he is solely desirous of directing our regard to his kinsman, yet we cannot be insensible to the illustration of his own excellencies presented in this sketch. His theological creed appears to be that of his relation. This creed, however, is not obtruded on the reader: nor is it defended with bitterness and rancour; and we can respect the motives which dictated the following paragraphs and the spirit which breathes in them— though we may not fully assent to the reasoning they contain: xvii.

"A most erroneous and unhappy idea has occupied the minds of some persons, that those views of Christianity which Cowper adopted, and of which, when enjoying the intervals of reason, he was so bright an ornament,* had actually contributed to excite the malady with which he was afflicted. It is capable of the clearest demonstration that nothing was

further from the truth. On the contrary, all those alleviations of sorrow, those delightful anticipations of heavenly rest, those healing consolations to a wounded spirit, of which he was permitted to taste at the periods when uninterrupted reason resumed its sway, were unequivocally to be ascribed to the operation of those very principles and views of religion, which, in the instance before us, have been charged with producing so opposite an effect. The primary aberrations of his mental faculties were wholly to be attributed to other causes. But the time was at hand, when, by the happy interposition of a gracious Providence, he was to be the favoured subject of a double emancipation. The captivity of his reason was about to terminate; and a bondage, though hitherto unmentioned, yet of a much longer standing, was on the point of being exchanged for the most delightful of all freedom."

The event to which the biographer of Cowper alludes, took place on July 25th, 1764: xix.

"—Before he left the room in which he had breakfasted, he observed a Bible lying in the window-seat. He took it up. Except in a single instance, and that two months before, he had not ventured to open one, since the early days of his abode at St. Alban's. But the time was now come when he might do it to purpose. The profitable perusal of that divine book had been provided for in the most effectual manner, by the restoration at once of the powers of his understanding, and the superadded gift of a spiritual discernment. Under these favourable circumstances, he opened the sacred volume at that passage of the epistle to the Romans where the apostle says, that Jesus Christ is 'set forth to be a propitiation through faith in his blood, to declare his righteousness for the remission of sins that are past, through the forbearance of God.' To use the expression employed by Cowper himself in a written document, from which this portion of his history is extracted, he *received strength to believe it*;† to see the suitableness of the atonement to his own necessity, and to embrace the gospel with gratitude and joy." xx.

We doubt not that "the *primary* aberrations of" this poet's "mental faculties were wholly to be attributed to other causes" than any theological sentiments whatever. But the return and the continuance of his disorder seem to have been owing, in some

---

* There is an incongruity between the words *views* and *ornament*. Rev.

† It appears that Cowper was prepared for the impression by previous trains of thought and feeling. Rev.

degree at least, to the peculiarities of his religious creed. What is the testimony of his last original composition in this volume—*The Cast-Away?* 329. We leave the decision with our readers; only remarking, in the language of Dr. Johnson, that Cowper's malady, " while for many subsequent years [after 1770] it admitted of his exhibiting the most masterly and delightful display of poetical, epistolary, and conversational ability, on the greatest variety of subjects, it constrained him from that period, both in his conversation and letters, studiously to abstain from every allusion of a religious nature." xxvii.

Our own acquaintance with Cowper's poetry, was occasioned by the publication of his *Task:* our admiration of it has been cherished and increased by a repeated perusal of his volumes. That as a writer he has some defects, it were useless to dispute : these however are of little account, when weighed against his excellencies. It is seldom, after all, that we meet with so much taste and genius united with a spirit so devotional, benevolent and pure. On this ground we recommend Cowper's pages to our younger readers in particular, and entreat them, in estimating his merits, to make just allowances for the occasional influence of a melancholy imagination and of what we humbly think an unscriptural theology. The improvement of the mental powers as well as of the heart, can scarcely fail to be the consequence of familiarity with a writer who is at once simple and correct, lively and energetic, moral and pious. In the present age we have no abundance of models of good composition, either in poetry or prose. Gaudiness is often substituted for ornament : and in many instances metaphors are pronounced *fine* merely on account of their being extravagant, unnatural and confused. *Propter hoc ipsum, quod sunt prava, laudantur.*[*]

━━━

ART. II.—*The History and Antiquities of Dissenting Churches and Meeting-Houses, in London, Westminster and Southwark ; including the Lives of their Ministers from the Rise of Nonconformity to the*

present time. With an Appendix on the Origin, Progress and Present State of Christianity in Britain. 8vo. 4 vols. Portraits. Button and Son. 1808—1814.

SOME of our periodical critics affect to smile at the application of the term " Antiquities" to Meeting-houses. Dr. Milner would be equally amused with its being bestowed on any thing belonging to the Protestant Church of England. Some meeting-houses are ancient compared with others that are modern. Protestant Episcopal Churches are of a little greyer age ; but for antiquity in its most venerable sense we must go to periods before the Reformation, and even before Christianity if not before Judaism itself. Westminster Abbey is of yesterday compared with the altars of Stonehenge and the pyramids of Egypt.

In point of age as well as of architecture, meeting-houses are indeed mean subjects of history ; and in this view, no one will condescend to regard them : but there is a light in which they are exceedingly interesting, and invite and will reward the historian : they have been places of voluntary assembly to such Christians as have followed the guidings of conscience, disdained and scorned the slavery of the mind, and asserted religious liberty, in the midst of perils and by the severest sacrifices. In such places have been found men of eminent biblical learning, of powerful eloquence and of unsullied lives ; the best advocates of divine revelation, the most successful expositors of evangelical truth, the truest benefactors of their species ; reformers, confessors, martyrs and saints. Their history is the history of the Bible, of sound faith and real virtue, and is in our judgment more abundant in all that awakens, purifies and exalts the mind than the history of churches spread over empires and ages in which implicit faith on the one part and ecclesiastical tyranny on the other have bound down the human mind in ignorance, and cramped and fettered the heart, and thus prevented the highest exercises of the understanding and the most kindly operation of the affections. The human mind awake and active, in the humblest condition of our nature, is a far nobler sight than it can present when laid asleep

━━━

[*] Quinct. Instit. L. ii. Sect. 5.

even in the soft and stately repose of palaces.

With this unfashionable association of ideas with meeting-houses, where the mind fashions the church and not the church the mind, we have been from the first not a little anxious for the success of Mr. Wilson's design. No history of " Dissenting Churches" was ever before drawn up, and it is evident that in a very little time all traces of some of them would have been worn out! All that could be collected by diligence is here recorded with regard to the churches in the cities of London and Westminster and the Borough of Southwark. The author's design extended farther ; he had planned and prepared materials for a history of all the Dissenting places of worship in the Metropolis and the circumjacent villages, which would have filled another volume ; but a scanty subscription-list, of scarcely three hundred persons, afforded not encouragement enough for the undertaking. This fact is by no means creditable to the Dissenters. It is not perhaps too late ·to repair the neglect, and we take up these volumes with some faint hope of exciting such attention to the work as may dispose the author to pursue and complete his design.

Mr. Wilson, we understand, is now pursuing a learned profession,· but was engaged at the period of the commencement of his work in a considerable book-trade in London, which we mention only to shew that he had opportunities rarely enjoyed by authors of collecting materials for his history, which lay scattered in numberless single sermons and pamphlets. These authorities are carefully acknowledged, and of themselves form an index to the literary history of the Dissenters.

The first qualification of the historian of Dissenting Churches is a spirit of religious impartiality. Of the value of this, our author is fully aware, and remarks very justly (Pref. p. v.), that " to arrive at truth, we must divest ourselves of sectarian prejudices, weigh well the opinions of others and be diffident of our own judgment," and that " true wisdom is always allied to modesty, and whilst it becomes us to be decided in our own opinions, a recollection of human fal-

libility will teach us a lesson. of candour to others." We ·shall have occasion, hereafter, to point out instances in which Mr. Wilson appears to us to have lost sight of these Christian sentiments ; but it is only justice to him to observe, that there is a growing liberality in the work as it advances, which we take as a pledge that should the public patronage ever induce the author to revise his volumes, he would correct some passages which in their present form offend such readers as consider History degraded when, instead of being the handmaid of truth, it is made the servant of a party.

At the same time we are willing to make allowances for prepossessions which spring from a sense of religion and a zeal for its promotion ; and we applaud that strong attachment to the common principles of dissent which our historian every ·where manifests. Without such an attachment, he could not have been expected to qualify himself for his laborious task or to accomplish it with credit. His own ardour, however, leads him to form an unfavourable, and we hope an unjust estimate of the temper of his fellow-dissenters. The compliment which in the following passage is paid to one denomination to the prejudice of the others is a hasty and censorious reflection :—

" A spirit of inquiry as to the distinguishing features of nonconformity, has, *with the exception of the Baptists, wholly fled from the different sects.* The Presbyterians have either deserted to the world or sunk under the influence of a lukewarm. ministry ; and the Independents have gone over in a body to the Methodists. Indifference and enthusiasm have thinned the ranks of the old stock, and those who remain behind are lost in the crowd of modern religionists." *Pref.* pp. xi, xii.

We have no wish to disparage the Baptists as Dissenters, but we 'fear that there are striking examples amongst them of an attempt to gain popularity by sinking the principles of nonconformity. They have not certainly been accustomed to take the lead in the assertion and defence of religious liberty ; nor do the Presbyterians and Independents of the present day yield to any generation of their fathers in zeal on behalf of the rights of conscience. And may it not be said that the Dissenters and Methodists have met each other half way, and that if Dissenters have seemed to become Methodists, the Methodists have really become Dissenters?

Mr. Wilson's plan is to trace the history of every particular place of worship, according to its situation, in the Metropolis, and then to give sketches of the lives of the ministers who have successively officiated in its pulpit, allotting of course the largest space to such as were distinguished by their activity or are still known by their writings: Where the same minister has been placed at different times over several congregations, reference is made from page to page, in the manner of a dictionary. This method is attended with inconveniences, but they were unavoidable.

A work like this can be viewed only in detail; and as we deem it worthy of particular notice we shall go through it carefully, extracting passages which are peculiarly interesting, and making such remarks as appear to us to be subservient to the cause of truth and liberty. Our review will extend through several numbers, but we do not fear that we shall try the patience of our readers, since every article will be complete in itself, or rather, every extract and every remark will be intelligible without further reference, and independent of what may go before and come after.

The first section of the History is on the " Rise of the first Nonconforming Churches :" it begins with an account of the Protestant congregation in London in the reign of Queen Mary, of persecuting memory. This church consisted of about two hundred members. Their meetings were held alternately near Aldgate and Blackfriars, in Thames Street, and in *ships upon the river.* Sometimes they assembled in the villages about London, and especially at Islington, that they might the more easily elude the bishop's officers and spies. For the same reason they often met in the night. A credulous martyrologist, Clark, has recorded some of their providential deliverances. Their ministers appear to have been, Dr. Edmund Scambler, afterwards Bishop

of Norwich, a Mr. Fowler, John Rough,* a Scotchman, Augustine Bernher, a foreigner, and Dr. Bentham, of whom we have (pp. 6, 7.) the following interesting account:—

" THOMAS BENTHAM, D.D.; born at Sherbourne, in Yorkshire, and educated at Magdalen College, Oxford. Upon Queen Mary's accession, he was deprived of his Fellowship ; when he retired to Zurich, and then to Bazil, where he became preacher to the English exiles. Afterwards, being recalled by his Protestant brethren, he was made superintendant of their congregation in London. In this situation he continued till the death of the Queen, encouraging and confirming his people in their faith by his pious discipline, constant preaching, and resolute behaviour in the Protestant cause. Under his care and direction, they often met by hundreds for divine worship, without discovery, notwithstanding they were under the nose of the vigilant and cruel Bonner.† Upon the accession of Elizabeth, he was nominated to the bishoprick of Litchfield and Coventry, which he filled with great moderation till his death, Feb. 21, 1578, 9.‡ Dr. Bentham was held in great repute for learning and piety. It was with considerable reluctance that he complied with the Queen's injunctions for suppressing *the prophecyings*. His letter to his archdeacon upon this subject,¶ bears strong marks of a pious mind ; but at the same time shews the extent to which the Queen carried her prerogative, and the blind obedience she exacted from her subjects. The Prophecyings were religious meetings instituted by the clergy, for explaining the scriptures and promoting knowledge and piety. One very important benefit arising from them was, that they occasioned a familiar intercourse between the clergy and their people, and excited a laudable emulation in watching over their respective flocks. The Queen complained of them to the Archbishop,§ as nurseries of Puritanism ; she said that the laity neglected their secular affairs by repairing to these meetings, which filled their heads with notions and might occasion disputes and seditions in the state. She moreover told him that it was good for the church

---

* Mr. Wilson's account of this reformer closes with an ill-timed pun. " At length, after much *rough* usage, he ended his life joyfully in the flames, Dec. 1577." The joke was probably borrowed.

† " Heylin's Hist. of the Reform. pp. 79, 80."

‡ " Wood's Athen. Oxon. i. 192, 704."

¶ " See Neal's Puritans. i. 239."

§ " Dr. Edmund Grindall."

to have but few preachers, three or four in a county being sufficient; and peremptorily commanded him to suppress them. The archbishop, however, thought that she had made some infringement upon his office, and wrote her a long and earnest letter, declaring that his conscience would not suffer him to comply with her injunctions. This so inflamed the Queen, that she sequestered the Archbishop from his office, and he never afterwards recovered her favour."*

Honourable mention is here made of Mr. *Cuthbert Simpson*, who was a deacon of this first Protestant church; a pious, faithful and zealous man, labouring incessantly to preserve the flock from the errors of Popery, and to secure them from the dangers of persecution. He was apprehended with Mr. Rough and several others, at a house in Islington, where the church were about to assemble, as was their custom, for prayer and preaching the word; and being taken before the council was sent to the Tower. It was the office of Mr. Simpson to keep a book containing the names of the persons belonging to the congregation, which book he always carried to their private assemblies; but it happened through the good providence of God, that on the day of his apprehension, he left it with Mrs. Rough, the minister's wife.†

During his confinement in the Tower,

" the Recorder of London examined him strictly as to the persons who attended the English service; and because he would discover neither the book, nor the names, he was cruelly racked three several times, but without effect. The Lieutenant of the Tower also caused an arrow to be tied between his two fore-fingers, and drew it out so violently as to cause the blood to gush forth. These marble-hearted men not being able to move the constancy of our Confessor, consigned him over to Bonner, who bore this testimony concerning him before a number of spectators : ' You see what a personable man this is ; and for his patience, if he were not an heretic, I should much commend him ; for he has been thrice racked in one day, and in my house he hath endured some sorrow, and yet I never saw his patience once moved !' But notwithstanding this, Bonner condemned him, ordering him first into the stocks in his coal-house, and from thence to Smithfield, where with Mr. Fox and

Mr. Devenish, two others of the church taken at Islington, he ended his life in the flames.‡

ART. III.—*A Letter to Trinitarian Christians.* By W. Marshall, Minister of the Unitarian Chapel, St. Alban's, Herts. Pp. 20. 12mo. Price 6*d.* Richardson, 91, Royal Exchange.

THIS Letter contains a forcible appeal to Trinitarian Christians, intended to excite them to a careful examination of the doctrines they profess. The writer asks, " Will you take in Christian charity my inviting you to a serious examination of your faith ? Will you permit me to remind you, your Trinitarian doctrine and Calvinistic creed, are not true because you have never questioned their truth ; are not true because you have been educated in the belief of them, nor because they form the popular faith : as far only as you sincerely believe they were taught by Jesus Christ and his apostles, can you have an honest conviction of their truth." How will Trinitarians answer the following questions? Yet it seems incumbent on them to do it. " Do you, Trinitarians, sincerely believe that God Almighty was in the form of a man upon earth ? That the Creator of the World was *an embryo in the womb?* That God was born ? That God was an infant at the breast;— that God passed through the stages of youth to manhood;—that *God worked as a carpenter;*—that God lived as a man, and at last died as a man, through excess of bodily pain and torture ?" P. 4.

ART. IV.—*A Father's Reflections on the Death of his Child.* Pp. 32. Law and Whitaker, Ave-Maria Lane.

THESE Reflections shew the practical influence of the views Unitarian Christians entertain of God and his government, in times of affliction. A father deeply affected by the death of a beloved child in its infancy, presents the reader with his meditations on the mournful occasion, which are truly edifying. He says, p. 10, "This sad disappointment of my fondest wishes I am bound to consider as the voice of Almighty God, inviting me to wean my affections from the world;

---

* " Neal, ubi supra, p. 239—40."

† This is ascribed by Clark to a " remarkable dream," but was nothing but an act of common prudence.

‡ " Clark's Martyrology, p. 497."

prudently to moderate my attachment to earthly objects; and diligently to prepare for that awful moment, when it will be my lot also to breathe my last, and to close my eyes for ever on terrestrial things." Throughout he discovers pious resignation, and devout confidence in God. P. 12, he says, " It is, I must confess, no slight satisfaction to me to be able to reflect that it was neither conceived nor born in sin." What must be the feelings of tender parents who entertain the opposite sentiment!

Art. V.—*A Vindication of the General Baptists*, from some aspersions cast on them in the Letters, published by the Rev. Joseph Ivimy, entitled, " Neutrality the proper Ground for Protestant Dissenters respecting the Catholic Claims." Being an Address, delivered at the General Baptist Meeting-House, Portsmouth. By a Member (Not a Minister). Pp. 24.

WITH much good sense this writer vindicates his brethren from the aspersions of Mr. Ivimy, and concludes with the following advice : " Let us take heed then, brethren, if we suffer reproach, that it be wrongfully ; otherwise it cannot be persecution. Then if we bear it patiently, our patience will be acceptable to God. Hear our beloved Master's cheering message—' Hold fast that which thou hast, that no man take thy crown.' Let us not be discouraged by the taunts, the sneers, the sarcasms, or the slanders of the sons of bigotry and enthusiasm. Our Master hath told us—' If they have persecuted me, they will also persecute you.' He hath also said—' Be of good cheer ; I have overcome the world ; and to him that overcometh will I give to eat of the tree of life, which is in the midst of the Paradise of God.'"

Art. VI.—*A Vindication of Unitarians and Unitarian Worship, in two Letters to a Clergyman.* By Thomas Payne. Pp. 27.

THE author of these Letters is an Unitarian preacher in Sussex. He wrote them, " As a check to censoriousness ;" in consequence of the unjust censures the clergyman, to whom they are addressed, had passed on Unitarians. In the first letter the writer appeals from *mystery* to *scripture :* and in a plain, concise, and forcible manner, alleges the testimony of Moses and the prophets, Jesus and his apostles, against the Trinity, and in support of the strict Unity of God. The clergyman having after this, from the pulpit, denounced the Unitarians under the inappropriate name of Socinians, as "*damnable* heretics ; damnable idolaters, and damnable apostates ;" Mr. Payne wrote his second letter ; in which he expostulates with his clerical adversary, on the illiberality and injustice of his conduct, with much earnestness, but without returning railing for railing : so far from it, he is careful to express his respect for the moral worth of his opponent, and praises him for his " commendable and truly Christian conduct, in behalf of the Bible Society." We are glad to find these letters are adopted by the Kent and Sussex Unitarian Tract Society ; as they are well calculated to promote the cause of truth and charity.

Art. VII.—*A Brief Statement of the Religious Sentiments of Unitarians, more particularly respecting the Person, Character and Offices of Jesus Christ ;* In a Letter to a Friend, who had expressed considerable regret and surprise at the writer, for having quitted the Church of England on Unitarian principles.

THIS writer follows the advice of the Apostle, " Be ready to give a reason for the hope that is in you." By a plain statement of his sentiments, which he supports by solid argument, he justifies his separation from the Established Church, and invites his friend to examine the subjects on which they differ. This pamphlet discovers much good sense and candour.

Art. VIII.—*The Opinions of Unitarians (or Modern Socinians) proved Unscriptural and Dangerous :* in a Sermon upon the Self-existence of Jesus Christ. By the late Rev. Wm. Romaine, M. A., &c. Pp. 35.

SIXTY years have elapsed since the first publication of this sermon, during which every thing its author insists on as evidence of the self-existence of Jesus Christ has been repeatedly answered and shewn to have no bearing on the subject; as often as the advocates for this notion have ventured to take the field, they have found their opponents ready to meet them, and after a few attempts at argument have been glad to take refuge in mystery. Its republication at this time is a proof that Trinitarians still rely more on appeals to the passions than to the understanding. The self-existence of a person who was actually born, and who actually died, (and that Jesus Christ was such a person the scriptures plainly teach, and no Christian can deny it) is a notion so directly contrary to reason, and involves such a seeming impossibility, that nothing contained in scripture ought to be supposed to teach it, if it will bear any other construction; but Mr. Romaine builds his conclusions on the mere sound of words, arbitrarily applied, and makes up for the want of argument by thundering out eternal damnation against those who differ from him. P. 10, he says, " If you deny him [Christ] to be God, your sins remain, and misery must be your portion—Misery, the greatest you can suffer, in soul and body, among the condemned spirits in hell for ever and ever." Where is Christian charity? Where the meekness and gentleness of Christ, when professed ministers of the gospel, thus condemn others, for what at most can be but an error in judgment?

ART. IX.—*Unitarianism Vindicated; in a Letter to the Editor of Mr. Romaine's Sermon, upon the Self-existence of Jesus Christ.* Pp. 53.

THE passages of scripture referred to by Mr. Romaine, as proofs of the self-existence of Jesus Christ, are here impartially examined, and shewn to have a very different meaning: and his uncharitable declamation animadverted upon, and justly censured. Nor has the writer confined himself to Mr. R's sermon ; but replied, with considerable ability, to the arguments of other writers in favour of the same hypothesis. He shews himself well acquainted with the subject on which he has written, and reasons in a clear and forcible manner. After having vindicated the Unitarian doctrine by scriptural argument, he asks, p. 44, " In what respect are the views of

Trinitarians more estimable than those of Unitarians ? Are we upon their principles to expect something greater than the favour of God and endless felicity ? Or are these prospects of greater importance if purchased by the sufferings of Christ, than if they are the unmerited *gift of God* to men through him?

" In many respects the views of the reputed orthodox are certainly far less cheering and consolatory than those of Unitarians. The first believe him to be a being of unrelaxing rigour and severity, when offended ; that he will severely punish every transgression, however unpremeditated, however forcible the temptation which led to its commission, or however sincerely it may be repented of, either in the sinner himself or in his substitute. The latter believe him to be ' merciful and gracious, slow to anger, and plenteous in mercy :' that he is ' not willing that *any* should perish, but that *all* should come to repentance.' These believe him to be the kind and compassionate Parent of the whole universe; those consider him as a partial, arbitrary, and vindictive sovereign. Which of the two systems would a wise and good man wish to be true? Which of the characters above described, namely, the God of the Calvinists, or the God of the Unitarians, is it the Christian's duty to imitate ?"

ART. X.—*The Influence of Bible Societies on the Temporal Necessities of the Poor.* By the Rev. Thomas Chalmers, Kilmany. Pp. 40. 8vo. W. White and Co., Edinburgh ; Longman and Co., London.

THIS well written pamphlet is an answer to the objections which, it seems, have been made to the Bible Societies in the North, as encroaching on the fund which charity provides for the relief of poverty, by diverting the contributions of benevolent persons to another object, and as taking from the comfort of the poor, by exciting them to form Bible associations, in which they contribute one penny a week to promote the circulation of the scriptures. He shews that the subscriptions of those who are above the class of mere labourers, may be taken from the fund employed in luxuries, without sensibly diminishing it: p. 3, and that, so far from the benevolent principle being exhausted by its operation in Bible Societies, it will be rendered more active in other directions. P. 9, he says,

" It is not so easy to awaken the benevolent principle out of its sleep, as, when once awakened in behalf of one object, to excite and to interest it in behalf of another. When the bar of selfishness is broken down, and the floodgates of the heart are once opened the stream of benevolence can be turned into a thousand directions." He contends that the poor man's being brought to participate in so good a work as the circulation of the scriptures, by contributing his penny, " puts him in the high attitude of a giver, and every feeling it inspires is on the side of independence and delicacy." P. 25. This advocate of the Bible Societies, consistently, and with equal earnestness, contends for the education of the children of the poor, the happy effects of which he shews to be fully exemplified in the independent feeling, industry, and aversion to becoming paupers, which prevail among the mass of the people in in Scotland.

Art. XI.—*Thoughts on the Probability of our being known to each other in a Future Life.* Pp. 33. 8vo. J. Johnson and Co., St. Paul's Church Yard.

WE think the observations of this writer authorize his conclusion, that " The more we consider this interesting subject, the more probable it appears, that the re-union of virtuous persons' in a future state, *does* form a part of the gracious design of Providence : and that, with such modifications only, as will be necessary to a new and more exalted state of existence, the benevolent affections which have constituted our happiness here, will continue to be the sources of bliss hereafter. An expectation so delightful tends to elevate the mind and purify the affections. It renders life more happy ; death more easy. It expands the heart in gratitude to God, and in good will to all mankind."

Art. XII.—*A Serious Address to Unitarians, on the Importance of maintaining a Conduct worthy of their Principles.* By a Seceder from the Establishment. Pp. 16. Eaton, 187, High Holborn.

THIS is a truly Christian exhortation to those who believe the Unitarian doctrine, to let their light shine before men, by an open profession of what they believe, by uniting in the worship of the one God only, and by shewing the holy influence of their faith in their temper and conduct. The following passage, p. 13, deserves the attention of those who conceal their sentiments. " Convinced as we are that the notion of three divine persons being each of them truly and properly God, is not only a gross and palpable delusion, but that it has been the means of bringing Christianity into contempt; is it not mean, is it not criminal, is it not inexcusable, to conceal our sentiments on a point of such infinite importance ; or to act as though we believed such a glaring and pernicious absurdity ?"

Art. XIII.—*The Divine Unity unambiguous ;* or, The Plain and Emphatic signification of the phrase JEHOVAH OUR GOD IS ONE JEHOVAH maintained, and Jesus Christ shewn to be the Chief of the Children of God according to the spirit of Holiness : including an Examination of John i. 1—14, Heb. i. Col. i. 15—18, &c. Pp. 40.

THE title fully expresses the contents of this pamphlet ; the writer understands his subject, and shews himself no feeble advocate of the important doctrines of the Unity of God, and the superiority of Jesus Christ in his office and character, though in his person simply a man.

Art. XIV.—*An Essay on the Impolicy of War.* By William Pitt Scargill. Pp. 16. 6d. Darton, Harvey and and Darton, Gracechurch Street.

AFTER shewing that the abolition of war is practicable, this sensible writer answers the pleas usually urged for its recurrence, states in a concise and forcible manner its evil nature and tendency, and suggests a plan to be adopted by the friends of peace for its prevention. Though we much fear the spirit of the gospel will not soon triumph over the spirit of war, we earnestly recommend Mr. S's. plan to the consideration of our readers. He says, p. 14, " Associations and societies have been formed for benevolent purposes in this country, and the objects for which they have been formed have been more or less answered. What prevents the formation of a society for this object? The great concern in the first instance is to circulate knowledge upon the subject, to communicate to the people at large a knowledge of their own interest. . When the nation feels that peace is its interest there will be an expression of that conviction in the general voice, that will be uttered in behalf of humanity and reason.

" It is alas too certain that war never will be abolished so long as men content themselves with deploring its evils and lamenting its prevalence : some definite and persevering exertions must be made before any hope can be entertained of its cessation. It is in vain for us to flatter ourselves with the hope that after a long and sanguinary war. we shall repose in profound peace and quiet ; if we do not take some steps to destroy the system of war altogether. Living as is our privilege, in a country where the utmost liberty of speech and discussion by press is allowed, so far as is consistent with decorum and good order, a mighty engine of benevolence is in the power of every friend of humanity. Would it not then be desirable to form associations in every part of the kingdom, whose object should be to raise a little fund for the necessary expences attending such unions, and that these associations should use their best endeavours to impress upon the minds of the people at large, the desirableness and practicability of abolishing the system of war altogether? Could the ministers of religion make a better use of their pulpits than to inculcate from them the doctrine of Jesus Christ—the doctrine of peace ? There is no need of making this a party question, it is an object in which all may unite, it is a concern of general and universal interest ; under whatever government men may live, whatever be their loyal attachment to their sovereign, they can conscientiously unite their endeavours for peace.

" Nor let us imagine that associations for this benevolent purpose will be confined to this country, the friends of humanity and religion in every part of Europe, in every quarter of the globe, would cheerfully contribute their assistance to an object so powerful in its tendency to ameliorate the human race and increase the comforts of mankind."

POETRY.

Reflections after reading Sir Robert Ker Porter's Account of the French Campaign in Russia, 1812.

I.

Again the Niemen's cross'd! with willing
   hand,   '
I'd close the Book so fraught with human
   · woe ;
Nor longer dwell on Gallia's warlike band;
By death in ev'ry horrid form laid low !

II.

But mem'ry will be brooding o'er the
   scene, '
Where discord, strife and horror reign'd
   around ;
Where with gigantic stride and dreadful
   mien,
Pale death with countless victims strew'd
   the ground.

III.

Welcome his fatal shafts ! 'twere they
   alone, ·
Reliev'd at once the dying man's despair ;
They hush'd the wounded soldier's stifled
   groan,
That on the midnight breeze assail'd the
   ear.

IV.

'Twere they reliev'd the agonizing pain,·
Shot thro' the soul, by Russia's northern
   blast ;

Turn'd to a bed of rest the snow-clad
   plain,
And in oblivion wrapp'd their sufferings
   past.

V.

Unheard of woes, for what were ye endured ?
Why these sad scenes beheld so wide and
   far ?
Had ye to all mankind long peace ensur'd !
Had freedom's cause led Gallia's sons to
   war !

VI.

Much might be said to mitigate the loss
That Parents, Widows, Orphans, long must
   bear ;
When o'er the mind the glorious cause
   should cross ;
'Twould soothe the pang for those .they
   held so dear. ·

VII.

But even this consoling thought's denied ;
And execrations from the mourners burst;
" Curs'd be the tyrant's overreaching
   pride ;
Curs'd his ambition, and his mem'ry
   curs'd."

VIII.

" But for this ruthless war, my boy had
   bless'd,
With youthful spirits, his paternal home ;

But now he's sunk, by unknown ills oppress'd,
And with his life my fondest hopes are
gone."

IX.

Thus mourns the parent whose ill-fated
son,
Back to his country never must return ;
The widow thus bewails her husband
gone ;
And for their Sires ten thousand orphans
mourn.

X.

" Ill-fated Host !" the Russian Patriot's
steel,
Was not unaided to ensure thy doom ;
A northern winter's frown thy ranks must
feel,
A northern snow must prove thy warrior's
tomb.

XI.

Such the effect of Heav'n's resistless laws;
Whose anger frown'd upon the ruthless
plan ;
Nor could the tyrant with unhallow'd
cause,
Encroach unpunish'd on the rights of
man.

Lewes, Feb. 9, 1816.

From the German of Schiller.

Wrapt in gloomy mist of even
All my joys are fled afar,
One bright ray in mem'ry's heaven
Lingers,—one immortal star.
See it beam celestial light;—
No ! 'tis but a gleam of night.

Death's long slumber hath o'erta'en thee,
Veil'd those lovely eyes of thine—
Can my sorrows, Emma, pain thee ?
Beats thy bosom now with mine ?
Ah ! thou liv'st in light above ;
But thou liv'st not for my love !

Love's emotions perish never :
Can they perish, Emma, say ?
All beneath is fleeting ever :
And must love too pass away ?
Can this flame of heav'nly fire
Like an earthly spark expire ?

A.

From the Portuguese of A. Ferreira.

To the beloved Disciple.

Celestial Eagle ! that on wing sublime,
Rose above heav'n in thy seraphic flight,
And brought the secrets of the stars to
light,
And gave eternal day to darksome time ;
That fill'd with heavenly gladness earthly
clime,

And tore away the veil from mortal sight,
While shewn by thee, th' ETERNAL's glory
bright
Is own'd,—felt,—seen,—ev'n in this world
of crime !

Thou, once a slumberer on the Saviour's
breast !
Deem'd worthy to be call'd the Virgin's
Son !
Fav'rite of Jesus !—lov'd and honour'd
best !
Whose brow now bears a martyr's golden
crown,
O let the fire of extacy divine
Which glow'd within thy bosom, influence
mine !

A.

To Spring.

Thrice welcome ! soul-reviving Spring,
That com'st with smiles ; and with thee
bring,
The Zephyrs bland, with balmy wing,
Gladding the plains,
And let the feather'd warblers sing,
Their softest strains.

Sweet Philomel's autumnal lay,
When tears hang trembling on the spray,
May softly hymn departed day,
With pensive voice ;
But when thou com'st enchanting May,
All hearts rejoice.

The violet, and the primrose pale,
Perfume with sweets the vernal gale,
Roses and lilies of the vale,
United bring,
Their choicest, fairest charms to hail
Returning Spring.

Ah ! I have seen a blushing rose,
At young-eyed morning just unclose,
Wafting with every gale that blows
Fragrance around,
Cropt off before it fully blows,
Fade on the ground.

This fate was thine, thou lovely maid !
'Twas faithless love that thee betray'd,
(Thou fairest flower of all the glade)
And yew trees wave,
Where oft with breaking heart I tread
Thy lowly grave !

C. S.

Epigram on Scott's Waterloo.

How prostrate lie the heaps of slain
On Waterloo's immortal plain !
But none by sabre or by shot,
Fell half so flat as WALTER SCOTT.
Yet who with magic spear or shield,
E'er fought like him on Flodden Field ?

Morn. Chron.

INTELLIGENCE.

FOREIGN.

French Protestants.

DOCUMENTS.

Royal Ordinance.

Louis, by the Grace of God, King of France and Navarre, &.

" We are informed that our Ordinance of the 21st of Nov. last, has received in the town of Nismes the respect and submission we expected ; that though the criminal whom justice demands is not yet secured, strict searches have been made ; that they have been seconded by the National Guard and the inhabitants; and that every thing announces that the assassin of General Lagarde has neither asylum nor protection at Nismes.

" On the other hand, the article of the Constitutional Charter, which, in recognizing the Catholic religion for the religion of the State, secures to other religions liberty and protection, has been faithfully executed. The temple of the Protestants is open, and they enjoy therein all the security which is guaranteed to them by the laws.

" After so marked a return to principles and order, we will no longer postpone the revocation of the rigorous measures which necessity drew from us.

" For these reasons we have ordered and do order what follows :—

" ART. 1. The troops quartered in garrison or on the inhabitants of Nismes, shall be without delay withdrawn, and distributed in the barracks, and in such parts of the department of the Gard, as our Military commandant may judge necessary.

" 2. Our Prefect shall declare to the inhabitants of Nismes, that we are satisfied with the zeal with which they concurred in the maintenance of tranquillity, and the re-establishment of order in our said good city.

" 3. Our Minister, Keeper of the Seals, and our Ministers for War, and the Interior, and General Police, are charged with the execution of the present Ordinance.

 (Signed)   " LOUIS."

" Given at Paris, Jan. 10, 1816."

Paris, Jan. 12.

The following is the Proclamation issued by the Mayor of Nismes, respecting the opening of the Protestant churches. The Marquis de Vallonques, by whom it is signed, was not appointed to his office by the King, but by M. de Bernis, one of the Commissaries of the Duc d'Angouleme, who displaced, for that purpose, M. Donant, a most faithful Royalist and Protestant, who had been nominated by the King immediately on his return :—

Notice to the Inhabitants of the City of Nismes.

" The laws of the realm and the will of the King secure the exercise of the Protestant worship. I tell you so, I, who am your magistrate, your mayor—I, who have surely some claims to your confidence. The Protestant churches will be opened on Thursday next, and that day will prove to the King, to France, and to Europe, who are our accusers, that the blindness of *a few women and children* is not the crime of the city of Nismes, which has distinguished itself on so many occasions, and even *recently*, by its fidelity and devotion to the King.

" Women who are blinded by your zeal, and perhaps excited by your enemies, you will not once more ruin your city, and gratify by your errors *the enemies of the Royal cause.* I am assured, and for that reason I have a pleasure in informing you, that conferences are opened, and nearly terminated, with the Consistory of the Protestant worship. Their object is to restore, by common consent, to the worship of the State, the churches which have been conceded to the Protestant worship. Two churches will be built, and that very shortly, in lieu of that concession. During that short interval, the Protestants may enjoy, undisturbed, the churches thus conceded. The people of Nismes need only know the will of the King, and hear the voice of the Royal Authorities, to do their duty.

" Marquis de VALLONQUES, Mayor."

" *Nismes, Dec.* 19, 1815."

The *Official Gazette* of this day announces, that tranquillity is restored in the South; notwithstanding which assertion, we have authentic accounts of the following transactions having recently taken place in that part of the kingdom :—

At Sommières, the Protestants, having attempted to celebrate their worship on the 24th of December, the power of which they had been deprived of since the month of July, they met with the most barbarous treatment on that account.

The royal troops, which do not cease to infest the environs of Nismes, exercise continual vexations on the Protestants. On the 22nd of December a detachment of about fifty men broke into the house of M. Mourier, a gentleman of property at St. Blancard, lately returned from emigration, who had just time to effect his escape. Failing in their main object, these brigands completely pillaged the premises, and daily continue their depredations in the neighbourhood.

Several families at Nismes have abjured their religion, the motive of which is evident. They are families of mechanics and workmen, who are without bread in consequence of the persecutions they have undergone. The Protestant manufacturers have, for the most part, fled, and the Catholics will not employ Protestant workmen ; besides which, the looms and frames of the latter have been destroyed, and they are reduced to the alternative of recanting or starving.

This system of persecution has extended to Bordeaux and its neighbourhood. Its effects have also been felt at Nantz, the President of the Consistory of that city having been sent into exile. Tristaillon, Quatretaillon, and another brigand of that party, made their entry lately into Lyons. They wore in their hats white cockades of a preposterous size, in the midst of which was displayed a large red cross, the characteristic badge of the fanatics of Nismes. These crusaders met with a very ill reception from the people of that city, several of whom have been arrested upon a charge of having insulted them. In consequence of the spirit of the Lyonnese being so unfavourable to these culprits, the latter have been transferred to some town in the province of Bourbonnais. The refugees from Nismes have been warmly greeted by the people of Lyons ; which circumstance has given great disgust to the Royal Authorities of that place. The Prefect of that city having learned that the President of the Protestant Consistory had received letters from the English Society for the Protection of Religious Liberty, called up that minister before him, compelled him to deliver them up, and threatened him with a criminal prosecution for corresponding with the enemies of the State.

It may not be unworthy of notice, that the soldiers, who, by the late Royal Ordonnance are removed from Nismes, were quartered solely on the Protestants during their stay in that city ; and that the whole weight of extraordinary contributions is made to fall upon the Protestants, of which the following is a striking instance : The Marquis de Calvieres, a Catholic gentleman, enjoying a landed estate of 60,000 livres a year, is assessed at 600 livres—while Mr. Brosse de Pierdon, a Protestant, whose income amounts to about 10,000 livres, has paid within this last year the sum of 15,000 livres towards those contributions.

(From the Journal des Débats.)
Protestant Society of London.

The anxiety and inquiries of the Protestant Society of London have at least produced one good effect.— These inquiries have become, to a very considerable class of Frenchmen, an opportunity for manifesting sentiments, respecting which the most perfidious malevolence cannot any longer express a doubt. From all sides, the heads and the members of the Consistories are eager to prove, by the most authentic protestations and the most formal declarations, that no real cause existed for the proceedings of the Society in London, and that an excess of zeal alone inspired that Society with its fears and suspicions. The following is the extract from a letter which M. Martineau de la Zalgue, President of the Consistory of the Reformed Church at Clairac, has written to his Excellency the Minister of the Interior, sending to him at the same time the letter which the Society of London had addressed to all the Consistories of France :—

" Full of an entire confidence in his Majesty Louis XVIII. my well-beloved King, I look for peace and tranquillity on the earth from him alone.

The finest promises of protection and aid from a foreign government cannot make any impression on my heart;— God, my country, and the Charter of my King, are my sacred signs of rallying, and I would die rather than abandon them.

"These, Sir, are the sentiments which I unceasingly endeavour to fortify by my discourses and my example, in the minds and hearts of my flock, and where they have long since been engraven; and I dare affirm, without fear of contradiction, that the King has not any subjects more devoted than the Protestants of Clairac."

We think it our duty to add to this new testimony, the following extract from an address sent to the King by the President, Pastors, and Members of the Reformed Consistories of the Department of the Ardeche.

" Sire, your faithful subjects, professing the reformed religion in the department of Ardeche, come to lay at the foot of the throne the respectful homage of their gratitude and love. They form no body in the State; they do not harbour the guilty thought of forming one; united together by the single bond of a common worship, they are also united to all your subjects by their sentiments for your august person; and the precious title of Frenchmen is sufficient for their happiness and glory.—It is in this quality, Sire, that they come to swear to your Majesty an unlimited fidelity.

" They have no complaints to make; no petition to offer : they rely implicitly on your justice and goodness. The tribute which they presume to offer to you is equally pure and disinterested; and their language must be that of unalterable gratitude and entire devotion. While the torch of fanaticism, repressed by your Majesty, has been shaken in less happy districts, they have constantly enjoyed all the liberty guaranteed by that Charter, the immortal offspring of your noble wisdom, and the pledge of your goodness. No attempt has been made to check the impulse of their conscience, to oppose their devotions which they publicly practise, and in which they fervently pray for your safety and happiness.

" You come, to secure to us for ever that internal tranquillity which can alone serve as the basis for the public prosperity. That tutelary am-

nesty, proposed in your name, by your ministers, has subdued all hatreds, dissipated all alarms, calmed all resentments, re-established universal confidence, and blended into one common sentiment of gratitude and love, the differences of opinion which party spirit had fomented.

" Sire, posterity will place the name of Louis XVIII. between those of Louis XII. and Henry IV. The latter, who was your ancestor and your model, has always been, to the Protestants of France, the object of a sort of adoration. We love, Sire, to discover him again in you; and if our ancestors had the glory of powerfully contributing towards placing him on a throne which has become your inheritance, we will prove, by our conduct towards your sacred person, that the Protestants of the present day have the same love and the same fidelity for the august family of the Bourbons which animated the Protestants of two centuries back.

" We are, Sire, with the most profound respect, your Majesty's most humble and most obedient servants and faithful subjects, the Presidents, Pastors, and Members of the Reformed Consistories of the Department of the Ardeche."

[Here follow the signatures.]

Proclamation of the Prefect to the Inhabitants and the National Guard of the City of Nismes.

Nismes, Jan. 20.

" At last, brave and loyal Inhabitants, and National Guards, after so much solicitude for your happiness and your renown, I perceive a bright day shine upon this city, whose population has given so many proofs of its unalterable fidelity to legitimate monarchy, to the August House which reigned so long over our happy ancestors, and who, if our vows are heard by the Supreme Arbiter of nations and monarchs, shall reign for ever over our descendants.

" The King is satisfied with your conduct; he has fulfilled all my wishes and rewarded all my efforts, by ordering me to make known his sovereign and paternal satisfaction.

" Thus are obliterated a few errors, into which perfidious agitators, abusing even your attachment to your king, had drawn you. Thus are annihilated those calumnious reports, which a vain attempt has been made to cir- culate in the bosom of our country, even to the foot of the throne of our august monarch; but which had been spread with too much success among foreign nations, which are now undeceived as to our true feel- ings.

"I conjure you then, brave Nis- mois, brave National Guards, continue to deserve, by your fidelity to the King, by your obedience to his sa- cred orders and the laws of the king- dom, by your respect for liberty of worship and conscience, the favour which the King has just conferred on you—and your justification in the face of all Europe, which his Majes- ty has not disdained himself to pro- claim, by his Royal Ordonnance of the 10th of this month. *Live the King! May our great, our good King live for ever!*

"The Prefect Marquis d'ARBAUD JOQUES."

Extract of a Letter of Jan. 12, 1816, *of his Excellency the Minister of the Interior to the Prefect of the Gard.*

"I learn with joy the happy con- valescence of M. the Count de La- garde. May this good servant of the King yet for a long period consecrate to him his loyal services."

Strasburg, Jan. 29.

The Journal of our department has published the following circular of the Minister of the Interior to the Pre- fects, dated Paris, Jan. 17.

"A circular, printed and dated at London, has been, Monsieur le Pre- fect, addressed by a pretended Pro- testant Society to the French Protes- tant Ministers. This paper, under the pretext of persecutions, to which it supposes the latter to be subjected, may spread disquietude amongst them, and induce them to emigrate.

"I have before me the answers of the Presidents of several Consistories; all of them are marked by the good disposition which prevails in them, and by the sentiments which they ex- press; and I doubt not that those which have not yet come to hand have repelled with the same indigna- tion these dangerous insinuations. I pray you, Monsieur, to send me co- pies of all these answers, which I shall lay before the King. His Majesty will see with satisfaction these une-

quivocal testimonies of the confidence of the Protestants in his paternal go- vernment, of their attachment to his person, and of their love for the coun- try.

"The Protestants may also rely up- on the Protection of the King, who only sees in his subjects, whatever may be their religion, children to whom he bears an equal affection.

"I have the honour, Monsieur le Prefect, &c.

"The Minister Secretary of State for the Department of the Interior, (Signed)   "VAUBLANC."

The following audacious calumny appeared in the French papers.

"The Prefect of Calvados has pub- lished at Caen a letter from M. de Vaublanc, Minister of the Interior, to the following effect:

Paris, Jan. 31, 1816.

"I received the letter which you missives from the Protestant Society of London. I have recognized with pleasure in this answer the patriot- ic sentiments which animate all Frenchmen of the Protestant commu- nion. They may depend on the pro- tection of the King; tell the Consis- tory, at the same time, that to my certain knowledge, the persons who have formed a society at London, in order to throw a correspondence into France, enjoy little credit or confi- dence in their own country; they are there justly considered as belonging to a party of jacobins, enemies of re- pose and of every government. The sessions of Parliament about to open, will furnish proofs of this."

This is the manner in which the avowed agents of the French govern- ment dare to speak of the respectable body of Dissenting ministers, and of the Parliament of England. In every way, and by all descriptions of the constituted authorities in France, England and Englishmen are treated with illiberality. The fact is, that while these proclamations are pub- lished, and that the unprotected vic- tims of persecution are forced to write letters denying the miseries they en- dure, every man who gets away from the horrid scene makes known to us the grievous truth, that their suffer- ings are not at an end, and that their only hope is in the exertions of the friends of civil and religious liberty in England.

Morn. Chron., Feb. 7.

A letter from Switzerland contains the following particulars :—

" During the last three months we have had here several persons, who had left Nismes on account of the persecutions to which they were exposed. Among others, I have conversed with four or five ministers ; they all agree in painting their situations as extremely critical ; they declare most solemnly that the present evils are not the result of any *political* misconduct on their part, but arise solely from the hatred and jealousy of their Catholic brethren ; that they are so surrounded by enemies, and all their actions so misrepresented, that they are afraid to take any steps, lest, on their proving insufficient, they should be exposed to an increase of malice and persecution ; they are therefore quite at a loss to know how their miseries are to be remedied. On a late occasion, when the Duke d'Angouleme visited Nismes, a memorial was drawn up, beseeching him, in the humblest manner, to grant them his protection, and to accept their assurances of loyalty ; but though not a single complaint was made of all they were actually suffering, their bitter enemies, who surrounded the Duke, intercepted the memorial, and threatened tenfold vengeance on its authors.

" The persons here are most anxious for the fullest investigation, but they decline furnishing any details in writing, lest they should commit their unfortunate companions. Such is the state of terror and alarm.

" Last week a letter was received here from a Protestant Minister in France, where he had officiated for twenty-five years, informing his friends that the French government had decreed that none but natives should continue in its offices, and that himself and many other Swiss ministers must leave their churches and throw themselves upon charity. This respectable man, between 50 and 60 years of age, is anxious to obtain bread for his children."

MISCELLANEOUS.
Rev. O. Desmond.
Williams's Library, Redcross Street,
SIR,   *Dec. 9,* 1815.
While the correspondence of every day accumulates the proofs of a desolating persecution in the southern provinces of France, it is a duty as grateful as indispensable, to prevent all unnecessary agitation and distress.

I embrace, therefore, the earliest moment, through your Magazine, to allay public apprehension as to the fate of the Rev. O. Desmond, President of the Consistory of Nismes.

From a letter received this day, the following paragraph is extracted :

" I render a sad homage to truth, by confirming the frightful accounts of the massacres in the South. How many widows inconsolable ! How many orphans wanting bread ! ! Notwithstanding the number of Protestants who have been assassinated is great, we cannot count among the victims the venerable Olivier Desmond, President of the Consistory."

Having been informed by another correspondent that the reformed churches have sustained a great loss by the death of the Rev. Mr. Armond, one of the pastors of Nismes, it appears probable, in the distracted state of the country, that the event has occasioned an erroneous report to obtain considerable circulation.

By order of the Committee,
T. MORGAN, Secretary.

Assassin of Gen. Lagarde.

The following paragraph from the French papers proves, what we suspected, that the military employed at Nismes to protect the liberties of the Protestants, are the volunteers, or national guard of the town, who swore, when the Protestants some months ago wished to shew their loyalty by joining that corps, that ' they would have no *Protestant rascal* among them.'

——" A notice, published by order of the Prefect of Vaucluse, says, that the assassin of Gen. Lagarde is a man of the name of *Boissin,* a grenadier of the national guard of that city."

The Times.

The most decent part of society must feel so instinctively and strongly, that any remarks of ours on the scurrilous language of *The Times* may be well omitted. We need only record the fact, that that Journal had the indecency (to say no worse) to describe the ministers of religion, who preside over the Dissenting congregations in the metropolis of the British empire, and any individual of whom would, we presume, incalculably outweigh that Journal in public confidence, as "*the treble faced rogues.*" What must be the character of that cause which dictates such abuse and employs such means?

We wish the Bourbons joy, with their agent in the Journal Department of this country; he may give articulation to their malignity, and display their taste as *legitimate* gentlemen, though he will precisely fail where they especially need his aid ; that is, in deterring the honourable and benevolent inhabitants of this kingdom from bringing to light, and resisting the shameful persecutions which have marked the short periods of their first and second reign.

The Times is exceedingly delighted at having disposed so soon of the company, called ' The Protestant Society,' and of course equal pleasure will be experienced at the Thuilleries. The task, by the bye, appeared so easy, that it was hardly worth the celebration : indeed we were always at a loss to discover what the Protestant or *Penitent* Society had done to excite the rage of the Bourbons and The Times. It certainly could only arise from neglect of a little explanation. Whether intentionally or not, its operations seemed calculated to secure their cause, and now it is evident that it is only anxious to make its peace, by preventing the exertions of others.

We suspect, however, that the Bourbons and their Editor will find, that the respectable persons whom they now vituperate with all their might, are made of more genuine and sterner stuff, and that a threefold cord will not easily be broken.

The contributions they cannot endure, but they cannot prevent them, and The Times may be assured that not a farthing of them will be given to it for *hush money*, nor will the advice, nor the consent of the French police be asked as to its disposal.

Europe will know, and history will record, that wise, upright, and charitable Christians in England assisted to relieve the sufferings of persecuted Protestants in France—in the second reign of LOUIS THE DESIRED.

M.Chron., Jan. 31.

Mr. Marron.

When Mr. Marron's letter was published by the Bourbon Journals, in this country, we stated as a fact which was before the public, that the respectable editor of a periodical work had mentioned, that Mr. Marron had written to this country in strains of high commendation of those who took an interest in the affairs of French Protestants.; and the fact is precisely as we stated it.

Mr. Marron now, it appears, sends another letter, in which he acknowledges that he wrote to the Rev. R. A. and with a profligacy of expression, unworthy of a minister of religion, and especially when connected with the calamities of his brethren, he says —" *he might have gilded the pill,* and *have softened the crudity of his refusal.*" That pill still exists, but the gold has disappeared.

If Mr. Marron feels sore at the gratuitous abuse of the " self-styled Protectors," he has much reason to bless the forbearance of the Committee at Williams's Library—but forbearance may have its limit ; and in the letter itself, which we hope will be published, the public may learn how to estimate the President's talents for *pill making* and *pill gilding.* No one need " be inclined to asperse him," for he takes care what with odes and pills, effectually to asperse himself.

As to the dictation of the police, we know the history of that business too well to assist Mr. Marron in his justification.—*M. Chron., Feb. 3.*

Protestant Society.

TO THE EDITOR OF THE MORNING CHRONICLE.

SIR,

Without entering at all into the consideration of the conduct of the Protestant Society for the Protection of Religious Liberty, in regard to the letter of the Duke of Wellington, I have thought it proper to address you, on purpose to distinguish the Society in question from the great mass of Dissenters in this country. It is the cause paragraphs have appeared in many of the papers, and, I believe, in your respectable Journal, assuming that this Society defeated Lord Sidmouth, obtained the enlargement of the Act of Toleration, and is composed of many members of the Church of England, and represents all the Dissenters of England and Wales. Now, Sir, this assumption deserves the severest reprobation.

On the occasion of Lord Sidmouth's Bill, all that worshiped under the Act of Toleration, made an instant movement; the Methodists in the connexion of the late Rev. John Wesley, particularly distinguished themselves, and a great proportion of the petitions was from that numerous body. A great many Dissenters also came forward at that time, who have not acted with any public body since. Some of the persons who were active in that affair formed a Society, and called it the Protestant Society; but others retired, and have neither contributed to the Society or been members of its Committee; it cannot, therefore, be said with truth that this Society defeated Lord Sidmouth, for it was not formed till after that event, and many who took part then have no connexion with it whatever. With respect to the enlargement of the Act of Toleration, the Methodists, also, were particularly employed to obtain that measure. The solicitor to that body, and Mr. Butterworth, M. P. I, myself, know to have been very active.

It is further stated, that the Committee is composed of several members of the Established Church. Now, Sir, the names of that Committee are published, I suppose officially, in a work called the Evangelical Miscellany; it appears that there are fifteen ministers and fifteen gentlemen—all the ministers are Dissenters, and I perceive the others are tradesmen in the Metropolis, and may therefore be easily known; and out of the fifteen I only see one to whom any doubt can attach of his being a Dissenter—and that is the individual whose name generally appears as Chairman, Mr. Mills. He does, I understand, receive the sacrament at the church occasionally—but all his family are Dissenters. He was brought up to attend a meeting in Spitalfields, and now attends himself principally at that in East Cheap, where the Rev. Mr. Clayton preaches—he is further a manager of a Dissenting Academy in Hoxton, for educating persons for the ministry among Dissenters. It seems to me therefore to be deceiving the public, to hold out that the Committee is composed of members of the Established Church. As to its representing all the Dissenters in England and Wales—there is and has

been in existence since 1782, a Committee of Deputies appointed by almost all the regular Dissenting churches in London, to protect and represent them in all matters respecting their religious freedom, and from an interesting volume lately published, containing the Proceedings of this body, it appears, that as long ago as 1745, they addressed a circular letter to the Dissenters throughout England to raise forces against the Pretender. They have also come to resolutions on the present question.

I learn, in fact, that very few of the London Dissenters, belong to this society, which assumes to represent all England and Wales. They represent none of the Methodists—the Quakers have a Committee of Sufferings—and indeed they only represent, according to their own plan, those congregations who subscribe annually a certain sum. The design of the Society, it appears, was to protect the persons so subscribing in their freedom, under the acts of toleration as existing from time to time, and to afford legal assistance in assault, riot, &c. Very important objects, no doubt, but how this Committee of thirty gentlemen, thus appointed from year to year, can assume to represent all the Dissenters, on the subject of a persecution in France, is to me inexplicable.

An Old Citizen and Dissenter.

Wahabees, Mahometan Reformers.
—Letters from Egypt state, that Mohammed Ali, the reigning Viceroy, who had undertaken an expedition against the Wahabee Arabs, had at length terminated it with complete success. After driving them from Mecca, Medina, and the ports along the coast of the Red Sea, taking possession of their great inland capital Tarabe, &c., the strong hold on which they chiefly depended, he effected their total defeat, by pursuing them to the remotest confines of their territory.

DOMESTIC.

The first Annual Meeting of the Southern Unitarian Fund Society will be held on Wednesday, 17th April, 1816, at the General Baptist Chapel, Thomas Street, Portsmouth. The Rev. W. J. Fox is expected to preach.

Manchester College, York.

The following benefactions have been received on account of this Institution.

	l.	s.	d.
Wm. Brodhurst, Jun., Esq., of Mansfield	5	5	0
Rev. Mr. Anstis, Bridport	2	0	0
Mrs. Markham, Shaw Hill, Halifax	5	5	0
Wm. Shore, Esq. Tapton Grove, near Sheffield	50	0	0
Rev. John Holland, Bolton	5	0	0
Rev. John Kentish, Birmingham	105	0	0
	£172	10	0

The following Congregational Collections have been likewise received.

	l.	s.	d.
KENDAL—Rev. John Harrison	5	13	0
CHESTERFIELD—After a sermon preached by the Rev. Wm. Parkinson	12	12	0
	£18	5	0

GEO. WM. WOOD, Treasurer.
Manchester, March 2, 1816.

Unitarian Chapel, Thorne, Yorkshire.
(See pp. 120, 121.)

Subscriptions at the Meeting at Elland, announced, p. 121.

	l.	s.	d.
Rev. R. Astley, Halifax	1	0	0
Rev. C. Wellbeloved, York	1	0	0
Rev. Thomas Jervis, Leeds	1	1	0
Rev. —— Donoughue	1	0	0
Dr. Thomson, Halifax	1	0	0
Ms. Robert Mathien	1	1	0
Mr. John Cartlidge	1	0	0
Mr. Joseph Darnton	1	0	0
Mr. Geo. Wm. Wood	1	1	0
Mr. Daniel Gaskill	1	1	0
Mr. Edward Ferguson	0	10	6
Mr. Thomas Kershaw	0	10	6
Mr. Richard Kershaw	0	10	6
Mr. Wm. Huntress	0	10	6
Mr. Charles Carthage	0	10	6
Mr. Robert Swaine	0	5	6
A Friend	0	10	0
Ditto	0	10	0

New Subscriptions.

	l.	s.	d.
Unitarian Fund	20	0	0
Richard Cooke, Esq., Bath, (By Mr. Aspland)	1	1	0
Viscountess Galway, Bawtry	1	0	0
Mr. John Marriott, Rawmarsh, near Rotherham	1	1	0
Mr. Thos. Eyre, Rawmarsh	1	1	0
I. A., by Rev. P. Wright	1	0	0
I. A., by Ditto	1	0	0
Mr. Richard Naylor, Sheffield	1	1	0
Rev. Wm. Foster, York	0	10	6
Rev. John Williams, Mansfield	0	10	6

NOTICES.

Preparing for the press, and to be published by Subscription, a volume of the mons. More particulars will be given next month.

The Rev. James Gilchrist, of Newington Green, has issued the following Prospectus of a Rational Grammar and Dictionary of the English Language.

The foregoing title is not pre-occupied and not merited by any system of grammar and lexicography already published. That of Dr. Johnson has been pronounced a disgrace to the English language by the most philosophic philologer of modern times. It is not however the intention of this Prospectus to point out the demerits of the philological works which already exist: that which is now offered to the public has nothing in common with them.

The Grammar is introductory to the Dictionary and contains, 1. The nature and origin of alphabetic signs explained. 2. A canon of etymology established. 3. The elements of speech; or, the few simple words collected into one view of which all the numerous compound words are formed. 4. The manner of their formation. 5. The common system of grammar examined and its absurdities exposed. 6. A standard of orthography established.

Though the Grammar be introductory to the Dictionary, yet it may be considered as a separate and independent work; and if it do not justify the pretensions of the Author and satisfy the expectations of Subscribers, they may withhold their encouragement from the Dictionary: they shall therefore in the first instance be considered as subscribing only to the Grammar.

It is expected to contain about 300 pages, demy 8vo., price 6s. to Subscribers, 8s. to Non-Subscribers; and will go to the press whenever a sufficient number of names has been obtained.

Those who intend to encourage the work are earnestly requested to notify their intention as soon as possible to the Author, Newington Green, or to any of the following Publishers and Booksellers: Mr. Hunter, St. Paul's Church Yard; Messrs. Longman and Co., Paternoster Row; Mr. Arch, Cornhill; Messrs. Ridgeway and Sons, Piccadilly; Mr. David Eaton, High Holborn.

Subscribers in the country will have the goodness to communicate their names through the medium of the nearest Bookseller.

The plan of the Dictionary is as follows:

1. All the different forms or spellings of the same word are brought together into one view. 2. The common meaning of

these different forms of the same word is clearly and concisely given; showing that while the same word has many applications both literal and metaphoric, it has uniformly one unvarying meaning. 3. The Dictionary here proposed being intended as a handmaid to philosophy rather than a mere vocabulary, those words which are fittest for the purposes of speech are recommended to the choice of clear thinkers; and obscure, indefinite, equivocal, unintelligible, unmeaning and false-meaning words or uses of them are proscribed. A leading object of the work is to promote clear and definite expression—to dissipate mysticism and jargon and put down sophistry. 4. The German, Italian, French, Spanish and Latin forms or spellings of the same word are presented to view with its English form or spelling. Thus the work is intended to serve as an easy introduction to universal lexicography. 5. All the words etymologically related are brought together and arranged according to their degrees of proximity: all the branches of the same stock or members of the same family are

clustered around the primitive stem or parent word. Competent judges will admit this to be the most philosophic plan of lexicography. It is attended however with one disadvantage—the difficulty of finding any word that may be wanted. To obviate this difficulty an *Index* will be given—all the words of the Dictionary will be alphabetically arranged, with the page referred to where each may be found in its proper etymological connexion. 6. The pronunciation of all those words which deviate from analogy will be marked and indicated in the manner of Mr. Walker's Dictionary; which shall be taken as the standard of English pronunciation. Thus with the principles and rules laid down in the grammar, the present work will serve as a guide to provincialists and foreigners for pronouncing the English language.

It is intended to publish the whole work in Five Parts, at 6s. each, to Subscribers; 8s. to Non-subscribers; but the Author means to wait the decision of the public respecting the Grammar before he send any part of the Dictionary to the press.

OBITUARY.

Died, Wednesday, March 13, 1816, in the 69th year of her age, Mrs. ANN MAR-SOM, wife of the Rev. John Marsom. She was born in the year 1747, received a religious education from her mother, and at an early age made a public profession of Christianity by baptism and an association with a church of the Calvinistic persuasion. She afterwards embraced the Unitarian doctrine, and in the year 1774 addressed a letter on that subject to the pastor of the church of which she was then a member, avowing and defending her sentiments, in consequence of which she was separated from their communion. This letter has been lately printed in the first number of the *Christian Reformer*. On some disputed points she could never fully make up her mind, but her views in general were rational and free from enthusiasm, and she entertained the most friendly sentiments towards those from whom she differed in opinion. On this subject she often repeated the words of the Apostle Peter, as containing a declaration which gave great satisfaction to her mind, *In every nation he that feareth God and worketh righteousness is accepted of him.* On the subject of the Divine Unity she frequently mentioned the 3rd verse of the 17th of John as having been decidedly convincing to the mind of her mother as well as herself. *This is life eternal that they might know thee, the only true God, and Jesus Christ whom thou hast sent.*

In her disposition she was remarkably affectionate and sympathizing; strongly affected by the sufferings of others and anxious for their relief. This temper continued with her even when the decay of her faculties rendered her incapable of the active exertion for which she had before been distinguished, and which had made her eminently useful in her family connexious, among whom her memory will long be cherished with tender and grateful recollection.

With respect to her hope of acceptance with God she always expressed it to be founded distinctly and solely on the mercy of God as revealed in the gospel of Jesus Christ, and professed to derive all her comfort from the promises of God contained in his word. She often repeated those two lines of Dr. Watts's,

" The voice that rolls the stars along
Speaks all the promises !"

She was often heard to say, " I never had a voice from heaven to tell me that I was a child of God ; but I trust I can say, *I know in whom I have believed*." She disclaimed all confidence in herself, and her mind seemed to rest for support on such declarations as these, *There is forgiveness with thee that thou mayest be feared. The Lord taketh pleasure in them that fear him, and in those that hope in his mercy.*

It was remarkable that in the latter years of her life, when she was in a state of great mental debility which particularly impaired her memory, she could nevertheless recollect and repeat whole psalms and chapters, besides a variety of detached verses of scripture on which she dwelt with delight. One of the last expressions she was heard to utter was, that passage Titus ii. 13, *Looking for that blessed hope, and the glorious appearing of the great God and our Saviour Jesus Christ.* From these words her Funeral Sermon was preached to a full congregation on Sunday, March 25th, at Worship Street, by the Rev. John Evans, who read the above character of the deceased from the pulpit —adding his own expressions of regard for her memory. Her remains had, on the preceding Tuesday, been interred by the Rev. R. Aspland in the adjoining cemetery.

15th, at Reading, aged 53 years, Mr. JAMES DROVER, an intelligent and active member of the Unitarian congregation of that place. His death was very sudden. He attended religious worship on Sunday the 10th; went on Monday the 11th to Oxford to exercise his musical profession, in one branch, of which he was very eminent, and in which he continued to practise from his attachment to it notwithstanding his being engaged in a considerable business of long standing; and returned home on Wednesday noon, the 13th, when he complained of a cold and took to his bed. His disorder rapidly increased and terminated in a mortification, of which he died on Friday evening, the 15th, to the unspeakable grief of his family and the consternation of his neighbours. He was buried on Friday, the 22nd inst.: his remains being followed to the grave by a vast concourse of people. On the following Sunday, the 24th inst., a funeral sermon was preached for him at the Unitarian Chapel, Reading, by his friend, Mr. Aspland, of Hackney; a crowd of his surviving townsmen, testified their respect for his character by attending this melancholy service. Great numbers returned from the chapel, unable to gain admittance, at an early hour. By desire of Mr. Drover's surviving family and friends, the Sermon is put into the press; some further particulars will be extracted from it in our next.

On Thursday, the 21st, at her son's house, Crown Street, Finsbury Square, aged fifty, Mrs. ELIZABETH EASLEY, widow, after having submitted to a most painful and lingering illness (with remarkable Christian fortitude) the foundation of which was laid by some severe domestic afflictions and bereavements. As a wife, parent and friend, few have fulfilled these important duties with more propriety. She has left two sons to lament her loss.

Her religious principles were strictly Unitarian: she was a convert of the late Mr. Lindsey's, and as long as she was able, a regular attendant on the ministry of Mr. Belsham, at Essex Street.   E.

At his house in Aldermanbury, early in the morning of Thursday, the 22nd of February, died SWAN DOWNER, Esq. aged 81 years. This worthy gentleman by habits of economy and diligence, acquired a considerable fortune, in the use of which he avoided all expensive and ostentatious parade, seeming to regard it as a talent, which he was bound to devote to purposes of usefulness and charity. His parents were Dissenters; he followed them in their dissent and conscientiously adhered to it, having made himself acquainted with its grounds, and being convinced of their solidity. He was, through a long series of years, a member of the Presbyterian church now assembling in Jewin Street, under the pastoral care of the Rev. Doctor Rees, on whose very able and interesting ministrations he attended with constancy, seriousness and entire satisfaction. He was the firm and ardent friend of civil and religious liberty, of peace in opposition to war, of freedom as opposed to slavery and the slave-trade, of men's emancipation from oppression and persecution in all parts of the globe, and of every practicable diminution of our national expenditure and burthens; and always approved the legislative measures, or the attempts in Parliament, the object of which was the attainment of these desirable ends. When he spake concerning religion, it was with a gravity demanded by its high and important nature; but he placed a just regard to it less in talking about it than in acting agreeably to its rules. The poor have lost in him a considerate and generous benefactor. He distributed his bounties among them not indiscriminately, but after a careful search and investigation, and with a due preference of the cases, which he judged most suitable and deserving. Strict and inflexible probity was always conspicuous in him, accompanied with remarkable strength and clearness of intellect. He retained his powers of recollection and discernment and of expressing his thoughts with precision to the last. He was interred on Wednesday the 28th of February in the vault containing the remains of his parents and sisters in the burying ground of the parish church at Brighthelmston, his native town; in which, by the provisions of his will, there will be permanent memorials of his benevolence and compassion. He has also bequeathed liberal sums to certain well known and valuable institutions; nor are his numerous though distant relations forgotten.

                 W. J.

Addition to the Obituary of MR. JAMES HENNELL, p. 111. (Extracted from the conclusion of Mr. Aspland's funeral sermon for him just published.)

" These animating prospects (of the improvement of mankind in the future world) supported and cheered our departed brother MR. JAMES HENNELL. He had enjoyed the unspeakable advantage of a religious education and had acquired in early life that habit of soul which may be called the *religious sense.* A favourite topic of his conversation in his last days was, his obligations, never to be sufficiently acknowledged, to pious parental counsel and example. After apostolic example, he reasoned upon his faith as a Christian, and reasoned well; but what is of more consequence, he felt deeply and felt correctly. In his varied and complicated transactions with the world he might err through the uncertainty of every thing human, but I am firmly persuaded he never erred from design. His, as he assured me, was on a death-bed, the testimony of a good conscience; yet he was conscious of imperfections and frailties and with sincere repentance he reposed on the mercy of his heavenly Father.

" It pleased the Sovereign Disposer of Life to lay him long on the bed of languishing. All hope of recovery had left him for months before his departure, during all which time he knew he had nothing to do but to die. But the prospect of certain death at so untimely an age, when in the course of nature he might have calculated on many years to come, and the thought of leaving in the world a large family to whom he was tenderly attached, never terrified or agitated him; for himself, he knew in whom he had believed and that he was able to keep that which he had committed to him, his eternal interest, against the last day, and, for his children, he could trust with confidence to the Father of the fatherless. Seldom has a death-bed been so calm, so cheerful, so instructive, I may even add so animating, as his. As he had done with the world, so, in his own language, he appeared to have risen above it. His conversation was in heaven. The greatest efforts of his sinking nature were put forth in exercises of parental duty and of piety. Whilst his strength lasted he was accustomed to lead the worship of his family, and his voice was often heard in the psalms that were sung upon these occasions with a fulness and vigour that bespoke the earnestness and the joy of his soul. Almost daily he assembled his children around him and gave them his counsels and his blessing. Soon after one of these edifying, exemplary exercises, the springs of life began to appear exhausted and he gently fell asleep, dying in the Lord, resting from his labours and awaiting that glorious day when them that sleep in Jesus God will bring with Him. The Lord grant that he may find the promised mercy of the Lord in that day; that his friends and children may according to his fervent prayers live the life and die the death of the righteous, precious in the sight of heaven; and that we all may so pass the time of our sojourning upon earth as to enjoy a peaceful end and to rise in the resurrection of the just, companions of all them that through faith and patience inherit the promises. *Amen* and *Amen.*"

MONTHLY RETROSPECT OF PUBLIC AFFAIRS;

OR,

The Christian's Survey of the Political World.

———

THE country has been in a considerable state of agitation since our last. The example set by the City of London has been followed by counties, cities, towns and boroughs, so that the table of the House was every night covered with petitions from various parts of England against the Income Tax. Even the county of York came forward upon this occasion, and as far as public sense can be known upon any measure, never has it been more decisively proclaimed, than in this instance. All orders and classes of men have united in reprobating this pernicious tax, and it was evident, that if the measure had been carried in the Houses, still so deeply rooted was the public odium against it, that it is not likely that commissioners could have been found to carry it into execution.

The petitions, as they were daily laid before the House, were generally accompanied with some remarks, so that each night produced increasing reprobation of the measure. The pertinacity of the Minister in his determination to submit it to the decision of the House after such marks of reprobation was a subject of general astonishment. Many persons of great consequence had withdrawn from him; but it was presumed, that he was still secure in a very considerable majority: How he should have been deceived in this last circumstance is matter of more surprise, for it is evident, that on the night when he brought on the debate, he had the fullest confidence in victory. Very little debate however arose, the parties seem to have been satisfied, that enough had been said upon both sides; and the question was called for with eagerness when a few speakers only had delivered their sentiments. The result was, that the Minister was left in a minority. The difference between the majority and minority being thirty seven.

Thus ended this great struggle, and it is evident that the declaration of the popular feeling had its share in the overthrow of the Minister. But people must not be led away with the idea, that it is in this country alone that a minister is kept in awe by popular feeling; the fact is, he knows with us its power, but he views it without dread or dismay. In despotic countries popular feeling finds a vent in a very different way. At Constantinople the head of the offending Vizier would have been thrown over the walls of the Seraglio : in Russia the Prime Minister would have exchanged the luxuries of a palace for the horrors of Siberia. In our country a question is discussed in court meetings, city halls, borough meetings. There may be energy and indignation, but animosity and ferocity are never seen there. If the general voice is heard, the minister retires from his station, or giving up the measure continues in it. The country is satisfied with its triumph, and has none of those base sentiments, which belong to the slaves of a despot.

Still it is difficult to account for the Minister's permitting his weakness to be made so manifest. He ought to have known better his own strength, and that of his adversaries. But there may be cases, which justify this sort of pertinacity. The measure was probably determined on in Cabinet, when it was presumed, that the utmost reliance might be placed on the House of Commons, and the great measures of government were formed on this consideration. There are some minds not easily convinced, and when a project has been once formed they will not be diverted from it by the clearest prognostics of its future ill success. Hence the voice of the country went for little, as indeed if other parties remain firm, it is not of great estimation. This might have done in ordinary questions, but in this it must be considered, that the voice of the country was in unison with the private interest of the voters, and however some might, from their offices under government compensate themselves for the tax on their private estates, yet this could not be the case generally, and it was a question, on which individuals

would exercise their private judgment. The curious ties, by which parliamentary connexions are bound together, render it a matter of amusing investigation to see by months before of a decisive majority feels himself unexpectedly in a minority.

The discontinuance of this odious and oppressive tax is a subject of joy not merely in a pecuniary but in a moral point of view. The decline of kingdoms from a state of great prosperity, is owing sometimes to foreign force; at others from the ruin introduced by the governors themselves. This ruin works gradually, and when its evil effects are at last discovered, it is too late to check the evil. Such would have been the case, if this pernicious tax had been continued. The whole character of Englishmen would have been changed. Every man would have his neighbour prying into his concerns, and financial *espionnage* would have prepared the way for *espionnage* of every kind. The noble independence of the English mercantile character would disappear, and when that is lost in vain are to be expected those riches, which have been derived from it. Let us hope that the sentiments which have displayed themselves every where upon this occasion, are a presage, that the horrible war in which this country has so long been engaged, will be followed by years, in which the ancient British honour, economy and industry will appear to great er advantage.

Symptoms of reviving spirit appear in the atttention paid by the House of Commons to that, which is indeed an important part of their business, the expenditure of the country. The Crown recommended economy in its speech, and the whole house is sensible of the necessity of it; but on entering into the details of the expenditure, little regard seems to have been paid to this virtue. Indeed the war establishment is of itself sufficient to confound all expectations that might have been entertained of substantial reform. Many of the petitions from the country were sensible of this inroad made upon our constitution, and spoke of it in appropriate terms. The apologies for it in the House were weak, yet the measure will, it is to be feared, be finally accomplished. An investigation stricter than usual is taking place into the estimates laid before parliament, and as yet the pretensions of ministry to economy appear but in very ludicrous colours. The fact is, the affairs of the country require a serious, dispassionate inquiry, an examination into the past to prevent future abuses, the placing of our finance system on a solid footing, such that it may be examined with the same ease as that of a merchant's counting-house, and every farthing of money may be traced through every channel from its receipt to its expenditure.

A short debate in the House gives rise to many melancholy reflections, and this was introduced by a member mentioning the number of persons confined at present in Newgate under sentence of death. This is owing to the fate of those convicted at each sessions, not having been regularly laid before the Regent in council, so that his next determination will be upon an accumulation of sessions. This destroys a great deal of that solemnity which ought to attend every execution under criminal law; and it becomes cruel at last to execute persons, who have been for a great length of time in suspense between life and death. The language used in the House of Commons upon this occasion will prevent in future the recurrence of a similar evil.

All accounts of France concur in their accounts of its degraded state. We may judge of their views of justice in that country by a prefect declaring his determination whenever a riot takes place in his district, to send out some one principal man from the class of agitators. By this title the prefect probably means some possessor of national domains, whom he may thus get rid of. We have an instance of the king's clemency in the pardon of General Boyer, who had hoisted the tri-coloured flag in the West Indies, on the news that the king had absconded, and Buonaparte had taken his place in the Thuilleries. The guilt of the general is very problematical; but however the Court-martial sentenced him to death; and out of regard to the many services of the general's family, and some good deeds of his own, to his evident contrition and various other items, the king commutes this sentence of death to imprisonment for twenty years. We need not wonder at the sentences of imprisonment for five, seven, ten and more years, so continually occurring in their tribunals. In fact it seems to be true, what they say of themselves, the nation is *demoralisée*, the same want of humanity prevails in all classes. Expatriations are very numerous, and the horrors of Europe will be the cause probably of a numerous establishment on the banks of the Ohio.

The House of Commons at Paris is engaged in a similar manner to ours. They examine the minister's budget with a degree of attention, which might be well imitated here. Every article goes through a committee. Items are not passed in the lump. Remarks are made upon each; and if a saving can be made there is no difficulty in suggesting it. All this it is to be observed is done not by the opposition, as would be the case in England, but by the majority, by that body of overzealous royalists, who are for making the crown every thing, yet in their superabundance of zeal are attacking its influence in the most violent manner. At present no idea can be formed of the future government of this strange people, which after such great exertions will probably fall back into its ancient frivolity, and be the jest of surrounding nations for its grand monarque and its wooden shoes.

Our countrymen have not yet been brought to their trial: but it seems that the plan of trying them for high treason did not succeed. It is a case of misdemeanor only. The curiosity of the public is great both as to the supposed offence itself, and the manner in which Englishmen will conduct themselves in such strangely constituted courts; courts in which every man is considered guilty till his innocence is proved, and every step in favour of innocence is resisted with the most indefatigable industry.

In France the tribunals are at any rate open. Spain retains its horrible Inquisition, and the inquisitor-general has issued a proclamation of no small import to that miserable country. It is probable, that this infamous tribunal could not have entered upon its functions, without creating too great a ferment in the country, and its prisons would not have been sufficient to contain the victims, that would have been brought in the first week within its grasp. An unexampled degree of clemency is therefore displayed. After deploring the wretched state to which the country had been subjected for so many years by the heretics contaminating its soul, and pointing out the necessity of a thorough cleansing and expiation, the falsely-called holy office allows a term for all that have lapsed in any degree from Catholic purity to return to the bosom of the church. This term expires with the close of this year, which will consequently be a busy one, and one very profitable to the Priests. Every one, who is conscious to himself, that he has used any free expressions, must make his bargain with his confessor, and they two together will settle an explanation with the Inquisition. Numbers will act in this manner, and be esteemed good Catholics. No small quantity will free themselves from trouble by becoming officers of the Inquisition, and probably at the end of the time many really good Catholics will be thrown into prison from the calumnies of their enemies. A total purgation of booksellers' shops takes place immediately. This is one of the wretched effects of what has been called the deliverance of Europe.

Of the remaining countries of Europe Prussia occupies most attention. The spirit of inquiry is there much alive, but before they can establish their desired constitution it must be seen, how it will suit the different parts of this straggling kingdom. They are dividing their country into departments, such as that of Saxony, which being dissevered from its former kingdom is now to be the department of Saxony in the kingdom of Prussia. Our country has shewn how easily such departments may be joined together by representation, for not one of them will form so great a mass as that of Scotland or Ireland. The difficulty will be to give a spirit of liberty and independence to the association when formed, that they may concur in making laws, which shall be equally useful to king and subject. However most parts of this straggling kingdom have in general been so ill governed, that we cannot but expect some good from their being united together, and if they get rid only of their military system, that basest of slaveries, they will gradually improve, and deserve a higher rank among the nations.

NEW PUBLICATIONS IN THEOLOGY AND GENERAL LITERATURE.

The Tendency of the Human Condition to Improvement, and its ultimate Perfection in Heaven. A Sermon, preached before the Unitarian Church, Hackney, on Sunday Morning, Feb. 18, 1816, on occasion of the lamented Death of Mr. James Hennell. By Robert Aspland, Minister of the Church. 8vo. 1s. 6d.

God the Author of Peace. A Sermon preached at Mill, Hill Chapel, Leeds, on the Thanksgiving Day, Jan. 18, 1816. By the Rev. Thomas Jervis.

The Happiness of Great Britain. A Sermon at Newbury on the Thanksgiving Day. By John Kitcat. 8vo. 1s.

Moral Discourses, principally intended for Young Persons. By Wm. Pitt Scargill. 12mo. 1s. 6d.

The Claims of Misery, or Benevolence its own Reward. A Sermon, preached at Marble Street, Hall, Liverpool, on Sunday, Dec. 31, 1815, in behalf of the Distressed Seamen. By John Wright. 8vo. 6d.

A New Edition of the Greek Testament, chiefly from Griesbach's Text. Containing copious Notes from Hardy, Raphel, Kypke, Schleusner, Rosenmuller, &c. in familiar Latin : together with parallel passages from the Classics, and with references to Vigerus for idioms and Bos for Ellipses. By the Rev. E. Valpy, B. D. Master of Norwich School. 3 vols. 8vo. 2l. 12s. 6d. L. P. £4.

The Origin of Pagan Idolatry, ascertained from Historical Testimony and circumstantial Evidence ; by the Rev. G. S. Faber, Rector of Long Newton, Yarmouth. 3 vols. 4to. £6. 15s.

CORRESPONDENCE.

Our Publisher has received a parcel from Mr. White, of Carmarthen, we presume a bookseller, containing a number of the Monthly Repository which was sent down imperfect. Mistakes unavoidably happen in the hurry of stitching up the sheets, and these are easily rectified by means of the booksellers. In the present instance, however, Mr. White has put us to the expense of a parcel by the Mail, amounting to *five shillings and twopence*. We might retaliate by sending down the number of the Magazine, set right, by the same conveyance; but we think it best to leave the parcel for him at Messrs. Lackington's, his booksellers, presuming that he will make good the unwarrantable expense to which he has put our publishers.

Mr. Howe's account of the late Francis Webb, Esq. ; the original Letter of Dr. Watts's, communicated by Mr. Kentish ; the paper on Natural Theology, and various other interesting articles too late for the present number will be given in our next.

THE

𝔐𝔬𝔫𝔱𝔥𝔩𝔶 𝔐𝔢𝔭𝔬𝔰𝔦𝔱𝔬𝔯𝔶,

&c.

No. CXXIV.]   APRIL, 1816.   [Vol. XI.

HISTORY AND BIOGRAPHY.

ORIGINAL LETTERS, &c.
*Sketch of the Life, Character and
Writings of the late Francis Webb,
Esq. By the Rev. T. Howe.*

Bridport, March 23, 1816.
MR. EDITOR,

SINCERELY do I join with your
correspondent in the Repository of
February, [p. 71.] in the regret he
expresses, that no *Memoir* of the life
of the late FRANCIS WEBB, Esq. has
yet been presented to the public. His
papers, I am informed, he left to an
intimate friend, the Rev. Mr. Racket,
a clergyman of liberal principles, great
scientific knowledge, various literature, and what is still more to his honour, of a pious and virtuous character, than whom no one is better qualified to become his biographer. Whether he intends to engage in this office
or is restrained by the wish expressed
by his deceased friend, that " he may
not be made the object of posthumous
praise," I cannot determine. An injunction or request of this nature, must
in the view of the present writer, be
greatly *outweighed* by the consideration of *utility* to the public, if a faithful memoir of departed worth be really
calculated to be both instructive and
gratifying. Should Mr. Webb have
kept a journal of the circumstances of
his varied life, (as I am told he did,
written in short-hand) a large volume
might be furnished, abounding no
doubt with interesting information and
rational entertainment. He was a native of Taunton ; but of his early days
I can say nothing. When he first
came out into the world, a dissenting
minister among the General Baptists,
it could not have been expected that
he would afterwards move in so different a sphere. The two little volumes of elegant Sermons he published,
to which your correspondent refers, do
credit both to his head and to his heart.
His inducements to resign the minis-

VOL. XI.   2 c

terial office must be a matter rather of
conjecture than absolute certainty.
Mankind in general are influenced,
I believe, by *mixed* motives. Conscious of talents which qualified him
for almost any department in the State,
it is not improbable that Mr. Webb
was actuated at that time of his youthful ardour, in some degree at least, by
the spirit of worldly ambition. Whether the change in his situation rendered him more useful to mankind,
or really happier in himself, than he
otherwise would have been, is a point
which the present writer will not attempt to decide. Many interesting circumstance of his life, I have heard
from his intimate friends and associates,
and some of them from himself,
though unable to state them in the
precise chronological order in which
they took place. Recommended to the
late Duke of Leeds, he was for some
time, I believe, Secretary to his Grace,
who greatly respected him for the
powers of his mind and the qualities
of his disposition. Sent by our government on a private embassy to one
of the petty Courts of Germany,* the
recital of the scenes he then passed
through has often fixed the attention
and interested the feelings of many a
social circle. One of the circumstances
I have heard him relate of his narrow
escape from robbery and murder, which
was prevented, under the Protection of
an overruling providence, by his courage and presence of mind, I shall en-

---

* To the Prince of Hesse, respecting the
treaty for some of his human subjects called
Christian soldiers, whom we British *Christians* had hired of him a *Christian* Prince to
kill or be killed in our service, fighting with
our *Christian* brethren in America ; all the
professed followers of a leader " meek and
lowly in heart," who has declared, " By
this shall all men know that ye are my disciples, if ye love one another."

deavour to state as accurately as my recollection will permit.

Travelling in Germany to the place of his destination, he was one day overtaken by the shades of night before he could reach the town where he had proposed to sleep. He therefore stopped at a solitary inn on the road. His bed-room was an inner chamber. He had the precaution, not only to lock his door, but also to secure it by some other contrivance. As he travelled armed, he put his sword and a brace of pistols, which he had with him, on the table. He kept a light burning in his chamber, and instead of undressing, he merely took off his coat, and wrapping himself up in his roquelaure, lay down on the bed. In the space of about two hours, he was roused by the sound of steps in the outer room, and a violent push at his door. He immediately started up, took his sword in one hand and a pistol in the other, and calling with a loud thundering voice to these disturbers of his repose to desist, he told them, " the first that entered was a dead man, and that he was prepared to encounter with half a dozen of them." Upon this they thought proper to withdraw. He then made the door still more secure, and expecting another attempt, " gave neither sleep to his eyes nor slumber to his eyelids," but sat down, waiting and preparing his mind for whatever might happen. In about an hour, he heard what appeared to him a greater number of footsteps in the outer chamber than before, and immediately an assault was made at his door with so much violence as would have forced it open in an instant, had it not been for the *additional security* which his prudence had devised. He again addressed them as before, when the villains retreated, some of them uttering the most horrid imprecations. As soon as the day began to dawn, he called his servants, and before he left the house told the attendant that he wished to speak with his master, who however excused himself from making his appearance by pretending he was very ill in bed. When Mr. Webb came to the next town he waited on the magistrate and acquainted him with the transaction, who promised that notice should be taken of it, and congratulated him on his deliverance from so imminent danger of losing his life; for murdering on the Conti-

nent more generally attends robbery, than in this country. Having fulfilled the object of his mission he returned to England, but how much time elapsed before he was again employed in a diplomatic capacity I cannot determine. After the peace of Amiens, however, in 1802, when Mr. Jackson was sent on his embassy to France, (Napoleon Bonaparte being then only Chief Consul) Mr. Webb was appointed his Secretary; but the state of his health obliged him to return at the end of a few weeks. During the short time he was in Paris, his office leading him to frequent intercourse with those persons who then made the most conspicuous figures in the French government, his penetrating genius enabled him to acquire considerable knowledge of their characters and political views, of which he used afterwards to communicate to his friends many interesting particulars.

From this period he retired wholly from public life. His places of residence have been various within the last thirty years. He took a house in the neighbourhood of Crewkerne, where he lived for a short time and attended the religious services of his beloved friend, and, if I mistake not, quondam fellow-student in the Daventry Academy, the late Rev. Wm. Blake, to whom was peculiarly applicable the character which the Apostle John gives of a pious and amiable man, " Demetrius hath good report of all men, and of the truth itself." For some years Mr. Webb resided at Litchet, a pleasant village between Poole and Wareham, and became an attendant on the worship of the Unitarian Dissenters (I use the term *Unitarian* in its most *extensive* signification, as distinguishing from *Trinitarian*) either in the former or latter place. Quitting Litchet in 1809, he went to Norton sub Hamdon, in the neighbourhood of South Petherton. In 1811 he removed to Lufton, in the vicinity of Yeovil, a delightful retreat which Mr. Webb would gladly have retained to the end of his life. Whilst in this place he joined the society of Unitarian Dissenters in the town last mentioned, under the pastoral care of my highly-valued friend, the Rev. S. Fawcett. His residence being a parsonage house, and the clergyman to whom it belonged giving him notice to quit it, his removal to Barrington, in 1814, was the last stage of his eventful journey, which, as you have already announced, was terminated on August 2, 1815, in either the 80th or 81st year of his age. About two years before his death he became a member of the Western Unitarian Society, and at its meeting in Yeovil in 1814, when the late venerable Dr. Toulmin preached, a respectable company of gentlemen dined together, and Mr. Webb was requested to take the chair. This office he discharged with much propriety, and with more spirit than might have been expected in a person on the verge of fourscore. He declared, that "though he had often presided at different meetings, be never did it with so much pleasure and satisfaction, as on the *present* occasion."

No man ever possessed a more *independent* mind than the subject of these remarks. He never hesitated to think freely on all subjects of human inquiry, and to speak unreservedly on proper occasions what he thought. In political sentiments he was a staunch Whig, though this did not prevent him from esteeming a conscientious Tory; in religion, a Unitarian Protestant Dissenter, though of too liberal and enlarged a mind to confine his friendly regards, much less the Divine favour and future salvation, to those merely of his own denomination. He was a man of a delicate moral taste and strong feelings, which led him to perceive clearly and to expose forcibly the deformity and baseness of vice in whomsoever found. A mean, cringing, time-serving disposition his soul utterly abhorred; while he could not refrain from expressing, in terms of rapture, his approbation of noble, generous, disinterested actions.

Cui pudor, et justitiæ soror
Incorrupta fides, nudaque veritas.
                                    Horace.

And where will equal justice find,
Where steady faith and naked truth,
So generous and so great a mind?
                                    Creech.

Warm in his friendships, he was ready, if occasion required, to make the greatest sacrifices to them. His benevolence also prompted him to serve any person who needed his aid to the best of his abilities, some pleasing instances of which are known to the present writer. His companionable powers were of the first class, and no man knew better how to unite the

utile et jocundum. His stock of information seemed to be inexhaustible. There was in his conversation always something new and interesting.

In manners, Mr. Webb had the address of the polished gentleman. In stature, he appeared to be not less than six feet high; of an athletic make; well proportioned; upright in his gait, with a fine, open, manly countenance, expressive both of intelligence and good humour.

The writings of Mr. Webb which have appeared before the public, (few in number) evince a lively imagination, elegant taste, an enlightened mind, and rational, fervent piety. The best Greek and Roman classics were familiar to him, and his memory was so retentive as enabled him to make appropriate quotations from them on all subjects. His allusions to them and the heathen mythology indeed are so frequent, as to cast a *veil of obscurity* over some parts of his poetic compositions, except to those who are themselves well versed in classic lore. The same however may be said of his favourite Milton, and many other poets; but which I think cannot be justly ranked among their greatest excellences. Besides the two volumes of sermons already mentioned, in the year 1790 he published a quarto pamphlet of poems, on Wisdom, on the Deity, and on Genius, the two first in blank verse, and the third in rhyme, enriched with many valuable notes, containing the sentiments of the most celebrated ancients on these sublime and important subjects. In the year 1811, appeared from the same pen, a Poem, termed Somerset, written in blank verse, with the spirit of a *young* Poet, (though he says "*time* has pluck'd my pinions,") and an enthusiastic admirer of Nature, through which he delighted to look up to Nature's God. The following lines will illustrate the truth of this observation, and furnish a specimen of his poetic powers and devotional feelings.

Hail, Nature! in whose various works appears
The fair-drawn transcript of the Mind
    Divine.
In Thee, whate'er is beautiful, sublime,
With correspondent transport we behold.
I worship thee without Idolatry.
Paying Thee homage, I my homage pay
To Him who form'd thee thus to be ador'd.
The Universe his Temple—human hearts

The Altars whence the incense should
    arise
To Him who fills all space; whose Spirit
    pure
Inspires the mind with thought, and guides
    the hand,
Else all unable to direct the plume,
That flutt'ring strives to wing his praise,
From this terrene, up to the radiant Sun,
Thro' all the countless orbs which flame in.
    heav'n,
If flight it could sustain.   But Seraph's
    wing
Would fail; and all too weak an Angel's
    voice
To hymn His glory, and His praise pro-
    claim.
P. 42.

A year or two before his death, Mr. Webb amused himself with preparing a curious work, which he terms Panharmonicon. It consists of a large engraved plate, (delineated by his ingenious friend, Mr. John Nicholetts of South Petherton,) with a quarto pamphlet, designed as an illustration of it. The author states it as his object, to prove that "the principles of Harmony more or less prevail throughout the whole sytem of Nature, but more especially in the *human frame*; and that where these principles can be applied to works of art, they excite the pleasing and satisfying ideas of proportion and beauty."

If it be true, as here maintained, that there is an harmonious connexion between lines of beauty in natural objects, and notes of music, it is evident that the latter, should the mode of application be correctly ascertained, would greatly contribute to exact proportions in the Painter's delineations. To prove that this is not a merely speculative idea, devoid of all utility to society, Mr. Webb makes his appeal to a well-attested *fact.* The ingenious artist, the late Giles Hussey, Esq. of Marnhull, in the County of Dorset, (who died suddenly in 1788,) an intimate friend of our author, used to correct and improve his drawings by applying them to the *musical scale.* His *mode* of doing it is particularly pointed out in a letter* of this celebrated painter. Mr. Webb, it appears, adopted in younger life the sentiment which he endeavours to prove and,

illustrate respecting the harmony of nature. "This work," says he, "was first undertaken merely for amusement, when the author, from bodily indisposition, was unable to exercise his mind by more serious study and closer appliication. The subject ever was, from his earliest days unto those of his present very advanced years, pleasing and attractive. He feels indeed at the present moment of recital, though with abated energy, the rapture which he experienced when, in the course of his juvenile studies, that beam of celestial light was first darted into his mind from the great luminary of science, Sir Isaac Newton, in the astonishing and beautiful discovery, that a ray of light transmitted through a prism; exactly answered in its differently refracted colours, to the divisions of a *musical chord*; or in other words, that the breadth of the seven original colours, were in the same proportion, as the seven musical intervals of the octave. And further delighted was he with the no less wonderful discovery, that if we suppose musical chords extended from the Sun to each Planet, in order that these chords may become unison, it will be requisite to increase or diminish their tension, in exactly the same proportion, as would be sufficient to render the gravities of the Planets equal." Webb's Parhon. p. 1.

As Mr. Webb was delighted in tracing out the beauty and harmony of the *natural* world, so he believed, and the persuasion afforded him still sublimer pleasure, that causes were in operation, appointed by the Sovereign Lord of Nature and Parent of Good, tending to correct the disorders of the *moral* world, and finally to produce universal virtue and happiness, the beauty and harmony of the moral creation of God, almighty, all-wise, and infinitely benevolent. What indeed were his sentiments respecting the result of the gracious plan of the divine government, the final glorious "consummation devoutly to be wished," appears from the concluding lines of his Poem on the Deity.

Nought can He will, but good—and what
    He wills
Must come to pass. All creatures in degree,
Answering his great idea, rise to good
Through countless forms and changes; and
    at last,
Looking complacent on his mighty Works,
As on creation's morn he look'd, and smil'd,

---

* This letter, which I hope other readers can understand better than myself, is also inserted in the late edition of Hutchins's History of Dorset.

(While shouted all the Sons of God for joy)
Pronouncing all was good, th' Almighty
   Sire
His awful consecrating nod shall give
Of final Approbation; and his Sons,
The sacred Hierarchies of Heav'n, shall sing
Triumphant Hallelujahs! Man shall join;
The Consummation of his mighty works,
Triumphant sing, when perfected the plan
Of sovereign Love—and God is All in All,
            WEBB's POEMS. p. 33.

Should this very imperfect sketch of the life, character and writings of the late Francis Webb, Esq. be in the least degree interesting to your readers, and induce any of them, qualified for the undertaking, to favour the public with a more particular and correct account of this ingenious and excellent man, the design of this communication will be fully answered.

    I am, Mr. Editor,
      Yours most respectfully,
        THOMAS HOWE.

N.B. Mr. Webb has left a widow behind him of a very advanced age, still residing at Barrington in Somersetshire.

A Letter of Dr. Watts, hitherto unpublished, on the Deity of Christ. Communicated by the Rev. J. Kentish.

    Birmingham, March 5th, 1816.
SIR,

THE autograph of the subjoined letter, is in the possession of a lineal descendant of the gentleman* to whom it was addressed: and I am permitted by its respectable owner to transcribe it for your pages. It's contents suggest many a reflection: I submit it however, without a comment, to the attention of your readers.

In the copy the orthography varies from that of the original, which otherwise is exactly followed.

      Yours, &c.
        JOHN KENTISH.

Copy of a Letter from Dr. Watts to the Rev. Mr. Alexander.

REV. SIR,
   I return you thanks for your Essay on Irenæus, wherein you have effectu-

---

* The Rev. John Alexander, of Stratford upon Avon, afterwards of Ireland, and father of the Rev. John Alexander, of Birmingham. A short notice of the elder Mr. A. will be found in the Biographia Britannica, (edited by Dr. Kippis), in a communication towards the end of the article *Benson*; where also is a fuller account of the son.

ally proved that Irenæus believed the proper Deity of Christ. As I frequently make remarks in perusing the books I read, I have taken the freedom to do the same thing with regard to this book: but having left both your book and these papers in the country, I cannot possibly send them by your friend. If you come to London this year, I should be very glad to talk them over with you, and enter into some further disquisitions on the same subject.

With regard to Irenæus, the only thing I shall mention at present, is that you have made it evi
contradiction, that Irenæus supposed the Logos, or divine nature of Christ, to be the very νᾶς or mind of the Father, and in that sense to be *the Father himself*, as in one place you yourself express it: and this is manifestly the sense of Irenæus in many places. There are also other passages in Irenæus wherein the Logos is represented as the Son of God, and as a distinct person, or distinct conscious mind or spirit.

Now I beg leave to inquire, 1st, Why the last of these senses, i. e. the Son of God, may not be interpreted into a figurative personality, and so be reduced to the first, as well as the first of these senses, viz. the νᾶς, be raised up to a real, proper, distinct personality, and so reduced to the last? Whether there is not as much reason for the one interpretation as for the other? I cannot but think that it is much more intelligible to represent the νᾶς or mind of God in a personal manner (which is very agreeable to the Scriptural idiom) than to make a real, proper, distinct person become the νᾶς of the Father, or the Father himself, as Irenæus speaks.

2. If Irenæus cannot be reconciled to himself this way, whether the proposal of reconciliation which I have offered, Dissertation 4. Sect. 7, does not bid as fair for it as any thing else?

Or, in the third place, whether there is any need of reconciling Irenæus to himself? For he is weak enough to speak inconsistencies sometimes, or at least to speak words without any ideas.

Now the same thing which you have proved, and I grant, concerning Irenæus may be manifested concerning several other of the primitive fathers; if any man would search into them with that diligence as you have done into Irenæus; and I might make the very same remarks concerning them. They sometimes express themselves like *the Arians*, sometimes like the Sabellians. Now the query is, which of their ways of speaking must be reduced to the other, and interpreted by the other? I know no intelligible medium but what I have proposed, Dissert. 4. Sect. 7.

With regard to the different explications of the doctrine of the Trinity, I am very much of your mind; that is, it is necessary to distinguish the doctrine itself from the human explications. Let us but suppose a divine communion between the Sacred Three sufficient to answer the divine titles and characters and honours given them in Scripture, and a sufficient distinction to answer their several offices, and this is abundantly enough for our salvation; though we be much at a loss about any farther determination.

Yet, amongst men of learning and inquiry, methinks 'tis not enough to say that *God is an infinite spirit,* which we all confess, and that *the Sacred Three are one God,* which we confess also, and yet that we cannot tell whether the Sacred Three be one infinite spirit or three infinite spirits. I would fain come something nearer to ideas. If we content ourselves with mere sounds without ideas, we may believe any thing: but if we seek after ideas, I think we must come to this determination, viz. that the great God is either one conscious mind or spirit, or he is three conscious minds or spirits. Now I have such arguments against the latter that I cannot at present assent to it. If therefore God be one infinite spirit, the word and Holy Ghost must either be the same whole and entire infinite spirit, with some relative distinctions, or they must be some really distinct principles in the one infinite spirit, and as much distinct as it is possible: now either of these two last agrees with my way of thinking: perhaps both these may be joined together; and there are some places of scripture wherein the word and spirit may be represented as the same entire godhead under relative distinctions, and other places of scripture where they may be represented as distinct principles of agency in the same one godhead. These are the best ideas I can yet arrive at, after all my humble and diligent searches into these deep

things of God: and I think both these have been counted orthodoxy these two hundred years. I am very sure that I can bring citations from several great writers, who have been counted very orthodox, to countenance and support both these explications; though of the scholastic account of generation and procession I have no idea.

Dear Sir, let us not always be content to keep these great points of our holy religion in a mysterious darkness, if it be possible to obtain ideas of what we believe. But if there be any scripture which declares this doctrine to be entirely unintelligible, I will then cheerfully acquiesce in the sacred determination of scripture, and submit to believe propositions without ideas. In the mean time, I shall be very glad to receive any hints from Mr. Alexander which may give me occasion to relinquish any opinions which I have proposed: for I acknowledge I am still an inquirer into truth, and ready to learn.

You may assure yourself, Sir, in affairs that relate to your great work, and in all other Christian offices,

I am, Sir,
Your most obedient servant,
I. WATTS.

From the Lady Abney's, in Lime Street, London, April 18, 1727.

Public Character of the late Rev. Joshua Toulmin, D.D.

[From the Sermon on his death, preached at Plymouth, by the Rev. Israel Worsley, and prefixed to "Observations on the Presbyterian Societies of England, &c." a duodecimo volume, just published.]

THE case of our friend, whose death we now contemplate, with mixed emotions of concern and of firm Christian hope, furnishes a striking instance of the sufferings of an upright man in the faithful discharge of his duty.

In order to form a proper opinion of the sufferings of himself, and of many others who were embarked in the sacred cause of integrity and of truth, at a period when this country was not prepared to do them justice or to hearken to their inspired voices, your recollection must be carried back at least twenty years of your lives, or perhaps a few more.* About that time a

---

* The period to which this refers, was the year 1792.

violent fermentation was excited in many parts of this kingdom, which partook of the character both of a political and of a religious persecution. And it is not a little remarkable that, although our religious views are entirely detached from all political considerations, yet it pleased some persons in this country to identify Unitarianism with a freedom of thinking which is inconsistent with the safety of the state. There is only one way in which I can conceive such a mistake to have originated. It is this :—The grounds upon which we form our religious opinions are the inductions of reason and the plain dictates of common sense. By these we interpret the word of God. And it is probable that by these also we interpret the word of man ; and that we are not previously disposed, as all time-serving men around us are, to submit our wills to the will of those in power, and to believe that only to be politically true and right which men in power have imperiously announced for the public approbation and support. There cannot be a doubt that, when a man dares to think freely and honestly upon subjects of the very first importance, upon those grand questions of duty which connect him with his God; and to act up to his thoughts and his principles on these; he will not for a moment hesitate to examine with freedom, and, if there is occasion for it, to expose without ceremony, the unjust pretensions of men in power. And therefore it may with the greater reason be admitted, that, amongst the class of English dissenters who have been generally known by the denomination of Rational Christians, there have been found very few who have been inclined to flatter the vices of great men, and avow themselves the approvers and the patrons of plans of government which would trench upon the liberties of the people, and lessen that influence which every good subject has a right to enjoy in a well-ordered society. There are some members of society who are naturally timid; there are others who are fawning and mean ; there are many who are anxious to obtain the profits of civil government, or afraid of losing what they already hold,* and there is, perhaps,

yet a larger portion of the community who wish only to remain quiet, and peaceably pursue the line they have marked out for themselves, in which they may exist and breathe out, without commotion, the few years which are allotted to them upon earth. I scarcely feel myself authorised to give to any one of these the honourable denomination of the righteous man. If to do the duty of an enlightened member of society be to be righteous—and what can be right but to do our duty in its fullest extent ?—neither he who is afraid of saying what he believes to be right, nor those who crouch before the great and powerful, nor those who sacrifice the slightest duty for the sake of reward, nor those who will spend their lives like moles or like bats, in an ignoble, in a despicable privacy, can possibly merit the title of the righteous man. He only can be righteous, whether we consider the question in an economical, in a political, or in a religious point of view, who says and does all that he believes to be right, after that he has taken pains to inform his mind, and to imbibe the principles of truth and of the general welfare.

I believe that, not the great body of serious thoughtful Christians alone, but also the great body of thinking people in this country, indulged, at the period to which I have alluded, an excessive joy upon the occasion of the French Revolution ;† in which they saw the promise of a mighty people, shaking off the yoke of ignorance, of superstition, and of slothfulness, about to form a constitution in which the rights of man, but more especially, in

---

* If those men who cloak their sentiments, and barter their religious principles for a maintenance, do not betray the best

interests of society, I cannot conceive what men do so. All human duties are marked upon a scale, which distinctly points out their relative importance. Some are of greater influence than others ; and those of the greatest influence demand the greatest care and the steadiest fulfilment. And who will say that the duties of religion are of the least importance ? They are indeed placed by some men very low in the scale ; and, while other duties are deemed imperious, the duties of religion and the support of truth may be tampered with at pleasure, or laid altogether aside. Precept is neglected by them, and their example is hurtful:— as though the world ought to be diligently taught the commandments of men, but it is no matter whether or no they are informed " what the Lord their God has said unto them." ! !

† Which took place in 1789.

which the rights of conscience would be respected and honoured, and under the influence of which they would rise from the state of degradation in which they had been long held by a race of princes, whose favourite maxim had been that *the people were made for them,* to the enjoyment of the rights and liberties of intelligent moral agents, and to a distinct view of the requirements and duties of revealed religion.

It happened also, that about the same time some of those conspicuous events took place which have been, under the blessing of God, the occasion of giving, in later years, a more extended spread to Unitarian principles. I refer particularly to the bold and fearless writings of Dr. PRIESTLEY;—to the establishment of the Unitarian Tract Society in London;—to the publication of various books and pamphlets upon Unitarian principles;—to the application which was made to parliament by a numerous and enlightened association of clergymen for an enlargement of the grounds of admission into the Established Church,—and to the departure, in consequence of a disappointment, of several highly respectable, learned, and popular men, from the pale of the church, and an open avowal, on their parts, of the principles of their dissent from a church whose foundation does not, as they conceived, rest upon the prophets, the apostles, and their great Master.

A considerable alarm was raised in consequence of these circumstances amongst all the orders of society in this kingdom.* It originated with the clergy, the motives of whose anxiety we scarcely need describe. The necessary connection of church and state with each other was then loudly vociferated throughout our island, and it was most industriously rumoured that a conspiracy was formed against the church and state, and that the most active in this rebellion were the Unitarian Dissenters. A pretext for this assertion was readily obtained from an admirable sermon, which had been

published just before by Dr. Priestley† on *The Importance of Free Inquiry,* accompanied with some *Reflections on the present State of Free Inquiry in this Country.* His object in that sermon, and in his reflections, was to shew the imperious duty, and the probable consequences of, a fair and candid investigation of religious truth. Nor do I see how any one can at the present time read what he wrote near thirty years ago, without acknowledging, that he appears to have been almost endowed with a spirit of prophecy, and without feeling a high gratification in the prospect which is held out in his just and irresistible reasoning, of the continued progress of religious scriptural truth, and the accelerated advance it will make, till it has overcome all the opposition of ignorance and of interest.

You will recollect that the riots at Birmingham were the immediate effect of this fermentation:‡ persons of distinguished character took the lead in them, who hoped to put down the accused party by noise, persecution and cruelty. The cause of religious truth was assuredly paralysed by these measures. For, although the same cruelties were not extended beyond the town of Birmingham, yet the terror of them spread throughout England; and many who were immediately connected with the church or the state seem to have " thought it writ down in their duty" to mark out, to stigmatize, and to silence all who avowed the religious principles which Dr. Priestley had publicly maintained.

It is not surprising, that a town of so great public importance as this, in which I have now the happiness, openly and without fear, to preach the doctrines of the gospel to a numerous and highly respectable society, should have felt this political and religious shock; nor that a neighbouring town, still more of a public character, and more under the influence of government, should have sustained the entire loss of an institution which the ignorance and the bigotry of that day deemed a profanation of Christianity and an enemy to the government of the country.‖

* Dr. Priestley's " Letter to Mr. Pitt" and various controversies he had with members of the establishment, and, perhaps most of all his admirable " Letters to the Inhabitants of Birmingham," in reply to Mr. Madan, contributed not a little to alarm and to move the partizans of the Establishment.

† Preached at the end of the year 1788.
‡ The riots took place 1791.
‖ In no part of his present Majesty's

On perusing the history of mankind, we find that such has been the

reign has there openly appeared, in those who immediately surround his person, a disposition to persecute on account of religious differences; which may fairly be ascribed to the antipathy of his mind to every thing like religious persecution. But it has not been uncommon for those who served under him at a distance, and who were not themselves aware of the purity of his mind, to misconceive his wishes, and to imagine that they should render a service to the state by vilifying and by injuring those who follow a religion different from the religion of the state. It has been thought, also, that they were secretly instigated by men high in power. Hence arose, in some parts of England, subsequent to the riots of Birmingham, a disposition to exclude from all public works those Dissenters whom hot-headed Churchmen have marked as obnoxious. Commissioners and other state-agents have been known, who have actually refused to admit to the public works any person who avowed dissenting principles; certainly through a most unaccountably mistaken idea, that, because they were not of the Established Church, they were not the friends of government. In the Dock-yards it is usual for the shipwrights and other workmen to have apprentices under them, who are brought up to their work within the yard. These apprentices must be approved by the commissioner, and must produce certificates of their baptism, in order that their age may be ascertained. In one of our dock-yards, in a subsequent year, all the youths were refused admittance into the yard who could not bring a certificate of baptism from the Established Church. This occasioned great alarm in a town, a considerable portion of whose population are Dissenters. It became necessary, therefore, to make application to government to remedy this cruel grievance; and Mr. William Smith very kindly undertook to do so. Upon a statement of the facts being made by him to Lord Melville, (1801) his lordship assured Mr. Smith that Government would sanction no such partiality, and that the commissioner should be immediately written to. He was forthwith directed to allow, in every respect, the same advantages to Dissenters of every denomination as to the professed members of the Establishment, and charged to make no distinction amongst his Majesty's subjects on account of religious opinions. But interest naturally sways in the minds of parents who are desirous of putting their children forward in the world. Before the decision of the ministers could be known, crowds of boys of all ages under fourteen, flocked to the church at ———, in order, by receiving *Christian baptism*, to be qualified for handling the hammer and

usual course of events. Persecution, of whatever kind, has chilled the energies of the friends of truth, and withheld many from uniting to promote it. But, in a little time, the storm has passed over, and has left behind it the fertilizing means of vigour, of animation and of increase.

Amongst the many who suffered in consequence of the violence of party-spirit at that period, was the friend whose memory we are now willing to consecrate. Residing at Taunton, in Somersetshire, he was at this time evil-intreated, reviled and persecuted; and, together with a highly esteemed medical friend,* a man as upright and as righteous as himself, he could seldom pass through the streets without insult:†—while to keep company with

the adze in the dock-yard of ———; and it is not a little amusing to think, that the clergyman received copies of registers from dissenting chapels and made them his own. And so much has this circumstance weighed on their minds since that period, that Dissenters generally, and avowed Unitarians amongst the number, have formed a sort of habit of taking their children to receive baptism by the hand of a clergyman of the Establishment. If these latter have any serious views of Unitarian principles, it may be questioned how they can, consistently with the principles of conscience, thus introduce their children into life by making a solemn mockery of a religious rite. If, to them, baptism be a rite of no essential importance, and if they think it should be discontinued, it were better to use no baptism at all, and to avow themselves Anti-baptists. But if it be with them a duty, or if they wish to have their children registered in a place to which they may at any time apply for a copy of it, it ought not to be altogether indifferent whether it is done in a manner consistent with their Christian principles, or in a manner which to them must appear ridiculous and absurd, if not impious. Dissenters are not perhaps generally aware, that the registers of a chapel are legal documents: and that there is a place in London (Dr. Williams's Library in Red-cross-street) where registers of the birth of Dissenters' children are kept. A copy of the register from this deposit, although it is not regarded as a legal instrument, yet is always received in our courts of law, and taken as valid evidence.

* Dr. Cox.

† "During this fiery period of persecution he experienced unremitted insult and misrepresentation. At one time Paine was burnt in effigy before his door, and but for the interference and remonstrance of parti-

him was deemed contagious and impossible. Deserving none of the calumny with which he was loaded, in truth the best friend of his king and of his country, his conscious integrity bore him up. He knew that, safe under the Almighty's eye, the rage of his enemies would soon be spent, that the motives of his conduct would be fairly appreciated, and that a far different opinion would ere long be formed both of him and of his conduct, that his enemies would be covered with shame, while he would rise superior to them all.

The man resolv'd and steady to his trust,
Inflexible to ill and obstinately just,
May the rude rabble's insolence despise,
Their senseless clamours and tumultuous
    cries.
The tyrant's fierceness he beguiles,
And the stern brow and the harsh voice
    defies,
And with superior greatness smiles.*

He lived to see things take a very different turn: nor did he quit the place in which he had been thus ill used and persecuted, till there was scarcely one within it who did not respect the independent principles upon which he had acted, and revere the man who could, under such trying circumstances, support and justify them, and triumph with them in the end. In him was seen, and confessed to be, THE RIGHTEOUS MAN ; and he enjoyed the high delight of knowing that he was recognized as such, and of receiving the respectful attentions, the friendly offices of many, who would once have been pleased to blot his name from the annals of the children of men.

Where could a man be found more worthy to succeed the upright, the undisguised Priestley, in the honourable and envied office of teacher to the congregation assembling in the New Meeting, at Birmingham ?

MISCELLANEOUS COMMUNICATIONS.

Exeter, March 12, 1816.

Sir,

THE following letter I received by post, too late for a communication to your last number ; but I solicit for it a place in the next. I am sure that if it had been addressed to you, (as it should have been,) it would have been readily admitted into the Repository. I trust it will never be said with justice, that the Monthly Repository refused admittance to a correction of its errors.

I regard your work as of high value to the cause of free inquiry and religious liberty. It has undoubtedly contributed, in an important degree, to the spread of Unitarianism, and to the union of those professing it: and we are ready to acknowledge our great obligations to you for the perseverance, exertion and ability with which you have so long conducted it. But the opponents of our religious views are widely mistaken when they consider the Unitarian body, or any individual among them, (except yourself and the writer of the particular article,) as answerable for the contents of the Monthly Repository.

When I looked at the article [p. 35] which led to the letter of my anonymous correspondent, I regretted the expression " *Popish* Renderings." The enlightened Catholics of our country at least disclaim the appellation *Papists :* and as among the illiberal, it is a kind

cular friends, he would have undergone a similar fate. The house of an interested neighbour was so closely connected with his, that, to save himself, he employed all his influence to save the doctor's premises from the devouring flames. But, although the persecuting spirit was in this instance repelled, it unhappily succeeded afterwards in breaking the windows of his house in every direction in which they could be assailed : and after he had been obliged, for the sake of peace, to quit his then abode, and to relinquish a concern in which Mrs. T. had been long engaged, he was still insecure, and was poisoned by the bitterest rancour. One evening a large stone was aimed at his head through his study window, where he was sitting, with an evident intention to strike a mortal blow. His agitation of spirits on this occasion was excessive ; because the act manifested such determined malice. His bed-room windows were nightly beset ; nor can one say what fatal event would have ensued if a professional friend had not taken up his cause, and, collecting a few more to assist him, watched these midnight foes, who finding they were thus watched, at length, through fear desisted."

LETTER FROM BIRMINGHAM.

* Justum et tenacem propositi virum, &c.
        HORACE.

of abusive nickname, those who know the wide difference between distinctive appellations and party names, and especially those who protest against a similar act of injustice towards themselves, ought not to employ such terms as are made the vehicle of bigotry and intolerant abuse.—I believe that where the general progress of knowledge has been shared by the Catholics, their religious system is greatly ameliorated. Certainly as Protestants, prizing the grand principles of the Reformation, and rejoicing in the light which it diffused where before there was more than Egyptian darkness, we should be injurious towards those to whose labours we owe so much, if we endeavoured to throw a veil over those great corruptions from which they cleared gospel truth; but we do a much greater injury, if we charge upon the enlightened Catholics of the present day, those corruptions, and that intolerance which, as far as they allow their existence, they join us in reprobating.

I doubt not that most readers of the Repository, who knew of no other Catholic translation of the New Testament into English, than the Rhemish, would, like myself, take for granted, that the renderings which Middleton cited are to be found in that Version. The Gleaner must have done the same. He has quoted Middleton accurately; but he would have done well to have examined into the truth of his statement. 'The simple fact is, that as far as respects the Rhemish Version,* it is utterly unfounded.' And it may furnish us with a useful warning, to consult all important references, as far as we have the power; especially if they wear a party aspect. If we fall into any error, however trifling and purely unintentional, our opponents seize it with avidity to disgrace our character and our cause. If they would place the case fairly before the public, it would signify but little; but it is the

system of the present tomahawk warfare against us, to write down our reputation as critics and as men, in order to wound Unitarianism through its advocates. Such is the nature of that ungenerous attack which Bishop Burgess has for some time been making against Mr. Belsham: and I may be permitted thus to express my congratulations with our veteran and respected friend, on his recent masterly and honorable termination to his share in that contest. We must all feel on what high ground he stands in this controversy, and how successfully he has maintained it.

Where is the recent opponent of Unitarianism who has taken up the grand question at issue, on the broad basis on which we rest it, and where it must stand immoveable, because our foundation consists of the plain, unambiguous, express, and often repeated declarations of the Scriptures, which, unless Revelation can contradict itself, render the common interpretations of a few dubious passages, utterly inadmissible?

The letter which has caused my present address to you, is as follows.

SIR,

No. 121, for January 1816, of the Monthly Repository, has accidentally fallen into my hands. I should not address myself to you on this occasion, but supposing you to be a friend to that work, and that possibly you may correspond with its Editor. Do desire him to be careful in what he publishes, and remember that great commandment, "Thou shalt not bear false witness against thy neighbour." I allude to an article, p. 35, "*Popish Renderings.*" The texts are stated wrong; I give you the exact words, as they are written in the English translation (a modern tongue) out of the Latin Vulgate, published by the English College at Rheims, 1582, published by Keating and Co., the only translation sanctioned by the Roman Catholic clergy. St. James v. 11, "Behold we account them blessed who have endured," &c. not a word about "beatify." Heb. xi. 30. "By faith the walls of Jericho fell down, by the going round them seven days," not "after a procession of seven days around it." 1 Tim. v. 10. says not a word about lodging "Pilgrims." 3 St. John 5. "Dearly beloved, thou dost faithfully whatsoever thou dost for the

---

* This was made by the English Catholic College at Rheims, in 1582. It retains many words which need translation; and it is merely a translation from the Vulgate: but it is worth consultation. The rendering of John xvii. 5, is important: "And now glorify thou me, O Father, with thyself, *with the glory which I had before the world was, with thee.*" This more readily allows the Unitarian interpretation, than the common rendering does.

brethren, and that for strangers:" no " Pilgrim" mentioned. Now, Sir, whenever you or your friends quote, do let me desire of you to keep in view our blessed Saviour's golden rule, " Do as you would be done by." As I wish no controversy with you, (but merely to set you right, that you fall not into the like again,) I subscribe myself your obedient servant,

✠

It seems best to add, that the handwriting of the above is unknown to me; but that I am persuaded it did not come from the respectable Catholic clergyman of this city, of whose Christian liberality we have had repeated and impressive proofs, and who would I am sure have taken a different mode of pointing out these errors.

I am, Sir,
Yours truly,
L. C.

———

Sir, *Bath, 10th December,* 1816.

IT will, I presume, be a high gratification to most of your readers, if some of your ingenious correspondents will favour them with a clear explication of the doctrine of angels which is contained in the whole scriptures. The angels who kept not their first estate to whom Jude refers, I take it for granted, were the lying spies who gave a false account of the land of Judea; and the angels who are mentioned in the first chapter of the epistle to the Hebrews, to be prophets who went before and predicted the coming and character of Christ.

"But what I intend at present, is to attempt an explanation of the word *angels*, which we find in Romans viii. 28. The apostle had declared in the context, that he was so fully satisfied of the truth of the Christian religion, and of all its promises to the righteous, that neither the fear of an immediate death, nor of the most tragical life, nor the malice of principalities or of their delegates, nor any afflictions which they could impose upon him at present or threaten him in future, nor any dangers present or to come, not even the being made a spectacle to the world in lofty situations, nor being drowned through violence in the sea, nor any possible occurrence in this world, should be able to separate him from the love of God which is in Christ Jesus our Lord. He said also, that

angels should not have this effect upon him. Expositors explain him, as saying evil angels, meaning exalted beings who surrounded the throne of God, and who were degraded because of their apostacy, but were now suffered to traverse the regions of the air, to tempt men to imitate them in their horrid degeneracy and disobedience. At first sight we may observe upon this explication, that the apostle knew nothing of such angels, and that instead of any such being invested with a power over men, in opposition to the great Creator, we learn that every man is tempted by the indulgence of his own lusts. We should consider, therefore, that the word *angels* always signifies *messengers*, and that if it had been always translated *messengers*, one great difficulty would have been removed out of our way. Now, what were the messengers whom the apostle had to encounter, but the messengers of persecuting princes and of others, who by their murdering threatenings endeavoured to reduce all Christian preachers to silence? Such messengers, therefore, with all the terrors which he here introduces, could, he asserts, make no impression upon him, whilst he knew in whom he believed, whilst he professed the gospel, and such should be the resolution of every one of us, whilst we look not at things seen and temporal, but at things unseen and eternal.

Hence, then, we should learn to employ ourselves in such studies as will most effectually terminate in our conviction of the truth of the gospel, and of the blessed hope which it sets before us, if we walk worthy of our heavenly calling. We should therefore search the scriptures with all piety and diligence, and be directed to lay hold upon that unfailing inheritance which will be the portion of all those who love God, and keep his commandments, when this world and all the things of this world shall be no more. We should, therefore, sedulously practise all the duties which are required from us as the disciples of Christ, worshiping God in spirit and in truth, and looking unto him as our only strength and refuge, whilst we do to all our fellow creatures, as we would have them do unto us; and we should particularly cultivate a charitable disposition towards those who most widely differ from us, blessing them whilst they curse us, and exercising every act of humanity, whilst they do us every injury in their power. We should give no room to the most rigid Athanasians to speak any evil of us. Whilst they judge us and pass the sentence of condemnation upon us, we should pity them and pray for them, and so make our light to shine in all purity, peace and benevolence, that even they may gradually learn truly to glorify our heavenly Father.

W. H.

Sir, *Norwich, 25th March,* 1816.

IT is the duty of every friend to religious truth, to assist in the preservation of those monuments of human intellect, which inculcate the importance of Free Inquiry and defend the Right of private Judgement, when these monuments are wasting under the destroying hand of time. On this subject I quite agree with Dr. Carpenter, that the republication of works of sterling value of this description "may have great efficacy in weakening the influence of religious bigotry;" and perhaps nothing is 'etter suited to this purpose than the works which he mentions in his letter, dated Jan. 8, in the Repository for that month.

Wishing therefore to lend my feeble aid in a cause which I deem highly important (particularly at a time when we seem to be relapsing into the bondage of a blind fanaticism,) I have sent to the press for republication, a Copy of *Dr. D. Whitby's Last Thoughts,* with his Discourses annexed thereto: to which will be added some Account of the Life and Writings of this learned Divine, the friend of *Hoadly.* As I hope soon to be enabled to announce its publication, I shall esteem myself greatly favoured by receiving such hints and communications from any of your Correspondents, as may assist me to render both the main work, and the biographical part as complete as I wish them to be.

I am, Sir,
Yours very sincerely,
JOHN TAYLOR.

Natural Theology. No. XIII.

Of the Face, Complexion and Speech.

THE face is particularly used to denominate the visage of an animal,

and especially of a man, as being in him the only part of the body that is usually visible. The great variety observable in men's faces, voices and hand-writing, furnishes a capital argument in defence of a Providence.

The human face has been denominated the image of the soul, as being the seat of the principal organs of sense, and the place where the ideas, motions, &c. of the soul are chiefly set to view. Besides the eyes, nose and ears, the other parts of the face present, separately, nothing very particular in their structure or uses. The forehead covers the greatest part of the frontal bone of the skull, on the inside of which lies the brain, descending as low as the orbits, and it is ornamented at its lower edge by the eye-brows, which also serve as defences to the eyes, and which are calculated to display the passions of pride and disdain. From the forehead the skin is continued to form the eyelids, whose uses, together with that of the beautiful row of hairs which grows from each of their edges have already been described. The cheeks serve as side-walls to the cavity of the mouth, and also constitute the principal share of the face: in many persons they are tinged with the bloom of health; and often in the fair sex exhibit a most beautiful and indescribable something denominated modesty. The cheeks are lined on the inside with a membrane full of small glands, for secreting a liquid to moisten the mouth. The lips complete the cavity of the mouth, and form its aperture; these are moved with several small muscles, and are covered at the edges with a fine red border, consisting of villous papillæ closely connected together and extremely sensible, being defended only by a very thin membrane. While the chin terminates the inferior boundary of the face, and completes the number of its divisions.

The features of the face viewed collectively, present a striking and beautiful characteristic of the superior nature of man. In the whole creation there is not another object, probably, which breathes so many, such various, and such elevated influences as does the human countenance. To this we naturally look in conversation for the full meaning of the words expressed, and by it we are enabled to anticipate the emotions and feelings of others, before they reach the tongue. "It speaks," says a good writer, "a language peculiar to itself; anticipating and outstripping all others in rapidity; which is general to all nations, and intelligible to every individual of the whole human race: by this language have our circum-navigators been able to hold converse with, and interchange civilities between themselves and the untutored inhabitants of remote regions. Even the brute animals, whom man has domesticated and made his occasional companions, are not ignorant of this kind of expression; when the dog wants to know the commands of his master, unable to understand them in the complicated sounds of his speech, he looks intently upon his face, and endeavours to collect from it his wishes, and the disposition with which he regards him. All the affections and passions of the mind are more or less pourtrayed in turn in this very limited but expressive field; love, pity, courage, fear, calmness, anger, and every other marked condition of the mind gives a peculiar disposition to either the whole or some features of the face; and when they are impressed by characters expressive of virtue and wretchedness, of injury and innocence, our feelings are awakened, and the noblest sympathies of our nature are called forth in favour of the sufferers."

It may be observed, that to the size and proportion of the bones underneath, and which constitute the basis of the face, the difference of features is to be principally attributed; youth, age, sickness, health, and even the stronger affections of the mind, no doubt have an effect in changing the countenance; but that diversity of feature consisting of the difference of length, breadth, or projection, depends chiefly upon the bony frame that lies below it. Hence arise the Aquiline, the Grecian and the African nose, &c. the high cheeks of the Tartars, and the more regular ones of the people inhabiting the West of Europe: the same may be said of the other features, and from this difference in them is that great diversity produced, which gives variety to the countenance, not only of nations but also of individuals ; so that no two of the whole family of mankind could be found exactly alike, But notwithstanding this wonderful diversity, we are not to suppose that the individual features composing each

face are different from those of all other faces; the features may be confined and limited to a certain number of kinds ; but each is; probably, capable of an indefinite number of combinations with other features; and, that as from twenty-four letters all the words composing a language are constituted, so are produced, from, perhaps, a very few kinds of features, by transposition and various composition, the astonishing and beautiful variety of faces we see around us.

We may observe here, that there are three things in connection with this subject which manifest the wisdom of the Creator; these are the great variety of men's faces, voices and hand-writing. Had not the human countenance been the result of Divine wisdom, the wise variety, of which we have been speaking, would never have existed, but all faces would have been cast in the same, or at least not in a very different, mould : the organs of speech would have sounded the same, or nearly so, and the same structure of muscles and nerves would have given the hand the same direction in writing. In this case, what confusion, what disturbance, to what mischiefs would the world have been subject ? No security could have been given to our persons; no certainty, no quiet enjoyment of our possessions. Our courts of justice can and do abundantly testify frequently the dreadful consequences of mistaking men's faces and of counterfeiting their hand-writing. But as the Creator has ordered the matter, every man's face has some character to mark it from others in the light, and his voice in the dark, and his handwriting can speak for him though absent, and be his witness, and secure his contracts to future generations. A manifest as well as admirable indication of the Divine superintendance and management !

Of the complexion. The colour of the skin has engaged the attention of naturalists, and it has sometimes given rise to opinions that were extremely injurious to the happiness of mankind; as directly asserting, that, in violation of the eternal principles of justice and the sacred rights of humanity, the people of one colour had a right to seize and enslave those of another. But now the seat of colour being discovered, and some of the circumstances which influence its changes being known, these erroneous opinions are exploded, and instead of seeing ground for the slavery and ill-treatment of our fellow-creatures, in the difference of their complexion from our own, the philosopher and the Christian contemplate the shades of the human countenance, as he does the variety of its features, and beholds alike in both the provident design and work of the Supreme Architect.

Dr. Hunter, who considered this subject more accurately than has commonly been done, determines absolutely against any specific difference among mankind. He introduces his subject by observing, that on the question whether all the human race constituted one or more species, much confusion has arisen from the sense in which the term species has been adopted. He accordingly defines the term, and includes under it all those animals which produce issue capable of propagating others resembling the original stock from whence they sprung; and in this sense of the term he concludes, that all of them are to be considered as belonging to the same species. And as in plants one species comprehends several varieties depending on climate, soil, culture, &c. so he considers the diversities of the human race to be merely varieties of the same species, produced by natural causes. Upon the whole, colour and figure may be styled habits of body. Like other habits they are created not by great and sudden impressions, but by continual and almost imperceptible touches. Of habits, both of mind and body, nations are susceptible as well as individuals. They are transmitted to their offspring and augmented by inheritance. Long in growing to maturity, national features, like national manners, become fixed only after a succession of ages. They become, however, fixed at last; and if we can ascertain any effect produced by a given state of climate, or other circumstances, it requires only a repetition during a sufficient length of time to augment and impress it with a permanent character.

It is ascertained that what we denominate the skin of the human body consists of three parts, separable from one another: viz. the scarf-skin, which is external, the thicker or true skin beneath it, and a coagulated substance which lies between both. This co-

agulated substance is the seat of colour in the skin, and that which causes the various shades of complexion in the different inhabitants of the globe, from the equator to the poles; being, in the highest latitudes of the temperate zone, generally fair, but becoming swarthy, olive, tawny and black, as we descend towards the south.

These different colours are without doubt best adapted to their respective zones, although we are ignorant how they act in fitting us for situations that are so different; and the capability of the human countenance to accommodate itself to every climate, by contracting after a due time the shade proper to it, affords a fine illustration of the benevolence of the Almighty. This pliancy of nature is favourable to the increase and extension of mankind and to the cultivation and settlement of the earth: it tends to unite the most distant nations—to facilitate the acquisition and improvement of science, which would otherwise be confined to a few objects and to a very limited range, and likewise by opening the way to an universal intercourse of men and things, to elevate the various nations of the earth to the feelings of a common nature and a common interest.

Of Speech. In addition to what has already been said on the human voice, we may observe, that the organs for effecting speech are the mouth, the windpipe and the lungs. The *mouth* needs no description. The windpipe is a passage commencing at the back part of the mouth, and thence descending along the neck, it opens into the lungs; at the upper part it is constructed of five thin cartilages, connected by ligaments and put into motion by small muscles. These cartilages form a kind of chamber at the head of the tube, which is situated at the root of the tongue. The opening of this chamber into the throat is a very narrow chink, which is dilated and contracted to produce every change in the modulation of the voice, by the muscles attached to the cartilages. To defend this opening there is a beautiful contrivance of an elastic valve which falls flat upon it whenever we swallow, like the key of a wind instrument, and which at other times rises up and leaves the aperture uncovered for the uninterrupted ingress and egress of the air into the lungs. The *windpipe,* or tube, leading to the lungs is so formed as to be always open, and to resist compression; at the same time it is quite flexible, and gives way to all the bendings of the neck; had it not been so we should have been in perpetual hazard of strangulation. The passage to the stomach, on the contrary, being intended only for occasional use, has its sides always collapsed, unless when distended by the passing of food. The lungs are two cellular bags for containing air; they are situated in the chest, and both open into the bottom of the windpipe.

In the act of inspiration the air dilates the lungs; these, like bellows, force it back in expiration into the windpipe: here the air is straitened in its passage, and made to rush with force along the tube towards its upper end, where it is variously modulated, and the sound of the voice is produced. In articulation the voice is required to pass through the mouth, where it is differently modified by the action of the tongue, which is either pushed against the teeth or upward against the palate, detaining it in its passage' or permitting it to flow freely by contracting or dilating the mouth. It has been remarked of the tongue, that it is the only muscle of the body under the controul of the will, which is not wearied by incessant use.

Speech is a high and distinguishing prerogative of man. By this noble faculty we are enabled to express all our feelings and inclinations; to communicate our thoughts, and blend our energies, our knowledge and discoveries, with those of others. In written language, form and permanence are given to evanescent sounds: the ideas and the improvements of one age are transmitted to a succeeding one: the superior acquirements of one country are scattered over distant regions, and knowledge, civilization and happiness diffused far and wide.

Sir,

YOUR correspondent I. W., p. 23, has quoted passages from several authors, in which he conceives the word but has been improperly used; and in order to give his notion of the meaning of the word, he says, "This is a conjunction, which when we meet with it is a kind of stop to the sense, and prepares the mind to expect a change of subject, or an opposition to what went before." He, however, modestly suspects he may be mistaken, and asks for information.

On reference to the "Diversions of Purley," Vol. i. p. 190, &c., I. W. and such other of your readers as are fond of language, may find a clear and copious exposition of the word but. Lest, however, I. W. should not have that inestimable work at hand, which it is evident he has never read, I will endeavour to give him in a few words a sketch of the learned author's luminous view of the subject. He says, "it was the corrupt use of this one word (but) in modern English, for two words (bot and but), originally (in the Anglo-Saxon) very different in signification, which misled John Locke, and which puzzled Johnson in his Dictionary, where he has numbered up eighteen different significations of the word." The first mentioned but or bot is the imperative of botan, and answers to sed in Latin and mais in French, and this appears to be the but to which I. W. has confined his definition or description—the other but is derived from bute, or butan, or be-utan, and answers to nisi in Latin—"this last but (as distinguished from bot) and without have both exactly the same meaning; that is, in modern English, neither more nor less than be-out."

It is this last but, the want of the knowledge of which has occasioned all the perplexity both in the mind of your correspondent and also of many of his *more learned* predecessors, and which knowledge was never clearly developed but by that man whose philological labours are an honour to his memory, and whose valuable papers, having been committed to the flames by himself in a fit of spleen, are an *irreparable* loss to the republic of letters, and operate as a serious visitation of the injuries he suffered, on generations yet unborn—a retaliation of injustice, not on those who committed it, but on innocent and unconscious inquirers. The omission of negation before *but* is one of the most blameable and corrupt abbreviations of construction in our language. In the example,' my intent is *but* to play, was formerly written, my intent is *not but* to play.

Most of the instances which I. W. has given of the improper use of the word *but* exhibit a perfect redundancy in which the total omission of the word actually clears the sense in the quotation.

" I trembling wak'd and for a season after
Could not believe *but that* I was in hell."

I think he will discover the evident difference between that *but* which answers to his description and the *but* which Mr. Tooke derives from *be-utan* and signifies *be out, nisi.*

S. W.

Mansfield, March 11, 1816.

SIR,

I BEG leave to propose to your correspondent W. H. to reconsider the ground upon which he has stated it as Dr. Chauncey's sentiment, "that *the righteous,* in successive ages, will pass through many deaths, or states of oblivion". (M. Rep. for Feb. p. 69). The Doctor's words, in his treatise " On the Salvation of all Men" (London, printed in 1784) are as follows : " Some will be disposed and enabled in this present state, to make such improvements in virtue, the only rational preparative for happiness, as that they shall enter upon the enjoyment of it in the next state. Others, who have proved incurable under the means which have been used with them in this state, instead of being happy in the next, will be awfully miserable ; not to continue so finally, but that they may be convinced of their folly and recovered to a virtuous frame of mind. And this, as I suppose, will be the effect of the future torments upon many ; the consequence whereof will be their salvation, they being thus fitted for it. And there may be yet *other states,* before the scheme of God may be perfected, and mankind universally cured of their moral disorders, and in this way qualified for, and finally instated in, eternal happiness," (p. 12.) He considers the " death," which is said (Rom. vi. 23,) to be " the wages of sin," as the same with what is called (Rev. ii. 11, xx. 14, xxi. 8.) " the second death" (p. 277). And, having asserted (p. 279) " that the first death is intended to put an end, not to our existence, but only to its present mode, with all its connections and dependencies," he maintains, that, " at the resurrection, the souls of wicked men will be again related or united to particular systems of matter, somehow adapted, by the wisdom of God, to render them capable of communication with the world they shall then be placed in ; that they will become fitted for sensations of pain, vastly more various in kind, and greater in degree, than at present, which yet they will be able to endure for a much longer continuance ; but that, in time, the torments they must endure, will (again) end in death, that is, in a (second) dissolution of the union between their souls and their bodies ; that, in God's time, their souls shall be (again) united to their bodies ; and if, by means of the torments of hell, they have been humbled, and so brought into subjection to the government of God, as that they are meet for his mercy in Jesus Christ, the bodies they shall be related to shall, by the Divine wisdom and power, be fitted for that glorious dispensation when God shall be all in all ; but, if not, they shall again, in some other form of existence, be put into a state of suffering and discipline, till at length they are, in a wise and rational way, prepared for final and everlasting happiness" (p. 281, 282). On the contrary, he maintains, in regard to " *the righteous,*" that they " will pass into that final dispensation (in which God himself will be immediately all in all), *not by dying again*, but probably in some way analogous to that in which the believers that are alive on the earth at Christ's second coming, shall pass into the resurrection state ; upon which account their *life* and happiness may properly be said never to have an end" (p. 283) ; in proof of which he refers to those passages which speak of their not being hurt by the second death, of their putting on incorruption and immortality, and especially to that declaration of Jesus that they can die no more. (Rev. ii. 11, 1 Cor. xv. 53, 54, Luke xx. 36—see p. 287). Without entering into a discussion of Dr. Chauncey's opinions concerning the nature of man, or the operation and effect of death, I presume that these quotations will sufficiently prove that the sentiment ascribed to him (that *the righteous* will, in successive ages, pass through many deaths) was not his.

J. T.

Bromley, Jan. 12, 1816.

SIR,

A COPY of the foregoing Resolutions of a Meeting* having been

---

* Inserted p. 50.——ED.

lately sent me by a much valued friend of mine, who took a prominent part in the proceedings of the day, I send the same to you, not doubting but they will be generally acceptable to your readers, as a gratifying proof how warmly " the cause of universal liberty of conscience" has been recently asserted in the sister kingdom, by persons of the most opposite sentiments on the doctrines of the Christian religion.

After expressing his preference for the 5th of those Resolutions as it was first moved, my friend in a letter annexed to them makes the following pertinent observations, which you are at liberty to present to your readers. "I do not," says he, "charge the British ministers with directly promoting persecution in France, but I certainly do conceive they were less susceptible of alarms on this subject than in their zeal against liberty and revolutionary principles. They were anxious to place the old dynasty on the throne of France; thus they risked the more than probable return of the bigotry which characterized many of this feeble race. In the present temper of the times, the governors intoxicated with their triumphs on the restoration of legitimate despotism, and the people meanly crouching to them, I should not be much surprised, if for a season, arbitrary power should again come into fashion, and by the people surrendering their rights, freedom, both civil and religious, should become ' Dream of a dream and shadow of a shade.'

"I embraced the opportunity of the persecution in France by Catholics to turn the public attention to the persecution at home of our Protestant Church and State mob against Catholics, and even against the liberal among the Protestants. Our domestic persecution is less severe than the late attacks in France, but in the course of twenty-two years many have fallen victims to it, and many Catholic chapels have been burned, as well as innumerable outrages of less magnitude committed. The Orangemen have also gone as far as the spirit of the times and the circumstances of the country would permit, and our Irish persecution has only differed from the French in being more limited in extent, but not in the spirit which actuated it. In short, I think it would have been hypocritical affectation in us to have cen-

sured the proceedings in the South of France if we had not impartially reprobated the conduct of our Irish Orangemen, as being alike hostile to the principles of civil and religious liberty."

Yesterday's post brought me the Belfast Commercial Chronicle of Saturday, Jan. 6, 1816, from which I send you the following interesting letters, and remain, sincerely yours,

THOMAS FOSTER

Friends of Civil and Religious Liberty.

The following correspondence on the subject of the Resolution passed at the Meeting held in this town on the 11th ult. has taken place. The Resolution ran thus:

Resolved Unanimously—That the thanks of this meeting be returned to DANIEL O'CONNELL, Esq. as being the first in Ireland to call public attention to the Persecution of the Protestants in France, at a meeting of the Catholic Association in Dublin; thus evincing, that in the honourable pursuit of Catholic emancipation, and protection from the hostility of Orange Outrages, he only sought for himself, and his fellow-Catholics, that Liberty which he was equally ready to grant to others."

Lisburn, 12th Month, 13th, 1815.

DEAR FRIEND—I have great satisfaction in communicating to thee the annexed resolution of a meeting held in Belfast on the 11th inst. It is a just tribute to thy honourable firmness and zeal in the cause of civil and religious liberty, which, after a close attention, I have always found to be displayed in thy public conduct, as well as in the private correspondence with which thou hast occasionally favoured me.

I am, with sincere respect, thine truly,
JOHN HANCOCK.

DAN. O'CONNELL, Dublin.

Merrion Square, 16th Dec. 1815.

MY DEAR SIR—The kind manner in which you have transmitted to me the vote " of the friends of civil and religious liberty in Belfast," demands my sincerest thanks. I am truly proud of that vote. It is a rich reward, infinitely beyond the value of my poor exertions in the sacred cause of freedom of conscience.

I have ever sought Catholic emancipation on principle, and as a matter of right. That principle, if established, would be equally useful to the Protestant in France and Italy, as to the Catholic in Ireland. It is a principle which would leave conscience free and unshackled in every country, and without which real liberty cannot, in my opinion, exist in any country.

As a Catholic I feel myself bound, not only by the genuine precepts of my religion, but by the glorious example of other Catholics, to be the first in my humble sphere to disclaim and oppose the persecution of Protestants. The state which first, after the reformation, established freedom of conscience, was a Roman Catholic State—that of Maryland, in North America. The only government in modern days that has granted total and unqualified emancipation to a religion different from its own, is the Roman Catholic Government of Hungary ; in which the Protestants were in our own times fully emancipated by their Roman Catholic countrymen.

Let us hope that the day is not distant, when those noble examples of justice and pure religion will be not only admired but imitated by Christians of all denominations. Let us hope that man shall at length be allowed to worship his Creator according to the dictates of his conscience, without the impious interference of penal laws ; and that bigotry and persecution may be banished from amongst nations boasting of Christianity and civilization.

I have the honour to be,
With sincere respect,
Your very faithful and obedient servant,
DANIEL O'CONNELL.
Johy Hancock, Lisburn.

Southampton, 13th March, 1816.

SIR,

I COULD wish to draw the attention of your readers to the great question of a *religious establishment*—is it *wise, just, necessary* or *politic ?* The Dissenters from the Establishment are *now* become so numerous and respectable as to challenge and deserve the serious attention of the legislature —let them then unite on the *broad ground* of *dissent*, and present a respectful petition to the House of Commons, that *they* may be no longer subject to the *payment of tythes.*

To be obliged to support a church whose doctrines we reprobate, as contrary to reason and scripture ; and to be punished and disgraced for our dissent, by being excluded from the discharge of civil offices, is no longer to be borne.

Let every congregation then be required only to support its own minister, as is the case in *America,* and elsewhere—particularly in *Prussia* ; and let not *one* sect be obliged to support *another*, by a tax levied upon the community at large.

The beneficial effects of such an arrangement, in whatever light we view them, are greater than many persons are aware of. One in particular would be, the abolition of *religious* distinctions, and the restoration of Dissenters

to their *proper* rank and station in the community.

The abolition of tythes would be also a *national* advantage, especially in the present distressed state of agriculture, whose *necessities* imperiously demand their remission.

Who are the persons that would consider themselves aggrieved ? Those who are not entitled to any favour or consideration from the public,—the *indolent* and *luxurious clergy,* the *"fruges consumere nati."* I compare this class to a large and increasing wen attached to the body politic, which is drawing off its nourishment, and will prevent its restoration to health until it be removed.

The money drawn annually from the industrious part of the community under the head of tythes is *enormous*, and the shameful manner in which it is distributed renders the burthen more grievous and intolerable.

With *civil* sinecures let us then get rid of *spiritual* ones, and it would strengthen us to raise the supplies for the year, and save us from the alarming apprehensions and dreadful consequences which our present *distressed* and *oppressed* state cannot fail to excite in the breast of every thinking man.

B. T.

SIR,

I COPY the subjoined from *Niles's Weekly Register*, published in Baltimore, America, Vol. II. p. 33, thinking it not unsuitable to your work.

A. B.

Legislature of Kentucky, Jan. 10, 1812.

Report of the Committee of Religion.

The Committee of Religion to whom was referred the petitions of sundry persons respecting the people called SHAKERS, have, according to order, had the subjects of the same under consideration, and beg leave to report—

Without regard to religious persuasions, sects or faith, of any particular denomination whatever, your committee recommend to the consideration and adoption of the house, the following Resolutions :

1st. Resolved—That an open renunciation of the marriage vow and contract and total abstinence from sexual and connubial intercourse, agreeably to the intentions and objects of matrimony, ought to be provided against by law.

2nd. Resolved—That provision ought to be made by law, for the competent support of the wife out of the husband's estate, when abandoned by him under such circumstances.

3rd. Resolved—That provision ought to be made by law, for the competent support of children out of their father's estate, where they shall be by such father abandoned under like circumstances.

4th. Resolved—That guardians ought to be appointed to the children of husbands so abandoning their wives, who should have the care of the persons and estates of such children.

5th. Resolved—That when a wife is so abandoned she ought by law to be permitted to acquire and hold property as a *femme sole*, as well as to have reasonable parental control over her children, by the husband so renouncing the marriage contract; and when prayed for, she should have divorce granted, without its benefits being extended to the husband so abandoning her.

In adopting the foregoing Resolutions, your Committee are not unmindful that religious tenets are not the subject of legislative or judicial interference.

They entertain too high respect for their country, this legislative body, and themselves to recommend any measure contravening those golden provisions of our constitutions, which declare—"That all men have a natural and indefeasible right to worship *Almighty God* according to the dictates of their own consciences ; and no human authority ought in any case whatever, to control or interfere with the right of conscience."

Your Committee can but regret, that in all ages and countries, individuals have been found too ready to condemn all other sects and persuasions, save that adopted by themselves, should they have adopted any.

These unfortunate individuals, wanting the benign influence of Christianity become odious themselves, by that interference which prompts their exertions to bring odium on others. It is the good fortune of the *real Christian*, that in our enlightened day, this intolerance recoils back on the intolerant ; and thus, while working their own destruction, they make the rays of Christianity shine but the brighter.

With these sentiments your Committee leave the Shakers, and all other sects, to pursue, uninterrupted, the dictates of their own consciences—leaving their religious creed to the approbation or disapprobation of themselves and their God.

Mr. Worsley on the Marriage Ceremony.

Plymouth, Feb. 16, 1816.

Sir,

I AM so perfectly aware of your wish to promote the investigation of all subjects which are interesting to Dissenters in general, that I scarcely conceive an apology to be necessary for requesting permission to call their attention through the medium of your pages, to a subject which has remained long enough, secretly wounding our peace, to a rite which has scandalized our profession, or is calculated to rob us of some of our most delicate enjoyments. I refer to the subject and to the rite of marriage, as this rite must of necessity be submitted to by the English Dissenters, if they have not made the bold resolution of not submitting to it at all. It happens to have fallen to my lot to fill the office of Secretary to the Devon and Cornwall Unitarian Association, which was established last midsummer twelvemonths. At our last July meeting, which took place at Tavistock, this was one of the subjects which engaged our attention, and it was rendered the more interesting from the circumstance of our having in company a more than usual proportion of those gentlemen who are known by the name of Old Bachelors. It did not appear whether these gentlemen had been influenced by Unitarian scruples, or by scruples of any other character, in determining thus to abandon the first duty of an active citizen ; but, Sir, we did not quit the room in which this interesting subject was discussed till I had received a charge in the character of secretary, to correspond with the Associations which meet in other parts of England, and endeavour to unite them all in resolute exertions to seek for relief on this point. It has occurred to me, however, that the better way of bringing this subject before the public, is by means of the Repository. Allow me then to offer some thoughts upon this very interesting subject, in the hope that they will call forth other and more interesting and useful ones, and that they will, ere long, bring about our wished-for end. It is interesting in the highest degree to all classes of Dissenters, who cannot but wish to be released from the necessity of taking their brides to the established church ; but to Unitarian Dissenters it is most of all important, and seems upon the ground of absolute duty to demand their serious consideration and their firm purpose.

This is a subject, Sir, which naturally unites the serious with the gay ; and it may be considered on the broad basis of general expediency and justice, or upon the more limited ground of private feeling.

We are not permitted to enjoy the privileges of wedded life unless we will go to the priest of a certain religion, which may be the religion we approve or not, as the matter happens to fall out; and without uttering certain words he dictates to us, which may or may not contain sentiments which we conceive to be indecent, absurd, nonsensical or idolatrous. Here then our rights as subjects of a free government, in which the people bear a respectable and powerful part, are certainly broken in upon. We expect indeed to give up some of our natural rights and privileges in order to enjoy those of social life; but there is no occasion for us to abandon any in the enjoyments by which we cannot injure the society in which we live; nor have we any occasion to submit to forms and ceremonies which to us appear absurd and mischievous. We shall not object to other men's being as absurd and as foolish as they please to be; but they have no claim upon us to justify their folly by following their example ourselves.

In the earlier periods of society the ceremony of marriage, though ever equally important, assumed a very different character to that which it now bears in our country. It was regarded as nothing more than a social engagement entered into by a man and a woman, to increase the virtuous pleasures of life, and to convey down to other creatures the privileges of human beings. It was then performed, as it generally still is in most parts of the world, by a man going to the house of the woman's parents, and there in the presence of the family and other friends taking her to wife; or by taking her from the house of her father to his own house, where he called in his friends and neighbours to bear witness that he had taken her for his wife. Christian priests appear to have been more skilful in cutting out work for themselves which would be profitable to their fraternity, than even the priests of the ancient Pagan systems or those of Jewish renown, celebrated as they were for gulling the people by an abundance of rites and ceremonies, and fattening upon their spoils. The ceremony of marriage was first converted into a religious rite and made one of the seven sacraments of the Church of Rome by Pope Innocent the third: and the Church of England, which in so many things adopted the plans of that Church, did not think it expedient to give up so profitable a concern, as that of being instrumental in administering to a man's pleasures, at a moment when he is usually most of all moved to be liberal to his benefactors.

But the Church of England did not at first take to itself the exclusive power of performing the ceremony of marriage. For when the principles of the reformation had spread in this country and different classes of Protestants sprang up, they all performed this rite for themselves; the Dissenters marrying in their respective places of worship. This general practice prevailed in this country till the year 1753, in the reign of George II., when the celebrated Marriage Act was passed; the object of which too plainly is to turn the attention from the pure act of marriage, to the ceremony which the priest performs, and which gives occasion to much deceit and wickedness.

By the English law, marriage is regarded as of divine institution. Now if the reader would know what is the ceremony of marriage as it has been ordained of God, and was recognised by the Levitical law, let him look into the 22d Chapter of Exodus, ver. 16, 17, and into Deut. xxii. 28, wherein the case is clearly and fully described; and then let him examine the laws of England, and refer to the various decisions of our Ecclesiastical Courts, he will find they are of a contrary character, and militate directly against the clear object of that law.

The marriage act declares, that "if a person shall solemnize marriage, except it be in Scotland, or except he be a Jew, or a Quaker, in any other place than in a Church or public Chapel after the publication of bans as therein directed, or by special licence from the archbishop's court, such marriage shall be null and void;" hereby completely taking away from all other Dissenters the privilege they had previously enjoyed, and giving all the power and benefits of the marriage ceremony to the Clergy of the Church of England.

But exceptions are made in favour of the Jews and the Quakers. It may be asked, how happens it that these two classes enjoy this high privilege, while other classes equally respectable do not? And is there any justice in granting so partial a favor? To the first question it can only be replied, it has happened, because these two large bodies of men have stood up firmly for their rights, and would not submit to any of the ceremonies of the established church; and because government men were aware that if these people were to be compelled to violate their consciences, in order to legalize their marriages, they must inevitably lose the whole body of them, and all the advantages of a political and social nature which are derived to this country by their residing within it. It is much to be regretted that this act was suffered to pass with so courteous a silence on the part of the other Dissenters, in which no provision was made for them.

For what possible reason can be assigned, why two classes of dissentients from the established church should follow the dictates of conscience in so high a civil concern, however respectable we must acknowledge them to be, while to us it is forbidden? What possible reason, except on the ground of a religious scruple? and that religious scruples equally strong do exist in the minds of other Dissenters will appear in our subsequent remarks; while if the Quakers and the Jews are competent to make registers of their marriage contracts, and in case of need to prove the validity of such engagements, the other dissenters are equally qualified, and may do it with as much safety to the state and to the public at large.

When the District Meetings of the united Dissenters took place in the year 1789 in all parts of England, there were three objects in their view: To obtain the repeal of the Test and Corporation Acts, which was their principal object; to obtain the repeal of the penal laws relative to religious professions, and to get an emendation of the Marriage Act. It was thought expedient, in consequence of circumstances which then occurred, to drop the design of those meetings. But, so much is the spirit of the times improved, and so much are the minds of the men of talent and authority in our country enlightened since that period, that the second of these objects

has been obtained in the most gentle and gratifying manner, in a manner highly honourable to the feelings and the liberality of our houses of parliament. The penal laws against certain religious opinions and professions are no longer a disgrace to our Statute Book: that which was an offence to a respectable and valuable body of the subjects of these realms has been removed being Now, certain Acts, now going to inquire; the question of the Marriage Ceremony stands exactly on the same ground as that of the penal laws. To the Government of this country it cannot be a matter of the smallest consequence in what way Dissenters form their marriage contract; nor can they wish the established clergy to be engaged in the celebration of that rite which unites a man to a woman until death, any more than in that which unites an infant to the Christian Church, or which consigns a human being to the land of forgetfulness. We are allowed to bury our dead and to baptise our children, and our registers of such acts are received as legal documents, why may we not also marry our young people by such rite as we shall approve, and give our legal certificate of such a marriage?

Great objections are made against the marriage ceremony itself as it is performed in our churches, because, although in point of fact it is a civil contract, it has been made by the laws of our land a religious rite,—thus completely changing its character and design, for no other purpose than to make it a source of wealth to the established clergy; for admitting that there is a propriety in a public avowal of a marriage contract in the society of religious professors to which the parties belong, according to the practice of both Jews and Quakers in this country, yet we have the greatest ground of complaint to our legislature of the service itself we are compelled to go through when entering into wedded life.

In the very exordium of that service we are struck with the following absurdity—"that matrimony is a honourable state, instituted by God in the time of man's innocency, signifying unto us the mystical union that is betwixt Christ and his Church." This, to say the least of it, is a most delicate refinement upon the other mysteries with which Christianity has been loaded, and by which it has been well nigh borne down; and truly nothing but the very love of mystery could have led the compilers of our Liturgy to compare the union of the person of a man and that of a woman with the union of Christ and his Church. Here one cannot say what one would, to expose the absurdity of such a comparison. We must be content with remarking, that mystery has been the great source of wealth to the priesthood of old times and all times, and that a more profitable mystery has not been devised than that which mixed up the purest pleasures of life with the interests of the Christian priesthood.

Next follow the three causes for which matrimony is said to have been ordained.

There is a manifest indecency in the first cause, which certainly need not be stated in the Christian assembly supposed to be present, and which, especially when the couple appear at the altar with their hoary locks, can excite no other than a smile.

The second appears to cast a slur upon the very "honourable state" itself as though it had been ordained, not as an act of pure benignity to the virtuous man, and good member of society, but as a covert into which the rogue may fly to escape an unavoidable crime.

The third is the only cause which can with propriety be assigned in a public company for entering the married state, and if it be necessary to offer any apology at all for the act, of which there may be a doubt, this is a sufficient one.

Although the solemn charge which follows these causes of matrimony, cannot on its own account be objected against, yet to the virtuous couple it is perfectly needless, while the violators of decency and of rectitude will disregard it.

I know not whether I may venture to object against the queries which follow " wilt thou have this woman, &c." " wilt thou have this man, &c." which are addressed by the priest, first to the man and then to the woman, on the ground that, as they meet on equal terms, the same solemn engagement should be entered into by both

of them. Yet in our service, while the man covenants "to love, comfort, honour and keep" the woman, she, is required to do more, "to obey and to serve the man." Is there any marked difference in the original formation of the two classes of the human species to justify a partiality of this kind? Or has it not happened that the law owes its birth to this circumstance, that the male part of the species have been, viva voce, the framers of human laws? Some years ago a Liturgy was used in an English Church on the Continent in which many marriages were celebrated; in that Church the man and the woman were required to enter into the same solemn promise and engagement with respect to each other, " to love, comfort, honour and keep in sickness and in health, and forsaking all other," &c. Your readers will judge, both male and female, whether that Church or the Church of England was the more just in its requirements. If, however, for a moment we wave the consideration of right to make such a statute, it may be allowed to the sceptical by-stander to ask, what is the good of it? is it not in most cases obliging an intelligent creature of God to make a solemn vow which she does not mean to fulfil? Let the Dunmow flitch of bacon maintain the argument.

The charm which follows in the marriage service is one of the most entertaining things one can well conceive of; for as we are not on these occasions in a humour to be horrified at any thing, we can scarcely keep our lips in a posture sufficiently steady to articulate the magical words "With this ring I thee wed, with my body I thee worship, and with all my worldly goods I thee endow." I must suppose that with most people these words are a mere abracadabra. They have always reminded me of the jan—van—tin—tan—tire—rare—litter—air—van —fain—well, of which, when I was a boy, I remember to have heard that these sounds were, under certain circumstances, calculated to produce a most surprising effect. A venerable Divine of the last age was accustomed to say of the words of this charm, that the man who repeats them is guilty of three of the greatest crimes which the Bible knows—" with this ring I thee wed;" that is witchcraft—with my

body I thee worship;" that is idolatry
—"with all all my worldly goods I
thee endow;" that is a lie. As a
proof however of the weakness of human nature, or perhaps still more of
the strength of human passions, we
are also told of the venerable Seer, that
he had been guilty of this three-fold
crime three several times.

We know so little of the lives of
Abraham and Sarah, or those of Isaac
and Rebecca, that there is more than
a doubt of the propriety of introducing
them into the marriage ceremony; while
we feel a persuasion that they would
be better left out; for in truth they
offer a facility of scoffing and banter
to those who are disposed to turn a
serious and a solemn compact into a
jest.

These are objections, Sir, to the
marriage ceremony of the Church of
England, which, it is presumed, are
felt by serious thinking men of all
societies of Christians, as well in the
Church as out of it. Surely the great
body of the people would be pleased
with being rid of so much nonsense
altogether.

But the most serious objection a-
mongst that class of religious professors
by whom these pages will be read, is,
the name in which this engagement
is entered into, "in the name of the
Father and of the Son and of the Holy
Ghost." We are obliged to make a religious rite of what numbers can regard
in no other point of view than as a
civil compact; we are obliged to go to
a church to celebrate this rite from
which we carefully and conscientiously
withhold ourselves on every other occasion, and we are obliged to contract an
alliance in a name, which either conveys no idea whatever to the mind,
or which we conceive to be an insult
upon common sense, and an offence to
the One Living and True God whom
we worship. This, this, is the severest cut of all. The folly of some
parts of this service, and the indecency
of other parts of it, we might perchance
upon such an occasion be inclined to
tolerate by a laugh of scorn; but when
we come to use a name which we conceive to be the foulest spot on the fair
face of Christianity, the great stumb-
ling block of its professors, and the
terror which excludes from its pale
thousands and tens of thousands of se-
rius persons, or which involves in such
a dreadful mist those who do enter,

that they can scarcely even see that two
and two make four; joking is at an
end, the countenance resumes its sobriety, and for a moment we are even
induced to doubt whether we ought
not to turn from an altar on which we
are compelled to sacrifice every best
feeling, every pious devotional thought.
Can it be, Sir, that under any other
circumstances than those in which
advantage is taken of our weakness,
we should consent thus to abandon
our religious principles, and act in
direct opposition to our most serious
convictions.

These thoughts will for the most
part appear just to dissenters of all
classes, and it is desirable they should
unite to obtain parliamentary relief;
but to Unitarians it most clearly belongs to consider this subject seriously,
and to act upon it with firmness; nor
can we doubt that their number, their
respectability, and the disposition
which is manifest in the best circles to
indulge their religious views and accommodate the laws to their prejudices,
will insure to them the right and privilege of every rational creature of God
in a natural or in a social state.

ISRAEL WORSLEY.

Newport, Isle of Wight, Feb. 7, 1816.
        SIR,

YOUR correspondent D. E. (p.
22.) has invited the discussion in
the Repository, of the question, how
far it is proper for Unitarians to be
married at Church, and has called
upon them to apply for legislative permission to marry among themselves,
as is the case with the society of
Friends and the Jews. I perfectly agree
with D. E. that it is extremely improper to oblige Unitarians to go to
church for this, or any other occasion;
because to the common objections to
the Church, which all Dissenters
have, they have the additional one arising from their different view of Christian doctrine. And consequently no
Unitarian can fairly join in the service. It is true they may stand quite
unconcerned while the Priest is performing his duty; they may be quite
inattentive, as far as devotion is concerned, to the ceremony, as we may
witness the ceremonies of the Roman
Catholics in conducting their worship
—and this I know has been done, at
least, in one instance. But still, as I very
much dislike having to do with reli-

gious services, unless the heart and mind are thoroughly disposed to enter into these services with purity and spirit. I must say, I think, to consecrate marriages at Church is a profanation of the holy religion which as Christians we profess. I object to it for all Christians, not merely for Unitarian Christians. I object to it, Sir, because it is lugging in religion with a matter which has nothing to do with religion, and which belongs to the civil magistrate, and not to the priest. It may be said in answer to this, that marriage is a divine institution, and that nothing can be so proper as to enter into it, with minds imbued with a spirit of devotion, and to ask upon the act, the blessing of heaven. That marriage is a Divine institution I readily grant. It has always appeared to me so. But the *contract* between the parties marrying, on the notification of this contract, is a matter of *civil* concern. And so it is regarded in this country. D. E. justly remarks, that the remedy for the breach of this contract is to be sought for in our courts of law ; for in this view the ecclesiastical court may be considered : but if we except this court, which regards only minor transgressions, or at least in a minor way—the remark is just. And it is observable that the marriage contract has been varied by different people. This any one may satisfy himself of, by going no further than to Calmet's account of it among the Jews, —who mentions a disagreement as to the ceremonies to subsist between Buxtorf, Selden, and Leo of Modena. The marriage therefore as a divine institution is one thing ; the contract between the parties quite another. It may however still be said, 'if the institution be divine, is it not right to keep up the idea of its being so, by celebrating the contract within the sacred walls used for the purposes of devotion ? Is it not right then to ask, as is done by the present ceremony, and as if in the more immediate presence of the Almighty, whether the parties are aware that there is any impediment why they may not be lawfully joined together in matrimony ; and to assure them that " so many as are coupled together otherwise, than God's word doth allow, are not joined together by God, neither is their matrimony lawful?" To which I reply, provided marriage were entered into as

a *religious obligation,* this might be well ; but as it is notoriously not so entered into, it appears to me to be a shameful farce of things holy, to put such questions ; more especially as the young people or the by-standers are not told what it is that God's word allows or forbids thereupon. And if they were told, would it in any probability have any effect?' Mr. Editor, the discussion of the subject of marriage is almost sure to give rise to some droll ideas ; and I feel that in handling it I may be thought fanciful ; but I must say there are two things omitted in the cautions given to young persons on this head which appear, to me at least, essentially to be avoided in marriage, provided it is expected that the Divine blessing will attend it. First then, I say, I think property, or consideration of property, should never be the basis of the marriage contract. I do not mean that a wife with forty thousand pounds may not be more convenient for many purposes than a wife with only one ; but I do mean that he who marries the woman with forty thousand pounds, while he really in his heart and judgment prefers the woman with only one, is a complete violator of the institution of marriage. For if, as appears both from the Old and New Testament, to be the case, the man and wife are to be as dear to each other as though they were one *flesh,* does not he thwart the design, and go contrary to the spirit of the institution who marries, what, in respect to his feelings of regard, is nothing but a statue of gold? It cannot be said that those enter into the benign spirit of this institution, who make it a matter of traffic, or political regulation. But further, those persons violate the marriage institution, who enter into it, having previously thereto been connected with any other man or woman, such man or woman being still alive. If I can read my Bible rightly, marriage is the connection between the sexes : and the first connection (in the eye of heaven) forms the man and wife. I consider those to be, in the estimation of heaven, *adulterers* and *adulteresses,* who take a wife or a husband at church, unless all those with whom they have been previously connected are dead. Some of your readers, Sir, will smile at this remark, and say, " who then will be saved?" To this question, which need not be answered, I shall only say, I hope, for the sake of my fellow-christians at large, that my views are wrong. If, however, I am right, what hypocrisy, what profanation is it for our marriage ceremonies to be performed in Church! It would be more in character for ninety-nine couples out of the hundred to be joined by the hangman rather than the priest. We talk much of Christianity having abolished *polygamy*. I am no friend to the practice; but of one thing I am certain, that it has no where so strongly prohibited polygamy as it has forbidden fornication : and when I look through the *Jewish* religion, and see how well female virtue was protected, I cannot believe that under the Christian system, those will be regarded with the favour of the Universal Parent, with whatever pomp their marriages may have been solemnized, to whom we owe the necessity of Penitentiary houses, Magdalen hospitals, &c. &c. From these observations, you will observe, Sir, that the devotional spirit which some people think so proper for persons to possess who are about to enter into holy matrimony, and which they also think the present mode of solemnizing it has a tendency to promote, I think should be felt before marriage is *thought of at all*. And the man who only feels devotionally in this matter just when the priest is going to tie him by a knot which cannot be undone for life, has the same sort of bastard devotion as the culprit feels, in the apprehension of encountering on the morrow the hangman's noose.

If these imperfect hints, Mr. Editor, should provoke a discussion, which, conducted with as much modesty as the subject will admit of, shall tend to make the institution of marriage more rightly understood, more devotionally sought after, and more religiously observed, I shall be satisfied in having brought it before the notice of your readers. At all events I shall be happy to see success attend the exertions and project of your correspondent D. E.   J. F.

———

Sir,   *Hackney, Feb.* 16, 1816.
WHEN I sent you the article, inserted Vol x. p. 741, I had not seen the advertisement of an intended Bible Meeting in Bethnal Green Church, which called forth the Rector's extraordinary letter. Having

since seen it posted up in many parts of the parish, and to-day another advertisement intended as a defence of the Rector, I send you copies of both.

The first will shew in what terms the meeting was advertized, which the Reverend Gentleman was, it seems, apprehensive might " convert so sacred an edifice" as his " freehold—the church, into a bear garden." The other exhibits an authentic exposition of his " great lenity and forbearance;" towards *one* of his parishioners, who did not understand, as is evident, the paper he signed, and *three* others whose confessions relate only to the alleged libel, and who may not be very competent judges, and especially under the dread of an impending prosecution, how far the large hand-bill contains any libel against the Rector, unless it be *his own letter.*

Prosecutions are however, I understand, going on against at least *eight* of the Rector's other parishioners, including the author of the imagined libel, all of whom refuse to make any similar acknowledgement, or to sign their names to any such paper. I forbear making any observations on their confession which the Rector has been authorized " to insert in one or more of the daily papers, or to publish in any other way which he may think advisable," than on a few plain matters of fact. I would in the first place observe, that to claim the right of *opposing* the circulation of the Holy Scriptures in the manner the Rector's letter to the Churchwardens proposes, and to which the said hand-bill refers, is not to attempt *opposing* their circulation *entirely*, or in any other manner. Nor is it to charge him with " attempting *to prevent* the circulation" of those writings amongst his parishioners *altogether*, but only through the medium of the Bible Society, which is well known to distribute them *without the Prayer-Book.* My introductory observations, which were published long before I had any knowledge, or even suspicion that such a prosecution was thought of, will evince that this was my impression of the extent of the Rector's objection to the circulation of the Scriptures by the Bethnal Green Bible Association, which surely his letter warrants, and he will not deny. One of his parishioners has since confessed that he has frequently calumniated, unjustly opposed, and wilfully misrepresented his motives, character and conduct; but all these private injuries, *however great,* seem very improperly brought forward on this occasion, having nothing to do with the libel alleged to be contained in the large hand-bill. The first notice of the intended meeting was expressed in the following terms.

Bethnal Green Bible Association.

"The First Annual Meeting of this Association will be held at the Parish Church of St. Matthew, Bethnal Green, on Thursday, November 14, 1815, at six o'clock in the evening precisely. George Byng, Esq. M. P. President, in the Chair.   **** The attendance of the labouring classes is earnestly requested."

After the Churchwarden received the Rector's very unexpected letter, at a late hour the evening before the meeting was appointed to be held, it was concluded "for the purpose of avoiding contention," and " to prevent the Church from being" in the Rector's apprehension *again* turned into a Conventicle, "that the meeting should not be held in the Church, but in Gibraltar Chapel." Of this adjournment it was necessary to inform the public *very promptly,* and this was done by the publication of the notice sent you, consisting of a very few introductory lines, and *of the Rector's Letter,* that his parishioners might see for themselves the true character and spirit of his opposition to the Bible Association, *as exhibited by himself.* About three months after these events, the following advertisement was published, and posted up throughout the Parish, in vindication of the Rector's "*character and conduct,*" while a prosecution was pending in the Court of King's Bench against a number of his other parishioners "for having posted up and otherwise distributed" the said notice of the adjourned Bible meeting, Viz.

"I, the undersigned Hilkiah Samuel Young, of Church Street, in the Parish of St. Matthew, Bethnal Green, in the County of Middlesex, Undertaker, belonging to the *Sect* of Methodists, and *lately* one of the Committee of the Bible Association, having frequently calumniated the Rector of the said Parish, unjustly opposed him, and wilfully misrepresented his motives, character and conduct, and having posted up and otherwise distributed and circulated large hand-bills, charging the Rector with a design of attempting 'to *prevent* the circulation of the Holy Scriptures amongst his parishioners.' And we, James Christopher Sanders, of 157, Church

Street, in the said Parish, *Painter and Glazier;* John Mouson, of Tyson Street, in the same Parish, *Publican;* John Pettit of. Bethnal Green Road, *Watchmaker* and *Collector to the Auxiliary Bible Association;* having inadvertently and imprudently suffered the said hand-bills to be posted up in conspicuous parts of our respective dwellings, and believing the same to contain a most gross, false and malicious Libel, tending to lower the Rector in the estimation of his Parishioners, and to sow the seeds of dissension in the Parish, do, in this public manner, and with feelings of the deepest contrition, express our sorrow for the offence; humbly begging the Rector's pardon for its commission, and *earnestly requesting* the peaceable and well-disposed part of the Parish *to attribute* this most shameful and wanton attack on the character of the Rector, *to the instigation of men,* who *ought* to have set us *a better example,* and who take this method to shew *their enmity to the Establishment.*

The Rector with great lenity and forbearance, of which we are *fully sensible,* having instructed his solicitor to withhold prosecutions against us, on the condition of our *giving up the Author of the Libel,* paying all expenses, and solemnly pledging ourselves to behave towards the Rector in future with the respect which we believe to be due to his character and conduct, and to avoid giving him any interruption in the future performance of his Sacred Duties, do hereby authorize him to insert this public expression of *our* pardon and sorrow, in one or more of the daily papers, or to publish it in any other way which he may think advisable."

HILKIAH SAMUEL YOUNG,
JAMES CHRISTOPHER SANDERS,
JOHN MOUSON,
JOHN PETTIT. *

---

* In the Times of Monday, Feb, 19, 1816, the above confession and *exhortation* was published, to which by way of preface, the following information was prefixed, concerning the hopeful progress of the prosecution, while it rests *only* on *ex parte evidence,* and the no less philosophic "contemplation," of an indefinite number of " other prosecutions," against "*the remainder* of *the Offenders,*" as they are termed, previous to being heard in their own defence, and to the judgment of the law being pronounced. "We have been credibly informed (say the Editors of this paper) that the libel, to which the following apology refers, has been widely and industriously circulated in a very extensive and populous Parish, and that a grand jury of the County of Middlesex have within the last few days, found a true bill against *eight* of the offenders, and that other prosecutions are *in contemplation against the remainder.*"

. Such are the conditions on which the Rector is desirous it should be *publicly known*, he forbears to prosecute these persons, who not only express their deep contrition and sorrow, for their offence, but earnestly request their "well-disposed" neighbours to attribute the supposed libel, not to "the author," whom they engage to give up to the vengeance of the law, which they were themselves so terrified at and so anxious to escape, but "to the instigation of men" who it seems ought to have set them "*a better example*." Who these men are does not *expressly appear*, but the Rector's letter, and this *intended* justification of his conduct, (which does not even once mention *his letter*) are both strongly marked with hostility to the Bible Association. It is therefore probable, at least, that its ostensible agents are the persons described therein as shewing "*their enmity to the Establishment*," by promoting the professed object of the society, the distribution of *the Scriptures alone*, "*without note or comment*."

I shall not presume to anticipate what the judgment of the Court of King's Bench may be on the case, after its real merits shall be sifted to the bottom, and fully investigated; but the article I sent you before on this subject having been inserted in your journal, its well-established character for impartiality appears to me to require I should also send you copies of the above documents. Patiently and respectfully waiting the result of the Rector's appeal to the law of the land,

I remain, sincerely yours,

PHILEMON.

Field of Waterloo.

SIR,   *April 2nd*, 1816.

I AM one of those who cannot pretend to rank with "the more intelligent class of your readers," such as your worthy correspondent (p. 185) designed to gratify by his remarks on *Waterloo*, and the two military Dukes.

I must, indeed, confess a taste so anti-martial, that I feel no interest in the discovery that the Duke of Marlborough first entertained the project of converting the peaceful field of *Waterloo* into an *Aceldama*. War, whether presented in the form of victory or defeat, still appears with *garments rolled in blood*, and equally affects my

mind as the *drum's discordant sound* affected the poet of Amwell :

To me it talks of ravaged plains, :
And burning towns and ruined swains, .
And mangled limbs, and dying groans,
And widows' tears, and Orphans' moans.

I am thus in some danger of estimating in the lowest *moral* rank of our species, however exalted by fortune, the mere soldier, who gives his nights and days to cultivate the science of human destruction, and whose *virtus* can only be translated *valour*.

Whether "the great troubler of Europe," whose blood-stained laurels were too often drenched with *widows' tears*, possess no other claim to distinction, let those who have considered the events of the last twenty years, or studied the *Code-Napoleon*, determine.

Your correspondent must allow me to suspect that he was deserted by his usual and justly acknowledged candour when he adopted this favourite *common-place* of priests and courtiers. The Pope and his Jesuits, the *beloved* Ferdinand and, his Inquisitors, and especially those *fruges consumere nati*, the family of Bourbon, will readily agree that Napoleon was *the great troubler of Europe*. Yet the lately persecuted Protestants, whose protection had been extensive as his power, and the French peasantry who, under the Imperial Government, had gradually acquired the comforts of independence, may be justly expected to demur. Nor will an impartial historian fail to discover some good reasons for suspecting that the wisdom rather than the violence of Napoleon, excited the late coalition of Europe.

When, in the revolution of ages, a great *man* rises from among the multitude and invests himself with power, he naturally excites the antipathy of his contemporaries, who are only great *Kings* and great *Emperors*, "waxen images of souls," as a poet expresses it, who must be conscious that to the mere accident of birth they owe all their distinction from the common crowd.

Your correspondent ascribes to the Duke of Wellington a sort of sacerdotal character, under which he was employed as priest, I suppose of Mars or Bellona, to "consecrate this same post of Waterloo by a signal victory." Here I cannot help recollecting "an Hymn for the consecration of Colours," which was printed, and came into my hands twenty years ago, and of which this first stanza runs in my head.

> All people that on earth do dwell,
> : Full sweetly let us sing '
> The praises of the God of War,
> For 'tis a comely thing.

As to the Dutch Deputies who forbad the Duke of Marlborough thus to *consecrate* the Field of *Waterloo*, their decision might, after all, be correct, considering the Duke of Wellington's acknowledged hair-breadth escape from a ruinous defeat by the unexpected attainment of a " signal victory."

I cannot take leave of your correspondent without giving full credit to his love of peace, and joining him in a wish for " permanent tranquillity," a good for which we can scarcely venture to hope. We differ only from the different aspects under which we have viewed our subject. He appears to have imbibed some portion of the enthusiasm produced by the late *heyday* of victory, and can contemplate " the pomp and circumstances of glorious war," while I have indulged the sober sadness produced by beholding the monster stripped of the specious habit which he wears in the *masquerade* of civilized, and especially of fashionable life, and appearing in native deformity, dreary and disgusting.

PACIFICUS.

On Poetical Scepticism.
No. II.*

SIR,

THERE is no subject on which the orthodox believer and the poetical sceptic more entirely coincide, than that of *mystery*. It cannot be denied that there is something congenial to the human mind in the contemplation of objects which it sees but in part; and this arises from its perpetual love of action, and its partiality for its own creations. When a magnificent object is placed before our eyes, in its full proportions, little more is left us but to gaze and admire. But when a gloom is thrown round it which half conceals it from actual observation, our higher faculties are called into exercise ; imagination fills up the void ; a thousand fantasies occupy the place of a single truth, which we delight in the more because they are our own. The love of mystery springs, therefore, not from humility

See p. 157.

but from pride—not from a desire to submit to superior wisdom but a craving after opportunity to exert our own creative powers. For this the spirit of inquiry has been too often resigned ; for it is always easier to feel than to think, to wonder than to examine. The love of mystery, so far as it excludes reason, is a sensual gratification, though of a noble kind ; for it is the absorption of perception in sensation; the triumph of the sensitive over the intellectual faculties.* Still it must

* In the notes to the last edition of his Poems Mr. Wordsworth has preferred a charge against Unitarians, which comes from too high a source to be passed over in silence. After observing, that the readers of religious poetry are liable to receive a strong prejudice in favour of an author whose sentiments coincide with theirs, and as violent an aversion to one who maintains different opinions, he thus proceeds : " To these excesses, they, who from their professions, ought to be most guarded against them, are perhaps the most liable; I mean those sects whose religion being from the *calculating understanding*, is cold and formal. For when Christianity, the religion of humility, is *founded upon the proudest quality of our nature*, what can be expected but contradictions ? Accordingly believers of *this cast* are, at one time, contemptuous; at another, being troubled as *they are and must be* with inward misgivings, they are jealous and suspicious ;— and, at all seasons, they are under temptation to supply, by the heat with which they defend their tenets, the animation which is wanting to the constitution of the religion itself." Here all the misgivings, jealousies, contempts, and contradictions imputed to Unitarians, are traced to the circumstance of their founding a religion of humility on the "calculating understanding," " the proudest quality of our nature." But how can any *quality* of our nature be termed *proud* ? Pride is a distinct quality of itself, and though it may be mingled with others in operation, cannot enter into their substance. Besides, reason is a power and not a quality ; it may possibly produce pride, but can no more be proud than sight, hearing or taste. All that can be said of it, even in correct language, is, that it has a tendency to make those proud who take most pleasure in its exercise. But is not the imagination liable to the same charge ? Nay, does it not lead more naturally to self-admiration when it enables its possessors to frame worlds of their own, to create the regions they are to revel in, to rise in the kindling majesty of their own conceptions? Truth, which is the object of the reasoner, exists independently of him, and he is only anxious to find and to enjoy it. The materials of the poet are stored within himself, and

be admitted, in the present condition of man, to be the source of many pure and elevated pleasures, and linked to some of the most divine speculations which we are capable of indulging. My design is, therefore, to inquire what advantage the Calvinist possesses by reason of his belief in the TRINITY, over those who maintain the proper unity of the Great First Cause of all things.

A mystery, in order to excite lofty emotions of any kind, must not be entirely a secret. It must not be " invisible," but " dimly seen." It must afford the materials, however visionary and slight, which fancy may mould into images beautiful or sublime. The joy it excites consists not in the absence but in the plenitude of ideas. We must, therefore, be able to form some conception respecting the objects of our wonder. A mere Gordian knot which we cannot untie; an enigma we cannot solve; a direct contradiction in terms which we are unable either to understand or explain, can never become the spring of imaginations either tremendous or delightful. If, for instance, a person ignorant of Algebra is informed that there are quantities less than nothing, he will derive nothing but perplexity from the information, though he may firmly

believe it on the credit of the speaker. It is just so with the believer in the Trinity. He says his creed is that one is three and that three are one; but has he the most faint idea of the wonders he receives? Does any dim vision of something unearthly, in which there is a distinction of persons combined with a unity of substance, swim before the eye of his fancy? No. Let him work up his powers of imagination to the utmost, he will still be able only to conceive of three separate beings, in which there is no mystery at all. All the wonder consists in their union, and of that he can imagine nothing. His idea must be either of three divine substances distinctly, or of one alone. In the latter case, he can have no associations, which the Unitarian does not enjoy; and, in the former, as plurality is his only advantage, he is far below the most ignorant inhabitants of Rome. All that is truly sublime in his creed arises from a contemplation of the Divine essence as embodied in a single form. His peculiar belief amounts only to this, that there is something about which he can believe nothing. He may use the term *Trinity*, or any other phrase of human invention, but it must come to this after all. He is precisely in the condition of a person unacquainted with the laws of nature, who should be told that there is a mysterious principle called *gravitation*, in which he must believe; but whose ideas respecting it, supposing him to give credit to his informer, would probably be as accurate as that of the blind man, who heard that scarlet was a brilliant colour, and then conjectured it must resemble the sound of a trumpet. A Trinitarian falls short even of this conception. He can surely derive no sublime ideas from belief in his favourite mystery, since it does not afford him even the dimmest image of the object he supposes it to conceal.

When the poetical champion of orthodoxy asserts that there is something more lofty in the contemplation of the Divine Being as a triune substance than as properly one, inasmuch as the former is more mysterious, he must admit that, in the latter, a degree of possible sublimity is wanting. No object can derive any additional grandeur from mystery unless it is imperfect. There must be a power in imagination to make it more awful than

---

his triumph is peculiarly his own. The love of fame is confessedly the passion he most ardently cherishes. Surely, then, the imagination is, to speak in Mr. W's. language, as *proud a quality* as the understanding. And, on what is his hypothesis founded but the very reason which the author endeavours to condemn? What does the word " accordingly" imply, but the deduction of a conclusion from its premises: So that here is a paragraph written in defence of humility, " founded upon the proudest quality of our nature;" and, in such a case, " what can be expected but contradictions?"

It is almost needless to observe, that these observations leave untouched the merits of Mr. W's. poetry. Here indeed he is far above my feeble praise. In acute sensibility, in the philosophy of nature, in the delineation of all that is gentle in man, and in the power of rendering earthly images ethereal, I believe him to be surpassed by none in ancient or modern times. But I would confine poetry and reason to their respective uses. I would no more allow the former to usurp the place of the latter, than I would suffer a spirit of conceited criticism to deprive me of my purest enjoyments.

it is in itself, or it must seem mightier in proportion as it becomes visible. When the object is so sublime as to transcend all human conception, the clearer we behold it, the more must we be filled with wonder and every power be called into exercise to comprehend, to admire, and to enjoy. This has been strikingly the case with the discoveries made by human skill respecting the systems that encircle us. When the Chaldean shepherd contemplated the glory of the starry heavens, he might have trembled at any attempt to investigate the qualities of those immortal lights whose mystery seemed to add to their lustre, and have apprehended that when truth was forced on him his loveliest fancies must vanish. And yet, though such a feeling would have been in perfect sympathy with that of a poetical believer, what shall we say of it now when science has given us a nearer view of these objects of mysterious wonder? Are our conceptions respecting them less majestic because instead of lamps fixed in the heavens for our delight we find them to be the centres of mighty systems—suns which give light to unnumbered worlds—and in their turn catch a distant gleam from ours? Has the region of imagination been contracted, as reason has drawn aside the veil from nature's perpetual miracles? On the contrary, the more we have known, the more, we have been convinced, there is yet to know. Reason has gone forth as the pioneer of imagination into untried regions; and whilst she has found some resting places on which she has kindled beacons that can never perish, she has formed them not only to cheer and direct her followers, but to shed a dim and religious light over a boundless space fitted for the dwelling of her immortal sister. And if this be true as it respects the creation of God, the heavens that are but " his footstool," and the " clouds and darkness that are about his throne," how much more truly may it be urged of the Deity himself! An increase of knowledge respecting him must at once expand and fill all the capacities of the mind; make every faculty overflow with intelligence, every passion still with wonder, and every pulse beat with joy. Yet the Trinitarian promises much sublime contemplation from a mystery respecting his nature, which in so far as it operates at all, must conceal him from us. And then he offers us in exchange for a glimpse of divine perfections, the images which, in the midst of darkness we may ourselves be able to create!

It is singular that those who speak of mysteries as the glory of their religion, represent them as intended to vanish in heaven. A state of knowledge is there anticipated as a state of bliss, and yet here there must be no joy but that of darkness. Surely we are at liberty to suppose that the nearer we can approach the perfections of our future being, the longer perspective we can attain of the regions beyond the grave, the clearer glimpses we catch of the beatitudes of eternity, the better we shall be prepared to enjoy them. The more we see of our divine Father " as he is," the more shall we " be like him." And yet we are told that " a religion without its mysteries would be a temple without its God." As a system then which leaves us most in the dark is most divine—has most of God in it—how preferable was the faith of the Jews to Christianity, and the Grecian mythologies to both of them! On the contrary, mystery is no more a part of religion than ignorance is of knowledge. The object of the former in divine, is the same as that of the latter in human things; to disclose what before was hidden. No uncertainty can exist now which did not exist always; revelation, indeed, when it made all manifest which it is essential to know, enabled us to perceive that we had much yet to discover. The mystery remains, no doubt for wise purposes, but not in consequence of our faith. The Calvinist, like the " poor Indian," " sees God in clouds;" but with this difference: the former traces him as far as he is able in the most ethereal of his works, the latter enshrouds him in darkness which he has himself created.

After all, if there is any thing pleasing in the contemplation of mystery, there are surely objects enough that we see but dimly without obscuring the light which heaven has given us. In the infancy of an eternal being we must necessarily be surrounded with wonders. We feel mighty stirrings within us, like the motions of Homer's Cyclop in his cavern, gigantic though in darkness. Possessed with desires which nothing visible can satisfy, we are elevated by aspirations after imaginary good, favoured by visitings which we cannot trace, and delighted with occasional glimpses of our future glorious condition. In the human soul itself, its strengths and its weaknesses, its high cravings and natural instincts, its depths and its sublimities, there is enough to tremble at and admire. The vast riches of nature are to man but the faint shadows of things that he shall behold hereafter; the sources whence his spiritual associations arise, the fore-ground of his ethereal perspective. The stars " tell him of the glory of God," the loveliness of earth gives him a dim vision of paradise, and he rises from the contemplation of transitory scenes,

> " to breathe in worlds
> " To which the heaven of heavens is but a
> veil."

And yet there are those who think he wants deeper mysteries—who can find no sublimity but in terms to which they can affix no idea—who, while they talk of the pride of human reason, wish to make the idea of God more sublime, by fancying contradictions in his existence, and think the universe itself too narrow for their lofty imaginations to inhabit!

S. N. D.

Sir, *April 5, 1816.*

I SUSPECT that Dr. Thomas Thomson, as quoted, p. 143, has brought, or at least credited, a charge against " Horsley, the Champion of the Trinity," which is not well supported. Whether in any other case he " found Newton's papers unfit for publication" I know not; but scriptural inquirers, and especially Unitarians, are indebted to him for the first correct printed copy of Newton's critical testimony against the interpolation 1 John v. 7, and the common reading of 1 Tim. iii. 16. I find it in Horsley's *Newtoni Opera quæ extant omnia.* 4to. 5 v. 1779—1785. The concluding article, p. 494, in the last volume, is entitled,

" An Historical Account of two notable Corruptions of Scripture, in a Letter to a Friend. Now first published from the MS. in the author's hand-writing, in the possession of Dr. Ekens, Dean of Carlisle." Prefixed is the following " Advertisement. A very imperfect copy of these Tracts, wanting both the beginning and the

end, and erroneous in many places, was published at London in the year 1754, under the title of Letters from Sir Isaac Newton to Mr. Le Clerc. But in the author's MS. the whole is one continued discourse, which, although it is conceived in the epistolary form, is not addressed to any particular person."

It is to be regretted, that the author of these papers should have avoided so cautiously any direct declaration of his opinion on the subject of the Trinity. He says indeed, in the beginning of the first paper, referring to 1 John v. 7, that " in the eastern nations, and for a long time in the western, the faith subsisted without this text," as if he would be understood to recognize the truth of the *orthodox* doctrine. Yet, in quoting the baptismal form in Matthew, he speaks of it as " the place from which they tried to derive the Trinity." And having observed that in Jerome's time, and both before and long enough after it, this text of *the three in heaven* was never once thought of," he adds, " it is now in every body's mouth, and accounted the main text for the business." Would a Trinitarian thus express himself, without taking some occasion to avow his *orthodoxy*, especially while he was exploding as " notable corruptions" two main pillars on which the doctrine of a Trinity had rested for ages.

These papers by Sir Isaac Newton are not dated, but they may be placed among his comparatively early productions, as he refers to a testimony of " Dr. Gilbert Burnet," as " lately" given " in the first letter of his Travels." Burnet's Travels were in 1685, and his Letters to Mr. Boyle describing them were first published in 1687.

N. L. T.

Attack on Unitarians in the last Quarterly Review.

A WRITER in the Quarterly Review for October, 1815, labouring in his vocation, makes a new attack on the Unitarians. The occasion of this onset is the publication of the Bp. of London's Charge and Mr. Belsham's Answer. The reviewer lauds very highly his lordship of London, and thinks he cannot laud him sufficiently; remembering perhaps Pope's climax of panegyric,

" A gownman learned; a Bishop—what you will!"

In his awe before the episcopal throne, he is utterly astonished at Mr. Belsham's presumption in looking up to so elevated a personage, and at his irreverent boldness in contradicting a Bishop uttering his commands to his clergy. He then falls into his common places. We have another outcry at the "scandalous deception" practised by the Unitarians in the publication of the "Improved Version;" they have republished an *Archbishop's* book with alterations and additions, and have still kept up his name in the title-page: it is true they carefully explain all the additions and alterations, but their explanation is of no use to those that will not read it, and what orthodox writer, be he monthly or quarterly, will do this? The Unitarians, again, are haters of the Church of England: the proof of this charge is, that they united with the other Dissenters and the Methodists in opposing Lord Sidmouth's bill, which was so wise a provision even for their own respectability! What had that bill to do with the Church by law established? Its object was to fritter down the Toleration Act and bring Dissenters more completely under the *surveillance* of the government. The Unitarians generally did exert themselves to oppose Lord Sidmouth's insidious project; but the Reviewer's anger with them on this account is surely *misfixed*, when vented at the moment in which he was employed upon what he and his friends no doubt meant as a castigation of Mr. Belsham; for this gentleman, alone, we believe, of all the Dissenters, vindicated and complimented Lord Sidmouth, maintaining that his lordship's design was good, and that his bill might have been shaped into a liberal and useful law. The Reviewer next takes up the old calumny; the Unitarians are Deists, or at least very much like them. They reject as much of revelation as they like! But what part of revelation do they reject, for the rejection of which they do not give a reason? They renounce the text 1 John v. 7, 8, and the Reviewer knows, or ought to know, that it is a forgery; and who are the better Christians, the Unitarians who explode this foul interpolation, or the governors of the Church of England who, with their eyes open, still impose it upon the multitude for genuine scripture? But the Unita-

rians resort to figurative interpretations of scripture! Of what sort is the Protestant interpretation of *This is my body?*—Still, Unitarians are chargeable with the pride of the understanding. All pride is bad, but the worst pride of all is the pride of folly; and it may be that some Unitarians in their wish to avoid this extreme have run into the other. They, moreover, claim great men as of their party, witness Bishops Law and Shipley, who were not Unitarians for two reasons, 1st, the Reviewer never knew of their being such, and 2ndly, there is positive evidence of the contrary,—in their having subscribed the Thirty-Nine Articles!

The main subject of the article is, however, the late repeal of the statutes against Unitarians, on which the Reviewer writes cautiously; on one side urged on by his zeal for the Church, on the other restrained by his reverence of the government. He complains that the Unitarians have misrepresented the act of repeal, as if the government had repealed the Trinity itself; whereas he is authorized to say that his Majesty's ministers are sound in the faith. What Unitarian ever doubted their orthodoxy? They are orthodox by virtue of their places.—The Reviewer cannot blame the repeal, for that would be to blame the government, which is not the business of a Quarterly Reviewer; but he thinks the Unitarians should not have sought it: it became them to be quiet and contented. To be sure, Toleration is agreeable to the spirit of the English Constitution, and if we bear with Jews and Quakers, we cannot consistently drive Unitarians out of the country. In justice to the Reviewer be it said, that he fully exposes the fallacy of the distinction of doctrines as *essential* or *non-essential*, with regard to Toleration; all dissent must be allowed or none, at least all within the limits of scripture, though this does but partially comprehend the Jews, towards whom this writer is benevolent beyond his own measures of charity.

Whether to account for the harmlessness of the repeal or to explain the grounds of his own attack, the Reviewer represents the Unitarians as few in number, cool and philosophical, fond of writing, but sure not to prevail to any great extent. The reason why they will not succeed is, that the consequence of discussion fairly conducted is the more complete developement of truth. This reason has led other minds to a different conclusion.

But apparently fearing lest his liberality should encourage the heretical Unitarians to greater daring, he concludes with a warning to them and a salvo for the orthodoxy of his own spirit. We quote the passage as a curiosity.

"There is one case, and one only, in which we should wish to see *legal penalties put in force against the Unitarians*;" and this is, when they *depart from the course of regular reasoning*, and have recourse to *light* and *indecent ribaldry* in assailing the received doctrines of Christianity. Instances have occurred of late, in which some writers of that party have *offended* in this respect: we trust that they are not likely to recur. At all events, we are convinced that, notwithstanding the late repeal, the legislature will never be found backward in framing *suitable enactments*, which may effectually *protect from ridicule* and insult those sacred truths which are and have been received with reverence and awe by the great body of Christians in all ages and countries."

Is the writer in earnest? Does he contend that the distinction cannot be made between *essential* and *non-essential* doctrines and at the same time assume to distinguish between "*regular*" and *irregular* "*reasoning*" and to hold out the latter as punishable? A conclusive argument against the Trinity must be *offensive* to a Trinitarian. "*Ribaldry*" is a vague expression; it may mean only the playfulness of Jortin, or the indecency of Swift, or the scurrility of Warburton. Unitarians are not accounted witty, nor are they chargeable with foul speech. The bitterest invectives against the system of orthodoxy are to be found in writers of the Reviewer's own church.

The Legislature protect the Church from *ridicule!* Idle. Men will laugh at folly and shake their heads at absurdity, in spite of Acts of Parliament. What enactments, ecclesiastical or civil, could save from ridicule the doctrines of Transubstantiation, of Regeneration by Infant Baptism, of the Infallibility of the Pope and of the validity of Holy Orders!

A Committee of the House of Commons would be curiously employed in

scrutinizing the writings of Unitarians and determining when they reason and when they scoff, when their arguments are regular and when irregular, when their wit is legitimate and when extravagant.

A bigot with penal statutes in his hand is formidable; a bigot, with no other weapon of offence than the pen (the Reviewer must pardon us) is *ridiculous*.

GLEANINGS; OR, SELECTIONS AND REFLECTIONS MADE IN A COURSE OF GENERAL READING.

No. CCXLVIII.
Death of James II.

That Prince died in exile at the palace of St. Germains, Sept. 6, 1701, of a lethargy, as our historians relate. The celebrated Madam Maintenon, in a letter written from the French Court to Philip V. of Spain, grandson of Louis XIVth. gives the following account of the death of James, and the circumstances which preceded his interment. The *Religio Medici* in the case of human *relics* must be allowed to be rather equivocal, and a *prepared* toe or finger of a King would dignify any collection of anatomical curiosities.

"We must not talk of deaths to your Majesty without mentioning one, which, however, you must already have heard of from others, and which must have been as pleasing to heaven, as it proved edifying to all those who witnessed it; I do not mean good and religious persons alone, but even the most profligate about the court have not beheld the King of England at this awful period, without surprise and admiration: during six days his life was entirely despaired of: all around him saw it; he took the sacrament twice, spoke to his son, to his Catholic and Protestant attendants, to our King, to the Queen, in short, to every person he knew; and all that he said evinced a presence of mind, a peaceful serenity, a zeal and fortitude which all were truly charmed in beholding. On his body being opened, the physicians and surgeons all took some particle of it to keep as a relic; his attendants dipped their handkerchiefs in his blood, others their chaplets." *Memoirs of Lewis the XIVth.* written by himself. Translated from the French 1806. ii. 184.

---

* The italics are not the Reviewer's.

No. CCXLIX.
Spanish Ambition.

When *Drake* took St. Domingo, "in the Town-Hall were to be seen, amongst other things, the King of Spain's arms,' and under them a globe of the world, out of which issued an horse with his fore-feet springing forward, with this inscription, *non sufficit orbis,* that is, the world sufficeth not. Which was laughed at, and looked upon as an argument of the boundless avarice and ambition of the Spaniards, as if nothing could suffice them."

Camden, An. 1585.

No. CCL.
Ordination of a Mechanic, by Archbishop Usher.

The following anecdote is related by Dr. Parr, and repeated by Dr. Aikin, in the Life of Archbishop Usher.

An English mechanic in his diocese, honest, pious, and much addicted to the perusal of works in practical divinity, applied to him, expressing an earnest wish to be ordained. The primate, regarding the inclination as the offspring of fancy or conceit, advised him to go home and adhere to his proper calling. The man, however, unable to resist his propensity, soon after renewed his application; when the primate discoursed with him, and finding that he had attained considerable knowledge in the fundamentals of the Christian religion, asked him if he understood the Irish language, at the same time telling him that he could do little good in those parts without such an acquisition. He acknowledged his ignorance of it, but professed himself ready to undertake the task of learning it if his Grace accounted it a necessary preliminary to his ordination. About a year after, he returned again, and acquainted the primate that he was now able to express himself tolerably in that language, and therefore hoped he might at length be admitted to orders. The primate, thinking that a man of his character, capable of speaking to the people in their own style and tongue, was more likely to be serviceable to the cause than a Latin scholar without that qualification, complied with his request; nor had he reason to repent of his condescension, since the new clergyman proved a respectable and useful minister, and was very successful in making converts from the Catholics, till the rebellion put a period to his labours.

No. CCLI.
"*The Learned Tradesman.*"

Mr. William Pate, the friend and correspondent of Dean Swift, was educated at Trinity Hall, Cambridge, where he regularly took the degree of LL.B. He afterwards became a most eminent woollen-draper, lived over against the Royal Exchange, and was commonly called "the learned tradesman." In 1734, he was one of the Sheriffs of London, and died in 1746. In the church-yard at Lee, in Kent, where he lived for many years, in a delightful house adjoining the rectory of that place in which he died, is the following epitaph to his memory:

Hic jacent reliquiæ
GULIELMI PATE,
Viri
propter ingenii fœcunditatem
et literarum peritiam
haud minus eximii,
quam
ob morum urbanitatem suavitatemque
dilecti ;
huuc lapidem
sequenti apophthegmate aureo incisum,
tumulo imponi jussit :
" Epicharmian illud teneto,
"Nervos atque Artus esse Sapientiæ,
"Non temere credere."
Obiit nono die Decembris
anno ætatis suæ octogesimo
æræ Christianæ
M.DCC.XLVI.

REVIEW.

" Still pleased to praise, yet not afraid to blame."

Art. I.—*Two Essays; one on the Effects of Christianity, the other on the Sabbath.* By the late John Simpson. London : Published* by Hunter. 1815. 8vo. pp. 125.

THE writings of the excellent author of these Essays, were directed to the illustration of the evidences of Revealed Religion, and to the developement of some peculiarities in the language of the books which record its doctrines and history. Few of our readers can be ignorant of the services which he has thus rendered to the best interests of mankind : nor will they be ungrateful to " the Editor† of this pamphlet," who " esteems it his most pleasing and bounden duty to comply with the wishes or intentions" of his deceased father, in laying " before the public in the same state in which he found them," the only papers which Mr. Simpson left behind him ready for the press.

In the former, the Essayist endeavours to shew, " that no reasonable objection can be brought against the divine authority of the religion of Jesus, from its not having been more effectual in reforming the lives of men." He begins with concisely illustrating the natural tendency of the gospel, which he regards as favourable in a high degree to good morals and pure religion. Then he proves, on the authority of facts, that Christianity has *actually* caused great improvements of this kind, that it has abolished many savage and inhuman national practices, and has considerably softened and decreased the barbarity of others. Its beneficial influence on public laws, is not overlooked ; nor its success in spreading the most proper means of increasing and diffusing these blessings. The obligations of sound learning to the gospel, are clearly and forcibly stated. A summary follows of the good effects of the Christian doctrine : and reasons are assigned for ascribing these to it and to no other cause. Having thus repelled the objection to

* Printed at Leicester, by Combe, and very neatly.

† J. W. Simpson, Esq. of Rearsby, Leicestershire.   Rev.

this revelation on account of its having produced *no* advantageous effects at all, Mr. Simpson next vindicates Christianity from the charge of having *fallen short* of that *degree of efficacy* in promoting the virtue and welfare of mankind, which might have been *expected* from a divine religion. He maintains that these expectations themselves are not reasonable. " They have no proper ground. They originate from ignorance. Even natural religion and the faculties of reason and conscience, have failed of improving the hearts and lives of men so much as we think we might have expected. Yet is it fair to conclude from hence, that all religion should be rejected, and that our mental faculties are not the gift of God?" To the allegation that the gospel " has not produced so *many*, nor such eminently good, effects, as it is *naturally fitted* to produce," he answers that " moral causes work only by persuasion." A good moral cause may be, and in many instances actually has been perverted, so as to be made the instrument and occasion of bringing about very ill effects." The excellence therefore of Christianity, as " a moral means of bringing men to repentance and holiness, may be manifest, though great numbers will not apply it to its proper purpose." This excellence indeed the objection supposes ; from this it argues, however inconclusively. A physician is not responsible for either the inattention or the obstinacy of his patient. Let it not, further, be forgotten that the first preachers of the gospel foretold its corruptions ; which predictions evince the sincerity of the views of Christ and his apostles and the truth of their pretensions. Social union, government, learning, arts and science, are manifestly good means of improving the noblest faculties of men. This is their natural tendency. And it is no sufficient reason for declining to employ them, that they are capable of being perverted to bad purposes, and have been the occasion of innumerable evils. " Why then should Christianity be rejected on this account? With what justice or impartiality do we make it answerable for consequences flowing from doctrines and institutions which, in truth, are not Christian ?

But, waving this argument, how can we prove that the religion of Jesus has produced more ill effects than good ones? In ecclesiastical as well as civil history, the baneful consequences of pride, ambition, and other evil passions are most dwelt upon. When peace and its attendant blessings prevail, these are not usually thought by historians to be subjects sufficiently interesting to engage the public regard. Now a computation, the truth and exactness of which is beyond the limit of human faculties to ascertain, cannot be a proper ground of human judgement and action. As to the allegation that a doctrine communicated by God for the best of purposes, can never be the occasion of iniquity in *any* instance, the principle which this objection assumes, namely, that a divine law or plan for the general good cannot be accompanied with any partial evil, is contradicted by the whole course of nature and Providence. 'To say that religion is not a restraining motive, because it does not always restrain, is equally absurd as to say, that the civil laws are not a restraining motive.'* Even Lord Bolingbroke has confessed the futility of this charge. Indeed, nothing can be more palpably unjust than to ascribe any consequence to a cause which has the strongest genuine tendency to prevent it. Yet whoever accuses the gospel of producing vice of any kind, adopts this false mode of reasoning. And no argument can be properly drawn from the conduct of the professors of any religion, either for or against the religion itself, unless the conduct naturally flows from its principles.

This is an abstract of Mr. Simpson's Essay on the Effects of Christianity. On a subject so often and so amply discussed, novelty was not to be expected. The author's reasoning is distinguished however by perspicuity, elegance, precision, correctness of method, extent of information and unaffected candour. In a small compass he has presented us with the substance of many bulky volumes: and he employs no other weapons against the opponents of the gospel than such as are congenial with its mild and gentle spirit, which he seems fully to have imbibed. His design and plan required him to discuss some objections of unbelievers rather than represent at large "the beneficial effects of Christianity on the temporal concerns of mankind:" these are "proved from history and from facts," in a tract of the late Bishop Porteus which bears that title.

As a specimen of our author's manner, we extract his remarks, on a sentence in the History of the Decline and Fall of the Roman Empire:

" 'By the industry and zeal of the Europeans, Christianity has been widely diffused to the most distant shores of Asia and Africa: and, by the means of their colonies, has been firmly established from Canada to Chili, *in a world unknown to the ancients.*' *Gibbon's Decl. and Fall*, &c. Ch. xxv. p. 535.†

"This observation of Mr. Gibbon was made long before the formation of the British and Foreign Bible Society; an institution by means of which the Christian Scriptures have been most rapidly and generally distributed throughout the earth. The very idea of forming a plan for disseminating those best instructions in pure religion and good morals that were ever delivered, to all nations of men, in their own respective languages, derives its origin from the gospel. It is the natural effect of that enlargement of mind which Christianity produces, and of that universal benevolence which is a characteristic feature of it. What more effectual means could have been employed for the speedy and universal diffusion of truth, righteousness and piety in the world; for refining and exalting the human character to its highest perfection; and for promoting the purest happiness of mankind in general, both in the present, and in the future life?" (39.)

We shall next attend to Mr. Simpson's thoughts "on the nature and obligation of the patriarchal, the Jewish and the Christian Sabbath." He appeals to Gen. ii. 2, 3, as "a positive law given to the first parents of our race;" with the view of determining "the fixed periods of time at which mankind should stately join together" in divine worship. Against this "positive evidence" it would be irrational to place the conjecture that Moses might have inserted the above order for sanctifying the seventh day, when he wrote the book of Genesis, as a reason for his giving a similar command to the Israelites; especially as

---

* Montesquieu's Spirit of Laws, b. 24. chap. 2.

† This reference is incorrect: at least, so far as concerns the chapter, which should be xv, the first paragraph. Rev.

" he seems evidently to have formed his narrative in general according to the series of events." From other considerations also we may fairly infer that he has recorded the precept in the just order of transactions, and at the period of the history in which it was given.

In our author's judgment, "there can be no doubt, when we consider the general piety of the patriarchs, but that they obeyed the command to worship God every seventh day." It is true, the history "does not specify any particular instance of this," but the conciseness of the narratives in the earliest ages may easily be explained. Oral tradition would first be employed. Afterwards, when either hieroglyphical or alphabetical writing came into use, an insertion of particular instances of what was a regular practice would naturally be omitted. In subsequent parts of the Jewish annals, and for a very long period, there is no mention or intimation of the Sabbath. For a much longer space their sacred books are silent concerning the observance of the rite of circumcision,* which unquestionably, continued to be practised. But " though there is no express account" of the regular appropriation of the seventh day to divine worship in the patriarchal ages, there are many passages that *allude* to, and imply such a custom. Such, in the opinion of some learned men, are Gen. iv. 3, and Job i. 6. ii. 1. Universal attention was paid in those early times to weeks of seven days: and Mr. Simpson thence infers the high probability of men's having "habitually met for social worship on every seventh day." He is aware, indeed, that to the foregoing arguments may be objected what is said, (Nehem. ix. 13, 14.) " From Sinai thou madest known unto them thy holy sabbath." The Hebrew term here rendered *to make known*, he therefore translates as follows; didst manifest to them *in a peculiar manner*." And in this sense he also understands Exod. xvi. 29. "The Lord hath *given you the Sabbath*," and Ezek. xx. 12. Thus Christ says

(John vii. 22) "that Moses *gave* them circumcision, though this rite was first instituted in the time of Abraham, Gen. xvii. 10." To this reasoning Mr. S. subjoins a review of the arguments by which he attempts to establish the existence of the patriarchal sabbath.

"The Hebrew Sabbath at the fall of Manna," is the subject to which he now proceeds. Express notice of " the actual observance of a seventh day's sabbath," occurs for the first time in Exod. xvi. 22, &c.

" It appears, however," says Mr. S. " to be mentioned as a well-known institution." This inference he deduces from the context.

Following the order of the history, he next treats of " the Jewish sabbath commanded at Mount Sinai.—Exod. xx. 8—11."; with which Deut. v. 12 —15. must be compared. On this article of the decalogue he observes, that, " though it is a ritual law, yet it is one of those ten select commandments which were first delivered by Jehovah himself, to all the people of Israel assembled together in the most solemn manner ;" that " it is the *only* ritual ordinance in these tables ;" that " there are, however, *ritual* circumstances *peculiar* to the law for a weekly Sabbath as promulgated at this time ;" and that it was a special sign of the covenant between Jehovah and the Israelites. Hence it is noticed with singular distinction in the Mosaic law, is introduced with the emphatical word, *remember*, and, in its nature and tendency, was a direct and powerful means of promoting the principal designs of the Jewish dispensation; it being a memorial that the true God was the creator of all things, a mark of his having selected the posterity of Jacob for his own people, and, at once, a preservative from idolatry, and an instrument "of cherishing and improving the knowledge, love and practice of pure religion and virtue, both in individuals and in the community."

The most interesting section of this Essay, is devoted to the consideration of " the Christian Sabbath, or the Lord's day appointed by Christ and his apostles." Here Mr. S. makes some preliminary remarks, intended to prepare his readers for admitting that Jesus, " as the great Messiah of God, asserted his claim to a dominion over the sabbath." For the truth of this

---

* Mr. Simpson refers here to Kennicott's Dissert. p. 156, ed. 2. The reference should have been to *Kennicott's* TWO *Dissert.* &c. otherwise the Dissert. &c. may be confounded with those on the state of the Hebrew text. REV.

statement our author appeals to Matt.
xii. 8. Mark ii. 28. Luke vi. 5 ; which
texts he understands as referring spe-
cifically and exclusively to Christ.
And he judges it inconsistent with
the habitual prudence of our Lord to
suppose that he would have frequently
endangered his life, by correcting the
abuses of the sabbath, if such an ordinance was to cease when the kingdom
of the Messiah was established. Our
Saviour, in the opinion of the Essayist,
authorized his apostles to change the
day on which it was kept from the
seventh to the *first day* of the week.
This he conceives him to have done
after his resurrection; though "the
brief narratives of the evangelists do
not particularize every single precept
that our master gave relative to religion
and morals, even before his crucifixion." The accounts of his instructions
after his resurrection, are still more
concise. He sometimes taught by
symbolical actions, instead of giving
verbal precepts. To this method he
had recourse as to the sabbath day.
For example, the Jews being habituated to instruction by visible representation, he chose, by the clear and
decisive action of his repeated presence
with his apostles at the time of their
assembling on the day of his resurrection, the first day of the week, to
authorize and countenance them in
appointing and appropriating this particular day, instead of the Jewish Sabbath, on the seventh day, for the worship of God. There are passages in the
New Testament which prove that it was
so employed by the apostles and the earliest believers : the most credible authors likewise bear testimony to the
continuation of the practices of assembling on the first day of the week for
public worship, and of then partaking
in the Lord's Supper and making charitable collections for the indigent.
Accordingly, this day was soon distinguished by the appellation of the *Lord's
day*.

Towards the conclusion of the Essay, Mr. Simpson puts these questions,
"Though there is no express verbal
precept for a sabbath on the Lord's-
day, can arguments be found equally
strong with those which have been
produced for the religious observance
of any other day of the week by Christians? Are not these reasons sufficiently clear and powerful to sway the
judgment and to direct the conduct?"

He points out the valuable ends to be
answered by such an observance of
the day, corresponding with that on
which Jesus, our Master, rose from
the dead, and finishes his undertaking
by a reply to the objection, " that public worship and rest from the common
business of life one day in every seven,
occasions such a frequent suspension
of labour, as to injure both the rich
and the poor " In a devotional and
moral view " a discontinuance of *regular public* acts of Christian piety, and
of public instruction from the scriptures," would be exceedingly injurious.
" Nor would either individuals or the
community derive any *worldly* advantage from the *additional* labour of the
poor on the *first* day of the week."
This position the enlightened author
argues from a comparison of the general stock of labour with the rate of
wages and from the average measure
of human strength: his reasoning here,
is highly satisfactory to us; and we
cannot but pronounce it at once ingenious and convincing.

We are far more desirous of giving
a faithful epitome of the sentiments of
Mr. Simpson than of declaring and
vindicating our own. So much however has been said and written on the
subject of the latter of the essays contained in this pamphlet, that our readers
will, probably, expect the present article of review to be something more
than analytical.

For the most part, we agree in the
conclusions of the worthy and judicious writer. But we have always hesitated, and still hesitate, to employ
such language as *The Christian* SAB-
BATH. The object of the investigation and controversy before us, is to
ascertain whether a *sabbatical* institution be obligatory under the Gospel?
Now it is not a little remarkable that,
except in cases which refer, evidently
and immediately, to the observance of
the seventh day by the Jews, the word
sabbath has no place in the New
Testament. In this discussion no
passage of Scripture is so important as
Coloss. ii. 16. " Let no man *judge you*
in meat or in drink, or *in respect* of an
holy day, or of the new moon, or *of
the Sabbath days!*"

It becomes us to notice Mr. Simpson's translation of a sentence from
Justin Martyr (Apol. 1st ed. Thirlby,
p. 98). According to the Essayist, this
father "affirms *that he observed the*

SUNDAY SABBATH, &c." The words in the original are, τὴν δὲ τοῦ ἡλίου ἡμέραν κοινῇ πάντες τὴν συνέλευσιν ποιούμεθα, κ. τ. λ. In the 97th page Justin makes a statement to the same effect. From neither of the passages do we learn that these early Christians observed the first day of the week *sabbatically;* but only that they then assembled for the purposes of social religious worship and instruction. Mr. S. therefore would, on re-consideration, have forborne to speak of *the Sunday* SABBATH.

This investigation, assuredly, is not unimportant; the different opinions of men concerning the proper result of it having a strong influence on their practice. We could wish to moderate between the contending parties; each of whom, we think, has somewhat mistaken the real nature of the question, and failed of doing justice to the views and reasonings of their antagonists. On the one hand, we plead for the consecration of no scanty portion of *the Lord's day* to social worship, &c.: on the other, we are of opinion that the strictly *sabbatical* observance of it is not enjoined by either the precepts or the spirit of Christianity. There is great force in the arguments brought by Mr. S. to establish the position that from an early period of the world mankind were in the habit of dedicating every seventh day more immediately to the public homage of the Creator: we are convinced that it was the custom of Christians in the apostolic age to assemble for this purpose on the *first* day of the week, or *the Lord's day*; and such is the nature of man, such the state of society, that, in Mr. Simpson's language, " the usual habits of labour and amusement on other days, if continued on a day appropriated to religious objects, would prevent or diminish the good effects of public devotion and instruction, by diverting the mind to a quite different train of ideas." These, we take leave to say, are our sentiments, and our practice is agreeable to them. At the same time, nothing which rests solely on *deduction* should be represented as a doctrine or institution of revealed religion: nor should *he who observeth the Lord's day* sabbatically, *condemn him who in that manner observeth it not.* If weight be allowed to names, we could enumerate some of highly respectable divines who have declined to speak concerning *the Christian* SABBATH!

Our readers will permit us to add, that *J. D. Michaelis*[*] looked on *the Sabbath day* as an ante-mosaical institution; yet believed that, among the Jews, and in its original purity, it was not intended to be a day of rigour.

In concluding this article, we must again offer our humble tribute of respect to the memory of the author of these Essays. *Il pense et fait penser.* He was himself a diligent inquirer after religious truth; and he excites and assists inquiry in others.

ART. II.—*On the late Persecution of the Protestants in the South of France.* By Helen Maria Williams. 8vo. pp. 62. Underwoods. 1816.

THE lady whose name stands in the title-page is well known as an early advocate of the French Revolution. She has resided for many years at Paris, and may therefore be supposed to take a lively interest in the affairs of France, and to be qualified to describe them correctly and to discuss them satisfactorily. Last year, she published a " Narrative of the Events which have lately taken place in that country," in which, to the surprise of every body, she stood forward the apologist and even panegyrist of the Bourbons. Some passage or passages were quoted from that work in a publication advertised in the English Newspapers, and referred to under the character of " H. M. Williams's Confession," meaning, we suppose, her allowing the existence, in France, of religious persecution. Startled at this statement, she has written this pamphlet in the form of a letter as a supplement to her " Narrative." From the title we expected at least more information. There is enough, however, to shew that the accounts published by the Dissenting ministers of the persecution of the Protestants are correct, or rather that they are below the truth; though not enough to exonerate the French Court from the suspicion of conniving at these iniquitous and detestable proceedings.

In the language which is now fashionable at Paris, Miss Williams refers to Buonaparte as " the tyrant"

---

[*] Commentaries on the Laws of Moses, (Translated by Dr. A. Smith) Vol. iii. 166, &c.

from whose oppression the world is freed ; yet she confesses (we can use no better word) that under him and " amidst all the various phases of the French Revolution, the star of religious liberty had moved calmly in its majestic orbit and cheered despairing humanity with a ray of celestial radiance. Amidst the violations of every other principle," she says, " the domain of conscience appeared to be consecrated ground, where tyranny feared to tread." No sooner, however, did the *legitimates*, in the popular phraseology, regain the ascendancy, than religious persecution burst out in all its horrors : an odd symptom, surely, of deliverance from oppression ! Let the fair author speak for herself.

" The French Protestants had, during a long succession of years, been seen *with brow erect in the senate, in the legislature, the army, at court—in every ceremonial of state holding their equal rank and marshalled beside their Catholic brethren.*

" But what became of the dream of personal security, and the proud consciousness of undisputed rights, when the ear was suddenly appalled by new and strange exclamations ? ' We are despoiled, we are devoted to slaughter, we are the victims of our profession of the faith of our fathers —of that faith once delivered to the saints !'

" The persecutors of the nineteenth century have not entered into the niceties of religious belief ; they have not, in the indulgent spirit of their predecessors under Lewis XIV. proposed the alternative of *La messe ou la mort*, Repent, or perish; become Catholics, or we kill you; *they have proceeded at once to execution : their victims were marked, and they have plundered and murdered as their fury directed, wherever they found Protestant property, or persons professing the Protestant faith.*

" Nor was it now on the inhabitants of villages, such as the abodes of the obscure and disseminated Vaudois, that these horrors were inflicted ; the citizens of opulent towns and their popular vicinages, have become the martyrs. Nismes has been the centre of this desolation, from whence it has spread into the country around, even to that which has been noted as the citadel of Protestantism in France, the mountains of the Cevennes.

" From whatever cause this violence proceeded, *the Protestants alone have been the victims.* Were it a local insurrection against property or lives, such as sometimes has desolated parts of France during the Revolution, the assailants would not have been *so discriminate in their choice. It is on Protestants only that their rage has fallen ;* and the selection of the professors of this faith

appears to them an unequivocal proof that it was *an organized religious persecution.* There is something so strange to all our habitudes and feelings, so horrible in the sound of religious persecution, that we cannot help doubting the fact, though it be committed at our very doors. *We were for a long time incredulous,* and, what added to our incredulity on this subject, was, that this persecution should have taken place while the country was in possession of *the Protestant powers of Europe, by either of which it might instantly have been crushed.*" Pp. 6—8.

Miss Williams, with the rest of the world, is *incredulous* no longer. But why did not the Protestant powers of Europe interfere ? They were too busy, says our author, in a subdued tone of sarcasm ; and " no French army existed." Even Napoleon's army, then, would, if in existence, ' have speedily crushed the persecution. The Protestant powers were unconcerned spectators while the knife was held to the throats of their fellow-protestants; but, it should have been added, that the troops of Austria, a Catholic power, did on one occasion step beyond their commission to check the crusaders of the south. A little of the same *virtuous irregularity* on the part of the Duke of Wellington and Lord Castlereagh would have effectually kept under the French bigots both in the court and the country.

In a long passage, forming a considerable part of the pamphlet, too oratorical to be instructive, Miss Williams pencils a rapid sketch of the varying fortunes of the French Protestants from the Reformation to the Revolution. She relates that during the momentous period comprehended under the latter term, the Catholic clergy made overtures to the Protestants for a junction of the two churches ! The proposal came to nothing, though the Catholic prelate chiefly concerned was complaisant, and the Protestant minister who treated with him was flexible. " We were acquainted," says Miss Williams, " with *the flexibility of our Protestant friend.*" Is M. Marron the person here intended ? and is there here a sly allusion to his *flexibility* on a later occasion ?

Instead of an alliance between Catholics and Protestants, one of a different description took place between Buonaparte and the Pope, which produced the celebrated *Concordat.*

" Whatever might have been the advantages to the Pope, the Church or Buonaparte from this compact, *the Protestants completely gained their cause. It was no longer the persecuted or the tolerated sect. They were at once enthroned in rights equal to those of the Catholic church, and became alike the objects of imperial favour.*" Pp. 37, 38.

Such is part of the history of " The Tyrant," the attachment of the Protestants to whom (though scarcely equal to the common measures of decent gratitude) is a crime to be expiated with blood !

" The Royal family of France returned. *By some oversight in the King's Charter, there was mention of a state-religion, and the Protestants consequently were obliged to sink back to Toleration.*" P. 38.

An " oversight"! Miss Williams has surely forgotten the meaning of English words. Such an abuse of language is happily disgusting to English understandings and English hearts. But the Protestants were " *secure in the virtues of the monarch,*" " *the protection of a pious and philosophical prince.*" The *philosophy* of Louis may be determined by the " oversight," and as to his *piety,* that may be estimated by processions and persecutions. How the Protestants felt at first is doubtful ; but how do they now feel ? If we may judge by our own feelings, sitting in the security of laws, they entertain sentiments more intolerable than persecution itself, whilst doomed to hear the slavish and hypocritical cant of *Bourbon piety and philosophy!* The department of the *Gard* became convulsed, and such convulsion, by Miss Williams's own shewing, was neither unnatural nor unexpected. It was ascribed to political contests ;

" But it was at length recognised that when the troubles which had prevailed in other provinces were hushed into peace, the department of the Gard was still the scene of violence and horror. It was found that some evil of a darker hue, and more portentous meaning than the desultory warfare of political parties, hung over the devoted city of Nismes. A fanatical multitude, breathing traditionary hatred, was let loose : —the cry of " Down with the Hugonists" resounded through the streets. Massacre and pillage prevailed ; but *Protestants alone were the victims. The National Guard of Nismes, composed of its most respectable citizens, had been dissolved, and a new enrolment of six times the number had taken place,*

and in which many of the fanatics had found admission. Here, and here only, by some cruel fatality, the national guard betrayed its trust, and abandoned its noble functions of protecting its fellow-citizens. In vain the unhappy Protestants invoked its aid ; no arm was stretched out to shelter or to save them !—*their property was devastated without resistance, and their murderers were undisturbed.*

" The government caught the alarm ; the complaints of the Protestants assailed its ear, and General La Garde was sent to Nismes to command the military force of the department, and protect the Protestants.

" On his arrival at Nismes, General La Garde ordered the temples to be opened, which was announced to the public at eight o'clock on the Sunday morning. The summons was obeyed with alacrity by the Protestants. They had long been deprived of the consolation of assembling together, and they felt with the Psalmist, ' How amiable are thy tabernacles, O Lord of hosts !'

" The church was crowded, but the congregation was almost entirely composed of the higher order of citizens ; who perhaps felt the obligation that their situation imposed on them of shewing an example of courage, and publicly displaying their steadfast and firm adherence to the faith which they professed. It appeared that a hightoned sentiment of duty, an enlightened feeling of what was right and fit towards the community, an abnegation of self, were in this awful conjuncture associated with that piety by which they were no doubt strengthened ; that sublime confidence, which looks calmly down on the injustice of earth, making its appeal to heaven.

" The holy service began ; but what must have been the emotions of the auditory, when in less than half an hour their solemnities were interrupted by the horrible vociferations of a frantic populace, and loud and repeated strokes assailed the doors, in order to burst them open. M. Juillera, the minister, continued the service with a firm voice, and the congregation listened with that calm, which is the privilege of those who feel that their witness is in heaven. The uproar increased ; the tumult became horrible : the preacher ceased, and his auditors recommended themselves to God. ' I held my little girl in my hand,' writes Madame Juillera, the wife of the minister, a woman of a superior mind, with whom I am personally acquainted : ' I held my little girl in my hand, and approached the foot of the pulpit,—my husband rejoined us,—I thought of my nursling boy, whom I had left at home, and should embrace no more ! I recollected that this day was the anniversary of my marriage. I believed that I was going to die, with my husband and my daughter. It was some consolation that we should die together ;

and it seemed to me that this was the moment in which we were best prepared to appear in the presence of God—the victims of a religious duty ; in the performance of which we had braved the fury of the wicked ; we had flown with eager footsteps to our temple ; we had clung to the altar of our God. without heeding that the assassin's dagger might cross our path and impede our purpose.'

" It was at this moment that General La Garde, who had hastened to the post of danger, received from one of the assassins a ball, which entered near his heart. He covered the blood, gushing from his wound, with his manteau, and protected the retreat of the Protestants from the temple. He was then conveyed to his house, where the bullet was with difficulty extracted. The fury of the populace was not satiated. In the evening of this day the temples of the Protestants were broken open, and every thing contained in them—the registers, psalm-books, the gowns of the ministers, were torn into shreds and burnt." Pp. 45 —51.

After this picture we have a panegyrical account of the measures of the Duke of Angouleme, also, we suppose, *philosophical* and *pious*. Nothing but the remonstrances of the Protestants prevented, and these scarcely prevented, his ordering the Protestant churches to be re-opened ! He and all the Court and all Catholics abhorred the outrages at Nismes ; " the Buonapartists alone exulted," and according to the doctrine of the Bourbon satellites in England these Buonapartists included all the Protestants !

Eager as it should seem to quit this subject, Miss Williams turns to England, and dwells with enthusiasm upon the bold proceedings of the English on behalf of their persecuted Protestant brethren. But who are the English whom she thus extols ? A part of the Protestant Dissenting Ministers of the Three Denominations, and their churches, who, forgetting all doctrinal differences, not lulled into slumber by the promises of Lord Liverpool, not deterred by the coarse calumnies of hireling prints, not kept back by the calculations or prognostics of some of their own body, not shaken by the cowardice and desertion of a sister society which had attempted to outrun them and to get *first to the sepulchre*, have made all England and all Europe ring with execrations upon the bigotry and insidious policy of the French government and the cruel and criminal neglect of the Allies !

" The period was now arrived when, England fixed her steadfast eye on the Protestants of the South of France. The story of their persecution had reached her ear. The feeling of their wrongs had penetrated her heart. *Indignation beat high in every British bosom.* Public meetings were called together. The various associations, which watch with wakeful jealousy over the civil and religious rights of mankind, expressed in their addresses and declarations all *the energy of virtuous resentment, impatient for redress.*

" Favoured and glorious England ! How poor are the trophies of other nations compared with those which encircle her brows ! She has ever the pre-eminence in all the counsels of philanthropy ; the arbitress of moral action ; the guardian of the wronged; whatever region they inhabit, with whatever colour they may be tinged. While England exists, justice will never want a sanctuary, nor the oppressed a refuge.

" Her annals proudly boast her long support *of the Protestant cause.* We see the court of Elizabeth receiving the apologizing Ambassador of Charles IX. in silence, and in mourning. We find the sympathies of the whole nation aroused by the moans of the Protestant vallies of Piedmont, when they " redoubled to the hills, and they to heaven."[*] But *Englishmen wait not the tardy spur of government to goad them into action when the tidings of religious persecution strike in their ear.* They are at their post when danger menaces their brethren. They pause not to inquire against what form of worship, or mode of faith, religious persecution be directed ; it is sufficient for them that this demon exercises its ravages. *The followers of Calvin, and the professors of a less difficult faith become the mutual guarantees of their common religious rights.* England is the natural guardian of Protestantism, and she will never betray her trust. Unwearied vigilance is the function of a tutelar divinity. *England knows, that if the Vatican no longer speaks in thunder, the efforts of that power are not less persevering.* In all its variations of shape, this Proteus, whether it be styled, as in the days of yore, the dissolute of Babylon, or the Hydra, with numerous heads and horns; or whether, as in latter times, it resemble the tortoise, retreating within its shell from the storm, sometimes stationary, but never receding—is still the same. What it appears to have forgotten it yet remembers ; and when it seems torpid, it does not slumber. Wrapped up in its own infallibility, it sees ages pass away, with their manners and their innovations, like the waves rolling at the foot of a rock, while its own principles and maxims remain unchanged.

---

[*] See Milton's 18th Sonnet, with Wharton's Notes.

" The high-toned and generous resolves, proceeding from the three denominations assembled in London, and which were re-echoed by all other denominations, were not unheard in France. The French Protestants, while they paid a just tribute to the upright intentions of their own government, in declining the proffered intervention, felt all its grandeur; it was rejected, but admired; it was discreetly repulsed, but enthusiastically applauded. This intervention was the calm commanding voice of a great people lifted up against persecutors, and claiming kindred with the persecuted. *Its sound in Paris was noble, and persuasive; and it glided over the South like that sacred harmony of the heavenly host which spoke to the watch of shepherds' of peace and of good-will.*' Pp. 55—59.

Again Miss Williams is led by inclination or prudence to the nauseating subject of the views of the French government, and in answer to the question, What did it do to crush the persecution? very coolly answers, "It did all its *position* admitted. It exerted *the full extent of its power, but its* power was then feebleness; *and some secret and evil influence rose between its purpose and its act.*" Could this sentence have been penned by an English hand, and not rather by some one of the reviving fraternity of Jesuits? Its real and its seeming meaning are at war. It amounts to this, that the verbal purpose of the government was contradicted by its actual measures. It could fill the gaols of France with Buonapartists, but could not apprehend a single murderer of the Protestants, It could deliberately kill the brave and generous Labédoyère and spill the blood of the heroic Ney, but it had no power to bring a sanguinary ruffian, who headed a small band of Catholic banditti, to justice. But it could do something; it could *disarm* all the Protestants whose property and lives were in danger; it could quarter soldiers upon the plundered impoverished Protestants by way of punishing their enemies; it could dictate letters to Protestant Consistories, full of praise of th government for its singular protection of the Protestants of France, and compel those Consistories to subscribe them on pain of banishment; it could drive into exile the least *flexible* of the Protestant pastors; it could shut up all the schools of general and cheap education which were in the hands of Protestants: all this it could do, for this it has done; and reviewing its mea-

sures we are authorized to pronounce it impotent to good and powerful to evil, weak to protect but strong to persecute.

———

Art. III.—*Memoirs of the Life and Writings of the Rev. Andrew Fuller, late Pastor of the Baptist Church at Kettering, and Secretary to the Baptist Missionary Society.* By J. W. Morris. 8vo. Pp. 504. Hamilton. 12s. 1816.

THE late Mr. Andrew Fuller was a man of considerable talents and of well-earned distinction in his denomination. " Memoirs" of him can scarcely fail to be interesting and instructive, and few persons had better opportunities of becoming thoroughly acquainted with him than his present biographer. The character of our miscellany would not justify us in making a large abstract of the memoirs, or in going into minute and circumstantial criticism on the work; but we shall put down some of the leading events of Mr. Fuller's life, and make a few remarks upon Mr. Morris's book.

Andrew Fuller was born of parents in humble life, at Wicken, a small village in Cambridgeshire, mid way between Newmarket and Ely, February 6, 1754. He received only an imperfect English education at the free-school of Soham. His parents were Dissenters of the Calvinistic persuasion. They were engaged in husbandry, which occupation he followed till the twentieth year of his age. In his seventeenth year, he entered by public baptism into the church at Soham under the pastoral care of Mr. John Eve; and at the same early period of life began to preach, In 1775, after a probation of more than twelve months, he became pastor of the Baptist Church at Soham, which then and for some time after assembled in a barn. His income from the church being very slender, he engaged in business and set up a school; but not succeeding in his temporal pursuits, and meeting also, amidst much usefulness, with many unpleasantnesses in his pastoral connection, owing chiefly to the extreme ignorance and the meddling disposition of the greater part of his flock, he removed, after many struggles of mind, to Kettering, in Northamptonshire, in October 1782, and undertook the charge of the Baptist congregation in that place, which he held till the time of his death. At Kettering, Mr. Fuller had, according to his own characteristic expression, "plenty of elbow room." He was brought upon a stage more suited to his talents and to his ambition; an ambition of public usefulness, for which Providence had plainly fitted him. The events of his life were not various or uncommon. His story consists, besides the usual domestic incidents, some of which, peculiarly painful, displayed the strength and goodness of his feelings, of successive publications and controversies and of extraordinary and unwearied efforts in the establishment, superintendence and promotion of the Baptist Mission to the East Indies; undoubtedly, the most important mission that has been undertaken in modern times. "Fuller," says Mr. Morris, "lived and died a martyr to the mission." He departed this life, after a long and painful illness, May 7, 1815, in the sixty-second year of his age. His death-bed was Christian; but it may read a lesson to those of his own sentiments that estimate the human character by the dying frame of the mind.

"The general vigour of his constitution providing a resistance to the violence of disease, rendered his sufferings peculiarly severe; and towards the last, the conflict assumed a most formidable aspect. Placing his hand on the diseased part, the sufferer exclaimed, 'Oh! this *deadly* wound!' At another time. 'All misery centres here!' Being asked whether he meant bodily misery, he replied, 'Oh yes: I can think of nothing else.'" P. 461.

"Frequently during his affliction, he said, 'My mind is calm: no raptures, no despondency.' At other times he said, 'I am not dismayed. My God, my Saviour, my Refuge, to thee I commit my spirit. Take me to thyself. Bless those I leave behind.'" P. 462.

This dying *experience* may not come up to the expectation of enthusiasts; but we apprehend that it will excite the deep sympathy of the more enlightened readers, and even increase the confidence of the public in Mr. Fuller, as a *natural Christian Character*. We admire the following passage on this subject from a sermon preached on the Sabbath after his decease by Mr. Toller, the truly respectable pastor of the Independent Church, at Kettering:

"———in no one point, either from his writings which I have read, or the sermons

I have heard from him, or the interviews and conversations I have had with him,—in nothing can I so fully join issue with him as in his manner of *dying*. Had he gone off full of rapture and transport, I might have said, 'Oh! let me die the triumphant death of the righteous!' But it would have been far more than I could have realized, or expected in my own case: but the state of his mind towards the last appears to have been, if I may so express it, 'after my own heart.' He died *as a penitent sinner at the foot of the cross.*" P. 466.

It may be supposed that we look back to one part of Mr. Fuller's history with no pleasant feelings; but we can truly say that all our displeasure is buried in his grave. Such of our readers as wish to know more fully the circumstances to which we allude may consult our Fourth Volume, p. 466, &c. We obtained our end, we believe, in public estimation; and the present biographer, though sufficiently tinctured with party-spirit, does us ample justice. With a quotation from the Memoirs, we shall let this matter drop. Mr. Morris having described Mr. Fuller's want of forbearance, adds—

"It is extremely painful to advert to particular instances of this kind of severity, and if truth, justice, honour, and impartiality did not imperiously demand it, we would not advert to the unhappy transactions in which he was concerned at Soham, in the year 1809, in a dispute between his former friends and a party of Socinians, who claimed a right to their place of worship; and to the incorrect and unsatisfactory statement he was induced to make of those transactions nearly eighteen months afterwards in defence of his own conduct. Under no pretence whatever can we attempt to justify those transactions, nor the part which Mr. Fuller took in them, nor the means which he afterwards employed to exculpate himself from the charge of wishing indirectly at least to avail himself of those disgraceful statutes since repealed by the legislature, to secure, what he considered, the right of the injured party; much less can we agree to consider him as having been influenced by any sinister or dishonourable motive of which he was utterly incapable. The whole was a downright and palpable mistake, founded indeed, as in many other cases, on a large quantity of misinformation, and a wilful design of accomplishing the supposed ends of public justice. There is no need of any farther comment. His "Narrative of Facts" relative to these occurrences, which we have consigned to oblivion, instead of classing it with his other publications, admits but of one apology. It was written long after the "facts" had taken place, and must be attributed, as his eloquent and judicious friend observed, to 'a most unhappy lapse of memory,' though unfortunately, there are some other 'facts' which demand a similar apology."* Pp. 492, 493.

Mr. Fuller appeared frequently before the public as an author. He was engaged in controversy with the *Socinians*, as he called them, the *Unitarians* as they call themselves, the high-Calvinists, the Universalists, the Sandemanians and the opposers of the Baptist Mission. His writings display no learning or taste, nor an affectation of either: but they are marked by strong sense, by acuteness and sometimes by bitterness and wrath. He was a man of war, and it is amusing to see how his feelings betray him into military, or we had almost said *pugilistic* language. He flattered himself with having obtained a complete triumph over the Unitarians; and although we consider his argument fallacious and his boast ridiculous, and indeed could point out instances of his writings having made, instead of unmaking, Unitarians, yet we cannot but confess our regret that his first book had not been answered at the time more fully, more in his own way and more to the conviction of that class of readers for whom he wrote, and wrote certainly with effect.

The diploma of Doctor in Divinity was conferred upon Mr. Fuller by the College of New Jersey, but he declined accepting it, partly from a modest sense of his want of qualification for an academical honour and partly from religious scruples.

As a preacher, Mr. Fuller was distinguished by a clear view of his subject, by the coherence of all the parts of his discourse, by the solidity of his remarks, and by the striking cases which he put to explain his meaning. The following reflection is quite in character.

* In reply to Mr. Fuller, appeared, "Bigotry and Intolerance Defeated: or, An account of the late prosecution of Mr. John Gisburne, Unitarian minister of Soham, Cambridgeshire: with an Exposure and Correction of the Defects and Mistakes of Mr. Andrew Fuller's Narrative of that affair: in Seven Letters to John Christie, Esq. Treasurer of the Unitarian Fund. By Robert Aspland, minister of the Gravel Pit Congregation, Hackney. 1810." 8vo.——A *second Edition* of this pamphlet was afterwards published.—Mr. Fuller made no answer.

Rev.

"When I have seen a pious young man marry an irreligious woman, it has occurred to me, how will you be able to bury her? You may lay your bones, or have them laid some day by her side, or even mingle dust with her: *but you will be parted at the resurrection.*" P. 67.

Mr. Fuller was strictly an *extempore* preacher.

"The composition of a sermon seldom cost Mr. Fuller much trouble; it was generally the easiest part of his labours. An hour or two at the close of the week, would commonly be sufficient; and, when much pressed for time, as he often was, his preparations would be made on the Sabbath, during the intervals of preaching." Pp. 70, 71.

This is surely a dangerous piece of information to young preachers. They may be assured that Mr. Fuller's excellencies in the pulpit, whatever they were, were not owing to this negligence (which perhaps is here overrated) but in spite of it. Few can presume upon the correctness of judgment, the even flow of ideas, and the readiness of language which enabled Mr. Fuller to speak to the purpose without much premeditation.

The insertion of this account without qualification or caution is only one out of many instances of Mr. Morris's want of *prudence*. While, for instance, he sometimes praises the subject of his book without bounds; he indulges, at other times, in insinuations and invectives which betray a soreness of feeling in the recollection of some unexplained difference between himself and Mr. Fuller. In general, too, he treats as personal enemies all the sects with whom Mr. Fuller had any controversy, and particularly the Universalists and the misnamed 'Socinians.' But imprudent as our author is in his strictures on the systems of these two bodies of Christians, his ridiculous vaunting and his vulgar slang, suited only to the champions of the fist, quite disarm us of anger. We really forget the antagonist and smile at the critic, when we read of the "*insidious attempts*" of Unitarians, when we see a *Baptist Dissenter* appealing or praising an appeal to the "friends of *orthodoxy*," and especially when we are told that "Dr. Toulmin was *scarcely a breakfast* for his powerful antagonist," and that "Dr. Toulmin and Mr. Kentish received *their quietus*." Still we agree with Mr. Morris, that "If Socinianism still lives, it owes its existence to controversy and maintaining itself by the logical dexterity of its defenders." The same cannot certainly be said of Mr. Morris's *orthodoxy*. But of this hated "Socinianism," he says, with rhetorical contempt, "Like the apocalyptic beast, it appears with its head wounded to death and is going fast to perdition." Now, we know not that it is quite charitable to break up his prophetic visions, but we will venture to assure him, be the effect what it may, that never since the Reformation was Unitarianism so much alive as at the present moment; that never were the 'Orthodox' generally so far from 'Orthodoxy,' and that never were there so many, even in Baptist churches, whose faith is *unsatisfactory*. Mr. Fuller's book, which has betrayed his biographer into such unseemly language, was an appeal to spiritual pride, to the holy temper of those whose holiness Mr. Morris knows is not invariable, and was besides made up of the most unfair assumptions and the grossest misrepresentations. A proper answer to it would have been the memoirs of some individuals who have been most distinguished in the outcry against the 'immoral tendency' of 'Socinianism.' Now that the political prejudices against the Unitarians have died away, there are, we believe, few Trinitarians of any intellectual consideration, that would wish to rescue Mr. Fuller's tedious indictment from the oblivion into which it is sinking.

Though we are obliged to rebuke our author as a heated partizan, we are most willing to allow that in this volume he has displayed some talent, a facility in composition, a bold exposure of what he considers to be error even in his own friends, a consistent regard to Dissenting principles, and a love of religious liberty. We suppose that he is a man of warm feelings, and we regret that he sent his work to press without cool revision.

A Portrait of Mr. Fuller, by Medley, is prefixed to the volume, which is a likeness, but not a happy one.

ART. IV.—*The Geneva Catechism: entitled Catechism, or, Instruction on the Christian Religion: prepared by the Pastors of Geneva, for the use of the Swiss and French Protestant Churches.* Translated from the French. A New Edition. 1814. 12mo. Pp. 228. Sherwood and Co. 1815.

ONE of the articles of 'The Ecclesiastical Discipline of the Reformed Churches in France," established on the same model as that of Geneva, was as follows,——"The churches are to be warned to use most frequently Catechizing, and the ministers are to handle and expound the same most diligently, by compendious, succinct, simple and familiar questions and answers, framing and fitting themselves unto the plainnesse and rudenesse of their people, and not entering into long tedious discourses of common-places."* Nothing could be wiser than this direction, which the "Pastors of Geneva" seem to have had in their eye, when compiling the work before us, which may be justly entitled "compendious, succinct, simple and familiar," plain and not tedious or common-place.

Whether the Geneva Pastors have equally attended in this work to "The Lawes and Statutes of Geneva,"† as we find them set forth by authority, the reader will presently determine. In explanation of those "Lawes and Statutes," it is said, "But first it is to be noted, that there bee crimes which utterly bee intollerable in a minister—the first be *Heresie, Schisme.*" The Pastors are not perhaps chargeable with either of these "crimes" directly, but they manifest a deplorable want of *orthodoxy* and of conformity to Calvin's model of "Ecclesiastical Regiment."

It is a striking proof of the progress of the Reformation, that in a Catechism printed on the spot where Servetus was burnt to ashes, and authorized by the legal successors of those that hurried that Unitarian martyr to the stake, there is not only no exposition or defence of the doctrine of the Trinity, but not even an allusion to it. For aught that appears in this work the Trinitarian scheme might never have been heard of at Geneva. The same may be said of all the *Five Points* in which Calvinism, properly so called, consists. Not one of them is here propounded or

---

* See "The Ecclesiastical Discipline, &c. Faithfully transcribed into English out of a French Copy. London. 1642." 4to. P. 5.

† See "The Lawes and Statutes, &c. Faithfully translated out of the French tongue wherein they are written in the Register Book of the same City. London 1643." 4to, P. 3.

contained by implication. In excuse, however, of the Genevan Divines, it may be truly alleged that they proposed to substantiate every answer to every question by one or more scriptural proofs, and that therefore they were obliged to confine themselves to doctrines for which the scriptures vouch, but amongst which are not the Five Points or the Trinity.

The Catechism is divided into *Three Parts*. The First Part consisting of ten Sections, contains an " Abstract of the Sacred History," which is judicious and abundant in instruction to the young and unlearned. The Second Part, consisting of Nineteen Sections, is, " On the Truths of the Christian Religion," and is in reality an admirable summary of divinity. The Third Part, consisting of Twenty-four Sections, is " On the Duties of the Christian Religion," and may, we think, be pronounced one of the best compendiums of Christian morals within the reach of the English reader. In families, in schools, in congregational libraries, and even on the desks of ministers preparing for the pulpit, the whole work, and especially this last Part, will be found extremely useful.

Some of the statements of Christian doctrine may be objected to by a rigid scripturist, though we know but of few which by a liberal interpretation may not be reconciled with the sacred volume. The Genevan Pastors are on the high road of Reformation, and their next Catechism may not merely omit but openly expose pretended orthodoxy.

This little volume will surprise and may perhaps instruct and improve the English disciples of the Reformer of Geneva, the majority of whom are, we apprehend, as little entitled as the Genevan Pastors to the name of Calvinists.

At the end are given the Formulary observed at Geneva in the admission of Catechumens to the Lord's Supper, and also some Forms of Prayer.

It is but just to observe, that the translation is correct and equal to the original in elegance.

Art. IV.—*The History and Antiquities of Dissenting Churches, &c.*

[Continued from p. 169.]

THE first Presbyterian Church in England was established in the year 1572, at Wandsworth, near London, by the Reformers who fled to the Continent on Mary's obtaining the Throne, and who returned on the accession of Elizabeth. During their residence abroad they were schooled in the Geneva doctrine and discipline, which on their return they attempted to set up in England. This attempt, however, did not accord with the policy of Elizabeth, who, like her father, aimed to be a Protestant Pope, and the Presbyterians were jealously watched and severely persecuted by the Court of High Commission, founded upon the very principle of the Inquisition.

Some of the Reformers, as was natural, pushed the principle of the Reformation to a greater extent than the Presbyterians were willing to allow, and amongst these stands foremost Robert Brown, a clergyman, who may be considered as the father of the English Independents: from him they were for a considerable time denominated Brownists. Brown began to assert his principles openly about the year 1580, but being a violent and unsteady man and no Puritan in his manners, he faltered in his profession, conformed to the Church of England, and died, A. D., 1630, in the 81st year of his age, in jail at Northampton, to which he had been committed in consequence of a parish squabble.

Brown's apostacy did not stop the spread of the principles which he had set afloat. The Reformer continued to make disciples whilst the renegade was forgotten. Sir Walter Raleigh declared in Parliament, that the Brownists, in Norfolk and Essex and the parts adjacent to London, were not fewer than 20,000.

The old expedient of persecution was resorted to in order to reduce them to ecclesiastical obedience. They were thrown into the jails of London, where many of them died of want and disease. On the coffin of one who perished in this manner, his fellow-prisoners wrote the following inscription :—

" This is the corps of ROGER RIPPON, a servant of Christ and her Majesty's faithful subject; who is the last of sixteen or seventeen, which that great enemy of God, the Archbishop of Canterbury (Dr. John Whitgift) with his high commissioners, have murdered in Newgate, within these five years,

manifestly for the testimony of Jesus Christ.
His soul is now with the Lord, and his
blood cries for vengeance against that great
enemy of the saints, and against Mr. Richard Young, (a justice of peace in London,)
who in this and many like points, hath
abused his power, for the upholding of the
Romish Antichrist, prelacy and priesthood.
He died A. D. 1592." Pp. 19, 20.

Amongst the heads of the Brownist
party were some men of considerable
learning and talents. *Henry Ainsworth,* the Commentator, was of the
number. He resided chiefly in Holland, whither the Brownists were banished. He translated into Latin, in
1598, the Brownist Confession of
Faith, and dedicated it to the Dutch
Universities.

"His great work, the 'Annotations on
the Five Books of Moses, the Psalms and
the Song of Songs, was published separately
in 4to in 1612, and some following years.
In 1627, they were collected together and
reprinted at London, in one volume folio,
and again in 1639. This last edition is said
to be very rare, and is inserted in all the
catalogues of scarce books. As to the execution of the work, its merit has been established by the strongest testimonies of
foreign as well as British Divines. Succeeding critics have adopted his remarks,
and he is frequently cited by modern commentators. Dr. Doddridge observes, 'Ainsworth on the Pentateuch is a good book,
full of very valuable Jewish learning; and
his translation is to be preferred to others,
especially in the Psalms.'* The whole work
was translated into Dutch, and printed at
Leuwarden, in 1690; as was a German
translation of the Song of Solomon, at
Frankfort, in 1692. It should be remarked
that Ainsworth's works are more valued
abroad than in his own country, insomuch
that it is not easy to produce an English
writer oftener quoted, or with greater testimonies to his merit, and this by the learned of all sects and opinions."† P. 25.

John Smyth, another leader of the
Brownists, seems to have been the
founder of the English *General Baptists.* He was a clergyman of the
Church of England, and is said to
have held the living of Gainsborough,
in Lincolnshire. Having well studied
the principles of the Brownists, he
joined this party, and established a
congregation, which he transplanted
to Holland, in order to skreen himself

and them from persecution. In his
newly adopted country, the land of
liberty, Smyth pursued his religious
inquiries, and in the end avowed his
conviction of the unlawfulness of infant baptism, and set himself in opposition to the doctrines of predestination and original sin. He is charged
with entertaining "some absurd and
enthusiastic notions," which is likely
enough; but amongst these we cannot agree with our present author in
reckoning the opinion, "that no
translation of the Bible was the Word
of God." He is laughed at for administering the rite of baptism upon
himself; but the folly, if it must be
such, has been re-acted in modern
times. Our own pages [M. Repos.
VI. 410,] record an amusing instance
of *Se-Baptism,* performed under the
sanction of Dr. Adam Clarke, the
learned Wesleian Methodist.

Smyth's successor in the pastoral
office was *Thomas Helwisse,* a member of his congregation. He returned
to England with the greater part of
the congregation and settled in London. This is said to have been the
occasion of the establishment of the
first *General Baptist Church* in England.

None of the Brownist exiles were
more distinguished than *John Robinson,* whom the Independents prefer
to Brown as their legitimate father.
He was more moderate than Brown,
and struck out a middle way between
the Brownists and Presbyterians. He
removed first from England to Amsterdam and then to Leyden, and was
preparing to emigrate to America, to
join a part of his congregation who
had gone thither under his sanction,
and to carry over to them the remainder of their brethren, when he was
taken to a more quiet world, A. D.
1626, in the fiftieth year of his age.
His address to that part of his congregation which sought religious liberty
in the wilds of America, delivered on
the eve of their taking ship for their
perilous voyage, is happily preserved,
and will perpetuate Robinson's name
as a wise, noble-minded and truly
Christian Reformer. We have great
pleasure in transcribing it into the
Monthly Repository.

"BRETHREN,
"We are now quickly to part from one
another, and whether I may ever live to
see your faces upon earth any more, the

God of heaven only knows; but whether the Lord has appointed that or no, I charge you before God and his blessed angels, that you follow me no farther than you have seen me follow the Lord Jesus Christ. If God reveal any thing to you by any other instrument of his, be as ready to receive it as ever you was to receive any truth by my ministry; for I am verily persuaded, the Lord has more truth yet to break forth out of his holy word. For my part, I cannot sufficiently bewail the condition of the Reformed Churches, who are come to a period in religion, and will go at present no further than the instruments of their reformation. The Lutherans cannot be drawn to go beyond what Luther said; whatever part of his will our God has revealed to Calvin, they will rather die than embrace it; and the Calvinists you see stick fast where they were left by that great man of God, who yet saw not all things. This is a misery much to be lamented, for though they were burning and shining lights in their times, yet they penetrated not into the whole counsel of God, but were they now living, would be as willing to embrace further light as that which they first received. I beseech you remember it is an article of your church covenant, that *you be ready to receive whatever truth shall be made known to you from the written word of God.* Remember that and every other article of your sacred covenant. But I must herewithal exhort you to take heed what you receive as truth; examine it, consider it, and compare it with other scriptures of truth, before you receive it; for it is not possible the Christian world should come so lately out of such thick antichristian darkness, and that perfection of knowledge should break forth at once, I must also advise you to abandon, avoid, and shake off the name of BROWNISTS; it is a mere nickname, and a brand for the 'making religion and the professors of it odious to the Christian world." Pp. 33, 34.

Robinson's scheme of Church Government was followed by *Henry Jacob* in his establishment of a Puritan congregation in London, in 1616; this is called the First Independent Church in England. Jacob was a divine of some eminence. With a view to further usefulness he went over to Virginia, America, 1624, and soon after died there. He was succeeded by *John Lathrop,* who in 1634, being driven by persecution from his native country, settled at Barnstaple, in New England. During his ministry a dispute concerning baptism agitated the church; the consequence of which was the secession of a part of the members, who united to form a

Calvinist-Baptist-Church, the first of that denomination in London. After Lathrop's removal, the Independent Church chose for their pastor, the learned *Henry Jessey,* who had been ejected from the living of Aughton, near York, for not using the ceremonies of the Church and for presuming to take down a crucifix. Under Mr. Jessey, also, the Baptist controversy divided the society. He was led by this circumstance to study it attentively, and in the end he himself became a Baptist. He continued however on good terms with his Pædobaptist brethren, preaching amongst them and admitting them to his communion.

At the present moment, when the current of opinion sets so strong against any *Improved Version* of the scriptures, it is seasonable to make known a fact, honorable to Mr. Jessey and to his age, and in the mode of its relation creditable to our Dissenting Historian:

"Besides his constant labours in the ministry, Mr. Jessey was employed many years upon a *new translation of the Bible,* in which he was assisted by many learned men both at home and abroad. This he made the great *master-study of his life;* and, in order to evince its necessity observed, that, *Archbishop Bancroft, who was supervisor of the present translation, altered it in fourteen places, to make it speak the language of prelacy.** Mr. Jessey had nearly completed this great work when the Restoration took place; but the subsequent turn to public affairs obliged him to lay it aside, and this noble design eventually proved abortive." P. 44.

Mr. Jessey was distinguished by his charities. Above thirty families are said to have depended upon him for subsistence. The following passage shews that his charity arose from no party-feeling:

"The year 1657 afforded Mr. Jessey a favourable opportunity of displaying his benevolence. The Swedes and Poles being engaged in war, *the poor Jews at Jerusalem* were in a most distressed state; all supplies from their rich brethren in other countries, upon whom they depended for subsistence, being cut off. This induced Mr. Jessey to raise *a collection for their relief;* and he sent

---

* "Dr. Miles Smith, afterwards Bishop of Gloucester, who was one of the translators of the Bible and wrote the Preface, complained of the Archbishop's unwarrantable alterations; but, says he, ' he is so potent, there is no contradicting him.'"

them 300l. with letters, strongly persuading them to embrace Christianity." P. 44.

This good man was a great sufferer at the *unhappy* Restoration, a period at which bad men and bad principles triumphed. Cotemporary with him, if not his colleague, was *Praise-God Barebone*, who is little known as a divine, but who is celebrated for having been an active member in Cromwell's parliament, and indeed for giving a name to it which is yet preserved in history. Praise-God Barebone had two brothers, namely, *Christ—came—into—the—world—to—save Barebone*, and *If—Christ—had—not—died—thou—hadst—been—damned Barebone*: some are said to have omitted the former part of the name of the latter, and to have called him only " Damned Barebone."*

" This .stile of naming individuals was exceedingly common in the time of the civil wars. It was said that the genealogy of our Saviour might be learned from the names in Cromwell's regiments, and that the muster-master used no other list than the first chapter of Matthew.

" A Jury was returned in the county of Sussex of the following names :
Accepted Trevor, of Horsham.
Redeemed Compton, of Battle.
Faint-not Hewet, of Heathfield.
Make-peace Heaton, of Hare.
God-reward Smart, of Fivehurst.
Stand-fast-on-high Stringer, of Crowhurst.
Earth Adams, of Warbleton.
Called Lower, of Warbleton.
Kill-Sin Pimple, of Witham.
Return Spelman, of Watling.
Be-faithful Joiner, of Britling.
Fly-debate Robert, of Britling.
Fight-the-good-fight-of-faith White, of Emer.
More-fruit Fowler, of East Hadley.
Hope-for Bending, of East Hadley.
Graceful Harding, of Lewes.
Weep-not Billings, of Lewes.
Meek Brewer, of Okeham." P. 49.

Art. V. *A Plain View of the Unitarian Christian Doctrine, in a Series of Essays on the One God, the Father, and the Mediator between God and men, the man Christ Jesus :* with an Appendix, containing an Explanation of the Principal Passages of Scripture, which are urged in Support of the Doctrine of the Trinity and the Deity of Christ: and an Answer to the Chief Objec-

" * Granger's Biog. Hist, of England. Vol. III. P, 68."

tions of Trinitarians. By Richard Wright, Unitarian Missionary. 12mo. Pp. 524. 8s. Eaton, 1815.

MR. WRIGHT is too well known as an author amongst our readers to need any recommendation of ours. His numerous little tracts have contributed in no small degree to the present revival of the Unitarian doctrine. Such of them as relate to the Unity of God and the nature of Jesus Christ are here collected into a volume, to which is added An Appendix, now published for the first time, the subjects of which are expressed in the Title-page, and which is inferior to none of the Essays in sound reasoning, in happy illustration, in agreement with plain scripture and in practical moral .tendency. For the accommodation of such as possess the single tracts the Appendix is published separately.

The following are the subjects of this volume of Tracts: Use of Reason in Religion ; First Principles of Religion ; Unity and Supremacy of One God, the Father ; the Object, Nature and Design of Religious Worship ; Humanity of Christ ; Miraculous Conception of Jesus Christ ; Doctrine of Two Natures in Christ ; Divinity of Christ as distinguished from his Deity ; Reasons for not being a Trinitarian.

This enumeration of Contents will suffice to shew Unitarians how serviceable they will find this little volume in the contention which they are carrying on for *the faith once delivered to the saints.*

Should the present publication meet with a sufficient number of purchasers to indemnify the author, it is his intention, we understand, to collect his other Tracts into a volume or volumes, which may serve as a cheap and portable body of Unitarian divinity. The statement of this design in our Review will, we hope, contribute to its accomplishment.

Art. VI.—*Peace and Persecution incompatible with each other. An Address on the Persecution of the Protestants in the South of France ;* delivered at Worship Street, Finsbury Square, Thursday, January 18, 1816, being the Thanksgiving Day, By John Evans, A. M. 8vo. Pp. 44. 1s. 6d. Sherwood and Co.

MR. EVANS made good use of the Thanksgiving Day by directing the attention and the charity of his audience. to our suffering Protestant Brethren in the South of France. We need not inform the reader that his Sermon abounds in those generous principles of religious liberty which he has so often and so effectually asserted.

ART. VII.—*God the Author of Peace.* A Sermon, preached in the Dissenting Chapel at Mill Hill, in Leeds, on Thursday, January 18, 1816, being the day of Public Thanksgiving on the Conclusion of a General Peace. By the Rev. Thomas Jervis, Minister of Mill-Hill Chapel. 8vo. Pp. 38. Longman and Co.

IN a strain of bold and manly eloquence, Mr. Jervis sets forth the blessings of peace by describing the plague and curse of war. He seems to have judged, in our opinion correctly, that the only way to make peace permanent is to cherish the spirit of peace. Hence, whilst he extols the national courage, and adverts with conscious pride to our military and naval achievements, he hesitates not to rebuke and condemn that hostile disposition, too-long prevalent in Great Britain, which has made Europe a field of blood.

ART. VIII.—*The Happiness of Great Britain.* A Sermon, delivered at Newbury, January 18, 1816, being the Day appointed for a General Thanksgiving. By John Kitcat. 8vo. Pp. 18. 1s. Hunter.

THIS Sermon breathes a military spirit which is rare in meeting-houses, where "the ever venerable Blucher, that noble veteran in the cause of national independence," (p. 5) and the "illustrious Commander, the ever-memorable, Field Martial" (*Marshal*) "Duke Wellington" (P. 6.) are, we believe, as yet, strange names. The preacher paints with a patriotic pencil the happy consequences of the battle of Waterloo; other consequences, might, we fear, be described by the French and Piedmontese Protestant, the Spaniard, the Saxon, the Genoese and the Pole. Even the English farmer and tradesman would have listened to Mr. Kitcat with some surprise and incredulity, whilst he described in words of large meaning, Great Britain as risen superior to her difficulties, and enjoying "the sunshine of pros-

perity!" (Pp. 8, 9.) At the same time, no hearer could have gone away from the sermon without a pleasing impression of the preacher's good sense and piety and love of freedom, or without feeling a stronger attachment to the political institutions of his own country.

ART. IX.—*A Letter to the Rev. T. Price, occasioned by his Speech delivered at the first Anniversary Meeting of the Isle of Sheppey Auxiliary Bible Society, held at Sheerness.* By M. Harding, Minister of the Unitarian Church, Miletown. 12mo. pp. 18. Sheerness, printed, and sold by E. Jacobs. 4d.

ART. X.—*An Address to the Committee of the Isle of Sheppey Auxiliary Bible Society, containing Animadversions on their Conduct, in having rejected a Donation. With a Copy of the Correspondence.* By M. Harding. 8vo. pp. 18. Rochester, printed. 8d.

THE Bible Society is on no account more worthy of support than that it promotes a spirit of charity amongst the several Christian denominations. Here and there, however, a bigot mistakes and perverts this happy tendency and design. "The Rev. T. Price," for instance, on the occasion described in the title-page of the first of these publications, miserably abused the privilege of a public speech by attacking the Unitarians, whom he represented "as the *Devil's Chaplains,*" sent by his Satanic Majesty to Sheerness "to *oppose the Bible.*" Mr. Harding, an Unitarian teacher, was an indignant hearer of this Bedlam jargon; which he afterwards exposed to his neighbours in the "Letter," on the title-page of which he advertised that "the profits arising from its sale would be given in aid of the Bible Society."

We may congratulate Mr. Harding as one of the few successful authors. His Letter netted a profit of *Eleven Shillings.* This sum he paid into the hands of the Treasurer of the Society, September the 18th, 1815, wishing it to be inserted in the Annual List of Subscriptions as "a Donation, being the profits, &c." The List appeared without any acknowledgement of the donation. Mr. Harding then addressed a note of inquiry to the secretary, who returned for answer that the sum alluded to was in the Bank, but that it was not passed into the account of the last year, because the Committee had not determined " on the propriety of receiving it." Wishing to save this body the trouble of further consultation, Mr. Harding then demanded that the contribution should be given back. In reply to this demand the secretary stated that it would be " most likely" complied with at the next meeting of the Committee, the matter having been debated but not decided at two previous meetings. At this announced meeting the Committee made up their minds and instructed their secretary to inform Mr. Harding that he might receive his *Eleven Shillings* " by applying to the bank where he left it." Mr. Harding pocketed the affront, and in return for the favour has *addressed* the Committee upon their conduct. The Address must, we should think, shame them, and will, no doubt, prevent the repetition of any such bigotted and mean proceedings. This affair ought to occupy a page of Mr. Owen's proposed History of the Bible Society.

Art. XI.—*The Trinitarian Catechised, and allowed to Answer for Himself.* 1815. pp. 15. 2d. or 2s. 6d per dozen. Hunter.

THE author says, " This small publication has no other object in view than to produce candid reflection, and destroy the influence of superstition, bigotry and prejudice, those grand enemies to the kingdom of Christ, and to peace on earth and good-will towards men." This important object we think it calculated to promote. The Questions proposed are pertinent, and the reader is left to form the Answers.

Art. XII.—*A Letter from an old Unitarian to a young Calvinist.* 1816. pp. 24. Hunter.

THIS letter contains just and pointed remarks on the Calvinistic doctrines, and wholesome advice to the young Calvinist; but we cannot agree with the writer, p. 7, " That Jesus Christ taught nothing except moral precepts." The whole of his doctrine is calculated to produce moral excellence, and all his precepts are enforced by evangelical motives, arising from what he taught concerning the gracious Father of all, and a future state of immortality. Had milder language been used in some passages the value of this letter would not have been diminished. It is apostolic advice, *Be gentle towards all men: in meekness instructing those who oppose themselves.*

POETRY.

SIR, *April 4, 1816.*

The following lines, to which I venture to add a translation, may not be uninteresting, as the composition of a learned Negro. They are the introductory stanzas of a Latin elegy, the fragment of which is preserved by the Abbe Gregoire in his work *de la literature des Negres.* Their similarity to the *Pallida Mors* of Horace makes it probable that they were thence suggested to the author. The elegy was written by the African *Jacques Elisa-Jean Capitein* on the death of his friend and master, *Manger,* a clergyman at the Hague. *Capitein* was bought and carried to Holland at about eight years of age; whence, having passed through several universities, with great celebrity, he was sent Calvinistic missionary to Guinea. M. Gregoire mentions the remarkable circumstance that, before his death, at the instigation of some Dutch

merchants, he became an advocate of the Slave Trade.

OTIOSA.

Invida mors totum vibrat sua tela per orbem:
Et gestit quemvis succubuisse sibi,
Illa, metùs expers, penetrat conclavia regum
Imperiùque manu ponere sceptra jubet.
Non sinit illa diù partos spectare triumphos
Linquere sed cogit, clara tropœa duces.
Divitis et gazas, aliis ut dividat, omnes,
Mendicique casam vindicat illa sibi.
Falce senes, juvenes, nullo discrimine, dura
Iustar aristarum, demittit illa simul.

Death's all unerring darts around are spread
At once the monarch's and the peasant's
    dread ;
In regal palaces her dire command
Wrests the bright sceptre from the nerveless hand :

She checks the warrior in his proud career,
And lays him vanquished on the trophied
   bier :
Or treasur'd hoards, or pen'ry's simple all,
A prey indiff'rent to the tyrant fall :
Alike indiff'rent hasten to the tomb
Or hoary age or childhood's op'ning bloom,
As the full ears beneath the reaper's sway,
Promiscuous fall with flow'rets of a day.

To a withering Rose that had been trans-
   planted by the Author, 1815.

Midst gayer flowers awhile to bloom,
I rais'd thee from thy native bed,
Alas! I but prepared a tomb ;
Already droops thy beauteous head.

Say, have the Sun's meridian rays
Beam'd on thee with resistless force,
And like the breath of flatt'ring praise
Blasted thy beauty at the source?

No ; morn and eve have scarcely flown,
Nor scorching noon has o'er thee past,
Yet low to earth thy stem is prone,
Thy life's bright morning all o'ercast.

Thus, by misjudging kindness torn
Reluctant, from its genial shades,
To sink the prey of fortune's scorn,
Full many an op'ning virtue fades.

How oft the hand of friendly pow'r
In mis'ry's aid arrives too late,
So vainly now this falling show'r
Would still arrest thy hapless fate.

To grace thee, lovely sight of woe,
In idle sorrow does it weep,
As glistening in their wonted shew
The crystal drops thy blossoms steep.
                OTIOSA.

To a Crocus,
Which has blown for thirty years on the same
    Spot.

Welcome, thrice welcome, little flower,
Blooming harbinger of Spring ;
With thee we hail the genial hour,
Borne on the vernal zephyr's wing.

Exhausted nature droops and dies,
Chill winter holds his dreary reign;
Thou blossom'st, and the earth revives,
The op'ning buds appear again.

Gay woodbines and the blushing rose,
On summer gales their fragrance shed ;
But thou, sweet flow'ret, 'mid the snows
Of winter, rear'st thy tender head.

Kind Nature's first-born darling child,
Chaste leader of the flow'ry host,

Not summer bright, nor autumn mild,
A lovelier ornament can boast.

The radiant sun in splendour drest,
Has thrice ten seasons led the day ;
And thou with constancy confess'd
His genial power and cheering ray.

Renew thy blossoms, lovely flower,
Inspiring hope and confidence ;
Though storms may rage and tempests
   low'r,
Fear not, thy shield is Innocence.
                A. C.

From the Portugueze of Camoens.

Thou lovely spirit that so soon hast fled
From this dark vale of solitude and woe,
In heaven's eternal peace to rest thy head,
While I must heave unceasing sighs below ;
If in the ethereal Courts thou honorest now,
A thought of earth may enter, heavenly
   maid !
Forget not the pure tears these eyes have
   shed,
The love which fill'd this breast with holiest
   glow !

And if the sorrow from my bosom driven,
The agony of losing thee, may rise
With thine own pray'rs, propitious, to the
   skies ;
Ask from the bounty of indulgent heaven
That I to meet thee from vain earth be
   riven,
Early as thou wert torn from these sad eyes.
                A.

Impromptu de M. Voltaire fait à Cirey, sur
la beauté du ciel, dans une nuit d'été.

" Tous ces vastes pays d'Azur et de Lu-
   miere
" Tirés du sein du vuide, et formés sans ma-
   tiere,
" Arrondis sans compas, et tournans sans
   pivot,
" Ont à peine conté la depense d'un mot."
    Memoires, &c. par Grimm et Diderot,
            Tom 2. p. 260.

TRANSLATION.

Impromptu by Voltaire, on the Beauty of the
Heavens on a fine Summer Night.

Regions of Azure, bright ethereal plains,
Sprung from the womb of space, of matter
   void,
Spher'd without compass, self-revolving,
Boundless all, and at a word created.
                A. C.

OBITUARY.

On Thursday, the 18th of January, at Doncaster, after a short indisposition, in the 81st year of his age, the Rev. RICHARD HODGSON, Unitarian Minister at that place, where in connexion with Long Houghton he continued preaching until six months before his death, for the last fifteen years. He was the son of the Rev. John Hodgson, the minister at Lincoln. He received his education at Glasgow and Warrington: on his removal from thence he married Miss Lightfoot, daughter of the Unitarian minister at Osset, at which place he commenced the ministry, succeeding his wife's father, and for sixty years faithfully and unremittingly preached the gospel. He had by her seven children, (two having since died) four of whom he had the satisfaction to see advantageously settled in Sheffield. From Osset he removed to Monton and continued to discharge the various duties of the ministry for many years. He afterwards went to Namptwich, where he preached thirty-one years. The former part of his time there he devoted to the education of a small number of young gentlemen. He then succeeded the Rev. Mr. Scott, at Doncaster. Although the smallness of the congregation there would often cause him a momentary concern, yet it proved no discouragement to his zeal and perseverance; he seldom suffered any thing except indisposition to interfere with the performance of his duty, and could not be prevailed upon by his children or friends (who long thought him unequal to the exertion) to retire, until he was completely incapacitated for public service. He was blessed with a strong constitution, uncommon vigour and activity at his advanced period of life, until the loss of his excellent wife, who died the 10th of October, 1812, in the 76th year of her age: that deprivation produced in him a material change, though he bowed with humble submission to the will of heaven; since that time his intellectual faculties lost their vigour, and his health was gradually on the decline. Throughout life, he exhibited a natural cheerfulness of mind united with sensibility of heart, and in his last illness he exemplified the true spirit of Christian fortitude, patience under his sufferings, and derived great consolation from those principles of faith he had imbibed himself, and endeavoured to instil into the minds of others—" The memory of the just is blessed." His children will ever remember his tender concern for their welfare, and his grandchildren his affectionate disposition and engaging manners.

The above is inserted as a tribute of affection and respect by a part of his surviving family.

Sheffield, March 19, 1816. K.

At Saffron Walden, on Friday, March 1st, 1816, in the 73d year of his age, Mr. JOSEPH EEDES, for many years a deacon of the General Baptist Church in that town. He was a worthy member of society in general, and particularly useful to the religious society to which he belonged. He was a bright and ornamental character as a Christian; loved and respected by persons of different persuasions in religion for his mild and peaceable temper, his charitable disposition and good-will to all. He truly adorned the doctrines of Christianity. His death was easy and calm; he was resigned to the will of heaven, and fell asleep without a sigh or groan. He was interred March 12, in his family vault, in the burial ground belonging to the General Baptists in Saffron Walden. An impressive sermon was preached on the occasion by his minister, the Rev. S. Philpot, from 1 Thessalonians iv. 13, 14, to a respectable and crowded audience, who testified their regard to the good man by paying this last tribute of respect to his memory: an appropriate Oration at the grave finished the last part of the solemn scene.

H.

Died, March 22d, 1816, in her fifty-second year, ANN, wife of Mr. Robert BLYTH, of Birmingham, (to whom she was married April 10, 1783), and daughter of the late Mr. George Brittain, merchant, of Sheffield. The best qualities of the understanding and of the heart were united in this valuable woman. A worshipper, on inquiry and from conviction, of the one God, the Father, in the name of the man Christ Jesus, she adorned her religious profession by the spirit of genuine meekness, humility, devotion and beneficence. Her estimable and liberal-minded parents had educated her in the principles of the Established Church. The events, however, of her early life, led her to examine the foundation of Unitarian Dissent: she reflected and read much on the subject; and, comparing with the scriptures what she heard respecting it in conversation and in public discourses, she saw reason to embrace that simple faith in the evidences and obligations of which she assiduously instructed her children; ten out of eleven, of whom survive to bless her memory and attempt the imitation of her virtues. In her family and neighbourhood, in a large circle of associates, through which the sweetness of her temper and manners uniformly shed delight, and in the religious community of which she was a distinguished ornament, her death has occasioned a vacancy that will not be easily supplied. All her duties were discharged with eminent wisdom, affection and fidelity. As a daughter and a wife, not less than as a mother, she was, above most, deservedly admired and beloved. To the voice of friendship and the feelings of enlightened piety she was ever alive : and her submission to the Divine Will, through many years of bodily languor, presented a truly engaging and edifying spectacle. Of such a character a sketch is now given, that the graces of it may be emulated : around such a tomb Christian mourners may join in two employments which are among the noblest, the most beneficial and the most soothing, of any that can occupy the contemplative mind—in *virtuous recollection* and in *the indulgence of sacred and even exulting hope !*

On the 29th of March, in the 60th year of his age, and exactly seven weeks after the death of his mother, (see p. 110,) Mr. JOSHUA JOYCE, of Essex Street, Strand, highly respected as well for the activity and usefulness of his talents as for the uprightness and integrity of his conduct in every relation of life. By the death of his father in 1778, when he was a very young man, the care of the junior branches of the family, in a great measure, devolved on him, whose concerns he managed with zeal and disinterestedness. The patrimony resulting to them was small, but to the younger brother, in addition to an equal share with the rest of the children, was bequeathed a small copyhold, supposed by his father, to be his right as youngest son. The subject of the present article was, however, informed, when he appeared in court to pay the usual fine, in behalf of his brother, that he might dispute his father's will and claim it for himself, the idea of which he instantly rejected. By this act of disinterestedness the youth, in whose favour it was done, was enabled, when he came of age, and had completed the term of his apprenticeship, in which he had been engaged about a year, to quit mechanical employments and to devote himself, under the patronage of the late Rev. Hugh Worthington, to those studies that are necessary qualifications for the profession of a dissenting minister. In 1794, when his brother was singled out by the late Mr. Pitt as a victim, with others, to be sacrificed at the shrine of his wicked ambition, Mr. Joshua Joyce zealously interested himself in his behalf, and that of the other state prisoners ; and the late Mr. John Herne Tooke has frequently asserted, that himself and friends were more indebted to his exertions than to those of any other man in defeating the projects of ministers, who, at that period, were conspiring to subvert the liberties and constitution of the country. The minister had hoped to perplex and confound the prisoners, by sending to each, or causing to be sent, an unheard of number of persons as jurymen, and to use his own phrase *a cloud of witnesses* whose cha-

racters it would be difficult, if not impossible to scrutinize in the short period of ten days; but by the constant and unwearied efforts of the subject of this article, with the aid of other persons of great respectability, who felt that on the issue of those trials depended the liberties and safety of every man in the realm, as well as the lives of the accused ; the characters and motives of four-hundred and twenty-one persons were fully investigated in the time allowed : the minister was baffled, his spies detected, and himself discomfited and disgraced.

Many private trusts were committed to the care of Mr. Joyce, which he executed with fidelity and to the satisfaction of those for whose interests he was engaged. He has left a widow and ten children to deplore his loss : the latter by imitating his virtues will do honour to the character of an excellent parent, and probably secure to themselves the reputation and success in the world which are, to the young and well disposed, always objects of laudable ambition.

Highgate.   J. J.

Addition to the Obituary of MR. JAMES DROVER, p 184. (Extracted from the conclusion of Mr. Aspland's Funeral Sermon for him, just published.)

Here I might conclude. But I shall be expected perhaps to say a few words on the sad occasion of this Sermon ; and I shall fulfil this expectation as far as appears to me consistent with propriety and serviceable to the cause of righteousness and truth. Funeral sermons are however for the benefit of the living only, and any further praise of the dead than may excite the virtuous imitation of survivors would be useless and even painful: within this limit I shall strictly confine myself.

The sentiments of the discourse which you have just heard were familiar to the mind of our departed brother, Mr. JAMES DROVER. He was in the constant habit of putting down his thoughts and feelings in writing ; and amongst his last-written manuscripts there has been found a paper, with this remarkable sentence, " *When I arrive at the closing period of my existence, if I can look back with as much satisfaction as I now look on my present sentiments, I shall die with confidence in the divine mercy.*"

Hence it appears, that though the death of our respected friend was sudden, it was not, in the most important sense of the word, untimely ; it did not find him unprepared. He was, in fact, a truly religious man. I know no one, not engaged in the study of divinity by the duties of a profession, who read and thought so much upon sacred subjects. He was accustomed to frequent retirement; and the papers which he has left behind show how his retirement was occupied, namely, in the inquiry after

Christian truth and in the cultivation of a pious temper. He was particularly conversant with the Holy Scriptures, and his family and nearest friends can bear witness how he prized this inestimable volume. His religious opinions underwent of late years some considerable change, and he is well-known to have embraced cordially and to have professed unreservedly the Unitarian faith. He thought himself the happier and the better for the change : nor was he singular in this persuasion. But whatever may be the judgment of the world upon his creed, it may be confidently affirmed that no one can ascribe his adoption of it to a want of examination or to a defect of religious feeling, much less to motives of self-interest. He sought for truth in the Holy scriptures, and, persuaded that he had found it, he held it firmly, and recommended it to the conscientious consideration of his fellow-christians.

His zeal was at the same time tempered by charity. He condemned no one for retaining opinions which he himself gave up. He esteemed and honoured highly many Christians, whom I see before me, whose faith was very different from his own. On the same paper from which I borrowed the sentence which I have just read, there is the following record of his liberality, which agrees with the tenour of all his conversations on the subject, " *I do think many are as sincerely wrong as others are sincerely right.*"

Our deceased Christian brother's piety was manifested by his regularly filling up his place in this House of Prayer, where he was an attentive hearer and a devout worshipper, and by his daily observance of the too much neglected duty of family devotion.

What he was in the intercourse of life, his neighbours and friends are best able to declare. But I know I shall not lay myself open to contradiction, when I say that though he had failings which he himself was the first to acknowledge and lament, and over which it was the business of his life to get the mastery, he was just in his dealings, temperate in his enjoyments, innocent in his discourse, ready to serve his fellow-creatures, especially such as were in trouble and distress, and of an independent and public spirit.

His last illness was so rapid and so enfeebling as to allow of few opportunities for the expression of his opinions and feelings ; but his dying hours were marked by patience under suffering, serenity in the midst of change, gratitude for conjugal and filial kind offices, and resignation and devotion to God.

Such is my honest view of his character, which I think it the part no less of religious duty than of friendship to hold up to public imitation. May we, my brethren, be followers of him, as far as we believe that he followed Christ ! May you especially that were his friends, take warning from his sudden departure, to prepare to meet your God, that you also may enjoy a peaceful end and sleep in Jesus! And may you, above all, that are mourning a relation, a father, a husband, be comforted by the remembrance of his faith and virtue, and be led by his example to live the life that you may die the death of the righteous! And may God Almighty of his infinite love and mercy through our Lord Jésus Christ grant that when time shall be no more, we may all rise with our sleeping brother in the resurrection of the just, to enjoy the blessedness of them that die in the Lord, and to enter together into that holy and heavenly state, where truth will be no more shaded by error, where piety will be no longer weakened by the influence of time and sense, where friendship will be interrupted by no cloud of imperfection, where there will be no more death nor sin nor separation nor pain ; where Jesus Christ, in the glory of his exaltation, will be our eternal companion and wonderful counsellor, and where God, the ever-living, ever-gracious Father, will be all and in all through endless ages. Amen and Amen.

———

At Bath, on Monday, the 15th instant, in the 70th year of his age, Mr. WILLIAM MATTHEWS, of the Society of Friends, and Secretary to the West of England Agricultural Society. The Newspapers, from which we extract this notice, state that Mr. Matthews was the author of a Tour in the manner of Sterne, and of some religious and moral Tracts. We hope to receive an authentic account of this gentleman from some one of our correspondents.

INTELLIGENCE.

DOMESTIC.
RELIGIOUS.
Christian Tract Society.

The seventh anniversary of this Society was held on Tuesday the 15th of February, at the Old London Tavern, Bishopsgate Street. At the meeting for business, W, Frend, Esq. was called to the chair. The report of the Committee, which was read by the Secretary, gave a favourable account of the continued prosperity of the Institution, and of the increasing approbation with which its labours are viewed by the religious public. It stated that three new tracts had been published in the course of the preceding year, by which the Committee had been able to complete a third volume. The entire number of Tracts printed and reprinted during this period, was mentioned to be ten thousand. It appeared that since the first establishment of the Society in the month of May, 1809, there had been printed in all 208,500 Tracts; and that the entire number circulated, was 162,600, of which 22,000 had been issued from the Society's warehouse during the last year.

The following statement was presented of the Society's property.

	l.	*s.*	*d.*
Estimated value of the stock on hand,	241	0	0
Due to the Society from the publishers, &c.	122	7	8
Balance in the Treasurer's hand,	66	13	0
	430	0	8
Due from the Society for printing, &c.	94	4	11
Amount of the Society's present property,	334	15	9

The Report announced that Messrs. Cradock and Joy having discontinued to act as the Society's publishers, Messrs. Sherwood, Neely and Jones, of Paternoster Row, had been appointed to be their successors.

The Resolution of the last meeting respecting the time of holding the annual meetings was re-considered, and it was agreed that in future the anniversaries should be held on the third Tuesday in January, in each year.

The thanks of the meeting were voted to Mrs. Mary Hughes and the other literary contributors to the Society; to Messrs. Cradock and Joy for their attention to the interests of the Society while they acted as its publishers, and to the officers of the Society for their services during the last year.

The following gentlemen were elected into office for the year ensuing:

TREASURER.—James Esdaile, Esq.

SECRETARY.—Rev. Thomas Rees.

COMMITTEE.—Messrs. Roberts, Titford Gibson, Hurt, Parker, Thomas Foster, Lean, Groper, Frend, Hall, Barton.

AUDITORS.—Messrs. Parks, Mackmurdo and J. Taylor.

The subscribers and other friends of the Society, to the number of seventy, dined together; Thomas Gibson, Esq. in the Chair. Although the meeting was deprived, through the state of the weather, and other circumstances, of the company of some of the friends of the institution whose presence has usually enlivened its assemblies, the evening past off with considerable spirit; and much interest was imparted to it by the speeches of several gentlemen who addressed the Chair on topics connected with the great objects, for the promotion of which

the Society was originally formed. Several names were added to the list of subscribers.

Unitarian Book Society.

The twenty-fifth anniversary of this Society was holden on Friday, March 29, at the Old London Tavern, Bishopsgate Street. In the morning the Society met at the Chapel in Essex Street, where an able discourse was delivered by the Secretary, the Rev. Jeremiah Joyce. As this discourse is already before the public, having been printed at the unanimous request of the general meeting, where upwards of four hundred copies were subscribed for, it is unnecessary to give any statement here of the preacher's subject and reasonings. Mr. Joyce was considerably agitated in the delivery, at the commencement, owing to the recent and sudden death of an esteemed brother, of whose decease he had been informed only a few hours previously; but the sympathy which he claimed he fully received from all who heard him, whose attention was amply repaid by the increased fervour and animation which this afflicting calamity imparted, as he proceeded, to his language and manner.

At the meeting for business, after the service, Mr. Rutt was called to the Chair. Mr. Belsham produced a letter which he had received from Mr. Joyce, (of whose company the society was unfortunately deprived after the close of the religious service,) notifying his resignation of the office of Secretary. This communication was received with deep regret by all present, who considered the Society as eminently indebted to the unremitting activity and laborious pains of Mr. Joyce for its prosperity during the last fourteen years. The following resolutions were then passed unanimously:

Resolved, on the motion of Mr. Belsham, That this resignation be accepted; but that Mr. Joyce be respectfully solicited to favour the Society, by continuing to perform the duties of the office until a successor can be appointed.

Resolved, on the motion of the same, That the cordial thanks of this meeting be returned to Mr. Joyce, for his long, able, and meritorious services as secretary; and that it receives with the liveliest regret his resignation of an office, the arduous duties of which he has during fourteen years, discharged in a manner so honourable to himself, and so highly advantageous to the Society.

Resolved, That the thanks of this meeting be returned to Mr. Joyce for his very appropriate, eloquent, and energetic discourse delivered this morning.

The members of the Society afterwards dined together, in number about seventy, at the Old London Tavern, Bishopsgate Street, Wm. Smith, Esq. M. P. in the Chair.

Various interesting topics were touched on by several speakers. Amongst others the proposed edition of Dr. Priestley's Works by Mr. Rott, to which several new subscribers were obtained. In his speech, on his health being given, the Chairman entered into the inquiry how far Religious Liberty had prevailed of late, and produced some interesting proofs (which we shall lay before our readers next month in another part of the work) of the Rights of Conscience being better than ever known and respected amongst the nations of Europe.

The Spring Quarterly Meeting of the ministers generally denominated Presbyterian, in the district of Manchester, was held on Good Friday, the 12th instant, at Dukinfield. Mr. Brettell introduced the service, and Mr. Elliot preached from 1 Tim. v. 22. the last clause: "Keep thyself pure." Though the day was very unfavourable, a considerable number of friends from a distance attended the meeting, especially from Stockport and Hyde. After the service, twelve ministers and between thirty and forty laygentlemen dined together, and passed the afternoon in a manner suitable to the occasion.

Though the Reporter does not undertake the task of giving a detailed account of the sentiments and speeches at each meeting, yet it is conceived, that such a brief notice as the present, with the addition of any interesting particulars when they happen to occur, must be pleasing and edifying to the friends of rational religion and primitive Christianity in other parts. By this mode of communication, when they are precluded from others, may the zealous friends of truth provoke one another to virtuous and unremitting activity in the sacred work of reformation.   J.

Manchester, April 16, 1816.

Southern Unitarian Fund.

The first General Meeting of the subscribers to the *Southern Unitarian Fund* was held on Wednesday, 17th of April, at the General Baptist Chapel in Portsmouth. In the morning the devotional exercises were conducted by the Rev. J. Fullagar, and the Rev. J. Lyons. The sermon was preached by the Rev. W. J. Fox, from John iv. 22, *Ye worship ye know not what; but we know what we worship.* After strongly contrasting the mystery and absurdity of Trinitarian worship with the simplicity and intelligibility of that which is addressed to the One God, the Father, the preacher applied his subject to the principles and objects of the institution, whose members were now, for the first time assembled together. The Southern Fund Society is formed on the broad basis of Unitarianism, disregarding all minor differences, and aiming simply at the promotion and encouragement of a pure and scriptural worship.

This end is pursued by establishing lectures in different places, and defraying the expenses of ministers by whose labours they are supported; assisting necessitous congregations by loans or donations; and inducing individuals who have become converts to Unitarianism to form themselves into religious societies. After the service the report of the Committee was read, by which it appeared that the short period which had elapsed since the commencement of their exertions, in September last, had been distinguished by the most encouraging success. To one congregation in the district very acceptable pecuniary aid has been advanced; and another, in a depressed state, has been cheered by an arrangement for the frequent visits of neighbouring preachers. A fortnightly lecture at Portsea has been numerously and respectably attended. A similar one at Gosport, where at first much opposition was experienced, has been attended with the happiest results, as several families have already united for the regular support of Unitarian worship. The effect of preaching has been aided by the judicious distribution of books furnished by the Southern Unitarian Society. The thanks of the Society were voted to Messrs. Brent, Fox, Fullagar, Lyons, Read, Saint, and Treleaven, for their services in these lectures.

About thirty gentlemen afterwards dined together at the Fountain Inn, where the Chair was ably filled by James Carter, Esq. Several new subscribers were announced; and the company was highly gratified by the able and animated discussion of topics connected with the institution by several gentlemen present. The Rev. J. Lyons, in particular, on the Chairman's proposing as a toast, "Success to the London Unitarian Fund," gave a pleasing account of various instances of its usefulness which had fallen under his own observation, and adverted to his own change of sentiments in a manner which deeply interested the feelings of all who heard him.

In the evening an impressive discourse was delivered by Mr. Lyons, from John viii. 31, 32, on the importance of religious truth, the difficulties to be encountered in its pursuit, and the characteristics by which it is distinguished. The friends of the *Southern Fund*, the first provincial society of the kind, separated with feelings of unmingled pleasure at the good already effected by their efforts, and its probable extension from the increase of their resources; and with ardent wishes that similar proceedings may speedily be adopted by their Unitarian brethren throughout the kingdom.

Letter from Dr. Thomson, respecting the Chapel at Thorne.

Sir,   *Halifax, April 20, 1816.*

The appeal of our brethren at Thorne

to the Unitarian public, (in your Number for February, p. 120,) requesting assistance in the building of their chapel, seconded as it has been by the recommendation of Mr. Wright, of Wisbeach, (p. 156) will, I trust, be kindly considered and promptly and liberally answered.

Your correspondent *Zelotes* (p. 134,) has made, in my opinion, some very sensible and just remarks, as to certain preliminaries which ought to be satisfactorily answered, before any appeal, similar to the one from Thorne, ought to be entertained by the Unitarian body. These preliminaries are briefly as follows :—1. That the Committee of the Unitarian Fund, or some other prominent and responsible body should certify that the case is a proper one for Unitarian liberality. 2. That in the event of a general subscription, it should be provided in the trust deed of the chapel, that on the discontinuance of public worship on Unitarian principles, the chapel shall come into the hands and be the property of some Unitarian body. 3. That the ground upon which the chapel stands and the burial-ground should be freehold. 4. That a burial-ground should be provided. Though these remarks of *Zelotes* are general, as I entirely concur in their justness, I shall briefly apply them to the case of our Unirian brethren at Thorne. 1. It appears to me that the testimony of neighbouring ministers, and of other friends, who from their local knowledge have better and surer means of information than the committee of the Unitarian Fund can, from the distant residence of its members, possibly have, is in all cases to be preferred ; and ought, henceforth, to be considered as indispensable. In a case submitted to the public (M. Repos. Vol. x. p. 313,) this mode was adopted. In the Thorne case, the testimony of Mr. Wright, and of several ministers and friends in the county of York, as borne in the subscription list (p. 182,) will be considered as satisfactory. We have a similar certificate from the Committee of the Unitarian Fund, in their grant of 20*l.* to the Thorne Chapel. 2. Our brethren at Thorne are desirous of the advice of friends respecting the provisions of their trust deed, that what may be built by Unitarian liberality, should in the event of discontinuance of worship on Unitarian principles, revert to that body ; and they will be obliged to any friend to furnish them with a clause providing for the same. 3. The tenure of the ground at Thorne is freehold. In this our brethren at Thorne have been very fortunate, as all the old enclosed land in the neighbourhood is copyhold ; but they have purchased for their chapel, and burial-ground an allotment of common land lately sold under an enclosure act, the powers of which convey the land as freehold of inheritance in fee simple.

4. The ground purchased is 10 yards by

20. The area of the chapel is 10 yards by 11. The remainder of the ground will be left for a burial-ground, and I am informed that if necessary, more ground adjoining this can be obtained. That it is desirable, in the first instance, to enlarge the burial-ground, few, I think, will doubt; and I hope the liberality of the subscription will enable our brethren at Thorne to do so.

I have thus, in order, adverted to the judicious remarks of *Zelotes* as applicable to the case at Thorne, and I hope what I have stated will so satisfy his mind that I shall see his name upon the subscription list. I take the liberty of adding a few particulars, on the authority of one of the brethren at Thorne, which I hope may tend to strengthen their appeal, and interest friends to assist them in the building of their chapel. The dimensions of the chapel have been already stated; our friends calculate that it will hold from three hundred to three hundred and fifty hearers. In this they appear to me to much over estimate its capability; but it is so planned as to admit of a gallery if necessary, large enough to hold from one hundred and fifty to two hundred people. At present the Unitarians in Thorne and its neighbourhood are estimated at from forty to fifty. "But," my informant adds, "we have generally about ninety or one hundred hearers.' It is *beyond all doubt* that the hearers will *greatly increase* when the chapel is opened." On their assembling for worship on the Lord's Day, the devotional part is conducted by an aged and venerable man, Francis Moate, who is the only member of the society with whom I am personally acquainted; two other members, by turns, read sermons. The society meets occasionally for religious conversation and prayer; "we generally have two or three such meetings in every month:" and it has been in agitation to hold these meetings regularly; an intention which it is to be hoped will be carried into effect. The chapel is expected to be finished by the first of June; and will be opened as soon afterwards as may suit the convenience of distant friends.

The society at Thorne is in a great measure insulated from other societies, who hold the same religious sentiments. This circumstance will not fail to be duly appreciated by distant friends, and is indeed one of the strongest points of the appeal. Every one must have read with the highest satisfaction the very handsome list of congregational subscriptions for the Oldham chapel (Vol. xi. p. 121,) from various Unitarian societies in Lancashire and Cheshire. But Thorne is very differently situated to what Oldham is. It has no near and powerful neighbours ; nor are the Unitarian Societies in the counties of York and Lincoln either so numerous, so large, or so affluent as those of Lancashire and Cheshire. I do not mean to insinuate the most distant doubt but that the societies in Yorkshire and Lincolnshire will do all in their power to assist their brethren at Thorne, but when they have done their utmost there will still be much for distant friends to do. I add the distance of Thorne from several other Unitarian Societies; but some of these are not in a condition to give any help to their neighbour. Thorne is distant from the following places (*about*) the number of miles specified; from Selby, 15; Doncaster, 10; York, 30; Lincoln, 40; Hull, 40; Rotheram, 22; Sheffield, 28; Wakefield, 25; Leeds, 30; Gainsborough, 20; Halifax, 45; Elland, 45; Bradford, 40.

With best wishes for the success of our brethren at Thorne,

I am, Sir,
Yours respectfully,
JOHN THOMSON.

Errata in the Thorne Subscription List, page 182.

For Mr. Robert Mathien *read* Mr. Malkin, Chesterfield.

For John Cartlidge, *read* James Cartledge.

For Charles Carthage, *read* Charles Cartledge.

New Subscription.

Mrs. M. Hughes, Hanwood, by Mr. Aspland, 2l.

Ecclesiastical Controversy.

" Strange such a difference should be
" 'Twixt Tweedle Dum and Tweedle Dee!"
SWIFT.

The momentous controversy which at present agitates, and seems likely to convulse, the Church of England as by law established, viz. " Whether the besprinkling an infant with water by the hand of a person episcopally ordained," (a *sine quâ non* it seems of the metamorphosis) determine or not his " moral character here, and his eternal destination hereafter," was decided, *ad interim*, a few days ago, in full

conclave at Bartlett's Buildings (present, the most Rev. the Archbishop of Canterbury, the Right Rev. the Bishop of London the Very Rev. the Dean of ——, and the plain Rev., the Anti-biblist Norris, and other illustrious Church and State Divines) by a majority of three only; the number for the affirmative of the question being thirty-seven; for the negative thirty-four. " Who shall decide when Doctors so disagree ?" Yet it has been thought by some profane clerks, that this portentous issue arises out of one of the most palpable interpolations that ever maintained its usurped station in a record, against the strongest internal evidence of its non-authenticity. Alas, what great events from little causes spring !

(*From a Correspondent.*)

Examiner, (Sunday Newspaper.) April 21, 1816.

NOTICES.

MRS. CAPPE has in the press a second edition of *Mr. Cappe's Sermons on Devotional Subjects*, which has been long out of print. It will be accompanied by the Memoir, &c. as first published in 1805. The volume is expected to be completed in June.

MR. COGAN, of Walthamstow, having resigned the pastoral charge of the Unitarian congregation in that place, proposes to present his friends, at their request, with Two Volumes of his Sermons. Those that have read Mr. Cogan's single sermons will look forward to this publication with much interest.

MR. MEADLEY, author of the Memoirs of Algernon Sydney and Dr. Paley, is collecting materials for a Life of John Hampden. Any gentleman possessing original letters or other documents, tending to illustrate this important subject, will oblige him much by either communicating them, or informing him where they may be found;

MONTHLY RETROSPECT OF PUBLIC AFFAIRS;

OR,

The Christian's Survey of the Political World.

EVERY day discovers more and more of the policy of the French cabinet. Twenty five years of revolution must have produced great effects in the minds of men, but it is presumed, that it is possible to bring them back to the same state, in which they were prior to these changes. One important point is doubtless education; and, if it were true of beings endued with reason as with trees, that as the

twig is bent the tree's inclined, it would be possible for a Government to debase in any manner it pleased the human race under its controul. But this is far from being the fact; and circumstances must concur to give the same effect to its institutions at one period, which they would have at another.

An attempt has been made to introduce into France the system of education, now, used for the poor, in this kingdom. Some schools had been established at Paris, but the clergy soon found, that they would be detrimental to their views, and they have succeeded at last in bringing them to suit their purpose. In fact, they have done no more than what the clergy of England have attempted, but without success in this country. With us the Lancasterian schools had scarcely been established, and the public at large was in general convinced of the benefit of instructing the younger minds in the grand principles of Christianity, rather than in the partial views of a petty sect, when the clergy of that established by law, a very small and insignificant sect when compared with the great body of Christians diffused throughout the world, excited a clamour against them; and in opposition set up their new establishment, which they had the presumption to stamp with the name of National schools, and in which instruction was to be given agreeable to their peculiar dogmas. However, in this country their sectarian principles did not avail so far as to destroy the schools on a more enlarged plan. The children of England, who are not of the sect established by law, have an opportunity of going to schools, where they will not be taught like parrots to repeat by rote a set of assertions, formed by men just emerged out of popery, and which will not bear the test of scriptural examination. It is not so in France. The question is there settled otherwise by an ordonnance of the king, who has decreed that in all the schools, the Catholic, Apostolic and Roman religion shall be taught, and no other. Consequently the children in that country must repeat like parrots, a certain set of notions, very different from those in which the children of our schools are instructed. They will be taught that the pope is the head of the church, that they must fall down before a consecrated wafer, and worship a triune god: that there is only one, true religion, and that theirs is that true one. How far the scheme will succeed time will shew. The education they receive in the schools will meet with some opposition at home; for, in consequence of the Revolution the attachment to the pope and to the clergy has very much diminished, and many of the notions of the schools will be dis-

cussed with freedom out of them. At any rate the children will learn to read, and the effect may be very different from what the cabinet expects. It seems scarcely possible, that popery should regain its ancient influence: but irreligion has had for so long a time its sway in France, that it may be replaced by superstition.

This circumstance of Government establishing opinions, in which children should be educated, and the contradiction there is between the opinions maintained on the different sides of the British Channel, ought to be a warning to us, who profess our attachment to scriptural religion only, how we inculcate upon our children, any thing, for which we have not the decisive warrant of scripture. Besides it is incumbent on us to be careful not to teach our children, as is the custom with the sectaries of Rome and England, to repeat things like parrots by rote. If we ask a child a question, the answer should not be put into its mouth, but it should be derived from its own reflection; and a very few trials will prove to every parent or teacher, how much easier and better this is than the common mode by catechisms, in which each sect teaches its particular notions; and consequently as these notions contradict each other, some of the children must imbibe falsehood instead of truth. Let the parable of our Saviour, the poor man that fell among thieves, be read by a child, and appropriate questions be asked from it. Its reason will be exercised by the answers, and its mind opened: and so it will be by all the plain passages of scripture, which indeed are the only ones, in which children should be instructed. The more difficult passages, on which in fact the sectaries ground their various opinions, ought to be reserved for a more distant period: and a child, brought up in the rational manner we have suggested, will be capable, at manhood of discerning the futility of the greater part of the doctrines, on which the sectaries lay so much stress, as well as the falsehood of some doctrines, in which the majority of professing Christians are united.

The farther views of the French cabinet are seen in the suppression of the National Institute and the Polytechnic School. The latter was admirably adapted for the instruction of the people in all the arts of civil life; but it seems that the pupils were not so attached to the reigning family as was desired. Whether the Government will adopt any thing in its stead, time will shew: but it is not likely that there will be the same encouragement held out to proficiency in the arts as under the former system.

A change is also likely to take place in the ecclesiastical system. The Concordat is to undergo a revision, and it is confidently asserted that the order of Jesuits is to be re-established. This order had at one time the education of youth chiefly in its hands, and in this line it displayed great talents ; but they were counterbalanced with such gross defects, that their re-establishment may be considered not only as an evil to the kingdom of France but to Europe in general. It would be a great advantage to this kingdom, if education in our universities and public schools were less confined than it is at present to the clergy. The monastic institution in the Universities particularly requires revision ; but it is not likely that any change will be effected for some time in this respect.

But the eyes of the public are turned to the trial of our countrymen, which will have probably taken place before this is published. The preparatory steps are already made known, and afford a good specimen of the ideas entertained by the French on justice. Their great object is to make the accused criminate himself, and if they do not gain this point, they extort from him a variety of circumstances, which may be converted to his injury. Their whole plan seems to be to destroy innocence; and wretched is the state of the poor man guiltless of crime, who is brought before their tribunal. Our countrymen have answered their interrogatories with the spirit of Englishmen, and the publication of the trial may do much good to France ; teaching that wretched country in what a miserable state is their criminal jurisprudence. The accusation is the favouring of the escape of a state criminal, and with this they wish to blend a plot against government. Nothing can appear more absurd to an Englishman than some of the interrogatories, in which they do not hesitate to take for granted the guilt of the accused : but we shall reserve our further remarks till the fate of our insulted countrymen is determined.

' As Europe is, or is said to be, delivered, a new object has arisen for the employment of the deliverers, which may lead to some new schemes of warfare. The Barbary powers have been harassing the coasts of Italy, and, it is said, have succeeded in carrying off a Neapolitan Princess, betrothed to the Duke of Berri, in her way from Palermo to Naples. Our chivalrous knight, Sir Sydney Smith has been endeavouring to excite the Christian powers to unite in a crusade against the Mahometans in Africa. The mode of warfare of the latter is certainly less defensible than that of the Christians, for they make slaves of the male prisoners, and enclose the females in their harems. But as to the grounds of their wars they are perhaps superior. They do not insult the Almighty with infamous appeals to justice, humanity and religion, in which, in the tergiversation of the Christian treaties, it is evident that all cannot be right, and that there must among some of the powers reign a contempt of religion and virtue entirely derogatory to the character they assume. It is a melancholy thing to reflect, that at one time the African shores of the Mediterranean acknowledged the authority of the gospel. At present the name of Christian is there held in abhorrence : and it is not by war that it will be restored to its former honours. Those shores were infected with the sectarian principles of Augustine long before the Mahometan invasion, and at the time of the Saracen successes had mixed with the religion of Christ the worship of images and a triune God. The faith is now changed; their places of worship are freed from images, and worship is addressed only to the Supreme Being : but they have set up Mahomet in opposition to our Saviour, and the Coran instead of the Gospel. But during the last twenty-five years they have not shed so much blood as the Christians. .

Our own country has since our last had one ground for consolation. The property tax was vainly attempted to be continued, in spite of the assurances, that it was a war tax, and to cease with the war. The opposition made throughout the country by petitions from all parts was very great, yet the conflict was expected to terminate in a different manner. The ministry to the last were pertinacious in their endeavours to continue the tax; but, to the surprise of every one, when the question came to a decision, they were left in a minority, the majority exceeding it by thirty-seven. Thus was an end put to this odious tax, which offended all the principles of just and equitable taxation, and could be maintained only on the same principles, that in a town besieged every man must part with his property of any kind according to the state of the place. One great objection to the tax was the advantage given to the landholder above the person who gained his livelihood by the sweat of his brow. Both were made to pay out of the same annual income the same sum to government, though their situations were materially different, and this advantage was given exactly contrary to true principles: for the landholder ought not to obtain an advantage over his countrymen, inasmuch as his security is so much the greater. But the world, and this country in particular, has much to learn on the subject of taxation, which when duly considered will introduce among the higher classes better principles of morality than they at present possess.

A strange infatuation now pervades the country. Formerly peace and plenty were considered as blessings, for which we could not be sufficiently thankful to Divine Providence. Different principles are now promulgated, and long faces are seen because corn is cheap. A smile covers them on the rise of the markets. These inconsiderate persons do not reflect, that plenty carries with it blessings on all classes. Could they raise the markets to the importation standard, the country would not be a gainer, and the only points would be to enable the landholder to keep up his war-rents and to increase the poor-rates. But the subject is of great extent. We shall continue to be thankful to God for plentiful harvests; and, notwithstanding all that we hear to the contrary, hope that the backward spring will be followed by a kindly summer, being persuaded that cheap corn is equally advantageous to the consumer and to the farmer.

NEW PUBLICATIONS IN THEOLOGY AND GENERAL LITERATURE.

Resignation to the will of God Illustrated and Enforced by the Example of Jesus Christ. A Sermon, preached at the Unitarian Chapel, Reading, Berks, on Sunday Evening, March 24, 1816, on occasion of the Death of Mr. James Drover. With an Appendix, containing some Thoughts on the Support and Consolations which the Unitarian System furnishes in seasons of affliction and trouble, and especially in the hour of death. By Robert Aspland, Pastor of the Unitarian Church, Hackney. 8vo. 1s. 6d.

Observations on the State and Changes in the Presbyterian Societies of England during the last Half Century: Also, on the Manufactures of Great Britain; which have been for the most part established and supported by the Protestant Dissenters; tending to illustrate the Importance of Religious Liberty and Free Inquiry to the Welfare and Prosperity of a People. Preceded by a Sermon on the Death of the Rev. Dr. Joshua Toulmin, in which his character as a Member of Civil Society is attempted to be improved. By Israel Worsley. 12mo. 3s. boards.

Remarks on the Rev. J. Harries's Treatise on the "Proper Deity of Christ," and the Doctrine of "Three distinct Persons in God." In a Letter to the Author. By a Layman. (John Rees, Swansea.) 8vo. 9d.

An Address to the Committee of the Isle of Sheppey Auxiliary Bible Society, containing Animadversions on their Conduct; with a Copy of the Correspondence which took place on the Occasion, for having rejected a Donation. By M. Harding. 8vo. 3d.

Illustrations of the Divine Government: tending to shew that every Thing is under the Direction of Infinite Wisdom and Goodness, and will terminate in the Production of Universal Purity and Happiness. By T. Southwood Smith. 12mo, extra boards. 6s.

THE

Monthly Repository,

&c.

No. CXXV.]   MAY, 1816.   [Vol. XI.

·HISTORY AND BIOGRAPHY.

Memoir relative to the Vaudois: communicated by Rev. T. Morgan.

Williams's Library, April, 1816.

SIR,

I SEND you some extracts from a Memoir relative to the Vaudois, delivered to me by a friend who was educated among them, and with whose family I have been acquainted many years. It is dated at Turin, Jan. 20th, 1816, and has been translated by me with difficulty from the French language, adulterated with the *Patois* of the valleys. Considered as supplemental to the Memoir respecting the Waldenses in the Monthly Repository for March last, (p. 129,) your readers, perhaps, will not think it unworthy of an admission into your pages.

I am, yours sincerely,

THOMAS MORGAN.

"The Vaudois, foreseeing by the events of 1814 what was likely to be their situation, thought it necessary to depute M. Paul Appia, then Judge of the Peace, and M. Peyran, Pastor of Pramol, to wait on his Excellency Lord Bentinck, Commander of the British Forces at Genoa, for the purpose of requesting that he would take us under his high protection, and recommend us to the king on his return from Sardinia, that we might receive the same good treatment from him with his other subjects. The king arrived at Genoa while the Vaudois deputies were in that city; and Lord Bentinck had indeed the goodness to speak concerning us to our sovereign, and to recommend us to his favour. This was about the 18th of May. Victor Emanuel arrived at Turin on the 20th; and on the 21st he published a manifesto, by which he put in force all the edicts which his predecessors had issued. The inhabitants of St. John, availing themselves of the liberty which the French go-

vernment granted them, had at length built a church in the centre of their commune. By the patents of Sept. 30, 1814, among other things, the king ordered the Intendant of the Province to compel us to shut up the church of St. John, as built beyond the strict boundaries to which we had been confined. This took place in consequence of a letter from that magistrate to the Moderator on the 25th Nov. 1814. Of such moment did Victor Emanuel consider the recommendation of Lord Bentinck, the representative of a great and generous nation, which had replaced him on the throne of his ancestors! He chose rather to be influenced by the perfidious insinuations of his ministers, or his fanatical confessors, than to comply with the request of Lord Bentinck.

"Immediately after the return of the king to his dominions, the Vaudois were deprived of all their employments, such as receiverships of the contributions, the places of salt-makers, secretaries of the communes, judges, &c. and their young men of merit, who had served with honour in France, were refused permission to enter the army, with the declaration that no Protestant officers would be received among the king's forces. About the beginning of May, 1794, the French had made themselves masters of the fort of Mireboue, situated at the extremity of the valley of Luzerne, and the Vaudois were accused of having been concerned in its surrender, though there was not one of them in the fort. But the fanatical Piedmontese laid hold of this accusation as a pretence for planning a second St. Bartholomew, to be carried into execution in the communes of St. John and La Tour, on the night of the 14th or 15th of May, 1794, by the murder of the old men, the women and the children who were left behind in the villages, while all the Vaudois who were able to bear arms were on the mountains, to oppose the invasion of the French troops. The venerable Curé of Luzerne, Don Briansa, was the first to put the Vaudois upon their guard; and a M. Odette, a captain of militia, and a rich person in the neighbourhood, repaired to Paul Vertu at La Tour, declaring that he would shed the last drop of his blood in their defence. Towards the night of the 14th of May, the house of the Curé of La Tour, the church, the convent of Recollects, and some Catholic houses were filled with assassins. While the fatal moment was approaching, seventeen expresses had been sent to general Godin, who commanded in the valley, and then had his head quarters five miles above La Tour, to give him information of these circumstances; but he could not believe that such horrors were in contemplation. At length, some persons of distinction having thrown themselves at the feet of the general, and entreated him to send some companies of Vaudois militia to La Tour, he entertained no further doubts on the subject, but complied with their request, and prepared to retreat with the rest of the army. The troops arrived at La Tour at the commencement of the night, when the rain was pouring in torrents, which, doubtless, had retarded the projected massacre. The assassins now took to flight; and after their departure, a list of the conspirators was discovered, which was sent to the Duke of Aosta, our present king. Not one of them, however, was either punished or sought after. Is not this evidence that the court did not disapprove of their execrable design? The brave general Godin was disgraced, without receiving any recompence for his long services, and retired to Nyon, in Switzerland, where he died.

" Charles Emanuel III., who called us *his good and faithful Vaudois*, would not revoke one of the oppressive edicts, and we could not have any physicians or advocates of our religion, nor any military promotion above the rank of serjeant, except in the militia; whilst under the last (French) government, three attained the rank of lieutenant-colonel, two or three that of major, and more those of chief of battalion, captain, lieutenant, and many received decorations. If they are

what shall they do, having no other resource than their military talents which the king will not value at all in Protestants? The Vaudois avow their having favoured the principles of liberty of conscience, and of breaking the chains by which they had been bound for ages. Posterity will judge whether this be a crime before God, or even before men. They had rendered services, most powerfully enjoined by humanity, to their deliverers (and masters), the commune of Bobbi alone having furnished, on the application of their very worthy pastor, the late M. Rostan, volunteers, who carried three hundred sick and wounded soldiers over the heights of the Alps. For this service they received the acknowledgements of the grand army of Italy, by an Order of the Day, dated 3rd Prim. An. 8, (24th Dec. 1799,) and signed by Suchet, General of Division, &c. This humane conduct was represented by the priests and other cruel enemies of the Vaudois, to have been the natural effect of their political opinions, notwithstanding that the Russians and Austrians met with a similar reception from them (never in the least interrupting their perfect liberty of conscience), as appears by the testimonials received from Marshal Suwarrow and Prince Bagration (who shewed the greatest favour), of Prince Kevenhuller, General Niemsell and, above all, the brave Count Nieper, who constantly interested himself on behalf of the Vaudois, and was respected by them as their benefactor,—at whose suggestion they sent to Count Bubna a short list of their requests, of which we give the substance :—

" 1. That they may have secured to them a perfect liberty of conscience, and of situation, in common with the other subjects of his Sardinian majesty.

" 2. That their religion may be no obstacle to their employment in civil and military offices, according to the scale of promotion.

" 3. That they may keep the property acquired beyond the limits to which they were confined, and that they may be permitted to make further acquisitions, should they meet with a fair opportunity.

" 4. That they may be permitted to settle in any of his Sardinian majesty's dominions, where they may find it their interest so to do.

" 5. That the support of their pastors may be established by the enjoyment of the property granted them by the French government (the salary of 1000 franks to each of the thirteen pastors), or in such mode as shall please his Sardinian majesty.

" 6. That they may be permitted to keep open the temple built at St. John's, beyond the ancient limits, as well as to build others, and to keep schools where it shall be found necessary for the pastors to reside.

" 7. That they may have liberty to print, within the dominions of his Sardinian majesty, such books as are necessary for conducting their public worship, or to bring them from abroad.

" 8. That persons educated in their religion may have perfect liberty to practise as physicians, apothecaries, surgeons, advocates and notaries.

" 9. That in forming the municipal councils, regard be paid in each commune to the proportion of the mixed population, and that strangers to the communes do not receive appointments, or indigent Catholics, without their consent.

" 10. That they may be permitted to inclose their burial places within walls, and to repair or build edifices adapted to public worship or instruction.

" 11. That children, under fifteen years of age, may not, under whatever pretence, be compelled or persuaded to change their religion.

" 12. That they may not be under the necessity of observing the festivals pointed out in the Almanack, which may render them idle, or seduce them to debauchery.

" 13. Finally, That they may wholly, and in every respect, partake of the privileges of the Catholic subjects of his majesty, in the same manner as they enjoyed them after the Revolution, until the restoration of his Sardinian majesty to the throne of his ancestors by English generosity!! Let the Status-quo of January 1813; be established with respect to whatever relates to the Vaudois.

" M. Count Bubna was not successful, any more than the English envoy, Mr. Hill, who, at the request of a deputation of Vaudois, (consisting of MM. Meille, Pegran and Ros-

taing, ministers, Brezzi and I. P. D. Vertu,) promised to take an active part on our behalf, but whose application appears to have been coldly received by the ministers, under the pretence that our situation was not worse than before the Revolution, without reflecting that our *slavery* could not in effect be worse than at that time. The king, also, received the deputation of the Vaudois; but he did not promise them any relief, and in truth granted them none, doubtless by the advice of his confessor. The Vaudois entertained hopes that the arrival of the queen would prove a favourable event for them, and the same deputation was appointed to wait on her majesty; but she would not deign to admit them to an audience, notwithstanding the positive assurance to the contrary of the Minister of the Interior, Count Vidua. The government has not made any public declaration respecting the purchases of national property and churches; and since opinions are divided on this subject, the state of uncertainty is fatal to those, whose pressing necessities render them desirous of parting with what they bought. Neither has any declaration been published respecting the Vaudois officers returned from France, and who have no other resource than their military talents. The following is a sketch of the population of the Vaudois communes, which measures are taking to render more exact:—

	PROTS.	CATHS.
P. La Tour - - -	1600	300
P. St. John - - -	2000	50
P. Angrogne - -	2000	100
P. Villar - - -	2000	200
P. Bobbi - - -	2000	20
P. Rora - - -	800	30
P. Prarustin - -	1500	30
P. Pramol - - -	1200	
P. Pral - - -	800s	25
P. St. Germain -	800	60
P. Pomaret - -	660	20
Anvers Pirache -	500	100
Massel - - -	500	40
Riclaret - - -	600	50
P. Ville Seche -	500	
Faet - - -	400	200
Roche Plate - -	400	20
Rodozet - - -	350	40
P. Manegle - -	300	50
Salsa - - -	300	60
Bovile - - -	150	100
Cheneviere - -	150	

St. Martin	- - -	100 -	150
Traverses	- - - -	100 -	30
Chabrant	- - - -	60 -	50
Total		19770	1725

" In this number are not comprised about 50 Protestant families of different nations, settled at Turin, who have no other pastor than the chaplain either of the English or Prussian envoy. The communes marked P. have Protestant churches; the others are obliged to attend the nearest church. But the church of St. John being shut up, the inhabitants are compelled to go to their ancient church (almost destroyed by an earthquake) in the commune of Angrogne, which has consequently two m its district. To the more distant parts of the country, and those seated among the summits of the mountains, the ministers can only go to exercise their functions once or twice a year, in the most favourable weather, and then preach in the open air. In order to re-establish the very small catholic parish of Bobbi, they compelled two poor widows of pastors who had an asylum in the house of the ancient curé, to quit their situation without notice in the middle of December, notwithstanding that all possible solicitations were made for a temporary indulgence, and the complaints which the writer of this paper preferred to Mr. Hill.

" This exposé, which has been drawn up in haste, contains only indisputable truths, as may be proved to conviction to those who will apply to M. Geymet, a pastor, and chaplain to Mr. Hill, English envoy at Turin (formerly moderator of the Vaudois churches) and the Ex-Sub-Prefect of Pignerol, of which all the Vaudois communes are dependencies. It is necessary to state that M. the pastor-Bert of La Tour, is at this time engaged in drawing up another account of the situation of the Vaudois, which cannot but confirm the contents of this, of which he has no knowledge. The Vaudois persuade themselves, that not only all the Protestant powers will favourably consider their case, but also the magnanimous emperors Alexander and Francis, and the other illustrious princes, if inform-

ed by the cabinet of London, the most powerful of all."

" *Turin, Jan. 20th, 1816.*" ·

Raynerus Sacco, an inquisitor, has published a book against the Vaudois, in which he gives them the name of *Leonists*, from one of their ancient leaders called Leon, who lived towards the end of the third century. You may also see the blasphemy of the church of Rome against the Vaudois in Gretzer's *Bibliotheque*, written against that people. Many writers pretend that the name Vaudois is derived from Peter Valdo, whose adherents, persecuted in France during the twelfth century, fled for refuge into the retreats of the obscure inhabitants of our valleys who they knew professed the same religion with themselves. They were known by this name, however, eighty years before the time of Valdo, as appears from a poem written in the Patois of the country : *illidison quel es Vaudose, e degne de morir.* This poem is entitled *La nobla Leiçon de 1100 ;* and it is said to exist in M. S. at Cambridge. The ancient history of the Vaudois appears like a dream to those who have no knowledge of the warlike valour of this small people, who have suffered persecutions, the recital of which must strike us with horror. The following is a list of the historians of this unhappy people. Boyer's (an Englishman's) short History of the Vaudois, 12mo. Perrin's History of the Vaudois and Albigenses, 8vo. Leger's General History of the Vaudois, folio. Giles's short History of the same people, 4to. Brez' Abridgment of the History of the Vaudois, 8vo. Maranda's Picture of Piedmont, imperfect.

The situation of the pastors is truly deplorable. For the government have condemned Messrs. Vertu and Brezzi (who rented from the Protestant ministers the property granted by the French government of the value of 1000 franks each) to reimburse the sum of about ten thousand franks, advanced by them to the Protestant ministers, as they were authorized to do, and to claim the same from the pastors, who are positively compelled to borrow the means of existence, and of course find it impossible to satisfy such a claim.

MISCELLANEOUS COMMUNICATIONS.

Mr. Belsham's Reply to the Animadver-sions of the Rev. Reginald Heber, in his Bampton Lectures.

Essex House, May 1, 1816.

Sir,

IN ancient days it was a subject of grave discussion among the fathers of the church, how it should happen that the Holy Spirit, who is the third person in the Trinity, of the same substance and equal in power and glory both with the Father and the Son, should be so little noticed in the New Testament, and that no act of worship, not even a single doxology, should be addressed to him. This controversy, however, unlike to many others, was, fortunately, soon set at rest, by the very natural suggestion, that the Holy Spirit being the author of the book, he could not, consistently with propriety and decorum, say much concerning himself, and especially in his own praise. Happily, however, for us, who live in these latter days, this deficiency in the sacred records is abundantly made up by the pious and learned lucubrations of the reverend Reginald Heber, M. A. and Rector of Hodney, who, in a series of discourses lately delivered before the University of Oxford, at the Bampton Lecture, has communicated all which it is necessary for orthodox Christians to know and believe concerning the Holy Spirit, and, which, from discretion or other considerations, the Holy Spirit has not thought fit to reveal concerning himself.

In truth, Sir, it is so clearly the doctrine of the New Testament, that the Spirit of God is God himself, as the spirit of a man is a man himself, and this is so obvious to all who are but moderately acquainted with scripture phraseology, that to institute an inquiry, in the present advanced state of theological science, whether the Spirit of God is a third part of God, or a third person in the godhead, appears to be much the same as to inquire, whether the spirit of man is the third part of a man, or a third person in the manhood.

This learned gentleman (for Mr. Reginald Heber is a very learned man, of which he has made an abundant display in his copious Notes, which would have stamped upon his work an inestimable value, had they been accompanied with a reasonable share of judgment and candour,) amongst other novelties, has started a question, whether the body of Christ was raised from the dead by his own divine nature, or by the operation of the Holy Spirit: and after discussing the subject with becoming gravity and diffidence, he decides in favour of the latter supposition.* Now, Sir, this decision is so diametrically opposite to that of Paul, who positively declares in the Epistle to the Romans, that "Christ was raised from the dead by the glory of the Father," that I cannot help suspecting that this learned gentleman may be a concealed Ebionite : a sect which did not hold that apostle's writings in the estimation to which they are entitled. And this suspicion would be greatly confirmed if it should appear that the learned lecturer, who is also said to be a great traveller, had extended his progress eastward as far as Palestine, where it is well known that this heretical sect flourished even in the age of the apostles. At any rate, I am sure you will allow that I have as good reason, upon the grounds which I have stated, to charge Mr. Heber, upon suspicion, of being an Ebionite, as he has to charge me with being an unbeliever, because I agree with the Theophilanthropists that the love of God and our neighbour is the sum and substance of religion, while, at the same time, I expressly condemn that novel and ephemeral sect, for having abandoned the Christian revela-

* "I am well aware," says the learned lecturer, p. 272, "of the reasonable doubt which may exist, whether the spirit whereby Christ, according to St. Peter, was raised from the dead, be the third person in the Trinity, or our Lord's own immortal nature. But it may be thought, perhaps without impropriety, that the awful Being whom, on this occasion, St. Matthew calls, not an angel simply, but the Angel of the Lord, who with might and glorious majesty descended, amid the throes of labouring nature, to bring back the Saviour from his tomb was, in truth, the same everlasting Spirit who had announced to the Virgin-Mother the character and name of her Son," &c. Does the learned lecturer dignify such trifling with the name of argument?

tion which is the only foundation of our immortal hopes.*

But passing over these baby-controversies, which are only fit for those *who have need of milk,' and who are not able to bear strong meat,* I proceed to the main business of my epistle, which is to explain and apologize for an erroneous representation which I have been understood to have made of the late Bishop Shipley's sentiments concerning the person of Christ in my Letters to the Bishop of London. I did indeed conceive, by what I had heard from my friends Mr. Lindsey and Dr. Priestley, that *their* friend the Bishop of St. Asaph, had been an Unitarian like themselves. I misunderstood them. I am now informed, from very high authority, that Bishop Shipley was an Arian, similar in his principles to his learned friends, Dr. Price and Sir William Jones. I regret to place the venerable prelate a degree lower in the scale of theological excellence than that to which I once believed him to be entitled. He is, indeed, still in very good company. But, like David's worthies of the second order, he does not reach the high pre-eminence of Lindsey, Lardner, Priestley and Law. I hope, however, that I have now done theological justice to the memory of Bishop Shipley: and that those whose feelings were hurt at his being classed with Unitarians, will accept of my public, and, I

own, reluctant recantation. For I can assure them, that no personal disrespect was intended to that learned and liberal prelate by placing him in the highest rank of enlightened Christian divines.

The learned lecturer, not content with advocating Bishop Shipley's orthodoxy, in confutation of my supposed erroneous statement, prompted by his overflowing zeal, travels a little out of his record and volunteers an assertion which, if I am not mistaken, many of the prelate's friends will not deem to be either necessary or prudent: I will cite his own words, p. 121:—

"Had Dr. Shipley's faith been inconsistent with that of the church to which he belonged, those who knew his utter disregard of worldly interest and his characteristic frankness of character, know that he would not have retained his preferment a single hour."

This paragraph will excite a smile in many of the readers of Mr. Heber's elaborate performance, and by many will be regarded as the eccentric flight of a juvenile imagination, more conversant with books than with the world. This gentleman talks of a bishop's resignation of his mitre as if it were an every-day exploit. I recollect, indeed, that Chrysostom states, that no man is worthy of the office of a bishop, who is not prepared to resign it whenever duty calls. But Chrysostom wrote fourteen centuries ago, and both he and his doctrine are become completely obsolete. A bishop resign his office for conscience sake!! Mr. Heber, Sir, I am told, is a young man. He is but entering the lists, as a candidate for ecclesiastical preferment. When he becomes a bishop himself he will know better.

Mr. Heber charges me, p. 289, as taxing Bishop Horsley with insincerity, because I have said in my Review of Mr. Wilberforce, " I strongly suspect that the prelate of Rochester would smile at the honest simplicity of the member for Yorkshire, in supposing that a sincere faith in creeds and homilies is at all necessary to the permanent prosperity of a national church." I deny that the learned gentleman's inference can be fairly drawn from the premises. For has not Popery stood for ages though popes and cardinals have been notoriously unbelievers? But to say the truth, though I desire to exercise that charity, in its

* "I wish," says this charitable writer, p. 290, "that he (Mr. B.) had not, in a note to p. 168 of his Review of Mr. Wilberforce, given us too good reason to apprehend that his private notions of Christianity are of a kind very faintly distinguished from Deism." The passage alluded to in the Review of Mr. W. is as follows : " Their professed principles comprehend the essence of the Christian religion : But not admitting the resurrection of Christ the Theophilanthropists deprive themselves of the only solid ground on which to build the hope of a future existence." With this passage before his eyes and quoting the former part of it, Mr. Heber presumes to represent me as an unbeliever in the Christian revelation ! and affects to wonder at my expostulation with the Bishop of London for charging the Unitarians with being Deists in their hearts ! Can that be the cause of truth and honour which requires such gross and palpable misrepresentations in its defence ?

fullest extent, which *hopeth all things and believeth all things*, I do confess that my charity is strained to its utmost limit when it is required to believe, that one learned and highly celebrated prelate is sincere when he maintains, that the Father begot the Son by contemplating his own perfections: and that another can be quite in earnest when he contends, that three non-entities make a perfect Being. When one is reduced to the hard alternative of believing that a divine of the highest order in the church is either —— or ——, which of the sides of this distressing dilemma would Mr. Heber advise a friend to choose?

One word more, Sir, and I have done. There are "Christian advocates" at Cambridge, "Bampton Lecturers" at Oxford, and "Senior Fellows" at Dublin, not to mention a herd of Reviewers in their train, who all with one accord write and preach and publish against me and my works, and who take infinite pains to convince the public that neither the one or the other are worthy of notice. From none of my numerous opponents do I meet with quarter, and scarcely with common civility, except from my worthy friend, professor Kidd, of Aberdeen; who does not represent me as altogether void of common sense, though I am unable to comprehend his super-sublime demonstration of the doctrine of the Trinity. Now, Sir, as an overweening vanity will extract nutriment even from what was intended as its bane, and as I once knew a bad poet console himself for the lampoons which were made upon his wretched verses, by observing that "even Homer had his Zoilus," so though I desire to keep myself as humble as my adversaries themselves endeavour to make me, yet unluckily this formidable combination against me operates, I know not how, as a temptation to think more highly of myself than I ought to think. For when I see that no less than four of our Universities, are discharging their tremendous artillery through their respective organs, against an insulated, unsheltered, unpatronized, untitled individual like myself, ἐμηδὲν εἰδὼς Οὐδίπες, I am vain enough to conclude that my humble efforts for the restoration of primitive doctrine are not quite so inefficient as my zealous opponents would have it believed. And to say the truth, if

these learned gentlemen thought of me as they profess to do, and as I think of them, they would surely act by me as I do by them, and would give themselves no sort of concern either about me or my works.

I am, Sir, &c.
T. BELSHAM.

P. S. The learned lecturer, who is ever ready to charge the Unitarians with that inaccuracy of which he himself exhibits many conspicuous examples, accuses me note p. 121. of representing Archdeacon Blackburne, as an Unitarian.* This charge I distinctly deny. I have a better opportunity of knowing what that venerable dignitary's sentiments really were than Mr. Heber can possibly have: for I am in possession of his confidential correspondence: they were not Calvinistic. But whatever his theological sentiments were, Archdeacon Blackburne, was a man of a truly honourable mind. Entitled by talent and learning, and warranted by connexion, to look up to the highest preferment which the church has to bestow, he refused to accept of any benefice which made it necessary for him to renew his subscription to the thirty-nine articles. For which he was blamed by some who thought as freely as himself, but who possessed more of the wisdom of this world: who loved truth well, but preferment better. But this venerable man did not think it necessary to relinquish his moderate preferment in the church notwithstanding the change in his theological opinions, because he regarded it as a station of more extensive usefulness than any which he could occupy among the Dissenters. And he was offended with those of his family who thought and acted upon a different principle.

It seems that now in the nineteenth century it is great offence to hazard a doubt concerning the entire assent of any learned divine to every proposition contained in the articles which he subscribes: which assent, according to Archdeacon Paley it would be most unreasonable to expect or to demand. In the better times of Clarke, and Hoadley, and Sykes, and Jortin, a libe-

---

* "This zealous partizan," says Mr. Heber, p. 121, speaking of Archdeacon Blackburne, "was not only a Trinitarian but a Calvinist."

ral interpretation of these numerous and complex propositions was not deemed a disgrace: and it was even thought to be countenanced by the articles themselves, which require that nothing should be insisted upon as an article of faith which cannot be proved by the holy scriptures. And many in those days were not ashamed to avow the principle, "that an unity of spirit in the bond of peace," was of far greater value than "an unity of faith in the bond of ignorance, or an unity of profession in the bond of hypocrisy." In our days the case is altered: and we are now bound to believe that every clergyman who subscribes the articles, assents to every proposition contained in them: and that to hint the contrary is both "false and injurious."

Letter to a Friend on the Atonement.

[Communicated from Ireland.]

Dear Sir,   *March*, 1816.

I INTEND to answer at some length the note which you were so obliging as to send me with Sandeman's Letters and Walker's Address, for I presume you wish that I should give you my opinion of these writers.

You say you do not subscribe to all the sentiments of Sandeman. He certainly goes a strange length in describing the corruption of man, particularly where he maintains, that "as to the matter of acceptance with God, there is no difference between one man and another," for instance "between the most revered judge, and the most odious criminal," &c. Yet in his reply to Hervey, and others whom he calls popular preachers, he argues with candour, and he shews that they are not true to their own principles. In general, I think he proves that a moderate Calvinist is an inconsistent character. Mr. Walker also appears to me to have an evident advantage over those with whom he reasons; for they concede to him what is a sufficient groundwork for his entire theory, and he knows well how to profit by their concession. But the remark which I make upon him and his opponents is, that they both build upon a wrong principle, which has no foundation in the gospel.

This principle, common to both parties, is the doctrine of the atonement, which leads necessarily to the opinion, that the favour of God depends on a circumstance entirely independent on the will of man. But the Arminians, opposed to Walker, contend notwithstanding, that man has a free-will; and that he is here in a state of trial; for which opinions they quote the whole body of scripture, and they are quite shocked at the opposite suppositions. Walker, in his various writings, shews that they maintain these opinions in opposition to the principle of atonement. He asks them in substance, with much reason,—As you not merely admit but strenuously maintain that the sins of men are forgiven, and that they are accounted just before God, only for the sake of the atonement made by Christ, how can you in the next breath attribute these effects to a different cause? If works be a necessary condition of God's favour, where is the necessity for the atonement? Must the infinite atonement made to God by a part of himself be abortive, unless it be aided by the puny efforts of miserable man? Can such a costly atonement be necessary or suitable, to render our good works acceptable, or to enable a man to atone for himself? Can it be in the power of any man to reverse the councils and decrees of God with respect to himself, the most important of which must relate to the atonement? In answer to these questions, Arminians appeal to scripture and reason for the freedom of man's will, leaving the principle of atonement to shift for itself.

But neither do Walker and his party abide by the fair consequences from this doctrine of atonement, as may be seen in a few instances. For if God d for mankind to a part of himself by an infinite sacrifice, why should the benefit of this infinite sacrifice be restricted to a few persons, who have no more free-will to please him, than those have from whom the benefit is withheld? Calvinists dispose of this question arbitrarily, not regarding their own description of the atonement as infinite, nor the justice and goodness of God, whose essence is love, and who is no respecter of persons. The case of the potter, to which we are often referred, can relate only to the various conditions of men in *this* world. There are other questions, in answer to which Walker will hesitate to do full justice to the doctrine of the atonement. If it be pride in man to suppose that any of his works can have the slightest effect to propitiate the Deity, and if such a notion shews farther his want of faith in the atonement, would it not be the safest plan to renounce all good works whatsoever, both in profession and practice? Do not these men prove that they have not much faith in the atonement, who spend their lives in making converts to this doctrine, that is, in presuming to help in his work the omnipotent God? How can Walker insist on the all-sufficiency of the atonement, and consequently maintain that there is no condition required for justification, while he insists on faith as the one thing needful, by which he means, an accepting of Christ as a proxy, or an apprehended exchange with him of our vices for his merits? While he maintains literally that it is given to some men exclusively to believe in such an exchange, his preaching must appear a mockery. One of the great objects of the gospel, he says, is to humble the pride of man, by convincing him that the atonement is all-sufficient, and that the intrusion of his own works in any form is impertinent; but what is so much calculated to defeat this object, and to puff men up with spiritual pride, as the notions that they are the favourites and Elect of God, and that all who oppose them are Reprobates?

Both Calvinists and Arminians have always been involved in inconsistencies by their faith in the atonement; still they are alike fearful lest their faith in it might be questioned, for notwithstanding their mutual jealousies, they have always agreed to brand those persons with the name of infidels, who do not believe in it implicitly. Here I may be permitted to say, that those men are much better entitled to this name, who repose implicit faith in mysteries. A sincere Christian who values rightly his Christian liberty, will think it is incumbent on him to prove this doctrine, to analyze it, and view it on all sides, without prejudice, influenced only by a regard for truth. Such a severe examination will probably be censured as irreverent, even by men who scruple not to decide, with great confidence, that the substance of God is complicated, and his councils partial; but before they can convict us of profaneness for questioning their decisions, they must prove them to be sacred and self-evident truths; whereas nothing

seems wanting to prove them to be extravagant fictions, most disparaging to the Divine Nature, but a simple and accurate detail of them. I shall attempt to give such a detail in the fewest words possible.

In consequence of the foreknowledge that the wiles of Satan would prevail over man in paradise, God, for the first time, found himself under a necessity of dividing himself, or of being divided into three, distinct, co-equal, almighty Persons, all of the same substance. These three Persons, being still but one God, held a council on the subsequent state of man; upon which occasion, the first Person expressed infinite wrath at the foresight of man's transgression, the natural effect of which wrath, if uncontrolled in all cases, would be most grievous torments, in soul and body, without intermission, in hell-fire, for ever, to Adam and Eve and all their posterity. The crime for which Adam's posterity was to suffer in this manner, is called original sin, which means literally, the sin of men before they existed. When Adam and Eve ate the forbidden fruit, their offspring by this act was guilty of so henious a sin, that all men, women and children who have ever existed, with a trifling exception, and the greater part of men who are still to be born must be punished for it with endless torments, by the first Person, to the praise of his glorious justice. No alteration for the better or worse can be effected in their destiny by their works, good or bad,—to hell they must go without a possibility of redemption. All men, without any exception, would go the same road, if a few of these delinquents did not experience unconditional favour and reward, to the praise of God's glorious grace. Reprobates, as they are called, are here tempted to ask, as all the descendants of Adam are equally guilty of his crime, why should such a distinction be made between them, as that a few should be made eternally happy, independent of their works, and all the rest eternally miserable? For this distinction, the reason assigned is the sovereign will and pleasure of God, not of the first Person, nor of the majority, but of the second Person's alone; for though they are all One in Deity and substance, still they differ widely in their dispositions, and in their ideas of justice and mercy. The second part of the substance of God did not give way to positive wrath against any part of mankind. While he was resolved to leave most men as he found them; he was inclined to reprieve a few, not indeed from the foresight of their faith or amiable qualities, but rather the contrary. His Elect would be greatly alarmed, if even any part of his infinite atonement should be turned aside from themselves; his inflexible justice in refusing all aid to Reprobates, who are just as good as themselves, is a principal source of their triumph; and they are delighted with his goodness, principally on account of its partiality. However, his favour did not extend to a greater number than to one person in two thousand, and with only this trifling exception, he had no commiseration for the lost state of mankind. Or, perhaps, benevolence toward them would not have been consistent with a prudent regard for himself; for as the office which he did undertake to execute for this small number proved to him a most grievous task; so, if he had enlarged their number to one half of mankind he would have drawn down on himself a thousand times more wrath. At the commencement of his very limited undertaking, what must have been his distress of mind, when no dignified or rational way occurred to him, or was communicated to him to avert from the Elect the Father's infinite wrath, excited and impelled as it was by his infinite justice. He had no choice but to adopt or decline the expedient pointed out to him. It was promulgated in heaven, that the Father's wrath and justice, with respect to mankind, might be expended, not on them, but on some innocent person, who would voluntarily undertake to appease him by assuming their guilt and punishment. From this circumstance we cannot suppose that justice in heaven can bear any analogy to justice on earth. An awful silence ensued. No angelic being offered to bear the brunt of this wrath and justice. On this ominous pause, the Son himself, part of the very substance of God, came forward, and offered himself; to be reputed a sinner for the Elect exclusively, and not only to atone by exquisite sufferings for all their sins, both original and actual, but also to impute all his own righteousness to them, without requiring from them any condition in return;

for he scorned to save them by halves. Agreeable to this offer, he is aptly described by the Elect as a physician, who cures his patients by prescribing regimen and physic, not to them, but to himself,—and as a judge who procures himself to be executed, in order to save the lives of felons condemned by his own sentence. His offer was accepted, and the bargain was accordingly concluded between these two infinite Persons of the one substance. It certainly appears a very dear bargain; particularly when we consider that it did not prevent the success of Satan over both Persons, with respect to mankind, in the enormous proportion of at least two thousand to one; and that it gave Satan the triumph of exacting an infinite sacrifice, distress and humiliation, in the reserved case of the Elect, wherein he was foiled. In vain do curious persons inquire from the Elect the reasons, why the Devil should be allowed to triumph in this manner,—why this bargain between two Co-equals, either such as the other, should be so partial in itself, and bear so hard on the second Person,—why one part of the substance of God should have infinite wrath to be appeased, and not another,—why the second Person should not require the First to atone to himself by exquisite sufferings for the Elect, or for an equal portion of men among the Reprobates, —why the partial sufferings of God should be an advantage to men alone, and to a very small proportion of them, why they should not, at the same time, purchase vegetable life for inert matter, sensation for vegetables, rationality for brutes, and higher powers for all mankind, since they are as much calculated to produce these effects, as to expunge unconditionally the sin of any man? But if there be any congruity between these sufferings, and the unconditional removal of sin, then—being of infinite value, why should they not remove unconditionally the sins of all men? To none of these questions do the Elect choose to reply either from scripture or reason.

One of the wonders of this bargain consisted in the contrivance by which the substance of God might be made to suffer. It was stipulated, that, in process of time, the second part of this substance should become an infant and a man upon this earth, should submit to all the infirmities of a man, and die upon a cross. Afterwards this partial substance of God should remain to the end of time a man-God or God-man. With all this stipu ated degradation and suffering of part of his own substance, the first Person was so well pleased, that he not only consented to forego his infinite wrath and justice toward the Elect, but to shower down favours on them without measure. For these favours he was paid more than an adequate price, by which mean he was saved the trouble of exercising the slightest degree of mercy; and indeed, with respect to him, there is no room for this attribute in the gospel scheme. When this bargain should take effect, that is, when Christianity should receive the gloss of Calvin, it would then appear, that the difference between the Elect and Reprobate lies in this, that to the former alone it is given to believe in this account of the atonement, to renounce all works, and humbly to accept the merits of the man-God, as their own exclusive, undoubted right, as well as righteousness. Consequently they challenge the justice of God and are entitled to their salvation. Reprobates, on the other hand, believe, with much simplicity, that God can forgive them without the sacrifice of any finite or infinite person. All their hopes are placed in the mercy of God, and in endeavouring to imitate the example of Jesus Christ: but as no portion of God has any favour or mercy for them, they must endure to eternity all the torments which can be inflicted by infinite wrath.

In this and every statement of the atonement, it may be noticed that two parts out of three of God, of his very substance, require no atonement, and the third Person is an unconcerned spectator.

Arminians, who, fortunately, are not consistent in many parts of their faith, will not agree to some minor parts of the above statement; and a distinct case would be requisite for them, whenever they can be prevailed on to define accurately and fully their ideas of the atonement: or rather, such a definition from them would render any other confutation unnecessary. So far as justification is concerned, I think they can hardly avoid to describe as a nullity, either the infinite sacrifice of Almighty God, or the free-will of man. To the question

whether faith in the atonement be essential to salvation, they answer so cautiously as to betray the doubt in their own minds. We can grapple with Calvinists, because they are more decided and consistent; and I believe these people will admit, that in stating their doctrine of the atonement, I have kept close to the sense of their language, and to their ideas. Sandeman, at least, will bear me out in the strongest parts of the statement; and he will furnish me with sufficient arguments, *ad hominem*, against the mincing, moderate Calvinist. Some of these may be inclined to modify one or two passages; but every Calvinist entertains such notions of the atonement, as constitute a most frightful theology, calculated to expel all charity from the breasts of those who can receive it, and to appal the hearts of all others, without holding out to them the smallest benefit. However, it can produce no effect on the mind of an enlightened Christian, but pity for those who preach it; for to him it will appear to be more offensive to the Deity than the idolatry of Heathens. The gospel of Christ inculcated a very different lesson, and is as opposite to it in its principles as light is to darkness. In that we learn, that the Lord our God is the FATHER of all men, and not the capricious tyrant, flattered by suitable favourites. Every single precept of Christ and his apostles is sufficient to confute the childish notion of atonement; though it has been divulged with infinite perseverance and ingenuity by highly-gifted men, yet surely by men under strong prejudices. No plain passage of scripture gives it the slightest countenance; and it is supported only by figurative language, which is perverted so as to make scripture contradict itself, and to promote in the world, not religion and humanity, but a gloomy enthusiasm, or a most unhappy scepticism. All these figurative expressions can be explained without the slightest difficulty. One instance here may suffice. St. John, in the Revelation, says of Christ, that he *hath washed us from our sins in his own blood.* Now, which is it more natural to suppose, that this language is figurative, intended to shew that the death and resurrection of Christ had furnished Christians with a powerful, and, in most cases, an effectual motive to forsake their sins; or to suppose that it relates literally to an atonement—that is, to actual blood, in which the sins of the Elect are steeped and rubbed, and then come out virtues? All the texts particularly relied on by Calvinists have been abundantly proved to be consistent with the remainder of scripture, and thus their fancied privileges, deducible from their notions of the atonement, are shewn to be illusory. This has been done even by John Wesley, who gave up the groundless fancy of the imputed righteousness of Christ. But an objection lies to this doctrine of atonement, which supersedes all necessity for arguing against it on the ground of its great absurdity. It supposes that the grand and peculiar doctrine of the gospel is, that the One God is a compounded Being, made up of various persons, with opposite dispositions, and heterogeneous natures; whereas, the uniform testimony of the whole Bible is, that *the Lord our God is one Lord*; and this One God and Father of All, who is above all, is most particularly stated in the New Testament to be— *the God and Father of our Lord Jesus Christ.*

I hope now, Dear Sir, that you will draw one very just conclusion from this long letter, which is, that I would not be at the trouble of writing it, if I did not entertain for you much respect, to which you are entitled from your character and professional labours.

I remain, therefore, &c. &c.
B—S.

Sir, *Exeter, March 19th, 1816.*
ON perusing your valuable miscellany for last February, (p. 65,) a few days since, I was not a little surprised and concerned, at perceiving an aspersion of no inconsiderable magnitude, cast on the moral character of the late Count Zinzendorf; being convinced that there is no foundation for such a charge, I feel it a duty incumbent on me to defend an injured character, that I much and deservedly esteem. I beg to add, that in this undertaking, I have purely followed the impulse of my own mind. I would here be considered as merely advocating the Count's moral character, and by no means espousing all his religious opinions, any more than defending his theological language. If he conscientiously held such opinions, he was unquestionably right in maintaining

them, and if he considered the phraseology he employed as best calculated to convey and illustrate them, who has a right to deny him this liberty?

Having received a considerable part of my education amongst the United Brethren, or Moravians, as they are often though improperly called, and having attentively studied their history, especially that of their late ordinary, and made myself pretty familiar with his religious ideas and the language in which they are couched, I conceive myself rather better qualified than your correspondent, to form a just estimate of the moral worth of that respectable individual. Had the writer in your Repository, instead of adopting the malignant and deceptive representations of a Rimius, (who, forsooth, styles his work a *Candid Narrative,*—how far it deserves such an appellation will presently appear,) attentively perused Crantz's History of the Brethren, or the ample and ingenuous Life of Zinzendorf by the learned and venerable Mr. Spangenberg, or had he duly examined several of the numerous writings of the Count himself, I have little doubt but he would have formed a very different opinion. Your correspondent appears to have dipped into one or two of their works, but I trust that is all; I myself have had access to all their performances, and have made considerable use of them. I have, besides, been favoured with various communications from esteemed individuals of undoubted veracity, who were about the Count's person, and intimately acquainted with his public and private character. But I have not formed my judgment of the late ordinary merely from the testimony of friends, or from his own writings, but have attentively examined the works of his opponents; and though I have been at considerable pains to investigate their charges, yet have I never been able to substantiate any one that affected his morals. If it be true that the moral worth of a man results from his intentions and the motives that actuate him, and that his intentions and motives are alone discoverable from his dispositions and conduct, I then feel no hesitation in affirming, that the late Count Zinzendorf is, in no inconsiderable degree, entitled to our esteem and respect. Every honest and unprejudiced person, who will be at the pains of entering into the detail of the Count's life, must,

I think, perceive, that the main spring of his religious career (and to this cause he devoted his life), was, "Love to him who first loved us, and gave himself for us;" that this love prompted him to cheerful compliance with what he believed the Bible taught of his Lord's will; constraining him to diffuse,, as widely as possible, what *he* regarded as the good tidings of salvation; and in the prosecution of this, to him all-important object, he shunned neither privations nor dangers, nor reproach nor poverty; though his rank, connexions and fortune would have enabled him to move in what the world regards an exalted sphere.

As the apologist of the moral character of the Count, I am now compelled to take some notice of a work long since consigned to merited oblivion. I termed that work malignant and deceptive; for, under the mask of candour, the author evidently endeavours to represent the Count and his coadjutors as inimical to the cause of virtue and even decorum; without attempting to allege any thing by way of extenuation, which charity would naturally have suggested, and for which abundant scope unquestionably remained: but his aim has invariably been to exhibit them in the blackest colouring; thus to render them objects of universal detestation.

But this writer is by no means to be implicitly relied on, for his statements not unfrequently rest on the authority of persons who seceded from the Brethren's congregation from worldly or selfish motives, and whose disaffection would render their representations at least suspicious: again, his translations are often inaccurate, by no means presenting the genuine meaning of the original, frequently eliciting meanings and hints which the text does not warrant, or at least does not require. Nor is this all; language is frequently charged to the Count with which he had no concern and which he was foremost to counteract. This *candid* author, moreover, discovers a wonderful propensity to attribute impurity of thought and conduct to impropriety of language. But Zinzendorf, we know, is not the only mysticizer of scripture. Have not our venerable Gill and others done the same? Yet, who would dare to tax the learned and estimable commentator on the Song of Solomon with impurity of mind and

conduct, because his phraseology would admit of such an exposition? But your correspondent argues, that if Rimius's charges were not founded, they would certainly have been replied to; according to him, silence necessarily involves guilt: if such be his opinion, mine it certainly is not: nor, let me add, that of many great and good men besides. To conclude—Rimius's work appears to me its own refuter; for were the horrid charges he alleges matters of fact, it is incredible how any society in civilized Europe could hold together; and the Brethren themselves seem to have been of the same opinion; for I have been credibly informed, that they might have bought up all the copies of that work if they had been so inclined, but they preferred, and I think wisely, to leave it to its fate. Your correspondent seems to think, that Maclaine's testimony, who merely quotes from Rimius, is of great weight in this affair; but he is, perhaps, not aware, that at that period it was as much the order of the day to slander the poor Moravians, as it is at present the Unitarians. With best wishes for the success of your excellent Repository, I remain,

Your obliged friend,
J. F. B.

SIR, *Hackney, April 3, 1816.*

LET justice be done to every man. Although I may have frequently lamented the apostacy of our Poet Laureat from some of the best sentiments of his earlier, *unpensioned* years, the mistake of your correspondent Pacificus, (p. 106,) ought to be rectified. The beautiful and instructive little piece "The Great Victory," is *not* omitted in the late edition of Southey's Poems, but inserted Vol. III. p. 167. What naturally led your correspondent to make the mistake alluded to is the blunder of the printer or reviser of the late edition, who, in the table of contents, has omitted to notice the poem of "The Great Victory," and of another "The Old Woman," &c. p. 193.

B. F.

SIR, *Harlow, April 17, 1816.*

AS I suppose a considerable number of your constant readers are *Anti-baptists*, will you permit me to submit to them a few questions concerning the ordinances, and principles of that religion, which we in common believe; and the duties of which I doubt not to the best of our knowledge we endeavour to practise. I am sure we shall agree that the commandment of Christ is supreme authority, both with respect to faith and practice. I presume that all those persons, who do not attend to any kind of baptism, may be classed under the two following descriptions; first, such as consider that ordinance as superseded by the baptism of the Spirit, which I believe is the sentiment of the respectable society of Christian Friends, called Quakers; and who also decline the ordinance of the Lord's Supper, on the principle of a religion wholly spiritual, to which they suppose these institutes are not now necessary. The second, such as do not consider baptism as extending beyond the pale of converts from Judaism to Christianity. To the first of these I shall only propose one question, when that is answered we shall be better able to judge of the scriptural propriety of their Anti-baptism.

The question is this; is the religion of Friends more spiritual than the religion of the Primitive Churches, Martyrs, Confessors, Apostles, and of Jesus Christ himself? Of the second class of Anti-baptists more questions will be asked; for the present the following. As I suppose it will be granted that baptism in, or with water, was enjoined by Jesus Christ: And as we are ready to admit that baptism, in some form, was practised by the Jews before the time of Christ; is it a fact that he adopted this ceremony, and, as our example, submitted to it himself? Was his baptism to be extended beyond the limits of converts to Christianity? Was this ordinance to be extended to all the proselytes to the Christian faith? Did Christ give authority to the Apostles, or to any of them, to preach the Gospel to *every* creature, to disciple *all* nations baptizing them? Did the Apostles preach the gospel to idolaters, did they convert such, and when the door of faith was opened to the Gentiles, were *they* Jewish converts previously, or idolatrous heathen? Were the common and unclean Gentiles, Acts x. 11, to whom Peter communicated the Gospel, previously to their conversion and baptism circumcised Jewish converts? If they were not, then what constituted a Jewish

convert? Were not some of the Corinthian professors, idolaters, before their reception of the Christian faith? Did Paul understand his 'commission? Does he regret having baptized Crispus, Gaius and the household of Stephanus; was not the character of Paul traduced by the professing Christians at Corinth, and were not many of them a disgrace to their profession? Did not the Corinthians either weakly or malignantly represent Paul and his fellow-labourers as founders of different religious sects? Was not this sufficient reason to induce the apostle to congratulate himself, that he had baptized no more of them? Does he not ask these *very* people in *whose* name *they* had been baptized; whether in the name of the Jewish Christian Apollos, or Jesus Christ? Did these Jews who thus baptized idolatrous Gentiles, exceed their commission? What does Paul mean when he says to these people; Cor. i. 6, 7, "Know ye not that idolaters, &c. shall not inherit the kingdom of God, and such were some of you, but ye are washed in the name of the Lord Jesus?" Was not baptism *always* practised in the Christian church from the first age, and was it not considered as a privilege? Have we any account of the admission of Gentile converts without it? When did the distinction between catechumens, and Christian professors first begin? Though Gentile converts rejected circumcision, were they ever refused baptism? Is it not said that as many as have been baptized into Christ, have put on Christ? Have not those who have put on Christ, thus publicly acknowledged HIM to be Lord, to the glory of God the Father, and therefore bound themselves to obey his Gospel? What is the scriptural way of publicly professing to be a Christian? Ought not such a profession to be made in a way that cannot be misunderstood? Was not baptism the Jewish and Christian mode of professing proselytism? Is the profession of Christianity a voluntary and public act? Is a man a Christian before he is satisfied of the truth of Christianity? Or are they convinced of its truth who have never examined its evidences? Was not the ordinance of the Lord's Supper originally administered to the Apostles exclusively? Did either the seventy elders, or any of the five hundred brethren, or any of the Christian women, partake of it? Admitting that Paul was mistaken in baptizing Gentiles, if he did baptize them, then, might he not be equally mistaken in giving the supper to Gentiles, to the laity, or to the female converts of the Christian faith? May not the form of words used in Christian baptism be objected to by some persons, though I think without any reason?

Sir, yours,
B. P. SEVERN.

St. Ardleon, April 30, 1816.

Sir,

I VERY lately met with a pamphlet, published more than sixty years ago, which contains some particulars respecting the sufferings of the French Protestants, and the attention they excited in this country at that period. A recollection of these may not be uninteresting at present : the publication is entitled ; .

" Two Discourses, occasioned by the cruel oppressions of the Protestants in France, and enlarged with a recent and particular account of the state of the persecution in that kingdom. To which are prefixed some serious reflections on the present situation of these nations, and our American Colonies : by Thomas Gibbons." 8vo. 1755.

The author of these Discourses which appear to have preceded a congregational collection was a Minister among the Independents. He died in 1785, aged 65, having been distinguished through life, as I can describe him from personal acquaintance, by practical piety and extensive benevolence. For the historical particulars Dr. Gibbons quotes " a pamphlet entitled *Annals of the Rise, Progress and Persecutions of the famous Reformed Churches in France,* published by the Reverend Mr. *Isaac Toms,* of Hadleigh, in Suffolk, in 1753," and an Appendix by the same "worthy and excellent friend,". in 1755. On these authorities, the author of the Discourses thus introduces the following details. .

" During the minority of Lewis XV., the Duke of Orleans being Regent, the government was more favourble to the Protestants than it had formerly been ;* but the administration

falling into the hands of a cardinal† devoted to the Jesuits, by their influence a new declaration was issued on the 14th of May, 1724, which contains in it whatever was most severe in the edicts of Lewis XIV.‡ On the first of February, 1745, Lewis XV. published his ordonnance against the Protestants, enforcing the former edicts, and making it death to the minister who officiated, and perpetual imprisonment for the women, and gallies for the men, who have been present at the meetings.§ And how dreadfully these cruel orders were obeyed, the attack of religious Protestant assemblies by soldiers who scrupled not to fire in among them, the condemnation of some who were apprehended to the prison, and of others to the gallies, and the murders of ministers from the year 1745 to 1750, dreadfully testify. In the year 1750, the French king published an ordonnance at Versailles, January 17, willing, that former edicts against the Protestants, and particularly that of 1724, should be executed ; and enjoining officers and judges to attend diligently to their execution. How rigorously these edicts have been executed, take in the following accounts :—

" *Extract of a Letter from Mr.* —— *a Protestant minister of Lower Languedoc, July* 26, 1754.

——" ' About July 5th, a religious assembly returning home, the garrison fell upon them, fired, put them to flight, and seized three men and five women.—Another assembly having broke up were attacked by a party of dragoons, who fired among them, wounded one man, and ended his life with their bayonets. Forty-five were taken prisoners.— Other accounts of the assembly inform us, that five or and took out of the gallies sixty-eight of these unhappy persons, to whom he gave full liberty to go out of the kingdom wherever they thought proper." Priv. Life of Lewis 15th. 1781. i. 135.—R. B.

† The Duke of Bourbon was prime minister on the Regent's death, in 1724; but Cardinal Fleury was supposed to influence the affairs of government, before his appointment to succeed the duke in 1726. Priv. Life, &c. i. 148, 9.---R. B.

‡ " See this edict in Laval's History, vol. iv. or in the appendix to a pamphlet entitled, *Popery always the same;* p. 76."

§ " *Popery always the same,* appendix, p. 76."

* " The Regent moderated the fury of the clergy,' [towards the Protestants,]

six were killed on the spot, and fourteen or 'fifteen 'wounded.—Towards the latter end of the same month, an assembly was 'surprised 'by a party. of dragoons, who fired upon them, and seized several of both sexes, who remain in prison.—The 17th instant, an officer and five gentlemen were taken up, for what reason we cannot yet certainly know. Some say it is for holding assemblies, and others for performing baptisms and marriages.'

" *Part of a Letter from Mr. —— a Protestant minister at —— Aug.* 8, 1754.,

'——" ' I am well acquainted with the affairs, of our churches, and the several unjust and cruel methods which are daily used to destroy them. Never before have they been so artfully attacked: they are beset on every side, and ravaged from every quarter. And it will be impossible to bear up under this heavy calamity, unless sustained and upheld by God himself. Let us, therefore, incessantly offer up our prayers to him for assistance, and, perhaps, sooner than we expect, a happy Providence may change the present awful appearance of things to scenes more happy and delightful. The provinces of this part of the kingdom, where the Protestant religion has most flourished, are crowded with troops, as I imagine to extirpate all the Protestants, if possible, for they are to quarter here for some time. And what strengthens my opinion is, that they have expended large sums of money to furnish beds and other necessaries sufficient for 20,000 troops. Expenses which are entirely needless, if they were stationed here only for the convenience of pasture. On the fourth instant they made a general sally. They plundered not only the houses in the country, but even those in the city did not escape their fury. A minister, who has taken upon him that office no more than two years, had the house surrounded where he was, and, attempting to escape, was shot by a fuzee, and was arrested, as was all the family where he was. He was carried prisoner to Montpellier, where, in all probability, he must suffer, as most of his predecessors have done before him.*

---

*, if He ,(by name M. la Fage) finished his course gloriously at Montpellier, on the 16th of the same month, after having gained the esteem of those who saw him

Myself must have shared the same fate had it not been for the kind protection of a Catholic friend. For I had no sooner left my house than it was surrounded by a numerous detachment, which made the most exact search for me. Since this fatal time my day is turned into night; and my people, seeing it is impossible for me to elude their diligent search, advise me to retire for some time into Switzerland, there to wait till more quiet and peaceable days; and, as our church is oppressed with taxes and impositions, and struggling with difficulties, it cannot be expected they should be any longer able to support their minister.—We have great reason to fear our enemies will exert all their power to disturb and molest, them, (the ministers and others that baptize, &c. in the desert,) since the Bishop of Alais has sent a letter for that purpose to all the curates of his diocese.'.

"*An Account of Mr. P——e, drawn up by himself.* J.

——" ' On the parish curate's (the same as rector here) taking my child by force, and baptizing it according to the rites of the Church of Rome during my absence, on my return home I expressed my resentment, and reproved the curate, who hereupon complained of me to the deputy, and a warrant was granted against me. I was accused, and, though innocent, condemned to death, as accessary to the murder of a woman found dead in the prison. I appealed to the parliament of Thoulouse, and thereby was acquitted and discharged from imprisonment; but after some time was again ordered to be arrested; but a friend gave me private intelligence. I immediately embraced the favourable opportunity, left my family the very same day, and fled for refuge to this *happy isle,* where, by the kind Providence of God, I am safely arrived.'

" *Extract of a Letter from Mr. Bourdillon, minister in London, Secretary to the Society for the Relief of the*

---

in prison by his discourse and courage; greatly affecting by his death all those, without distinction, who were spectators of it. Every body was extremely edified by his piety, his meekness, his resignation to the divine will, his resolution and firmness. Toms's Appendix, p. 3."

French Refugees, dated Nov. 14, 1754.

"' Our dear brethren are more and more persecuted in France. They increase every day; and by the last letters which were read the day before yesterday at our society, we hear that the troops in Languedoc search in the night-time, not only for the pastors, who are mostly fled to woods and dens, but for their defenceless flock. A great many of the faithful have been taken and confined to prisons. The terror is spread every where. The worship of the Lord suspended. Few congregations meet together. Courage is abated. Zeal slackens. They have nothing left but their private prayers in the midst of their alarms and sorrows.'

"*Extract of a Letter from the Rev. Mr. Isaac Toms, minister at Hadleigh in Suffolk, dated Dec.* 30, 1754.

——"' Very affecting accounts from France. Does a spirit of concern for the dear sufferers increase? One minister says, I have been these five weeks like a wild goat going from rock to rock, and have not lain in a house. And this to attend the interests of his persecuted flock, when he might have lived at ease in a city; but he says, We are accustomed to pursuits, and rejoice that we are counted worthy to suffer for the common faith.'

"*Extract of a Letter from the same gentleman, dated March* 13, 1755.

"' I have to acquaint you that Mr. ——has informed me by last post but one, that in Normandy things are more quiet, but that they have very few ministers for above 100,000 souls. In Languedoc things are worse and worse. Ministers are so closely followed, that, there being no possibility of being useful to the flocks, they are retired to Switzerland, &c. There are near eighty men now in the gallies for their religious zeal, and very many, great numbers, in prisons and fetters.'

"*From the Appendix to the Rev. Mr. Isaac Toms's Annals under the Month of April,* 1755, p. 8.

"' We have heard that in February last an assembly of Protestants being held for divine service towards Bourdeaux, the enemy had notice of it, sent soldiers, who fired upon the poor people, killed some of them, and took some prisoners. The persecutions are going on in many other parts with great severity. The prisoners upon the gallies* earnestly desire our prayers, and are sent from Marseilles to Toulon, where they are far from their friends, who used now and then to give them some help.'

" Such was the situation of the persecution in France but a few months ago. I have learnt since, from the Rev. Mr. Bourdillon, the Secretary to the Society for the Relief of the Protestants that fly into this kingdom for the sake of religion, that there is no remission of the cruel edicts; that the people have been miserably exhausted by taxes, &c.; that the ministers are driven away by the severity of the persecution; and that religious assemblies have been in a manner totally suspended. Such is the mournful state of the Protestants in France, whose number is computed at 3,000,000 of souls."

Such were some of the blessings which distinguished the reign of *Louis le bien aimé,* from whom the modern *Louis le desiré* delights to trace his descent and his royal authority. A few years after in 1761, occurred the horrid tragedy of the *Calas* family, a striking result of the prejudices excited against the Protestants. The *Continuation des Causes Célébres* (Vol. 4, 18mo. Amst. 1771), in addition to the interesting details respecting *Calas,* records other proofs of the antipathy excited against the Protestants at the same period; particularly noticing (p. 308), the pleasure with which some ladies at Tholouse attended the execution of a Protestant minister who was hanged in that city and of three

* " A galley is a low-decked vessel, generally from 120 to 132 feet long, 18 feet broad, and 6 feet deep. They are navigated by oars, and chiefly used in the Mediterranean sea. The slaves are chained to the oars, their shirts being stripped down to their waist, and exposed to all weathers. They must strike the oars all together, or they are severely handled. The chains sometimes gnaw them to the bone, and occasion gangrenes. The slaves, excepting Protestants for their religion, are notorious malefactors, who, having escaped the sentence of death, are condemned to this punishment for a time, or for life. See Toms's Annals, p. 30."

merchants who were, at the same time beheaded. Returning to the pamphlet I quote, from page 33, the following account of a "paper published Sept. 1755."

"The gentlemen who three years ago engaged in a society for the relief of those Protestants that fly into this kingdom for religion's sake, think themselves in duty bound to acquaint the benefactors to this charity with their proceedings, success and present situation:—

"Out of two thousand one hundred and forty-four pounds, thirteen shillings and nine pence received, they have expended one thousand nine hundred and twenty-four pounds, one shilling and ten pence, so that no more remains in cash than two hundred and twenty pounds, eleven shillings and eleven pence.

"To this time they have relieved three hundred and eighty-nine persons, most of whom are actually settled in England, and now subsist by their industry and labour, viz. one hundred and seventy-three men, ninety women, and one hundred and twenty-six children; the greatest part of these last have been put to apprenticeships: besides a very large number whose expenses the society defrayed in their journey through Switzerland and Holland to Ireland."

Your readers may compare the statements in this paper with the recent exertions in the same cause.

R. B.

'Sir ---   *April 9.*

WILL you allow me a few columns in your valuable Repository, to call the attention of our Unitarian brethren to the peculiar situation in which they are placed, and the duties which this peculiar situation appears to me most imperiously to call upon them to perform?

We are fully persuaded that our views of the gospel dispensation are more simple, more sublime, more rational, and far more scriptural, than those of our fellow-christians; that Unitarianism is "the faith once delivered to the saints;" the "tidings of great joy" to all nations, which shall carry salvation even unto the ends of the earth! We believe all this,—and is it not then our bounden duty to use every mean within our power, to give the pure word of God "free course"? to spread it widely amongst our fellow-

creatures? Surely no heart can be so cold and selfish as to doubt of this; and no one who has the desire, can in his measure, want means; for the most powerful of all, lies within the reach of every one;—each in his own station whether high or low, may so conspicuously let his "light shine before men," that seeing his good works, they will inquire from whence they spring, and what the tree is, which bears such heavenly fruits.

If we have indeed more perfectly "learned Christ," it becomes us to remember that we are accountable for the treasure, the "pearl of great price," which is committed to our charge; and not satisfied with a cold, heartless profession of our faith, we should zealously endeavour, by a constant manifestation of every Christian virtue, to "*live down*" the evil reports which ignorance and prejudice are ever ready to raise against men who venture to think for themselves, and doctrines which they fear to inquire into, and therefore do not understand.

It is vain, I had almost said it is absurd, and must appear hypocritical, to withdraw ourselves from what we account false and unscriptural modes of worship, if in all other points we conform to the selfish, vain, and frivolous pursuits of the world. If we "worship the Father" acceptably, we must do it "in spirit and in truth"; for devotion is enthusiastic, and faith dead and unprofitable, in the heart of that man, in whom it fails to produce *true Christian practice.* And in what does true Christian practice consist? Not in merely passing harmlessly through life, and just avoiding those gross faults which would call down upon us the censures of our fellow men! A child of worldly wisdom would do this; but the disciple of Jesus stands on higher ground, has nobler motives, and acts on other principles. Harshly as it may sound in the ears of some, a conformity with the world, even in this nation which so much boasts of the decorum and propriety of its manners, may often be too justly denominated, "enmity with God." According to the standard of the former we may feel ourselves justified in a course of conduct, which, weighed in the Christian balance, will be "found *wanting.*"

And is this less the case in Unitarians than in other men? Would to God that I could clearly see it so;—

would to God that those who hold the faith of the gospel, in its original purity, would bring salvation to themselves, and convert their fellow-christians, by reviving the simple and virtuous manners of the primitive believers! All eyes would then be turned, and all hearts be drawn towards them! Let us look amongst the members of our numerous congregations, and see whether they display in their words and actions that purity, that simplicity, that heavenly-mindedness, which ought to flow from their clear and sublime views of gospel truth. Do they in their intercourse with each other, set aside the low distinctions which pride and folly have created, and show that brotherly love, and that union of heart and affections, which becomes those who so often meet together to worship a *common Father.* Do they *more than others* "take sweet counsel together," and go up to the house of God *as friends?* Are the rich "zealous of good works," the benefactors, the advisers, the comforters of their poor brethren? And do they take a real and affectionate interest in their 1 welfare?' 'I have often and anxiously looked for *marked* appearances of this kind; but alas! I have too generally found, that they who think with Newton and Locke, Priestley and Lindsey, and numerous other great and good men who have assisted in restoring our holy faith to its genuine purity, conform their lives to the common standard of those whose errors and misconceptions on the subject of religion, are, in part, an apology for the imperfections of their practice.

Unitarians would do well to consider, that all will, at the solemn day of retribution, be judged according to the degree of illumination which has shone upon their minds: and if our views are more sublime and beautiful, and more powerfully incitive to the practice of all that is excellent, than those entertained by other Christians; shall we not be expected and *required* to walk according to our light? Shall we who behold in our Maker "the Lord, merciful and gracious, long-suffering, and abundant in mercy and truth;" who "hath no pleasure in the death of sinners," but "*willeth* that *all men* should be saved, and come to the knowledge of the truth!"—shall we, who see in the holy scriptures

these heart-cheering and most attractive views of our great Creator plainly set forth; love him *no more,* and obey him *no better,* than others? Cold indeed must be our affections and hard our hearts if it be so!

I would warn you, I would earnestly warn you, as Christians, and more especially as Unitarian Christians, against *religious negligence.* "To whomsoever much is given, of him will much be required." If the pure doctrines of the gospel are happily opened to our understandings, let them sink deep into our hearts and be powerfully set forth in our lives. The Christian warfare cannot be made a mere secondary concern of life, a matter that is only now and then, at stated times, or in the hours of sickness or of sorrow to occupy our thoughts. What the good Dr. Barrow says of virtue, may be well applied to that purest form of it, *Christianity:*—" It is not a mushroom that springeth up in one night, when we are asleep or regard it not; but a delicate plant that groweth slowly and tenderly, needing much pains to cultivate it, much care to guard it, much time to mature it, in our untoward soil, in this world's unkindly weather: happiness is a thing too precious to be purchased at an easy rate; heaven is too high to be come at without much climbing; the crown of bliss is a prize too noble to be won without a long and tough conflict."

This is confirmed both by the precepts and the example of our Lord; "He that will come after me," says this great Teacher, "must *take up his cross* and follow me." We must "*strive* to enter in at the strait gate," for "*narrow* is the way which leadeth unto life." It is not the wide and beaten road which, because so much frequented, seems safe and pleasant to the thoughtless multitude. The fashions of this world speedily pass away and their followers will at length find, that they have been pursuing shadows; airy phantoms; while the great end and purpose of existence has been overlooked and cast aside, as a thing of little value or importance. Oh that Unitarians would come out from amongst the sons and daughters of vanity and selfishness, and prove to the world that they have higher aims than this uncertain life can satisfy; that they consider themselves as "strangers and pilgrims upon earth," seeking a

" better country," an " abiding place,"
a " city which *hath foundations!*" and
using all the powers which have been
entrusted to them to extend the knowledge of that great salvation which
God has graciously offered to the
world by Jesus, the " author and finisher of our faith." Then would every
form of idolatry vanish from amongst
the sons of men; all would see and
acknowledge that " the Lord is One
and his *name one*," and unite to worship the infinite Jehovah, as the disciples of his Son Jesus Christ.

Let that sect which has hitherto
been " every where spoken against,"
set themselves in earnest about this
great work, this " consummation, so
devoutly to be wished;" and may the
great Being whom *alone* we adore,
give a blessing to our zealous endeavours, and grant that by reviving the
genuine doctrines of our Master, and
diligently striving to exemplify them
in our lives, we may bring salvation to
ourselves, and forward the progress of
gospel truth amongst our brethren of
mankind!

M. H.

SIR, *Lower Clapton.*

THE following queries involve controversies of infinite importance,
which still divide the Christian world.
I shall be happy if any of your readers
of the popularly orthodox faith shall
think them, or any of them, deserving
of their notice; and offer such a solution of them to my understanding, as
appears to be satisfactory to their own.

First. If to deny the personality of
the power which we call divine, is
atheism, and to assert it Theism, is it
not Tritheism to ascribe personality to
three persons, each of them divine?

Secondly. If the existence of a mind
implies personality, must not two
minds constitute two persons; two infinite minds, two persons both infinite;
and two minds, one finite and one infinite, two persons, one finite and the
other infinite? If then Christ be both
God, and man, is he one person or
two persons?

Thirdly. If it is universally true
that a finite being cannot have attributes that are infinite, since guilt is
an attribute of finite beings only, is
not infinite guilt impossible, and to assert it a contradiction?

Fourthly. If guilt can be expiated
by the suffering of substituted inno-

cence, either it is not necessary under
the divine constitution that guilt be
punished, or the guilty have been punished when the innocent only has suffered: which ought we to affirm?

Fifthly. Is personal identity intrans-
ferable, and can personal attributes,
such as merit and demerit, be trans-
ferable?

Sixthly. Can Christians pray consistently as Christ commanded they
should pray, for the forgiveness of sins,
if the orthodox doctrine of atonement
be the doctrine of the scriptures; unless, not to punish what has been once
adequately punished, not to demand a
penalty which has been already paid,
be to forgive sins?

Seventhly. If depravity implies guilt,
is not innate depravity impossible, unless it be a crime to be born? Or is
the same being at once depraved and
innocent? And then, is it just that
he be punished for the necessary consequences of an innocent depravity?

Eighthly. Since the exertion of divine power, in the regeneration of all
who are regenerated, is acknowledged
to be an act of special grace,—or an
interposition of divine power not in
the course of nature,—the event is a
miraculous one: is it then true, that,
under the Christian dispensation, a
dispensation of mercy, every man is
born into the world subject to a divine
government so constituted, that nothing but a miracle can save him from
remediless and infinite woe, at the
same time that this miracle is in fact
performed in favour of but a small
part of men, born notwithstanding
under a dispensation of mercy?

I observe annexed to the Clergyman's Letter to the Bishop of St. David's, (see M. Rep. x. 590,) the following postscript: " I have taken the unusual liberty of sending a copy of this
letter to the bench of bishops; I hope
they will excuse it; my motive is good.
Their sentiments on the subject are of
the utmost consequence. If they agree
with you, that a belief in the Athanasian Trinity and Creed makes us Christians, and is necessary to salvation,
they will confirm your opinion in their
future charges and publications, and
enforce it with much greater zeal than
has hitherto been done. If they differ from your lordship, they will, I
am persuaded, act in a manner becoming the character of Christians and
Christian bishops." That they do

agree is not to be doubted, as long as they are sworn to think as their church has decreed that they shall think, that is, that he who does not acknowledge the Athanasian Trinity as the true God shall without doubt perish everlastingly. "If they agree with his lordship they will confirm their opinion, and enforce it with greater zeal than has hitherto been done." This is certainly what ought to be done; and it has often appeared to me extraordinary, that so many Christian bishops, and so many Christian preachers of different denominations, should profess their conviction that the doctrine of the Trinity is inseparable from Christian doctrine, and essential to the evangelical system, and that, notwithstanding, the term is seldom heard to escape their lips in the course of their public instruction. Is it that they hold the doctrine with a feeble faith? This cannot be supposed without impeaching their veracity, for they affirm their conviction to be entire. Is it that the word "Trinity," is not found in the Christian scriptures, and that they have no example for the use of it either in Christ or in any of his immediate followers? This is true, but it cannot be pleaded with reason by Christian preachers, who have admitted the barbarous and unwarranted name into their form of sound doctrine; and, least of all, by those who build their religion upon the foundation of Athanasiuses, and pseudo-Athanasiuses, and other doctors of the Papal or Protestant church, the "Trinity" being laid as the chief cornerstone. If the bench of bishops agree with their brother of St. David's, it behoves them to display the same courage and consistency which he has shewn. Let them rally round the Ajax of their church. It is not generous and it is not pious to stand aloof from the champion of their creeds, engaged in a conflict, which even they cannot think an equal one if they have taken the trouble to mark the thrusts of his adversaries:

Στῆτ᾽ ἐλελιχθέντες, καὶ ἀμύνετε
. νηλεὲς ἦμαρ
Αἴανθ᾽, ὃς βελέεσσι βιάζεται· οὐδέ ἐ
φημὶ
Φεύξεσθ᾽ ἐκ πολέμοιο δυσηχέος·

I am, Sir,
Yours, &c.
J. M.

SIR, *April* 12, 1816.

THE man who ventures to arraign his neighbour for *misrepresentation*, should be careful of the accuracy of his own statements: were it only from respect to himself and the cause which he espouses, however incapable he may be of other views. And yet, when Mr. Norris speaks of the *revision of Dr. Watts's Hymns*, as "bearing all the outward semblance of the genuine edition," he deviates widely from the fact. The original work is entitled, "Divine Songs attempted in easy Language for the Use of Children, by I. Watts, D. D.;" whereas, the little book which has been so clamorously and unjustly assailed, bears the title of "Dr. Watts's Hymns and Moral Songs for Children, revised and altered by a Lady." How is it possible, then, that these two works should be *designedly* confounded, where the slightest attention is sufficient to prevent mistake? "The same course has, *indeed*, been taken with that popular tract 'Melmoth's Great Importance of a Religious Life;'" but it is the course of honour and of fairness, carefully stating in the *preface* wherein the alterations consist. Neither of these works have been "palmed upon the public," otherwise than as *revisions* of books of acknowledged merit and general excellence, although containing views of Christianity in which the *revisers* could not acquiesce. They are consequently adapted to the use of a very different class of readers; and were offered to the public with the most correct and benevolent design. Is it not a high compliment to the devotional writers of the Church of England, that Christians of any other denomination should acknowledge their excellence, by making use of their works as far as they can consistently with their own sentiments, and frankly avowing the obligation? And with what propriety can that practice be censured in Unitarians, which has been repeatedly sanctioned by the example of orthodox Churchmen, with respect to the devotional compositions of the Church of Rome? I trust, therefore, that these unwarranted attacks will no longer disgrace the writings of the strenuous friends of the Establishment, or, at least, that their more liberal brethren will openly discountenance the ungenerous charge.

DETECTOR.

P. S. I will thank you to *notice* as *errata* the word *lawfully* for *carefully*, in my last letter, p. 151, col. ii. l. 37 ; and the omission of *afterwards* before *arraigned* in l. 37 of the succeeding column.

Effect of the Portrait of Washington on some Indian Chiefs.

[Extract of a Letter from New York.]

I CALLED to-day on Trumbull, the great artist, and saw him and his exquisite paintings. On my observing how much an Indian would be struck with his first sight of a painting, he told me, " that having painted a portrait of General Washington, the General invited him to dinner to meet a deputation of the Creek Chiefs : after dinner they were shewn into a room where the General's portrait was placed, the General accompanying them, dressed as there represented, and with Mr. Trumbull. The Indians were lost in astonishment ; they alternately looked at General Washington and at the portrait with many signs of wonder, and finding, on approaching it, that there was no projection, and that it was quite flat, were convinced it was a piece of enchantment. In fact, they sat up in council all that night to resolve how it was possible for " *the man*," (Trumbull,) to work a like piece of magic. Mr. T. endeavoured to prevail on them to let him take one of their portraits, but nothing could induce them to consent to it, as they were firmly persuaded, that when once he had wrought the phantom, they would be evermore entirely under the influence of his infernal agency."

Mr. Parkes's Account of a Visit to Birstal, Dr. Priestley's Native Place.

SIR,   London, *May* 8*th*, 1816.

IN consequence of your having suggested that the public would be gratified by an account of an incident which occurred to me during a journey in the summer of the last year, I now sit down to comply with your request, being happy that I have it in my power to contribute, in any degree, towards illustrating the character of one who is already so dear to the lovers of science, truth and virtue.

Having occasion, on the 31st day of last July to pass through the village of Birstal, in Yorkshire, I was very desirous of seeing the house, situated at Birstal-field Head, where Dr. Priestley was born, and accordingly I stopped at the inn, for the purpose of obtaining the necessary directions. The man informed us, that the house was two miles distant, but that the chaiseman would have a good opportunity of pointing it out to us from the top of a hill which we should have to pass over, and being pressed for time I was under the necessity of resting satisfied with a distant view of a mansion which had acquired so much celebrity from the peculiar character of one of its earliest occupants.

" Do you know, Sir," said the landlord, " that a brother of Dr. Priestley lives in this place ?" This question very much surprised me, for I had no idea that any brother of the Doctor's was then living. " Yes," said the landlord, " Mr. Priestley, who is a younger brother of the Doctor's, has resided here the greatest part of his life, and he is as worthy a man, and has always been as much respected as any person in the village." " I should be very glad," replied I, " if I could see this neighbour of yours ; would it be possible for me to be introduced to him ?" " If you respect the character of his brother," added the host, " I am sure, although you are strangers, he will be very glad to see you ; and this person," said he, pointing to a respectable looking man, who sat by, " will, I dare say, think it no trouble to shew you the way to his house." The man having, with great good nature, acquiesced, I immediately set out, accompanied by my daughter, who was travelling with me ; and I believe the circumstance of having discovered so near a relative of Dr. Priestley in so obscure a situation, afforded both of us more pleasure than any unexpected event which, till then, had occurred to us during the whole of our journey.

As we passed through the village, Mr. Joshua Priestley met us, and our guide introduced us to him. Having informed him that we were desirous of paying our respects to him in consequence of our regard for the memory of his brother, he kindly invited us to his house, and in the way introduced us to one of his sons, who joined us, and walked in with us.

When we arrived, we found it a very neat, cleanly cottage, quite in the style of simple country life ; and in an antique chair sat a respectable-looking, aged female, who proved to be the wife of the Mr. Priestley to whom our visit was intended.

We had not been long within the house before Mr. Priestley introduced us to his wife, and when he told her that we called to see them out of respect to the character of his brother, the Doctor, the good old woman burst into tears and sobbed violently. This behaviour very much astonished us, and the more so, because she was for a long time quite unable to speak. However, when the good old lady could articulate, she apologized for her weakness by saying, that " she could never hear the name of that good man (meaning Dr. Priestley) mentioned, without being overcome in a similar way."

This sudden, unpremeditated, involuntary tribute to the memory of an excellent individual, whom we both esteemed, struck us exceedingly, so much so that both of us were glad to sit down, to talk further with these good old people, and inquire more of their history.

During the course of the conversation, I learnt that Mr. Priestley, if he lived to the end of that week, would be eighty years of age; and that his wife, the individual whom I have already spoken of as being so singularly affected at the mention of Dr. Priestley's name, was in her eighty-fourth year.

Mr. Priestley told me, that he had had thirteen children by his present wife, and that one of his daughters had fifteen children. He said he had now only five children living, viz. three sons and two daughters, and that his sons are all married, and have each many children. He added, that he had now living nearly fifty grandchildren and more than twenty great grandchildren. The old man told me also, that he was healthy and well, and still able to walk to the Dissenting chapel at Hickmondwicke, which is two miles distant from his house, every Sunday, and back again.

Mr. Priestley and his wife both gave us a very pressing invitation to partake of their dinner, but this our other engagements prevented us from accepting. When we were taking leave and about to depart, Mr. Priestley, jun., son of Mr. Joshua Priestley, said, very kindly, that we should probably like to see the burial place

of Dr. Priestley's father and some of his more remote ancestors, as many of them were interred in Birstal church-yard; and he would walk with us and show us the spot with pleasure. This offer we accepted; and in our walk to the church, had a good deal of conversation with Mr. Priestley, jun. whom we found to be a sensible and well-informed man, for the sphere of life in which he moves.

While we were in the church-yard, we were joined by a youth of eleven years of age, a son of Mr. Priestley's, a smart, lively little fellow; and when I asked him his name and he replied, Joseph Priestley, his father added, with great animation and much self-complacency, that as he was born about the time that Doctor Priestley died, they had thought it right to name him *Joseph* after him and in remembrance of him.

From the retired manner in which Mr. Joshua Priestley appeared to live, I was apprehensive that he might be in straitened circumstances, and therefore took the liberty of questioning his son on that point; who immediately said, that he had great pleasure in informing me, that his father and mother were as comfortable as to the state of their pecuniary affairs as their best friends could wish; adding, that the Doctor had taken care of that, he having given them some canal shares, which had made them as independent as their circumscribed wants required. I am glad to have it in my power to make the public acquainted with this circumstance, as it redounds very much to the credit of Dr. Priestley, especially as it is well known that he had several children of his own to provide for, and was himself never rich. The intimate friends of Dr. Priestley were well acquainted with his generous temper and disposition, but I do not think that this particular instance of his benevolence was known to any of them. I doubt, indeed, if it was known to his son, Mr. Joseph Priestley, for if it had, he surely could not have omitted, in the Memoirs which he published, to have mentioned a circumstance so highly honourable to the memory of a revered and beloved father.

In the church-yard of Birstal, our attention was directed to three handsome tombs, made entirely of stone, and were told, that this was the burial place of Dr. Priestley's ancestors, and some of his contemporary relatives. I would gladly have copied all the inscriptions, but being much pressed for time, I transcribed only those which are upon the tomb belonging to the Doctor's father. They read as follows :—

" TO THE MEMORY OF JONAS PRIESTLEY,* THE SON OF JOSEPH PRIESTLEY, OF FIELD-HEAD, WHO DIED FEBRUARY 18TH, 1779, AGED 79 YEARS. ALSO, MARY, HIS WIFE,† WHO DIED DECEMBER 28TH, 1739. ALSO, ANN,‡ HIS DAUGHTER, WHO DIED JANUARY 8TH, 1763, AGED 20 YEARS. WHO ALL LIE INTERRED NEAR THIS PLACE. THIS CORRUPTIBLE MUST PUT ON INCORRUPTION, AND THIS MORTAL, IMMORTALITY."

On the flat stone which covers the same tomb is the following inscription :—

· " HERE LIETH THE BODY OF SARAH,§ WIFE OF JOSEPH PRIESTLEY, OF BIRSTAL-HEAD, WHO DIED 29TH DECEMBER, 1728, AGED 68 YEARS. HERE ALSO IS INTERRED THE BODY OF JOSEPH PRIESTLEY,‖ OF BIRSTAL FIELD-HEAD, WHO DEPARTED THIS LIFE THE 2ND DAY OF AUGUST, IN THE 85TH YEAR OF HIS AGE. ANNO DOMINI 1745."

The two other tombs were erected to the memory of Dr. Priestley's uncles, and their descendants. They are close to each other, and close to the tomb first mentioned.

Before I left Birstal, Mr. Priestley, jun. informed me, that theirs was one of the largest and most extended families in Yorkshire, and in confirmation of it said, that as we were going through Hickmondwicke, if we would call at the old chapel yard in that place, we might satisfy ourselves of the truth of what he said. Accordingly, as we had occasion to pass close

---

* The Mr. Jonas Priestley here mentioned was the father of Dr. Priestley.

† Dr. Priestley's mother.

‡ A half sister of the Doctor's.

§ This person was Dr. Priestley's grandmother, a woman of excellent character, so much so, that the Doctor named his only daughter, Mrs. Finch, after her.

‖ Dr. Priestley's grandfather, a manufacturer of woollen cloths and cloth finisher, and resided at the family house at Birstal Field-head, Yorkshire.

---

to the chapel, we directed the chaiseman to stop at the place, and as the keeper of the chapel lived very near to it, we procured the keys without difficulty. Here we saw a row of eight very handsome tombs all built alike and entirely of stone, belonging to the Priestley family; but as we had no one with us who could explain the exact relationship of any of the deceased to the late Dr. Priestley, I did not take the trouble of copying any of the inscriptions.

Thus, Sir, have I endeavoured to comply with your request, and I do flatter myself that those persons who value the character of the late Dr. Priestley, either as a man, as an author, or as a successful and industrious chemical philosopher, will thank me for my attempt to rescue these few unpublished facts respecting his family, from oblivion.

' I am, Sir, yours, &c.

SAMUEL PARKES.

The Philosophy of Calvinism.

SIR,

YOUR most learned correspondent Mr. Cogan, and others, have recently exposed the absurdities and inhumanity of this dreadful system. Now this system consists not of plain declarations of scripture, which contain no system expressed in connected arrangement, but is in fact a system of reasoning and deductions from certain expressions in the writings of St. Paul. It is at least as much a system of reasoning as the Unitarian system. Its advocates find in the writings of Paul, the doctrine of the divine prescience, and infer the divine predetermination. From the prescience of God and his uncontroulable power, they infer that all his determinations are accomplished. They infer from their doctrine of original sin, and some declarations on few that are saved, that all that are saved, are so by divine favour, and all the rest lost, by divine appointment. Their system is evidently a system of reasoning from the divine attributes, collected from detached passages in scripture ; and yet they decry reason and all philosophy! I ask them for a scriptural statement of their system, as such, in direct and scriptural language. As to distinct passages in the writings of scripture, if they be our guide, every opposite system may be proved. Who will deny that distinct expressions may be found favourable to necessity, to free-will, to general, to particular redemption, to salvation by grace and by works, to endless torments, to extinction of the being of the wicked, and to the final salvation of all men! The fundamental error seems to be, the reasoning from particular expressions, instead of the general tenour of scripture. Away, then, with all pretensions of systems founded on scripture without reason, and away with the pretensions of Calvinists, that they are more evangelical than Unitarians!

SEARCH.

P. S. Can there be a more pregnant instance of the vain philosophy of the Calvinists, than their whole reasoning in justification of eternal misery? Where do they find their reasoning about sin being an infinite evil, because it is committed against an infinite Being? I find no such statement in scripture; it is a mere invention, to gratify malignity, in asserting the miserable destination of man! Yet they are wise as serpents, for they know that in religion fear is more predominant than hope, and they thus obtain hearers, and gain their end!

SIR, *London, 15th April,* 1816.

I WISH to call the attention of some of your intelligent correspondents to a subject which has been thought of importance in vindication of the divine government—which is the state of human beings, as to happiness and misery, in the present life. The late Mr. Lindsey, and many other excellent men, have contended that the happiness of every human being greatly exceeds his misery here; which I think, however, they have not proved. In contemplating human society, the first consideration that offers itself is, that men, like all other animals, increase in number, or multiply much faster than their means of subsistence. This renders death a necessary occurrence in this economy, and accordingly it is calculated that not less than one fourth part of the human species perish before they become moral agents, before four years of age. Now it cannot be doubted that many of these perish by diseases brought on by want; and what more agonizing to the paternal heart can

be conceived than the observation that children are perishing through wants which they cannot supply? It is a consequence of this principle that extreme poverty must be, as we see it actually is, the lot of an immense majority of mankind. It has been suggested, as a remedy for this tremendous evil, that man should not marry. But the Christian religion strictly prohibits fornication, and we have apostolical authority for declaring that the gift of continence is not the lot of all, and it may be inferred from the practice of the world that it is the lot of very few. Take, then, the other side of this dilemma, and man is doomed either to a miserable existence, or to the violation of his duty, an existence full of misery. We see man, then, at the first step, involved in misery by the very constitution of his nature; nor have any writers on this subject attempted to answer this argument. If any of your numerous and intelligent correspondents can answer it, I shall be glad to see it answered; for it appears with so dreadful an aspect that the statement of it is horrible.

This is no modern discovery; it was not left to Wallace and Malthus and others of late date to find this out; it projects, it meets the eye, in every nation and age of the world: hence the common practice of exposing infants at all times and in almost all countries.—Now let us proceed on our observations. Where extreme poverty does not press upon families, how often are the tenderest connexions broken? How ill assorted are often the parties in married life? And when this is otherwise, and a happy union takes place, how seldom does this state of human life, the only one that seems desirable, continue long? Disease and death come, and the survivor is doomed to wear out a wretched life in aggravated solitude; or if there be children, anxiety attends every step to the grave, which is but too often increased by observing those children unhappy! Mr. Lindsey seems to think that those who die by their own hands being few, it is a proof that the world in general is not unhappy. But let it be considered, that in Christian countries this mode of dying is disreputable, that it involves too often the misery of survivors, and that it is thought to be a crime, and to expose to future punishment. Reverse this, and let suicide be not disreputable, let a general conviction exist that this world ends all human feeling, and I apprehend that hundreds of thousands would thus die. I am persuaded that a great part of mankind, after the age of thirty, and many before that age, would prefer, if it were a matter of choice, annihilation to the existence they support. All that has been said about the horrors of annihilation is downright rant, as I think your able correspondent Mr. Belsham has somewhere called it, and I cannot but be astonished at what Dr. Cogan has said about the dread of annihilation amongst mankind. A careful survey of the world, I think, will soon convince us that whatever be the end of God in creating man, it is not to make him happy in this world; and I firmly believe that the balance is against the majority of human beings here. Those philosophers who said the best thing possible was never to be born, and the next best, to die the hour of one's birth—appear to me to have spoken wisely.

A modern philosopher ordered to be inscribed on his tomb that he was with life contented and thankful. Now, I knew this philosopher, and have heard him say that he was perplexed at first how to dispose of his children, of which he unfortunately had many, until he found out an old man and woman who took them at their birth for ten pounds each and he never heard more of them! Contented and thankful! But had the children reason to be thankful? Who would not rather never have existence than purchase pleasure at such a sacrifice of humanity? I dare say that there is not one of your correspondents who would not prefer annihilation to such a life as this. Hoping that some notice will be taken of these remarks, I remain,

Your humble Servant,
Y. N.

On Poetical Scepticism.
No. III.

"Heaven lies about us in our infancy."
WORDSWORTH.

SIR,

THOSE who regard the peculiar doctrines of modern orthodoxy as the sources of poetical delight must surely forget "original sin," which forms the basis of them all. It seems scarcely possible to link any thing which is beautiful or exalted with the belief that the heart of man is naturally corrupt, his faculties morally depraved, and his earliest emotions sinful. Nor does it seem an enviable creed which teaches us that the infant is under the wrath and curse of God," when the smile first begins to dawn over its features. This doctrine is not a mere incident associated with certain noble speculations, but easily separated from them; it is the ground-work on which the whole edifice of Calvinism is erected. Hence is deduced the emptiness of mere human virtue, the necessity of miraculous influence from above, the occasion of a vicarious sacrifice. Hence, election and reprobation, the eternal torments of hell, and the mighty spirit of evil. Those, therefore who admire the fantastic ornaments of this vast building, and rejoice in the chillness of its shadow, must be prepared to estimate also the solidity and grandeur of its foundation.

And this too is something for imagination to doat upon—something to be enjoyed as a glorious vision—something for the heart to rest upon amidst the uncertainties of life! This is the faith for whose gentle consolations our reason is to be despised as worthless! For this, not only the understanding is to be laid aside, but the sweet visions of childhood, and the kindling memory of original innocence are for ever to be rendered dim. The doctrine which is the main support of the Calvinistic system disturbs the holiest spring of poetical joy. For there is no theme by which those who are blest with a true feeling of poetry are kindled into a brighter and more delicious enthusiasm than the joyousness and purity of childhood. They can remember when they wandered through this world as a fairy-land—when it seemed less a material thing than an enchanting vision—when they appeared hardly to tread on an earth from whose follies they were yet unsoiled. Then nature poured forth its blessings, with over-flowing measure, to greet them. Then saintly thoughts, pure desires, and holy aspirations after perfection, made their soul a consecrated dwelling. Then first they felt the touch of sympathy the consciousness, of belonging to a universal brotherhood, the first exercise of the benevolent and social affections. Then they walked with God as fit companions with angels. Since those happy times they have become inhabitants of a world where virtue is compelled to struggle, where joy is shaded by affliction, where experience too often chills the heart, and its fine bloom is injured by too ungentle collision. Yet the moments when they remember what they were are the greenest spots of their journey. In the seasons, when, as from some little eminence, they catch a glimpse of the happy scenes in which they once delighted to wander, they are filled with a delight too rapturous for smiles, and too deep even for tears. It is like the ravishment of the pilgrims on the delectable mountains, when they saw the gate of heaven from afar. This holy sympathy with ourselves in former times is one of the most cordial refreshments earth can afford us—a feeling which can sustain us amidst toil and suffering—a pure gush of joy, which we shall recognize in heaven. The recollections of early innocence and pleasure are, of all our possessions, the brightest and most lasting. Amidst the vicissitudes of fortune they will not wither, in the changes of friends they will not forsake us, in the chillness of age they will not grow cold. They will live and kindle even in our ashes. The sun of life, in its holiest decline, will throw its parting rays on the hills from which it arose, and still fondly linger over them. And these are the affections over which Calvinism casts its shadow! We are to be told that our cherished innocence was a fiction; that we were guilty even from the cradle; that our first aspirations after virtue, "without doubt did partake of the nature of sin;" and that our souls were polluted at the very season when the tenderest heart earth ever knew, would have said of us "of such is the kingdom of heaven." Thus the system which assumes the name of the gospel, blights our young virtues in their early blossom. It will not spare even those enchanted regions which seem fresh and glorious to us still;— the only spots of life on which we can dwell with an undisturbed sense of joy. It enters them like a withered enchantress, to change their loveliness

into a melancholy waste, to extinguish the pure and heavenly light shed over them, and to enshroud them with a gloom relieved by nothing but a fitful gleam from beneath.

Nothing surely need be said to prove the near connexion of the loftiest sublimities of poetry with the sacred feelings of childhood. The first touch of inspiration—the beautiful dawnings of fancy—the bright visions of celestial beauty—the shapes of unearthly loveliness, dimly seen—the reverential awe, and the mounting hopes which nothing on earth could satisfy— are the darling treasures of genius. They are "the fountain light of all its day." Perhaps a poet may almost be defined as one who possesses all those feelings of childhood with the expanded intellect of maturer years. He is one who preserves all the images of his early life in the inmost sanctuary of his soul. The emotion of primal innocence lives for ever, as a pure flame on the 'altar of that holy of holies; and forms the vital principle of all his moral and intellectual being. And this true "spark of heavenly flame" it is the first object of Calvinism to extinguish!

But this is not the only way in which the doctrine of *original sin* strikes deadness into the heart. It teaches us that all human virtue, before conversion, is a mere shadow: because man is, in his natural state, "dead in trespasses and sins," and is, therefore, utterly incapable of any thing really excellent. All, therefore, which we have been accustomed to revere in the history of past ages, those lovely or magnificent pictures of goodness which so delightfully relieve the sad story of human frailties, must be viewed with admiration no longer. We must no more draw kindling hopes of the improvement of mankind from the noble qualities we can discern, even in savage bosoms, from the kindliness that greets us every where, from the touches of goodness by which even the worst are visited. Surely this cannot be a poetical creed. On the contrary it is the peculiar delight of a true poet to trace out the kindly emotions in the midst of their holiest seclusion, to exhibit pictures of lowly goodness on which the soul can repose, as well as to kindle it into a sympathy and almost participation with the deeds of sublimer virtue.

He sees a "spirit of good even in things evil." To him the human mind appears majestic, even in ruins. He rejoices to find that there are some feelings, and those the holiest with which heaven has blessed us, to be found in every land where the dwellings of man can be traced—high instincts of conjugal devotion, of parental tenderness, of filial love, of romantic affection, and of veneration, however blind, for a superior intelligence—which prove to him "that we have all of us ONE HUMAN HEART." *

---

* Mr. Wordsworth arrives at this conclusion, in his "Old Cumberland Beggar," after a vein of philosophical poetry, as beautiful as ever the purest heart and the holiest imagination suggested. He takes as mean an object as the country in which his scene is laid could supply. A poor aged mendicant regularly visiting the scattered hamlets to receive alms, and traces out his importance to the general welfare, and the useful purposes for which he lives. He exhibits him as a record which binds together the memory of past charities, as impelling the villagers to goodness by "the mild necessity of use," and as giving "the first kind touch of sympathy and love" to the youth amidst the mountains.—In the midst of these reflections he exclaims,

"Man is dear to man;---the poorest poor
Long for some moments in a weary life
When they can know and feel that they
    have been
Themselves the carvers, and the dealers
    out
Of some small blessings;---have been
    kind to those
Who needed kindness---for this single
    cause,
That we have all of us one human heart."

In the same poem, as an example of the blessedness of this humble charity, he gives the picture of one poor woman who, "though prest herself with her own wants," as the mendicant makes his weekly call, "takes one unsparing handful for his scrip," and

"Returning with invigorated heart
Sits by her fire and builds her hope in
    heaven."

This is finer than the finest things in Cowper. It comes over the heart with an absolute conviction of its reality; and fills it at once with a cordial love for its species. No one can read the whole of this exquisite poem, and be *for the time* a Calvinist. If Mr. Wilberforce should write for ages on the total corruption of man---

None of these emotions can a Calvinist enjoy; except in spite of his creed. True it is that nature, more powerful than opinion, makes him feel all these things at peculiar seasons: but his view of them is perpetually shaded by the dreary colouring of his faith; his soul is checked in the midst of its noblest impulses. Surely then that system which has its origin in a belief that man is radically corrupt, must be less an object of pleasure, even to the imagination, than one which has its foundation in the original purity of our nature, and which cherishes the grandest hopes of our future condition.

The Calvinists and their sceptical allies are perpetually exhorting us not to build our religion on the cold understanding, but on the feelings and intuitions of the heart. In this case, we may triumphantly employ their own language. If there is any ground for the fond veneration with which we contemplate the mighty deeds of the times of old—if the grandest efforts of human virtue are not empty shadows—if the sweetest recollections of childhood are not mere delusions—then is the main doctrine of Calvinism FALSE, by how specious arguments soever it may be supported. Before one touch of genuine emotion from the joys of infancy—one gush of innocent delight round a heart oppressed with the fever of the world—how do the scholastic reasonings, the ingenious quibbles, the strained constructions of scripture, by which the original guilt of man is maintained, crumble and vanish! We take our stand on the best affections of man; on the deepest of his feelings; on the most universal and deathless of his sympathies. And we trust the foundation on which we rest is not to be despised merely because the understanding may be also with us.

S. N. D.

Sir,   *Bridport, May* 17, 1816.

I AM happy to correct any mistakes, which, in consequence of either inaccurate information or failure of my recollection, I may have made, in my imperfect sketch of the life, character, and writings of the late Francis

---

these lines would be more than an answer to the most eloquent exaggerations he could produce.

Webb, Esq. contained in last month's Repository [p. 189—193]. This purpose will be effected, by the publication of the following obliging letter, sent to me by his most intimate friend (with whom I have not the pleasure of personal acquaintance), which I have transcribed for insertion, should it suit your convenience, in the next month's Repository. THOMAS HOWE.

"DEAR SIR, *May* 14, 1816.

"As your letter to the Editor of the Monthly Repository discovers an esteem for the late Mr. Webb's character, I doubt not you will do it justice, by rectifying the mistake in your account of the Panharmonicon. This, I assure you, Sir, was *delineated by him* many years before he resided in Somersetshire, where his intimacy commenced with Mr. Nicholetts; and as the plate in some parts of it appeared almost obliterated, Mr. Webb was greatly obliged to that gentleman, for taking an elegant copy of the whole plate, from which the engraver performed his work.

"I must also wish you to correct the mistake contained in a note. Mr. Webb was not sent on any private embassy; he went merely as Secretary to Sir Isaac Heard, who was sent to invest the Prince of Hesse with the Order of the Garter.

"I flatter myself that your goodness will pardon this trouble. As your having been misinformed will appear from yourself with more propriety, in the same publication, than from any other hand, I thought it a duty due to your character, to make you this communication, several friends having already observed the mistake, and wished you to be informed of it. I am, Sir, with great respect and esteem,

·Your unknown friend."

SIR, · *April* 27, 1816.

OWING to circumstances not worth relating, I had not, till last night, observed the notice taken by Dr. Carpenter [p. 34] of my offer to publish a reply to Dr. Middleton, as far as he has applied his *Doctrine* of the Greek article to the Deity of Jesus Christ. Your correspondent refers me to Gregory Blunt and Winstanley, both of whom wrote *before* Dr. Middleton. My opinion of the former is, that his work is altogether unsatisfactory, in itself, and because of its irrelevancy to the matured argument as stated by the Indian prelate; as well as unworthy of the illustrious scholar to whom, surely, it is falsely ascribed. I have not seen Mr. Winstanley's work, but intend to consult it, though it cannot be expected to furnish a reply to Dr. Middleton, who himself had that author in his hands when he composed his ponderous volume. The same observation applies to Dr. Carpenter's own publication, the *second* edition of which I have perused. A sufficient account is thus given of my having taken no notice of any answers to the "Doctrine of the Greek Article," and for my having supposed that it "maintains its triumph unopposed," and that "nothing has yet been done with effect against it."

Mr. Granville Sharp ushered forth his system in a crude form: Dr. Middleton has lopped off its unseemly and mis-shapen excrescences, and trimmed it into a measure of comeliness and favour. Although he be himself, *atrox, truculentus,* υπερηφανος, lofty and overbearing, he has justly chastised the coarseness and insufficiency of Gregory Blunt, and is, in effect, at this day, left master of the field. The orthodox pulpits very properly resound with his victory, which has been silently conceded by one side, and supported and rewarded by the other. The reviews alone have attempted to dispute his pretensions to recompense and glory, and they have done it with more good-will than success. Indeed they have oppugned his *general* doctrine, which is irrefutable, while they have left its application to the support of the Deity of Christ unassailed. The first is of no perceptible value; the last is big with the most important consequence to Christian verity. The one derives all its consequence from the other, and, without its connexion with it, would never, probably, have been undertaken. Affectation of contempt for the argument has been assumed; but it is evidently assumed for want of better resource, and never has affectation been more misplaced. I am neither ashamed nor afraid to confess that if the application of the "Doctrine" to the Deity of Christ cannot be satisfactorily disproved, that Deity is established as an object of apostolic faith. Yet, while I believe that the "Doctrine" is well-founded, I propose, with no ordinary measure of certainty, to demonstrate the fallacy of its application. As the matter now stands,—both the doctrine and its application being unrefuted, because the former is sound and because the rottenness of the latter is not perceived,—there is no alternative but to admit that Jesus is *the only true God,* or to deny the authority of the apostolic writings. I thank the Almighty that I am not reduced to this dilemma, because my consolation under the afflictions of this state, the visitations of God and the malignity of men, is the evangelical hope of eternal life, of which I should be despoiled by the election which would be forced on my mind.

It is a long while since I intimated, in a note to one of my papers on Acts xx. 28, that Dr. Middleton's, "Doctrine" appeared to be generally true. In my letter, given in your number for November last, it is asserted, that "the argument" deduced from that doctrine, "is totally unfounded," and that "I can *demonstrate* that the new doctrine of the *Greek Article* fails to prove the Divinity or Deity of Christ." I am at a loss to guess what new *facts* Dr. Carpenter can expect on a question of criticism, or what facts *he* has adduced to which he requires an addition. The *principles* on which I rely are not designed as *additions* to those maintained by former writers, but are independent of them. Without giving an exposition of them, I will repeat, that I admit the chief principles of Dr. Middleton, thinking, however, that "nothing has yet been done with effect against" the conclusion which he infers, though I hold it altogether inadmissible.

Ready to assign "honour to whom honour is due," I have to observe that the ground on which I proceed has been discovered by two independent inquirers, and is probably unknown to all others. I am happy to have this opportunity of bearing my humble testimony to the perspicuity of one of the most unassuming and best informed friends of the Unitarian cause. It gave me no small pleasure to find, on explaining to Mr. Richard Taylor my view of the irrelevancy of Dr. Middleton's "Doctrine" to the only question which confers on it the slightest importance, that *he* also had been impressed with precisely the same idea,—an idea equally simple and decisive. Mr.

Taylor has higher claims to esteem than those which the profoundest learning alone would furnish, to which neither he nor I presume to urge any pretensions. His genuine simplicity, his modest manners, his diligence of inquiry and love of the truth, add grace and ornament to the clearness of his perception, and to the respectable learning which distinguishes him in his profession. These have contributed their full share towards securing to him the attention and patronage of the most renowned scholars of our times. It is a great satisfaction to me to be able to appeal to him for the originality of the principles on which my argument proceeds, and for the complete conviction which results from them. I may be able to bring forward some collateral considerations to fortify it, that have not presented themselves to his mind; but have no hesitation in saying, that he will fully support my declaration, that "all the learning called to the aid of the argument from the Greek article by Middleton, Wordsworth, &c. is altogether wasted."

At the same time, I am compelled to observe, that there is no appearance of any desire among the Unitarians to countenance *my* efforts on this question. In love of the truth I yield to none: thousands may boast of much greater zeal for the interest of the party, which, like others, is not exempt from weakness, or divested of a partiality towards those who, at least, unite devotedness to the one, with an attachment to the other. Indeed, the utmost indifference to the present subject has been indicated. This might excite no small surprise on a moment's consideration of the humiliating state to which Mr. Yates was reduced in his controversy with Mr. Wardlaw. Having no other resource, he was under the necessity of transcribing the miserable and evasive gloss of a popular writer, which, to say the least, is any thing but satisfactory,—a gloss which may serve as a specimen of polemic dexterity in a case that had no remedy at command, but which is by no means a fair sample of the general ability of its author, who seldom takes in hand a subject on which he does not spread all the light yet emitted from the orb of truth.

I am, however, content. The refutation of Dr. Middleton must, as it seems, remain uncommunicated except to a few, whom envy may not render incapable of apprehending it, by means of personal explanation. Be it so. As I seek no recompense, I will not, certainly, publish by subscription, which is the mode suggested by Dr. Carpenter in your magazine, and by an intelligent and learned friend in a private letter,—the only persons who have considered my proposal as deserving of notice. I am ready "to offer my labour on the altar of the God of truth." But if the truth be not worth countenance, *as truth*, I withdraw, willing neither to undergo a useless loss, nor to accept of any ungraceful obligation. If the truth be lightly esteemed on its own account and unconnected with the exaltation of a favoured individual or of a favoured party, considerations of prudence and feeling must justify me in withholding it. If, however, any person will undertake to procure the necessary subscriptions and to publish my work, the copy shall be at his service, and the profit at the service of any institution that may appear to merit support.

I am, &c.

CHARLES LLOYD.

GLEANINGS; OR, SELECTIONS AND REFLECTIONS MADE IN A COURSE OF GENERAL READING.

No. CCLII.

Heterodoxy. Heresy.

To be of a different persuasion (ἕτερος, other, and δόξα, faith), constitutes heterodoxy; to have chosen a faith for oneself (αἵρεσις, choice), constitutes heresy. Heterodoxy is negative, heresy is positive dissent. The heterodox differs, the heretic separates. Heterodoxy endangers conformity; heresy destroy union. Extensive heterodoxies produce heresy.

All distinct sects are heterodox with respect to each other; Jew, Catholic, Calvinist and Socinian. That sect only is heretical which has a newer creed than the party from which it dissents. In Christian countries the Jews are not heretics; but they are heterodox. In Protestant countries, the Church of Rome is not a heresy; but it is a heterodoxy. Socinianism, while secretly entertained, is but a heterodoxy; when embodied as an Unitarian sect, it is a heresy.

Truth may form a heresy, and so may error. Christianity was a Jewish heresy, until it became established by law. Heresy begins in schism, and ends in the sanction of the magistrate.

W. Taylor's English Synonyms.

No. CCLIII.

Religion. Devotion. Piety. Sanctity.

Religion is the bond which ties us to the Deity; it is the external contract, the alliance made by others. Devotion is the wish to become obedient to the Deity; it is the internal subjection of man to his God. Piety is that filial sentiment which we feel for the Father of all. Sanctity is the habit of interior coercion, which a constant sense of duty to the Godhead inspires.

He is religious who adheres to the ordinances of his country or his sect. He is devout whom this adherence has trained to allegiance. He is pious who regards the Deity as his Father. Sanctity is to piety what devotion is to religion—the state of mind which results from acquiescence in the feeling.

Some men are pious without being religious; and some are religious without being pious. For a worldly person it is sufficient to be religious. Those are devout whose purposes embrace their interests in other worlds. There is a fear of God observable in these times among the Calvinists, which is no less hostile to piety, than that rude familiarity with the Almighty which is observable among Methodists. Yet all these sentiments grow out of religion.

Religion is considered as a duty; piety as a merit; devotion and sanctity as equivocal excesses. This arises from the scepticism of the world, which questions the eventual retribution of the industry spent in devotion, or of the privations incurred from sanctity. One may infer a man's creed from his using the words devotion and sanctity with deference or with a sneer.

The Same.

No. CCLIV.

Superstition. Credulity. Bigotry. Enthusiasm. Fanaticism.

Those are called superstitious who are too much attached to ritual observances of religion. Those are credulous who are too easy of belief; those are bigoted who are too obstinate in their creed. Enthusiasm is the zeal of credulity, and fanaticism the zeal of bigotry.

Of our sects, the Catholics tend most to superstition; the Methodists to credulity; and the Calvinists to bigotry. Enthusiasm is commonly a solitary, and fanaticism a social passion. Credulity is the reverse of scepticism, and bigotry of indifference. Superstition is humble and industrious; enthusiasm proud and capricious. Credulity is the most inconstant; fanaticism the most intolerant of the religious affections.

The Same.

No. CCLV.

Tiberius a Royal Pattern.

William Penn, in his *No Cross no Crown*, cites Tiberius in his list of witnesses to *the just principle, the principle of life.* As far as the citation extends, would to heaven that Christian kings, (as some kings are called) would lay to heart this *testimony* of a Heathen emperor!

"Tiberius would not suffer himself to be called *Lord,* nor yet *His Sacred Majesty;* for, (says he) *they are divine titles,* and *belong not to man.* The commissioners of his treasury advising him, *To increase his taxes upon the people,* he answered, *No, it was fit to shear, but not to flea the sheep.*"

No. CCLVI.

John Fox, the Martyrologist.

When the famous John Fox, the martyrologist, was summoned to subscribe, by the queen's direction, the venerable old man produced his *Greek Testament,* and said, *"To this I will subscribe."* And when a subscription to the canons was required, he refused it, saying, "I have nothing in the church, save a prebend at *Salisbury,* and so much good may it do you, if you will take it away from me."

Fuller's Ch. Hist. B. ix. p. 76.

No. CCLVII.

An eminent Lay Preacher.

"After lamenting the dispersion of the scholars on account of the plague, and the low ebb to which learning was reduced in consequence of it, he proceeds thus:—'Preachers I am sure were so rare, that there were but two in the University that preached on

the Lord's day (yet not constantly) to the academians: those were Mr. Thomas Sampson, Dean of Christ Church, and Dr. Lawrence Humphrey, President of Magdalen College. Nay, Sir Henry Saville hath often reported to certain intelligent persons, that have told me the same, that when he first came to the University, about 1561, there was but one constant preacher in Oxon, and he only a Bachelor of All Soul's College. These, I say, preaching for the most part to the academians, their puritanical doctrine took such deep root among their auditors, that it never could be quite extirpated. When Mr. Sampson left the University, and Dr. Humphrey often absent upon occasions, and none left, perhaps, to execute the office of preaching rightly, Richard Taverner, of Woodeaton, near Oxford, Esq. did several times preach in Oxford, and when he was High Sheriff of this county (which was a few years after this,) came into St. Mary's church, out of pure charity, with a golden chain about his neck, and a sword, as 'tis said, by his side, (but false, without doubt, for he always preached in a damask gown,) and gave the academians, destitute of evangelical advice, a sermon beginning with these words:—

"'Arriving at the Mount of St. Mary's in the stony stage,[*] where I now stand, I have brought you some fyne biskets baked in the oven of charitie, carefully conserved for the chickens of the church, the sparrows of the spirit, and the sweet swallowes of salvation, &c.'

"He was some time of Cardinal College, in Oxford, afterwards Master of Arts and at length Clerk of the Signet to King Henry VIII. and Edward VI., from the last of whom he obtained Letters (though a mere layman) to preach the word of God in any church of his majesty's dominions. A good scholar he was of his time, but an enemy not only to the Catholic religion, but to the ceremonies of the Church of England now in their infancy."

Wood's Annals, 1563, 5, 6 Eliz. vol. ii. quoted in *Letters of Eminent Persons, from the Bodleian Library,* vol. i. p. 67, '68. *Note.*

---

[*] "St. Mary's pulpit was then of fine carved Ashler stone."

REVIEW.

"Still pleased to praise, yet not afraid to blame."---POPE.

Art. I.—*The Village School Improved; or, the new System of Education practically explained, and adapted to the Case of Country Parishes.* The third edition, with additions. To which is added, an *Appendix*, containing Specimens of Catechetical Exercises; an Account of the Method of teaching Arithmetic in Classes, and by the Agency of the Scholars themselves; Mental Arithmetic on a new and simple Principle, &c. By John Poole, M. A. Late Fellow of Oriel College, Oxford, Rector of Enmore and Swainswick, Somerset, and Chaplain to the Right Hon. the Earl of Egmont. Oxford: at the University Press. Sold, in London, by Messrs. Rivington and by J. Hatchard. 1815. 12mo. pp. 188.

TO the large, and, we trust, increasing, body of persons who exert themselves, in various ways, for the success of *popular* education, we cordially recommend this volume: it is the result of the inquiries of a cultivated mind, accustomed to patient, attentive observation, and instructed by much individual experience; and it constitutes, on the whole, the most valuable and interesting of all the publications on the subject.

Enmore; from the parsonage of which the author dates the "Advertisement to the third edition," is a village four miles west from Bridgewater in Somersetshire. Here a day-school had for some time been established, which Mr. Poole was in the practice of occasionally visiting. "It consisted generally of about twenty-five or thirty children of both sexes; all of whom were taught to read; some few to write; and such of the girls as were old enough were instructed in needlework. The schoolmistress was an active, intelligent woman; who appeared desirous of doing all in her power to bring on the children in their learning: but her plan of instruction being that which is followed in most of the old village schools, the progress made by the children, though equal to what is usually made in such schools, was by no means such as satisfied" their kind and intelligent visitor. Hence he "formed the resolution of attempting to introduce into the school some of the recent improvements in education."

For a detailed account of the Enmore school, we must refer our readers to the publication before us. In the general plan of this seminary there are two circumstances which deserve more immediately our notice and applause: we mean, "the method of teaching" and the rank of life of some of the children who receive instruction.

"The method of teaching is a compound of Dr. Bell's and Mr. Lancaster's systems, with alterations and additions. In what respects it agrees, and in what it differs from each, may be seen at once in the subjoined table."

"I. It agrees with both—

"In the division of the school into classes; each under the tuition of one of the scholars.

"II. It agrees with Dr. Bell's—

"1. In the use of small, cheap books, in preference to cards.

"2. In reading word by word, backwards, and sometimes syllabically.

"3. In unreiterated spelling.

"4. In the reading and ciphering lessons being accompanied with questions.

"5. In keeping a register of the business done in each class.

"6. In the interrogative mode of communicating religious instruction.

"7. In the religious instruction being according to the principles of the Established Church.

"III. It agrees with Mr. Lancaster's—

"1. In all the children being seated at single desks, facing one way.

"2. In all the children being taught to write.

"3. In all the children being taught to spell, by writing on slates words dictated by the teachers.

"4. In all the children, when of a proper age, being taught to cipher in classes.

"IV. The Enmore school differs from the greater part of those, both on Dr. Bell's and Mr. Lancaster's systems—

"In not being a free school.

"V. The following modifications and additions have been introduced:*

---

* Some farther modifications and additions are described in the notes to this third edition.

" 1. Writing from dictation connected, in various ways, with every reading lesson.

" 2. Numerals, punctuation, &c. taught by writing from dictation.

" 3. Sets of questions and answers provided for many of the reading lessons.

" 4. Sets of questions and answers provided for the ciphering lessons;—and for other things taught in the school.

" 5. Nothing repeated from memory, until first read, with all the accompanying exercises.

" 6. Mr. Lancaster's method of teaching arithmetic considerably modified and extended: tables, in some rules, given on a peculiar construction," &c. &c.

This table is important, as it exhibits the nature and extent of the instruction communicated in the Enmore school, which "now (1815) consists of a hundred children." A synoptical view, moreover, is thus presented of the respective systems of Dr. Bell and Mr. Lancaster. Many persons suppose that the mechanism of the schools denominated severally after those two individuals, is, in substance, the same. No opinion can be more contrary to the fact. Some of the points in regard to which their plans differ, are here described: and others will be visible on an inspection of a Madras and of a Lancasterian seminary; although the chief of the variations have not been overlooked by Mr. Poole. Of the schools somewhat improperly termed " national," it is a remarkable feature that the method of instruction observed in them is strictly uniform; no deviations being permitted from the rules and order prescribed by Dr. Bell. In the other class of popular schools, on the contrary, all those improvements take place which experience suggests or local circumstances demand. The Royal Lancasterian institutions, in most large towns of the kingdom, are conducted, it is true, agreeably to the leading principles first exemplified in this nation by the active and benevolent person whose name those seminaries deservedly perpetuate: but the apparatus is not identical with what may have been seen at the Borough school.* In the majority of the provincial schools time and labour are saved, and the

proficiency of the pupils advanced, by means of not a few very simple and ingenious contrivances: silence, too, is secured, and the necessity of the frequent recurrence of punishment obviated, by well-devised modes of appealing to some of the best feelings of the youthful breast. The teachers and superintendants are eager to acquire information from any quarter, and to adopt every judicious hint or scheme in regard to practical and popular education. On looking into the last report of the British and Foreign School Society,* we perceive, with much satisfaction, that in this respect the labours of Mr. Poole have not been useless: in the second of his classes " a skewer is given to each child, with which he is instructed, by the teacher of the class, to form the letters in the sand"—and availing himself of this intimation, the industrious and skilful master of a school in one of our large manufacturing towns furnishes " each boy" of the second class, " with a style to write the small letters and figures in sand." We are also sanguine enough to indulge the hope that our present notice of The Village School, &c. may excite in some of our readers a desire of studying Mr. P.'s account of it; and may thus assist, in no small degree, the instruction of the children of the poor.

The Enmore school is divided into eight classes. He who shall make himself acquainted with its general arrangement, as described in this little volume, and with the business of each class (of which Mr. P. likewise gives a distinct account), will find his trouble well rewarded. We shall not undertake an abridgement of the author's chapters: this could not be done without injury to them; and they merit a repeated and diligent perusal. His Village School, &c. whether it be viewed through the mirror of his publication, or actually visited, cannot but present a most engaging scene to the eye of the benevolent reader or traveller. It is, no doubt, possible, and even probable, that different persons will pronounce opinions more or less favourable to some of the parts of the plan of instruction, which he has detailed. But his zeal, intelligence and kindness, his unaffected candour

---

* Nothing more is intended by these remarks than to shew, that the Lancasterian schools may, and do, receive improvements.

and liberality, will, we presume, be *universally* admired.

Our author gives it as his judgment, in which we fully concur, that " no school will be popular, or will long continue so, from which writing and arithmetic are excluded." Accordingly, we have perceived that " in the Enmore school all the children, when of a proper age, are instructed in arithmetic; which is taught in classes, each under the direction and tuition of its teacher." And the progress made by them in this valuable article of knowledge, " is not only far beyond what the old method is capable of effecting; but is even greater than" Mr. P. has " ever witnessed in any of the schools conducted upon the new system." He has found that " in the course of two years, children, who were before entirely unacquainted with figures, may be thoroughly instructed in the four first rules, simple and compound; reduction; the rule of three, direct, inverse, and double; practice; tare and tret; interest, and its dependent rules; cross multiplication, or duodecimals; and the extraction of the square and cube roots; and may obtain some knowledge of vulgar and decimal fractions. In nothing, however, is their progress so conspicuous and extraordinary as in mental arithmetic—a branch of the science which has hitherto been little attended to in schools; but which, in the business of life, is of great importance."

It may be added that *mental arithmetic* is perhaps the best of all instruments for bringing forth and strengthening the intellectual faculties. In particular, it has a tendency to bestow " that power of determined undeviating attention, which is the fundamental principle of all considerable attainments, and to which even Newton ascribed the great philosophical discoveries by which his name is immortalized." * There is no part of the Rector of Enmore's publication, which we so much admire as those of its pages that treat of *arithmetic*; those especially in which some account is given of the " method of calculation", prescribed for his village scholars— " which, though easy and simple, is somewhat peculiar."

Mr. Poole " has no hesitation whatever in saying, that in the new plan

* Mon. Repos. vol. iii. 538.

of instruction, which he has had the happiness of establishing in his parish, there is nothing which affords him greater satisfaction" than its comprehensiveness. His system brings together under the same roof the rising generation of the labouring poor and those who will probably be their future masters or mistresses." We consider such an arrangement as calculated 'for the benefit of both descriptions" of scholars; and much prefer it to those inferior boarding schools, to which the children of farmers are frequently sent, " where, if their morals escape corruption, they are at least in danger of acquiring, and often do acquire, a distaste for country employments."

The several boys and girls in the Enmore school, are, we presume, of families belonging to the church of England; " the religious instruction being according to the principles" of that church. Whether the offspring of dissenting parents are admissible, and on what conditions, we know not: Mr. Poole appears to be exceedingly zealous for what he styles " the church of England schools"; nor will we reproach any conscientious clergyman with his attachment to the ecclesiastical discipline under which he has solemnly enlisted. The education however, of the infant poor, is an object of paramount importance: it is worthy of being promoted, and will be best promoted, by the united efforts of men of various denominations of religion. And of the volume under our review, so little is exclusively applicable to schools for *one* church, or *sect* (the Romish communion looking on *Protestants without exception* as *Sectarians*), that we do not shrink from urging its claims on an attention still more general than what it already has obtained.

How signally useful would be those of the clergy, and of our country-gentlemen, who should imitate Mr. Poole's example! We are astonished, mortified and grieved, that men of wealth and leisure and education, men too, who profess a belief in the Christian religion, are so careless of the mental improvement of the children of their less affluent parishioners and neighbours. Hostility to the instruction of the great body of the people, is not, it would seem, quite so common among us as it was a few years since. Many however of those who avow themselves its friends, should be urged to more active efforts in its behalf. There is scarcely a village in which *an Enmore school* might not be seen, if persons of property, influence and talents, would but apply them to this object.

Intellectual and religious education, may be intrusted with most safety and advantage to the voluntary exertions of individuals; to their wisdom, experience and zeal. This remark forces itself on us, in consequence of our being made acquainted with *the Village School Improved*: and the correctness of it receives an illustration from numerous facts. What Mr. Poole has done, other intelligent and public-spirited and able men may also execute. Of the legislator all which we can justly and prudently ask is that he will place no obstacles in the way of "national instruction": * the *productive or creative* power by which "the dormant seeds of genius and virtue" are vivified, belongs not to *him!*

Art. II.—ΑΙΡΕΣΕΩΝ ΑΝΑΣΤΑ-ΣΙΣ: or, *A New Way of deciding Old Controversies.* By Basanistes. 3rd ed. enlarged. 8vo. pp. 246. Johnson and Co. 1815.

BASANISTES is said to be a clergyman of the Established Church. His "New Way" is an attempt to explode the doctrines of the Trinity, and the divinity of Christ, by shewing that the arguments usually brought forward on their behalf, may be applied with equal fairness and success to the most absurd and ridiculous doctrines, such for instance as the divinity of Moses, and, by the addition of him to the godhead, the *Quaternity* of persons in the divine nature.

This is not altogether a "New Way;" it is more properly Αἱρέσεων *ανάστασις*, the revival of an old argument, or rather joke. The first suggestion of it was made in the first volume of the Unitarian Tracts, 4to. printed in the year 1691, in a paper, entitled "Some notes taken from Mr. Bidle's mouth whilst he was in Newgate." The argument is followed through a page and a half, with the following pertinent introduction: "As

* Supplement to the 4th and 5th ed. of the Encyclop. Brit. vol. 1, p. 1. First Diss. p. 58.

for the business of Attribution, when men argue that Christ is God, because what is attributed to God in one place, is attributed unto Christ in another, this arguing is very fallacious; for according to that (though the usual way of proving when men speak of Christ,) Moses, as a man, will also be God; because what is attributed to God in one place, is attributed to Moses' in another."—The argument was taken up and enlarged in an *Appendix* to "Six more Letters to Granville Sharpe, Esq. on his Remarks upon the Uses of the Article in the Greek Testament. By Gregory Blunt, Esq." an 8vo. pamphlet of great learning and wit, published in the year 1803. The Appendix is entitled, "Table of Evidences of the Divinity of Moses," constructed on the plan of Mr. Sharp's "Table of Evidences of Christ's Divinity," "in order to shew him the *validity* of this mode of arguing by inference and deduction, from detached passages and figurative expressions."—*Basanistes* has spread out the argument into the volume before us, and quite exhausted it. The *reductio ad absurdum*, the design of which is to prove an adversary's principles false, by shewing that they necessarily lead to a conclusion, which in itself is confessedly a false proposition, was never more complete. Sometimes, indeed, the author pushes his reasonings to an extreme which startles the reader; but, whatever may be thought or felt concerning particular passages, the work, considered as a whole, shews that the popular and most approved reasonings on the subject of the divinity of Christ and the Trinity, are certainly false, because they prove infinitely too much. This is the answer to the question of *Cui bono*? which every one asks on taking up the work.

The allowableness of ridicule on sacred subjects is a problem of difficult solution. On the one side, there is danger of breaking up those habits of reverence for certain names and things which are the safeguard of religion; on the other, there is an impossibility of forbearing laughter at downright absurdity and nonsense. We generally determine the matter according to our prejudices and party-interests. Every man uses ridicule, as he does reason, when he supposes that it makes for his own creed; but every man deprecates it as far as it spoils some favorite notion. The Roman Catholic laughs at Luther's dogmas on the subject of predestination; the Protestant makes merry with the Roman Catholic's breaden God: the mirth is to one party, of the nature of argument, to the other, of the nature of blasphemy. Both parties arraign the Unitarians as impious when they presume to be witty upon the Trinity. There appears however to be no fairness in Trinitarians having one law for themselves, and imposing another law upon Unitarians. If the grave *Tillotson* be allowed, in that grave thing, a Sermon, to sport with the doctrine of Transubstantiation, why should not *Basanistes* make equally free with the doctrine of the Trinity, which he considers no less absurd and ridiculous? The breach of charity is as great in the former case as in the latter; for the pious Catholic is as much shocked at *Tillotson*, as the pious Trinitarian is at *Basanistes.*—It must be conceded then, we apprehend, that the right and wrong in this case depend upon the manner of the writer. A good Christian will not suffer even wit to transport him beyond the bounds of modesty, and to hurry him into a transgression of that respect which he owes to religion in every form: he will certainly reckon a laugh bought at too high a price, if it be at the expence of truth and charity. *Ea quæ dicit vir bonus, omnia salvâ dignitate et verecundiâ dicet: nimium enim risus pretium est, si probitatis impendio constat.*

How far *Basanistes* has conformed to this rhetorical canon, we may even say this law of Christian morals, must be left to the reader's determination. The argument is, we confess, less agreeable to our own taste, than to that of some of our friends, whose judgment and moral sense we always respect; but we are ready to acknowledge that our author has handled it like a master, and that they who can enjoy his humour, without any checks from old habits of feeling, have here a rich treat. *Basanistes*, true to his assumed name, has put orthodoxy to the rack, and extorted some odd and not very creditable confessions. Abstracted from the general argument, there are many passages in the work which cannot fail to be admired for judicious criticism or powerful rea-

soning. We subjoin one passage, (a *note* in the *Additional Preface to the third edition,* p. xxix—xxxii,) relating to Dr. Magee's work on the Atonement, as a specimen of the writer's talents and style:—

"The Author confesses that he had not paid much attention to the doctrine of the atonement, and that he was rather partial to it, on Arian principles, until he read the celebrated work of Doctor Magee upon this subject. From the perusal of this very work he began to suspect that this doctrine is altogether "groundless'; and he now thinks that the only way in which the sacrifice of Christ removes the sins of men, is by supplying a powerful motive to repentance and good works. Every kind of argument is attempted by the Doctor, except the "argumentum ad judicium:" and throughout the whole of his work may be seen the dexterity of the determined advocate, whose object is victory more than truth. He makes a great parade of logical precision, the whole of which may be passed over, as none of it applies to the main question; and he has himself so little confidence in it, that he prepares his readers for his doctrine, by praising a "reverence for the mysterious sublimities of religion;" and he asserts, after much declamation— "assuredly, if our pride of understanding, and self-sufficiency of reason are not made to prostrate themselves before the awfully mysterious truths of revelation, we want the essence of Christianity." This is precisely the language of Romanists when they defend transubstantiation; and it will always be adopted by men who dread any rational test, and propagate their faith by spiritual tyranny. Such are the men, and not those whom the Doctor somewhere describes, who press the figurative language of scripture into their service as literal truth, and represent the literal truth as figurative. The Doctor admits that there is no discoverable connexion between the sacrifice of Christ, as he understands it, and the forgiveness of sins. He has also failed to shew, if he had any such intention, that there is a discoverable connexion between the forgiveness of sins and faith, in the atonement; or that this faith is declared in scripture to be any condition or token of forgiveness. By this singularly cautious management, he certainly avoids many absurd consequences with which the Calvinists are pressed, and to which they have never given a satisfactory reply; but, at the same time, his greatest admirers must admit, that he proposes no more advantage to mankind from the success of his labours, and the decision of the abstract question, than if he were to ascertain our Lord's stature, or the colour of his hair. It appears now that he has exerted his utmost talents, for a series of years, with much bitterness of language, upon a subject which he allows to be altogether speculative---unconnected with morality, or with our duty in any shape. As if he were aware of this objection, he sets up "humility" as "the soul and substance of all Christian virtue." What he means by it may be accurately known from his observation that a "reverence for the mysterious sublimities of religion teaches humility," and from his description already quoted of "the essence of Christianity." This species of humility he enjoys and recommends, in common with the most haughty advocates for spiritual tyranny; who place the utmost perfection of a Christian in his repeating these words, with most humble devotion,---"I renounce the evidence of my senses, and all human understanding." If Christ had been *meek and lowly*, in their sense of the word humility, he would have been perfectly obsequious to the jewish priests and rulers, and Christianity would have died with him; and if the humility which he admires prevailed universally, priests alone would reign, and be as gods on the earth. No, the humility which is uppermost in his mind, is not charity, nor sober thoughts of our works and situation, nor any Christian virtue; but it is an implicit acquiescence with him in these senseless opinions, that man has no power to do or to will any thing which is pleasing in the sight of God, but that the blood of God Almighty washes away, in a literal sense, the sins of those men who rely on that alone. With these right humble notions in his head, a man may live in the breach of all the commandments, and yet be flattered by the Doctor that he has "the soul and substance of all Christian virtue," and "the essence of Christianity." To favour the same notions he has produced a string of texts, relating to the sacrifice of Christ, the true meaning of which the reader may learn by the following experiment: Let him try how they will all bear to be explained according to the two opposite suppositions of a figurative and a literal sense. On the first supposition, the meaning is abundantly supported by parallel figurative language; and the Doctor himself must admit that all these passages contain nothing but truth, are replete with beauty and harmony, and are free from difficulties and absurdities. On the other supposition, the candid and judicious reader will find, that the entire New Testament is at variance with itself; that it states different exclusive grounds

of our acceptance with God, and that, for no apparent object, it teaches the most unnatural and monstrous doctrines. The Doctor says, that no one can point out any congruity in the measure of a literal sacrifice; and he contends for this sense, solely because it suits his prejudices or inclinations, that we should submit our reason, implicitly, to the literal meaning of scripture, upon this particular subject. When we are thus called on to put out the light of reason, which is the first revelation from God, we may fairly presume that it is not for the purpose of substituting the undoubted revelation of the gospel, but some manifest perversion of it. Upon what principle can he blame or refute those who profess to renounce their reason and senses, in order that they may understand literally these words of our Lord---*this is my body ?* It will farther appear to the reader, who will make the experiment here recommended, that the notion of the literal sacrifice of Christ to appease the infinite wrath of another person, implies or supposes the doctrine of a Deity strangely compounded of different persons, with opposite dispositions, one of whom became and remains incarnate; a doctrine which no reflecting man can believe, though there are many violent advocates for it. Will not 'the most steadfast of the orthodox be offended, if the question be put to him,' whether he really believes this doctrine? and will he not apologize for his faith by under-statements and appeals to mystery? Dr. Magee wishes to rank among the most zealous of the orthodox; yet he exposes his orthodoxy with such caution, that it is plain he is ashamed to confess that his God is composed of three persons. If he does believe this doctrine, would it not be incumbent on him to shew the reason why two-thirds of his God should be refused an infinite atonement for the sins of men? He was aware of this objection, and from his silence we may conclude he was unable to answer it. But the truth is, he no more believes there are three persons in Almighty God, than the generality of Romish priests believe they can re-produce their Maker; and his belief in the atonement, so far at least as it depends on this idolatrous notion of three persons, is, after all, nothing more than the belief of a partisan, whose views are confined to this world. He will probably have his reward."

ART. III.—*The History and Antiquities of Dissenting Churches, &c.*
[Continued from p. 239.]

THE "English Presbyterian" congregation in Poor Jewry Lane,

now extinct, was distinguished by a succession of able ministers, of whom the following is a list: Timothy Cruso, M.A. Francis Fuller, M.A. William Harris, D.D. Samuel Rosewell, John Billingsley, Samuel Harvey, Nathaniel Lardner, D.D. George Benson, D.D. Ebenezer Radcliffe, Richard Price, D.D. John Calder, D.D.

Timothy Cruso, of whom a handsome portrait is given, was a learned, able and faithful Dissenting pastor. Our historian having indulged a conjecture (p. 57) that " he spent some time as chaplain or tutor in a private family, a very usual practice for young ministers at that time," remarks very truly that " the Dissenters have derived no advantage by *(from)* discontinuing so laudable a custom." At the time when students leave their academies they are commonly too young to undertake the pastoral office; and by being hurried at once into the duties of a laborious profession and the cares of life, they are in great danger of dropping or at least of becoming irregular in their studies.

Francis Fuller was the son of " Mr. John Fuller, a pious and eminent minister in London, who was ejected in 1662, from St. Martin's, Ironmonger Lane," and brother to Dr. Thomas and Dr. Samuel Fuller, also eminent scholars and preachers, who conformed at the Restoration. This family was celebrated for facetiousness. Jere. White, one of Oliver Cromwell's chaplains, was the friend of Francis Fuller, and preached his funeral sermon, which was afterwards published.

A full account is given (pp. 66—75), with a pleasing portrait, of *Dr. William Harris.* He was an author of some note in his day, but none of his works have maintained their ground in public estimation. His name will be preserved, however, as one of the continuators of Matthew Henry's Exposition: he drew up the Commentary upon the Epistles to the Philippians and Colossians. He made an extensive collection of books, which he bequeathed to Dr. Williams's Library, in Red Cross Street, where there is preserved a very fine painting of him. It is to his honour that he was one of those that resisted subscription to articles, at the Salters' Hall Synod, in 1719.

Here Mr. Wilson introduces a short notice of another Dissenting minister of the same name, which we shall extract:

" Besides the above Dr. William Harris, there was another writer of the same name, also a Dissenting minister, and a celebrated historian. The latter was a native of Salisbury, and received his academical learning under Mr. Grove and Dr. Amory, at Taunton. At that period, he was remarkable for pregnant parts and a love of books. He began to preach when very young—it is apprehended, before he was nineteen years of age. His first settlement was with a dissenting congregation at St. Loo, in Cornwall. From thence he removed to the city of Wells, where he was ordained April 15, 1741. Mr. Samuel Billingsley, of Ashwick, and Dr. Amory, of Taunton, assisted on the occasion. Mr. Harris did not continue many years at Wells; but, on marrying Miss Bovet, of Honiton, he removed to that town, to reside with two uncles of that lady, and preached the remainder of his life to a small society at Luppit, in the neighbourhood. In September 1765, the University of Glasgow conferred upon him the degree of Doctor of Divinity, through the interest of his friend, the late Thomas Hollis, Esq.

" Dr. Harris's first essay in the walk of literature, in which he afterwards made a distinguished figure, was the Life of Hugh Peters, after the manner of Bayle. In 1753, he published ' An historical and critical Account of the Life and Writings of James I.' upon the model of the forementioned writer, drawn from state papers and original documents. This was followed in 1758, by the Life of Charles I. upon the same plan. These publications attracted the notice, and secured him the friendship, of the munificent Mr. Thomas Hollis, who, from time to time, assisteu him with many valuable books and papers for the furtherance of his design. In the year 1762, he gave to the public, the Life of Oliver Cromwell, in one large volume octavo; and in 1766, the Life of Charles II. in two volumes octavo. Both were executed in the same manner, and gained the author increasing reputation. The characteristic qualities of Dr. Harris as an historian, are diligence in collecting materials; exact fidelity in quoting authorities; impartiality in stating facts; and an ardent zeal for civil and religious liberty. It has been justly observed, that while Eachard, Hume and Smollet [*Smollett*], and other writers of their stamp, composed their histories for the use of kings, or rather tyrants, to instruct them how to rule at pleasure; Rapin, Harris, Wilson, Osborne, &c. wrote for the use of the people, to show them that they could claim an equal protection in their privileges and liberties, by a right anterior to the authority conferred upon kings.* Dr. Harris adopted the manner of Bayle, as it gave him an opportunity to enter into disquisitions; and to indulge reflections in the notes, which, in the text, would have interrupted the narrative. His abilities and merits as an historian, introduced him to an acquaintance and correspondence with some of the most eminent characters of his day; as Lord Orford, Archdeacon Blackburn [Blackburne], Dr. Birch, Mrs. Macauley, Dr. Mayhew of Boston, Mr. Theophilus Lindsey, &c. Besides the foregoing works, it is conjectured that he was the author of a tract, without his name, in answer to, 'An Essay on Establishments in Religion;' which passed as the work of Mr. Rotherham, but was suspected to have been dictated, or at least revised, by Archbishop Secker. He was, likewise, the editor of a volume of Sermons, by the late Mr. William West, of Exeter. An ill state of health, brought on by nocturnal studies, when the mornings had been spent in relaxation, and converse with neighbouring friends, impeded his application to further historical investigations, and terminated his life, on February 4, 1770, when he was only 50 years of age. *Monthly Magazine for August,* 1800." Pp. 75—77. Note.

Samuel Rosewell was the son of the celebrated Thomas Rosewell who was tried for high treason before Judge Jefferies, and found guilty, but whose condemnation was so palpably iniquitous, that even in those base times the capital part of the sentence was remitted.

John Billingsley was one of the nonsubscribers at Salters' Hall.

Samuel Harvey died young; but not before he had excited amongst his friends the liveliest expectation of his future usefulness in the church. The following epitaph was composed in honour of him, by his friend Dr. Watts:

" Here lie the ruins of a lowly tent,
Where the seraphic soul of Harvey spent
Its mortal years. How did his genius
    shine
Like heaven's bright envoy clad in powers
    divine !
When from his lips the grace or vengeance
    broke,
'Twas majesty in arms, 'twas melting mercy spoke.

* " Memoirs of Thomas Hollis, Esq. vol. i. p. 210."

What worlds of worth lay crowded in the breast !
Too strait the mansion for th' illustrious guest !
Zeal, like a flame, shot from the realms of day,
Aids the slow fever to consume the clay,
And bears the saint up through the starry road
Triumphant : so Elijah went to God.
What happy prophet shall his mantle find,
Heir to the double portion of his mind ?"

ART. IV.—*Observations on the State and Changes in the Presbyterian Societies of England during the last half Century.* Also, on the Manufactures of Great Britain, which have been for the most part established and supported by the Protestant Dissenters. Tending to illustrate the Importance of Religious Liberty and Free Inquiry to the Welfare and Prosperity of a People : preceded by a *Sermon* on the Death of the *Rev. Dr. Joshua Toulmin,* in which his Character as a Member of Civil Society is attempted to be improved. By Israel Worsley. 12mo. pp. 134. Longman and Co. 3s. 1816.

FROM Mr. Worsley's Funeral Sermon we have already extracted a passage of some length, [M. Repos. xi. 194—198] containing a description of the Public Character of the late truly reverend Dr. Toulmin. But the Sermon is the least portion of the work : the *Addenda* are very copious, and relate to subjects of deep interest, which are well stated in the title-page.

Mr. Worsley is a zealous nonconformist. He makes his boast of principles which some that hold them are disposed to hide. He puts in a large claim for his denomination with respect to patriotic services. Few readers will we think condemn him as presumptuous. However it may be explained, it is a fact that the Protestant Dissenters have been for a century and a half a very active part of the population of England. The detail here given of their labours and improvements will surprise such as are not familiar with their history. Whilst Mr. Worsley renders honour to Protestant Dissenters, he freely exposes their defects. He is the friend of Dissent, but more the friend of Truth and Liberty.

In reading this amusing and instructive little work, we could not help regarding it as the ground-work of a

History of Nonconformists, more comprehensive, more minute and therefore more instructive than has yet been contemplated : in such a history, all that is here stated of their ability and enterprise in trade should have a place, together with much more that could be stated, but the work should likewise embrace their literary labour., their political influence and the weight of their character on public manners. We recommend this thought to Mr. Worsley's notice. He has our thanks for his present performance, and will, we are persuaded, receive the same from our readers.

ART. V.—*A Second Letter to the Bishop of St. David's.* By A Lay Seceder. 8vo. pp. 36. Hunter. 1816.

AN account of the Lay Seceder's First Letter was given in our last volume [x. 373—375];* the Second Letter is written with the same ability, and in the same temper, fearless but not uncandid.

If the bishop be not too old in prejudice and bigotry to be a learner, the Lay Seceder may teach him both scriptural divinity and good manners. The following passage is a fair specimen of the Letter, which exhibits internal evidence of coming from a pen not wholly strange to our readers :

"The interpretations, on which your Lordship's acquiescence in the doctrines of the Church of England is founded, appear to me repugnant to the general sense of scripture, and altogether insufficient to support the scheme. The more I examine the subject, and I have not failed as you suppose in due *enquiry*, the more firmly am I fixed in the ground of my reluctant, but strictly conscientious secession from that Church. But why, my Lord, in matters of opinion, should you require the interference of a *penal law?* Why should I be condemned to *imprisonment* and *disqualification*, because, finding no satisfactory solution of the difficulties which surround contested doctrines, I confine my assent to those only, which are clearly and explicitly revealed? How is society injured by my conduct; how is it benefited by your own? The honours and emoluments of your pro-

---

* The article, with the exception of the conclusion of the last paragraph, was written by our respected friend, the late Dr. Toulmin, the loss of whose valuable communications we sensibly feel.

fession have rewarded your Lordship's adherence to the established system : let those honours and emoluments content you : enjoy your own opinions in peace and affluence ; but presume not to infringe the sacred rights of conscience, and cease to invoke the aid of those *disgraceful statutes*, which the unanimous voice of the legislature has repealed." Pp. 6, 7.

ART. VI.—*Morning Meditations for every Lord's Day in the Year.* To which are added, *Twelve Sacramental Meditations.* By Josiah Townsend, Minister of the Gospel. 12mo. pp. 72. Baldwin and Co. 2s. boards. 1815.

THIS is a laudable attempt to supply that want of devotional books which is so much felt amongst Unitarians. The "Meditations" occupy a page each, and conclude with one or more suitable verses from well-known hymns. Controversy is properly lost sight of in the work, which is a good companion for *Tremlett's Reflections*, and together with those little volumes, will be acceptable to such Christians as observe the duties of the closet, and are intent upon the acquirement of a devotional spirit.

We observe with pleasure that Mr. Townsend is preparing for the press, " Meditations for every Day in the Year, on different Texts of Scripture, selected and arranged so as to comprise a System of Religious Truth and Duty."

ART. VII.—*An Essay on Miracles.* In Two Parts. Pt. I. Observations on Miracles in general. Pt. II. On the Credibility of the Miracles of Jesus and his Apostles. By R. Wright. 12mo. pp. 24. Eaton. 6d. 1816.

NONE of Mr. Wright's judicious and valuable Tracts appear to us to promise more advantage to his readers than this. It does not aspire to the praise of originality, but it condenses and simplifies the arguments of the best writers on the subject. Mr. Wright justly contends that a miracle is not a *violation* of the laws of nature; he defines it "an effect produced independently of the laws of nature, without the use of natural means, by the power of God." Is not a miracle, a prophecy instantly fulfilled, of an event out of the ordinary course of nature, and not to be foreseen by human sagacity?

ART. VIII.—*An Essay on the Universal Restoration*: tending to shew that the Final Happiness of all Men is a Doctrine of Divine Revelation. By Richard Wright. 12mo. pp. 24. 6d. Eaton. 1816.

THIS Essay is divided into six sections, which are thus headed: The Promise to Abraham—Passages in the Old Testament—The 'Universal Restoration a Doctrine of the Gospel—The Apostle Paul an Universalist—The Universal Restoration a Doctrine according to Godliness—An Address to Universalists.

Section IV. entitled, "The Apostle Paul an Universalist," is perhaps the best part of the argument, though the whole demands the attention of such as believe, we wish we could say *fear*, that Almighty God will torture some of his children for ever; or by torture reduce them to nothing.

———

ART. IX.—*The Subserviency of Free Inquiry and Religious Knowledge, among the lower Classes of Society, to the Prosperity and Permanence of a State*: attempted to be shewn in a *Discourse*, delivered before the Unitarian Society for promoting Christian Knowledge, at Essex Street Chapel, on Friday, March 29, 1816. By the Rev. J. Joyce. 8vo. pp. 40. Hunter. 1816.

OUR reporter (p. 246) has already given the character of this Sermon from the Journal of the Unitarian Society: and though we think that it would for the most part have been heard with much interest before many other Societies, as well as this,* we cannot withhold our testimony of unqualified approbation to its bold and at the same time benevolent spirit, and to the unreserved declaration which it makes of the great principles of Christian truth.

————

* The Unitarian Society has a benevolent and charitable object in view, but can scarcely be considered as a *Benevolent* or *Charitable Society*: much less, we apprehend, can it be regarded as established for the benefit of "*the lower Classes of Society*." Were the Sermon less excellent we should not suggest these doubts, which, however, scarcely affect its worth.

With a too faithful pencil, Mr. Joyce paints the unhappy condition of the poor. In one short sentence he points out a mass of wretchedness—*The voice of the poor man for peace is never heard by those who make war*. Until that voice is obeyed by legislatures and courts, little will have been done for the prevention or abatement of national misery.

In the conclusion of the Sermon, the preacher draws an animated sketch of the history and purposes of the Unitarian Society, and states briefly but forcibly some arguments on behalf of Unitarianism. The following observation is of great weight:

"The word *Trinity* is of human origin; and no degree of sanctity has been, it may be presumed, at any time attached to it.—The name of Almighty God is guarded in the Holy Scriptures by the most awful sanctions.—Now if there had been a Trinity of persons, and if that Trinity had included all the perfections of the Deity himself, one might have supposed that the name would have been guarded by equally solemn sanctions. So far from it, it is used in all sorts of connexions, and no one feels shocked at the profanation. In our own country we have Trinity colleges, Trinity churches, Trinity corporations, Trinity squares and Trinity lanes:—Now can it be believed for a moment, that the word could have been so used, had it been originally meant to designate the attributes of Almighty God? Who would not be shocked—who could endure to hear the awful name of God attached to places of this kind and used for such purposes!" Pp. 28, 29.

————

ART. X.—*The final Prevalence of Unitarianism a Rational Expectation.* A Discourse delivered at Palgrave, Dec. 19, 1815. By John Fullagar. 8vo. pp. 60. Eaton.

MR. FULLAGAR, who has been for some years the active Secretary of the Southern Unitarian Society, has undertaken the pastoral office at Palgrave, in Suffolk, and this is his Inaugural Sermon. He lays down several weighty reasons for the expectation expressed in the title-page, and endeavours to explain why the expectation has not yet been realized. The Sermon is followed by several pages of interesting Notes.

POETRY.

A TRIBUTE

To the Memory of Joseph Fox.

And is thy course of earthly glory past,
And still that glowing pulse that throbb'd
   too fast?
Has eager death, in unrelenting haste,
His glorious prize, with trembling joy, em-
   brac'd,
As jealous of those never-resting pow'rs
That liv'd whole years when others reckon
   hours?
Sunk is that strength no adverse pow'r
   could bow,
And cold that heart that never froze till
   now?

Yet if there be in nature's ebb and
   flow,
Ought that no dimness and no change can
   know;
If impulse high the conscious bosom
   thrill,
With ought of heav'n that death can never
   chill;
If energy there be whose vestal fire
Lights ages on when mortal pow'rs ex-
   pire—
Farewell the plaintive notes of fond re-
   gret,
Thy spirit walks in deathless grandeur
   yet;
Nor to the skies alone new gladness gives,
But still on earth in holiest freshness
   lives;
Wakes up the tend'rest joys that youth
   beguile,
And glows and brightens in the infant's
   smile.

See, while thy ashes scarce unconscious
   burn,
Angelic mourners gather round thy urn;
There silent kneel in childhood's holiest
   mood,
The deepest bliss of opening gratitude;
Their hands, in thankful joy, together
   prest—
The rapture-breathing sigh, the heaving
   breast;
Smiles lighted up with bliss thy deeds
   have lent,
Shall be thy everlasting monument:
In eyes that beam of heav'n is writ thy
   fame,
In infant's lispings sacred is thy name;
And mounting hopes that gen'rous souls
   employ,
Make thy renown immortal in their joy.
For thee are cheeks, by earth uninjur'd,
   wet,
The light of heav'n is round thy mourners
   yet;

So cherub-like they bend, around thy
   tomb,
Time scarcely throws his shadow on their
   bloom,
Stops his own fatal ravage to condemn,
And rests upon his scythe to gaze on
   them.

Methinks in some sweet ev'ning's ho-
   liest calm,
When every sinking breeze is charg'd
   with balm,
Some youth, with genius dawning o'er his
   cheek,
To think of thee his best-lov'd path shall
   seek,
And 'neath some jagged oak's eternal
   shade,
In holy dream of things unearthly laid,
Hear angel voices whispering from on
   high,
And trace bright visions in the Western
   sky;
Till borne upon etherial clouds he roam,
To catch a glimpse of thy immortal home.
Then, when with joy the pulse of life is
   still,
Thy deeds his heart with impulse high
   shall thrill,
Light there a flame through life's dark
   scenes to burn,
And with mild radiance settle on his urn.

Forgive this humble off'ring to thy
   bier,
An honest boon; though no " melodious
   tear;"*
But hands yet rude shall weave thee
   greener bays,
And harps yet silent give thee worthier
   praise:
Harps, in sweet vales no British steps have
   trod,
Wak'd when across them sweeps the breath
   of God—
When heav'nly truths spontaneous notes
   inspire,
Like morning rays on Memnon's sacred
   lyre!
Then on each breathing of the joyous air,
Thy name shall mingle with the Indian's
   pray'r;
Oft with the song of praise to heav'n pre-
   ferr'd,
In strains like those which Bethle'm's shep-
   herds heard.

                T. N. T.

Ode to Solitude.

Far from ambition's selfish train,
Where avarice rules the busy day,

---

* Lycidas.

And patient folly "hugs his chain,"＊
Enslav'd by custom's ruthless sway,
Lead me, calm spirit, to some still retreat,
Where silence shares with thee the bloom-
   ing mead,
Save when at distance heard in cadence
   sweet,
The village minstrel tunes his simple reed;
There free from cares; from jarring pas-
   sions free,
Oft may I strike the lyre, sweet Solitude,
   to thee.

When orient morn in blushing pride,
Profusely sheds the glist'ning dew,
Oft let me climb the mountain's side,
And raptur'd mark the varied view.
When noon directs on earth his parching
   ray,
Then let me find the cool, the peaceful
   shade,
Form'd by embow'ring oaks, in firm ar-
   ray,
O'er some small stream that rustles through
   the glade.
Thither let fancy lead her magic band,
And o'er my senses wave her soul-in-
   trancing wand.

† But when at eve the curfew's knell
Winds slowly through the dusky grove,
Pensive I'll seek the rural cell,
Or 'midst the gloom in silence rove:
And when from village spire the solemn
   toll
Yields its sad tribute to the breathless
   clay,
As calm reflection steals upon my soul,
The tear unmark'd shall take its silent
   way;
And mournful oft I'll cull the violet's
   bloom,
Heave the sad, soothing sigh, and dress
   the clay-cold tomb.

When midnight spreads her blackest
   robe,
And shrouds in sullen mists the sky,
When terror rules the silent globe,
And phantoms mock the fearful eye;
Parent of All! whose voice the winds
   obey,
The raving ocean, and the black'ning
   storm,
Yet stoop'st to guide the sparrow on his
   way,
And shed'st thy mercy on the struggling
   worm—
To thee, great God, to thee my voice I'll
   raise,
Trembling I'll strike the lyre, and hymn
   thy boundless praise.

                  W. A.

＊ Gray.
†. This idea and the last in the preceding stanza are taken from the "Pense-
roso" of Milton.

Anticipations.

When shall the bell toll over me;
When shall the green sod cover me;
   Peace dry the eyelids that weep;
Sunshine play over the dreary one,
Slumber and rest bless the weary one,
   Low on earth's bosom asleep?

Say, shall a tear softly falling there;
Say, shall a mem'ry recalling there
   Thoughts of the pilgrim at rest;
(Visions of fancy still cherishing)
Visit the spot where lies perishing
   Nature's fond child on her breast?

And in the great desolation day,
(Heaven and earth's new creation day,)＊
   Calm 'midst the wreck—shall my eye,
Fix'd on my God, and discovering
Pardon and mercy there hovering,
   Find welcome in happier skies?

                  A.

Soliloquy of Alphonso IV. of Portugal.
TRANSLATION.

Proud sceptre! thou art bright and beau-
   tiful
To those who know thee not;—but he
   who knows
The curses hanging round thy treacherous
   form,
Rather than lift thee from the damned dust
Which gave thee being, with a soul of
   scorn
Would spurn thee, trample thee indig-
   nantly.
Dazzling, delusive, gaudy, gilded toy!
But earth at best—and heaviest, dullest
   earth!
O blissful life of the poor labourer,
Sheltered in his cottage from the thorns
   of fate;
The cares, the tumults of proud royalty!
Who less a king than he who kingdoms
   rules!
And is this state, and is this dignity
Whose glare all covet, but whose misery
But few can tell?---A pompous servitude!
A wearying, watchful toil, misnamed re-
   pose!
He is a monarch (such an one as he
A court's wide circuit never held) who
   lives
Passionless,---free from hope, desire or
   fear;
Whose hours (O blissful hours!) glide
   softly on,
Lucid and lovely. O for hours like these
What years of kingly pomp my soul would
   give!
Kings must be lengued with vice; they
   hate, they fear,
But cannot, dare not punish! Kings can
   feel,
And feign, and weep too! Where's the
   suffering slave
More captive than a king?   A.

＊ Revelation xxi.

OBITUARY.

Short Sketch of the Character of the late Mr. Joseph Fox.

SIR,

It would give me great pleasure could I communicate to you a satisfactory account of the life of Mr. JOSEPH FOX, which I am persuaded would be interesting to your readers. My acquaintance with him was too short to enable me to state any facts respecting him with which they are not generally acquainted. But there are some deeds which speak for themselves, which require no minute acquaintance to recommend them, and which all ages and capacities may estimate. In such as these Mr. Fox's memory is sure to survive. The single fact, indeed, that in the infancy of the British System of Education, at the critical moment when it was on the point of expiring, he advanced nearly the whole of his property to save it, is, I fondly hope, enough to preserve his name in undying remembrance. When we reflect that this sacrifice was made in the commencement of life; on the eve of settling in the world; and that he had no other resource than the profits of a laborious profession, we shall be incited to believe that it will be blessed by generations yet unborn, when the trophies of ambition and bloodshed are forgotten.

But Mr. Fox was not content with this single act of beneficence. During the remainder of his life he gave unceasing attention to the advancement of his favourite object. His toils were restless and unceasing. As his success in his profession increased, he seemed even more ready to resign himself to the good work he had undertaken, and to forego the bright prospects which opened around him. And though the education of the poor, unmingled with bigotry, was the aim at which his efforts were chiefly directed, a multitude of other schemes for the welfare of his fellow creatures perpetually roused him to fresh exertions. Many of these proved abortive, perhaps from the excess of zeal with which they were pursued. But he was never for a moment appalled; with wonderful elasticity of mind he passed from one generous plan to another, starting up with new energy from every defeat, and deriving fresh spirit from the difficulties of his aspiring career. His life was a perpetual contest—a ceaseless warfare with bigotry which knew no pause, and never suffered him to rest on his arms. It was the ruling passion of his soul to be useful. One

might almost term him a knight-errant in the cause of universal good. No corruption was too high for his attack, no individual too low for his sympathy. He would have been another Clarkson had there been another slave trade to abolish. Like that great benefactor of his species he was by no means possessed of extraordinary talents, except in the line of his profession. It was the energy of his soul that distinguished him from ordinary men. He appeared to have no ambition for personal fame—no desire for making speeches or obtaining applause—but forgot himself in his cause, and was contented to be known only by the blessings he shed around him. The enthusiasm of benevolence kindled a sacred flame within him, supplying the place of the loftiest intellectual faculties. And the honour with which he will hereafter shine in the annals of human improvement will afford an able proof of what the simple energy of virtue is capable of atchieving.

The religious opinions of Mr. Fox were, in general, what is termed orthodox: But, he was a man whom no sect could claim as its own. He never gave up to party "what was meant for mankind." His enthusiasm operated on his sentiments as genius influences all with which it is connected—it threw a peculiar tint over them, softening their asperities and bringing them all into a certain keeping and harmony, as imagination lends its loveliness to the passions over which it broods and leaves its light wherever it lingers. The abuses of the Evangelical world met with no indulgence from him, nor were the virtues and charities of the heterodox for a moment forgotten. He associated with men of all denominations to work out his holy purposes: and the Missionary Society, through all its hierarchies trembled before him.

On the great cause with which his name will for ever be associated, I forbear to dwell. At the term Universal Education such a crowd of blessings rush over the heart, that one is more disposed to enjoy their delicious confusion, than to analyse or to display them. It was the enthusiasm of Mr. Fox which so intimately connected him with that immortal cause; that enthusiasm which is the spring of every thing truly great; which can elevate ordinary beings to the level of genius, and attire man in a brightness not his own.

I venture to add a few lines as an humble tribute to the memory of my friend.* I am sorry they are not more worthy of him whom they attempt to celebrate. For I can never forget that I first knew him by his kind attentions to me when at school; and those I regard as among the most sacred claims upon gratitude.　　　　　　T. N. T.

*, Temple, 16th May, 1816.

On Wednesday the 10th of April, 1816, died at his house in Chichester, in the 43d year of his age, THOMAS PETTER POWELL, M. D.. He was the second son of an eminent surgeon at Smarden, in Kent, and was born there on the 30th of July, 1773. When seven years old he was sent to a day school in that town, where, under the superintendance of his father, he made some progress in the Latin grammar. At the age of ten he was placed under the tuition of the Rev. Mr. Cherry, of Maidstone. At thirteen he was removed to the King's School at Canterbury, but was not put on the foundation. In this ancient and respectable seminary he remained four years; and his proficiency was such as to render him a favourite of the learned master, the Rev. Dr. Naylor, and to enable him to read with facility and pleasure the Greek tragic poets. Leaving the King's School he returned to Smarden, and, under his father's roof, was initiated in the rudiments of his future profession, his leisure hours being devoted to keeping up and improving his classical attainments. In the year 1792, he entered on his medical studies at Edinburgh, and prosecuted them with singular diligence and success. His respected preceptor, Professor Duncan, sen. promoted him to the honourable and advantageous office of clinical clerk; and, in the last year of his academical course, the Royal Physical Society elected him one of their presidents. In 1795, he took his degree of Doctor of Physic, having chosen for the subject of his thesis the disease called acute Hydrocephalus; and this difficult topic he treated with much skill and discrimination. Having thoroughly availed himself of all the advantages afforded by his residence at Edinburgh, he passed one winter in attendance on the lectures and medical and chirurgical practice of Guy's and St. Thomas's Hospitals, and in 1796 entered into partnership with his father. In December, 1797, he married Miss WOOLDRIDGE, of Chichester, a young lady whose personal and mental qualifications fully justified his choice. In 1801, he quitted Smarden, and fixed himself at Northiam, a large and populous village near the eastern extremity of Sussex. Here he resided more than twelve years, dividing his time between

the labours and harassing duties of his calling, the care of a fast increasing family, and very assiduous application to study both professional and general. At length, finding his extensive practice as a medical surgeon and accoucheur too fatiguing, he removed in the beginning of the year 1814, to Chichester, with the purpose of confining himself to that department for which both his acquirements and his professional rank so well fitted him: In that city he hoped, with less emolument, to find more ease, more opportunity to study, and the enjoyment of more varied and desirable society. But Providence, doubtless for the wisest and kindest ends, often sees fit to disappoint the most reasonable expectations of man. Although in his youth Dr. Powell was extremely active, and capable of sustaining great and long continued exertions, there is reason to believe that his constitution was not of the firmest and most robust kind: and the incessant toil of thirteen years, added to the injurious effects of some accidents which had befallen him, had so fatally undermined it, that the more favourable circumstances of his residence at Chichester were altogether inadequate to its reparation. From the time of his arrival there, and, more remarkably from the autumn of last year, his health and habit were observed gradually to decline. The earnest efforts of his medical friends, his own suggestions, and the ablest assistance which this country can furnish, and which he received in the very particular attention paid by Dr. Baillie to his case, were all unavailing. He continued, however, notwithstanding his various oppressive maladies, to labour in his profession with undimished zeal till within a month of his decease, which was preceded by many days of unusual pain and suffering.

It is difficult to estimate Dr. Powell's character too highly. In his professional capacity he was eminently conspicuous for indefatigable diligence in the pursuit of knowledge, and for the prompt and judicious application of what he thus acquired in his practice. He was thoroughly instructed in all the branches of his business and in the sciences subsidiary to it. To be a good surgeon is the readiest and surest way to become a good physician. Of the truth of this remark Dr. P. afforded a striking example. Like his illustrious countryman, Dr. Harvey, he was peculiarly fond of the study of anatomy; and his acquaintance with this science was comprehensive and correct to a degree seldom found in a practitioner placed at a distance from opportunities of maintaining and improving it; but being accustomed to make extracts from what he read, or references to it, and being happy in the possession of a retentive memory, and skil-

---

* See Poetry, p. 295.

ful in managing it's treasures, he found his acquisitions always at hand, and ready for use. Such was his ardour for study, that neither fatigue, nor affliction, nor sickness (if not violent) prevented his application to it. With him, as with the President *Montesquieu*, it was a " never failing remedy for all the ills of life." From his knowledge of different languages and in the dialects of his native tongue, he was an eminently good judge in points relative to the derivation and filiation of words, and to phraseology in general. On subjects of metaphysical inquiry he had much acuteness and discrimination ; and if his skill in these topics was greater than his attachment to them, this was probably owing to his preference of studies in which certainty, or, at least, conviction was more easily to be attained, and of which the useful application was more obvious to his mind. With almost all subjects of history, civil and ecclesiastical, of rural and national economy, and of philosophy, natural and moral, he was conversant. Very few indeed were the topics of discussion to which Dr. P. did not bring a mind copiously stored with ideas, well assorted, and embodied into a comprehensive and instructive system. His amusements were those of a scholar and a man of taste. He wrote lively *vers de Société* with great facility and success. In music, both vocal and instrumental, he was no inferior proficient; and his fertile vein of wit and humour was a source of great entertainment to his familiar friends.

Dr. *Powell's* family, as well as that into which he married, were members of the society of *General Baptists*; but there is reason to believe that the rapidly increasing sect of *Anti-baptists* might fairly claim him as one of their own number. The *Baptists*, having no place of public worship open at *Chichester*, most of the very estimable individuals of that denomination have been for several years past attendants on the ministry of the Rev. Mr. *Fox*, the able and eminent pastor of the congregation of Unitarian dissenters in that city. Dr. P. was also one of Mr. Fox's constant hearers, not one of whom was better qualified to appreciate, or, in fact, more highly valued his services. It is believed that, in his religious opinions, he differed very little from his friend. It is certain that topics of controversial divinity had engaged no small portion of his attention, and he had fitted himself in a peculiar manner to judge of such topics by diligently studying the phraseology of the *New Testament* in its original language, which his philological skill enabled him to interpret in the most rational and satisfactory manner. That this, in conjunction with a thorough knowledge of the customs, modes of thinking, &c. prevalent among the Jews and first converts

to Christianity, and not the assiduous contemplation of discordant systems, or a partial attachment to any one system, is the proper foundation for the study of theology, has been most clearly shewn by the late *Professor Campbell*, in his *Introductory Lectures*, and sufficiently exemplified in the character and result of most of the controversies which have agitated the Christian world.

While at *Edinburgh*, Dr. P. was the spectator of a very stormy scene of political contention, and if he was not an actor in it, this arose from no want of zeal in favour of the party which, in his opinion, comprehended the friends of liberty and of popular claims. Through life he retained the same partiality, regulated, however, and repressed by the good sense and sound judgment which he applied to all subjects. Still it may be doubted whether he was sufficiently aware of a fact, the belief of which must be impressed on every calm and unprejudiced mind by even a superficial knowledge of history, and by a slight view of what, during the last five and twenty years, has passed under our own eyes. The fact alluded to is, that there are not in the world wise and virtuous people enough, to keep the foolish and vicious in order. One would imagine that this truth is too obvious to be overlooked and too important to be neglected, and that if it was duly attended to by reformers as well as anti-reformers, it would suggest a salutary lesson of moderation to both. It seems, to be the plan of Providence to restrain and check one class of crimes and delinquents by the counteraction of another. The *Ovidian* hemistich, *ponderibus librata suis*, is not more applicable to the system of the universe, and to the British constitution, than it is to the general frame of society, composed (as is the majority of it) of short-sighted, wilful and selfish human beings.

In his personal, social and domestic character, Dr. *Powell* was most exemplary. His anxiety for the welfare of his family impelled him to exertions beyond his strength. His benevolence was conspicuous in the professional attention which he bestowed on the poor, and which was not at all inferior to what he paid to the rich. He had the highest ideas of what is due to integrity and honour; and his conduct was altogether correspondent to his ideas. Before sickness had begun its ravages on his bodily frame, and rendered him somewhat querulous and irritable, he was remarkable for equanimity and sweetness of temper. To all but his familiar acquaintance his deportment was rather distant and reserved, and this made him less acceptable, than he otherwise would have been, to strangers.

Such was this able physician and excellent man, who devoted his life to useful and almost incessant labour in a situation where the hope of fame could not animate his exertions, or the acquisition of wealth reward them; but he is gone to a reward infinitely more valuable than the highest earthly distinctions.

His saltem accumulem donis, et fungar
    inani
Munere.   T. S.
   Chichester, May 2, 1816.

Lately, at Alphington, near Exeter, EDMUND CALAMY, Esq.——*Edmund Calamy* is a name ever-memorable in the annals of Nonconformity in this country, and dear to all the real friends of religious liberty and truth. The gentleman who is the subject of this memoir was bred to the profession of the law, and was in early life called to the bar; and after having, as a counsel, attended the courts in Westminster Hall for several years, he at length quitted his residence in the metropolis, and sought and found in the retirement of the country, that tranquillity and quietude which were suited to the habits of his mind. In private and domestic life, his conduct exhibited a pattern of those united virtues of humanity which are best calculated to render it amiable, useful and happy. His native urbanity and kindness, his obliging temper, and accommodating manners, together with the genuine humility, candour, courtesy and benevolence which marked his general deportment, rendered him beloved and respected by all those who were best acquainted with his character and the virtues of his heart: as they will ever endear his memory to an amiable family who are deploring his loss.——Mr. Calamy was for many years, during his residence in London, a highly respected member of the principal public Trusts amongst the Dissenters; as he was also concerned in the execution of several private Trusts which were committed to him in consequence of the high estimation in which he was justly held by a numerous circle of friends, for

uprightness, integrity and honour.—— Having been in a declining state of health for some time past, he finished his course on Sunday, the 12th of May, and was interred in a family vault in the burial-ground attached to the Protestant Dissenting Chapel at Gulliford, near Lympston, in Devonshire, his funeral being attended by several respectable friends.   ˈ

                              I. J.

On the 18th instant, Mr. STEPHEN PAUL, Engraver, of Blackman Street, Borough: he died (says a Correspondent) confiding to the care and protection of the *one and indivisible God,* a wife and seven children, the youngest only three months old, utterly unprovided for, and deprived of the means (by his long and protracted illness) of continuing the establishment.
                          Examiner.

On Thursday the 23rd instant, at his house, Brooksby's Walk, Homerton, aged 38 years, Mr. CALEB STOWER, the Printer of this Magazine from its commencement in 1806, and author of the Printer's Grammar and other Typographical works. He had been for some time drooping under a constitutional, pulmonary complaint, and was at length carried off in a rapid and distressing manner by a brain fever, which no medical directions or friendly attentions could abate. Difficulties in business probably aggravated his disorder, and clouded the last weeks of his life. He has left a widow and four children, to struggle with the world, without the help of an active-minded, kind-hearted husband and father.

April 12, at Draveil, near Paris, Mr. W. STONE, formerly of Rutland-Place Wharf and of Old Ford.

The Republic of Letters has just sustained a loss by the death of SIR HERBERT CROFT, who lived in *France,* for the last fifteen years.

INTELLIGENCE.

FOREIGN.

MISCELLANEOUS.

HERISAU, April 4.—The Government of Appenzel has expressed by a proclamation its grief on account of the emigration of a considerable number of weavers and other manufacturers, who carry with them branches of industry valuable to the Canton. Until a legislative decision, the *Préposés* of the Communes are invited to refuse passports to persons who desire them.

A second proclamation of the same date

is directed against the religious fanaticism, the excesses of which have excited the attention of Government. The Curés in particular are desired to be sedulously watchful as to the execution of the Ordonnances of moral police, and not to tolerate the introduction of fanatic or irreligious works.

Index Expurgatorius.——NICE, April 12. The Curés of this place have demanded that an Index should be published by authority of books to be read by the inhabitants. This demand is made on the ground of the dangerous tendency of the French principles of politics and philosophy which have spread amongst all classes.

They write from the *Hague* that the French Refugees have received orders to retire to the towns situated in the northern parts of the Netherlands.

ROME, April 17.—The reform in the Tribunals of the Inquisition and the Holy Office is continuing with activity, and will extend to all the countries where this institution exists. In the briefs addressed by his Holiness to the congregation charged with the labour, his Holiness says, "Do not forget that the way to render religion powerful in all States is to shew her divine and bringing to mankind only consolation and benefits; the precepts of our Divine Master, Love each other, ought to be the law of the universe."—All legal proceedings in religious matters shall be subjected to the forms of proceeding in civil and criminal matters: accusation, denunciation and inquisition, in matters of faith, cannot serve to begin a legal proceeding; it cannot be founded except in facts. Persons under a judicial sentence, the accomplices of the accused persons declared infamous by a court of justice, cannot be heard as witnesses. All persons, of whatever theological communion they may be, shall be admitted if they are called in exculpation by the accused. The relations and servants are excluded from being heard either for or against the accused. The proceedings shall be public, and no witnesses shall ever be allowed to adduce hearsay evidence.—His Eminence Cardinal Fontana has greatly contributed to get these judicial forms adopted, and it is an essential service which he has rendered to humanity and to religion. It is affirmed that as soon as the New Code is finished, it will be sent to all the Courts.

French Fanaticism.—The ceremonies of the Last Supper being too painful for his Majesty, who would have been obliged to remain long standing, it was Monsieur who filled the place of the King in this act of piety, practised by our Monarchs, from time immemorial, on Holy Thursday. Thirteen children of poor but honest parents were admitted to the honour of representing the Apostles. They were all in red tunics, and placed on benches sufficiently raised to enable the Prince, without stooping, to wash their feet, wipe them, and kiss them. Every child received from the hands of Monsieur a loaf, a small cruse of wine, thirteen plates, and thirteen five-franc pieces. The Dukes D'Angouleme and Berri performed the functions of waiters, and brought the bread, the wine and the meats. All these

ceremonies were gone through with piety and collectedness worthy the descendants of St. Louis. *Times, April 17.*

DOMESTIC.

RELIGIOUS.

Protest against the Marriage Ceremony.

April 28th was married Mr. Isaac Carter, of Shoreditch, to Miss Charlotte Southworth, when they delivered the following protest into the hands of the minister.

"To Mr.———, commonly called the Rev. Mr.———.—The undersigned, being Unitarian dissenters, present to you the following *protest* against the marriage ceremony, to which, according to the law of the land, they are compelled to subscribe; they disclaim all intention of acting disrespectfully to the legislature, or it's civil officer before whom they stand; they lament that they are placed in a situation so unnatural, as that even forbearance to what they consider as established error, would be a formal recantation of opinions, which they received on conviction, and which they will only renounce on similar grounds. Against the marriage ceremony then, they can but most solemnly protest, *Because* it makes marriage a religious instead of a civil act.

Because, as Christians and Protestant Dissenters, it is impossible we can allow of the interference of any human institution in matters which concern our faith and consciences.

Because, as knowing nothing of a priesthood in Christianity, the submission to a ceremony performed by a person "in holy orders, or pretended holy orders," is painful and humiliating to our feelings.

Because, as servants of Jesus, we worship the One living and True God, his God and our God, his Father and our Father, and disbelieve and abominate the doctrine of the *Trinity,* in whose name the marriage ceremony is performed.

Signed { ISAAC CARTER,
CHARLOTTE SOUTHWORTH,

members of the church of God, meeting at the Crescent, Jewin Street, and known by the names of Free-Thinking Christians."

Manchester College, York.

The following sums have been received on account of this Institution since the last report.

Mr. William Duckworth, Manchester. Annual Subscription, — — — — 3 3 0
Mr. Thomas Patter, Manchester, ditto, — — — — 2 2 0
Mr. Isaac Harrop, Altringham, ditto, — — — — 2 2 0
Mr. John Lees, Duckinfield, do. — 2 2 0
Mr. John Leech, ditto, ditto, — 2 2 0
Mr. George Cheetham, ditto, ditto, — — — — 3 3 0

Mr. Robert Lees, ditto, ditto,	2	2	0
Rev. Josiah Ashton, ditto, ditto, additional, - - - - -	1	1	0
Miss B. Lees, ditto, ditto, ditto,	1	1	0
Rev. William Whitelegg, Manchester, Annual Subscription,	1	1	0
Rev. Thomas Madge, Norwich, ditto, - - - - - -	2	2	0
Rev. W. J. Bakewell, Chester, ditto, - - - - - -	1	1	0
	23	2	0
Collection at Rochdale, by Rev. Mr. Elliott, - - - - -	10	0	0
Mrs. Markham, Shawhill, near Halifax, second benefaction	20	0	0
Thomas Berry Rowe, Esq. Brentford, benefaction, - -	25	0	0
A friend to the Rev. Charles Wellbeloved, - - - -	50	0	0
Mrs. Jones, Greenhill, near Manchester, for the purchase of books, - - - - -	50	0	0
Legacy from the late Swann Downer, Esq., London, paid in full, - - - - -	200	0	0
	£378	2	0

G. W. WOOD, TREASURER.
Manchester, May 11th, 1816.

Unitarian Chapel, Thorne, Yorkshire.
(Subscriptions continued from pp. 182 and 249.)

Amount of collection at Halifax, April 28th, by Rev. R. Astley,	11	10	6
Rev. John Kenrick, (York) -	0	10	6
Anonymous, by Mr. J. W. Morris, (York,) - - - -	1	1	0
A Friend, by ditto, - - -	0	10	6
Miss Rawdon, - - - - -	0	5	0
Rev. N. Philipps, (Sheffield,) -	1	1	0
Mr. Fox, (Sheffield,) - - -	1	1	0
Senex Cornubiensis, - - -	1	0	0
Rev. T. Smith, (Selby,) - -	0	5	0
Mr. Walker, (Leeds,) - - -	2	2	0
T. W. Tottie, Esq. (Leeds,) -	1	1	0
Robert Philipps, Esq. (Manchester,) - - - - -	5	5	0
Rev. Thomas Johnstone, (Wakefield,) - - - - -	1	0	0
Rev. B. Evans, Stockton, (by Mr. Aspland,) - - -	1	1	0

N.B. The Chapel will be opened on the 28th of June. There will be two services, one at 12 at noon and the other at 7 in the evening. There will be a collection after each service in aid of the expenses of the building. An economical dinner will be provided at the Royal Oak Inn, at 2 o'clock.

Opening of the New Chapel at Neath.
(From the Cambrian, Swansea Newspaper.)

On Thursday the 16th instant the New Unitarian Chapel at Neath, was opened for Divine worship. After an introductory address on the occasion, by the Rev. D. Davis, Mr. Aubrey read Matth. xx. and conducted the devotional part of the service, and preached from Rev. xviii. 4. A discourse in Welsh, on 1 Kings, viii. 18, was delivered by the Rev. T. Davies, of Coedycymmar, who concluded with prayer. The ability, candour, and charitable spirit evinced in the sermons, and the very impressive manner with which they were delivered, commanded profound attention from a numerous and most respectable audience. Although the day was very unfavourable, a great many attended from Swansea and its vicinity, and other parts, and contributed very liberally to the collection, which exceeded twenty pounds.

From the Cork Advertiser.—The following curious dialogue took place in Skibbereen Chapel, between a Mr. O'Driscol and the Rev. Michael Collins.—The priest was preaching a sermon, when he was addressed by Mr. O'Driscol; great animosities subsist between the parties in consequence of the question about the Veto :

"While I was speaking, a voice from the opposite gallery said something about the Pope; it was Mr. O'Driscol's. It struck me that he said the Pope had sanctioned the Veto. I denied the fact, and begged not to be interrupted." Mr. O'D. "I will interrupt you, as often as you allude to me or to my friends." Mr. C. "I have disclaimed personal allusions." Mr. O'D. "You are deluding the blind multitude; the poor creatures; a thousand millions have declared for the Veto." Mr. C. "A thousand millions! puh!" Mr. O'D. "Here is Lord Trimbleston's petition; read it." Mr. C. "Sir, I shall use my own discretion, and choose my own topics; do not interrupt me. I am here in the discharge of my lawful duties; no man has a *legal* right to obstruct me. If any man disapproves of what I say, let him withdraw; but let him not interrupt me." Mr. O'D. "You have no right to introduce *politics* here." Mr. C. "You are a magistrate?" Mr. O'D. "Yes." Mr. C. "If I say any thing illegal, prosecute me according to law." Mr. O'D. "If I saw you acting against the law, I would wink at it." Mr. C. "I don't want your winking, nor would I trust to it; but now I warn you, that in thus persisting to interrupt me, you are acting against law, and breaking the peace. The Catholic clergy have been charged with a design to subvert the constitution." Mr. O'D. "I did not charge them with that, I said, that in *meddling* with politics, they must have *other* intentions." Mr. C. "This is not a political question; I have not discussed it as such. I have treated it as it regards religion; I have a *right* to treat it in that view." Mr. O'D. "You have no right to talk *politics*." Mr. C. "Sir, I must tell you that you are very presumptuous." Mr. O'D. "I am not presumptuous; in any other place I would say something else." Mr. C. "I would tell you so here, or elsewhere. Strange doctrines have been introduced by persons retaining the name of Catholics, and renouncing the principles of that religion. It has been said that Lords Fingal and Trimbleston are as competent judges of ecclesiastical subjects as the Bishops or the Pope. According to the principles of the Catholic Church, no individual has a right to interpret the Scriptures, save in the sense of that church, nor to act or decide in matters of religious concern otherwise than according to ecclesiastical laws and discipline. This is the doctrine of the church; any individual denying this doctrine ceases to be a Catholic." Mr. O'D. "I differ with you; it is no such thing." Mr. C. "Sir, I have taken some pains to acquire a competent knowledge of the religion, which, as a pastor, I am bound to teach; I have taken more pains in that way than you have, and I believe I am not over-rating my slender powers by saying, that I am as capable of acquiring knowledge as you are. You will therefore allow me to state those principles. If you dissent from the tenets of the Catholic church, you have a right to separate from her communion. But you have no right to impugn those tenets in the face of a Catholic congregation, and to the obstruction of their pastor."—Here the dialogue ceased.

MISCELLANEOUS.

Prince Regent's Notice of French Protestants.—On Monday, April 29, the address and petition of the city of London with respect to the French Protestants was presented to his Royal Highness, who returned the following answer:—

"The just sense entertained by his Majesty's subjects of the value and importance of religious toleration is necessarily calculated to excite in their minds strong feelings of uneasiness and regret, at any appearance of the want of it in other nations of the world.

"In such feelings, *when called for and justified by the occasion*, I shall ever participate, and whilst I lament the circumstances which led to your address, I derive great satisfaction from the persuasion, that they are in no degree to be attributed to an indisposition on the part of the Government of France, to afford to the freedom of religious worship, the benefit of its promised protection and support."

The rector of Framlingham, in Suffolk,

soon after the battle, wrote to the Duke of Wellington, stating, that in his opinion, the non-commissioned officers of the British army, had by their valorous conduct on that day entitled themselves to some distinct marks of their country's approbation, and therefore he felt disposed for one, to offer his humble tribute to their merit. In order that this might be properly applied, he requested the favour of his Grace to point out to him the non-commissioned officer, whose heroic conduct, from the representations which his Grace had received, appeared the most prominent, to whom he, the rector, meant to convey in perpetuity, a freehold farm, value 10l. per annum. The Duke set the enquiry immediately on foot, through all the commanding officers of the line, and, in consequence, learnt that a serjeant of the Coldstream, and a corporal of the 1st regiment of Guards, had so distinguished themselves, that it was felt difficult to point out the most meritorious; but that there had been displayed by the serjeant an exploit arising out of fraternal affection, which he felt it a duty on this occasion to represent, viz:— That near the close of the dreadful conflict, this distinguished serjeant impatiently solicited the officer commanding his company, for permission to retire from the ranks for a few minutes; the latter expressed some surprise at this request, the other said, "Your honour need not doubt of my immediate return." Permission being given him, he flew to an adjoining barn, to which the enemy in their retreat had set fire, and from thence bore on his shoulders his wounded brother, who he knew lay helpless in the midst of the flames. Having deposited him safely for the moment, under a hedge, he returned to his post in time to share in the victorious pursuit of the routed enemy; we need scarcely add, that the superior merit of this gallant non-commissioned officer was thus established.

Battle of Waterloo, 8*th. ed. p.* 84.

NOTICES.

The Annual Meeting of the Members of the *Unitarian Tract Society* established in *Birmingham,* for *Warwickshire* and the neighbouring counties, will be holden at Oldbury, in Shropshire, on Wednesday, June 19, 1816. The Rev. John Small, of Coseley, has engaged to preach on the occasion.

The Devon and Cornwall Unitarian Association and Tract Society will be held at Moreton Hampstead, on the first Wednesday in July next, when Mr. Worsley, of Plymouth, is appointed to preach, and it is hoped Mr. Butcher, of Sidmouth, will conduct the devotional part of the service.

We are informed, that the minister at Lynn and his friends having declined receiving the members of the *North-eastern Unitarian Association*, to hold their annual meeting in that town, according to a former notice, that association will be held at *Wisbeach*, on *Thursday, June - the Twenty-seventh.* There will also be a public service on Wednesday evening, June 26.

Manchester College, York.

The annual examination of students will take place as usual at the close of the session, in the College Library, York, on Tuesday, Wednesday and Thursday, the 25th, 26th and 27th of June. The York annual meeting of trustees will be held at Etridge's Hotel, on the evening of Wednesday, the 26th, when all applications for the admission of divinity students on the foundation will be taken into consideration and decided upon.

'The friends of the institution will dine together at Etridge's Hotel, at the close of the second and third days' examination.'

As a considerable accession of new students is expected next session, it is particularly requested, that gentlemen intending to enter as lay students will make application as early as possible, in order that the necessary accommodation may be provided for them.

THOMAS HENRY ROBINSON, } Secretaries.
J. G. ROBBERDS, }

Manchester, May 11, 1816.

MONTHLY RETROSPECT OF PUBLIC AFFAIRS;

OR,

The Christian's Survey of the Political World.

THE situation of the Protestants in France has long been a subject of great uneasiness to the friends of true religion. The bloodshed in Nismes and its district excited the commiseration of every British heart that was not led away by the base calumny that Protestantism was only another word for Jacobinism. Under this latter word it is well known that the speaker means to convey an idea of all the horrors perpetrated in the violent stages of the French revolution. Strange, however, it is, that crimes attended with such infamy should not deter others from the imitation of so horrible a conduct; yet future ages may perhaps class Jacobinism and Bourbonism together as the parents of enormities at which humanity shudders.

The efforts made by various bodies in England to place this subject in its proper colours before the public are well known. A subscription was raised and information was procured which might satisfy the most incredulous. Still it was the interest of certain persons to stifle the discussion, and discourage the benevolence of England, and, to a certain degree, their measures succeeded. It was contended that the whole was a political feud, that religious opinions had nothing to do with it, that our government could not possibly interfere, or if it did, that its interference would be only disadvantageous to the suffering party. Above all, it was contended that the Bourbons could not be at all to blame in this matter as they were perfectly friendly to religious freedom.

A debate in the House of Commons has enabled every person to form an accurate judgment on all these points; and we are much indebted to Sir Samuel Romilly for taking up the question, for stating facts as they really occurred and for making those comments on the celebrated letter of the Duke of Wellington which it really deserved. Lord Castlereagh took, as might be imagined, the other side of the question; but in spite of all his sophisms he corroborated these facts in such a manner, that it can be no longer a doubt that murders and massacres to an incredible amount were perpetrated at Nismes and its neighbourhood, and that the murderers were suffered to escape with impunity, though the government is strong enough to repress inferior crimes without difficulty.

We will not repeat here all the horrors committed by the Bourbonites upon this occasion. We trust that the speeches of Sir Samuel Romilly, Lord Castlereagh and Mr. Brougham will be faithfully reported in a separate publication with such notes as may tend still more to excite an horror of religious persecution. Notwithstanding the solicitude that our papers should not have a free circulation in France, we have no doubt that the debate will find its way into that country; and at any rate the other nations of Europe will feel for the unhappy sufferers in France, and hold in abhorrence that anti-christian spirit which leads a man to injure, insult and murder his neighbour on account of his religious opinions.

Above all the reflection on what has happened in France ought to make us grateful to Providence for the comparative ease which we enjoy in this country. Though our opinions differ so widely from those of the sects established by law in this island, and we who bow to no authority but that of Christ in matters of religion, are so small a body compared with those who blend with the precepts of our Saviour rules derived from human tradition and the laws or fashion of the country, yet how happy is our state compared with that of the early Christians under the Roman emperors. We are not called upon as they were to sacrifice our lives in support of our faith, and the danger we have to apprehend is not from persecution, but the indifference which such a state of ease is apt to create. The fascinations of the world may be as dangerous as its hatred, and if we do not impress upon our children the importance of our religious faith, it may be undermined by the seductions of interest. The Israelites did not all at once fall down before Baal; yet when his worship was supported by the court, by fashion, by interest, the worshippers of the true God gradually diminished till there were left only seven thousand men who had not bowed the knee to the idol. In fact, nothing can preserve us and our children but the full conviction that as our Saviour has said, "to know the Father as the only true God, and to acknowledge the Christ sent by him is eternal life," and that to leave our Saviour on account of fashion or interest, or the palpable deceit of innocent compliance with a false worship, is a dereliction of duty disgraceful to ourselves and attended with most dangerous consequences. We cannot serve God and Mammon. We cannot adore one God in our hearts and with our lips offer up prayers to three Gods. Let those who pretend to be Unitarians and yet frequent Trinitarian worship consider this.

A subject of a temporal nature was introduced into the House, and though it did not lead to immediate amendment, yet at a future time the change recommended will probably be adopted. The word usury conveys an odious impression which is encouraged by the absurd epithets annexed to it in our laws. The use of money is supposed to be essentially different from that of any other commodity, and the divine and the landholder have united their forces together to establish the prejudice. The former grounds his opinion upon some passages in scripture perverted from their real meaning, the latter from selfish motives wished to secure to

himself advantages above the rest of the community to which least of all men is he entitled. The consequence of this false policy is, that the landholder cannot at present obtain a loan of money but at a much greater rate of interest than the state of the money market requires. As the law stands, five per cent is the utmost annual sum that can be received for a loan of money, but as the holders of money can make more of it than by lending at this rate, a borrower is put to his shifts to obtain a loan. The law is avoided in this manner. The borrower grants an annuity to the lender during the life of the longest of three lives named by him, redeemable on a notice specified by the deed. This annuity amounts in general to ten per cent, though sometimes the money may be got at nine, and thus in another name the borrower pays from nine to ten per cent for that sum which he might obtain, if it were not for the law, at six or seven per cent. The borrower also pays all the law expences on the transaction, which are considerable.

The absurdity of the law is evident from its not distinguishing between the different securities on which money is lent. Thus, if five per cent is a fair price for money secured on land, a greater rate is certainly to be required if it is lent merely on simple bond. Many have been the merchants and tradesmen ruined by this law, for a loan at a certain time would have preserved them, though they paid for it at the rate of ten or fifteen per cent, and the injury done to the landed and commercial interests by it may be estimated at many millions annually.

In support of this law it is argued by administration that their loans would not be so cheaply made as they are at present. But it is not considered that the trifling gain upon their loans bears no proportion to the injury occasioned to the community by the losses which it sustains. The landholder also thinks it a preventative to spend-thrifts whose estates might be swallowed up by their improvident bargains, as if it were of consequence to the state what became of such wretches, and the interest of a few individual families is not to be put in competition with the general good of the country. The real fact is, that the landholders in this as in some other instances, take an unfair advantage of their situation. They have looked too much to their own supposed interests, and have paid too little attention to what is due to the community at large.

A still more important question was brought forward, but the agitation of it is deferred till the next sessions of parliament, and if the promoters of the bill succeed, the consequence to the kingdom may be in a high degree detrimental. The readers of this report were favourable to the abolition of the slave trade, and with just reason, but the abolition of that trade and the emancipation of the blacks in the West Indies are two distinct questions. In the former case the right and propriety of parliament to legislate cannot be doubted, for it is a question intelligible by every member of the House. But the emancipation of the blacks or measures tending to it are questions of a very different nature, and involve the knowledge of the relations of several classes of people to each other in our West India islands. The abolition of slavery throughout the world is a desirable object, but care must be taken not to increase the evil nor to obtain our end by unjustifiable means. Mr. Wilberforce announces his intention to bring in a bill next sessions for registering all the slaves in the West India islands, and this is to be done under technical forms of law very oppressive to proprietors and very expensive to the colonies. Many a good job will be created by them, and salaries here and abroad are to be multiplied. The intended measure has created very great alarm in the colonies, for it strikes at the root of their internal legislation, and excites among the slaves a restlessness which renders the masters apprehensive of similar scenes being acted in their islands as, have taken place in St. Domingo: The promoters of the bill out of parliament have not in the mean time been inactive; they have published writings teeming with false and injurious accusations of the planters for their conduct towards the slaves, and endeavouring to make them odious to their fellow subjects in England. Under the specious head of humanity to one class of mankind, they are guilty of inhumanity to another class; and laying hold of the interest taken by this country in the abolition of the slave trade, they aim at a new species of legislation which shall put the planters at their mercy, and hasten their object of emancipation. It is necessary that the humane should be put on their guard against these false pretences, and be particularly careful not to be led away on this subject by the appeal made to Christianity; for the language of Scripture is very different from that used ou this occasion by the supporters of this intended bill, and our religion was never intended to interfere rudely between the master and slave, but to introduce such dispositions as would gradually overcome every evil belonging to servitude.

Both Houses were occupied in a debate, on what, though trifling at first sight, is of great importance: This was the stationing of the military in various places adjoining to the palace on certain court days. Military parade is the great feature of arbitrary governments, and cannot be permitted in a free state without danger to its constitution. For by being accustomed to see soldiers performing the duty of constables, the people will gradually lose the distinction between those two characters; and thus the military will, in time, as was the case in France, usurp all the employments of the civil power, be seen in the corners of every street, and the nation will be enslaved, and no slavery is so bad as that exercised by one part over the other of the fellow subjects. In submitting to the bayonet of a foreign soldier, a tacit respect is paid to the right of conquest; but in crouching under the sabre of ones own countrymen, the mind is degraded, rendered abject and vile, and he is fit only to lord it in his turn on similar degraded beings. This was felt by two noble lords whose progress in the open streets had been resisted by soldiers, and they complained of this outrage in their respective Houses. Both Houses entered into their feelings, and the result was a promise on the part of administration that care should be taken to remedy the evil by placing the whole under the controul of the civil power, and at a following court day the constables were seen in their proper places.

But the measure of the greatest consequence has been introduced by Lord Stanhope, which is to digest our laws in such a manner that they may be intelligible to lawyers and people. At present it is well known that the latter have no chance of understanding them, and of the former very few indeed have time, application and abilities to do it. A committee is to be formed of both Houses with proper assistants for the laborious task, which if properly executed will be highly beneficial to the country.

Disturbances have appeared in France, but to what extent it is not easy to determine. Grenoble is said to have been taken at one time by the insurgents, whose defeat was attended with executions of some and high rewards for the apprehensions of other ringleaders. The French press is so completely subjugated, that an insurrection might extend over half of the kingdom without the good people of Paris knowing any thing about it but by private information, or on its defeat by government. Their parliament has been prorogued and our three countrymen have been tried. Whatever opinion may be entertained of the nature of the misdemeanour for which they were indicted, all parties concurred in applauding their spirited and manly conduct in their defence. The court was crowded by the principal people of both nations, English and French, at Paris, who were admitted only by tickets, and the French had an opportunity of seeing the difference between minds formed under English liberty and French slavery. The sentence was three-months' imprisonment, and it is to be hoped that this interesting trial will, on the return home of our countrymen, be given faithfully to the public.

The eye recoils with horror on a view of Spain. The officers of the Inquisition boarding ships to examine books, and the defenders of their country suffering torture, are objects too shocking to humanity. It seems as if the legitimate sovereigns were determined to convince mankind that usurpation and exclusion were highly justifiable actions. Where success attends the Spaniards in America, cruelty harrows up the feelings in the rear of their armies.

At home the satisfaction was general on the marriage of the presumptive Heiress to the Crown to a young prince of a respectable family in Germany, the head of which was made royal by Buonaparte. Such a marriage does not involve with it foreign alliances or foreign subsidies. But this event was followed by the distressing intelligence of dissatisfaction in several counties on the price of corn, which had broken into tumultuous riotings. These were chiefly confined to parts of Suffolk, Norfolk and Cambridgeshire. They who are at the head of affairs will follow Lord Bacon's advice we trust upon such subjects.

NEW PUBLICATIONS IN THEOLOGY AND GENERAL LITERATURE.

History of the Origin and First Ten Years of the British and Foreign Bible Society. By J. Owen, A. M. 2 vols. 8vo. 1l. 4s. Royal 1l. 15s.

A Second Letter to the Bishop of St. David's. By a Lay Seceder.

Prospectus of a Polyglott Bible, in Six Languages. In 4 pocket volumes or 1 volume 4to. with the Prefaces and Specimens of each Language.—12mo. 1s.

Religious Freedom in Danger; or the Toleration Act invaded by Parochial Assessments on Places of Religious Worship. By Rowland Hill, M.A. 8vo. 1s.

The Sequel to an Appeal to the Yearly Meeting of Friends, on Thomas Foster's Excommunication for asserting the Unity, Supremacy and Sole Deity of God the Father. 8vo. 4s.

Persecution of French Protestants.

Resolutions and Statements, relative to the Persecution of the French Protestants, extracted from the Proceedings of the General Body of Protestant Dissenting Ministers of the Three Denominations in and about the Cities of London and Westminster. 8vo. 6d.

Statement of the Persecution of the Protestants in France since the Restoration of the Bourbon Family. By the Rev. Ingram Cobbin. 3rd edition. 8vo. 4s.

The Cause of the French Protestants Defended against the Attacks of the Christian Observer. By the Rev. I. Cobbin. 8vo. 1s.

Peace and Persecution incompatible with each other: An Address on the Persecution of the Protestants in the South of France, delivered at Worship Street, Finsbury Square, Thursday, January 18, 1816, the Thanksgiving Day for the Peace. By John Evans, A.M. 8vo. 1s. 6d.

The Fatal Effects of Religious Intolerance: A Sermon preached at Gateacre Chapel, Sunday, Dec. 17, 1815, in recommendation of a Subscription for the Relief of the Persecuted Protestants in France, and published for their Benefit. By the Rev. William Shepherd. 8vo. 1s. 6d.

A Sermon on Universal Benevolence, containing some Reflections on Religious Persecution and the alleged Proceedings at Nismes. By the Rev. James Archer. (Catholic Priest.) 8vo.

Perfect Religious Liberty the Right of Every Human Being, and Persecution for Conscience' Sake the most atrocious of Crimes: Proved in a Sermon, preached on Dec. 10, at Hemel Hempstead, for the Benefit of the Persecuted Protestants in France. By John Liddon. 1s.

Notes, intended as Materials for a Memoir, on the Affairs of the Protestants of the Department Du Gard. By the Committee of Dissenting Ministers at Williams's Library. 8vo. 1s. 6d.

The French Preacher; containing Select Discourses, translated from the Works of the most eminent French Divines, Catholic and Protestant, with

Biographical Notices of the Authors, and a Characteristical Account of many distinguished French Preachers. To which is prefixed, An Historical View of the Reformed Church of France, from its Origin to the present Time. By Ingram Cobbin. 8vo. 12s.

On the late Persecution of the Protestants in the South of France. By Helen Maria Williams. 3s. 6d.

Baptism.

Two Tracts, intended to convey correct notions of Regeneration and Conversion, according to the Sense of the Holy Scriptures and the Church of England. Extracted from the Bampton Lectures of 1812. By Richard Mant, D.D. Chaplain to the Archbishop of Canterbury, and Rector of St. Botolph's, Bishopsgate. 1s. 6d.

An Enquiry into the Effect of Baptism, according to the Sense of Holy Scripture and of the Church of England; In Answer to the above. By the Rev. John Scott, M.A. Vicar of North Ferriby, &c. 8vo. 5s. sewed.

Baptism a Seal of the Christian Covenant, or Remarks on Regeneration, &c. In Answer to the same. By T.T. Biddulph, A.M. Minister of St. James's, Bristol. 8vc. 5s. sewed.

On Terms of Communion, with a Particular View to the Case of the Baptists and Pædobaptists. By the Rev. Robert Hall, A.M. 8vo. 5s. 3d edition.

The Essential Difference between Christian Baptism and the Baptism of John, more fully stated and confirmed; In Reply to a Pamphlet, entitled "A Plea for Primitive Communion." By Robert Hall, A.M. 8vo. 2s.

Baptism, a Term of Communion at the Lord's Supper. By J. Kinghorn. 8vo. 4s.,

A Practical View of Christian Baptism, addressed particularly to Parents intending to devote their Children to God in that Ordinance. By William Harris. 1s. fine. 6d. common.

Scriptural Regeneration not necessarily connected with Baptism, in answer to Dr. Mant. By G. Bugg, A.B. 3s.

CORRESPONDENCE.

In consequence of the calamitous event recorded in our Obituary department (p. 300), we are constrained to shorten some articles and to omit others designed for the present Number.

Our *Bristol* correspondent, J. B. is referred to, *Bp. Law's. Considerations* for an answer to his question.

J. T. is informed that the names of the publishers of new works cannot be introduced into the monthly list without subjecting them to a charge from the Stamp Office as advertisements.

ERRATA.

THE

𝔐onthly 𝔑epository,
&c.

| No. CXXVI.] | JUNE, 1816. | [Vol. XI. |

HISTORY AND BIOGRAPHY.

Oration delivered at the Library, Red-Cross-Street, London, February 7, 1816, being the Centenary of the Founder's Death; by James Lindsay, D. D.

· BRETHREN AND FRIENDS,

I SHOULD justly incur the charge of presumption, if I did not state the circumstances to which I am indebted for an unmerited precedence among so many colleagues, who could have addressed you on the present occasion with greater talent and better effect. To our visitors this statement is especially due. The father of our Trust, who has been more than forty years its most efficient member; whose fame is coextensive with the world of science; whose learning and virtues shed lustre upon our body, and to whom we all look up with respect and affection—is present, and in the chair.* The question naturally occurs, why he has not been selected to celebrate the memory of his own countryman, and to distinguish this day, as it ought to be distinguished, by weight of character and elegance of panegyric? I am bound to exculpate the members of the Trust from what might otherwise be imputed to the want of discrimination :—Our united voice would have called him to a post, which no other can fill with equal dignity; but in pleading precarious health and urgent avocations, he resisted *our* importunities, and has disappointed *your* expectations. Next to our father in standing as a trustee, and in all the qualifications which would entitle him to be the eulogist of our excellent founder, is that venerable brother who, with a mental eye yet clear and strong, can unfortunately claim exemption on the lamented ground of bodily darkness.† I am third in the order of seniority;

and to that cause alone do I owe an office, which I should feel as an honour if it were not for the painful consciousness that I am addressing men in every respect so much my superiors. Happily the occasion does not demand those arts of an ostentatious oratory, so often employed to deck out vice in the garb of virtue. We are not here to bestow the praise of talent upon the baseness of political intrigue; or to exalt into heroes the scourges of the human race; or to canonize monks and hermits, because they have been the ignorant tools or the hired advocates of ecclesiastical domination. We burn no incense at the shrine of ambition, and heap no praises upon those who consecrate ambition by naming it religion :—those restless spirits who embroil the world to enrich or to immortalize themselves ;—princes, who in extending the boundaries of empire contract the limits of freedom and happiness ;—statesmen who plan, and warriors who fight, that they may found a name upon the ruins of honest industry and the destruction of human life ;—priests who, instead of being messengers of peace, to allay the angry passions of mankind, become, whenever it suits the purposes of the state which supports them, the trumpeters of discord to irritate the phrensy which it is their duty to restrain. These may constitute fit themes of panegyric to pensioned orators and venal poets :—the praises of an enlightened piety and an honest patriotism will be reserved for very different subjects.

He who came not to destroy men's lives, but to save them, has imparted to us far other views of that glory which ought to be the chosen object of a Christian's ambition. He who shared the secret counsels of divine wisdom, and knew what true and lasting glory is, has instructed us in the means by which he obtained himself, —by which every one of us, in our

---

* The Rev. Abraham Rees, D. D.
† Rev. Thomas Tayler.

measure, may obtain,—that honour which cometh only from God. He aspired not at that baneful fame which is seized by diabolical skill and animal courage in fields of death,—which history records in blood, which charity defaces with tears; which, if there is justice in heaven, will be the subject of an awful retribution in that world where the destroyers of life will meet themselves a more terrible destruction. To the desire of such fame as this the doctrine and the life of Jesus are directly opposed. His was the glory of pouring the light of divine truth into the dark and bewildered mind, and of delivering it, by just conceptions of the moral government of God, from that bondage of ignorance and superstition, which constitutes its degradation and its misery. His was the glory of speaking promises of rest to the weary and the heavy-laden; of taking the desponding penitent by the hand, and leading him direct, without the intervention of priests or sacrifices, to the mercy-seat of a Father ever ready to forgive, ever anxious to bless even his prodigal child. His was the glory of exposing that pride and covetousness, which establishes an usurped dominion over the rights of conscience, under the hypocritical pretence of zeal for God;—an usurpation which was, and unhappily yet is, employed by men in power, to exalt the few, enslave the many, and defeat the efforts of enlightened benevolence for the peace and improvement of the human race:—to break down every wall of partition which divides man from his brother, and to bind the rational creation of God together by the tie of a common faith, a common hope, and a common charity; to extirpate the base passions which embroil the world, by implanting in the heart that love of God and virtue which elevates and sanctifies all its affections; and thus to spread a divine influence over the pursuits and enjoyments of mortality: —in one word, to restore simplicity to religion, purity to morals, dignity to the minds, and immortality to the hopes of rational beings:—this was the ambition, this the glory of the great Captain of our Salvation,—the joy set before him; for which he endured the cross, despising the shame, and is in consequence set down at the right hand of the Majesty on high.

But it may be asked, How is this connected with the occasion of our meeting? In my judgment, closely. We must know the true nature of Christian glory, before we can select the proper objects of Christian admiration, or confer a suitable tribute of Christian eulogy. He only who imbibes a portion of the same spirit, who acts upon the same views, who co-operates according to his abilities in promoting the same ends to which we have just alluded, as the ends of our great Master;—he only merits the name and the honours of a Christian hero; and it is upon this ground alone that we have assembled to express our veneration for the character and memory of Dr. Daniel Williams. It is not by splendour of birth, of brilliancy of genius, or any of those qualities or deeds which dazzle a vain imagination, that this veneration is excited. No. But it is because our founder voluntarily abridged even that splendour which his fortune might have commanded;—it is because he voluntarily devoted solid talents and useful learning to the duties of a profession which the world despised, and from which he expected and received no worldly advantage;—it is because he preferred the simplicity of dissenting worship, and the full possession of Christian liberty, to the favours of the great, which he might have enjoyed ;— because he chose rather to be the honest, disinterested champion of truth and freedom, than to bask in the sunshine of courts and churches ;—because he thus formed one in that illustrious band, who have maintained the rights of conscience against the usurpations of power, and blessed their posterity with greater privileges than they themselves inherited ;—it is because, after establishing so many claims to respect by an upright and honourable life, he perpetuated the effect of his beneficence, in devoting his worldly substance, upon a wise and liberal plan, to the instruction of ignorance, the diffusion of knowledge, and the encouragement of rational religion. It is because Dr. Williams acted thus piously, thus nobly, living and dying, that the trustees of his bounty, after the lapse of a century, during which his bequests have been the means of instructing, and we hope of saving thousands, meet themselves, and have brought their friends with them, to express their own thankfulness to Providence for having raised him up, and to venerate those virtues which have given him a name by rendering him a benefactor to mankind. These are the peaceful claims of a private man, which, in the eye of the thoughtless and the proud, are destitute of interest. But they are, in fact, and I hope and believe in your estimation, above all Greek—above all Roman praise.

It may be expected, perhaps, that I should enter into some details relative to the life of Dr. Williams; but this would not be consistent with the brevity of such an address: besides, the necessity is precluded by a short memoir,* written, with his usual perspicuity and information, by our excellent friend and librarian.† I shall therefore merely observe, that, judging from his writings, our founder was evidently a man of strong natural powers, of considerable learning and acuteness; and, what is still more to his credit, whilst he steadily defends what he conceived to be important truth, he discovers that spirit of candour which ought ever to distinguish, though it too seldom has distinguished, the Christian controversialist. His religious sentiments were orthodox, according to the common acceptation of that word, though not orthodox enough to satisfy the bigots of his time, by whom he was accused of the horrid crime of Socinianism. Had he lived till now amidst increasing light, there is reason to believe that he would have imbibed what we think more rational and enlarged views of the Christian doctrine: and from the candour which he exhibited, when candour was not very common, we may pronounce with assurance, that, whatever might have been his religious opinions, he would have yielded to none of us in liberality towards those who might have held a different creed. In character he stood high, not only in his own immediate connexion, but among Dissenters in every part of the British dominions. And no wonder. For his labours were abundant and disinterested. He very properly insisted, indeed, upon his annual salary from his congregation, who could well afford it; but none of it went to increase his own fortune. It was wholly devoted

to purposes of charity, and he showed them at the end of the year how it had been expended;—an example of generosity which, whilst it enhances his honour, should put to the blush those miserable creatures who, with coffers running over, are deaf to every call, either of public benefit or private distress. His politics were those of freedom. Fearful lest the machinations of the High Church party should defeat the Protestant succession, he remonstrated boldly on that subject with Lord Oxford, to whom he was well known, and incurred his resentment because he communicated his fears to others. But his principles were, to him more dear than the favour of the great; and his adherence to rectitude on this occasion received an appropriate reward. For the displeasure of a tory minister was soon compensated by the approbation of a constitutional king, to whom, at the head of the dissenting body of ministers, he delivered a congratulatory address on his accession to the throne. He had formerly been consulted by William III., one of the few princes who have had the wisdom and the manly condescension of mind to advise with such a character. His counsels were congenial to the private opinions of that truly great man, who, had he been permitted to follow his own inclinations, would have extended the limits of religious freedom much further than the prevailing toryism of the country would permit. But Dr. Williams's solid claim to fame rests upon the favour or displeasure of the great, only as these were indications of his unshaken and disinterested integrity. With us he stands upon higher ground. · Though dead, he yet speaketh. His best monument is that charity which for a century has been communicating instruction to youth, administering the consolations of religion to age, and giving relief to indigence and deprivation. This charity embraces various objects; but these so wisely combined, that they all concur in promoting one great end—the spread of religious knowledge, in connexion with that liberty which alone can render it efficient as the means of promoting rational piety and social happiness. His first object was to establish schools in the different parts of the country where his different properties lay; and in these schools more than

* Communicated to *Mon. Repos.* and inserted Vol. X. p. 201---203.

† The Rev. Thomas Morgan.

200 poor children receive annually that kind of education which is suited to their circumstances; whilst the endowment for this purpose, forms an important addition to the little stipend of those dissenting ministers to whose care our schools are committed. His next aim was to furnish a few young men seriously disposed to embrace the profession of religious teachers among Protestant Dissenters, with those advantages from which they are excluded by the universities of this country. With this view he established exhibitions at the college of Glasgow; and, owing to the increased value of his estates, and the care and fidelity with which the produce of them is husbanded and applied by this trust, we are now enabled to assist eight young men annually at that college, besides giving occasional aid to several more at other institutions. Thus numerous students derive from our funds the means of that liberal education which qualifies them for being honourable and useful ministers of Christ, among Protestant Dissenters in England and Wales. It was the intention of our founder in this bequest to provide a succession of men who, subjected to no test, and acknowledging no ecclesiastical jurisdiction, might be nursed in the very bosom of freedom; might be encouraged to think without bias or constraint, and to speak conscientiously and boldly what they think. This is the inestimable advantage of our dissent. It was seen and appreciated by our founder, and he was anxious to do his part that it might be rendered perpetual: nor have his efforts been vain. Many of those who, for almost a century, have distinguished themselves amongst us as the advocates of a simple worship, a rational belief, and a truly gospel liberty, have been indebted to his funds for that learning which enabled them in their day to uphold the cause of truth and piety. These are considerations which cannot but speak to the judgment of any impartial man who looks into our history. For there he will see, how much freedom, and the consequent prosperity of the kingdom, have been owing to the barrier erected by Dissenters against those encroachments on the rights of conscience to which even the most moderate establishments have a natural tendency. How much more power-

fully then should such considerations speak to the heart of that Protestant Dissenter, who regards religious freedom as the best foundation of all that is truly excellent and dignified in the moral nature of man? If we set any value upon our own principles, if we believe what some of our adversaries have been forced to confess, that to these principles, asserted by our forefathers at the expense of persecution and blood, our country itself is chiefly indebted for that share of civil and religious privileges which it enjoys; if we are persuaded that the same principles, more generally understood and more widely diffused, would extend and perfect this liberty with all the rational views of truth and piety that are connected with it;—then what respect, what gratitude do we not owe to the memory of a man who has done so much, living and dying, to encourage and propagate these principles, and to render them efficient for the great purposes of godliness and virtue?

One thing more was necessary to complete the beneficent design of our pious founder. There was no public library in this great metropolis, to which Dissenters, as Dissenters, might have easy access. The sagacity of Dr. Williams perceived, and his munificent love of learning supplied, the defect. He purchased the curious books of Dr. Bates, and adding them to his own, formed a valuable collection, which, by the donations of Dissenters, and even of liberal Churchmen, and recently by an annual sum of 50l. from our funds, has been greatly increased. Every lay Trustee gives a donation of ten guineas when he enters upon the trust; and if other wealthy individuals amongst us, who have the honour of our institution at heart, would remember it as they ought, we might soon have to boast one of the most valuable and magnificent collections in this capital. This is not all. The house in which we are now assembled, built in compliance with our founder's will, has become, through the liberality of the trustees, the place of public business to the collective body of Dissenters in this great city; a place, in which noble stands have often been made against ecclesiastical usurpation; in which generous efforts have originated to promote the extension of religious privileges to men of all persuasions;—a central point, round which the friends of religious freedom in every part of Britain rally, and from which even recently a spirit has gone forth, by which the bigots and persecutors of another country are abashed, at least, if not finally overcome.

Having thus laid before you a short account of the objects which Dr. Williams contemplated, in a scheme so wisely planned, so nobly endowed,—permit me to say, (and from the small share of merit that I can claim in the management, I trust I may be exempted from the imputation of vanity, when I do say confidently,) that no trust was ever discharged with more care, or applied with more disinterested fidelity to fulfil the intentions of the founder. If that founder could have foreseen that men who were to be the ornaments of science as well as of religion,—the Chandlers and Kippises, —the Prices and Priestleys, — the Reeses and Belshams of the coming age;—the future champions of that learning and freedom which he loved: —if he could have foreseen that such men would have given their time and labour to promote the objects of his piety, it would have added one delightful feeling more to those which must have passed through his mind, in contemplating the probable effects of his own beneficence.

It is difficult indeed to conceive a more exquisite satisfaction to a pious and good heart, than that which our founder must have enjoyed at the close of a life devoted to virtue, and the approach of a death, after which he was to become, under God, a powerful and constant agent in promoting the kingdom of his Son. It is a satisfaction compared with which all the pleasures of selfishness are less than nothing and vanity; a satisfaction which every man who is conscious of having a soul to exalt and save, should covet as his richest treasure. We may not, indeed, possess the means of that extensive usefulness which has dignified the name of Dr. Williams:—but every one of us, by being an advocate for truth and freedom in his own age; by speaking, acting and giving for the support of those institutions by which knowledge is diffused and liberty promoted, may form, and is bound to form, one link in that chain upon which the future destiny of social man depends. Despicable are the pretences

by which so many excuse themselves from taking any active part in those public labours which are essential to the improvement of the world. They, forsooth, are not public men. It is enough for them to attend to their private concerns. They leave the civil and religious affairs of their country to princes and statesmen, and wonder that private individuals should be officious enough to meddle in such matters. It is a language too common; sometimes heard even in the mouth of Dissenters. But from whatever quarter it may proceed, I can never hear it without indignation. True, we must mind our private concerns; but have we not likewise a duty to discharge to that social state of which we are members? Are we not bound to watch over that liberty which we inherit from our fathers, and to see that this inheritance is not tarnished or diminished in passing down to our posterity? And is it not by the combination of individual exertion that all great effects must be produced? No man who has enjoyed the advantage of education is so insignificant, but that by uniting his own efforts with those of others, he may withstand the inroads of civil and ecclesiastical power, and extend the limits of that religious knowledge and civil freedom which must ultimately enlighten and bless mankind. A Priestley in his closet communicates those ideas of liberty which a Smith[*] carries with him into the senate, and renders triumphant, at last, over narrow views and impolitic laws. And a Wood,[†] under the like influence of education and principle, goes into the magistracy, and I trust will one day go into the legislature, with the determined purpose of becoming the advocate of popular rights and of the reform and improvement of popular institutions. Thus the student co-operates with the man of active life, and from this co-operation no individual can justly plead an exemption. He who will not lend his arm to the work of purification, because, forsooth, he has not the arm of a Hercules, is a selfish dastard, who, under the cover of weakness, hides corruption, and deserves to suffer the worst

---

[*] Wm. Smith, Esq. M. P. for Norwich, present.

[†] Matthew Wood, Esq. the Right Hon. the Lord Mayor, present.

evils that the most abject slavery can   our prin
inflict upon him. What would have   diffusion
been our state if Dr. Williams and   tages. I
our Puritanic ancestors had been thus   founder.
but   different

and be zealous for the maintenance of

MISCELLANEOUS COMMUNICATIONS.

than a

· in · the

are not
sessing a
the · pos-
r reward,
ent and
h degree

by
we
fer-
the
in
are
constantly complaining of the labour
and toil we are subjected to, and ex-

of every individual. The characters,
situations, abilities natural or ac-
duties,
various.
ent and
imprac-

our present situation exposes us.
When we examine human life however a little more attentively, we shall

are more
such as
dulgence.
he insup-

may be safely hazarded, since, though
the situations of different individuals
are extremely various, yet the general

portable burden of idleness, we often
see them have recourse to the most
childish and frivolous amusements;

and moral constitution of man, is in
a great measure the same in all ages
and nations. It can never cease to
be true for example that the active
man *cæteris paribus*, is more likely to
be happy than the lounger; or that
a serene and cheerful temper is more

health and vigour as well as in many other things of much greater importance. The idle man is commonly low-spirited, peevish and splenetic; every little inconvenience or obstacle to the accomplishment of his desires, vexes him and ruffles his temper; but since he is not thus excited to exert himself in its removal, his life is rendered an endless scene of petty troubles and vexations, which if he had any habits of enterprise or activity would be removed without difficulty as soon as they made their appearance, and before they had had time to occasion any material inconvenience. But when allowed to remain and accumulate, they grow up to a serious amount; which one more accustomed to look difficulties in the face might contemplate with apprehension, and which fill him with absolute despair. Still, though he despairs of getting rid of them, they are not on that account the less felt; they produce a permanent effect upon his temper, he contracts a sour, morose, complaining disposition; and thus, from being at first merely indolent, he becomes a thoroughly discontented, dissatisfied creature, caring for no one but himself, and despised or disliked by every one else. Even when it does not operate in this manner; when circumstances are not such as to throw any of these petty miseries in his way, yet the necessary effect of laziness is to bring on ill-humour and disquiet; a temper of mind which is most destructive of his own peace, and must greatly impede his usefulness to others.

To correct this unhappy disposition, there is no remedy more effectual than *employment*; perhaps no sovereign remedy but this. In so far as its efficacy in promoting this object is concerned it is of little consequence what the employment is; provided it interests the mind and presents it with some other object on which it can dwell with more complacency than on its own grievances and complaints. If the employment be one which is fitted at the same time to answer some valuable end, to contribute to his own comfort or convenience; to promote his improvement in useful knowledge; or still more to promote the comfort or relief of others; so much the better. It is scarcely necessary to dwell on the obvious tendency

of idleness to concentrate the thoughts on self, in a manner which is utterly inconsistent with the cultivation of any elevated or enlarged sentiment, and destructive of all real enjoyment; while on the other hand, an active disposition is continually carrying us beyond these narrow bounds; and thus, as it is often first excited by benevolent and amiable feelings, so it has commonly the happiest effect in continuing, enlivening and purifying these feelings, converting them into habitual states of mind, and ruling principles of conduct. " The necessity of action," says Dr. Johnson, " is not only demonstrable from the fabric of the human body, but is also evident from the universal practice of mankind; since all men, for the preservation of their health, for pleasure and enjoyment, even when exempted by circumstances from the necessity of pursuing any kind of lucrative labour, have invented sports and diversions which though not equally useful to the world with the mechanical or menial arts, yet equal them in the fatigue they occasion to those who practise them; differing from them only as acts of choice differ from those which are attended by the painful sense of compulsion." Even this sense of compulsion which is the general subject of complaint, may nevertheless be of considerable service, by excluding that undecided, vacillating state of mind which often attends those who are aware that their laborious exertions are merely the objects of their own free choice, and than which nothing can be more mortifying and humiliating to those who are conscious of its influence yet cannot shake off its power. This is another reason why it is a most wise and excellent appointment of Providence, that in most cases it is not left to our own choice whether we will exert ourselves or no; but that we are most of us compelled, in order to gain the means of comfortable subsistence, to devote ourselves to some regular employment. Dr. Johnson himself seems to have furnished a striking illustration of the truth of this remark;—though abundantly active in the earlier part of his life, his latter years which were spent in ease and comparative affluence were clouded with melancholy, occasioned it would seem in a great measure by the absence of *imperious* motive to exertion. I have no doubt that he was much happier when compiling his Dictionary, or even when writing the parliamentary debates in a garret in Grub Street, than in the luxurious indolence of Streatham.

I have said that employment, *constant regular* employment of any kind, cannot fail to have a most beneficial effect upon the spirits and temper; but it is evident that this effect must be greatly heightened, if it be directed towards honourable pursuits, or arise from the prosecution of objects suggested by a generous and benevolent disposition. It may therefore be added in the *second* place, that the happiness of man must materially depend on the gratification of the more enlarged and benevolent feelings of his nature. It is scarce possible for any man to be happy in a state of absolute solitude. I do not speak here of those occasional seclusions from social intercourse which are useful to promote meditation and thought, and which may thus tend greatly to exalt and improve the benevolent feelings, and suggest to us additional opportunities and modes of calling them into action, but an entire and permanent separation from all intercourse with our fellow-creatures. The happiest men probably are they who enjoy the most frequent and constant opportunities of cultivating the sentiments which belong to and arise out of domestic society. What picture of human felicity can equal that which is often enjoyed in the simple scenes of private life; where every one is deeply interested in the general welfare; where every heart glows with delight in contemplating the enjoyment of all; where every one is actively employed in ministering to the general good of the little society. Such feelings thus generated and improved, in a mind otherwise well disposed, are the best means of introducing and nourishing more exalted and extensive affections and of leading to a complete forgetfulness of self in an habitual regard through the whole conduct of life to the general welfare and improvement of the human race.

Closely allied to benevolence is what is commonly called *a good temper.* Though nearly connected, how-

ever, these qualities are sometimes seen separated, and may easily be distinguished from each other. There are many persons of great and eminent worth, and who possess abundance of benevolence, or who are at least continually performing acts of the most disinterested and even profuse beneficence, who are yet destitute of all command of temper; who either administer their good offices with a sour moroseness of manner which takes from them their most powerful charms, or are liable to sudden fits and starts of passion which sometimes induce them to inflict serious evils upon the very persons whom but a moment before they had cherished and assisted. Thus their kindness even towards those whom they wish to serve, is interrupted or prevented, and all its happy effects both on the giver and the receiver are in a great measure destroyed. A temper of this kind is one of the greatest bars to happiness in those who are afflicted with it:—it becomes therefore one of our most important personal duties to be strenuous in our endeavours to restrain and sweeten it. There is an apology, but a very imperfect one, which is sometimes made for this unhappy irritability of temper, which ascribes it to a morbid sensibility in the original constitution of such persons. This apology might be made with nearly equal justice for every moral defect and for every intellectual folly whatever; and if admitted, puts a stop to all sorts of improvement. It is true that original temperament, or rather, perhaps, improper management in early life, may occasionally give rise to an unusual degree of this disposition; but this can be no justification of it; it cannot render it less inconsistent with our enjoyment of life and society; and rather furnishes an additional motive to such persons as have laboured under these disadvantages, to be more than ordinarily solicitous to keep it in check. And let no one imagine that this is impossible;—that his own case is so peculiar as not to yield to the ordinary influence of moral medicine. There is a course of discipline before which the most inveterate mental disorders will give way. The remedy, however, it must be admitted, is often more easily perceived and pointed out than applied. To perceive it only requires good sense and discernment; to apply it steadily and effectually requires often a great share of self-government and self-denial, and the frequent mortification and disappointment of our strongest propensities.

By the unreflecting at all times, and by some sects among philosophers, much more than their due weight is attributed to original differences in mental and bodily constitutions. That such differences do exist, no one I think can doubt who observes the very great variety of character and disposition, which frequently appear in persons whose circumstances and education, so far as we have been able to trace, or as human means were able to controul them, have been as nearly similar as possible. We are not either formed or educated after one common standard; nor is it desirable that we should: a dull, uniform sameness would doubtless take away greatly from the enjoyment of human life, and would be inconsistent with the proper discharge of the various duties which the convenience or the subsistence of mankind requires. Though however we admit that such original diversities do exist, yet by much the greater part of the actual diversity observable in human character is to be ascribed to those circumstances which we call accidental or adventitious; that is, they are the result of education and experience, and are in some considerable measure subject to government and controul. The contrary opinion appears not only inconsistent with a just theory of the history of the human mind, but also leads to dangerous practical consequences, and ought therefore to be diligently guarded against. But to return to our proper subject.

The weakness and irritability of temper which I have alluded to, is so inconsistent with our happiness, that it is necessary to take all possible methods to restrain it. For this purpose it is very desirable to cultivate a habit of looking always in preference on the *bright side* of every character, and indeed of every object which attracts our notice. I would not recommend a total blindness to the defects and errors of others, for that might be fatal to our own personal security, and injurious to the important interests of those whose welfare it is our more immediate duty to promote; but a

disposition to observe with satisfaction and duly to appreciate such good qualities as are possessed even by the worst men, and to place in their due light all the excellencies of the really deserving, and which when justly estimated are sufficient to cast into the shade the infirmities or failings by which they may be accompanied. Candour in acknowledging all these would greatly contribute to the formation of an even and gentle disposition. Again, a habit, which may soon be acquired by care and practice, of checking the *external signs* of those emotions of contempt and anger to which we feel ourselves peculiarly liable, will succeed in time in preventing the inordinate rise of the emotions themselves. Such efforts at first produce nothing more than the external appearance of decorum and propriety of behaviour; but the influence soon becomes more extensive. Between the outward signs and the feelings which are represented by them, there is a surprising connection; and as, on the one hand, the assumed language of violent emotion will, in many cases, excite a considerable degree of the emotion itself—so, on the other, the constant endeavour to check the external symptoms, soon chokes up and even entirely removes the source from whence they flow.

The species of ill-humour which arises from a morbid sensibility to our own miseries, is equally inconsistent with real enjoyment. Nothing is more destructive of pleasure than a constant habit of complaining and grumbling; which leads a man to look in preference on those circumstances of his lot which are the least inviting, and is eternally brooding over them so as to preclude all attention to those which are more favourable and encouraging, and to magnify the others to such a degree in his disordered imagination, that what might have been but trifling grievances are exalted into evils of the first magnitude. A habit therefore of dwelling on whatever is in its nature fitted to give pleasure, and of endeavouring to look out for the beneficial consequences which are to flow even from those which cannot, in the first instance, be regarded with satisfaction, is exceedingly well calculated to secure and increase our happiness. This is the disposition which every sincere Christian, every believer in the constant superintendance of an infinitely wise and kind Providence, will naturally cherish; and he will be led to this, by a sense not merely of its propriety, but of its immediate and direct influence on his present enjoyments. Let the more serious afflictions of life then teach us patience and resignation. As for the lighter grievances and petty miseries by which so many suffer their tempers to be ruffled and their cheerfulness destroyed, let them be regarded as fitter subjects of a laugh or jest than of any graver reflections. A very amusing book—which had a great run some years ago, but seems now almost forgotten—the "Miseries of Human Life," may perhaps show us the right way of dealing with these minor troubles. To allow them to destroy one's comfort would be the extreme of folly; and to talk about philosophy or resignation in connexion with such trifles would be equally absurd; the only method left therefore is to treat them with their own characteristic levity.

Another circumstance of great importance to human happiness, is a wise management and distribution of our habits. The capacity of acquiring habits, both bodily and mental, is a most important and valuable part of our constitution. By its means we acquire and continually improve our skill in those occupations which are to be the means of our subsistence or the source of our usefulness to our fellow-creatures; and our various necessary employments become, through the operation of the same general principle, not only easy but agreeable to us. Every thing however depends on the right application of this principle. It may minister to virtue or be made subservient to vice; it may contribute to happiness or greatly aggravate our misery, according as it is wisely or injudiciously directed. The object therefore in the regulation of our habits must be that those things be rendered easy and agreeable through frequent practice, which are most essentially requisite to our comfort and permanent well-being; and that we render our pleasures dependent, as much as possible, on those sources which are most easily attainable. Now all this may be done by habit. A habit of moderation in our desires will enable us to take as much delight in the cheaper, more ordinary means gratification, as others do in those

which are most difficult to be procured. In absolute enjoyment we are nearly upon a level; but the difference in our favour consists in this, that our pleasures are more secure and permanent than theirs, and also that almost every change is with us a change from contented tranquillity to a state of high enjoyment, while they, having foolishly placed their habitual station at the summit of all, cannot remove from it without descending.

Such then are some of those sources from which the wise and prudent man may, in ordinary cases, depend upon deriving an abundant and secure supply of happiness;—from innocent, or still better, from beneficent, activity—from the exercise of the benevolent affections either towards those with whom he is peculiarly connected by the ties of kindred or friendship, or as delighting in the more enlarged, expanded views of universal philanthropy—from a serene and even temper, unruffled either by trifling offences on the part of others, or by those petty miseries and vexations which occasionally occur to himself. From these, and such as these, the wise man may draw a never-failing supply of enjoyment. Not that he is to be always in transport or extacy, for this is inconsistent with human nature, and indeed is not in itself desirable; but a steady, uniform cheerfulness and tranquillity which, from its permanence and security, will certainly furnish in the end a much greater sum of real happiness. The enumeration is not by any means complete; for such is the admirable constitution of things, that, to the truly wise man, every object in nature, and almost every circumstance of life, may be made the source of pleasure. All the provinces of external nature—all the powers, desires and affections of his own mind, will contribute to his felicity: the powers of taste and imagination—the search after, and discovery of, knowledge—the interest he takes in the events which diversify the history of his species,—all these, and a thousand other pleasures of the mind, which, though nothing can in this uncertain state be pronounced absolutely imperishable and constantly within reach, may yet be said to be in general firmly secured to wise and good men as a just reward of intellectual and moral happiness.

Mr. Wright's Remarks on Two Passages in Dr. Adam Clarke's Notes on the Holy Scriptures.

IN his remarks on 1 Cor. i. 8, the Doctor relates two Jewish stories to illustrate the faithfulness of God : the following is one of them :—" Rabbi *Simeon*, the son of *Shetach*, bought an ass from some Edomites, at whose neck his disciples saw a *diamond* hanging: they said unto him, Rabbi, *the blessing of the Lord maketh rich*, Prov. x. 22. But he answered, The *ass* I have bought, but the *diamond* I have not bought : therefore he returned the diamond to the Edomites." To this story Dr. C. has added the following illiberal remark :—" This was an instance of rare honesty, not to be paralleled among the *Jews* of the present day; and probably among few *Gentiles*." On what authority the *Gentiles* are supposed to be so much better than the *Jews*, and the whole of the latter, as well as the greater part of the former, to be destitute of strict honesty, the Doctor has not stated. It is certain every strictly honest man would act as Rabbi *Simeon* is said to have acted. It has been too much the practice for Christians to speak of the Jews, because they do not believe that Jesus is the Christ, as men destitute of all piety and virtue ; though proofs of the contrary might be produced. To treat a whole people as altogether depraved and worthless, is the way to debase them, and injure their moral character. It is inconsistent with Christian charity, and even with common justice, to represent a whole nation as not furnishing, in the present day, a single instance of the strictest honesty. I have been credibly informed of an instance of what the Doctor calls *rare honesty*, in the conduct of a *Jew*, with whom I was well acquainted, which may be paralleled with the case he has stated. The Jew I refer to, travelling with his box, happened to call at a house where he was asked if he would purchase a watch which was presented to him: he inquired what price the person who offered to sell him the watch required for it, and being told, he asked if the seller knew what the watch was, and was answered " Yes, it is a gilt one ;" he replied, " No, you are mistaken, it is a gold one, and worth much more than you ask for it."—Will Dr. C. take upon him to say that none of the Jews, in the present day, are or

can be conscientiously such ? And if conscientiously Jews, according to the law of Moses, will they not be men of strict integrity ? Is he sufficiently acquainted with the conduct of all the Jews, to justify the censure he passes upon them ?

In his notes on 1 Cor. xvth. chap. the Doctor says, " One remark I cannot help making; the doctrine of the *resurrection*, appears to have been thought of much more consequence among the primitive Christians than it is *now!* How is this? The apostles were continually insisting on it, and exciting the followers of God to diligence, obedience and cheerfulness through it. And their successors in the present day seldom mention it ! So apostles preached ; and so primitive Christians believed : so we preach ; and so our hearers believe. There is not a doctrine in the gospel on which more stress is laid : and there is not a doctrine in the present system of preaching which is treated with more neglect !" Is not this an acknowledgment that what is called evangelical preaching in the present day is essentially different from the preaching of the apostles ? Dr. C. asserts that the doctrine which the apostles were continually insisting on, is seldom mentioned by those he calls their successors; but he does not state the reasons for this difference. He will not say the doctrine of the resurrection is of less importance *now* than it was in the days of the apostles. He does not attempt to justify the neglect of their doctrine by modern preachers. Surely if those who take to themselves the name of evangelical ministers in the present day had the same views of the gospel as the apostles had, they would preach as the apostles preached. Ought not Dr. C. and his readers to inquire whether the primitive doctrine of the gospel be not neglected on account of other doctrines being insisted on, as leading articles of faith, which the apostles did not preach, and which cannot be found in their discourses, of which we have an account in the book of Acts? There are ministers, but I fear the Doctor would hardly allow them to be evangelical, who insist more on the doctrine of the resurrection than all their more numerous brethren who disown them as legal teachers.

R. WRIGHT.

Shore Place, Hackney,
SIR,   *May 22, 1816.*

I OBSERVE in the public papers an account of Lord Grosvenor having dismissed a number of his poor labourers from his employ because they could not conscientiously attend the Established Church... I have now to relate to you another circumstance of a similar description in the walks of humbler life. My niece, about the age of eighteen, left me, about a fortnight ago, to take a situation as dressmaker to two maiden ladies, who have been long established in business, at Newport, in the Isle of Wight: both parties were perfectly satisfied with each other as far as related to business; but on the Sunday morning after her arrival at Newport, it was inquired of my niece, what place of worship she had attended; she answered, she had lately gone to an Unitarian chapel at Hackney: she was told, *they* attended the Established Church, to which she said she had no objections, and went with them twice on that day and once on the following Sunday. Nothing more was said to her on the subject, but on the Friday following I received a letter from one of the ladies (A. F.) saying, my niece must immediately return, assigning as a reason, *that as she was of a different religion to themselves they must be under the necessity of parting with her, for it would be very uncomfortable to be disunited not only in their places of worship but in their ideas.* They regret they did not know this before, "more particularly as they think her a very nice young lady," I replied, wishing her to remain; but to no purpose: and she accordingly returned to me, in company with one of the ladies on her usual visit to London for the purposes of business. It does not appear that Unitarian worship is the particular objection, but the crime of attending *any chapel*; for they informed my niece they had before turned off a young female *because she was a methodist.* So you see, Sir, that though we hear so much of the liberality of the present age, the breed of a persecuting spirit is not yet extinct.

J. W.

P. S. I observe this morning in the Public Ledger that Lord Grosvenor's affair is contradicted.

SIR,   *Ditchling, May 28, 1816.*

IN number CXXIV. of the Monthly Repository, for April last, p. 199, is a letter purporting to come from the pen of a Roman Catholic to Dr. Carpenter, as a complaint against you. This letter seems to me, to have been written in an arrogant style, with a considerable degree of pettishness. I suppose an editor of a periodical work is not bound to examine all the authorities which his correspondents may quote; therefore, no great blame belongs to you, if any of them should blunder or make mistakes: if you are always ready to admit corrections, as I believe you always are, it is as much as can reasonably be required.

But what I would particularly wish to take notice of in the Roman Catholic's letter, is his account of the Rheimish version of the New Testament, as it respects its reception among the Roman Catholic clergy. He says it is "the only translation *sanctioned* by the Roman Catholic clergy." This translation, then, is *sanctioned* by the Roman Catholic clergy!

Now, Sir, I wish to inquire, for really I feel myself a little alarmed, though I have always been a friend to Catholic emancipation, I wish to inquire, whether the sanction of the Roman Catholic clergy to the Rheimish translation extends to all the annotations annexed to each chapter? If it do, pity my weakness, I am afraid I see in it the direful demon of persecution. The following is the Rheimish rendering of Luke ix. 56:— "The Son of Man came not to destroy souls, but to save." The annotation on these words is :—"Not justice nor *all rigorous punishment* of sinners is here forbidden, nor Elias, in fact, reprehended, nor the *church* or *Christian princes* blamed for putting *heretics to death:* but that none of these should be done for a desire of our particular revenge, or without discretion, and regard of their amendment, and example of others. Therefore St. Peter used *his power* upon Ananias and Sapphira, when he struck them both down to death for defrauding the church." We all know, that in the Church of Rome's idea of heretics are included all those who differ and separate from her: according to the above annotation these may be *rigorously* punished; or, if it be said that the sinners are to be confined to those who commit civil offences, yet heretics, both by the *church* and *Christian princes* may be put to death. Is not this persecution? Would not Roman Catholics call it so if they were the victims?

So also Luke xiv. 23, the Rheimish translation is: "Compel them to enter, that my house may be filled." In the annotation we are told, "St. Augustine also referreth this compelling to the *penal laws* which Catholic Princes do *justly use* against heretics and schismatics, proving that they who are by their former profession in baptism subject to the Catholic church and are departed from the same after sects, *may and ought* to be compelled into the unity and society of the universal church again."

Can any one be so blind as not to see to what this leads? If it be supposed, that these annotations were written by the spirit of infallibility, and if the sanction of the Roman Catholic clergy extends to them, and that by the same spirit, I see not how the church of Rome can give up the doctrine they contain, which is persecution.

If, Sir, you permit this to have a place in the Monthly Repository, it will give an opportunity for any Roman Catholic, and particularly the writer of the letter who has been the occasion of these lines, to inform the public, whether the sentiments of persecution contained in the above annotations, are now sanctioned by the Roman Catholic clergy or not. I for one should be glad to hear on this subject.

A. BENNETT.

SIR,

NOT being satisfied with the explanation generally given of the blasphemy against the Holy Spirit, (see Matt. xii. 31, 32. Mark iii. 28, 29.) I beg leave to submit the following queries on the subject to the consideration of your readers, and shall be thankful to any one who will candidly answer them.

1. Have we sufficient authority from the above passages to conclude that any of the Jews had, at the time when our Lord uttered the words, blasphemed against the Holy Spirit; as he does not charge this crime upon them, but warns them of the danger of committing it?

2. As the Jews had not been previously warned of a sin which would be unpardonable, if they had already uttered this blasphemy when the condemnation to which it exposed them was declared, would not their total exclusion from forgiveness be the same as proceeding against men on the ground of an *ex post facto* law? Is it not more consistent with the character of Jesus, and the conduct of God towards his creatures, to suppose the above passages contain an awful warning, than to construe them as expressive of the penalty of a crime already committed?

3. Were not the most malignant expressions which the Jews had uttered at the time spoken against Jesus personally, against the Son of man; for they did not admit that he had the spirit of God? Is it not contrary to the whole account to say the blasphemy they had uttered was directed against the spirit; did they not evidently intend to degrade the character, and invalidate the pretensions of Jesus; was not this their whole object, and is it not the intention that characterizes the action under a moral view?

4. If the blasphemy they had already uttered was against the Spirit, how are we to distinguish between their speaking against the Son of man and their speaking against the Holy Spirit?

5. Are we not told that the Holy Spirit was not given till Christ was glorified: John vii. 39. Acts ii. 33. and could they blaspheme against the Holy Spirit before it was given in the sense in which the expression is used in the evangelical writings?

6. The Editors of the Improved Version, in a note on the place, say, "They who ascribed the miracles of Jesus and his apostles to demoniacal agency, resisted the strongest possible evidence of the Christian religion, and were therefore incapable of being converted to the belief of it." But can this observation be just, if restricted to the miracles wrought during our Lord's personal ministry; for he said to his Apostles, "He that believeth on me, the works that I do shall he do also, and greater works than these shall he do because I go unto my Father?" John xiv. 12. Did not the resurrection of Jesus, and the Holy Spirit given to the apostles,

furnish stronger evidence than any that had preceded? ""

7. Can the supposition that some of the Jews had sinned beyond the possibility of forgiveness during our Lord's personal ministry, be reconciled with the accounts at large? Did not Jesus after his resurrection direct that forgiveness should be preached to them indiscriminately; and was their condemnation finally sealed before they rejected the gospel, contradicting and blaspheming, when preached by the Apostles with the Holy Spirit sent down from heaven?

A SCRIPTURIST.

Sir May 6, 1816.

IN Repository for February, (p. 74) two schemes of the Divine government are offered to consideration as alone consistent in themselves, or as having any pretensions to reason or the common apprehensions of mankind.

The first holds forth that all things are subjected to fixed laws;—that all is an universal settled scheme of Providence; every thing was foreseen and determined, and happens as the Author of all appointed that it should.

Now I do suppose that *all* events, *all* effects of power, are not subjects of intellectual determination, or objects of appointment; but on the contrary, that there are many natural results of force, which are not parts of any scheme, or any matters of device or ordination whatever.

Indeed all things are *necessarily what* and *as* they are: but we need distinct evidence of appointment—that all events are, or ever were, *objects* of divine contemplation, or devised, determined parts of provident plan. No doubt, Deity is source of all order, all systematic work, all management.

But is God actually the *designing cause* of all movement and result? Is all movement and consequence, issue of *intellect*, pure offspring of wisdom and good-will? True, the natural standing order of the world indisputably betokens wise and good design; and all men must be agreeably affected thereby—by the beauty and benefit of the provident succession of things; the orderly, eligible course which actually prevails throughout the system of nature. Every man

must be more or less impressed with those characters of design and contrivance with which he is constantly surrounded and upheld. But sure *every* successive fact that we witness, cannot be justly considered a necessary component, or requisite mean, to any purposed end whatever. Can we reasonably think that all movement is *judicious* change; and all operation *intentional* effect?

If this is "Inquirer's" view of Providence, I must say that all men do not decidedly think with him. Under this notion I cannot believe it possible to form a consistent character of Deity. The laws of nature indeed, are divine emanation, and of course perfectly characteristic of Deity, and terminate on universal good; on the accomodation and final welfare of his sentient creatures.

But fully admitting this providential order of things, I apprehend not that it amounts to destiny, or positive assignment of every separate atom in respect of every other in the universe; all possible relation and state of being: but rather suppose that it does *not necessarily* follow, from hence, that all states and relations of being and every consequent result are subjects of divine device, or any mental concern whatever. It seems to me, and it is my present opinion, that though every phenomenon in nature is (essentially natural) necessary issue of eternal principle, nevertheless all bearing of objects, every event, every movement and consequence, is not a part of divine scheme; not a link, or distinct subject of direct *will*, *device*, *purpose* and *ordination*. And that man's personal character and end, is not (it may be) absolutely prescribed and preordained. I suppose that it is *by divine* pleasure and purpose that I am constituted capable of a certain measure of action: but must or may I thence infer and affirm, that I cannot do more or less than was the pleasure and purpose of God in my make? This seems to me tantamount to saying that all efficiency is strictly divine will-deed; that every instant motion and operation is personal act of Deity, to all intents and purposes. However, I do suppose, think and believe that we are not justly authorized to affirm that the supreme legislator of the universe actually appointed every temporary fact—all events whatever, that take place through the action of man or other (provident ordination, or) creature energy. Finally, I will repeat, that I cannot think that every natural effect is *subject* or *object* of *purpose* and *appointment.*

This said scheme of divine determination and ordination, now lies before us simple say-so. But as it is seriously thought that facts do not altogether answer to the tale, the matter demands some elucidation. And it is hoped, Sir, that this ingenious theoretic correspondent will engage himself herein to our common interest, and he will oblige an

OLD INQUIRER.

Whether natural evil be the cause of moral evil.

January, 1816.

IT is commonly said that if moral evil could not injure sensible beings, or produce misery, it would be no evil at all, and I see no reason to dispute this position. There is another question, however, connected with this subject, and that is, if the previous existence of natural evil be not the cause of the subsequent existence of moral evil, or whether if there were no natural evil moral evil could be possible in man? Now, all natural evil, is to sensible beings, unhappiness; so the question will be, if men were all perfectly happy, could an immoral volition or act take place? I think not. Every immoral act appears to be produced by the imperfection of the agent's happiness. He is stimulated by some apprehended good which he has not and which he desires, and if he were perfectly happy he could have no desires, and therefore could have nothing to draw forth an immoral wish. If the will be determined by desire, take away that desire, and no volition will be exerted. A human being perfectly happy, can do no immoral act, because he can have no desire to change his condition. Take away from man in his present state, uneasy passions, bodily and mental, and all wants, and the dread of want, and all moral evil must cease. The first pair are represented as not perfectly happy, they had uneasy desires, and criminal volition followed. Moral evil, therefore, is caused by natural evil, and indeed in proportion to the extent of natural evil; moral evil exists in a very limited

degree. Take away the natural evil and it would cease to exist at all. Will this reasoning apply to the Deity? If we conceive that the Deity is really the Creator of all things, which all men now allow; that he must be *perfectly happy,* possessing all things, and having nothing to counteract his views, seems to be an undeniable inference, the contrary of which cannot be conceived, but seems to involve a contradiction. If the Deity then be a perfectly happy being, it will follow that he can have no desire, contrary to the happiness of any Being. It will now be asked, why then has this happy being produced natural evil, and that moral, in a word, why has he made any suffering and unhappy beings? I cannot answer this question. The usual solution of thinking men is, that all beings which he has made are or will be happy, and I confess that if this be not true, the difficulty admits of no solution whatever. Without this, all is a riddle, an inexplicable mystery, all reasoning on the divine character and conduct, vain. This is universally, or nearly so, the doctrine held by Unitarians, and no other has the appearance of common sense, connected with the present condition of man and the belief of a perfectly happy Creator.

SEARCH.

P. S. May I be permitted to ask your correspondent, Mr. Belsham, who is one of the most diligent students in the scriptures now living, if he have found any prophecy in the Old Testament, which speaks of the Messiah's dying and rising again the third day, which seems to be clearly designated by Jesus after his resurrection, as recorded in Luke.

SIR, *March* 28, 1816.

THE suggestion in a late number, if I take it right, that the Author of "Armageddon," [M. Repos. X. 649] probably intended in that poem, indirectly to *oppose* the common notion of future punishment, hath induced me to send you a few scattered thoughts drawn up under a similar idea, somewhat amplified, a few years ago: an idea, with which I was forcibly impressed, on perusing Dr. Young's Poem "On the Last Day." They are part of others on the subject in general, much too long on the whole, for a periodical work. If the present fragment be not out of time or unacceptable, it is at your service.

AN OCCASIONAL READER.

Apparent Inconsistencies of great Minds, exemplified in a series of Extracts on Future Punishment.

There yet remains one *collateral* argument, of great weight and importance in the writer's opinion, against both the schemes already treated of, namely, the indiscriminate notion of future punishment, as represented by some, or the doctrine of absolute, eternal and unremitting torments; and secondly, that of punishment *limited*, in degree, but strictly everlasting, in duration—an argument, distinct in itself, and not much adverted to in books; and that is—the indeterminate and equivocal language employed by the advocates of eternal punishment, either in explaining their ideas of the doctrine itself, or of circumstances connected with it. If a writer lays down a specific opinion, and presently shuns the investigation of it, and elsewhere, perhaps in the next page, expresses a sentiment diametrically opposite, or utterly inconsistent with the former one; we may fairly conclude, either that he hath not formed any precise ideas upon the subject; or that he means to compound with different parties; or wishes to retract in some measure what he had before advanced. Nothing can be a surer proof of a weak argument, than a man's authority *against himself*. A prodigious mass of evidence might be furnished of this kind; at present we shall produce only a few instances, without regard to chronology.

Calvin, in his Institutions, B. III. Ch. 25, Section 5, having slightly mentioned some of the common arguments for eternal punishment; as to the contrary opinions, only says, "Let us leave these trifles, lest we should seem to consider such dotages as worthy of confutation." No doubt many a zealous Romanist has said the same, respecting any sentiments contrary to the peculiar dogmas of his community: nevertheless, of the greater part of *these*, this pious reformer justly thought it necessary to enter into the most minute and laborious investigation.

The *Rev. W. Wisheart*, a profound divine of the church of Scotland, in his "*Theologia*," 1716, a work, which, allowing for some parts of the author's creed, contains an inexhaustable fund of theological matter, treating of the *divine patience*, says: "Of all the other perfections of the divine nature, this of *patience* hath the shortest time to act its part, having *no other stage but this world to act in*: after the end of which, it will remain, *shut up* in the Deity, without any further operation. The time of this life is the only time of *long suffering*." Yet, he afterwards tells us, that the consideration of the divine patience is to be used as an argument, "to manifest the gracious, merciful, and *reconcileable nature* of the Deity, and to *clear and justify* the divine judgments in *a future world*;—an abundant patience, called *the riches of forbearance and long suffering*, far beyond the patience of good men, of glorified saints, or angels." Not to advert here to the singular freedom of speech in the former part of this quotation, it may be observed, than which nothing can be plainer, that the divine *patience* and *long suffering*, are often very *limited* in their exercise in the present life. The Deity doth not often interpose, that we know of, by miracles, or by remarkable deviations from the common course of nature and Providence, to prevent the usual, or the accidental effects as they are called, of transgression. The pious author himself observes, "How many candles have we seen put out, before they were half burnt!" War and pestilence, famine and intemperance, destroy their thousands and ten thousands in the first acts of sin, and many of them perhaps in the possession of a previously moral, if not religious character: now, to propose that, as a *general argument*, which at present applies only to *particular cases*, is a false and absurd method of reasoning. Again, under the head of *divine justice*, he tells us, "The justice of God, in a future state, is *inexorable*:" but afterwards, that "This vindictive justice, though essential to the nature of God, is not *natural* to him, as heat is to the fire, though it be necessary that he should punish sin, because of his righteous nature; yet, not by a natural, or *physical* necessity, as the fire burns, but by a *moral*, or *rational* necessity.

The fire burns, without any influence of a free and rational principle, but the Deity is a *free agent*, and therefore determines the mode, seasons, *degree*, and other circumstances of punishment by his sovereign will and pleasure. Further, when we say that God *cannot* let sin go unpunished, we do not thereby limit *the power* of God, but it is the justice and righteousness of his own nature that bounds him. As he cannot lie or deny himself, so he cannot do any thing *unjust*, and it would be unjust to let sin go unpunished."

These sentiments are strictly just, but utterly inconsistent with the foregoing assertion: for if we are to argue upon the grounds of " a *moral* or *rational necessity*," as to the proceedings of the Supreme Being as sovereign judge in a future world; how does it thence appear, that his primitive justice will be "inexorable?" Or where is it said in scripture that it will be so? Rather, as his patience and longsuffering are only, so to speak, *branches* of his infinite goodness, which is essential to his nature, is it not far more probable, that *these* will continue as long as *that* ?—that is, be coeval with his being? For, as our author well observes on the *Divine Eternity*, " God always is what he was, and always will be what he is!"

Sir *Thomas Brown*, in his " Religio Medici," treating of future punishment according to the high orthodox system of his day, among some exquisite passages,* introduces others which, separately considered, might lead a hasty reader to conclude that the au-

thor had possessed neither grace, reason nor humanity: he closes his remarks thus: " the one," the eternity of happiness, " being so far beyond our deserts; the other," the eternity of suffering, " being so infinitely below our demerits!" What did this good man require further, or what could he expect, more than *all?*

Sir *Kenelm Digby*, his annotator, expresses upon this occasion a little alleviation of sentiment: he tells us, that the victim of divine anger, deprived of former criminal enjoyments, restless and insatiable, " will neglect all other contentments he *might have*, for want of a due taste and relish; hating whatsoever good is in *his power*, and thus pining away a long eternity:" hereby plainly supposing, that there is some *real good* to be obtained in that state, if the proper *means* could be discovered and adopted.

The luminous author of " A Gentleman's Religion" dismisses this subject in a very summary way. " Eternal damnation, of which we have fair warning given us, and may therefore avoid if we please, is *as little as can be threatened*, and often is but *too little* to keep us back from all manner of sin and wickedness." Thus taking for granted the question proposed, and confounding a supposed divine threatening with its execution; though, to do the author justice, he clearly holds out the difference of *degrees*.

Richard *Baxter*, in his Treatise of Universal Redemption, or the Sufficiency of the Gospel in itself to save all Mankind, has the following passage:—" All divines that I know, say that God loveth those in *hell*, as his creatures and as men. Aquinas and the schoolmen have it frequently; and many Protestant divines say, that he punisheth those in hell short of their deserving, and so sheweth some mercy there. *That I will not meddle with*." There might be some reason for this: the pious and laborious minister was branded as *a heretic* by many of his brethren; and would probably have been still farther advanced on the black catalogue had he hinted at the possibility of *universal restoration*. But let us attend to his sentiments in another part of this work, which should be deeply impressed upon our minds. " If any say that God followeth not the rules of human laws; I answer, He is the

* " I thank God, that, with joy I mention it, I was never afraid of hell, nor ever grew pale at its description: I have so fixed my contemplation on heaven, that I have almost forgot the idea of its contrary, and am afraid rather to lose the joys of the one, than endure the sufferings of the other ! To be deprived of *them*, is a perfect hell, and needs, methinks, no addition to complete our affliction! That terrible term hath never detained me from sin, nor do I owe any good action to the name thereof: I fear God, yet am not afraid of him; his mercies make me ashamed of my sins, before his judgments alarm me for their consequences. These are but the forced and secondary methods of his wisdom; a course rather to deter the wicked, than incite the virtuous to his service."---*Rel. Medic.*

fountain of all *right-laws*, and reason and justice. 'Tis an ill pretence for men to judge their Maker by, when they will not allow him that reasonable apology, nor make that construction of his ways, according to common undeniable *equity*, as they will do of the ways of men. *Right reason* and the laws made thereby, are a beam of God's perfect wisdom and justice.

Jeremy Taylor, that truly Christian bishop, or overseer of souls, " himself an host, the Homer among preachers," though he appears in general to adopt the common notions on this subject, (especially in his Treatise "On Man,") probably the only weak book he ever wrote, and some of the sentiments of which, if true, would almost justify the scheme of Anthropomorphitism,) yet, has many passages quite inconsistent with them. In his "Life of Christ," treating of temporal judgments, he observes of Ananias and Sapphira, Uzzah the prophet slain by the lion, and other cases of sudden surprisals in the commission of sinful acts, where the sufferers were in the main upright characters, that "We must not conclude such persons perishing and miserable to all eternity; it were a sad sentence to think God would not impute the untimely death for a punishment great enough to that deflexion from duty, and judge the man according to the constant tenor of his former life; unless the act were of malice enough to outweigh the former habits, and interrupt the whole state of acceptation and grace. For as God takes off our sins and punishments *by parts*, remitting to some the sentence of death, and inflicting only the fine of a temporal loss, or the gentle scourge of a lesser sickness; so also, *he lays it on by parts* and suitable proportions; and every transgression and lesser deviation from duty does not drag the soul to death eternal; but he suffers our repentance, though imperfect, to have an imperfect effect, knocking off the fetters by degrees, leading us in some cases to *the council*, in some to *judgment*, and in some to *hell-fire*; but it is not always certain, that he who is led to the prison doors shall there lie entombed, and a man may by a judgment be brought to the gates of hell, and yet those gates shall not prevail against him."

This passage is not cited as any

indirect argument against eternal punishment, but only as proving by the way, that this great divine did not interpret too strictly those texts in Ezekiel, where it is said that the righteous shall perish in his present sin, notwithstanding his former attainments; and as proving, most unequivocally, that, like the favoured disciple, his soul was so wrapt and absorbed in the contemplation of the divine character, as *the God of love*, and probably, at the same time, so shocked, or at least dismayed, by the common notion of future punishment, that he could not allow himself to believe, that any would prove the victims of this dire, ineffable doom, but the most flagrant, enormous and incorrigible transgressors. This is further evident, from another passage in the same work, where he tells us that there is "but *one*" individual of the human race, *Judas Iscariot*, of whom we may affirm, without breach of Christian charity, that he is "certainly damned:" nay, he goes farther yet, and says, even of this delinquent, "his sin stuck close, and it is *thought* to a sad eternity." But, we do not insist upon this latter passage; the good bishop often indulges in a laxity of phrase common in his day, but which, the literary taste of the present times, superior in this respect, will not admit of. The foregoing sentiment, however, is delivered in plain and decided terms: let us attend, for a moment, to the *singular idea*, and to the instruction which it may afford us.

If Christian charity will not allow us to affirm that any man but Judas Iscariot is " *certainly damned*," it most assuredly will *not* require us to believe, on the other hand, that every man besides him is *certainly saved*: taking salvation in the common sense of the word, for the state of happiness *immediately* succeeding the general judgment. This would be *enthusiasm*, and not charity, or charity carried to a degree of enthusiasm.[*] We cannot doubt, from the history of the world and our own experience,—happy if we have no reason to fear it respecting ourselves!—that many go out of life utterly unfit, as far as appears, without considerable degree of *purification*, for the Christian heaven; judging, not

---

[*] "Enthusiastic doctrines---good things strained out of their wits." *Whichcote.*

from the manner of their *death*, which, of all the extravagancies of theological dreamers, is one of the most strange and unaccountable, but from the manner of their *life*: Now, how are we to determine between these *two extremes?* If, according to the reasoning of this profound writer, we should form such exalted ideas of the divine benignity, *in a general view*, as exercised in the character of Supreme Judge; how is it conceivable, that, after the future awards of his justice, this benignity, as to the objects of it, should be *eternally suspended?*

It is difficult to ascertain precisely, what were the sentiments of *Archbishop King* upon this important subject. In the Appendix to his Treatise on "The Origin of Evil," a work abounding with many weighty truths, he adopts, in a great measure, the orthodox notion, and endeavours to obviate some of the arguments against it in the usual way:—such as the sufferings of the damned tending to *enhance* the blessedness of glorified saints, by way of comparison and contemplation; a sentiment which, as applicable to the *adequate* and *limited* suffering of transgressors in a future state, may be allowed to have some weight; but which, if applied to the doctrine of strictly *eternal* punishment, confutes itself. The eternity of this state, however, he observes, is not a doctrine of *reason*, but of pure *revelation.* "It appears from the light of nature that there shall be future punishments, but not that they shall be eternal." He further informs us, that they "do not proceed from the *vengeance*, but from the *goodness* of the Deity;" and then proceeds to offer some opinions which seem to be peculiarly his own :—

"As to another objection, the matter is still in debate, whether it were better to be miserable than not to be at all; and there are arguments on both sides. 'Tis manifest, indeed, that those evils which overbalance the desire and happiness of life, commonly put an end to life itself; and that such objects as are hurtful to the sense, at length destroy it. The same seems to hold good in thinking substances, viz. those things which affect the mind to a higher degree than it can bear, may in like manner put an end to it: for they may be supposed either to drive us to *madness*; or so far to disorder the thinking faculty, as to make us think

of *nothing at all.* Who can tell, then, whether the punishment of the wicked may not lead them into a kind of *phrenzy* and *madness?* Thus they may indeed be very miserable, and become a sad spectacle to others; they may be sensible of their misery also, and *strive against it* with all their power; but while they do not observe or believe that it is founded in *perverse election*, they may hug *themselves in the cause, the effects of which they abhor*; being still wise in their own opinion, and, as it were, *pleasing themselves in their misery.*"

"Thus, the more they labour under it, the more they embrace the cause of it, and thereby become *their own hindrance from ever getting free*; and *will not suffer themselves to be any thing but what they are*. This we see daily done by mad and frantic persons, and reckon it a part of their unhappiness. The divine goodness, therefore, is not to be charged with *cruelty* for *letting them continue* in that existence, though it be very miserable, when they themselves *will not have it removed*; or, for not altering their condition, *which they utterly refuse to have altered*. 'Tis better indeed for them not to be; but this, in the opinion only of wise men, to which they do not *assent*; for they indulge themselves in their obstinate *election*, and though every where surrounded and oppressed with woes, yet will they not *alter* what they have once embraced, and had *rather endure all* than *repent*: as men that are desparately in love, ambitious, envious, choose to bear torments, loss of estate, and hazard of life, rather than lay aside these foolish and bewitching affections. We may easily conceive, then, how the wicked in hell may be in very great misery, upon the increase of their obstinacy and folly, and yet *unwilling to be freed from them.*"

The reader will make his own comment upon these passages, and more of the same kind, in the original: for the writer's part, he professes only to regard them as constituting *an inextricable labyrinth*, from which, it is probable, he should not readily escape, and into which he hath certainly no inclination to enter: he has, therefore, only to observe, that awful instances of the prevalence of evil habits in the present life, can furnish no criterion as to their influence in the next, where all the objects of sinful gratification shall, be done away, where. " *hell is open before them, and destruction hath no covering!*" that we shall search in vain for this system of *insanity* in the *Bible*; and that we should receive with caution some of the opinions of an author, however learned and pious, who could conclude his elaborate and justly celebrated work, in the following manner:—

" But I offer all these things to the *censure of the learned*: I submit them entirely to the judgment of the Catholic church, especially to the *governors* of those parts of it, which constitute the churches of England and Ireland. If there be any thing herein which seems not perfectly agreeable to *their faith*, as I hope there is not, and would not have it; I desire that may be looked upon as *absolutely unsaid* and retracted!"

The only prose divine remaining, whose sentiments upon this subject we shall briefly consider, is the pious, learned and candid *Dr. Doddridge.* In his Theological Lectures, Prop. 163, Ed. 1776, he proposes the question with great fairness and impartiality. We cannot enter into all the arguments he has produced on both sides, which would be to repeat much of what hath already been offered : our inquiry here is only respecting his *consistency.*

He acknowledges that " We cannot pretend to *decide, à priori,* or previous to the event, so far as to say, that the punishments of hell must and will certainly be eternal;" but gives it as his opinion, on a review of the arguments, "That there is at least so much force on the affirmative side of the question, and in the solution of the preceding objections, as to render it both imprudent and unsafe to go out of the way of scripture upon this head; or to explain those expressions in such a manner, as positively to determine that future eternal punishments, in strict propriety of speech, are not to be apprehended."

Now there is evidently *a chasm* in this way of reasoning : for if we *cannot* decide that eternal punishments will take place ; and *must not* be persuaded or express our conviction,— that is, according to our conceptions of things,—that they will not; we must remain all our lives in a state of *tortuous suspense* as to one of the leading *motives* of the gospel, in one

of its principal characteristics ; and be utterly unable, *in this view,* either to understand it ourselves, or to preach or explain it to others, and consequently unable, *thus far,* to believe it ; since we can believe nothing which we do not, *in some measure, apprehend :* and this, in a question involving our ideas of the moral attributes of the Deity, is a circumstance of prodigious importance. This is not a matter of mere abstract speculation, as to which it is of little consequence on which side the truth lies :—doubtfulness, in such a case, is *death!*

But it will be said, alas! what can we know of the extent of the divine plans and operations in a future state? "Who can by searching find out God, who can find out the Almighty to perfection?" Shall the Omnipotent be arraigned at the bar of a worm? Shall the delinquent sit in judgment upon the Judge himself? These objections are plausible, and the sentiments themselves founded in truth; but they do not altogether apply, in the present case. We are not to renounce our understandings in the contemplation of subjects in which we are so deeply interested, under a false notion of humility and self-abasement. " We may have *true* conceptions of God, though not full and *adequate* conceptions."*

For be it recollected, that in all our reasonings concerning the Deity, we can reason only as to his perfections and attributes ; of his abstract nature and essence, we can, at present, know nothing : and moreover, that if the ideas of those perfections which we derive from his works and his word, should be supposed to deceive us, there are *no others to be had :* we must begin anew, and launch out into a fathomless ocean, without a pilot, without a helm, and probably without a shore! But it has long been determined as the only legitimate criterion we have whereby to regulate our notions of the Divine Being, to consider the highest perfections of created natures, to subtract every thing imperfect from them, and then to add infinitude to those ideas: " It would, indeed, be a high presumption to determine, whether the Supreme Being has not many more attributes, than those which enter into our conceptions of him;

----

* Wisheart.

but it is impossible that we should have any ideas of any kind of perfection, except those of which we have some small rays, and short, imperfect strokes in ourselves."[*] "It is foolish," says Archbishop Tillotson, "for any man to pretend that he cannot know what justice, and goodness, and truth, in God are; for if we do not know this, it is all one to us, whether God be good or not, nor could we imitate his goodness; for he that imitates, endeavours to be like something that he knows, and must have some idea of that to which he aims to be like: so that if we had no certain and settled notion of the justice, goodness and truth of God, he would be altogether an *unintelligible* Being, and religion, which consists in the imitation of him, be utterly impossible."

Thus it is plain, that though we cannot comprehend the extent and mode of operation of the divine attributes,—for how can finite comprehend infinite?—yet, we have a sufficient idea of the attributes themselves, that is, of those which relate to us, and of their nature and properties—of what, *upon the whole*, appear to be consistent or inconsistent therewith: and that, although it would be highly improper and irreverent to say, with some weak persons, if such a thing take place, God must be so and so; or, if such a thing be true, " then you may burn your Bibles," &c.—yet there is no irreverence at all in saying, such or such a thing is absolutely inconsistent with all our ideas of the divine perfections, and utterly impossible if those ideas be founded in truth. Thus we have clear ideas of the divine *benignity* and *power*; and if we take these attributes in connexion, may easily conceive, that the Almighty could instantly and for ever annihilate all sin and suffering, and make his moral creation universally holy and happy; but we know, that though such a process, this holiness by *influx*, might indeed render intelligent beings happy, it could never constitute them *worthy of praise*; and that, therefore, this desirable event must be brought about by the co-operation of their own powers, in order to render it consistent with his wisdom and justice, as well as with his holiness. Again, with respect to the attribute of *infinite power*, simply con-

sidered, we know that it extends to every *object* of power—to every thing, that doth not imply a contradiction—and yet, we may be more than morally certain, that there are many things *simply possible*, which the Deity will never bring to pass: as, for instance, to *create a world in one instant and destroy it the next*; because this would be, according to all our notions, *a capricious act*, a mark of imperfection,[1] and of the creature, and therefore not to be predicated of the Divinity; all whose attributes are in perfect unison, and who cannot for a moment be supposed to magnify his power at the expense of his wisdom and goodness.

But this pious and benevolent divine (Dr. Doddridge), when emancipated from the trammels of system, and attending to the silent operations of his own sublime and capacious mind, could give his opinion decidedly enough on this point. Thus, though he seems in one place to adopt the common notion, that "the punishment of the damned may be an instructive spectacle to glorified saints;" yet he asks, Prop. 45, "How can the view or experience of misery be necessary to give a virtuous being a more exquisite relish of happiness?" Again, he observes, that "if it appear the scriptures declare the eternity of future punishment, these considerations may serve to *balance the difficulties* arising from principles of the light of nature." Yet, in Prop. 95, on the internal evidences of a divine revelation, he tells us, "We may be *sure* such a revelation can contain *nothing apparently contrary* to the light of nature, because that is *the law of God*, and he is too wise and too faithful to contradict himself." Then, as to what this light of nature *really teaches* concerning this doctrine, he observes, Prop. 82, that, "As for eternal punishments, though some of the Heathen did assert them, and many have undertaken to infer them from natural principles; yet it seems, that our natural apprehensions would rather encourage us to hope, that the Deity would leave some room for *amendment* and *recovery of happiness* in a future state; or, by *annihilation*, put an end to men's misery, when they appeared *humbled* by their punishment."[!] An argument, surely, for annihilation, of all others the most *inconclusive!*

He afterwards proceeds to consider

---

[*] Addison.

a further notion of some of the old divines, of perpetually succeeding sins and punishments; but this, he says in another place, is not reconcileable to scripture; which uniformly represents the punishments of futurity as inflicted for sins " *done in the body.*"

Such are the inconsistencies into which the greatest minds may fall when treating upon subjects not perhaps wholly mysterious and inexplicable in themselves, but rendered so by the intricate and unscriptural jargon of disputants and systematical writers, to whom they are often inclined to pay a degree of attention and deference far beyond their real deserts. In speculation, therefore, as well as in practice, " Let our eyes look right on, and let our eye-lids look straight before us."

[*To be continued.*]

Ryde, Isle of Wight,
Sir,   15th May, 1816.

I HAVE always considered the memory of great and good men as a sacred deposit which cannot be too highly cherished and too carefully preserved; and when the reputation which they have justly acquired has been violated, I have attributed it to the grossest ignorance of their exalted worth.

In this light I regard the attack of Sir G. Hill on the character of that illustrious man, the late Rev. Dr. Priestley, in the Committee of Supply, on Friday, the 10th instant, respecting an academical institution at Belfast, in which the reporter of his speech informs us, that he remarked, "That this institution was likely to be perverted, as persons of a desperate character had wormed themselves into that school with the view of promoting the politics and religion of Paine and Priestley; hoping, by these insidious means, to promote their abominable principles by inculcating them into the minds of the young. The visitors," he added, " have not been perhaps sufficiently active—and many good men have declined interfering."

If the above report be correct, (which, for the credit of Sir G. Hill and the reputation of the honourable the House of Commons, I much question) I am at a loss to account for the silence of those members who could patiently suffer so illustrious a name to be so vilely traduced—and by their silence apparently confirm the truth of his remarks.

The superior merits of Dr. Priestley, both as a divine and a philosopher, are well known and acknowledged by every candid inquirer after truth; and no man was ever actuated by a stronger desire to promote the best interests of his fellow-creatures, by means the most gentle, peaceable and praise-worthy. I speak from knowledge; for I was intimately acquainted with him. He had a soul endued with the most benevolent affections, comprehending, in its grasp, the whole human race; wholly unlike those narrow and illiberal men who, from want of education or early prejudice, have been led to embrace the doctrines and to conform to the worship of an established church, and to despise and consider as dangerous enemies to the state, all those who dissent from it.

What the character of Sir G. Hill may be, I know not; but I hope, and have no reason to believe it otherwise than respectable, notwithstanding this attempt to lower the opinion which every candid and well-informed man entertains of the late Dr. Priestley. We are none of us perfect, and Sir G. Hill has his weak side; let us pity and pray for him.

Country 'squires (and titles are no exemption) labour under great disadvantages. How superficial is their education! how low and groveling their pursuits! Their days spent in hunting and shooting, and their nights in carousing!

Study has no charms for them; and literary characters, who dare to investigate truth and to think for themselves in matters of the highest importance—who refuse to subscribe to articles which they are convinced are false, though imposed by the highest human authority, are, in their judgment, persons entertaining the most abominable principles.

I rejoice to think that we are no longer the slaves of a feudal aristocracy. The mind of man is now beginning to work; it will be found a most powerful engine, and eventually exterminate the deep-rooted errors and prejudices both of religion and politics.

We cannot raise our expectations too high. In the mean time let us aid the progress of truth in every way which lies in our power; recollecting that we are the *salt* of the earth, and the *light* of the world, and though for a short time we may be reviled and persecuted and our names cast out and trodden under foot by ignorant and slanderous men, we shall in no case fail of our reward. I am, Sir,

Your obedient Servant,

B. T.

Sir, *Bath, June,* 1816.

I WISH that you could furnish us with more particulars concerning the late Francis Webb, Esq. I wish therefore that Miss Milner, of Islington, would grant you her assistance. I was glad to see the mistake corrected, that he was secretary to an embassy sent to the prince of Hesse to hire troops to fight against the Americans. I knew that to be an unfounded assertion, as he was always a most strenuous advocate for the cause of American resistance. The history of his defence against the attempt to rob him was not worth recording. Let your correspondents furnish us with matters of more moment.

Your correspondent who wishes to know where I learned Dr. Chauncey's particular doctrine concerning the successive states of oblivion of the righteous in their passing to higher degrees of glory in a future world, must be informed that I learned it in a long private conversation with himself, which he began by saying, I must pass through many sleeps. The Dr. thought highly of my liberality, and was perhaps more open in his communications with me than with any person except his son , Charles. Though we did not always agree, I always greatly esteemed and loved him.

Lord Stanhope's speech is very interesting. To make us a truly glorious nation, very many of our laws must be abolished. I have been informed of a gentleman who lived about seventy years ago at Birmingham, who in the younger part of his life was guilty of some transgressions which led him to fly into Holland: not being yet cured of his follies, he committed some acts for which he was committed to the Rasp-house, where he must either work or be drowned: the rasping not suiting him, and he being informed that he might pursue any trade for which he was fitted, and that all his earnings beyond a weekly allowance for his

board should be regularly paid him, he chose to make a species of boxes which he learned to execute when at Birmingham. This being what his employers much approved, at the end of every week he received what he thought a considerable sum. He proceeded in this way until the time of his imprisonment expired. Being then told that he was at liberty to go where he pleased, he requested that he might be allowed to continue in the Rasp-house until he should earn a sufficiency to support himself elsewhere. His petition was acceded to, and after remaining there some years, he found himself in possession of money enough to live without labour. He returned to Birmingham and took a neat house in its neighbourhood, and, being found a thoroughly reformed and intelligent man, some gentlemen became acquainted with him, and frequently dined at his table. To them he generally related his whole history, and the circumstances which contributed to implant in his breast honesty and integrity and generosity; and he always concluded the feast with toasting the master of the Rasp-house.

If we would only study how to employ the licentious and profligate in some such way, and to impress them at the same time with the principles of true religion, we should soon see purity reign in all our island. We should no longer be shocked with accounts of murders, executions, &c. At present when we go to Morocco, we express our horror at the sight of heads of human beings in the entrances to their palaces, but forget what was seen at Temple Bar some years ago, and what is still seen in some places in the country.

The memorialist of Mr. Calamy in your last number, was very defective in not mentioning his age, his relationship to the great Calamy, his wife, and what children survive him. Many other particulars would be satisfactory to your readers.

W. H.

Bury St. Edmunds, 3d June, 1816.

Sir,

THE friends of peace in this country will be happy to hear, that exertions are making in America for the diffusion of pacific principles. On Saturday the first of June, I received a packet from Boston, containing some pamphlets on the subject, and a letter from the Rev. W. E. Channing. (A copy of which I herewith transmit to you.) The pamphlets, five in number, consist of "A Solemn Review of the Custom of War," a work which has been already reprinted in this country. Numbers 1, 2, and 3, of a work published quarterly, called, "The Friend of Peace." And Number 34, of a periodical publication, called, "The Christian Disciple." There also accompanied these pamphlets a printed statement of "The Constitution of the Massachusetts Peace Society." (A written copy of which I also send you.) Number 1, of "The Friend of Peace," containing 42 pages, consists of "A Special Interview between the President of the United States and Omar, an Officer dismissed for Duelling." "Six Letters from Omar to the President, with a View of the Power assumed by Rulers over the Laws of God and the Lives of Men in making War, and Omar's Solitary Reflections. The whole reported by Philo Pacificus, Author of a Solemn Review, &c." Number 2, contains "A Review of the Arguments of Lord Kaimes in Favour of War." Number 3, "The Horrors of Napoleon's Campaign in Russia." This article is formed of extracts from Porter and Labaume; with some remarks by the Editor: it is followed by "An Estimate of Human Sacrifices in the Russian Campaign." A Paper, "On Estimating the Characters of Men who have been concerned in Sanguinary Customs." "A Solemn Appeal to the Consciences of Professed Christians." And "A memorable and affecting Contrast between the peaceable Conduct of William Penn, and the opposite Behaviour of some other Settlers." In each of these, is much that is truly valuable and interesting: and I do hope that some steps may be taken for reprinting and circulating them in this country. In America, the "Solemn Review" has gone through three large editions in different states. One in Connecticut, one in New York, and another in Philadelphia—the latter amounting to twelve thousand copies, for gratuitous distribution. From Number 1, of "The Friend of Peace," I quote the Author's own words. "The writer

has devoted six months to careful and almost incessant inquiries in relation to the dreadful custom, its origin and popularity among Christians, its causes, principles and means of support; its tremendous havoc, and miseries, its opposition to Christianity, its moral influence on nations and individuals, and the means by which it may be abolished. The more he has examined the more he has been astonished that a custom so horrible has been so long popular among Christians. For he has been more and more convinced, that it is in its nature perfectly hostile to the principles, the precepts and the spirit of the Christian religion. He is also confident that such light may be offered on the subject as will bring reflecting Christians of every sect to this alternative,—either to renounce Christianity as a vile imposture inconsistent with the best interests of mankind, or to renounce the custom of war as indefensible and anti-Christian." From "The Christian Disciple," I transcribe "Facts relating to the Massachusetts Peace Society." "In consequence of an arrangement made by four individuals, who are now members of the Massachusetts Peace Society, a meeting of seventeen persons took place in Boston on the eighteenth of December last, to consult on the subject of forming a Peace Society. It was the wish of the projectors of the plan to form a society on such principles as would embrace *the real friends of society*, without any regard to difference of opinion on other subjects whether religious or political. But it was not known how extensively the sentiments in favour of such a society had been embraced, and of course but a few persons were requested to attend. At the first meeting a committee was chosen to form a constitution, and the meeting was adjourned to the twenty-eighth of the same month to be held in Chauncey place, immediately after the Thursday Lecture; at which time the committee reported a constitution. This was read, discussed, adopted, and subscribed by a considerable number of persons. The choice of officers was postponed to January 11, 1816, in the hope that the number of subscribers would be increased. The number of subscribers has indeed been increasing; and some of the officers have been chosen, but the list is not completed. We shall therefore defer giving the names of the officers to a future number. But we have the pleasure of stating that in the list of subscribers may be seen the names of the governor of Massachusetts, the chief justice of the supreme court, the president and several of the professors of Harvard University, twenty ministers of the gospel and a considerable number of respectable laymen."

I have not now time nor room for further extracts from these very interesting publications, and I sincerely regret that I have it not in my power to give greater publicity to them by reprinting: should, however, any persons feel disposed to give their assistance towards the object, I shall be happy to hear from them, and to devote my attention to superintending the press.

Your's very respectfully,
W. PITT SCARGILL.

Sir,   *Boston, Feb: 12, 1816.*
Your letter dated June 1, 1815, which you did me the honour to address to me, was received some time ago, together with the pamphlet which you had published on the subject of *War*. I have deferred writing you, in the hope that I should be able to communicate to you some gratifying information in regard to the diffusion of pacific principles in this country. Before your letter reached me, the subject of *War* had begun to draw the attention of Christians. Some interesting pamphlets had been extensively circulated for the purpose of awakening public sensibility to the guilt and calamities of that barbarous custom; and a proposition had been distinctly made that "Peace Societies" should be established to give uniformity and energy to the exertions of the friends of peace. The prospect which your letter afforded of the formation of similar institutions in Europe, gave new animation to the author of these pamphlets, and to those who adopted his views; and the subject of a "Peace Society" continued to be agitated, until in the course of last month the desirable object was effected. Several gentlemen of Boston and its vicinity assembled to consider the expediency of combining their efforts for the diffusion of pacific sentiments. A degree of zeal, which the best friends of the cause had not anticipated, was expressed, and the society was formed and organized. I enclose you the constitution, and several pamphlets which have been distributed on the subject, together

with a number of the "Christian Disciple," a work devoted to peace. These publications are chiefly from the pen of the Rev. Noah Worcester, a gentleman of great respectabity of character and distinguished by his benignant, amiable and philanthropic spirit. He is, as you will perceive, the corresponding Secretary of the Peace Society, and will be happy to open a correspondence with you or with any gentleman or societies who have espoused the cause of peace.

In this country many of us have a strong confidence that a favourable impression can be made on the public mind. We regard the abolition of the slave trade as a practical proof, that great and long established abuses may be resisted and extirpated by persevering and disinterested exertion; and whilst we feel that war has a strong and deep foundation in some of the principles of human nature, we believe that there are other principles, which, when invigorated and directed by the light of the gospel, may and will avail to its gradual subversion. The incredulity of men as to the practicability of happy and important changes in the condition of society is certainly diminished. The idea of a more improved state of the world is no longer dismissed with a smile or a sneer as the dream of enthusiasm. It seems to be one of the characteristics of this age, that men cherish more generous hopes in regard to the human race. I regard this as a most happy omen, and when combined with the predictions of revelation, and with the benevolent administration of God, it ought to awaken an unconquerable zeal in the friends of humanity.

Very respectfully,
Your obedient Servant,
W. E. CHANNING.
W. Pitt Scargill.

Constitution of the Massachusetts Peace Society.

In forming a society, which it is hoped may have an extensive influence, we, the subscribers, deem it proper to make a concise declaration of our motives and objects.

We have been strongly impressed, by considering the manifold crimes and tremendous calamities of public war, and the melancholy insensibility which has been induced by education and habit, in regard to this most barbarous, destructive, and unchristian custom. Our earnest wish is, that men may be brought to view war in a just light, to see clearly its baleful influence on the political, moral, and religious condition of communities, and its opposition to the design and spirit of the gospel. Most earnestly do we desire that men may be brought to feel that a spirit of conquest is among. the most atrocious of crimes ; that the thirst for military glory is inhuman, and ruinous ; and that the true dignity and happiness of a people result from impartial justice towards all nations, and the spirit and virtues of peace.

Various facts and considerations have conspired in exciting a hope, that a change may be effected in public sentiment, and a more happy state of society introduced. It is evidently the design and tendency of the gospel, to subdue the lusts and passions from which wars and fightings originate ; and encouragement is given that a time will come when the nations will learn war no more. We believe that a great majority of the people in every civilized country, when free from the delusions of party passions and prejudices, have such an aversion to public hostilities, that they would rejoice if any plan could be devised which would both secure their rights and absolve them from the burdens and sufferings of war. A late treaty of peace has suggested the practicability of such a plan, and given us an admirable lesson on the subject.

We now see, that when two governments are *inclined to peace*, they can make some friendly power the umpire and last resort, for settling points of controversy. For this ray of pacific light we are grateful, and we hope that it will be like " the shining light which shineth more and more unto the perfect day." This hope is strengthened by reflecting on the animating fact, that the horrid custom of *private wars*, which for ages desolated Europe, was finally abolished by a similar project.

Besides, it is clear that every popular custom must depend on public opinion ; and we also know, from history, that many customs and usages, which were formerly considered as honourable, useful and even necessary, have since been abolished as inhuman and barbarous, and are now regarded with detestation and horror.

To the list of encouraging facts we may add, that by their late dreadful sufferings, the attention of the European nations is unusually excited to the guilt and miseries of war ; and with joy we have learned that Peace Societies have been proposed, if not already established, on the other side of the Atlantic. These things not only encourage our hearts and strengthen our hands, but preclude the objection which might arise, that it is dangerous to cultivate the spirit of peace in one nation, whilst others retain the spirit of war. A co-operation in different countries is joyfully anticipated in this great work of promoting peace on earth and good-will among men.

But above all other sources of encouragement, we contemplate the benevolent character of our heavenly Father, as displayed in the gospel of his beloved Son. We there behold him as " the God of peace," and we have a cheering hope that he will own and prosper a society of peace-makers.

It is well known that a diversity of sentiment has existed among Christians on the question, whether war be not in all cases prohibited by the gospel. But we intend that this society shall be established on principles so broad, as to embrace the friends of peace who differ on this as well as on other subjects. We wish to promote the cause of peace by methods which all Christians must approve—by exhibiting with all clearness and distinctness the pacific nature of the gospel, and by turning the attention of the community to the nature, spirit, causes and effects of war. We hope that by the concurrence of the friends of peace in all nations, and by the gradual illumination of the Christian world, a pacific spirit may be communicated to governments, and that, in this way, the occasions of war, and the belief of its necessity, will be constantly diminishing, till it shall be regarded by all Christians with the same horror with which we now look back on the exploded and barbarous customs of former ages.

On these principles, and with these hopes we adopt the following

ARTICLES.

I. The name of this society shall be *The Massachusetts Peace Society.*

II. The government of this society shall consist of a president, a vice-president, a treasurer, a recording secretary, a corresponding secretary, and six trustees, who shall be annually chosen, three of whom shall constitute a quorum.

III. The funds of the society shall be under the direction of the trustees, to be employed for the diffusion of light on the subject of war, and in cultivating the principles and spirit of peace. The trustees shall have power to appoint an executive committee, and counsellors to advise with the corresponding secretary, and to make regulations for the dispatch of business.

IV. Each subscriber of one dollar annually shall be a member.

V. Each subscriber of twenty-five dollars shall be a member for life.

VI. All donations to the society shall be recorded ; and every donor of fifty dollars or upwards, shall be an honorary member of the society and of the board of trustees.

VII. Each member of the society shall receive one half his annual subscription in such books or tracts as the trustees shall approve, and at the lowest prices of the society.

VIII. The annual meeting of the society shall be on the last Thursday in every year ; at which time reports shall be made by the trustees and treasurer.

IX. This society will encourage the forming of similar societies in this country and in foreign countries, by the dispersion of tracts, by correspondence, and by other suitable means. They will encourage mutual aid and co-operation among all the friends of peace of every denomination.

X. Should any person become a member of this society whose residence is remote from Boston, it shall be regarded as honourable for him to encourage the establishment of a similar society in his own vicinity.

XI. No change in the objects of the society shall ever be made; but the articles may be amended, and new articles may be added as occasion shall require; provided that no alteration be made except at the annual meeting, and by the consent of two thirds of the members who may then be present.

Sir,   *June* 8, 1816.

THOUGH your Repository is not intended to contain much political discussion, yet there are some points so intimately connected with the well-being of mankind, that I think some of your pages may be very usefully occupied with the subject.

I have been much pleased with your correspondent, T. S.'s account of the late Dr. Powell: but there is one paragraph in the Obituary, p. 299, where, after speaking of Dr. P.'s love of liberty and popular claims, he mentions some of his own political sentiments, on which I should be much gratified by his giving some farther explanation. Your correspondent says:

"While at *Edinburgh*, Dr. P. was the spectator of a very stormy scene of political contention, and if he was not an actor in it, this arose from no want of zeal in favour of the party which, in his opinion, comprehended the friends of liberty and popular claims. Through life he retained the same partiality, regulated, however, and repressed by the good sense and sound judgment which he applied to all subjects. Still it may be doubted, whether he was sufficiently aware of a fact, the belief of which must be impressed on every calm and unprejudiced mind by even a superficial knowledge of history, and by a slight view of what, during the last five and twenty years, has passed under our own eyes. The fact alluded to is, that there are not in the world wise and virtuous people enough, to keep the foolish and vicious in order. One

would imagine, that this truth is too obvious to be overlooked and too important to be neglected, and that if it was duly attended to by reformers as well as anti-reformers, it would suggest a salutary lesson of moderation to both. It seems to be the plan of Providence to restrain and check one class of crimes and delinquents by the counteraction of another. The *Ovidian* hemistich, *ponderibus librata suis*, is not more applicable to the system of the universe, and to the British constitution, than it is to the general frame of society, composed (as is the majority of it) of short-sighted, wilful and selfish human beings."

Now I think, Sir, there cannot be a stronger argument for reform, than the fact, that "there are not in the world wise and virtuous people enough to keep the foolish and vicious in order:" it shews how diligently we should strive to keep our constitution so adapted that the senate may contain the greatest possible number of wise and virtuous persons; and it appears to me a "truth too obvious to be overlooked and too important to be neglected," that it is impossible such should be the case so long as seats in parliament are bought and sold like stalls in a fair, which must necessarily lead to a great deal of corruption, and have a tendency to fill the senate with men who are more anxious to fill their own coffers, than to promote the general benefit and good order of society.

I think the last twenty-five years which have passed under our own eyes, have clearly shewn how very impolitic it is to neglect the people's voice till too late, when the whole fabric of society may be destroyed in attempting to bring about a reform, which, if attended to as the times demanded, would have had a gradual and very salutary operation. All history shews, and more particularly the last two years, how very unfit kings and their ministers are to have the management of affairs entirely at their disposal, without the beneficial influence of the people, expressed through a constitutional representation; which is, I believe, the best method that can be devised of collecting together "wise and virtuous people enough to keep the foolish and vicious in order:" for I suppose no person will contend, at this time of day, that courts or *congresses* are less liable to be infected with vice and folly, or want less keeping in order, than other parts of society.

I agree with your correspondent, that the majority of society is comprised of "short-sighted, wilful and selfish human beings;" but if he suppose that those qualities reside in general more amongst the governed than those who govern, I certainly dissent from that opinion.

If T. S. will do me the favour to inform me how far I may have mistaken his sentiments, it will oblige

Your constant reader,
J.

Mrs. Sarah Toms's (Daughter of the Rev. Samuel Say, of Westminster) Account of Mr. Hopton Haynes, in a Letter to her Son, Samuel Say Toms, Framlingham.

MR. HAYNES was Assay Master in the Mint. He married his second wife out of the Joslin (Josselyn) family (the first knight baronet in England—the title is now lost in a a higher). They lived in Queen's Square, Westminster, which lies between the Broadway and the Park, Mrs. Haynes attended upon Mr. Say, my father, as her minister, and in consequence they visited at each other's houses. Mr. Haynes was of the Established Church. He had a son, by a former wife, who was rector of Elmset (about four miles from Hadleigh in Suffolk). I often dined at Mr. Hopton Haynes's off turkeys that were sent from him. He was living at Elmset when I came to reside at Hadleigh, about the year 1746.

Mr. Hopton Haynes thought that those who addressed any but God the Father were idolaters. Upon which my father asked him, how he could join in the established service, where it was so often done. His reply was, that he *sat down* to show his dislike. My father saying, "he thought that was not sufficient," Mr. Haynes never after attended any place of worship, and it gave my father much concern that he had hinted it to him. There was no particular intimacy between them.

A grandson of Hopton Haynes, a venerable clergyman, is now resident at Cretingham, a village about five miles from Framling He previously resided at Ipswich, and officiated at Swilling, a small village, if

not elsewhere. He has a living or livings at a considerable distance.

Some years since, visiting at a friend's house near to Mr. Haynes's present residence, I met the old gentleman, and entering into conversation, I mentioned that I had often heard my mother speak of a clergyman at Elmset of his name: he replied, "he was my father;" and of Mr. Hopton H. "yes, he was my grandfather;" and said, his writings were very differently thought of now from what they were at their first publication, and some years after. They are now in high repute with many as giving a just and rational interpretation of the scripture doctrine concerning Jesus Christ. There were warm contenders on both sides of the question. It became every one to examine and think for himself and speak and act from conviction; but some were of opinion that religion was a plain simple thing, and that it was of more importance to insist on it practically than to enter upon the minutiæ of controversy. "He hath taught thee, O man, what is good and what," &c. "Thou shalt love the Lord thy God," &c. "The grace of God which bringeth salvation, hath appeared unto all men, teaching," &c. On these things hang all the law and the prophets, and they think they best preach Christ by laying the main stress on them.

Mr. H. is a very liberal minded gentleman—leads a very retired life—is a bachelor.

S. S. T.

Bromley, May 17, 1816.

SIR,

I LATELY found, among some long forgotten papers, the enclosed which I remember to have received soon after the date of the letter, from a friend who was well assured of its authenticity. The date must have been in 1792, when "about the 20th September the French General Montesquieu entered the territories of Savoy. A deputation from Chambery waited on him almost as soon as he passed the boundary, and on the 21st he proceeded with a detachment to take possession of that city."—(New Ann. Reg. XIII. 193.) Savoy was soon after annexed to France, under the name of the Department of *Mont Blanc*. Of the Marquis of Bellegarde, I am not aware that I ever before met with any account.

I suspect that history will not sustain Mr. Sharp's opinion that " the Crown of France has offered *more* support to the" papacy, " than any other of the" European Powers. My venerable acquaintance appears not to have recollected the frequent contentions of that Crown with the Court of Rome for the liberties of the Gallican Church, the absence of an *Inquisition*, and the Toleration of Protestants, under the name of the Pretended Reformed, from the time of Henry IV. through a large part of the 17th century, though the Toleration was gradually infringed and at length abolished by the revocation of the Edict of Nantes, in 1685. Nor, whatever the *Church* might desire, can it be correctly alleged that the *State*, in France, generally interfered, as in Spain, Portugal, and perhaps *papal* Germany, " to deprive the common people of the Holy Scriptures." I have in my possession two evidences to the contrary. One is the French Testament of the Protestants, printed in 1668 : to which is annexed Marot and Beza's Version of the Psalms, and the Prayers, Catechism, &c. used by the French Protestant Churches. This volume, as appears by the titlepage, was publicly sold by a bookseller at Charenton and Paris. But the other evidence is still more to the purpose; it is a French Testament published at Paris in 1764, with the customary *privilege du Roi.* The Mass is prefixed, with a French translation. Short notes are added to the text of the New Testament; and besides the common division into chapters, there is a more rational arrangement, by sections and paragraphs, and a preface, recommending the study of the Scriptures. This edition of 1764 is described as a re-publication of one that had been printed in 1746. Thus, seventy years ago, at least, any Frenchman might have purchased, at Paris, the New Testament and the Service of his national Church, in his native language, as freely as an Englishman could purchase in London the Liturgy of his Church and the authorized Version, so falsely described, by a favourite *pious fraud*, as *without note or comment.*

I cannot help adding the testimony of Dr. Geddes, in his *Prospectus.* Having censured the opinion " that the Scripture should not be translated into vulgar tongues," he remarks, p. 102, " that this doctrine has chiefly obtained in those countries where the *Inquisition* has been established." He adds, that " in France and Germany a different system has at all times, more or less, prevailed."

Having this occasion again to mention Mr. Sharp, I recollect, what I ought to have noticed sooner, the letter of L. H. (p. 27) occasioned by my former communication. After all, your respectable correspondent's difference with Mr. Jenyns, like that of Mr. Sharp, appears to be little more than verbal. The reference which he makes to the great exemplar of Christians, may well serve to settle the question. L. H. considers Christ as a *patriot*, because he wept over Jerusalem, the metropolis of his native land. But would he not have wept as freely over Rome or Athens, had he been commissioned, a messenger of divine judgments, to either of those cities? The disciples of Christ were indeed *patriots*, according to the constitution and practice of all our *Christian* governments. In one case they wondered that their Master talked with a woman who was a stranger to the commonwealth of Israel, and on another occasion they asked for *fire from heaven*, to revenge an incivility offered by their *natural enemies*, the Samaritans.

I remain, Sir,

Your's,

J. T. RUTT.

Extract of a Letter from Granville Sharp to W. Gill.

" I feel great concern for the distresses which must necessarily be occasioned to the Marquis of Bellegarde, and his amiable family, by the eruption of the French Army into Savoy ; they were in possession not only of Chambery, where the Marquis has a house, but also of the *Chateau des Marches*, the superb seat of the family, and probably in possession also of most of the Marquis's estate, so that undoubtedly the family must have been obliged to fly.

" The retreat of the combined army is stated in a variety of accounts, so that there is now no doubt of the fact, : and of course the French Revolution must be established. The progress of it has been more extraordinary than any event in the history of France, or any other nation for many ages, and contains a variety of very singular instances of God's providence in the timely discovery of secret plots and intended insurrections which the present Atheistical state of that nation prevents them from observing, for they ignorantly impute all their success to their own valour and philosophy.

"The infidelity that pervades France is the natural effect of the long continued exertions of their apostate church and state to deprive the common people of the Holy Scriptures, which were witnesses against their usurpations, and without which men become *brutes* by being unguarded against the sudden and secret impulses of spiritual enemies, which know how to take advantage of every sudden occasion of fear, passion or lust, to stifle the knowledge of good and evil in man——but without this infidelity and the occasional demoniacal phrenzies of some of them (to which Infidels are always liable) they would not have been proper instruments in God's hand for a retribution *in blood* to their more bloody deceivers, of whom the prophet has declared "they have shed the blood of saints and prophets, and thou (O God) hast given them blood to drink, for they are worthy:" thus the very worst of men and even demons are made instruments of God's justice and providence to fulfil his word.

"France was certainly the eminent tenth part of the Roman empire, and the crown of France has offered more support to the anti-christian Pontifex of Rome, than any other of the ten horns of the Beast; so that when the city of Rome was deprived of that support, the prophecy of John was certainly fulfilled, that *a tenth part of the city fell* in a great earthquake or σεισμος, the popular commotion which preceded the event, in which were to be slain "the names of men seven thousand." The names of men could not be slain, otherwise than by a civil death, by a law to extinguish human titles, of which before the time of accomplishment our English translators of the apocalypse could form no conception, nor could they make any sense of the passage; which difficulty induced them to curtail it, and to omit the expression that the names of men were slain, though all the Greek copies have it: and as seven thousand is a prophetic number of perfection, it means a total extinction of all titles, which suddenly and wonderfully happened in an immense nation, more remarkably attached for ages to titles, vanity and arbitrary power, than any other nation on earth; and this wonderful prophetic mark is so strongly impressed upon the nation at present, that they will not even allow the ordinary title of Monsieur to be used among them.

It is remarkable that the army of the French emigrants, consisting chiefly of nobility and titled men, is exactly seven thousand eight hundred, so that if that army should be cut off (and it seems at present in deplorable danger) the number is just sufficient to afford even a literal accomplishment, and to leave a remnant to be affrighted and give glory to the God of

heaven, according to the express terms of the prophecy. But the civil death or total extinction of all titles by law, is amply sufficient to prove the prophetic mark upon that nation, and to enable us to judge by the context of the prophecy (see 11th chapter) in what an awful period of time we stand at present. Excuse these remarks; the accidental mention of our mutual friend the Marquis of Bellegarde insensibly led me to them, and as I have a real satisfaction in being aware of the times, I naturally wish my friends to partake of it. Be pleased to present my respectful compliments to your mother and the ladies.

I remain with great esteem, Dear Sir,
Your humble Servant, G. S."

GLEANINGS; OR, SELECTIONS AND REFLECTIONS MADE IN A COURSE OF GENERAL READING.

No. CCLVIII.
Saint Thomas à Becket.

Gervase, of Canterbury, says, that two volumes of miracles, performed by the dead archbishop, were extant at Christ Church, in Canterbury, when he wrote, and affirms, that *they equalled all those in the gospel.* In proof of which he tells us, that not only diseases of all kinds were healed by the invocation of his name, but members cut off and eyes pulled out *(genitalibus abscissis et oculis effosis)* were restored to the bodies from which they had been separated, and the dead were raised to life.—To which Matthew Paris adds, that he also restored life to dead birds and other animals. This, I presume, he did at idle times for his amusement.—His *blood* was accounted a sovereign

and formed

articles of traffic to the monks of Canterbury.—The archbishop of Sens, in a letter to the pope, delivered to posterity by Roger de Hoveden, told his holiness very gravely, that the wax-lights which were placed about the corpse of Becket, before his interment, happening to go out in the night, he rose up and lighted them again himself.

No. CCLIX.
Short and Long Prayers.

In the reign of Abd'ullah the Third, surnamed Meemoun, Bagdad was afflicted with a great drought. The caliph enjoined a public penance, and went himself in procession, at the head of his Mussulman subjects, to perform, in the neighbouring plains, the prayers prescribed by religion on such occasions. The ceremony was repeated on three succeeding days, but without effect. Heaven withheld its blessings and rejected their petitions. The caliph then ordered the Jews and Christians to unite their supplications with those of the faithful; when, lo! to the great scandal of Islamim, the rain fell in abundance, and the earth was refreshed. The caliph was astounded: he felt the affront even more than he acknowledged the favour, and his faith staggered with resentment. The *Ulema** were assembled, and the caliph proposed his doubts; when a reverend doctor, no less learned than pious, arose, and enforcing his reasonings with the seductions of eloquence, calmed his disquietude, and brought him back into the stedfastness of truth. The Mahometan doctors attribute to inspiration the discourse which he pronounced. "What is there," said the holy man, "so extraordinary in this event, or so inimical to the religion of Mahomet? God," continued he, "so loves the Mussulmans, his chosen people, their prayers and their petitions are so grateful to his ear, that he even abstains from an immediate compliance with their request, to compel them to renew their pious addresses: but the voice of infidels is harsh and dissonant; and if he grant their petitions, it is from disgust at their nauseous supplications, and to rid himself of their importunities."

No. CCLX.
Ancients and Moderns.

" *God* hath given wisdom unto all, according to a competent measure, that they might both find out things unheard of before, and weigh things already found out. Neither because they had the start of us in time, doth it likewise follow that they have it also in wisdom, which, if it be indifferently granted to all, it cannot l e forestalled by them that went before. It is unimpareable, like the light and brightness of the sun, it being the light of man's heart, as the sun is of his eyes. Since then to be wise, that is, to search the truth, is a disposition inbred in every man, they debar themselves of wisdom, who, without any examination, approve the inventions of their ancestors, and, like unreasonable creatures, are wholly led by others.

* The Turkish Court of Doctors' Commons.

But this is it which deceives them, the name of *ancestors* being once set in the front, they think it cannot be that either themselves should be wiser, because they are called *punies*, or the others should in any thing be mistaken, because they are called their *ancestors*." From Lactantius, *Div. Inst.* l. ii. c. 8, by Hakewill. *Apologie*, 1630. l. iii. ad fin.

No. CCLXI.
Magnanimity of the Royal Family.

When the Princess of Wales, mother of his present Majesty, mentioned, with some appearance of censure, the conduct of Lady Margaret M'Donald of Sleat, who harboured and concealed the Prince when in the extremity of peril, he threw himself on her protection—"And would not you, Madam," answered Prince Frederick, "have done the same in the like circumstances? I hope—I am sure you would." Besides the great measure of restoring the forfeited estates of the chiefs, our venerable sovereign shewed, on many occasions, how little his heart was capable of nourishing dislike against those who had acted upon principle against the authority of his family. The support which he afforded to the exiled branch of the Stuarts, will form a bright trait in his history; and secluded as he now is from his government and people, we may as of a deceased monarch relate one of those trifling *traits* which marked the generous kindness of his disposition. His Majesty was told of a gentleman of family and fortune, in ————shire, that, far from taking the oath of allegiance to him, he had never been known to name or permit him to be named as king in his presence.— "Carry my compliments to him," said the king, "and say that I respect his steadiness of principle; or, as he may not receive my compliments as King of England, present them as those of the Elector of Hanover." And he never afterwards saw the gentleman from whom the anecdote is derived, without enquiring after the health of the venerable recusant, and reiterating his wish to be remembered to him. The same kindness to the memory of those who hazarded themselves for the Stuart cause, has been inherited by the present administrator of royal authority; and to him as to his father, their descendants have been and are prompt to repay it.
Quarterly Review.

REVIEW.

"Still pleased to praise, yet not afraid to blame."---POPE.

ART. I.—*The General Prayer-Book*; containing Forms of Prayer on Principles common to all Christians, for Religious Societies, for Families, and for Individuals: chiefly selected from the Scriptures, the Book of Common Prayer, and the Writings of various Authors. By John Prior Estlin, LL. D. Cr. 8vo. pp. 236. Longman and Co. 6s. 6d. 1815.

PRAYER-BOOKS have too often been the mere symbols of party, serving to instruct the several sects in their *Shibboleths.* One of these compilations has been the occasion of more misery than any other hundred volumes which were ever published. From St. Bartholomew Day, 1662, to the present time, its influence has been manifested by divisions and excommunications, wounded consciences and broken hearts.

We therefore hail the appearance of a Book of Common Prayer, the design of which is to unite and not to divide, to support Christianity and not human systems, and to promote charity and piety and not what the compiler may deem *orthodoxy.*

" Of the following collection of prayers, the first form is taken entirely from the Scriptures; the second is taken chiefly from a Paraphrase on the Lord's Prayer by the Rev. John Simpson; the third, from some Services published about fifty years ago, for the use of a congregation in Liverpool; the fourth and fifth, from alterations of the Common Prayer; and the sixth, which preserves the mode generally in use among Dissenters, from a Prayer written for a Fast-day, and published by request of the congregation with which the writer is connected. It consequently contains both the religious and political sentiments of that respectable society. The prayers for Families, for Individuals and for Young Persons, are partly original and partly taken from the Essex-street Liturgy, from the services of Dr. Enfield, Mr. Kingsbury, Mr. Merivale, and the Prayers published by the Unitarian Society." *Pref.* Pp. xvi. xvii.

Both the original and the selected forms in this volume appear to us answerable to the professions of the compiler, and to be drawn up " on Principles common to all Christians." They will be found of great use to such societies of Christians (if such there be) as, agreeing in the general doctrines of the gospel, in the desire to unite on this foundation, and in the expediency of a liturgy, are yet of different persuasions on some of the controverted points of faith. Churches of this description, alone Catholic, will feel the value of this manual of charity and devotion.

In the *Preface*, Dr. Estlin states, in a very frank and solemn manner, his sentiments on some of the most interesting topics of Christian morality. He thus explains the reasons of his nonconformity:

" Approving of the occasional use of printed forms of prayer, both in public and in private, and admiring the style and manner of the Liturgy of the Church of England, he laments that he is precluded from joining in it, by a disbelief of some of the doctrines which it contains, and a disapprobation of the claim to infallibility, and the intolerant spirit which characterize one of its fundamental creeds.

" In connecting himself with Dissenters, he was influenced by no sectarian spirit; for the first wish of his heart, until he was nearly twenty years of age, was to officiate in the Established Church, and to procure for himself that share of its emoluments and honours which was to be obtained by a fair competition, by professional industry, and by consistency of character.

" It has often been a painful consideration to him, and has led to a most unpleasant general inference, that *his close attention to the subject,* and *his fixed determination never to sacrifice principle to inclination,* should have operated as the *cause* of his exclusion. With every pious mind he would cordially sympathize, if it could be made to appear that the opposite qualities—that *ignorance* and *want of principle,* not only presented no bar, but afforded a facility to admission.

" Further consideration, instead of removing, only *increased* his difficulties, until he was forced at last to rest in the conviction, that as conformity to the mode of religion established in this country would require him to subscribe about two hundred and fifty propositions, many of which he did not believe, and to read creeds which he considered as unscriptural and intolerant, and above all, to lead the devotions of a congregation when he could not accompany them with his heart; such conformity in him, would be nonconformity.

to the first principles of Christianity and Protestantism, and to the eternal laws of truth, as well as to every principle of Christian humility and charity." Pp. iv. v.

The following thoughts on " Subscription," are worthy of serious consideration :

" It is an idea which has forcibly taken possession of his mind, that a subscription to articles of religion which are *not* believed, as the condition of obtaining any worldly advantage—the subscription to and repetition of creeds which are so far from being the actual creed of the subscriber or repeater, that he himself is sentenced by them to everlasting 'perdition—above all, *professing* to worship the God of Truth, when the heart is at variance with the lips, —if it be not that *specific* crime for the commission of which *two persons were stricken dead by an apostle,* is a *species of crime* comprehended under that *generic character* which is laid down by the apostle to excite a suitable horror on this awful occasion.

" If there be any foundation for this apprehension, if moral evils of this nature actually exist, as soon as their existence is generally known and adverted to, it is presumed that the integrity of the nation will be as steadily directed to the means of removing them, as the benevolence of the nation was to the means of effecting the abolition of the slave-trade. The causes are obvious; the remedies may be applied with perfect facility, and they *cannot,* from the nature of things (for they are agreeable to the nature of things which has been obstructed only because they were not applied before, *they cannot) be attended with any inconvenience whatever.*

" Such changes have been produced in men's religious opinions by that great innovator *Time,* that, notwithstanding some symptoms of a retrograde march of mind to the darkest ages, the understanding of a *man* cannot be moulded into an acquiescence in the infallibility of the composers of our articles and liturgy, or of the infallibility of Elizabeth and her parliament, under whom they received the sanction of law, or of Charles the Second and his parliament, by whom this sanction was confirmed. The absurdity of a similar establishment in medicine every person would immediately perceive; and it is presumed that few physicians at present, whatever might have been the case among the ancient Egyptians, would submit to be members of such an establishment. Institutions supposed useful in certain circumstances (not that the utility of sanctioning by law human creeds or human articles in any circumstances is acknowledged) may survive their utility. It is hard to conceive

that some hundreds of propositions on the most abstruse points of theology, should for centuries constitute the faith of so many thousands as from some motive or other are induced to subscribe what are called the thirty-nine articles.

" An alarming, and a justly to be dreaded effect of this adherence to ancient establishments is, that it will probably lead to attempts to *bring down the standard of morality to human institutions,* instead of endeavouring to *raise human institutions to the standard of morality.* And if this be not a national corruption of morals, what is ?" Pp. v. vii.

Dr. Estlin considers, and we think justly, that he only is a *Church-man,* who believes the Athanasian Creed.

" It would seem to be a question of easy solution, what is it which constitutes a churchman ? Can it be any thing else than *a belief in the creeds and articles of the church, manifested by a correspondent conduct ?* It is true a man may *profess* himself a churchman, without this belief. It is equally true, a man who disbelieves the divine mission of our Saviour, or even an Atheist, may profess himself a Christian.

" A churchman, then, is one who embraces the following creed. " Whosoever will be saved, before all things, it is necessary that he hold the Catholic faith. Which faith, except every one do keep whole and undefiled, without doubt he shall perish everlastingly." A man who *believes* this may undoubtedly, consistently with religious integrity, read it or join in it, and be a member of a church of which this forms a constituent part. But nothing appears clearer to the compiler of these forms of prayer, than that the person who attends the service of the church *without* believing this, is by profession a churchman, but in principle a dissenter." P. ix.

The author expresses himself very strongly, but who will say too strongly? on Dr. Paley's celebrated chapter in the Moral Philosophy.

" The writer of these remarks wishes, however, to add one word more on the subject of *religious integrity.* It is with the sentiment of disapprobation that he always reads Dr. Paley's Chapter on *Lies.* It is with unspeakable pain that he reads that on *Oaths to observe local Statutes.* It is with horror that he reads that on *Subscription to Articles of Religion.* Excellent as the works of this author are in general, it appears to him, that in these instances he has surrendered the citadel of truth. The united exertions of men of religious integrity, from all denominations of Christians, he trusts will soon regain it. Farther this accommodating writer could not go: the pen dropt; and no chapter is to be found in his work, in which an attempt is made to defend *insincerity in the worship of Almighty God.*

" The appeal is made to every pious parent, and to every ingenuous youth, whether the taking of oaths which are not to be observed, and the subscription to articles which are not believed, as the first step of a preparation for the Christian ministry, would not be succeeded, as its second step, by joining in the worship of God with lying lips; and whether such a repetition of sounds can be called the worship of God at all." P. x.

Every enlightened mind will take pleasure in the author's benevolent speculations with regard to the progress of " pure and undefiled religion."

" The return of peace; the general circulation of the Bible and the extension of the ability to read it; the recognition and the bringing into exercise of many general principles, which in former ages were only occasionally discerned, and soon obscured by the clouds of ignorance and prejudice, are most auspicious circumstances; and in the midst of so much enthusiasm, superstition and bigotry on the one side, and indifference on the other, are highly consolatory and grateful to the feeling mind.

" There is a rotation of intellectual taste, as well as of outward fashion. The attributes of God; the character of his administration; the everlasting state of mankind; the means of obtaining and enjoying that felicity for which God has designed us; the obligations of religious integrity, and Christian humility and charity; in a word, the science of religion and morals, with a view to its practical application, will not, in every period of the world, be considered as the least important of all the subjects which can employ the attention of the human mind." P. xvi.

ART. II.—*The History and Antiquities of Dissenting Churches, &c.*
[Continued from p. 292.]

NATHANIEL LARDNER, D. D. is one of the few names of which all the Dissenters make their boast. A full account of him is here given from the memoirs already existing. It is a circumstance not generally known, says Mr. Wilson, I. 91, that he commenced his stated labours in the ministry at an ancient meeting-house in Hoxton Square. Here he preached for a few years as assistant to his father, Mr. Richard Lardner.

" In the year 1757, Dr. Lardner, in conjunction with the Rev. Caleb Fleming, revised for publication and introduced with

a preface, a posthumous tract of Mr. Thomas Moore, entitled, ' An Inquiry into the Nature of our Saviour's Agony in the Garden.'—Mr. Moore was a woollen-draper in Holywell Street, Strand; a thinking man and studious in the scriptures. The design of his pamphlet is to account for our Lord's agony, from the series of events which befel him during the latter part of his ministry, without supposing it to have been the result of any preternatural inflictions." Pp. 103, 104; and *note.*

We take notice of this tract in order to suggest that if any person possessing it will entrust it to our care by means of our publishers, we will cause it to be re-printed. There is a sermon, also, on the same subject, which we beg leave to inquire after, with the same view: the following character of it and of the author is taken from *Wakefield's Evidences of Christianity,* 2nd edit. 8vo. 1793, pp. 136, 137:—

" But I forbear to enlarge on this subject of our Lord's *agony,* because it has been discussed with much good sense and perspicuity, by my venerable friend, the *Rev. Timothy Wylde, late master* of the *free-school* in *Nottingham,* in a *sermon* preached almost sixty-three years ago at that place, upon Matt. xxvi. 39,[*] from which I shall quote the *three* reasons assigned for this extraordinary emotion of our Saviour:

" 1. The first ground of *Christ's* fear and agony I shall mention, is his *knowing beforehand* the particular circumstances of his torment and death.

" 2. Another reason of our Saviour's fear and disorder was, the *remarkable severity* of his sufferings, and the many circumstances of cruelty with which his death was attended.

" 3. The only other reason I assign for our Saviour's fear of death (and what I principally rely on), is his sense of the *important consequences* which depended on his dying well.

" Thus far this intelligent preacher, who reasons on each of these propositions in a rational, convincing and instructive manner."

To return to the *History*: Mr. Wilson having given an account of the publication of Dr. Lardner's *Letter on the Logos,* drops a reflection which we cannot pass over:

---

[*] " The author is still alive, and has the full enjoyment of his intellect, in extreme old age. The sermon well deserves re-publication."

" It is with extreme concern that we place so great a man as Dr. Lardner on the list of Socinian authors, who, however respectable, on account of their labours in the cause of literature, have contributed by their writings to poison the streams of divine truth and promote an universal scepticism in matters of belief." P. 105.

To this uncharitable assertion is added a still more uncharitable note :

" We have somewhere met with an observation of the celebrated Dr. Taylor of Norwich, which is much to our present purpose. The Doctor, who was a zealous Socinian, and a learned tutor at Warrington, expressed his surprise ' how it happened that most of his pupils turned Deists.' The fact, it seems, he admitted ; but he never thought of accounting for it from the sceptical tendency of Socinian principles." *Ib.*

It is an unfavourable augury when an historian is *extremely concerned* and manifestly reluctant to relate historical truth. Dr. Lardner was in opinion what he saw reason for being ; and it is not for his biographers either to hide his faith or to sit in judgment upon it. Such a man could not believe *without*, much less *against*, evidence.

The pleasure of vilifying " Socinian authors" is, we believe, very great : still, it was hardly to be expected that, with Lardner at their head, they should be characterized as a class of men who " have contributed by their writings to *poison the streams of divine truth and promote an universal scepticism in matters of belief!*" The citation of such a sentence is reprobation enough.

Mr. Wilson must excuse our doubting the truth of the anecdote relating to Dr. Taylor. He should not have told such a story without being prepared to allege his authority. His " somewhere" will, we suspect, turn out to be *no-where*. If we wrong him, he may set himself right with our readers in the department of our work allotted to Correspondence.

We have no satisfaction in making objections to Mr. Wilson's work, which, upon the whole, we consider highly valuable and interesting, but we feel it to be a duty to endeavour to prevent his *poisoning the streams of historic truth and promoting an universal scepticism in matters of* ecclesiastical history ; and therefore we cannot pass by the account of Mr. Paul Cardale without animadversion. The name

of this gentleman is introduced into the History, in consequence of Dr. Lardner's having revised the manuscript of his Treatise on the True Doctrine of the New Testament concerning Jesus Christ, and the following biographical note is subjoined :—

" Mr. Cardale was educated for the ministry under Dr. Latham, at Findern, in Derbyshire. About the year 1735, he settled at Evesham, where he preached about forty years, till his death, early in 1775. At the last, he had about twenty people to hear him, having ruined a fine congregation by his very learned, dry and critical discourses, an extreme heaviness in the pulpit, and an almost total neglect of pastoral visits and private instruction.[*] He wrote several pieces in a dull, tedious way in favour of Socinianism. In common with other writers of his stamp, he endeavours to impress his readers with an idea that every creed promulgated under the name of Christian, is equally acceptable to the Divine Being ; or, in other words, that *there is no such thing as religious truth.* His publications, according to Dr. Kippis,[†] had considerable influence in drawing over persons to his own opinions." P. 106.

There is great indecorum in the attack upon the ministerial character of Mr. Cardale, who we know was respected and beloved by his hearers. Job Orton's authority is not sufficient for the charge : Orton was subject to fits of ill-humour, and many of his letters bear the marks of severity and intolerance.

Did not Mr. Wilson perceive the inconsistency of describing Cardale as *a dull, tedious* writer, and at the same time of admitting, on the representation of Dr. Kippis, that he was successful in making converts by his publications? Let the historian read the works which he has censured and he will find that they display learning and judgment and talents, and that the author occupies, if not the first rank as a writer, yet one which will ever secure him the respect and confidence of his readers.

Mr. Cardale, says the historian, in common with other " Socinians," endeavours to shew that *there is no such thing as truth !* Astounded at this assertion, we took down from its shelf

---

* " Orton's Letters to Dissenting Ministers, vol. i. p. 154."

† " Life of Lardner, p. 67."

our copy of The True Doctrine, and almost the first passage which met our eye, was the following, which we extract for Mr. Wilson's information:—

"The principal thing, therefore, that I would recommend and inculcate, is, a *love of truth.* This is the most promising and likely way to be led into it, the best preparative for receiving it, and, in all cases, the best preservative against every dangerous error and delusion. It is for want of this, that there are multitudes in the world who labour under mental slavery and oppression, and are hardly. ever sensible of it. Reason must always be dormant, and in a state of captivity, when there is no disposition and relish for free inquiry. And I cannot but lay the greater stress upon this, as the apostle, when speaking of the *grand apostacy,* thus accounts for it, telling us, that, because men *received not the love of truth,* they erred to their own destruction. See that remarkable passage in 2 Thess. ii. 10, 11, &c. where the apostle strongly intimates, that persons *need not,* or rather *cannot* be deluded, by the lying wonders, the unrighteous and fraudulent wiles of the *man of sin,* if they are lovers of truth and virtue. It is only upon other characters, that God, at any time, sendeth strong delusion, so that they should believe a lie, or embrace the most absurd and foolish things, &c. whereas the mind of a truly honest man, who sincerely loves and seeks the truth, being free from every corrupt and criminal bias, will seldom, if ever, err, in any matters of real importance. Truth of every kind, and especially religious truth, will be always dear to him. He will, e. g. inquire after and cordially embrace whatever appears to be the truth of the gospel, however contrary it may be to his former opinions, to the faith of his own, or to the articles of any other church.—Upon the same principle, he will always act as conscience persuades, and be strictly just and true to the light and sentiments of his own mind; knowing that, how light a matter soever some persons make of it, conscience is very much concerned in stedfastly adhering to what we apprehend to be the truth, how wide or different soever it may be from the apprehensions of others." Pref. Ess. pp. 68, 69.

Having read this passage, our concern for the Historian led us to look into Mr. Cardale's other principal work, The Gospel Sanctuary; where we were equally at a loss for any one sentence to justify Mr. Wilson's censure: we found one passage, however, which, though it does not bear him out in his condemnatory criticism, may possibly set him right in spirit:

" Christians, as such, would do well to consider, that one eminent branch or precept of this gospel is *charity,* *(charity* in respect to other men's opinions, and our own temper and conduct towards them that differ from us,) and that the *peculiar* doctrines of Christianity do, in the strongest manner, recommend and enforce it. All *uncharitableness* is *unrighteousness :* it is *iniquity ;* or a manifest breach of the *gospel rule,* which is a rule of *equity,* and contrary to the very spirit and design of it.— When professed Christians, in open defiance of this noble *maxim,* grow *angry* with those that differ from them, call in question their *honesty,* deny them the rights of *common humanity,* and are for propagating what they call *truths* in the way of the *Alcoran,* not of the *Bible;* this is the *bane* of Christianity, and inconsistent with all *true religion :* or, this is that *bitter zeal,* (as the *apostle* truly describes it,) which is *earthly, sensual,* and *devilish,* and ought never to have a *place,* or a *name,* amongst Christians, amongst *Protestants.*" Pref. pp. xx. xxi.

The historian sinks into the partizan in the description of Dr. Lardner's character, (p. 111.) It is needless to quote Mr. Wilson's words: the purport of them is that he wishes Dr. Lardner had believed as he (Mr. W.) believes, regrets that Dr. Lardner should have assisted in *the destruction of the faith* of Christians, and disavows moderation and charity where " Socinianism" is concerned ! " Charity, for a system that stabs at the very vitals of Christianity, is no longer a virtue, but *a crime!*" Were the History disgraced with many passages of this ridiculous, insolent character, we should take little interest in it; but regarding Mr. Wilson's intolerance as occasional and as an exception to the usual spirit which he breathes in these pages, we deem ourselves not ill-employed in pointing out places where he may employ the pruning-knife with credit to himself.

George Benson, D.D. was another of the eminent men who preached in

Poor Jewry Lane. He was educated in Calvinism, and was first settled over a congregation professing that system at Abingdon, in Berkshire. Whilst here, he published three practical Discourses to young persons, which he afterwards suppressed, Mr. Wilson says, " on account of their *evangelical* tendency," meaning, we suppose, on account of their inculcating the doctrines of John Calvin, which Dr. Benson in the maturity of his understanding renounced as odious corruptions of the gospel.

Mr. Wilson charges Dr. Benson's "Account of Calvin's causing Servetus to be burned" with exaggeration. We think the charge groundless. The death of the Unitarian martyr is brought home by a chain of unquestionable evidence to the Genevan dogmatist, whose language concerning the murdered Spaniard, after the tragical deed, convicts him of a barbarousness of heart which is rare even in the annals of persecution. It is due to Mr. Wilson to state that he avows in measured terms his disapprobation of Calvin's conduct in this affair.

In delineating Dr. Benson's character, the historian is betrayed by his zeal for his own system of faith into reflections, resembling those which deform the picture which he has given of Dr. Lardner.

Ebenezer Radcliff [Radcliffe,] who changed the style of *Reverend* for that of *Esquire*, was living when Mr. Wilson drew up the account of him, but died shortly after. We inserted (V. 707—711) an interesting Memoir of him from the pen of a near friend. His first settlement as a minister is there said to have been at Boston, not at Stamford, as stated by Mr. Wilson. Mr. Radcliffe's Sermon on the refusal of the repeal of the Test Act in 1772, is said by our Author, with apparent acquiescence, to have been "considered at the time much too violent:" but what publication against injustice and oppression ever escaped this accusation? It has been humourously said that the verb *reform* has no present tense; and the efforts of reformers have been always pronounced by such as are *wise in their generation* to be ill-timed and imprudent.

Richard Price, D. D. was afternoon [or evening?*] preacher at Poor Jewry

Lane at the same time that he was pastor at Newington Green : he continued here till his acceptance of the pastorship, in 1770, at the Gravel Pit, Hackney.

John Calder, D. D. is the last name on this distinguished list. We extract Mr. Wilson's account of him :

" Upon the resignation of Dr. Price, the afternoon service in Poor Jewry Lane was undertaken by Dr. Calder. This gentleman (who is still living) is a native of Scotland, and received his education in the University of Aberdeen, from whence he received his degree. He was settled some time with a congregation at Alnwick, in Northumberland, where he married a lady of considerable fortune. From thence he removed to London, and succeeded Dr. Price as already mentioned. After the dissolution of the society in Poor Jewry Lane, Dr. Calder retired to Hammersmith, where he devoted himself chiefly to his literary labours. Since that time he has not undertaken any stated work in the ministry, and he is now a member of Mr. Belsham's congregation in Essex Street."*

Dr. Calder is since dead. He left a valuable library, chiefly numismatic, which was not long ago sold, together with the late Dr. Towers's, by public auction. For a short period, Dr. Calder was Librarian of Dr. Williams's Library, Red-Cross Street.

This brief notice may possibly induce some of his surviving friends to furnish a complete memoir.

The latter end of Poor Jewry Lane Meeting-House exhibits a melancholy instance of the mutability of all that is human and of the degeneracy of institutions which depend upon the talents of successive individuals. After having been shut up a short time it was reopened by a new people, termed a chapel, furnished with an organ and a Common Prayer-Book, and the other attractive *et cetera* of *Calvinistic Methodists*, the name itself of Poor Jewry Lane giving place to that of Jewry Street.

Our author manifestly droops with his subject; his account of the converted place of worship is scarcely above the style of the Obituary of the Evangelical Magazine. He takes apparently as much pleasure in the minute biography of obscure, however virtuous, preachers as of Lardner and Benson. A short memoir is given in a note of *Henry Mead*, who "was very

---

* See Review of Morgan's Life of Price, Mon. Repos. X. 505.

* " Private information."

near becoming minister of Jewry Street Chapel, and had *purchased the organ, which was built for the little Minories Church.*" The names of the actual ministers of this *Chapel*, from the period of its becoming such to that of this publication, are *William Aldridge, Richard Povah,* and *John Ball.*

Mr. Aldridge was one of Lady Huntingdon's students. He left her connexion and became in 1776 stated minister at Jewry Street, where he continued till his death in 1797. He published a funeral sermon on the death of his patroness, the Countess of Huntingdon; and "The Doctrine of the Trinity stated, proved, and defended." He was occasionally assisted by "a Mr. Bryan," also a student at Trevecca, who obtained holy orders from Erasmus; a Greek Bishop, who visited London in the year 1763, and ordained several persons that could not procure ordination from the English Bishops. Mr. Bryan became minister of a congregation at Sheffield, but "was afflicted for many years, at intervals, with an unhappy dejection of spirits, which bordered upon derangement."

Mr. *Povah* was introduced to the ministry by means of Lady Huntingdon: after his settlement at Jewry Street, he conformed to the Church of England and endeavoured to put the chapel under the jurisdiction of the Bishop of London; this being resisted by the trustees, led to the resignation of his charge. He then became curate and lecturer of St. James's, Duke's Place; and has since, we believe, been harassed by proceedings against him in the spiritual court on the ground of his being heretical in his notions of baptism.

Mr. John Ball was "designed for the water," and "spent a part of his youth upon the river Thames," but, diverted from his original calling, entered Dr. Addington's Academy at Mile End, and after various ministerial engagements settled at Jewry Street, where the History leaves him. "In 1807, Mr. Ball *took up the cudgels* in defence of the Rev. Rowland Hill," in a pamphlet in answer to "An Admonitory Epistle." (See M. Repos. II. 437.) This pamphlet is said by Mr. Wilson to have been written "in an ill temper."

The importance of the former part of this article in the History, must plead our apology for devoting to it so many of our pages. Our notices of the remaining historical and biographical articles will be more brief; we anticipate less and less occasion for animadversions on the historian.

ART. III.—*A Solemn Review of the Custom of War;* shewing that War is the Effect of popular Delusion; with a Proposal for a Remedy. 8vo. pp. 16. [Price 3d. or 2s. 6d. per Dozen.] Souter, Paternoster Row.

THIS is the first number of the *Tracts of the Society for preventing War.* We hail the rise of such a Society, and insert with pleasure the three first Resolutions of the persons composing it, explanatory of its object:—

"*London Coffee House,*
"*March* 20, 1816.

"At a meeting of friends to the principle of this Society, Sir Richard Phillips having been invited to take the chair, the following Resolutions were passed:—

"1. That a Society be now formed whose object it shall be to circulate knowledge among all nations, on subjects of public morality, on the folly, inutility and wickedness of war, and on the obligations of governments not to appeal to the sword on slight occasions, on questions of equivocal policy, or for the gratification of pride, revenge or ambition.

"2. That to guard the proposed Society against misrepresentations, it is deemed proper to declare that its purpose is of a nature *purely moral*; that it addresses itself to no particular party, either religious or political; and that it will on no occasion mix itself with questions of temporary and local politics.

"3. That some approved tract, tending to promote the objects of this Society, shall be published every three months.

The only name as yet published in connexion with the Society is that of the Chairman, who offers to give information concerning the Institution to such as may apply to him for it. The same information may be obtained of the publisher of this tract, who is also appointed general publisher to the Society.

We trust, however, that more efficient means will be adopted to make the Society known, and to secure the patronage of the moral and Christian public. Subscriptions are invited for the sake of enabling the Society to make a gratuitous distribution of their publications; these will not we dare say, be withheld; but they cannot be expected to any great amount, unless the several officers of the Society give their names to the world. This step, therefore, we recommend them instantly to adop ; taking it for granted that the names are wisely selected, so as to preclude the suspicion of party views and interested motives.

The *Solemn Review*, as we learn from our correspondent, Mr. Scargill (see p. 332), is an American publication, the first-fruits of the *Massachusett's Peace Society*. The English Society could not have chosen a better tract to head their publications. It is well-written and ably argued, and though temperate, contains such appeals to the better feelings of mankind in favour of peace as can scarcely be resisted. We hope that there are few of our readers who will not procure it and put it in circulation.

The American Peace Societies (for we reckon that they have multiplied since the date of the last dispatches from America) have originated in New England, amongst that part of the people of the United States, who opposed the late war with England, and who have generally been distinguished from the majority of their countrymen by their Anglican predilections and politics. If in England the same institutions should be established by persons not usually concurring in the public policy of the government, the fair conclusion will be, not that peace and republicanism are kindred objects of desire (history has shewn them commonly dissociated), but that the objection, on whatever grounds, to any particular war, sharpens the understanding and quickens the feelings, to a perception of the injustice and an abhorrence of the iniquity of all war, by whomsoever and wheresoever and for what purposes soever waged. The English have for years been accustomed to extol the wisdom and virtue of the American New Englanders, and we trust that they will not abate in their admiration and esteem of that portion of the population of the United States, now that they are happily converting

their politics into morality, and sublimating the spirit of party into pure philanthropy.

The Society announce for publication on the first of August a second Tract, consisting of Extracts from Grotius on Peace and War, in the same form and at the same price, as the "Solemn Review."

ART. IV.—*The Value of a Child; or, Motives to the good Education of Children. In a Letter to a Daughter. By* John Taylor, *D. D. of Norwich.* 12mo. pp. 34. *Printed by* Richard *and* Arthur Taylor. *Sold by* R. Hunter, *St. Paul's Church Yard.* 1816.

THIS treatise, now presented anew to the public in a very elegant form, by the hand of filial piety, was written by Dr. Taylor in 1748, and addressed to his daughter, Mrs. Rigby, of Chowbent in Lancashire, and his daughter-in-law, Mrs. Taylor, of Norwich, on the birth of their first children. It has been long out of print and sometimes anxiously inquired after. In so small a compass, it is impossible to imagine more sound moral instruction. We recommend the tract especially to those who are entering, or have but lately entered, into the parental relation.

The following maxim is worthy of Dr. Taylor's well known liberality of spirit:—

" The justest notions attended with the virulence of bigotry are but as generous wine turned into the sourest vinegar." P. 28.

ART. V.—*A Sermon* delivered at the Unitarian Chapel, Chichester, April the 21st, 1816, *on occasion of the Death of* Thomas P. Powell, M.D. *By* W. J. Fox. 4to. pp. 32.

THIS is an elegant tribute of affection and respect to the memory of a gentleman who seems to have been worthy of the choicest offerings of friendship. There is prefixed to the sermon the interesting sketch of Dr. Powell's life and character, by an able pen, which appeared in the obituary of our last number (p. 293).

POETRY.

To a Wife,

On the Anniversary of her Marriage.

See Time, *Serena*, close our thirtieth year
Since, first, the bliss was mine to greet
    thee Wife,
And breathe the vow, to mem'ry ever dear,
With thee to share th' allotted hours of
    life.

Blest hours! thy love has well essay'd to
    fill
With sweet content, alone by virtue giv'n,
Grateful the good enjoy'd, endur'd the ill,
Submissive to th' all-just dispose of heav'n.

And now, affection's soothing arts to prove,
O'er age's honour'd couch I see thee bend,
And sure some fond remembrance of thy
    love,
Shall with thy sire's departing pray'r as-
    cend.

Nor vainly lavish'd thy maternal care,
Tho' fortune lend no more her gladd'ning
    rays;
If virtue, knowledge, health, our offspring
    share,
And, haply, theirs to welcome brighter
    days.

Yet meddling mem'ry, busy o'er the past,
Will oft revive a parent's tender woe ;
Such as when, hope still ling'ring to the
    last,
The truth severe 'twas ours, alas! to
    know.

And still the silent sorrow we partake,
Till number'd days expend our tale of
    time ;
Oft as lov'd scenes regretful thoughts
    awake,
That widely wander o'er a distant clime.

Yet, hail the light from heav'n—the vision
    fair,
That raptur'd seers to human hope dis-
    play ;
Lo! man restor'd—the end of pain and
    care,
For all the former things are pass'd
away.

        SENILIUS.

Elegy

Written at Thorpe Hall, Essex, 1794.

Blithe Spring now leads the jocund hours
    of May,
Again the hills, the laughing vallies bloom;

Yet, pensive, o'er the beauteous scene
    stray,
For sad affection points to yonder tomb:

Where sleeps Sarissa, she whose gen
    care,
Bade on her guests the friendly mansi
    smile ;
A husband's happy hours who late wor
    share,
Or every grief with lenient arts beguile.

Her's was the charming sympathy of joy,
Yet her's full many a piercing pang
    feel,
As long beside a sister's hapless boy,
She watch'd life's quiv'ring lamp with
    a parent's zeal.

E'en where the stranger, sorrow's frien
    less child,
O'er pen'ry's gloomy desert rov'd forlorn
His tale she would inquire, in accen
    mild,
Nor dealt the boon with pride's oppressi
    scorn.

Foster'd by heav'n her modest virtu
    grew,
Unlike the themes of flatt'ry's loud a
    claim ;
Virtues that time's primeval children kne
Ere plum'd ambition wak'd the trump
    fame.

Heroes avaunt! my grief-tun'd lyre sh
    praise,
" The tender sister, daughter, friend a
    wife,"
Whose gentle passions shed no banef
    rays,
But cheer'd the scenes of calm, domest
    life.

Ah, Spring! thy balmy gales, thy bloomin
    flow'rs,
Suit not the pensive musings of my soul
Led by sad sympathy to leafless bow'rs,
To dreary wilds, where wint'ry tempes
    howl.

Yet hark! what strains the heav'n-taugl
    sages sing :
Nature! I envy not thy vernal glow ;
For when no more thy winter yields
    spring,
With fadeless charms the human flow
    shall blow.

Nor ill the lot of mortals will I deem,
Though, Paradise! thy plants can ne'
    be found ;

That erst, by Tigris' or Euphrates' stream,
Bloom'd life unwith'ring o'er the favour'd
   ground :

Since hope, illumin'd by a ray divine,
Can the new Eden's verdant bow'rs ex-
   plore :
There shall, again, earth's sever'd pilgrims
   join,
To fear, to suffer, and to part no more.

              . FRATERNUS.

An Aspiration.

If 'twere but to retire from woe,
  To undisturb'd, eternal rest—
How passing sweet to sleep below,
  On nature's fair and flow'ry breast !

But when faith's finger points on high
  From death's decaying dismall cell ;
O, 'tis a privilege to die—
  To dream of bliss ineffable !

In balmy sleep our eyes to close,
  When life's last sunshine gilds our ev'n ;
And then to wake from long repose,
  When dawns the glorious day of heav'n !
                      A.

The Evening of an Unimproved Day.

Beyond the western bound'ry bright,
  The radiant sun retires ;
And fading with the fading light,
  Another day expires.
Now deep'ning shadows veil the sky,
And night and sacred sleep are nigh ;
Yet, ere I count the midnight hour,
Or yield me to the slumb'rous pow'r,
Let truth's unfalt'ring hand pourtray
The features of the parted day.

And if in fair proportion just,
  The pictur'd form appear ;
Thou, conscience ! faithful to thy trust,
  Wilt yield the joy sincere.
If passion's wild distorted mien
Deform the visionary scene ;
If sloth be there, with languid eye,
With nerveless hand, with coward sigh ;
O ! faithful still, thy pow'r shall dart
Reproof and anguish to my heart.

The heav'nly pencil, dipt in flame,
  Unerring takes its way ;
And forms of sorrow and of shame
  Its rapid touch obey.
Lo—thrall'd by sloth, enchantress strong,
Each hour dejected moves along ;
No graceful deed to virtue dear,
No vows to wisdom paid, appear :
Life droops, in weak pursuits employ'd ;
And time is wasted—not enjoy'd.

Thus year by year, in mercy lent,
  All unimprov'd have past ;
What if this day, so vainly spent,
  Should be decreed thy last ?

Say,—could'st thou, fearless, yield thy
  breath,
And, tranquil, lay thee down in death ?
Say,—in that future hour, unknown,
When justice shall assume her throne,
Couldst thou affirm, with steady pace,
Thy feet have run th' appointed race ?

O rouse thee yet ! while yet from heav'n
  Is lent a day—an hour !
Thou know'st that not to thee was giv'n
  A mind of meanest pow'r.
Spell-bound, in death-like sleep it lies ;
Awake, command its energies !
Burst with strong hand the galling chain,
Nor shrink from salutary pain.
Bow to the rod ;—the tears that start
Fall blest—they fertilize the heart.

Look up to thy Almighty Friend,
  His sov'reign aid implore ;
All good, all perfect gifts descend
  From his benignant pow'r.
And may his strength new grace impart ;
Guide in the way of truth thy heart ;
And guard, indulgent to thy pray'r,
From weak'ning sorrow, from despair,
From rash presumption, cold delay,—
Misleaders of thy early day.

Now to thy silent couch retire,
  And sink in soft repose ;
And may these thoughts thy breast in-
  spire
  When new-born morning glows.
Nor may thy nobler purpose fail,
Nor sloth's unhallow'd charms prevail ;
Proceed, instructed by the past,
Each day improving on the last ;
And humbly in his presence move,
Whose pow'r is boundless as his love.

                      S.

Vale Crucis,

Written for The Welsh Songs, by Wil-
  liam Stanley Roscoe, Esq.

Vale of the cross, the shepherds tell,
'Tis sweet within thy woods to dwell,
For there are sainted shadows seen
That frequent haunt thy dewy green ;
In wand'ring winds the dirge is sung,
The convent bell by spirits rung,
And matin hymns and vesper pray'r
Break softly on the tranquil air.

Vale of the cross, the shepherds tell,
'Tis sweet within thy woods to dwell,
For peace hath there her spotless throne,
And pleasures to the world unknown ;
The murmur of the distant rills,
The sabbath silence of the hills,
And all the quiet God hath giv'n
Without the golden gates of heav'n.

OBITUARY.

On Tuesday the 28th May, at Belvedere House, Bath, aged 12 years and 9 months, FRANCES, youngest daughter of Mr. THOMAS FISHER, of Dorchester, a child in whose ingenuous mind the opening buds of every virtue had promised an abundant source of comfort and enjoyment to her affectionate parents and friends. She was for the first time absent from the paternal roof, and had been under the tuition of Mrs. Broadhurst only two months, when, apparently in good health, she experienced an attack of epilepsy, which soon terminated her happy life: two days after the first seizure, unconscious of the presence of her affectionate relatives who surrounded the dying pillow, her pure spirit bade an eternal adieu to the sorrows of mortality, and returned to God who gave it. Her afflicted parents do not—cannot murmur that this choice blessing is withdrawn from them; it is the will of heaven, and they desire calmly to resign her to her God.

It is not wished ostentatiously to eulogise the memory of so young a person, by describing the attractions of a peculiarly amiable disposition, engaging manners, and a sweet susceptibility to all that was endearing, virtuous and good, but the recollection of these interesting characteristics is highly consolatory to her parents. Over such a tomb nature and affection are allowed to weep, and longer would they weep, but, thanks to the infinite goodness of our gracious God! the sun of righteousness arises to dissipate the sepulchral gloom, and the exulting hope of immortality leads parents, children and friends to anticipate the glorious morning of that eternal day which will reunite them in the regions of permanent and purer love.

An additional consolation would it afford them, if this instance of sudden removal from the bosom of earthly affection, should induce any young persons so to regulate their tempers and habits, so to cultivate a fitness for the future state, as to ensure their surviving relatives the delightful hope of witnessing and enjoying their progressive improvement and perfection in another and a better world, which is to them the greatest possible source of comfort.

Long as the memory of this lamented object of their affection will be cherished by her parents and their surviving children, they cannot fail to associate with it the kind and sympathizing attention of those to whose care she was entrusted, and the affectionate solicitude, the maternal tenderness of her instructress, which so well compensated for an own mother's love, will ever claim their warmest gratitude and respect.

" June 14, after a short illness, at *Winkfield Green*, near Bradford, aged 67, the Rev. DAVID EVANS, of Bath, upwards of forty years Minister to the Society of Unitarian Dissenters at Marshfield, Gloucestershire. A correspondent says, " the remembrance of his virtues through life, and pious resignation in the hour of death, is the only consolation that can be offered to those now mourning his loss." His life was spent in the acquisition of liberal and useful knowledge, and in the cultivation of those strong and vigorous powers of intellect with which he was endowed. He was a firm believer in Christianity, not upon the authority of creeds and councils, but from an attentive and diligent perusal of the Sacred Writings. In him civil and religious liberty, and freedom of inquiry, have lost one of their most zealous and enlightened advocates." *Examiner*, June 23.

We have the melancholy task of inserting among the Deaths of the month, that of our respected friend and valued correspondent, the Rev. JEREMIAH JOYCE, of Highgate, Minister of the Unitarian Congregation, Hampstead, Secretary of the Unitarian Society, and Author of many useful and popular Works. He died quite suddenly on Friday evening, the 21st instant. In the morning of the same day, he had written to us a friendly letter on the subject of the article on *Natural Theology*, of which he was the author, and which he promised to continue next month! How strikingly is vanity written upon all that is human! We shall hereafter, doubtless, insert a more full account of our lamented friend.

INTELLIGENCE.

DOMESTIC.
RELIGIOUS.
Unitarian Fund.

The Anniversary of this Society was held on Wednesday the 5th instant. The religious service was carried on as usual in Mr. Vidler's Chapel, Parliament Court, Artillery Lane. In the absence of Mr. Vidler, through ill health, which we lament to say has been of long continuance, Mr. Rees officiated in the desk. Mr. B. Goodier, late of the Unitarian Academy, prayed and read the Scriptures. Mr. Fox, of Chichester, the preacher-elect, delivered the second prayer. Mr. Broadbent, of Warrington, preached the sermon, and concluded the devotional exercises. The sermon contained an able and energetic defence of the duty of avowing and supporting the truth. It was received with great interest by the Society, who resolved, with the permission of the preacher, which has since been obtained, to publish it: in a little time, it will come under our notice, in another part of our work, and therefore we shall say no more of it at present, than that it was truly appropriate and will form a suitable addition to the valuable discourses by Doctors Toulmin and Carpenter, and Messrs. Lyons, Butcher, Kentish and Madge, which the Unitarian Fund has already given to the world. The collection at the doors exceeded that of any year except the last.

The Society proceeded to business after divine service, Mr. Edward Taylor, of Norwich, in the chair, The Treasurer's Report was satisfactory. The Report of the Committee was read by the Secretary—an abstract of it shall be given in the next number. It was shorter than on most former occasions, the business of the Society being, in a great measure, the same every year, and there being of course less novelty in their proceedings. The Committee express themselves delighted with the openings of truth in every direction, and recommend persevering and increased labours in the great and good cause. Mr. Christie was re-chosen Treasurer, Mr. Aspland, Secretary: and the following gentlemen were appointed the Committee, viz. Messrs. Bailey, Eaton, Gilchrist, S. Hart, Ives, Hurry, John Taylor and William Titford.

After the Unitarian Fund business was concluded, there was a general meeting of the governors, subscribers and friends of the *Unitarian Academy*, Mr. William Cooke, of the Isle of Wight, in the chair: a report of this meeting will be given in our next number.

The subscribers to the Unitarian Fund and their friends afterwards dined together, in number two hundred and sixty, at the London Tavern. By request of the Committee and the Stewards, *Mr. Frend* took the chair,

and he ably supported his station. Many admirable sentiments were brought forward and enlarged upon by the chairman and other gentlemen. The meeting was throughout harmonious and pleasant. Considerable additions were announced to the list of subscribers. Amongst the contributions we heard with great pleasure of the sum of £2. " from a few persons in humble life, at Leeds, who wish prosperity to the doctrine of Unitarianism." We cannot close this brief account without saying that much of the agreeableness of the afternoon is to be ascribed to the judicious arrangements and the activity of the Stewards.

General Baptist Society.

The Annual Assembly of the Old General Baptists was held, as usual, on Whit-Tuesday, June 4th, in the Meeting-House, Worship Street, London.

The Elders and Representatives of the churches in connexion with the Assembly, met early for business. At eleven o'clock the public service commenced. Mr. Evans, of Islington, read the scriptures and gave out the hymns; Mr. Treleaven, of Dorchester, offered up prayer; and Mr. Samuel Dobell, of Cranbrook, Kent, delivered the sermon, and concluded the devotional service.—The preacher's text was Ephes. iv. 15, 16, " But speaking the truth in love," &c. The discourse was delivered with an animation which excited great attention. The authority of Jesus Christ as Supreme Head of the church was proved by a judicious appeal to the sacred scriptures; the equality of all the members of a Christian church zealously vindicated; and that equality shown to consist not only in a common right to participate in the privileges and blessings of Christianity —but also in an indispensable obligation to advance by individual exertion the interests of *truth*, and to promote to the utmost in their power, each other's welfare.

The letters from most of the churches were of a satisfactory nature—the different congregations are rather increasing than diminishing, the accession of their new members being, on the whole, more than adequate to compensate for their losses by deaths or removals. The General Baptist church at Selby, Yorkshire, was received into connexion with the Assembly, and that of York will, in all probability, be united with it next year. Since the last annual meeting several of the churches have established Sunday-schools with success; while those which existed previously were represented as being in a flourishing condition. The letter from the church at Cranbrook, Kent, stated that, "Agreeably to the recommendation of the last Assembly, they had established a Sunday-school, and though it is not more than eight months from its commencement, yet more than 220 children have been admitted. The school was opened upon the liberal plan of admitting the children of parents of every denomination; and hitherto teachers have been procured out of the different societies, who undertake to conduct the children orderly to their respective places of worship."

The Committee, appointed by the Assembly, two years since, recommended in their Report to this Assembly, the adoption of more vigorous measures for the revival of the General Baptist cause. Among other measures was that of raising a fund to defray the expenses of a more extended distribution of tracts tending to the promotion of morals in general, and the dissemination of their peculiar tenets in particular—of local preaching wherever there appeared a prospect of usefulness—and of lending pecuniary aid to poor or newly-formed societies. A resolution was passed by the Assembly, in approbation of the recommendation; it will, therefore, be submitted to the consideration of all the churches in the Assembly's Proceedings.

After the business was finished, the ministers, representatives and their friends (about sixty in number) retired to the White Hart Inn; Bishopsgate Street, to dinner.—Several sentiments were given from the chair, which called forth very animated and appropriate speeches. The following were the principal: "The worthy Preacher"—"Religious Liberty complete and universal"—"The Old General Baptist Cause"—"The Union of all Christians"—"Mr. Rees and the Christian Tract Society," &c.

The ministers and their friends separated at an early hour.

Report of the Committee of the Southern Unitarian Fund, read at the First General Meeting of the Subscribers, at Portsmouth, April 17, 1816.

The age in which we live is honourably distinguished by the formation of numerous associations for benevolent purposes. The friends of religion and humanity by combining their efforts, have multiplied their usefulness. Relief has been administered to the bodily wants and infirmities of man; education has been provided for the ignorant, and knowledge placed within the reach of the inquiring. Nor have endeavours been wanting to bring back theological opinions to the simplicity of the New Testament. In many districts societies have been instituted for promoting the knowledge of the scriptures and the practice of virtue by the distribution of books. The London Unitarian Fund has forwarded the same object by the encouragement of missionary preaching. Still it was felt by the friends of genuine Christianity in this neighbourhood, that something more was desirable. Missionaries have paid us but rare and transient visits. Our tracts have too often lain dormant in the libraries of subscribers. In some places small congregations have been formed which needed the countenance and assistance of their brethren. In others a disposition to hear Unitarian preaching existed, which it was impossible for individual ministers to gratify, however desirous, on account of the attendant expense, and the want of co-operation. In the desire to remedy or alleviate these evils this Society originated; and your Committee have the gratification of announcing, that, in the short period which has elapsed since the commencement of its labours in September last, they have all been attended to with encouraging success. In one instance pecuniary assistance has been afforded to a necessitous congregation, towards the maintenance of public worship. A number of useful works, with which we were liberally furnished by the Southern Unitarian Society, has been distributed in such a way as was deemed most likely to secure their perusal. By the union of preaching with the dissemination of tracts, there is reason to believe that the impression which each was calculated to produce has been rendered more deep and lasting.

On the 28th of September a lecture was opened at the school-room of Mr. Stockman, Bishop Street, Portsea, by the Rev. W. J. Fox, which has been regularly continued, once a fortnight, and attended always by respectable, and on several occasions by very numerous congregations.

Public notice was given for the following evening of a similar lecture at Gosport, where a room had been engaged for that purpose. Our intention was, however, frustrated. Bigotry had taken the alarm, and the person in whose house the meeting was to have been held had been so intimidated by the denunciation of both temporal and spiritual evils, that it was judged expedient to desist. A second attempt, shortly after, was equally unsuccessful. It is just and gratifying to record, that the measures adopted to prevent our assembling by some professing Calvinists were, by respectable persons of that denomination, indignantly disclaimed. At length the Old Poor-house was obtained, and on the 10th November Unitarian Christianity was first preached in Gosport, to an attentive and overflowing auditory, by the Rev. W. J. Fox, from Numbers x. 29, "Come thou with us and we will do thee good." Our subsequent efforts have been attended with considerable success. A room has been permanently engaged at Mr. Stubbington's, corner of Bemister's-lane; where several families, forming, it is hoped, the germ of a regular congregation, assemble every Lord's day for the worship of the only God.

For the continued and regular support of these lectures, the Society is indebted to the services of Messrs. Brent, Fox, Fullagar, Lyons, Read, Saint, Travers, and Treleaven, who have cheerfully contributed their labours towards the great objects for which we are united.

The ministers in connexion with the Society have also engaged to preach alternately, on the first Tuesday in every month, at Fareham. This measure has been adopted in conformity with the earnest wishes of the Unitarians in that place, and is expected to prove very useful in promoting their comfort, establishment and increase.

The attention of your Committee has been much engaged by the situation of the congregation at Southampton, collected by the exertions of Mr. Travers, who has unfortunately been compelled by illness to relinquish his station. The chapel has been kept open on Sundays by Messrs. Fullagar, Saint and Read, and there is reason to expect that permanent arrangements will soon be made for the support of Unitarian worship in that town.

The amount of subscriptions actually received during the past year has been 25*l*. 5*s*. 6*d*., of donations, 38*l*. 18*s*. 6*d*. The expenditure, of which the different items have been sanctioned by the Committee, and are submitted to your inspection, is 53*l*. 6*s*. 9*d*. leaving a balance of 10*l*. 12*s*. 2*d*. in the hands of the treasurer.

It would have been easy for the Committee to extend its operations, had the funds of the Society permitted. Limited however as they were, much has been done. Our brethren have been cheered by encouragement and assistance, and the pure word of life has been dispensed to numbers of willing hearers, to whom, but for this Society, it would only have been offered with the adulteration of human inventions. We rejoice that we have not laboured in vain, while we still look anxiously at the wide field of usefulness which remains to be cultivated. Aiming only at the divine glory and the good of man, we hope for the continued and increased support of our brethren, and the blessing of the God and Father of our Lord Jesus Christ.

May the Southern Fund be an humble instrument, in the hands of Providence, of accelerating the time, announced by inspired prophecy, *when there shall be One Lord and his name One, in all the earth!*

Proceedings of the Scottish Unitarian Association.

Sheffield, June 10, 1816.

MY DEAR SIR,

I am desired, by the Committee of the SCOTTISH UNITARIAN CHRISTIAN ASSOCIATION, to transmit to you the following account of the Proceedings at the Fourth Anniversary of the Institution, held on Sunday and Monday, May 12th and 13th, in the Unitarian Church, Glasgow. Delegates were present from Edinburgh, Paisley, Dundee, Greenock, Blackford, Daley, Port-Glasgow, &c.

On Sunday, the devotional part of the morning service was conducted by Mr. YATES; and Mr. TORRENS, of York, delivered an excellent Discourse, on the Tendency of the Unitarian Doctrine to promote Love to God and Man, from the text, 2 Corinthians, chap. v. ver. 20. In the afternoon, Mr. YATES delivered his farewell Sermon, from the words, Philippians, chap. ii. verses 14, 15, and 16, "Do all things without murmurings and disputings, that ye may be blameless and harmless, the sons of God without rebuke, in the midst of a crooked and perverse nation, among whom ye shine as lights in the world, holding forth the word of life; that I may rejoice in the day of Christ, that I have not run in vain, neither laboured in vain." In the evening, Mr. SMITH, Minister of the Unitarian Church, Edinburgh, preached the Annual Sermon in aid of the Institution; the subject, the Tendency of the Unitarian Doctrine to promote Benevolence, from John, chap. xiii. ver. 35. The congregations throughout the day were very numerous and respectable. Between the morning and afternoon worship, the friends from the country, and many of those in Glasgow, both male and female, to the number of seventy, partook of some refreshment; and, between the afternoon and evening worship, about sixty persons, of both sexes, drank tea together.

On Monday, the Society met in the Church at 12 o'clock, when, after joining in prayer, Mr. AULD, of Leith, was elected President of the Meeting. The Report of the Committee for the past year was then read by Mr. GEORGE HARRIS, the Secretary. It stated, that two editions of Mr. Yates's Sermon, on the Duty and Manner of deciding the more important Religious Controversies, preached at the last Anniversary, had been printed; that Messrs. GASKELL, RUSSELL, and HARRIS, had, in the course of the year, volunteered their Services as Missionaries to the Institution, and had preached, with great success, at Cathcart, Renfrew, Partic,

Rutherglen, and Greenock; that Mr. SYME had undertaken a mission last summer, and preached at Hamilton, Lanark, Carnwarth, Melrose, &c.; that the Society have had in their hands, since the last anniversary, 3248 Tracts, of various kinds, nearly 2000 of which they have sold or distributed; and that ten corresponding members had this year been added to the Institution, making altogether forty-two places in Scotland in which Unitarians are at present known to reside. Letters were then read from the corresponding members of the Society, most of which were very satisfactory and encouraging, particularly those from Greenock, Blackford, and Dundee; and gave an additional stimulus to the friends of the Institution to proceed, with vigour, in the good work they had begun.

The following Resolutions were severally proposed, and unanimously adopted:

"That the cordial thanks of this Meeting be presented to Mr. George Harris, for the distinguished zeal, ability, and perseverance, with which he has continued to discharge the office of Secretary during the past year; also to Mr. Potter, and the members of the Committee, for their co-operation in promoting the objects of the Association.

"That it is the opinion of this Society, that the attention of the Association should be particularly directed towards Dundee, during the ensuing year; that the Committee be requested to use every exertion in their power to send them supplies as often as possible; and that the Society there be requested to institute a Penny Weekly Society, in aid of the Association; or of the promotion of Unitarianism in any other way they may deem proper.

"That it likewise be recommended to the Committee to supply Blackford with preaching as often as possible.

"That this Meeting express their most cordial thanks, congratulations, and good wishes, to Mr. George Harris for his exertions in preaching at Greenock, as the Missionary of this Society; and to the regular attendants on his services in that place, who have exposed themselves in the cause of pure and undefiled religion, to the great discouragements and obstacles attending the first introduction of unpopular truth.

"That the thanks of this Society be given to the London Unitarian Fund for their Donation of Ten Guineas to Mr. Syme, in order to enable him to continue his services to the Paisley Church.

" That the thanks of this Meeting be presented to Mr. Smith, of Edinburgh, and to the Edinburgh Unitarian Association Fund, for their Donations of Books, Tracts, and Money; also to the Glasgow Unitarian Association Fund, for their Donation of 20*l*.; to the Greenock and Port-Glasgow Unitarian Association Fund, for their Donation of 5*l*. 5*s*. and to all the other contributors.

" That Mr. George Harris be earnestly requested again to undertake the office of Secretary to the General Association of Unitarians of Scotland.

" That the cordial thanks of this Meeting be given to Mr. Torrens, Mr. Yates, and Mr. Smith, who so ably conducted the religious services of yesterday.

" That the Association have heard, with pleasure, of Mr. Syme's acceptableness and usefulness, and return him their thanks for his conduct.

" That the cordial thanks of this Meeting be presented to the Rev. Dr. Rees, and the Committee of the Dissenting Ministers of the three denominations in London and the neighbourhood, for their able, zealous, undaunted, and persevering exertions, in calling the attention of the British public to the condition of the persecuted Protestants in France, in exhorting us to perform towards them the Christian duties of sympathy and aid, and in maintaining the great cause of Religious Liberty."

The following persons, resident in Glasgow, were elected the Committee for the ensuing year :—

Secretary,
Mr. George Harris.
Treasurer,
Mr. William Shirley.
Committee:

Mr. G. M'Leod	Mr. J. Lawson
Mr. J. M'Kenzie	Mr. J. H. Burn
Mr. D. Potter	Mr. G. Wilson
Mr. J. Lambe	

The thanks of the Meeting were then unanimously voted to the Chairman for his able conduct in the Chair, and the Meeting adjourned.

At five o'clock a numerous and respectable company sat down to an economical dinner in the Trades' Hall. In the course of the evening many excellent sentiments were given, and many able speeches delivered, and the company separated at an early hour, every one appearing to be impressed with a desire of supporting, to the utmost of his power, an Institution, which has already, with its very limited resources, produced much

good, and which, if enabled to extend its benevolent exertions, would assuredly produce great and incalculable benefits to society.

I remain in behalf of the Committee of the Scottish Unitarian Christian Association,

Your's sincerely,
GEORGE HARRIS, *Secretary.*

FRENCH PROTESTANTS.

Williams's Library, Red-Cross Street,
April 24, 1816.

At a Special Meeting of the Committee of the Dissenting Ministers of the Three Denominations, appointed by the General Body for Inquiry— Superintendance and Distribution of the Funds collected for the French Protestant Sufferers for conscience sake —summoned to receive the Report of the Rev. Clement Perrot; who, from his eminent qualifications, the respectability of his character, and his personal acquaintance with the most distinguished Protestants in the South of France, had been requested to repair to that country, for the purpose of examining in the capital, and on the spot, the real situation of the Protestants, collecting evidence of their persecution, and arranging plans for the distribution of the money contributed for their relief:

Rev. J. RIPPON, D. D.
IN THE CHAIR:

It was unanimously resolved—

I. That the interesting and luminous Report now presented by the Rev. Clement Perrot, of his personal investigation into the past sufferings, and present situation of the Protestants, be received, approved and printed: and that the various verified documents, and articles of intelligence, illustrative of the Report, and forming an historical relation of the sufferings which the Protestants have endured, and are enduring, be prepared for the press, under the direction of the Rev. C. Perrot, and published with all possible dispatch.

II. That the Rev. Clement Perrot, for the promptitude with which he complied with the request of this Committee, and undertook a long, fatiguing, and dangerous journey—for the diligence, the prudence, and the zeal with which he has executed the objects of his important mission—for the generous sacrifice of his time, his engagements, and his personal safety—for the display his conduct has afforded, of those liberal and enlightened principles which have distinguished Protestant Dissenters among the benefactors of mankind—for the important services which he has rendered to the cause of the French Protestants in particular, and to the interests of truth, liberty, humanity, and religion in general; merits the warmest gratitude and esteem, and that he be requested, to accept the most sincere and affectionate acknowledgments of this Committee.

III. That this Committee recognizing the sacred right of every man to adopt his religious creed, and to profess his religious faith without molestation, insult, or privation—considering the re- of this right by human governments to be essential to the tranquillity and happiness of the world, and esteeming it as the first duty of Rulers and Magistrates to preserve inviolate that right themselves, and to guarantee its enjoyment to all classes of society, free from outrage, interruption, or disquietude—cannot review the whole history of the persecutions which the Protestants of the South of France have endured, and are enduring, without horror and indignation. That from the verification of documents before possessed, (the truth of which was never questionable,) and especially from the evidence now produced by their respectable friend, it is perfectly evident to them, that the persecutions so long and so disgracefully continued, have been instigated by bigotry and intolerance, and have been excited and directed by powerful leaders, against the Protestants, as the depositories of those religious and social principles, which must always render their possessors efficient and honourable in society;—that political opinions have only been the pretexts under which the odious projects of their enemies were concealed, as Protestants were as prompt, and as sincere in their acceptance of the restored dynasty, as any class of Frenchmen whatever;—that the impious, rapacious, and barbarous conduct of their persecutors, has exceeded the representations which have been made by the Committee, and has equalled in criminality that of the most guilty persecutors of ancient times;—that it is impossible to exculpate, at least from connivance, the local, civil, and military authorities, because the extent of the outrages—the length of their duration

—the publicity of the crimes—the notoriety of the criminals—the uselessness of complaints from the sufferers, and the vexations to which they have been exposed—the confidence with which the robbers and murderers have acted, and the impunity and protection they have experienced, are equally unknown, in any country, where the magistracy, however feeble, has been active and sincere. That it is equally evident, that from some cause, which this Committee do not intend to assign, the higher departments of the Government have not taken a suitable interest in the dreadful calamities, which have been sustained by its faithful and honourable subjects—have not maintained equal security for the professors of the Protestant and Catholic religions;—but have appeared to entertain the most lively jealousy of the unsolicited interference of benevolent persons in this country—have neglected to give to the Protestants, and to Europe, any satisfaction, by demanding an account of their conduct from the local or extraordinary authorities—and, finally, have left the victims of persecution at the mercy of prevotal courts, composed of their enemies, who have inflicted on Protestants the most degrading and cruel punishments for alleged trifling crimes, and have *honourably* acquitted Catholics—covered with blood, and guilty of numerous and horrid murders.

IV. That it was not the design of this Committee to procure for the Protestants a temporary alleviation of their public miseries; or to raise an useless clamour, and then leave them a prey to persecutions more dreadful, because they are more secret; and because they assume the character of judicial punishments, instead of the outrages of banditti; but they were resolved to contribute, by every honourable means, to reinstate them in that security and comfort they had so long enjoyed, and their title to which they have never forfeited. While, therefore, the objects of their unabated solicitude are living under the most dreadful apprehension—exposed to the violence of hostile authorities—cut off from the enjoyments of civil society—fugitives from their homes—deprived of their sources of support, and prevented from exercising, on account of their religious opinions, their industry and talents—while many, from the absence of their pastors, the loss of their temples, or the fear of their enemies, are destitute of the public supports and consolations of their religion; and especially encouraged and stimulated by the voice of the General Body, lately expressed at their Annual Meeting, this Committee will not relax in its vigilance or activity, but will endeavour to direct public attention to the situation of the French Protestants—to enlighten public opinion on the true character and extent of their sufferings—to excite public sympathy and benevolence for the alleviation of their calamities, and public indignation against the authors of their distress:—and although they will seize with eagerness the first opportunity to announce any improvement in the situation of their brethren, or their full restoration to their former state of happiness as professors of religion, they will not remit their humble efforts, nor abandon the sacred cause to any delusive promises or violent opposition, but will persevere, till to the gratitude of their fellow Protestants, shall be added, their congratulations and repose.

V. That, grateful for the numerous and liberal contributions which have been already received, not only as they display the generous emotions of Christian benevolence, and provide relief and comfort for the miserable, but as they afford also a strong expression of attachment to the unalterable principles of truth and freedom; this Committee renew their solicitations to those who have not to this period remitted to the Secretary the amount of their subscriptions or collections, and assure all their friends, that a punctual and faithful attention will be paid to the distribution of the funds which may be entrusted to their care.

Signed by order of the Committee,
THOMAS MORGAN,
SECRETARY.

MISCELLANEOUS.

Debate in the House of Commons, on the French Protestants, May 23, 1816.

Sir S. ROMILLY rose, in pursuance of notice, to bring this subject under the consideration of the House. He had waited for some time in the hope that there would have been no occasion for such a motion as that which he was now about to propose to the

House; but, considering the impression which had been made throughout the whole country, it appeared to him that it would be extremely to be lamented if the session were to pass over without any notice having been taken of the subject. Reports had reached this country of dreadful acts of riot, violence and oppression in the southern departments of France; they had made a deep impression upon the public; public meetings were called, resolutions were formed, subscriptions were opened with that liberality which had always characterized the British nation; and the House would recollect the progress that was making in the public feelings, when a sudden turn took place, and the face of affairs was changed. Although these meetings had not taken place without a previous communication being had on the subject with his Majesty's ministers, yet those meetings were discouraged, and he was most sorry to have seen that a very successful turn was given to that meritorious course of proceeding. In a letter written by the Duke of Wellington to one of these meetings, his Grace had said, that he felt satisfied that every thing possible had been done on the part of the French government to prevent these disturbances; that the King of France had extended his protection to his subjects of all persuasions, and had secured them in the exercise of their religious rights. The effect of that letter was very strong upon the minds of the people. The Common Council of the City of London had considered this subject, and had voted an address to the Prince Regent: much delay occurred in its presentation, and although his Royal Highness had said that it could be received by him on any occasion on his arrival in London, that occasion had never arrived, and the address had never been presented. He was not bringing this question forward to criminate his Majesty's ministers; and he most sincerely assured the House, that he had not such an opinion of them as to believe, that if they had been acquainted with what had really taken place, or had seriously considered what the interposition of the French government amounted to, and had known in what manner it had been demonstrated, they would have acted as they had done. He never could think that it could have been in human nature to have conducted themselves in such a manner, if they had known the real facts of the case. All that he imputed to his Majesty's ministers was, that they had too credulously believed, and too lightly judged upon, all the stories they had received. He could also assure the House, if indeed it were necessary, that in introducing this matter to its consideration he was actuated by no party or personal feelings, but by motives of justice and humanity to an injured and disheartened people; and after having received information from various quarters, after having had the means of conversing with many persons that had been on the spot, he did think it would have been a dereliction of the duty he owed to oppressed and injured individuals, had he not drawn the attention of the House to the subject.—The letter of the Duke of Wellington had been published at Nismes, and was scattered about the town with the greatest joy and exultation by the Catholics; but it filled the Protestants with the utmost consternation; it took from the oppressors the only restraint imposed upon them, and from the oppressed their last hope. So completely were they oppressed, that they were looked upon as mere slaves, under the controul, and subject to the passions, of an enraged master—without hope, without comfort and without relief. In considering, then, this important subject, there were three principal questions to be discussed: 1st. whether any and what punishment had been inflicted on these murderers and assassins; 2dly, whether these offences had been committed against law and nature from political or religious motives; and 3dly, whether the French government had afforded any protection to the injured. Unless these three questions were considered, it would be impossible to give a distinct idea of the disgraceful transactions which had taken place in the department of the Gard, to which the distressing scenes were almost wholly confined. There could be no doubt that there had been a most unjust persecution of the Protestants in the South of France, and that Nismes was the principal scene of horror and of bloodshed; but in order that the subject might be fully comprehended by the House, it would be necessary for him to put it in possession of the situation in which the Protestants were placed previous to the restoration of his present Majesty, Louis XVIII. on the throne of France. The department of the Gard was the first part of France, and, he believed, of Europe, where the doctrines of the reformed religion were promulgated; and it was in the mountains of the Cevennes that, in the twelfth century, heresy, as it was then termed, first took its root, distinguished by the piety of the doctrines of those who professed it. In this situation they remained unmolested to the time of the Reformation; but by the unhappy communication between the leaders of the two parties at the latter end of the reign of Francis I. a dreadful destruction of the Protestants took place at Aix. This was the first appearance of that bitter animosity which afterwards spread devastation throughout the whole of France, and the commencement of those dreadful wars between the Hugonots and Catholics, so disgraceful to human nature. At last religious peace was restored under the reign of Henry IV. when the Protestants enjoyed the most perfect liberty. Nismes was then the city to which the Protestants resorted. So matters rested until the revocation of the edict of Nantes, when those bloody orders were issued, the object of which was to convert the whole province of the Gard by a regiment of dragoons. The face of things was immediately changed; all France became a Catholic country, and not a Protestant was to be seen in it. In the time of Louis XIV. and XV. the Protestants again began to rear up their heads; and of so novel a description were they, that the term of "*les noveax convertis,*" was applied to them. Proceeding in his statement of the grievances under which the Protestants laboured, the Hon. Gentleman mentioned that, it had been stated as an instance of comparative lenity by one writer, that from the year 1745 to 1770 only eight of their ministers were hanged. In all this period their marriages were declared null, their children of fourteen years old, who professed the Catholic religion, were taken from the care of their parents: instances might be mentioned of husbands being sent to the galleys for marrying according to the Protestant forms, and their wives to a receptacle of prostitutes. Such by law was the condition of the Protestants in France—ameliorated, no doubt, by the increasing toleration of the age. Louis XVI. had the distinguished merit of remedying many of those grievances from the earliest years of his reign. There were extant memorials presented to him by the lamented M. Malesherbe and others, on this subject; and their remaining grievances would, doubtless, have been removed by that unfortunate sovereign, had not his throne been overthrown by the torrent of the revolution, amidst his wishes to establish a constitutional liberty. One of the first acts of the revolution was to restore the Protestants to a perfect equality of privileges. They were declared admissible to all civil offices without distinction; and one of their ministers, Rabaut St. Etienne, was president of the national assembly. The Protestants, with the feelings natural to men, could not but applaud and admire a work, by which they were raised, from being outcasts of society, and from a state of degradation and infamy, to that of citizens with equal rights. This, however, had been objected to them by some persons as matter of reproach; but he trusted he should be able to show, to the satisfaction of the House, that all that had been said of their being revolutionists and Buonapartists, in a peculiar degree was perverted and misrepresented. He would assert, that in those scenes of horror which soon disgraced the progress of the revolution, not one Protestant was found to be an actor. Of course he must here be supposed to speak generally, as far as his information extended. He acknowledged, indeed, that some of them who were members of the convention voted for the death of the king, but all of them with the addition of the appeal to the people, which, if not displaying due firmness, at least discovered their wish to save the monarch. There was not one Protestant a member of the revolutionary tribunal of the department of the Gard; and, of the 130 persons who were guillotined by its orders at Nismes, more than 100 were Protestants, though the Protestants formed only about one third of the population. He might say, that amidst the horrors of the revolution they were always found on the side of modera-

tion and justice. He did not speak this invidiously, but, as was usual in a sect which formed the minority, many of whom were opulent, greater regularity of conduct and correctness of morals were generally found to prevail. The Protestants being thus restored to the rank of citizens, all religious animosities seemed to subside in the South of France. In 1802, Buonaparte, being then First Consul, procured the enactment of a law which placed their religion precisely on the same footing with the Catholic faith in point of establishment, and privilege. Could it be matter of reproach to them that they were grateful for this favour?—it was not possible but that they must have felt attachment to him for it. Hence, however, it was deemed proper by some that they should be stigmatized as Buonapartists. There was no foundation for the assertion that any partiality was shown to them by Buonaparte. There was not one Protestant prefect or commandant of department appointed by him; none of them filled the tribunal of justice; and probably one reason of this might be, that before the revolution they were not allowed to follow the profession of the law. It was not improbable, however, that the circumstance of the Protestants being thus placed on a level with their former masters, might excite a rankling jealousy in the latter, which would break out on the first convenient opportunity. This state of things continued until Louis XVIII. was restored to his kingdom in April 1814. At this period Buonaparte had become odious to the Protestants at Nismes, both from the weight of taxation with which they were loaded, and from the incessant demands of the conscription. The taxes fell with peculiar hardship on the Protestants, as, generally speaking, there was more property in their hands; and leading, as they generally did, retired, domestic-lives, the conscription, which tore from them their children, was peculiarly felt by them as a hardship of the greatest severity. He believed that the Protestants were, under these circumstances, unanimous in the joy which they expressed on the restoration of Louis XVIII. Unfortunately, however, during the course of the succeeding ten months, a considerable change of opinion took place. Persons who had been long absent returned with their old prejudices, and the lower orders of the people began to threaten the Protestants, who conceived on their part that there was a strong tendency to go back to the old regime. They were not much alarmed by the circumstance of the charter issued by Louis, declaring the Catholic the established religion of France, because the other guards which it afforded appeared sufficient to protect their rights: they could not forget also that the king had just returned from a residence in a land of Protestants, where he must have witnessed the effects of religious toleration; and they looked forward to a season of tranquillity and enjoyment. But circumstances soon compelled them to change their ideas. They were insulted by the populace on the ground of their religion; songs were sung publicly in the streets of Nismes, in which they were threatened with the renewal of the horrors of St. Bartholomew; gibbets were drawn on their doors. In this situation of things, Buonaparte suddenly made his appearance in France, in the month of March 1815. It was a trying occurrence for the Protestants at Nismes: but uniting with the established authorities, they declared their determination to support the government. He had in his possession the original declaration to this effect made at Nismes on the 13th of March last year, and which was signed by the principal Protestants, the five Catholic clergy, and three Protestant ministers of the town. The list of Protestants who signed it was greater in proportion to their respective numbers than that of the Catholics. It contained an expression of the warmest attachment to the government of the king, and called upon the people of the department for their support. Soon after this the Duke d'Angouleme fixed his head-quarters at Nismes, and here it was alleged that the Protestants did not join the Duke with much alacrity. They were in truth deterred from so acting by the previous alarm which had been excited among them; and perhaps it was not surprising that they did not zealously join the Duke's army. Some of them, however, offered their sons to join him. On the 3d of April the authority of Buonaparte was declared in the town of Nismes: the few soldiers in the garrison there were called out, and shouted *Vive l'Empereur.* It had been represented, that during the second reign of Buonaparte, acts of the greatest violence were committed by the Protestants; and that when Nismes again became a royal town on the 17th of July, the atrocities which ensued were merely retaliative. The fact was, however, that no acts of violence were committed during this interval—no persons were insulted—no houses attacked—none were killed, at least in the town of Nismes, though it was said that some stragglers of the Duke d'Angouleme's army were murdered by the peasants. Upon the 15th July many of the royal volunteers, as they were called, returned to Nismes; numbers of armed men flocked in from the country, and required the garrison which held it in Buonaparte's name to surrender. This garrison, consisting of about 200 men, consented to lay down their arms; but they were all of them, with the exception of a few who contrived to make their escape, massacred as they came out of their barracks. For some successive days the whole of the Protestants of Nismes were exposed to outrages of every kind; their houses were plundered or pulled down, the rich were laid under contributions, the looms of the poor manufacturers were destroyed, women were stripped and scourged in the streets; no less than 30 females were subjected to this atrocity, one of whom was far advanced in pregnancy. He would repeat what he had stated on a former occasion, that 200 persons were murdered in cold blood, besides 2,000 individuals who were persecuted in their persons and property. One man, a Mr. Lafond, far advanced in life, these wretches threw from the balustrades of his own staircase, and, on still discovering some signs of life, they cut him to pieces with their sabres. The seven sons of a Mr. Leblanc, and the five sons of a Mr. Chivar, were murdered. A wretch of the name of Trestaillon was the chief leader in these atrocities. This man, hearing that Chivar, the father, was confined to his bed, came to his house, and asked the wife to let him see her husband, affecting to feel for him; but immediately on being introduced, he shot the old man dead with a pistol. This monster in human shape had been taken twice into custody, but he had never yet been punished by the French government. [Hear!] He had boasted of the murders he had committed. One of the first acts after the 17th of July, the period when Nismes reverted under the royal government, was to disarm the urban guard, which it was declared should exclusively consist of Catholics: and he should have to state an order of the new authorities, that all persons should be disarmed who could not belong to the national guard, which was equivalent to declaring that their intended victims should be disarmed, in order to their execution. In one place these infuriated persons dug up the body of a young man, and burnt it, together with the house of his father. In short, every kind of atrocity was committed. He was speaking now of persons who were murdered in cold blood, and not taken with arms in their hands. It was proper here to inquire what steps were taken by the French government to prevent these excesses. The king had appointed the Marquis d'Arbaud Joucques prefect of the department of the Gard. He arrived on the 30th of July, and issued a proclamation for the purpose of protecting the Protestants from the fury of their persecutors. In consequence of this he was ill-treated on his appearance at the theatre. They insisted that Trestaillon should be released, which was accordingly done. This prefect was still continued; and under such circumstances could any man say, in the language of the Duke of Wellington, that the French government had done every thing to protect its Protestant subjects? The disturbances at Nismes still continued. The 21st of August was the important day fixed for the election of deputies to the legislature. He read from the official journal of the Gard, the proclamation of Devallon, the mayor of Nismes, on the eve of the feast of St. Louis, recommending to the people to abstain from the employment of squibs and crackers, and reminding them that the least disturbance would throw great responsibility on the magistrates. What was the amount of force which this mayor, then, had at his disposal? It was twenty-four companies of national guards and three of cavalry. There was another proclamation issued on the 30th of August, in which he states, that many murders

had been committed, the perpetrators of which concealed themselves in darkness. These, he said, had profoundly wounded his heart; but he ascribed them all to unknown agitators, who in this way abused their love for their king. What were we to think of a government which ascribed these murders to misguided demonstrations of loyalty? They are then reminded that such crimes could not be justified, because crimes of the same kind had been committed during an usurpation blasted by heaven, and detested by man. But what was the fact? The national guard which was at the disposal of the mayor, had never exerted themselves during all these days to prevent the perpetration of the murders. It might be worth mentioning, that M. Trinquelaque, a lawyer, who was chosen one of the deputies to the legislature, and lately appointed secretary general to the minister of justice, was the person who, after the first restoration, proposed that a silver image should be dedicated to the Virgin, in the event of the pregnancy of the Duchess d'Angouleme. It was also worthy of remark, that on the 24th of August, another military force entered Nismes, exclusive of the national guard, when tranquillity was restored, and continued as long as they remained. The national guard was marched into the mountains of the Cevennes, where the people had remained in perfect tranquillity, though they were now treated by the national guard as in a state of rebellion. The Austrian troops that were soon after sent into the Cevennes, in order to disarm the inhabitants, declared, on the contrary, they had never seen a people more peaceably disposed. They quitted the country on the 25th of October, and the same system of murder was recommenced. Besides the infamous Trestaillon, there was another notorious murderer, of the name of Quatretaillon. Trestaillon had been sent away from that part of the country, but punished he had never been. In fact, not one of the persons concerned in these numerous atrocities had been brought to punishment; they still roamed about at large, though well known to most of the inhabitants of Nismes. He had to notice another proclamation of the prefect, in which he spoke of an indignation, too natural not to be excusable, having burst on the heads of the disaffected; but, illegal as it was, he adds, it was not stained by plunder, and popular indignation had not been disgraced by robbery. The Honourable Gentleman then proceeded to advert to the opening of the Protestant churches at Nismes, on the 12th of November, when General Legarde was severely wounded. 'Many of the congregation were besides wounded and maltreated. On the 1st of September, 1815, another proclamation was issued, which still used the language of 'persuasion to murderers. He made no doubt that the Noble Lord was much better acquainted than himself with all these facts; but the House would take into its consideration the extreme difficulty of procuring authentic information. There had been no difficulty, indeed, in publishing any thing against the Protestants; the conductors of the journals were permitted, nay, they were even courted, to publish statements against those persons; but the police would not suffer a single paragraph to be inserted with regard to their sufferings. He was himself present in the Chamber of Deputies, when a discussion took place on the personal liberty of the subject; and because one of the representatives, Monsieur d'Argenson, stated, that there had been persecutions in the South of France, a great part of the assembly rose in a most tumultuous manner, and in the coarsest terms insisted that he should be called to order. He (Sir Samuel Romilly) then saw a gentleman in his place who was present in the French Chamber on that occasion; and he appealed to that Honourable Member to corroborate this statement. The President yielded to the cry of the House, and Monsieur d'Argenson was called to order. It was notorious, however, that only six days before he made that speech, the blood of the Protestants was flowing down the streets of Nismes, and it was only a fortnight before that the king's general was wounded; and yet he was called to order for stating that there had been a persecution in the South. [Hear, hear!] When General Legarde was wounded at Nismes, the king published a proclamation on the subject; and

Sir GERARD NOEL rose to call the Honourable and Learned Gentleman to order. It seemed to him, that the House would act very unwisely, if they should allow the Honourable and Learned Gentleman to proceed with these details. He had been admitted into the Chamber of Deputies by courtesy, as an English gentleman on his travels; and he had no right to make use of what he then heard for the purpose of grounding an inquiry in the English House of Commons. It would be a great breach of confidence in the Honourable and Learned Gentleman, [a laugh,] and was derogatory to the high character and dignity of the House. [Repeated laughter and loud calls to Sir Samuel Romilly to proceed.]

Sir SAMUEL ROMILLY said, "he could easily remove all embarrassment from the mind of the Honourable Baronet, with respect to being guilty of any breach of confidence, as he was only stating what the French government itself had permitted to be published in all the newspapers on the following day. [Hear, hear!] He repeated, that there was no hesitation whatever on the part of that government in publishing every thing against the Protestants. The four deputies of the department of La Gard published in the *Quotidienne* a sort of protest against the king's proclamation, and declared that the tumult was excited only by a few old women. On the 12th of November the prefect issued a proclamation, and, in the name of the department, promised a reward of 3,000 francs to any person who should make known the name of the individual who had shot the General, and bring him before him. This man, however, had not been prosecuted or punished; nay, he had not been seized, though his name was well known to be Boisset. The proclamation of the king said, that an atrocious crime had been committed; but what followed? It called upon the magistrates to disarm all the Protestants; and why? Because, as the prefect stated, a tumult had been excited by a few old women! On the 19th of December, the mayor published a proclamation, stating, that the Protestant churches should be re-opened on the following Thursday, and an assurance was given to the people that the Protestants should have churches built out of the city. Of the two churches of the Protestants at Nismes, one had been bought by themselves, and the other was given to them by the government; but, instead of these, they were to be permitted to build two new ones beyond the walls of the town at their own expense. Now, he would ask, what had this to do with politics? What had this to do with Buonaparte? The House would see that all this was purely religious. On the 9th of January the king published another proclamation, stating, in the first place, "that his orders had met with that respect and submission which he had a right to expect." But what was the nature of this respect and submission?—only that the Protestants had been disarmed. It then declared, "that the temple of the Protestants was open, and that they enjoyed all the protection of the law;" and it concluded with "his Majesty's thanks to his good people of the city of Nismes." This must be considered as a kind of general amnesty; and the fact really was, that not a single individual had been prosecuted or punished. The present condition of the Protestants certainly was so far in a state of security, that since the month of December no murder or cruelty had been committed; but he had been informed by a gentleman who had recently arrived from the city of Nismes, and on whose veracity he could place the utmost reliance, that the Protestants were continually driven away from the public walks. Whenever they ventured to appear in such places, they were jostled by the very persons who had murdered their wives, their husbands, brothers, sisters, and dearest relations. The prisons were now filled with Protestants who had been apprehended on the charge of sedition. In the several departments of France there were not less than 19,000 Protestants in custody upon this pretence. Some were imprisoned for five years, some for ten years, and others for longer periods, on the charge of having sung improper songs. [Hear, hear!] It seemed a most extraordinary thing, that crimes so atrocious as those which he had mentioned should be suffered to pass unpunished, and that such trifling offences as singing a few songs, should be visited in this terrible manner. It was a strange feature of the administration of justice in any country; but that on which he most relied was,

that no person had been yet brought to trial. He did not intend to move that there should be any immediate address to the crown on this subject; but he contended that the Protestants had suffered, not for seditious conduct, but only on the suspicion of entertaining particular opinions. All that he meant to ask for was, that an humble address should be presented to the Prince Regent, that he would be graciously pleased to lay before the House copies or extracts of all correspondence between his Majesty's government and the government of France, relative to the Protestants in the South of France. He made this motion in no spirit of hostility against ministers, but to give them an opportunity of making a statement more in detail, than had yet been done. He could give a long list of names of persons who had been murdered at Nismes, but he did not consider it necessary in this stage of the business. Because they were Protestants, they were said to be Buonapartists; and the Catholics, who had been suffered to persecute them, were called Bourbonists. The Noble Lord would have an opportunity of correcting this error, if it were one; and he should be glad to hear that government had used all the means in its power to put a stop to these crimes. In concluding his remarks, he might advert to what had been done by our ancestors on similar occasions: and if precedents were necessary, he need only recall to the recollection of the House what it had recently done for the negroes of Africa. But surely the Protestants of the South of France had equal claims upon our generosity and benevolence, and we ought not to suffer them to be persecuted, imprisoned, and murdered, without some remonstrance to the government which was bound to protect them. At the very moment when these dreadful scenes were acting in Languedoc, Paris was in possession of three Protestant armies, and the king could not look out of the windows of his palace without seeing the cannon that was planted before it. He did not state this for the purpose of bringing a charge against his Majesty; but if he neglected to send assistance to his Protestant subjects, it was the duty of those who commanded the foreign armies to protect and defend them. The

French government did nothing but give words and make professions; but it was still in our power to interpose all good offices in this case. Tumults had recently arisen in various parts of France; and if disorders should again break out, who could tell what might be the situation of the unhappy inhabitants of Nismes? He trusted that the House would consider what a heavy responsibility was then upon them, and that, as they would answer to God and their consciences, they would not refuse protection when it was in their power to afford it. [Hear, hear!]

Lord CASTLEREAGH said, that the House must have listened with great pain to the speech of the Honourable and Learned Gentleman, as they must certainly lament to hear that persecutions for religious opinions were still practised in any part of Europe. He did not mean to make any invidious reflection, but he must take leave to say, that the Honourable and Learned Gentleman had drawn a most exaggerated and unfairly coloured picture. The Honourable and Learned Gentleman had placed him in a most embarrassing and painful situation. He had addressed himself to the House as to a tribunal that had jurisdiction to inquire into all the circumstances; but if they had even the means of arriving at the truth, they had not the means of applying a remedy to the evils. He must enter his protest against the false policy of interfering with the internal situation of the affairs of other countries, more especially with respect to religious opinions. The Honourable and Learned Gentleman had dwelt with great pains upon the centuries that were gone by, as if he wished to rouse all those bad passions which, he should hope, had been long buried in oblivion. He had also adverted to the impression made on the public mind by the conduct of certain individuals; and had stated, that a sort of countenance was given to their exertions by his Majesty's ministers. If he imagined, however, that government was disposed to encourage those persons, he was certainly incorrect; for they were satisfied, that, notwithstanding the benevolent motives by which those bodies might have been actuated, they had done more harm than good to the cause in which they interposed. He knew that it was not possible to discourage the efforts of individuals, but he was confident that his Majesty's government would have lost sight of their duty if they had encouraged them. It was a question of prudence to look at the cases of former interference, and every man who viewed them with an impartial eye, would consider what the spirit of toleration was working in favour of religion. There was a time, indeed, when religion was made a pretence for imposing a system of government, and then the Protestant powers were obliged to stand together: but we were now placed in a situation in which we might suffer Christianity to effect its own work. He did not say that one government could not communicate on this subject with another; but he did say, that if one government at this day would suffer a foreign state to interfere with it because it administered its laws according to its own conception, that government would be degraded in the eyes of all the world. But suppose we should be rash enough to interfere with another state on this account; if we were not listened to, what would become of our dignity? Was the Honourable and Learned Gentleman prepared to state, that he wished an appeal to arms?—[Hear, hear!] He was the more astonished at the Honourable and Learned Gentleman's proposal, when he found he had not laid the ground for it in the general situation of the Protestants: on the contrary, he had told the House that his was not a charge of religious persecution; he had told them that the evil was local—that it was confined to the department of the Gard—that the Protestants derived their liberty from that man who owed the loss of his life and crown to his benevolence: had he been more vigorous, the world would have been spared those scenes of calamity that had since overwhelmed the whole of the civilized globe. He had commented on the acts of the French government and the proclamation of the king himself. It would be invidious for him (Lord C.) to enter into critical disquisitions on that proclamation, but he was persuaded that the king felt the most sincere desire to put down the hostile feeling against the Protestants: he had not only tolerated but indulged them, and their miseries were only the result of a local feud, such as we had but too often seen in parts of this empire, and which all the force of government could not put down at once. Was he (Lord C.) to tell the House, that in the country to which he belonged, a feud, a dispute, which appeared religious, but which was totally unconnected with religion, would often disturb a province for years? In the county of Armagh sects had for two years been waging war with each other, and the whole power of the arm of the law was found insufficient to repress them. Did the House forget the present state of things in Ireland, and would they have us advise a foreign country to interfere in the cause of the Catholics of this country?—[Hear, hear!] He was sure that such an interference would not be endured. Whilst there was but one common feeling—that of deep grief on the unhappy calamities in France, and an anxious desire to see them terminated; whilst the Honourable and Learned Gentleman himself admitted that no outrages had been committed since December, and now, after such a lapse of time, he came to harrow up the feelings of the House with the recital of calamities we could not redress, he (Lord C.) had hoped that he would lay the question at peace, instead of colouring the proceedings on one side as highly as he might, if he had pleased, those of the other—instead of inflaming the passions of two sects who were tearing each other to pieces. This was an act of disrespect to the French people, and not an act of benevolence, whatever might be the motives of the Honourable and Learned Gentleman. He (Lord C.) could not consistently with his public duty acquiesce in producing to the House all the correspondence that had passed on this subject. If ever there was a question on which parliament and every good man should be silent, it was this. He did not mean to deny that communications had passed which had convinced his Majesty's ministers, that though the French government was in the exercise of a power so recent that it could hardly be productive of any great and immediate results, yet that his most Christian Majesty had been most serious in his efforts to repress all persecution. He agreed with the Hon. and Learned Gentleman, that the situation of the Protestants of France had for a long time been a source of pain to every liberal mind; but the emancipation of the Protestants commenced early in the

Revolution; it had been followed up; and they enjoyed a degree of freedom they had never known before. Without imputing blame to the sect, without denying that they were a most enlightened people, he should contend that having acquired an extent of power, and that from Buonaparte, they felt interested in the continuance of his power: their conduct showed that they felt this, and had led to a jealousy which was the cause of the present disturbances. If he were to believe the Honourable and Learned Gentleman, and the various publications on the subject, he must imagine that the Catholics had not suffered or been provoked at all, and that this was a gratuitous persecution of the Protestants. Indeed, the Honourable and Learned Gentleman had touched so slightly on the wrongs or provocations of the other side, that though he admitted a few individuals had been sacrificed, yet it would appear from his statement, that in general they had no cause for complaint. He (Lord C.) did not mean to give official information to the House, but he would read a passage from a letter which he believed to be written in a fair and impartial spirit. It contained the opinions of an individual whose sentiments he wished to receive, because he went out with a mind pure and unbiassed. This letter would bring one point on which the Honourable and Learned Gentleman had touched slightly—the provocations and wrongs of the Catholics—into open view. "Both parties are to a certain degree right;" that was, the Protestants were mixed up with Buonaparte, and imputed to the Catholics jealousy and political dislike; while the Catholics, who adhered to the Bourbons, were afraid of the designs of the Protestants.

[To be continued.]

Schools for All.

The Anniversary Meeting of this grand British Institution, was held on Monday, the 13th of May, at the London Tavern, the spacious ball-room of which was thronged, and had a large proportion of respectable females.

The Duke of Bedford was expected to take the chair; but not arriving, the Right Hon. Lord Mayor took it *pro tempore*, and being obliged to wait on the Prince Regent, resigned to Sir

J. Jackson, who also, on the arrival of the Duke of Kent, resigned it to his Royal Highness.

The Rev. Dr. Collyer read the Report, which paid some well-merited compliments to the memory of the late Secretary, Joseph Fox, Esq. by whose noble benevolence the great cause had been rescued from failure, he having taken upon himself the engagements which Mr. Lancaster had entered into, but could not meet to a very considerable amount. The Report quoted the exertions making in Southwark, as an example to the City of London, and to the rest of the United Kingdom; stated that the invested subscription, which was accumulating for the purpose of raising £10,000, had arisen to £7,000, and that the remaining £3,000 was expected to be raised, as first hoped for, within the present year. The funds of the Institution were still lamentably narrow, when compared with the great object in view :—but the Report recommended perseverance, and the union of all good men of all persuasions, and the great object would be attained. The harvest was generally promising. . . . . . . The vast empire of Russia was of good promise; its government felt the value of general education, and was preparing for a hearty co-operation with this Society. A society was establishing in that empire for the purpose. It was with very mingled emotions that the Society looked to France, whose public schools, once on a footing of liberality, now refused instruction to any but professed Catholics, though its population contained at least sixteen millions, who could neither read or write! All the masters, who conscientiously could not be Papists, were, whatever their talents, dismissed from the schools, to which they had been great ornaments. This was a source of deep regret. Much good, nevertheless, had been done. The British system had been transplanted into France, and exhibited in its beauty and strength to the admiring eyes of Frenchmen.

Switzerland was busily opening schools for general education, under the patronage of the Plenipotentiary of that country to the Congress at Vienna,—a gentleman, to whose praise it should be known, that when offered a national recompence for his high

services, he declined it; but prayed that the amount, with an addition from himself, might become the beginning of a national fund for a free-school, on the model of the British free-school.

Through the lamented loss of Mr. Fox, who was, when taken ill, engaged on the business of the Foreign part of the Report, but a scanty account could be given of Asia.

In Africa the cause had received a severe check. Mrs. Sutherland had yielded to the pressure of the climate, and Mr. S. had returned ill; but yet, under the fostering care of Lieut. Col. M'Carthy, the Governor of Sierra Leone, between two and three hundred children were receiving education, and this under the superintendence of the eldest African youth trained by this Society.

Unshackled by prejudice, America was progressing in education. She had shown her wisdom by the adoption of a liberal system, and a school on the principle of exclusion was not known in the United States. The legislature of New York had given repeated encouragement by grants. A society was formed there for the education of all the children not provided for by some religious establishment. On a Sunday morning between eight and nine hundred children assembled under that society, and branched off at a given hour to the respective places of public worship appointed by their parents. Female associations were forming for instruction of the girls in needle-work.

The legislature of Halifax had voted £400 to the schools there, in token of approbation of the very manifest change for the better, in the character and conduct of the children.

Very great emotions of pleasure appeared to agitate the assembly, when that part of the Report which regards Hayti was read. The Chief, Christophe, deeply penetrated with the benefits of knowledge and the diffusion of the Scriptures, invites among his people, all those who could contribute to their improvement. In a proclamation in the gazette of Hayti, he says,— " I invite professors of all sciences— no difference of religion shall be deemed an exclusion. Merit and ability alone shall be considered, without regard to the nation which gave birth, or the creed which may be preferred. After twenty-six years of revolution and thirteen years possession of hard-earned independence, we are not (says the gazette) the same people. Formerly, as brutes, we bowed under the lash of a cruel and ignorant master—as men we were dead—our faculties all crushed; but we burst our chains, and, again erect, we look upward toward heaven —as men—as social beings! A new career is now before us—thanks to thee, O God of heaven! Haytians! (says the Chief) be it ours to shew, by our lives, that blacks, equally with whites, are the work of Omnipotence, and the objects of the kind regard of the Father of all!"

Mr. Allen (of the Society of Friends, and Treasurer) felt under strong depression from the loss of his late co-adjutor, Mr. Fox. Beside the original debt, there was last year a balance of £336 against the Institution. Mr. Allen urged forcibly the cause he advocated. Even in London, education was more needed than any, who would not inquire closely, could be persuaded to believe. The object of the Institution was to interest the poor themselves—not to receive the high blessing of education as an *alms*, but, by doing something themselves, to let it have more the semblance of a purchase. They wanted to raise the moral character of the poor. Parents became benefited through the children; and instances are on record where the parents have been admitted to the schools at their own request, when they have seen their good effects on the children.

Mr. Adams, Minister at the British Court from the American States, said, that he appreciated the compliment paid to the country he had the honour to represent, and which felt the necessity, and knew the advantages, of education. Education is knowledge, and it leads to virtue.

Mr. Williams (banker) gloried in the prospect that, through this Institution, there was a chance of making some adequate return to the people of colour. The sons of Africa were much indebted to a most honourable man then in his eye (Mr. Wilberforce, who had just entered) for the cessation of slavery. That horrid traffic had by him been shown in its detestable colours; but it appeared how in darker shades, since we learn from Hayti such proofs of intellectual capacity in those whom our avarice and cruelty had held as inferior to our species.

The Earl of Darnley noticed, that the Institution was one for universal benevolence. He would remind the assembly that their venerable Sovereign was its prompt, and first and zealous patron. They would remember the good Monarch's wish,—' That he might live to see every poor child in the kingdom able to read his Bible.' But had Providence permitted his continued presence among us, this wish could not have its accomplishment, but from schools not built on the principle of religious exclusion. His R. H. the Prince Regent was a liberal contributor to this Institution; and so were their R. Hs. the Dukes of Sussex and Kent. His Lordship moved the thanks to the Royal Personages, which was seconded by the Rev. Rowland Hill, who thought that education, being an universal blessing, should be as universally as possible bestowed.

Sir J. Swinburne assured the meeting that his Grace of Bedford would have been present, but that indispensable business had taken him out into a distant county.

Rev. Dr. Lindsay said, It was to be regretted that an unity of faith, which *could never be found*, was sought after, to the neglect of the unity of the spirit in the bond of peace, which could be obtained.

Rev. Dr. Collyer then read the Ladies' Report, which announced progress in various places; and in one (if we heard right) there were 1800 female children. Knitting was introduced into the school, but the ladies lamented that the parents, in many instances, were insensible to the blessings of education.

The Russian Envoy to Portugal (through the medium of Dr. Schwabe) declared, that his Sovereign was sensible of the value of the object of the British and Foreign School Society, and was ready to give it the most warm co-operation.

Rev. J. Townsend was happy to advocate so great and good a cause. He rejoiced to hear that a king of Hayti could read such an admirable lesson, and give such excellent admonitions—even to Christian princes!

Sir J. Jackson, bart. moved thanks to the Committee; which were seconded by the Rev. Mr. Cox, in a speech of much eloquence.

Mr. Marten, in moving thanks to the Subscribers to the invested Fund, spoke of the necessity of supplies, without which, the cause of education of the poor could not proceed. The £10,000 were to be raised in two years, and if not completed in the present year, the money was to be returned to the subscribers. The fund was to pay a debt, and the surplus of it to build a suitable central school for the metropolis. The commencement of the subscription for investment and accumulation, till it reached £10,000, was, by various zealous friends, each according to his ability, undertaken to raise in their different connexions, some £100, and others smaller amounts: but still these sums were inconvenient for others who moved in narrow circles; and therefore he took the liberty to recommend, that those of either sex who felt the importance of this cause, and who could raise but £5 among their friends, would be volunteers in aid of this Society. Many of these small additions would form an aggregate of consequence to the Society, and go far toward completing the sum originally proposed. He then urged the completion of this undertaking on the ground of its utility. It was Christian education which was afforded. The minds of children were early imbued with lessons from the Bible, inculcating the fear of God, leading away from vice, and drawing to virtue.—He had to inform the meeting that a Mr. Owen, of Scotland—that land of bright example of the benefits of education—had presented the society with £1000.

Mr. Rowcroft, in seconding the motion, felt chagrined, that while, on another occasion, in ten months, £500,000 had been subscribed, he should have to plead *in London*, for so pitiful a sum as £3000 to make up a sum of £10,000 begged for all over the kingdom, for the education of the poor. "But I ask it (said he) for the education of children who may hereby know what a country theirs is, and if against any future tyrant they may have to defend it, they may feel the firmer in the trying hour."

His R. H. the Duke of Kent said,

"The attendance to-day surpasses my most sanguine expectations. I have at former meetings looked forward to preside at the next returns.—Not so now.—I am about to leave my beloved country. Perhaps years may elapse before I meet you again. Let me hear while I am abroad that this cause prospers, and I pledge myself, that when the purposes of my absence are accomplished—when I return, I will place *One Thousand Guineas* at the disposal and use of this Institution. If I have not done it before, it is because I had it not in my power. I am desirous that this last act—this pledge of my love to it should be upon record. I feel gratified that this motion came from the Minister of the United States. I have lived long in the neighbourhood of the United States, and it was ever a grief to me that the two countries should be at variance. Their language and their interest is the same, and their friendship should be inviolable. I return my thanks to this assembly."

Lady Darnley and the Lady Mayoress held the plates at the door, and the collection exceeded £105.

BARON MASERES.—Mr. Baron Maseres, who is eighty-five, is much younger than many men are at fifty. He performs all his duties as Cursitor Baron of the Exchequer, which duties are various and important, with as much regularity and in every respect as well, as he performed those of Attorney-General in Canada fifty years ago. Few men in England write or speak with more fluency, more precision or more force; to which I take this opportunity of adding, that very few indeed have acted, as to politics, so disinterested, or, in any respect, so honourable a part. Degenerate and base as the times are, there are still some worthy men left in England; and if their names should ever be collected, that of *Maseres* will certainly occupy a prominent place.
Cobbett. W. Reg. June 1.

LORD GROSVENOR.—There appeared lately in the *Chester Courant* a paragraph, stating, that thirty-one men employed in *Lord Grosvenor's* mine at Halkin, in Flintshire, had been turned out of work because they were Dissenters from the Church of England. We understand that the dismissal originated entirely in a mistake of his Lordship's agent. His Lordship had simply desired that his workmen should be encouraged to go to church (instead of wasting their time and spending their earnings idly on Sundays); and his aim would have been equally gained by pressing those of his workmen who were Dissenters, to regularly attend their own place of worship; but the agent taking the recommendation in its literal sense, dismissed the latter. It is said that orders have since been given by his Lordship, that no person shall be excluded from employment on account of his religious opinions.

Examiner. June 2.

· THE JEWS.—If it be true that the Senate of Lubeck have ordered the Jews settled there to leave that city, we can only remark that Lubeck deserves to be deprived of her title and privileges as a free and independent city. In the first place, it is a direct violation of the 16th Article of the German Confederation, by which it is declared that the Jews should continue in the full enjoyment of all their present rights and privileges, and await a further decision. In the second place, it is a shocking outrage upon the principles of humanity and hospitality. It is not pretended that this expulsion is for any crimes committed. But even that charge could not apply to a whole community—to the aged, the infirm, the female and the infant. We have ever thought that the treatment which the Jews have received has been a disgrace to all countries and to all nations. The fate of never having a home—of being a people without a people's country—of being dispersed over every part of the world, is hard enough: but to have superadded the fate of being treated as criminals and outcasts—of having the punishment of guilt without the commission of guilt—of having their very names pass into a synonym for all that is bad and tricking, and false and foul—to be the mock and scorn of the rabble—to have the " very dogs bark at them"

as they pass, is a degree of suffering to which no other race were ever exposed from the creation of the world.—And this has been their lot for ages. If they have been hard and griping in their dealings, may it not have been occasioned by the treatment they have received? To treat men as if they were incapable of virtue, is to make them so.

Examiner. June 23. ·

Collections at the late Missionary Meeting of the Calvinistic Dissenters and Methodists.

	£.	s.	d.
Surry Chapel - - - -	380	0	0
Tabernacle - - - - -	157	10	3
Spa-Fields Chapel - -	104	12	1
Tottenham Court Chapel	171	0	0
St. Bride's Church - -	120	0	0
Sion Chapel - - - - -	109	2	2
Silver Street Chapel - -	55	0	0
Orange Street Chapel -	68	0	0
Total - - - £1165	4	6	

NOTICES.

The Anniversary of the Kent and Sussex Christian Unitarian Association will be held at Maidstone, on Wednesday, July the 10th: Mr. Aspland to preach the sermon.

The Southern Unitarian Society will hold its Annual Meeting at Newport, in the Isle of Wight, on Wednesday, July 24th, 1816. The Rev. Robert Aspland is expected to preach the sermon.

T. Cooke, Jun. Secretary.

A Second Edition of Mr. Cappe's Sermons, chiefly on Devotional Subjects, is just published by Messrs. Longman and Co.

· Mr. Thomas Rees proposes to publish shortly his long projected Translation of the Racovian Catechism.

MONTHLY RETROSPECT of PUBLIC AFFAIRS;

OR,

The Christian's Survey of the Political World.

THE explosion has taken place which has been so long dreaded. Every one connected with the West Indies had prognosticated that the efforts used by Mr. Wilberforce and his friends to get a bill passed by the parliament of the empire to enforce certain regulations respecting the blacks, must produce some fatal effects in the colonies. The language used by the favourers of the measure was of a most unhappy tendency. It raised expectations in the slaves that there was an authority here highly paramount above. that of their masters, and that Mr. Wilberforce was so great a man, and so much their friend, that their servitude was soon to be broken, and a general emancipation was to take place. Highly culpable indeed was the language of some of the writers upon this question. They took a delight in representing the planter in the most odious colours, in exaggerating every instance of ill-treatment that might have occurred, concealing all the kindness that is continually displayed, and has for many years been increasing, in the islands; and in fact doing every thing to excite a spirit of discontent in the minds of the slaves, and depreciating the character of the masters.

That man in every part of the world, whatever may be his colour, should attain to the dignity of his nature, should be free in the highest sense of the word, is the great object of Christianity, and the desire of every reader of this Miscellany. But till his mind is improved and he is capable of understanding and appreciating the blessings of this freedom, it is in vain that he is released from certain yokes laid upon him by the rules of civil society. Many a king upon his throne is as much an object of our pity as the slave under the lash of his driver; and who would wish to enjoy the liberty of the savage in the wilds of America? It is an old and a good adage, *Natura nihil facit per saltum*. A greater evil could not possibly befall the blacks, than that they should be instantly declared free, for the only result of this freedom would be the tearing of each other to pieces and the destruction of the masters. In what manner they are best to be brought forward to a higher degree in the scale of nature, is a problem worthy of the consideration of the true politician; but of this we may be sure, that Mr. Wilberforce and his friends are taking the worst methods possible for the attainment of this end. If

the slave is to look up to the authority of this island, and to conceive that he has a party in the House of Commons in his favour, if Mr. Wilberforce is to be his patron and the local legislature to be set at nought, it will be in vain to expect any thing but what has already taken place—the burning of plantations and the destruction of life.

The error of Mr. Wilberforce consists in not attending to the state of society which exists in that country over which he attempts to regulate. He does not recollect that slavery existed at the first propagation of Christianity, and that it took several ages before the maxims of our holy religion could prevail over the principles of the world. In this state, however, no violent efforts were used by the apostles and first teachers of Christianity. They did not attempt to excite an outcry against the holders of slaves, nor to use any irritating language respecting slavery. They saw clearly that the emancipation would be produced in a better manner by teaching slaves to obey their masters, not from eye-service, but from a regard to duty, and in like manner by inculcating on the masters the duty of being kind to their slaves. Thus gradually both parties were brought nearer to each other, and at last slavish services were exchanged for a better tenure—the compact between master and servant.

The abolition of the slave trade and the emancipation of the blacks are two distinct questions, and they ought to be kept entirely distinct in our minds. On the first question the parliament of the kingdom had an undoubted right to interfere, for it might assuredly dictate that an Englishman should not carry on a trade in the persons of blacks, as well as it prohibited his trading in other articles. To this law the West Indians submitted equally with all other subjects; and the advocates for the abolition of the slave trade having gained this point, were interested only in seeing that the law was not broken. But the emancipation of the blacks involves a variety of questions on which the residents of England are not competent judges. There are three conditions in the West Indies, that of the white, who must be the ruler—the freed man—and the slave. The white enjoys all the privileges of Englishmen, the other two parties are necessarily deprived of some of them; but all are under certain laws liable to be changed at the discretion of the governor of the two houses of assembly in the island. Here as in England is a proper place for improvement: and it is unjust to say that great improvements have not been gradually taking place under the local legislatures. All has not been done that the sanguine emancipator may expect; but it would be time for Mr. Wilberforce and his friends to call on a superior authority when, having proposed to the colonial legislatures a regulation, it had been rejected by them without cause. The rude attempt to legislate for all the islands is such an attack upon the local legislations as cannot but excite dismay and distrust; and if a similar thing had been attempted in England, interfering with all our corporate bodies, the table of the House of Commons would have been overwhelmed with petitions from every part of England.

The spirit of insurrection first appeared in the island of Barbadoes, and it displayed itself in the burning of plantations to a very great extent. From the energy of the whites the misled blacks were brought into subjection, but not without considerable slaughter of the latter in the field, and the execution of others by the hand of justice. The island, however, is in that state that the whites are compelled to keep a strict watch over their dependents. The proclamations issued by the governors of other islands indicate that a similar watchfulness is necessary in them; but it is hoped that as the whites are now every where on the alert the intended mischief may be prevented.

In this state of things Mr. Wilberforce's motion was coming forward, but it was delayed till government had received its dispatches; and after they had arrived, Mr. Wilberforce made a long speech tending rather to inflame than to appease the existing troubles. He was replied to by a gentleman connected with the West Indies, who contented himself with a plain representation of facts, which pointed out the inevitable loss of the colonies unless speedy measures were taken to make it clear to the blacks that no such measure was in agitation as their emancipation. He proposed that an address should be presented to the Prince Regent to request that the governors of the islands might be directed to issue proclamations testifying his high displeasure at the late outrages and the insidious attempts of those who were exciting hopes of emancipation, since no such measure was in contemplation, though every effort should be encouraged which had in view their moral and religious improvement. All sides of the House saw the necessity and propriety of this measure, which was unanimously voted, and we trust that it will have the desired effect, though it must not be concealed that, at this moment, the holders of property in the West Indies are in fear for its security, as well as for the lives of their friends and relatives in those regions. The mischief that has already been done will make the legislature pause before it gives its countenance to a set of persons so little acquainted with our West India islands and deriving their information from very suspicious quarters.

The spirit of discontent has appeared in our own country. Great outrages have been committed in the isle of Ely; the alleged cause—the distresses of the poor from want of work and want of proper pay. By a due degree of spirit these infatuated people were brought under, and a number of rioters were committed to prison. A special commission was appointed of two judges to sit with the judge of the isle of Ely upon this occasion, and after the trial and condemnation of a few of the ringleaders, the crown very humanely stopped farther prosecutions, letting the rest go out upon recognizances for future appearance and bail for their good behaviour.

An occurrence has taken place of a singular nature, which might give room for many comments. A meeting of the county of Kent took place at Maidstone for the purpose of congratulation on the late royal marriage. An address was moved and seconded, but on taking the show of hands scarcely any hands were held up in its favour and the meeting was dissolved. The principal gentlemen retired to an inn and requested the High Sheriff to take the chair, which he with great propriety declined, and the company resolved that copies of the address should be sent to the principal towns for signatures. Addresses so signed want the legitimate stamp and can convey only the sentiments of individuals; and the expression of popular feeling at the meeting cannot be construed into any intended affront to the young couple, in whose happiness all must be interested, though it is indicatory of a discontent which it will be the duty of government to examine, and if there are just causes for it to endeavour to remove the grounds of it.

In France all is quiet, if we are to believe government reports. The principal instigators to the insurrection in Dauphiny have been executed. The court has been occupied with two grand events—the marriage of the Duke of Berri and the celebration of their grand feast called by them the Feast of God. On the day for this feast processions are made in every parish of the Catholic world. The wafer god is paraded about the streets—altars are erected at various places—and the deluded multitude falls prostrate as it passes before this miserable emblem and other abominations of their strange idolatry. The whole represents a heathen rite. During the reign of Buonaparte such exhibitions were prohibited, but 'they are now revived with all their ancient folly and superstition.

Symptoms of some new régulations with respect to the Barbary powers have made their appearance. They have for too long a time been permitted to exercise a tyranny over their captives in war, which is disgraceful even to the religion they profess. The Americans have shown what may be done with them, and England has interfered to procure the liberation of a number of Christians from a wretched captivity in which some of them had been held for many 'years. A project was on foot for the union of the Christian powers to put

an end to these disorders, and it is i a melancholy thing that the fine sho the Mediterranean should be subjec race of men little better than pirates.

Germany goes on very slowly in it constitution. Spain indicates no ai ration. It has had some successes colonies, but still it remains doubtful ther its ancient influence can be res Wherever its power extends its ma disfigured by cruelty. Vast emigr: are taking place from all parts of E to America. There is land enough fc and it is to be hoped, that in quittin; supposed civilized part of the world, will leave behind them the vices by \ it is peculiarly distinguished.

NEW PUBLICATIONS IN THEOLOG AND GENERAL LITERATURE.

An Essay on the Existence of a Supreme Creator possessed of Infinite Power, Wisdom and Goodness. (To which Mr. Burnett's First Prize of Twelve Hundred Pounds was adjudged.) By Wiliam Lawrence Brown, D. D. Principal of Marischal College, Aberdeen. To which is prefixed a Memoir relating to the Founder of the Prizes. 2 vols. 8vo. 1*l.* 1*s.* boards.

A Sermon delivered at the Unitarian Chapel, Chichester, April the 21st, 1816, on Occasion of the Death of Thomas P. Powell, M. D. By W. J. Fox. 4to.

The Value of a Child ; or Motives to the Good Education of Children. In a Letter to a Daughter. By John Taylor, D. D. of Norwich. 2nd. ed. 12mo.

Ecclesiastical Claims Investigated and the Liberty of the Pulpit Defended. By Daniel Isaac.

The Christian Doctrines of the Trinity and Incarnation considered and maintain-

éd, on the Principles of Judaism. B Rev. J. Oxlee. Vol. I. 8vo. 12*s.*

History of the Inquisition, abri from Limborch ; with an Historical S: of the Christian Church. 8vo. 13*s.*

Persecution of French Protestant: Report on the Persecution of the Fr Protestants, presented to the Comm of Dissenting Ministers of the Three D minations. By the Rev. Clement Pe 8vo. 2*s.* 6*d.*

Sketch of the Past and Present Sta' the Vaudois or Waldenses, inhabitin; Vallies of Piedmont. By the Rev. ' mas Morgan. (Published by order ol Committee of Dissenting Ministers o Three Denominations.) 8vo. 6*d.*

An Historical View of the Refo: Church of France, from its Origin t Present Time. With an Appendix, taining Documents and Remarks on ! Castlereagh's Speech. 8vo. 5*s.*

CORRESPONDENCE.

Our correspondent *Liberus* is informed that the article of *Public Affairs* is al written by the same gentleman, who expresses in it his own sentiments wit assuming to represent those of the Editor, correspondents or readers. The Edit too sensible of his obligations to this gentleman to attempt to interfere with the statement of his views of public events. The *Slave Registry Bill* is a measure t decided not by the feelings but by a cool judgment on the state of the West I Islands. To such as wish to understand the question, we recommend an able pam just published, entitled, " The British Legislature's Interference respecting Slav the West India Islands deprecated."

The paper on *Poetical Scepticism*, with various other articles, was too late insertion the present month.

ERRATUM.

P. 191. col. ii. l. 1. for " jocundum," read *jucundum.*

THE

𝕸𝖔𝖓𝖙𝖍𝖑𝖞 𝕽𝖊𝖕𝖔𝖘𝖎𝖙𝖔𝖗𝖞,

&c.

HISTORY AND BIOGRAPHY.

*Biographical Account of the Negro An-
gelo Solimann.*

[Translated from "Literature des Negres,"
by M. Gregoire. (p. 130.) Paris, 1808.]

THOUGH Angelo Solimann
never published any thing,[*] he
merits one of the chief places among
Negroes distinguished by a high degree of cultivation, and extensive
knowledge, and still more, by moral
excellence.

He was the son of an African prince,
the sovereign of *Gangusilang*, and his
family name *Magni-Famori*. Besides
the little *Mmadi-Maké*, (which was
Angelo's name in his own country)
his parents had a younger child, a
daughter. He used to relate with
what deference his father was treated,
being surrounded by a great number
of servants. Like all the children of
princes in that country, he had
characters imprinted on each thigh,
and long did he indulge the hope
that he should be known by those
characters and discovered to his parents. The recollections of childhood,

---

. [*] It is my duty publicly to mention the
names of those to whom I owe the biography of this estimable African, who was first
mentioned to me by Dr. Gall. On the
application of my countrymen of *Hautefort*,
attached here to the foreign *relations*, and
Dudun, first secretary to the French legation
in Austria, great zeal was discovered to satisfy my curiosity. Two respectable ladies
of Vienna, Madame *de Stief* and Madame
de Picler paid the greatest attention to it,
carefully collecting the accounts furnished
by the friends of the deceased Angelo.
From these materials this interesting
narrative has been compiled. In the
French translation it loses much elegance
of style; for Madame *de Picler*, who
drew it up in German, possessed the rare
talent of writing equally well in prose and
verse. I have great pleasure in expressing
to these obliging persons my just gratitude.

especially of his first attempts to draw
the bow, in which he surpassed his
companions, the remembrance of the
simple manners, and the fine sky of
his country often produced in his
mind a pensive pleasure, even to old age.
He could never sing his country's
songs, which his excellent memory
had retained, without being deeply affected.

It appears, from the recollections of
Angelo, that his nation had then attained to some degree of civilization.
His father possessed many elephants,
and even horses, which are rare in
those countries. Money was unknown, but the commerce of exchange was regularly conducted, and
they had sales by auction. They worshipped the stars, and practised circumcision. Two families of whites
resided in the country:

Authors who have published their
travels mention perpetual wars among
the nations of Africa, of which the
objects are revenge, plunder, or the
most shameful species of avarice; the
conqueror haling his prisoners to the
nearest market, to sell them to the
whites. A war of this kind, against
the people of *Mmadi Maké*, broke out
so unexpectedly that his father had
no suspicion of danger. The child, at
the age of seven years, one day, standing by the side of his mother, who was
suckling his sister, they suddenly perceived the clash of arms and hurling
of arrows. The grandfather of *Mmadi
Maké*, seized with terror, rushed into
the house crying out the enemy is at
hand. Fatuma started up alarmed,
the father seized his arms, and the
little boy, terrified, fled with the swift-
ness of an arrow. His mother called
to him loudly, where are you going
Mmadi Maké? The child answered,
there where God wills. In advanced
age he often reflected on the important
meaning of those words. Having fled
from the house he looked back and saw

his mother, and many of his father's people, fall under the blows of the enemy. With another boy he crept under a tree, terrified and covering his eyes with his hands. The tumult increased, the enemy who already assumed the victory, seized and held him up in token of triumph. At this sight the countrymen of *Mmadi Maké* made a last effort and rallied to recover the son of their king. The combat was renewed around the child. In the end the enemies remained conquerors, and he became unquestionably their prey. His master exchanged him with another Negro, for a fine horse, and the child was conveyed to the place of embarkation. He there found many of his countrymen, all, like himself, prisoners, and condemned to slavery. They recognised him with unavailing sorrow, but were even forbidden to speak to him.

The prisoners, having been thus conveyed in small boats to the sea, *Mmadi Maké* saw with astonishment large floating houses, into one of which he entered and found a third master. He conjectured that this was a Spanish vessel. After escaping a tempest, they came on shore, and his master promised to conduct him to his mother. This delightful hope soon vanished, on finding, instead of his mother, his master's wife, who received him affectionately and treated him with much kindness. The husband gave him the name of Andre, and employed him to lead the camels to pasture and take charge of them.

The master's country is unknown or how long the boy remained with him. Angelo has been dead twelve years; and this account has been lately collected from the information of his friends. It is only known that after a considerable time his master proposed taking him to a country where his condition would be improved. *Mmadi Maké* was well pleased, but his mistress parted from him with regret. They embarked and arrived at Messina. He was brought to the house of a rich lady who was expecting him. She treated him with much kindness, had him instructed in the language of the country which he easily acquired. His affability conciliated the affection of the numerous domestics, among whom he distinguished a Negress, named *Angelina*, for her gentleness and kind attentions.

He fell dangerously ill, the marchioness, his mistress, felt for him all the anxiety of a mother, so that she sat up with him a part of every night. The most skilful physicians were called in. His bed was surrounded by a crowd of persons who waited his orders. The marchioness had long wished that he might be baptized. After repeated refusals, one day during his convalescence he himself requested baptism, when his mistress, highly gratified, ordered the most magnificent preparations. In a saloon, a richly embroidered canopy was suspended over a bed of state. All the family and friends of the house were present, *Mmadi Maké* reclining on this bed was consulted on the name he would have. From gratitude and friendship to the Negress *Angelina* he wished to be called *Angelo*. His wish was gratified and for a family name he had Solimann. He annually celebrated the 11th of September, the day of his entrance into Christianity, with the same pious feelings as if it had been the anniversary of his birth.

His good conduct, complaisance, and excellent understanding, endeared him to all. The Prince Lobkowitz, then the imperial general in Sicily, frequented the house where this child lived, of whom he became so fond that he requested him of the marchioness. From her regard for Angelo, she reluctantly yielded to considerations of interest and prudence, which determined her to make that present to the general. Many tears were shed by her on parting with the little Negro, who entered with regret into the service of a new master.

The functions of the prince were incompatible with a long residence in that country. He loved Angelo, but his manner of life, and perhaps the spirit of the times, induced him to attend very little to his education. Angelo became wild and choleric. He passed his days in idleness and childish sports. An old house-steward of the prince, perceiving his good disposition and other excellent qualities, notwithstanding his idleness, provided him a tutor, under whom Angelo learned, in the space of seventeen days, to write German. The grateful affection of the child, and his rapid progress in every branch of knowledge, amply rewarded the old man's care.

Thus Angelo grew up in the prince's family. He accompanied him in all his travels, partaking with him the perils of war. He fought by the side of his master, whom once when wounded, he bore on his shoulders out of the field of battle. Angelo distinguished himself on these occasions, not only as a servant and faithful friend, but likewise as an intrepid warrior and an experienced officer, especially in tactics, though he never obtained any military promotion. Marshal Lascy, who valued him highly, pronounced in the presence of a number of officers the most honourable eulogium on his bravery, made him a present of a superb Turkish sabre, and offered him the command of a company, which he refused.

His master died, bequeathing Angelo to Prince Wenceslaus de Lichtenstein, who had long desired to have him. He however inquired if he were satisfied and would willingly live with him. Angelo gave his word and made the necessary preparations for his new situation. In the interval the Emperor Francis I. made him the same offer, with very flattering conditions. But the word of Angelo was sacred. He remained with the Prince of Lichtenstein. Here, as with General Lobkowitz, he became the guardian genius of the unfortunate. He conveyed to the prince the cases of those who sought his bounty. His pockets were always full of memorials and petitions. Indisposed to ask for any thing, on his own account, he could, with more hope of success, pursue his applications for others.

Angelo accompanied his master in his travels, and was at Francfort, during the coronation of the Emperor Joseph as the King of the Romans [in 1764.] One day, by the persuasion of his prince he tried his fortune in a faro bank and gained twenty thousand florins. He offered to his opponent to try another game, by which he lost twenty thousand florins more. Making him one offer more, Angelo contrived to manage the game so that the loser regained that last sum. This delicate conduct on the part of Angelo was much admired, and gained for him numerous expressions of esteem. The accidental favours of fortune did not beguile him. On the contrary, aware of her caprices, he never again hazarded any considerable sum. He amused himself with chess, and had the reputation of being an adept.

At the age of . . . . . he married a widow, Madame de Christiani, whose maiden name was Kellerman, of a Belgic family. The prince was not informed of the marriage. Angelo might have reasons for concealing it. A subsequent event justified his silence. The Emperor Joseph II. who took a lively interest in all that concerned Angelo, distinguishing him so as to take his arm in the public walks, discovered one day, without being aware of the consequences, Angelo's secret to the Prince of Lichtenstein. He sent for him and questioned him. Angelo avowed his marriage. The prince informed him that he should banish him from his house and erase his name from his will. He had designed for him diamonds of considerable value, which Angelo used to wear when on gala days he attended his master.

Angelo, who had so often interceded for others, said nothing for himself. He left the palace to inhabit in a distant suburb, a small house, which he had purchased for the accomodation of his wife. He lived with her in that retreat, enjoying domestic happiness. The careful education of his only daughter, Madam the Baroness of Heuchtersleben, who is dead, the culture of his garden, the society of some enlightened and virtuous men, such were his amusements and occupations.

About two years after the death of Prince Wenceslaus de Lichtenstein, his nephew and heir, Prince Francis, perceived Angelo in the street. He stopped his carriage, took him into it, and told him that, fully convinced of his innocence, he was determined to make reparation for his uncle's injustice. He then assigned to Angelo an income to be paid, in case of his death, as an annual pension to Madam Solimann. All that the prince required of Angelo was that he should superintend the education of his son, Louis de Lichtenstein.

Angelo punctually performed the duties of that new employment; and every day attended the prince, to watch over the pupil entrusted to his care. The prince observing that the distance was troublesome to Angelo, especially in bad weather, offered him a residence. Thus Angelo was fixed a second time in the palace Lichten-stein. But he brought his family with him and lived as retired as before in the society of a few friends and learned men, and devoted to polite literature, which he cultivated with ardour. His favourite study was history, being much assisted by his excellent memory. He could cite the names of eminent persons with the years of their birth, and the dates of all considerable events.

His wife, whose health had been long declining, survived a few years by the tender attentions of a husband who procured for her all the succours of art, but at length she sunk under her disease. From that time Angelo altered the arrangements of his family. He no longer invited friends to his table, and drank nothing but water, to give an example to his daughter, whose finished education was entirely his work. Perhaps also he wished, by rigid economy, to secure a fortune for his only child.

Angelo still performed many journies, in advanced age, either on his own business or that of others, esteemed and beloved every where. Acts of courtesy and benefits which he bestowed are still recollected in these already distant times. His concerns having led him to Milan, the late Archduke Ferdinand, who was the governor, paid him the most friendly attentions.

He enjoyed to the close of life a robust constitution. His exterior discovered scarcely any symptoms of old age, which occasioned mistakes and friendly disputes; for often persons who had not seen him for twenty or thirty years have taken him for his own son and addressed him accordingly.

Struck with apoplexy in the street, at the age of seventy-five, assistance was procured for him, but in vain. He died November 21, 1796, regretted by all his friends, who could not recollect him without being affected even to tears. The esteem of all the worthy followed him to the tomb.

Angelo was of middle stature and well proportioned. The regularity of his features and the nobleness of his figure, formed by their beauty, a contrast to the unfavourable ideas commonly entertained of Negro physiognomy. An extraordinary readiness in all bodily exercises gave to his motions an air of grace and agility. To all the

delicacy of taste uniting a sound judgment, formed by extended and solid attainments, he possessed six languages, the Italian, the French, the German, the Latin, the Bohemian, the English, and spoke the three first with fluency and correctness.

Like all his countrymen, he was born with an impetuous temper. His unalterable serenity and gentleness were consequently so much more laudable, as the fruit of difficult combats and many victories gained over himself. There never escaped him, even when irritated, any improper expression. Angelo was pious, without being superstitious. He punctually observed all the precepts of religion, and did not judge it below him to give an example to his family. His word, his resolution taken on mature reflection were immutable, and nothing could turn him from his purpose. He always used the dress of his country. It was a habit very simple, after the Turkish fashion, and generally of a dazzling whiteness which set off the black and shining colour of his skin. His portrait, which has been engraved at Augsburg, is in the gallery of Lichtenstein.

N. L. T. A.

Abstract of the History of Dr. Williams's Trust. [Appendix to the Account of his Life. Mon. Repos. X. 201.] By the Rev. Thomas Morgan, Librarian.

WHEN Dr. Williams's will came to be examined by his trustees, it was found to be dated June 26, 1711. Since that time he had purchased several estates, which by a codicil with his signature, dated August 22, 1712, he appointed to be applied to the same uses with those formerly devised by him. The execution of this codicil, however, was not attested by any witnesses, on which account the estates mentioned in it became the legal property of the testator's heir at law, his sister, Mrs. Roberts, of Wrexham. Of this circumstance, Mrs. Roberts, in the first instance, declared herself not desirous of taking any advantage, but, on the contrary, stated that she was determined, on certain conditions to which the trustees agreed, to confirm her brother's charitable design, so far as lay in her power. Relying on this declaration, the trustees gave orders for the preparation of the deeds necessary to be executed by her: but in the mean time the lady had changed her intentions, and insisted upon having those estates at her own disposal, or at least an equivalent of two hundred pounds per annum. As the trustees had it not in their power, any more than in their inclination, to submit to either of her demands, they found themselves under the necessity, in the year 1717, of filing a bill in Chancery against Mrs. Roberts, and afterwards a supplemental bill against the attorney-general, to have the will and codicil of the testator established, and the trust carried into execution. During the progress of these bills, Mrs. Roberts relinquished her former claims, and consented to confirm her brother's will, on the condition of receiving sixty pounds per annum, commencing from the time of his decease, to dispose of in charities in North Wales, as she should see fit; with which the Trustees agreed to comply, upon the report of the master in Chancery that it was for the interest of the charities that they should come into this proposal. Accordingly, by indentures of the 24th of March 1719, and 25th of March 1720, Mrs. Roberts granted and released to the trustees and their heirs all the estates of which the testator was possessed before making his will, as well as those described in his codicil, subject to the payment of sixty pounds per annum, as she should by deed or will direct, and for want of such direction to Mrs. Roberts herself. This grand obstacle to the proving of Dr. Williams's will having been removed, on the 26th of July 1721, a decree was obtained at the Rolls, by which the above-mentioned indentures and the testator's will were established, and his various charities were directed to be executed and performed. By the result of these proceedings, the trustees have a legal estate of inheritance, in fee-simple, in Temple Manor in Essex; Beech-Lane and Glover's-Court estates; Coleman-street estate, and Clerkenwell-green estate; and in all the rest of the Doctor's real and personal property, not specially devised, an equitable term of two thousand years.

One of the first steps taken by the trustees, after obtaining this decree, was to propose schemes to the master in Chancery for settling the charities,

and carrying them into execution; which were approved of, and continue to be followed to the present time, with such alterations as they have found it necessary to introduce, which have received the sanction of the Court.

The founder's will directs, that the trustees whom he appoints, and their assigns and successors, shall meet at least once a quarter in London, for the management of his estates; and that if any of them, or their successors, shall remove to a considerable distance from London, or voluntarily neglect or betray their trust, or be rendered incapable faithfully and diligently to answer the ends of it, then the residue of the said trustees and successors, from time to time, shall choose others in the room of such, and the disallowed be deprived of all power and right to intermeddle in any part of the trust. The will also directs that the vote of the major part of the trustees present shall conclude any matter; but that twelve of them shall be always present, (if so many are alive and near London, free from violent restraint,) in granting leases, electing successors, and other very important matters. And that in the aforesaid cases of death, &c. all about London being summoned to two successive meetings, what is concluded in the first meeting, notice thereof being sent to the absent in and near London, and confirmed in the second meeting, shall stand and be valid if the number be seven; provided they have not wilfully omitted to fill up the numbers by electing others to succeed the dead, and such as reject the management of the trust after they had accepted it, or inhabit above ten miles from London, and such as shall be voted by fifteen of the trustees to endeavour to betray or frustrate the scope and purpose intended by the testator in any considerable part of his will; for these last are to be succeeded as if dead, and others elected by his trustees in their stead.

After various legacies to individuals, and to charitable institutions, Dr. Williams devised estates at Barnet in Hertfordshire, and Totham in Essex, together with one hundred pounds in money to the College of Glasgow, towards the maintenance of such students from South Britain as his trustees should appoint and nominate from time to time, to be removed at their discretion, and successors appointed by them to supply their place. Having pointed out students, then at Glasgow, to be his first beneficiaries; who while under-graduates were, to receive six pounds per annum from the said College, and when admitted masters of arts, ten pounds, or fifteen pounds for three years, as his trustees should direct; he enjoined the latter in filling up of vacancies, to prefer the sons of poor presbyterian ministers, equally qualified, before others. The College, however, was ordered to send every year to the trustees in London an account of their receipts and distributions; and the testator ordained that the grant should be no longer valid than while the present constitution of the church of Scotland continues, and that should the episcopal hierarchy or popery be established in North Britain, the beqnest shall become null and void, and revert to his trustees, to be applied to the other uses of his will. In the year 1725, the then trustees of Dr. Williams conveyed to the then professors of the College of Glasgow, and their successors, the estates before mentioned; but by this conveyance the professors took only estates for *life* in the presentations, the fee and inheritance remaining in Dr Williams's trustees. In the year 1754, the trustees passed a resolution, that all persons who shall hereafter be presented to exhibitions in the College of Glasgow shall be entered as under-graduates, and shall wear the gown, and be subject to the rules of the college, in order to their being admitted to the degree of M. A. and that a clause be for the future inserted in the presentations of the exhibitioners for that purpose. In 1755, the professors of Glasgow brought an amicable bill against Dr. Williams's trustees, praying that they and the surviving professors might convey the devised estates to all the members and professors of the university in their natural capacity, and their heirs. As the trustees did not oppose it, a decree was made accordingly at the Rolls. During subsequent years the income of the college estates has increased so much by savings and improved rents, that at the present time (1816) exhibitions are granted to eight students of forty pounds per annum, while under-graduates, and of forty-five pounds per annum when

graduates. By the regulations of the trustees, no exhibition is to be made to any of the students who are absent during the terms, or times of reading lectures, unless leave of absence be previously granted by them, or by the principal or faculty of the university. The qualifications of students, as to their knowledge in the languages, should be attended to while under-graduates, and testimonials are to be sent at the end of each session of their progress: if any exhibitioner wishes to continue another session beyond what is usually allowed, he must apply at least six months before the close of the expiring session. Students are not eligible till sixteen years of age, and are required at certain periods to declare their intention of pursuing the Christian ministry in South Britain. On the value of such an institution, and the enlarged liberal views of the founder, this is not the place in which to expatiate, and they will be found amply illustrated in another department of this treatise.

The same spirit prompted Dr. Williams to give to the Society in Scotland for Propagating Christian Knowledge, an estate at Catworth in Huntingdonshire, together with one hundred pounds in money, to possess at the end of one year after they should send three qualified ministers on missions for the conversion of foreign infidel countries to the Christian faith; with the proviso, in the event of the Society's becoming dissolved, or subjected to restraint, or neglecting to name such ministers, that the possession of those estates should be resumed by his trustees. From the minutes of the trust it appears, that a variety of obstacles arose in negotiating the settlement of this business with the Scots Society, which were not removed for several years: but at length the conditions on which the grant was made by the testator having been satisfactorily complied with, and a deed of conveyance drawn up, which met with the approbation of all parties concerned, it was executed by the trustees on the 4th of July, 1737.

- The reversion of another estate called Beeknam Hall, in Essex, Dr. Williams bequeathed to the Society for the Propagation of the Gospel in New England, upon the condition that sixty pounds per annum should be allowed to two properly qualified persons to preach as itinerants in the English Plantations in the West Indies; and that the remainder of the income should be paid to the College of Cambridge in New England, towards the support of persons engaged in the conversion of the Indians. In the year 1740, by the death of the person who had a life interest in that estate, it fell to the Society, and in 1746 the writings relating to it were delivered to the treasurer for the time being.

Dr. Williams was also fully aware of the state of barbarism and superstition which prevailed among the lower classes in Ireland, where he had his earliest settlement, and formed that matrimonial connexion to which he was chiefly indebted for his means of benevolence. With a view to promote their reformation, he charged his estates with a grant of fifty pounds per annum, to be paid in Dublin to a preacher of the gospel, being a Protestant, and skilful in the Irish tongue, who should be willing as an itinerant, diligently to preach in Irish, wherever he might find an opportunity, so long as he should be approved of by four gentlemen whom he nominated in Ireland, and their assigns from time to time, as well as by his trustees.

But Dr. Williams's bequests for the instruction and improvement of the poor were made on the most extensive scale, on behalf of that class in his native country, and at Chelmsford, in Essex. His trustees were directed to choose and appoint some pious grave persons, with salaries of eight pounds per annum, for the purpose of teaching twenty poor children to read English, and of instructing them in the principles of the Christian religion, in several towns which he named, so long as they should conduct themselves in a manner to meet with their approbation. Among other towns he had selected Flint, Beaumaris, and Conway. When, however, the trustees made proposals to the clergy and principal inhabitants of those towns for the settlement of such schools in them, they were rejected, on the supposition that the children were to be taught the Assembly's Catechism, and to be under the tuition of Dissenters from the Church of England. The trustees resolved, therefore, to establish schools at Newmarket in Flintshire, and Pullhely in Caernarvonshire, in their stead; and their resolution was confirmed by the Court of Chancery. In consequence of considerable improvements in the trust estates, the salaries of the respective masters have of late years been raised to sixteen pounds per annum; and the benefits of this branch of the testator's charitable benefactions extend, *communibus annis*, to more than two hundred children.

The advantage of the rising generation was also consulted in another part of Dr. Williams's will, which directs the appropriation of the surplus of the income of his estates, after the other purposes and uses of his will have been fulfilled. Among the schemes for settling the testator's benefactions approved of by the Court, the following relates to such surplus:—Whenever it shall be found to amount to five hundred pounds, it shall be divided according to the proportion which he prescribes: one eighth for the purchase of bibles, catechisms, &c, to be distributed by his trustees; one tenth among the widows of ministers, and one fifth among ministers respectively nominated by them; one eighth for the purpose of apprenticing poor boys; one eighth among the students of three years standing in seminaries of education for the ministry, for aid during two years additional study either in Scotland, or in England, at the discretion of the trustees; one hundred and eight pounds six shillings and eight pence among approved ministers in North Wales; and fifty-four pounds three shillings and four-pence among approved ministers in South Wales. The amount of the nomination to ministers and ministers' widows is always to be determined by the number of trustees present on the day of the distribution.

Dr. Williams's last bequest of any magnitude, was that of his books, including the purchased collection of Dr. Bates, which he appointed for a public library, accessible to such persons as should be approved of by his trustees, "for the perusal of any books in the place where they are lodged." For the reception of this library, he directed his trustees to "purchase or build a fit edifice, not pompous, or too large," and to pay ten pounds per annum to a library keeper, " giving security for his fidelity and attendance at such times as they appoint." In a parenthesis he intimated that a young preacher seemed to him the fittest for such a situation; but by not binding them with respect to the object of their choice, submitted it to their discretion. When the trustees found themselves in circumstances which permitted them to carry the founder's design for a public library into execution, they appointed a deputation to examine several buildings and situations which were recommended as well adapted to their purpose; but none of them met with their approbation. At length, in September 1727, they purchased the piece of ground in Red-Cross Street on which the present building stands; for the sum of four hundred and fifty pounds, and appointed a committee to consult with proper persons respecting the erection of such a house, and to procure an estimate of the requisite expense. The estimate delivered in to them amounted to fifteen hundred and eighteen pounds, which they were empowered by the Court of Chancery to apply to the purpose out of the founder's estates. However, owing to mismanagement somewhere or other, the whole money was expended before the building was finished, and the trustees were compelled to desist from its completion. Thus circumstanced, they consulted about the propriety of making application to the Court of Chancery, for leave to appropriate an additional sum from the Doctor's estates; but were dissuaded by their legal advisers from adopting such a measure. They afterwards agreed, at a general meeting on the 25th of March 1729, to circulate the following notice among their members, with the view, doubtless, of its being communicated to their friends.

" Dr. Williams's Library, being near finished, some additions of general advantage to the common interest it is apprehended may be made upon the foundation of that building, consistent with the Doctor's design of additions and of general use, which will require a considerable expense, and yet cannot be defrayed out of his estate according to the allowance made by the Court of Chancery for erecting the library. It is therefore proposed, that any who are inclined to forward that service, would contribute what they see proper for such a service."

This appeal to liberal-minded men fully answered their expectations. One gentleman defrayed the expense of wainscoting and furnishing the room on the left hand next the outer door, now the librarian's parlour; another paid for the iron gates and iron palisades before the windows; a third expended upwards of forty pounds, contributed by himself and friends, in finishing two stalls in the library; a charitable society (most probably the managers of the presbyterian fund) paid upwards of sixty pounds for fitting up and furnishing what is now called the committee room; and various gentlemen contributed sums of money towards finishing the library and useful additions to the building. The names of Thos. Hollis, Esq.; Joseph Andrews, Esq.; the Rev. Dr. Samuel Wright; Samuel Lessingham, Esq.; the Rev. Mr. Neal; the Rev. Mr. G. Smith; the Rev. Mr. J. Newman; and the Rev. Jos. Bayes, are conspicuous in the list of benefactors on this occasion. By such honourable exertions was this building completed to the state in which it continued till about the year 1760, when two of the trustees, Mr. South and Mr. Bowden, worthily emulated the liberal deeds of their predecessors, by presenting the mahogany glazed book-cases in the large front room, as well as the mahogany glazed doors to that room and the library. Within our own times, the improved revenues of the founder's estates have enabled the trustees to render the whole establishment greatly more respectable and commodious. The trustees held their first meeting at the library on the 8th of December, 1729; and on the 20th of April 1730 the first librarian was chosen, (with inul salary of ten pounds per annum, to which the trustees added fifteen pounds) and the institution opened to the public under the regulations which the trustees thought it proper to prescribe. Since that day great accessions have been made to it, by bequests of whole libraries, donations of money for the purchase of books, and the respectable presents of numerous individuals. Our limits will not permit us to insert here the names of all the benefactors; but we may be allowed to mention that of the Rev. Mr. Davies, who presented to the library many scarce and useful volumes; that of the Rev. Thomas Rowe, which stands at the head of a long list of valuable books; that of the Rev. Dr. Harris, who bequeathed 1959 volumes; that of the Rev. Mr. Archer, who bequeathed 473 volumes; that of the Rev. Mr. Sheldon, who bequeathed 214 volumes; that of Mr. Wastfield, who bequeathed a valuable collection of books; that of Thomas Hollis, Esq. which often occurs in the book of benefactions, under the title of an unknown hand; and those of Dr. Horsman, the Rev. Mr. Calamy, the Rev. Dr. Evans, the Rev. Dr. Lardner, Mr. Neal, the Rev. Mr. Walburgh, the Rev. Mr. Lowman, the Rev. Dr. Benson, William Mount, Esq., the Rev. Mr. Lindsay, and Thomas Brand Hollis, Esq. We could with pleasure enrich our list by the insertion of names of many living benefactors, who will be honoured by posterity, were we not checked by the recollection of the beautiful and classical apology which Dr. Jortin makes for not panegyrizing his patron Archbishop Herring, then alive, "that it was a custom amongst the ancients *not to sacrifice to heroes till after sun-set.*" In the records of our gratitude those names are faithfully preserved; and far, very far distant be the period, when the trust shall have to offer the tribute of praise to their memory!

MISCELLANEOUS COMMUNICATIONS.

SIR,   *June* 22, 1816.

I HAVE been, I dare say, by no means singular in entertaining some curiosity respecting the religious opinions of the author of *Sandford and Merton,* whose talents, so wisely and benevolently employed, during his comparatively short term of life, would have done credit to any *mode of faith* which he might have adopted. This curiosity was lately revived, by a circumstance which occurred in a course of very miscellaneous reading. I made what inquiries were in my power, and now offer you the result.

There are two biographies of Mr. Day. One, his friend Mr. Keir's *Account,* published in 1791, the other, by Dr. Kippis, in the *Biographia Britannica,* Vol. V. 1793, p. 21. From both it appears that he "entered as a gentleman-commoner at *Corpus Christi College,* Oxford, at the age of sixteen." He must then have subscribed the thirty-nine articles, probably considering such a subscription as a mere form. He took no *degrees* at Oxford, and is described by Mr. Keir as proposing for "the main object of his academical pursuits, the discovery of moral truths, which he investigated with the severity of logical induction and the depth of metaphysical research." (P. 6.)

The early, warm, and apparently unqualified admiration of J. J. Rousseau which Mr. Day indulged in the dedication of *the Dying Negro,* in 1773, may, I suspect, sometimes have given occasion to a doubt whether he were a Christian. It is to be regretted that the only hint on this subject which Dr. Kippis affords, is where he refers, with high approbation, to the first volume of *Sandford and Merton,* for "some observations concerning the excellency of the Christian religion as adapted to the instruction and comfort of the poor, in a conversation between Mr. Merton, sen. and the tutor." This can hardly be considered as decisive, for Rousseau himself, who panegyrised Jesus Christ, in his letter to the Archbishop of Paris, would not have scrupled such a compliment to Christianity. Mr. Keir has, I think, settled the question, for had Mr. Day been an unbeliever in the Christian revelation, he could not have imitated too many unbelievers, who scrupled no Christian pretensions to serve their interest; but would have proved himself *an honest Deist.* Yet Mr. Keir describing "with what veneration the people in Mr. Day's neighbourhood beheld him," adds, "he conversed much with them in a familiar style adapted to their capacities, and confirmed them in their respective duties. Being at a considerable distance from the parish church where he resided in Surry, and finding that many of his neighbours were thereby prevented from attending the service on Sundays, he used to invite them to his house, where he read prayers to them and to his own family, and strongly recommended to their practice the excellent morality of the gospel." (P. 134.)

While Mr. Day thus formed a *church in his own house*, in which he led the devotions and filled the office of a Christian instructor, the question naturally arises whether he could satisfy himself with the liturgy as it is still established on the credit of the theological wisdom of the sixteenth century. I think he could not, and I ground my opinion on the sentiments which occur in his political pamphlet published in 1784, and entitled, *The Letters of Marius.* The three first letters are addressed to his friend Dr. Jebb, in which the following passages are introduced for the purpose of illustrating some political opinions. At page 3, he speaks of " a saving faith, according to the true orthodox form of *Credo quia impossibile.*" At page 13, is the following passage :

" I have often thought it a wonderful fallacy of some divines to depreciate human reason in order to exalt religion : for unless that religion be imparted by particular inspiration to every individual, what other method is there of establishing it, than proofs adapted to his reason ? The more therefore you convince him of the weakness and fallibility of that faculty, the more you must incline him, were he consistent, to doubt his power of judging concerning the particular evidence you propose." He adds, p. 15: " Here is the general fallacy both of divines and politicians : both begin by teaching you to distrust yourself, and address themselves, if I may use the expression, to the hypocondriacism of human nature. When their representations have succeeded to a certain degree, they give you to understand that the only cure for all your evils is to adopt their own particular system of faith or government."

The following passage, p. 19, contains language worthy of an enlightened Christian. I need not say how congenial to the views of that excellent man to whom these letters were addressed.

" The first apostles of Christianity were mild and lowly, like the founder of their faith. They addressed themselves to the reason of men and propagated their religion by persuasion. They abjured the luxuries and the

enjoyments of sense ; they submitted to every insult ; they refused the offered benefits of their friends, and deprecated only by prayers and blessings the malice of their enemies. But mark the change! The instant a royal convert has given the clergy entrance to a court, they abjure every principle of their religion. Then we lose sight of a suffering, and begin the era of a triumphant church. The immediate successors of fishermen and mechanics consent to be clothed in purple and scarlet, to wallow in all the sensualities of the most abandoned age and country, and to disgrace the simplicity of the most spiritual religion, by the rites and ceremonies of the grossest. The power of consulting about the interpretation of the articles of their religion, which was expressly given to the whole body of Christians, is, in a short time, monopolized by the clergy; and the power of choosing their pastors and bishops, a right equally deducible from equity, history, reason, and the scriptures, taken from the laity, and shared between the hierarchy and the civil power. And this system of practice and belief, so grossly adulterated, so totally unlike the original, is called Christianity, and enforced by racks, and flames and gibbets; the ancient supporters of civil, and now the welcome auxiliaries of ecclesiastical power. What may we suppose would have been the state of Christianity, at the present hour, had not the daring and original genius of Luther reduced it something nearer to its original principles in the sixteenth century ? What may we suppose will be its state in the twentieth, should no new Luther arise to teach our clergy the distance between the house of the Lord and the courts of princes, the difference between the service of God and mammon ?"

Mr. Day presently supposes an objector to exclaim, " you are writing upon government and political liberty, why then deviate to the abuses and corruptions of Christianity ?" He answers, " because the history of Christianity, a perfect and recorded succession of facts, which every man may consider at his leisure, is the best illustration in the universe of the subject on which I am writing. Because, if neither the immediate doctrines of heaven itself, nor its positive com-

mands, have been able to preserve
even a Christian clergy from every
corruption which can grow upon the
selfish passions, what are we to expect
will be the fate of institutions merely
human, if once abandoned to the
avarice, ambition, and insolence of
those who have an equal interest to
pervert them.".

It thus appears that Mr. Day was
not only a political but also a Christian
reformer, though, probably, he had
never extended his enquiries into the
corruptions of Christianity, like his
friend Dr. Jebb, whom he survived
only a very few years. His death was
premature, as we inaccurately speak
while we forget that

" Before our birth, our funeral was
decreed."

According to Mr. Keir's *Account*,
(p. 97,) "On the 28th day of December 1789, as Mr. Day was riding
from his house in Surry, to his
mother's seat at Barehill, [Berks,] an
end was put to his valuable life at the
age of forty-one years. His horse
having taken fright, threw him to a
considerable distance. By this fall
his brain suffered such a concussion
that he never afterwards spoke."

What Mr. Day has justly attributed
to Dr. Jebb, may be recorded as his
own praise, "a consistency of life and
manners, the delicate colouring of
private honesty and integrity, to fill
up the flowing outline of public profession, and to make it worthy of a
people's admiration." We scarcely
know how to turn from the contemplation of such characters; one
sacrificing to the claims of conscience
the fair prospects of early years, and
devoting himself, for an honourable
subsistence, to an arduous profession
which would also afford him the
means of extensive benevolence: the
other, with an ample fortune, sparing
of personal gratifications, that he might
abound in benefits to others—both
blessed with consorts who cherished
their memories, as they had encouraged
and assisted their exertions, and possessed and deserved their tenderest
affections. If the world is to improve,
the time must surely arrive when, as
to such men—*the people will tell of
their wisdom, and the congregation will
shew forth their praise.*

IGNOTUS.

" On horror's head, horrors accumulate—
" For thou canst nothing to DAMNATION
   add
" Greater than this."   SHAKSPEARE.

SIR,

THE doctrine of *eternal torments* has
more appearance of grandeur than
any other article of the orthodox creed.
Sometimes it is displayed in all the
horrible minuteness and variety in
which it is possible to contemplate
pain ; at others more artfully veiled to
heighten its effect, and expressed by
distant hints and broken images which
make even a sceptic shudder. It enables those who believe it " to shake
this world with the thunders of the
next." It rouses the most ignorant to
energy if not to eloquence. It "makes
mad the guilty, and appals the free."
But admitting that it is attended with
all these advantages, I think it may
be argued that there is nothing in
it essentially poetical—nothing which
has a tendency to purify or refine—
nothing which can elevate the mind
above itself, and add to the stock of
its sublime conceptions.

There is, I apprehend, no poetry in
the mere excitement of terror, or in
the display of mental or bodily suffering. Pain and horror, considered in
the abstract, can be objects only of
pity and disgust ; and the more they
are realized to the mind, the more
they tear or oppress it. It is a mistake to suppose that because they have
been associated with magnificent and
pleasing images, they have any thing
in themselves on which our contemplations can repose. No doubt sorrow
has been made the source of some of
the most delicious sensations which
we are capable of enjoying. But then
it has been by associations not its own
—by the tender and solemn images
with which it has been encircled, and
the sympathy we delight to indulge.
Thus meditations on the instability of
all earthly things derive their touching
interest from our perceptions of a
resting place that can never perish.
We feel that our consciousness of
mortality proves us to be immortal.
There is a melancholy " ill bartered
for the garishness of joy ;" but we do
not love it because it is painful. The
memory of buried friendship—the

prospect of beauty cut down like a flower—the recollection of past afflictions and joys, all come mellowed over the heart by a thousand tender remembrances which take all that is earthly from sorrow. So even death itself is softened in the anticipation, not only by the holy hopes which look beyond it, but the images with which fancy encircles its victims. We think of it as of a placid slumber—as a shadow thrown from a passing cloud—as a humbler of human pride that levels artificial distinctions, and gathers all the children of men to rest together. The garlands of affection are hung gracefully on the tomb where the weary reclines from his labours; beauty looks most lovely in the tears it sheds there; and all the malevolent passions and uncharitable thoughts of the bitterest foe are melted into tenderness beside it. Images of funereal pomp have charms for the imagination, as well as solace for the heart. This appears the true secret of that mysterious pleasure which we sometimes feel at the exhibition of fictitious guilt or distress. They are the mere materials on which the poet works—the back ground of the pictures that delight us. We are not gratified because we see our fellow creatures in suffering, but because from their suffering they rise triumphant—because in grief the mighty energies of the soul are called forth in the fulness of their strength, or the sweet instances of affection receive a holier tinge. It is not the province of a poet merely to draw tears or make us shudder: rather it is his triumph to render grief soothing—to shed a tender enchantment over the scenes of woe—to break the force of affliction by the gentleness of his own imagination, through which he enables us to survey it. If this be not the case, why is the " Gamester" inferior to "Lear," or " George Barnwell" to " Macbeth" or " Othello ?" Why are not the works of Mrs. Opie preferable to those of Richardson? If mere horror be required, how inferior is the tale of Duncan's murder to many examples of atrocity with which the Newgate calendar will supply us! The truth is that if a man of real genius choose materials of mere human interest, he will so adorn them with mild and joyous associations, and so interweave them with the sweetest

emotions of the heart, that the darker shades which remain will seem rather to blend in harmony than to operate as a contrast.

The doctrine of eternal torments is a theme for eloquence, for energy, for passion. But imagination is formed of no elements of human passion; it enters not into the intensity of suffering; it is too celestial in its movements to beat with the pulse of agony. It " broods over the vast abyss and makes it pregnant." It throws its own lovely radiance over all the objects which it contemplates. It softens down all the asperities of things, lightens the sad realities of actual existence, and makes us view a broken and discordant world silent and harmonious as a picture. The popular ideas, therefore, of eternal misery are no themes on which a poet can dwell.*

Some perhaps may think that these observations may be answered by the word Milton. But a little reflection will convince them that the works of that great poet furnish the best example of the position I have ventured to develope. He has indeed the words "Satan" and "Hell," but O, how unlike are his descriptions of them from the ideas which the orthodox receive! It was impossible for a genius like his to paint the hell of a bigot. Setting out with a vague description of its misery, as if he meant to suit it to the taste of the Assembly

---

* The most popular writer in verse of the present day has, however, thought fit occasionally to hint at eternal torments, merely to add energy to his verse or to point his curses. As it is evident from various parts of his writings that he utterly disbelieves in the doctrine, he must do it from a mere taste for the shocking. Destitute of any spirit of joy, he is incapable of entering into the true sources of delight, and can, at best, only strew a few flowers over objects of repulsiveness and horror. In one of his late poems—if so it can be termed—he has wished that the grave of a human being may be sleepless. He descends into the regions of darkness, not to break in with the glories of imagination,—not to leave there the imperishable monuments of talent—but to light the torch of personal animosity at the flames of the furies! The use he makes of the doctrine of undying woe is a fit example of what its abstract poetical merits are, when it is not moulded and softened by the magic influences of genius.

Treatment of the Insane, 1561.

of reverend divines, he ends with making it almost a paradise. We lose the idea of horror in that of grandeur. We pass over the burning marl without pain when Pandemonium rises in its beauty. In the very catalogue of the satanic armies we are carried to all the solemn temples and glorious images of the ancient world. And for the "leader of these armies bright," who ever felt any thing but admiration and sympathy? To make a stand against omnipotence makes him more than conqueror. If the doctrines of Calvinism were ever so true, Paradise Lost would remain as pure a fiction as ever was written. Those worlds of heaven and hell, that magnificent chaos through which the hero makes so sublime a progress in a hundred lines,— those angels whether successful or defeated—the gorgeous palaces of hell, and that everlasting throne, which have so real a presence in the poem—have no existence in any creed which has ever been invented. They are the mighty creation of the poet's own genius, assoiled from all encumbrance of systems, untrammelled even by any distinctions of matter and spirit, and orthodox in nothing but in name.

At all events the doctrine of endless misery, if it has any thing sublime about it, must be disbelieved in order to be enjoyed. Indeed how is it possible to enter into any of the enjoyments of life with an idea of such a reality present with us. While we think that the people among whom we live and move, those with whom we are holding daily intercourse by the perpetual courtesies of life, those perhaps whom we love with an affection that death cannot extinguish—will be tormented in unspeakable agonies for ever, we can scarcely derive gratification from the sublimity of our own conceptions. A man might rather exult in having witnessed the mortal agonies of a friend, to shew in what dreadful colouring he could paint them.

In this world, thank God, there are no beings of this description. That any one can talk of the sublimity of his contemplation on eternal torture, shews that he does not in heart believe it. The man who, in the mansions of blessedness, could derive satisfaction from the miseries of his brethren, must be truly unfit for heaven. Even the emperor who fiddled on a tower

while Rome was in flames, would become humane in comparison with one who could thus smile over the wreck of a world.

Next month I will reverse the picture.

S. N. D.

Sir, *June 23*, 1816.

THE following historical extract may serve to compare, or rather to contrast the wise and humane treatment of the insane which is now peculiarly encouraged, with the ignorance and barbarity formerly displayed towards that afflicted portion of our race. It may well be expected to moderate the admiration of *the golden days of good Queen Bess* and to excite the admonition, *Say not that the former days were better than these.* Bedlam, which had been for many years a receptacle for lunatics, was then on the spot which is now called *Old Bethlem.* The Marshalsea, in Southwark, appears always to have been a prison.

"1561.—The 10th of April was one William Geffrie whipped from the Marshalsea in Southwark, to Bedlem without Bishopsgate of London, for that he professed one John Moore to be Christ our Saviour. On his head was set a paper, wherein was written as followeth: *William Geffrie, a most blasphemous heretic, denying Christ our Saviour in heaven.* The said Geffrie being stayed at Bedlem gate, John Moore was brought forth, before whom William Geffrie was whipped, till he confessed Christ to be in heaven. Then the said John Moore being examined, and answering overthwartly, was commanded to put off his coat, doublet, and shirt, which he seemed to do very willingly, and after being tied to the cart, was whipped an arrow's shot from Bedlem, where at the last he also confessed Christ to be in heaven and himself to be a sinful man. Then was John Moore sent again into Bedlem, and Geffrie to the Marshalsea, where they had lain prisoners nigh a year and a half, the one for professing himself to be Christ, the other a disciple of the same Christ." Hollingshed, 111. 1194.

Such were the moral discernment and the Christian spirit of an age which had undertaken the extraordinary task of forming articles and imposing creeds to save posterity, Christians and Protestants, the trouble of examining the Scriptures and choosing a religion for themselves.

BREVIS.

Family Sermons.

SIR,

IT has long been a subject of regret with me that I cannot find any book of sermons which appears to me to be adapted to the use of families. The works which I have made use of I have found deficient in some quality or other which I think essential, in compositions intended for that purpose. In some, the language is too lofty, and the style too much ornamented; others are logical and argumentative, abounding in nice distinctions; and others contain mere moral essays, devoid of those all-important motives which are only to be derived from the gospel.

The work I am desirous of possessing is one plain and simple in the style, persuasive rather than argumentative, abounding in scriptural motives and illustrations, and dwelling frequently upon those glorious promises, and those awful threatenings, which appear in almost every page of the gospel, and elevate Christianity far above every other system.

Such a publication is, I think, a *desideratum* in all Unitarian families. It would be extremely useful among persons of the middle ranks of life, whose education has been confined, and whose daily employments preclude them from much reading. It would also be much more beneficial to servants, and the younger branches of families, than the books which are generally made use of. And there is another description of persons, for whose use such a publication is, I think, particularly required. I mean those who have departed from the prevailing creeds of the day, and embraced Unitarianism. Such persons must be, I suppose, wholly at a loss for books to substitute in the place of those numerous publications, which are circulated with zeal by Christians of other denominations. This may not be the case with persons of liberal education and cultivated minds, for whom there is an ample supply in the many elegant and perspicuous works which have been written by Unitarians; but for the poor (I mean the unlearned) to whom, at least *equally*.

with others, the gospel should be preached, the food is scanty indeed. I might enlarge upon the advantages to be expected from a publication of sermons such as I have described; but, not to occupy any more space in your valuable Work, I will conclude with a hope that if any of your correspondents can point out such a work, he will do so; and if that cannot be done, that some one will endeavour to supply the deficiency; and besides the satisfaction of being extensively useful, I have little doubt that he would reap an ample pecuniary reward for his labour.

I am, &c.
J. H.

P. S. Is not this subject worthy the attention of the Unitarian Tract Society; and would not the offer of a small reward soon furnish ample materials from which such a publication might speedily be made?

Mr. Rutt's Edition of Dr. Priestley's Works.

SIR,

AMIDST the general satisfaction which was manifested by the company at the last Anniversary of the Unitarian Fund, there was one circumstance referred to, at which I felt considerable regret, viz. the fear expressed by Mr. Rutt, that he should be under the necessity (for want of encouragement) of relinquishing his project for publishing by subscription the Theological Works of the late Dr. Priestley.

Anxious to promote (though in a feeble manner) so desirable a purpose, I have taken the trouble to transcribe two extracts from the very interesting "Memoirs of the late Rev. Theophilus Lindsey, M. A." by Mr. Belsham, which appear to me particularly suitable and deserving of notice at the present moment, and which, with the few remarks that follow, I shall be obliged by your inserting.

The first is taken from the fourth chapter of that work, in which the author giving an account of the earliest hearers of Mr. Lindsey at the chapel in Essex-street, mentions "Mrs. Rayner, a near relation of the Dutchess of Northumberland and of Lord Gwydir, a liberal patroness of the cause of truth," of which the following (p. 120) is but "one instance out of many." That "to this lady the Christian world is indebted for the publication of one of the most learned and most useful theological works which the age has produced—Dr. Priestley's History of Early Opinions concerning Christ: a work which demonstrates in a manner which never has been, and never can be confuted, that from the earliest age of the Christian religion down to the fourth century, and to the time of Athanasius himself, the great body of unlearned Christians were strictly Unitarians, and consequently that this was the original doctrine concerning the person of Christ. This most valuable treatise was a work of great labour and expense, the demand for which could by no means have defrayed the charge of the publication. But Mrs. Rayner, with exemplary generosity, supplied the money, and to her the work is with great propriety dedicated."

The other extract is from a note in page 447, in which the writer of the Memoirs, " apprehensive lest the Christian world might be deprived of the benefit of his (Dr. Priestley's) most valuable labours for want of a sufficient fund to enable him to publish the work, it occurred to him that if a hundred persons could be found to subscribe five pounds each for a copy of the whole of both the works, and to pay their subscriptions in advance, every difficulty would be surmounted." The proposal was " adopted with great ardour and zeal by Dr. Priestley's numerous friends, *so that the sum wanted was very soon far exceeded.* The list of subscribers was numerous and respectable. The Duke of Grafton subscribed fifty pounds, Lord Clarendon twenty, and Robert Slaney, Esq. of Tong Lodge, thirty guineas, *with a promise of more, if more should be wanted.*" And the late Rt. Rev. Dr. John Law, Bishop of Elphin, inclosed a draft for one hundred pounds in a letter to Mr. Lindsey, to be applied in aid of Dr. Priestley's publication, in any way he chose.

I trust, Sir, that those friends to the memory of Dr. Priestley, who are in affluent circumstances, and who appreciate his valuable labours, will not fail to imitate as far as is necessary, such bright examples of liberality; and afford that support to Mr. Rutt, who is so well qualified for the work, which will ensure the success of his design.

Not, however, to throw an undue portion of the burden upon the wealthy friends to the cause, I beg

further to state, that there are at present about one hundred subscribers to the proposed work, and I understand that with two hundred Mr. R. would venture to proceed. Now, Sir, if each of the present subscribers would use their influence with their friends to obtain one or more new subscribers, that number would soon be completed. I have the pleasure to announce two new subscribers—and trust that at a time when the principles so ably defended by Dr. Priestley are widely extending, all alarm for the failure of so desirable a purpose will be entirely dissipated. That increasing success may attend your valuable Repository, is the sincere wish of

J. CORDELL.

Mechanism; an Allegory.
Section I.

A GENIUS of a superior order having constructed a great number of very curious machines, but of a somewhat complicated structure, put them under the management of a corresponding number of individuals, with the view of gradually training them to the employment of working these instruments, after the most advantageous and beneficial manner.[*] He accustomed them from their childhood to some of their more simple and necessary movements, and admonished them of the sad consequences of neglecting his instructions, to pursue the impulse of their own fancies and humours. But youthful inexperience and vivacity soon precipitating them into considerable errors, he took occasion from a palpable breach of an express injunction[†] to acquaint them that they must be kept to their business by a severe course of discipline, and that, anticipating their mismanagement, he had made the machines of a fragile structure so that they would last but for a time; the length of which, and the benefits of which they would be productive, would depend very much upon the use which they made of them.[‡] He however gave them some kind intimations of their future success, and of the blessings which might ultimately result from it.[§]

---

[*] Gen. i. 27, 28.   Psalm viii. 5—9.
[†] Gen. iii. 6.   [‡] Ib. 17—19, and iii. 7.
[§] Ib. iii. 15.

A long course of experience and discipline, accordingly ensued, in which the genius occasionally interposed, to maintain his authority, to remove hurtful errors, to impart the necessary instructions, and to cultivate among the operators in general an increasing skill in their employment, a comprehensive acquaintance with its true nature and design, and a growing estimation of its beneficial effects; and consequently a just principle of obedience and gratitude to himself, as their beneficiary and instructor.

At length when they had made considerable attainments, but had nevertheless from neglecting his instructions, and following the devices of their own imaginations, fallen into some capital errors, more especially with regard to the higher movements of the machines, it pleased the genius to select one of the greatest proficients and the most docile to his instructions, as his leading instrument, in removing those errors, and more fully unfolding his designs. Through this person he imparted many instructions remarkable for their perspicuity and comprehensive utility; and such was the extraordinary manner in which the powers of the genius were exerted on this occasion, that many of the particular evils resulting from the fragile structure of the machines, and the mismanagement of the operators, suddenly disappeared, like the pestilential vapour before the breath of heaven: machines which had been injured, were repaired with astonishing rapidity, and some which had been thrown aside as useless, and were actually dropping to pieces, quickly resumed their wonted functions. All these words and deeds of beneficence but served to usher in the grateful intelligence, that the genius at an appointed time would re-fabricate after an improved plan the whole system of the machines; and that then those operators who duly kept in view his designs in constructing them, carefully adhering to the spirit of his instructions, and working them after that admirable pattern which this distinguished operator had exhibited in his own practice, would reap inestimable advantages from the use of machines of such superior excellence and durability; but that those who scornfully or heedlessly rejected this gracious

intelligence, and preferred the gratification of their own humours to the wise instructions of the genius, would quickly experience the consequences of their obstinacy and ingratitude, in their incapacity to operate upon instruments of such powerful efficacy, to which however they must be trained by a much severer course of discipline than any which they had hitherto experienced. He indeed gave strong intimations that the designs of the genius being purely beneficent, would be pursued till all the operators became duly trained to their employment, and were well skilled in the art of working their machines to the greatest advantage, when they would all conspire in the production of benefits of immense magnitude.

To confirm more fully his assertions, by an actual specimen, and as the commencement of what he announced, which in his case was to be effected immediately, on account of his superior attainments, he voluntarily submitted to have his own machine wholly taken, or rather beaten to pieces, by the mad fury of some neighbouring operators; after which within the space of three days, it was reconstructed by the genius upon that highly improved plan which he had described. From this time it has been constantly held forth as the pledge and pattern of that universal effort of the genius, in re-fabricating the system of the machines, the annunciation of which constituted the great object of this extraordinary errand.

A long interval again passed, in which great numbers of operators were successively trained up in the anticipation of this event, and in that improved method of operation, which accorded with the instructions and pattern which had been given. The influence of the genius was still conspicuous, in the first instance, in promoting the exertions which were now made for the circulation of the intelligence, and in aiding the first efforts of the operators upon the new plan. But when the intelligence, with every requisite instruction, had been widely spread, and preserved in authentic writings, and many operators had been sufficiently introduced to the new method, this extraordinary influence, was withdrawn. The operators were now left to make the best use of their instructions and acquisitions, in advancing their own improvements, and in training up new operators upon the same plan.

But as time advanced, many began to shew symptoms of their former propensity, to consult fancy and to follow its wayward dictates, rather than their understandings, in adhering to the plain course which had been pointed out to them. Not content with the gracious intelligence which they had received, they were fond of mingling certain imaginary discoveries of their own with it; and even sometimes conceited themselves that these fancies, for their obscurity and, inconsistency plainly shew that they were no other than fancies, were the immediate suggestions of the genius himself. This was a kind of lazy amusement, which they found easier than a well directed application of their powers in substantiating and circulating the genuine intelligence, and applying its principles to practice, which was a work of considerable though salutary exertion. These vain imaginations soon began to affect the minds of the operators, like a mist and darkness, obscuring the light of heaven. Amid the gathering mist, the genius, and the distinguished operator whose machine he had re-constructed, and who was now pursuing his employment in the most gloriously beneficial manner, became absolutely confounded in the view of the gazing multitude. And even the invisible *influence* of the genius seemed occasionally to assume the appearance of a *third person* distinct from the genius himself. With these phenomena some were mightily pleased; and so much was this strange confused phenomenon preferred to a distinct view of the genius, and of this deserving object of his beneficence, each in his proper person, character and relations, that it soon came to be regarded as the height of presumption to attempt the latter; and nothing would do, but every body must use a contradictory, or *at least* an unintelligible assemblage of words, in describing the mystic representation in which they gloried. It was moreover reported from some ancient legends, that the machines possessed an inherent vital activity;* that it was only the

outward case, or visible frame work which would be broken and dissolved, and that though after this their movements would be *imperceptible*, yet that they would be more efficient than ever. Uniting with this notion the figurative idea of a *fiery trial†* contained in the instructions, they fancied they continually saw, in the mist in

sented more particularly to the rude uncultivated mind, particularly in dreams and reveries. What is the whole history of ghosts, but the detail of the workings of the "untutored" imagination, mistaking its fancies for realities? And what is the doctrine of the separate existence of the soul or percipient principle, after that the vital functions have ceased, and man is "*returned to his dust,*" but the same creature of the imagination, attempted to be realized by metaphysical refinements, but which in fact eludes the grasp of reason, and by refining vanishes into a nonentity, devoid of all those properties, which are essential to our very idea of existence? Can there be any two opinions more opposed to each other, than that of the Psalmist, that in the very day in which man ceases to breathe *his thoughts perish*, and that of Psychologists, that the soul "will never die!" Does not Christianity "bring life and immortality to light," by "*abolishing* death," not by representing that the soul remains untouched by the fatal stroke? By forgetting that the same fate "*befalleth the sons of men which befalleth beasts,*" that "*all are of the dust, and all turn to dust again,*" have, not dead men been represented "*as gods*" "usurping or sharing the throne of the Creator, or as demons" and "fiends incarnate" destined to a state of endless burnings? While the Scriptures constantly hold forth the doctrine that man is dust, and that Jehovah is "the only *living* and true God," who at his *appointed day* will raise all men up from the "dust of death" into which they are sunk to the "glorious light of" renewed "life;" how have mankind been troubled with mere phantoms of life and immortality and with "chimeras dire," while biblical truth in its simplicity has been in a great degree hidden from their eyes! Who can doubt the beneficent designs of that God who after wiping away sin by death, its "finishing" stroke, at length proclaims an universal abolition of this "king of terrors" and brings life and immortality to light; and yet further reveals to us that our great "adversary" sin, with his angels, death and his attendants, shall be cast into the lake of destruction?

* The doctrine of the immortality of the soul probably originated in those lively images of the defunct, which are pre-

† 1 Peter iv. 12. See also Matt. xxv. 41.

which they were enveloped, many of the former machines throwing out incessant vollies of liquid fire and brimstone on their respective operators. Many others they imagined as instantaneously and automatically, on their separation from their visible exterior, shedding the most beneficial influences, and that in such *superabundance*, that the overplus gradually accumulated into a large stock, under the care of certain managers, who made a lucrative trade, by placing it in portions duly estimated, to the credit of those debits had become formidable. It is somewhat extraordinary that such a superabundance of beneficial effects should be accumulated in circumstances where so little could be seen doing, when the operators instead of pursuing their employment, agreeably to their instructions, occupied so much of their time in gazing and wondering, while the remaining portions of it were applied to those servile occupations about the inferior movements of their machines, by which they might best gratify the pampered appetites of these *managers* and their friends and dependants, who in their turn, like drones in a hive were eagerly absorbing all the real produce on which they set any value, and occasionally entertaining the operators with *phantasmagoria*, which served only to bewilder their minds and palsy their hands from useful activity.

Thus the genius and his instructions were almost wholly lost sight of. His distinguishing powers were absurdly distributed among worn out and broken machines of his own construction. And the writing which contained his instructions was carelessly thrown aside and buried amid ridiculous tales about the *phantasmagoria*; or if occasionally brought forward by the managers, to whose sole care it was consigned, so murdered in the reading, so dressed up in unintelligible phraseology, or so broken into bits and scraps and intermingled with foreign matter, that it scarcely served any other purpose than that of promoting the delusions, and supporting the ascendancy of these pretenders.

[*To be concluded in the next No.*]

---

part, of having brought a groundless insinuation against Count Zinzendorf, but because my evidence, for an obvious reason, is not producible in a work designed for general readers. Yet I cannot suffer your respectable correspondent, who is scarcely *anonymous* to me, to remain longer without some reply.

I assure him that I have no desire to think unfavourably of Count Zinzendorf, my exceptions to whose character rest entirely on the highly improper tendency of passages quoted from his alleged Hymns and Sermons. If your correspondent will examine them, especially from p. 55—68 of *the Candid Narrative*, he must, I think, agree with me as to this tendency. Those passages, indeed, exhibit a shameless intrusion on the most sacred privacies of life and a violation of decency, in language and allusion, scarcely ever equalled, certainly never exceeded, under a *Christian* profession, and which the decorum of heathiens might serve to condemn. Even of the Spectators, Dr. Watts complained that they "now and then, though rarely, introduce a sentence that would raise a blush in the face of strict virtue." He also commended Tillotson for having proposed the omission of some "parts of the Bible," on the ground of decorum, "in the public lessons of the church." What would Watts or Tillotson have thought of the phraseology attributed to the Christian hymns and sermons of Count Zinzendorf?

Yet Cicero has shewn that a man need not be a Christian to express himself justly on this subject. Many of your readers will recollect the passage to which I refer, near the end of the first book *de Officiis*. He is guarding his son against the sophistry of the cynics and the stoics [whom he terms cynical.[*] Their *theory* Count Zinzendorf, if fairly quoted, seems to have adopted, how correct soever may have been his own practice. Dr. Jortin, who was no calumniator, describes the Count, judging

---

Sir,   *Bromley, July 7, 1816.*

THE letter of J. F. B. (p. 264,) has remained so long unnoticed, not from any consciousness, on my

---

[*] " Nec vero audiendi sunt cynici, aut si qui fuerunt stoici pene cynici, qui reprehendunt, et irrident, quod ea quæ turpia, re non sunt, verbis flagitiosa dicamus; illa, autem quæ turpia sint, nominibus appellemus suis.——Nos autem naturam sequamur, et ab omni quod abhorret, ab ipsa oculorum, auriumque comprobatione fugiamus." *M. T. Cic. de Officiis, &c.* 18mo. 1698. p. 52.

probably only from the impure tendency of his alleged writings, as " one of the vilest of men;" yet I am not unwilling, however inexplicable, to attribute to him that singular *hypocrisy,* a heart and life of purity, with an occasional phraseology, too gross, to be repeated in decent society.

Your correspondent, however, considers the author of *the Candid Narrative* as " by no means to be implicitly relied on." From the years elapsed since his publication in 1753, that author has probably long had a claim to the justice included in the trite maxim *de mortuis nil nisi verum.* As *true* I am disposed to receive whatever J. F. B. can allege against Mr. Rimius, *on his own knowledge,* but that I apprehend cannot go back far enough to settle the question. Certainly no author ever more deserved exposure if he misquoted Count Zinzendorf, yet no one ever laid himself more open to detection. Mr. Rimius has constantly referred to the number and page of the Count's published sermons and to the numbers and verses of the hymns for every passage introduced. Of these passages he has always given the professed German original and added an English translation, a task which he ought to have performed correctly from his knowledge of both languages.

Yet these quotations thus connected with minute references to " the writings of the Count himself," and therefore peculiarly exposed to detection, are left unimpeached, as to, *text* and *version,* both by the German historian *Crantz* and his English translator *La-Trobe,* while your correspondent, without detecting a single forgery or mis-translation, describes the " representations of a Rimius" as " malignant and deceptive," and his book, now rarely to be met with, as " long since consigned to merited oblivion." He adds, whether *on his own knowledge* or the representations of others does not appear, that Rimius's " translations are often inaccurate, by no means presenting the genuine meaning of the original, frequently eliciting meanings and hints which the text does not warrant, or at least does not require." Does your worthy correspondent consider such a charge as requiring no proof, only assertion, not even a single reference? I confess I differ from him, but will here leave

that difference to the judgment of our readers.

I have been greatly misunderstood by J. F. B. if he regarded me as charging the *indiscretions* of Count Zinzendorf on the Moravians of our time. They possess, I doubt not, the decorum and Christian consistency to avoid, though not yet the magnanimity publicly to explode them. To their conduct, as a community, I willingly add the testimony of an intimate acquaintance, who like your correspondent was educated and passed his early life among them, but who has long left their society. He has often assured me, to use his own words, that if they are charged as a sect with any practices, *contra bonos mores,* the charge is unfounded.

Dr. Gill and other writers, to whom J. F. B. refers, who have adopted an *amatory* style in religion, have very little if any connexion with this subject. Other Christians differ from them not because their phraseology, excusing some rare inadvertence, violates decorum, but because even the pure and becoming language of human passion appears ill adapted to subjects so serious as the faith and hope of the gospel. Thus when *Watts* in his juvenile " Meditation in a Grove," sings

" I'll carve our passion on the bark,
  And ev'ry wounded tree
Shall drop and bear some mystic mark
  That Jesus dy'd for me,"

he may be supposed, I think justly, to degrade his subject, by expressing in a style of pastoral fondness, his reliance on *the author and finisher of our faith,* yet he cannot be fairly charged with an offence against decorum. Nor would any thing besides the taste and judgment of Count Zinzendorf have been brought into question, had he been content to describe a Christian's connexion with his Saviour as in the following verse quoted from his 33d hymn, in *The Enthusiasm of Methodists and Papists Compared,* 1754, vol. 1, pt. 2, p. 5:

" Chicken blessed, and caressed,
  Little Bee, on *Jesu's* breast
From the hurry
And the flurry
  Of the earth thou'rt now at rest."

I would give your correspondent

every satisfaction in my power, but I am not aware that I ought to trouble him or any of your readers further on the disagreeable subject which has been very unexpectedly forced on my attention. I still think that it was my duty to guard the memories of such men as Watts and Doddridge from the imputation of an unqualified approbation of Count Zinzendorf. A nobleman exchanging the luxury of a court for the labours of a missionary, whatever be his creed or his ritual, presents an interesting character. Yet if the Count really made the representations attributed to his Hymns and Sermons, I know not how to discover in that character the sober-mindedness becoming a Christian, or a disposition to seek after "virtue and praise" in the manner recommended by an apostle. If, on the other hand, the Count has been wronged, as J. F. B. supposes, by forgeries and mis-translations, no man ever left behind him in the world friends and followers more strangely regardless of his just reputation.

I remain Sir, Your's,
J. T. RUTT.

P. S. I take this opportunity of requesting any of your readers who design to encourage the publication of Priestley's Theological Works by their subscriptions, to subscribe directly, as from present appearances the publication must be delayed much longer than I wished or intended, or the early promoters of the design had reason to expect.

Opinions of the Early Quakers.

SIR,

IN looking over the " Athenian Oracle," a work published above a century ago, I was struck with a curious passage relating to the Quakers, which may serve to shew what idea prevailed at that time respecting their religious sentiments, and will in part confirm the observations of several of your correspondents that their original opinions were pretty far removed from modern orthodoxy.—In answer to the question "may not a Quaker expect happiness after this life?" it is said "we are sure that many, or most of them, have held very dangerous and detestable opinions. They generally speak contemptibly of the Bible, and will by no means allow it to be *God's word*: they have turned it into an odd sort of a jejune allegory, even the highest and most sacred truths therein contained, and have spoken, not very honourably of our Saviour, and *almost generally deny the trinity, and many, if not all, embrace the other Socinian dream of the soul's sleeping till the resurrection.* Besides they use neither of the sacraments, and if our most authentic accounts don't impose upon us, were at their first appearance in England commonly actuated by a worse spirit than that they pretend to. These 'tis hard to hope well of, nor can we see how with any manner of propriety they can be called Christians. But if there be any of them who have left their first principles, and are *degenerated into Christianity* (we ask pardon for the harshness of the expression) and grown more religious, as well as more mannerly, there may be more hopes of them."

In the same work the following question is asked, and to my mind not satisfactorily answered : should any of your correspondents think proper to give an opinion on the subject, I shall feel highly gratified, conceiving it to be one well worthy of the serious attention of professing Christians, and a fit subject for discussion in the Monthly Repository. The question is as follows, " Our jurors that try in cases of life and death are obliged to be (or at least to tell the court that they are) all of one mind, before they can give or the court receive their verdict; and it being but reasonable to suppose that it may so happen that one or more of the twelve may dissent from the major part, as being of deeper judgment, &c. or by building upon false notions, which yet he believes, and cannot be persuaded otherwise, but that they are the truth, &c. In short we'll suppose him to act according to his conscience, whether otherwise he be in the right or no, and then query, how must such a man act, so as to keep a good conscience towards God and man, so as not to be guilty of the blood of the prisoner, as well as of perjury, if he bring him in guilty and he is not," &c. &c.

I shall feel obliged by your insertion of the above,

And remain, Sir,
Your constant Reader,
T. R. S.

P. S. It will greatly oblige several of your readers, if Mr. Rees will inform them through the medium of the Repository what progress he has made in his proposed " History of Foreign

Unitarians" (see M. Repos. Vol. VI. p. 105,) or whether he has abandoned it altogether; also, whether the Racovian Catechism, which he was sometime ago said to be preparing for the press, has been published or not, as I do not recollect seeing it advertised.[*]

Unitarian Baptists in the City of York.

. ` Sir,

WE beg leave through the medium of your valuable Miscellany to lay before our Unitarian brethren the case of the Unitarian Baptists in the city of York, confident of their disposition to assist us in the laudable undertaking of propagating primitive Christianity, and removing those misconceptions which originated in the dark ages of heathen and popish superstition. We have laboured upwards of thirty years, under considerable disadvantage, in this great cause for want of suitable accomodation and a central situation; we have at length met with the object of our wishes. A chapel in the centre of York now occupied by the Independents was ' to be disposed of by public auction; we made an offer for it, the consequence was it became ours for the sum of three hundred pounds, one hundred of which was paid on the 2nd February last as a deposit, which we borrowed upon interest, the remaining two hundred pounds are to be paid on the 2nd November next, at which time possession will be given. The chapel is well fitted up with pews and gallery, and will seat upwards of four hundred ' people. The sum we are able to raise amongst our own friends is sixty pounds; we hope our Unitarian brethren will not think the sum too small, considering our pecuniary circumstances, as we are all labouring people, so that with the sum of sixty pounds already subscribed, and twenty pounds which the Committee of the Unitarian Fund has been pleased to bestow upon us, making a total of eighty pounds, there will remain a debt of two hundred and twenty pounds upon the chapel, besides other necessary expences incident to the purchase of such property: this debt will be felt by us as a great incumbrance, but becomes as nothing when divided and shared by the Unitarian public. Donations however small will be thankfully received, and with your leave, Mr. Editor, the subscriptions may, from time to time be acknowledged in the Monthly Repository, a mode of acknowledgment which will save some trouble and expense both to the subscribers and receivers.

Subscriptions in aid of liquidating the debt of £220 upon the Unitarian Baptist Chapel in York, will be received by the Rev. C. Wellbeloved, York.

As you, Sir, have a knowledge of the most proper characters in various parts of the country, and if to the favours already conferred upon us, you will add this one of appointing receivers at such places as you may judge necessary, you will much oblige,

Sir,

Your obedient humble Servants, ·

JAMES TORRANCE, Minister.

RICHARD HANDS, } *Deacons.*
JOSEPH RICHARDSON, }

N. B. As to the rise and progress of this Society we beg leave to refer your readers to a work published in the year 1800, by Mr. David Eaton, and re-published by him in London, entitled, "Scripture the only Guide to Religious Truth, or a Narrative of the Proceedings of a Society of Baptists in York."

·
SIR, *June* 25, 1816.

AT the late meeting of the friends to the Unitarian Academy I understood with much satisfaction that the pro s on for communicating classical knowledge to the students was likely to be extended. I hope these students when they become ministers will attend to a duty now much neglected, and occupy that talent by which they may . be distinguished from the *unlearned.* The latter respectable and highly useful class of Christian teachers would well employ any leisure they could command, in comparing different English translations, and thus forming one which appeared to them to give the best connected sense of scripture. But as to · *learned* ministers, by their general practice of adopting King James's Bible, do they not contribute, in a high degree, from the pulpit and the press, to preserve and increase a superstitious regard for that version which is the

---

[*] For an answer to the latter question, our correspondent is referred to the notice in our last No. p. 369.

unavoidable effect of early associations?

"A. bad effect, but from a noble cause."

They also deprive their hearers or readers of opportunities, which would otherwise frequently occur, of distinguishing the true *sense* from the customary *sound* of a difficult passage, by attending to it in a new phraseology.

Yet when *learned* ministers determine to act up to their proper character, I hope they will not content themselves with the use of any version of the Scriptures, however improved, but their own. What lecturer on Cicero or Demosthenes, who claimed or received credit for having spent years in acquiring the languages of those orators, and ascertaining the force and beauty of their expressions, would be endured; or rather, what would be thought of his pretensions to learning or of his application, if he always quoted the translations of Duncan or of Leland?

Here I am reminded of learned ministers in earlier times, who neglecting, like the moderns, to use their learning on a proper occasion, were justly reproved by a profoundly learned layman. The story is thus told by Whitelock.

"Divers members of both houses, whereof I was one, were members of the assembly of divines, and had the same liberty with the divines to sit and debate, and give their votes in any matter which was in consideration amongst them. In which debate *Mr. Selden* spake admirably, and confuted divers of them in their own learning. And, sometimes, when they cited a text of Scripture, to prove their assertion, he would tell them, *perhaps in your little pocket Bibles, with gilt leaves*, (which they would often pull out and read,) *the translation may be thus; but the Greek or the Hebrew signifies thus or thus*; and so would totally silence them." Mem. (1732) p. 71.

Notwithstanding this passage, I am persuaded neither *Whitelock* nor *Selden* regarded the *Assembly of Divines* as illiterate or unworthy of respect. It was reserved for the bigotry of Lord Clarendon to disgrace his History by thus describing that *Assembly* (I. 530). "Some of them infamous in their lives and conversations, and most of them of very mean parts in learning,

if not of scandalous ignorance and of no other reputation than of malice to the church of England."*

The late Dr. Zouch, one of the prependaries of Durham, in a note to his edition of Walton's Lives, quoted the passage from Whitelock and appears to have given it *con amore*. In a later work, his "Life of Sir P. Sidney," he attempted to degrade as low as possible the literature of the Puritans, though they had long ceased to interfere with Durham's golden prebends. From his want of knowledge on this subject I suspect that Dr. Zouch was too much like the clergyman censured by Bishop Watson in the preface to his Theological Tracts, who "never read Dissenting Divinity."

LAICUS.

SIR, *Chichester, July 3, 1816.*

ALTHOUGH the greater part of your readers and correspondents, as well as yourself, are of quiet and pacific dispositions and habits, far re-

---

* On this passage Dr. Calamy well remarks in his "Life of Baxter," &c. (I. 82): "Who can give credit to him as an historian, that shall represent such men as Dr. Twiss, Mr. Gataker, Bishop Reynolds, Dr. Arrowsmith, Dr. Tuckney, Dr. Lightfoot, &c. as men of scandalous ignorance or mean parts? Or who runs down such men as Dr. Gouge, Mr. Oliver Bowles, Mr. Vines, Mr. Herle, Dr. Spurstow, Mr. Newcomen, Mr. Coleman, &c. as persons of no other reputation than of malice to the church of England?"

Calamy in his *Continuation* (I. 14) also thus refers to Whitelock's story, which, it seems, other writers had been fond of repeating. "It is easy to observe how the generality of our historians take pleasure in representing *Mr. Selden* as insulting the members of that assembly, when he sat among them, about their *little English Bibles with gilt leaves*, and attacking them with *Greek* and *Hebrew*; as to which there were many among them that were both able and ready enough to answer him. But, methinks, they should not, as, upon this occasion, they seem willing, forget that the same learned man, in his *History of Tithes* where he deals with the gentlemen of the hierarchy, freely reproaches them with *ignorance* and *laziness*, and upbraids them with *having nothing to keep up their credit but beard, title and habit*, intimating that their *studies reached no farther than the Breviary, the Postil, and the Polyanthea*."

moved from the follies and crimes of fashionable life, and calmly though strenuously employed in the investigation and diffusion of useful knowledge, neither they nor you are ignorant that when, either in fictitious history, or in real life, *Sir* X. Y. demands of *Lord* Z. an explanation, the inevitable result is a combat, and sometimes a mortal one. He who requires the explanation is desirous of nothing less than that it should be given, and he, from whom it is required, finds in the requisition itself the strongest possible reason for not complying with it.

Very different from any thing like this are the feelings and situation of the ingenious writer, whose letter in your last number [pp. 335, 336,] is subscribed with the signature J. and myself. He courteously asks an explanation, because he sincerely desires it; and if I decline doing as he desires, this arises from the apprehension that the giving and not the witholding the explanation may lead to a combat, in which I may receive a mortal wound; a mischance, this, ill compensated by any reputation I may thus obtain for rash and adventurous valour.

After all, I am so much gratified by the approbation expressed by your correspondent of the scrap of biography which you honoured with a place in your Obituary for May last, that I would willingly oblige him with the more detailed statement he wishes for, could I flatter myself that such an *explanation* would tend either to confirm in his mind correct notions, or to rectify erroneous ones in my own.

Referring to the supposed political opinions of the late lamented Dr. POWELL, I hazarded one or two positions of an import so general, and of a tendency (as I hoped) so conciliatory, as to afford no possible ground for debate or offence. The questions relative to a reform in the present constitution of the lower house of parliament, to the supposed superiority of a limited monarchy to a republic, or of both to an aristocratical form of government, &c. &c., are no more involved in these general positions than any particular and subordinate theorem must be included in the universal and superior one; and of theorems of this latter kind the application to individual cases is a matter far too

difficult to be profitably discussed by a politician so rude and uninstructed as myself.

I must therefore respectfully decline the polite invitation of J. to state in any explicit form my sentiments on " the beneficial influence of the people expressed through a constitutional representation," as well as on the manifest liability of " courts or *congresses*" to the pernicious infection which he specifies, and will only venture to mention the inseparable concomitants and not unfrequent result of a *popular election* of a representative in parliament, as one of the most remarkable examples of the triumph of wisdom and virtue over vice and folly.

About eight years ago I was indulged by the admission into your respectable Miscellany [M. Repos. III. p. 584,] of a paper in which (under a different signature) I endeavoured to shew that *political right* is founded in *power*, and that it has no other solid foundation. If your able correspondent J. would have the goodness *to take that paper in hand*, and point out the mistakes of the writer, he would confer a much greater favour than, he could possibly receive from the happiest efforts at *explanation* of his and your much obliged and

obedient Servant,
T. S.

SIR, *July* 6, 1816.

ACCORDING to Lord Castlereagh's reply to Sir S. Romilly, [M. Repos. p. 364] how little influence in favour of the Protestants of France has been acquired by our *royal* Protestant government from the gratitude of Louis XVIII.! Yet that prince was pushed up to the throne by British bayonets, and were he to lose their support must probably sink into his former insignificance

" By nature's law, as sure as plummets fall."

Allow me, in this connection, to draw from the oblivion of 160 years a tale of other times, and to shew what security was attained for the Protestants of France, by the *Protector of the Commonwealth of England,* from the policy or apprehensions of the French government, during the minority of Louis XIV.

I have now before me an Appendix of historical documents annexed to

Essays on the Balance of Power, &c. 8vo. 1701. The last piece consists of "Secret Articles agreed upon between Cromwell and Cardinal Mazarin," in addition to their "Public Treaty," which "bears date the 3d of November, 1655." The following are the concluding articles.

ART. VI.

"Qu'en toutes les villes et bourgs de ce royaume, ou il y aura des havres, et des ports, la nation Angloise y aura commerce, et y pourra faire bastir des temples pour l'exercice de la religion, et sera permis aux Francois de la religion, qui y seront aux environs, d'y faire prescher en Francois."

That, in all the cities and towns of the kingdom where there are harbours and ports, the English nation shall carry on their commerce, and may erect temples for the exercise of the [Protestant] religion, and that the French of the religion residing in the neighbourhood may have preaching there in French.

ART. VII.

"Que les edits de Janvier et de Nantes seront executez selon leurs formes et teneurs et toute la nation Angloise demeurera caution pour l'execution des dits edits."

That the edicts of January and of Nantes shall be executed according to their full import, and that the whole English nation shall be a perpetual guarantee for the execution of those edicts.

I am at a loss to know what was the edict of *January*. That description is not singular, for Sully (I. 99) names the edict in 1585, in favour of the League, "the famous edict of July." The edict of January might be the same as "the edict of 63 Articles" in 1576, by which, according to a note in *Sully*, (I. 49) "Chambers of justice, composed equally of Protestants and Catholics, were granted in the principal parliaments." The edict of Nantes was finally *verified* in 1599.

The memory of Cromwell has been treated with no small injustice respecting that transaction of the Protectorate, of which these quoted articles form a part. Historians and biographers, so far as I have been able to observe, have been content to follow, in a train, censuring the Protector for a supposed sacrifice of the permanent interests of England and Europe to the temporary security of his own power, by uniting

with France rather than with Spain. Had these censurers read the public *treaty*, as it is given in *A General Collection*, 1732, (III. 149) translated, probably, from Milton's Latin, they must, I think, have at least described it as displaying a manly style, neither haughty nor submissive, providing for the fair reciprocations of commerce, and, if not preventing war, designing to shelter the people on both sides from being immediately overwhelmed by its horrors. And if such historians and biographers had sought till they found these *Secret* Articles, which, I apprehend, because secret, were allowed to be originally, in French, they could scarcely have denied their commendation to the Protector.—Nor is the praise inconsiderable of having placed his nation singularly eminent on the page of history, among those whose power has been exerted to succour the oppressed.

HISTORICUS.

Sir, *Hackney, July 6, 1816.*

IT has often been ignorantly stated and as ignorantly believed, that the governments of the Peninsula have always made it a part of their policy to prevent the circulation of the Scriptures. The assertion has been repeated in a singular letter from one of your correspondents, (p. 336) who is marvellously fond of expatiating. I beg leave to state a few facts connected with this subject, merely premising that general error prevails as to the biblical literature of Spain and Portugal.

Before the early part of the 13th century, many copies of the Scriptures must have existed in the vulgar tongue, for we find King Jayme of Arragon, in 1233, prohibiting their circulation.

In 1260, Alfonso the Wise *ordered* a translation of the Bible to be made into Castilian (Spanish) and the original MS. yet exists in the Escurial;—and about the same period King Denir, of Portugal, caused the sacred books to be rendered into Portugueze, of which work, too, a copy is still preserved. In the following century John I. engaged the most learned men of his time to translate the Gospels, the Acts of the Apostles, and the Epistles of Paul, and himself translated the Psalms into the language of his country. Near this time two other versions of the Old Testament were made, besides translations of the Acts, Epistles, and Apocalypse of the

Epistles *from a French version*, and of the Gospels and the Epistles from the original Greek, by Father Julian.

In 1478, the well known translation into the Catalonian (or Valencian) provincial tongue, by Boniface Ferreira, was printed: and in 1485, Garcia de Santa Maria published in Zaragoza his " Gospels and Epistles" in Spanish. An admirable translation of Matthew's Gospel, and Extracts from the other Evangelists, by Bernard Alcobaga, was printed in Lisbon in 1495, as part of " the Life of Christ." Of the Psalms there is preserved a printed Spanish copy, in Gothic letters, without date, supposed to have issued from the Toledo press. It is believed that Alfonso V. encouraged the publication of another Spanish translation of the Bible, which was followed by yet another in the succeeding century. At the request of King Manuel, the Psalms were again translated and printed in 1529, and a Portugueze version of the Proverbs came from the Lisbon press in 1544.

In very modern times many have been the translations of the Bible published in Portugal. Their circulation has been wide, and manifest their beneficent influence. The best of them is that of Anto. Perreira de Figueiredo, of which a second edition (I think in 16 vols.) was printed in Lisbon in 1805. Notwithstanding the expense of this work, it is eagerly inquired for by the middling classes and best instructed part of the lower, and it continues silently diffusing its blessings, in spite of the concealed, but decided opposition of monks and priests. I need not add that no book whatever is printed in Portugal without the " authority of the king" and of the most holy inquisition.

Your's, &c.

J. B.

SIR   *June* 27, 1816.

I WAS gratified to observe, in your last No. pp. 295, 6, the respect so elegantly paid, in two different forms, to the memory of Mr. Joseph Fox. I had the pleasure of acting with him, several years ago, in promoting some objects which promised and have since effected no small public good, and can bear a very impartial testimony to his ardour and pure intentions, as I had the misfortune to differ from him, widely and warmly, on some points of

internal arrangement in the society to which I allude. Our differences, however, we were disposed to forget as soon as possible, and happily they never interrupted our mutual goodwill.

I had just heard of the death of that excellent man, who lived so much for the benefit of others, when I met with a striking and satisfactory evidence of the improvement which a century has produced among us, " in the greatest of all manufactures, the formation of human minds," to borrow the happy expression of the late Mr. Christie, in his *Miscellanies*, 1789, p. 213.

Having occasion to consult the 3d volume of *Magna Britannia*, published in 1724, I observed, p. 224, an account of " the charity schools," under the article *London*, including Westminster and Southwark. Distributed among 45 wards or parishes, there were 87 schools, educating 3737 children, consisting of 2357 boys and 1380 girls. So that supposing 263 children within the same district to be educated by the Dissenters, and it is probably, a sufficient computation, no more than 4000 children of the poor could then gain the commonest education, by any public charitable provision, in the *metropolis*, even according to its most extended description.

Yet this number of 3737, inconsiderable as it now appears, was indeed a large increase upon the number computed about sixteen years before. There was published in 1708, in 2 vols. 8vo. *A New View of London*, anonymous, but generally ascribed to Mr. Hatton. It is regarded as a work of merit in its way, and the author declares in his preface that in it was " nothing taken upon trust that admitted of inspection." In the sixth section is an enumeration of the " charity schools within the cities of London, Westminster and Southwark." I have collected the number of children belonging to these schools, and find their amount in 1708 to have been only 2041, being 1310 boys and 731 girls. I have, of course, omitted in both cases the *free grammar* schools.

After 1708 there appears to have been some zeal excited for the promotion of charity schools. The author whom I have just mentioned found one or two new schools building.

The Spectator, No. 294, in 1712, was written expressly to encourage subscriptions to what was then thought a great object, a school for 50 boys. The second letter in No. 430, is on the same subject, as is the Guardian, No. 105.

At this period, and long after, there seems to have been no thought entertained of educating poor children, unless they could be also provided for, at least with cloathing. It was Mr. Raikes who, nearly forty years ago, produced a new era in education by admitting to his sunday schools clean hands and faces, though in rags, a fine popular improvement of Erasmus's resolve, in favour of classic lore, first, to buy Greek books, and then, cloaths.

PLEBEIUS.

St. Ardleon,
SIR, *June 20, 1816.*

I OBSERVED (p. 257) that the misrepresentations of a young, though learned *orthodox* lecturer, had obliged my old friend Mr. Belsham to notice the *Theophilanthropists.* I had thought little about them for some years, but now recollected that, among a few curiosities, I possessed what may be called their *liturgy*, or rather *directory*, which a friend brought to me from the continent soon after it was printed. The *Theophilanthropists* had ceased to attract any notice, if indeed they existed in a connected form, when your work commenced, and have, I believe, never been described in your pages. You may therefore be disposed to accept the following account.

The publication to which I have referred is neatly printed in 18mo. extending to 78 pages, and thus entitled : —"Le Culte des Theophilanthropes, ou Adorateurs de Dieu et Amis des Hommes ; contenant leur Manuel et un Recueil de Discours, Lectures, Hymnes, et Cantiques pour toutes leurs fetes religieuses et morales. Seconde edition. A Basle de l'imprimirie de J. Decker. 1797."

From a short history prefixed, we learn that the origin of this society was in September 1796, when a little work appeared at Paris, under the title of "Manuel des Theanthophiles, &c. publie par C——." They then consisted of a few persons who carried on worship and instruction in separate families.

The publication of the *Manuel* excited so much attention, that these families determined to unite for public worship. This assembly, formed by five heads of families, was first opened in the month of *Nivose*, year 5, (January 1797) at Paris, in the street of St. Denis. Instead of *Theanthrophiles* they took the name of *Theophilanthropes*, as a more pleasant sound, and equally describing those who love God and men. They chose for their day of meeting the *Sunday*, without interfering with the choice of another day by any other society. And here I cannot help remarking how the language of these Theophilanthropists assimilates, on this subject, to that of their countryman *Calvin*, in his Institutes, (B. II. C. viii. S. 34). After describing the utility of substituting the Lord's day for the Jewish Sabbath, to remind Christians that the ceremonies of the former dispensation are abolished, Calvin adds—nor do I rely upon the number *seven* so as to consider the church as bound to its rigid observance, nor would I condemn churches that use any other solemn days of assembling, so that they abstain from superstitition.* The part of the Institutes from which I have taken this passage, was that I suppose to which Mr. Peirce thus refers in his letter to Dr. Snape, 1718. p. 30. "You cannot but know, that as we never professed to make *Calvin's* judgment the standard of truth, so we have always testified our dislike of some of his opinions. I will here mention one opinion of his, which 'tis well known has been always disagreeable to us, and that is concerning the Lord's day. You never knew any of us profess an approbation of his doctrine in this respect, or the practice of the church of Geneva, which is founded thereon."

The Theophilanthropists had a committee who were expected to employ an hour in each week to examine the lectures designed for delivery at the ensuing general meeting. Their meetings were called religious and moral festivals—*fetes religieuses et morales*. In these they proposed to introduce

---

* "Neque sic tamen septenarium numerum moror, ut ejus servituti Ecclesiam astringam, neque enim Ecclesias damnavero, quæ alios conventibus suis solennes dies habeunt, modó à superstitione ab sint." Institutio, Genevæ, 1602. fol. 131.

whatever of good is common to all religions, omitting what is peculiar to any. The Theophilanthropists professed not to be disciples of a particular man, but to avail themselves of the counsels of wisdom transmitted by writers of all countries, and all times. From these they would combine the injunctions of moralists, both ancient and modern, separated from maxims either too severe and refined, or contrary to the duties of piety towards God or men.

Such is a sketch of the information communicated in this preface, the *Précis Historique sur la Société des Theophilanthropes.* Some detail respecting their course of worship and instruction must be reserved to another occasion.

R. B.

SIR, *July* 1, 1816.

THERE is too much reason to believe that what has been so common may have happened in the case of Mr. Cardale, and that, though a learned, he may have been an unattractive preacher. Had Mr. Orton, however, expressed this fact with more kindness, he had done more credit to himself. As to the character of Mr. Cardale's writings, (p. 343) I beg leave to demur to the authority of Mr. Wilson. His censure reminds me of a more favourable opinion, given soon after the publication of the *True Doctrine,* by a writer who differed from the author, but whose learned competence will not be disputed, whatever may be thought of his uncommon and seemingly extravagant theories.

I refer to Mr. Holwell, who had filled a very high, if not the highest place in the administration of Bengal, and published a variety of curious Tracts on the civil and sacred antiquities, as well as on the British government of India. His Theological System is directly at issue with that of Mr. Maurice on the Hindoo and the Christian Trinity, rejecting both, as equally opposed to the proper Unitarian doctrine, which he supposes to have been revealed alike to Moses, Birmah, and Christ. He rejects the *miraculous conception,* for the reasons which have been frequently adduced against that doctrine, but maintains a pre-existence of the soul of Christ, consistently with his notions of the pre-existence of man and of all other animals and of a *metempsychosis.* He appears

to set the authority of the Gospels above that of the Epistles, and to defer least of all to the authority of Paul, whom he even charges with *reveries.* Yet amidst his freest remarks Mr. Holwell deprecates, with apparent sincerity and seriousness, the imputation of *Deism,* or a design "with *Hobbes, Tindal, Bolingbroke* and others, to sap the foundation or injure the root of Christianity." Such is a hasty but, I hope, not an unfair representation of this singular theologian, who speaks of Mr. Cardale's book, without appearing to know the author, in the following terms:

"A treatise which we never saw or heard of before we had closed our second general head, (although published in 1767) entitled, *The True Doctrine of the New Testament concerning Jesus Christ considered,* contains a plausible chain of objections to his supposed *pre-existence.* In that book, and the appendix, we have the singular pleasure of finding our sentiments upon the evil tendency of the Athanasian doctrine, and the true meaning, and reading of the first chapter of St. John's Gospel, supported by so learned and judicious an advocate for truth. We concur in sentiment with this writer, and feel very distinct ideas respecting the *deity* of the Father and the *divinity* of the Son, but we cannot conceive why he should stumble at allowing the pre-existence of the divine spirit of Christ. When this learned and ingenious writer gives an unprejudiced hearing, and full force to the doctrines of the *metempsychosis,* and duly weighs the insufficiency of every other human hypothesis, to account for the phenomena of our present existence, and indeed of all nature, he will, we flatter ourselves, receive full conviction, that his doubts and disbelief of the pre-existent state and original dignity of Christ, were ill-founded, and not *the True Doctrine of the New Testament.*" Pp. 145, 6, Part 3, dated Milford Haven, 1st November, 1770.

Mr. Holwell died in 1798. He must have reached a very advanced age as he resided in India as early as 1742, and filled a considerable station in 1756, when he was one of the few surviving sufferers in the *black hole* at Calcutta. Of the horrible scenes in that prison he published a very affecting *Narrative.*

N. L. T.

GLEANINGS; OR, SELECTIONS AND REFLECTIONS MADE IN A COURSE OF GENERAL READING.

No. CCLXII.
On the Use of Tea.

The Chinese first used tea as a necessary result of the badness of the water *hoang-ho,* or yellow river. They *must* employ some corrective to render the water of that river potable, for this purpose they used tea. This made the plant popular; hence it has been adopted where the same cause did not exist, and fashion has rendered it almost a necessary of life, in countries in the east, distant from China, and in the west, where the very existence of the yellow river and its qualities is not so much as thought of. That the Chinese use it so much as they do, is probably ewing to their having nothing better; for when the Dutch carried them *sage,* nicely dried and prepared, it appeared, so far preferable that they gave in, exchange three boxes of tea for one of sage.

No. CCLXIII.
Love of Children.

"It forms (says Mr. Wakefield, *Evidences of Christianity,* pp. 99, 100, *Note*) one of the most amiable traits in the character of Sir Isaac Newton, who was indeed *all-accomplished* beyond any of his species, that he was fond of *little children,* and delighted to see them playing about his study. Such was the simplicity, the sweetness, the condecension of a mind, that could expatiate through the universe,

And pass the flaming bounds of place and time!

resembling in this respect also the affectionate tenderness of the *Nazarene,* who fondled *little children in his arms, laid his hands upon them,* and recommended their innocent and artless manners to the imitation of his disciples. And yet (that I may lose no opportunity of shaming corrupted *churches,* which *make* and *love* and *believe* a LIE [2 Thess. ii. 11. Rev. xx. 15.] and, of disgracing *Anti-Christian* principles, wherever I discover them) these very *infants* are strenuously maintained by *sound divines,* tho spiritual pastors and teachers of this goodly land! to be CHILDREN of WRATH and BORN in SIN; till the hallowed drops from their *disinterested* fingers have purged away the defilements of nativity, and made the *creature* fit for the acceptance of its *Creator.*"

CCLXIV.
Highland Revenge.

A Highlander who made the *amende honorable* to an enemy, came to his dwelling, laid his head upon the block, or offered him his sword held by the point. It was deemed unworthy to refuse the clemency implored, but it might be legally done. We recollect an instance in Highland history:—William M'Intosh, a leader if not chief of that ancient clan, upon some quarrel with the Gordons, burnt the castle of Auchendown, belonging to this powerful family; and was, in the feud which followed, reduced to such extremities by the persevering vengeance of the Earl of Huntley, that he was at length compelled to surrender himself at discretion. He came to the castle of Strathbogie, choosing his time when the Earl was absent, and yielded himself up to the countess. She informed him that Huntley had sworn never to forgive him the offence he had committed, until he should see his head upon the block. The humbled chieftain kneeled down, and laid his head upon the kitchen dresser, where the oxen were cut up for the baron's feast. No sooner had he made this humiliation, than the cook, who stood behind him with his cleaver uplifted, at a sign from the inexorable countess, severed M'Intosh's head from his body at a stroke. So deep was this thirst of vengeance impressed on the minds of the Highlanders, that when a clergyman informed a dying chief of the unlawfulness of the sentiment, urged the necessity of his forgiving an inveterate enemy, and quoted the scriptural expression, "Vengeance is mine, saith the Lord," the acquiescing penitent said, with a deep sigh,—'To be sure, it is too sweet a morsel for a mortal.' Then added, 'Well I forgive him; but the De'il take you, Donald, (turning to his son) if you forgive him.'

Another extraordinary instance occurred in Aberdeenshire. In the sixteenth century, Muat of Abergeldie, then a powerful baron, made an agreement to meet with Cameron of Brux, with whom he was at feud, each being attended with twelve horse only. But Muat, treacherously taking advantage of the literal meaning of the words, came with two riders on each horse. They met at Drumguadruin, a hill near the river Don, and in the unequal conflict which ensued, Brux fell with most of his friends. The estate descended to an only daughter, Catherine, whose hand the widowed lady Brux, with a spirit well suited to the times, offered as a reward to one who would avenge her husband's death. Robert Forbes, a younger son of the chief of that family undertook the adventure; and having challenged Muat to single combat, fought with and slew him at a place called Badewyon, near the head of Glenbucket. A stone called Clachmuat (i. e. Muat's stone) still marks the place of combat. When the victor presented himself to claim the reward of his valour, and to deprecate any delay of his happipiness, Lady Brux at once cut short all ceremonial by declaring that Kate Cameron should go to Robert Forbes's bed while Muat's blood was yet recking upon his gully (i. e. knife.) The victor expressed no disapprobation of this arrangement, nor did the maiden scruples of the bride impede her filial obedience.

One more example (and we could add an hundred) of that insatiable thirst of revenge, which attended northern feuds. One of the Leslies, a strong and active young man, chanced to be in company with a number of the clan of Leith, the feudal enemies of his own. The place where they met being the hall of a powerful and neutral neighbour, Leslie, was, like Shakspeare's Tybalt, in a similar situation, compelled to endure his presence. Still he held the opinion of the angry Capulet, even in the midst of the entertainment,

"Now by the stock and honour of
: his kin,
To strike him dead to hold it not a
' sin."

Accordingly, when they stood up to dance, when he found himself compelled to touch the hands and approach the persons of his detested enemies, the deadly feud broke forth. He unsheathed his dagger as he went down the dance—struck on the right and left—laid some dead and many wounded on the floor—threw up the window, leaped into the castle court, and escaped in the general confusion.

Such were the unsettled principles of the time, that the perfidy of the action was lost in its boldness; it was applauded by his kinsmen who united themselves to defend what he had done; and the fact is commemorated in the well known tune of triumph called *Leslie among the Leiths.*

No. CCLXV.
Cardinal Turquemada.

"The inquisition is nothing but the highest improvement of persecution which begins with tests and negative penalties but ends in fires and halters. Cardinal Turquemada, the first inquisitor-general in Spain, even in the infancy of the inquisition, brought an hundred thousand souls into it in the small space of fourteen years. Of these six thousand were burnt alive." Trenchard and Gordon's Tracts, 1751, ii. 290.

No. CCLXVI.
Palmer and Pilgrim.

"Palmers differ from Pilgrims, in that the Pilgrim has some home or dwelling-place, but the Palmer none. The Pilgrim travels to some certain designed place, or places, but the Palmer to all. The Pilgrim goes on his own charges, the Palmer professes wilful poverty, and lives on alms. The Pilgrim may give over his profession and return home, but the Palmer must be constant till he hath obtained the palm, that is victory over all his ghostly enemies and life by death; and thence is his name *Palmer*; or else from a staff or bough of *palm*, which he always carries along with him." History of Popery, 4to. 1735, i. 113.

No. CCLXVII.
A Dutch Bible imprisoned in the Inqui-
" *sition.*

"The brave old Marshal *Schonberg*, when he was last at *Lisbon*, told a friend of mine, with tears in his eyes, that having when he came ashore there, left a *Dutch* Bible, which had been his grandfather's, upon the table of his cabin, it had been carried from the custom-house to the inquisition; and that though he had sent to the chief inquisitor, and had spoken to him himself for it, he had not been able to recover it." Independent Whig, 1720. 7th Ed. ii. 47.

BIBLICAL CRITICISM.

On the Priesthood of Christ.
June 22, 1816.

IN this paper I shall place, at one view, before my readers, those texts of Scripture which speak of Jesus Christ as a *priest*: I shall then compare them together, and with some other passages; and, finally, I shall state, in a few distinct remarks, the result of my investigation.

I. (1.) Heb. ii. 17.—" in all things it behoved him to be made, like unto his brethren, that he might be *a merciful and faithful high priest*, in things pertaining to God, to make reconciliation for the sins of the people."

(2.) — iii. 1.—" consider the apostle and *high priest* of our profession, Christ Jesus."

(3.) — iv. 14. " Seeing then that we have *a great high priest, that is passed into the heavens, Jesus, the Son of God,* let us hold fast our profession."

(4.)—iv. 15.—" we have not *an high priest* who cannot be touched with the feeling of our infirmities: but was in all points tempted as we are, yet without sin."

(5.)—v. 5.—" Christ glorified not himself to be made *an high priest*."

(6.) — v. 10 " *Called of God, an high priest,* after the order of Melchisedec."

(7.) — vi. 20. " Whither the forerunner is for us entered; even *Jesus* made *an high priest for ever,* after the order of Melchisedec." Thus, too, vii. 15, 16, &c.

(8.) — vii. 3.—" made like unto *the Son of God,* abideth *a priest* continually." So verses 15, 16, 17, 21.

(9.)———24.—" this man, because he continueth ever, hath *an unchangeable priesthood.*"

(10.) ——— 26.—" such *an high priest* became us, who is holy, harmless, undefiled, separate from sinners, and *made* higher than the heavens."

(11.) ——— 27, 28. " Who needeth not daily, as those high priests [under the Law], to offer up sacrifice first for his own sins, and then for the people's: for this he did once when he offered up himself. For the Law maketh men high priests who have infirmity: but the word of the oath,

which was since the Law, *maketh* the Son, who is *consecrated for evermore.*" So x. 11—13.

(12.)—viii. 1. " Now of the things which we have spoken, this is the sum : we have such *an high priest, who is set on the right hand of the throne of the Majesty in the heavens.*"

(13.)———4.—" *if he were on earth, he should not be a priest.*"

(14.) — ix. 11.—" Christ — *an high priest of good things to come.*"

(15.) ——— 12.—" *by his own blood* —entered in once INTO THE HOLY PLACE, having obtained eternal redemption for us."

(16.) — x. 21, 22.—" having *an high priest* over the house of God, Let us draw near with a true heart, in full assurance of faith."

II. The texts thus cited, may be distributed into four classes : (1) those which simply represent Jesus Christ as a *priest* or *high priest,* (2) those which describe his qualifications for that character, (3) those which speak of his *appointment* to the office, and (4) finally, those which direct our regard to the *characteristic excellence* of his priesthood.

To the first class we refer Nos. 2, 14, 16; to the second, Nos. 1, 4, 10; to the third, Nos. 5, 6, 11; and to the fourth, Nos. 3, 7, 8, 9, 12, 13, 15.

The allusion, in all the passages, being to priests under former dispensations of religion, it will be requisite to add a few texts from the Old Testament :

Gen. xiv. 18, 19.—" Melchisedec, king of Salem, brought forth bread and wine : and he was the *priest of the Most High God.* And he blessed him [Abram], &c." Psalm cx. 4.

Lev. xvi. 2.—" the Lord said unto Moses, Speak unto Aaron thy brother, that he come not *at all times* into the holy place within the vail ;" See, likewise, ver. 15, &c.

Deut. x. 8.—" the Lord separated *the tribe of Levi,* to bear the ark of the covenant of the Lord, to stand before the Lord, to *minister* unto him, and to bless in his name."

These passages will explain, in particular, the first, third and fourth classes of the texts quoted above: on the second of them light will be thrown by the commands respecting the priests in the books of Leviticus and Numbers; and all receive illustration from

1 Pet. ii. 5. " Ye [Christians] are *an holy priesthood*, to offer up spiritual sacrifice, acceptable to God by Jesus Christ."

———9. " Ye are *a royal priesthood*."

Rev. i. 6.—"hath *made* us [i. e. Christ hath made us] *kings and priests* unto God and his Father."

— xx. 6.—"they shall be *priests* * of God and of Christ."

III. We are now, I trust, prepared, for discerning the Scriptural doctrine of the priesthood of Jesus Christ.

And, in the first place, this tenet is altogether unrelated to the *popular* tenet concerning his intercession. Not one of the passages transcribed, speaks of his *interposing* in behalf of mankind: not one of them implies that he so interposes. His *priesthood* is not of his own appointment, but of God's.

Secondly; The great point of resemblance between Jesus and the Jewish high priest, is *our Lord's having presented himself before God in. the spiritual holy of holies.* Of the chief of the priests under the law it was the special duty, the characteristic privilege, to enter, once a year, the most holy place: he did not go into it more frequently; he did not remain there long. Christians have a high priest to whom far greater honour is appropriated. And the benefits derived by them from our Saviour's priesthood are precisely those which they derive from his death, resurrection and ascension.

In the third place; Jesus *makes reconciliation for the sins of the people*. How? Not by dying in their stead (for this was not required from the high priest, and formed no part of his office); but by duly appearing in the presence of God on their behalf. The high priest among the Israelites offered

their prayers to God.† Particularly, on one solemn day in the year, after assisting in the *sacrifices of the people*, he entered the holy of holies, and finished, by the act of his appearance in that spot, the great work of *making reconciliation* [ιλασκεϑαι] : it was the reconciliation of the people, together with the altar, &c. to God, not of God to the people, and instead of implying the existence of wrath in the mind of the Supreme Being, it denoted his mercy and forbearance.

Fourthly; Nothing can be more evident than that our Lord is a priest allusively and figuratively. In John x. 11. he styles himself a *shepherd*, language which also is metaphorical. According to the Scriptural representation, his *priesthood* is not a distinct office, but *a connected view of his ministry, his death, and his resurrection to* an IMMORTAL life. Hence the Hebrew Christians are exhorted to perseverance: *they* are members of an undecaying dispensation.

Lastly; Christ never speaks of himself as a priest. Nor is he ever so spoken of by his apostles, in their discourses or epistles; unless indeed the letter to the Hebrews be the production of Paul, which, at least, is very doubtful.

Admitting however that it was dictated by this great teacher of Christianity, still it must be interpreted with reference to its occasion, design and readers. The author's object is to preserve the Jewish converts from apostacy: one method therefore which he employs for this purpose, is to shew that the Gospel has in all respects a vast superiority to the Law; and this argument he in part illustrates by a comparison of the Levitical high priest with the high priest of the " new and better covenant."

It will now be easily understood *why* and *how* Jesus Christ is " the apostle and high priest of our profession." And the foregoing observations are respectfully submitted to those persons who, like the writer, make the sacred volume its own expositor.   N.

---

* " Regni ejus sunt administri, uti olim sacerdotes Israelitarum." Eichhorn. Comment: in Apoc: 289.

† " Munus sacerdotale eo maxime a prophetico atque etiam apostolico differret, quod sacerdotarum et apostolorum esset res Dei apud homines agere, Sacerdotam autem res hominum apud Deum." Outram de Sacrif: (1677) p. 220.

REVIEW.

" Still pleased to praise, yet not afraid to blame."---POPE.

ART. I.—*The Literary and Scientific Pursuits which are encouraged and enforced in the University of Cambridge, briefly described and vindicated.* By the Rev. Latham Wainewright, A.M. F.A.S. of Emanuel College in that University, and Rector of Great-Brickhill, Bucks.

NOTHING shows more decisively the influence which public opinion is constantly acquiring in this country, than the deference paid to it by those great chartered bodies, whose constitution seems designed to enable them to set it at defiance. It is chiefly this, which has enabled the friends of humanity to carry the light of investigation and reform into the worse than inquisitional cells of Bedlam; it is this which makes the Church of England circulate the Scriptures, and educate the poor, and even submit to hear the commutation of tythes made the subject of parliamentary discussion. The French Revolution, of which some persons seem to think that they can never speak in terms too strongly expressive of their abhorrence, has been one great cause of this remarkable characteristic of the present times. The evils which resulted from that tremendous collision between the spirit of reform, and the " morosa morum retentio,"* have left a deep, though unavowed impression upon the minds of those who are interested in the support of existing institutions, and have moderated that high and disdainful tone, with which they were accustomed to plead antiquity against reason, and privilege against justice. They remember what was in France the consequence of despising those murmurs, which public opinion had long uttered against a corrupt hierarchy and a despotic government— it spoke once again, and heaven and earth were shaken with the voice. The horror of reform, which was the first result of the excesses of the Revolution, has in great measure subsided; impe-

tuosity of innovation has been diminished on the one hand, and tenacity of abuse on the other; and the whole effect has been a calm determination in the public mind towards investigation and improvement, which, notwithstanding the failure of some enthusiastic hopes, may still console the patriot and the philanthropist.

Among the other indications of a change of views, in those who are interested in the preservation of existing establishments, we may reckon those vindications which have appeared within the last few years, of the discipline and studies of our two Universities. Placed as these bodies appear to be, " above the fear of a rival and below the confession of a fault,"* they have evidently begun to feel that the public requires from them some account of the manner in which they discharge the high trust reposed in them, and how they repay to their country the endowments, immunities and privileges which she has conferred upon them. Our readers probably remember the vindication of Oxford by Mr. Copleston,† occasioned by the animadversions of the Edinburgh Reviewers, who came just too late with their censures. After wasting the time of its students for we know not how many generations, in an absurd and useless course of studies, the University of Oxford had at length condescended to adapt its pursuits to the altered condition of the world, and to ensure attention to them by a very strict and efficient system of examinations. Cambridge, as being of less ancient establishment, and far inferior in independent revenues, had always been less bigotted to ancient forms and obsolete doctrines, and had therefore less that required alteration. Yet whoever will compare the proposals for improvements of various kinds, made by Dr. John Jebb, and then

---

* Lord Bacon.

* Gibbon.
† Now we believe LL.D. and Provost of Oriel College.

most vehemently opposed, with the statements contained in the work before us, will perceive here too what a change a very few years have made in the disposition to reform. The work of Mr. Wainewright, which is dedicated to Lord Palmerston, one of the Representatives of the University, does not appear with quite so official a character as Mr. Copleston's. He informs us, however, that it has been written chiefly in compliance with the suggestions of others, and that it has been " submitted to the inspection of two members of the University, of learning and station, upon whose judgment he could place implicit reliance." It may, therefore, be considered as *demi-official.* To those of our readers who know nothing of the studies which are cultivated at Cambridge, this work, diffuse, ill-written, and ill-reasoned as it is, may afford some interesting information; and we are very ready to assent to the panegyrics which he bestows on many parts of its literary pursuits. No man who is acquainted with the history of learning and science, of enlightened scriptural criticism and liberal political principles, will deny the share which Cambridge has borne in promoting them. May that day never arrive, when the prevalence of Calvinistic bigotry among one set of its members, and an affectation of orthodoxy among another, shall make the University desirous of blotting from its *fasti* the names of these illustrious friends of the human race! We frankly give notice to our readers, however, that our design in calling their attention to Mr. W.'s work, is not so much to enter into its general merits, as to animadvert upon some very unfounded and unwarrantable reflections which he has taken occasion to throw out, upon the system of academical education among the Dissenters, and especially those whom he calls the rational and Socinian Dissenters. Coming forward as he does in the cause, and almost in the name of the University, it is not fit that he should be allowed to circulate his assertions, without such a contradiction as this channel can convey.

Under a consciousness of the inferiority in some branches of learning, which from necessary causes must always characterize Dissenters, who are debarred by religious scruples, not only from universities but even from public

schools,[*] we have been accustomed to console ourselves with the idea that theological studies, at least, were carried on amongst us in a manner consonant to that unfettered freedom of inquiry which we profess, and with as careful a research into the original sources of theological doctrines, as it is possible to institute. Our academical institutions have always made it their primary object to educate ministers, and their failure must indeed have been complete, if they have not attained even this. It will be seen, by the following passage from Mr. W.'s book, pp. 66, 67, how little cause he thinks we have for this self-congratulation:

" As so large a proportion of the students of the University are designed for the *sacerdotal order*, it will naturally be expected that an ample provision has been made for the acquirement of that species of learning, which this important profession peculiarly demands. Complaints, however, have been sometimes made, that this provision is in many respects defective, and that it is by no means commensurate with the wishes of those, to whom the ordination of the clergy is assigned by the church. Whatever cause for objection may formerly have existed on this point, it has for many years been almost entirely removed, and an opportunity is now afforded to every intended ecclesiastic, I do not say of completing the character of a profound theologian, which can never be effected during any academical course of studies, but of acquiring such a competent knowledge of the various branches of divinity, as will qualify him for passing a very respectable examination, previously to his admission into holy orders. In some colleges one term of every year and in others one day in the week, is appropriated in the lecture-room to the Greek Testament; and unless counteracted by particular circumstances, the critical remarks of the lecturer, and his judicious use of the labours of former scholars and commentators, must be the means of exciting a desire for biblical information, and of forming a taste for biblical pursuits. *And here we cannot but observe, the vast superiority of the mode of studying the Sacred Writings, recommended and enforced on these occasions, to the careless*

---

[*] In a case which lately fell under our own knowledge, a lad, who, from his father's scruples on the subject of infant-baptism, had never undergone this rite, was informed by the master of one of our public schools that he must either be baptized or leave the place.

and superficial manner, so common in dissenting institutions, where a notorious deficiency in classical and oriental literature, and a general ignorance of the laws of just criticism, must obviously give rise to a mistaken interpretation of the original text, and to the consequent formation of erroneous opinions."*

Ἐὰν πρότερός τις εἴποι τα προσόντ' ἑαυτῷ περὶ ἄλλου, καὶ δὴ ταῖς ὅτως ἔχει καὶ ἐκέτι οἱ ἀκέοντες σκέψονται, τίς ποτ' αὐτός ἐςιν ὁ ταῦτα λεγών;

Such appears to have been the expectation of Mr. W. who has either asserted that of which he knew nothing, or that which he knew not to be. We very readily allow him 'the milder half' of the alternative, believing that he has only spoken here in the plenitude of that dignified ignorance which Churchmen affect, in regard to the internal concerns of the Dissenters. We are far from complaining of this ignorance which it is their privilege to enjoy and our fate to suffer; but let them at least " neither bless us at all nor curse us at all," or if they will stoop to censure us, let them also humble themselves to learn what it is they are censuring. They would hardly admit it as an excuse on our parts, for a misrepresentation of an university, that it was raised too high above us, for us to see it distinctly: yet the distance from which we look up to Mr. W. is exactly that from which he looks down upon us. He should both in justice and in prudence have informed himself a little better, before he ventured to commit the honour of his University, and even the credit of orthodoxy, to such a comparison as he has provoked. As a reply to the reflections contained in the paragraph which we have quoted, we shall beg leave to lay before our readers a statement of the course of *Biblical study* pursued in an academical institution, which till lately was the only one in which ministers among the Unitarian Dissenters received their education. We are persuaded that we shall the more readily obtain this indulgence from them, as it will afford us an opportunity of doing justice to

one, to whom justice will never be done, but by some other hand than his own.

In the first year of his course, the theological student, who is required to have reached the age of sixteen at his admission, and to be able to read Homer and Horace, begins, upon his first entrance, the study of the Hebrew language, in which it will generally be found, that at the end of a session of nine months, he has made sufficient progress to have read, with tolerable ease, considerable portions of the historical books of the Old Testament. In the second year he reads the Prelections of Lowth, with the notes of Michaëlis, grammatically resolving the passages which are quoted in the text; and, in addition to this, some of the devotional and prophetic books, comparing the Hebrew throughout with the Septuagint. In the third year, he continues to read other parts of the Hebrew Scriptures in the same critical and grammatical manner as before. Syriac and Chaldee do not make an invariable part of the course, but are taught to those, whose ability for learning languages promises that the knowledge of them will be useful. The reader will observe, that through the three first years, theological studies are subordinate to the cultivation of the languages, history, mathematics and philosophy, while in the two last, theology forms the chief, and almost the exclusive business. The course of the fourth year begins with the critical examination of the sources whence the text of the Old Testament is derived, including the various ancient versions, the history and authority of which and their relation to the Hebrew, are more or less minutely investigated, according to their importance to the commentator. When the way is thus prepared, the Scriptures of the Old Testament are separately examined, as the records of the Jewish Revelation; the laws of Moses are presented in a systematic view, that their wisdom and divine origin may appear more conspicuous, and all the light is thrown upon them which can be supplied by oriental manners and a comparison with other systems, of ancient jurisprudence. A similar course is pursued with regard to the other historical, to the devotional, and the prophetic books. It is impossible to make use of the original text, where so large a space must be gone

---

* That we may not escape under cover of these general reflections, the charge is brought home to us in the next page:— "The very scanty portion of critical skill possessed by the disciples of Socinus, in common with every class of dissidents." P. 68. Note.

ever; but wherever any thing depends upon critical interpretation or various readings, the original is referred to, and is compared with the versions, and with what commentators have written for its illustration. In this way, seven or eight hours in every week are occupied in the lecture-room, besides what the private preparation of the student requires. The fifth year is chiefly devoted to the reading of the New Testament, with the same scrupulous attention to every thing which can elucidate its meaning, without imposing any doctrinal interpretation; but as it is of the highest importance in the institution of a Christian minister, that he be thoroughly acquainted with this part of the sacred volume, the whole, or nearly the whole, is read over in the original.

We have purposely confined ourselves to a statement of the means employed to give the students educated in the institution in question, *a critical knowledge of the Scriptures*, since it is to this that Mr. W.'s charge refers. And we now request the reader to turn back to the passage marked in italics in our quotation from him, and to say, if he ever saw a charge which more violently recoiled on the head of the accuser, than that which Mr. W. has so unadvisedly advanced. 'The fling at the Dissenters for their deficiency in *oriental* literature is the more strange, as we meet with the following passage at p. 76. "It is sometimes asked, what useful purpose is promoted by the professorships of Hebrew and Arabic established in both Universities, when no lectures are delivered upon the subject?* To this we reply, that though lectures are occasionally read on these topics, *as is the case* with the present Arabic professor at Cambridge, yet the design of these institutions is not regularly to teach the elements of the languages in question, which is best effected by private tuition, but to afford encouragement to the pursuit of an object which presents but few attractions, and to the critical examination of those oriental dialects, *which* would otherwise perhaps be speedily neglected, if not utterly lost." Besides the curious fact here stated, viz. that the present Arabic professor

is sometimes read as a lecture to the under-graduates, the reasoning of this passage is worthy the attention of our readers. The title of these oriental scholars to the emoluments of their offices, arises from the unpopularity of oriental studies; of course they would forfeit this title by doing any thing to render them more easy or more attractive. The paradise of placemen is surely an appointment which not only allows inactivity but makes it a condition. Silent, however, as the operation of these oriental professorships is, it is not the less powerful on that account; not the knowledge only of the oriental dialects, but *the dialects themselves*, Mr. W. assures us, would speedily be lost, did not a gentleman at Oxford and another at Cambridge receive salaries for doing nothing to diffuse them. Certainly nothing can equal the cogency of our author's reasoning, unless it be the accuracy of his style.

The deficiency in classical learning, which Mr. W. alleges as another source of the heresies of the Socinians, we are not inclined to deny; but we wonder that a Cambridge man should suppose it a necessary consequence, that if we had more learning we should have more orthodoxy. If the learning of Porson and his orthodoxy[*] together could be transferred to us, we fear we should be still at a lamentable distance from Mr. W.'s standard. In Porson's days it had not become the fashion of the great scholars of Cambridge (for there is a fashion in keeping or laying down a conscience) to affect a political adherence to the church as by law established. On the other hand, there is a species of learning which we should be sorry to purchase by the renunciation of common sense, in applying it to the interpretation of the Scriptures. Of this sacrifice we might produce numberless examples, but while Bishop

---

* "Though Hebrew is considered as a requisite qualification for a fellowship in some colleges, it does not constitute a regular and an essential part of collegiate literature." P. 74. Note.

---

[*] "You may say that his religious creed resembled that of Dr. Samuel Clarke. You are at liberty to think so. Was Dr. Clarke not a Christian?"—Kidd's Imperfect Outline of the Life of Richard Porson, prefixed to his Miscellaneous Tracts and Criticisms, p. xxx. It may be interesting to our readers to be informed, on the authority of the same intimate friend, that Porson, though not the author of "Gregory Blunt's Letters;" nor well pleased to have been suspected of it, thought the new doctrine of the Greek article, as applied to the support of the divinity of Christ, to be untenable.

Burgess lives and writes (may he long continue to do both!) he will be himself a host to prove, how little a man may be the better Scripture critic for his learning. Who could have believed that the editor of the *Pentalogia* and the *Miscellanea Critica*, would propose, on the authority of Suidas, to render ἐν μορφῇ Θεῦ ὑπάρχων " pre-existing in the nature of God?" " *I poach in Suidas for unlicens'd Greek!*"

Let not our readers, however, imagine that we mean, without further explanation, to surrender the classical learning of the Dissenters to all the sarcasms which Mr. W. and others are pleased to bestow upon it. Perhaps, even among ourselves, it has not always been duly considered what place it is possible to allot to classical studies, in the education of a minister (for of that only are we now speaking), without encroaching upon other things. A young man, who has devoted himself to the ministry, goes to the academy to prepare himself for the discharge of a practical and a laborious profession; and all his *literary* studies have a direct reference to this object. If among these studies there be some, which appear to have but little connexion either with the duties of the preacher or those of the expounder of Scripture, they find a place, because experience has shown, that next to a fervent piety and active benevolence (qualities in which we shall be surprised if even Mr. W. claim a superiority for Churchmen over Dissenters), nothing is more essential to the due influence of a pastor's character over the minds of his people, and his ability to take the lead among them in plans of general usefulness, than that he should possess a well-stored and well-cultivated understanding. Were this object lost sight of, in an age like the present, when the intellect of society is upon the rise, the consequences must be very prejudicial, not only to the respectability of the ministerial character, but to the prosperity of the Dissenting interest and to the influence of those principles of civil and religious liberty, which have been nurtured in the bosom of English nonconformity, and which still find among us their most steady advocates. But though these considerations to our minds satisfactorily prove the propriety of making a course of academical study, and especially of the study of the ancient languages, as ample and complete as pos-

sible, it must still be borne in mind, that these things are the *means* and not the *end*—means to the discharge of the active duties of a laborious profession. A clergyman when he leaves college, may have a living in waiting for him, where, with a well-arranged cycle of other mens' sermons, (many probably purloined from the works of those Dissenters on whom he looks down) and Nares and Magee to furnish out a visitation philippic against the Unitarians, year after year may find him wholly devoted to his literary occupations, and not at all reproaching himself for being absorbed in them. A Dissenting minister who should thus sacrifice his professional duties to his taste, would be admonished by the failing numbers and languishing zeal of his congregation, of the folly of forsaking his proper character to assume another incompatible with it. The ultimate destination of those under their care, can never be lost sight of by those entrusted with the academical instruction of our youth, without neglecting their duty and exposing themselves to much severer reflections than the sarcasms of university-men. Whatever can be done, to render that portion of time which can be given to classical studies, either at school or afterwards, more efficacious, to encourage the diligence and emulation of the young, to secure the attainment of such a portion of knowledge in *all* their ministers, as may enable them to read and explain the Scriptures, and to provide for those who have more than ordinary talents for such pursuits, the means of qualifying themselves to be the teachers of the rising generation, the past and present conduct of the Dissenters give us reason to believe they will not neglect. With less than this they ought not to be contented—at more than this we should be sorry to see them aim. Indeed when we look at what Mr. W. states as the common course of classical reading at Cambridge, we do not see that it is above all hope of imitation, even by Dissenters. If a young man enters an academical institution, already able to read Homer and Horace, and continues five years there, pursuing his classical studies during the whole time, is it impossible for him, if he and his teachers are tolerably diligent, to read " the finest Plays of the Greek Tragedians, Plato's Dialogues, the Histories of Herodotus and Thucydides, Cicero's Philosophical Works, and the two Treatises of Tacitus;" nay even to master the difficulties of Aristotle's Treatise of Poetry, and learn to call it by its proper name?*.

Whatever humiliation it behoves the Socinian dissidents to feel, when they compare their own armour, χαλκεια, εννεαβοια, with the golden " panoply divine, in which have issued forth a Porson, a Parr, a Burney and a Wakefield," (p. 83, Note) it is clear that the attainments of Mr. W. himself are by no means of that colossal magnitude, beneath which the pigmy scholarship of the Dissenters must peep about to seek itself a dishonourable grave. A man who takes upon him to school others for their deficiencies in Latin and Greek, should be very sure that he himself can write English. But did it ever befal a literary body before, to be defended by an advocate, who could print such a sentence, nay many such sentences, as the following? " *Respecting* Dr. Hartley's celebrated *theory of solving* the phenomena of the human mind by the agency of vibration and association, the former of these doctrines is certainly subject to great difficulty of actual proof," &c. (P. 64, Note.) Had such a sentence occurred in the theme of a student in the first half of his first session · at a dissenting academy, we hardly think he could have escaped a rebuke for prefixing a " respecting" to that which nothing *respected*; and he would certainly have been informed that a *theory of solving* was a combination of English words, which " *non Di, non homines, non concessere columnæ.*"

The short duration of dissenting academies is another circumstance on which Mr. W. dwells, and he contrasts it with complacency with the antiquity of universities. " Let any one direct his view to the seminaries projected at various times for the education of those who call themselves Rational Dissenters, (to say nothing of similar foundations for the Independents and Methodists) in which the defects and corruptions of the English universities were professed to be avoided, and the acquirements† of learning to be ac-

complished with infinitely less toil and consumption of time; let him observe the success of these visionary attempts, and ask where are now the academies of Warrington, Daventry and Hackney, and what is the condition of the few which have escaped the wreck of their companions, and he will be less disposed to indulge in unreasonable declamations against those venerable and magnificent institutions which have endured the trial of so many ages, or to be led away by the chimerical dreams of the possibility of exemption from practical error."

We were aware that it had been, and still is, an object with the Dissenters, to provide the means of giving education to their youth, without sending them to the universities. Were the studies pursued at these places, as well adapted to secure the great objects of education, and their discipline as favourable to morals, as Mr. W. alleges them to be, still no Dissenter could be admitted to partake of these privileges, at Oxford, without trampling on the faith of his forefathers, nor at Cambridge, without joining in a worship, the form and invocations of which he must deem unscriptural. But at the time when the Dissenters formed those institutions, in whose decline Mr. W. triumphs, Oxford was still covered with the thick darkness of the scholastic ages, and not one of those reforms had been made, which have since placed her at least upon a footing of equality with Cambridge, in intellectual and moral discipline. Was it then an unpardonable presumption in the Dissenters, to have perceived, half a century earlier, the unfitness of university plans to the true objects of education, and while they preserved their youth from the evils of relaxed discipline, and temptations to dishonest conformity, to attempt to provide for them a course of study, more likely to qualify them for the duties of real life? That it was their object to abridge that *needless infinity of toil* to which young men would be exposed at an university, we never heard, and we require better evidence of the fact than the assertions of one who writes so much at random as

* " The Poetics of Aristotle," as Mr. W. has it. Did he learn at Cambridge to speak of his Rhetorics?

† The blows which Mr. W. aims at the Dissenters generally fall upon Priscian. The acquirement of learning is an act which

may be accomplished; the acquirements of learning are things which may be attained or purchased but not *accomplished.* Και ταυτα, ημιπτες τι τα στηματα ταυτα. See last note. *Xen. Hist. Gr.* IV. 4. 10.

Mr. W. Dissenters have, we think, rather been prone to the opposite fault from that with which he charges them, and have suffered from attempting to make their institutions too much like the universities; and they have been respectable and prosperous, in proportion as they have known, and adhered to their own proper character. In magnificence it will readily be conceded that they are as much inferior to Cambridge, as Cambridge is to Oxford, but they are adapted to the wants and the means of those to whom they belong, and are the fruits of their generous and voluntary zeal. "Parva, sed apta mihi, sed nulli obnoxia."[*]

The Dissenters are as ready to acknowledge the errors which have caused the decline of their academical institutions, as Mr. W. to lay them to their charge. Yet some of the vicissitudes to which he alludes had no connexion with this cause. The *removal* of the academy from Daventry (for it still exists) was owing to the conscientious scruples which made its able and exemplary (would that the time were more remote when we might say its venerable!) Theological Tutor resign his charge. Before we can allow Mr. W. to exult over the errors which caused the decline of Warrington and Hackney, we must request him to answer us this question: Would either of our universities have been at this moment in existence, if they must have fallen, as soon as the opinion of the public pronounced, that their professors made sinecures of their offices, that their discipline was imperfect and relaxed, and their plans of study antiquated and barbarous? We are very sure that this question cannot be honestly answered in the affirmative; and into what then does their boasted perpetuity resolve itself, but into a power of holding out against public disapprobation, of slowly admitting the light which has long pervaded every place besides, of being the last strong-hold of exploded prejudices? It is the natural tendency of the independent revenues and exclusive privileges possessed by universities, to make them all this; and if Oxford is superior to Salamanca, it is less owing to any difference in her own constitution, than to that free and manly national spirit, of which she has

been reluctantly compelled to inhale a portion—which has quickened her indolent circulation, and sweetened the acrid humours of her bigotry—a spirit which has been cherished chiefly by those who have never been either within her walls, or those of her sister University, and which she herself has done her utmost to extinguish.

To the imagination there is no doubt something imposing in an institution, whose identity is prolonged through so many reigns and centuries; and he who has walked up the High-street of Oxford, without feeling such emotions, may assure himself that he was not born to be an orator or a poet. The judgment, however, pronounces, that changes which destroy the chain of antiquarian associations, may be useful and even necessary. Founders bequeath their prejudiced and partial views along with their estates, and take upon them to legislate for future ages, of whose condition and wants they can have no conception: institutions which each successive age forms for itself will be adapted to the wants of each. In the mortality of the individual, Providence has taken a method to break the entail of error and prejudice; and frequent renovations seem necessary to produce a similar effect on public institutions. The boasted perpetuity of endowed and chartered bodies is generally only the immortality of a *Struldbrug*—a perpetuity of decrepitude, an eternity of dotage.

Academical establishments among the Dissenters have risen and fallen during the last fifty years, but the DISSENTING PRINCIPLE survives their vicissitudes, and re-appears with undiminished vigour. It is the same undying, though transmigrating spirit, that has successively animated them, which still lives in those, from which the present generation, and the next must expect a supply of ministers, to carry on the work of recalling Christians to the undivided worship of the One True God; and if, as is reasonable to hope, some portion of original imperfection have been left behind, in every mortal vehicle which it has occupied, we have warrant for expecting that they will attain to a longer term than their predecessors. We are, however, far from saying to them, *estote perpetuæ*; the failure of some past applications of the pious wish might seem to have converted it into a phrase of evil omen, and

---

[*] Ariosto's inscription over his own house.

we might be praying for what would be rather an injury than a blessing. We are rather disposed to take leave of this subject by congratulating them, that whatever be their duration they can never survive their usefulness, and that as soon as they become negligent of their work, it will be transferred to abler and more faithful hands.

ART. II.—*The History and Antiquities of Dissenting Churches, &c.*

[Continued from p. 346.]

IN the history of "Turner's Hall, Philpot Lane," we have an amusing account of *Joseph Jacob*, who was brought up a Quaker, but became an Independent minister. He displayed his zeal on behalf of civil liberty in the year 1688, by mounting a horse and going to meet the Prince of Orange in the West of England. He was however no blind admirer of William IH.: he frequently took occasion to animadvert in public upon such of the measures of the government as he considered blameable. He did this in a Lecture which he preached at Mr. Gouge's Meeting-house, near the Three Cranes, Thames Street: the report of his disloyalty reached the House of Commons; and, says Mr. Wilson, "Mr. Shallet, one of Mr. Gouge's people, being then a member of parliament, took up the business at a *Church-meeting*, complained loudly of Mr. Jacob's behaviour, and insisted upon his being dismissed from his lecture at that place, which was complied with."—Mr. Jacob, like most other reformers, assumed no little church-authority: he obliged his congregation to stand during the singing, discarded periwigs, introduced, on the part of the men, whiskers on the upper lip, of which he set the example, and proceeded even to regulate the dress of the women. He forbade the members of his church to attend any other worship than his own, and made it an offence, to be visited with excommunication, for any of them to intermarry with persons not in church-connexion. These singularities were urged to an extreme: had Mr. Jacob been a little more temperate, his sect might have lasted (the spirit of the sect still lives in many different communions that we could name) and his name might have been preserved among the heresiarchs. The inscrip-

tion on his tomb, in Bunhill Fields, is pleasing from its simplicity:

In hopes of a part in the First Resurrection.

To the Memory
Of Mr. JOSEPH JACOB,
An Apostolic Preacher,
Who died the 26th of 4 mo. 1722.
Aged 55.

We learn from the subsequent history of "Turner's Hall," that the practice of singing in public worship was, about this time, introduced amongst the Baptists: but it was an innovation, and in one particular case occasioned a schism, the seceders, who objected to the novelty, claiming to themselves the title of the *Old Church*. How uniform is human nature!

Mr. Wilson is to be considered in a higher rank than that of a compiler, and therefore his readers may justly complain that he has sometimes slavishly copied the language of sermons and pamphlets from which he drew his materials. Who can now endure such quaintnesses as the following, which occur pp. 145 and 147, in the account of two ordinations: " Mr. Wallin *opened the work of the day*, and was *the mouth of the church* upon the occasion:" " they were not in connexion with *any board*. Mr Boeket, one of the deacons, was deputed by the church *to be their mouth*." " Mr. Dewhurst then *closed the work of the day*."

" Intolerance is always the same. Orthodoxy, creeds, and persecution are natural allies.

" In the year 1719, the Dissenting Churches in the West of England, were thrown into a flame, in consequence of some of their ministers having embraced Arianism. This produced a long controversy, which was carried on with great bitterness on both sides. At length the matter being referred to the London ministers, they met together in a synod at Salters' Hall, to consider of advices to be sent to their brethren in the West, with a view of composing the differences. But it so happened that they could not agree among themselves; and, as is generally the case with large bodies, they split into parties and still further widened the breach. It being proposed in this assembly, that, in order to support their orthodox brethren in the West, the ministers present should make a declaration of their own sentiments with regard to the Trinity, by subscribing the first article of the Church of England, and the answers to the fifth and sixth questions in the Assembly's Catechism, the matter was violently opposed, as an infringement of Christian liberty, and they divided into two parties of subscribers and non-subscribers." I. 162, 163.

The decision of the synod was worthy of nonconformists! On dividing, it appeared that there were *for* subscribing articles of faith 53, *against* it 57! This ever-memorable majority stamped an honour upon the cause of Dissent, and have redeemed ecclesiastical assemblies from disgrace. Coldly as Mr. Wilson writes of the triumphant party in this part of his work, he uses, in another place, II. 6—8, the language of warm approbation which becomes the friend of liberty.

Amongst the voters at Salter's Hall were Thomas Reynolds, pastor of the Weigh-house, and James Read, his assistant: Reynolds was in favour of subscription, Read in opposition to it. The vote given by Read caused his orthodoxy to be suspected, and he was persecuted with artful questions; and not giving answers satisfactory to Reynolds and his orthodox party in the church, which was the majority, was at length dismissed. Two of the questions urged by the inquisitors on this occasion deserve to be recorded as a model for such as may in future be desirous of screwing and racking conscience: they were,

"1. Whether a person that pays religions worship to Christ, but at the same time disowns him to be truly and properly God, (that is, in the strictest and strongest sense of the word) be chargeable with downright idolatry? 2. Whether such a one has forfeited his claim to Christian communion?" I. 170.

In this connexion, our historian uses gravely, and without a note of admiration, the phrase "Arian heresy!" Protestant Dissenters ought surely to have learnt by this time the folly of language which implies on the part of the speaker or writer theological infallibility.

The occasional mention of, " Mr. Jollie's church at Sheffield," leads Mr. Wilson (p. 177. *Note*) to name Archbishop Secker, who, in early life was a member of that church, and who afterwards studied for the Dissenting ministry under the learned Mr. Jones, of Tewkesbury. Secker delivered a probationary Sermon in the meeting-house at Bolsover, Derbyshire. And

yet the late Bishop Porteus, in his life of the Archbishop, his patron, asserted that " he never was in communion with the Dissenters!"—The Primate is *convicted* of having been a Presbyterian minister, in " A Collection of Letters and Essays in favour of Public Liberty,"·published in 1774; in 3 vols. duodecimo; but he appears to have purified and prepared himself for the church of England by a course of scepticism and medical study and practice (midwifery?) " The Archbishop had a dissenting education, was designed for the pulpit among that people; but had not so much freedom from doubtings, as to allow him to engage in the service of a public instructor in the Christian religion; and therefore turned his thoughts to the study of physic. Bishop Talbot's arguments reconciled him to the faith of the civil church-establishment, in April, 1721, and he became more and more confirmed in that faith as bermade: his advances in the church, till he reached the See of Canterbury." Collection, &c. III. 34.

One of the most interesting biographical sketches in the History, is that of *Samuel Wilton, D. D.* pastor of the church, formerly Presbyterian, now Independent, at the Weigh-house. Dr. Wilton distinguished himself as an ardent friend and able advocate of religious liberty. He took an active part in the application of the Dissenting ministers to parliament for relief from subscription, and published in 1773 " An Apology for the Renewal of an Application," and in 1774, " A Review of some of the Articles of the Church of England, to which a Subscription is required of Protestant Dissenting Ministers." The latter publication is still read and admired and will never be out of date whilst the articles continue to be imposed as a test of orthodoxy in the parliamentary church. With other eminent faculties of mind, Dr. Wilton possessed a very strong and retentive memory; it was partly from his memory, as well as that of Dr. Furneaux, that Lord Mansfield's celebrated speech, establishing the right of Dissenters to exemption from office in corporations, was published. A good portrait of him ornaments this part of the History.

Dr. Wilton's public character is the more observable, on account of the different part in religious politics which has been taken by his successor, *John Clayton*, whose Sermon on the Birmingham Riots has been preserved from oblivion by the eloquent Answer to it by *Robert Hall*, M. A. the celebrated Baptist minister, then of Cambridge, now of Leicester. Mr. Clayton was educated under the patronage of the late Countess of Huntingdon, and was some time assistant to *"the Rev. Sir Harry Trelawney, who was pastor of an Independent congregation at West Loo, Cornwall."* The reverend Baronet after various changes settled down into a parish priest in the national church. An account of his religious progress is given by Mr. Dyer, in his Life of Robert Robinson, p. 179, &c. It has been said that Sir Harry has not taken his rest in the Church of England.

An opposite course to Sir Harry Trelawney's is described by the historian in the Memoir (I. 205) of *Carolus Maria de Veil, D. D.* who was born at Metz, in Lorrain, of Jewish parents, and educated in that religion, but embraced Christianity and became first a Roman Catholic, and held distinguished stations in that church, next a Protestant, and obtained orders in the Church of England, and lastly a Dissenter of the Baptist denomination. He latterly practised physic for a maintenance, and being poor, received an annual stipend from his Baptist brethren. He published several learned works, exhibiting his opinions in the several stages of his belief. A brother of his, *Lewis De Compeigne De Veil*, also became a Christian, and was interpreter of the oriental languages to the king of France, but turning Protestant, came over to England.

Mr. Wilson is not likely to rise to fame, as a translator. He gives, for instance, the English of a Latin epitaph on the monument of Mr. Nathaniel Mather, in Bunhill Fields, and the phrase *"Laude dignissimus"* is thus *done into English,* " *meritorious of the highest praise !"* I. 233, 234.

The character of *Robert Bragge*, as a preacher, may be a useful admonition to some of Mr. Wilson's readers :—

" It was his custom, as we are informed, to make the most of his subject, by preaching several discourses upon the same text.

There is a story related of him, but for the truth of which we cannot be responsible, that, in one part of his life, he was employed no less than four months in developing the mysteries of Joseph's coat, from Genesis xxxvii. 8. *And he made him a coat of many colours.* In allusion to this circumstance, Mr. Bragge was thus characterized, in some lines descriptive of the Dissenting ministers, at that period :

" Eternal Bragge, in never-ending strains,
Unfolds the wonders Joseph's coat contains ;
Of ev'ry hue describes a different cause,
And from each patch a solemn myst'ry draws." I. 247.

The decline of Presbyterian congregations is commonly imputed to the Unitarian doctrine, though, in fact, no peculiar doctrine has been advanced in the greater part of them : but to what cause is the decline of the old Independent "Evangelical" churches to be attributed ? That decline in London, at least, is unquestionable. *Ex uno disce omnes.*

" This church (Bury Street, St. Mary Axe) is remarkable for the number of ejected ministers who have presided over it. We have an account of no less than eight of those worthies, in this connexion. *There has been a considerable variation in the state of the Society for the last century and upwards.* Prior to Dr. Chauncey, it appears to have been in a flourishing condition ; but in his time it declined. There was a great revival under Dr. Watts, who had a large and respectable audience. During the latter part of Dr. Savage's time the interest was in a very low state. Though a learned man and a judicious *as well as Evangelical* preacher, *his labours were not attended with* that *success* which frequently accompanies meaner abilities. At the settlement of the present pastor, it was expected that his popular talents would have a considerable influence in reviving the congregation ; *but they have failed of that desired effect."* I. 253.

There are particular circumstances which more than any general causes affect the condition of Dissenting congregations : one thing is plain, that the ready way to success is to consult the taste of the public, which is ever varying. There is now a love of novelty, variety, life and bustle in religion. Methodism did not create this taste, it was a happy concurrence with it : regular preaching and church order will not now satisfy the bulk of Christian hearers and communicants. Hence Independent churches, that have not been cast anew in the methodistic mould, have in very few instances kept up their reputation and numbers.

Mr. Wilson takes a great liberty in coining a word, p. 262, viz. *Laudensian,* by which he means *belonging to* (Archbishop) *Laud.* The adjective warranted by usage is *Laudean;* although a circumlocution would be better than even this term.

In the memoir of *Dr. John Owen,* the historian writes *con amore.* Owen was a great man, and we are disposed to make but few abatements in Mr. Wilson's panegyric. It is indeed honourable to this patriarch of Independency, that he was one of the first advocates in England of liberty of conscience, on the right principle. Bishop Jeremy Taylor went before him in this noble course: Richard Baxter, with all his boldness, dared not follow these eminent leaders of the public mind. There was a remarkable consistency in Dr. Owen's nonconformity: he scrupled to give the popish title of *saint* to the apostles, and he shewed a praiseworthy indifference to the usual clerical titles.

" Upon a certain high-churchman refusing to style him *Reverend,* he wrote thus : ' For the title of *Reverend,* I do give him notice that I have very little valued it, ever since I have considered the saying of Luther, *Nunquam periclitatur Religio nisi inter Reverendissimos.* (Religion never was endangered except among the most Reverends.) So that he may, as to me, forbear it for the future, and call me, as the Quakers do, and it shall suffice. And, for that of *Doctor,* it was conferred on me by the University, in my absence, and against my consent, as they have expressed it under their public seal : nor doth any thing but gratitude and respect unto them, make me once own it ; and freed from that obligation, I should never use it more : nor did I use it, until some were offended with me and blamed me for my neglect.' *Defence of Review of Schism, prefixed to Mr. Cotton's Defence against Cawdry,* pp. 97, 98." I. 265. Note.

Dr. Watts's father is said (I. 292) to have been " *a Dissenter from principle.*" The meaning of the phrase is evident, but it has been so often turned into a joke that we doubt the propriety of repeating it ; and there are so few temptations of a worldly kind to nonconformity, that it is for the most part needless to say that a Dissenter is not swayed in his religious choice by a love of ease or lucre or honour.

The historian does not conceal Dr. Watts's heresy on the subject of the Trinity, but he is careful to represent it as less alarming than has sometimes been imagined. Of the " solemn address" he says nothing.[*] The Doctor is commended by this biographer for keeping reason out of the province of religion : but had he suffered his own excellent understanding to exercise itself on points of faith, could he have fallen into the strange notion that non-elect infants, dying in infancy, sink into *annihilation?* (I. 308.)

Art. III—*Substance of a Speech delivered in the Court of Common Council, on a Motion to address his Royal Highness the Prince Regent to accede to the late Treaty concluded between the Emperors of Russia and of Austria and the King of Prussia.* By Mr. Favell. To which are added other Papers on the Subject of Peace. 8vo. pp. 54. Conder. 1816.

MR. FAVELL is well known in London as the zealous and consistent friend of civil and religious liberty and of peace. In the evening of life, and apparently meditating a retreat from public business, he publishes this speech as a testimony in behalf of the principles which, with various success, he has avowed and defended for forty years. He delivers a flattering opinion of his old associates " the Reformers of England—a class of high spirited and independent men, who have maintained the cause of freedom, and have dared be honest in the worst of times." We cordially wish the public attention may be drawn to Mr. Favell's sensible and manly plea for Peace and Reform.

---

[*] The question of Dr. Watts's last religious opinions is largely discussed in our eighth volume.

POETRY.

EPITAPH,

In a Church-yard in Wales, over the Grave of a faithful Servant.

In memory of Mrs. Mary Carryl, deceased 22nd November, 1809. This monument was erected by Elenor Butler and Sarah Ponsonby, of Plasnewydd, in this parish.

Released from earth, and all its transient woes,
She, whose remains beneath this stone repose,
Stedfast in faith resign'd her parting breath,
Look'd up with Christian joy, and smil'd in death.
Patient, industrious, faithful, gen'rous, kind,
Her conduct left the proudest far behind;
Her virtues dignified her humble birth,
And rais'd her mind above this sordid earth.
Attachment, sacred bond of grateful breasts,
Extinguish'd but with life, this tomb attests,
Rear'd by two friends who will her loss bemoan,
Till, with her ashes, here, shall rest their own.

CONCLUDING SONNET.
By Sir Philip Sidney.

Splendidis longum valedico nugis.
To splendid trifles, now, a long farewell.

Leave me, O Love! which reachest but to dust;
And thou, my mind, aspire to higher things:
Grow rich in that which never taketh rust;
Whatever fades, but fading pleasure brings.
Draw in thy beams, and humble all thy might
To that sweet yoke, where lasting freedoms be,
Which breaks the clouds, and opens forth the light,
That doth both shine, and give us sight to see.
O take fast hold! let that light be thy guide,
In this small course, which birth draws out to death;
And think how ill-becometh him to slide,
Who seeketh heav'n, and comes of heav'nly breath.
Then farewell, world, thy uttermost I see,
Eternal love, maintain thy love in me.

From the Italian of Frugoni.

And shall we turn a deaf and careless ear,
To Thy dread voice, OMNIPOTENT,—
nor bow
Our daring foreheads to the dust, when
Thou
Hurlest Thy thunders round the trembling sphere?
What!—shall we grasp our fatal pleasures dear,
Till that dark, des'late hour of helpless woe,
When the pale spectre, death, shall strike the blow,
And we the victims?—Then appalling fear
Shall scatter dew drops on our brow;—a blast,
A chilling blast, shall freeze our veins,—and chase
The spirit of life that trembles on our tongue;
Now, now rebel, presumptuous ones,—now face
The frownings of THE TERRIBLE;——'tis past!
O fearful, frightful hour, forgot too long!

A.

THE SOLDIER.

[*From the Cabinet,* 1795.]

Who hath beene a soldier, O,
Who hath soughten glorie?
Who hath thronged with archers bolde,
Till his lockes were hoarie?

I have beene a soldier, O,
Seekinge ever glorie,
Facinge death, with my archers bolde,
Till my lockes be hoarie.

My bodie is well seam'd with scarrs,
Though ne'er a limbe be wantinge;
But let me not the braggart seeme,
True valour is not vauntinge.

Good Lorde! and though thy haires be gray,
And thy bodie roughe and seamed,
Hath thy greene manhood dedes achieved,
To make thine age esteemed.

Tygres that doe thirste for blood,
Through forestes wilde are raginge;
Ah me! that man, like tygre gaunte
With man should warre be waginge.

Grieslie demons sprong from hell,
Fraught with accursed vengeance,
Lead on grimm discorde through the world,
And hurle their slaughtering engines.

Townes they sack, and realmes despoyle,
　Maidens are defloured,　.
Babes doe bleed and age doth groane
　Contemned and orepowred.

Swaines that fed their sev'ral flocke,
　Nor thought of other harminge,
Now foot to foot and hand to hand,
　In breache or scarpe are storminge.

What the angrie surrde did leave,
　Sharpe battel axe, or bowmen,
Fire and wastinge must complete,
　For warre is ever foaming.

Where shall hie th' affrayed dame,
　With infante offspring clinginge?
Not farre off is the fatal storme,
　Eche gale its terrours bringinge.

Tell me now thou gallante soldier
　Now thy lockes with age be hoarie,
Can'st thou praise thy wilde carriere,
　Can'st thou call thy madnesse gloric?

To upholde some lordlinge proud,
　Or king with curst ambition,
What foule murders hast thou done!
　Sweet Christ, give thee contrition.

Amen, amen, thou reverent priest,
　Thy counsaile is most holie;
Thy wordes do teache repentaute age,
　To curse its manhood's follie.

But doubly curst be kinglie pride,
　Makinge erthe one charnel,
Millions of masses dailie sayde
　Stay not hell's paynes eternal.

INTELLIGENCE.

DOMESTIC.

Religious.

Manchester College, York.

On Tuesday, Wednesday, and Thursday, the 25th, 26th, and 27th June, the Trustees held their Annual Examination of the Students educated in this Seminary; (present, Messrs. Broadhurst, Crompton, Falla, Falla, jun. Fletcher, Jevons, Kershaw, Leo, Malkin, Martin, Needham, S. R. Philips, Sanderson, Shore, jun. Stanger, Stanger, jun. Thomson, M. D. and G. W. Wood, *Treasurer,* and the Rev. Messrs. Ashton, Astley, Beattie, Heineken, Hutton, Jevons, Johnstone, Jones, G. Kenrick, Kentish, Lamport, Robberds, *Secretary,* H. Turner, P. Wright, Wallace, and Turner, *Visitor,*) on Tuesday the junior Greek and Hebrew Classes, the senior Mathematics and Modern History Classes, and on Wednesday the senior Hebrew, junior Latin, and second Mathematical Classes; after which Mr. Samuel Wood read an Oration on the Origin of Evil, and Mr. James Taylor on the Causes which have led to the Differences between the English and Continental Constitutions. The Examination then proceeded of the second Greek and Latin, junior Mathematics, Ancient History, Evidences, and Natural Philosophy, and concluded for that day with a Discourse by Mr. Haslam, to shew that the Apostles were not Enthusiasts, and an Oration by Mr. John Tayler, on the reciprocal Influence of Taste and Morals. On Thursday, Messrs.

Mardon, Morris and Cannon, went through a long critical examination on the New Testament, with a particular view to shew the Use of the Septuagint Version of the Old Testament, and the Syriac of the New, in the illustration of the latter, and also to exemplify the application of Paley's argument for the genuineness of the books, by a comparison of the historical and epistolary writings. They were afterwards examined in Church History, and the various controversies which had arisen in the several ages, with the principal writers who had distinguished themselves on both sides down to the present time. The classes in Logic and Metaphysics, and in Ethics and Political Economy, were then examined, as was also the senior Latin Class; after which Mr. John Taylor read a Latin Oration on the Poetical Merits of Lucretius; Mr. John Wellbeloved on the Hope of a Future Life; and Mr. Fletcher on the Early Periods of the Greek and Roman History; Mr. Cannon an English Oration on the Influence of Mental Cultivation in producing good Morals in the Individual; and Mr. Morris a Sermon on John ix. 4. The remaining Classes examined were those in Hebrew Poetry, the Belles Lettres, and the higher Greek Classics and the Greek Metres; after which Mr. Stratton read a Discourse on the respective Influences of Civilized and Savage Life on Virtue and Happiness, and Mr. Mardon a Sermon on the Love of Truth, from 2 Thess. ii. 10.

It ought to be observed, that in these

examinations, the students are not previously apprized of any question that will be asked them, or of any passage (which they will be called upon to explain, and that their orations and discourses are uncorrected, and indeed unseen by any of their tutors. Considering this, and the number of young students who were now for the first time to appear before so numerous and respectable an assembly, the result was highly satisfactory.

The examination was closed by an address from the Visitor, which, at the request of the Trustees present, is sent for insertion in the Monthly Repository. A part of it was also ordered to be separately printed, and a copy given to each student on his admission.

"Gentlemen,

"In commencing my annual address to you at the close of this gratifying exercise, I am naturally led to express the regret which I am sure we all feel at the absence of our late excellent and venerable president, so distinguished by his uniform attachment, through the course of a long life, to the promotion of virtue, truth, and science, and to the cause of religious and civil liberty; by his steady friendship and substantial countenance of some of its most eminent confessors; and by his munificent patronage of the places of public education devoted to it, particularly of this Institution; where we have seen his cheerful and encouraging manners add a grace to the dignity and excellence of his character, and a sanction to his judicious suggestions; and, while they have commanded the esteem and respect of those of maturest age, engage the love and admiration of the young. I am sure I shall express the general wish that this may be only an occasional absence; and that though he has ceased to hold the connexion with us which it was every where our pride to avow, he will still continue to adorn our annual meetings, so long as it shall please a kind Providence to continue to him the blessing of a healthy and vigorous old age, the consequence and reward of a well spent life.

"It has been usual, in taking leave of our young friends, at the close of each session, to address a few words to those, with whom our academical connexion is concluded. To both our friends who are going out to the exer-

cise of the Christian ministry we wish the best success,—the success of eminent usefulness in the promotion of truth and practical religion, the native union of which one of them has just so well described. I hope that neither of them needs to be reminded by me, that the eyes of the world will be upon them—of many with no favourable intentions; and that for whatever they do or say not only themselves, but the cause which they serve, will be made answerable. Great prudence and circumspection, therefore, will be requisite, to avoid every reasonable, and often even unreasonable cause of offence. One of our young friends will have the difficult task of maintaining high credit already obtained by a former associate in the studies of this place, in one of the most eminent seats of learning in the sister-kingdom. The charge is a weighty and important, and in some respects an awful one: for it will subject the man who holds it to the risk of dishonour as well as honour, of evil as well as of good report. It will, of course, be an object of his constant study, that the former be in no case deservedly incurred.—But into whatever situation either of our friends may be thrown, they will both of them, I hope, be careful to recollect, that great self-attention and caution will be necessary, in the common intercourses of life, as well as in their preparations for, and conduct in the pulpit, to insure their respectability and usefulness; and the utmost care to avoid giving any handle to those who will be ready enough to take it, of perverting ill-considered expressions to the disadvantage of the speaker and his cause; of taking offence at petulant or provoking words; and setting themselves in decided hostility to whatever may border on abuse or violence.—The sun will prevail to strip off the cloak of prejudice, much sooner than the north wind.

"I hope Mr. Stratton will believe he has our best wishes in the further progress of his studies, and in the course of his future life. He will excuse my reminding him, for I am persuaded he needs only to be reminded—the reflection must often have occurred to himself, while composing the excellent Essay which we have just heard of the obligation which lies upon those whom Providence has placed in easy circumstances, to so much superior exertion; in order that they may discharge the various additional duties which enlarged opportunities of usefulness to the world impose upon every man in proportion to his rank in life:—of course I need not remind him of the necessity in this precious period of life, of a proportionally diligent preparation, for he knows that whatever we have is not our own, but lent; and we must pay an interest proportioned to the loan.

"To our younger friends who are to return to us, especially to the lay-students, I would also beg leave to address a few words.

"As your connexion with this Institution is comparatively recent, and I have never had the pleasure of meeting you here before, perhaps it may not be uninteresting to explain to you, gentlemen, in a few words, the nature and intention of my office of Visitor, which I have now had the honour to hold for the last nine years. Such an officer was appointed, at the suggestion of my venerable predecessor in it,* first, as a coadjutor to the Tutors in the enforcement of discipline and the correction of abuses, and secondly, as an assessor to the President in this annual business of examination and advice. The former branch of my office as has been my frequent boast, on recommending this Institution to my friends, has, happily, been a sinecure: and that it may continue so, I would take advantage of my privilege in my latter capacity, to offer you a few words of advice.

"What I have said to Mr. Stratton, on the necessity of exertion in order to future respectability and usefulness, you may, each, with great propriety, apply to yourselves.

"But as you are, in general, so much younger, I would urge the same advice in a somewhat different way; by suggesting to you a few considerations more particularly applicable to your age and late situation.

"I have no doubt that you have been frequently urged to diligence in your respective studies at school, by the several judicious and learned persons who have conducted your school-education.

"But this is a different place from

school; where you are necessarily placed, in several respects, under a different discipline: and it is my duty, as well as that of your parents and tutors, to represent it to you in such a light as may induce you not to abuse it.

"At school, your attention was chiefly confined to words, to abstract numbers, and to other things, the ultimate advantage, or even intention of which you, often, did not perceive. You had therefore compulsatory tasks assigned you; and you performed the tasks very much upon the principle of compulsion.

"But here you pursue a course of study, much of which, at least, yourselves may clearly perceive, not only to be a useful application of what you have already learned, but also to be applicable to the purposes of future life, by qualifying you for important offices in society. I trust, therefore, you will see the necessity of laying aside the principle of task-work; and that you will never set yourselves to the preparation of the exercises prescribed to you by your tutors, or to the perusal of the authors to whom they refer you, merely that you may get your work passably done, or qualify yourselves for answering questions at lecture, so as just to escape your tutor's censure; but that you will rather consider yourselves as entered on a voluntary course of studies which it is your determination to pursue with alacrity, and constantly keep in mind that though, in the prosecution of this purpose, you avail yourselves of the assistance and direction of your tutors, as to the proper sources of information, yet it must depend upon yourselves what advantage you make of them. And give me leave to assure you from pretty long experience and observation, that according as you improve or neglect present advantages, in the same proportion you will look back, in future life, on the period of education with satisfaction or regret.

"There is another difference between the scholastic and academical periods of life, concerning which it is necessary for me to drop a hint, and I hope I shall do it in such a way as to avoid giving offence, either to you, or to any of your parents or friends; but rather so as to deserve, and I hope obtain, your thanks.

"At school you were under the entire control and management of those

---

* The Rev. William Wood, of Leeds.

entrusted with your education: whereas here, instead of being treated as children, and having every thing managed for you, you make a step, as it were, into the world, and are, to a certain degree, entrusted with the management of yourselves: your friends in this way making the experiment, how far you are qualified for being afterwards left more entirely to your own direction. On the use which you make of this privilege will depend its continuance and further extension. If abused, it may be necessary for your parents or other friends to recal it; particularly with regard to the article of expense.

"To prevent the possibility of one particular source of abuse, in this respect, the trustees have determined to follow in future the salutary rule of both our Universities, viz. to prohibit all credit with the trades-people of the city, unless with the previous knowledge and consent of the tutors. They think it proper that both you and your friends should be explicitly informed of this; and they assure themselves that it will meet with their cordial approbation and concurrence.

"At the same time your tutors desire me expressly to state to this assembly, that, while these arrangements are adopted by the trustees as a necessary measure of precaution, there has been nothing morally wrong among you that they have observed or even suspect: on the contrary, they cheerfully bear testimony to your general good behaviour. And we trust that you will all, my young friends, in a succeeding session, join to the natural vivacity of youth, the thought and manliness of those who feel that they are approaching the period of active usefulness; and exemplify in all your future conduct the truth of the proposition so well supported by your fellow-student, "that mental cultivation has a powerful influence to promote good morals" in every individual among you.

"For myself, it is always much more agreeable to me to commend than to censure, to encourage than to caution or admonish. And I assure you, that when I consider the great number of you who have now for the first time been thus publicly examined, I have been extremely pleased with the result of this week's business. I

only wish we could have prevailed with some of you to speak more distinctly; and I am sorry to hear from your tutors a complaint of a too general inattention, through the whole of the session, to the article of elocution. The importance of a distinct and audible utterance to persons of every rank is so obvious, that I should have expected it would be an object of prime ambition, and that you would have endeavoured to avail yourselves of the judicious directions which I had the honour to convey to you last year from my friend Dr. Thomson; and in this case I should have had better encouragement to add to them a useful observation lately pointed out to me, by another friend, in Mr. Jones's Life of Bishop Horne. The observation is this; "Every speaker wishes to be understood as well as heard; but many are deficient in this respect for want of a distinct articulation, which might easily be acquired if they would attend to a simple rule, without the observance of which no man's delivery can be perfect. It is well known that a piece of writing may be understood if all the vowels be omitted; but if the vowels are set down, and the consonants are omitted, nothing can be made of it. It is the same in speaking as in writing; the vowels make a noise, but they discriminate nothing. Many speakers think that they are heard if they bellow them out; and so they are, but they are not understood; because the discrimination of words depends upon a distinct articulation of their consonants; for want of considering which many speakers spend their breath to little effect. The late Bishop of Peterborough, Dr. Hinchliffe, was one of the most pleasing preachers of his time. His melodious voice was the gift of nature, and he spoke with the accent of a man of sense; but it was remarkable, and to those who did not know the cause, mysterious, that there was not a corner of the church in which he could not be heard distinctly. By watching him attentively I perceived that it was an invariable rule with him to do full justice to every consonant, knowing that the vowels would be sure to speak for themselves. And thus he became the surest and clearest of speakers; his enunciation was perfect, and never disappointed the audience. And in this respect most speakers have it in their power to follow him." (*Preface to Horne's Works, p.* 143.)

"The gentlemen who have most eminently distinguished themselves by their diligence, regularity, and proficiency, are Mr. John Tayler of Nottingham, and Mr. Samuel Wood of Liverpool: and I am particularly desired to state, that Mr. Tayler's name is mentioned first only as he is already in possession of the first place by his excellent conduct during the last session; in the present, the merits of these two gentlemen have been so nearly equal, that it is impossible to assign the absolute preference to either. The prize for elocution, also, is awarded to Mr. John Tayler.—In future years this prize will be given, as formerly, for improvement in elocution during the session.

"Before I conclude, I am directed to state, that the trustees, at their last annual meeting in Manchester, agreed to propose an annual prize of five guineas in books, to those students in divinity who shall have completed a course of education in this college during the three former years, for the best essay on some subject connected with theology, to be annually prescribed by the tutors. The intention of this proposal is to encourage the continuance of a habit of theological study among the young ministers who have here received their education. The subject proposed for the first prize was "the Origin and Design of Sacrifices, and the Influence of the Jewish Institutions relating to Sacrifices on the Language of the New Testament." The persons intrusted with the adjudication of this prize have awarded it to an essay, the note bearing a motto corresponding to which is found to be the production of Mr. Henry Turner, who will believe that I have peculiar pleasure in declaring his name on such an occasion."—

The examination was then closed with a short devotional exercise, after which the company adjourned to dinner at Etridge's, where much interesting conversation took place on the business of the three days. Several other interesting topics prevented much being said on the subject of Union, proposed at the last annual meeting; but a sort of general report was made by the committee then appointed, who undertook to draw up a set of queries with the view of ascertaining certain facts illustrative of the present state of their societies in the North of England, in the hope that it a "statistical account" of this sort can be accomplished for one district, it may easily be afterwards extended.

The next session opens on Thursday the nineteenth of September, on which day it is extremely desirable that all the students should be at York, in order that the rooms may be chosen, and all the arrangements made, previous to the commencement of actual business on the Monday following.

V. F.

New Chapel at Thorne.

The New Unitarian Chapel at Thorne, in Yorkshire, was opened on the 28th ult. The Sermon in the morning was preached by the Rev. Dr. Philipps, of Sheffield, from 1 Cor. xi. 19. "There must also be heresies among you, that they who are approved may be made manifest." That in the evening by the Rev. William Turner of Newcastle, from Psalm xxvi. 8. "Lord, I have loved the habitation of thy house, and the place where thine honour dwelleth." The ministers engaged, besides the preachers, were the Rev. Mr. Astley of Halifax, Rev. Mr. Hutton of Nottingham, Rev. Mr. Heineken of Gainsborough, Rev Mr. Wright of Stannington, near Sheffield, Rev. Mr. Turner of Bradford, and the Rev. Mr. Kenrick of Hull: the congregations, particularly in the evening, were very large and attentive. We understand that Dr. Philipps's Sermon will be published, at the request of the hearers, and is now in the press.

At half past 2 o'clock about 50 gentlemen sat down to an economical dinner at the Royal Oak Inn. Dr. Thomson, the chairman, improved this friendly cheerful meeting into an occasion of giving the newly-formed church much excellent advice, on the necessity of church-order, on their conduct towards their fellow-members in their respective families, towards their fellow-townsmen of a different persuasion, and towards the world at large. Many interesting speeches were made by other persons, particularly by Francis Moat, "the patriarch of Thorne," who gave a circumstantial detail of the steps by which they had been led to the knowledge of the truth. The chairman proposed that Mr. Turner should examine the accounts and report thereon, when the certificate, of which a copy follows, was drawn up and signed:—

We, whose names are underwritten, being ministers and *others* present at the opening of the New Unitarian Chapel at Thorne, having examined the account of monies contributed by the members of the society there, and hitherto subscribed by others, and also the sums expended by them in the building of their plain, but neat and convenient place of worship, beg leave to submit to the Unitarian public the following general statement, and respectfully to recommend the case of their friends at Thorne to public notice; not doubting that the debt at present upon the chapel will in no long time be liquidated.

	l.	*s.*	*d.*
Subscriptions in the Neighbourhood of Thorne,	91	11	6
Other Subscriptions received or promised,	86	1	0
	177	11	6
Costs of the Unitarian Chapel at Thorne,	408	1	3
To be provided for	230	9	9

Nathaniel Philipps, *Sheffield;* W. Turner, *Newcastle;* N. T. Heineken, *Gainsbro';* P. Wright, *Sheffield;* Richard Astley, *Halifax;* John Beattie, *Elland;* Henry Turner, *Bradford;* Joseph Hutton, *Nottingham;* George Kenrick, *Hull;* F. W. Everet, *Sheffield;* W. Jevons, *Altringham;* John Thomson, *Halifax;* Samuel Martin, *Hull;* John Fox, *Sheffield.*

Subscriptions received at Thorne, June 28th, 1816.

Rev. W. Turner, Newcastle,	1	1	0
—— George Harris,	1	1	0
—— Benjamin Marden,	0	10	6
—— John Kentish,	1	1	0
—— N. T. Heineken,	1	1	0
Samuel Martin, Esq.	1	1	0

Association of the West Riding of Yorkshire.

The Meeting of the *Dissenting Ministers of the West Riding of Yorkshire,* as they have been wont to term themselves, took place at Halifax the 6th of this month. This is a very ancient association, and has undergone in the course of its progress, considerable fluctuations in point of number,

and great changes in the religious views of its members. It has never altered its name, and perhaps on some accounts it may be better that it should preserve its original appellation. That appellation, however, it must be confessed, but very imperfectly delineates the real complexion of the meeting, the members of which are nearly all professedly Unitarians, as the term has been explained by Dr. Priestley. The meeting appeared to afford peculiar satisfaction to every one present: the cause of truth and religion was the predominant impression upon the mind, and it was accompanied with every kind and good-tempered feeling of the heart. If there are times when it may be said that "righteousness and peace have kissed each other," the present would seem to have been an occasion when a salutation of a similar nature had taken place; for piety, friendliness, and cheerfulness, appeared to have met in very pleasing union.

The religious services of the day were conducted by the Rev. Jeremiah Donoughue, of Lidget, and the Rev. John Gooch Robberds, of Manchester, the former taking the devotional part, the latter the Sermon. The words of the discourse were from John xiv. 15. "If ye love me, keep my commandments." Nothing could be more interesting, impressive, and improving than this discourse: the style of its composition was simple, elegant, manly, and forcible; the manner of the preacher solemn and impressive. It has sometimes been complained, that piety seems not in very close union with Unitarianism: the Sermon of Mr. Robberds would sufficiently redeem the cause from this reproach: never did there appear a more happy and engaging alliance. To enlarge is to endanger an encroachment upon delicacy of feeling in that quarter where it is our last wish to give offence: where the eulogium is most due, it is sometimes the least desired, and that we are assured is the case in the present instance. A violation, however, would be done to our feelings not to advert to one idea upon which the preacher very beautifully enlarged—the decisive advantage which the Unitarian view of the character of Christ possessed over every other system for the fulfilment of that love which is considered by all as due to the blessed Saviour. Every other system distracted in some degree. the feeling of regard. Calvinism utterly confounded the whole thing, or if not that, it did worse, for whatever of love it conferred upon Christ, it necessarily stole from the Father. Two of the persons of the triune Godhead, the Father and Son, were ever placed in opposite scales, and as the one rose the other inevitably fell. It was in contemplating a being who in every respect was made like unto his brethren, who was tempted as those brethren are, yet without sin, who was familiar with the same emotions of the heart, felt a similar influence from the objects of life, was as alive to scenes of pleasure, and as sensible to those of suffering, yet, throughout the whole, was perfectly pure, resigned, and firm, that we could both understand and feel the principle of affection that was due to the Saviour of men: beholding him "a man of sorrows and acquainted with grief," yet "made perfect through suffering," we contemplate a definite and engaging object of regard—we understand the nature of the sacrifice, what it must have cost, and how to value it, and prompt do we find ourselves ready to confess with an apostle, greater love hath no man than this, that a man lay down his life for his friends.

There was another idea most happily adverted to by the preacher in connexion with his subject, not indeed as a matter of certain belief, but of pleasing probability, viz. that the blessed Jesus might be still present, though invisible, with his churches, and might he at that time a witness to their expressions of regard, and their earnest wish to shew their love agreeably to the test he had prescribed, by keeping his commandments. The very mention of the circumstance seemed at once to warm the heart, to spread a more than common sanctity over the place, to impart to the countenance of the speaker, and of many others, that animated irradiation which intimates an almost actual vision of the revered personage the mind was contemplating. These and similar thoughts were brought forward upon the subject, and rendered the whole discourse a most interesting service. We have to regret that we do not recollect the words of the preacher, and therefore can only very imperfectly convey those sentiments,

which, being beautifully clothed, and solemnly and earnestly delivered, very deeply affected the audience.

At the close of the service, the business of the *Tract Society* lately established in the West Riding of Yorkshire came to be considered, and the Rev. T. Jervis, of Leeds, being called to the chair, the Secretary to the Society (the Rev. H. Turner, of Bradford) proceeded to read the first Annual Report (and stated the following particulars) which gave a very encouraging account of the progress of this Society, during the short period that had elapsed since it was first instituted. It was stated that at the last annual meeting of the association, &c. held at Leeds, June 8th, 1815, it had been resolved to institute a Society for the Distribution of Religious Tracts, in the congregations of the West Riding, and that at a subsequent meeting at Elland in September, (See M. Repos. Sept. 1815) the Rules of the Society had been agreed upon, and ordered to be printed: since that time printed copies of the Rules and Catalogues had been widely circulated, and that local Tract Societies had been formed in the following places; York, Leeds, Wakefield, Bradford, Halifax, Elland, and Lidgate. The Secretaries appointed in those places had communicated with the Secretary to the Tract Society, under whose care the Depository of Tracts was placed, and had reported the number of subscribers, and the amount of donations, and the following is an abstract of the affairs of the Tract Society. The rate of subscription was fixed at a penny a week, or 4s. 4d. a year: the number of subscribers reported from the different local societies 330: the total amount of donations £26. 5s. 6d. the total number of the Tracts sold from the Depository 1243. Most encouraging accounts had been received from various quarters, of the acceptableness of the institution, and of the good which it had done, and was likely to do. It has been regarded as an acceptable opportunity of supplying a deficiency which had been long felt in our Societies, of the means of obtaining a more general and exact idea of the grounds and principles of rational theology. And from the variety of useful works of a strictly practical nature, which it affords the opportunity of procuring, it will doubtless be the means, under the blessing of God, of a more general diffusion of the spirit and practice of the Christian life. But truth and virtue are natural, though not inseparable companions, and never thrive so much as when they are cultivated together. This is what it has been our endeavour to connect, in the formation of this Society, and it is hoped that it is one of those institutions, of which there are so many in the present day, highly tending to the moral and religious improvement of mankind.

The report was ordered to be printed, additions to the catalogue proposed, &c.

On this occasion, certain speeches were made, particularly one by Dr. Thomson, of Halifax, to which we are truly sorry it is not in our power to do justice. One particular point which the Doctor dwelt upon should certainly be noticed, viz. that the Tract Society had fully redeemed its pledge. Its catalogue of books, though in some respects not all that could be wished, arising from circumstances that could not be avoided, was yet of a nature to do ample justice to every promise it had made.

It possessed those Tracts it is true which gave a very clear view of Unitarian sentiments; and this, from the nature of the Societies which had joined together, might be expected to be the case; but it also possessed those which were separate from any doctrinal tenets, and which were purely of a practical nature, while it was open to any recommendation of Tracts, of other views, which its members might bring forward. In a word, every applicant might be accommodated agreeably to his wishes. The Doctor intermingled with the subject of discussion many interesting thoughts. Contemplating the progress of truth, as it had advanced in the North, he glanced his imagination back to the time of Wickliffe, that day-star of reformation, who, he believed, was born in the county of York. A Priestley, too, was born not far distant from the spot where his friends were then meeting. This reformist would become a yet brighter star. He was hourly gaining the ascendant with an increasing lustre. The mists of ignorance and error were gradually departing, and permitting the pure light of the gospel to be seen and felt. The Tract Society

was acting in the same cause. Here the speaker could not but contemplate with satisfaction the idea that he had been the first promoter of this Institution. No father could view the success of his child with more anxiety. He breathed the wish that if his name were destined to be hereafter repeated, it might be in connexion with the West Riding Tract Society. May it be that the latest posterity shall own the parent and the offspring! The name of Thomson is worthy of the purest cause of benevolence and truth that can be associated with it. The Doctor also took up in a peculiarly interesting manner the idea which the preacher had advanced of the possible presence, though invisible to mortal eye, of the blessed Jesus, and under that impression begged to call to mind the nearly last injunction of their master to his disciples, "Feed my sheep. Feed my lambs," and again "Feed my sheep," a command so reiterated yet discriminating, that it would seem to indicate that provision should be made in the Christian church, both for the mature and the young. In this point of view, the Tract Society very strikingly met the injunction, and the blessed Jesus might be now supposed to be casting his smile upon it.

After the business of the Tract Society was over, an adjournment took place to the Talbot Inn, where a dinner was provided for the occasion, to which 68 gentlemen sat down—24 ministers and 44 lay brethren. After dinner, many toasts congenial with the objects of the day were given by the Chairman, the Rev. R. Astley, which produced very animated speeches. Accounts were imparted of the progress of Unitarianism in various places, particularly in Scotland, by the Secretary to the General Association of the North, in Rossendale, Thorne, Selby and Huddersfield, by the different ministers, whose labours in these places had been pleasingly blessed. If, in the ardour of feeling, a more sanguine colouring might be occasionally imparted, than the stubborn and slow progress of change may at present justify, still that much is doing is beyond a question. After every deduction the most suspicious and sober-minded calculation can exact, there is sufficient cause for congratulation, and for rejoicing in the assurance that the great doctrine of the Divine Unity is gradually advancing, till at length it shall be the one Universal Faith. This at least is the polar star of our creed, that to which we believe the great lawgiver of the Jews pointed, and to which the founder of the Christian faith as clearly pointed. And we have no doubt that although, like the polar star of the natural firmament, it may at present be but dimly seen by some Christians, yet that ere long it shall be as clearly viewed as a star of the first magnitude in the brightest night, and prove, in connexion with those pleasing hopes of the gospel to which it is attached, a safe guide to all who are sailing the ocean of life, to the blissful shores of eternity.

Wakefield.   T. J.

Kent and Sussex Unitarian Association.

The fifth Anniversary of the Kent and Sussex Unitarian Association, was held at Maidstone, on Wednesday the 10th instant, when it is but justice to Mr. Aspland to observe that his truly excellent discourse excited a very lively interest in the minds of his auditory, and that it is sincerely hoped that he will yield to the warm expression of their wishes in favour of its publication, and thus enable them to derive the full benefit from his generous labours, by its extensive distribution. The service commenced with an appropriate prayer by Mr. Harris; while the principal part of the devotions, by Mr. Holden, presented a beautiful delineation of the universal beneficence and tender mercies of our heavenly Father, with a most fervent expression of gratitude and obedience. The annual report of the proceedings of the Committee, which has been appointed to superintend the distribution of Tracts, and to direct their attention to whatever relates to the general interests of our associated body, was read at the close of the service, and was followed by the reports and communications from the several congregations, some of which have chosen committees from their respective subscribers, denominated District Committees, which maintain a correspondence with the general Committee, through their Secretaries. Nearly 2000 small Tracts have been distributed during the last year; upwards of 1000 of which consist of practical publications, by the Christian Tract Society in Lon-

don, and the remainder are immediately directed to the promotion of rational views concerning scripture doctrine, with exhortations to consistency of conduct in all who are convinced of the strict Unity, the unrivalled supremacy, and the spontaneous and universal benignity of GOD.

The melancholy case of Mr. C. Herbert, who has lately been warned out of his school, on which he depends for the subsistence of a family of eight children, for his integrity in maintaining the divine Unity with the plain and inestimable truths connected with it, was laid before the Society, and as he possesses considerable merit as a teacher, and is particularly desirous of inculcating just and generous views of religion and virtue upon the minds of children, it is hoped that should any opening of this kind be afforded, or indeed should *any* source by which an upright man skilled in the arts of writing, arithmetic, &c. may provide, or be assisted in providing for a numerous, and still increasing family, reach the knowledge of any of our Unitarian friends, or of the friends of liberality and humanity in general, who may be acquainted with his case, they will not fail to communicate the particulars either immediately to Mr. Herbert himself, or through the medium of some friend. There is evidently no object of our unanimity so pressing as the endeavour to remove or alleviate those sufferings or inconveniences to which a friend may occasionally be subjected, from a conscientious adherence to his principles.

From the communications of several of our friends from different parts of the counties, it appeared that the spirit of inquiry has been making considerable progress. Our Battle Secretary observes that "it is become almost universal: men begin to think concerning religion, and are no longer content to rest in an implicit faith. This, therefore," he observes, "is the time to exhibit Christianity to their view in its native purity and simplicity, that they may see its excellence and be convinced of its truth, and that its effects may appear in their character and deportment in life." A scarcely less pleasing account was presented in the narrative of a friend from Dover, whose exertions have been a principal means of establishing a conference in the General Baptist Meeting-house of that place, by which no small degree of attention has been excited to the great question at issue between Unitarians and their opponents. Our Secretary for the Maidstone district observes that "we have every evidence of the number of Unitarians being much greater than it appears to be ; the extreme difficulties, the force of fashion, and a false shame, deter many from expressing their belief of the sublime and despised truths of Unitarianism." He acquainted the Society with a plan which has been adopted at Maidstone for conveying religious instruction to children in a language and manner adapted to their tender capacities. The boys on one part of each Sunday, and the girls on the other, are taken apart from the congregation to be familiarized with the leading principles of religion, and the plainest practical admonitions.

The Society adopted some resolutions with a view to the more prompt dispatch of its business, and to the keeping up of a more perfect intercourse between its branches, as it is hoped that every step which tends to engage us in the mutual pursuit of the common objects, will contribute in every point of view to increase the advantages of our Association.

With an expression of the deepest regret at the horrid persecution of which our Protestant brethren in the department of the Gard, have so long been the unoffending and unprotected victims, a vote of thanks was unanimously passed to the Committee of the Dissenting Ministers of the Three Denominations, for their unwearied exertions in their behalf; to Mr. C. Perrot for his Christian intrepidity in encountering every hazard and every difficulty to arrive at the first sources of information, and for the luminous report by which he has established the dreadful detail of ferocious cruelties and merciless oppression ; and to Sir Samuel Romily for the able, manly, and Christian-like conduct, which he has shewn in pleading that cause in the British House of Commons.

The company afterwards adjourned to the Star Inn, where 134 persons sat down to a plain dinner, a larger number than had assembled at any previous meeting of the Society. Several appropriate sentiments were given by the chairman (Mr. Aspland) which he prefaced with some interesting remarks, and which drew forth observations from several persons present. The company being composed of both ladies and gentlemen, the inconsistency of the marriage ceremony with the general principles of Dissenters, and especially of Unitarians, became the subject of some animated discussion, and perseverance in applications to Parliament for release from this ceremony, as the only legal bond of union, was strenuously recommended. The utmost harmony prevailed, the company in general appearing impressed with the obligation, as well of imitating their master in his entire devotion to the will of his Father and his God, as in his brotherly-love and charity. May these social meetings in which we sit down to one table, as the worshippers of one common and only God and Father, in obedience to one Lord, be attended with the happy effect of diminishing our attachment to all sublunary distinctions, remembering that, as the disciples of Christ, we must strive to be distinguished by those qualities of the heart and life which it was his sole object to inculcate upon mankind of every rank and condition, and by our proficiency in which, alone we can attain to distinction in his heavenly kingdom !

THOMAS PINE,
Maidstone,   Secretary.
July 16, 1816.

Eastern Unitarian Society.

The Yearly Meeting of this Society was held at Ipswich, on Wednesday and Thursday, the 26th and 27th of June. On Wednesday evening Mr. George Harris of Greenock introduced the service by prayer, and reading the Scriptures, and Mr. Fullagar of Palgrave preached from 2 Peter i. 10. "Wherefore, the rather, brethren, give diligence to make your calling and election sure." On Thursday morning Mr. Scargill, of Bury, introduced the service, and read the Scriptures; Mr. Toms, of Framlingham, prayed ; and Mr. Thomas Rees, of London, preached from Isaiah xl. 25. "To whom then will ye liken me, or shall I be equal ? saith the Holy One." It is much to be regretted that Mr. Rees declined complying with the wish of the Society to print a sermon so admirably adapted to expose the pernicious tendency of the doctrine of the Trinity. By the report of the Committee it appeared that the funds of the Society were in a flourishing state. The following resolutions were passed unanimously:—That Is. L. Marsh, Esq. and Mr. Edward Taylor be continued in the offices of Treasurer, and Secretary for the year ensuing. That a number of Tracts, at the discretion of the Committee, be placed at the disposal of the different ministers in the association. That the next yearly meeting be held at Framlingham, on the last Wednesday and Thursday in June, 1817, and that Mr Scargill be requested to preach. Thirty-seven members and friends to the Society afterwards dined together at the Bear and Crown, Mr. J. D. Harmer in the chair. The toasts and sentiments which were given, called forth observations from several gentlemen present, particularly Mr. Rees, Mr. Toms, Mr. Harris, Mr. Scargill, Mr. Fullagar, and Mr. Taylor. On " the memory of our departed friend, Mr. Joyce," being given, Mr. Rees took occasion to pay a just and affecting tribute of respect to the character of that excellent man, and steady friend to the cause of civil and religious liberty. Several subjects connected with the spread of Unitarian principles in this district were discussed, and some measures adopted for the attainment of so important and highly desirable an event. The greatest cordiality and harmony pervaded the meeting, and the company separated with feelings of Christian affection and sincere pleasure.

North-Eastern Unitarian Association.

This Association comprehends the Unitarian Churches in *Wisbeach*, *Sutton*, *Boston*, and *Lincoln*. They held their annual meeting at *Wisbeach*, on Wednesday, June the 26th, and Thursday the 27th. Mr. Platts, of Boston, preached on the Wednesday evening, " On Salvation by Jesus Christ, on Unitarian Principles." On Thursday morning Mr. Wright, the Missionary, preached the Association Sermon, " On the Import and Practical Tendency of the Doctrine of the Unity of God :" after which the Annual Business of the North-Eastern Unitarian Book Society was transacted. At two o'clock more than 100 friends

dined together; after the dinner a number of sentiments were given, which called up different speakers, and the afternoon was spent in an animated and truly Christian manner, much to the edification of the whole company. At seven o'clock the congregation re-assembled, and Mr. Hawkes, of Lincoln, preached. " On the Nature of Heresy." The public services were numerously attended. The Unitarian cause in this district is still advancing. The Association will be held next year at *Boston.*   R. W.

Nottinghamshire, Derbyshire, &c. Association.

At Nottingham, on Friday, 21st of June, 1816, was holden the Annual Meeting of the Unitarian Ministers of Nottinghamshire, Derbyshire, and the Southern part of Yorkshire. The devotional service was conducted by the Rev. J. P. Wright, of Stannington, near Sheffield : and the Sermon was preached by the Rev. John Williams, of Mansfield, from Matt. xiii. 52.

In this Sermon, which produced a strong impression on the audience, the preacher pointed out the necessity of a well-educated ministry ; and shewed what qualifications are essential to constitute a well-educated minister. Much general knowledge, and especially a thorough acquaintance with the Scriptures in the original tongues, he deemed indispensable, to a scribe thoroughly instructed unto the kingdom of heaven. He concluded with a display of the advantages resulting from such a ministry: adding, that from an ill-educated ministry, much positive evil results to religion and society.

The number of ministers present was small; yet, by the respectable attendance of lay friends, a company of about thirty lay-men and ministers dined together. The place of meeting announced for next year is Sheffield.

Devon and Cornwall Annual Meeting of Unitarian Christians.

July 5.—The Annual Meeting of "the Association of Unitarian Christians in Devon and Cornwall, established for the purpose of promoting the cause of Christian Truth and Practice, by the Distribution of Books, and effecting a more intimate Union among the Professors of the Unitarian

Doctrine in those Counties," was held at Moretonhampstead, on the 3d instant, when the Rev. T. Cooper opened the service of the day, by reading a psalm, which was sung in an excellent stile by the choir, after which the devotional service was conducted by the Rev. Dr. Carpenter in his usually impressive and serious manner. The annual Sermon was delivered by the Rev. I. Worsley, founded on the 40th chapter of Isaiah and the 18th verse, "To whom then will ye liken God?" The discourse was somewhat original and highly impressive, and pointed out some of the various erroneous notions entertained by reputed orthodoxy concerning the Divine Being, and his messenger of love to the human race, the holy Jesus. After the conclusion of the service, the members of the Association went through the business of the day with zeal, and unanimity, which was highly edifying, and admitted several new members. After a very plain dinner, at which nearly 60 members sat with apparent satisfaction, the memory of the late venerable Dr. Priestley was solemnly drank, standing; nor were the names of Lindsey, Kenrick, and Toulmin, and some others still living for the benefit of the cause of religious truth, forgotten; and with a feeling which was affecting and impressive, the members were reminded of their obligations to "the friends of Unitarianism both *in* and *out* of the establishment," who, though they have not yet avowed themselves as such, have by rational instruction and virtuous examples, been for years rooting out the weed, and preparing the ground, in which the enlightened Unitarian is now encouraged to sow with diligence the good seed, which, by producing an abundant crop, will ere long cause the nations of the earth to rejoice;—and, by one respected member of the Society, the effects of the improving liberality of some of the most distinguished advocates of reputed orthodoxy on the cause of Unitarianism, and of the exertions of the friends of the latter on the former, were with Christian benevolence pointed out as tending to spread religious enquiry and the cause of divine truth, as well as to diminish and prevent asperity, on both sides of the question. In short, the zeal and liberality displayed by

every speaker, seemed to give delight and animation to all, and to prove the happiness which brethren, who in some respects differ in opinion, may enjoy, when they meet together to promote the cause of divine truth and religion.　　　　　　　　J. I.

South Wales Unitarian Book Society.

The Annual Meeting of the South Wales Unitarian Book Society was held at Swansea, on Wednesday the 26th, and at Gellyonen, on Thursday the 27th of June. The Rev. J. Rowe, of Bristol, preached, on Wednesday morning, from John xx. 31, a very manly and seasonable Discourse, which he was afterwards requested to print, but declined. The Rev. D. Davis, of Neath, followed him, in Welsh, from 1 Tim. ii. 5.: and in the evening the Rev. J. Evans, of Carmarthen, delivered, in English, a very ingenious Discourse, from John i. 1. Between thirty and forty gentlemen dined together at the Bush Inn, and sixteen new subscribers were added to the Book Society.

On Thursday morning, at Gellyonen, the Rev. Thomas Evans, of Aberdare, preached from Colossians iii. 4.; and the Rev. J. Evans, of Carmarthen, the Sermon before the Society, from 1 Cor. viii. 6. The Rev. Mr. Thomas, a pupil of Mr. Evans, of Islington, and the Rev. B. Philips, of St. Clear's, conducted the devotional part of the Service. The whole of the Services of this day were in Welsh; and Mr. J. Evans's Sermon, at the request of the Society, is to be printed.

When the business of the Book Society was closed, the attendants, who were very numerous and respectable, and among whom were eighteen ministers, formed themselves into "A Meeting of Unitarian Christians from different parts of South Wales," at which

GEORGE THOMAS, Esq.

Being in the Chair,

IT WAS UNANIMOUSLY RESOLVED,

" 1. That the thanks of this meeting be given to the Rev. Thomas Belsham, for his seasonable and very useful publication, entitled, " A Letter to the Unitarian Christians in South Wales."

. " 2. That it is not known to this meeting that any injury whatever, but on the contrary very eminent service, has been done to the " Cause of Unitarianism in Wales" by Mr. Belsham's writings.

" 3. That the Chairman be requested to transmit the above Resolutions to Mr. Belsham.

" 4. That the thanks of this meeting be given to the Rev. Richard Awbrey, for his several excellent publications in defence of Unitarianism.

" 5. That the Chairman be requested to transmit the last Resolution to Mr. Awbrey.

"(Signed) GEO. THOMAS,
    " Chairman."

MISCELLANEOUS.

Debate in the House of Commons on the French Protestants.
[Concluded from p. 365.]

Lord CASTLEREAGH continued :— The Protestants had risen to power since the revolution, and had secured to themselves the majority of public offices. [A laugh.] This power they enjoyed under Bonaparte, while the return of the Bourbons gave the Catholics hopes of supplanting them, which from their numbers, loyalty, and patriotism, they considered themselves justly entitled to do. The Noble Lord then proceeded to read many more passages, among which the most striking were, " that previously to the return of Bonaparte several songs had been sung, insulting to the feelings of the Protestants, and exciting rancour and animosity. The Duke of Angouleme, who was then in the country, hastened to meet Bonaparte at Lyons, but he was stopped by the treachery of General Mallet; his followers then dispersed, and fell victims to the fury of the Protestants or the adherents of Bonaparte." [Mark the synonyme, said Sir SAMUEL ROMILLY, the Protestants, *or* the adherents of Bonaparte.] " During the four following months the Protestants committed great excesses on the royalists ; at this period commenced the reaction, and the excesses were retaliated after the news of the battle of Waterloo : the disturbances at Nismes were carried to a perilous extent, but those who committed them were of the lowest class of Catholics; the richer Protestants suffered in their property and houses. However, the crimes were greatly exaggerated, and many accounts in the English newspapers were entirely forged. The number of lives lost in the department were under 1,000, and at Nismes under 200." The House

must see that the King had no authority, no army, here. There were details in the management of government, of which no man sitting here tranquilly in parliament could form a judgment. " A considerable number of houses were plundered and burnt; and though there was little doubt that encouragement was given to these crimes, yet many of the magistrates were disposed to resist : but they were provided with no military force. Matters stood thus, when on the arrival of Prince Stahremberg in August, measures were taken, by which a general distrust was excited among the Protestants; they were 120,000 in number, and it was in vain to expect tranquillity at once. The officer best qualified to restore peace was General Lagarde." This did not argue illiberality in the government to choose a Protestant for the command of the province, and, therefore, it did look a little as if the Honourable and Learned Gentleman was seeking for a case, when he attributed to a general want of toleration measures taken for one troubled district. " General Lagarde's assassination was considered a public calamity ; the Protestants had lost a friend who alone could give a free opinion to the Duke of Angouleme. The neighbouring departments, and the Protestants in them, with the exception of Cevennes, were in a state of tranquillity ; and, after every inquiry, it appeared that the disturbances at Nismes were a local and partial feud." This then was the error of the societies in this country; they took the matter up as a general disturbance, and sent out their papers to places in perfect tranquillity ; they further sent a respectable clergyman to the disturbed district, he published a pamphlet, which the Honourable and Learned Gentleman repeated, and this was the way in which it was attempted to harrow up the feelings of the House. " In the neighbouring districts there was no disturbance ; in Montpelier there was no interruption of the communication between the two persuasions; intermarriages were celebrated between them, and the Protestant public functionaries continued in office. In Lyons there was no interruption of peace, and there was one minister of the reformed church so admired, that many Catholics attended to hear him." Did this savour of general intolerance, or did it warrant the interference of the city of London ? " It could not be wondered at, that in the department of the Gard the King should not choose to place authority in those hands which had so lately been raised against him. There was not a conscientious Protestant who expected more liberality than had been exercised towards them : his Majesty was surely justifiable in refusing to place power in the hands of the Protestants at the present crisis, but it would be proper for him to adopt mild and conciliatory measures." If this was the case, our interference was more likely to produce evil than good. " The disturbances were quite local, and had been greatly exaggerated." The Learned Gentleman would not recommend prosecuting one side, without also attacking the other [Loud cries from the Opposition] ; he had admitted that no outrages had occurred since December, and he now wished to revive the disputes; but by making ourselves a party, we should only increase the evil. " There was no hope of tranquillity without a change of ministry." But with this parliament could not interfere. " A late communication from Nismes complained of severity towards the Protestants, and assigned as a reason the letters received from the Protestant Society in London." [Hear, hear!] " They caused a strong feeling of dissatisfaction and uneasiness among the Protestants themselves." It was impossible that foreign interference could produce any effect but the contrary of what was wished: the present had been productive of injury, by exciting false hopes on the one side, and jealousy on the other; and the best informed Protestants, though they respected the motive, dreaded the consequences of such interference. The House would see that there was no ground to charge the French with systematic persecution and intolerance ; that the disturbances were completely local, and the departments on the very borders of it were tranquil and unaffected: he had reason to hope, therefore, that this serious mischief would soon find an end. He did not deny that the mischief was serious; but it was not by blowing a trumpet, and telling a tale, to make people believe that we were returned to the bigotry of the 9th century—it was not by highly colouring the violences of one party, that we could put an end to these religious struggles. It was on these grounds—on a persuasion that the French government had but one feeling

and one interest (for who would be benefitted, or what rational object could be gained, by fomenting these disturbances?)—that he thought any proposal impolitic which would lead parliament to interfere, on the notion that we stood in a relation with respect to France, which justified our demanding some concessions. He denied that we stood in any such relation ; we were obliged to keep a military force there, because we were persuaded that the government of Louis XVIII. was the most likely to ensure peace. We were pledged to support him against any revolutionary spirit that remained, but we had not given a pledge that we should interfere or administer the internal jurisprudence of France : we were the protectors of our own rights, not of the government of France. He hoped, and was indeed satisfied that the Honourable Gentleman could have no design to cast obloquy on the members of that government; but he knew that there were others who promoted such designs : there were spirits abroad who were anxious to overturn the power of Louis XVIII. and the peace which had placed their prospects at an immediate distance. He warned the country against the proposals that had been made : there was no prospect of happiness but in peace, and no peace but in the present government of France. He acquitted the Honourable and Learned Gentleman of any bad intentions, but his speech would certainly be attended with bad consequences, containing, as it did, such exaggerated statements, dressed up with all the eloquence of which the subject was capable. His Lordship would not give his consent to a motion so injurious. [Hear, hear!]

Mr. BROUGHAM complained that the tone and manner of the Noble Lord was not at all justified by any thing that had fallen from his Honourable and Learned Friend (Sir S. Romilly.) He begged leave to put in a distinct disclaimer to the objects and principles imputed by the Noble Lord—first, as to the hostility of the supporters of the motion to the family of Bourbon; next, as to their wish to disturb the peace of Europe by destroying the tranquillity of France; and thirdly, as to their intention of enforcing a direct and offensive interference with the internal regulations of the French government—an interference alien to the plainest principles of policy, and upon a subject that could be touched only with a most cautious and delicate hand. For the information of the Noble Lord, who appeared to be most singularly ignorant upon this subject, he begged to state, that it was possible to moot a question of this kind, to ask for accounts of the state of our persecuted Protestant brethren, and what steps had been taken for their relief and protection, without danger of exposing the country to the calamity of a new war. The whole scope of the proposition was to obtain information, that, if deemed necessary by parliament, steps might be taken: and although the Noble Lord might refuse his assent, a very important object had been accomplished, for in the course of his speech the Noble Lord had given most ample and valuable information, which more than confirmed the statement made of the horrible atrocities of which the deluded Catholics had been guilty in the department of La Gard. While the Noble Lord, with such exultation among his friends, was reading the statement, which he had produced to the House, every man, not blinded by admiration of the stupendous abilities of his Lordship, must have seen that it completely proved the case in favour of the motion: the Noble Lord was partially aware of the fact, and had interlarded his document with such observations as he thought calculated to remove the unfavourable impression. So far from showing that the assertions of the Honourable Mover had been exaggerated, it proved directly the contrary. The House had heard with astonishment, that no less than 1,000 murders had been committed,—a number far exceeding the calculation of other men. The Noble Lord had next endeavoured to alarm the House, by referring to a period not long past, when religious controversy had produced unhappy consequences in the county of Armagh; but did he mean to say, that even during the rebellion of 1798 and 1799, the outrages had equalled those of La Gard? [Lord Castlereagh said across the table that he did not refer to the date mentioned.] If the Noble Lord did not allude to the rebellion, his argument was the weaker; for if not during the period of rebellion, where could be found any thing like a parallel to the horrors of La Gard? Within the space of three months a thousand murders had been committed: where could similar atro-

cities be found in the history almost of any country? What had fallen from the Noble Lord regarding the ten thousand men who had oppressed a part of France by their adherence to Bonaparte did not at all apply, because at that period hostilities had not ceased. The motion did not require that this country should draw the sword in favour of the Protestants: other means of redress were in our hands, which might be used without any breach of amity. It was the duty of England to use them peacefully, and delicately, in proportion to the importance and delicacy of the subject. It was the duty of government to make such representations to the authorities in France, as became the situation of that country, and the attitude we were entitled to assume. A renewal of hostilities would not necessarily be the consequence: on the contrary, in former times, when we had felt called upon to interpose in favour of those who were unjustly suffering, our sympathy had been frequently rewarded by the accomplishment of the desired object. The Noble Lord had frequently reverted to a favourite topic—the injury done to the cause of the Protestants by the humane interference of their brethren in this country; and the example of those benevolent persons was held up as a warning to the House. "Though your ancestors have frequently interposed with effect, you must not think of endeavouring to rescue these unhappy people from destruction," said the Noble Lord; and what was the reason assigned? "I admit (added his Lordship) that their persecutors inflict upon them inhuman cruelties; that they are tortured—that they are murdered; that in three months 1,000 murders for conscience-sake have been perpetrated, and not one offender executed or even brought to trial: but you must not interfere, because the generous sympathy of the people of England will only draw down upon the Protestants of France new calamities." [Hear, hear!] Such was the argument of the Noble Lord: and he (Mr. Brougham) had heard it with more regret, because it was not the last time it would be employed. The subject of the Slave Trade was shortly to be brought before the House: another attempt would be made to ameliorate the condition of those with whom we had, in common, neither manners, language, religion, nor complexion;

but, what would be the answer of the Noble Lord to such a proposition? He had given a foretaste of it to-night. " Do not interfere (he would say)—do not endeavour to promote the happiness of the slaves; it is true they are now whipped with scourges, but if you interpose they will be flogged with scorpions." Such an argument would not impose upon the understanding of Parliament. The Noble Lord had stated, that he was no friend to peace who diminished the stability of the present government of France: it was true that conflicting opinions had been entertained as to the propriety of our interference in the establishment of the Bourbons, but both parties might now join sincerely in the prayer that that family might not be disturbed. That it should continue on the throne of France, presenting a firm front to its enemies, and a benevolent countenance to its friends, must be the nearest and dearest wish of every man who rejoiced in the happiness of France, and in the tranquillity of Europe; but he was at a loss to imagine how this government was prevented from remonstrating on the subject of the Protestants at a time when we had an army in France, and a general with powers little less than sovereign. He trusted that the present discussion would operate as a spur to those who had authority in our neighbour kingdom; at least it would show, that there were a few persons in Great Britain who felt the ancient sympathy of their forefathers, and who felt equal pity for the persecuted, and indignation at the authors of their calamities.

Lord Binning maintained that Protestants and Bonapartists were in truth synonimous; and that interference was most of all to be avoided at a time when we had an imposing force in France, because then it would be most likely to give umbrage.

Mr. W. Smith supported the motion.

Sir Samuel Romilly, in reply, said, that it was not his intention to divide the House upon the question. He had never known more flagrant injustice done to an individual, than he had experienced in the course of this debate. Never having himself intentionally given offence, he was at a loss to account for the marked and designed injustice done him by the Noble Lord. [Order, order, from Lord Castlereagh.] He had no wish to give personal offence

to the Noble Lord, but he thought he had not been fairly treated. Principles and motives had been attributed to him which he had never entertained, both with regard to the government of France, and to the dangerous interference which he was supposed to require. The kind of interference which he recommended was one merely of amicable suggestion and good offices; and it was admitted on the other side, that ministers had already interfered to a certain extent. The Noble Lord had accused him of exaggeration; but he was extremely happy that the report to which the Noble Lord had alluded as authority, bore ample testimony to the truth of all his statements. The Noble Lord must know that he abstained from mentioning many circumstances of horror, which, if it had been his wish to inflame the feelings or imagination of the House, he might have derived from the same source of information. He was not conscious of any intention to heighten the colour of those descriptions, because the mention of them was abhorrent to his nature, or because he could not express himself with the same coolness as others, in touching upon such subjects. [Hear, hear!]. In consequence, however, of what had fallen from the other side, he must remind the Noble Lord, that whilst the town of Nismes was in the possession of the Bonapartists, not a single murder had been committed. The latter party never directed their hostility against religion as a distinctive characteristic of political inclination. The persecution carried on by the emissaries, partisans of the present government of France, had been aimed against the Protestants as such. He certainly thought the proclamation of the government, describing these outrages as excusable acts of vengeance, entirely without justification. He was quite sure that the present discussion would be attended with happy effects, and that it would serve to exhibit to the world, that there was at least one place in which the enormities of such monsters as he had described, however they might be countenanced or rewarded elsewhere, were sure to be stamped with the infamy which belonged to them. Was it because it was only in the department of the Gard, containing a population of 160,000 persons, where these disorders prevailed, that they were to be regarded as unworthy of notice? As the Noble Lord had thought proper to refer to the period of 1780, he would also remind him that although a religious mob then domineered, they did not commit a single murder; but that, on the other hand, government acted with an extraordinary severity. Much blood was shed both in the streets and on the scaffold, and it was not the fault of government that Lord George Gordon was not brought to a public execution. He had certainly as good a right to comment on the proclamation of Louis as on a proclamation of his own king. He felt great respect for the personal character of Louis; but he considered that he, as well as our own Prince Regent, had the misfortune to be dependent on others. After hearing the whole case made out by the Noble Lord, he had no doubt that, under all its circumstances, the letter of the Duke of Wellington was wholly unjustifiable on the facts. He would not divide the House, but he felt satisfied that the result of this discussion would be beneficial.

After a few words of explanation from Lord Binning and Lord Castlereagh, the question was put and negatived.

Bible Society.

The following Statement represents the Receipts and Expenditure, together with the number of Bibles and Testaments issued within the year, as mentioned in their Report.

The Issue of Copies of the Scriptures, from March 31, 1815, to March 31, 1816, had been

138,163 Bibles, | 110,063 Test.

Making the total issued, from the commencement of the Institution, to the last mentioned period,

654,427 Bibles, | 828,546 Test.

In all, 1,482,973 copies, exclusive of about 75,500 copies circulated at the charge of the Society, from Depositories abroad, making a grand total of *one million, five hundred and fifty-seven thousand, nine hundred and seventy-three* copies, already circulated by the British and Foreign Bible Society.

The Receipts of the Year have been

	l.	*s.*	*d.*
Annual Subscriptions,	3058	8	0
Donations and Life ditto,	1248	18	3
Congregational Collections,	811	7	3
	5118	13	6
Legacies,	878	18	8
Dividends on Stocks (less Prop. Tax),	476	3	10
Property Tax returned on ditto, to January 5, 1816,	78	7	4
Interest on Exchequer Bills, &c.	1430	3	3
Contributions from Auxiliary Societies,	55450	3	9
	62932	10	4
For Bibles and Testaments, the greater part of which were purchased by Bible Associations,	29927	12	5
Total,	92860	2	9
The Expenditure of the Year,	103680	13	3
Obligations of the Society, including Orders given for Bibles and Testaments, about	36000	0	0

The Chancellor of the Exchequer, in the course of an excellent speech, at the Annual Meeting, expressed himself to the following effect:—

"You will perceive, my Lord, that I am particularly alluding to a very remarkable transaction, which has distinguished the past year; and which differed so widely from diplomatic forms, and from the principles of ordinary policy, that it is not surprising that at first it should have excited some degree of jealousy and suspicion—I mean the Secret Treaty, concluded and signed at Paris, by the Emperors of Austria and Russia, and the King of Prussia. The confused and imperfect notions of this proceeding, which at first crept out, naturally occasioned curiosity, and even alarm, rather than confidence; but to those who had the opportunity of being acquainted with the real and genuine history of this arrangement, and of knowing the sincerity and integrity of the principles from which it originated, it afforded the gratifying, and hitherto unprecedented spectacle, of a union of Christian Sovereigns, differing in their respective modes of religious persuasion, but agreeing in a public recognition of the divine authority of the gospel, and binding themselves, by a solemn compact, to adopt its precepts as the rules of their policy and conduct. I feel it my duty to add, that, though legal and constitutional difficulties prevented the Sovereign of this country from acceding in form to this Treaty, yet this Government was confidentially acquainted with every stage of the proceeding, and fully concurred in its principles and spirit. It was not, however, till the return of the Emperor of Russia to St. Petersburg, that it received the fullest elucidation. When we learn, from the Report we have heard, the zeal with which that great Sovereign entered into the concerns of the Bible Society, it becomes impossible longer to hesitate as to the real sentiments and intentions of his heart, in the transaction we have been considering. In giving the Bible to every nation of his vast dominions, in its own language, he fixed the real and most appropriate ratification to the Christian Treaty."

The impression made by the late Anniversary of this Society, is well expressed in the following passage, from the conclusion of the Report:—

" It is indeed impossible to contemplate the effects produced by the British and Foreign Bible Society, so conspicuously displayed in the attention which it has excited to the supreme importance of the holy Scriptures, in the unparalleled efforts for the diffusion of them, and in the extension and enlargement of charitable feeling, without emotions of the purest delight, the warmest gratitude, and the most cheering anticipation.

" In humble dependence on the favour of Almighty God, deriving efficiency from the public bounty, and with no other recommendation than the simplicity of its principle, and the benevolence of its design, the British and Foreign Bible Society has gone forth from strength to strength, triumphantly opposing the attempts of Infidelity to discountenance the truths of Divine Revelation, imparting its spirit to Christians all over the world, animating their zeal, and aiding their exertions, accompanied by their prayers, and rewarded by their benedictions. The Members of the Institution have the amplest grounds for rejoicing in the glorious privilege which they exercise of dispensing the bounty of the Most High. The charity to which they have devoted themselves, in humble imitation of that divine love which, in its dispensation of mercy, offered the gospel of salvation to all mankind, embraces the whole human race, without distinction of colour or country, of friend or foe; connecting the scattered members of the Christian community by the sacred ties of a religion which considers all men as brethren, the children of one common Father; and exhibiting, by this union, a practical exemplification of the apostolic precept, ' To keep the unity of the spirit in the bond of peace.'

" It is a charity no less ennobled by its object, than sanctified in its means, which enriches those who bestow, as well as those who receive; and the Christian, who knows the word of God to be the savour of life unto life, and the power of God unto salvation, puts forth his hand to the work with heartfelt delight, thankful that God has blessed him with the ability, as well as inclination, to render others partakers of the heavenly banquet on which he has feasted, and to enable them to gather with him, the fruit of immortality from the tree of life."

" *Secession from the Church.*—A few weeks since we announced the baptism, by immersion, of two respectable clergymen, the Rev. Mr. Snow and the Rev. Mr. Bevan, who, from conscientious motives, have lately resigned their connection with the Established Church. [See M. Repos. XI. 143.] We have now to notice that on the 14th ult. two of their colleagues, who have also resigned valuable preferments, the Rev. George Baring and the Rev. Mr. Evans, with —— Grange, Esq. were baptized by the Rev. Mr. Bevan, at the Octagon Chapel in this town, which has been purchased for their accommodation."

Taunton Courier.

NOTICES.

Mr. Wright, of Liverpool, whose attachment to the principles of liberty are well known and deservedly respected, announces a new weekly publication, to be entitled The Liverpool Freeman, with this excellent motto, from Mr. Fox:

"If to inform the people of England of their actual situation is to inflame them, the fault is in those who have brought them into that situation, and not in those who only tell them the truth."

It will partake of the character of a Magazine; Political Intelligence and Discussion will be the primary objects: but, by compressing the events and reserving the space occupied with advertisements, a large portion of the paper will be appropriated to a greater variety of subjects, and to communications of merit. It will be printed on a sheet of demy, in octavo pages.

As an addition to the slender means left in the hands of the people for resisting the flood of political corruption, we heartily wish Mr. Wright the success which his good intentions merit.

In the press, Historical Relations of the Persecutions of the Protestants of Languedoc, by the Rev. Clement Perrot: prepared at the request of the Committee of the Three Denominations.

Mr. Boothroyd, who has just completed his Hebrew Bible, has circulated a quarto pamphlet, entitled Reflections on the Authorised Version of the Holy Scriptures, with a Specimen of an Attempt to improve it, with a view to collect Subscribers for an improved Version, with Notes, intended to be comprised in 2 or 3 vols. royal quarto.

OBITUARY.

The Late Mr. Joyce.—By the friends of civil and religious liberty, and the advocates for freedom of enquiry, the death of the Rev. Jeremiah Joyce cannot be contemplated without deep interest and unfeigned regret. He was possessed of no ordinary share of merit as a man, a scholar, and a member of society. Ardent in temper, and unsophisticated in principle, he was always solicitous to promote the spread of truth, the love of liberty, and the interests of humanity. In every virtuous cause that came within the scope of his exertions, he was prompt and persevering. And it is not his least praise, that his heart, warm, generous, and open, was highly susceptible of the friendly and sympathetic affections; that he was active, zealous and unwearied in offices of kindness, and the great duties of benevolence. His faculties were all awake, and his mind constantly on the alert, full of energy, and fruitful of resource. His talents, highly respectable, were versatile and various. Distinguished by his attainments in philosophy and general literature, he possessed the peculiarly happy art of turning his talents to account, by applying them to the purposes of general utility. With these qualifications, aided by great industry, indefatigable assiduity, and unremitting attention, he rendered eminent services to the rising generation, by the publication of several useful works for their benefit and instruction. Amongst these, his "*Scientific*

Dialogues" hold a distinguished place; a work happily calculated to communicate knowledge to the youthful mind, and to illustrate and exemplify the principles of natural science in an easy and familiar manner. He had a kind of original aptitude to the business of education; and was accordingly most usefully and honourably engaged in this arduous and important occupation; having been entrusted with the education of several young persons of high rank and condition.

In all his engagements, it is due to the memory of Mr. Joyce to observe, that he was upright and strictly conscientious, actuated by a nice regard to the purest principles of probity and honour. Though he had lived among the great, he was no respecter of persons; he never forgot what was due to his own character; he never dissembled his sentiments, nor compromised his principles, nor forfeited the independence of his own mind; much less did he ever descend to the baseness of personal adulation and servility. He was remarkable for a native frankness, simplicity, and manliness of mind, devoid of art, and incapable of duplicity and disguise.

Thus gifted, thus endowed, the name of Mr. Joyce will live long in the recollection of his friends—endeared, honoured, and lamented. He will ever be remembered by them with grateful respect and affection. And by the disinterested, the impartial, and the unprejudiced public, his merits will be justly appreciated and highly esteemed, as long as uncorrupted virtue, inflexible integrity, and undeviating consistency of character, shall continue to be held in moral estimation.

Mr. Joyce was a very active and useful member of " The Unitarian Society," and had for a great number of years acted as its Secretary ; which office he had resigned but a very short time before his decease. This worthy and excellent man died at his house at Highgate, on Friday the 21st of June.—Having dined from home on that day with some friends, amongst whom he conversed with his usual frankness and cheerfulness of temper ; on his return to his family in the evening between nine and ten o'clock, he complained of pain in the stomach ; and, after he had lain on a sofa for a little time, in a dosing posture, Mrs. Joyce, on going near him, soon made the awful discovery of the affecting change which had already taken place. He had breathed his last.

Leeds.   T. J.

June 29, in the 78th year of his age, after a protracted suffering of near five years under a severe paralytic affection, DAVID WILLIAMS, Esq. Founder of the Literary Fund. The writings of this gentleman were, as to several of them, on subjects so important, that we hope to be able to take further notice of the Author.

July 4. At his seat, *Calgarth Park, Westmoreland,* at a very advanced age, Dr. RICHARD WATSON, Bishop of Llandaff, Regius Professor of Divinity in the University of Cambridge, and Archdeacon of Ely. Of the life and writings of this eminent man we hope to give some account in a future Number.

July 7. RICHARD BRINSLEY SHERIDAN, Esq. early and justly celebrated for his literary accomplishments, and especially his dramatic genius, and for more than 30 years a member of the British Senate.

He was born in 1751, at Quilca, near Dublin, of a family long connected with the literary history of Ireland. At 6 years of age he was brought to England and placed at Harrow School, under the tuition of Dr. Sumner. He entered at the Middle Temple, but declined being called to the Bar, having attached himself very early to classical and dramatic literature. When only 18 he engaged with a friend in translating from the Greek the Epistles of Aristæus. In 1775 he produced his first play, *The Rivals,* and the next year commenced his long connection with Drury-Lane Theatre, as one of the Proprietors.

In 1780, Mr. Sheridan came into Parliament, where, it is but justice to recollect, that he was generally found sup-

porting the great interests of civil and religious liberty. Soon as he had taken his seat he distinguished himself by animadverting on the unconstitutional employment of the military during the *riots.* The *Regency* and the *Trial of Hastings* afterwards called forth his shining talents. His speeches on the latter occasion, especially that in Westminster Hall, have been applauded by all political parties. During the short periods in which Mr. Fox was Minister, Mr. Sheridan shared in the administration, first as his private Secretary, and afterwards as Treasurer of the Navy.

Such was the *public* life of this possessor of many talents. We will not *reverse the medal* and describe a life which has been too justly represented as " rather a warning than an example ;"

" *Nor draw his frailties from their dread abode.*"

Those who have been blessed with a more favoured, though less brilliant lot, and who possess

" *The single talent well employed,*" let such be content and grateful.

At *Manchester,* aged 82, THOMAS HENRY, Esq. President of the Literary and Philosophical Society of Manchester, Fellow of the Royal Society of London, and Member of several other learned Societies both in this country and abroad. As a practical and philosophical Chemist, he obtained a high and merited reputation. His contributions to that science, besides a small volume of Essays, and his Translations of the early Writings of Lavoisier, which he first introduced to the notice of the English public, consist of Memoirs, dispersed through the Transactions of the various Societies to which he belonged, and relative to those parts of Chemistry that are purely scientific, and to those which have reference to the useful arts. On a subject intimately connected with the success of the Cotton Manufacture (the employment of Mordaunts or Bases in Dyeing), Mr Henry was the first who thought and wrote philosophically. In the Introduction of the new mode of Bleaching, which has worked an entire revolution in that art, and occasioned an incomparably quicker circulation of capital, he was one of the earliest and most successful agents. In addition to the attainments connected with his profession, he had cultivated, to no inconsiderable degree, a taste for the Fine Arts ; he had acquired a knowledge of historical events remarkable for its extent and accuracy ; and he had derived, from reading and reflection, opinions, to which he was steadily attached, on topics of political, moral, and religious enquiry. Several years ago, he retired from the practice of Medicine, to which he had been extensively engaged, with credit and success, for more than half a century; and, from delicate health, he had long ceased to take an active share in the practical cultivation of science. But possessing, almost unimpaired, his faculties of memory and judgment, he continued to feel a lively interest in the advancement of literature and philosophy. Retaining, also, in their full vigour, those kind affections of the heart that gave birth to the most estimable moral conduct, and secured him the faithful attachment of his friends, he passed through a long and serene old age, experiencing little but its comforts and its honours, and habitually thankful for the blessings with which Providence indulged him.

July 13. At *Aberdeen*, in the 84th year of his Episcopate, the Rt. Rev. JOHN SKINNER, Primate of the Episcopal Church in Scotland.

Lately, aged, 75, Mr. H. D. SYMONDS, many years an active and considerable bookseller in Paternoster-Row; having a few years since retired in favour of Messrs. Sherwood, Neely, and Jones. In the commencement of the crusade against the French Revolution, he suffered four years imprisonment in Newgate, and paid a heavy fine for vending some political pamphlets.

NEW PUBLICATIONS IN THEOLOGY AND GENERAL LITERATURE.

Dissertations on Various Interesting Subjects, with a View to illustrate the Amiable and Moral Spirit of Christ's Religion. By the Rev. T. Watson. 8vo. 6s.

Philosophic Etymology, or Rational Grammar. By James Gilchrist. 8vo. 5s.

An Open and Fearless Avowal of the Unitarian Doctrine Recommended and Enforced: a Sermon preached before the Friends and Supporters of the Unitarian Fund, on Wednesday, June 5th, 1816. By William Broadbent, Minister of the Unitarian Chapel at Warrington. 12mo. 1s.

Farewell Sermons of some of the most Eminent of the Nonconformist Ministers in 1662, with an Historical and Biographical Preface. 8vo. 11s.

Essays in Rhyme, on Morals and Manners. By Jane Taylor. Foolscap 8vo. 6s.

Commentaries and Annotations on the Holy Scriptures. By the Rev. John Hewlett, B. D. 5 vols. 8vo. 3l.

The Connection between the Sacred Writings and the Literature of the Jewish and Heathen Authors. By Robert Gray, D. D. Prebendary of Durham and of Chichester. 8vo. 12s.

Liberty, Civil and Religious. By the Rev. T. Bowdler, A. M. 8vo. 3s.

Substance of a Speech delivered in the Court of Common Council, on a Motion to address his Royal Highness the Prince Regent to accede to the late Treaty concluded between the Emperors of Russia and of Austria and the King of Prussia. By Mr. Favell. To which are added other Papers on the Subject of Peace. 8vo. 2s.

The Panegyric of the Late Samuel Whitbread, Esq. M. P. by the Rev. J. Whitehouse, formerly of St John's College, Cambridge, and Rector of Orlingsbury, Northamptonshire. 8vo. 2s. 6d.

John Bull's Bible; or Memoirs of the Stewardship and Stewards of John Bull's Manor of Great Albion, from the earliest Times to the present. By Demodocus Poplicola. 8vo. 9s.

Baptism.

Considerations on the Doctrine of Baptism and on Conversion, as connected with the subject of Baptismal Regeneration, and with the Legitimate Discharge of the Pastoral Function. (Reprinted from the *Eclectic Review*, May and June, 1816.) 2s.

A Brief Statement of the Nature of Baptism. By Robert Hardy, A. M. 6d.

Dr. Mant's Sermon on Regeneration Vindicated from the Remarks of the Rev. T. T. Biddulph. 1s. 6d.

The Doctrine of the Church of England upon the Efficacy of Baptism, Vindicated from Misrepresentation. By Richard Laurence, LL. D. 8vo. 5s.

CORRESPONDENCE.

The *Report* of the *Unitarian Fund* is postponed till next month—the *Intelligence* for the present month being unusually extended.

The letter from our respectable Correspondent at Norwich respecting Dr. John Taylor, and the Accounts of *Dudley Double Lecture* and of the Meeting of the *Warwickshire Unitarian Tract Society*, came too late for insertion this month. These shall all appear in the next Number, with articles of *Review* and other communications very lately received.

THE

𝕸𝖔𝖓𝖙𝖍𝖑𝖞 𝕽𝖊𝖕𝖔𝖘𝖎𝖙𝖔𝖗𝖞,
&c.

No. CXXVIII.]   AUGUST, 1816.   [Vol. XI.

HISTORY AND BIOGRAPHY.

*Memoir relative to John Burnett, Esq. of Dens, Founder of the Prizes for the two best Essays on the Existence and Perfections of God, lately awarded to Dr. Brown and Mr. Sumner.**

[Extracted from Dr. Brown's Essay, just published in two vols. 8vo.]

JOHN BURNETT, of DENS, Esq. was born in Aberdeen, in the year 1729. The month and day of his birth have not been ascertained. His father was an eminent merchant in that city, and gave his son a liberal education in the place of his nativity. In the year 1750, the son entered into business, on his own account, without any other fortune, but that which, though a young man, he seems to have possessed in a distinguished degree—the *esteem, confidence,* and *support* of friends. For about that time, his father had *failed* in his circumstances, not from any imprudence, or misconduct, on his part, but from a sudden, unusual, and, to him, most unfortunate decline in the prices of the articles of merchandize in which he dealt, while he himself was obliged, by contract, for a number of years, to purchase these articles, from others, at fixed and higher rates.

This circumstance principally arose from the war, in which this country had been engaged. It is, hence, evident that, if war produces, to some, temporary advantages, it is, at last, productive of equal *evils,* even to that class who have profited by it. Let our own times proclaim this awful truth. It is just, it is salutary, that this should be the case, in order to impress, even on those whose object

is gain, a detestation of war, one of the greatest scourges of humanity.

The business of the younger Burnett was that of a general merchant; but, he was chiefly engaged in *fisheries* and *manufactures.* In the former of these, his father had also been much concerned, and from this circumstance his misfortunes chiefly arose. The son profited by the experience which he had acquired from his father's case. His success in business was certainly considerable, but exceeded not those expectations which might have been naturally entertained, when his application, prudence, and caution, in the conduct of his affairs, were considered.

His parents were of the *Episcopal Communion,* in which it is most probable that he was educated, as far as related to his religious instruction. In his younger days, it is certain that he attended divine worship in St. Paul's Chapel, of Aberdeen, which is connected with the Church of England, and whose clergymen are in the orders of that church. On some religious points, however, as commonly professed by most Christian communities, he entertained, in more advanced years, certain doubts and scruples, nor could fully assent to the public standards of any particular communion. For this reason, during many years before his death, he ceased to attend public worship, because he supposed that such attendance implied an unqualified and complete assent to every tenet which was professed by the religious community in whose worship he joined; and he could never bear the idea of assuming the *appearance* of a *profession,* the *reality* of which was not sanctioned by his *understanding* and his *heart.* In this notion he seems to have resembled *Milton,* who abstained from public worship on account of his conceptions

---

* For an account of Mr. Burnett (whom *Maty* in his *Review,* VIII. 446, 447. represented as an Unitarian) and of the wording of the proposed Essays, see Mon. Repos. II. 110. and X. 596, 597.

of Christianity, which he found realized in no Christian community or church, existing in his days. Perhaps, *pure, primitive, vital* Christianity is to be found only in the Sacred Scriptures, and no small degree of purification must probably take place, before its genuine form, with all its celestial features, can be restored to this earth.

Although this circumstance does infinite credit to Mr. Burnett's *integrity,* his *understanding* seems, on this point, to have been misinformed. He appears not, at this period of his life, to have reflected on the general obligation, resting upon all men, to worship their Creator, both in *public* and in *private;* nor to have rightly distinguished between the *fundamental articles of Christianity,* and *those points* which are of *subordinate importance ;* between those which are *essential to its existence,* and those which are, comparatively, *less momentous.* He seems not to have reflected on the truly judicious and divinely liberal sentiments of the Apostle Paul, on this, and other similar subjects. " Him, that is weak in the faith," says he, " receive ye, but not unto doubtful disputations.* One man esteemeth one day above another; another esteemeth every day alike. Let every man be fully persuaded in his own mind. He, that regardeth the day, regardeth it unto the Lord ; and he that regardeth not the day, to the Lord he doth not regard it. He that eateth, eateth to the Lord, for he giveth God thanks ; and he that eateth not, to the Lord he eateth not, and giveth God thanks. The kingdom of God is not meat and drink, but righteousness, and peace, and joy in the Holy Ghost. Hast thou faith? Have it to thyself before God. Happy is he that condemneth not himself in that thing which he alloweth. Whatsoever is not of faith, is sin."†

The spirit of those passages is to this purpose ; that pure Christianity consists not in points comparatively *indifferent,* but in certain grand and important views ; and that whatever is subservient to these, or connected with them, constitutes its essence,

advances its sublime objects, and must be firmly and unalterably maintained ; but, that matters of smaller moment, in which, however, the generality of mankind have, in all ages, been disposed to place the very substance of *religion,* ought to produce no schism among Christians, but must be viewed with mutual forbearance and charity. It would have been happy for the Christian church, if these apostolical sentiments, which have, in fact characterized also the ablest and best men, since the apostolic times, had been generally adopted. Much confusion would have been prevented, and one great cause of *intolerance* and *persecution* would have ceased to operate. Now, as the *fundamentals* of Christianity seem to be preserved among all Protestants, with the exception of such as exclude, from *salvation,* those who differ from them in the most minute article of *order,* or *worship,* there appears to be no solid reason for withdrawing from any *Protestant communion,* in which a person has been educated, and refusing to join with any other, on this sole ground, that assent cannot be given to every individual tenet which its members may profess. On the same principle, there could hardly be any society among men. For, there exist not, perhaps, any two individuals whose opinions are, on all subjects, perfectly conformable to each other. Such conformity of sentiment would not, on the whole, be conducive to the advancement of *truth,* or to the attainment of *happiness.* It is by *diversity of opinion,* by the different aspects in which the same object is viewed by different minds, that a variety of information is collected, and that the stores of knowledge are increased. The real bond of union, therefore, is not *exact conformity of opinion,* but, mutual *charity, freedom of discussion,* and *true,* not *pretended, liberality of mind ;* is the *subjugation of pride,* the *renunciation of tyrannical supremacy,* and the *unqualified acknowledgment of those rights, in religious matters, as belonging to others, which we claim to ourselves.* If Mr. Burnett had reflected on these principles, his excellent heart would have prohibited his withdrawing from *public worship* in every religious community. In fact, we shall immediately see that

---

* Rom. xiv. 1.
† Rom. xiv. 6. 17. 22, 23.

his mind, ever open to conviction, afterwards assumed, on this subject, the complexion which reason appears to dictate.

While he entertained this erroneous opinion, which was certainly, on his part, most *sincere*, he seems to have fallen into one of those inconsistencies incident to the human character, even in its most amiable forms. He would not allow his servants to be absent from church, on any occasion, although he interfered not with their general adherence to any religious profession. Now, while he himself abstained from attendance on public worship, because he could not assent to all the tenets of any church, or sect whatever, it seems not to have occurred to him that any of his servants might, on the ground of conscientious scruples, have urged the same plea for his non-attendance. The celebrated Mr. Howard was a strict *predestinarian.* He had been threatened with the *Bastille*, if he ever ventured again to pass through France. He had resolved, for a certain object which he judged to be of the first importance, to traverse the whole extent of that country. When I strongly urged on him, the danger to which he exposed himself, he asserted his firm belief in *predestination*, as a ground for his proceeding. He said, however, that he would not expose his *servant* to the same danger, sent him round by Italy, and, as he himself was resolved to go to *Toulon*, ordered him to meet his master at *Nice*. The *servant* was just as much secured, by *predestination*, as his *master*; yet *Mr. Howard* would not venture to apply the doctrine to the *poor fellow*. The master, nevertheless, escaped all danger, accomplished the object of his journey, and, afterwards related to me the wonderful particulars of his perilous adventure. Such are the inconsistencies to which the most vigorous and noblest minds are, sometimes, liable.

Mr. Burnett called his servants together, regularly, every *Sunday evening*, and read prayers to them. Although, *on some points*, he had peculiar doubts, he was far from being a *sceptic* in regard to the *grand doctrines* of the Christian religion. By diligent reading, accurate examination, and serious reflection, he endeavoured to acquire that information which he deemed to be of the highest importance to his present comfort, and to his eternal happiness. Nor were his pains unsuccessful. Some time before his death, he had obtained clearer and more satisfactory views of those doctrines, in regard to which he had experienced the greatest difficulties. If his life had been prolonged, he would, in all probability, have again joined in public worship. He was remarkable for his scrupulous observance of the Lord's day. On that day, during many years, he never opened any letters on business. This is, at least, a striking proof of the *sincerity* of his religious sentiments, whatever opinion may be entertained, by some, of their enlargement. I cannot pretend to say how he could discover, before opening a letter, if it was on *business*, or on *some subject* connected with *religion*. He probably knew the hands of his correspondents.

Punctuality and *integrity*, in all his dealings, were prominent features of his character. He was, indeed, considered, as difficult and hard in making bargains. When, however, they produced greater advantage than he expected, or than he deemed to be fair and just profit, he returned, to his correspondents, *as a gratuity*, the surplusage of his honest computation. In this manner, during the course of his mercantile career, some thousand pounds were restored. When the question was put to him, if he thought that his correspondents would have treated him in the same manner, had the bargain been equally unfavourable, as it had been favourable to him; and, when the severity, which his father had experienced, was brought to his recollection; his reply uniformly was—" With the *conduct* of others I have nothing to do.—It is my duty to regulate my own by the rules of equity, as they appear to me."

This was an answer expressive of a great mind. It is, to me, a proof of the strength of his *religious principles*. For, these only could have dictated such sentiments and conduct. I would fain hope that, however different the general sentiments may be, there are several instances of a similar kind, in the mercantile world, which may not be generally known. To the best interests of mankind the *fact*, which I have just now recorded, is of high importance. For, selfish minds, actuated by groveling and sordid opinions, have a strong tendency to ascribe their own characters to the whole human race, and to regard, as *visionary*, feelings of a more exalted description. To all such Mr. Burnett's *conduct* and *principles*, and those of a similar complexion, may be triumphantly opposed, and serve, on the ground of experience, to vindicate, from the imputation of being mere *theorists*, those who applaud and recommend more *generous*, and, therefore, *better* principles of action, than are entertained by the herd of *ignoble moralists*.

His affection for his relatives was also warm and constant. His humanity was expansive and vigorous, and particularly interested in the wants of the poor. During many years, he appropriated one or two hours every day, to the hearing of their cases, and to their relief. In this manner, he applied more than 300l. yearly.

On the return of his brother, James, from India, about the year 1773, they resolved to discharge their father's debts, each of them paying one half. The only exceptions, which they made, were in the case of one or two creditors, who had been, in the first instance, chiefly instrumental in ruining their father's credit, and then, after his failure was accomplished, treated him with the greatest harshness, and severity. This important *fact*, so honourable both to the subject of this Memoir, and to his brother, proves that strict integrity and honour were inherent in the family. As family-likenesses are exhibited in the *countenance*; so, we often find them in the *moral* and *intellectual* character. Those two brothers thus paid, on their father's account, about 7000l. or 8000l. This sum, which, compared with modern failures, may appear insignificant, was, when the failure of Mr. Burnett, sen. happened, and even at the time his debts were paid by his conscientious sons, considered as of no trivial magnitude.

The younger Burnett was never married, and, at the age of 55 years, died on the 9th of November, 1784. He possessed a small landed estate, lying in Buchan, in Aberdeenshire, and situated about 25 miles northward of Aberdeen, which he inherited from his mother. In this property he was succeeded by a brother, a clergyman in the Church of England, who died without issue. It devolved to a nephew, son of another brother of Mr. Burnett, who, now, possesses it. With the exception of this property, and of moderate legacies and annuities to various relatives, the residue of his fortune was appointed by him to be applied to charitable purposes.

Since his death, these charitable destinations have increased in value, and may, now, produce, altogether, about 700l. of annual income. They were, by the testator, appointed to be applied in the following manner.

I. For the relief of the poor in the city of Aberdeen, with a preference to those who may be *bed-rid*, or may labour under diseases deemed *incurable*.

II. For the relief of the poor residing on his own landed property, descending to his heirs.

III. For behoof of all the poor within the bounds of the county and synod of Aberdeen, which last contains 96 parishes, a sum, not less than 20l. and not exceeding 50l. in proportion to the extent of each parish, and to its peculiar circumstances, is to be paid annually, in rotation, till this payment has extended over all the parishes within the jurisdiction of the synod. When this rotation has taken place, it is to begin anew, and circulate, in this manner, in constant succession. The donation to each parish is to be applied, for the benefit of its poor, according to the discretion of its minister, or ministers, and elders.

IV. A sum is appropriated for the benefit of *lunatics*, or persons deprived of *reason*.

V. Another portion is destined to promote *inoculation* among the children of the poor. This money is, now, applied in support of a *Vaccine Institution* in Aberdeen—an improvement of *inoculation* unknown at the time of the donor's death.

VI. A small sum is appropriated to the benefit of the prisoners in the jail of Aberdeen, and, especially, to assist in procuring, to them, the consolations and correctives of religion, by the regular performance of divine worship within the walls of their confinement.

VII. A small part of this general fund is appointed to be set apart annually, and allowed to accumulate, for a two-fold purpose—*1st*; for his *Two Prizes*: *2dly*; for an addition to the provision previously made for the poor of Aberdeen. This accumulating fund is, for ever, to be applied to its objects, at the end of every fortieth year. The accumulation of the first 25 years, if not less than 1600l. is destined for Prizes to the authors of the two best Essays, on the subjects which he prescribed, and the following Work discusses. Three fourths are assigned to the first, and one fourth to the second in merit. Whatever exceeds these sums, allotted to the *Prizes*, is to be added to the fund for the use of the poor of Aberdeen. What this fund may produce, in the course of a long period of years, it is impossible to determine. In all probability, it will amount to a very large sum.

His motives for founding his two *Prizes* can be collected only from the terms in which the *foundation of them*, and his other benevolent destinations, are expressed. It can hardly be doubted that he was chiefly influenced by the strong impression, resting on his mind, of the high importance of the subjects proposed, and of the benefits likely to result, to mankind, from the comprehensive and able discussion of them. This appears chiefly from what is expressed in his *Deed of Settlement*, in behalf of the poor of Aberdeen, and in his *Provision for the Prizes*, contained in the same deed. To these he subjoins the following sentences :—" And I make the above *Destination*, with an hearty desire to be sincerely thankful to the Providence of Almighty God, for having conferred, upon me, the power to do so; and with an humble hope that the same will, in some degree, be acceptable in his sight; and as becoming a disciple, and conformable to the precepts of the Holy Jesus, being' intended for the relief of the distressed; and to promote a thorough conviction of those truths, which are of the greatest consequence to mankind."

Again; in a codicil, he adds—" I see it a great duty to be impressed with the inexpressible love of the Lord Jesus to mankind; and with a sense of the invaluable benefits they receive by him. Some unhappily do not acknowledge *Revelation*, and think

all is doubtful. To such, considerations, independent of *Revelation*, are necessary. To bring them to a conviction of a Deity is of the utmost consequence, and a step to a belief in *Revelation*. The considerations on the subject may be beneficial to all.".

From the words, last stated, it is not improbable that Mr. Burnett had been frequently in company, with persons who attacked Revelation, on *Atheistical principles*; and, as, from his being unavoidably much engaged in business, he could not be supposed to have studied such subjects with philosophical accuracy, that he found himself perplexed to reply to their distorted *metaphysics*. This conjecture, which is merely that of the writer of this *Memoir*, will acquire more probability, when it is considered that, when Mr. Burnett must have been in the prime of life, *Mr. Hume's Philosophy*, which did so much mischief to the young and volatile, was in high fashion in Scotland. To sneer at religion was deemed to be genteel. *That Philosophy*, as far as it relates to *religion*, and *morals*, has been exposed, as utterly false, by men of the most distinguished talents. Whether, or not, religious principle be, now, more firmly established, and more generally diffused, than was the case in Mr. Burnett's time, I pretend not to determine. The French Revolution exhibited the most ferocious aspects of *infidelity*, as connected with *politics*. An alarm was, hence, spread; and, although it be evident, to the smallest reflection, that *irreligion* has a tendency to subvert, the best interests of *society*, if not to dissolve it; still, no *reasoning*, or *persuasion*, could have excited the terror occasioned by this *revolutionary convulsion.* Hence, greater *external* respect, at least, has been shewn to religious institutions; and *infidelity*, is, now, generally connected with *licentious political opinions*. This may probably procure a fair hearing to the Gospel, and obtain a candid examination of its principles and tenets. To a mind, habituated to refer all events to the direction of Providence, it will appear that, to produce this result, was probably one reason for the permission of such horrible convulsions, and tremendous calamities, as have characterized our own times. On the other hand, it must be acknowledged that men's minds have been so much engaged by *war*, and *politics*, whose influence is far from being auspicious to the cultivation of *rational piety*, that they have had little leisure, and, perhaps, less inclination, to attend to the great concerns of *Religion*. Her voice, however, must, and will be heard, at last, if not in the calm tone of argument, or in the mild and affectionate language of admonition, at least, in the *thunder* of general calamity.

Mr. Burnett's opinion, relative to the effect that the *conviction of a Deity has in leading men to a belief of the truth of Revelation*, will appear perfectly just to every person who understands, and reflects on the subject. In fact, *Infidelity* and *Atheism*, in some form or other, are more intimately connected than may be generally supposed. It will be found that the greater part of modern *infidels* have had, and still have, no religious principle at all. *Christianity* admits, establishes, and expands all the just principles of *Natural Religion;* and enforces them by sanctions which no human authority could pretend to enact. To reject *Christianity* is, therefore, to reject *Natural Religion herself*, invested with her fairest, most engaging, and most venerable aspect. The truth is, that by far the greater part of *infidels* never give themselves the trouble to make any inquiry concerning *religious subjects*. Under the impression of certain vague, indefinite, and hastily assumed notions, they discard the *Christian faith*, by reason of a secret aversion from its *purity of principle*, and exalted *moral complexion*.

The peculiar nature of Mr. Burnett's *religious scruples* has not been ascertained. It is evident, however, that they could not relate to the *fundamental* articles of Christianity. For, of these he not only professes, in *his will*, his firm belief, but also his *deep sense of the inexpressible love of the Lord Jesus, and of the invaluable benefits which mankind receive by him*. That there are *difficulties in Revelation* itself no rational divine will deny. But, these affect neither the *essential* doctrines, such as they exist in the Sacred Scriptures, nor the moral precepts of Christianity. The Apostle Peter says, "that, in the Epistles of his beloved brother, Paul, are some things hard

to be understood, which they that are unlearned and unstable wrest, as they do also the other Scriptures, unto their own destruction." [*]

Mr. Burnett's *scruples* evinced that he was a conscientious believer, and an anxious inquirer after truth. I have, already, pointed out one *erroneous* conclusion which, at a certain period, they led him to adopt. But, even this was *sincerely erroneous*, and it appears that his mind, afterwards, embraced a juster view of the subject, in respect to which he erred. It is only persons of *some discernment*, and of *upright hearts*, that ever entertain religious scruples. The *profligate*, the *indifferent*, the *bigot*, the *enthusiast*, and the *hypocrite*, never have their minds perplexed in this manner. The *profligate* and the *indifferent* are utterly regardless whether the whole, or any part of the religious system, which is professed, be true, or false. The *bigot* and the *enthusiast* adopt, without examination, any set of opinions, and neither entertain *doubts* themselves, nor suffer others to entertain them, with regard to their *professed creed*. The *hypocrite pretends* to believe whatever is subservient to his *temporal interests*. The *honest inquirer* will, sometimes, experience *doubts*, with respect to certain points, and, ever open to conviction, will be anxious to obtain their solution.

The preceding narrative, and the quotations with which it is interspersed, evince the subject of it to have been a character of no ordinary stamp, in regard whether to his *intellectual*, or to his *moral qualities*. Though assiduously occupied in business, he, nevertheless, directed his mind to the most important and noblest objects that can fix the attention of man. Though employed in merchandise, and attentive to its chief aim—the *acquisition of wealth*—he expanded his heart to the most generous and comprehensive impressions of benevolence, and, in the midst of an increasing fortune, was constantly mindful of the indigent ; in the enjoyment of ease and comfort, felt for the distresses of those who " had none to help them." [†] Active in the discharge of the duties of his

---

* 2 Pet. iii. 16.   †
† Job xxix. 12.

terrestrial sphere, he raised his views to heaven, and, as the best preparation for its happiness, practised those virtues, in the completion of which this happiness must chiefly consist; made provision for the elucidation and extension of the *fundamental* principles of *religion*, which comforts man by the prospects of *eternity*; and, as far as lay in his power, endeavoured to sooth his *earthly* sorrows, and to supply the *present necessities* of his brethren.

The admiration of mankind is commonly excited by the splendour of *talent*, or by the celebrity of *exploit*. They seem to pay little regard to the objects for which the former has been displayed, or the latter performed. *Understanding, skill*, and *courage*, even when *mind* is applauded, engross their attention, while the *will*, and the *affections*, which are the springs of human action, are commonly overlooked, or disregarded, as of no moment. It is, however, the *principle* that imparts any real value to every exertion of the human faculties, and if the original view be *erroneous*, or *vicious*, the whole conduct, which it dictates, must be proportionably vitiated, and debased. *Wisdom* consists in the selection of the *best ends*, and of the adoption of the *best means* of their attainment. If the *end* be *absurd*, or *wicked*, all the *means* for its prosecution, however effectual they may be, ought only to produce the deeper regret, or the stronger reprobation. That Mr. Burnett's *views* were virtuous and noble, will not be contested; nor can it be denied that he devised very effectual *means* for their execution. Tried, then, by this equitable standard, he is certainly entitled to no common portion of applause.

Mankind generally admire what is *rare* and *unusual*. *Genuine probity*, and *pure benevolence*, united with *soundness of judgment*, are, I hesitate not to affirm, as uncommon as *genius*, and *acuteness of intellect*. By *probity* I understand not merely the *will*, the *inclination*, the *desire* to act a *virtuous part*, but also the right apprehension of what a *virtuous part* implies; and, when it has been clearly apprehended, the *courage* to adopt and to maintain it, without fear of *detriment*, or of *profligate ridicule*. For, it often happens that those, who are called *good men*, are *weak, uninformed*, and *compliant* personages, and have obtained

the character of *goodness* by their easy sacrifice of the interests of *virtue* and *truth*. On this account, they frequently do more mischief than the openly *profane* and *profligate*, who are hated, or despised, and cannot, therefore, produce any effect extensively pernicious. The *good man, as he is styled*, who, for the sake of what he terms *peace*, saying, in the words of the Prophet, " Peace, peace, when there is no peace,"[*] is always prepared to make concessions, and to surrender, to *deceit*, or to *violence*, some important cause, induces mankind, misled by his specious appearances, to suppose that the distinction between *virtue* and *vice* is very small, and that, on account of the *former*, no effort ought to be made, and no hardship endured.

Real *probity*, then, enlightened by *clearness of judgment*, and supported by the energy of *courage*, constitutes a very uncommon character, and is, therefore, on this ground, entitled to the highest commendation.

This *high-toned probity* bears a stronger resemblance to *genius*, than is commonly apprehended, and ought, on the ground on which *genius* is so much admired, to obtain a proportionable degree of admiration. *Genius* is the *gift of heaven*, and seems to possess a species of *inspiration*. Those, therefore, who are endowed with it, are considered as, in some respects, the favourites of the Deity; although, like other favourites, they often abuse their pre-eminence. *Exalted probity* may surely, with a far better title—a title sanctioned by Scripture—refer its origin to heaven. " It is that wisdom, which is from above, and is first pure, then peaceable, gentle, and easy to be intreated, full of mercy and good fruits, without partiality, and without hypocrisy."[†] It is certain that there is, in some minds, an inherent natural propensity to virtuous sentiments and conduct, a certain *susceptibility* of generous, affectionate, and noble impressions, by which they are distinguished from the ordinary, and *morally* groveling herd of their species. This seems to depend, in a great measure, on the peculiar complexion of the *imagination*; and this circumstance

---

[*] Jer. vi. 14.

[†] James iii. 17.

chiefly. asserts its analogy to genius. Some minds, even from their most early years, dwell, with peculiar pleasure, on descriptions of noble characters, and image them with delight. They will, hence, be prompted to imitate, and, if possible, to surpass them, in the moral qualities which they most admire. To such impressions the generality of mankind are totally insensible, and are wholly engrossed by self interest, or ignoble ambition, and hug themselves in the conceit of their prudence, and their policy. They cannot discover, with their feeble eyes, that region, in which the man, who is really virtuous, dwells, and, although they were translated into it, the purity of its atmosphere would be too keen for their asthmatic lungs.

There is another point of resemblance between genius and high probity. As the former embraces objects of a character, raised above ordinary life; so, it cannot always stoop to the minute consideration of these, and is liable to be deceived by that low, and microscopical cunning, whose attention is exclusively devoted to such objects. The case is the same with distinguished Probity. She can, with difficulty, conceive the mean and contemptible arts, the complete degradation of moral character, to which Improbity often descends; and she is, thus, sometimes, for a short time, deceived by these ignoble and reptile devices. This leads the race, who practise them, to value themselves on their childish sagacity. But, no man of genius, or of real worth, will envy them their creeping distinction.

It were much to be wished that these, and similar, considerations, had, on mankind, their due influence. If they possessed it, admiration and applause would not be exclusively appropriated to brilliancy of genius, or to grandeur of achievement; but, genuine moral excellence would obtain its legitimate share. Genius often flatters powerful and opulent Vice, or, by the display of metaphysical acumen, distorts truth, and recommends error. Heroism, vulgarly so called, has deluged the earth with blood, and laid waste the habitations of men. Moral excellence is "the salt of the earth,"* which prevents the putrefaction of the human

species. This is so much the case, that, were it not for those virtuous individuals, whom divine Providence supporting truth and virtue, has in every age, stationed in different parts of the world, human corruption would proceed with such accumulated aggravation, that the condition of our species would be desperate. It is to the wisdom, the beneficence, and the perseverance of such men, that the world is indebted for every salutary plan which has been adopted, and for every good institution which has ever been established. Notwithstanding the opposition with which they have had to struggle, the noblest title that any mortal can obtain, is that of being the friend of God, and the benefactor of mankind.

Let those who pervert their power for the purposes of oppressive pride, or lavish their wealth in dissipation, in sensuality, in frivolous amusement, and in all that degrades the individual, and injures society; let such institute a fair comparison between themselves, and Mr. Burnett, and learn to acknowledge that, in spite of their ostentatious assumption, and ridiculous vanity, they sink into utter insignificance, and ought to be satisfied if they are allowed to pass, with silent contempt. As soon as their bodies are consigned to the grave, their names are either buried in oblivion—their most fortunate posthumous condition—or are mentioned with derision, or disgust. His is recorded, as that of the patron of exalted and salutary science, as the reliever of indigence, as the comforter of distress; and will be transmitted, with undiminished applause, to remote posterity. To him may be justly applied Pope's beautiful lines, in which he describes the character of the MAN OF ROSS.

W. L. BROWN.

Origin and History of Benefit of Clergy, from CHITTY's "Practical Treatise on the Criminal Law." I. 667.

BY far the most important circumstance intervening between conviction and judgment, is the claim and allowance of the benefit of clergy, in those cases where it is by law to be granted. It is of course claimed immediately before judgment at the assizes. This is one of the most

* Matt. v. 13.

singular relics of old superstition, and certainly the most important. That, by a mere form, without the shadow of existing reason to support it, the severity of the common law should be tempered, may seem strange to those who have been accustomed to regard our criminal law as a regular fabric, not only attaining great practical benefit, but built upon solid and consistent principles. The benefit of clergy is, no doubt, of great practical advantage, compared to the dreadful list of offences which would otherwise be punished as capital; but it would be well worthy of an enlightened age to forsake such a subterfuge, and at once, without resorting to it, to apportion the degree of suffering to the atrocity and the danger of the crimes.*

The history of this singular mode of pardon, if so it can be termed, is both curious and instructive. In the early periods of European civilization, after the final destruction of the Roman empire, the church obtained an influence in the political affairs of nations, which threw a peculiar colouring over their original institutions. Monarchs who were desirous of atoning for atrocious offences, or of obtaining the sanction of heaven to their projects of ambition, were easily persuaded to confer immunities on the clergy, whom they regarded as the vicegerents of heaven. Presuming on these favours, that aspiring body soon began to claim as a right what had been originally conferred as a boon, and to found their demand to civil exemptions on a divine and indefeasible charter, derived from the text of Scripture, " touch not mine anointed and do my prophets no harm."† It need excite no surprise that they were anxious to take advantage of their dominion over the conscience, to exempt themselves from the usual consequences of crime. To the priests impunity was a privilege of no inconsiderable value. And so successful was the pious zeal to shield those who were dedicated to religion, from the consequences of any breach of temporal enactments, that in several countries they obtained a complete exemption from all civil

liabilities, and declared themselves responsible only to the pope and his ecclesiastical ministers.‡ They erected themselves into an independent community, and even laid the temporal authorities under subjection.§ Nobles were intimidated into vast pecuniary benefactions, and princes trembled at the terrors of spiritual denunciation. In England, however, this authority was always comparatively feeble. The complete exemption of the clergy from secular punishments, though often claimed, was never universally admitted. ‖ For repeated objections were made to the demand of the bishop and ordinary to have the clerks remitted to them as soon as they were indicted.¶ At length, however, it was finally settled in the reign of Henry VI. that the prisoner should first be arraigned, and might then claim the benefit of clergy as an excuse for pleading, or might demand it after conviction: and the latter of these courses has been almost invariably adopted to allow the prisoner the chance of a verdict of acquittal.

But if the privileges of the church were less dangerous in England than on the continent, they soon became more extensive. They not only embraced every order of clergymen; but were claimed for every subordinate officer of religious houses, with the numerous classes of their retainers: And so liberal was the application of these dangerous benefits, that, at length, every one who, in those days of ignorance was able to read, though not even initiated in holy orders, became entitled to demand them, such reading being deemed evidence of his clerical profession.** The privileges of the clergy were recognized and confirmed by statute in the reign of Edward the Third.†† It was then enacted, that all manner of clerks, secular as well as religious, should enjoy the privileges of holy church for all treasons or felonies except those immediately affecting his Majesty. To

---

* See Observations, Fest. C. L. 305, 306.

† Keilw. 181. P. S. 105, 15.

---

‡ 2 Hale, 324.   4 Bla. Com. 366. Burn, J. Clergy, II. Williams, J. Felony, V.

§ 2 Hale, 324.

‖ Keilw. 180.   2 Hale, 372, 377. 4 Bla. Com. 366.

¶ 2 Hale, 377.   4 Bla. Com. 366.

** 2 Hale, 372.

†† 25 Edw. III. c. 4.

the advantage of this provision all who could read were admitted. * But as learning became more common, this extensive interpretation was found so injurious to the security of social life, that the legislature, notwithstanding the opposition of the church, were compelled, to afford a partial remedy. In the reign of Henry the Seventh,† a distinction was drawn between persons actually in holy orders, and those who, in other respects, secular, were able to read, by which the latter were only allowed the benefit of their learning once, and on receiving it to be branded in the left thumb with a hot iron, in order to afford evidence against them on any future occasion. The church seems to have lost ground in the succeeding reign, probably in consequence of the separation of England from the sway of the Roman Pontiff; for all persons, though actually in orders, were rendered liable to be branded, in the same way as the learned class of laymen. ‡ But, in the time of Edward the Sixth, the clergy were restored to all the rights of which they were deprived by his predecessor, except as to certain atrocious crimes which it became necessary more uniformly to punish. § At the same time, some of the more enormous evils attendant on this general impunity were done away. Murder, poisoning, burglary, highway robbery, and sacrilege, were excepted from all that privilege which was confirmed as to inferior offences. ‖ But peers of the realm for the first offence were to be discharged in every case, except murder and poisoning, even though unable to read.¶

But here we must pause before we proceed to follow the gradual improvement of this privilege, to enquire what was originally done with an offender to whom it was allowed, by those ecclesiastical authorities who claimed the right of judging

him, and in what manner the power of the church in this respect was ultimately destroyed. It appears that after a layman was burnt in the hand, a clerk discharged on reading, or a peer without either burning or penalty, he was delivered to the ordinary to be dealt with according to the ecclesiastical canons. ** Upon this, the clerical authorities instituted a kind of purgation, the real object of which was to make him appear innocent, who had been already shown to be guilty, and to restore him to all those capacities of which his conviction had deprived him.†† To effect this the party himself was required to make oath of his innocence, though before he might have confessed himself guilty. Then twelve compurgators were called to testify their belief in the falsehood of the charges. Afterwards he brought forward witnesses completely to establish that innocence of which he had induced so weighty a presumption. Finally, it was the office of the jury to acquit him; and they seldom failed in their duty.‡‡ If, however, from any singular circumstance they agreed in the justice of the conviction, the culprit was degraded and compelled to do penance. §§ As this seldom occurred, and the most daring perjuries were thus perpetually committed, the courts of common law were soon aroused to abridge the power of these clerical tribunals. They, therefore, sometimes delivered over the privileged of felony, when his guilt was very atrocious, without allowing him to make purgation; the effect of which proceedings was his perpetual imprisonment and incapacity to acquire personal or to enjoy real estate, unless released by his Majesty's pardon.‖‖ But the severity of this proceeding almost rendered it useless; and it became absolutely necessary for the legislature to interfere in order to prevent the contemptible perjuries which this absurd ceremony produced under the sanction and pretence of religion. This desirable object was

---

* 2 Hale, 272, 3. Kel. 100, 101, 102. Hawk. b. 2. c. 33. s. 5. Williams, J. Felony, V. See Mode of Admission of Defendant convicted of Manslaughter. 1 Salk. 61.

† 4 Hen. VII. c. 13.

‡ 28 Hen. VIII. c. 1. s. 7. 32 Hen. VIII. c. 3. s. 8.

§ 1 Edw. VI. c. 12. s. 10.

‖ Id. Ibid.

¶ 1 Edw. VI. c. 12. s. 14.

** Hob. 291. 4 Bla. Com. 368.

†† Hob. 291. 3 P. Wms. 447, 8. 4 Blu. Com. 368.

‡‡ Hob. 291. 3 Pr. Wms. 447, 8. 4 Bla. Com. 364.

§§ Hob. 289. 4 Bla. Com. 364.

‖‖ 3 Pr. Wms. 448, 9. 4 Bla. Com. 368.

effected in the reign of Elizabeth, and the party, after being allowed his clergy and burnt in the hand, was to be discharged without any interference of the church to annul his conviction.*

The clerical process being thus abolished, it was thought proper, at the same time, to empower the temporal judges to inflict a further punishment where they should regard it as proper. The 18 Eliz. c. 7. empowered them, therefore, to direct the convict to be imprisoned for a year or any shorter period. But the law on this subject was still in many respects imperfect. Females were still liable to the punishment of death without any exemption, in all cases of simple felony; because being never eligible to the clerical office, they were not included in any of the extensions of the benefit of clergy. No other proof need be adduced to show the absurdity of the very foundations of the system.† At length it was enacted that women convicted of simple larcenies under the value of 10s. should be punished with burning in the hand and whipping, exposure in the stocks, or imprisonment for any period less than a year.‡ And in the reign of William and Mary they were admitted to all the privileges of men, in clergyable felonies, on praying the benefit of the statute;§ though they can only once be allowed this means of escaping.‖ In the same reign, the punishment of burning in the hand was changed for a more visible stigma on the cheek,¶ but was soon afterwards brought back to the original practice.**

Hitherto all laymen except peers, who, on their conviction, were found unable to read, were liable to suffer death for every clergyable felony. But it was at length discovered, that ignorance instead of an aggravation was an excuse for guilt, and that the ability to read was no extenuation of

crime;†† and, therefore, by 5 Ann, c. 6, the idle ceremony of reading was abolished,‡‡ and all those who were before entitled to clergy on reading, were now to be admitted without any such form to its benefits. At the same time it was sensibly felt that the branding, which had dwindled into a mere form, and the year's imprisonment which the judges were impowered to inflict, were very inadequate punishments for many clergyable offences; and, therefore, the court were authorized to commit the offenders to the house of correction, for any time not less than six months nor exceeding two years, and to double it in case of escaping.§§ Further alterations have since been made in the penalties consequent upon clergy. The 4 Geo. I. c. 11,‖‖ and 6 Geo. I. c. 23, provide, that the court on the allowance of this benefit, for any larceny whether grand or petit, or other felonious theft not excluded from the statutable indulgence, may, instead of judgment of burning in case of men, and whipping in that of females, direct the offender to be transported for seven years to America, which has been since altered to any part of his majesty's colonies.¶¶ To return within the period was, at the same time, made felony without benefit of clergy. And by several subsequent provisions, many wise alterations have been made respecting transportation, and the mode of treating offenders while under its sentence.*** At length the burning in the hand was entirely done away, and the judges are empowered to sentence the criminal, in its room and in addition to the former penalties, to a pecuniary fine, or, except in the case of manslaughter, to private whipping, not more than thrice to be inflicted, in the presence of three witnesses.††† Provisions were at the same time made for the employment of this description of convicts in penitentiary houses,

---

* 18 Eliz. c. 7. 2 Sess. C. 265 to 282. 3 P. W. 444, 5, 6.
 † Fost. C. L. 305, 6. 2 Hale, 371, 372.
 ‡ 21 Jac. I. c. 6. Fost. 305, 6.
 § 3 & 4 W. & M. c. 9. s. 5. Fost. 306.
 ‖ 4 & 5 W. & M. c. 24. s. 13.
 ¶ 10 & 11 W. III. c. 23. 3 P. W. 451.
 ** 5 Ann, c. 6. 3 P. W. 451.

†† Fost. 305, 6.
 ‡‡ Fost. 305, 6. 3 P. W. 443, 4.
 §§ 5 Ann, c. 6. s. 2.
 ‖‖ See observations on this statute, 3 P. W. 490.
 ¶¶ 19 Geo. III. c. 74.
 *** 16 Geo. II. c. 15. 8 Geo. III. c. 15. 19 Geo. III. c. 74. 31 Geo. III. c. 46. 24 Geo. III. Sess. 2. c. 56.
 ††† 19 Geo. III. c. 74. s. 6.

where a system of reformation might be adopted, and an experiment made how far punishment might become conducive to its noblest and most legitimate use—the reformation and benefit of the offender.* But this regulation, though applauded by Blackstone,† and other humane writers,‡ after having been continued by several subsequent acts, § was recently suffered to expire.‖ It appears from these several modern regulations; that, as observed by Mr. Justice Foster, we now consider benefit of clergy, or rather the benefit of the statutes, as a relaxation of the rigour of the law, a condescension to the infirmities of the human frame, exempting offending individuals in some cases from the punishment of death, and subjecting them to milder punishment; and therefore in the case of clergyable felonies, we now profess to measure the degree of punishment by the real enormity of the offence, and not as the ignorance and superstition of former times suggested, by a blind respect for sacred persons or sacred functions, nor by an absurd distinction between subject and subject originally owing to impudent pretension on one hand, and to mere fanaticism on the other.¶

MISCELLANEOUS COMMUNICATIONS.

Kilworthy, near Tavistock,
SIR,   *July* 30, 1816.

HAD the modern Bishop of Calcutta's notion of the Greek Article been stated to the ancient Philosophers of Athens, they would probably have inquired—" May we know what this new doctrine, whereof thou speakest, is?" Aristotle regarded the Article as a term of no signification in itself, detached from the sentence in which it occurs. ἄρθρον δέ ἐστι φωνὴ ἄσημος, ἣ λόγου ἀρχὴν, ἢ τέλος, ἢ διορισμὸν δηλοῖ. C. 20, De Poetica. In his estimation, the Article served only as indicative of a certain object of sense, or of intelligence.

Apollonius, the grammarian, remarks that some indications are ocular, and some are mental.—τὰς μὲν τὴν ὄψεων εἶναι δείξεις, τὰς δὲ τὸ νε. De Syntaxi, L. 2, C. 3.

The primary force of the definite Article consists merely in directing the eye, or the attention t the definitive power assigned to it is rather an effect of the sight, where the object is present, or of the mind in drawing the necessary inference, where the object is previously described, or specified. The Article is only an index; having indicated the thing intended, it does no more: thus the index of a barometer points to the mercury, but the eye ascertains the degree of its elevation. Mr. Tooke, in his "Diversions of Purley," says that the Article is "a mere substitute for a particular term"—to do that which, on the contrary is done by another principle; namely the eye or the mind.

" Sed pulchrum est Digito Monstrari, et dicier, Hic est."   PERSIUS.

It is perhaps worthy of observation, that both Aristotle and Euclid frequently omit the Article in their respective definitions as to the subject, and predicate. θεῦ δὲ ἐνέργεια, ἀθανασία· τῦτο δὲ ἐστι ζωὴ ἀίδιος? Arist. de Cœlo, L. 2, C. 3.

The inscription on the Altar at Athens, to which the Apostle alluded in his speech on Marshill, was without the Article—Αγνωστω θεω· but Paul applies the Article to the name of the Deity, which he announced.

Dr. Middleton asserts that the Greek Article is the pronoun relative 'ο, which, he thinks, has no resemblance to the definitive Article—the—in English; but though it be granted that 'ο was originally a pronoun, it is no more a pronoun now, than it is a verb or adjective. The Monthly Reviewer of his book, has justly maintained the superiority of the English over the Greek

---

* 19 Geo. III. c. 74. s. 5 to 27.

† 4 Bla. Com. 371, 2.

‡ See Montague's Collection of Opinions on the Punishment of Death, vol. 2.

§ 24 Geo. III. st. 2. c. 56. 28 Geo. III. c. 24. 34 Geo. III. c. 60. 39 Geo. III. c. 52.

‖ 25 March, 1802. 2 Will. J. 443. Id. 448.

¶ Post. 305, 6.

in precision, by the means of the indefinite—an—in combination with the definitive.

Dr. Carpenter has truly remarked, that Dr. Middleton's exceptions and limitations furnish sufficient testimonies that Mr. Sharp's construction of the controverted passages is not required by the Greek idiom. Dr. M. says "that all nouns are excluded from the rule, except those which are significant of character." When Θεος is subject to the rule, it signifies nothing more than a divine character; to which every Christian ought to aspire.

I am desirous of expressing a hope that your able correspondent, Dr. Charles Lloyd, will not allow "the victory to be silently conceded." Silence is not always an occasion of triumph. The Trojan Chief, though clad in the armour of Achilles, boasted not of victory, while the Grecian Hero was silent in his tent.

Why will not Dr. Lloyd himself, or his worthy friend, Mr. R. Taylor, promote the interests of Biblical criticism, by communicating to your Repository their view of those principles, which prove to demonstration that the Deity of Christ is not to be inferred by any right application of the Article to passages in the New Testament.— "Truth," says Berkeley, "is the cry of all, but the game of a few." If they interfere to decide this controversy, we may then say with the bard—

"This battle fares like to the morning's war,
When dying clouds contend with growing light."

A doctrine that depends, like the Deity of the Logos, on the application of an Article, in a dead language, while in living languages it varies with the thoughts of men, and their natural idioms, may be pronounced, in the Latin of Papal Benediction, to be

"*In articulo mortis.*"

I am, Sir, with great respect, &c.
WILLIAM EVANS.

P.S. Such a contribution as I have thus solicited would not supersede a separate publication, prepared by Dr. Lloyd, on the Greek pre-positive Article. Professor Porson communicated seven of his "Letters to Travis," to be inserted in the Gentleman's Magazine.

Sir, Bridport, July 5, 1816.

THE following communication contains a plan for elevating all the subjects of these realms, even the poorest among them, to the honourable rank of kings, without endangering their allegiance to our rightful sovereign King George. Should it on the perusal meet with your approbation, it is very much at your service for insertion in your valuable Repository.

Your occasional Correspondent,
T. HOWE.

AMBITION is natural to man, and the mind destitute of all species of it, (if such a supposition may be admitted) would be dormant and inactive. Feeling no stimulus for exertion, it would remain stationary, and make no improvement in science, or any other excellent attainment. It would resemble a vessel on the bosom of the ocean, so becalmed as to make no progress in any direction. Motives of ambition of some kind or other are as necessary to put the mind in motion, and call forth its latent energies, as the wind at sea to waft the sailing ships to their desired ports. Whether in any supposed case it be *censurable* or *laudable*, depends upon the object to which it is directed. From early association of ideas, from hearing the pleasures, riches and honours of the world highly extolled, young persons are led to estimate them beyond their due value. As they advance in years, some or other of these objects present themselves to excite their ambition.

Rank and pre-eminence among their fellow creatures, are the wish of most persons, and the *aim* of those who are placed in such situations, as to give them a chance of obtaining them. To be, however, in some of the highest conditions of society, is the lot but of few. To sit on the throne and wear the crown of royalty, is the peculiar honour of one only of our fellow mortals, till incapacity or death makes way for his successor. This at least is the constitution of our own country. It may therefore at the first view excite the astonishment of my readers to be told, that the present writer has a plan to communicate to the public, (which indeed did not originate with himself,) whereby *all persons* may become kings, and exercise regal government. Let not the zealous royalist be alarmed; he may be assured that there is no treason in the proposal; it does not interfere with the allegiance due to his Majesty. The plan, indeed, if duly executed, would make persons of all classes of the community *kings* (even the meanest beggars); but instead of inspiring them with the spirit of rebellion against our lawful Chief Magistrate, it would render them more peaceable subjects, more worthy and useful members of society, and unspeakably happier in themselves: it would confer a noble dignity on them, to which the highest peers of the realm, even its illustrious princes, have no claim, if they do not adopt the same mode:—without this every man is a *slave*, however exalted may be his external rank. This however does not come to men by hereditary succession, like the crown of the United Kingdom, but is to be attained by the individual's own exertions. He must acquire a signal and complete victory over those whom he is destined to rule, before he can reign in safety and in peace. Yea he must become an *absolute monarch*, whose will is not to be controlled, or he himself will be led captive, and doomed to the worst kind of bondage, by those who ought to be his obedient subjects. When the latter has been the case, it has made my heart bleed, to see him degraded from his throne, trampled as it were in the dust, treated with every mark of indignity, and made to submit to the most servile employments. What shocking scenes of riot and outrage, wretchedness and misery, have then succeeded each other! According to the constitution of our country, the *people* take part in the government, by their representatives chosen by themselves: this is a right which they may justly claim. In the other kingdom, however, to which I refer, *none* of its subjects are qualified to be admitted to any share in the government; and whenever this be done, confusion and disorder immediately ensue. That the sovereign should be the sole ruler according to his discretion, and that any indulgence granted to his subjects should be sanctioned by his authority, is as necessary for *their* preservation and safety, as for his own dignity and happiness.

By this time, no doubt, my sagacious readers perceive in what sense every man may be a *king*, that the kingdom is *within* him, and that his *humours* and *fancies*, his *appetites* and *passions* are his subjects, whom he is to govern according to the laws prescribed by that great and good Being, from whom all authority emanates.

I was led to these reflections, by the perusal of the following lines of a Poem, composed by a learned and pious Divine, nearly, I believe, a century ago. These I shall transcribe with a little alteration.

    " Rex est, qui metuit nihil,
       Rex est, qui cupit nihil,
       Hoc regnum sibi quisque dat."
                   SEN.

" What ails the mortals! See their rage
For empire, on life's little stage: *
When he's a *prince*, and well may vie,
With loudest name in monarchy,
Who sways with sweet and soft control,
The wide dominions of his soul;
Who with a free despotic hand,
Has all his passions at command;
Makes appetites and humours wait,
At reason's throne and wisdom's gate;
Who nothing fears, save to molest
The spring of peace within his breast;
Lives unconcern'd at what may be
Lock'd up in dark futurity;
Whose just desires are still confin'd
To noble treasures of the mind,
Nor hunts for wealth, nor covets more
Than frugal state of earthly store:
Who thus with sails and streamers whirl'd,
Rides master of the lesser world,
Has more of king, and royal robe,
Than he that governs half the globe.
And now what's strange, believe it you,
'Tis not more strange, my friend, than true,
There's none but may, howe'er so low,
This kingdom on himself bestow—
A kingdom that more pleasure sheds,
Than all the pomp of crowned heads."

     A View of Death, a Poem,
               By J. REYNOLDS.

SIR,   *Norwich, July 20, 1816.*

DURING the lifetime of Dr. John Taylor, he was followed about the streets of this city, with cries of " there goes the old heretick!" and very soon after his death appeared a pamphlet, called *The Arian and Socinian's Monitor*, in which he was represented as tossing on the waves of Hell, and suffering the most exquisite tortures, on account of his religious opinions. This work has been, and yet is industriously circulated. The last edition which I saw was accompanied with an engraving, representing him in the situation above described. Such being the methods which Calvinists have adopted, in order to prevent the circulation of his opinions, and such

---

        * *Instead of*
   " What ails the mortals, that they so
Contend for empire here below?"

the kind of warfare they have chosen, I was not at all surprised to see the following quotation from a work, which was reviewed in the Monthly Repository for June, entitled, *Wilson's History and Antiquities of Dissenting Churches:* "We have somewhere met with an observation of Dr. Taylor, of Norwich, which is much to our present purpose. The Doctor, who was a zealous Socinian, and a learned tutor at Warrington, expressed his surprise how it happened that most of his pupils turned Deists. The fact it seems he admitted, but he never thought of accounting for it from the sceptical tendency of Socinian principles."

I thank your Reviewer for this quotation. I should most probably else have never seen the passage, or even heard of the work; and I trust you will allow me to occupy a small part of the Repository, in exposing the falsehood of some of the assertions which it contains. 1st. *Dr. Taylor was a zealous Socinian.* Now it is certain that Mr. Wilson is either completely unacquainted with Dr. Taylor's writings, or that he is entirely ignorant of the meaning of the term *Socinian.* If the former, how dares he to make any assertion about Dr. Taylor's creed; if the latter, let him study some dictionary before he sets himself up as the historian of Dissenting Churches. That Dr. Taylor was an Arian is very well known to all who have read his works. The following passage (which I copy from his own handwriting) is sufficient evidence to this fact. "The Scriptures tell us that there is such a being as the only begotten Son of God; the first born of every creature, by whom he made all things: whereby I understand that this being is the first or most excellent production of the divine power. This being is called 'the Word,' John i. 1, 'the Word of God,' Rev. xix. 3, probably because God by him spake and declared his will to his creatures, especially to us. This being, called 'the Word,' existed in the beginning (or at the creation of the world, Gen. i. 1,) in a state of great glory, and was then with the Supreme God and Father, John xvii. 5.; and he was God, or *a God:* i. e. in a state of great glory and power. For the term *God* is applied to any being to whom power is given, not only to angels, but also to men. And that we might not mistake

the Evangelist as to whom he meant as the Supreme God, he repeats it again, ver. 2, ' the same was in the beginning with God,' for God who was with the Supreme God, cannot be the Supreme God with whom he was. Further, this being, called the ' Son of God,' or the ' Word,' is that being or agent by whom God made every thing (Ephes. iii. 9, Heb. i. 2) so universally, that all the rest of the creation, without exception, was made by him, i. e. by that power and wisdom which he had received from God: so that he, himself alone was immediately produced by the power of God, and all the rest, without exception, were made by his instrumentality. And as it pleased God to employ him as the creator of the world, so also it is his further pleasure that he should be our final judge." These were Dr. Taylor's sentiments; how far they are consistent with Mr. Wilson's assertion that he was a *zealous Socinian,* your readers will easily determine for themselves.

2d. But Dr. Taylor, notwithstanding he was *a learned tutor and a zealous Socinian,* "expressed his surprise how it happened that most of his pupils turned Deists." This assertion proves Mr. Wilson to have been as ignorant of the events of Dr. Taylor's life, as of his theological opinions. Dr. Taylor went to Warrington in November, 1757, and he died in March, 1761. So far, therefore, from his having "expressed his surprise how it happened that most of his pupils turned Deists;" he did not live to see any of them even complete their course of education; so that, as your Reviewer conjectures, this "somewhere" of Mr. Wilson's turns out to be "no where." The whole story is a gross falsehood, coined by a spirit of bigotry and malice, and circulated with the hope of defaming and vilifying the pious dead. I don't mean to charge Mr. Wilson with being its author; it is probably very current among his brethren, and he might think it (as indeed he intimates) so much to his purpose, as to insert it in his "History of Dissenting Churches." He is probably only a retailer of scandal and falsehood. But, Sir, what else can be expected from a man who could have the unblushing effrontery to write and to publish the following sentence: that "Dr. Lardner, among other Socinian authors, "has contributed to poison the streams of divine truth, and promote an universal scepticism in matters of belief."

To such persons as Mr. Wilson, I should use the words of Dr. Harwood, in his Funeral Sermon for Dr. Taylor: " Let those whose Christian principles could teach them to abuse him, and deny him salvation, heap upon his memory all the execrations that enthusiasm can very religiously and piously utter. Let them spurn his ashes and insult over his grave with the same ridiculous wildness, the same frantic postures, and the same low revenge, as it is well known some of them did over Dr. James Foster's after his interment. Such treatment *now* can no more affect his happiness, than it ever affected his arguments. He now enjoys a calm undisturbed repose, under the protection and guardianship of him, *who has the keys of death, and the invisible world:* and in the morning of the resurrection, *when those who sleep in the dust of the earth shall awake,* will rise from the ruins of the grave, the first in immortal glory, splendour and blessedness." I am, Sir,

Your's, respectfully,
EDWARD TAYLOR.

Mechanism ; an Allegory.
[Concluded from p. 390.]
Section II.

IN the mean time the Genius so ordered it, that while the mists of illusion continued to accumulate on one side of the horizon, the beams of light began to break in from the opposite hemisphere. Some of the operators now began to rouse out of their lethargy, and to resume the use of their faculties. An honest spirited fellow, who was not altogether averse to his employment, and had luckily discovered a copy of the original instructions, began to protest stoutly against the gainful trade of the managers ; and by degrees discovered that the superabundant blessings which they pretended to dispense, on certain terms, had no existence but in their crafty imaginations. The mist, however, continued to be so great, that he could by no means distinguish between the Genius and the eminent Operator with whom he had been so strangely confounded ; nor could he distinctly see to read the book of instructions. But from what he could trace, he concluded

that the machines, when worn out and broken, lost their *activity*, though he could not divest himself of the idea that their *essences* remained. This conclusion did away at once the pretensions of the managers ; but the admission that these essences remained indestructible, though their action was suspended, proved the fruitful source of numerous errors. This notion being directly opposed to the purport of the promise, that the machines having been destroyed would be reconstructed, led to conclusions no less opposed to it. It was supposed that they would be recalled to action and retain their activity, amid the continued fury of the most intense flames, serving but as the instruments of their violence. It was even believed that the language in the instructions, which plainly expressed the temporary *destruction* of the machines, purported their *continued action*, in vomiting incessant flames upon their respective operators ; and also that all of them except the very first that had been made, were for one single offence of that operator, of which all the other operators were wholly unconscious, constructed for this very purpose. So far did many of them carry this persuasion, that they thought it the height of presumption to expect the least beneficial effects, by any exertions, or attention to the instructions of the Genius, of which they were capable. Both his machines and his instructions, according to their ideas, were the very reverse of being useful : nor did they think they could be better employed, than in making strong protestations that they were vile instruments, fit for nothing but mischief, and that it was impossible for them to do any real good whatever with them, and therefore that they hoped he would be pleased entirely to change their structure, and moreover, so to overrule and direct all their own operations, that they would in future shower down nothing but perpetual benefits upon themselves, whatever might be the fate of the great majority of their companions. This kind of language they considered as expressive of proper dispositions in the presence of the Genius, and such as he would be very likely to reward in that extraordinary, not to say most extravagant manner which they requested. It might have been well had they considered how they would have liked to have workmen of their own, coming before them with similar complaints, and expecting to be rewarded ever after with the like liberality, without any further exertions on their part. They were intent only on obtaining deliverance from this imaginary calamity; and concluded that the great business of that operator, whom they confounded with the Genius himself, was to effect this deliverance; by making the essence of his machine, while it was in the act of being broken to pieces, to discharge its fury so powerfully upon his own person, that the misery which it inflicted upon him, would *compensate* for that of as many of the sufferers as he thought fit; while the rest, for no other purpose than his own *pleasure* or *glory*, would be left the ceaseless victims of their mischief working machines. In consequence of this strange compensation, the essences of the machines of the *chosen* few were supposed to sustain the total change desired, and ever after to work in such a manner, as would no less inevitably shower down immense blessings upon them; so that from this time forward, they would have little to do, but to hymn praises to the Genius, and to pipe perpetual songs of joy and rejoicing, while their unfortunate companions were incessantly uttering the most dreadful groans and shrieks, from the agonizing sufferings to which they would be devoted. In all this there was little to encourage the operators in the sober pursuit of their employment, or to cultivate in their minds a proper sense of their obligations to their great Benefactor. His gracious promise of the future re-fabrication of their machines, was little understood or attended to; and the dreadful circumstances, both real and imaginary, attending the breaking to pieces of the distinguished Operator's machine, though an event common to the whole system of mechanism, was much more the subject of attention and triumph, on account of the supposed *substitution*, than those of its glorious re-construction, though this was the only pattern which had been presented of those improved machines, which were hereafter to be placed in the hands of the operators for their use.

The day, however, was advancing, and copies of the instructions written in plain characters were now freely and extensively circulated; and though

the *root* of the evil * was not very soon detected, yet many of its principal branches were by degrees lopped off. It was indeed long before the great body of the operators found proper opportunities of thinking and acting for themselves; and those who were employed as their guides, were too apt to throw obstacles in the way of their exertions and discoveries. Some of them even endeavoured to obstruct the free circulation of the instructions, and

---

* The writer cannot help conceiving that the doctrine of the immortality of the soul lies at the foundation of theological error. It appears to deny the reality of man's primitive doom, "dust thou art, and unto dust shalt thou return;" since it maintains the uninterrupted existence of the perceptive, conscious principle, *without* which man is indeed dust, but *with which* alone he may be said to be pure intelligence. It fabricates a new doom for him of a very different nature, viz. that *he is destined to live and suffer the most exquisite torments amid flames to all eternity.* - It provides a new deliverance from this new calamity, by representing the mind of the man Jesus, not merely as *a ray* of divine intelligence, according to the more modest conceptions of the heathens, but as the infinite Intelligence itself; and then maintaining that this infinite nature underwent, in its sufferings on the cross, all the miseries, which the immortal souls of the *elect* were destined to undergo in hell, as a *substitute* for those miseries. Thus this doctrine is continually amusing the majority of its votaries, with different natures, different destinies, and different deliverances from those about which the Scriptures are conversant. Without this persuasion, it is highly probable, that the idea of a God-man, of endless torments, and of the infinite Deity suffering in lieu of some of the rays of his immortal nature, with the change of nature, arising from the infusion of the *Holy Ghost, a third person* in the *God-head* would never have entered into the human mind. Admit that the whole man " *returns to his dust,*" and " the glorious gospel of the blessed God," reversing this sad doom, and proclaiming the blessings of the second estate of man, when he shall become a " *quickening*" or " *vivifying spirit,*" over which " death hath *no dominion,*" shines forth in its genuine lustre. " *The wages of sin*" indeed " *is death;*" and it is therefore the object of the resurrection from death, and the judgment which will follow, to effect our deliverance from both these evils, to *destroy him that hath the power of death, that is the Devil,* or sin our deadly adversary.

many of them enjoined under the heaviest pains and penalties, that they should be understood precisely in the sense which they thought fit to prescribe. They were all, excepting a small numbe who had imbibed the true spirit of the instructions, decidedly against any persons, excepting themselves, presuming to open their mouths in public assemblies, so that *their* decisions for the most part assumed the character of laws; and the body of the operators, who, alas! in general, were too little disposed to it, were much prevented from reasoning, or *holding sweet converse together,* upon the subjects which related to their common employment. This conduct, of the few who undertook to expound the instructions, was the more extraordinary, as by so doing, they were themselves in the constant habit of violating an express injunction of the common Master.[*]

Notwithstanding these obstacles, light gradually broke in often through the medium of some of those guides who felt its salutary influence. A large body of the operators under one of them (for they generally moved in bodies like a flock too implicitly following a shepherd), embraced the persuasion, that more depended upon the will of the operators, than some had represented. Hence though they supposed the nature of their calamities, and the means of their deliverance to be much as has been above described, and were even remarkable for insisting much on the great and sudden change in the machines, which they imagined was conspicuous in certain violent movements, in reality occasioned by the agitated state of the operators; yet they certainly laid more stress on their attention to their business than many others. And though while following their employment they were continually fancying that either the good or an evil genius was operating upon their machines, and were often relating to each other curious particulars about their *experiences,* yet as all these were in reality their own doings, they gradually learnt many just, with some very injudicious distinctions, between the right and wrong movements of the machine. Upon the whole they made considerable progress both in point of skill and industry, though not without giving a very unfavourable bent to the operations of their machines upon some neighbouring operators, who could not enter into their fancies.

The time would fail were I to attempt to particularize the various discoveries and improvements which have been made and are still in progress. The attention of a few only has yet been directed to obtain a more distinct view of the Genius, and of the operator whose merits have been so signally rewarded. In this attempt, notwithstanding the opposition and annoyance which they have met with from the lovers of mystery and enchantment, they have succeeded, first in distinguishing them from each other, and then in recognising each of them in his true character. They have also learnt that each operator will reap benefits, precisely in proportion to the grateful and proper use which he makes of the excellent piece of mechanism which has been kindly placed in his hands. And by availing themselves of the advantageous circumstances in which they stand for apprehending the true structure of the machines, and the genuine purport of the instructions, with the necessity of applying closely to their business, actuated by a principle of gratitude to the Genius, of generous regard to the interests of each other, and of all their fellow operators, whatever may be their progress or want of progress either in knowledge, skill or industry, there is every reason to conclude, that they may rise to distinguished eminence in their employment. Then when this great Genius both of power and beneficence, shall perform his promise of re-fabricating the whole system of mechanism, upon that highly improved plan of which a pattern has been given, they will find little difficulty in applying their respective instruments to the most lastingly beneficial uses.

SIR, *August* 6, 1816.

A CORRESPONDENT in your last number, [p. 392, 393.] who signs himself T. R. S. proposes two questions, which he wishes me to answer through the medium of your Repository;—the one respecting my projected History of Unitarianism, the other concerning the translation of the Racovian Catechism, which was long ago announced as in preparation. With your leave, Sir, I will in a few

---

[*] Matt. xxiii. 8—11.

words give him all the satisfaction in my power on both these points.

I have certainly not abandoned the History to which your Correspondent refers. Ever since the first public notice was given of my design, my attention has been directed to the subject; and I have been engaged, as opportunity offered, in searching after and collecting materials for its execution. A variety of circumstances, which need not be here detailed, and, above all, a severe and long protracted bodily indisposition, have hitherto put it out of my power to digest and arrange the multiform mass of materials which I have succeeded in bringing together. I can, however, assure your Correspondent, that it is my fixed purpose, if Providence vouchsafe me health, to proceed with the work; and to devote to it as large a portion of time as I can spare, after the imperative demands of my professional and other avocations have been answered.

It affords me satisfaction to be able to inform your correspondent, that the Translation of the Racovian Catechism after which he inquires, is in such a state of forwardness, that by the time this paper meets his eye, it will, most probably, be in the hands of the printer: and unless some unforeseen accident occur to interrupt its progress, through the press, I have no doubt of its being before the public by the month of December.

In my original announcement of this work I stated my intention to be, to make the translation from the most recent authorized edition; but, at the same time, to collate the text with that of the preceding editions, in order to mark the alterations which had, at successive periods been made, and thus exhibit the changes, which had taken place, in the opinions of the Polish Unitarians. I have deemed it adviseable, however, on re-consideration, to abandon this part of my design. On a minute comparison, of the several editions, and I believe I am in possession of every one that was published, in Latin, I observed that no material alteration, in respect to any matter of religious belief, had been introduced, by the learned editors of those which were last printed. The chief differences consist of explanatory additions, when the subjects appeared to be obscurely stated or insufficiently explained; and of some considerable improvements in the language and style of the original text.

Instead of the marginal notes with which such a collation would have disfigured and burthened the pages of the Translation, without answering any purpose of utility, I shall substitute some short remarks in those parts of the work that relate to points of doctrine, respecting which modern Unitarians differ in opinion from the authors of this formulary. By this method of annotation, the reader will be furnished with a comparative view of the two systems; that is, of Unitarianism as it is now generally professed, and of Unitarianism as it was held by those great and venerable men, who formed so brilliant a constellation in Poland at the era of the reformation, and to whom, under Providence, the cause of divine truth is so signally indebted. This course was thought to be in some measure necessary, in order to guard those persons, who have yet to learn what Unitarianism is, against attributing to its professors in the present day opinions which have long been abandoned, in this part of the world at least, as unwarranted by the Scriptures. A few other notes will be occasionally introduced, containing references to approved modern writers upon some of the topics discussed in the Catechism; and furnishing notices of additional authorities for particular emendations of the Greek text of the New Testament, which have been supplied, since the publication even of the last edition of this work, by the laborious researches of Griesbach and others, and the present highly improved state of Biblical criticism and Biblical knowledge. These are to be considered as supplementary to the learned and curious notes which were published by the last editors of the Catechism, and which will be given with the Translation. I shall only observe farther, for the information of your Correspondent, that there will be prefixed to the work a Brief Sketch of the History of Unitarianism on the Continent, from its first appearance in Poland, until the final expulsion of its professors from that country in the year 1660. This will exhibit a faint outline of what the larger History is intended to comprize.

I am Sir,

Your's, &c.

THOMAS REES.

Sir,   July 5, 1816.

I BELIEVE it is very generally imputed as a fault to the liberal Dissenters, (most of whom are now denominated Unitarians) both by their orthodox brethren, and even by many of their own body, that controversial, or doctrinal preaching is becoming too prevalent among them. I have frequently of late heard this style of preaching severely condemned, and considered as a grievance by some of those who attend on it.

That our opponents should complain of this style of preaching is not to be wondered at; as by its means the errors of the prevailing systems are exposed to view, and it seems to be the fashion of the day to belabour the poor Unitarians with every kind of accusation that may be *conceived* rather than *proved.* Thus by a writer in the Quarterly Review they are accused of *indecency* and *ribaldry;* though without quoting chapter and verse. But my surprise is, that any who are in the main with us, and who have embraced at least a comparatively-pure system of Christian doctrines, should object to the occasional use of that kind of public instruction, which is the most effectual means of diffusing the knowledge of them in the world. As I have in some instances heard this objection strongly urged by people of great respectability, and cultivated minds, and as possibly it may be more generally extended than many are aware of, I have thought it my duty to draw the attention of your readers to the subject, that it may be fully discussed, and by that means become better, and more generally understood. "In a multitude of counsellors there is wisdom."

It has rather excited my surprise to hear this style of preaching objected, *exclusively,* against the Unitarians, as if it were much more reprehensible in them than in others. I believe it may be correctly stated as a matter of fact, that it does not prevail to half the extent (to speak within compass) among those who have been called rational Dissenters, as it does among the orthodox, both within and without the pale of the church. Indeed the discourses of the evangelical party in the church, of the whole body of Methodists, and of the Orthodox Dissenters in general, consist almost entirely of controversial materials;

and I know of no party in the Church that is not occasionally loud and bitter enough against all Schismatics (i. e. Dissenters) and Unitarians παρ 'εξοχην. Now, to attribute a fault (supposing it to be a fault) to those who are least chargeable with it, appears to me very much like " pulling out the mote out of thy brother's eye, and behold a beam is in thine own eye." I cannot help again expressing my surprise, that the demerit of controversial preaching (if it has demerit) should be most laid to the charge of those who least practise it.

I know that a bad construction must of course be laid on every thing done by the Unitarians, even on things praiseworthy in others. Thus, an Unitarian, who avows his religious opinions, and declares his reasons for doing so, is unpardonably arrogant and presumptuous, destitute of a real religious principle, devoid of charity, and neglectful of piety and a devotional spirit. But let us now for a moment suppose the Unitarian religiously to follow the course chalked out for him by his friends. While the practice of controversial preaching is general and incessant against him, let him wholly withhold all controversial subjects from the pulpit; while others on every hand are denouncing his religious sentiments as heretical and damnable; while he is represented as belonging to the fraternity of Deists, and a more dangerous enemy to religion than Atheists because more concealed; while all this and much more is going on on every side of him, let not a word drop from his lips which shall lead any one to suppose that he is conscious of any difference, of any offence, of any opposition, or any denunciations against him; while others are zealously contending for error (as in his opinion they must be) let him not open his mouth even for the truth—let the unclean spirit of dumbness incurably possess him. Now let us suppose that the Unitarian were to follow this good advice of his friends, what construction would they in *that case* put on his conduct? They would then with much reason urge against him, that he is conscious that his principles are bad and false, and that he is ashamed to avow them; that they do not bear to be brought forth to the light, and to be made manifest : and they would say this with a great appearance of truth. For, suppose two persons sold manufactured goods, and one of them exposed his wares in the most public manner, and shewed them in the best light, but the other very carefully deposited them in the darkest corner of his warehouse, and shewed the greatest reluctance to expose them to view—it is not difficult to guess in what manner even unprejudiced persons would be disposed to construe their motives respectively.

I have been told by those who are averse to the introduction of controversial subjects into the pulpit, that the practice is a sure mark of bigotry. Be it so. " If I by Beelzebub cast out demons, by whom do your children cast them out?" Let every denomination take as much as belongs to them of this bigotry, and let not other sects throw a stone against the Unitarians, I will not say till they are themselves without sin, but only till they have as little as the Unitarians in this respect.

"This as an *argumentum ad hominem* is as conclusive as I can wish. But I will not rest the matter here. I contend that occasional preaching on the doctrines of Christianity is both proper and necessary. How are the Scriptures to be explained if not from the pulpit? How are we to get rid of the anti-christian doctrines which have been so long received, if we are not to utter a syllable against them? How are the minds of those who read but little to be informed and enlightened? and the bulk of all congregations consists of such persons : and, it may be asked finally, what are we to teach if not Christian truth; the preaching of which, of course, is controversial preaching, if it has been controverted?

1. The answer which I have heard made to this last interrogatory may be considered as another argument against controversial preaching worthy of brief notice.

We do not go, it is replied, to a place of worship ready prepared with our critical scales to weigh arguments ; we do not go there to be puzzled with definitions and syllogisms; we do not go for the exercise of our intellectual powers; but we go for the sake of cherishing devout affections towards the Deity, and to be more deeply

impressed with the obligations which we are under to perform our duty. We go not to inform our reason, but to excite and improve our feelings—not to be informed, but to be persuaded.

As to the affirmative part of your object in going to a place of worship, well and good ; and are not proper means made use of to answer it? The Scriptures are read ; devout hymns and psalms are sung ; and your wants and devout wishes are made known unto God by the common prayers and supplications of the congregation. Yet more—the sermons are *generally* of a moral and practical tendency. But is it reasonable that your feelings be *exclusively* regarded—that public worship should monopolize your affections, and banish your reason? Must your pious affections and devotional feelings be necessarily injured, and the word become unprofitable to you, if sometimes your minds be informed concerning the doctrines of Christianity, if your intellectual powers, those which make you rank among the higher order of beings, be called into exercise? Has God in the institution of public worship, made provision only for your affections, and left your reason to shift for itself?

As to the bigotry of controversy, it is a quality which does not necessarily belong to it. Controversy may be, and ought to be managed with a charitable and even brotherly spirit towards those whose opinions we oppose. The manner and the spirit constitute bigotry, not the opposition of sentiment. There is no bigotry in a liberal exposition of our opinions; the essence of bigotry consists in the damnatory spirit, the exasperation of feeling, the evil surmises, the ungenerous suspicions and the unkind propensities which are attendant on controversy conducted in an unchristianlike manner.

I have been told by the opposers of all controversial preaching, we have a sufficient knowledge of the doctrines of religion, but we want constantly to be impressed with a sense of our duty, and to have our devotional feelings habitually exercised.

I cannot admit the correctness of the first part of the argument. Very few indeed have a comprehensive knowledge of the christian Scriptures, and the doctrines which they contain. The corruption of Christianity has been so radical, and the language of the Scriptures has been so systematically misinterpreted, that the reading of a few meditations and prayers, and a few select sermons, written in a liberal style, can neither discover the error, nor manifest the truth; both of which are equally necessary for the perfect emancipation of the mind. Most persons, it is true, have a general superficial knowledge of Christianity; and were a preacher to take a superficial common-place view of any doctrine, there would be some justice in the objection, as far as it regards those who are *really* well informed. But the truth of the case too generally is, that even of those who will resort to this argument, few, I fear, have more than a superficial knowledge of different systems of religion, or of the interpretation of the Scriptures. I have certainly a strong suspicion that their dislike of attending to the doctrines of religion, and the arguments by which they may be defended or assailed, arises immediately and entirely from their unacquaintedness with them. I believe it to be always a plain matter of fact, that those who are least acquainted with the subjects of controversy, are least interested in the discussion of them, and *vice versa.*

Involved in religious error as men have been for ages, systematically perverted as the language of the Scriptures has been from time immemorial, so completely changed as almost every expression of the Sacred Writings has been from its original intention; is it at all probable that general readers, those who have a dislike for all controversy, those whose reading is trifling and fashionable, those who deem it a mark of great ignorance of the world and rusticity of manners to avow undisguisedly and publicly singularity of religious profession or opinion, and exhibit independence of religious character; that those who never think of reading any thing on religious subjects but a prayer and a chapter, or perchance a volume of sermons, or lectures, or sacred dramas, by some popular writer, which the *aura popularis* may have sufficiently consecrated, with perhaps a treatise on education in which religion is forgotten—that these should be sufficiently acquainted

with the doctrines of Christianity? I do not believe it. These persons surely have a dislike of strong meats, because they are by them indigestible. But grant there are some who are well informed on such topics—will they be so interested in their feelings as not occasionally to allow what is suitable and necessary for others—the ignorant? There is certainly a numerous class that wants information concerning the doctrines of Christianity. Those whose education and situation in life, whose daily necessary attention to the concerns of life, to their daily bread, preclude the acquisition of much knowledge by reading and books, are they never to be instructed in the fundamental truths of religion, and never to be informed of and guarded against erroneous opinions, lest fastidious ears should be offended? The young people in most societies are without much elementary knowledge on the subject of religion. Are they, too, to be led to suppose by the quality of the matter that always descends from the pulpit, that the Christian religion is sufficiently taught and inculcated by a few well-turned sentiments about the amiableness of virtue, the pleasures of refined emotions, and the harmony of well-tuned affections? I have no damnatory clauses in my creed; but I know very well what dependence is to be placed on this kind of Christian institution. For one thing—our most notable defections, of which I scarcely ever knew an instance which was grounded upon avowed principle, are to be attributed to the policy which dictates this kind of public instruction.

It has been asserted, that controversial preaching necessarily scandalizes the minds of those who differ from us, and that thus frequently the most excellent and worthy men, even friends and relations, are disunited in charity and estranged in affection from one another; and that, therefore, for the sake of peace and charity, controversial subjects should never be introduced into the pulpit.

Peace and charity are certainly most excellent things, and, well understood, are to be considered among the essentials of religion; but they are not the only essentials, nor should we suffer, that to be sacrificed to them, which is more important and essential than themselves—truth.

It is a thing of general notoriety, that great difference of opinion exists between very worthy and good men. Now, is human nature, improved by religion too, really so constituted, that the avowal of our belief, and the defence of our principles, must necessarily lead us to hate and injure one another? And must wise and good men mutually conceal their sentiments with great care, and religiously forbear to urge their claims on the attention of mankind, lest they should be scandalized, and be led into disputes? And would this kind of forbearance and concealment be that thing which we call Christian charity?

Surely, a very false notion of charity and peace is implied in the above argument. Jesus Christ said, that he came to set a man at variance with his neighbour, the father against the son, and the son against the father, &c. Here is an undoubted breach of charity. But surely *he* is not guilty of it, though he be the occasion, who believes in Christ, and follows him; but *he* is guilty of it, who suffers the conscious integrity of him who honestly avows his belief in Christ to be the occasion of enmity and variance. "Offences must come;" but the woe is to him by whom they unreasonably come, not to him who is the innocent occasion of them.

If we allow its full scope to this argument, it proves too much, and is plainly inadmissible. If peace and harmony are the only things to be consulted, Jesus Christ should not have preached repentance, a change of religious sentiment and practice, to the world, nor should he have so vehemently attacked the Jewish Scribes and Pharisees because he differed from them. The apostles acted very wrong in unsettling the minds of men, and setting them at variance by their novel opinions, and, as it were, turning the world upside down. All missionary undertakings, since the days of the apostles to our own, must be regarded as crusades against peace and charity. We should never assail the idolatry and superstition of the Heathen, because their minds, of course, are scandalized and offended: the Mahometans must be left in quiet and peaceable possession of the errors of their false prophet, of their seven heavens, their beautiful virgins, &c.: the Catholics must be quietly suffered to retain a

barbarous and priestly-tyrannical superstition substituted for the religion of Christ: and, in a word, if this argument means any thing, we must leave the world for peace and harmony's sake in quiet possession of all its multifarious idolatries, errors, superstitions, vices. O all ye holy martyrs and confessors, what infernal enemies were you to the peace and tranquillity of the world: the holy zeal with which your noble army was animated, was a brand from Hell. Thou Martin Luther, with thy undaunted host of reformers, what a pest wert thou to the world:—how much malignity was displayed in consequence of thy reformation; how many bloody wars were kindled; how many cities reduced to ruins; and how many fair provinces laid waste and depopulated. And thou, O Priestley, *(famam qui terminet astris,)* whose uncommon sagacity in discovering, and unappalled courage in publishing to the world, truths long obscured and lost, naturally attracted the enmity of mobs and interested priests; though thou hadst enlightened and benefited Europe by thy discoveries, and thy native country might be proud of numbering thee amongst her most honoured sons; yet, enemy of tranquillity, well didst thou deserve thy fate: laudable was the design of the infuriated mob, instigated to burn thee, together with thy library and apparatus; holy were the maledictions, lies and calumnies of thy interested enemies; and glorious for the conclusion of the eighteenth century was thy banishment to a distant region, beyond the confines of civilized inhumanity.

I am afraid that the spirit of rational inquiry has been long declining among the Presbyterian and rational Dissenters; and the richer class, I am well aware, are exceedingly averse to every innovation, to every improvement, to all church-discipline, to doctrinal preaching, to the exposition of the Scriptures: they will give no countenance to catechizing, to lectures, to associations for information. It is no wonder that our societies in many places are in a depressed state, in some extinct. They will become extinct in many more, without a renovation. I could disclose more of the evil, if this were the proper place. I think I could point out as radical causes of our decay as have yet appeared in any of the communications you have published, but this does not belong to my present subject, and I must return.

The richer members of Presbyterian congregations appear to be ashamed to belong to a sect, and they wish their ministers to conform as much as possible to the more liberal party in the Church. They must say their prayers from a book in a monotonous manner, and they must read for sermons short moral essays, without any reference to the peculiar doctrines of the gospel, or the anti-christian errors and delusions of the age. These persons have too long continued to give the *ton* to our Presbyterian congregations: they have damped and half extinguished free and liberal inquiry: they have tied the hands of our ministers: they have numbed the energies of our people: they mistakenly imagine that a zeal for their religious profession and opinions would disqualify them for the general society of men of their own rank in the world. Hence they become ashamed of the peculiarities of the conventicle, like a rich man of his poor relations; and their ingenuity from this time is wasted on devising means how to serve God and Mammon, or how most speciously to desert the former for the latter. It would be much better for the Presbyterians if such persons would leave them at once, as a thing of course, as soon as they became rich : for as it is, they not only will not enter themselves into the kingdom of heaven, but they hinder others from entering.

This process has been gradually going on since the Restoration. At that time the Nonconformists consisted of many persons of rank and influence: at this time, I believe, they cannot lay claim to an individual of the nobility or gentry. We perfectly, however, understand the process by which this transformation has been effected—by means of the prevalence of a worldly spirit over religious principle. Though many men, of property still remain among us, yet the too general spirit of conformity to the world, and the dread of being suspected partial to the peculiarities of a sect, and zealous in propagating heresy, are sad presentiments of still further defections. But we hope that the defection of the degenerate will be well supplied by the virtue and courage of fresh accessions: for I am not ashamed to avow my prayer and desire that truth and righteousness should prevail. I shall never be ashamed

of the reproach of proselytism, while reason and persuasion are my only weapons of conversion.

In justice to a numerous class of opulent Presbyterians and Unitarians, it gives me great pleasure to observe, before I conclude, that there are many most honourable exceptions to a too common rule. Many are truly consistent in their conduct; and by their consistency they maintain that respectability and dignity of character, which the others never fail to sacrifice, by aping the manners of the world, and sacrificing independence of principle: still, many to whom this praise truly belongs, might do more, much more, by a renewed attention to the interests of religious truth—by their example, by their wealth, by their personal exertions and general influence.

Sir,—If these remarks should induce any of your readers duly to consider the subject, more especially, if they should excite amicable discussion, and promote practical improvement, my object will be fully answered. I am, your's, &c,

HOMILY.

Apparent Inconsistencies of great Minds, exemplified in a Series of Extracts on Future Punishment.

[Concluded from p. 330.]

BUT the fore-cited authors are not generally read: it may be proper, therefore, in the same view, to mention a few of those, which are universally celebrated and admired.

The classic moralists of the United Kingdoms, though the most profound reasoners in matters of *practice*, yet, seldom deviate from the strait line of orthodoxy, so called, in matters of *theory*. Though the avowed friends of toleration, and enemies to bigotry and persecution in every form, they never censure the ecclesiastical establishments of their own country, either in doctrine, constitution, or discipline. No doubt they either thought all these things right and as they should be, or they had their reasons for proceeding no farther, into which we do not now inquire. But there is one circumstance here which deserves notice: notwithstanding all their wit and all their wisdom, they sometimes, in their theological essays, adopt a kind of phraseology, neither called for by the occasion, justifiable by the common use of figurative language, nor even upon their own religious principles.

and which should not be drawn into precedent. In *The Guardian*, No. 88, the writer, representing the advantages of revealed religion, above those of natural, observes, " It is owing to the God of truth, who came down from heaven, and condescended to be himself our Teacher !" This is neither sense nor orthodoxy: it is the language of a modern *Swedenborgian.* Thus, likewise, *Mr. Addison* concludes a sublime paper on the Passion, with this extraordinary sentiment :—" Sure, Nature, all Nature, is departing with her Creator !" But this by the way.

These admirable writers also appear, in general, to adopt the popular ideas of future punishment. We shall only quote one passage from *The Guardian*, on the opposite side of the question.

In this work, No. 158, the author, under the similitude of a dream, introduces his readers into the court of *Rhadamanthus*, one of the supposed heathen judges of men after death. Among the rest, a certain female was brought before him, who, to his first question, replied, that " she had done no hurt;" but when it was asked, " what good she had been doing?" made no answer, and appeared in much confusion; when immediately one of the attendants took her by the hand to convey her to *Elysium*, and another with the intention of conveying her to *Erebus*: but " *Rhadamanthus*, observing an ingenuous modesty in her countenance and behaviour, bid them both *let her loose*, and set her aside for a *re-examination*, when he was more at leisure." Here, the ingenious writer evidently suggests, that there are characters, which, after death, may be considered as neither fit for heaven or hell; and that such will assuredly meet with a correspondent treatment, from a righteous and impartial Judge.

Mrs. Chapone, in her elegant *Letters*, (L. 3.) after describing the judgment day, and the sentence of the wicked, as that which must "determine their fate to all eternity," instead of entering into *the reasons* of this supposed irreversible sentence, presently adds—" Let us turn from this horrid, this insupportable view !" What! a doctrine of the gospel, " horrid and insupportable" even in idea—that will scarcely bear *a moment's reflection*—that cannot admit of being *impressed* upon the juvenile and tender mind for a single instant, without danger of benumbing its faculties!

VOL. XL.   3 O

Surely, this can never be the religion of *Jesus !* " Whom should we teach knowledge, and cause to receive instruction? Them that are weaned from the milk, and drawn from the breasts."

Dr. Kippis, the late pious and learned editor of the *Biographia Britannica*, to the life of *Daniel de Foe*, written by his colleague, Dr. *Towers*, adds a note, the substance of which we shall here insert. " Many fine displays of natural sentiment occur in Robinson Crusoe's man, *Friday*, one of which is particularly striking. In a conversation with his master concerning *the Devil*, being told that God is stronger than he; he inquires, in his broken dialect, why, if this be the case, the Almighty doth not destroy this evil being, and so put an end to his wickedness? To this *Crusoe* replied, that God would at last punish the Devil severely; that he is reserved for judgment, and is to be cast into the bottomless pit, to dwell with everlasting fire. *Friday*, however, still dissatisfied, returns upon his master— ' *Reserve at last ?*'—and thinks it unaccountable why such a malevolent being was not ' *destroyed long ago !*'— ' You may as well ask me,' replied *Crusoe*, ' why God doth not destroy you and me, when we do wicked things that offend him; we are preserved to repent, and be pardoned.' At this, *Friday* appears highly pleased, and goes on to express his satisfaction in being persuaded, that both wicked men and devils are preserved *to repent*, and that God will finally *pardon all !*"

The annotator adds, " Perhaps it would be going too far to assert, that *De Foe* here intended covertly to insinuate, that there might be a more merciful distribution of things in the final results of Divine Providence, than he dared, at that time, openly to exhibit."

It is presumed from this specimen, few of our readers will doubt, that the pious biographer was fully justified in suggesting these ideas of *De Foe's* real sentiments, which, also, the present writer hath every reason to believe, from a long, happy, and personal acquaintance and intercourse with him, were fully congenial with his own. [*]

There are, however, many modern professors, who appear far inferior, in

---

[*] See also, in this view, the Life of the Earl of Shaftsbury, in the new edition of the B. B.

the exercise of Christian sympathy and benevolence, to this *simple African*; who seem to envy the prince of apostates the very possibility of a restoration, and who, perhaps, would scarcely be reconciled to him, were he in reality, as well as in appearance, to be again "*transformed into an angel of light.*"

We shall close these observations upon authors, with a few remarks on the sentiments of *two* of the greatest of any age and nation, *Milton* and *Young*.

Of the general merit of that "Divine Poem," as it is emphatically styled by *Mr. Addison* and others, *Paradise Lost*, there can be but one opinion: that eminent writer hath admirably illustrated its beauties, and pointed out some of its blemishes. Our inquiry here, is only as to *the consistency* of some of the sentiments contained in it, with the doctrine of *eternal punishment*, which, in its highest possible sense, the sublime poet is commonly supposed to have adopted.

In the astonishing description of the consequences of the War in Heaven, in the 1st book, though we behold "Cherub and Seraph rolling in the flood," it is "with scattered arms and ensigns;" and "the superior Fiend" is represented "with his ponderous shield, whose broad circumference hung on his shoulders like the moon," at whose tremendous call, the multitude of apostate spirits are aroused "from their slumber on the fiery couch," to attend his summons. At his command, "The mighty standard" is upreared by the Cherub Azazel:

　　—— "Which full high advanced,
Shone like a meteor streaming to the wind,
With *gems* and *golden lustre* rich emblaz'd,
Seraphic arms and trophies : all the while
Sonorous metal blowing martial sounds."

Being now arranged

　　　　"In thick array,
Of depth immeasurable; anon they move
In perfect phalanx, to the Dorian mood
Of flutes, and soft recorders; such as raised
To height of noblest temper, heroes old
Arming to battle, and instead of rage,
Deliberate valour breathed; firm and unmoved
With dread of death, to flight or foul retreat;
Nor wanting power, *to mitigate and swage
With solemn touches, troubled thoughts,
　　and chase
Anguish and doubt, and fear, and sorrow,
　　and pain
From mortal, or immortal minds?* Thus they,

Breathing *united force, with fixed thought;
Mov'd on in silence to soft pipes, that
　　charm'd
Their painful steps* o'er the burnt soil—".

Then, as to *the place* to which they were consigned, one of the chiefs, in the council of *Pandæmonium*, employs this language :—

　　"As He our darkness, cannot we *His*
　　　　light
Imitate when we please ? This desert soil,
Wants not her *hidden lustre*, gems and
　　gold,
Nor want we skill or art from whence to
　　raise
Magnificence; and what can Heaven shew
　　more !"

After the close of the *Stygian Council*, the poet gives the following account of the *amusements* and *diversions* of the fallen spirits, "till their great Chief's return :"

　　"Part on the plain, or in the air sublime
Upon the wing, or in swift race contend ;
As at the Olympic games, or Pythian fields :
Part curb their fiery steeds ; or shun the
　　goal
With rapid wheels, or fronted brigades form;
Others, with vast Typhæan rage, more fell,
Rend up both rocks and hills, and ride the
　　air
In whirlwind : Hell scarce holds the wild
　　uproar !
　——　—— Others, more mild,
Retreated in a silent valley, *sing
With notes angelical* to many a harp
Their own heroic deeds, and hapless fall
By doom of battle : and complain that fate
Free virtue should enthral to force or
　　chance.
Their song was partial; *but the harmony
(What could it less, when spirits immortal
sing ?)
Suspended Hell*, and took with ravishment
The thronging audience. *In discourse
more sweet*,
(For eloquence the soul, song charms the
　　sense,)
Others apart sat on a hill retir'd,
In thoughts more elevate, and reason'd high
Of Providence, foreknowledge, will, and
fate——"

Soon after we are told, another part proceed to explore the regions of their wide domain, who at length meet with "a frozen continent," whither,

　　"At certain revolutions, all the damned
Are brought, and feel by turns the bitter
　　change
Of fierce extremes, extremes by change
　　more fierce
From beds of raging fire, to starve in ice

Their soft ethereal warmth, and there to
  pine,
Immoveable, infixed, and frozen round
Periods of time; thence hurried back to
  fire!"

Now, however we may be transported, as we ought to be, by these magical sounds, we should not suffer them to bereave us of our *understandings.* It is certain, that if they had been composed by a *Hume* or a *Voltaire,* instead of a pious Christian poet, they would have been deemed a species of *solemn bombast,* and as intended to ridicule and expose the doctrine of future punishment altogether. It is well, if they may not have frequently produced this effect, though nothing was farther from the design of the pious author, in the minds of superficial persons—the moral instruction lying far too deep for common observation. We shall not enter into particulars, as one would wish to avoid every thing *ludicrous* in a serious discussion: one thing is obvious—that the writer who could give so great a scope to his imagination, and introduce so many *lenient circumstances* into the supposed state of punishment of fallen angels, could not possibly believe in the doctrine of *unremitting torments,* which here, indeed, he expressly contradicts; nor, probably, even in that of the *eternal duration* of future punishment, though *limited in degree.* Perhaps these very passages might be intended covertly to insinuate the contrary. Reasoning from analogy, he could not suppose a more tremendous and dreadful hell, for impenitent rebels of the race of *Adam,* than for apostate spirits; and moreover, that in this view, he is to be read with great latitude of interpretation, and a due regard to the *poetic license,* even when he appears to be the most *serious.* That admired passage, in his description of Hell, " Hope never comes, that comes to all," is, in itself, *equivocal,* and would have been so regarded in the mouth of an heathen oracle. The poet might mean no more, than that " Hope never comes" to some *for a long period,* " which comes to all" *at last;* for, as he tells us in the 2d book :

  " Neither do the spirits damned,
   Lose all their *virtue!*"

Dr. *Young* is, perhaps, scarcely inferior to Milton, either as a poet or as a divine, alluding here chiefly to his practical divinity and his poetical ge-

nius.* He transports us to regions beyond the stars, elevates us to the empyrean heaven, or plunges us into the unfathomable abyss! In his " Universal Passion," he glances at the sentiments of Origen, Tillotson, and others, respecting future punishment, and is much too ludicrous to quote in this place, for the reasons just mentioned. Whenever writers have recourse to *jesting* and *sneering,* in opposing any religious opinions, it is a shrewd sign that they have either a weak head or a weak argument. The *former* circumstance no one will think of applying to Dr. *Young.* But—perhaps we forget, in this particular case, that " the love of fame" is " a *satire.*†

In his poem on " The Last Day," the author appears to be serious throughout. And here, if any where, one would naturally have expected, from so great a reasoner, a series of irrefragable arguments in proof of the doctrine which he appears to espouse: and indeed he gives us arguments enough, but they are *all* on the other side of

---

* " With all his faults, Young was a man of genius, and a poet."—

         Dr. Johnson.

† Nothing can justify the mixture of *frivolity,* either in opposing what we deem religious *errors,* or in recommending and enforcing religious *truths* and *duties.* In the Bible, we have instances of the severest irony and sarcasm, but nothing like *buffoonry;* and even these allowed instruments should be employed by *us,* with the greatest circumspection. It should be recollected, that *we* are neither prophets nor apostles; and although *they,* in general, and the great Author of our religion, at all times, had an intuitive knowledge and perception of mental error, yet, they seldom apply the severity of rebuke in this particular case, but chiefly in cases of enormous moral delinquency, such as idolatry, hypocrisy, a persecuting spirit, carelessness, presumption, and obstinate infidelity. We should reflect, that no honest mind embraces error, *as such,* but, under the semblance of truth; and that they, who think themselves " strong, ought to bear the infirmities of the weak."

In enforcing the truths of religion, we have some eminent preachers who grievously offend in this way. Where this arises from an *idiosyncrasy,* or is the effect of constitution, and counterbalanced by a thousand useful and valuable qualities, it must be borne with, as men never get entirely rid of their natural tempers; but—— let the humble imitators beware!

the question. Let the impartial reader judge. It will be necessary, for the sake of those who may not have the book at hand, to cite a few passages, and then offer some remarks on the several parts.

The following are the sentiments which the victims of divine anger are supposed to utter, in the state of future punishment.

" Who burst the barriers of my peaceful
 grave ?
Ah ! cruel Death, that would no longer
 save ;
But grudg'd me e'en that narrow dark
 ş abode,
And cast me out, into the wrath of God !

Must all these pow'rs, Heav'n gave me to
 supply
My soul with pleasure, and bring in my joy,
Rise up in arms against me, join the foe,
Sense, reason, memory, increase my woe ?
And shall my voice, ordain'd on hymns to
 dwell,
Corrupt to groans, and blow the fires of
 Hell ?
What, no reprieve, no least indulgence
 giv'n,
No beam of hope from any point of Heav'n ?
Ah ! mercy, mercy, art thou dead above ?
Is love extinguish'd in the Source of love ?
Bold that I am,—did Heav'n stoop down
 to Hell,
Th' expiring Lord of Life my ransom seal ?
Have I not been industrious to provoke,
From his embraces obstinately broke ?
Pursu'd and panted for his mortal hate,
Earn'd my destruction, labour'd for my
 fate ;
And dare I, on *extinguish'd love* exclaim ?
Take, take full vengeance, rouse the
 slack'ning flame ;
Just is my lot—but, oh ! *must it transcend
The reach of time ? despair a distant end !*
With dreadful growth shoot forward and
 arise,
Where thought can't follow, and bold fancy
 dies !
Never !—where falls the soul at that dread
 sound !
Down an abyss, how dark and how pro-
 found !
Down, down I still am falling ; horrid pain !
Ten thousand, thousand fathom still re-
 main !
My plunge still *but begun*—and this for sin ?
Could I offend, if I had never been ?
But still increas'd the senseless happy mass,
Flow'd in the stream, or flourish'd in the
 grass ;
Father of mercies ! why, *from silent earth,*
Didst Thou awake, and *curse me into birth ?*
Tear me from quiet, ravish me from night ;
And make a *thankless present of Thy light ?*

Push into being—a *reverse of Thee,*
And animate a clod with misery !

As our dire punishment, for ever strong,
Our constitution too, *for ever young,*
Curs'd with returns of vigour still the same,
Pow'rful to bear, and satisfy the flame ; ş
Still to be caught, and still to be pursued,
To perish still, and still to be renewed !
And this my King ! my God ! *at thy decree,
Nature is chang'd, and Hell should succour
 me !*
And canst Thou, then, look down from *per-
 fect bliss,*
And see me plunging in the dark abyss ;
Calling Thee *Father !* in a sea of fire ;
Or pouring blasphemies, *at Thy desire ?*
With mortals' anguish, wilt *Thou raise Thy
 name,*
And by *my pangs, Omnipotence proclaim ?*
Call back Thy thunders, Lord ! hold in thy
 rage,
Nor, with a speck of wretchedness, engage :
Forget me quite, nor stoop a worm to blame,
But lose me, *in the greatness of Thy name.*
Thou art all love, all mercy, all divine,
And shall I make those glories *cease to
 shine ?*
Shall sinful man grow great by his offence,
And from its course, *turn back Omni-
 potence ?*
Forbid it, and oh ! grant, great God, at least,
This one, this slender, *almost no request*—
When I have wept a thousand lives away ; ş
When torment is grown weary of its prey ;
When I have rav'd ten thousand years in
 fire ;
Ten thousand thousands, *let me then
 expire !*
Deep anguish ! but too late—the hopeless
 soul,
Bound to the bottom of the burning pool,
To toss, to wreathe, to pant beneath his load,
And bear the weight of an offended God !"

This is evidently the high *Drexelian* system, in irreproveable poetry. It is essentially different from *Milton's* Hell, and, perhaps, on that account, the more consistent. Here are no *lenitives,* or occasional diversions ; no " dulcet harmony of sound ;" no gymnastic exercises ; no *disputations,* rational or irrational, wise or vain, to recreate and calm their perturbed spirits ; nor, as far as appears, any *discrimination of character ;*—but the antediluvian sinner, and the transgressor of slender age, who has but *just looked* into existence, and who, in an unguarded moment, hath unwittingly slipped through the first hidden snare, on the fatal bridge of human life ; the wicked servant, who shall be beaten " *with many stripes,*" and the ignorant servant, who shall be beaten " *with few;*" are all consigned together, in one undistinguished mass, to never-ending torments! Such a representation of things can be neither true nor wholesome: the last cited text, in full unison with the dictates of nature, proves its *falsity*; and what is not true can never be useful. Such a scheme may amaze and terrify, but can never satisfy and convince. To *believe* a thing, is to be *persuaded* of it, and to be able to give some solid reasons for such a belief. That which hath no hold on the understanding, can work no conviction on the heart.

But, let us briefly examine *the pleas*, which the victim of eternal wrath is here supposed to urge, in the midst of his sufferings. We shall pass over those passages which justly and awfully display the self-accusations of the hitherto impenitent transgressor: they need no comment. " It is a fearful thing to fall into the hands of the living God!" when manifested as a God of judgment, and when his mercy and loving kindness, as to individuals, shall appear for a season to be suspended! The *pleas*, here supposed to be urged, arise from the consideration of the strict *eternity* of punishment, represented in different views.

" What, no reprieve, no least indulgence giv'n,
No beam of hope from any point of Heav'n?
Ah! mercy, mercy, art thou dead above,
Is love extinguish'd in the Source of love?"

This is a very important question, and, upon the supposition of eternal punishment, absolutely unanswerable. It is not a *mere difficulty*, but an *insuperable objection*. If individuals shall suffer strictly to all eternity, then divine mercy, as to them, is *for ever dead*, and love extinguished in its original source. The very supposition appears to be *profane.*

But, says the advocate of this opinion, we allow that the divine goodness and mercy are, *in themselves*, always the same, that is, in their *essence* and *nature*, but *eternally restrained* in their exercise, in this particular case. The *unchangeableness* of the Deity is an everlasting bar to any change in their state: " because God is eternal, therefore the torments of the damned are so also."[*]

This, however, is mere assertion; without the possibility of a proof.

Metaphysical writers sometimes reason and subtilize as to the *immutability* of the Deity, till, from their zeal to avoid *anthropomorphitism*, they appear, as it were, almost to divest him of *sensations:* and though neither this term, or any others that we know of, are adequate to the description of his matchless and adorable excellencies, yet, having no better, we must be content to employ them. Now the immutability of the Deity is the unchangeableness of *all* his perfections: " one divine attribute is not exercised to the prejudice or wrong of another."[*] As he is infinitely holy and just, so he is also infinitely gracious and merciful; and there is the same proportion of infinite to infinite, as of one to one. His mercy cannot impede his justice, nor can his justice obstruct or diminish the exercise of his mercy, only with this distinction, that " mercy is his darling attribute, and judgment his strange work," and that in many cases, " mercy rejoiceth against judgment."

Moreover, this *unchangeableness* of the Deity is consistent with infinite *variety:* " As, therefore, God is present every where, knows and perceives every thing, he must be supposed also, in a way infinitely superior to our comprehensions, *to feel every where for all his creatures.*"[†] The immutability of God, is, therefore, so far from implying the eternity of future punishment, that, as we have formerly observed of his *power*, it rather implies the contrary.

The poet goes on to represent the sinner, as checking himself in the midst of these reflections, magnifying the former mercy and forbearance of the Almighty, and endeavouring to reconcile his present dealings with him, to his own conceptions of his moral character and government. Yet, still the plea is repeated—must his punishment " transcend the reach of time," and shoot forward beyond the limits of thought and imagination? In this view he proceeds to urge, that it would have been far more merciful in the Deity not to have given him existence, which, if succeeded by eternal suffering, would render all *the blessings of his prior state a nullity, and " a curse,"* and the light of Heaven "a thankless present," which would be for the Almighty not

---

[*] Wisheart.

[*] Wisheart. [†] Hartley.

only to " animate a clod with misery,"
but, as it were, to " push into being a
reverse of himself!" What are we to
think of a doctrine, which necessarily
involves such *consequences?* . But let
us proceed.

The following lines exceed, perhaps,
in horror, any thing that ever was
written : ,

" And this my help ! my God ! at thy de-
        cree,
Nature is chang'd, and Hell should succour
        me !"

The sentiment, in plain prose, is this
—*The foundations are out of course*; the
ideas which we have been led to form
in yonder world, of the divine character
and government, are rooted in error;
and we must appeal *(horrendum dictu !)*
from the justice of Heaven to the justice of Hell !

But we may be certain "that the
victim of divine justice, in any period
of his existence, will never be able to
urge such a profane plea as this. " Is
God unrighteous? How then shall God
judge the world? . He is the rock, his
work is perfect, for all his ways are
judgment: a God of truth, and without
iniquity, just and right is he: and
though clouds and darkness are round
about him, yet righteousness and judgment are the foundations of his throne."

The succeeding lines, describe the
ever blessed Deity as an *infinite Tor-
mentor*, (thus confounding vengeance
with justice,) looking down from his
seat of " perfect bliss," and proclaiming his own " omnipotence," at the
expense of the pangs and anguish of
a feeble mortal, " a speck of wretchedness !"

" Calling Thee Father ! in a sea of fire;
Or pouring blasphemies, at Thy desire !"

The first line implies *penitence,*
which the advocates of this system, in
general, deny, but which the poet is
here constrained to admit of. The
other implies contumely, which, on
the part of the transgressor, in a state
of future punishment, seems to be
highly improbable.

Contumely, as regarding our Creator,
in the present life, springs from absolute, or partial *infidelity.* The greatest
sinner upon earth, when sensible of a
present Deity, was never contumeli-
ous. We can draw no rules of judgment in this case, from the agitations
or triumphs of a death-bed repentance,
or the ravings of a death-bed despair,

many records of both which we meet
with in books; and where, frequently,
the superstition, ignorance, or bigotry
of the priest, the overweening kindness of the by-standers, the mental
imbecility of the *clinick*, and the
fumes of deleterious medicines, may
all conspire to produce an unreasonable confidence, or, an unreasonable
despondency. In the parable of Dives
and Lazarus, which, besides its principal object, that of inculcating the folly
of expecting new revelations, may be
partly intended to designate somewhat
of future punishment, we meet with
nothing but patient suffering and
supplication. But if it be said, that,
from the nature of the human mind,
contumely, in these circumstances,
must at length arise; or, in the
tremendous language of the poet, that
the sinner will continue to " pour out
blasphemies at the desire of his
Maker !" then, this is an irrefragable
argument against the proper *eternity*
of such a state, (heretofore fully discussed,) as utterly inconsistent with
all our ideas of the majesty, holiness,
and glory of God.

The same ideas are afterwards pursued, in language, which, had it not
proceeded from a *privileged, writer,*
might, under some political adminis-
trations, have been thought worthy of
a litttle *wholesome correction*; and may
be considered, even by candid minds,
as tending, in itself, rather to promote
irreligion and profaneness, than the
contrary, though nothing could have
been farther from the mind of the
pious author.

" Thou art all love, all mercy, all divine,
And shall I make those glories *cease to
        shine?*
Shall sinful man grow great by his offence,
And from its course, *turn back Omni-
        potence?*"

The proper answer is—certainly not.
This is impossible. What proves too
much, proves *nothing.*

The only reply which the poet and
divine condescends to give to these
objections against the doctrine which
he appears to espouse, is, that derived
from the *sovereignty* of the judge, and
the supposed *certainty* of the doctrine
itself: the latter is begging the question, and, as we have seen, incapable
of proof, *à priori*, by the confession of
its professed advocates. The former,
though a legitimate argument *in itself,*

strictly applicable in many cases, and especially to the plans and operations of divine *wisdom*, in nature and providence, of which we are not competent judges; yet, is not to be urged *by itself*, in this particular case, since, as we have before endeavoured to illustrate, and as it hath been often shewn from reason and scripture, the Deity in the exercise of this attribute, acts by known and established rules, and " will do nothing by his right of sovereignty, but what is unquestionably agreeable with the other perfections of his nature."*

Further remarks might be made upon those passages of Dr. Young, which the reader's judgment will supply: and, upon the whole, we have reason to conclude, that the admired author was ashamed of the popular system of future punishment, and adopted this method of secretly exposing it, apprehending, perhaps, that the times in which he lived, were not ripe enough for a more open confession. How far this was consistent with Christian simplicity, is a question which we do not now enter into; but, surely, had he firmly believed it, he would never have taken such pains, in reality, if not in appearance, to demonstrate the contrary, and, in immortal strains, to perpetuate the glaring defects of his own system !

If this be thought a hasty and unwarrantable conclusion, let the poet speak for himself, in other parts of his great work, the "Night Thoughts," one specimen of which shall here suffice.

" Who, without pain's advice, would e'er
  be good ?
Who, without death, but would be good in
  . vain ?
Pain, is to *save* from pain; *all punishment*,
To make for *peace*; and death, to save from
  death :
And *second death*, to guard immortal life !
By the same tenderness divine ordain'd,
That planted Eden, and high bloom'd for
  man,
A fairer Eden, endless in the skies !——
Great Source of *Good alone*, how kind in
  all !
In vengeance kind! Pain, death, Gehenna save !"

It will be said, the poet only meant, that *the threat* of Gehenna saved: but

Wisheart.

the contrary is far more probable. There is evidently a *climax* here employed—pain and death, not the threat only, but the *infliction*—for we experience them both—these, *save* : that is they are instruments in the divine hand, for the most important and salutary purposes. But, they do not save, *all* : therefore, a wise and gracious Creator, who originally designed his rational offspring for happiness and for himself, must have other means, salutary and medicinal, in future worlds, to accomplish his benevolent purposes ; and in this view, *Gehenna*, or the punishments of the invisible state, will be instrumental, under the same divine direction, of producing those necessary moral qualifications, and that alteration of character, in another period of existence, which the former failed of accomplishing in the present.

But whatever were the real sentiments of this great writer, of one thing we may be certain : that, as all the attributes of the Deity, are coeval with his Being, and cannot be separated from it; so, they will continue to be exercised throughout everlasting ages. As he has been *from all* eternity, infinitely wise, powerful, holy, just, and benevolent ; so, *he will be to* all eternity the same, in every part and period of his universal dominion. . " If I ascend up to heaven, thou art there !" of this, there can be no doubt : but, are heaven and earth alone the spheres of thy divine activity ? by no means. " If I make my bed in hell," or, in the invisible state of punishment, "behold thou art there also !" Thou art there, as an avenger of the impious, as a punisher of the incorrigible transgressor. But, in what sense, great God ! art thou an avenger, or a punisher ? Is it to seal them up under a sentence of misery, commensurate with thine own existence, without any possibility of restitution and recovery ? Are they prevented from repenting, by an act of thy sovereign will, or wilt thou never *accept* of their repentance ?· Hast thou appointed them to be monuments of thine infinite power, trophies of thine everlasting vengeance, or, perpetual arguments of happiness to the saints in glory ? Where were then, the exercise of thy mercy and benevolence, which thou hast taught us to consider, as well as thy holiness and justice, as over all thy works? Where were then the exercise of thy *long-suffering*, which, with respect to *some* of thy creatures, hath been in this world scarcely experienced? Hast thou not sent thy well-beloved Son into the world, " the second Adam, the Lord from heaven," to restore the ruins of the first, " to seek and to save, that which was lost?" And shall his original intentions, and thine through him, be finally frustrated? Hath not thine holy apostle assured us, that " not as is the original offence, so is the free gift?" O Lord! all things are possible with thee! We commit the condemned criminal, as well as the accepted saint, into thine hands, fully persuaded, that though thou wilt reward us infinitely beyond our deserts, thou wilt punish us only in proportion to our demerits: that " thou wilt be justified when thou speakest, and overcome when thou art judged!" Rom. iii. 4.

" Learn, therefore, to refine, spiritualize and elevate all your notions and conceptions of God: rise in your contemplation from those perfections and excellencies that are in the creatures, and mount up by degrees to a knowledge of his nature by these several helps, and conceive of him by these divided excellencies, since you cannot conceive of him in the simplicity of his own being and undivided essence. Even when you endeavour to frame the highest notions of the Almighty, there will be a similitude of something corporeal in your fancy; therefore, what is offered to your *imagination*, should be purified by your *reason*. Endeavour to refine every representation of God, by separating therefrom in your idea, whatever is *unworthy of him.* Labour to have your apprehensions still more purified, and to rise higher and higher in your conceptions of him. Remember, that whatever God is, he is *infinitely so!* Conceive of him, as excellent without any imperfection; as great, without quantity; as perfect, without quality; as every where, without place; as powerful, without members; as wise, without reasoning; as light, without darkness: and when you have risen to the highest, conceive him to be yet infinitely above all this, and humbly acknowledge the weakness and in-

firmity of your own minds. Say, with respect to the highest and purest conception you can attain to,—this is not God!. God is infinitely more than this! If I could conceive him, then he were not God, for he is incomprehensibly above all that I can either think or conceive!"*

Sir,

ALTHOUGH *I* am the party who is in danger of being wounded, and not your very able Correspondent, T. S. (394) by my venturing to enter the lists with him, yet as I think good humoured discussion has a tendency to throw light upon every subject, and none can be much more important than the liberty or slavery of mankind, as regarding its well-being in every point of view, physical, moral and religious, I am sorry he has declined to entertain and instruct your readers by any further explanation. But though I cannot obtain any additional information respecting his political allusions, I have at least learned one very agreeable fact, that it is possible to animadvert on the writing of a man of benevolent character, and to bring forward opposite opinions, and yet to meet with politeness and liberality, and to have such contrariety of opinion ascribed to its real motive, a wish to elucidate the truth with every desire not to give offence, and being encouraged by such generous treatment, I will once more trouble you, Mr. Editor, with a few remarks, some of them applicable to the letter of T. S. trusting to your editorial discretion to lay them aside, if you think the insertion had better be omitted.

Since the French Revolution, many persons, who have been spectators of it, and have been disappointed at its conclusion, are so terrified at every discussion connected with the rights of the people, that they appear to be willing tacitly to suffer a despotism, even if it were like that of Turkey, rather than advocate any *innovation*; whereas the events of the last twenty-five years should teach us *a great moral lesson*, that making timely reforms, is the way to prevent great and sudden revolutions, or in the great Lord Chatham's words, " reform yourselves from within, or you will be

* Wisheart.

reformed from without with a vengeance." We have the opinion of Algernon Sydney, " in his Discourses on Government,"* that nothing but abuses and corruption can make a people wish for change: he remarks that the inhabitants of a country never wish for, nor will exert themselves to procure any great change in the government so long as it is conducted with tolerable equity and moderation; but all history gives proof that courts will always become more and more corrupt, unless they are constantly checked by the influence and control of the people.

I am quite aware, as indeed who is not, that the present system of choosing representatives to serve in parliament is very faulty and productive of much disorder, as your Correspondent, T. S. ironically infers, page 395; yet these abuses might no doubt be removed, and perhaps all the difficulties remedied by another plan of collecting the votes: but I am afraid that the lovers of, and gainers by corruption, amongst whom I certainly do not include T. S. are glad to perpetuate these evils, as a preventative against a more complete representation of the people, as these election excesses are brought forward as shewing the evil dispositions of the people; but I believe that very many of the vices of the governed, are caused by the selfishness and consequent misrule of the governors.

T. S. observes, p. 394, 5, that your Correspondents, and yourself, Mr. Editor, are calmly though strenuously employed in the investigation and diffusion of useful knowledge; but can any one suppose, that we should at this time be freely writing, or you, Sir, publishing our religious and political opinions, if it had not been for such patriotic men as Pym, Russell, Hampden and Sydney, who struggled in the cause of freedom and paved the way for us! How is it in Spain and Portugal? and yet we are informed that Mr. Gibbon, who had been friendly to freedom before the French Revolution, doubted after that event whether so great an innovation as the

removal of the Inquisition in Spain would be a safe and wise political experiment. But if I understand your Correspondent, T. S. rightly, he seems to hint that a kind of *passive obedience* is most becoming to the wise and virtuous, and that it is not advisable for them to exert themselves to restrain bad government, or indeed any great evil; for he remarks, p. 229, " It seems to be the plan of Providence to restrain and check one class of crimes and delinquents by the counteraction of another;" but might not such a principle as this lead us into a state of the most dangerous apathy if carried to its full extent? The excesses of the French Revolution appear to have had in many respects the same effects upon the liberties of the present generation, as the fanatical excesses of the Puritans had upon the religion and morals of the English people in that day: in both instances a re-action has been produced and a strong disposition to run into the opposite extreme; for after the period which has been ironically called the reign of the saints, followed in quick succession the reign of the sinners: but I have always thought that a very great proportion of the crimes, that were committed by the French, are to be ascribed to the sanguinary manifestoes of the surrounding despots, and their entrance into France at the head of immense armies, which turned the nation into a great military camp, and excited the most violent animosities amongst men of all parties; and in the end, turned their attention from the love of liberty to that of ambition and conquest.

And thus, in the present day, after the dreadful struggle of the French for liberty, has followed a time remarkable for high monarchical declarations, in which the divine right of kings has again been openly avowed and acted upon. And even in this land of comparative freedom, I think many persons attend the Established Church who are not at all attached to its principles, and do not believe in its doctrines, because they fear that if they attended a Dissenting place of worship, they would be ranked amongst the disaffected and jacobinical. To conclude, Sir, although no person can more regret than I, the excesses which have been committed by bad men under the assumed ban-

---

* A work that I earnestly recommend every person to read, as one of the very best treatises that was ever written upon this subject.

ners of civil and religious liberty; yet I cannot respect freedom or religion the less, because ambition, knavery and hypocrisy have used these sacred names as cloaks to cover their own designs.

                       J.

P. S. Since writing my last letter, I have read the extracts from "Old-field's Representative History of Great Britain and Ireland," in the Supplement for the Monthly Magazine for July, which I would recommend to every person who wishes to learn the true state of our representation, and has not an opportunity of seeing the valuable original.

Sir,   *Clapton, Aug.* 4, 1816.

I OBSERVE, at page 386 of your last Number, a letter from a gentleman who was first known to me as one of the earliest encouragers of my projected Edition of Dr. Priestley's Theological Works. On Mr. Cordell's concluding proposal, the result of great good will to my design, it does not become me to make any remark, except that he is correct in stating that I intend to proceed with the undertaking, if two hundred subscriptions can be procured. I now think it proper to add, that no copies will be printed, except for subscribers. Thus their copies will not be depreciated, as they might apprehend, by a number being reserved for sale.

So far as I can ascertain their amount, the *subscriptions* already received do not exceed sixty. Of reported *subscribers,* who have not yet paid their subscriptions, there appears to be about the same number. Should those subscriptions be paid, and eighty more be added to them, by November next, so as to complete the number of two hundred subscriptions, which is now scarcely to be expected, I purpose, immediately, to put the first volume to the p,ess, and to bring out the edition with all the accuracy and dispatch in my power.

Should it appear by November next, which will complete one year since I first proposed the subject, in your work, that the subscriptions have not amounted to two hundred, I shall think myself justified, to the promoters of the undertaking, in abandoning it, and will immediately return their subscriptions. Their names, by your leave, I shall, in that case, record in your pages.

as a justification of my project, and from respect to those who would have united with me, to offer that tribute to Dr. Priestley's memory, which has always been considered as paid by the publication of a correct edition of an author's works.

My expectations of success in this project were always moderate. Experience has still further restrained them. I must now leave the question to be determined by the Unitarians, and shall never be likely to regret, whatever may be the result, that I have connected my name with such an attempt.

        I remain, Sir, your's,
               J. T. RUTT.

P. S. A young friend who, though a lawyer, has not, like Blackstone, bid *farewell to his muse,* and who is much more conversant with Shakspeare than myself, has referred me to a passage in *As You Like It,* from which Watts appears to have taken a hint for the lines, which I quoted (p. 391). It is in the 2d Scene of the 3d Act, where *Orlando* in a soliloquy exclaims:

" O Rosalind! these trees shall be my
     books,
     And in their barks my thoughts I'll
       character;
     That every eye, which in this forest
       looks,
     Shall see thy virtue witness'd every
       where.
Run, run, Orlando; carve on every tree,
The fair, the chaste, and unexpressive she."

My friend's conjecture is strengthened by this verse of Watts, which immediately follows that I quoted:

" The swains shall wonder when they
     read,
     Inscrib'd on all the grove;
     That heav'n itself came down and bled,
     To win a mortal love."

The Reviewer (p. 405) has, perhaps, understood too generally the difficulties occurring to *Dissenters,* on attempting to place their sons at *public schools.* Unless my memory serves me very ill, there were no inquiries but of a literary kind, when I entered St. Paul's School in 1771. I observe in Knight's Life of *Colet* (p. 364), among the founder's statutes, that he bade *the children learne first above all the catechizon in Englishe;* but this rule I apprehend had been long neglected, as well as that which enjoined the reading *specially Cristen autors, that wrote theire wisdome with* clean and chaste Laten. In the 6th and 7th classes, which were those I passed through, we indeed repeated the Church catechism, in Greek, as a school exercise; and thus the children of Nonconformists were frequently uttering falsehoods, though in a dead language, about supposed benefits from pretended godfathers and godmothers.

There are other difficulties, not peculiar to Dissenters, but which must, I think, occur to any parent, educated in a public school, who has since acquired a conviction that moral habits are of more value than classical attainments.

SIR, *August* 5, 1816.

I HAVE been informed that Mr. Belsham has, in a state of readiness for the press, Notes by himself on the Epistles of Paul. As one of the many admirers of his most excellent works illustrative of the meaning of the writers of the New Testament, especially with reference to the doctrines about which Christians are so much divided in opinion, I most sincerely hope that, if my information is correct, he will be induced to add to the important services which he has already rendered to the good cause which he advocates, by publishing them for the benefit of the public.

Such a work is a great *desideratum.* It would form a valuable addition to the late excellent Mr. Kenrick's "Illustrations of the Gospels and Acts of the Apostles;" and coming from the masterly pen of Mr. Belsham, it would be purchased and read with avidity. Mr. Belsham will, I trust, favour the public with information on the subject, through the medium of your valuable Repository.

D. D.

New Mode of Diffusing Knowledge.

A CORRESPONDENT in the Monthly Magazine (Aug. 1816), suggests a new, but not extravagant mode, of disseminating useful and important truths. It may be applied to other articles of manufacture besides earthenware, and to other articles of earthenware besides those which he specifies. The watch-seal with the engraving of the negro in the attitude of supplicating mercy, with the words, "Am I not a man and a brother!"

proceeding from his lips, was not without effect in the great work of the abolition of the slave trade.

The Monthly Magazine Correspondent, who signs himself T. H. S. and dates *Nottingham*, June 20, 1816, explains himself as follows:

" If instead of the silly castles in the air which principally cover the earthenware in present use, there were a wise saying or an immutable truth on every plate and tea-cup and saucer; what a fund of sententious wisdom might be introduced into every family, particularly the middle and lower classes of society. What admirable topics for conversation would thus be introduced, and what useful and early associations would be formed!—It seems to me that this system of communicating moral instruction, would be much superior to that of communicating it through the medium of tracts."

No. CCLXVIII.
Improvements in Moral and Political Science.

" It is chiefly in judging of questions ' coming home to their business and bosoms,' that casual associations lead mankind astray; and of such associations how incalculable is the number arising from false systems of religion, oppressive forms of government, and absurd plans of education! The consequence is, that while the physical and mathematical discoveries of former ages present themselves to the hand of the historian, like masses of pure and native gold, the truths which we are here in quest of may be compared to *iron*, which, although at once the most necessary and the most widely diffused of all the metals, commonly requires a discriminating eye to detect its existence, and a tedious as well as nice process to extract it from the ore.

" To the same circumstance it is owing, that improvements in Moral and in Political Science do not strike the imagination with nearly so great force as the discoveries of the Mathematician or of the Chemist. When an inveterate prejudice is destroyed by extirpating the casual associations on which it was grafted, how powerful is the new impulse given to the intellectual faculties of man! Yet how slow and silent the process by which the effect is accomplished! Were it not, indeed, for a certain class of learned authors, who, from time to time, heave the log into the deep, we should hardly believe that the reason of the species is progressive. In this respect, the religious and academical establishments in some parts of Europe, are not without their use to the historian of the Human Mind. Immoveably moored to the same station by the strength of their cables and the weight of their anchors, they enable him to measure the rapidity of the current by which the rest of the world are borne along.

. " *This* too is remarkable in the history of our prejudices; that as soon as the film falls from the intellectual eye, we are apt to lose all recollection of our former blindness. Like the fantastic and giant shapes, which, in a thick fog, the imagination lends to a block of stone, or to the stump of a tree, they produce, while the illusion lasts, the same effect with truths and realities; but the moment the eye has caught the exact form and dimensions of its object, the spell is broken for ever; nor can any effort of thought again conjure up the spectres which have vanished."

Dugald Stewart's Pref. to Diss. prefixed to Supplement to Encyclop. Britann. p. 16.

No. CCLXIX.
Grotius's Chaplains.

" Grotius, when ambassador for Sweden in France, had two Chaplains, a Calvinist and a Lutheran, who preached by turns. What they principally laboured was to revile one another, and their sermons were only invectives. The ambassador, tired and ashamed of the extravagancies of these reverend madmen, begged them to explain the gospel, without wounding Christian charity. This good advice neither of them relished. His Lutheran chaplain particularly replied, that *he must preach what God inspired*; and went on in the old strain.—Grotius at last ordered him either to forbear railing or preaching. The meek preacher turned away in

great wrath, expressing his amazement that a *Christian ambassador should shut the mouth of the Holy Ghost*."

Trenchard and Gordon's Tracts, 1751, ii. 296. ˴

No. CCLXX.
ANECDOTES RELATING TO CRIMINAL LAW.
The Rack.

" Judge Foster relates, from Whitlock, that the Bishop of London having said to Felton, who had assassinated the Duke of Buckingham—' If you will not confess, *you must go to the rack*;' the man replied, ' If it must be so, I know not whom I may accuse in the extremity of the torture, Bishop Laud perhaps, or any Lord at this board.'

" Sound sense (adds Foster) in the mouth of an enthusiast and ruffian'! ˌ

" Laud having proposed the rack, the matter was shortly debated at the board, and it ended in a reference to the judges, who unanimously resolved that the rack could not be legally used."

De Lolme on Eng. Const. Vol. I. B. 1. Ch. 11.

No. CCLXXI.
Universal Providence. ˌ

" GOD, says *Newton*, is all EYE, and EAR, and SENSE.

" *Schol. Gen. in Princip.* The whole passage deserves quotation. *Totus est sui similis, totus oculus, totus auris, totus cerebrum, totus brachium, totus vis sentiendi, intelligendi et agendi, sed more minimè humano, more minimè corporeo, more nobis prorsùs incognito.*

. " With this passage, one from *Pliny*, Nat. Hist. ii. 7, may very properly be compared. *Quisquis est Deus, totus est sensus, totus visus, totus auditus, totus animæ, totus animi, totus sui.*

" But this prince of philosophers, this glory, not of our nation only, but our species, refined his notions of the Divinity from the favourite volume of his meditations; that volume, which had declared, that a *sparrow*, nay even a *hair of the head* could not *fall to the ground*, without vibrating through the remotest corner of God's creation."

. *Wakefield's Evidences of Christianity,* p. 40.

REVIEW.

Art. I.—*Illustrations of the Divine Government; tending to show, that every Thing is under the Direction of Infinite Wisdom and Goodness, and will terminate in the Production of Universal Purity and Happiness.* By T. Southwood Smith.* Sold by Sherwood, Neely, and Jones, Paternoster Row, and D. Eaton, 187, High Holborn, London; and by Bryce and Co. South Bridge Street, Edinburgh. 1816. pp. 240. 12mo. price 6s. extra boards.

AMONG all the truths, which engage the attention of mankind, there are two of supreme importance, the Unity of God, and his Infinite Benevolence. These doctrines are intimately connected together; for the former cannot be fully apprehended without leading to a firm belief of the latter. The evidence for the strict Unity of God having been previously presented to the minds of religious inquirers in Scotland, Mr. Southwood Smith, has in the work before us, called their attention to the sublime and delightful consequences, which flow from that doctrine, and which relate to the Character and Government of the One God and Father of all.

Our author commences his treatise by a brief view of the evidence for the existence, perfections, and providence of the Supreme Being. From arguments, stated much in the manner of Dr. S. Clarke, he concludes, that " nothing can happen without the knowledge and permission of unerring wisdom and perfect goodness, and that all the vast affairs of the universe, in every particular circumstance, and in every instant of time, are under the wisest and the best direction." P. 18. He then shows that upon these points revelation confirms the deductions of reason; and, after quoting our Saviour's admirable proof of the universal and minute Providence of God,

derived from his care over the lilies of the field, he annexes the following observations: "The argument, which our Lord here employs, is beautiful and affecting. Every one must have felt its force. When in a solitary ramble our eye has been struck with a little flower blooming in a secluded spot—when we have examined the perfection of all its parts, the richness, the variety, the exquisite beauty of its tints; when we have considered the care that has been taken of this humble plant, and the inimitable skill employed upon its construction, which of us has not been deeply impressed with the truth, which our divine Instructor would here teach us? Which of us has not said to himself,—can so much care have been spent upon this little flower, and can I, humble and insignificant though I am, be overlooked by the Author of my being? It is impossible. There must be a God, there must be a Providence, and I, and the myriads of creatures, who in common with me enjoy the boon of existence, have reason to rejoice!" Pp. 20, 21.

Here Mr. Smith properly introduces the doctrine of Philosophical Necessity, which represents the Deity as appointing and producing every event in the moral, as well as in the natural world, but in such a manner as is consistent with the nature of man as a rational and accountable agent. Having shown that all events are continually directed and immediately produced by the agency of God, and having hence inferred that they must conspire to the accomplishment of some wise and benevolent *end*, he advances the grand doctrine of his volume, that the great design of the Deity in the creation and government of the world is TO BRING ALL HIS INTELLIGENT OFFSPRING TO A STATE OF PURITY AND BLISS.

Before adducing the evidence in favour of this opinion, Mr. Smith considers the preliminary question respecting the *kind of proof*, by which it ought to be established. Some Christians object to the admission of any doctrine, which is not expressly

* Since this work was published, Mr. Smith has graduated at Edinburgh, M.D. His inaugural thesis, which is printed and dedicated to Mr. Belsham, is entitled " De Mente Morbis læsa." Ed.

affirmed in Scripture. Others contend that this evidence is not absolutely necessary. The history of the corruptions of Christianity, should not doubt make us exceedingly *cautious* in the reception of doctrines, which revelation does not directly inculcate. But this caution need not in our opinion be carried to such an extreme, as to lead us to refuse our assent to a doctrine upon this ground alone, if it be supported by competent evidence, of a different description, and be *in perfect consistency* with the declarations of the Scriptures. The whole spirit and design of the Christian religion, and the example and authority of Jesus Christ and the apostles, instead of discouraging, favour and enjoin the free exercise of the understanding upon religious subjects; and we probably coincide most entirely with the design of the Almighty Author of the gospel, when we habitually contemplate the light of nature and the light of revelation as streaming alike from himself and in parallel rays—every object, upon which they fall, being the most brightly and beautifully illuminated by their united action. We need not therefore hesitate to receive any doctrine, which, upon the most careful and attentive examination, appears to be a fair or necessary inference from other doctrines, admitted upon the authority either of revelation, or of the religion of nature, or of both combined. But at the same time, we should keep in mind, "that arguments may in reality be derived from Scripture, which do not at first sight appear to be so. Revelation has poured so much light upon the mind, and has led us into such a just way of reasoning concerning God, concerning his design in creation, and his government of the world, that our conceptions and arguments, even when they do not appear at all to depend upon this heavenly Guide, attain a degree of sublimity and truth, to which they would never have arrived without it; and we often appear to be following the deductions of our own understanding, when, in reality, we are only repeating in other words, and with other associations, the declarations of Scripture." P. 36.

Mr. Smith first argues in favour of the doctrine of Universal Restoration from the *perfections of the Deity,* and especially from his *goodness.* "He

proves this attribute from the nature and condition of man and other animals, in that interesting and pleasing manner, which is to be expected from a pious, well-informed, and enlightened mind. He infers, that the Almighty could not have created mankind with any other view but to render them happy, and observes, that the motive often ascribed, namely, that he created the world in order to display his own glory, coincides with that here assigned, since the glory of God can be nothing but the happiness of his creatures. But, since many Christians allow, that the goodness of God moved him to the work of creation, and consequently that he must have originally designed the ultimate felicity of at least the majority of mankind, while they nevertheless suppose that the eternal punishment of a portion of them may be decreed by his wisdom in subserviency to this end, it was necessary to prove further the *universality* of the divine benevolence. This is pehaps the point of Mr. Smith's argument, upon which his doctrine chiefly depends. He appears to us to have completely succeeded in it. He has vindicated the *impartiality* of the great Father of all the families of the earth, by reasonings so masterly, facts so various, and illustrations so beautiful, that we cannot here attempt an abridgment, but must request our readers to turn to the book itself; pp. 57—65. He further argues, that nothing can frustrate the design of the Deity, which has been stated, and that all his other perfections, instead of presenting any opposition, must harmonize with his benevolence in the production of this glorious result.

In the next place, our author argues with great force and ingenuity *from the natural capacities of the human mind,* maintaining that a structure so vast and so noble, cannot have been raised to afford to the universe an eternal spectacle of majestic desolation, but that it must have been formed to answer some use proportionate to its grandeur. In the constitution of all the inferior animals we see means adapted to promote the ends which are accomplished. "Why then is man the only creature in the universe, who possesses a nature that falsifies every appearance and disappoints every expectation; a capacity, that enables him to soar with the seraph, and a destiny, that levels him with the brute?" It is answered, "that there are many cases, in which the apparent object of nature is evidently and completely defeated; that every blossom does not ripen into fruit, nor every embryo attain the maturity, of which it was capable, and for which it was obviously designed." It is sufficient to reply to this objection, that "there is no parallel between the two cases. Every blossom, it is true, does not ripen into its proper fruit, nor every embryo grow into a perfect animal, yet neither is any blossom or embryo, perverted from its genuine nature into one that is opposite. Every blossom of an apple does not ultimately form an apple, but neither does it become a poisonous fruit: every embryo does not grow into a perfect animal, but neither does it degenerate into a disgusting monster. But the doctrine which teaches that man was created for purity and happiness, but that he will continue for ever vicious and miserable, and that which teaches that he will remain so for unknown ages, and then be destroyed, not only suppose, that he does not attain his proper nature, but that it becomes perverted into that which is directly opposite." P. 86.

Mr. Smith further confirms his doctrine, by considering *the nature of punishment*. Revenge and punishment both imply the infliction of pain on account of the violation of duty. They differ in the *ends*, which they are respectively designed to answer. The object of the former is simply to gratify a malignant passion; that of the latter is to prevent the recurrence of the evil. Nothing therefore but a vengeful disposition could induce the Almighty to inflict upon his creatures torments, which being eternal are necessarily unavailing. But if the sufferings of the guilty in a future state be punishment, and not revenge, they must be intended to produce reformation, and must cease when they have accomplished their object. If this be their nature, they are analogous to the privations and pains which ensue from guilt, and tend to effect its removal in the present state.

The writer of this very valuable work proceeds to reply to the arguments, usually produced to support the doctrines of everlasting punishment, and of limited punishment,

terminated by destruction. He is thus led to a critical investigation of the words translated "everlasting" and "for ever," and of other Scriptural expressions, referring to the future punishments of the wicked. He has here availed himself of the candid, learned, and accurate writings of the late Mr. Simpson, and has proved that the language of the Holy Scriptures, correctly interpreted, instead of containing any thing adverse to the doctrine of universal restoration, presents intimations in its favour in the use of the word "*Fire*," which is in Scripture a common emblem of *purification*, and also in the use of the term Κολασις, translated "Punishment," which always means *chastisement for the purpose of reformation*. In this part of his volume (pp. 125—130), Mr. Smith admirably illustrates the *moral tendency* of the doctrine which he supports, and shows that it not only does not weaken the dread of vice, but is peculiarly adapted to engender love to God and a habit of cheerful and entire compliance with his will.

Passing over several minor topics, we shall only notice the reasoning advanced (pp. 163—166), in opposition to the popular tenet of the *infinite evil of sin*, as being singularly ingenious, as well as lucid and conclusive. Nor must we omit to remark (although the narrowness of our limits scarcely allows us to do justice to Mr. Smith's work) that he has examined the Scriptural evidence alleged in support of the *destruction* of the wicked, as well as that which is adduced to prove their eternal misery. He justly observes, that the doctrine of the destructionists is established rather upon the *sound* of certain passages of Scripture than upon their sense: for the Greek terms, translated literally by the English words *destruction*, *death*, &c. only signify the infliction of intense pain, and are so explained by Schleusner in his Lexicon. Those therefore, which speak of the "everlasting *punishment*," and those which assert "the "eternal *destruction*" of the wicked, convey the very same meaning, and are all perfectly consistent with the doctrine of universal restoration.

Our author concludes his argument by endeavouring to show, that this tenet is supported by the express authority of the Sacred Scriptures. Here his observations are more questionable than in the former parts of his treatise. With Newcome and some other critics, he supposes the New Testament phrase "all men," or "all things," to denote all intelligent creatures. If however we judge of its meaning by the rules of strict criticism, we shall probably see reason to interpret it as signifying both Jews and Gentiles, in opposition to Jews only. In former times God appeared as the Saviour, or peculiar Benefactor, of the Jews; but, at the introduction of the gospel, as the Saviour of all men; both Jews and Gentiles. Although this may be the sense intended by the Apostle Paul in those passages, which Mr. Smith has quoted from him, yet his writings, as well as every other part of the Bible, not only accord with the doctrine of universal restoration, but strongly countenance it, by the grand and affecting views which they present of the unlimited benignity, the impartiality, the wisdom, and the justice of the universal Parent. Although Mr. Smith may not be correct in these criticisms, yet he has established his doctrine by other evidence, in our opinion completely decisive and unanswerable. We would earnestly recommend his treatise as a work, distinguished by clear, masterly, and convincing argument—by unaffected and powerful eloquence—by its suitableness to the capacities of all who are in the habits of inquiry and reflection upon religious subjects, and its adaptation to cherish and increase those habits; and lastly, by the strong impressions of piety to God, and benevolence to man, which the attentive perusal of it must make upon every susceptible heart.

Y.

Art. II.—Four Sermons on Christian Peace and Unity, with a Pastoral Address to the Congregation at Stourbridge. By the Rev. B. Carpenter. Second Edition. With Notes and Anecdotes. Birmingham, Printed and Sold. 1816. 12mo. pp. 104.

WE know not whether these Sermons are likely to obtain more than a local circulation. However, since the author is evidently desirous of their being regarded as an Irenicum, we deem it important to inquire, whether they be really calculated to promote that Christian peace and unity of which they treat?

"In discoursing on the apostolic exhortation," Ephes. iv. 3, "Endeavouring to keep the unity of the spirit in the bond of peace," Mr. Carpenter purposes——

"I. To shew that men never will think alike on religious subjects.

"II. That it is not desirable they should.

"III. That they do think alike on the most important articles.

"IV. That these considerations are sufficient to induce them to keep the unity of the spirit in the bond of peace."

In proof of his first position, he cites an observation which he ascribes to "a sensible and acute writer on ecclesiastical history:" it is this, "that in order to have persons think alike, they must either possess more light or less liberty." Unfortunately, the worthy preacher has not here made a specific reference or an accurate quotation. Jortin is the author whom he has in view: and Jortin's words are, "diversity of opinion is the unavoidable result of human imperfection and human liberty, and is not to be removed unless we had more light or less agency."* Speaking of a current theological tenets, Mr. C. says (p. 6),

"The deep and mysterious nature of these doctrines, supposing them to be revealed, is such, that, persons of the most accurate judgment, the greatest learning, and the most pious dispositions, will always entertain different opinions concerning them."

Supposing them to be revealed! Why will the preacher thus reason from an assumption, a supposition? The point to be ascertained, is, are any such doctrines revealed or not? And this, surely, is a question of fact. It is the very question respecting which opposite denominations of Christians are at issue. If the doctrines to which this writer adverts are indeed revealed, they must be embraced, whether they be "high and mysterious", or plain and simple. But we repeat that the previous inquiry should be, where are they found?——in the Scriptures, or only in symbols and catechisms of man's device? In another passage (5) this gentleman speaks of "the obscure manner

* Pref. to Remarks on Eccles. Hist. XIV.

in which these" doctrines "are revealed." What the ideas are which he affixes to such language; what he understands by the terms *revealed* and *revelation*, we presume not to define. Does he believe that light and obscurity, that discovery, and concealment, are the same thing? If there exist any conventional relation between words and the objects signified by words, *a divine revelation is complete, so far as it professes to be a revelation*: although it makes no disclosure of truths of a certain class, yet its disclosure of those which come within its limits is unreserved. To intimate that a revelation from God is, as such, partial and *obscure*, what is this but to reflect injuriously on the Divine Attributes? What is it but to misstate, we will not say, misrepresent, the claims of revelation and of its records? We conjecture that Mr. Carpenter has not justly informed himself of the import of the term *mystery* in the Bible. Has he yet to learn that it *never* signifies *there*, whatever be its sense when employed elsewhere, something *unintelligible*—but *an event or design hitherto kept secret?* What is *mysterious*, according to its Scriptural meaning, with which alone we have at present any concern, is that which has been in no degree revealed: once revealed, it ceases to be *mysterious* and obscure.*

Of the whole of Mr. C.'s argument under his first head the following consideration is destructive: an apostle of Jesus Christ† declares it to be practicable for *all* Christians to come in *the unity of* THE FAITH [or, as Archbishop Newcome translates the words, *in the same faith*] "and of the knowledge of the Son of God, unto a perfect man," &c." This passage is even found in the chapter whence our author selects his text; though it seems not to have gained his attention. Now Paul was no visionary, no enthusiast, but well acquainted with the Gospel and with human nature.

In Mr. Carpenter's judgment, it is not *desirable* that Christians should think alike on religious doctrines. And he trusts (7) "that it will be no difficult matter to establish the truth of the assertion;" though, he confesses, it will not be readily allowed by "the

bigot who is violently attached to his own system or his own party," and by "the zealot who will compass sea and land to make one proselyte."

The imputation of bigotry we should be extremely grieved to incur: and our zeal, we would hope, is "according to knowledge" and associated with charity. At the risk however of falling under this well intentioned author's censure, we demur to his unqualified proposition, and must own that we are dissatisfied with his reasoning.

"If," observes he, "it were necessary to salvation, or if it were at all desirable, that men should think alike on religious subjects, the All-wise and Merciful Creator would have ordered things differently from what he has done."

Doubtless, the interval is very wide between what is "necessary to salvation" and what is "at all desirable." Arguments therefore which apply to one of these cases, do not always and of course, apply to the other. Great care must be employed in reasoning from human imperfection to the design and proceedings of the Deity. We read, in a volume not less revered by Mr. C. than by ourselves, that "the living God would have *all men to come to the knowledge of the truth.*"‡ Now is not this declaration more clearly significant of the divine purpose than any evidence besides? Shall we oppose to it the preacher's inference from a gratuitous assumption? A diversity then of religious opinion among mankind, is rather attributable to their not studying the Scriptures with impartiality and diligence than either to the diversity of their minds or to an imagined obscurity in revelation itself. There are some respects in which unity of faith would be exceedingly "desirable."

Not more satisfactory is Mr. Carpenter's second argument: "as a variety in the natural world is pleasing, so also is a variety in the moral world;" whence he concludes "that it is not desirable that all men should think alike" (8).

But the analogies of fancy must not be substituted for the exercise and the reasonings of the judgment. "That diversity which is found in the

* See Dan. ii. 22. 1 Cor. ii. 10.
† Ephes. iv. 13.
‡ 1 Tim. ii. 4. iv. 10.

vegetable creation," and in the animal kingdom, possesses just as much connexion with the variety prevailing "in the religious sentiments and opinions of mankind" as the revival of nature in spring does with the resurrection of the human body. In both instances there may exist, or appear to exist, a mutual *resemblance*; which however will not furnish, in either case, an *argument* to the sound philosopher or divine. These supposed analogies are far more obvious to men of a particular cast of imagination and taste than they are to persons of another temperament: and they supply us with little, if any, assistance in the investigation of important truth or in ascertaining the rule and measure of human duty.

Mr. C. (9) is desirous of communicating to his hearers and readers his recent pleasure, at Bristol, in seeing "the great number of people whom he met or who overtook him in going to different places of religious worship." And it is curious to perceive him assigning as the cause of his satisfaction at this spectacle not so much the *variety* as the *unity* of their sentiments. The pious and benevolent preacher exclaims, "How pleasing and animating the thought! These persons are all going to worship the *same* God, through the *same* Mediator. They are all going to partake of that bread which cometh down from Heaven, and to drink of the *same* fountain of living waters, though at different streams." Evidently, Mr. Carpenter's admiration and delight were awakened rather by the *union* of these several inhabitants of Bristol in points of primary moment than by a regard to the dissonance in their creeds and discipline! He should, either not have introduced this fact in illustration of his subject or have introduced it in another part of his discourses.

His third plea for diversity of sentiment among Christians is that it "has produced and doth produce several good effects" (10). And, undoubtedly, the Providence of God renders human imperfection instrumental to valuable purposes. This admission, nevertheless, will not prove the *desirableness* of variety of religious opinion; although it is a very powerful argument for the exercise of mutual candour and forbearance. The Supreme Ruler causes the wrath of man to praise him: even vice itself gives scope for the cultivation and improvement of moral dispositions on the part of those who lament it's ascendancy and experience it's injurious effects; yet we must not thence infer that it is *desirable* for some persons to be the slaves of fierce and lawless passions.

The preacher endeavours to shew (17) "that Christians do think, alike on the most important articles of religion," that "they agree in their belief of those truths which are of the greatest moment," and that "their difference in other points is not so great as they are ready to imagine."

Among the truths which are of the highest moment Mr. C. ranks one which we consider as perfectly unscriptural, and in the belief of which, *all* Christians, most assuredly, do *not* agree. In paraphrasing the verses with which his text is connected, he gives the following gloss on part of the apostle's language:—"Him who is the Father of angels and men; who is over all, Supreme in majesty, perfection and dominion; even above him who is the one Lord of Christians; *by whom he made the world.*"

Now although this be the preacher's creed, and, as we conclude from p. 20, his worthy colleague's "Mr. Scott," we cannot receive it without and against the testimony of the Sacred Writers: and we are grieved that Mr. Carpenter has in this instance not only *added*[*] to the words of Paul, but has even numbered the tenet asserted in this unauthorized exposition among "the principal and most important articles of the Christian faith." This conduct is the more extraordinary as in another passage (53), he recommends that we be "*satisfied with the use of Scriptural language on controversial points*," and as he admits (pp. 30, 36, &c.) the decline of his own, that is, of the "Arian," denomination, of the zeal and the numbers of those who regard Christ as under God, "the Maker and Governor of the world," and, as, nevertheless "becoming an infant, and liable to all the wants of mortality" (31).

The writer before us allows that, "there is a real difference in the religious sentiments of Christians" (21), and, in our turn, we concede to

---

him that sometimes their diversities of opinion are only verbal and apparent. Those we deem to be least reconcileable to each other which regard the object of worship, and the popular doctrine of *atonement* or vicarious satisfaction, which, it seems, however, Mr. Carpenter does not hold (26, 67); though he more than once employs this term, never used in the Christian Scriptures, and leaves it unexplained.*

If we suspect that his metaphysical and his theological learning are somewhat inaccurate, the following sentence awakens, and, perhaps, may justify, the suspicion (19):

"——the high Calvinists who maintain that all the actions of men are foreordained by God, and that man is not a free agent, exactly agree with many who are esteemed most wide in their sentiments, and who believe in the necessity of all human actions."

"That all the actions of men are foreordained by God," is a position admitted, we conceive, by every class of believers in the Divine Government and in the records of revelation, and not exclusively by High Calvinists and by Philosophical Necessitarians. Nor do any of them deny the free agency of man, in the just and consistent sense of that expression. The doctrine of what Mr. C styles "the *necessity* of all human actions," is not *fatalism*, or an approach to fatalism: it is the *certainty* of actions, agreeably to the nature and the force of the motives which dictate them; and this tenet cannot be disproved, however it be misunderstood. Of philosophical necessity (for it is a *metaphysical*, and not a *theological*, opinion) the bulk of Calvinists—whether high or low—have no knowledge: and their characteristic notions of arbitrary decrees and influences are incompatible with it's simplicity and fatal to it's proper and natural operation.

Concerning his "worthy colleague" and himself the preacher affirms (20), —"in every religious service, we either directly or indirectly profess our faith in Christ as the Son of God and the Saviour of men." Of the justness

* Scriptural doctrines may be stated in Scriptural language. Here the proper word is *reconciliation.* Rom. v. 11. 2 Cor. v. 18, &c.

of this declaration we are convinced. Not less confident is our persuasion that *all* classes of Christians profess the same creed: and we heartily wish that "other foundation" would "no man lay!"

This gentleman admires (21) the conduct of the Quakers in fairly and openly placing their principles before their Christian brethren, and leaving them to judge for themselves, but discovering "no great zeal for making proselytes." Now in several members of this society we have witnessed a considerable zeal to enlarge it's bounds. Be the fact however as it may—we have yet to learn that proselytizing zeal is an offence against the Christian law and spirit. Ridicule, we know, is thrown on it by unbelievers and by men of the world: but that any professors and ministers of the Gospel should attempt to brand it with disgrace, is a sad illustration of human weakness and inconsistency. Is proselytizing zeal, as *such*, condemned by our Lord and his apostles? Unquestionably, *not.* They denounce it only when it takes an ill direction, or is accompanied by a malignant temper. Of proselytizing zeal in it's purest form they were themselves examples. No doubt, the zeal of *some* men for making converts "will adopt every method, fair or unfair, to accomplish it's purposes." This is "mischievous and accursed;" not however because it is a "proselyting" but because it is a spurious zeal.

"It is no uncommon thing, both in politics and in religion (so Mr. C. informs us, 22), for persons who are of the middle party to be regarded with a suspicious or an evil eye by those bigots who belong to the two opposite extremes."

Bigots, of every party, whether of the middle or the two opposite extremes, regard with a suspicious or an evil eye those to whom they consider themselves as being opposed. Yet, after all, who and what are the middle party? There is no denomination which does not claim, and which may not successfully claim, to be the *middle* party, in respect of certain other denominations. This fact however is no test, no presumption, of such middle party, being in possession of the truth.

As a motive to peace and unity, Mr. C. urges the consideration "that there is something good in all the different denominations of Christians as well as something defective.". He praises the *soi-disant* " orthodox or evangelical denomination" for their zealous attention to the instrumental duties of religion, which, nevertheless, he adds, some of them are too apt to substitute " for the weightier matters of the law, such as fidelity, integrity and mercy." Passing over, for the present, " the middle party,' he tells us, what is strictly true, that the body of Unitarian Christians has also it's excepjencies and defects : " It is distinguished," he is pleased to say, " for honour, probity, integrity and liberality, but is less exemplary for it's observance of the instrumental duties of religion than the opposite party." A charge still more serious, we imagine, in Mr. C.'s estimation, and certainly in our own, succeeds :

" Of late years it [the Unitarian denomination] has manifested a great proselyting zeal, and some, I apprehend, are more solicitous to make converts to their grand doctrine of the Unity of the Godhead, than to teach men to fear God and keep his commands ; though many, I know, make this their great object, and are of a truly serious spirit." 26, 27.

It is a very small thing for us to be judged by this preacher, or by 'man's judgment : he who judgeth us, is the Lord. The grand doctrine of the Unity of the Godhead, so prominent in the Scriptures, so neglected, obscured and corrupted in human creeds, possesses an importance which demands no ordinary measure of " proselyting zeal." Still, the dissemination of it is an object of inferior moment to that of teaching men to fear God and keep his commandments. He then who accuses the Unitarians of making the latter only a secondary end, ought to produce strong evidence in support of so weighty an accusation : nor will his hearers or his readers admit it on his bare assertion or intimation.

In his portrait of Unitarians Mr. C.'s pencil is unfaithful, and his colours are inappropriate :

" They are often superstitiously afraid of superstition ; and while they are obliged to acknowledge that there are mysteries in the works of creation and in the dispensations of Providence, they feel a great aversion to the word mystery when applied to the dispensations of divine grace."

He would have expressed himself with more discrimination, and with not less of equity and candour, had he subjoined, ' that their aversion from the word *mystery*, as here employed by Mr. Carpenter, arises from their firm conviction that this language has no such use and application in the volume of Revelation ; and that their alleged superstitious fear of superstition, is really a dread of adopting, in their theological discussions, terms and ideas which cannot be discovered in the Scriptures.

But the picture is not yet finished :

" They are too prone to look down with pity or contempt on those who believe that the Gospel contains more than they are willing to allow [read, *than they are able to find*]. And though they are happily free from that uncharitable spirit which consigns persons of different sentiments from themselves to future punishment, yet some of them are not altogether free from that supercilious and dogmatical spirit which arises from the pride of human reason."

A supercilious and dogmatical spirit may proceed from other and additional causes—v. g. from the temper or the creed which says, ' Stand by thyself ; for I am holier than thou.' Men who stigmatize the exercise of human reason, may evince, in that very act, the pride of reason : and the advocates of *mysteries*, in the unscriptural sense of that expression, may be quite as dogmatical and supercilious as those who are willing to make the Sacred Writers their own commentators.

On the Methodists our author bestows a mixture of panegyric and of censure : but the former is the principal ingredient. The Established Church he regards (29) as " tolerant in it's practice and useful in it's institutions." And then he pays this Church and her sons a very singular and equivocal compliment :

" The private sentiments of it's members are various. Some are Calvinists and others Arminians. Most of them are Trinitarians, not a few Arians, and some perhaps Socinians. But they obey the exhortation of the Apostle, *Hast thou faith ? Have it to thyself.*"

Say rather, they in practice pervert and misapply it, as much as Mr. Carpenter does by his quoting it in reference to this matter. Certain, too, we 'are that, whatever apostolic ex-

hortation they either obey or disregard,
they do violence, by this diversity of
opinion, to the articles and the spirit of
the Church of England. If we ask,
for what purpose were those articles
framed, and subscription to them enjoined, the reply must be, *for the avoiding diversity of opinions, and for the
establishing of consent touching true religion.** This consent however a religious establishment cannot secure, cannot indeed produce: and that variety
of sentiment among it's officiating as
well as it's private members which Mr.
C. appears to eulogize, betrays it's
weakness and manifests it's evil tendency; that unity of spirit and that
bond of peace of which he here boasts,
are not in truth preserved —— and,
while the restriction of *articles* continues, they cannot be preserved (as
existing controversies prove they cannot) except by the aid of some other
bond, that of ignorance or of insincerity.

If the Established Church be tolerant
in its practice, we are indebted, under
God, for her tolerance to the progress
of knowledge, inquiry and rational
freedom, and to the spirit of the British constitution: if her institutions are
useful, they are those of them which
she maintains in common with almost
every Christian denomination. To
obtain the approbation of a consistent
Nonconformist, she must be reformed
in a degree that we cannot expect to
witness.

Concerning the denomination to
which himself belongs, Mr. C. allows
(30) that it has it's defects as well as
it's excellencies, that it has conformed
too much to the world, and that it has
declined in it's zeal and consequently
in it's numbers. But he tells us that
there are still many highly valuable
and respectable characters to be found
in it. It's zeal, we conclude, has not
been a " proselyting zeal!"

In our author's judgment, " every
system of opinion has it's difficulties as
well as it's advantages:"

" The candid and thoughtful Calvinist
must allow that his system in appearance
is somewhat harsh, and militates against
the justice and goodness of God. The
candid Trinitarian must allow that there
are many passages of Scripture which speak
of the Son of God as a derived being and

dependent on his Father. The candid Socinian must concede that it is not very
easy to reconcile some declarations of the
Gospel with the notion of the simple humanity of Christ: and I, as an Arian, am
ready to acknowledge that my system is
not free from difficulties. Indeed the idea
of that exalted Person whom, under God, I
regard as the Maker and Governor of the
world, becoming an infant, and liable to
all the wants of mortality, appears to some
so strange that they cannot embrace it."

Very strange, and even wonderful,
it appears to ourselves! Yet this is
not the reason of our refusing to embrace it: for could Mr. C. prove his
tenet to be the doctrine of the Scriptures, it should instantly be the subject
of our faith. The whole paragraph
might provoke and warrant animadversion: but we are not particularly
disposed to extend the limits of this
article.

In the third sermon the preacher
makes these further remarks on the
religious denomination to which he
belongs, and in which he would comprehend the Presbyterians and moderate Independents (36):

" When I call to mind the illustrious
names and characters which have adorned
this body of Christians, the two Henrys,
with Watts and Doddridge ; Chandler and
Barker and Pickard; Price and Farmer and
Furneaux; Towgood, Urwick and the two
Worthingtons, with others that might be
mentioned; I feel it an honour to belong
to this denomination of Christians."

The grouping is somewhat incon-
gruous. Not stopping however to take
critical exceptions, we acknowledge
the high respectability of these names :
and, with a zeal of admiration not inferior to Mr. Carpenter's, we could
eulogize almost every one of these characters. If names were concerned,
and not evidence, such an array would
be truly formidable.

Our author goes on :

" When I consider the numerous and
flourishing congregations which belonged
to this respectable body from the beginning
to the middle of the last century, and the
greater or less decline of almost all those
congregations since that period, I ask,
whence arises this decline? It cannot be
from death. That has equally attacked
other societies. Has it arisen from persecution? No: for except in a partial and
solitary instance, we have had the full liberty of worshipping God without molestation. The temples of the living God have
been open to us, but our hearts have been

---

* *Neal's Hist. of the Puritans* (edited
by Toulmin), I. 160.

too much shut against them. I will again ask, are those principles which wrought in the minds of such men as Watts and Doddridge so deep a conviction of the malignity of sin, and so high a sense of the Divine justice and mercy in the redemption of sinners by the death of Christ, are those principles a mere delusion? Have they no foundation in the Gospel? Do they cease to pull down the strong holds of sin, and to convert transgressors to God, because some choice spirits of the present day chuse to call them superstitious and absurd? To these questions I am strongly disposed to answer in the negative." 37.

Here amidst a few remarks which are just, and one or two inquiries which are pertinent, we find others that demand our strictures. To argument, where it is employed, argument may perhaps be opposed. But what course shall we take when the prejudices of men are addressed, instead of their understandings, and when an imposing tone and an unwarrantable sneer are substituted for fair discussion? Principles embraced even by a Watts and a Doddridge, may, nevertheless, be errors, may have no foundation in the Gospel. One is our Master: and that Master is Christ. Let not those who speak of certain opinions (which, it may be, have the sanction of great names), as unscriptural, be sarcastically denominated *choice spirits.* Some Trinitarians would bestow the sarcasm on Mr. Carpenter himself for denying the essential, underived Deity of Christ: and some Calvinists, for his calling in question the doctrine of the Saviour's *vicarious* sacrifice. Of needlessly offensive language in any class of controversialists we shall not be the advocates: in this gentleman it is eminently censurable on account of his reiterated professions of candour, moderation and liberality.

We are far from believing that the decline of a serious spirit has preceded the change of sentiment among the Presbyterians. Indifference to religious truth and to the examination of the Scriptures, is, on the other hand, a symptom and a cause of decaying piety. There is no surer indication of the existence of " a serious spirit" than a fearless regard to tenets which, however the world frown on them, are inculcated, as is our humble conviction, in the Sacred Volume. At the shrine of Religion numerous and costly sacrifices are made by several Unitarians: for

the sake of what they deem the genuine faith of the Gospel, they have been contented to surrender temporal blessings of no trifling value, and to have their names cast out as evil. We do not remind our readers of this fact by way of boasting, but in order to repel the insinuation, from whatever quarter it proceed, in whatever style it be conveyed, that Unitarianism is inauspicious to " a serious spirit." 13.

When Mr. C. asks (38), " have we any better commentators on the Scriptures than Henry and Whitby and Doddridge and Orton?" We answer distinctly *Yes.* Of Henry and Whitby and Doddridge and Orton we think with high veneration: and most of their works we read with much satisfaction and improvement. But we repeat, without hesitation, and, we trust, without a bias for or against particular systems of theology, that many better commentators on the Scriptures may be consulted. On the New Testament especially Bishop Pearce, Peirce of Exeter, Hallet, Benson, Lowman and Dean Woodhouse are more accurate (and, with an exception, perhaps, in the instance of Whitby, more learned) expositors.[*] To shew our impartiality, we have purposely mentioned writers whose religious sentiments accord more nearly with the preacher's than with our's. For the correctness of our statement and our choice, we appeal to the knowledge and experience of those who are in the habit of *studying* the Scriptures.

" Have they" [the moderns], further asks this gentleman, " found out by the examination of ancient M.S.S. that all those passages which speak of the divine nature and atonement of Christ are interpolations?"

The difference between Mr. C. and the Unitarian Christian, is chiefly in respect of *interpretation.* No Unitarian concedes that the passages adverted to by our author " speak of the divine nature and atonement of Christ:" and if there be any texts which the Unitarian considers as *interpolations*, he so considers them on those principles of Biblical criticism which are admitted

* Of the books of the Old Testament, there has been a series of translations, executed during the reign of his present Majesty. These, for the most part, are accompanied by *notes,* and possess, in general, superior merit.

by theological scholars of all denominations. With the history and progress of this science for the larger proportion of the last half century Mr. C. would seem to be unacquainted: to ascertain the genuine text of Scripture, is one object; to interpret it, when ascertained, is another.

It is a misfortune belonging to these and similar inquiries on the part of Mr. C. that his brethren, and not least his Trinitarian and Calvinistic brethren, may retort them on himself. For example, *he* may be asked, "Has any new revelation been sent us from heaven? Or have we any better commentators on the Scriptures than" *Gill, Guyse, &c.?* The writer before us, employs the words, *the divine nature and atonement of Christ,* in a very different import from that in which they are used by the *orthodox* denomination of Christians; though such of them as are ignorant of his real sentiments will perhaps rank him among their sect, on account of his adopting their current phraseology.

We profess *our* ignorance of the connexion of his next remark with his subject:

"Of those ministers who have changed their sentiments within these few years, I have known some who used to express themselves very strongly in favour of the doctrines which I have mentioned, and declare that they never could give them up as long as they found some passages in the New Testament which they mentioned. I cannot therefore account for the change which has taken place; and they will say it is no business of your's to account for it; I acknowledge the truth of this remark, and remain silent."

But Mr. C. will excuse *us* for not maintaining the silence which, no doubt, *he* has good reason to preserve. We are of opinion that an account may and ought to be given of the change which he has stated: we believe that the gentlemen in whom it has been produced, are desirous of it's being satisfactorily explained by him. And we cannot solve the phenomenon otherwise than by inferring that a conviction of the unscriptural nature and pretensions of the Arian, or reputed Arian, doctrine has been daily gaining ground. As to the *confidence* of these ministers—this, in itself, will prove nothing: their confidence might *formerly* be unfounded, and *now* it may rest on the firmer basis of careful reading and rigorous examination. This preacher, too, can be *confident* in assertion.

" —— there is one question of great importance which" Mr. Carpenter (39) would intreat " the converts to Socinian principles to ask themselves,—Have they received any benefit from their change of sentiment?" We beg permission to join in this intreaty. Of what the answer will be we have no apprehension: and we wish that the inquiry may be seriously weighed and impartially applied.

Some of the best observations in his second discourse, regard the practice of Christians ascribing to each other " sentiments which they do not maintain, and consequences which they do not allow" (40). Yet even here he exhibits some incorrectness:

"How prone," he says, "are Unitarians to charge Trinitarians with contradiction and absurdity in maintaining that one is three and three are one."

"The Trinitarians constitute a great majority of the Christian church; yet not one of them will say that three are one and one three, in the same sense—and that the same person or the same thing may be one and three in different senses, we must all allow—thus, for instance, the same person may be a clergyman, a justice of peace and a farmer, and it is in some such manner as this that some of them explain their notions of the doctrine of the Trinity."

Be it known however to Mr. C. that such explanations are not *commonly* received by Trinitarians. Let us hear the language of a recent, a dexterous and, we presume, a popular writer " on the principal points of the Socinian controversy."[*] " We do not," says he, " consider them [i.e. the ' distinguishing appellations,' the Father, the Son and the Holy Spirit] as expressive of a distinction that is *merely official,* or as exhibiting the same Divine *person under three different aspects;* but as implying *a real personal distinction,* which has subsisted from eternity, and is essential to the nature of Deity."

We must bestow unreserved commendation on the picture, which Mr. Carpenter places before us (44), of the union of Zeal, Prudence and Charity:

" When those three heavenly sisters, Zeal, Prudence and Charity, walk hand in hand, what a lovely groupe do they form!

---

[*] Wardlaw's Disc. &c. (2d edit.) p. 11.

The admiration of men, the delight of angels, the beloved of God! As they proceed, the flowers spring up under their feet, the rose of Sharon blossoms around them, and the lily of the vallies sheds it's sweetest perfume. The dew of Hermon and of the Mountains of Zion descends upon them, and the precious ointment goes down to the skirt of their garments. As they advance, the mountains and the hills break forth before them into singing, and all the trees of the field clap their hands. Instead of the thorn comes up the fir tree, and instead of the briar comes up the myrtle tree. They will enter every house that is open to receive them, they will enter every heart that is not shut against them. Let us throw open the doors of our houses, let us open wide the avenues of our hearts for their reception : for they will bless us in our temporal and they will bless us in our spiritual concerns. They will bless us in our basket and in our store, they will bless us in the city, and they will bless us in the field, they will bless us in our going out and in our coming in, they will bless us in our domestic relations, in our family connections and in our friendly associations, and they will conduct us to the presence of the Prince of Peace and the God of Love."

There is little which calls for notice in the fourth discourse. One observation we transcribe without a comment (52) :

" If Christians would but use words in the same sense, not mistake each other's meaning, and not deem small variations of sentiment ground for separation, I think they would find about seven divisions sufficient to comprehend them all ; but now they are divided into I know not how many denominations, I believe not less than ten times seven."

The *pastoral address, &c.* is pious and affectionate. To some however of the observations which it contains we must refuse our assent ; though it will be less necessary to animadvert on them, in consequence of our ample review of the Discourses. We quote only a very few sentences (69) :

" The Socinian scheme may do for a few philosophic and well disposed minds ; but I am persuaded will not do, for the generality of Christians. They must have a Saviour who is more than human : they must have an atoning sacrifice : they must have a throne of grace, where they may apply not only for mercy to pardon, but for grace to help them in their time of need : and they must have a high priest, who is touched with the feeling of their infirmities to intercede for them."

In note 13 (101) Mr. C. explains a part of this language :

" *A throne of grace, &c.*"

" Some of my Unitarian brethren have objected to the sentence in which these words are found, and allege that I have not given a fair statement of their sentiments. They say that they do believe and rejoice that there is a throne of grace, at which we may obtain mercy and find grace ; and also that we have a high priest, who is touched with the feeling of our infirmities. It was not my intention to deny this, but I am now sensible that I was not sufficiently accurate or sufficiently full in the statement which I made. I would therefore make the following alteration, which I apprehend will meet the ideas of those gentlemen who were present when this subject was discussed."

" The generality of Christians must have a Saviour who is more than human : they must have an atoning sacrifice ; they must have a throne of grace, where they may apply not only for mercy to pardon (as the Socinians allow) : but also for grace to help them in time of need, (which many of them do not allow if by grace we mean the immediate assistance of the Holy Spirit) and they must have a high priest who is touched with the feeling of their infirmities, (which the Socinians allow that they have, and also that he is now actively employed in promoting the welfare of Christians, but they do not allow that he intercedes for them or pleads their cause in the common acceptation of the word)."

On the whole of this statement and explanation Mr. Carpenter's " Unitarian brethren" will, doubtless, observe, that numbers of Christians, besides the few of *philosophic minds*, actually entertain the views which our author pronounces unsuitable to *their wants and habits* ; that to say *the generality of Christians must have a throne of grace*, is to deny that the Unitarians have such a throne ; that this denial is itself unjust, and is made in a manner fitted to be offensive and injurious ; that when Mr. C. became sensible of his inaccuracy, he should, in his second edition, either have expunged the obnoxious clause or have incorporated his note with the text ; that, after all, his amendment and his illustration are unsatisfactory ; inasmuch as they prove nothing more than that he and the Unitarians differ in their interpretation of some Scriptural terms ; that the throne of *grace* is the throne of *favour* ; that Divine *favour*, however dispensed, is earnestly supplicated by Unitarian.

Christians; and, finally, that the priesthood of Christ and his intercession are never connected together by the Sacred Writers; so that it may now be easily determined, whether Mr. C. or his "Unitarian brethren" shew the greater reverence for the volume of revelation?

Are *they* deficient in this reverence who study to quote the Scriptures faithfully, and to expound them with an uniform regard to the subject and the context? The same process of interpretation, would have conducted our preacher to the real meaning of Matt. xi. 27, 'No man knoweth the Son but the Father:' it would have shewn him that our Lord there speaks not of the person of either the Son or the Father, but solely of *the extent of the dispensation of the Gospel* (66). It is a much easier undertaking to explain Scripture by it's sound, and in conformity with a previous hypothesis, than by a strict comparison of one passage with another.

Most of Mr. C.'s *notes and anecdotes*, might have been omitted without any loss of reputation to the author or of advantage to the reader. To be "narrative with age," is not the character of the great *Clarendon* alone. The *anecdotes* which the writer under our review has appended to the second edition of his discourses, are chiefly of the nature of *table talk*, and, however good-humoured, possess little general interest and exhibit little discrimination—— *dicenda, tacenda locutus.* We extract some few biographical *memoranda* of "the late Rev. Thomas Urwick." 91.

"He was born of respectable parents in the neighbourhood of Shrewsbury, and, having attained [*obtained*] a competent share of classical learning, spent part of his academical course under the tuition of Dr. Doddridge, at Northampton."

"The remainder of it was [*was passed*] at Glasgow, under Dr. Leechman, whose celebrity as Divinity professor attracted many students to enjoy the benefit of his lectures."

"The first place at which he settled was Worcester. Here he resided for many years, respected and beloved: till at length sighing after retirement he went and settled at Narborough, a village near Leicester."

"But retirement was not suited to his active mind: and his ministerial talents were too well known to suffer him to remain long in obscurity. He received an invitation from the respectable congregation at Clapham to succeed their late pastor Dr. Furneaux."

"His distinguishing characteristic was simplicity.—He was born Dec. 8, 1727; died Feb. 26, 1807, and was twenty-six years pastor of the congregation at Clapham."

We have reason to believe that Mr. Urwick became a student at Northampton, about the year 1747 or 1748. Here, and subsequently at Glasgow, the late Rev. *Newcome Cappe* was one of his academical companions and most intimate friends. And Mr. U. was the "venerable minister of the gospel" who, in 1802, attested, with all the eloquence of the heart, the excellencies of his former associate.[*] Praise more honourable to the memory of it's object as well as to the judgment and feelings of the giver was never bestowed; and none could be more soothing and gratifying to surviving relatives.

During his residence at Clapham, Mr. Urwick "was particularly serviceable to young men (92), in advising and directing them to proper situations; and amongst the rest to the celebrated Joseph Lancaster," from whom, a few weeks ago, our author received the following particulars of his life:"

"He was born of pious parents in London, and when he was about fifteen years old, felt so deep though misguided a sense of religion that he resolved to retire from the world and devote himself to God in some remote and secluded part of the earth. With this view he went to Bristol. But the little substance he took with him being soon exhausted, he was obliged to enter on board a tender. Here he commenced a preacher to the sailors; and though at first he was treated with ridicule, yet afterwards his plain and heartfelt addresses made a serious impression on their minds. In the mean time, his parents were much afflicted at his loss [*at losing him*], and though they were acquainted with his situation could afford him no relief. At this time, it accidentally or rather providentially happened that Mr. Urwick going into the shop of his father to purchase some trifling article, found his mother in tears, and inquiring the cause, was so much affected with the account she gave him of her son, that he made application to persons of influence, and obtained an order for his release. Lancaster was surprised to see an officer of rank come on board, and not only take him on shore, but supply him with money and clothes for his journey from

* In a letter to the highly valuable relict of Mr. Cappe. Memoirs of his Life, prefixed to *Discourses, &c.* (1805) xxiii.

Plymouth to London. By this time he was convinced, as he told me, that no life can be pleasing to God which is not useful to man. Accordingly, he set up a school; but though the number of his scholars soon became considerable, his pay was so small and so often withheld, that necessity led him by degrees to find out that plan of education which has been so useful and which goes by his name.".

In the tenth note (97) Mr. C. makes this declaration :

"—— if I were ever to change my sentiments, I should sooner yield to the mild persuasion of a Lindsey or a Toulmin than to the bold and decisive, not to say dogmatical, assertions of authors of a more confident tone and a more sanguine temperament."

An *Irenicum*, in order to produce it's desired effect, should be written with solid judgment and with a conciliatory temper. In the former of these qualifications we are humbly of opinion that Mr. Carpenter is defective : the grand Scriptural bond of union among all Christians is, or ought to be, their common belief *that Jesus their Master*

is the Christ :* and to this principle the preacher has been less attentive than his topic and the connexion of his text demanded. Unhappily, too, the frequent absence of precision from his statements and reasonings, prevents the fulfilment of his evident wish to be just and kind in his representations of the sentiments of those of his brethren who have the fortune to differ from himself. Sometimes he even appears to forget that there are the same laws of controversy for both Arians and Unitarians !

Reluctantly therefore we must pronounce that these Sermons are ill calculated to promote *Christian peace and unity*; which objects, it is our persuasion, are more likely to be advanced by Mr. Carpenter's life and character than by his present labours in theological literature.

* It is remarkable that *Hobbes*, " de Cive" (Amsterd. 1669), thus expresses himself. " Dico alium articulum fidei præter hunc, JESUM ESSE CHRISTUM, homini Christiano, ut *necessarium* ad salutem requiri nullum." P. 386.

OBITUARY.

On Friday the 5th of July last, at *Laurenmney*, in the county of Monmouth, calmly fell asleep in Jesus, ere long to awake to eternal life and happiness, in the 21st year of her age, SARAH, the eldest daughter of JOHN H. MOGGRIDGE, Esq.

At a period like the present, when religion, which ought to constitute " our being's end and aim," possesses so weak a hold on the thoughts, the affections, and the pursuits of the human race, it may perhaps in some degree contribute to the spread and influence of genuine Christianity (identified in the mind of the writer with the undivided unity and the un-purchased love of the Universal Parent), briefly to state a few particulars respecting the lovely and excellent young person, whose removal from this state of trial and discipline is now announced to the public.

In the possession and *prospect* of a rich variety of earthly blessings, she was enabled by those just and elevated conceptions which an excellent understanding, applied to the study of sacred truth, had induced her to form of the character and perfections of the Supreme Being, and by the glorious prospect of a happy immortality, meekly to resign herself into the hands of her heavenly Father ; and with a degree of self-annihilation and Christian fortitude truly admirable,

to administer such consolation and advice to the objects of her affectionate solicitude, as could only have been expected from the ripened judgment of maturer years.

Consoled by the recollection of her virtues, animated by her bright example, and mindful of her last request, the surviving objects of her tenderest affection " sorrow not as those without hope ;" firmly believing " that as Jesus died and rose again, even so those also who sleep in Jesus, will God bring with him in that glorious day, when this corruptible shall put on incorruption, this mortal be clothed with immortality, and death be swallowed up in victory !"

" When loveliness array'd in op'ning bloom,
　Fram'd to delight the sense, the heart to
　　cheer,
Sinks early blasted to the silent tomb,
　Who can suppress the sigh, restrain the
　　tear !
But faith sheds comfort o'er the troubled
　　mind,
　And gratitude recounts what once was
　　giv'n ;
To him who lent it be the boon resign'd,
　What soul too spotless, kind and good
　　for Heav'n !"

E. H. P.

Penmain, Aug. 14, 1816.

Brighton, 8th August, 1816.
To the Editor of the Monthly Repository.
Sir,

On the 31st of July, died at *Scamel Hill*, in the parish of Lindfield, in the county of Sussex, at the good old age of 77 years, Mr. NATHANIEL DRAWBRIDGE, a worthy character, well known and much respected in this neighbourhood, and whose memory I judge deserves to be handed down to posterity through your valuable Repository.

He was buried in the General Baptist burial-ground at Cuckfield, on Tuesday last, August 6th, and a very appropriate sermon on the occasion was preached by Mr. Bennett, of Ditchling, from a text of the deceased's own chusing, Psalm xxxvii. and part of verse 3,—" Trust in the Lord and do good." In these two points of Christian exercise I believe but few of any denomination exceeded him, particularly in the former; for as for the latter, no man however well-disposed, can go beyond his ability.

Though for three or four years past he laboured under an infirm state of body, yet he was highly favoured in his intellectual powers, which he retained in their full exercise to the last moment of his life.

Permit me now to say a few things in reference to his general views of Christian truth. He was not only a firm friend to the rights and liberties of man in a general point of view, and shrunk from every idea of restraint upon private judgment; but particularly upon matters of religion it was a fixed principle with him, that every man had an equal right with himself to form his own opinion in matters of theology; and never condemned any man's eternal state on account of his creed, however it might differ from his own. Though he condemned their creeds he was tender over their persons, and ready to serve them upon every occasion, as far as in his power. The last observation he made on this head, a little before his death, was this: he said, " Oh God! dispose of me as thou seest fit:" a relative answered, " God is merciful to us:" he answered, " *there can be no doubt of that, but mankind make the Deity like themselves, a mere human being, all passion and prejudice.*"

He was a firm believer in the Unity of God, and had embraced this doctrine with every other in unison with it, I believe from an early period of his life. He had studied nature as well as revelation, and was fully persuaded that both natural and revealed religion concurred to prove and confirm the doctrine of One God and Father of all. He was also a firm believer in the mission of Jesus as the true Messiah and sent of God the Father; and he most conscientiously believed him to be truly

and properly man, and no other as it respected his person; yet he considered him every way qualified and adequate to all the purposes to which he was sent. He considered him as the greatest of all the prophets and the most dignified and most exalted character of the human race, and that through him life and immortality was brought to light, and that his precepts and conduct were not only worthy but incumbent upon all Christians to imitate. He had deeply studied and contemplated the character of the One Supreme Jehovah, and I believe has written much on the subject, which I hope will some day appear in public. He entertained some ideas upon the government of God that were probably peculiar to himself. He believed God to be the primary cause of all things, but could not suppose him to be the designing cause of all events: but for fear I should misunderstand him, I will give you his ideas in his own words, as I have collected them from your Repository for last June, (p. 322,) in a letter signed an " Old Inquirer," which I knew to be his when I read it, and have since had it confirmed by himself. His words are as follow:

" Now I do suppose that *all* events, *all* effects of power, are not subjects of intellectual determination, or objects of appointment; but on the contrary, that there are many natural results of force, which are not parts of any scheme, or any matters of device or ordination whatever." " No doubt, Deity is the source of all order, all systematic work, all management." He then asks—" But is God the *designing* cause of all movement and result?"

I have quoted thus much as a specimen of his ideas upon this critical subject. I shall conclude by saying that he was a good husband, a tender parent, a quiet neighbour, a faithful friend, and a pious man. I could say more, but think were he living he would not have wished me to say so much, for he coveted not honour from man, but that only which cometh from God, and was peculiarly circumspect in his words as well as actions. May every reader of your valuable publication imitate his virtues, and leave behind him as good a testimony of his faith, disposition, and conduct, as this our old and worthy friend.

I remain, Sir, your obedient Servant,
THOMAS VINE.

On Wednesday Morning, August 7, 1816, Mr. JOHN NEIGHBOUR, eldest son of Mr. Thomas Neighbour, Wine Merchant, *Smithfield.* The following character of him formed the conclusion of a Funeral Sermon preached for him at Worship Street, from Eccles. xii. 1, by the Rev. J. Evans, who interred his remains in the adjoining cemetery.

"The *beloved youth* whose decease we now lament, and endeavour to improve, ought to have a tribute of respect paid to his memory: He died in the 22d year of his age, of a consumption, which, prying upon his vitals these three years, brought him down to the grave. He bore his tedious illness with exemplary patience and resignation—knowing that his HEA-VENLY FATHER *did all things well!* Nor must it be omitted, that worn out by the ravages of this cruel disease, he was at length blessed with an easy dismissal from the pains and sufferings of mortality. Having had the superintendence of the closing part of his education, I am enabled to say that he possessed a good understanding, and an amiable temper, combined with a warm and generous heart. His love of knowledge, so commendable a trait in every youthful character, never forsook him, but continued with him to the last. He was gratified by every accession made to his little library; and never more happy than when conversing with a friend on topics conducive to mental improvement. As to RELIGION, he was regular and devout in his attendance on public worship in this place, as well as anxious to understand the *Holy Scriptures*, which are the sole rule both of our faith and practice. Nothing excited his disapprobation more than a spirit of ostentation exhibited in the exercise of prayer : to this purpose were the remarks he made to me on the very day previous to his death ; and I was particularly pleased with them, because the circumstance shewed the just ideas he entertained of a scriptural and rational piety ;—indeed my last interview on this occasion was of a devotional nature, and from which even in his extreme state of weakness he appeared to derive peculiar satisfaction. Without entering into further particulars respecting his character, it is sufficient to say, that by *his* death has been lost a dutiful son, an amiable brother, and a promising member of society.

" Return my soul—the works of life attend,
A little time to labour here is given ;
Meanwhile a *new attractive* thou shalt find
To draw thee hence and fix thine heart in HEAVEN !"

"Honourable age is not that which standeth in length of time, nor that is measured by number of years ; but wisdom is the grey hairs unto man, and an unspotted life is old age'."*

J. E.

* Wisdom of Solomon, chap. iv. 8, 9.

ADDITION TO THE ACCOUNTS OF REV. SAMUEL CARY, X. 656 and 729.
[*Extracts from a Discourse, delivered 17th Dec. 1815, on Occasion of the Death of the Rev. Samuel Cary. By the Rev. Mr. Colman, one of the Ministers of Boston.*]

I mean not on this occasion to attempt a studied eulogium of the character of our departed friend Cary, but to speak of him, as you would ever wish to remember him, as he was and as I knew him: a simple and faithful delineation of his character will be a sufficient and most honourable eulogy.

I knew Mr. Cary well. He was my friend. I promised myself much satisfaction and benefit from his friendship; the more intimately I became acquainted with him, the more were my esteem and respect for him increased.

Mr. Cary's talents were of a superior character; his intellectual attainments were considerable, and afforded an honourable testimony of his application and industry. His tract in defence of Christianity* was in the opinion of competent judges, able and convincing; though we must always regret that any thing personal should be mingled in our discussions of a subject of such immense importance and dignity as the truth of our religion, yet this production reflects high credit upon his good principles and learning.

As a preacher he was deservedly eminent. I have heard him often, and always with pleasure and improvement. His style was perspicuous and nervous; his discourses instructive and practical; not highly but sufficiently ornamented, discovering ever a pure and refined taste, and distinguished more by a rare solidity of judgment and a noble simplicity, than by a brilliancy of imagination. His manner was unaffected, serious, impressive; and suitable to the dignity of the pulpit.

Of his religious opinions, I need not speak particularly; you heard him yourselves, and he had too much integrity and simplicity of heart, ever to be guilty of equivocation, of a dishonourable concealment of his sentiments, or of a reluctance to express them, when he deemed it proper. His views of Christianity, in my opinion, and in such cases we ought only to speak for ourselves, were highly rational. Of the Unity of the Deity and the propriety of paying religious homage to the Supreme Being only, he was seriously convinced. He might, I believe, be denominated a strict Unitarian, but those persons from whom he differed found him, though a strenuous, yet an honourable

* Review of " The Grounds of Christianity Examined." Boston, 1813.

opponent. Correctness of religious belief is no evidence of moral goodness; and when we consider the innumerable invisible and indescribable influences to which the human understanding is subject, and the infinite variety of absurd and false opinions, which have been embraced and defended by the most distinguished men, it furnishes an equivocal proof of a man's wisdom or learning. Had Mr. Cary been a Calvinist or a Papist, I think, with his perfect rectitude of moral principle and exemplary life, I should not have esteemed or respected him less. Our friend had a liberal and honourable mind; and, with a just regard for the inalienable and sacred rights of conscience and private judgment, he was always ready to maintain the liberties, defend the characters, and assist the inquiries of others.

The correctness of his faith was attested by the purity and goodness of his life. He was a man of singular integrity, frankness, and generosity, with an entire freedom from avarice, or any low and sordid passion; evincing a nobleness of spirit, a high sense of honour, and a peculiar delicacy and refinement of moral sentiment. He possessed a serious and devout mind: he had no affectation in his religion, and anxiously endeavoured to guard against the appearance of ostentation in his piety.

He was a good son: while his father lived he served him with kindness and fidelity; he dwelt upon his memory with singular veneration; his death inflicted a wound which time had not healed: and he cherished his mother in her solitary old age with filial duty, love, and gratitude. In his family he was remarkably hospitable. His children, though the time was short during which he was permitted to enjoy them, had a strong hold on his affections; and his wife, who indeed deserved every thing from him, was the object of his faithful, affectionate, and courteous attention.

Such, as far as I knew him, was the character of our lamented friend. I have endeavoured to delineate it with fidelity. I pretend not that he was without his faults,—for what human being is?—perfection belongs not to man in his present state; and if he might sometimes be thought impetuous in his feelings and language, we must remember that this same temper was the spring of that generous enthusiasm, with which he cherished every honourable purpose.

The death of so excellent a man, in the morning of life, while his path yet glittered with all the lustre of promise, and our hearts exulted in the prospect of an increasing brightness, is an event to be deeply deplored. The privation of his

talents, the loss of his society and friendship, the cessation of his labours in behalf of virtue and piety, the rupture of those ties by which he was connected with this religious society, the interruption of so much domestic comfort, the dispersion of so many animating hopes,—it cannot be that these events should not fill our hearts with sorrow. Our religion does not forbid our sorrow; the stubbornness of a brutal philosophy makes no part of Christian resignation; but we are not permitted to nourish and prolong our grief, which, when excessive, indicates a distrust of the wisdom and rectitude of Divine Providence.

Divine Providence!—there is something in these words to reconcile us to any event, however dissonant to our wishes, however disastrous to our hopes. The world with all its concerns, we ourselves and all that is dear to us, are ever at the disposal and control of God. The government of God is truly paternal; the exercise of his authority is never arbitrary, capricious, or wanton, but the discipline of a most wise and faithful friend, suited to train the subjects of it to virtue and felicity. His knowledge embraces alike the past, the present, and the future, all things actual and all things possible; his power is adequate to any effect; his wisdom is unerring; his goodness and mercy are perfect and unchangeable. Is this the Being who presides over the destinies of mankind? and may we not confide in him with perfect security?—can we receive from God any thing but good, and that, the highest good attainable by our nature and condition?

These would have been the sentiments of our departed friend, if God had demanded of him such a sacrifice, as he has required of us. He displayed in this respect a truly Christian example. If any sentiments were predominant in his mind, they were sentiments of entire acquiescence in the will of heaven. When God took from him his first child under circumstances of peculiar trial, he submitted to the event with calm resignation. From the commencement of his last sickness, he seems to have been fully impressed with a conviction of its fatal issue; yet he bore it with Christian fortitude. I am persuaded that I shall gratify you by an extract from a letter, which I received from a friend* in Philadelphia after his last visit to that hospitable city.

"When I spoke to him," this friend writes, "of leaving Boston next spring, so as to avoid the unpleasant weather at that season of the year, he said with perfect

* Mr. James Taylor, one of the ministers of the First Unitarian Society, Philadelphia.

composure, that long before that time, he should be in his grave; that he had always been subject to inward fever, and that he had already lived as long as he expected; that when he was stout and hearty he was impressed with the persuasion, that he had not long to live; that he had only one petition to offer on this subject, 'Father, thy will be done'. He then conversed in an admirable manner on the good providence of God, which he was persuaded would dispose of his wife and his little child in the best possible manner; and particularly said, that even on their account he had no solicitude about life; that if such was the will of God that he should now be taken away, his death would be good for them as well as for himself."

Our friend made no boast of his submission; these sentiments were uttered in all the ingenuousness and confidence of friendship. They show a temper most truly evangelical, the exercise of which, in life and death is blessed and magnanimous. It is the same sublime spirit which burst from the soul of the apostle in that rapturous exclamation, O Death! where is thy sting! O grave, where is thy victory!——

SKENANDON, THE ONEIDA CHIEF.

[*From an American Paper.*]

At his residence near *Oneida Castle,* on Monday, the 11th of March, SKENANDON, the Celebrated *Oneida Chief,* aged 110 years; well known in the wars which occurred while we were British colonies, and in the contest which issued in our independence, as the undeviating friend of the people of the United States. He was very savage, and addicted to drunkenness in his youth[*], but by his own reflections, and the benevolent instructions of the late Rev. Mr. Kirkland, missionary to his tribe, he lived a reformed man for more than sixty years, and died in Christian hope.

From attachment to Mr. Kirkland, he had always expressed a strong desire to be buried near his minister and his father, that he might (to use his own expression) *go up with him at the great resurrection.* At the approach of death, after listening to the prayers which were read at his bedside by his great grand-daughter, he again repeated this request. Accordingly, the family of Mr. Kirkland, having received

information, by a runner, that Skenandon, was dead, in compliance with a previous promise, sent assistance to the Indians, that the corpse might be conveyed to the village of Clinton for burial. Divine service was attended at the meeting-house in Clinton, on Wednesday, at 2 o'clock, p. m. An address was made to the Indians, by the Rev. Dr. Backus, President of Hamilton College; which was interpreted by Judge Dean, of Westmoreland. Prayer was then offered, and appropiate psalms sung. After service, the concourse which had assembled from respect to the deceased Chief, from the singularity of the occasion, moved to the grave in the following order:—

Students of Hamilton College,
Corpse,
Indians,
Mrs. Kirkland and family,
Judge Dean, Rev. Dr. Norton,
Rev. Mr. Ayer,
Officers of Hamilton College,
Citizens.

After interment, the only surviving son of the deceased, self-moved, returned thanks through Judge Dean, as interpreter, to the people, for the respect shown to his father on the occasion, and to Mrs. Kirkland and family for their kind and friendly attentions.

Skenandon's person was tall and brawny, but well made; his countenance was intelligent, and beamed with all the indigenous dignity of an Indian Chief. In his youth he was a brave and intrepid warrior, and in his riper years one of the ablest counsellors among the North American tribes. He possessed a strong and vigorous mind; and though terrible as the tornado in war, he was bland and mild as the zephyr in peace. With the cunning of the fox, the hungry perseverance of the wolf and the agility of the mountain cat, he watched and repelled Canadian invasions. His vigilance once preserved from massacre the inhabitants of the infant settlement of German-flats. His influence brought his tribe to our assistance in the war of the Revolution. How many of the living and the dead have been saved from the tomahawk and scalping knife, by his friendly aid, is not known; but individuals, and villages have expressed gratitude for his benevolent interpositions; and among the Indian tribes he was distinguished by the appellation of the *White Man's Friend.*

Although he could speak but little English, and in his extreme old age was blind, yet his company was sought. In conversation he was highly decorous, evincing that he had profited by seeing civilized and polished society, and by mingling with good company in his better days.

* In the year 1755, Skenandon was present at a treaty made in Albany. At night he was excessively drunk; and in the morning found himself in the street, stripped of all his ornaments and every article of clothing. His pride revolted at his self-degradation, and he resolved that he would never again deliver himself over to the power of *strong water.*

' To a friend, who called on him a short time since, he thus expressed himself by an interpreter :—

' " I am an aged hemlock—the winds of an hundred winters have whistled through my branches; I am dead at the top.' The generation to which I belonged, have run away and left me; why I live, the Great Good Spirit only knows. · Pray to my Jesus, that I may have patience to wait for my appointed time to die.

· Honoured Chief! his prayer was answered! he was cheerful and resigned to the last. For several years he kept his dress for the grave prepared. Once, and again, and again, he came to Clinton, to die, longing that his soul might be with Christ, and his body in the narrow house, near his beloved Christian teacher.

While the ambitious but vulgar great, look principally to sculptured monuments, and to niches in the temple of earthly fame, Skenandon, in the spirit of the only real nobility, stood with his loins girded, waiting the coming of his Lord.   · 1 ·

· His Lord has come! and the day approaches when the green hillock that covers his dust, will be more respected than the pyramids, the mansolea, and the

pantheons of the proud and imperious. His simple ' turf and stone' will be viewed with affection and veneration, when their tawdry ornaments of human apotheosis shall awaken only pity and disgust.

" Indulge, my native land, indulge the
    tear,
That steals impassion'd o'er a nation's
    doom ;
To me each twig from Adam's stock is
    dear,
And sorrows fall upon an Indian's tomb."
   Clinton, March 14, 1816.

Lately, at *Harrowgate*, Mrs. E. HA-MILTON, well known by her works on Education, &c. [Of this lady we shall be glad to receive some account.]

We are called in the course of our duty to record the melancholy event of the death of the REV. WILLIAM VIDLER. He expired 'on Friday the 23rd inst. after long and grievous sufferings. His faculties were entire to the last, and his feelings and conversation were worthy of a Christian teacher.——[Further particulars in our next.}   · ·   ·   · · ·

INTELLIGENCE.

DOMESTIC.
RELIGIOUS.

UNITARIAN FUND.

[*Extracts from the Report of the Com-
i mittee delivered to the General Meeting,
· June* 5, 1816.]   · · ·   · · ·

The Committee have witnessed with pleasure during the last year many new and striking proofs of the spread of a spirit of religious inquiry, and of the sure though gradual success which must attend all prudent and zealous efforts to enlighten the public mind. Their correspondence with persons in various parts of the kingdom emboldens them to state, that never was there so great a disposition in the public, to look seriously and dispassion-ately into the Scriptures, to hear the doctrines of those who have been too often reviled, instead of being heard with patience and candour, to receive Unitarian mission-aries and to associate for the formation of churches on true evangelical principles.' In some particular cases the cause of truth may appear to be declining, and in many it may be at a stand ; whilst it is flourish-ing upon the whole. One certain evidence of the success of the labours of this and other Unitarian Societies, is, that scarcely a town in Great Britain is now to be found where there are not avowed Unitarians, even though they have no places of wor-

ship. As their numbers increase, they will no doubt form themselves into Christ-ian Societies. The object of the Unitarian Fund is to collect them into assemblies, and to encourage them in the exercise of social worship, on the principles of the New Testament. As yet the great work of Christian Reformation is but commen-cing; the Unitarians of the present day are- laying the foundation on which the next generation will build the Temple of Truth, sacred to the God and Father of our Lord Jesus Christ.

The Report of the last year announced that the Committee had engaged Mr. Wright to undertake another missionary tour into Cornwall, and that he was to be accompanied by Mr. Cooper, who had received his education at the Unitarian Academy. This journey was accomplished and a full account of it was extracted from Mr. Wright's Journals into the Monthly Repository. It was extremely laborious to the missionaries and proportionably successful. In almost every place the people were impatient to hear Unitarian preaching, and inquisitive after books, of which a great number were distributed. Cornwall appears to the Committee to be a most promising soil for the reception of the seed of Christian Truth, and they have engaged Mr. Wright to re-visit it during the present summer. He is to be accompanied at his request by one of the junior Students of the Unitarian Academy. This plan of sending out a companion with a missionary is of great advantage, especially to the young men who are thus sent, who acquire habits of religious exertion and are educating for public service.

Since his return from Cornwall, Mr. Cooper has been supplying the long destitute congregation of Moreton Hampstead, in Devonshire, of which he has undertaken the charge for the next twelve months. The congregation have submitted to the Committee a plan by which a preacher may settle with them and employ the summer months in missionary excursions, particularly into Cornwall. This plan suggested by Mr. Wright, may, it is hoped, be hereafter carried into effect.

With this mission into Cornwall, Mr. Wright will connect one into Wales, whither he has never yet gone, but where there is a great desire to see him. There can be no doubt that in those towns, in which the English language is spoken or understood, his labours will be exceedingly useful.

It was in contemplation at the last Anniversary to authorize Messrs. Wright and Cooper to devote the spring and summer of the present year to a mission into Ireland, recommended by a respectable subscriber at Dublin. Upon mature consideration however and further correspondence with the gentleman referred to, it was deemed expedient to drop the design for the present. As the Committee never doubt of the sanctions of the Society to any scheme which requires or indicates zeal, so neither do they question their concurrence in any measure of prudence.

In this connexion the Committee judge it proper to state that a proposal was submitted to them by Mr. Wright, of a mission to the United States of America, of which he entertained the desire and had formed the plan. This proposal was taken into consideration at a meeting specially appointed for the occasion, when the following Resolution was passed.

"Resolved unanimously—That the Committee have deliberated on Mr. Wright's proposal with a seriousness proportioned to its importance; that they regard it as a new and decisive proof of his zeal in the cause of truth and virtue: but that, at the same time, they consider an American mission scarcely within the object of the Unitarian Fund, and are so impressed with a conviction of the great services to which Divine Providence has called Mr. Wright in this country, that they think they should be departing from the plain path of duty, were they to be

instrumental in removing him from his present sphere of usefulness."

Mr. Wright's candid interpretation of this resolution, ought to be considered as an additional sacrifice and service to the Society. His reply to the letter of the Secretary communicating it, is so grateful to their feelings, that the Committee cannot refrain from breaking through the rule which they had laid down of not lengthening their Report with extracts of correspondence, and laying a part of it before the Meeting. The extract which they meditate is as follows:

"Accept my thanks for your favour of the 20th inst. containing the decision of the Committee on my projected mission to the United States of America. Though it is contrary to the decision I had anticipated, I neither question the superior wisdom nor the truly Christian zeal of the Gentlemen of the Committee, in negativing a plan which I took the liberty of submitting to them; and am truly thankful to them for the expression of esteem contained in their resolution. I had fully made up my mind to the undertaking which I contemplated, as a difficult and arduous one, and did not think my uninterrupted continuance in this country of the importance which the Committee seem to suppose, but conceived I might be very well spared for two or three years, without any injury to the great cause in which we are engaged: however, as it seems to be scarcely within the objects of the Fund, and the decision shows that in the opinion of those for whose judgment I have a very high respect, I ought not to leave England for so long a time, I acquiesce; and, if God be pleased to give me strength, will endeavour to render my services worthy of the opinion they form of them. I wish to state distinctly, that I most sincerely thank you; my dear Sir, and the whole of the Committee, for the kind attention paid and the serious consideration given to the plan which, from a deliberate sense of duty, I submitted to them: that the approbation of my labours which they have so kindly expressed, will, I trust, be a motive to further exertion: that I esteem it a blessing, for which I thank the Almighty, that I can have the judgment and advice of such judicious persons respecting plans which suggest themselves to me: and that I am deeply sensible my services in the best of causes, of whatever value they may be, derive no small part of it from their support and countenance, without which many of them could not have been undertaken."

The Committee have great satisfaction in reporting, that one measure of a novel kind, which they pursued during part of the past year, has been attended with complete success. It occurred to them that as the

Sunday Evening Unitarian Lectures at St. Thomas's and Parliament Court had answered the expectation of those that set them on foot, there was great probability that a Unitarian Lecture on a Week-day would also be well attended. They therefore appointed a Sub-Committee to make due inquiry, and report to them the result: in consequence, a Lecture was established on the Thursday Evening, in the Meeting-House in Worship-street, which was gratuitously lent to the Unitarian Fund for this purpose. The following preachers gave their services in this good work: Messrs. Gilchrist, Vidler, Rees, Broadbent, Flower, Treleaven and the Secretary. The Lecture was continued during four months. All means consistent with decorum were taken to make it known. The congregations were generally good and sometimes large. Private subscriptions and public collections enabled the Committee to discharge the expense, without drawing upon the Fund for more than the small balance of 6l. 14s. 11d.

The success of the plan leads the Committee to recommend that it be hereafter followed up with zeal, and extended. In order to strengthen the hands of the Lecturers resident in London, unhappily weakened by the illness of some gentlemen who were at first calculated on for most valuable assistance, they invited Mr. Treleaven, of Dorchester, to London for a few weeks in the winter, and the Society is indebted to that gentleman for his ready compliance with the invitation. It appears most desirable to the Committee, that a succession of ministers from the country should be engaged for the London Winter Evening Lectures. They cannot doubt of their willingness to concur in the plan, and they anticipate that the weight of expense which would lie upon such a proceeding, would be in great measure borne by subscriptions and collections for this particular purpose: though should the Fund be required to make good even a large deficiency, they consider that whilst the Treasurer's Report continues to be so satisfactory, a better use could not possibly be made of the Society's wealth. Were this plan to be adopted, all the late Lectures might be renewed with spirit, and others instituted, particularly at the West End of the Town, to which the attention of the Committee had been long directed in vain, but to which the Society, if it should concur in the present proposal, may look with very high expectations of success.

The missionaries have not been inactive during the past year. In Wales, Mr. Benjamin Phillips and Mr. Davies, of Carmarthen, have made frequent journies, of which the report is pleasing. Mr. Winder has gone out preaching with great acceptance,

in the neighbourhood of Wisbeach. The usual labours of Mr. Bennett, in Sussex, have been continued, and appear to be progressively valuable and important. And, besides the mission already described, Mr. Wright has visited numerous places which have been named in the Reports of preceding years.

On the recommendation of Dr. Thomson, of Halifax, the Committee have voted ten pounds, to defray the expense of the hire of a room for the experiment of Unitarian preaching for one year, in the populous town of Huddersfield, in Yorkshire; two neighbouring ministers having zealously offered their services for this purpose, namely, Messrs. Donoghue and Beattie.

Assistance has been rendered to various congregations during the year; to Edinburgh, which has hitherto had the able services of Mr. Smith, but which will soon be without a pastor; to Paisley, where the Unitarian cause is prospering under the ministry of Mr. Syme, who has been for several years patronised by the Fund; and to Brighton, which is supplied on Sunday evenings by Mr. Bennett, but which is in want of a Sunday morning preacher.

This want the Committee are able to provide for, during the months of July and August next, by the liberality of the Governors of the Unitarian Academy, who have consented that one of the senior Students should spend the ensuing vacation at Brighton. One of the junior Students will also be able to assist Mr. Bennett at Ditchling; and thus Mr. Bennett may be set free for some more extended plan of missionary labour, to be hereafter determined on.

Considerable pecuniary grants have been made by the Committee to new Unitarian places of worship; not indeed the first objects contemplated by the Unitarian Fund, but still objects which the Committee, with means in their hands, have not thought it allowable to neglect.

The interesting case of *Rossendale* was reported from Dr. Thomson at the last Anniversary, and the Committee have observed with pleasure that the sanction of the Fund has contributed greatly to the relief of the zealous body of Unitarian Christians in that place.

A new chapel has been lately built at Oldham, a town of considerable population, in the neighbourhood of Manchester. In this town Mr. Wright preached the first Unitarian sermon, on his journey into Lancashire, the time before the last. A congregation has been since collected, and a neat and commodious chapel erected, capable of holding nearly 300 people, and so built as to admit a gallery hereafter if necessary. The building cost 550l. and about 530l. had been raised when application was made to the Committee. They voted 20l. It is but justice to an individual to state, that the raising of a congregation at Oldham, and the providing of the means of building a new chapel, are chiefly owing to the zealous but wise and prudent exertions of Mr. B. Goodier, late a student in the Unitarian Academy.

Another new chapel has also engaged the attention of the Committee—that at *Thorne* in Yorkshire. The Unitarian doctrine was introduced into this town and neighbourhood about ten years ago, by your missionary, Mr. Wright, and has been taught by him in repeated journeys, described in preceding years. Amidst some discouragements the cause of Truth has continued to prosper, until it has been found necessary that the worshippers of the One God, the Father, should have a capacious building in which to assemble. The chapel is to be finished by the end of this month. The plan appears to be commendably economical. It is calculated that the cost will be 350l. of which 120l. have been subscribed in the immediate neighbourhood. The Committee gave 20l. to this case. Many private subscriptions has since been received. In the judgment of several judicious correspondents, Thorne is an important station; and Mr. Wright has impressed upon the Committee, that it would form a proper centre for the labours of a missionary.

The only remaining case of this kind which the Committee think of sufficient importance to report, is that of the Unitarian Baptists at York, whose early history has been so well made known by Mr. David Eaton, in his "Narrative." This people, consisting of persons in humble life, had laboured under great inconvenience from the narrowness, obscurity and unpleasant situation of the room in which they had been wont to assemble. At length, a commodious chapel, formerly occupied by another denomination of Christians, became vacant; and with the advice of judicious friends they ventured to purchase it at the price of 300l. though of this sum they could raise amongst themselves no more than 60l. The case was strongly recommended to the Committee by the respectable name of Mr. Wellbeloved, of York: and they voted to it the sum of 20l. hoping from the representations made to them, that the whole debt may be speedily liquidated. In no instance would the Committee sanction any congregation in the contracting of a burdensome debt.

A former Report advised the preparation of a Trust Deed, under which places of worship might be held by the Fund; but the Committee have found this so difficult, and in some cases which they have duly considered there appeared such great danger

of expensive law proceedings, that they have been able as yet to take no steps towards the accomplishment of this object, nor are they certain that it would be for the interest of the Society to hold this species of cumbersome and uncertain property.

The names of Trustees are upon the books of the Fund for taking care of any monies that may be bequeathed to the Society; and the Committee have reason to expect that in the course of time their means, will be recruited and enlarged by this kind of liberality.

In looking back to the receipts of the last year, the Committee see many instances of individual and some of congregational zeal which they gladly acknowledge; but they cannot help recommending strongly to congregations in general, to adopt some plan of contribution, by which the resources and consequently the exertions of the Society may be increased.

The Committee find a perpetually growing demand for Tracts, of which they have distributed many hundreds in the course of the last year; in which they have been assisted by the Unitarian Society and the Christian Tract Society and other Book Societies; though the cost of Tracts will still be found a considerable item in the year's expenditure.

The Committee have great pleasure in announcing Mr. Fox, of Chichester, as the next year's preacher.

In concluding their Report, the Committee have only to express their wish that the Society may continue to proceed upon the principles by which it has been hitherto guided, uniting zeal for truth with prudence in exertion, and boldness in the great cause with delicacy towards individuals; and their prayer that the God and Father of our Lord Jesus Christ may own and prosper the labours of the Society, and make it an effectual instrument of promoting the purity of evangelical truth, the improvement of the human mind, and the glory of the Divine character and name.

Unitarian Academy.

The Annual Meeting of the Governors of this Institution was held in the Chapel, Parliament Court, Artillery Lane, on Wednesday, June 5th, 1816, after the Meeting of the Subscribers to the Unitarian Fund, William Cooke, Esq. of the Isle of Wight, in the Chair, when the following Report was read and adopted:

The Committee of the Unitarian Academy report with much pleasure to this General Meeting the proceedings of the Institution through the past year.

The four students who have been in the Academy throughout the present session have continued to prosecute their studies to the entire satisfaction of the tutors and of the committee. Mr. Goodier has not been able to resume his situation, from the precarious state of his health; but the committee have the satisfaction to state, that the time he passed in the Academy has not been lost, for he continues to prosecute his studies though absent, and should his health and strength be restored, he promises to be a zealous and useful preacher of the gospel pure and undefiled.

The Rev. R. Aspland and the Rev. T. Broadbent have continued their able assistance through the session now closing, to the great advantage of the institution and of the pupils. The committee have also availed themselves of the assistance of Dr. Morell in the mathematical department.

The thanks of this meeting are justly due to these gentlemen for their care and assiduity, as the funds of this institution have not yet been able to offer any adequate remuneration to them for the time and labour they have devoted to the improvement of the students.

It is in the recollection of this meeting that two years was the term appointed for the course of study of each student, with power given to the committee to extend it. But many inconveniences have been found to result from this method; for in every instance the tutors and the committee have found two years too short to accomplish the objects of the institution; and the committee have uniformly extended the time to the longest period in their power: so that the term of three years instead of two, may now be considered the rule not the exception. From the experience of the tutors they have learned that this extension of time at the end of two years has been attended with great inconvenience to them and has proved a hinderance to the progress of the students; as the tutors have not been able to arrange their course of instruction to the longer period, from the uncertainty of the committee acceding to their request to continue the students under their care beyond the period of two years. Thus it appears from the experience of the committee and of the tutors that the plan originally designed has not been found advantageous or practicable.

The committee therefore recommend that the course of education be extended to four years. Though at the same time the original plan of the institution need not be lost sight of, as a course of instruction limited to two years may be arranged, in order to prepare students for the Christian ministry, by instructing them in general theology and English literature only. The students admitted into the Academy on this plan ought not to be permitted to continue longer than two years.

For admission to the larger course of instruction the committee recommend three months should be fixed for probation, and that no young man be admitted under the age of seventeen or above the age of twenty, nor any who have not previously attained the rudiments of the Greek and Latin languages. For the shorter course a probation of six weeks, and from the age of eighteen to twenty-three, and that no one be admitted who has not previously received an adequate English education.

The committee also beg leave to add, that they trust a fitness for pulpit services will at all times be considered an indispensible qualification for all candidates for admission on the foundation of this Academy, whether for the longer or the shorter period: as it is the fundamental principle of this institution to offer its assistance to such young men only who appear to be qualified to be useful and zealous Christian ministers.

The committee wish they were able to close their report with a favourable account of the funds of the Academy: but with every possible attention to economy, they are obliged to declare them inadequate to the objects of the institution. The committee cheerfully offer their services to maintain and direct the establishment, but these will not be effective unless the funds for the support of the Academy are considerably increased. And here they cannot refuse the opportunity to direct the thanks of this meeting to the Rev. T. Belsham, who has been through the past year a most liberal promoter of the Academy in regard to its pecuniary resources. They recommend to the serious consideration of the Unitarian public the advantages an institution in the neighbourhood of London, like the new Unitarian Academy offers, for the promotion of the general interests of true religion and virtue. Hitherto it has been supported by a very few of the friends of free inquiry in matters of religion; but it demands the liberal support of all to continue its existence and to make it effective.

THOMAS GIBSON, Secretary.

Dudley Double Lecture.

On Whit-Tuesday, June 4th, 1816, the Annual Meeting of Ministers, denominated " The Double Lecture," took place at Dudley. The Rev. Robert Kell conducted the devotional service. Two excellent discourses were delivered to a very numerous congregation : the former by the Rev. James Yates "on the historical argument in favour of the truth of Christianity, arising from the progress

which it has made in reforming and
ameliorating the state of the world,"—
from Isaiah lv. 10, 11,—*For as the rain
cometh down, and the snow from heaven,
and returneth not thither, but watereth
the earth, and maketh it bring forth and
bud, that it may give seed to the sower,
and bread to the eater: So shall my word
be that goeth forth out of my mouth: it
shall not return unto me void, but it shall
accomplish that which I please, and it
shall prosper in the thing whereto I sent
it:*—the latter by the Rev. James Scott,
" on the duties of the Christian ministry," from 2 Cor. viii. 23,——*they are
the messengers of the church, and the
glory of Christ.*

Fifteen ministers were present: viz.
Rev. Messrs. Guy, Kell, and Kentish, of
Birmingham; Small, of Coseley; Davis,
of Coventry; Scott, of Cradley; Bransby,
of Dudley; Davis, of Evesham; James
Yates, lately of Glasgow; Corrie, of
Handsworth; Bristowe, of Hinckley;
Fry, of Kidderminster; Davis, of Old-
bury; Carpenter, of Stourbridge; and
Steward, of Wolverhampton.

In the course of the afternoon, Mr.
Bransby read the following extract from a
most affecting letter addressed to him by
his lamented friend, Dr. Toulmin, in
reference to one of the resolutions at the
last anniversary.*

" *London, No. 2, Pump Court, Temple,*
May 23, 1815.

" Dear Bransby.—My mind is variously
affected with the unexpected and united
testimonies of respect and affection, and
of approbation of my work from my worthy
brethren, assembled at the Double Lecture at Dudley on Whit-Tuesday, and
with the cordial interest you express in
the communication of their resolutions:—
on which I shall ever place a high value,
and ever recollect with lively gratitude.
As they do not meet again under the same
circumstances till next Whitsuntide, when
probably my intercourses of a friendly and
ministerial kind, and my days may be
terminated, it must remain uncertain
whether I shall ever have an opportunity
to offer them, as a body, my sentiments
of affectionate respect, and my warm
thanks for these expressions of their estimation of my imperfect labours and
character. But, as they fall in your way,
I would request the favour of you to
express to them individually, my sentiments of brotherly attachment to them, as
ministers, my sense of the honour they
have done me and the sincere pleasure
with which I entertain the thought of

spending the remainder of my days in the
circle of such characters and friends as I
am cordially united to in the neighbourhood of Birmingham.

*   *   *

Dear Bransby,
Your obliged and sincerely affectionate
Friend and Brother,
JOSHUA TOULMIN."

Warwickshire Unitarian Tract Society.

The Members of the Unitarian Tract
Society, established in Birmingham for
Warwickshire and the neighbouring counties, held their Annual Meeting at Oldbury, in Shropshire, on Wednesday, June
19th. In the morning, the Rev. Richard
Fry, of Kidderminster, read the Scriptures
and conducted the devotional service. The
Rev. John Small, of Coseley, delivered a
very argumentative and interesting discourse on the Unity of God, from John
viii. 54.—"*It is my Father that honoureth
me; of whom ye say, that he is your God.*"
The sermon was heard with the most
marked attention. Two passages, in particular, the one referring to the preacher's
emancipation from Calvinism, and the
other offering a tribute of affection to the
memory of Dr. Toulmin, exhibited specimens of the finest eloquence. Mr. Small
has kindly consented to favour the Society
with a copy of his sermon to be printed
for distribution among the members.

At the conclusion of the service, Mr.
Samuel Kenrick, of West Bromwich,
(second son of the late Rev. Timothy Kenrick, of Exeter,) being called to the chair,
the minutes of the last general meeting
and of the subsequent committee meetings
were read by the Secretary. After the
usual business had been transacted, upwards of forty members and friends of the
Society dined together. In the course of
the afternoon several gentlemen addressed
the meeting on topics connected with the
objects of the Society, and the day was
spent in a way that could scarcely fail to
exercise and improve the best emotions of
the heart.

It was resolved, " That the warmest
thanks of this meeting be presented to the
Rev. Jeremiah Joyce, the Secretary of the
London Unitarian Book Society, (an office
which after having ably discharged its
duties for fourteen years, he has signified an
intention of resigning,) for his uniform
punctuality and kindness in furnishing the
tracts ordered from time to time by the
Committee, and for the lively interest
which he has always taken in the welfare
of this Society."

It is impossible to record this vote of
thanks (passed only two days before Mr.
Joyce's lamented death) without feelings
of mournful regret. Mr. Bransby, in

---

* See Monthly Repository, Vol. X. p.
319.

moving it, stated Mr. Joyce's claims to the gratitude of the Society, and availed himself of the opportunity to express his own personal esteem; and Mr. Kentish observed that he had for a long series of years had the pleasure of calling Mr. Joyce his friend, and that he never knew the bosom in which glowed a warmer or a kinder heart.

In the evening Mr. Bransby conducted the devotional service and the Rev. James Yates delivered an eloquent discourse from Ps. civ. 31: " The Lord shall rejoice in his works."

J. H. B.

Southern Unitarian Society.

On Wednesday the 24th of July, the Annual Meeting of the Southern Unitarian Society, was held at the Unitarian Chapel in Newport, Isle of Wight. The object of this Society is to promote the knowledge and practice of evangelical Christianity, by the distribution of books. Mr. Aspland preached a sermon adapted to the occasion of the meeting, from Rev. xiv. 6, 7. The Society voted thanks to Mr. Aspland for his sermon, with a request to be allowed to print the same. They re-appointed Thomas Cooke, Jun. Esq. the Secretary; voted several new books; and determined that the Society shall meet next year at Poole, in Dorsetshire, and that Mr. Bennett be requested to preach. Afterwards a numerous and respectable company met to dine at the Bugle Inn, in Newport, when Mr. Samuel Parkes was unanimously called to the chair. After dinner several appropriate addresses were delivered by different gentlemen; and the afternoon was spent in a truly pleasant and harmonious manner.

The meeting was dissolved at an early hour, and the company adjourned to the chapel, where Mr. Fox delivered to a numerous and attentive audience a very impressive discourse from John viii. 32: " The truth shall make you free."

N. B. After the morning service, the names of several gentlemen were enrolled as new members of the Southern Unitarian Society.

Manchester College, York.

The Manchester Annual Meeting of Trustees and Friends to this Institution was intended to be held on Friday, the 30th of August. The anniversary dinner was to be at the Spread Eagle Inn, in Manchester, on the same day, Nathaniel Philips, of the Dales, Esq. in the Chair. We hope to give an account of the proceedings in a future number.

Manchester College, York.

The following sums have been received on account of this Institution.

	£	s.	d.
Collection at Stannington Chapel, near Sheffield, by the Rev. P. Wright.	7	0	0
Do. at Wakefield Chapel, by the Rev. Thomas Johnstone.	30	2	1
Do. at Upper Chapel, Sheffield, by the Rev. Dr. Philipps.	14	3	0
Do. at Plymouth, by the Rev. Israel Worsley.	10	10	0
Do. at Norwich, by the Rev. Thomas Madge,	13	6	6
Do. at Newcastle, by the Rev. William Turner.	13	2	8
Do. at Leeds, by the Rev. Thomas Jervis.	15	17	9
Two Collections at Gainsborough, by the Rev. N. T. H. Heinekin.——In 1815.	5	5	0
In 1816.	5	0	0
Benefaction from the Rev. Mr. Anstis, of Bridport.	2	0	0
Do. from George Bayly, Esq. Plymouth.	25	0	0
	141	7	0

Manchester, August 17, 1816.
G. W. WOOD, Treasurer.

State of the Finances of the Oldham Unitarian Society.

ADDITIONAL BENEFACTIONS.

	£	s.	d.
S. Jones, Esq. near Manchester	5	0	0
Legacy from the late Mr. Rd. Mason,	5	0	0
Donation from the Unitarian Fund,	20	0	0
	30	0	0
Amount of Contributions including the above	560	1	9½
By Loan from the Rev. W. Johns,	100	0	0
Money in advance per J. Taylor,	7	5	2
	667	6	11½

Amount of bills discharged, including every expense connected with the building of the new Chapel - 667 6 11½

There is a deficiency to the amount of 107l. 5s. 2d. which remains to be provided for.

The Unitarian friends at Oldham are gratefully sensible of the liberal aid which they have experienced, and beg leave, through the medium of their Treasurer, to renew their acknowledgments. In recalling the attention of the Unitarian public to the present state of their finances, they by no means wish to trespass upon that liberality in which they have so largely participated. They merely desire it to be known, that their own resources are very inadequate to the provision which they are called upon to make, and that the smallest donations with which they may be favoured will be most thankfully received.

         W. HARRISON.

Any persons disposed to contribute to the assistance of the Oldham brethren, may transmit their donations, either to the Rev. R. Aspland, Hackney, or to the Rev. W. Harrison, 29, Brazen-nose Street, Manchester.

For particulars of the different contributions to the Oldham Chapel, *vide* M. Rep. for Feb. 1816, p. 123.

DOMESTIC.

MISCELLANEOUS.

Dr. Herbert Marsh, Margaret Professor at Cambridge, is promoted to the See of Llandaff, vacant by the death of Dr. Watson. This appointment is probably designed to preserve an equilibrium on the Episcopal bench; the last gentleman raised to this dignity, Dr. Ryder, Dean of Wells, made Bishop of Gloucester, being a zealous member of the Bible Society,

and Dr. Marsh being known as its warm opponent. We can hardly suppose that the Professor has been rewarded with the mitre for his political publications, tending to promote the war against Republican France: the results of that war are now so clearly seen and so, *strongly felt*, that even the Pitt party must, one should think, look back upon its promoters with sentiments very different from gratitude. We can still, less imagine, in these times of professed orthodoxy, that Dr. Marsh is advanced to his present dignity on account of his services to Biblical Literature. Those services are in the eye of a true Churchman of very questionable merit; since they have contributed (in spite of Dr. Marsh's own protestations) to take away the supports of some of the fundamental doctrines of the *soi disant* orthodox church. Whatever be the cause of the new Bishop's creation, it will be honourable to him and gratifying to the lovers of Biblical learning, if he proceed in the course which he has so successfully entered upon, and lay open the road to a thorough knowledge of Scriptural divinity. He has displayed on some occasions an independence of mind and a spirit which are an earnest to his friends that the See of Llandaff will still be eminent for the public virtue as well as talents of its bishop.

MONTHLY RETROSPECT of PUBLIC AFFAIRS;
OR,
The Christian's Survey of the Political World:

A great fleet is gone out to chastise it is said the Algerines, for their mode of warfare, which differs from that pursued by the states which call themselves Christian. The papers are in consequence full of bitterness against the Corsairs, not reflecting how very little superior to theirs is the conduct of more civilized life. Some allowance is also to be made for those wretched men, who have not the advantages which we possess of more improved instruction from the Scriptures, from the liberty of the press, and a better system of government. It is to be recollected also what cause of hatred to the Christian name they inherit from their ancestors; for they are the descendants of the Moors, whom the wicked policy of the Spaniards drove with unexampled barbarity from the country in which they had been settled for several hundred years. Besides, if the Christians complain of slavery in Africa, it is to be recollected that the Africans in their turn, when taken slaves, have been subjected to a very great degree of hardship on board the Christian gallies.

Far be it from us to vindicate the Africans, or to deny the propriety of bringing

them if possible to a superior line of conduct. It is a beautiful trait in the history of the Romans, that in a treaty with the Carthaginians, they insisted on the abolition of human sacrifices. We may readily conceive what influence the religion of Moloch must have had on the temper and manners of his worshippers. Traces of it may be seen in the writings of St. Augustine, whose divinity was warped by the feelings of his country; and we are not to be surprised that Calvin should have beheld with joy the torturing of Servetus, without reflecting that this inhuman sentiment sprang from the Carthaginian Moloch, not from the God and Father of our Lord Jesus Christ, who is distinctly proclaimed to us under the endearing epithet of a loving Father. This reflection merits to be impressed on every mind subjugated to Calvin; for the same cause produces the same effects, provided the circumstances are the same: and however meliorated by the spirit of the times is the Calvinistic spirit, yet its basis remains the same, derived from Moloch, not from him of whom it is said—God is Love.

This new warfare will lead to many re-

rections on the conduct of Christians towards each other. For nearly a quarter of a century they, who profess this holy name, have been living in a state, which is the direct opposite to what the name implies. Every Christian is directed to address his heavenly Father in a prayer, that his kingdom may come: but this is a kingdom of peace, and it cannot be conceived that, if this prayer which was repeated so frequently by so many millions of tongues, had really come from the heart, the nations of Europe could have lived in the state of warfare, which it has been our melancholy fate to experience. We know that it has been and is urged continually, that war has existed from the earliest times, and will continue as long as there are men on earth. True it has existed for too long a period, and will exist as long as the spirit of the first-born Cain, the first murderer, continues to be the theme of general applause. But let it be recollected, that this spirit is entirely opposite to the spirit of Christianity: and as real Christianity makes a progress in the world, the spirit of Cain will give way to it, and at last be entirely subdued. In the mean time it is the duty of Christians to oppose it to the utmost of their power, and to hail with satisfaction every attempt to bring men to a just knowledge and abhorrence of war, and at any rate to endeavour to alleviate as much as possible its horrors. The events of the last years shew how little is to be gained by blood: conquerors and conquered on calculating their respective gains and losses, have reason to regret that the voice of religion had not its due effect on all parties.

Let us hope that the new Christian treaty, as it is called, may have some effect. The eyes of Europe are turned to the congress of sovereigns united on this occasion. Mankind has been so often deceived by professions, that apprehensions are entertained that under cover of religious zeal greater inroads may be made on civil liberty. Yet who knows whether God may not have turned the hearts of sovereigns towards their people, and reflecting on the miseries which they have occasioned to each other, and to their subjects, too often upon frivolous occasions, they may be led to embrace a system, which shall prevent in future unnecessary effusion of blood. The page of history bears too ample testimony to the poet's exclamation—

Delirant reges plectuntur Achivi:
and the converse is also true

Delirant Achivi, plectuntur reges.

The hearts of all parties must be changed; and if they have rendered themselves up as servants of iniquity to iniquity, it is an encouraging thought that the time is at hand when they will render themselves up as servants of holiness to the perfecting of human life. At any rate it is now the time for all men of enlightened minds and liberal dispositions to forward the designs of these sovereigns, and to encourage their undertakings. As they express their determination to act upon Christian principles, too much care cannot be taken to place those principles before them in their proper light; and one of the first objects should be so to regulate the relations of states to each other, that they may not hereafter rush heedlessly into war, but take every previous step which prudence dictates and religion requires, before they run into the danger of calling upon themselves or their subjects the Avenger of blood.

France appears to be approaching to a more settled state. It has been said of the Bourbons, that they neither learned any thing nor forgot any thing during the years of their adversity. But whatever might be their state, whether that of dreaming, or dozing, or attending in some degree to the changes in their nation, they cannot avoid the general rule; they must submit to circumstances. They cannot bring the nation to what it was before the Revolution, and they must accommodate themselves to the change. One great point has been submitted to by them: The Legion of Honour formed by Buonaparte has been adopted by them, and the consequence is, that the flattering distinctions of ancient nobility will bend to the new honours, more suited to the present times. In fact they now find that it is impossible to restore the nobility and the clergy to their ancient privileges. The minds of men are so changed in this respect, that the deference formerly exacted would now appear ridiculous. But it must be long before the French can adapt themselves suitably to the new order of things. The court now sees that in governing twenty millions of people, used for twenty-five years to a freedom of sentiment, unknown in the times of the Bourbons, cannot be ruled by the few that were devoted to their cause. The old Royalists may be offended, but the necessity of the case requires that men in office should be selected from other parties; and whatever may be deemed the crimes of the Revolutionists, some of them must be admitted into the management of public affairs, or there will be no rule at all. By degrees party spirit may subside. Each party should look a little more to its own faults, and not to the faults of their neighbours: and of all spirits, that which is the most dangerous to the kingly authority is the military. Happy will it be for all nations and for all sovereigns, when they see this subject in its true light. A sovereign, who is despotic by means of the military, is only a slave to the military, and holds his throne on a very precarious tenure.

Such contradictory accounts arrive from Spanish America, that it is impossible to form a decisive opinion of its state. One event in the Northern part seems fatal to the Spanish power. It is said, that General Humboldt, with a great body of French officers, has entered into the service of the insurgents of Mexico, and with such instructors in the art of war, they will find no great difficulty in overcoming their opponents. In the South, apprehensions are entertained for the independence of Buenos Ayres; and the kingdom of Brazil is reported to have sent considerable forces towards La Plata, if not to attack the rising republic, to secure at least the territory North of its banks. Enough is to be done by the court of Brazil in its own kingdom, without interfering in this contest; for by looking well to its own internal government, it may soon become a power of far greater consequence than it can be by a return to Europe.

At home a great gloom overhangs the country, from the distresses of the agricultural, commercial, and manufacturing interests. This was foreseen by those who considered the artificial state in which we lived during the war; and it must be some time before things return into their natural channel. A mistaken policy gave way perhaps too much on the alarm, and a strange alarm it was, on the comparative cheapness of provisions; but the hopes raised by their becoming dearer have been falsified. The evil took its rise from another source, which no prohibitions could remedy. We had lived with an artificial circulating medium, which could not bear the sudden shock that was given to it by the peace. The restoration of payment in gold will put things on a proper footing; but in the return to it, the sufferings of individuals must be great. Notwithstanding the unfavourable season we have experienced, we may yet look to a plentiful harvest; and it is fortunate for us that government need not be apprehensive of any financial difficulties.

The riots in the Isle of Ely terminated in the execution of five of the ringleaders, and a few more were subjected to inferior punishments. The conduct of the unhappy men in taking leave of the world, and the solemnity which so judiciously took place upon the occasion, will, it is to be hoped, prevent a recurrence to similar interpositions of the law. An extraordinary course was taken by some of the persons employed in collieries. They dragged heavy waggons along the road, laden with coals, moving very peaceably, but bending their course to the metropolis. They were happily prevented, but in a mild way, from arriving to the end of the journey, which could not but

have been productive of riot and tumult. There seems to be a general disposition on the part of the higher to attend to the wants of the lower classes; and as long as this is cultivated, however we may feel for the present calamities, we may rest confident that time will do much towards the relief of them. There has been distress at the end of every war, but peace brings healing in its wings. Only let us not be wanting to ourselves, nor think too slightingly of its blessings.

Meetings have been held in town and in several parts of the country, for the relief of the poor. One at the London Tavern was presided over by the Duke of York, accompanied by two of his brothers, the Archbishop of Canterbury, several other members of the Houses of Lords and Commons, and a very respectable body of members and tradesmen of the city of London. The purport of the meeting was to raise a subscription, but the framers of the motions gave an erroneous statement of the causes of the distress, which led to a sharp discussion, ending in the alteration of the motion and the withdrawing of the amendment. The latter entered into a political disquisition, in which a very great majority of the room concurred, censuring the lavish expenditure of the public money, and calling for reform in various particulars. There was much truth in the assertions of all parties, for it is to a complication of causes that the present distress is owing, among which the injudicious act, under the name of the corn-bill, is apprehended by many to bear no inconsiderable share. The fact is, that whatever may have been the causes, the distress actually exists; and though a society of this kind can go but little way towards the general relief, yet the spirit of benevolence which it engenders cannot be too highly commended, and in many instances its assistance will be efficacious. A Common Hall has also been held, which has determined on a petition to the Prince Regent on his Throne, a resolution which requires the assent of two parties before it can be carried into execution. A strong objection was made to the petitioning of the House of Commons, from an evident disapprobation of the proceedings of that House. But perhaps it is not duly considered, that the right of petitioning is a very great advantage possessed by the people of this country; and that if petitions were general, and they are not likely to be general unless a strong case is made out, it is not likely that the House of Commons would resist the unanimous feeling of the nation. At any rate, whatever may be our political differences, Charity is not of a party.

Various Articles of Intelligence, &c. *stand over for insertion next month.*

THE

𝕸𝖔𝖓𝖙𝖍𝖑𝖞 𝕽𝖊𝖕𝖔𝖘𝖎𝖙𝖔𝖗𝖞,

&c.

No. CXXIX.]   SEPTEMBER, 1816.   [Vol. XI.

HISTORY AND BIOGRAPHY.

Estimate of the Philosophical Character of Lord Bacon. [*]
[From Dissertation I. by Dugald Stewart, prefixed to Supplement to Encyclopædia Britannica, Vol. I. p. 48—59.]

THE state of science towards the close of the sixteenth century, presented a field of observation singularly calculated to attract the curiosity, and to awaken the genius of Bacon; nor was it the least of his personal advantages, that, as the son of one of Queen Elizabeth's ministers, he had a ready access, wherever he went, to the most enlightened society in Europe. While yet only in the seventeenth year of his age, he was removed by his father from Cambridge to Paris, where it is not to be doubted, that the novelty of the literary scene must have largely contributed to cherish the natural liberality and independence of his mind. Sir Joshua Reynolds has remarked, in one of his academical Discourses, that "every seminary of learning is surrounded with an atmosphere of floating knowledge, where every mind may imbibe somewhat congenial to its own original conceptions."[†] He might have added, with still greater truth, that it is an atmosphere, of which it is more peculiarly salutary for those who have been elsewhere reared to breathe the air. The remark is applicable to higher pursuits than were in the contemplation of this philosophical artist; and it suggests a hint of no inconsiderable value for the education of youth.

The merits of Bacon, as the father of experimental philosophy, are so universally acknowledged, that it would be superfluous to touch upon them here. The lights which he has struck out in various branches of the philosophy of mind, have been much less attended to; although the whole scope and tenor of his speculations shew, that to *this* study his genius was far more strongly and happily turned, than to that of the material world. It was not, as some seem to have imagined, by sagacious anticipations of particular discoveries afterwards to be made in physics, that his writings have had so powerful an influence in accelerating the advancement of that science. In the extent and accuracy of his *physical* knowledge, he was far inferior to many of his predecessors; but he surpassed them all in his knowledge of the laws, the resources and the limits of the human understanding. The sanguine expectations with which he looked forwards to the future, were founded solely on his confidence in the untried *capacities of the mind*; and on a conviction of the possibility of invigorating and guiding, by means of logical rules, those faculties which, in all our researches after truth, are the organs or instruments to be employed. " Such rules," as he himself has observed, " do in some sort equal men's wits, and leave no great advantage or pre-eminence to the perfect and excellent motions of the spirit. To draw a straight line, or to describe a circle, by aim of hand only, there must be a great difference between an unsteady and unpractised hand, and a steady and practised; but to do it by rule or compass it is much alike."

Nor is it merely as a logician that Bacon is entitled to notice on the present occasion. It would be difficult to name another writer prior to Locke, whose works are enriched with so many just observations on the intellectual phenomena. Among these, the most valuable relate to the laws of memory, and of imagination; the latter of which subjects he seems to

---

[*] Born 1561, died 1626.
[†] Discourse delivered at the opening of the Royal Academy, January 2, 1769.

have studied with peculiar care. In one short but beautiful paragraph concerning *poetry* (under which title may be comprehended all the various creations of this faculty), he has exhausted every thing that philosophy and good sense have yet had to offer, on what has been since called the *beau idéal*; a topic, which has furnished occasion to so many over-refinements among the French critics, and to so much extravagance and mysticism in the *cloud-capt* metaphysics of the new German school.* In considering imagination as connected with the nervous system, more particularly as connected with that species of sympathy to which medical writers have given the name of *imitation*, he has suggested some very important hints, which none of his successors have hitherto prosecuted; and has, at the same time, left an example of cautious inquiry, worthy to be studied by all who may attempt to investigate the laws regulating the union between mind and body.† His illustration of

the different classes of prejudices incident to human nature, is, in point of practical utility, at least equal to any thing on that head to be found in Locke; of whom it is impossible to forbear remarking, as a circumstance not easily explicable, that he should have resumed this important discussion, without once mentioning the name of his great predecessor. The chief improvement made by Locke, in the farther prosecution of the argument, is the application of Hobbes's theory of association, to explain in what manner these prejudices are originally generated.

In Bacon's scattered hints on topics connected with the philosophy of the mind, strictly so called, nothing is more remarkable than the precise and just ideas they display of the proper aim of this science. He had manifestly reflected much and successfully on the operations of his own understanding, and had studied with uncommon sagacity the intellectual characters of others. Of his reflections and observations on both subjects, he has recorded many important results; and has in general stated them without the slightest reference to any phy-

---

* "Cum mundus sensibilis sit anima rationali dignitate inferior, videtur *Poësis* hæc humanæ naturæ largiri duæ historia denegat; atque animo umbris rerum utcunque satisfacere, cum solida haberi non possint. Si quis enim rem acutius introspiciat, firmum ex *Poësi* sumitur argumentum, magnitudinem rerum magis illustrem, ordinem magis perfectum, et varietatem magis pulcram, animæ humanæ complacere, quam in natura ipsa, post lapsum, reperiri ullo modo possit. Quapropter, cum res gestæ et eventus, qui veræ historiæ subjiciuntur, non sint ejus amplitudinis, in qua anima humana sibi satisfaciat, præsto est *Poësis*, quæ facta magis heroica confingat. Cum historia vera successus rerum, minime pro meritis virtutum et scelerum narret, corrigit eam *Poësis*, et exitus, et fortunas, secundum merita, et ex lege Nemeseos, exhibet. Cum historia vera obvia rerum satietate et similitudine, animæ humanæ fastidio sit, reficit eam *Poësis*, inexpectata, et varia, et vicissitudinum plena canens. Adeo ut *Poësis* ista non solum ad delectationem, sed ad animi magnitudinem, et ad mores conferat." *(De Aug. Scient.* Lib. ii. cap. xiii.)

† To this branch of the philosophy of mind, Bacon gives the title of *Doctrina de fœdere, sive de communi vinculo animæ et corporis. (De Aug. Scient.* Lib. iv. cap. i.) Under this article, he mentions, among other *desiderata*, an inquiry (which he recommends to physicians) concerning

the influence of imagination over the body. His own words are very remarkable; more particularly, the clause in which he remarks the effect of fixing and concentrating the attention, in giving to ideal objects the power of realities over the belief. "Ad aliud quippiam, quod huc pertinet, parce admodum, nec pro rei subtilitate, vel utilitate, inquisitum est; quatenus scilicet *ipsa imaginatio animæ vel cogitatio perquam fixa, et veluti in fidem quandam exaltata*, valeat ad immutandum corpus imaginantis." (Ibid.) He suggests also, as a curious problem, to ascertain how far it is possible to fortify and exalt the imagination; and by what means this may most effectually be done. The class of facts here alluded to, are manifestly of the same description with those to which the attention of philosophers has been lately called by the pretensions of Mesmer and of Perkins: "Atque huic conjuncta est disquisitio, quomodo imaginatio intendi et fortificari possit? Quippe, si imaginatio fortis tantarum sit virium, operæ pretium fuerit nosse, quibus modis eam exaltari, et se ipsa majorem fieri datur? Atque hic oblique, nec minus periculose se insinuat palliatio quædam et defensio maximæ partis *Magiæ Ceremonialis.*" &c. &c. *(De Aug. Scient.* Lib. iv. cap. iii.)

siological theory concerning their causes, or to any analogical explanations founded on the caprices of metaphorical language. If, on some occasions, he assumes the existence of *animal spirits*, as the medium of communication between soul and body, it must be remembered, that this was *then* the universal belief of the learned; and that it was at a much later period not less confidently avowed by Locke. Nor ought it to be overlooked (I mention it to the credit of *both* authors), that in such instances the *fact* is commonly so stated, as to render it easy for the reader to detach it from the *theory*: As to the scholastic questions concerning the nature and essence of mind,—whether it be extended or unextended? whether it have any relation to space or to time? or whether (as was contended by others) it exist in *every ubi*, but in *no place ?*—Bacon has uniformly passed them over with silent contempt; and has probably contributed not less effectually to bring them into general discredit, by this indirect intimation of his own opinion, than if he had descended to the ungrateful task of exposing their absurdity.*

While Bacon, however, so cautiously avoids these unprofitable dis-

cussions about the nature of mind, he decidedly states his conviction, that the *faculties* of man differ not merely in degree, but in kind, from the instincts of the brutes. " I do not, therefore," he observes in one occasion, " approve of that confused and promiscuous method in which philosophers are accustomed to treat of pneumatology; as if the human soul ranked above those of brutes, merely like the sun above the stars, or like gold above other metals."

Among the various topics started by Bacon for the consideration of future logicians, he did not overlook (what may be justly regarded, in a practical view, as the most interesting of all logical problems) the question concerning the mutual influence of thought and of language on each other. " Men believe," says he, " that their reason governs their words; but, it often happens, that words have power enough to *re-act* upon reason." This aphorism may be considered as the text of by far the most valuable part of Locke's Essay,—*that* which relates to the imperfections and abuse of words; but it was not till within the last twenty years, that its depth and importance were perceived in all their extent. I need scarcely say, that I allude to the excellent Memoirs of M. Prevost and of M. Degerando, on " Signs considered in their connection with the Intellectual Operations." The anticipations formed by Bacon, of that branch of modern logic which relates to *Universal Grammar*, do no less honour to his sagacity. " Grammar," he observes, " is of two kinds, the one literary, the other philosophical. The former has for its object to trace the analogies running through the structure of a particular tongue, so as to facilitate its acquisition to a foreigner, or to enable him to speak it with correctness and purity. The latter directs the attention, *not* to the analogies which words bear to words, but to the analogies which words bear to things;"† or, as he afterwards explains himself more clearly, " to language considered as the sensible portraiture or image of the mental processes." In farther illustration of these hints, he takes notice of the lights which the different genius of

---

* Notwithstanding the extravagance of Spinoza's own philosophical creed, he is one of the very few among Bacon's successors, who seem to have been fully aware of the justness, importance, and originality of the method pointed out in the *Novum Organon* for the study of the mind. " Ad hæc intelligenda, non est opus *naturam mentis* cognoscere, sed sufficit, mentis sive *perceptionum* historiolam concinnare modo illo quo VERULAMIUS docet." *Spin. Epist.* 42.

In order to comprehend the whole merit of this remark, it is necessary to know that, according to the Cartesian phraseology, which is here adopted by Spinoza, the word *perception* is a general term, equally applicable to all the intellectual operations. The words of Descartes himself are these: " Omnes modi cogitandi, quos in nobis experimur, ad duos generales referri possunt: quorum unus est, *perceptio*, sive operatio intellectus; alius verò, *volitio*, sive operatio voluntatis. *Nam sentire, imaginari, et pure intelligere, sunt tantum diversi modi percipiendi;* ut et cupere, aversari, affirmare, negare, dubitare, sunt diversi modi volendi." *Princ. Phil.* Pars. I. § 32.

† *De Aug. Scient.* Lib. vi. cap. 1.

different languages reflect on the characters and habits of those by whom they were respectively spoken. "Thus," says he, " it is easy to perceive, that the Greeks were addicted to the culture of the arts, the Romans engrossed with the conduct of affairs; inasmuch, as the technical distinctions introduced in the progress of refinement require the aid of compounded words; while the real business of life stands in no need of so artificial a phraseology."* Ideas of this sort have, in the course of a very few years, already become common, and almost tritical; but how different was the case two centuries ago!

With these sound and enlarged views concerning the philosophy of the mind, it will not appear surprising to those who have attended to the slow and irregular advances of human reason, that Bacon should occasionally blend incidental remarks, savouring of the habits of thinking prevalent in his time. A curious example of this occurs in the same chapter which contains his excellent definition or description of universal grammar "This too," he observes, " is worthy of notice, that the ancient languages were full of declensions, of cases, of conjugations, of tenses, and of other similar inflections; while the modern, almost entirely destitute of these, indolently accomplish the same purpose by the help of prepositions, and of auxiliary verbs. Whence," he continues, " may be inferred (however we may flatter ourselves with the idea of our own superiority), that the human intellect was much more acute and subtile in ancient, than it now is in modern times."† How very unlike is this last reflection to the usual strain of Bacon's writings!. It seems, indeed, much more congenial to the philosophy of Mr. Harris and of Lord Monboddo; and it has accordingly been sanctioned with the approbation of both these learned authors. If my memory does not deceive me, it is the only passage in Bacon's works, which Lord Monboddo has any where condescended to quote.

These observations afford me a convenient opportunity for remarking the progress and diffusion of *the philosophical spirit*, since the beginning

of the seventeenth century. In the short passage just cited from Bacon, there are involved no less than two capital errors, which are now almost universally ranked, by men of education, among the grossest prejudices of the multitude. The one, that the declensions and conjugations of the ancient languages, and the modern substitution in their place, of prepositions and auxiliary verbs, are, both of them, the deliberate and systematical contrivances of speculative grammarians; the other (still less analogous to Bacon's general style of reasoning), that the faculties of man have declined, as the world has grown older. Both of these errors may be now said to have disappeared entirely. The latter, more particularly, must, to the rising generation, seem so absurd, that it almost requires an apology to have mentioned it. That the capacities of the human mind have been in all ages the same; and that the diversity of phenomena exhibited by our species, is the result merely of the different circumstances in which men are placed, has been long received as an incontrovertible logical maxim; or rather, such is the influence of early instruction, that we are apt to regard it as one of the most obvious suggestions of common sense. And yet, till about the time of Montesquieu, it was by no means so generally recognized by the learned, as to have a sensible influence on the fashionable tone of thinking over Europe. The application of this fundamental and leading idea to the natural or *theoretical history* of society in all its various aspects;—to the history of languages, of the arts, of the sciences, of laws, of government, of manners, and of religion,—is the peculiar glory of the latter half of the eighteenth century; and forms a characteristical feature in its philosophy, which even the imagination of Bacon was unable to foresee.

It would be endless to particularize the original suggestions thrown out by Bacon on topics connected with the science of mind. The few passages of this sort already quoted, are produced merely as a specimen of the rest. They are by no means selected as the most important in his writings; but, as they happened to be those which had left the strongest impression on my memory, I thought them as likely

---

* *De Aug. Scient.* Lib. vi. cap. i.
† Ibid.

as any other, to invite the curiosity of my readers to a careful examination of the rich mine from which they are extracted.

The ethical disquisitions of Bacon are almost entirely of a practical nature. Of the two theoretical questions so much agitated, in both parts of this island, during the eighteenth century, concerning the *principle* and the *object* of moral approbation, he has said nothing; but he has opened some new and interesting views with respect to the influence of *custom* and the formation of *habits*;—a most important article of moral philosophy, on which he has enlarged more ably and more usefully than any writer since Aristotle.* Under the same head of *Ethics* may be mentioned the small volume to which he has given the title of *Essays*; the best known and the most popular of all his works. It is also one of those where the superiority of his genius appears to the greatest advantage; the novelty and depth of his reflections often receiving a strong relief from the triteness of his subject. It may be read from beginning to end in a few hours,—and yet, after the twentieth perusal, one seldom fails to remark in it something overlooked before. This, indeed, is a characteristic of all Bacon's writings, and is only to be accounted for by the inexhaustible aliment they furnish to our own thoughts, and the sympathetic activity they impart to our torpid faculties.

The suggestions of Bacon for the improvement of political philosophy, exhibit as strong a contrast to the narrow systems of contemporary statesmen, as the inductive logic to that of the schools. How profound and comprehensive are the views opened in the following passages, when compared with the scope of the celebrated treatise *De Jure Belli et Pacis*; a work which was first published about a year before Bacon's death, and which continued, for a hundred and fifty years afterwards, to be regarded in all the Protestant universities of Europe as an inexhaustible treasure of moral and jurisprudential wisdom !

"The ultimate object which legislators ought to have in view, and to which all their enactments and sanctions ought to be subservient, is, *that*

the citizens may live happily.* For this purpose, it is necessary that they should receive a religious and pious education; that they should be trained to good morals; that they should be secured from foreign enemies by proper military arrangements; that they should be guarded by an effectual police against seditions and private injuries; that they should be loyal to government, and obedient to magistrates; and finally, that they should abound in wealth, and in other national resources."*—"The science of such matters certainly belongs more particularly to the province of men, who, by habits of public business, have been led to take a comprehensive survey of the social order; of the interests of the community at large; of the rules of natural equity; of the manners of nations; of the different forms of government; and who are thus prepared to reason concerning the wisdom of laws, both from considerations of justice and of policy. The great desideratum, accordingly, is, by investigating the principles of *natural justice*, and those of *political expediency*, to exhibit a theoretical model of legislation, which, while it serves as a standard for estimating the comparative excellence of municipal codes, may suggest hints for their correction and improvement, to such as have at heart the welfare of mankind."†

How precise the notion was that Bacon had formed of a philosophical system of jurisprudence (with which as a standard the municipal laws of different nations might be compared), appears from a remarkable expression, in which he mentions it as the proper business of those who might attempt to carry his plan into execution, to investigate those "LEGES LEGUM,

---

* *De Aug. Scient.* Lib. vii. cap. iii.

* *Exemplum Tractatus de Fontibus Juris,* Aphor. 5. This enumeration of the different objects of law approaches very nearly to Mr. Smith's ideas on the same subject, as expressed by himself in the concluding sentence of his *Theory of Moral Sentiments.* "In another discourse, I shall endeavour to give an account of the general principles of law and government, and of the different revolutions they have undergone in the different ages and periods of society; not only in what concerns justice, but in what concerns police, revenue, and arms, and whatever else is the object of law."

† *De Aug. Scient.* Lib. viii. cap. iii.

ex quibus informatio peti possit, quid in singulis legibus bene aut perperam positum aut constitutum sit."* I do not know if, in Bacon's prophetic anticipations of the future progress of physics, there be any thing more characteristical, both of the grandeur and of the justness of his conceptions, than this short definition; more particularly, when we consider how widely Grotius, in a work professedly devoted to this very inquiry, was soon after to wander from the right path, in consequence of his vague and wavering idea of the aim of his researches.

The sagacity, however, displayed in these and various other passages of a similar import, can by no means be duly appreciated, without attending, at the same time, to the cautious and

---

* *De Fontibus Juris,* Aphor. 6.
· From the preface to a small tract of Bacon's, entitled *The Elements of the Common Laws of England,* (written while he was Solicitor-General to Queen Elizabeth), we learn, that the phrase *legum leges* had been previously used by some "great civilian." To what *civilian* Bacon here alludes, I know not; but, whoever he was, I doubt much if he annexed to it the comprehensive and philosophical meaning, so precisely explained in the above definition. Bacon himself, when he wrote his Tract on the Common Laws, does not seem to have yet risen to this vantage-ground of universal jurisprudence. His great object (he tells us) was "to collect the rules and grounds dispersed throughout the body of the same laws, in order to see more profoundly into the reason of such judgments and ruled cases, and thereby to make more use of them for the decision of other cases more doubtful; so that the uncertainty of law, which is the principal and most just challenge that is made to the laws of our nation at this time, will, by this new strength laid to the foundation, be somewhat the more settled and corrected." In this passage, no reference whatever is made to the *universal justice* spoken of in the aphorisms *de Fontibus Juris*; but merely to the leading and governing rules which give to a municipal system whatever it possesses of analogy and consistency. To these rules Bacon gives the title of *leges legum:* but the meaning of the phrase, on this occasion, differs from that in which he afterwards employed it, not less widely than the rules of Latin or of Greek syntax differ from the principles of universal grammar.

temperate maxims so frequently inculcated by the author, on the subject of political innovation. . "A stubborn retention of customs is a turbulent thing, not less than the introduction of new."—"Time is the greatest innovator; shall we then not imitate time, which innovates so silently as to mock the sense?" Nearly connected with these aphorisms, are the profound reflections in the first book *De Augmentis Scientiarum,* on the necessity of accommodating every new institution to the character and circumstances of the people for whom it is intended; and on the peculiar danger which literary men run of overlooking this consideration, from the familiar acquaintance they acquire, in the course of their early studies, with the ideas and sentiments of the ancient classics.

The remark of Bacon on the systematical policy of Henry VII. was manifestly suggested by the same train of thinking. "His laws (whoso marks them well) were deep and not vulgar; not made on the spur of a particular occasion for the present, but out of providence for the future; to make the estate of his people still more and more happy, after the manner of the legislators in ancient and heroic times." How far this noble eulogy was merited, either by the legislators of antiquity, or by the modern Prince on whom Bacon has bestowed it, is a question of little moment. I quote it merely on account of the important philosophical distinction which it indirectly marks, between "deep and vulgar laws;" the former invariably aiming to accomplish their end, not by giving any sudden shock to the feelings and interests of the existing generation, but by allowing to natural causes time and opportunity to operate; and by removing those artificial obstacles which check the progressive tendencies of society. It is probable, that, on this occasion, Bacon had an eye more particularly to the memorable *statute of alienation;* to the effects of which (whatever were the motives of its author) the above description certainly applies in an eminent degree.

After all, however, it must be acknowledged, that it is rather in his general views and maxims, than in the details of his political theories, that Bacon's sagacity appears to advantage. His notions with respect to commercial policy seem to have been more peculiarly erroneous; originating in an overweening opinion of the efficacy of law, in matters where natural causes ought to be allowed a free operation. It is observed by Mr. Hume, that the statutes of Henry VII. relating to the police of his kingdom, are generally contrived with more judgment than his commercial regulations. The same writer adds, that "the more simple ideas of order and equity are sufficient to guide a legislator in every thing that regards the internal administration of justice; but that the principles of commerce are much more complicated, and require long experience and deep reflection to be well understood in any state. The real consequence is *there* often contrary to first appearances. No wonder, that, during the reign of Henry VII. these matters were frequently mistaken; and it may safely be affirmed, that, even in the age of Lord Bacon, very imperfect and erroneous ideas were formed on that subject."

The instances mentioned by Hume in confirmation of these general remarks, are peculiarly gratifying to those who have a pleasure in tracing the slow but certain progress of reason and liberality. "During the reign," says he, "of Henry VII. it was prohibited to export horses, as if that exportation did not encourage the breed, and make them more plentiful in the kingdom. Prices were also affixed to woollen cloths, to caps and hats, and the wages of labourers were regulated by law. IT IS EVIDENT, *that these matters ought always to be left free, and be entrusted to the common course of business and commerce.*"—"For a like reason," the historian continues, "the law enacted against inclosures, and for the keeping up of farm-houses, scarcely deserves the praises bestowed on it by Lord Bacon. If husbandmen understand agriculture, and have a ready vent for their commodities, we need not dread a diminution of the people employed in the country. During a century and a half after this period, there was a frequent renewal of laws and edicts against depopulation; whence we may infer, that none of them were ever executed. *The natural course of improvement at last provided a remedy.*"

These acute and decisive strictures on the impolicy of some laws highly applauded by Bacon, while they strongly illustrate the narrow and mistaken views in political economy entertained by the wisest statesmen and philosophers two centuries ago, afford, at the same time, a proof of the general diffusion which has since taken place among the people of Great Britain, of juster and more enlightened opinions on this important branch of legislation. Wherever such doctrines find their way into the page of history, it may be safely inferred, that the public mind is not indisposed to give them a welcome reception.

The ideas of Bacon concerning the education of youth, were such as might be expected from a philosophical statesman. On the conduct of education in general, with a view to the developement and improvement of the intellectual character, he has suggested various useful hints in different parts of his works; but what I wish chiefly to remark at present is, the paramount importance which he has attached to the education of the people,—comparing (as he has repeatedly done) the effects of early culture on the understanding and the heart, to the abundant harvest which rewards the diligent husbandman for the toils of the spring. To this analogy he seems to have been particularly anxious to attract the attention of his readers, by bestowing on education the title of *the georgics of the mind*; identifying, by a happy and impressive metaphor, the two proudest functions entrusted to the legislator,—the encouragement of agricultural industry, and the care of national instruction. In both instances, the legislator exerts a power which is literally *productive* or *creative*; compelling, in the one case, the unprofitable desert to pour forth its latent riches; and in the other, vivifying the dormant seeds of genius and virtue, and redeeming from the neglected wastes of human intellect, a new and unexpected accession to the common inheritance of mankind.

When from such speculations as these we descend to the treatise *De Jure Belli et Pacis*, the contrast is mortifying indeed. And yet, so much better suited were the talents and accomplishments of Grotius to the taste, not only of his contemporaries, but of their remote descendants, that, while the merits of Bacon failed, for a century and a half, to command the general admiration of Europe,[*] Grotius continued, even in our British universities, the acknowledged oracle of jurisprudence and of ethics, till long after the death of Montesquieu. Nor was Bacon himself unapprised of the slow growth of his posthumous fame.

No writer seems ever to have felt more deeply, that he properly belonged to a later and more enlightened age;—a sentiment which he has pathetically expressed in that clause of his testament, where he "bequeaths his name to posterity, after some generations shall be past." ·

MISCELLANEOUS COMMUNICATIONS.

On Poetical Scepticism.
No. V.
(See pp. 157, 217, 278, 383.)

——— " I must tread on shadowy ground,
　　　and sink
Deep: and aloft ascending breathe in
　　　worlds
To which the heaven of heavens is but a
　　　veil."

　　　　　　　　　　　　WORDSWORTH.

　　　　　——— " I cannot go
Where universal love shines not around,
Sustaining all these worlds and all their
　　　suns
From seeming evil still educing good,
And better thence again and better still
In infinite progression."

　　　　　　　　　　　　THOMSON.

SIR,

THOSE who contend for the affinities of religion and poetry, can scarcely refuse to give the preference to that system which teaches that all the children of men are destined to be finally and immortally happy. This doctrine has more of the grand, the beautiful and the joyous: it opens to imagination more glorious vistas; it encircles us with more beatific visions; it supplies more firm and abiding objects on which the soul can repose, than any other hope of future joy which " it has entered into the heart of man to conceive;" it bursts upon us in all " the glory and the freshness of a dream;" it enables us to extend our anticipations far into the abyss of futurity without trembling, to dwell on the idea of God with nothing but delight, to identify the feeling of immortality with that of joy; it does that for the species which the orthodox system of Christianity does only for the individual who receives it; it robs death of its sting and deprives the grave of its victory.

The happiness which the most confident believer in the doctrines of Calvin anticipates in heaven is both selfish and imperfect: it is built on the ruins of the best and tenderest affections, for it implies an eternal separation from many who are objects of regard now, from some perhaps who have been more passionately loved even for their errors, or who are knit to the heart by ties so strong and sacred that no human frailty can sever them. In order to enjoy it, the most disinterested of all emotions must be torn from the heart, attachments cemented by the courtesies and the distresses of life must be rent in twain, early loves must lose their charm, and the holiest instincts of nature must wither and die within us! Not only must the profligate child, on whom the heart delighted, as it were, to waste its tenderness—the Absalom loved in the midst of rebellion and vice above his brethren—be dear to us no more; but we must forget the friend who, though associating with us in deeds of charity, professed not to have experienced any supernatural change; we must learn to think with tranquillity on the sufferings of him, who, though the benefactor of earth, was not the favourite of heaven; we must be callous to the misery of an old and dear companion, who, endowed with all that could render life delightful, did not agree with us in certain speculative points of faith! With those who cheered our passage through this vale of tears we must sympathize no longer. The deathless agonies of those on whose

　* " La célébrité en France des écrits du Chancelier Bacon n'a guere pour date que celle de l'Encyclopédie." *(Histoire des Mathématiques par Montucla,* Preface, p. ix.) It is an extraordinary circumstance, that Bayle, who has so often wasted his erudition and acuteness on the most insignificant characters, and to whom Le Clerc has very justly ascribed the merit of *une exactitude étonnante dans des choses de néant,* should have devoted to Bacon only twelve lines of his Dictionary.

bosoms we have leaned as a sacred resting place, must have no power to break our blissful repose.* We must, in short, become different beings, not merely in being purified from the pollutions of earth, but in losing our best and most virtuous affections, our most serene and unfading joys. Our human hearts must die away within us. I confess myself I have no interest in another life, if it is to bring with it such a change. It is not *I* who am to be happy hereafter—this heart which is to beat, these sympathies that are to flourish, these powers that are to be unfolded, these tastes by which I am to enjoy. And who is there who would change his individuality for that of another, even to be made better, wiser, or happier? Who would resign his friends and relatives for those who would be greater or worthier of his esteem? Who, that is worthy the name of man, would forget for ever those who have loved and cherished him, to be the companion of saints and martyrs, or the favourite of angels?

Not such are the everlasting hopes which the doctrine of Universal Restoration awakens within those who receive it. This belief not only assures us of personal happiness, but it makes that happiness consist, in a great degree, in its diffusion on all around us: it enables us to associate all whom we esteem in our Joys: it opens to us the grandest prospects of human improvement, discloses the statelier vistas of increasing knowledge, happiness and virtue, and gives us the noblest ideas of the dignity of our nature which is preparing for such glorious destinies: it realizes youth's most gorgeous and visionary dreams: it enables us to look back on the mighty deeds of past times with a new interest, for it displays them as so many deathless monuments of the innate dignity of man, and as glorious

proofs of what he will be hereafter: but it is chiefly welcome to the heart, as making its sweetest emotions deathless, and leaving its own peculiar objects of desire to rest on the splendid prospects which it reveals. It is this principle and this alone which renders friendship and love immortal.

According to the orthodox system of future punishment, the noblest and most divine faculties must, in many instances, be left to perish.* The "strong divinity of soul" has sometimes been mingled with human frailties, and the intoxication of heart produced by poetical inspiration has caused the poet to overleap the virtuous usages of life, and to follow without moderation the impulse of his pleasurable sensations. The pure and deep spring of celestial delight has been sullied in its passage through the world: and yet the generous would discern, even amidst irregularity and vice, the stirrings of a principle allied to the noblest sublimities of virtue, vast capacities for excellence, and bright indications of a celestial origin. "The light that led astray was light from heaven." The kindliest virtues and the most sublime energies have been too often linked with imperfections which have shaded or rendered them useless. But how inspiring is the belief that these powers and these excellencies shall yet be immortal, assoiled from the corruptions of earth when its temptations are removed from them, and tuned to heighten the joys of Paradise! How cheering is the thought that the heroes and sages of ancient story, who, amidst error and darkness, displayed a majesty of soul which has awed distant generations, are destined to obtain yet greener lau-

---

* The orthodox heaven would be an exact realization of Mr. Godwin's theory of Political Justice. As recommended by that ingenious speculator, all peculiar regards must cease, gratitude must be done away, natural affection must be extinguished, and we must love and esteem only according to the abstract merit or godliness of the individual. The Calvinist may perhaps be surprised to find that the system against which on its promulgation, he lavished every expression of scorn and disgust, is to be realized by himself—in heaven!

* Soon after the commencement of the Eclectic Review, some writer opposing theatrical entertainments, with something more than usual zeal, alluded to the spirit of Shakspeare as mourning in the everlasting torments of hell the evils caused by his writings. It was formerly said with reference to the disposition of the two reformers, "that it would be better to go to hell with Melancthon than to heaven with Calvin;" and some perhaps would be inclined to make the same choice between Shakspeare and the Reviewer. It is but just to add, that the Eclectic Review has since that time greatly improved both in talent and feeling, and would now probably treat the fate of the greatest poet who ever lived only with a mysterious silence.

rels, and to rise up again in the light of a holier virtue! How glorious is the prospect of mighty minds, on earth benighted, bursting into the full enjoyment of truth—of unknown energies unfolding their native grandeur—of genius here debased or unknown, tasting of ever fresh inspiration from " Siloa's brook that flows fast by the oracle of God!"

Around those who are enabled to realize the doctrine of Universal Restoration the arrows of misfortune fall harmless. The malignant passions can find no resting place in their bosoms. They look on the most wretched and depraved of the human race as brethren, as ultimately destined to become worthy of their esteem and affection, as erring children of their own Father, who will finally bring all the wanderers home. The ills of life and the burden of all material things are lightened to them by the fond belief that all are parts of one generous system of fatherly compassion. To them the face of nature seems enlivened by new smiles, for all the beauties which surround them appear indications of that universal goodness which will harmonize all the jarring notes of this discordant world. Every summer breeze whispers to them of unutterable love. The " splendour in the grass, the glory in the flower," which delighted them in childhood, seem almost to sparkle again before them. Their virtue is unimpelled by fear and unmingled with pride, for its origin and its essence is joy. Death seems to them as a placid slumber, as a genial repose which will take away all evil thoughts and desires, and will leave them refreshed from their labours, and purified and fitted for heaven. When they weep over friends whose eyes they have closed for awhile, no sad misgivings will disturb the serenity of their sorrow, or cloud over the sweet remembrances which they delight to cherish. To them the memory of buried love will have all its unearthly charms, for the sanctity of their grief will be unbroken. They will be elevated above the world, and yet taste with more exquisite relish all its genuine blessings. Their delight will be to look on the better and more engaging parts of human nature; they will follow the domestic affections to their loveliest seclusion, trace out the nice and delicate indications of good-

ness, which others pass by unheeded, and derive from them all fresh proofs of the noble destiny for which we were created. They will rejoice in the joy of all men, trace the progressive advancement of truth and virtue with honest pride, and catch, as if it were the music of angels, the low breathed voice of humble gratitude, or the first lispings of infant prayer—

> —— " to which God's own ear
> Listens delighted."

Here I might conclude these Essays. I trust I have, in some degree, shewn that the poetry of religion is not confined to the orthodox creed, nor the best feelings of the heart exclusively possessed by the followers of Calvin. But let me not offend my Unitarian friends, if I entreat them to cultivate and cherish those emotions to which, I apprehend, their opinions should conduct them. Let them not think that man is ennobled by his reason alone, or that abstract truth is the only object he ought to pursue. Let them remember that he has imagination to be called into exercise, veneration to be bestowed, and tender affections to gratify. Let them not return persecution with scorn. Let them never despise prejudices which are honest, or speak with contempt of doctrines which have consoled the hearts of thousands, because they regard them as erroneous. Let not the pride of reason or the fastidiousness of criticism pollute the sources of their joys. Let them remember that the toleration is imperfect which is not extended to intolerance itself; and that even in the bigotry of those who think their opinions dangerous, there is a feeling of zeal for their welfare to venerate and esteem. While engaged in the defence of truth let them remember that it is of more consequence to feel right than to argue well; that the best orthodoxy is that of the heart; and that while sentiments and creeds and systems perish, the best and purest feelings of the soul remain unchanged—the same in all sects, countries and generations—and that they will continue while God himself endures.   S. N. D.

Sir,   *July* 1, 1816.

YOUR Correspondent, *An Occasional Reader,* (p. 323,) refers, I apprehend, to the 3d Book of " The

Last Day" and the expostulation of the
damned soul, which thus begins—

" Who burst the barriers of my peaceful
grave ?
Ah ! cruel Death ! that would no longer
save,
But grudg'd me e'en that narrow, dark
abode,
And cast me out into the wrath of God."

Towards the close of his address, the
miserable victim of divine vengeance is
thus made to recollect the paternal character of God:

"'And canst thou then look down from
perfect bliss,
And see me plunging in the dark abyss,
Calling thee *Father*, in a sea of fire,
Or pouring blasphemies at thy desire ?"

Mr. John Wesley, many years before his death, and during the life of
Young, re-published, in a Collection
of English Poems, (3 vols. 8vo.) "The
Last Day." He was aware of the inconsistency into which the orthodox
poet had fallen, and annexed to the
lines I have just quoted the following
note, in substance, if my memory has
failed me as to the exact words: " Impossible ! Could a damned soul speak
thus, would he not in a moment be in
Abraham's bosom ?"

Your Correspondent (p. 326) appears
not to be aware of the question which
has been raised whether the Treatise to
which he refers was written by *Jeremy
Taylor*. I suppose he intends the
" Contemplations of the State of Man
in this Life and in that which is to
come," the eighth edition of which,
8vo. 1718, is now before me. It is
confessedly *posthumous*. Prefixed are
two Addresses to the Reader. The
first signed B. Hale, D.D. is highly com-
mendatory, without a word as to authenticity: the second Address, signed
Robert Harris, describes Bishop Taylor
as " having left these *Holy Contemplations* in the hands of a worthy friend of
his, with a full purpose to have printed
them if he had lived."

I have understood, on the best authority, that the Editor of " Specimens
of Early Dramatic Poets," a gentleman
critically versed in the fine writers of
Jeremy Taylor's age, is of opinion that
the *Contemplations*, though containing
passages in his manner, were not written by the Bishop. There appears no
evidence for assigning them to him,

except the testimonies of the unknown
Robert Harris and the equally unknown
worthy friend to whom they are said to
have been entrusted.

J.O.U.

Sir, *Bath, Aug.* 13, 1816.
I BEG leave to transmit to you a
short extract from a letter of an enlightened clergyman of the Establishment to a Dissenting minister, whose
Unitarianism lately compelled him to
resign his congregation, with whom
he was connected almost twenty-six
years.

" Dear Sir.——Those who wish to
worship any more Gods than one,
ought to go to the East Indies, and
prostrate themselves before the idol of
that country."

The whole letter is written in the
same strain, virtually acknowledging
no God but the One God and Father
of our Lord Jesus Christ, and condemning all encroachments upon the
dictates of reason, and all impositions
upon the rights of conscience, as diametrically opposite to the glorious doctrines of the gospel. As there are well
known to be a great number of clergymen of the same sentiments, why do
they not unite in petitioning the legislature, and, to use the language of
sailors when they are aroused to exert
their utmost exertions, with a long
pull, a strong pull, and a pull all
together, claim the privileges of the
children of God, and desire to be permitted to obey his voice, in the language of their own hearts, and according to their most strenuous endeavours
to understand and propagate the revelation he has given them. Our legislators are not at present Calvinists or
Laudeans. Many of them are lovers
of truth, and none of them can stand
up and say that this or that Shibboleth
should be required of men, when contrary to the light of their own minds,
and what they believe to be the word
of God. Whatever erroneous sentiments many of them may entertain at
present, let them all be allowed to declare themselves unequivocally, and
truth will be a gainer in the end. It
will shine with glory by a free discussion. Or if any subscription be yet
thought necessary in those who undertake the office of minister, let it
be this only,—" I believe in the Holy
Scriptures, and by the divine blessing

will endeavour to explain them in their original purity, according to the uniform declarations of the unadulterated Bible." But this latitude, it will be said, will produce almost as many creeds as there are men. I think, on the contrary, that it will soon terminate in the universal reception of the good word of truth, and lead all men to embrace that holy church, in which there is no spot, nor wrinkle, nor any such thing. Voltaire, notwithstanding his great infidelity, believed that there is one God, one great and good God, the God of all beings, of all worlds, and of all ages: and, had he not supposed, without making that inquiry which became him, that the Trinity and some other unfounded doctrines were contained in the Bible; or, had he perceived that the Divine Unity, and that true holiness, &c. contained in the New Testament, were the real doctrines which the Lord Jesus taught, he never could have become an infidel, nor have ridiculed what he did not rightly examine, and therefore did not understand. A NEW TESTAMENT CHRISTIAN.

SIR, *August* 1, 1816.

I HAVE heard it occasionally remarked, that at one period of the history of the Christian church, it was in agitation, by some synod or council, to place the Virgin Mary as a person of the Trinity, in the room of the Holy Ghost. In referring to the remarks of *Theototus*, M. Repos. Vol. VI. page 399, I find some confirmation of it, as represented by the Novogorod Idol, and in the censures of such a Trinity by the Arabian Impostor: but setting aside such authorities, I should be glad be informed by your more learned readers, if there be any other and better authority for such an assumption. J. W.

SIR, *August* 2, 1816.

IN this our sad season of logomachy, may I take the liberty of requesting from some of your more polemically given Correspondents, the proper name for a denomination of fellow interrogators with Pilate—" What is the truth?" Who, (*not more firmly assured of the existence of the Christ than of the divinity of his mission*), while, on the one hand, sitting at the feet of Jesus and hearing from his own lips

that he knew not the precise date of an event which he was yet empowered to predict (Mark xiii. 32); that he might well assume the very title about which so much controversy has arisen, and found his apology for assuming it on the ground that other missionaries of God had in Elohim arrogated a higher one than he did in that of Ben Elohim, John x. 36; that *of himself* he *could* do *nothing*, viii. 54; that if he bare witness of himself his witness were not true, v. 31; that the very words he spake, he spake not *of himself*, xii. 49, xiv. 10; hearing him, in short, referring every thing he said, and did, and was, as unequivocally, as invariably, as absolutely to that Being whom he called his Father, as any other pious man whom he had taught to address by the same endearing appellation could have done:—then superadding to this unimpeachable testimony the still (if possible) more unambiguous attestations of the Most Highest Himself at the several periods of his baptism, transfiguration and crucifixion, so admirably adapted in kind and in degree to the " beloved Son," in whom of all human kind God deigned to express himself emphatically " well pleased," so palpably *infra dig.* to a Being of an infinitely superior order:—and last and least, recollecting the remarkable incidents of the temptation, when this heavenly personage is accosted by another (whom later ages have almost invested with the character of omniscient) as a " Son of God," who might haply not only be seduced from his allegiance to his Father by such a consideration as the kingdoms of this atom of the universe, yclept our world, but to transfer it, and with it the homage of religious worship, to his seducer, as the donor of them:—who, ruminating I say over thus much, and more that might be adduced of a kindred description, regard the Christ in no other light the Son of God than as figuratively so constituted, or at most so miraculously born as no other human being ever was before him. Yet, on the other hand, reading the proem of St. John's Gospel, surprising as they think they do the interpolation of the reporter at the 16th verse of his third chapter, not to mention a multitude of appositions, turns and probable emendations, sufficiently indicative as they hold of the historian's construction of the more genuine phraseology—looking indeed at the *general tenour* of our Saviour's discourses as edited by that Evangelist, and collating them with the subsequent original letters of the same author: then again turning to the Epistles of St. Paul, observing his repeated classifications at the beginning of them, his closing sentence to the 2d Corinth. his Lord of Glory, his 5th and seq. verses 2d chapter Philippians, in spite even of their unlucky υπεευψωσε—remembering too the exclamation of Thomas, the prayer of Stephen—can scarcely dispossess themselves of something very much like a conviction that these first disciples of their heavenly Master recognized in him (consistently however always as they thought at least, *with their · most palpably fundamental doctrine of the unity of their ancestors' Jehovah in the sole person of his God and Father*) a Θεος προς (apud) HIM their One ο Θεος, an homousian the subordinate *Logos*, an only begotten Son from the beginning, the same yesterday, to-day, and for ever, a *One Lord by* whom are all things, the Associate of a *One God of* whom are all things, HIS co-eternal but not co-equal image, delegate, minister, representative.

How indeed these excellent men could reconcile some of these doctrines with others; how they could make up their minds to believe (as in the opinion of our inquirers they most unquestionably did, not more unquestionably any one tenet they published) that *such* a Son of God *died, such* a Lord of Glory was *crucified,* in the person of Jesus, or how (compatibly with their hypothesis) one of them could *dispose* of *such* a Being in the manner he does in the 15th chapter 1st Corinthians, they avow themselves quite incompetent to conjecture. Not less perplexed, aghast rather, (their reason and faith both utterly confounded) do they confess themselves upon the recollection of the familiarity, the chit chat, the rebuke, the lying on the bosom, the probable concurrence in the opinion that HE was beside himself, of these HIS contemporaries. As willingly do they avow themselves unable to reconcile the argumentation in the 1st chapter of Hebrews with the Scripture on which it professes to be founded, or that in the chapter of the Philippians already quoted, with the antecedently sempiternal claims of *such* a " Christ Jesus."

The Orthodox now would perhaps look no further than 2 Tim. iii. for a title for our Catechumens, but *illi in nos sæviant* if they will! You will not I hope be so short or severe with an almost conscious semi-proselyte to their heresy, in your Correspondent and Constant Reader,

TE TACE.

P. S. And *quære* against our heretics —On what Son of God does St. John suppose the Chief Rulers to have *believed,* when he *expressly states,* that though they did *believe on him,* they had not the consistency to confess him, John xii. 43, on a *præsens Deus* of any kind, or in the anointed Messenger of their One only true God? Could so monstrous a practical faith have ever existed in any human breast? And again, Martha, when she took it for granted HE had no power to bring back her brother from the grave though he might have prevented his going thither? Or the Disciples when they all forsook him and fled?

SIR,   *August* 1, 1816.

IT is pleasing to know that there is *one* publication connected with religious inquiry, which has for its main object the reconciliation of the doctrines of revelation with the conclusions of reason. It appears to be one of the great evils of establishments, that they often operate in the prevention of their members, from speaking fully their convictions, on the most important subjects. Thus we see Paley, when he reviews the popular objections to Christianity, wholly silent about the only weighty objection which exists— its future punishments. His situation, I think, must have been the cause of this, for there is nothing in all his writings which shews his belief in lasting or everlasting misery. We see those men who were independent of establishments, Hartley, Priestley, Simpson and others, quite explicit on this great subject. Paley says at the end of his " Natural Theology," that man lives in God's continual presence, and that death resigns him to his merciful disposal. This is language scarcely consistent with the popular doctrine concerning the final destination of mankind. Indeed this is the one fundamental objection to Christianity, for if the popular idea of its punishment be true, every human being must wish it to be false.

There are certain facts with which we are all acquainted that fill us with dismay, if this popular objection be the doctrine of revelation: That the great majority of human beings have not lived up to the acquirements of Christianity: That sensuality and selfishness (the true original sin of nature) have generally prevailed: That natural evil (of which our native passions and appetites are the greatest beyond all estimation) has universally produced moral evil: That the Scriptures seem to say that there are few that be saved, and if only those be who have completely overcome animal nature, the language of Scripture appears to be correct. Now when we take into the account the original strength of human appetites, and the unfavourable circumstances in which men are placed for their innocent gratification, the final lot of mankind becomes a most tremendous question. There is so much misery in this life, that it is a momentous question whether, considering this life alone, it be right for a man to become the father of a human being; but if the popular doctrine concerning futurity be true, no man that exists should in any case or circumstances become a father. This is the one moral duty, which must swallow up every other. And that men become fathers, professing this belief, shews that no one does indeed believe it to be true; for a man believing it true, and becoming a father, is a monster, little better, though not indeed so bad as the God whom he professes to worship.

Unprejudiced reason tells us, that although it may be right that the obtaining of eternal felicity should be very difficult, yet that the escape from eternal misery should at least be very easy, if in any case a Creator could be justified in making it possible for any being to involve himself in such a calamity. Besides what is this world and what are its enjoyments? Taken singly and of itself it is what no human being would have on such a condition, and very few would have it upon no other condition, than what their present circumstances impose.

It may be proper that very few should be saved, but it never can be just, that any should be damned, if by that be meant any thing more than destruction. A human legislator can only punish, a divine can reward and, to an extent more than equal to any difference of character. How can then the popular doctrine stand—and if it be Christianity—how can that religion be defended. All other objections are as dust in the balance, this is first, last, amidst, around and above them all, and I should hope that your publication would ever keep it in its eye, for the time will soon come, that this doctrine must be otherwise explained, or Christianity will be universally discarded.

SENEX.

Sir,　　　　*July* 30, 1816.

AS truth ought to be the sole object of religious as well as philosophical inquiry, men who pretend to be friends to the human race, will not be permitted by those who really are so, to impose their conjectures on the world as so many facts. The art of thinking justly on interesting subjects, especially on religion, is nevertheless generally speaking, but little understood. The multitude are dazzled too much by authority and prejudice, to view with steadiness, or to measure correctly the perfect symmetry of unveiled truth. They are used to think as they have been taught, and believe what they have been told; thus many things which are received, as obvious and essential truths, concerning natural and revealed religion, are certainly no better than vulgar prejudices;—often, pernicious errors, as dishonourable to God as they are contradictory to the concurring dictates of reason and revelation. Commonly these errors lie at the root of a system, consequently the data being false, the reasoning from them is sophistry, and its moral tendency often detrimental to the interest of virtue. Such, I am fully convinced, are the popular opinions concerning original sin. In this paper I purpose with your permission to lay before some of the occasional readers of your Miscellany who hold that doctrine, my reasons for rejecting it. Educated as I was in the Established Church, where the Calvinistic articles of that Church were constantly enforced, as well in the domestic circle as from the pulpit, it was natural that till I began to examine for myself, I should receive them as others do, without hesitation. I supposed that they were believed by all people who had any title to the Christian name. Time however convinced me, chiefly by study of the Scriptures, that amongst the rest this doctrine of original sin, was not to be found in revelation. Experience and observation, equally led me to feel, and think, that its tendency was very bad, dishonourable to God, and productive of much evil to men ; that it was not merely a doctrine on which Scripture was silent, and that therefore it might be true, but that it was an error which both Scripture and reason condemn. I would advise my friends, who are the subjects of religious depression, arising out of this soul-harrowing doctrine, to take the method that succeeded with me: if they can find a better I shall not object to it. My method was this: I took the sacred volume and determined to abide by its dictates whatever they might be; I kept my mind as indifferent as I could to every thing except the decision of truth ; I would not admit during the investigation for a moment, that the belief or rejection of this doctrine was of any consequence whatever with respect to my future state, for had interest or fear prevailed while the question was pending, the decision would have been dictated not by reason, but passion. I kept all my thoughts together, as much as possible, upon the one point I was investigating, and I tried to dismiss every thing foreign to it. I had no business with the existence of moral evil, nor with the universal mortality of creatures, nor with the frailties, follies, and imperfections of mankind. I had nothing to do with catechisms, creeds, the opinions or impertinences of fathers, priests or expositors. I cared as little for the mere assertions of those about me on either side: when they quoted texts, I compared them with others, and suffered no hypothetical explanation to contradict plain evidence ; I was to see and examine for myself; I prayed to God as a believer in Jesus Christ, for his assistance and blessing, and opened the Bible. I began with the Mosaic account of the creation of man. There I read, Gen. ii. 7, that "the Lord God formed man of the dust of the ground, and breathed into his nostrils the breath of life, and man became a living soul," and that he placed him in circumstances suited to

his nature. I read of a tree of life, and a tree of knowledge which grew in the garden of Eden, that to the former man had free access, and that from the latter he was prohibited ; but I read nothing of the natural immortality of his creature, made of the dust, nor of any powers, either of body or mind, that he possessed in a superior degree over many of his descendants. He appeared to me to be the same frail, fallible and peccable creature in his original state that his posterity have ever been. My reason told me that he could have but few wants, few ideas, very limited knowledge, that his language must have been barren, that he could have no acquaintance with either science or arts, that without a miraculous communication of ideas from the fountain of intelligence, he would have continued in this state of imbecility and ignorance, till he slowly, and by degrees, acquired ideas. I saw that his positive duties were but few, and that as his nature was frail, the test of his obedience was simple. I conceived of him as a youth whose capacity is indeed good,. whose passions are strong, whose experience is nothing. His passions prevailed, his reason was vanquished, he took of the forbidden fruit, he sought happiness, more happiness, a higher degree of glory, he fell, and found death ; he was told by his Creator the consequence of his disobedience, he was capable of understanding what he was told, but in an evil moment he transgressed. Were a man to be found with an equal simplicity of nature, and placed in the same circumstances, he would doubtless act in the same manner, and precisely the same consequences would follow. Reason weak, passion strong, temptation urgent, the man falls, and the sinner dies. " All die for that all have sinned." " It is appointed to all men once to die." It appeared to me therefore that death is an ordinance of nature and that it is only an evil to an accountable creature, who has broken the laws of God. " Dust thou art and to dust thou shalt return." As I read nothing of the death of the soul in this account of the fall of man, I found nothing there to support the modern doctrine of destruction or that of eternal future torment, nor indeed could I gather from any thing in that history, the evidence of a future state.

and I saw nothing there to induce me to think that a just God would impart any moral incapacity, or radical and inherent depravity to Adam's descendants, much less the imputation of his sin. By a necessity of nature, I perceived, that the first man must produce creatures in his own image, by which I understood frail, fallible, and peccable beings like himself, liable to sorrows and death, but possessed of equally high mental powers of reason and conscience, the image and superscription of God; and therefore accountable like their original parent for their moral actions, and in many instances more than he was, because placed in different and more favourable circumstances. I therefore think, that to represent, as some have done, the venerable parent of the human race as the greatest of all sinners, is an instance of the folly of hypothesis, and of shameful disrespect to the first of men, nor is it at all calculated to give glory to God his Creator. Josephus says well, that Moses spake philosophically concerning the fall of man, he meant I suppose figuratively. Many truths historical and moral were thus according to the eastern wisdom, given to the world by the ancient sages. To take the story literally, is to receive a fable without its moral, the account would be very lame and absurd. It is indeed a description of the triumph of passion over reason and conscience, and thus the birth of sin, misery, and death. Read the subject in this light, and it is intelligible, the imagery awfully sublime, well adapted and beautiful, and the moral in the highest degree impressive. Let our sons contemplate Adam, and our daughters their first mother, in their happy state of simple and satisfied nature, before the riotous passions began their wild uproar, before irregular desire awoke in their bosoms, before reason quitted her throne, and sensation assumed the sceptre. Then let them consider these parents of the world the victims of remorse, dissatisfaction, guilt and death. And let them fly with horror the pursuing and fascinating serpent, the first temptation to vice. Child of the dust! to taste is death. "Enter not into the path of the wicked, and go not in the way of evil men, avoid it, pass not by it, turn from it, and pass away."

I then proceeded to the examination of such other passages of Scripture, as I knew were advanced with a view to establish this doctrine of original sin. The next I considered was that awful one recorded in Gen. iv. 8, 9, the murder of Abel, the fruit of envy and revenge; but I hear the Creator exhorting Cain to do well, and promising him acceptance on that condition; and I read, Heb. xi. that Abel obtained witness that he was righteous: he believed and obeyed—"God testifying of his gifts;" yet both were the sons of the same parents, consequently both partook of the same nature. I supposed that both had the same moral capacity, and were therefore liable to the same degree of responsibility. I saw no difference in the brothers in the eye of God, beside moral difference evinced by their conduct; hence I concluded that not nature but habits made one brother a murderer and the other a righteous man. The next portion of Scripture I considered was the account of the moral state of the world before the flood—Gen. vi. 5, 11, &c. "And God saw that the wickedness of man was great upon the earth, and that every imagination of the thoughts of his heart was only evil continually. T before God, and with violence." This passage I knew was advanced as a stock text, to prove the radical and inherent corruption of human nature, derived from the fallen Adam; yet, while I admitted all this strong language, as giving a just description of universal degeneracy, of manners and corruption of hearts, I saw nothing in it to prove the original and radical corruption of nature; I knew that bad habits deprave the heart and imagination, and that if partial corruption of principles existed, universal corruption might also prevail, that men might become desperately wicked, that the voice of conscience might be stifled, and a moral death ensue. I knew that when men "like not to retain God in their knowledge," he might "give them over to a reprobate mind." I knew that "what may be known of God is nevertheless manifest in them," for "God hath shewed it to them." I knew that "the invisible things of him from the creation of the world (before and after the fall of man) are clearly seen being understood by the things that are made, even his eternal power and Godhead, so they are without excuse." I was convinced therefore that the Antediluvians could not lay their sins to the door of Adam, or their Creator, by pleading the original and radical corruption of their nature as the cause why "their foolish hearts were darkened, and every imagination evil continually." I found also that Noah was a preacher of righteousness, and a just man before God even in these bad times.

I read in Gen. viii. 2, that "the imagination of man's heart is evil from his youth," (not from his birth or nature,) a sad proof this of human frailty and the proneness of man to degenerate, like Adam, from that nature, at an early period of his existence. Accordingly this is assigned as a reason not for judgment, but for mercy, "I will not again curse the ground any more for man's sake, neither will I again smite any more, every living thing as I have done." I suppose the most ancient portion of the Bible except Genesis is the Book of Job. Some have quoted a passage in the fifteenth chapter of that poem, to prove the doctrine of the total depravity of nature. "What is man that he should be clean, or he who is born of a woman that he should be righteous, behold he (God) putteth no trust in his saints, yea, the heavens are not clean in his sight, how much more abominable and filthy is man who drinketh iniquity like water." Thus speaks Eliphaz, and the Lord said to Eliphaz the Temanite, "my wrath is kindled against thee, and against thy two friends, for ye have not spoken of me the thing that is right as my servant Job hath." Job xlii. 7. It would be therefore highly improper to exalt the reveries and dogmas of this man into the language of unerring revelation; but suppose his assertion to be strictly true, we are not attempting to disprove that all men are sinners, but to know whether all men are so by a necessity of nature, whether they are born one entire mass of moral corruption derived from Adam. If a man "drink iniquity like water," the poisoned beverage is no part of his nature, and to drink is a voluntary act. In this instance we have an old trite proverb verified.

The next passage I turned to, is read in Psalm li. 5. "Behold I was

shapen in iniquity, and in sin did my mother conceive me." I always thought that "sin was any transgression of or want of conformity to the law of God." I knew that this definition was totally inapplicable to the condition of a new born infant, or to the conception of a human being. I knew that God "made us and not we ourselves." I read Job x. 8, 12, that "God's hands had made and fashioned him, granted him life and favour, and that his visitation had preserved his spirit." I heard the same man asking (Job xxxi. 15,) concerning the poor slave, "did not he that made me in the womb, make him, and did not one fashion us in the womb?" I shuddered at the idea that God was the author of sin, I considered the situation of the man who used the language quoted in Psalm li. I supposed it to be David, an adulterer, a murderer, but an humble penitent, and I could not think that he was seeking to palliate the enormity of his crimes. I knew nothing of the character of his parents, but I supposed that all he derived from them, with his animal nature, were a human soul subject to constitutional frailty and strong passions, peculiarly prone to excess, peculiarly susceptible of certain impressions, which if not restrained by reason and conscience, were liable to carry him away from the path of rectitude. I read his history; I saw this man a potent and ambitious monarch, with a great soul, but I never saw him so great as when he humbled himself before God, and confessed, and forsook his sin. I was sure that he knew better than to excuse it by condemning the nature of his parents, much less the nature of man formed by that God "who fashioneth the hearts of men alike," who hath done whatsoever he pleased, "and whose tender mercies are over all his works."

In the strong, and figurative language of Eastern poetry, the Psalmist describes the constitutional weakness which plunged him into guilt, and he justly censures himself, but not his parents nor his God. I had not lived so long in the world, without observing that human beings constitutionally differed, that one man was heavy, phlegmatic, and stupid, a second sanguine, a third irritable, a fourth a mean, poor and timid animal, some were cold and barren spirits without capacity, and destitute of invention, that others were unable to compare two ideas together and draw a rational conclusion; that some were as destitute of memory as others of invention, I had seen idiots and creditors with good memories, and poets and debtors with none at all; I had seen souls of fire and souls of ice. Seriously, I accounted for the poetic imagery of David in Psalm li. from the depth of his guilt, the strength of his feelings, and the radical nature of his penitence, expressed in the figurative language of an highly wrought Eastern imagination.

I knew that there was nothing to be found in the sacred records which David possessed to justify the literal sense of his remark, a sense as contradictory to the tenor of his own writings as to reason. I could not therefore help rejecting that passage considered as a proof of the universal propagation of a radical and corrupt moral nature, derived from the first sinner or the imputation of his guilt to all his descendants. I turned over the pages of revelation till I came to Psalm lviii. 3. There I read that "the *wicked* are estranged from the womb, they go astray as soon as they be born, speaking lies." This passage I had heard frequently quoted to prove the universal and original depravity of the heart of human beings. I could not accept this as a proof of it; I knew that new born infants had no power to do good or evil, that they were incapable of a moral choice, that they were destitute of the faculty of speech, that they were too helpless to go astray, and that so far from speaking lies, they could not speak at all. I was free to admit that the children of the wicked might be corrupted in early life by the bad example of their parents, that they might go astray from nature and virtue, and thus be estranged from the womb, and I had been often grieved to see the direful contagion of vice spreading itself, like a fatal plague, infecting the very souls of youth and childhood. I had seen with terror lying, deceit, dishonesty, debauchery, villainy, pride, illiberality and hypocrisy, propagated in the heart's core of the rising generation, by the wickedness and folly of parents. But I was directed also, (blessed be

God for his goodness) to "train up a child in the way he should go," and was encouraged by the delightful hope that when he shall "come to be old, he will not depart from it."

I had seen that "a wise son useth his father's instruction and maketh a glad father," therefore I said "My son be wise and make my heart glad that I may answer him that reproaches me:" I said to my neighbour "correct thy son and he shall give thee rest, yea he shall give delight unto thy soul." I read Prov. x. 7, that the just man walketh in his integrity, his children are blessed after him,—that "even a child is known by his doings whether his work be pure and whether it be right," ver. 11. I read Psalm cxxxvii. that "Children are an heritage of the Lord, and the fruit of the womb is his reward." I knew who had said, "Suffer little children to come unto me and forbid them not, for of such is the kingdom of heaven." "Except ye be converted, and become as little children, ye shall not see the kingdom of heaven." I therefore began to think that they did not "as soon as they were born deserve God's wrath and eternal damnation."

I now looked around me with pleasure: I thought I had travelled through half my journey, that the prospect was clearing up, the clouds dispersing, light rising out of obscurity, the heart-cheering sun began to spread around me its life-nourishing beams; but a Reverend Gentleman quoted a passage in Jer. xvii. 9, on the deceitfulness of the heart: he asserted indeed that all who did not believe his explanation must be bad men; he seemed to glory in the baseness of his nature; he told me that the will, the conscience, the understanding, all the powers of the mind, and all the propensities of the heart of every man under the sun were by nature deceitful above all things, and desperately wicked; he added that whoever denied this fact, proved it by the very denial! I read the passage, and context. There I found, Jer. xvii. 1, that "the sin of Judah is written with a pen of iron, and with the point of a diamond, graven upon the table of their hearts, and upon the horns of the altar." I saw that the man whose heart departs from the Lord and trusts in man shall be like the heath of the desert, inhabiting the parched places of the wilderness, where falls no dew, no former nor latter rain, whose sandy plain yields no nourishment, produces no green thing, and no seed for the support of the famished traveller, no spring, no purling brook to quench his thirst, where only the dry and worthless sand moss, "the heath of the desert," preserved the semblance of vegetation,—like that moss, he shall never partake of the gentle dew from heaven, nor of the blessings of the fertile earth, "he shall not see when good cometh." I saw that sinners were ingenious to deceive themselves and others: I saw that the heart of Judah with sin engraved upon it thus must be deeply and desperately wicked, and that the altars upon which sin in its blackest colours was written (altars consecrated to idols) "whilst their children remembered them, and their groves by the green trees upon the high hills," where they worshipped Baal and Moloch and the Queen of heaven, must be an abomination in the sight of God, "who searches the heart, and tries the reins, even to give every man according to his ways, and according to the fruit of his doings." I might err, I was not infallible, my heart might deceive me, but I sought evidence, I think I was not influenced either by hope or fear to reject this passage, like the rest that went before it, as wholly inconclusive testimony when produced to witness the universal, radical, original and moral corruption of human nature.

I went on, I opened the New Testament, I read Christ's Sermon on the Mount: there I found every thing to prove that man was a frail, sinful mortal, but not a vessel filled by nature to the very brim with moral corruption, made under the wrath and curse of God. I read of the pure in heart, of the merciful, of inherent righteousness, of a righteousness that must be produced, very far beyond that of the Scribes and Pharisees, to fit a man for the kingdom of heaven. I read of attainable perfection, of a good tree producing good fruit, and a corrupt tree evil fruit: I read of doing the will of God, and hearing, and doing the sayings of Jesus Christ, that the wise man built his house upon *this* rock. I read John ix. of a blind man restored to sight by Jesus Christ, and was surprised to hear the disciples asking him "whether this man had

sinned or his parents that he was born blind," but I wondered not at all, at Christ's answer, "Neither hath this man sinned nor his parents." I read of evil thoughts and evil deeds proceeding out of the heart of man, and I knew that nothing upon earth besides could produce them.

I heard the human heart described, Matt. xii. 35, as a treasury. "A good man out of the good treasure of his heart bringeth forth good things, and an evil man out of the evil treasure of his heart bringeth forth evil things." I read in the parable of the sower, Luke xv. of seed "sown in the good ground of an honest and good heart." I saw the man Jesus, the son of Adam, Abraham, Judah, David, Manasseh, one of the wickedest tyrants that ever lived, and traced among his ancestors many great sinners, and I was sure that he derived *his* nature from his parents, yet I believed that he was "without sin," touched with a feeling of our infirmities, tempted in all points as we are, our brother, partaker of our flesh and blood. Here a good old lady interrupted me; she said that she was satisfied of the existence of corrupt nature, because infants cry when they are born! Good old lady! If you could be literally born a second time, and have all your teeth to cut over again, you would cry too, but they evince passion before they can speak; yes, they are not blocks of marble, they have nerves and feel, they express their sense of uneasiness, hunger, cold and pain: blind puppies, too, whine from the same causes; but if you cannot distinguish between the natural expression of animal feeling, want, and passion, and original sin, neither probably do you see the difference between a sinner and a fool by nature, an unhappy circumstance, which will effectually prevent us from plunging together into this deep subject.

I certainly found nothing in the Old Testament to support this doctrine; but I am again interrupted. A philosophical Calvinist, one of the rational brethren, who accounts for every thing, came forward with his text, "He answered and said, verily, no one can bring a clean thing out of an unclean," Job xiv. 4, and context. "Certainly not, therefore God will not require more of such a creature, than he is capable of performing, nor cause him to suffer more than is necessary and salutary." "His days are determined, the number of his months are with thee, thou hast appointed his bounds that he cannot pass, turn from him that he may accomplish as an hireling his day." Corrupt nature, he replied, is produced by natural generation, for all men existed in Adam, and all fell in him. So then, may it please your reverence, moral evil is propagated, like the king's evil. I thought a flame nourished by fœtid oil, and glimmering in a dirty lamp, might kindle a thousand gems of light, as pure as the flame of an altar produced by the lightning of heaven. I had no conception before that moral qualities were animal secretions. I read the four Gospels, not a word nor a hint did I find in them to countenance this strange opinion of corrupt nature, but much, completely to destroy it. Man is addressed there as a free moral agent, and as an accountable being; his reason and conscience are addressed, his sins are laid at the door of his inclinations, "Why do ye not of yourselves judge that which is right;" — "men love darkness rather than light, because their *deeds* are evil;" "ye will not come to me;" "every one that doeth evil hateth the light neither cometh to the light, lest his deeds should be reproved, but he that doeth truth cometh to the light, that his deeds may be made manifest that they are wrought in God." "The hour is coming when all that are in their graves shall hear the voice of Jesus Christ, and shall come forth, they that have done good unto the resurrection of life, and they that have done evil to the resurrection of damnation." "If thou wilt enter into life, keep the commandments." Thus our Lord taught, nor could I reconcile these truths with the unaccountable doctrine of radical, total, universal, moral corruption. I examined the Book of Acts: there I saw nothing about the fall of man, nothing about corrupt nature, though I read much of the wickedness of the world, of the sin of idolatry, many exhortations to faith and repentance, and the practice of righteousness. I heard Paul addressing the reason and consciences of his hearers, at Lycaonia, at Athens, at Ephesus, at Jerusalem, and at Rome. Yes, he *reasoned* with them

out of the Scriptures, he told them that "forasmuch as we are the offspring of God in whom we live, move, and have our being, we ought not to think that the Godhead is like unto gold or silver, or stone graven by art, and men's device, that God overlooked the times of ignorance but now commandeth all men every where to repent." I thought that if some had preached to these Heathen they would have begun with the total depravity of human nature, as the cause of all their idolatry and vices; that they would have shewn them the need of a Saviour by teaching their utter helplessness as dead sinners; that they would have taught them that they had no hearts to understand and obey the gospel; and that therefore it was in vain to preach it to them, that such sinners have no business with it, and that in consequence (the consistency of these people is complete) they have no Christ to offer them.

Others more inconsistently would teach them the universal corruption of nature by the fall, and yet spur on these dead sinners to faith, repentance, and all the moral duties enjoined by Jesus Christ; that, instead of God's "winking at" (overlooking) the ignorance of these idolaters in times past, they were all born so ignorant and sottishly opposed to the true God, as to be by nature not the objects of his forbearance but of his abhorrence; that it was yet their duty to love this God, and to serve him perfectly, which as they neither could, nor would do, they must perish everlastingly; yet if they believed and did what they by nature could not believe and do, they might be saved; that somehow or other there is a natural ability, and a moral inability, both arising out of nature as it now is, but that his moral inability is total, and universal, completely preventing all men from taking a step in the narrow road that leads to life; that even the will and choice are by nature wholly blind, and corrupt, so that no man can choose what is good, though his judgment may perceive it. I thought if Paul had believed all this he would not have preached as he is recorded to have done.

I now proceeded to examine the apostolic writings: I read in Paul's Epistles an awful description of the state of the world, at the time of our

Lord's appearance, but I did not see that he complained of nature but of the abuse of it. He tells us that when men knew God, they glorified him not as God neither were thankful. He taught that all had sinned, and all needed mercy: he shews to what an extent vice prevailed among the idolatrous Gentiles, and superstitious and bigoted Jews. He says nevertheless, that "man is the image and glory of God." 1 Cor. xi. 7. He tells us that glory, honour and peace shall be to every man that worketh good, that when the Gentiles who have not the law do *by nature* the things contained in the law, these having not the law are a law unto themselves, their consciences also bearing witness, and their thoughts the mean while accusing or else excusing one another: and I thought that these facts were wholly subversive of the doctrine of original, universal and total depravity. I read of the reconciliation of sinners to God, of the carnal mind, of the works of the flesh, and of men dead in trespasses and sins, and that in this state the people at Ephesus, and the Jews among the rest, were by nature the children of wrath even as others in similar circumstances: I was certain that a man destitute of revealed religion, and one whose morals had been neglected, would grow up a savage, a victim to numberless evil passions, and I was not surprised to hear Paul describing the condition of the Jews as not being much better than that of the Gentiles "fulfilling the desires of the flesh and of the mind," for I had read their history, and did not doubt that a state of uncultivated nature would produce this evil fruit: I saw an instance of it in Adam, I read of sin entering into the world by one man and death by sin, and that by one man's disobedience many were made sinners. I knew that the carnal mind was enmity against God: I had seen and felt it to be so; I had suffered by it, and I thought that if men were less carnally minded, they would not be so ready to find excuses for their sins, be more humble before God, and not plead their nature as an hardened criminal pleads an *alibi*. I thought that this would be but a poor excuse at the day of judgment: I knew that where bad habits and the love of sin governed the heart, men were dead to

God and righteousness. I thought of that passage in Jer. xiii. 23—"Can the Ethiopian change his skin, or the leopard his spots? then may ye also do well that are accustomed to do evil." I knew that the first man was the first sinner, and that death entered by sin. I doubted not that many became or were made sinners by this man's disobedience, that his posterity were exposed to a thousand natural evils, and consequently temptations to the commission of moral evil, which would never have existed had Adam never transgressed. I saw that men were naturally prone to wander from God; the conduct of our first parents proved that they were; therefore I was the less astonished at the abounding wickedness and folly of mankind. "Lo, this only have I found, that God hath made man upright; but they have sought out many inventions." Eccles. vii. 29. I read through the Epistles, but I could find nothing in them to countenance the doctrine of a nature universally, totally, and radically corrupt. Nothing in Paul, nothing in Peter, James and John, not omitting Jude.

I wondered with great astonishment! Where could this doctrine originate? I thought it began in the synagogue, that it was a refinement upon the Braminical doctrine of the metempsychosis: I suspected that the apostles were tainted with this error till better taught by Jesus Christ, or why did they ask that strange question—John ix. 2. I traced it to Africa, to Europe, to the Vatican, to Lambeth Palace, to the convocation, to the synod;—I saw original sin approaching me in the habit of the holy office, an inquisitor of the order of St. Dominic, I bowed not, but I thought it high time to retire. SIGMA.

Sir, *August* 12, 1816.
UPON perusing with usual interest the last Number of your valuable Repository, I was sensibly affected by the indirect information contained in page 386, (and the more official intelligence page 392), that the proposal of Mr. Rutt for a New Edition of Dr. Priestley's Theological Works is languishing for want of sufficient support from the Unitarian public. Allow me to state that when I first became acquainted with the proposal, by means

of the Repository, I experienced the genuine pleasure which results from the contemplation of the noble and dignified character of Dr. Priestley, and the probability that by this additional means the world would become still better acquainted with his excellencies, and still more enlightened by his serious and sagacious investigation into true religion. From that period to the present I have had little opportunity of learning what progress might be made towards the accomplishment of the design, except by the occasional hints which have been given in the Repository. Confiding in the high sense which is so generally and deservedly maintained among us of Dr. Priestley's religious and theological character, I had continued to cherish the expectation that the plan would ere long be in actual preparation, and had on various occasions contributed, I venture to say, to excite the interest I felt myself in the minds of others.—Let it not be supposed that I am induced to occupy your present attention by the selfish feeling of disappointment in my individual and anxious hope. I have no doubt whatever that the information which your last Number contained has produced similar regret in the breasts of many of your readers; and whether they adopt the same plan as myself, are ready to pronounce sentence upon that *indifference* to which alone the possible failure of such an object among us can be owing. Happy should I be if by any thing which I can offer, in conjunction with the appropriate suggestions of your worthy Correspondent in your last Number, such feelings may be inspired into the breasts of our *young laymen*, as may place the projected plan beyond the probability of failure.

There are *four classes* of persons to whom we might appeal for assistance in the publication of the new edition of Dr. Priestley's Works.—The *respectable laymen* in our connexion, who duly prize the importance of rational information on religious subjects; the *ministers of some standing*, who have had much experience in the prevalent opinion, and have learned duly to estimate these Works, which have been so great a means in the hands of Providence of contributing to the reformation which is going on; the *young ministers*, who have been taught indeed to make the Bible their chief book of theology, but are aware how much they are indebted to Dr. Priestley for the present improved principles of theological education; and lastly, the *sons of our respectable laymen*, many of whom, I doubt not, have the cause of rational religion at heart, and who are from time to time collecting those books by which they will store their minds with the most valuable materials for future reflection and meditation.

With respect to the first class, many have Dr. Priestley's Works already in their possession; and though probably a fair proportion of the hundred subscribers which have hitherto been procured, are from this class, yet it is not perhaps from them that the prosecution of the object may be expected. The second class have probably nearly all the Theological and Miscellaneous Works of Dr. Priestley in their present collection; and as a superfluity of money can seldom fall to their lot, their personal contribution would hardly secure the plan under consideration. The third class, or young ministers, no doubt feel peculiar interest in the object under consideration; but of these, the greater proportion, having it may be but recently surmounted the difficulties of an expensive education, however they could wish it, are not in a condition to spare the ten or eleven guineas out of their scanty salaries. The object devolves then pretty much upon the fourth class, consisting of the sons of respectable and wealthy laymen, to whom the expense, divided probably into two or three years, can be no hinderance whatever, and who would by their assistance, have a most excellent opportunity of testifying their concern for the religious welfare of their fellow men. This appeal is not made to those young men, who, attracted by the false glare of fashion, are, to the unspeakable regret of their families, in danger of forsaking those principles and that cause, which their fathers after much patient investigation, and severe sacrifices of family consideration, have nobly supported: such can hardly be expected to lend their helping hand to the cause of virtue and truth:—the appeal is more to the truly interesting (and it is hoped numerous) class of young persons, who, blessed with the means of benevolent exertion and with the inestimable blessing of a liberal education, have conceived a deep interest in the religion of Jesus, soberly and rationally explained—who have derived from the perusal of the Bible, and the works which are calculated to illustrate and authenticate its contents, the utmost improvement and delight, and who have resolved to devote a part of their leisure time in extending their acquaintance with such productions:—to these the appeal is made in favour of the proposed edition of Dr. Priestley's Works, and it is ardently hoped it will not be made in vain.

Two or three trivial objections have been made to the Proposal in the course of my conversation; and as these may possibly prevent some of your readers from yielding to the natural impulse of generous feeling, it may be well to bestow upon each a passing consideration.

1. There may be and probably are some copies of the larger Theological Works on hand; but this is no real objection to the proposed edition. This must have been the case with Dr. Lardner's Works, which consist almost entirely of two or three principal works; and yet happily for the celebrity of that useful critic, and for the progress of theological science in general, this was considered no sufficient obstacle to Dr. Kippis's edition. The fact is, that a great proportion of the eighteen volumes which it is computed Dr. Priestley's Works will occupy, would be made up of the smaller publications, many of which are little if any thing inferior in importance to the larger works; and many of these are almost inaccessible:—this is particularly the case with one of the most valuable, " The Letters to a Philosophical Unbeliever." The consequence of the new edition will be a reduction in the price of the former ones, which will thus become accessible to that interesting class of the community—men who, amid the daily toils for their subsistence, find time to ruminate on the grand truths of religion, and whose minds are often more enlightened on these subjects, than many of those who are favoured with a higher place in the scale of society. Every suitable exertion should certainly be made to secure the efforts of such persons who labour to convey to those of their own rank a knowledge of the truth as it is in Jesus.

2. Are there not some of Dr. Priestley's theological writings which partake rather of the nature of ingenious conjecture, than of sound and mature investigation? And would it be advisable, when the Christian world is so extensively combined in warfare against our little (but daily increasing) band, to place in their way any of those parts, of the Doctor's writings, which may have already afforded occasion for our opponents to cavil? If the objection had not been actually made, it would not have been deemed deserving of consideration in this connexion. Your present Correspondent, Sir, has learned too highly to prize Dr. Priestley's excellencies both of heart and head, to entertain any apprehensions of the general effect that would arise from a perusal of his works. Let a man of ordinary understanding do this with candour and seriousness, and I pronounce it impossible that he should rise from the employment without being a much wiser and better man than he was before. The state of the case is indeed this: occasion has been taken to revile Dr. Priestley's character, and to shudder at the thought of giving him a place in company with others of considerable name, (but in reality vastly inferior to him[*]), from a very partial acquaintance with his writings, and the unjustifiable selection (according to the too common practice of orthodox men) of a few passages out of their connection, upon which they found their erroneous and unjust conclusions. Present the whole of the Doctor's gigantic labours in morals and religion before the eyes of the discerning public, and no other refutation will be needed of the vile clamours so industriously circulated. The candid will be struck with the piety and intelligence evinced in his numerous productions; the bigot will be suffused with shame from a comparison of his own littleness; and the fair fame of Priestley burst from the ignoble chains in which she is at present confined, and soar aloft amidst the general shout of admiration and gratitude.

---

[*] " Who, that was not bent on giving his system popularity and *eclat*, would ever have thought of classing together in the same theological list the names of Dr. Isaac Watts and Dr. Joseph Priestley? Have there existed two men antipodes in religious sentiment and religious feeling, these are the two."—*Wardlaw's Unitarianism incapable of Vindication.*

The only remaining objection that I know of, arises from the depression to which trade is at present subject.

If the appeal in this letter had been made to the lower classes of the community, it is admitted the objection would have had its force. If it had been made solely to our laymen of easy fortunes, but who have themselves families to provide for, and whose benevolent hearts deeply commiserate the sad condition of the poor around them, there would still perhaps be some appearance of reason :—but the appeal is made, as before stated, to the young men of fortune either in or out of trade who have yet little of the cares of the world, who have just passed through their elementary education, whose minds are deeply impressed with the value and efficacy of truth, and who can easily spare a small portion of their spending money, to the promotion of the noble object which is now contemplated. To such of our body, all who feel interested in the progress of our plans for improvement in knowledge and religion, must look with the utmost confidence. The preachers who are successively educated in our seminaries, may raise their voices in the support of truth, they may contribute by their labours in public and private to the respectability of the cause; but after all, their success will very much depend upon their lay brethren who possess wealth to strengthen the hands of their ministers, and give them their sanction and assistance. If any such, influenced by these friendly and well-intended suggestions, should come forwards to raise this monument to the memory of one who laboured incessantly for the young in particular, to contribute their individual efforts to rescue eminent talents from abuse and calumny, to dissipate the mists of prejudice, bigotry and superstition which envelope the religious atmosphere,—happy will the writer of this letter deem himself to be, and fully compensated for the little trouble which it has occasioned him ; though this has been already sufficiently rewarded by the mere prospect of the disinterested efforts which he has now contemplated.

I am, Sir, with best wishes for the success of your very useful Repository,

A SUBSCRIBER OF THE
THIRD CLASS,

The Gipsies.

[From the Liverpool Freeman ; or Weekly Magazine. Price 6d. No. 6. Aug 6, 1816.]

OF late years some attempts have been made to reduce the numbers or at any rate to civilize the habits, of that vagabond and useless race, the Gipsies. In pursuance of such purpose, a society of gentlemen have been making all the preliminary inquiries requisite to a proper understanding of the subject. A series of questions have been proposed to competent persons in the different counties of England and Scotland ; and answers have been received. Our readers will, we think, be amused with the following specimen of these answers :—

1. All Gipsies suppose the first of them came from Egypt.

2. They cannot form any idea of the number in England.

3. The Gipsies of Bedfordshire, Hertfordshire, parts of Buckinghamshire, Cambridge and Huntingdonshire, are continually making revolutions within the ranges of those counties.

4. They are either ignorant of the number of Gipsies in the counties through which they travel, or unwilling to disclose their knowledge.

5. The most common names are Smith, Cooper, Draper, Taylor, Boswell, Lee, Lovell, Loversedge, Allen, Mansfield, Glover, Williams, Carew, Martin, Stanley, Buckley, Plunkett, and Corrie.

6 and 7. The gangs in different towns have not any regular connexion or organization ; but those who take up their winter quarters in the same city or town appear to have some knowledge of the different routes each horde will pursue ; probably with a desire to prevent interference.

8. In the county of Herts it is computed there may be sixty families having many children. Whether they are quite so numerous in Buckinghamshire, Bedfordshire, and Northamptonshire, the answers are not sufficiently definite to determine. In Cambridgeshire, Oxfordshire, Warwickshire, Wiltshire, and Dorsetshire, greater numbers are calculated upon. In various counties, the attention has not been competent to the procuring data for any estimate of families or individuals.

9. More than half their number follow no business: others are dealers in horses and asses: farriers, smiths, tinkers, braziers, grinders of cutlery, basket-makers, chair-bottomers, and musicians.

10. Children are brought up in the habits of their parents, particularly to music and dancing, and are of dissolute conduct.

11. The women mostly carry baskets with trinkets and small wares; and tell fortunes.

12. Too ignorant to have acquired accounts of genealogy, and perhaps indisposed by the irregularity of their habits.

13. In most counties there are particular situations to which they are partial. In Berkshire is a marsh, near Newbury, much frequented by them; and Dr. Clarke states, that in Cambridgeshire, their principal rendezvous is near the western villages.

14. It cannot be ascertained whether, from their first coming into the nation, attachment to particular places has prevailed.

15, 16, and 17. When among strangers, they elude inquiries respecting their peculiar language, calling it gibberish. Don't know of any person that can write it, or of any written specimen of it.

18. Their habits and customs in all places are peculiar.

19. Those who profess any religion represent it to be that of the country in which they reside: but their description of it seldom goes beyond repeating the Lord's Prayer; and only few of them are capable of that. Instances of their attending any place for worship are very rare.

20. They marry for the most part by pledging to each other, without any ceremony. A few exceptions have occurred when money was plentiful.

21. They do not teach their children religion.

22 and 23. Not *one in a thousand* can read.

Sir,   *Exeter, Aug.* 7, 1816.

I HOPED to have had no further occasion to engage the attention of yourself, or your readers, to the subject of my former paper, (p. 264;) but your Correspondent's reply in the last Number of your estimable Repository, (p. 390,) seems to require my

taking notice of some of his statements; in doing which I shall endeavour to be as brief as the subject admits.

To expose to the world the failings of a fellow-creature, must necessarily prove a painful task to a benevolent mind; but publicly to advance, or even insinuate, a charge of *immorality* against an individual unable to defend himself, without substantiating such allegation, appears to me a procedure altogether unwarrantable. Your Correspondent, however, seems to me placed in this awkward predicament, by his unnecessary and unproved insinuation against the Count. The injurious reflection he threw out in his first paper, I am sorry to find reiterated by him, after what had been advanced by myself. Since what he regards as evidence is not produceable in a work designed for general readers, why advert to so ungrateful a topic at all? Christian charity, not to mention justice, would in my opinion have here dictated silence. But your Correspondent assigns the following reason for his insinuation to the prejudice of the Count. "I considered it my duty, to guard the memories of such men as Watts and Doddridge, from the imputation of an unqualified approbation of Count Zinzendorf." A strange mode of acting this, to exalt one character by depreciating another! But whoever regarded the Count with unqualified admiration? That he was a great and good man I have no doubt, but he had his defects and weaknesses; and in persons of his ardent cast of mind they are always most prominent.

In reference to the religious poems to which your Correspondent alludes, (for they were *not* used as *hymns*,) let me inform him that scarcely any had the Count for their author; and, as already noticed, as soon as he perceived that they were open to misrepresentation, he checked their further circulation. Yet even these poems, objectionable as their original phraseology is, become far more so in Rimius's hands; and I affirm cannot be justly appreciated from his exhibition of them: his illegitimate renderings, and utter neglect of the connexion in which the passages quoted by him stand, necessarily preclude his work from implicit credit. Permit me, Sir, to add, that the only clue to a just exposition of such phraseology, is to be found in an intimate acquaintance with the theological and moral views of Count Zinzendorf and the brethren of that day. Such phraseology, though open to abuse, was, however, I am warranted in affirming, only employed in a spiritual sense by the brethren themselves, and I am satisfied, from experience and observation, gave rise amongst them to no other than the purest ideas and emotions. Had the excellent Jortin been aware of this circumstance, however he might reprehend "such language, he would have refrained from implicating in his censure the *character* of the Count.

But I am blamed by your Correspondent for not having verified my allegations against Rimius; in answer permit me to adopt his own words: " I did not conceive such a discussion adapted to a work designed for general readers." Your Correspondent and myself are here placed in similar circumstances; however with one material difference: my estimate of Rimius's work appeared necessary, whereas your Correspondent's attack on the Count's character may be considered optional. That I may not however be thought to have advanced charges wholly without foundation, I shall take the liberty of adverting to one instance amongst others of Rimius's unfairness, would I could say incapacity, as a translator: the example I select is his unjustifiable rendering of the German termination *lein* by *little*, instead of *dear* or *precious*; as in the words *laemlein, wundlein*; the literal rendering of these words is I admit *little lamb, little wound*; but the connexion in which they stand, plainly pointed out to Rimius that they ought to be translated *precious lamb, precious wound*; Christ and his sufferings being the theme, and the brethren of that time being in the habit of using that termination to express *holy endearment*. Thus a translator, deficient in ability, or in rectitude, may pervert an author's meaning without infringing any grammatical rules.*

---

* In my last paper I noticed the line of conduct the brethren thought proper to adopt, with regard to Rimius's publication; though your Correspondent seems

Your Correspondent tells his readers, that my appeal to the case of Dr. Gill " has very little, if any connexion with the subject;" but let me notwithstanding, still adduce it a well calculated to confirm my position, viz. that there is no necessary connexion between impropriety of language and impropriety of thought and feeling; though I would decidedly protest against the use of any such language myself. On this account cannot approve of your Correspondent's use of the word *amatory*, where *divine love* is the subject, because that word being usually expressive of *sensual attachment*, will be thus associated in the mind.

The compliment paid by your Correspondent, to the brethren of the present day, at the expense of their esteemed predecessors, will I apprehend scarcely be accepted by them.

It remains for me only to apologize for the length of this paper, and in conclusion (to avail myself once more of your Correspondent's words) will say that " I am not aware that I ought to trouble him, or any of your readers, further on the disagreeable subject which has very unexpectedly been forced on my attention," but which a sense of duty prompted me to undertake, in behalf of an esteemed individual, whose character I consider unjustly aspersed.

With every sentiment of regard,
J. T. B.

On the Divine Government.

SIR,

I FEAR that I do not fully understand your Correspondent, *An Old Inquirer*,† in the Repository for June (p. 322,) who animadverts upon the first scheme of Divine Providence to have overlooked what I there said, for he observes, " Crantz and La Trobe have left it unimpeached." As *historians*, an answer to that work did not fall within their province, had they been so inclined; but I will inform him that he may find full, and I think according to the Count's view of Bible truth, a satisfactory reply to all the charges brought against him, a quarto volume published in the German language about the year 1754.

† It will have been seen that the Correspondent has ceased from his labours and fallen into his place in our *Obituary*, p. 487. ED.

without touching upon the second, (p. 74,) which I should have presumed would have had his approbation.

If we admit the existence of God, as the Creator of all things, I think it will follow as an unavoidable consequence, that all lifeless matter that he has formed must obey the laws with which it is impressed, and that therefore not an atom is to be found, which did not necessarily occupy the station and perform the office for which it was appointed. I mean when such atom has not been acted upon or influenced by living existence. So far we seem to proceed, without the intervention of hypothesis, upon grounds absolutely certain, taking for granted only, that matter and its laws were created and made by an intelligent being. If *An Old Inquirer* deem this a gratuitous hypothesis, namely, that intelligent being created all matter, and impressed it with its laws, I confess it to be an hypothesis—but one, which seems not only reasonable, but what is now generally admitted. So far then, as lifeless matter is concerned, I think we need not enter upon any farther illustration. A vast class of living beings, which we do not deem rational and moral agents, next invite our inquiry, the birds in the air, the fishes in the sea, and the innumerable irrational animals on the earth. The question then will be, do these ever act, or can they act, in contrariety to the laws to which their Creator has subjected them? Have they independent powers, or do they necessarily follow the laws of their nature? For it will not, cannot be denied that they are created subject to certain laws. They have feeling, feel pleasure and pain, and necessarily avoid the one and choose the other. Their actions, are they the simple result of those feelings, or have they a liberty of self-determination? In as far as we can judge from observation, they appear to follow their feelings simply, for we cannot perceive that they have any thing to oppose to these feelings. We kill the tyger because he destroys us, not because in so doing, we imagine him to abuse his liberty and act contrary to his nature. All the actions of these immense tribes of animals, if they be the simple result of the laws of their nature, and not

the effect of independent powers, are therefore as much the appointment of God, as the place and action of every atom of lifeless matter. We may be confounded by the variety of effect, and wonder how any mind could comprehend such a vast machinery; but we are no less confounded by the powers of creation. Thus then all matter and its effects, and all animals which we see, and their actions, are of divine appointment, or the necessary effects of creating power; except indeed the actions of men, which must now be examined.

Either man is governed in his whole conduct by the fixed laws of his nature, or he is emphatically free in all his voluntary conduct—there is no middle supposition which is tenable, and under these opposite suppositions, the greatest names have arranged themselves in argument and disputation. I presume not to determine the question, but only to reason upon the consequences of either supposition. If man then be an agent perfectly free in all his voluntary conduct, it will follow that he possesses a power from his Creator, which he exerts at pleasure, concerning the effect of which nothing can be predicated. Whatever evils men occasion by their voluntary conduct, and whatever good, is ascribable to them, and not to their Creator.

If God formed the first male and female with such powers, then he appointed not the existence of the human race, for it depended upon their voluntary co-operation whether the race should proceed. God gave the powers, the use or abuse of them belongs only to man. According to this reasoning, the maximum of happiness and misery may be fixed; but whatever of happiness or misery be the effect of the voluntary powers of men, as these are free and independent powers, are not of divine appointment, but arrange themselves under Dr. Paley's scheme of chance. Whatever sufferings come upon brute animals, by the voluntary conduct of man, as it was not foreseen or appointed, is not resolvable into the will of God. This supposition places man in an awful situation, and he cannot but wish that the first pair had died without issue.

On the opposite supposition that

the actions of man, are the necessary result of his nature and circumstances, he has the consolation of a less tremendous responsibility, but then it is in contradiction to all the general systems of religion.

AN INQUIRER.

P. S. I will take the liberty of adding a few remarks upon Dr. Paley's Scheme of Chance. He says that there may be chance in the midst of design; two men travelling by design between London and York, meet by accident, or chance, on the road. Here is chance in the midst of design. This principle must be admitted to its full extent, when human design only is contemplated. Thus the consequences of nine tenths of the actions of men are consequences of chance. No man by design injures his circumstances, few by design injure their health, thus every man's death nearly, is by chance. Very few men when they marry design children, this is not their motive or design, therefore, every man's birth is by chance. There is according to this scheme, very little that affects the being or happiness of sensible beings the effect of design. And this is perfectly agreeable to my second scheme of the Divine government, which is the only doctrine consistent with the philosophical free agency of man, and which, as it excludes foreknowledge of effect from the Deity completely as to whatever relates to man in this world, excludes also effective design. God wills that if men are born, they should possess a definite organization, and be subject to certain general circumstances, and there the design of the Deity stops. Their future, not their present destination, depends entirely on his will, and if there be either justice or goodness in it, must be as various as the variety of human character. This is Dr. Paley's doctrine of chance, and seems to be agreeable to appearances, and the common apprehensions of mankind.

Every middle scheme is a system of confusion and contradiction, or of constant miracle, so that there appears to be no alternative between Paley's Chance, and Hobbes's Necessity. This is the full extent of my assertion, I meddle not with the question as to which scheme is the true one.

Newington Green,
SIR,   *September* 10*th,* 1816.

I OFFER a few remarks on a communication in your last Number, (p. 448), respecting the Greek Article, but without the smallest intention of stepping in between your Correspondent and Dr. Charles Lloyd. I have not the least doubt that a gentleman of the Doctor's learning can "prove to demonstration that the Deity of Christ is not to be inferred by any right application of the Article to passages in the New Testament;" and shall be glad to see such proof in the Monthly Repository or in a separate publication.

Your respectable Correspondent will not, I trust, be offended with my remarks on some parts of his letter. His object seems to be useful knowledge, and therefore I presume that my notice of his communication will be as well received as it is well intended. "The Article (your Correspondent remarks) is only an index." I thought so when I wrote the following sentence in *Reason the Arbiter of Language:* "*This* and *that* are merely two *indexes* or *pointers,* such as we often see on way-posts or buildings to direct the eye to some object, and which are properly printed as a *hand,* because they supply its place. So *that* or *this* supplies the place of a *hand,* or rather of a *finger,* and was originally nothing but its name." Such was my opinion at that time: whether I invented or borrowed it I cannot now ascertain; but I recollect well that even then the nature and origin of the *parts of speech* had cost me much hard thinking and tiresome searching. But on further inquiry (and, I trust, clearer, deeper reflection), I was compelled (somewhat reluctantly, for I had published an opinion), by what I deemed convincing evidence, to abandon the idea of *index,* and proclaim the fallibility of my understanding. The final decision of my erring judgment is expressed very fully in *Philosophic Etymology.* If your Correspondent will favour my Work with a perusal, he will find that my opinion coincides with that of Aristotle and that of Dr. Middleton at the same time. In representing the Greek as having no resemblance to the English Article, indeed I suspect the Doctor knew not what he said nor whereof he affirmed. He was right in saying that the Greek Article is the pronoun relative 'ο; but he would have been equally right had he said that the relative pronoun is the Article. The terms *relative* and *article* seem both to have originated in just conception.

Your Correspondent remarks:—"though it be granted that 'o was originally a pronoun, it is no more a pronoun now than it is a verb or adjective." Dugald Stewart employs similar language in his remarks upon the Diversions of Purley, which I do not wonder at; but I would submit to the re-consideration of your Correspondent, whether such language be suited to rigorous inquiry and just conception. The question of any importance, is not what technical names have been applied to 'o' but what it is. What is its nature or use? Will your Correspondent have the goodness to explain what a pronoun or a verb is? I can assure him the question is not captious, for if he can give a simpler, more intelligible and satisfactory account of these matters than I have endeavoured to give, he shall have my best and sincerest thanks. "The Monthly Reviewer (it is said) has justly maintained the superiority of the English over the Greek in precision, by the means of the indefinite—*an*—in combination with the definitive." But I suspect if the Monthly Reviewer were asked this simple question—what is the definite or what is the indefinite article? he would not give a very ready or very intelligible answer. What is called the definite article has no necessary connection with *definiteness*; and what is absurdly called the indefinite article is merely a varied spelling and pronunciation of the numeral *one.*

There is a gentleman with whose remarks on these subjects I should be extremely glad to see your pages enriched, for I consider his understanding of a much higher order than that of either the mere linguist or the mere metaphysician. He has only to think as freely, clearly and profoundly on philology, as on Philosophical Necessity, to render important services to true grammar and sound logic. He has with much candour (I ought perhaps to say generosity after the poignancy of some of my strictures) acknowledged that I have successfully illustrated several obscure points; and if he will point out some of the more essential particulars wherein I may have failed

in developing the principles of language satisfactorily, I trust that I shall treat his remarks with becoming respect.

He may have more reverence for scholastic authority than I can admire, but I feel confident that he will be at the trouble of understanding my meaning, though I fear much that some of my readers will resemble those alluded to in the following sentence: "When men have once acquiesced in untrue opinions, and registered them as authentical records in their minds, it is no less impossible to speak intelligibly (or convincingly) to them, than to write legibly upon a paper already scribbled over." Unfortunately for useful learning and true science, the minds of many teachers are scribbled over with school-boy nonsense; but as the judicious Locke justly remarks: "It is not strange that methods of learning which scholars have been accustomed to in their beginning and entrance upon the sciences, should influence them all their lives, and be settled in their minds by an overruling reverence, especially if they be such as universal use has established. Learners must at first be believers, and their master's rules having been once made axioms to them, it is no wonder they should keep that dignity, and, by the authority they have once got, mislead those, who think it sufficient to excuse them, if they go out of their way in a well beaten tract. And when fashion hath once established what folly began, custom makes it sacred, and it will be thought impudence or madness to contradict or question it."

If I have not already occupied too much of the room allotted in the Repository to communications of this nature, I should be glad to have some queries inserted in reference to a subject which has received some notice in your pages, hoping that some of your readers will be induced to reply to them.

What are the principal advantages and disadvantages of the different forms of *government*? Wherein consists true national prosperity? Is the doctrine of Malthus an insurmountable obstacle to the perfectibility or *improvableness* to any great degree of human society? In other words, are vice and misery necessary to keep population down to the level of the means of subsistence?

Are private vices public benefits? In other words, is what is called a great, powerful and flourishing state of society, necessarily corrupt or vicious? What are the advantages and disadvantages of foreign commerce? What are the advantages and disadvantages of luxury—of the fine arts—of large towns—of immense fortunes—of hereditary wealth and titles—of abridging labour by machinery, &c. &c.? Have public amusements, as the theatre, the opera, &c. a good or bad tendency? Have works of *fiction*, as plays, novels, poesies, &c. a good or bad tendency? What are the true origin, nature and tendency of gallantry, cicisbeism, &c.? What are the origin, nature and tendency of politeness? Is it (as Mandeville represents it) essentially insincere or hypocritical, the slavish offspring of despotic courts? What is the real value of what are called accomplishments? What are the advantages and disadvantages of the modern plan of education? What parts of modern education are useful—what parts are useless—what parts are mischievous? What are the advantages and disadvantages respectively of universities, colleges, day-schools, boarding-schools, &c.? Is it probable that there might be more of useful learning and true science without any of them? Whether are maxims and manners or laws and institutions of greatest importance to the well-being of commonwealths? Is it possible to have a system of laws so simple as to preclude the necessity of professional lawyers? Is it possible to have justice administered in a well ordered commonwealth without a code of laws? Are there any absolute or abstract principles of justice? What is the firmest and broadest basis of equity? What is the fairest or least arbitrary title to property? What are the best preventives of faction, commotion, fraud, violence, discontent, &c. in a commonwealth? What are the most effectual means of preserving a commonwealth in the even tenour of progressive improvement, equi-distant from despotism and anarchy? What is the great central principle, round which a commonwealth must constantly revolve, to have the greatest sum of freedom, dignity and happiness, and most security from despotism and anarchy—external and internal war? Is it possible and desirable to raise a whole people into a philosophical society? What are the best means for that purpose? What are the advantages and disadvantages of ecclesiastical establishments? Are they compatible with the peace, security and progressive improvement of a well-ordered commonwealth? Are any religious sects or factions (two or more congregations united into one body), whether established or tolerated, compatible with the well-being of commonwealths? Are *charities* of any description benefits or injuries to society?

These, Sir, are a few of such queries as I should be glad to see well answered in your pages. Crude thoughts in loose remarks will serve no good purpose; but if some of your readers will digest or *think* any of the above queries into simple, clear, distinct, self-evident, or demonstrable propositions, they will confer a benefit on society, and very much oblige

Your Correspondent,
JAMES GILCHRIST.

GLEANINGS; OR, SELECTIONS AND REFLECTIONS MADE IN A COURSE OF GENERAL READING.

No. CCLXXII.
Lord Clarendon's Character of the Emperor Julian.

".And now succeeded Julian in the Empire; whether an apostate or no, may for aught I know be lawfully doubted. That he was a great enemy to the Christians, and that he found a way more to discredit and dishonour Christianity by his wit and mirth and scoffs and discountenance, (which made a greater impression upon the Christians of that age, and made more of them to renounce their faith, than any one of the fiery and bloody persecutions had done) is very clear: yet I have never seen ground enough to conclude that he ever embraced the Christian faith, or was instructed in it; for though he had conformed in some outward appearance, to the commands of his uncle the Emperor Constantine, yet he appeared always addicted to the religion of the Gentiles, in which he was very learned; and taking him as a Gentile, he may well be looked upon as a prince of extraordinary virtue, and one, who if he had not been carried by a wonderful providence, and against all the advice of his friends and several predictions (to which he was naturally superstitious enough) into that war where he was slain, it is probable might have extended his empire to as great an extent of dominion and reputation as ever it had under any of his predecessors. And here it may not be unfit (though I believe it will be very unpopular) to observe how much passion and prejudice contribute to the corruption of history: for we know not to what else to impute all those relations of the manner of his death, and his last speech in contempt of our Saviour, than to the over zeal of religious persons of that age; who, believing his apostacy, thought they could not load his memory with too many reproaches, nor sufficiently celebrate God's mercy in the vengeance acted upon him in so extraordinary a manner. And ' the Spaniards do still believe that he was killed by Saint Mercurius with one of the lances which was always kept in that Saint's tomb, as it was missed on the day in which Julian was killed, and found again the next day in its place, all bloody. Whereas, if we will believe Ammianus Marcellinus, (who is incomparably the best writer of that age and was himself in that battle,) he was hurt in a very sharp charge of the enemy when great numbers fell on both sides; and being carried out of the field into his tent, where he lived some days after he found his wound to be mortal, he sent for the principal officers of his army, made a long discourse to them of the public affairs and of his particular person and his actions and intentions, full of wisdom and magnanimity, and died with as great serenity and tranquillity of mind as any Roman general of whom we have received very good account in story."

Religion and Policy, 8vo. 1811. I. 23—25.

No. CCLXXIII.
Magnanimity of a Scottish Prince.

Malcolm the Third having received information, that one of his nobles had conceived a design against his life, he enjoined the strictest silence to the informer, and took no notice of it himself, till the person accused of this execrable treason came to his court, in order to execute his intention. The next morning he went to hunt, with all the train of his courtiers, and when they were got into the deepest woods of the forest, drew that nobleman away from the rest of the company, and spoke to him thus: " Behold! we are here alone, armed and mounted alike. Nobody sees or hears us, or can give either of us aid against the other. If then you are a brave man, if you have courage and spirit, perform your purpose; accomplish the promise you have made to my enemies. If you think I ought to be killed by you, when can you do it better? when more opportunely? when more manfully?—Have you prepared poison for me? that is a womanish treason. Or would you murder me in my bed? an adulteress could do that. Or have you hid a dagger to stab me secretly? that is the deed of a ruffian. Rather act like a soldier; act like a man; and fight with me hand to hand; that your treason may at least be free from baseness."—At these words, the traitor, as if he had been struck with a thunderbolt, fell at his feet and implored his pardon. " Fear nothing: you shall not suffer any evil from me," replied the king, and kept his word.

The above story is related (from the mouth of Malcolm's own son, David the First, to Henry II. of England, his great grandson,) by Ethelred, Abbot of Rivaux. [De Genealogia Reg. Angl. p. 367.]

See *Lord Lyttelton's Henry II.* 8vo. I. pp. 94, 95.

No. CCLXXIV.
Spiritual Comedy at Rome.

" The Father-Jesuits at *Rome* have had a play, or spiritual comedy, acted in their *Casa Professa* (or part of their college where they read their lectures) concerning the conversion of *Japan*. In the first scene of which there appeared a Jesuit making a sermon to the pit about this subject. That God, being upon the work of renewing the world, has in this age raised up their society, which his Divine Majesty hath been so gracious to, that no human power has been able to oppose it, and such other *jimcracks*, which they brought in a *Japanese* to reply to: who said, that they did not believe that God sent them thither, but that some enemy of mankind wafted them over into their country, and there they make it their business to set people together by the ears, and to spy out the nakedness of their country, and divers others such conceits. And so the play went on, with divers other remarkable passages spoken by the actors, all against them. And I cannot imagine how this came into their heads, unless it be to tell the world to their teeth, that they know what folks talk and think of them ; and that they value no man a farthing for it."

Father Paul's Letters, p. 326, *Venice,* 1612.

No. CCLXXV.
Jesuits Outwitted.

" At Palermo these sweet fathers have met with a pretty accident. A certain wealthy gentleman died there, that was hugely devoted to them ; and having made his will, and left *his only son* and *those fathers* together, his heirs, making them his executors, with a power of dividing the estate as they pleased, and of giving the son what they should see convenient; the fathers have divided it all into ten parts, and fairly given one part to the son, and kept the other nine for themselves. The son hereupon has made his complaint to the Duke of Ossuna (the viceroy) of this great inequality ; who hearing both parties, has made good the division that the Jesuits made of the whole estate ; but changing the terms, has ordered that the nine parts do (by the will) belong to the son, and one part (and no more) to the fathers, because they were to *give him* what *pleased them.*"

The Same, p. 326.

No. CCLXXVI.
A Canonization.

Not many years ago, a Dominican of Toledo was ranked among the Saints *for having remained thirty years in his cell alone and without smiling or speaking.*

BIBLICAL CRITICISM.

July 27th, 1816.
Observations on Matt. xi. 27.

WHERE Mystery exists, there is no Revelation: and, again, in points which are *revealed* there can be no *mystery.* If the sun burst on us in his splendour, darkness is immediately put to flight. To speak of the mysteries of Revelation, is at once to employ phraseology as incorrect as can well be conceived, and to arraign the Divine wisdom, goodness and fidelity in the doctrine of the Gospel. It is to say that God, having professed to give mankind the most important knowledge respecting himself, and the designs which he executes by Jesus Christ, has, nevertheless, failed of his intention, has withholden what, according to the persons whom I have in view, is yet essential to be believed ; inasmuch as without the belief of it we can have no salvation.

The question concerning this supposed alliance of mystery with Revelation, may be brought within a short compass and to an easy issue. Let all those passages of Scripture where the word *mystery* occurs be collected and compared together. This being done, if a single text can be produced which asserts the mysteriousness of any revealed doctrines, I will consent to retract as erroneous my opinion on the utter irreconcilableness of the term *mystery* with the term *revelation.*

What then, it may be asked, is the import of the passage to which reference is made at the head of this paper? Must we not pronounce it somewhat favourable to the notion that even Revelation has its mysteries? So it may be thought, when torn away from it's context, when interpreted by readers whose minds have received a bias from human creeds: so it will not be considered after it has been thoroughly examined.

As error is best confuted by the establishment of truth, I begin with endeavouring to ascertain the just sense of our Lord's declaration, " All things are delivered unto me of my Father: and no man knoweth the Son but the Father; neither knoweth any man the Father, save the Son, and he to whomsoever the Son will reveal him."

The Gospel was rejected by numbers

of those to whom it had been first offered, and especially by the leading persons in the Jewish nation, by the sect who possessed the chief honour and influence among them. It was a consolation however to the benevolent mind of Jesus Christ that some of the lower classes of the people had received his doctrine with willing hearts, and that he could look forward to the further diffusion of it, particularly beyond the limits of Judæa. On this account, he, accordingly, presented to the God whom he worshipped the following devout acknowledgment: " I thank thee, O Father, Lord of heaven and earth, because thou hast hidden these things from the wise and prudent," from men who are such in their own conceit, " and hast revealed them unto babes," to persons of humbler attainments and pretensions, and of teachable dispositions——" Even so, Father, for so it seemed good in thy sight." Here it is observable that our Lord expressly distinguishes between what is *hidden* and what is *revealed:* and to this admirable devotional address succeeds the declaration, " all things, &c. &c."

From this reference of the passage to it's *connexion,* we learn that Jesus is speaking throughout of *the designs* of the Father, and of *the instrumentality and commission* of the Son, in the scheme of the Gospel.

Let us now consider somewhat more minutely *the words themselves :*

" All things," all matters relative to the Christian dispensation, all *persons* of every nation, who are to be the subjects of it, " are delivered unto me of my Father," committed unto me by God, the only possessor of underived and essential power : or, as the same fact is expressed, John iii. 35, " the Father loveth the Son, and hath given all things into his hand." " And no man knoweth the Son," or is as yet acquainted with the comprehensive object of his office, " but the Father," who putteth the times and seasons in his own power, and worketh according to the counsel of his own will : " neither knoweth any man the Father," no one is in possession of the extent of the plans of Divine grace, " save the Son, and he to whomsoever the Son will reveal him ;" which latter sentiment is illustrated and supported by our Lord's words in John vi. 46—' not that any man hath seen the Father—save he who is of God, he hath seen

the Father'——where the term *seen* is manifestly equivalent with *known.*

To justify this exposition, which, in it's principle, agrees with Dr. S. Clarke's,[*] and with Rosenmuller's,[†] it may be remarked that in the New Testament *persons* are not unfrequently denoted by the word *things,*[‡] as in 1 Cor. i. 27, 28 ; that *the Father* is the appropriate name of God under the dispensation of the Gospel, and expressive of his parental relation to *all* mankind ; that *the Son* is a title of office ; that nothing is more common than to state general propositions in an absolute form ; and that the concise modes of speech in use among the Eastern people admit and receive light from the occasions and the subjects in respect of which they are employed.

The true sense then of the passage before us I take to be the following, ' that at the time when these words were uttered, no one, but the Father, the only God, knew the extent of our Saviour's commission, including, as it really did, the whole human race : and, on the other hand, that no man save the Son, none but Jesus Christ, possessed a knowledge of the merciful designs of the Father being thus unlimited ——although it was a truth which the Messiah had the privilege of communicating at his pleasure.' How well this interpretation accords with facts, and with our Lord's character and circumstances, it is unnecessary to represent.

Of a double meaning the passage does not appear to be susceptible. Consequently, if I have succeeded in ascertaining it's just signification, all other paraphrases of it must be erroneous.

If, for example, any persons will infer from these words that the nature or the essence of the Father and of the Son are known mutually to themselves, and to those who are favoured with this knowledge by Jesus Christ, let such expositors be informed that they substitute their own imaginations for the language and the meaning of the Bible. The Bible does not profess to instruct us in the essence of the Deity, but declares that he is a perfect spirit, and conveys to mankind the most valuable knowledge with regard to his character,

* *A Paraphrase, &c.* in loc :
† *Scholia in N. T.* in loc :
‡ *Hammond, &c.* in loc :

government and will. And of the great Messiah, the Mediator of the covenant of the Gospel, it invariably speaks as *the man Christ Jesus*; never even intimating that his nature and person are mysterious, and certainly holding forth no such intelligence in the sentences on which I am commenting.

Further; It ought not to be concluded from the last clause, 'he to whomsoever the Son will reveal him,' that Jesus communicates to any of his followers a private or individual revelation of the nature or the mind of God. This mistake is very current, and tends to produce in some men spiritual pride, in others religious despondency. It is a *public* revelation which our Lord here mentions; one that was made in part by his own instrumentality, in part by that of his apostles. There are two passages in the New Testament with which the words before us ought especially to be compared : John i. 18, " No man hath seen God at any time; the only begotten Son, who is in the bosom of the Father," i. e. who has a compleat acquaintance with the Divine counsels for the salvation of the world, " he hath declared him :" Matt. xiii. 16, 17, " — verily, I say unto you that blessed are your eyes, &c.; for many prophets and righteous men have desired to see those things which ye see, and have not seen them, and to hear those things which ye hear, and have not heard them."

So far therefore is the phraseology which has been the subject of these remarks from stating or implying the existence of a mysterious union between the Father and the Son, that it declares a plain and most interesting truth : I mean, the concurrence of God and Christ as to the grand objects and vast extent of the Christian Revelation ; a truth particularly valuable to those professors of the Gospel who are of Gentile parentage! **N.**

August 7th, 1816.
Supplementary Remarks on the Priesthood of Christ.
[See pp. 402, 403.]

IT is usual with writers on systematic theology to represent Jesus Christ as sustaining the several offices of *prophet, priest* and *king*. This division, though not exactly this arrangement,

of his characters, is adopted in *The Racovian Catechism* ;[*] a manual which I hope, will soon be more extensively known among my readers, and from which I shall now make two extracts on a subject to which their attention has lately been directed :[†]

" — was he [Christ] not a priest till he entered into the heaven? not when he hung upon the cross ?"

" A. At no hand ; for, as you hear even now, the divine author to the Hebrews, ch. viii. 4, expressly saith that if Christ were upon the earth, he would not be a priest. Besides, forasmuch as the same author testifieth that Christ ought in all things to be made like unto his brethren, that he might become a faithful and merciful high priest to God ward, it is evident that until he had been made like unto his brethren in all things, that is in afflictions and death, he was not our merciful and faithful high priest."

The following question and answer deserve the notice of careful inquirers into the sense of Scripture :

" Why doth the Scripture, treating of Christ's priesthood, say that he intercedeth for us ?".

" A. Both that the care which Christ takes of our salvation might, the requests which he is said to make to God, appear to us ; and also that the prerogative and eminency of the Father above Christ might remain entire and inviolate.".

Here the compiler of the Catechism alludes to Heb. vii. 24, 25. But the word *intercession*, which occurs in this passage, does not necessarily and exclusively import *the act of offering supplications for the welfare of others*. It is a term of very extensive significance, and means *the management of the concerns of our fellow men.*

The intercession of Christ, therefore, is not his pleading with offended justice, or his interposing to avert Divine wrath : it is *a part of his mediation ministry, as the* **APPOINTED** Messenger of God and Saviour of mankind ; and thus, in the language of this Catechism, it illustrates " the prerogative and eminency of the Father." **N**

---

* Translated into English. Amsterdam 1652. pp. 163, &c. Catechesis Ecclesiarum Polonicarum. 325, &c.

† M. Repos. XI. 402, 403.

REVIEW.

ART. I.—*An Essay on the Existence of a Supreme Creator, possessed of Infinite Power, Wisdom and Goodness:* containing also the Refutation from Reason and Revelation of the Objections urged against His Wisdom and Goodness; and deducing from the whole Subject the most important Practical Inferences. By William Laurence Brown, D. D. Principal of Marischal-College and University of Aberdeen, &c. &c. 2 vol. 8vo. pp. 782. Hamilton.

WE opened this book with considerable expectation: After the great minds which have engaged in the investigation of the subject of which it treats, the number and importance of the facts which they have left upon record relative to it, and the variety and beauty of the illustrations with which they have adorned it; though we did not anticipate much that was new, yet we did allow ourselves to hope that the benevolent and pious bequest of Mr. Burnett would call forth a work of ability and usefulness, possessing at least closeness of reasoning and clearness of illustration—a work which the philosopher might read with pleasure, and the theological student and the general reader with profit: When we heard that the prize had been adjudged to the Essay of the Principal of Marischal-College, we were still willing to believe that our expectation was well founded: page after page, notwithstanding the misgivings which soon began to gather on our minds, we clung fondly to this hope, trusting that the author would rise with the interest and importance of the subject;—but after having read to the end, we closed the book with the melancholy regret that the munificence of the worthy founder of this prize should only have added another proof to the sad catalogue which shows that the best efforts of benevolence are doomed in this world to disappointment.

The Reverend Principal divides his Essay into Three Books. The First treats of the Evidence of the Being of God; the Second of his Perfections, namely, his Power, Wisdom and Goodness, and enters particularly into

the consideration of the objections to the two latter, arising from the existence of natural and moral evil; and the Third comprehends the solution given to these difficulties by Revelation; especially by the Gospel, together with some Practical Inferences deducible from the speculative part of the Essay.

After some observations on the meaning of the terms Necessary Existence, Cause and Effect, the author arranges his proofs of the existence of God into the metaphysical proof; the proof from design; from the constitution of the faculties of the human mind: from the almost universal assent of mankind to the truth of this opinion; from the appearances which the world exhibits of a recent origin; and the traditions concerning it; and from the testimony of Scripture.

The metaphysical proof stated originally by Clarke with an acuteness and force, which, notwithstanding an extreme prolixity, and even when his arguments fail to produce conviction, awe the mind into veneration of the strength and profoundness of the understanding that conceived them, is here given without closeness and without ability: it extends through nearly thirty pages with an uncommon feebleness; it has scarcely the strength of the echo of an echo; and in the very midst of an argument which supposes the greatest precision and accuracy, there occur such affirmations as the following:

" We have evidence *equally* strong for the existence of mind as a *substance entirely distinct* from the body, as we have for the existence of this last, and of its peculiar properties, namely, consciousness and the internal perception of our mental energies; as entirely distinct from any quality of matter. Nay, perhaps this evidence is *stronger* than that of our *external senses*, by which we ascertain corporeal substance and the properties belonging to it."—P. 64.

And again:

" Nor in reality is it *more difficult* to admit the creation of matter, that is, its original production, than the production of any thing which did not exist before. The only difference lies in the superior power required and in the nature of the effects.

To all genius a species of creative power, that is, a faculty of producing something new is ascribed. A fine statue is indeed hewn out of a block of marble ; but where were the beauty, the symmetry, the proportion and exquisite composition which the statue displays ?"

Again :

" In fact, if the case be accurately examined, it displayed perhaps a *greater* exertion of divine power to superinduce on rude, uninformed matter, that symmetry, beauty and admirable construction which the universe exhibits, than to call into being the chaotic mass."—Pp. 70. 72.

So that according to the learned Principal, it is more difficult to conceive how a beautiful statue should be hewn out of a block of marble, than how marble itself should be produced out of nothing.

The proof of the being of God, from the manifestation of design in the works of nature, is in itself complete and decisive. On this rock the Theist may take his stand ; and it is not possible for all the artifice which human ingenuity can employ, to shake for a moment the firm foundation of his faith. Wherever there is design there must have been a designer ; wherever there is contrivance there must have been a contriver. This simple argument is level to the comprehension of every capacity ; and to him who is worthy of the name of a philosopher, it appears with an evidence which is absolutely irresistible. Show to any rational being a piece of mechanism, explain to him how one part is adapted to another, and how all the various parts are fitted to bring about some one particular result ; and he must admit the existence of a wisdom to conceive and of a power to execute that result. If he affirm that he does not, all reasoning must be at an end with him ; for it is no longer possible to hold an argument with a person who declares that he does not perceive the relation between what is admitted to be contrivance and what is termed a contriver. In the great controversy therefore between the Theist and the Atheist, the only question of real importance is—Are there or are there not indications of design in the works of nature ? Doctor Brown says there are, and he *refers* in general to several things in evidence of the fact, but he does not *prove* the fact. He does not give, and he does not attempt to give any illustration of it, any instance which brings it home to the understanding with irresistible persuasion, and upon which the mind may rest in those moments of doubt and difficulty which sometimes come to all. Nothing it is true was more easy ; it had indeed been perfectly done before ; but Paley by no means exhausted the subject ; and if Doctor Brown did not chuse to repeat what this admirable writer has said about the structure of the valves of the human heart, or the ligament attached to the head of the thigh bone, all nature was open before him—the sublime and most interesting adaptations of objects to each other on the most magnificent and on the humblest scale with which chemistry has made us acquainted ; the structure of the simplest flower or the formation and the fall of the dew of heaven that ministers to its sustenance. And the omission to state in detail at least some one of those striking and wonderful adaptations with which by the light of philosophy we know that every part of nature abounds, and the simple statement of which baffles the sceptic and silences his sophisms in the same manner as the philosopher by the act of walking silenced the sciolist who endeavoured to persuade him that there was no such thing as motion in the world, appears to us to be a capital defect, because it is neglecting by far the most convincing argument in support of the truth, for the clear and popular illustration of which the prize was instituted.

In the next chapter Doctor Brown, wonderful as it may seem, endeavours to prove the existence of God from the *immateriality* of the soul. Now without entering into the dark and difficult dispute which has been agitated about the nature of matter and of mind, we are humbly of opinion that no judicious person who has at all attended to that controversy, or who is even acquainted with the opinions of Metaphysicians and Theists in the present age, would have ventured to ground such a truth upon such a basis. But indeed there is in every part of this work a looseness, an inattention to the strict accuracy of the statements, the appositeness of the illustrations, the proper selection and the judicious application of the arguments, which take from it all its value as a philosophical, and much, very much, of its usefulness as a popular work. What is to be thought of the acuteness of the man as a philosopher, and of his attainments as the Principal of a University, who could give the following account of conscience, and endeavour to confirm it by the illustration with which it is concluded!

" By conscience, or a moral sense, I understand that internal perception which we have of right and wrong, of moral good and evil, of virtue and vice, antecedently to any reasoning concerning the more remote consequences of habits and actions, either to individuals or to society. This internal sense furnishes principles for judging of moral subjects, as intellect. affords principles for truth and error. The exercise of the moral faculty, however, it is to be remarked, is always accompanied by certain feelings either of complacence or disgust."

" We feel contempt or indignation rising in our minds towards those who have acted in an unworthy and base manner, and love and esteem for such as maintain a conduct just and beneficent. These principles, whether of morals or of speculative reason, *are not* the mere effect 'of education, but are *implanted* in the soul. *For without study or inquiry they present themselves to the mind.* Nay, what is more, if they were not *innate* principles, education could no more be carried on, than a building could be raised without a foundation, or a tree produced without its original seed. All that education does is to direct, improve and enlarge these original principles, and to lead them to their proper results. *Whoever contests this affirmation, may try to instruct a dog or a horse in morality !"*— Pp. 112. 116.

Here the learned Principal affirms that conscience, or as he terms it the moral sense, is . an *innate* principle; and his proof is that if it were not so, education could no more be carried on than a tree could be produced without its seed : and why ? Because do what you will you cannot instruct a dog in morality ! But the worthy Principal would find it rather a difficult task to teach a dog mathematics, or even to make it enunciate his favourite proposition that the whole is greater than a part : yet because his labour would be entirely thrown away upon such a pupil, but would not be wasted upon a boy, the learned Principal must admit, upon his own showing, that mathematics and even the very faculty of speech are in the boy innate principles.

Passing over the chapters on the proof of the being of God, from the almost universal assent of mankind to this opinion, which is not a very solid argument; from the appearance which the world exhibits of a recent origin, and from the tradititions concerning it, which is equally equivocal and inconclusive; from the Scriptures, which in this argument cannot be referred to as affording any proof without really, not apparently, reasoning in a circle; and omitting also the chapters on the conclusion which follows these various proofs of the existence of God, and on the causes of Atheism, which are the common-place observations of a thousand sermons expressed in a most commonplace manner; we come to the Second Book, which treats of the perfections of the Deity, namely, his infinite power, wisdom and goodness. And here we are happy to say the author writes with somewhat more closeness and accuracy. He seems to have formed .in the abstract a just conception of the divine goodness, for he defines it to be—

" That affection and habit of mind which prompts to communicate and to diffuse happiness, which is gratified by the contemplation of it ; and is averse from the infliction and the view of misery."——
" The goodness of the Deity being an attribute strictly moral must be a constant and immutable disposition to communicate and extend the highest measure of happiness *to all his creatures.* This definition when applied to omnipotence and infinite wisdom implies the communication of *all possible happiness to the whole and to every part of his sensitive creation."*——
" If it could be shewn that in any case such faculties were clearly designed for *misery,* and the beings to which they belonged were irresistibly impelled to the exercise of them, the inference would be unavoidable t*hat the Supreme Power was malevolent.* But the first branch of this supposition is contrary to universal fact, and the second is in itself incomprehensible. For it is impossible to conceive that any being, endued with activity, would delight to exercise powers which were constantly attended with pain and misery. Inactivity must in this case be the inevitable result. We must therefore conclude that he also has bestowed on every sensitive being its powers of perception and action; must desire those to be exercised and to produce their natural results ; and since in the exercise and gratification of those the happiness of every such being

in, reality consists, *that he intended the utmost happiness of which every living creature was susceptible;* that is, he is infinitely good."—Pp. 222, 223, 228.

After this will any intelligent person believe that Principal Brown advocates the cause of Endless Torments, and endeavours to show that it is not inconsistent with the infinite goodness of him who possesses Almighty power, while the very notion of infinite goodness comprehends, according to Doctor Brown, the design to promote the *utmost happiness of which any living creature is susceptible.* Admitting the sincerity, what can be thought of the understanding of a man who can assert with all the gravity of the philosopher such a palpable contradiction. In the senseless declaimer of the tabernacle, who despising the aid of human learning and reflection to qualify him for the office he assumes, and following only " the inspiration from above," suspends his hearers rightly over a bottomless gulph, foaming with fire and brimstone, prepared for all who despise the message of the man of God, for all heretics of all sorts, as well as for all who plume themselves on being adorned with " the whitewash of morality;"* in this man we do not wonder at inconsistencies and contradictions, for we know that they have taken such possession of his mind that he does not perceive even the impieties which he continually utters, and that he has most solemnly and piously renounced reason ; but in the man who pretends to have taken her as his guide and by the light with which she has illumined his mind to have investigated the wonders of nature, to have looked through them up to their great Author, and to have contemplated his excellencies till he has come to the sublime conclusion that it must be his constant and immutable disposition to communicate all possible happiness to the whole and to every part of his sensitive creation,—for him to affirm that it is perfectly consistent with this constant and immutable disposition to doom myriads and myriads of his creatures to unutterable torments in hell-fire for ever, awakens our pity at the weakness which can thus permit

* A favourite phrase of the Rev. Rowland Hill's.

his prepossessions to impose upon his own understanding, or our indignation at the insult which he presumes to offer to that of his reader. But the occasion on which these absurdities are affirmed, together with several others connected with them, much more than the ability with which they are defended, appears to us to justify a more particular comment; and we shall endeavour to show the utter fallacy of the reasoning, if reasoning it can be called, attempted by Doctor Brown. The learned Principal of the University of Aberdeen has undertaken the task of clearing up all the difficulties which rest on the works and the dispensations of the Deity; and of reconciling with his constant and immutable disposition to communicate all possible happiness to the whole and to every part of the sensitive creation, the doctrine of the endless misery of the great majority of mankind, by the aid of free agency! We shall see what he makes of it.

S. S.

[To be Continued.]

Art. II.—*Philosophic Etymology, of Rational Grammar.* By James Gilchrist. 8vo. pp. 270. Hunter. 1816.

BY the title prefixed to his work, our author, who loves to speak out, intends it should be understood that Grammar is no where else to be found in company with reason. Perhaps, there is not in the history of letters an instance that can parallel the arrogant manner in which Mr. Gilchrist advances to demand audience of the public. He steps forwards with an air of bold superiority, plants himself firmly at the bar of opinion, and requires that his book be " rigorously examined, well and truly tried." This indeed is right; but if his own book should not have a fair and impartial trial, he will have principally himself to blame. Mr. Gilchrist's peculiar manner has made it impossible that his work should be tried dispassionately by many of those who are (if any are) qualified to sit in judgment upon it. He who writes for the instruction of the public must chuse his own manner, or rather if he possesses original powers, nature has determined it for him;—but it is unfortunate for the writer, and for the reader too, when instruction is given, if the manner be such as must disgust many and offend all. Our author's manner is precisely of that kind, and in so remarkable a degree as to make it probable that the merits of his production may never be fairly examined. It is the insolence of triumph before the battle is won. Such vaunting of his own powers and contempt of all who have gone before him or who stand beside him, have made it impossible that he should fail without utter disgrace. For him μεγαλως ἀπολισθανειν ὁμως ευγενες ἁμαρτημα would be an insufficient apology, and one which he would disdain to make even if it had not classical authority. Like some performers whom we have seen, he moves to the front of the stage with so confident an air, that wonder or ridicule, applauses or hisses must pursue him as he withdraws. We introduce our notice of this extraordinary production with these remarks both from regard to justice, and with a view to prevent those who may open the book from throwing it down instantly in disgust. As to the writer himself, we fear that animadversion will be lost upon him. His feeling is that of a man, who has risen upon a dark world to enlighten and astonish it by his brightness. The voice of rebuke may provoke a smile at the admonisher; but the man who thinks it an act of condescension on his part to instruct his kind, is a hopeless subject of correction. Indeed, Mr. Gilchrist appears to anticipate with great satisfaction censure and condemnation from the greater part of literary men.

"I mean to use great freedoms with some of the literary idols; and to deliver some very *illegitimate* doctrines concerning *style*: the giants of taste, criticism and learning may be expected to rise in a body; if, however, they will stipulate to keep lightness and delicacy out of the fray, I will undertake single-handed to put them all down with such weapons only as etymology supplies: I have some confidence in myself—much confidence in my weapons—very great confidence in the goodness of my cause."—P. 204.

Again, in yet more chosen phrase:

"I expect a thousand classical tongues to be darted at me for my provoking doctrines; and much literary dribble—many roted morsels and critical crudities; with the very 'quintessence of established

opinion and general consent to be spitefully spit in my face: but delicate mouths never spit fire; and the saliva of polite taste has the singular property of taking away all the dangerous and deadly qualities of the venom of classical hostility; so that the bite of a well-trained literary viper is as harmless as the hiss of a goose. Perhaps some great critical gander will come flapping and flourishing out of the flock to peck at the legs of the present author; but a single kick or two (and it cannot surely be unpolite to kick *gander*-champions), will send the hero back into his own crowd and muddy hole. I know what courtly simperers will think and say (or rather *hint*—for the timid things dare not speak out), of this contemptuous, uncharitable, unpolite, *unphilosophic* style of writing; but I should despise myself if I could admire what they admire, or praise what they praise; and I should loathe my existence with consciousness of hypocritically cloaking my real opinions and feelings to appear orthodox, or become popular among a canting, mystical, visionary race of roters, eternally saying after consecrated authorities."—Pp. 216, 217.

If the present volume had contained nothing better than invective of this sort against schools and scholars, we should have left to others, if any should think it worth their while, to invite attention to such odious effusions of angry vanity. But the author believes that he has made a great discovery, that he has solved the problem of language in all its varieties, that, in short, he has in his hand the key of grammar, and he is graciously willing, though in a most ungracious manner, to put it into the hands of as many as are not too much stultified by scholarship to make use of it. Our readers will not be displeased to hear him speak for himself on this subject; for though, meaning to be the plain blunt man he continually violates the respect which man owes to man, still there is matter in him, and his coarseness is not without originality. Mr. Gilchrist has introduced his discoveries by a history of his own mind in its progress to knowledge.

"When the author of the following work began to study philology, it was with a logical rather than grammatical view. He had found his learning, such as it was, an inconvenience and intellectual cumbrance: nor was it merely *foreign speech* that he found as a vail of obscurity or net of entanglement upon his understanding; even the English language was to him as Saul's armour to David—cumbersome because it had not been proved. He had wandered ten years (for he became a student somewhat late in life) in the wilderness of words ; often looking wistfully up the hill of knowledge, but as often despairing of climbing to the summit. Frequently indeed he returned to his fruitless efforts with a kind of desperate courage ; but as frequently did he retire from the hopeless contest, under a mortifying sense of disappointment and useless effort.

"The truth is, he at last sunk into despair of ever knowing even the English language to his own satisfaction ; or so as to be able to experiment with it accurately as an instrument of science ; and it had actually become one of his fixed opinions, that man is fated to be the dupe of his own inventions ; that *language* of which he so much boasts is the greatest of all impostors ; and that no remedy could be found for verbal, that is metaphysical deception and mischief. Thus for a considerable time he heartily despised not only the systems of learning that owe their origin to language, but language itself, as a mere Babel-jargon intended or calculated to be a curse rather than a blessing—the parent of error, metaphysical nonsense, false-reasoning, endless controversy, contention and animosity.

"With this opinion and contempt of language, it is probable that the author would have been content to pity and deride the learning that prevails, without endeavouring to rectify it, had not an incident which it is unnecessary to name, roused him into a resolution of attempting to rid the world of intellectual bondage and metaphysical imposture. He had always (he means from the time he became a student) a kind of intuitive perception and conviction that all the systems of grammar, rhetoric, logic, &c. which prevail, are wrong ; but believing the origin of all learned absurdities to be language itself, he perceived not how the evil could be remedied ; and supposed that learned men must go on as they had done, boasting of their technical nonsense. He at last, however, perceived, he thought, how the labyrinth might be demolished, and the Babel-systems confounded into silence. As the radical evil was perceived to be in language, it was evident that there the remedy must be applied. He resolved therefore to create another kind of grammar and lexicography than had hitherto prevailed ; in attempting which, the principles he laid down were as follow :—

1. That language was a human invention. 2. That it was a simple invention. 3. That the true nature of true philology

must lie on the very surface of obviousness. 4. That all the dialects must be essentially but one language. 5. That the whole wilderness of words must have arisen from a few expressive signs originally connected with sensible objects. 6. That therefore the whole multitude of parts and varieties in language, or that all words must be resolvable into a few simple elements, indicating by resemblance visible objects. 7. That there could be nothing arbitrary about language. 8. That no words could be primarily or properly insignificant."—Introd. pp. i.—iii.

"As the author continued to study his subject, it became progressively more simple to his perceptions than he thought it could possibly be in its own nature ; for we are so educated and disciplined into the belief of abstruseness and ingenious mysticalness, connected with learned and philosophic questions, as to be constantly overlooking obvious truth, or deeming it not worth finding and raising into the dignity of science. Every man of any pretension to philosophic thinking, would blush to refuse for his motto : Simplicity is the seal of truth. But who does not seem to consider it the badge of intellectual poverty ? Frequently has the author felt over his discoveries as Bruce did at the source of the Nile. Frequently has he been ready to exclaim with the good Parisians, who had anticipated a grand spectacle at the *entrée* of the allies : Is this all !

"As may be supposed, the more that he studied words in different dialects, the more did he ascertain their true nature and origin. It was not, however, till he analized the alphabet and resolved its diversities into their primary form, that he could experiment with certainty on etymology. It was now discovered and proved at every step, that as men have few ideas, few senses, and are familiar with few objects, so there are few primitive words."—Introd. pp. v. vi.

That our readers may see at once the object of the present work, we shall lay before them the author's analysis of his philological principles, " which, he says, he has given in his introduction, that they may be seen and examined in their most naked form."

"1. There is nothing arbitrary about language. 2. All the dialects as Hebrew, Celtic, Greek, Latin, &c. are essentially but one language. They have such diversities as may be termed idioms ; but with all their circumstantial varieties, they have substantial uniformity : they proceed on the same principles and have the same origin. The philosophic grammar and lexicography of one, is in reality that of all. 3. There are no words primarily and properly insignificant. 4. There are many words that have ceased to be significant, as they are commonly employed. Many of the particles, including affixes and prefixes, conjunctions, prepositions, articles, &c. are of this description, and may be termed the *mummies* of language. 5. Every word that cannot be identified with the name of a sensible object, is either partly or wholly *mummified.* 6. The use of insignificant words, or using words insignificantly, is the chief, if not the only cause of verbal, that is metaphysical imposture; and all unintelligible or false reasoning is merely metaphysical imposture. Metaphysics as a science could have never existed but for the *mummies* of language, and the relics and ghosts of meaning. 7. All words are primarily and properly metaphorical; or to vary the expression,—language whether spoken or written, originated in simile; and metaphor is commonly explained to be—" a simile comprised in a word." The author does not wish to dispute about such unmeaning or half-meaning terms as metaphor, &c.; but he wishes it to be distinctly understood, that the vulgar errors—he means the errors of the literary vulgar, respecting metaphorical and literal terms, are the cause of much metaphysical imposture, much critical, logical, grammatical and rhetorical nonsense. What are called literal terms, such as *time, space, mind, spirit,* &c., are like worn out coin, or effaced inscriptions, the meaning or value of which, being never ascertained, occasions everlasting conjecture and controversy. 8. Almost every sentence is elliptical. 9. Almost every word is put elliptically. 10. Almost every word is a compound of two or more words. 11. All words are resolvable into a few primitives; or thus, all the seeming multitude of words are merely various spellings and pronunciations of the names of a few striking and familiar objects; as the head, foot, hand, eye, ear, mouth, &c. 12. As all words are resolvable into the letters of the alphabet, so all the letters of the alphabet are resolvable into one primary form. 13. That primary form was employed as a sign or representation of visible objects. 14. This method of significancy by similitude, is the origin of all written language. 15. There are very few words, which were primarily unwritten, or which originated in an imitation of natural sounds.

" If these principles can be overturned, the philology of the author will prove of course a baseless fabric."——Introd. pp. xx.—xxii.

It has been and is still the opinion of many men of sound understanding,

and not more guilty of fanaticism than our author is of modesty, that language had a divine origin. Since it is plain that man must soon have perished had he been thrown at his creation naked upon the earth, abandoned to the unassisted efforts of his own untutored powers, it might seem to require no great stretch of faith to believe that the Being who fostered him, gave him also language. But an opinion so unphilosophical and childish our author has refuted in his arrogant and easy way, simply by declaring that " as for those who still continue to consider language as arbitrary, or as invented and taught by the Deity, they must not be offended if I tell them that they are unworthy of notice."

We may venture to assure the writer that they will not be offended. Their vanity must exceed, if possible, the measure of his own, could they be offended, that they are not thought worthy of notice by a man of such lofty genius that to his mind " Virgil is a dull versifier, and Tully a petty rhetorician;" and whose taste is so exquisite, that he is able to say—

"Twenty times have I attempted to read the writings of Addison, but I could never succeed in getting through a single volume. I did get twice through Virgil by the gracious aid of an etymological motive; but I believe twenty etymological motives would not drag me through the volumes of Addison; and I declare, upon my honour and conscience, as an author, that I would rather fairly eat them up and digest them down, (all, saving and excepting the boards,) than give them my precious days and nights."—P. 215.

In reviewing a work written in the intolerant and supercilious manner of our author, it is difficult to refrain from making at every step such remarks upon the spirit and style of the production as may create prejudice against the substance and argument of the book. Since, however, it is to the interest of knowledge, that, if any advance has been made in illustrating the principles and history of language, the discovery should be known, and circulated as soon as possible, we shall present our readers with a few extracts that will shew what has been done or attempted in the present treatise on grammar; having first taken leave of the writer by recommending to his notice what his faith and calling must have taught him to respect, the apostolic exhortation to Christians and Christian teachers, "Think not more highly of yourselves than ye ought to think, but think soberly."

The work is divided into five parts: in the first, the nature and origin of Alphabetic Signs is considered; in the second the canon of Etymology is established; in the third, the principles laid down in the two first parts are applied to unfold the component parts of speech; in the fourth, the common system of English grammar is considered; and in the fifth, a standard of Orthography is established. The reader, whose object is knowledge, will read the three first parts with that awakened attention which is natural, when we expect continually some great light to break in upon the mind. The fourth part will afford entertainment to those who read principally to be amused; they will acknowledge that, whether right or wrong, the author is not dull. In the first part, which respects the origin of the alphabet, the following propositions are maintained;—that " letters of smoother and easier utterance are to be considered as growing out of those of harsher and more difficult utterance, but not *vice versa*. Thus gutturals (or letters formed in the throat) become dentals (letters formed by putting the teeth together); dentals become labials (letters formed by closing the *lips*); consonants become vowels; but vowels do not become consonants, nor labials gutturals." That " those forms of letters most speedily and most easily written, or rather graved, (for graving on leaves of trees, on stone, wood, lead, brass, &c., was the first mode of writing and printing,) are to be considered as derivatives, varieties, or corruptions of those forms graved most slowly and difficulty, but not *vice versa*." That " significancy by signs was prior to any significancy by sounds"—and that " the first attempt at articulate sounds or speech was, by expressing with the mouth the form of curiologic signs, that is of circular marks or variations of the circle." For the proof of these propositions we must refer to the treatise itself, in which the curious will find enough to entertain, if not to convince them; for though Mr. Gilchrist deals much in assertion, he does not merely assert.

In the second part the following propositions are laid down. That "*meaning*, rather than *pronunciation* and *spelling*, is to be considered as the great guide of etymologic investigation ;"—that " every word is to be considered significant;" that " every syllable of every word is to be considered significant;" that " every letter of every syllable is to be considered significant;" that " all words are primarily and properly the *signs* of *visible* objects;" that " every word is primarily an adjective, [that is expressive of some quality, circumstance, or manner of being;" that " almost every word is a compound ;" that " the constant tendency of words in passing from mouth to mouth is to contract, not to dilate—to lose, not to assume letters;" that " all the vowels, labials, dentals, in brief, all the letters of the alphabet are resolvable into gutturals, and all the gutturals into one character." " When I say one character," the author adds, " I mean one form of character or kind of sign, namely, the circular form; but there might be originally many *sizes*, bearing some proportion real or supposed to the magnitude of visible objects, with other contrivances to distinguish one particular visible object from another, as a whole circle to represent the sun, and a half circle to represent the moon ; and the sign might be repeated or compounded into two, three, or any number." The result is, which we give in Mr. G.'s own words, to shew that he has honesty as well as rudeness :

" The whole of written language, or that system of alphabetic signs, originally addressed to the eye, is resolvable into CR, CL; or LC, RC, &c. signifying round or *roundlike*. This is the foundation of what shall hereafter be called the New Philology. If this can be overturned, my system of language must fall, and therefore I show its opponents (if it shall be opposed) where to strike ; only, if they would not retire from the attack with disgrace, they must proceed with judgment, and must not rashly infer that because *they* cannot resolve all the parts of written language into such a simple origin, the above proposition is false. But that no one may, through misconception, enter upon useless controversy and verbosities, let it be observed that there are many names given to objects, whose form (the form of the objects) is not round or round-

.ish, and whose form was not contemplated in the imposition of their names ; yet their names are after all resolvable into 'CR, &c., signifying round or roundish."— Pp. 75, 76.

We cannot forbear to insert the author's note at this place, for it is a literary curiosity.

"I hesitated for some time, whether I should not leave the *eighteenth* (I ought to apologize for giving so many) proposition wholly unsheltered by explanation and proof, to invite attack, and draw on controversy ; for I do not expect it to be generally admitted without resistance : but on further reflection, it appeared unwise to induce war, which comes soon enough through all precautions for peace." —*Note*, P. 76.

As the contents of the third part, which consists of an application of the above principles to the analysis of the component parts of speech, could not be presented in a form very much abridged with fairness, we shall content ourselves with an extract which our readers may consider as a fair sample of the whole dissertation.

"*The verbal terminations are merely connective.*—There is strictly but one verbal termination, though it be diversified by various spelling and pronunciation : ath, (the very same as the Hebrew ath,) aith, eth, or ith, &c. was the older form, which became ed, et, es, est, an, en, &c. ; *en* (which is now in Dutch the conjunction answering to our *and*) is still connected with many words ; as *seen, known,* &c. in what is called the past participle : it is also firmly grafted into many words, as brighten, lighten, drown, &c. ; nay, it is both prefixed and postfixed to some words, as enlighten, enliven. The reader will perceive in these instances how liable words are to be used superfluously and insignificantly : in enliven the connective is put twice ; in enliveneth is is put thrice ; in enlivenedst it is put four times."—P. 99.

"It is always a certain sign of idolatry, or of a Babel-system, when the tongues of those employed about it are divided. There has been wonderful gibbering about the wonders of THE VERB ; and among the rest Dr. Crombie is seriously alarmed lest this important part of speech be degraded from its true dignity into a mere participle.

"It would be superfluous to explain *eth* to the intelligent reader ; he must perceive that like *en, ed, es,* it is merely a connective, whether affixed to what is called a verb, an adjective, a noun, or any word whatever ; and it would be easy to convince him that this is the primary use of

all verbal terminations in all the dialects. It has been the fashion of late, indeed, with some Greek and Latin grammarians, to consider them as primarily pronouns : in this they are nearer the truth than themselves are aware of, (for *eth* however diversified, is originally the same as what are called pronouns,) yet it is not as they mean it. Horne Tooke seems to have considered *th, do* and *to,* as the same word, but what he considered *do* he did not communicate. In Hebrew, ath, the grammarians say truly, "seldom admits of translation into English after an active verb, (nor does the verbal termination *eth* in English, admit of translation into any other language) : when prefixed to a person it commonly signifies *with.*'· Wilson's Hebrew Grammar.—This is always its signification when it has any signification, whether it be called a preposition, as *ad, at ;* or a conjunction, as *and, et ;* a termination as in amat, amat-us, amans, amant-is, &c. The reader must be now convinced that verbal, participial and simple adjective terminations, (those which do not denote negation, diminution or augmentation,) are all alike merely connective, and in fact the same *copula,* somewhat varied in its form by the accidents of pronunciation and spelling."—Pp. 100—102.

Whether our author has or has not solved the great problem of language, whether he has untied the knot or merely cut it, we shall leave to the sagacity of his readers to determine. He has, as he is fully persuaded, followed up the most remote parts of speech, through every winding, and sometimes up passages sufficiently rugged and abrupt, to one common channel ; he has also pursued that to its fountain, the supposed source of all written language, and he declares it to be neither more nor less than the cypher which is raised from insignificance into significancy almost infinite, or the circle, under all its variations into greater or less, single or double, more or less regular, &c. We do not certainly intend prediction ; but as the author in a moment of extraordinary diffidence has imagined what may happen, we shall annex the passage, both as it shews that he is prepared for the worst, and as it presents him to the reader in a gentle and even tender and elegiac mood.——" He," (meaning the author of *Etymologicon Magnum,* to whom in very gratitude our author owed an elegy)—

"He was almost within sight of the proper starting post of etymological investigation, yet deviated far from the right way

> ' And found no end in wandering mazes lost.'

This notice which I have been led unintentionally to take of the labours of Mr. Whiter, diffuses a tender melancholy over my mind ; for in turning from them I have often said to myself with an involuntary sigh, what a poor fallible thing is the human understanding ! Perhaps after all this anxious thinking and toilsome inquiry I shall only make a book to lie on the same shelf, or to be thrown to the same heap, with Etymologicon Magnum."—P. 78.

Art. III.—*A Unitarian Christian's Statement and Defence of his Principles with reference particularly to the Charges of the Rt. Rev. the Ld. Bp. of St. David's.* A Discourse, delivered at Langyndeirn, near Carmarthen, on Thursday the 6th of July, 1815, at the Annual Meeting of the Society of Unitarian Christians in South Wales, and published at their request, with Notes. By John Prior Estlin, LL. D. 8vo. pp. 88. Hunter. 1815.

BISHOP BURGESS is entitled to the thanks of the Unitarians for keeping alive the Trinitarian controversy. He means not, certainly, to confer any favour upon them, but he cannot write against them without making their principles known, which is all they ask. Even his gross misrepresentations and wretched personalities have in one view a good effect, for they lead honest, candid and intelligent minds to suspect very properly that the prelate is conscious of the weakness of his cause, and is afraid to let it rest upon its own merits.

The good Bishop may see the impotence of episcopal fulminations by looking around his diocese. There Unitarian churches have been recently formed and they hold their associations under his lordship's eye. This sermon preached before one of these may shew Dr. Burgess that elevated as he is in his own church, he is esteemed by his Unitarian neighbours like any other writer, and that the mitre cannot give weight to idle declamation or hide the meanness and malignity of slander.

Not confining himself to the ordinary plan of a sermon, Dr. Estlin takes occasion from Acts xxiv. 14, to state, defend and enforce the prin-

ciples of Unitarians, and to vindicate himself and his brethren from the charges of their opponents, and particularly Bishop Burgess. The discourse is marked by so much sound sense, so much becoming solemnity and such correct Scriptural knowledge, and contains so many passages of great beauty, that we cannot but wish it were in the hands of all those readers that have been taught by the Bishop of St. David's and a few like-minded writers, that Unitarians are not entitled to the privileges of Christians, the courtesy of scholars or the rights of men.

" In the name of justice, of humanity and of Christianity, what is that great *superiority* of intellectual and moral worth, which he who has received the Trinitarian system, or who professes to have received it, enjoys over the person whose understanding can only admit the Unitarian system ; that wealth and honours, and all the advantages of this life should be open to the one, and that the other should not only be subject to the most degrading privations, but " be every where spoken against ;" and to crown all, that one should be admitted into the regions of everlasting happiness, and the other be exposed to the curse of God for ever ?

" O Lord ! how long !"—P. 41.

Dr. Estlin speaks thus " comfortably" to the Unitarians on the subject of *fashion,* the whole current of which he admits is now against them :

" This last circumstance we know is of a temporary nature ; and although we consider it as the circumstance which operates *most powerfully* against us, yet we feel a full confidence from the general circulation of the Bible and the increasing light and liberality which that occasions that its operation will soon cease. Nothing is more changeable than fashion. If ever the ideas of superiority of intellect should be associated with the religious tenets of Newton and a Locke—of coarseness, inconsistency and even nonsense with some modern systems which have attracted the notice of the gaping crowd—of sublimity of conception, correctness of taste and propriety of feeling with unadulterated Christianity ; if ever this period should arrive—surely it cannot be very remote the *thousands* who now only *think* with us, will *speak* and *act* with us ; and those whose minds are composed of " matter too soft a lasting mark to bear," will then exhibit the visible impression of Unitarianism. In the mean time, all that we want is, that the soil of the human mind should not be suffered to lie fallow or to produce only tares. That the seeds of truth may be sown, is all we ask. The harvest we leave to Heaven."—P. 5.

The Doctor considers the Unity of God and the humanity of Christ as doctrines totally distinct, and (p. 68,) retracts an opinion which he formerly advanced " that the proper humanity of Christ should be a necessary article of belief in a Christian society." On this controverted point, he says,

" In a conversation which I once had with Dr. Priestley on the very point, I took the liberty of telling him that his definition of Unitarianism in excluding those who hold the pre-existence of Christ appeared to my mind an illogical definition, and that Dr. Price, with whom I then coincided in opinion, was as much a Unitarian as himself. At that time I did not foresee that prejudice would proceed so far as to affix an odium to the very word. I thought that the definition itself was incorrect; that justice was not done by it to those who hold the pre-existence of Christ, but do not worship him, and that their exclusion was dividing and weakening a party, the union and strength of which could not be too sedulously promoted. I once for all enter my protest against the *exclusive* use of the word : and what I always mean by it is expressed in the following definition.

" A UNITARIAN IS A PERSON WHO BELIEVES IN AND WORSHIPS ONE GOD ONLY.

" I add *another* definition, for the denial of which, or the substitution of any other for it, I demand the authority of Scripture.

" A CHRISTIAN IS A PERSON WHO BELIEVES THE DIVINE MISSION OF JESUS CHRIST.

" In the sense of these definitions, I claim for myself, and I doubt not that each of you will claim for himself, the appellation of a *Unitarian Christian*."—Pp. 25, 26.

The following observations on *the miraculous conception* appear to us worthy of attention :

" The authenticity of the two first chapters of St. Matthew and St. Luke, on which so much has been written, and on one side with so much acrimony, has nothing to do with the subject of Unitarianism. And even the *pre-existence* of Christ, a doctrine which many Unitarians hold, is no more connected with the *miraculous conception* than it is with the miraculous *appearances* which were seen, or the miraculous *voice* which was heard at the baptism of our Lord. Many Unita-

rians have believed the miraculous conception, and others from some interesting texts in the narrative, and an apprehended *consistency* in the circumstance, that the *second Adam* should have been produced without an earthly father as the first was, have *wished* it to be true. Griesbach, however, it is thought by some, has not proved these chapters to be authentic : nor do Unitarians profess to follow him implicitly, although they have a high opinion of his learning, his assiduity and his impartiality. See Dr. Priestley's History of Early Opinions, Vol. IV ; and Grundy's Lectures on this subject."—Pp. 33, 34.

The reader will peruse with some interest, Dr. Estlin's explanation of his view of the *Sabbath* :

" Unitarians can agree to differ. I am not a materialist, and I disagree in opinion with Mr. Belsham and my nephew, Mr. Grundy, on the subject of the Sabbath. The statement of my particular view of the case will probably not be deemed a digression, as I have been informed that what Mr. Belsham has said on this subject in his Letters to Mr. Wilberforce, has injured the cause of Unitarianism in Wales. I beg leave then, just to state, that it appears to me, that the institution of a Sabbath has made a part of every dispensation of Revealed Religion ; that there was a Patriarchal and a Jewish Sabbath ; and that there is a Christian Sabbath called the Lord's Day ; that Christ himself instituted a rite in commemoration of his death, and that his Apostles after his ascension, when they were authorised legislators in his kingdom, appointed a day to be set apart to commemorate his resurrection as well as to answer the general purposes of a Sabbath ; and that they instituted it by their *conduct*, which speaks a language stronger than words, at a time when any other mode of institution would have subjected them to endless disputes with the Jews."—*Notes*, pp. 62, 63.

Referring to Bishop Burgess's arguments, Dr. Estlin says, in a beautiful passage with which this article must conclude—

" If such are the weapons of orthodoxy, Unitarianism may stand unarmed before her without fear of injury. I express myself with confidence, because I know, that if in the intellectual world it is still twilight, it is the twilight *of morning*. The fogs which linger in the West will be scattered by the rays of the rising Sun. The Eastern horizon is clear, and bright will be the day."—*Notes*, p. 48.

ART. IV.—*The History and Antiquities of Dissenting Churches, &c.*

[Continued from p. 414.]

THE successive ministers at *Crosby Square,* a Presbyterian church, now extinct, furnish us with a series of interesting biographical articles. The following relates to a worthy man little known :

" John Hodge, D. D. a learned and respectable minister of the Presbyterian denomination, of whose life it is not in our power to lay before the reader many particulars. He received his academical education at Taunton, under the learned Mr. Henry Grove, for whom he ever afterwards retained an affectionate remembrance. The place where he spent the first years of his ministry was, we believe, at Deal, in the county of Kent. From thence he removed to Glocester, where he continued to labour with great reputation, for a considerable period. Dr. Grosvenor being disabled for public service, which made it expedient for him to resign the pastoral office in 1749, Dr. Hodge accepted an invitation to succeed him at Crosby-Square. At the time of his settlement in that place, the congregation was in a very low state. And notwithstanding his pulpit composures were very sensible and devotional, and his manner of delivery just, though not striking, he was not so happy as to raise the church ; but as the old members died, or families removed, it continued sinking. At length, the infirmities of advanced life, obliged him to resign the pastoral relation, about the year 1761 or 1762. After this, he lived for some time in retirement, preaching only occasionally, till he was removed by death, August 18, 1767. As an acknowledgment of the benefits he received during the course of his academical studies, he bequeathed to the academy of Taunton, his valuable library of books. Upon the dissolution of that seminary, they were removed to Exeter.

" Dr. Hodge was a learned and respectable man, of moderate sentiments, and an excellent preacher. He favoured the republic of letters with a valuable set of discourses, in one volume, octavo, upon the Evidences of Christianity. They are written in a comprehensive, judicious, and nervous manner, and have been highly spoken of by good judges. He also published several single sermons : as one upon New-year's day, at St. Thomas's, Southwark—another at the morning lecture, Little St. Helen's, August 1, 1751 —and a third occasioned by the death of the Rev. John Mason, author of the treatise on Self-knowledge, preached at

Cheshunt, Herts, Feb. 2⁰, 1769. Dr. Hodge also drew up an account of Mr. May's Life, prefixed to his sermons. 1755.'' —Pp. 354, 355.

In the memoirs of Mr. *Benjamin Robinson,* minister of the Presbyterian congregation, *Little St. Helen's,* which no longer exists, we have an account of a controversy once esteemed of importance by the Nonconformists :

" In 1709, he published, " A Review of the case of Liturgies, and their imposition ; in answer to Mr. Bennet's Brief History of bre-composed set Forms of Prayer, and his Discourse of joint Prayer." To this Mr. Bennet wrote a reply, which was answered by Mr. Robinson, and produced a second letter from Mr. Bennet. This was a controversy of some importance, and called forth no inconsiderable talent. Some sentiments advanced by Mr. Bennet, were considered not only contrary to the general sense of Dissenters, but as a shock upon the reason of mankind. It is no wonder, therefore, that his book met with animadversion. Two pamphlets by way of answer to it, were written by Mr. John Horsley, ancestor to the late bishop of that name. It was also severely reprehended by some of his own brethren, particularly by Dr. Wainewright, Mr. Ollyffe, and Dr. John Edwards, in his " Christian Preacher."—Pp. 379, 380.

Few names in the Dissenting *Fasti* are more respectable than that of Mr. *Samuel Jones.* We are obliged to Mr. Wilson for a sketch of his life in a note affixed to the memoir of one of his pupils, Mr. *Edward Godwin,* the grandfather of Mr. *William Godwin,* the celebrated author, now living.

" Mr. Samuel Jones, who was of Welsh extraction, received his education in Holland, under the learned Perizonius. He kept his academy first at Glocester, from whence, in 1712, he removed to Tewkesbury, where, we believe, he was also pastor of a congregation. Of his method of education, a very interesting account may be seen, in a letter written in 1711, by Mr. (afterwards Archbishop) Secker, then one of Mr. Jones's pupils, to the celebrated Dr. Isaac Watts.* Mr. Secker speaks highly of the advantages he enjoyed at this seminary, which he calls " an extraordinary place of education." Mr. Jones obliged his pupils to rise at five o'clock every morning, and always to speak Latin, except when they mixed with the family. —" We pass our time very agreeably (says

_____

* " See Gibbons's Memoirs of Watts, p. 346.''

Mr. Secker) betwixt study and conversation with our tutor, who is always ready to discourse freely of any thing that is useful, and allows us either then, or at lecture, all imaginable liberty of making objections against his opinions, and prosecuting them as far as we can. In this and every thing else, he shews himself so much a gentleman, and manifests so great an affection and tenderness for his pupils, as cannot but command respect and love."—When Dr. Doddridge set on foot his academy, his friend Dr. Clark communicated to him Mr Jones's Lectures on Jewish Antiquities. A copy of these, very neatly written, in two volumes octavo, is preserved in Dr. Williams's library. Of Mr. Jones's ability as a tutor, we cannot but form a very high opinion from the merit and eminence of many of his pupils, among whom were the following:—Dr. Samuel Chandler and Dr. Andrew Gifford, of London; Mr. Thomas Mole, of Hackney; Mr. Richard Pearsall, of Taunton; Mr. Henry Francis, of Southampton; Mr. Jeremiah Jones, the learned author of "A new and full Method of settling the Canonical Authority of the New Testament;" Dr. Daniel Scott, well known to the world by his learned and valuable writings; Dr. Joseph Butler, afterwards Bishop of Durham, the author of that most learned and valuable performance, "The Analogy of Natural and Revealed Religion;" and Dr. Thomas Secker, who also conforming to the Church of England, rose to the See of Canterbury."—Pp. 381, 382.

Under the head "Devonshire Square—Particular Baptist," we have a very full biographical account of Mr. *William Kiffin*, the first pastor in that place, who was an eminent and wealthy merchant. He had been apprentice to John Lilburn, the brewer, who in the civil war held a colonel's commission in the parliament service. Casting his lot amongst the Nonconformists, Kiffin endured a variety of persecutions, religious and political, under the hateful reigns of the Second Charles and James, from some of which he extricated himself only by means of his riches. It is related that on one occasion the prodigal and needy Charles sent to Kiffin to borrow of him *forty thousand pounds*. The "Anabaptist" teacher apologised for not having it in his power to lend his Majesty so much, but told the messenger that if it would be of any service he would *present* him with *ten thousand*. The offer was accepted, and Kiffin used afterwards to boast that he had saved thirty thousand pounds.

In Monmouth's unfortunate rebellion, two grandsons of Mr. Kiffin, Benjamin and William Hewling, took part, and being taken prisoners were put to death, under circumstances of great barbarity. We are told that their sister going to court to present a petition to the king on their behalf, was admonished by Churchill, afterwards Duke of Marlborough, not to indulge hope, for, said he, pointing to the chimney-piece, "that marble is as capable of feeling compassion as the king's heart."

James, who was as foolish as he was heartless, afterwards applied to Kiffin with a request that he would promote his designs in the city, and received the same sort of rebuke which was given him on an application for support to the old Earl of Bedford, father to Lord Russell. Having pleaded his age and infirmities, Kiffin added, his eyes fixed steadfastly on the king, and tears running down his cheeks,—"besides, Sire, the death of my grandsons gave a wound to my heart, which is still bleeding, and never will close but in the grave." The king shrunk from this manly refusal and cutting reproach into silence.

Kiffin survived the Revolution. He died in peace Dec. 29, 1701, in the 86th year of his age. Mr. Wilson has given a good portrait of him.

It should have been mentioned in a memoir of Kiffin, that he had a controversy with John Bunyan on the subject of adult baptism by immersion being a term of Christian fellowship. Mr. Wilson, however, takes no notice of this, but simply states in a note, p. 430, that Mr. Kiffin published only "*A Sober Discourse of Right to Church Communion*, in which he pleads for strict communion." This was not Kiffin's only publication, but it may be observed that it was the first piece published professedly on this subject. Robert Robinson, in his ingenious tract entitled "The Doctrine of Toleration applied to Free Communion," [Works, III. 143,] gives the following account of another work in which Kiffin had a share: "In 1672, Mr. Bunyan, then in prison, published his *Confession of Faith*, and in it pleaded warmly for mixed communion. In answer to this, Messieurs Kiffin and

Paul published a piece entitled—*Some Serious Reflections on that part of Mr. Bunyan's Confession of Faith touching Church Communion with Unbaptized Believers.* These gentlemen treated John very cavalierly. Your *conclusion*, say they, is *devilish topfull of ignorance and prejudice*: but this we forgive them, for John was a tinker without dish or spoon, and at best but a country teacher, and the Rev. Mr. William Kiffin was a London minister and worth forty thousand pounds." The interest which we take in this controversy, and our regard to the name of Bunyan, induce us to lengthen this extract from Robinson. "The next year, Mr. Bunyan published an answer, entitled *Differences in Judgment about Water Baptism no Bar to Communion.* To this piece of Mr. Bunyan's, Messieurs Danvers and Paul replied, and John answered them in 1674, in about two sheets in twelves, entitled *Peaceable Principles and True.* In all these he continued uniform in his sentiments, declaring he would abide by his faith and practice till *the moss should grow upon his eye-brows.* I mention this because the editors of his Works in folio have inserted a Discourse entitled *An Exhortation to Peace and Unity,* in which it is declared that baptism is essential to church communion; but it is evident Bunyan never wrote this piece."

Our author is a friend to religious inquiry and discussion, but he is not always consistent. For example he says truly and well, p. 428, " It is a distinguishing feature of truth that it invites inquiry : to stifle it is the mark of a bad cause, and the certain resort of bigots." In two pages afterwards, however, he relates of Kiffin's second son, that " having an inclination to travel abroad, he was accompanied by a young minister as far as Leghorn, and proceeding by himself to Venice, there *entered too freely into conversation upon religious subjects, and was poisoned by a Popish priest.*" This narrow-minded reflection we are willing to believe that Mr. Wilson has injudiciously copied from some one of his old authorities.

We meet in the History with frequent stories of the judgments of God upon persecutors, and in p. 436 there is an apology for them. We must remark, once for all, that such narrations

betray great credulity and an evident inattention to the ordinary course of Divine Providence, under which *all things come alike to all.*

There is an offensive vulgarism, in p. 441, where, relating a journey which *Sayer Rudd* made to France without the consent of his congregation (Devonshire Square), Mr. Wilson says " he took which [*what*] is commonly called *French leave.*"

In the account of *John Macgowan,* pastor in the place last-mentioned, who is known by his audacious and malignant pamphlets against reputed "Socinianism," Mr. Wilson is not sparing of his censures on controversial outrageousness and artifice : he says very judiciously, p. 453, " We have better evidence for the doctrines of the gospel than those afforded by ghosts and spectres." This refers to a piece of Macgowan's, entitled " The Arian's and Socinian's Monitor," in which a story is told of a young minister who saw his tutor (the learned and venerable Dr. John Taylor) rolling in hell-flames, and received of course due warning against ' damnable heresies.' Is it credible that Trinitarians should still circulate this abominable libel, and that any readers should be found (as we are informed there are) of such depraved understandings, as to receive the impudent and wicked fiction for truth ?

Macgowan published another notable piece, in letters to Dr. Priestley, entitled *Christ proved to be the Adorable God or a Notorious Impostor.* On this instance of polemic craft, the decorum to which we are constrained forbids us to, make the proper comment. It is akin to the wisdom of certain disputants in conversation, who declare, if some favourite notion be not scriptural *they will burn their Bibles.* In the same temper and with, the same degree of understanding, the Pagans, when their prayers were unanswered, in the rage of disappointment demolished their gods.

Of Macgowan, Mr. Wilson yet declares, p. 451, " his humility was very remarkable !"

A fact related of the Meeting-house in *Miles's Lane* reminds us of the late proceedings against the Protestants in France : it has been said of *popery,* but may more truly be said of *persecution,* that it is *always the same.*

"Though the exact date of the building is not now to be obtained, there is good evidence that it must have been erected very soon after the restoration of Charles the Second. Being a large and commodious place, it was fixed upon as a prey to the parish minister, when his church was consumed in the fire of London, A. D. 1666; nor could the rightful owners regain possession till the new church was built. This was the fate of many other meeting-houses, at that time, and places in a strong light the unprincipled power of the ecclesiastical government, during the reign of Charles the Second."—P. 462.

Art. V.—*The London Society for Promoting Christianity amongst the Jews Examined, and the Pretensions of the Converted Jew Investigated, &c. &c.* By B. R. Goakman, late Printer to the Institution. 8vo. pp. 64. Simpkin and Marshall. 1816.

WE know not what degree of credit is due to the "late Printer to the Institution" for converting the Jews, but if the tenth part of what he relates be true, the conductors of the society owe an apology to the public for the costly delusion which they have been the means of supporting. According to this statement, almost the only Jew of fair character who has been connected with the society was one who never professed conversion and who, wanting the qualification of hypocrisy, was ill-used by the managers.

One short story will explain the design of this pamphlet:

"A man of the name of *Marinus* came from Germany into this country, for the purpose of obtaining a sale for some *Cologne Water*, of which he professed to be the Inventor. Finding himself run short of cash, he applied to the London Society for assistance. I asked him if he had embraced Christianity; his reply was,

I am not yet converted, but if I can get a good sale for my Cologne Water I soon shall be."—P. 64.

The "late Printer" sums up his pleadings against the Society, in a few words:

"What has the London Society done? ——expended 70,000*l.* and have made their proselytes worse characters than they were before!"—P. 64.

Art. VI.—*On Persecution.* A Discourse delivered in the Protestant Dissenting Chapel, Lewin's Mead, Bristol, June 16, 1816, in recommendation of a Subscription for the Relief of the Protestant Sufferers for Conscience-Sake in the South of France. By John Prior Estlin, LL.D. 8vo. pp. 38. Longman and Co. 1816.

THE benevolent preacher exposes and reprobates Persecution, as pre-supposing "that a perfect knowledge of religious subjects is attainable by all men, and consequently, that an uniformity of belief is practicable; that those who practise it have attained this knowledge and are infallible; that errors of the understanding merely are criminal; that those who have arrived at speculative perfection themselves have a right to compel others to come into the truth; and that pains and penalties are the means to accomplish this purpose."

An opinion is stated in p. 20, which is well worthy of discussion; and we insert the statement of it to invite the notice of our Correspondents, viz. "Wherever the doctrines of *the eternity of hell-torments,* of *inspiration* or *infallibility,* and of *exclusive salvation* or *salvation depending on opinions,* are received together in a heart prepared for their reception, *a persecuting spirit appears to me to be a natural and legitimate consequence.*"

POETRY.

TO THE EDITOR.
Sir, *Reading, Sept.* 15, 1816.

THE humble tribute I send you for insertion in the Repository, to the memory of Mr. Vidler, is but a very feeble attempt to express the emotions of respect with which his memory is cherished by those who had the pleasure of his acquaintance here.

From his conversation they not only derived the highest intellectual gratification, but have to date the best and holiest feelings which Christian truth is calculated to inspire. They remember him with an enthusiasm of reverence, which it would be impossible for much higher powers than mine to express. It is gratifying to reflect that as this town was among the last scenes of his labours, so it was one in which they were most eminently successful. In future times, when the cause of truth may have advanced to a much greater eminence than it has yet attained in this place, his name will be recollected with gratitude as its first supporter; and of him, in the midst of the Unitarian congregation, might be most truly applied the epitaph on a celebrated architect—" *Si monumentum requiris, circumspice.*"*

T. N. T.

A Tribute to the Memory of
THE REV. WILLIAM VIDLER.

Hush! 'twas no strain of anguish or despair
That softly floats on ev'ning's stillest air,
Celestial bliss the distant note·reveals,
Though from the grave the solemn music steals;
An angel's lyre, through shades of fun'ral gloom,
More sweetly mild from sweeping o'er the tomb.

Yes; there remov'd from mortal cares, he sleeps,
Whose soft repose affection scarcely weeps,
Whose earthly days in such sweet concord ran,
Earth sunk from view ere death's control began;
Who, 'mid the storms of life, with cloudless brow,
As calmly rested as he slumbers now;
To evil dead while here he drew his breath,
And living yet triumphant in his death.

Here long shall friendship's tend'rest mem'ry trace
The mild effulgence of his speaking face—
The eye where kindness beam'd, and fires of youth
Still kindled joyous at the voice of truth—
Li't up, not dim'd by care or quench'd by years,
Sparkling with joy or eloquent in tears;—
The conscious dignity by nature giv'n,
The hope that had its resting-place in heav'n,
The heart-felt eloquence, the manly sense,
The genial wit that gave no ear offence;
The courteous mien that, grac'd by rev'rend age,
Disarm'd the bigot in his fiercest rage,
The pow'r that flash'd conviction on the mind,
The heart that knew no party but mankind:

* If you require a monument, look around you.

All live more tender seen through friendship's tear,
While gen'rous hearts shall feel and kindle here.

Methinks I see, by hope's great theme inspir'd,
That form rever'd in sudden light attir'd,
Pursue the path immortal prophets trod,
To trace the deepest charities of God.
Then as delight his raptur'd eye bedew'd,
Each mind amaz'd the glorious prospect view'd,
Death's icy fetters seem'd by mercy broke,
And sorrow dropt her sceptre as he spoke.
Deep 'mid the fading gloom as man could trace
Shone vistas fair of universal grace;
Heav'n seem'd all op'ning to the ravish'd sight
With fanes half viewless from " excessive bright;"
Hell sunk a trembling spectre 'mid the blaze,
And earth bloom'd ever young 'mid joy and praise.
Then notes of gladness from the vision clear,
Stole in sweet whispers on the list'ning ear;
Prophetic strains of bliss to reign on high,
Join'd with the mellow voice of years gone by;
Then light from heav'n seem'd freshly still to glow,
Like pure enchantment o'er these realms of woe,
Gleam'd like a holier moon-beam through the bow'rs,
Blush'd in the clouds and sparkled in the flow'rs,
Shed on the genial earth a softer green,
And gleam'd on angel's wings at distance seen,
Cast on the woods a tint of gentler spring,
Till earth appear'd a visionary thing:
Man seem'd again in hope and bliss a boy,
And life one cloudless dream of love and joy.

Then let no tear, save such as hope may shed,
Bedew the flow'rs that deck his lowly bed;
But there let breezy whispers greet the ear
Like first sweet concords of a jarring sphere;
There let young hearts pursue his glorious theme,
And sink absorb'd in virtue's holiest dream;
There let the soul oppress'd delight to stay,
Think on his name and muse its griefs away;
Let artless childhood lisp its earliest pray'r,
And contrite sinners taste forgiveness there:

And when the soul all mortal cares above,
Is wrapt in thoughts of universal love,
From eyes uprais'd with tearful rapture dim,
The purest, tend'rest drop shall flow for him.

From the Portuguese.
THE MANIAC.

Look at yon sad mourner there!
 Chilling thoughts bedew his cheeks,
 And in rapt loneliness he seeks
Comfort in despair!
In midnight cold—and noontide heat
He wanders o'er the mountain wild,
The rude crags wound his weary feet;—
 Yes, that is mis'ry's child!

He wants no guide, he owns no friend,
 No voice of joy he hears;
Darkness and dread his steps attend;
 He hates the morning's loveliest
 beam,
 And the sun never shines for him
Except in clouds and tears!

Brightest to him the blackest gloom;
His only paradise, the tomb:—
 Pity yon child of woe!
Pray that he soon may lay his head
Where his own hands have made his bed,
 And weeds and flow'rets grow,
Water'd by tears himself has shed;—
 Those tears have ceas'd to flow.

That troubled, madden'd soul hath been
Composed, and happy, and serene,
 As 'tis abandon'd now:
 Poor mis'ry's child,
 The tempest wild
Is calmer far than thou!

But it shall blast, and rage and roar
 When sweet repose shall still thy breast,
When thy mind's tempest beats no more,
 And thy lov'd grave shall give thee rest,
 So long denied before.
A little while, sad maniac! and thou'rt
 free—
Nor woe, nor thought of woe, shall visit
 thee.
 A.

DESPAIR.
From Bocage.

What! scathed with desolate curses,—no-
 thing left;
Of hope, of heav'n, of ev'ry thing bereft?
 O no! I still may rage and weep and
 sigh:
Pour forth the bitterness that blasts my
 mind,
Tell all my agony to the list'ning wind,
 And (O! most privileged of blessings,)
 die!
 A.

MORNING.

See the new light in ruddy mantle clad
 Come dancing o'er the mountains;
 darkness flies
From its gay footsteps; trees, and plants,
 and flow'rs
 Put on their brightest, richest liv'ries:
Smiles gild the path of early morning
 hours,
And heav'n is full of joy—and earth is
 glad.
 A.

OBITUARY.

REV. WM. VIDLER.

WE announced in our last (p. 491) the death of this able and truly respectable Christian preacher. He had scarcely outlived the usual period of the vigour of man. His age was 58. He had long suffered under an asthma, arising from internal disorganization. His affliction was extreme and his death slow. His conversation to the very last day of his life was characteristic of his mind: he felt no raptures, but he yielded not to despondency; he looked forward with Christian hope, and, in nearly his last expression, *his heart was fixed on God.* Throughout his illness and death he derived great satisfaction from the system of divine truth which he had publicly professed and taught, and took peculiar pleasure in dwelling on the character of Christ, as the son of man, the friend and brother of his disciples, and on the universal, inexhaustible love of God.

By his particular desire, he was interred by Mr. Aspland in the Burial-ground belonging to the Unitarian Church, Hackney. The funeral took place on Wednesday, August the 28th. A long train of mourning coaches and a great crowd of spectators attested the sensation created by the melancholy event. The corpse was carried into the Gravel Pit Meeting-House, and an address was delivered over it, the substance of which will be found in the *Christian Reformer.*

On the following Sunday Evening, Mr. Aspland, in fulfilment of the last request of the deceased, preached the funeral sermon, at the Chapel in Parliament Court, to a vast concourse of

sorrowing friends. The text was
2 Tim. iv. 6, 7, 8, which was used as
an introduction to a memoir and character of Mr. Vidler. His congregation
had caused the pulpit and galleries to
be hung in black, and had adopted
other measures of respect towards their
lamented pastor.

Mr. Vidler has left behind him some
manuscripts, which he has consigned
to the discretion of Mr. Aspland; and
it is in contemplation to publish a selection from these, with as ample a
memoir as can be compiled. A memoir will also appear in this work,
and it is hoped that a *portrait* will be
obtained for an accompaniment. Probably both may appear in the opening
number of the next volume.

In the mean time, we are happy
to gratify the affectionate curiosity of
Mr. Vidler's numerous friends, by the
following character of him, being
the conclusion of a funeral sermon,
preached by Mr. Evans, on the Sunday following Mr. Aspland's funeral
sermon.

———

*A Tribute of Respect to the Memory
of the* Rev. William Vidler, being
the conclusion of an Address delivered by *John Evans*, at *Worship
Street*, Sunday Morning, Sept. 8th,
1816, founded on Luke ix. 26—
" Whosoever shall be ashamed of me
and of my words, of him shall the Son
of man be ashamed, when he shall
come in his own glory, and in his
Father's, and of the holy angels."*

These remarks (illustrative of the
passage on which my Address is
founded,) lead me to notice the
character and conduct of my worthy
deceased friend, the *Rev. William
Vidler.* I had the pleasure of being
acquainted with him for these *twenty
years* past, and my knowledge of him
enables me to declare that he acted
upon the principles I have described.
He endeavoured to attain just views of
the Christian religion, and assuredly
he without disguise communicated
them to mankind.

Possessing naturally a vigorous mind,
my friend applied himself to the study

of the Old and New Testament.
Unaided by education, he exercised his
faculties in the best manner he was able
for the acquisition of truth. *Persuaded*
thus far in *his mind*, he laboured to
instruct and improve his fellow-creatures according to the views he then
entertained of the principles and practices of Christianity.

But when on further inquiry he
had reason to believe that the tenets of
Calvinism which he had adopted were
false, he relinquished them. His first
step was the renunciation of the doctrine of the *eternal misery of the wicked*,
and the adoption of the heart-exhilara-
ting tenet of universal restoration! Much esteemed for his talents
and zeal by his brethren, he was upon
his change of sentiment subjected to
their reprobation. The charge of
heresy was thundered against him in
every direction—he was said to be led
astray by the snares of Satan; and
suspicions of his safety in another
world were scattered about in pro-
fusion. One would have thought
from this treatment of an erring
brother, that forbearance formed no
part of the religion of Jesus Christ.†

It is somewhat singular that one
of Mr. Vidler's bitterest opponents
lately deceased (the Rev. A. Fuller,)
has in his diary just published in his
Life by Dr. Ryland, acknowledged
the *great corruption* of the Christian
religion, and confessed that accounts
of *Heretics* should be received with
caution. His words are these—" I
cannot help lamenting in reading

———

* The crowded attendance on the delivery of the Address is here acknowledged as respectful to the preacher, and
as an honourable token of regard to the
memory of the deceased.

† A delectable specimen of this anti-
christian spirit may be seen in a review of
the controversy between Mr. Fuller and
Mr. Vidler, in the Life of the former
gentleman, by *J. W. Morris*, late of
Dunstable; a man from whom Mr. Fuller
thought it " his duty" to withdraw his
friendship, and who ought not to forget
that it is possible for individuals to be
eager in pointing out the faults of others
while " they refuse to acknowledge any of
their own !" See page 560 of the *Life
of the Rev. Andrew Fuller*, by John
Ryland, D. D. This same Mr. Morris
declares very authoritatively that some of
the *sects* are grossly misrepresented in the
Sketch of the Denominations: but his
gratuitous assertion cannot be admitted
for proof; and the unparalleled success
of that little work, constitutes a sufficient
refutation of the falsehood, with the more
intelligent classes of the Christian world.

Mosheim's Church History, *how soon* and *how much* was the religion of Jesus corrupted from its primitive simplicity. And the partial account of the *English Baptists* leads me to indulge a better opinion of various sects who have been deemed *Heretics!"* Much indeed must the religion of Jesus have been corrupted from its primitive simplicity, since other tests of Christian fellowship are imposed than that of acknowledging CHRIST to be the *Messiah* or *the Son of God*; and surely the writer who makes the declaration contained in the concluding sentence of the above paragraph, might have indulged more tenderness towards the reputedly *heretical* advocates of universal restoration. It is a curious phenomenon in the annals of theology, that those who as to their *faith* take most pains to be right should be generally declared most wrong; and that those who as to *practice* abound most in the exercise of Christian charity should be pronounced destitute of true piety. But certain it is that without free inquiry and a patient, candid investigation of opposite systems of faith—we the inhabitants of this highly favoured island, might have been at this day "plucking misletoe with the Druid or mixing a little flour and water into the substance of the incomprehensible God!"

My deceased friend, however, was not deterred by the unchristian treatment of his brethren from holding fast what he deemed Scriptural truth. He even pushed his inquiries still further so as to renounce other popular errors and to maintain the glorious doctrines of *the Divine Unity*, and the *unpurchased love* of the Supreme Being in the redemption of the world. "Blessed be the GOD and FATHER of our Lord Jesus Christ, who hath blessed us with all spiritual blessings in heavenly things in Christ: In whom we have redemption through his blood, the forgiveness of sins, according to the riches of his grace."† On doctrines contained in this as well as similar passages of the New Testament, he dwelt with satisfaction and delight. Contrary views are to be found only in creeds and confessions of faith, which with him were in no estimation. Embodying human error

and consecrating human infirmity, he justly deemed them encumbrances to the progress of truth. And yet, strange to tell, for attaching themselves to the above Scriptural views of the character of the Supreme Being, Dr. Ryland in his *Life of Fuller*, declares a certain class of *General Baptists*, (to whom I and my deceased friend have the honour to belong), "to have gone from GENERAL REDEMPTION to *no redemption !!*" Such are the gross and abominable misrepresentations in which party writers indulge at the expense of truth and to the utter destruction of Christian charity.‡

It should be added that our venerable brother, whilst he maintained the prime leading doctrines of revelation, did not relinquish the ordinance of *Christian Baptism* by immersion, but administered it to its only proper objects, those who make a profession of their faith. Having preached for him more than once on those occasions, I have witnessed his administration of it in this place with pleasure. He conducted it with a solemnity which became its importance, making candid allowance for those otherwise minded, and pointing out its happy tendency in promoting the purity of the professors of Christianity.

As the treatment received by this good man from his particular Baptist brethren, on account of difference of sentiment, has been mentioned, it is but justice to add that he was similarly treated by a minister of that class who style themselves *Free Grace General Baptists!* This Reverend brother from whom better things were to be expected, endeavoured to prevent Mr. Vidler from becoming a member of the respectable GENERAL BODY of Dissenting ministers of the Three Denominations meeting at Red-cross Street. It is with no small pleasure that I now recollect the successful exertions made by me in his behalf on that occasion. An end was soon put to this unwarrantable and odious ebullition of bigotry.

Thus like his great Master, *through good report* and *through evil report*, did my friend pursue the even tenor of

---

† Ephes. i. 3, 7.

‡ In the Second Edition of my *Letter to Dr. Hawker*, will be found a discussion of the doctrine of GENERAL REDEMPTION.

his way, till resting from his labours he was laid in the peaceful tomb. The particulars of his life, and of his last long severe illness, which he bore with exemplary resignation, have been laid before his congregation by a friend every way capable of rendering justice to his benevolence and piety. I have thought proper to touch only on the leading traits of his character as a minister of Jesus Christ. His love of free inquiry, his endeavour to divest himself of prejudice, and his intrepid avowal of his religious creed, are creditable to his memory. These are essential requisites of ministerial fidelity. Though we agreed in many important articles of faith, yet as to others we were agreed to differ. Friendly and cheerful, he often conversed with freedom on religious topics, but never to the breach of Christian charity. He could bear with those who did not accompany him in all his convictions. And we both heartily acquiesced in the sublime and awful asseveration of Jesus Christ—" Whosoever shall be ashamed of me and of my words, of him shall the Son of man be ashamed, when he shall come in his own glory, and in his Father's, and of the holy angels."

To conclude—the minister of Jesus Christ, be he *Churchman* or *Dissenter*, *Trinitarian* or *Unitarian*, who, imploring the blessing of heaven, indulges free inquiry, endeavours to divest his mind of prejudice, and honestly proclaims his convictions, on every proper occasion, sanctioned and emblazoned by a correspondent temper and practice, will receive the final eulogy of the Saviour — " *Well done good and faithful servant, enter thou into the joy of thy Lord.*"

"Lo! with a mighty Host HE comes,
I see the parted clouds give way,
I see the banner of the cross display;
Death's *conqueror* in pomp appears—
In his right hand, a palm he bears,
And in his looks—REDEMPTION wears!"

"The souls of the righteous are in the hand of God, and there shall no torment touch them. In the sight of the unwise they seem to die, and their departure is taken for misery, and their going from us to be utter destruction; but they are in peace, for though they be punished in the sight of men,

yet is their hope full of immortality: and having been a little chastised, they shall be greatly rewarded, for GOD proved them and found them worthy of himself.*

September 10, at *Cheltenham,* having nearly completed his 81st year, RICHARD REYNOLDS, of *Bristol,* a highly respected member of the Society of Friends. For a long series of years in the possession of an ample fortune, he made it subservient to the purposes of benevolence. His numerous charities, public and private, rank him among the most eminent philanthropists of the present age. After a gradual decline, he closed a life of great usefulness in the faith and hope of a Christian.

MRS. ELIZABETH HAMILTON.—It would be with feelings of sincere sorrow, for a private and a public loss, that the lovers of elegant literature heard of the death of one of the most amiable, useful and popular of the female writers of the present age; one who has done honour to her sex and to her country.

Mrs. Elizabeth Hamilton was born at Belfast, in Ireland; and the affection for her country, which she constantly expressed, proved that she had a true Irish heart. She was well known to the public as the author of " The Cottagers of Glenburnie," " The Modern Philosophers," " Letters on Female Education," and various other works. She has obtained, in different departments of literature, just celebrity, and has established a reputation that will strengthen and consolidate from the duration of time—that destroyer of all that is false and superficial.

The most popular of her lesser works is " the Cottagers of Glenburnie," a lively and humorous picture of the slovenly habits, the indolent *winna-be-fashed* temper, the baneful content which prevails among some of the lower class of people in Scotland. It is a proof of the great merit of this book, that it has, in spite of the Scottish dialect with which it abounds, been universally read in England and Ireland, as well as in Scotland. It is a faithful representation of human nature in general, as well as of local manners and cus-

* Wisdom iii. 1, 5.

toms; the maxims of economy and industry, the principles of truth, justice, family affection and religion, which it inculcates by striking examples, and by exquisite strokes of pathos, mixed with humour, are independent of all local peculiarity of manner or language, and operate upon the feelings of every class of readers, in all countries. In Ireland in particular, the history of "the Cottagers of Glenburnie" has been read with peculiar avidity; and it has probably done as much good to the Irish as to the Scotch. While the Irish have seized and enjoyed the opportunity it afforded of a good-humoured laugh at their Scotch neighbours, they have secretly seen, through shades of difference, a resemblance to themselves; and are conscious that, changing the names, the tale might be told of them. In this tale, both the difference and the resemblance between Scottish and Hibernian faults or foibles are advantageous to its popularity in Ireland. The difference is sufficient to give an air of novelty that awakens curiosity; while the resemblance fixes attention, and creates a new species of interest. Besides this, the self-love of the Hibernian reader being happily relieved from all apprehension that the lesson was intended for him, his good sense takes and profits by the advice that is offered to another. The humour in this book is peculiarly suited to the Irish, because it is, in every sense of the word, *good humour*. The satire, if satire it can be called, is benevolent; its object is to mend, and not wound, the heart. Even the Scotch themselves, however national they are supposed to be, can bear "the Cottagers of Glenburnie." Nations, like individuals, can with decent patience endure to be told of their faults, if those faults, instead of being represented as forming their established unchangeable character, are considered as arising, as in fact they usually do arise, from those passing circumstances which characterize rather a certain period of civilization than any particular people. If our national faults are pointed out as indelible stains, inherent in the texture of the character, from which it cannot by art or time be bleached or purified, we are justly provoked and offended; but, if a friend warns us of some little accidental spots, which we had, perhaps, overlooked, and which we can,

at a moment's notice, efface, we smile, and are grateful.

In "the Modern Philosophers," where the spirit of system and party interfered with the design of the work, it was difficult to preserve throughout the tone of good-humoured raillery and candour: this could scarcely have been accomplished by any talents or prudence, had not the habitual temper and real disposition of the writer been candid and benevolent. Though this work is a professed satire upon a system, yet it avoids all satire of individuals; and it shews none of that cynical contempt of the human race which some satirists seem to feel, or affect, in order to give poignancy to their wit.

Our author has none of that misanthropy which derides the infirmities of human nature, and which laughs while it cauterizes. There appears always some adequate object for any pain that she inflicts: it is done with a steady view to future good, and with a humane and tender, as well as with a skilful and courageous hand.

The object of "the Modern Philosophers" was to expose those whose theory and practice differ; to point out the difficulty of applying high-flown principles to the ordinary, but necessary, concerns of human life; and to shew the danger of trusting every man to become his own moralist and legislator. When this novel first appeared, it was, perhaps, more read, and more admired, than any of Mrs. Hamilton's works: the name and character of Brigettina Botheram passed into every company, and became a standing jest —a proverbial point in conversation. The ridicule answered its purpose; it reduced to measure and reason those who, in the novelty and zeal of system, had overleaped the bounds of common sense.

"The Modern Philosophers," "the Cottagers of Glenburnie," and "the Letters of the Hindoo Rajah," the first book, we believe, that our author published, have all been highly and steadily approved by the public. These works, alike in principle and in benevolence of design, yet with each a different grace of style and invention, have established Mrs. Hamilton's character as an original, agreeable and successful writer of fiction. But her claims to literary reputation, as a useful, philosophic, moral and religious author, are of a higher sort, and rest upon works of a more solid and durable nature; upon her works on education, especially her " Letters on Female Education." In these she not only shews that she has studied the history of the human mind, and that she has made herself acquainted with what has been written on this subject by the best moral and metaphysical writers, but she adds new value to their knowledge by rendering it practically useful. She has thrown open to all classes of readers those metaphysical discoveries or observations, which had been confined chiefly to the learned. To a sort of knowledge, which had been considered more as a matter of curiosity than of use, she has given real value and actual currency: she has shewn how the knowledge of metaphysics can be made serviceable to the art of education; she has shewn, for instance, how the doctrine of the association of ideas may be applied, in early education, to the formation of the habits of temper, and of the principles of taste and morals; she has considered how all that metaphysicians know of sensation, abstraction, &c. can be applied to the cultivation of the judgment and the imaginations of children. No matter how little is actually ascertained on these subjects: she has done much in wakening the attention of parents, and of mothers especially, to future inquiry; she has done much by directing their inquiries rightly; much by exciting them to reflect upon their own minds, and to observe what passes in the minds of their children. She has opened a new field of investigation to women, a field fitted to their domestic habits, to their duties as mothers, and to their business as preceptors of youth; to whom it belongs to give the minds of children those first impressions and ideas, which remain the longest, and which influence them often the most powerfully, through the whole course of life. In recommending to her own sex the study of metaphysics, as far as it relates to education, Mrs. Hamilton has been judiciously careful to avoid all that can lead to that species of " vain debate," of which there is no end. She, knowing the limits of the human understanding, does not attempt to go beyond them into that which can be at best but a dispute about terms. She does not aim at making women expert in the " wordy war;" nor does

she teach them to astonish learned by their acquaintance various vocabularies of met system-makers.

Such jugglers' tricks she but she has not, on the oth been deceived or overawed who would represent the stu human mind as a study that no practical purpose, and tha and unsafe for her sex. Had milton set ladies on metaphysi merely to shew their paces, sl have made herself and them i and troublesome; but she ha how they may, by slow an steps, advance to a useful obje dark, intricate and dangerous l; she has converted into a clear, practicable road; a road not o ticable, but pleasant, and not o sant but, what is of far mor quence to women, safe.

Mrs. Elizabeth Hamilton known to be not only a mor pious, writer; and in all her as in all her conversation, reli pears in the most engaging view. Her religion was since ful and tolerant; joining, in piest manner, faith, hope and All who had the happiness this amiable woman will, v accord, bear testimony to the that feeling of affection which nevolence, kindness and che of temper inspired. She th little of herself, so much o that it was impossible she cou rior as she was, excite envy. every body at ease in her com good humour and good spii themselves. So far from bei straint on the young and li encouraged, by her sympath openness and gaiety. She n tered, but she always formed favourable opinion, that truth sense would permit, of every i who came near her; ther instead of fearing and shun penetration, loved and cou society.

Her loss will be long reg her private friends; her mei long live in public estimation

Much as Mrs. Elizabeth I has served and honoured the female literature by her writ has done still higher and more benefit to that cause by her li ting the example, through the whole of that uniform propriety of conduct, and of all those virtues which ought to characterize her sex, which form the charm and happiness of domestic life, and which in her united gracefully with that superiority of talent and knowledge that commanded the admiration of the public.—*Monthly Magazine.*

INTELLIGENCE.

DOMESTIC.
RELIGIOUS.
. *Manchester College, York.*

THE REV. WILLIAM SHEPHERD, of Gateacre, has offered a prize of five guineas for the best classical scholar in this Institution, in the ensuing session. The merits of the candidates to be decided on at the examination at the close of the session.

Manchester, August 21, 1816.

The following sums have been received on account of this Institution.

	£	s.	d.
Collection at Chesterfield Chapel, by the Rev. R. W. Wallace.	11	10	7
Rev. Israel Worsley, Plymouth (Annual).	1	1	0
Mr. T. Holt, Liverpool, An.	1	1	0
W. Ridge, Esq. Chichester, do.	1	1	0
Mr. W. Bayley, Chichester, do.	0	10	6
Hinton Castle, Esq. Clifton, do.	2	2	0
Mr. Richmond, Temple, London. do.	1	1	0
	18	7	1

G. W. WOOD, Treasurer.
Manchester, September 6, 1816.

The thirtieth Annual Meeting of Trustees of Manchester College, York, was held at Cross Street Chapel Rooms, in Manchester, on Friday August 30, 1816, Abraham Crompton, of Lune Villa, near Lancaster, Esq. in the chair.

The proceedings of the Committee during the past year were read over, and confirmed, and the Treasurer's Accounts were laid before the Meeting, approved of, and passed.

Benjamin Gaskell, Esq. M. P. of Thorns House, Yorkshire, was re-elected President, and James Touchet, Esq. of Manchester, Joseph Strutt, Esq. of Derby, Peter Martineau, Esq. of Canonbury, and Daniel Gaskell, Esq. of Lupsett, were re-elected Vice Presidents. Mr. George William Wood, of Manchester, was re-chosen Treasurer, and Mr. Edward Baxter, Mr. Jonathan Brookes, and Mr. William Duckworth, of Manchester, and the Rev. Joseph Ashton, of Duckinfield, were added to the Committee, to supply the places of the Gentlemen ineligible from non-attendance.

The Deputy Treasurers for the past year were re-elected, with the addition of Mr. Robert Philips, Jun. of Manchester, and Mr. Cyrus Armitage, of Duckinfield.

Mr. Thomas Henry Robinson and the Rev. John Gooch Robberds, of Manchester, were re-appointed Secretaries.

The thanks of the Meeting were voted to the President, Vice-Presidents, and other Officers of the College, for their services during the past year.

The Report made of the state of the Funds was encouraging and satisfactory. The Trustees have been enabled to discharge the debt that was owing to the Treasurer at the commencement of the year; to appropriate 400*l.* to the farther liquidation of the debt on the York Buildings, and to make a small addition to the Permanent Fund.

The means of accomplishing these desirable objects have been principally afforded by the receipt of several considerable benefactions, and of a legacy of 200*l.* bequeathed to the College by the late Swann Downer, Esq. of London. The Trustees have likewise made arrangements for the admission of twelve Divinity Students on the foundation next session, and for an addition to the emoluments of the Tutors.

The number of Students in the College during the last session was reported to have been 21, viz. 11 Lay-students, and 10 intended for the ministry; of the latter Mr. Mardon and Mr. Merris have finally left the College, and Mr. Mardon is settled with the Unitarian Congregation at Glasgow, as successor to the Rev. James Yates.

Thirteen Divinity Students and seventeen Lay-Students are expected in the College next session.

When the business of the meeting was closed, the chair was taken by Isaac Harrop, Esq. of Altringham; and the thanks of the meeting were unanimously voted to Abraham Crompton, Esq. for his services as Chairman.

The Trustees and friends of the College afterwards dined together at the Spread Eagle Inn; Nathaniel Philips, Esq. of the Dales, in the chair. The attendance was not so numerous as on former occasions, but the day was spent with much hilarity and interest.

Manchester, September 4, 1816.

Meeting of Ministers at Coventry.

On the 6tb instant, a *Meeting of Ministers* was holden at *Coventry*, and a religious service was performed in the great Meeting, in that city. The Rev. James Scott conducted the devotional parts ; and the Rev. John Yates delivered the Sermon, from 2 Cor. vi. 1. It is not intended to analize this learned and singularly excellent discourse, nor will it be attempted to point out its numerous and various merits ; but it may be permitted to say—that it discovered an extensive acquaintance with the writings of the ancients, and the several systems of philosophy which have prevailed in the world; and which, however they may have been extolled by some, were yet clearly proved by the preacher to be as inferior to Christianity as the light of the twinkling star is to the refulgent light of the midday sun : Mr. Yates disapproved of our British youth learning their morality from the pages of Homer, (the beauties of whose poetry, however, he freely allowed) while the Christian religion furnished a far superior and purer system of moral conduct. And it was finely remarked, that sooner than the heroes of Homer could become disciples of the mild, the forgiving, the benevolent religion of Jesus, should Satan and Beelzebub and Moloch have retained their stations in heaven ! The preacher pathetically described the vast difference between the effects produced by the orations of the Pagan philosophers and the discourses of the ministers of Christ ; and while the former could boast the mighty consequences that followed their eloquence, the latter had often cause to lament the little influence which their labours had upon the conduct of their auditors ! The *reason* of this difference is a subject of serious inquiry to both ministers and people. Some judicious and kind advice was given to the ministers on the subjects of their preaching ; which, coming warm from the heart, and flowing from a quarter, in every point of view, so highly respectable, and delivered with so much energy and feeling, could not fail of making a deep impression on the hearts of those to whom it was addressed. Nor was the congregation overlooked ; but exhorted diligently to improve the superior light and means of virtue and knowledge with which they were favoured : the hearers were respectable in point of number, and appeared unusually attentive. The following ministers were present on this interesting occasion—Messrs. Bransby, of Dudley ; Bull and Bristowe, of Hinckley ; Davies, of Coventry, (who gave out the hymns) ; Field, of Warwick ; Kell and Kentish, of Birmingham ; Keurick, of York College ; Lloyd, of Kingswood ; Scott, of Cradley ;

Small, of Coseley ; Yates, of Liverpool ; and James Yates, late of Glasgow.

The writer of this hasty, brief and defective account cannot withhold the expression of the great satisfaction and pleasure, which he felt during the day ; and he has reason to believe that similar sentiments were experienced by others of his respected brethren in the ministry. .   J. B. B.

Hinckley, Aug. 11, 1816.

Additional Subscriptions to the Unitarian Chapel, at Thorne.

At Altringham, by the Rev. W. Jevons:

Mr. Rigby, - - - - - -	5	0 0
Mrs. Worthington - - -	3	0 0
Mr. Hugo Worthington, - -	3	0 0
Mr. J. Worthington, - -	3	0 0
Mr. Js. Harrop, - - - -	2	2 0
Mr. W. Whitelegg, - - -	1	0 0
Mr. C. Hankinson, - - -	1	0 0
Rev. W. Jevons, - - - -	1	1 0
Mr. Burgess, - - - - -	0	10 6
Anonymous, - - - - -	0	6 6
Joseph Dobson, (London,) -	1	1 0

By Mr. Aspland:

Mr. David Walker, Hoxton, -	1	1 0
Mrs. Severn, Broughton, Notts,	1	0 0

Unitarian Chapel, New Church, Rossendale.

[See M. Repos. X. 343. 392. 458. 461. 527. 596. 660. 721. XI. 124.

Donations in aid of liquidating the debt, (350*l.*) upon this Chapel, will be thankfully received by the Rev. R. Aspland, Hackney Road ; Rev. R. Astley, Halifax ; Rev. W. Johns, Manchester ; Mr. W. Walker, Rochdale ; and Dr. Thomson, Halifax.

It is intended to proceed to liquidate the debt as soon as may be, and as far as the liberality of the public may enable the above-mentioned gentlemen to do so ; to whom all who have entrusted themselves in behalf of the Rossendale brethren are requested to report the Subscriptions in their hands without delay.

An accurate account of the Subscription and of its appropriation will be given in the Monthly Repository.

Amount Reported, XI. 124. -	249	5	0
A Legacy from the late Mr. Mason, of Bolton. - -	5	0	0
Unitarian Fund. - - - -	20	0	0
	274	5	0

MISCELLANEOUS.

Curious and Important Recent Religious Prosecution.

Religious liberty is so well established in Great Britain, that we rarely hear of *persecutions* or *prosecutions* on the ground of faith or worship. When Lord Grosvenor was lately charged with an indirect persecution of some of his labourers who were Dissenters, his friends came forward to explain away the charge. How Lord Romney's friends will proceed remains to be seen: his Lordship has acted the part of an Informer against, prosecuted and convicted, (not a Dissenter, but) a brother Churchman, for *unlawful religious worship!* The Penal Statutes regarding religion have been repealed with respect to Dissenters, and are in force only against the members of the Establishment!

But the reader will be better pleased with a history than a commentary, and therefore we extract the following account of this curious case from a pamphlet just published at Maidstone, entitled " A Narrative of the Prosecution of the Honourable Charles Noel——Intended as a Friendly Caution, by a Friend to Religion, Order and Law." The writer of the pamphlet appears to be a friend of Mr. Noel's, and to be intimately acquainted with all the circumstances of the case.

" The Honourable Charles Noel having travelled some time on the Continent for the recovery of his health; on his return to England, he came to reside at the family mansion, Barham Court, in the parish of Teston, where it was the first wish of his heart to render his influence, from his rank and situation, subservient to the best and most essential interests of all who were dependant upon him,— tradesmen and labourers; and being duly sensible that family religion is a most important part of practical Christianity, and that family worship is a duty that may be practised by persons of every rank in life, and that without the observance of this privilege, as well as duty, every other duty will be regarded with luke-warmness:—it was a reasonable hope and expectation that example would have its use, and prove productive of religious improvement in the parish.

" It may here be necessary to remark, that it is Mr. Noel's constant practice, and his general rule of conduct, to assemble his domestics and servants the mornings and evenings of every day for the exercise of this duty. When alone, he is his own chaplain; when favoured with the company of any friend on whom with propriety it can devolve, it is resigned to such friend.

" Such a commitment of this duty occurred on Sunday the 31st of December, 1815, and on Sunday the 7th of January, 1816—the two Sundays named in the complaint and information made against him, when the family worship at Barham Court devolved on Mr. Noel's friend: and from the attendance of this friend on every Sunday, at the parish church, during the whole of his visit at Teston, it would justly have been thought a breach of Christian charity, to have considered

this friend of Mr. Noel's as a person hostile to the establishment, or to have suspected him of forming designs injurious to the interests of the church.

" But however pure and unmixed were Mr. Noel's motives, it has been proved that he erred in his judgment, in the intimation given to his tradesmen and the workmen upon his estate, that they were allowed the privilege of attending at his family worship; as the law prohibits any congregation or assembly of Protestants for religious worship, exceeding the number of twenty, in addition to servants and domestics in any unlicensed place; of which limitation Mr. Noel was not aware, and has expressed his regret that he should unintentionally, or from the purest motives have violated any law.

" What contributed to lead Mr. Noel into this error, was the constant, uninterrupted, unopposed practice of the late Lord Barham, who, for a considerable number of years, had himself attended some religious services on a Sunday evening, at a school his Lordship had erected in the village for the instruction of the poor of those parishes where he had any interest, at which the parents of the children, and any other of the inhabitants might attend, and where his Lordship was very generally accompanied by any friends, visitors at Barham Court.

" As no objections had ever been heard against this practice, and Mr. Noel's state of health not rendering it prudent to be out in the evening air, at that season of the year, he was not aware that the transferring this long continued practice at the school, countenanced by the presence of Lord Barham and his friends in general, to his own house for a few evenings, was in contradiction to any existing law.

" In Mr. Noel's first intentions, the privilege of attending the evening service at Barham Court was limited to his own dependants, and that it extended beyond this, arose from circumstances not under his control. But soon after this had occurred at Barham Court, a rumour was in circulation, that a nobleman of high rank had commenced a prosecution against Mr. Noel, a report pretty generally discredited: strong reasons were urged by many against its being worthy of any credit, and it seemed to be dying away; when a second report positively stated that the same nobleman had called upon a most respectable solicitor, desiring to put into his hands the conducting the intended prosecution, which, by this solicitor was politely declined:—this second report seemed to rest on some evidence, but the solicitor applied to having declined the conducting the prosecution, it was supposed it would not be persevered in—when a third report came into circulation that a very respect-

...ble solicitor from Maidstone had actually been to Wateringbury to take the deposition of John King, lately a servant at Teston Vicarage, and who had asked and obtained permission to attend the family worship at Barham Court, on the two Sundays mentioned in the information. This report was soon proved to be founded on fact. By duplicates of a summons, one for each offence being served upon the Honourable Charles Noel, upon David Thompson, steward to the estate, upon the Rev. John Kennedy, vicar of Teston, upon the Rev. Richard Wood, curate of Nettlested, upon —— Nettlefold, parish clerk of Teston, upon John King, servant to the Rev. John Kennedy, and upon Gardiner Jeffery, of Yalding, gentleman, a copy of which is here added :—

"*Kent to wit.—To the Constable of the Lower Half Hundred of Twyford; to Edward George Buds, and to all others His Majesty's Officers of the Peace for the said County, and to each and every of them.*

"Whereas information and complaint have been made before us, his Majesty's justices of the peace for the said county, by the Right Honourable Charles, Earl of Romney, that the Honourable Charles Noel, of Barham Court, in the parish of Teston, in the said county, the occupier of the mansion house and premises called Barham Court aforesaid, situate in the said parish of Teston, and county of Kent aforesaid, did on Sunday the seventh day of January last past, knowingly permit and suffer a certain congregation or assembly for religious worship of Protestants (at which there were present more than twenty persons, (to wit) thirty or thereabouts, besides the immediate family and servants of the said Charles Noel), to meet in the said mansion house and premises, occupied by him the said Charles Noel as aforesaid, in the parish and county aforesaid, the said mansion house and premises not having been duly certified and registered under any former act or acts of parliament relating to registering places of religious worship, nor having been certified to the bishop of the diocese, nor to the archdeacon of the archdeaconry, nor to the justices of the peace at the general or quarter sessions of the peace for the county, riding, division, or place in which such meeting was held, according to the directions of the statutes in such case made and provided, whereby he, the said Charles Noel hath forfeited for the said offence a sum not exceeding twenty pounds, nor less than twenty shillings, at the discretion of the justices who shall convict the said Charles Noel of the said offence, if he shall be by them thereof convicted—and that the Rev. John Kennedy, vicar of

Teston aforesaid, the Rev. Richa curate of Nettlested, in the sai —— Nettlefold, clerk of the s: of Teston, David Thompson, s Barham Court aforesaid, James Jeffery, of Yalding, in the sai gentleman, and John King, la to the said John Kennedy, and vant to the Rev. Dr. Willis, of ' bury, in the said county, are witnesses to be examined conc same.—These are therefore t you, or any one of you, forthwit mon the said John Kennedy Wood, —— Nettlefold, David 'I James Gardiner Jeffery, and J(severally to be and appear bef such other of his Majesty's justi peace for the said county, as sl sembled at the Swan, in West N the said county, on Monday th of April next, at the hour of ele forenoon of the same day, then to testify their several knowledg ing the premises.—And be you to certify what you shall have d premises. Herein fail you nc under our hands and seals, the of March, 1816. *John Larkb Hawley, G. Moore, Thomas Col Brooke.*

"When this cause came t bench of magistrates at their meeting, held at the Swan I1 Malling, the six witnesses att whom, only Mr. Thompson, th of the estate, and the Rev. John vicar of Teston, were called.

"Mr. Thompson having prov cupancy of the house by Mr. delivered a letter from him to man of the sitting—which being as far as can be recollected, ex regret that any mistaken views privileges had led to the violat law enacted for the regulation conduct, and leaving to the deci bench to what degree of pena mistake, he had made himself li as far as can be recollected, wa stance of the letter.

"When Mr. Kennedy, bei was asked by the chairman wh than twenty persons, in additi vants and domestics were prese Lord Romney, whether any pers the parishioners of Teston were To both which questions, he a the affirmative.

"As the witness from freque sations with the Honourable was well acquainted with his views, and sentiments, he req mission of the bench to offer a f to their observation ; which bei he began by observing, that t the Noble Lord at the head of the Paper he held in his hand————

"Here Mr. Kennedy was interrupted by the Noble Lord himself, saying he could not permit Mr. Kennedy to proceed; and this interruption appeared to arise from an entertained idea that some censure was intended against his Lordship, for the part his Lordship had taken in this prosecution;—but such an idea, if entertained, was immediately removed by an immediate appeal from Mr. Kennedy to the Earl of Romney, whether in any one instance during the many years he had been known to his Lordship, he had ever given any ground for a suspicion, that he was capable of any disrespect to his Lordship; that what he meant to observe was—that from the name of the Noble Lord at the head of the summons he held in his hand, it was impossible to ascribe any but the best motives that actuated his Lordship in this prosecution.—Here Lord Romney observed, that Mr. Kennedy's remarks had taken a different turn to what he expected, and he had no objection to his proceeding; but that he thought it necessary here to state, that as complainant and informer he took the whole matter upon himself, and added he had learned with surprise and astonishment that Mr. Kennedy and Mr. Wood, two clergymen of the church of England, should countenance by their presence the illegal proceedings at Barham Court. To this, Mr. Kennedy begged leave to impress upon the minds of his Lordship and the bench, that for the reasons assigned in the letter read by the chairman, he was equally unconscious with Mr. Noel, that the assembly at Barham court was *illegal*—and referred to what had been the practice at the school, during the life of Lord Barham.

"Here it was observed from the bench, that by Mr. Kennedy's reference to the practice of the school, Mr. Kennedy was injuring the cause he meant to serve— and Lord Romney remarked, that the master of the school was not content with reading to his scholars a chapter in the New Testament, but that he actually preached.

"Mr. Kennedy was about to proceed in his observations, when Mr. Brooke, a magistrate, whose name is affixed to the summons, objected to his being heard any further upon the subject.

"As this required the determination of the bench, Mr. Kennedy was requested by the chairman to withdraw, and being soon recalled was informed that the bench acquiesced in his proceeding, as it was not his intention to justify any breach of the law, but merely to speak in mitigation of any penalty incurred.

"Mr. Kennedy now observed he had little more to say in addition to what Mr. Noel had addressed to the bench—that he

could assert from Mr. Noel's authority, and from the conversations with him, that no one could more venerate our laws, or was more desirous to pay all due respect to magistrates; that his error had been unintentional and arose from misconception, and respecting his public sentiments he need not intrude more upon their time. But as Mr. Noel was not present, being called to attend the death-bed of a beloved sister in a distant county, he requested the indulgence of the bench, to speak a few words upon his private character, to which, in his absence, he could speak more freely. He had known him from infancy to manhood, and hesitated not to say, that a person of more solid practical Christianity, of more amiable manners, of more humane benevolence, of greater generosity of mind, or with a greater degree of the milk of human kindness, he had never known—and he was persuaded he might affirm, he would not knowingly do the least injury to any human being, but would rejoice in any opportunity of doing good to all, and more especially in that good that ended not with the present life: in a word, he was the gentleman and the Christian.

"With such dispositions, such views, and such intentions, the degree of criminality attached to an error in his judgment; and the degree of punishment it merited, might cheerfully be submitted to the judgment and decision of the bench.

"Mr. Kennedy now begged a further indulgence for a few moments, to make an observation he considered as due to himself.

"He must confess that when the summons was delivered to him by a clerk to Messrs. Burr and Hoar, he read the names of the selected witnesses with some degree of surprise, as being classed with his servant boy, to give evidence against Mr. Noel.

"Here Mr. Kennedy was interrupted by Earl Romney, who remarked that Mr. Kennedy was the first person he had ever heard object against a servant and his superior being required to give evidence to a fact in a court of law; where, to prove the fact, a nobleman and his groom might be equally necessary, and he did not suppose Mr. Kennedy or Mr. Wood would appear as voluntary witnesses.

"Mr. Kennedy observed, that where a peer of the realm and his groom were equally necessary to prove a fact, certainly no objection could reasonably be made; but where more than an hundred other persons were equally competent to prove the fact, it had been thought singular by many that out of five selected witnesses— Mr. Kennedy, Mr. Noel's parish priest, Mr. Wood, his curate, Mr. Nettlefold, his parish clerk, and John King, his servant boy, were four out of the live summoned to appear before the bench to give evidence against a person he considered as his patron and his friend.

"The Earl of Romney here remarked, that to exonerate Mr. Hoar, the solicitor in this cause, he thought it right to declare that he was the sole selector of the witnesses, as well as being the complainant and informant. It was his wish to have avoided all discussion ;—simply to have proved the offence, and to have left to the magistrates the amount of the penalty ; but on this point his mind was now changed :—Mr. Kennedy had objected to being called to give evidence against Mr. Noel, whom he termed his patron and his friend. Mr. Noel was not his patron, nor had Mr. Kennedy ever received any benefits from that family, as he well knew.

"To this Mr. Kennedy replied—that for every favour he had received from Mrs. Bouverie, he stood indebted to the friendship of the late Lady Middleton.

"Here the discussion ended, and Mr. Kennedy and Mr. Thompson were desired to withdraw, but in a few minutes were recalled, and informed that the bench had convicted Mr. Noel in the *full* penalty of *forty pounds*, which was immediately paid into the hands of the chairman by Mr. Thompson, with an enquiry whether one moiety of the penalty did not belong to the poor of Teston parish ; and was answered by the chairman, that when the expences of the prosecution were paid, of what remained, one half went to the informer, and the other half to the poor of the parish where the offence was committed."

MONTHLY RETROSPECT of PUBLIC AFFAIRS;
OR,
The Christian's Survey of the Political World.

THE conflict at Algiers is over, and it has terminated with a treaty of peace, highly honourable to this country. For the time it lasted, and the small space in which the combatants were engaged, it may be considered as one of the great actions for which an eventful period will be celebrated in the annals of history. The Algerines, confident in the strength of their batteries, kept up the fight for above six hours ; but nothing could stand against the bravery and skill of the English sailor. Their batteries were demolished, their ships burnt, and great part of the town became a mass of ruins. This severe chastisement brought the sovereign to his senses, and fearing a worse disaster, he complied with the terms proposed to him.

The first article of the treaty abolishes the infamous traffic that had subsisted for many centuries, of selling for slaves the unfortunate persons that the chance of war had thrown into the hands of these barbarians. Whatever contempt we may cast upon the name of infidel in this country, it is a thousand fold greater at Algiers : but there the term of infidelity is appropriated to a confession of the Christian faith. Slavery in all its forms is wretched enough, but the Christian slave amongst the Algerines was treated worse than and called by the name of a Christian dog. The system is now changed : the States of Barbary are no longer to indulge in this horrid custom : their prisoners of war are not to be subjected to the horrors of slavery. This article is beneficial to the conquered as well as the conquerors ; for instead of their abominable piracy, the former may in time be brought to exercise their talents in honest industry.

A strict eye will of course be kept upon the execution of this article of the treaty; and it will be an honour to England to have acted more for the benefit of Europe than for its own—for few if any of the English had been kept in these disgraceful chains of bondage.

Another article provided for the release of all the Christians held in slavery, who thus through our means have been restored to their country and their friends. Many a captive now made free will, whilst gratitude remains, offer up prayers for the welfare of that power which has conferred on him the greatest kindness ; and the prayers of our fellow creatures are to the generous mind a source of the greatest satisfaction. Besides this the Dey was compelled to refund a considerable sum sent to him by European powers for the redemption of slaves ; and now for some time at least the Mediterranean will be freed from the ravages of the pirates. Its shores will however remain subject to the Mahometan name, and Christianity will lament that the bad conduct of its professors drove them from a country, which they disgraced by their contemptible disputes, and disregard of all that is most valuable in religion.

France presents to us a new picture. The sovereign seems at last to be sensible that he can no longer govern his country on the principles of faction : that the benefit of the whole must be consulted, not that of the few who arrogate to themselves the exclusive title of royalists. He has dissolved his parliament ; a new one is to be called, according to the charter, which he now declares to be the rule of his conduct.

Germany is on the point of entering in

good earnest into the consideration of a constitution, fitted for their present wants. The deliberation of their diets have always been noted for their slowness; and the variety of interests to be consulted will probably make their present a work of great difficulty. The King of Wurtemburgh, one of Buonaparte's kings, still keeps at variance with his subjects. Their dissentions tend however to promote a spirit of inquiry among the neighbouring states; and it is evident that they will no longer be governed in their former despotic manner. Their nobility must consent to consider themselves men, and their distinctions, which have longer been held in contempt, will no longer serve to separate them from the great body of their countrymen. Prussia has not yet obtained a constitution, but the courage of their Landwehr will in due time procure it.

The legislature of the Netherlands is employed on a very important object, namely, to reconcile together the interests of commerce, manufactures and finance. As the greater part of this nation was at one time commercial in a very high degree, it may be supposed to be well acquainted with every circumstance relative to trade; and thence we may derive lessons by which this country may be much benefited. Here we have an interest, lately much talked of, namely, the agricultural interest, and its policy has been seen in that very injudicious measure, the Corn Bill. With a view to bolster up its own interest, the landholders forgot their real situation, namely, that their wealth and importance depend on the flourishing state of our commerce and manufactures, and that cheapness of provisions is essential to their success. A landholder from a false view of his own interest looks to the dearness of provisions as his summum bonum; thence he conceives that his rents will be increased, and that he will enjoy increasing prosperity: but his view of the subject is fallacious: all the advantages of commerce and manufactures ultimately tend to the profit of the land owner; his lands are better tilled, and are thence capable of producing him a greater rent. If he is content to derive this advantage in the proper manner, then all parties flourish; but if he looks to his own aggrandizement merely, he injures himself and all parties. Without commerce and manufactures the land will fall to what it was a few centuries back, to ten or twelve years purchase, the roads will be unfrequented, the canals dry: every thing will stagnate. A few landholders may consume in sullen luxury the produce of their estates on their own backs and bellies and those of needy dependents, but all spur to industry and improvement will be lost. Besides, the term agricultural in-

terest is very much misunderstood with us. In conversing with the people, who are fond of using this term, it is easily discovered that they mean only the interest of the land owners, not of the cultivators of the land: but the latter are the true agriculturists, and the land owner stands to them exactly in the same situation, as what is called the monied does to the mercantile interest. The report, which is now in circulation, proceeding from the board of agriculture, must be read therefore with great caution. It is under the direction not of agriculturists, but of land owners; and the latter are little calculated to understand the complicated interests of such a kingdom as ours. A land owner talks of ruin when his rents are lowered, not recollecting that during the late war those rents had been raised out of all proportion to the profits of the other classes of society; and if he has derived for many years a very great advantage over his countrymen, it does not become him to grumble when the change of the times reduces him nearer to his pristine situation. How many are there in this class of life, who, by prudently applying the inordinate profits of the late years, have so increased their estates, that, if they were now let at the rate they went at before the war, still from the accumulation of land their yearly income will be increased doubly, trebly and more. But we shall be curious to see in what manner the great question is settled by the legislature of the Netherlands. We may persist, if the land owners please, for they are the legislators of this country, in pursuing their misunderstood interest. We may keep up the price of bread, but it must be recollected that other nations are not bound by our decisions. The road to commerce and manufactures is open to them, and they will not fail to avail themselves of it. Providence has supplied checks to imprudent and inordinate desires. We have been highly favoured. If we give up the advantages which industry will procure us, we shall only afford to the world another example, that riches make to themselves wings and fly away. Commerce and manufactures dwell only in those countries, where they are duly protected and held in honour.

The Americans are making claims on the Court of Naples for property which had been seized under the late regime, and it is said that they will be content, by way of compensation, with some island, which will afford them a secure harbour for their ships and a good depot for their commodities. This may occasion a new era in the commerce of the Mediterranean. We have the island of Malta, which is highly beneficial to us, and the Americans will look to similar advantages from a port of the same nature. In what manner this matter is considered by the Court of Naples and the other European powers time will shew.

Spain has promulgated its successes in the new world, but we may be allowed to doubt whether they will be permanent. It will take time before the natives are assisted by arms and ammunition, and a sufficient number of French military can make head against the discipline of European troops; but the experiment will shortly be tried, and no one except a Spaniard can contemplate the independence of the Spanish colonies in any other light than as a gain to the world at large. An English ship has been carried it is said into Spain, which had a cargo from Buenos Ayres. This may occasion a correspondence between the two courts, and settle the question relative to the true situation of the inhabitants on the Southern banks of La Plata.

A considerable sensation has been experienced by the publication and general circulation of a report of the House of Commons relative to the police of this country, and many extraordinary facts have been produced on the licensing of publi houses. The matter will probably engag the attention of parliament at its next ses sion, for when a grievance is universall felt and very generally understood an complained of, a change in the system i not far distant. This is a great advantag of our country, that by the free circulatio of opinions, every matter is brought unde general inspection.

A temporary alarm has been excited o the subject of the silver coinage, but i soon subsided. Its defects have been lon, known, and in due time a new coinage wil sweep before it the miserable pieces whic are now in circulation. It is to be hope that the nation will learn from the expe rience of the past, and never suffer thei coin to fall again into so miserable a state The time must come, when a bad coinag must give place to a good one; but in th change many will be the sufferers. Ho much better would it not be to preven the recurrence of such an evil, by neve permitting a piece of coin to pass, whic has not upon its face the legal stamp.

CORRESPONDENCE.

We are requested by the Treasurer of the *Unitarian Fund* to say that in the publishe list of Subscribers, the name of *Mrs. Severn*, of Broughton, Notts, has been by mis take omitted; and that the notification of any other errors in the list, will be esteeme a favour.

In our next Number we shall be able to give a *Memoir of the late Mr. Willian Matthews, of Bath.*

We have received a variety of interesting communications from America, of whic we shall make an early use.

A Correspondent, familiar with Spanish literature, has furnished us with a curiou account of an *Auto de Fé*, compiled from official documents.

"*Recent Case of Bigotry in Private Life.*"—The reader probably recollects a lette under this title in the Monthly Repository for June, p. 320. The persons who suppos that they are referred to by our Correspondent, J. W. have shewn a very laudabl anxiety to clear themselves of the suspicion of bigotry; but we are sorry to say tha their defence leaves the principal part of the charge in its full force. The only part o their correspondence with us which is to the point is the following paragraph, which w print as we received it: "but it is due to the public weal that we shoud [*should*] answe the imputation of crime:—One branch of our family has for these fourteen years pas attended a chapel: a present inmate in our service has long been and now is a regula attendant at a chapel. The *facts* are now before the public: we anticipate the result.' We are enjoined, indeed, to publish the whole of the letter from which this extract i made, and in spite of the manner in which the injunction is laid upon us, we shoul have inserted it if, with the exception of the part already copied, it were not wholl irrelevant and scarcely intelligible; not to mention that it contains insinuations of dark and serious nature. A plain fact is plainly stated by J. W. and that fact is n disproved but confirmed by the correspondence. We have said thus much to shew th we have not been inattentive to the subject, though we might have fairly stood excuse for passing by a correspondent who concludes a letter with the threat "that *if there any reply* or further notice of this transaction," the persons referred to "will see redress in another form.

A Correspondent wishes us to insert the following notice: "If the person who i the July Repository subscribed himself J. H. will please to inquire at the shop of Sher wood, Neely, and Jones, in Paternoster Row, he will find a small parcel directed f Mr. J. H. containing some small sets of sermons, such as he is desirous of seeing."

ERRATUM.
XI. 403. 2d. col. 3d. line from the bottom, for *sacerdotam*, read *sacerdotum*.

THE

Monthly Repository,

&c.

| No. CXXX.] | OCTOBER, 1816. | [Vol. XI. |

BIOGRAPHY AND ORIGINAL LETTERS.

Memoir of Mr. William Mathews.

IN the Obituary of the Monthly Magazine for May last, p. 383, a brief account is given of Mr. Mathews, "for many years the much distinguished and enlightened Secretary of the Bath and West of England Agricultural Society;" with an intimation from a Correspondent "that their next volume will contain a correct memoir of his life and useful labours." His publications in the volumes of the transactions of the Society, are said to "manifest his various useful attainments," and that in the station of Secretary, "he contributed in no small degree, to raise that excellent institution to the pre-eminence it has attained." The announced memoir will, it may be presumed, relate principally to these commendable efforts. Yet as he was well known to many of its members, and justly esteemed by them as a worthy, upright and actively benevolent man, and a warm friend to the great cause of civil and religious liberty, it may also advert to these features of his mind. My object is to give your readers some just ideas of my friend as a religious character.

WILLIAM MATHEWS was born at Milton, near Burford, in Oxfordshire, November 1, 1747. His father, Mr. John Mathews, was a man of strict piety, and much esteemed as a minister in the Society of Friends. He was of a benevolent disposition, and seems to have possessed something of the same spirit of freedom in his religious inquiries, by which his son William was so much distinguished. Some of the publications of the Rev. Theophilus Lindsey fell into his hands, and were not only perused by him, but approved and recommended to at least *one* of his children, as a plain assertion and Scriptural defence of the Christian doctrine of the Unity of God.

VOL XI.

4 D

He paid close attention to business and was careful to procure for a numerous family of children, as good an education as his circumstances and the village where he lived afforded. He also from an earnest wish to promote their welfare, encouraged their attendance of such meetings for worship and discipline, as lay within a convenient distance. The principles and economy of the Society became the early objects of his son William's serious consideration, who soon discovered an inclination and capacity for learning; and when about fourteen years of age, he was sent to London, where he remained in an exemplary Friend's family several years, and during that time became still farther improved in learning, and deeply impressed with the love of virtue and religion.[*]

In consequence of a severe illness he returned home, and soon after became a tutor in a Mr. Huntley's school, at Burford, where he remained some years, and acquitted himself much to the satisfaction of his employer. In the year 1768, he opened a boarding-school at Coggeshall, in Essex, in a large house which was soon quite filled. He was assiduous and successful in the education of his pupils, and their moral improvement lay very near to his heart. He often addressed them in pathetic and affectionate language, in order to establish in their minds religious and moral principles for their future benefit: and some of his pupils who are yet living still retain a lively and grateful

---

[*] This happy bent of his mind in early life be partly attributed to the eloquent and impressive preaching of a Mr. Letchworth, who was a man of distinguished talents, a uniform advocate for civil and religious freedom, yet a much esteemed minister among the Quakers, of whose life and character, in 1796, Mr. Mathews published a brief but very interesting memoir.

rememBrance of those labours of love. His school was continued with increasing reputation and success about eight years.

In the same year in which he removed to Coggeshall, he married Miss Mary Huntley, of Burford, a member of the Society of Friends, and sister to the Mr. Huntley before mentioned; and while he resided here formed an intimate acquaintance with several persons of superior intellect, and particularly with the late Mr. Edmund Rack, then of Bardfield, in Essex, but who removed to Bath about the year 1775, and Mr. Mathews soon after; the close confinement of his school proving injurious to his health. Both of them lived at Bath the remainder of their lives. Another of Mr. Mathews's most intimate friends at this time was the late Mr. Portsmouth, of Basingstoke, in Hampshire, "a man of great respectability as a practitioner in medicine, as a scholar, and as a gospel minister among *Friends.*" He was much older than Mr. Mathews, and had, like Mr. Letchworth, "suffered much pain of mind from what he had observed of the narrow and intolerant spirit," which prevailed among the ruling disciplinarians in the Society. In the hope it might do something "towards the removal of so great an evil," this worthy man wrote "An Essay on the Simplicity of Truth," and the Use and Extent of Discipline in the Church of Christ, particularly addressed to the People called Quakers," and confided the perusal of his MS. to Mr. Mathews, desiring his opinion as to the propriety of its publication. Mr. Mathews not only approved publishing the tract, but undertook to superintend the press at Bath on the author's behalf, and with his free consent annexed a P. S. to it, on Tithes, and the practice of disowning those members of the Society of Friends who paid them.

This temperate work was no sooner published, under the signature of "Catholicus," than it caused much inquiry in the Society after the author. Mr. Mathews was of course suspected, "and though I was," says he, "not restrained by *fear*, from avowing the facts as they stood, I thought it unnecessary to do so, and hoped the attempt to diffuse liberality of sentiment, might be somewhat increased by preserving

the secret. But my growing dissatisfaction with some articles in the discipline of *Friends*, induced me shortly after to take such steps in my own person, as led to the conclusion, that if I was not the author, I was completely of his school; and as the event soon proved, was no longer to be tolerated as a member of the Society."

How justly the disownment of Mr. Mathews, which took place in 1783, was attributed by him to the *ruling individuals* in the district of his residence, and how much he was previously esteemed as a minister, may be inferred from the following anecdote. "I was not hasty," says he, "in the discontinuance of my public ministry at Bath; where I reside, even after a minute of rejection from membership had been recorded in the monthly meeting book; both because I found the spring of love frequently flow in my mind towards my little audience, and because the far greater part of them had signed and sent me a written testimony of their regard for me in that character, *with hopes that it might continue.* But my knowledge of the consequences to *them*, of exposing, determined me to conceal their names. Many of them are now dead [in 1802] or removed to other situations. The *constitutional* irregularity of continuing my public appearances [as a minister] was a sufficient inducement to me soon to desist: and it was not long before I found myself most disposed to discontinue also a regular attendance of Friends' meetings."

Nearly twenty years after, Mr. M. described his feelings towards the Society, and his attachment to the simplicity of their peculiar form of public worship, in the following terms. It is then no matter for surprise that he continued an occasional attendant on their meetings for worship for the remainder of his life. "A man educated, habituated, and principled as I was, is very unfit to find satisfaction in the communion of any *other* religious Society; and I have hitherto found more content in remaining a solitary retired character, than in resuming religious attendances among those whom (though I very affectionately regard them) I cannot have full unity with as a body. Mere external appearances of fellowship produce but little satisfaction on either side. And there are situations in which I might find more freedom than where I now reside, in associating for the purpose of public worship, under the form peculiar to our Friends—and to which *I am strongly attached* on account of its simplicity, and the solemnity of its design."

In 1786, Mr. Mathews published "The Miscellaneous Companions." The first volume consists of "a short Tour of Observation and Sentiment through a part of South Wales." But even this part of his work, evinces his benevolent and virtuous disposition. Most of his remarks on the incidents of the journey, or on the objects that attracted his attention, are calculated to guard against some moral evil, or to promote some practical good. Thus, in passing through Bristol, at a time when the merchants of that city were deeply engaged in the African slave-trade, before the public mind was awakened to its enormity; more than twenty years before the act passed for its abolition; and previous to the first efforts of the philanthropic Clarkson in this great cause of humanity;—Mr. Mathews, after some interesting remarks on the arts of ship-building and navigation, observes, "The evidences of superior skill and elegance, in the construction of shipping which so strongly mark the present days, however flattering to the pride of modern ingenuity, and however ornamental to our trading cities, like many other boasted improvements and embellishments, are far from being evidences of superior virtue: and where virtue and moral usefulness are wanting, in the ingenuity of contrivance, or the applications and uses of art, much is wanting to charm the mind of a dispassionate and virtuous man. Thus, while we survey with astonishment and delight, those productions of mechanic genius, which we have been treating of; and consider their adaption to carry on an intercourse with foreign and remote countries, which, under virtuous regulations, might be at once pleasant and beneficial; who but must lament their subserviency also to slavery and distress! Who, without horror, can behold the clean, gilded, and ornamented vessel, riding at her anchors, and reflect that her hold has been made the dungeon, and the grave, of

many a poor innocent and mournful African, violently dragged on board from his native fields and every tender connexion! Who, without blushing for his country, and for human infamy, can survey the splendid engine of rapacious power without shuddering to the heart, at the thought of the pangs, the sorrows, and the suffocations which have existed beneath its gaudy ensigns! Who, that is worthy the name of man, but must deplore that the best principles of nature and all that is benevolent in the human heart should be so wantonly violated! That any calling himself a *Christian*, should commence the tyrant, and become the murderer, of distant unoffending fellow-creatures, whom he never saw, merely to have a chance of augmenting wealth, which, when gotten, must prove a shame, if not a curse to his generation!"

In the course of this journey Mr. Mathews availed himself of a ludicrous misapplication of a common word, by a genteel young man of good natural talents and disposition, who rode with him several miles, to give his readers some useful " thoughts on education." From these I shall select a passage or two before I quit this volume. " The division of empires and provinces," says he, " the general principles of the laws of nations—the rise, progress and importance of discoveries in arts and sciences, as well as the general history of mankind.:—these, or at least the *elements* of these should undoubtedly form parts of a liberal education. These, inculcated with a view to store the mind with important subjects for future reflection, will have the most enlarging and beneficial tendency, especially as they may powerfully come in aid of a frequent and serious contemplation of the great Governor of all things, and of all events; which in proportion as the heavens are higher than the earth, is the supreme good of a right education, and the sacred pre-eminence of all knowledge.

" With respect to *religion*, without an inward experience of the power of which no man can be happy, the simple and unchangeable doctrines of the New Testament can never be too strongly enforced. This observation holds true with regard to youth of every class, because to every class a reformation from the evil propensities of human nature, is of positive necessity and obligation: but particularly with regard to those, who, from beginning with classical studies, have been unavoidably accustomed to ideas of heathen mythology and heathen errors, which, it is to be feared are in some degree ever subversive, in young minds, of those reverential ideas respecting GOD and his glorious attributes, which are so essential to the faith of Christians."

After recommending two hours in a day to be set apart for a lecture on those subjects, he says, " children in general do not want for curiosity, they do not want a readiness of conception, they are seldom wanting in admiration at a new and curious discovery. Neither (which is the most animating consideration of all) are they unsusceptible of the most lively and reverential impressions of the Supreme Being. The doctrines of his fatherly goodness, and of his exalted and most adorable attributes, are subjects within the reach of their quick and lively conceptions, when treated with a suitable seriousness and concern for their well being. And it may well be considered as one of the most lamentable defects of common education, that so little use is made of the wonders of natural philosophy, to instil into, and advance the principles of real religion, in the tender and comparatively unpolluted minds of the rising generation !"

The 2nd volume consists of " Miscellaneous Maxims and Thoughts," arranged under more than a hundred heads, and of some Serious Reflections on fifteen select Passages of Scripture.

The 3rd volume opens with a Dissertation on Marriage, which young persons may peruse with much advantage, and especially those who are in danger of forming hasty, imprudent or unwarrantable engagements. The next article is entitled " Considerations on the Last Day," and is a candid inquiry, how far the general and popular opinions are revealed truths, and are " sanctioned or refuted by that reason which is one chief privilege and glory of human nature." The result of this examination with Mr. Mathews was, that to every individual " the day of death is the

solemn *last day,* the day when the spirits of those that go down to the graves finally hear the voice of the Son of GOD, and pass to their great account. The body returns unto the earth as it was, and the spirit unto GOD who gave it."

The succeeding and longest treatise in these volumes is on " Everlasting Punishment," which Mr. Mathews expected would probably " meet some strong objections among the more timorous and inconsiderate part of mankind." But he had suffered early in life too much, by having been prevailed on, by that species of discipline in the Society of Friends called *private dealing,* to condemn the freedom of his religious sentiments, when the object and end of them was to vindicate the ways of God to man, as the all-benevolent Parent of the universe, to withhold the full expression of his sentiments any longer, now he was happily freed from such baneful ecclesiastical imposition. His account is as follows : " I think it right to say, in this place, that under my own full persuasions respecting the subject, I could not with an easy mind, avoid treating on it in the manner I have done. In my childhood I found it impossible to fix my belief in the common notion of endless torments; as I grew older, my sentiments occasionally became known: I was assailed, in consequence, by some few zealous and implicit believers among my friends, particularly by one, for whom, on account of his moral character, I had a considerable respect. And being under the common frailty of human nature, I was influenced for a short time, to doubt of my right to profess, even contractedly, my belief in the future dispensation of universal refinement from iniquity.

" In this interval, and at the instance of the person to whom I allude, I was prevailed on to sign something like a condemnation of the freedom of my sentiments. But though this was not a declaration of my belief in a partial ultimate salvation, I soon found condemnation of mind for my wavering and timidity : and I can truly say, that no other single circumstance of my whole life hath ever given me so much uneasiness. I am now cheered with the rational, Scriptural, and as I think, glorious doctrine of the punishment of divine justice being eventually subservient to an universal purification and fitness for heavenly habitations!"

I wave giving even a summary of the arguments in this treatise, as unnecessary to your readers. It may suffice to repeat the author's observation, that "*five* places only occur in the whole New Testament, wherein the future misery of the wicked is described as *eternal* or *everlasting*; Matt. xviii. 8. xxv. 41. 46. Mark iii. 29, and 2 Thess. i. 9. That the original and derivative Greek words *αιων, eternity*, and *αιωνιος, eternal* or *everlasting*, may in general, as in many places they necessarily do, signify only a limited duration: and that their import is certainly much more general and indefinite than the English words *eternity* and *everlasting* are understood to be in our language."

An instructive dialogue follows between four persons, two of whom thought the author a well-meaning man, who had argued the subject with candour and piety; and the others that he was a sceptic and little better than an Infidel. To this are added a few pages of judicious quotations from some of the best writers in illustration of the author's views, and a well imagined dialogue in the world of spirits, between Theophilus, Zelotes, and another person named Purgatus, whom neither of them, while on earth, considered "as an heir of salvation," and Zelotes had rashly pronounced to be "a co-worker with the prince of the bottomless pit, in which his inheritance shall be for ever."

Mr. Mathews next gives a much more rational picture of a future state of punishment adapted to produce a gradual reformation of the worst of mankind, than that of endless torments exhibits, in a dialogue supposed to have taken place between Henry VIII. and the Dukes of Somerset and Northumberland, his cotemporaries, all of whom are represented as sensible of their former vices, as condemning them, and as acquiring by degrees more virtuous dispositions.

The volume ends with an appropriate dialogue between the Apostle Paul and a Protestant Martyr, each of whom acknowledges the imperfection of their state on earth when compared to their present advancement in heavenly wisdom and knowledge. The martyr concludes by saying, "as universal love and simplicity of devotion are within the fiat of our most wise and merciful Father, we are privileged to hope, at least, that this our heavenly society will be ultimately joined by all beings that are capable of receiving refinement from an infinite influence! Such are the sentiments on which I dwell with delight, when I contemplate the possibilities of heavenly goodness. To the source eternal of all felicity, and of all glory, be ascribed thanksgiving and praise! Such," adds the apostle, "is the proper theme of heaven, of all happy gradations of created existences, up to the nearest resemblance of the nature of GOD himself!"

In 1798, Mr. M. published "a new and seasonable Address to the people called Quakers relative to Tithes and Taxes," under the signature of *Catholicus*. The object he aimed at was to render the Society more consistent, tolerant and Christian, by contrasting their professed scruples against tithes, with their general payment of war taxes, laid on expressly for its support, and strictly appropriated to that purpose. A few years after he published several small tracts relative to the Society's treatment of Hannah Barnard, of Hudson, in North America, who was first silenced as a minister and afterwards excommunicated, for objecting to the practice of war as contrary to the will of God, in every age of the world, and on such other charges of erroneous faith, as the investigation of the original accusation upon the most inquisitorial principles enabled them to bring forward.

Soon after these events, which excited much attention among the Friends, Mr. Mathews published the first volume of his "Recorder," and in the next year, 1803, a second volume. The plan of the work is such as to invite its continuance by other hands, but whether it be continued or not, the author and editor of the first two volumes has conferred a benefit upon such of his readers as are friends to free inquiry and lovers of primitive Christianity.

The 1st volume of this work contains, 1. Mr. Portsmouth's Essay on

Church Discipline. 2. Mr. M.'s Postscript on Tithes. 3. A Detail of Ensuing Occurrences. 4. An Article " to Exemplify the Narrow, Bigotted and Mischievous Spirit, which becomes tolerated and fostered in the Society of Friends by the continuance of the mistaken Testimony with regard to Tithes." 5. Extracts from the second Pamphlet of Catholicus. 6 to 10. Sundry Pieces relative to the Case and Treatment of Hannah Barnard. 11. Plain Arguments from Reason and Scripture, against the presumptuous Doctrine of Eternal Punishment. 12. Of the Divinity of Christ, as stated by Robert Barclay, the Apologist for the Quakers, shewing that he did not profess to believe " the co-eternity and co-equality of the Son with the Father, as an uncreated, self originated, and eternal God!" 13. Of God the Father. This small tract exhibits, 1. Those passages in the New Testament wherein HE is styled the *one* or *only* GOD. They are about *seventeen.* 2. The chief passages about 320 wherein HE is styled GOD absolutely, by way of eminence and supremacy. 3. Passages wherein HE is styled GOD, with peculiarly high titles, &c. about 105. 4. About ninety passages wherein it is declared that all *prayers* and *praises* ought *primarily* to be offered to HIM, and that every thing ought to be *ultimately* directed to *his* honour and glory. A few notes are annexed principally from Hopton Haynes and Dr. Samuel Clarke. 14. Of the SON of GOD. Under this head Mr. Mathews exhibits, 1. About twelve passages in the New Testament wherein the *Son*, in certain senses, is styled, or supposed to be styled GOD. 2. About *eight* passages wherein it is declared that the world was made by (or through) him. 3. About 136 passages wherein are contained the other highest *titles*, *perfections* and *powers*, ascribed or ascribable to the *Son* in the New Testament, either positively, or by probable, or by doubtful construction. 4. Passages wherein are set forth the honour and reverence which are to be paid to the *Son.* These (but uniformly not implying supreme adoration) are about 70. 5. Three hundred and ten passages in the New Testament quoted at length wherein the SON is declared, positively, and by the clearest implication, to be

subordinate to the *Father,* deriving his being *from* Him, *receiving from* Him his divine *power*, *authority;* and other *attributes,* and acting in all things wholly according to the *will* of the *Father.*" 15. Of the Holy Ghost or Spirit. Under this head, the last in the volume, Mr. Mathews first exhibits 28 passages, in which the *Holy Spirit* is represented as the *author* and *worker* of *miracles,* even of those done by, or by means of *our Lord himself,* in the principal actions of his life on earth. 2. Fifty-two passages wherein the *Holy Spirit* is declared to be the *inspirer* of the prophets and apostles, and the *director* and *teacher* of the apostles, in the work of their ministry. 3. *Forty seven* passages wherein the *Holy Spirit* is declared to be the *sanctifier* of all hearts, and the *comforter* and *supporter* of good men, in the practice of their duty. 4. *Eighteen* passages wherein are contained the other *highest* expressions, concerning the Holy Spirit in the New Testament. 5. *Eleven* passages wherein is declared what *honour* is due to the *Holy Spirit,* and how his good motions are to be diligently *obeyed,* and not *resisted.* 6. *Fifty* passages wherein it is expressly declared that the *Holy Spirit* is *subordinate* to the *Father,* derives his *being* from him, is sent by him, and *acts in all things* according to his supreme will and pleasure. 7. Twelve passages wherein the *Holy Spirit* is represented as being *subordinate* to the *Son*, being his *spirit*, and *sent* or *given* by him. 8. Forty-three passages wherein the FATHER, Son, and Holy Spirit are mentioned in various ways *together.* Well might the author in the preface to this volume say that in the latter part of it, " the reader will find such a weight of sacred testimony, as must bear down all the notional irreverent cavils, of all opposers of the simple unity of God, the supreme adorable Father of the universe."

After the introduction to the second volume, the first article is, a Brief Biographical Account of Mr. Thomas Emlyn, with some Extracts from his Works. 2. His Humble Inquiry into the Scriptural Account of Jesus Christ, a scarce but valuable tract of above forty pages. 3. The Sandy Foundation Shaken, by William Penn, with Remarks by the Editor. 4. The Last Thoughts of Dr. Whitby, containing his Correction of several Passages in his Commentary on the New Testament. 5. An Historical Account of two Notable Corruptions of Scripture, (1 John v. 7. and 1 Tim. iii. 16.) by Sir Isaac Newton, pp. 70, with remarks on both by the Editor. The latter of these valuable works was first published entire from the MS. in the author's hand writing, in the possession of Dr. Ekens, Dean of Carlisle, in Dr. Horsley's splendid edition of Sir Isaac's Mathematical and Philosophical Works, and has never since been printed except in this volume. The sixth article consists of " Extracts and Reflections on the Scripture Doctrine of Future Punishments." The extracts are from STONEHOUSE. Then follows a Letter from Mr. Samuel Bourn, of Norwich, to the Rev. Samuel Chandler, D.D. in favour of the doctrine of *annihilation*, not as true, but as more consistent with the moral character of God, than the doctrine of endless torment. The two next Essays are mostly from *Stonehouse.* The first treats of that death which the Scripture calls our LORD'S last enemy: the second is intended to shew that the lake which is the second, and most properly called, death, will, as our LORD's last enemy, be ultimately disannulled. The concluding article is extracted from a pamphlet then recently published " on the Scripture Doctrine of Universal Redemption, by John Simpson, M.A. a minister of the Gospel, and one of the most amiable of men. The work itself," says the Editor, " evinces an intimate acquaintance with the subject, which he has treated with that learning, accuracy, clearness of arrangement and seriousness, which, while they do him the highest credit as a scholar, must render him equally estimable as a Christian."

In January, 1805, Mr. Mathews's wife died. Soon after this event, in a letter to a friend he says, " My poor long-afflicted, ever-affectionate wife has been taken from me. She departed *this*, in well-grounded hope of *a better life* on the 13th instant, and on the 19th I attended her remains to the silent grave: that house of final obscurity appointed for all living! But such was the preparation of her mind, such the refinement of her immortal spirit, that in her view

death had no terrors! I have no doubt but she had an all-sufficient share in that divine dependance which breathes forth the language ' O Death, where is thy sting? O Grave where is thy victory?' On the morning of her last day, her little grandson about seven months old being brought to her, she embraced and kissed him, then dozed on her sofa till near five, when she was carried to her bed again, where she lay composed and almost motionless till near seven, when we ascertained that imperceptibly to us she had passed out of mortality, and I have no doubt into the realms of ' immortality and eternal life.'

" Such was the sweet deliverance of my invaluable companion from all her pains and exercises, which during the last ten years had been frequent and hard to bear. A companion she was to me of unceasing affection and sympathy, through every adversity of six and thirty years! I feel affected with her absence in proportion to the strength of my attachment. But I repine not. All is well with her. All has been done in mercy, and in the exercise of infinite wisdom. And my desire is, that the short portion of time that can now remain to me, may be spent in reverence and the fear of God!"

Mr. Mathews some time after this, once more engaged himself in the duties of a Christian minister, by entering into a kind of social engagement to prepare a religious discourse in MS. twice in a month, and to deliver the same in his turn, with other brethren at the Bath Penitentiary. " In this employ," says he, in a letter to a friend, written in 1808, " I have some satisfaction: but it will add nothing to my credit among the professors of immediate inspiration ' for every good word and work.' "

The following extract of another letter, written in April, 1809, when " in poor health," exhibits briefly and clearly his serious objection to the leading doctrines of reputed orthodoxy, and the genuine humility of his mind.

" I have lived now," says he, " upwards of sixty-two years, and though by temperance and regularity of labour I have been favoured to maintain a comfortable share of bodily and mental abilities, I cannot expect to last much longer. The sands of life must soon be run. This consideration, with the removal of almost all the friends of my early life (dear Joseph Woods excepted), powerfully admonish me to prepare for the final allotment!—Whenever, in Divine wisdom, which is ever connected with Divine goodness, it shall arrive, I expect to find it an awful period: and but for the hopes of Divine mercy, how unspeakably awful would it be!

"I cannot after long and most serious meditation venture to place salvation to the account of "the meritorious blood of the atonement," about which I hear so much continually from different professors. No! Convicted I stand, as well as many of them, of great unworthiness, and that nothing short of the Divine mercy can cancel the demerits of a life of infirmities and transgressions! But I cannot (and I humbly trust I ought not so to do) seek a covering, however sacred in its character, which the wise and humble of all antient generations knew nothing of. The broad and sacred foundation of the mercy of God, humbly implored, was the foundation of prophets and apostles; and though Jesus Christ became the chief corner stone of the spiritual building, in his universal church, yet was the foundation never changed, nor can it change, for ever and ever! The testimony of all the gospels proclaim in substance *this*; the testimony of the blessed Jesus abundantly confirms the doctrine. Of all the enthusiasm which has prevailed among Christian professors, surely the orthodox artificial system of salvation is the most unaccountable. But of these things we have too long reflected with reverence, to have any disagreement."

It seems, however, that a rumour had been circulated among the Quakers, that he had at length seen and confessed his errors, and sought to be reunited to their Church. Under this impression, a respectable member of the Society wrote to inquire whether such was the fact. His reply is as follows:

"Bath, Aug. 19, 1815.

"Esteemed Friend,

"I received thy letter of the 16th, and am obliged by thy frank inquiries. I shall answer them very briefly. From the time I published my "Ex-planatory Appeal," to the present day (now thirty years), I am not conscious of having changed one religious opinion. Certainly no person could report with truth, that I had applied for re-admission into the Society of Friends. Membership in any particular society is of small account to me. I sometimes attend the meetings of Friends, because I love their simplicity and silence: but I would not join any society under heaven which holds or favours the doctrine of a Trinity of Gods! or that does not explicitly declare its belief in the plain Scripture doctrine of *One God*, and of Jesus Christ his Son, as the *created* and *sent* of the Father, deriving all power from him.

"With respect to that excellent Christian, *Hannah Barnard*, I continue to think she was shamefully treated.

"With best respects, though personally unknown, I remain thy sincere friend,　WILLIAM MATHEWS."

As the autumn approached, his infirmities gradually increased; but he was able to attend the funeral of his aged and venerable friend, Mr. Elijah Waring, at Witney, in the latter part of November. From this time his health still more rapidly declined, and very much disabled him from discharging the duties of an executor to Mr. Waring's will. He was however not confined to his chamber but a few days, and died at his house in Grosvenor Buildings, Bath, on the 12th of April, leaving only one daughter, and his grandson above-mentioned. He was universally esteemed by all who had the happiness of being well acquainted with his worth, and most by those who knew him best. His funeral was attended by many members of the Bath and West of England Agricultural Society, as well as by many members of the Society of Friends, and others of his acquaintance, out of sincere respect to his memory. I cannot perhaps close this memoir better than by annexing to it some elegant lines which Mr. Mathews wrote without intending them for the public eye; but as they afford so just and pleasing a picture of a pious mind calmly viewing the near approach of that change, which is destined to waft the whole human race to the shores of eternity, I would not withhold them from your readers. They were "oc-

casioned by the sudden fading of an
avenue of lime trees, (behind the
author's residence,) in the autumn of
1815.": .

" Ye russet shades, which late were seen
Array'd in summer's cheerful green,
   Alas, how chang'd your hue!
Your verdant vesture now no more
Can charm the solitary hour,
   So brown and cheerless you !

And yet methinks your ev'ry tree
Stands emblematical of me,
   Fast with'ring to decay;
This awful diff'rence still appears
You'll renovate in *future* years,
   Soon comes my latest day !

Such is the lot of feeble man,
Of time; prescribed a little span
   More wise and good to grow,
But to direct his course aright,
His Maker gives of gracious light,
   An intellectual flow !

And, lo ! th' unheeded sacred page
Proclaims aloud, from age to age,
   A great and glorious theme ;
Good men, with *new* celestial breath,
Shall triumph o'er the bed of death,
   And rise to bliss supreme !

Then let me ne'er at death repine,
But, bless'd with pow'r and grace
   divine,
(As fleeting hours decrease)
Improve each solemn day and night,
In humble hope of vision bright,
   And pure eternal peace !

Peace underiv'd from works of time,
Or mental means, howe'er sublime,
   Unsanctified by heav'n ;
The boon is *mercy* most entire,
To crown our deep devout desire,
   In heav'nly goodness giv'n !

Let then, glad hosts of men and angels
   bring
Their hallow'd incense, sweet, and
   Hallelujah sing."

                              T. F.

*Letter from Dr. Watson, the late Bishop
of Llandaff, to the Secretary of the
Society for Erecting a Monument in
St. Paul's, to the Memory of Mr.
Locke.*

                Calgarth Park, Kendal,
SIR,   *June 8,* 1809.

M R. LOCKE has by his works
     erected to himself a monu-
ment, which will remain whilst and
wherever there shall remain a veneration for revealed religion or an attachment to the civil liberty of mankind.

· VOL. XI.   ɪ

Notwithstanding this *ære perennius
monumentum*, I will contribute my
mite towards the erecting one of more
perishable materials; because it will
convey an intimation to some amongst
ourselves, and afford a proof to surrounding states, that amid all their
corruptions, true patriotism and rational religion are still held in the
highest estimation by the liberal and
enlightened inhabitants of Great Britain.   I am, Sir,
              Your faithful Servant,
To Mr. Mortimer.   LLANDAFF.

*Letter, &c. on the Doctrine of Jesus,
by an Eminent American Statesman.*
   [We have received a packet of
valuable communications from a venerable Correspondent in America, of
which the following is a part. No. I.
is an introductory Letter by our Correspondent, who adopts the signature
which he affixed to Letters on the Life
of Servetus, in our Fifth Volume.
Nos. II. and III. are a Letter and
Syllabus, by an eminent American
Statesman, whose name we are not
at liberty to mention, but who will
probably be recognized by such of our
readers as are acquainted with the
characters of the leading men in the
American revolution. Other communications from our valuable Trans-
atlantic Correspondent will follow.
                                 ED.]

            No. I.
   Oldenbarneveld, S. of New York,
SIR,   *July 1,* 1816.
P LEASED with the liberal plan
    which you have adopted in your
Repository, I deem it a duty to contribute to its success, as far as my
retirement will permit. The only
thing I regret, is, that I find it not
more generally encouraged. Every
lover of truth is interested in its success ; and a fair defence of any reprobated opinion ought to meet an
equally ready admittance, as an unadorned exposition of what is reputed
a revelation from heaven. The truth
of the gospel doctrine is built on a
rock, and cannot want the feeble or
crafty support of frail men ; and infidelity will blush, when, struck by its
native purity and lustre, it discovers
that its darts were aimed at human
inventions only. Perhaps you will
not disagree with me, that infidels,
moderns as well as ancients, have in
their most virulent and artful attacks

upon the religion of Jesus, done less injury to it, than its reputed friends by bigotry and false zeal. It is from this conviction that I have long wished to see the uncontrovertible facts of the gospel history placed in one lucid point of view, and in a similar manner the gospel doctrine fully explained, without the smallest mixture of any controverted tenet, or even the incidental admission of or allusion to any one, embraced by any Christian sect; and, this solid basis having once been adopted by friend and foe, the discussion might gradually proceed to collateral topics.

In this mood I was gratified with the perusal of *a letter* and *sketch*, which bear the stamp of candour and that of profound research. He would deserve well of his country, and the gospel doctrine, could he find leisure to execute the plan, whose outlines he so masterly delineated. But, accept it as it is. There are I hope many in your happy isle equal to this task. In this question is a Churchman as much interested as a Dissenter; and he, who shall have accomplished it, will have done more in defence of the religion of Jesus, than a host of well-meaning though misguided apologists.

SINCERUS.

No. II.

DEAR SIR,

In some of the delightful conversations with you in the evenings of 1798 and 1799, the Christian religion was sometimes our topic; and then I promised you that, one day or other, I would give you my views of it. They are the result of a life of inquiry and reflection, and very different from that anti-christian system imputed to me by those who know nothing of my opinions. To the corruptions of Christianity I am indeed opposed, but not to the genuine precepts of Jesus himself. I am a Christian, in the only sense in which he wished any one to be; sincerely attached to his doctrines, in preference to all others, ascribing to himself all human excellence, and believing he never claimed any other. At the intervals since these conversations, when I could justifiably abstract myself from other affairs, this subject has been under my contemplation: but the more I

considered it, the more it expanded beyond the measure of either my time or information. In the moment of setting out on a late journey, I received from Dr. Priestley his little treatise of "Socrates and Jesus Compared." This being a section of the general view I had taken of the field, it became a subject of reflection, while on the road, and unoccupied otherwise. The result was, to arrange in my mind a syllabus or outline of such an estimate of the comparative merits of Christianity, as I wished to see executed by some one of more leisure and information for the task than myself. This I now send you, as the only discharge of my promise I can probably ever execute; and in confiding it to you, I know it will not be exposed to the malignant perversions of those, who make of every work on the subject of religion a text for misrepresentations and calumnies. I am moreover averse to the communication of my religious tenets to the public, because it would countenance the presumption of those who have endeavoured to draw them before that tribunal, and to seduce public opinion to erect itself into that inquisition over the rights of conscience, which the laws have so justly prescribed. It behoves every man, who values liberty of conscience for himself, to resist invasions of it in the case of others; it behoves him too, in his own case, to give no example of concession, betraying the common right of independent opinion, by answering questions of faith, which the laws have left between God and himself.

To Mr. —— CRITO.

No. III.
Syllabus of an Estimate of the Doctrine of Jesus, compared with those of others.

In a comparative view of the ethics of the enlightened nations of antiquity, of the Jews and of Jesus, no notice should be taken of the corruptions of reason among the ancients, to wit, the idolatry and superstition of their vulgar, nor of the corruptions of Christianity by the overlearned among its professors.

Let a just view be taken of the moral principles inculcated by the most esteemed of the sects of ancient philosophy, or of their individuals, particularly Pythagoras, Socrates, Epicurus, Cicero, Epictetus, Seneca, Antoninus.

I. PHILOSOPHERS.

1. Their precepts related chiefly to ourselves and the government of those passions, which, unrestrained, would disturb our tranquillity of mind.* In this branch of philosophy they were really great.

2. In developing our duty to others they were short and defective : they embraced indeed the circles of kindred and friends, and inculcated patriotism, or the love of our country, in the aggregate, as a primary obligation; towards our neighbours and countrymen they taught justice, but scarcely viewed them as within the circle of benevolence; still less have they inculcated peace, charity and love to all our fellow-men, or embraced with benevolence the whole family of mankind.

II. JEWS.

1. Their system was Deism, that is, the belief in one only God, but their ideas of him and his attributes were degrading and injurious.

2. Their ethics were not only imperfect, but often irreconcileable with the sound dictates of reason and morality, as they respect intercourse with those around us.

III. JESUS.

In this state of things among the Jews, Jesus appeared.

His parentage was obscure; his condition poor; his education null; his natural endowments great.

His life correct and innocent; he was meek, benevolent, patient, firm,

---

* To explain, I will exhibit the heads of Seneca and Cicero's Philosophical works, the most extensive of any we have received from the ancients. Of *ten* heads in Seneca seven relate to ourselves, de Ira, Consolatio, de Tranquillitate, de Constantia Sapientis, de Otio Sapientis, de Vita Beata, de Brevitate Vitæ. Two relate to others, de Clementia, de Beneficiis; and one relates to the government of the world, de Providentia. Of eleven tracts of Cicero, five respect ourselves, viz. de Finibus, Tusculana, Academica, Paradoxa, de Senectute. One, de Officiis, partly to ourselves, partly to others. One, de Amicitia, relates to others, and four are on different subjects, to wit, de Natura Deorum, de Divinatione, de Fato, and Somnium Scipionis.

disinterested, and of the sublimest eloquence.

The disadvantages under which his doctrine appear are remarkable.

1. Like Socrates and Epictetus he wrote nothing himself.

2. But he had not like them a Xenophon or Arrian to write for him. On the contrary, all the learned of his country, entrenched in its power and riches, were opposed to him, lest his labours should undermine their advantages. And the committing to writing his life and doctrines fell on the most unlettered and ignorant of men, who wrote too from memory, and not till long after the transactions had passed.

3. According to the ordinary fate of those, who attempt to enlighten and reform mankind, he fell an early victim to the jealousy and combination of the altar and the throne at about thirty-three years of age, his reason having not yet attained the maximum of its energy; nor the course of his preaching, which was but of about three years, presented occasions of developing a complete system of moral duties.

4. Hence the doctrines, which he really delivered, were defective as a whole, and fragments only of what he did deliver, have come to us, mutilated, misstated, and often unintelligible.

5. They have been still more disfigured by the corruptions of schismatising followers, who have found an interest in sophisticating and perverting the simple doctrines he taught, by engrafting on them the mysticisms of a Grecian sophist, frittering them into subtleties, and obscuring them with jargon, until they have caused good men to reject the whole in disgust, and to view Jesus himself as an impostor.

Notwithstanding these disadvantages, a system of morals is presented to us, which, if filled up in the true style and spirit of the rich fragments he left us, would be the most perfect and sublime that has ever been taught by man.

The question of his being a member of the Godhead, or, in direct communication with it, claimed for him by some of his followers, and denied by others, is foreign to the present view, which is merely an estimate of the intrinsic merit of his doctrines.

1. He corrected the Deism of the Jews, confirming them in their belief of one only God, and giving them juster notions of his attributes and government.

2. His moral doctrines, relating to kindred and friends, were more pure and perfect than those of the most correct of the philosophers, and greatly more so than those of the Jews. And they went far beyond both in inculcating universal philanthropy, not only to kindred and friends, to neighbours and countrymen, but to all mankind, gathering all into one family, under the bonds of love, charity and peace, common wants

and common aids. A developement of this head will evince the peculiar superiority of the system of Jesus over all others.

3. The precepts of philosophy and of the Hebrew code laid hold of actions only. He pushed his scrutinies into the heart of man, erected his tribunal in the region of his thoughts, and purified the waters at the fountain head.

4. He taught emphatically the doctrine of a future state, which was doubted or disbelieved by the Jews, and wielded it with efficacy as an important incentive; supplementary to the other motives to moral conduct.

MISCELLANEOUS COMMUNICATIONS.

Narrative of a celebrated Auto de Fé, in the City of Logrono.

[That the following Narrative may not be suspected of having been coloured by Protestant prejudice, we think it right to preface it, by an extract from the private letter of our Correspondent, who will, we trust, excuse this freedom. " I am not at all sure that the enclosed deserves a place in the Monthly Repository; but I think I can promise you that what is meant to follow, will have more that is extraordinary and interesting—*if it be* interesting to trace the extravagancies, the worse than extravagancies, of the human character. The deeds of the inquisition have usually been narrated by its enemies: this is its own authorized official narrative. The documents I examined had been scrutinized with the utmost care, and every individual sentence was marked with the rubric of one of the inquisitors. They were signed by the different individuals who were employed in the commission, and addressed, I think, to the Cardinal Archbishop of Toledo, Dr. B. de Sandobal y Rojas, who was at that time at the head of the holy office." ED.]

IN the most illustrious period of the literary annals of Spain (the beginning of the 17th century), an ecclesiastical commission was sent by the holy office to celebrate an auto de fé in the city of Logrono. The writer of the present article has had an opportunity of examining the original documents of its proceedings (as they escaped from the archives of the inqui-

sition in the confusion accompanying the late invasion of Spain), and he can vouch for the general correctness of the following narrative.

The extirpation of witchcraft was the main object of this religious embassy; but it was commissioned to extend its fearful power to every thing in the shape of heresy. An account of its proceedings was printed in 1611 by a zealous Catholic, " desirous (as he informs his readers) that they being aware of the iniquities of the devilish sect of witches," may " watch over the safety of their houses and families." The Cortes, who saw that to unmask spiritual tyranny would be to subdue it, encouraged a re-publication of the pamphlet (of which four editions have been printed); but bigotry has now succeeded in consigning it to temporary oblivion. The writer, however, has the pleasure of knowing that many of the MSS. containing the official narratives of the foul and ferocious deeds of the inquisition have escaped from its dark and secret chambers. They are lodged in security, and will one day instruct and shame the world

The relation of the proceedings of the Logrono commission is prepared by the recommendation of a Franciscan friar, who says that " the book contains nothing against our holy religion and *good Christian customs*," (in timating of course that to torture and burn heretics is a very " good Christian custom"), " but on the contrary what is very true and necessary to be told to all the faithful, to undeceive the deceits of Satan."

The celebration of " this most famous and holy auto" was attended by such multitudes of priests, monks and friars, and by such crowds of the devout, who came " even from far distant countries," as had never been collected on any former occasion. A host of " minstrels, musicians and ministers" accompanied the procession of the " holy green cross" (the standard of the inquisition), which was afterwards planted on a high scaffold, and surrounded by torches. A religious guard paraded about it till the dawn of the following day, when fifty-three culprits were brought forth from the prisons of " the holy office." Twenty-one, who had recanted, marched first in " the vestments of degradation," and some with ropes round their necks, with which they were to be scourged. Twenty-one others followed, condemned to various punishments. Next came the bones and the figures in effigy of five individuals who had been already executed; and at last six other persons, who, at the end of the ceremony, were to be delivered up to be burnt alive. " They were all so appropriately and beautifully clad" (the relation says), " that it was truly well worth seeing." A mule bearing a coffer covered with velvet, in which the sentences were enclosed, was next in rank, and then the inquisitors, the magistrates and the different religious orders, all arranged with " great authority and gravity."

On arriving at the scaffold, the " worst criminals were stationed at the top, and the rest at different elevations according to their crimes." The inquisitors, officers of the civil power, ecclesiastics of rank and other dignified individuals to the number of a thousand, were seated in the lower benches of the scaffold; and a place was erected for the criminals after they had been long enough exhibited, in which were two pulpits from whence their sentences were to be read to them.

After a sermon from a Dominican friar, the whole of the first day was employed in reading the sentences of eleven of the most atrocious of the capitally condemned, six of whom were given up to be immediately burnt, and of these no further mention is made.

On the following Monday the other criminals were brought forth; every thing was arranged as before; a sermon was preached by a Franciscan monk, and the reading the sentences was continued—first, of " two famous cheats" who had " committed great enormities in the name of the holy inquisition," (as if the imitators could exceed the original!) one was fined and expatriated, the other received two hundred lashes and was condemned to be kept five years at the galley-oar. Fourteen were variously punished for different blasphemies and heretical opinions. " Six of a Jewish sect of Christians, who put on clean shirts on Saturdays, and performed other ceremonies of the law of Moses," after having abjured their errors, were ordered to suffer banishment and other punishments. One was transported for having sung, " Yes, the promised Christ is come, no! yes! no!" Another who " had been Judaizing for five and twenty years," having sued for pardon " with tears and true repentance," was " only imprisoned for life." A Moor (Mahometan) who owned he had apostatized, was reconciled and condemned to receive one hundred lashes. In the details of the evidence against these convicts, " such fearful and horrible things were related as had never before reached the ears of man;" and though a great deal of the narrative was omitted, they could hardly finish by close of day. The reporter goes on to say, " towards all these wretches the *greatest mercy* was shown, and more account was taken of their penitence than of their crimes."

Eighteen persons who were to be reconciled, were next brought to the highest floor of the scaffold, and while they were on their knees, they were " received into the communion of the church by a most devout and solemn service." All who witnessed it were inspired by the holiest feelings; " nor did they cease giving grateful praises to God and to the most holy inquisition." And thus the auto was concluded. The " green cross" was borne to the church amidst anthems of " Te Deum laudamus;" the convicted were handed over to the civil power to receive " the merciful award" of their devout judges; and so the day closed upon the pious actors in this dark tragedy.

In another communication some detail shall be given of the incredible evidence which was received against these victims of superstition—the evidence indeed of a host of witnesses. The records of human credulity can perhaps furnish no parallel.   B.

Halifax, September 17, 1816.

Sir,

IN the "Account of the opening of the New Unitarian Chapel, at Oldham, in Lancashire," in your Number for February, (XI. p. 121,) the reporter has taken notice of a few observations which I took that opportunity of making on the propriety of establishing a *Fellowship Fund* in connexion with Unitarian congregations. As several friends have approved of the idea, and have applied to me to detail my proposal, I have done so, and offer the following plan for insertion in the Monthly Repository or Christian Reformer.

PROPOSED REGULATIONS.

1. That there be established in the society of Unitarian Christians assembling at * * * * * a *fellowship fund*.

2. That its objects are : (1.) to assist the members of the society with occasional relief under the pressure of sickness, infirmity or want ; (2.) to defray the expenses (such as fire, candles, &c.) incidental to the meetings for religious edification and prayer* in the society ; (3.) to present such occasional contributions as the fund may allow to Unitarian chapels about to be erected or enlarged ; to the academies in our persuasion established at York and Hackney ; to the Unitarian Fund, and to any other institution now existing, or which may hereafter be formed, which may seem calculated to promote the diffusion of Christian truth, and to inculcate holiness of heart and life.

3. That the fund be supplied by voluntary donations and subscriptions.

4. That every donor of five shillings annually, or subscriber of one penny

---

* The second object is specified in this rule from such a fund having been needed (and supported by a small weekly contribution of the members) in the religious society to which the proposer belongs. This object may be omitted and others specified according to the local circumstances of particular societies : such as, to assist infant societies in obtaining regular public worship and in defraying the expenses of rent and of fitting up a place for that purpose ; to form or assist in defraying the expenses of plans for establishing plain and Scriptural preaching in districts, or circuits ; the support of a vestry library, tract society, Sunday school, &c. the purchase of Bibles and hymn books for the poor in the society, &c. &c.

---

per week (not in arrears) be entitled to vote on any case brought before the members of the fund.

5. That a president, secretary, treasurer, two auditors, and one collector for every ten donors or subscribers, be appointed ; the election to these offices to be annual, with the exception of that of president, which shall be offered permanently to the minister for the time being.

6. That when a case is to be offered for consideration and assistance, the secretary, on receiving a requisition signed by five members, shall call a meeting of the fund to be held immediately after the afternoon's service in the vestry (school-room or chapel as may be), to take the case into consideration and the sum proposed to be voted.

7. That no case shall be finally decided till a *second* meeting has been held on the Lord's day afternoon (after service) next following the first meeting, except in cases of infirmity, sickness, or want requiring *immediate* relief.

8. That in all cases a majority of the members entitled to vote (Rule 4.) shall decide, the president, and in his absence the chairman, having a casting vote.

9. That the subscriptions and donations as received by the treasurer, shall be put into the *bank for savings*, [or into the hands of such person as a majority shall deem trust-worthy] in the joint names of the president, secretary and treasurer ; and that all orders for payment shall be signed by not less than two of these officers.

10. That the secretary keep a book for minutes of the meetings, and the treasurer an account book : That these be open at every meeting for the inspection of donors and subscribers (not in arrears). That a statement of the accounts examined and attested by the auditors be submitted to the general annual meeting, and if approved be hung up in a conspicuous part of the vestry (or other place of meeting) for not less than one month.

11. That an annual meeting be held after afternoon service on the first Lord's day in January, of each year, and that notice shall be given of the same on the preceding Lord's day, as well as on the day of meeting : that at this meeting the officers

be elected, the accounts passed, and other business be transacted.

FORMS OF NOTICE.

We, the undersigned, request you to call a meeting of the members of the fellowship fund to be held the next Lord's day (the instant) immediately after afternoon's service, to take into consideration the propriety of voting a sum of money to [assist our Unitarian brethren at Thorne in Building their Chapel] (signed) AB. CD. EF. GH. IJ. dated To Mr. Secretary to the Fellowship Fund.

Notice from the secretary, to be read by the minister or clerk.

The members of the Fellowship Fund are requested to meet in the vestry this afternoon immediately after service.

By a plan of this kind, Mr. Editor, union and co-operation in individual societies would be promoted; a state of things in every point of view desirable, and preliminary to any good to be expected from a general association of the Unitarian body. The progress of Unitarianism, and the efforts made for its advancement, would be detailed in these societies, and carried home to and again discussed at the firesides of the members. Thus accurate information would be circulated, and an increased interest in and attachment to the cause excited, not only amongst the members of the same congregation, but between the scattered societies of the Unitarian body. The calls upon Unitarian liberality, for the erection of new chapels and other important objects, have of late happily been frequent. But if continued, which I trust will be the case, they cannot be so promptly met, and so effectually answered as they ought to be. The willing giver will from prudential motives be obliged however reluctantly to withhold his aid. We must therefore look out for other and multiplied sources of supply, and call in the many in aid of the few. Before you is a plan for that purpose, which whilst it organizes a fresh set of contributors, and falls so easily upon all as not to be felt by any, does not interfere with nor supersede the exercise of liberality on the part of the affluent members of the Unitarian body. I will only add of this project, that I shall be truly glad to see it superseded by a better.

There is indeed one objection which

deserves particular notice, viz. that these plans for raising additional sums of money in any congregation, do in fact detract from the stipend of the stated minister; or where that stipend is low and insufficient, tend to keep it so. I allow this objection in all its force as applied to many of the topics of sermons on particular occasions and to subsequent congregational collections; but I deny the assumption upon which this objection proceeds, as applied to the project detailed above. It will be found (except in cases of endowment) that a small salary bears a direct proportion to the smallness of a congregation. If this be so, all plans that tend to increase the numbers of a religious society, tend to the increase of the minister's salary; and this tendency must be granted to all means likely to convey information, excite additional interest, and promote personal attachment and intercourse and congregational union and co-operation.

By some an objection may be felt to the term *fellowship* fund. I care little about the name, and have not any objection to its being termed an auxiliary fund, a common fund, or any other name, provided the end be kept in view. It certainly is always desirable to call things by their right names, and I do not propose the project or the designation as at all corresponding with the κοινωνία, the "*fellowship*" of the primitive Christian church, nor as at all wishing to interfere with that apostolical institution wherein it is observed. Such a Christian contribution, were it universal, would be more efficient; and most earnestly would I wish to see it supersede the proposal before you, which is simply a project to organize a new and permanent set of contributors, and which must stand or fall on the ground of expediency alone. One word as to the *productiveness* of such a plan, and I have done. So far as I know, we have not any data to form any tolerably correct estimate of the Unitarian population of the United Kingdom; but if for the sake of illustration, we suppose a plan to be adopted which would associate one hundred thousand contributors throughout the empire, at *one penny a week each*, it would produce nearly *twenty-two thousand pounds* per annum, (21,666*l.* 13*s.* 4*d.*); when probably at present not so many *hundreds* are raised from the same sources for the same purposes.

JOHN THOMSON.

P. S. A friend, whose name is well known to your readers, and which, did I feel at liberty without his permission to mention, would insure attention to the subject, favoured me with the following remarks in reply to a rough sketch of the project detailed above. " The increase of calls on Unitarian benevolence is a pleasing sign of the advancement of truth; but I agree with you that as at present carried on they must exhaust and weary. To all religious societies, indeed, the advice is applicable; but to small associations of detached converts who are at too great a distance to join an established congregation, and not yet sufficiently numerous or opulent to build a place and maintain a minister, I would particularly recommend St. Paul's advice to the Corinthians about ' collecting for the saints,' (1 Cor. xvi. 2.) ' On every first day of the week let every one lay by as God hath prospered him.' Let them never fail to meet regularly for public worship every Lord's day, &c. Let there be a box with a slit in the lid into which every one may put in according to individual discretion and convenience, from a halfpenny upwards, and without any one knowing its amount but himself. Let it be periodically opened by appointed officers, and a regular account kept of its produce. What is more than is wanted for the relief of occasional distress, or for benevolence to other charities, should be carefully put out to interest and managed to the best advantage: and thus without any burden upon them, a fund would in time be raised equal to all their wants. In already established larger congregations, I greatly approve your regulations for the fellowship fund."

Sir,   *Bridport, Sept. 26, 1816.*

IF you think the following observations calculated to obviate the objections to the divine government, of one of your Correspondents, whose signature is Y. N. [p. 277,] and " to vindicate the ways of God to man," by inserting them in your truly liberal Repository, you will oblige,

Your's respectfully,

THOMAS HOWE.

THAT human life is a chequered scene of good and evil, of pleasure and pain, of the exhilarations of hope and the mortification of disappointment, is a point of no doubtful disputation. The most unfortunate of our fellow creatures have some comforts or other remaining, to sweeten the bitter cup which is given them to drink, whilst imperfection and uncertainty characterize the enjoyments of the most prosperous. The estimate of the happiness or infelicity of the present condition of men, is much influenced, I think, by the peculiar constitution and state of mind of the person who makes it, and the *views* he entertains of the divine government. If he be subject to depression of the animal spirits, and also has embraced a *rigid system* of *religion*, looking on the Deity as an object rather of *dread* than of *love*, dooming the greatest part of mankind, by an eternal and irreversible decree, for the offence of their first progenitor, to unavoidable and endless misery; the estimate of human life formed by such a one will probably partake of the gloom of his disposition and the rigour of his creed. Good Dr. Watts was in one of his melancholy moods, and had not the most cheerful views of religion, when he composed the hymn containing the following lines.

" Lord, what a wretched land is this,
    That yields us no supply,
No cheering fruits, no wholesome trees,
    Nor streams of living joy !

But pricking thorns through all the ground,
    And mortal poisons grow,
And all the rivers that are found,
    With dang'rous waters flow.

Yet the dear path to thine abode,
    Lies through this horrid land.

Long nights and darkness dwell below,
    With scarce a twinkling ray."
                        Watts, H. 53. B. 2.

Your Correspondent, Y. N. in the Monthly Repository for May last, p. 277, seems to me to have thoroughly imbibed the spirit of the lines just quoted. He looks at human life through a gloomy medium, and sees nothing in it but evil. As to the inquiry he proposes for discussion, whether happiness or misery prevails in the present state (but which he does not hesitate to decide himself in a manner most unfavourable for mankind) it must be determined by the knowledge of the *actual feelings* of *men* in *general*, during the whole of their mortal existence, as far as these can by any means be ascertained. Should it appear that good preponderates over evil, and happiness outweighs the miseries of life, a strong presumptive argument is hereby furnished for *perfect ultimate felicity*, when the scheme of the divine government respecting man is completed. Should the *reverse* however be established, and it be clearly shewn that evil prevails more than good, pain and distress more than ease and comfort; even in this case so many proofs present themselves of the benevolence of God in the constitution of nature, and the salutary tendencies of evils themselves, that we should be justified in inferring the *necessity* of them to such an extent, in this introductory scene, but not in concluding that therefore evil will *eventually* triumph over good. As to the estimate of which I am treating, let the comparison be fairly made on an enlarged view of the aggregate of mankind, and the evidence, I think, appears in favour of the comforts of life exceeding its infelicities. On this extensive scale should the inquiry be conducted, and not confined to the peculiarly sad condition of certain individual sufferers, or to such *times* as the *present*, when more than *usual* distress prevails. Neither is it necessary, in order to vindicate the wisdom and goodness of our heavenly Father, or to prove the prevalence of happiness over misery, to assert that the pleasing sensations of *every human being*, whether he remains on the stage of life for a longer or shorter period, exceed his painful feelings. That in some *particular cases* the latter should exceed the former seems unavoidable, unless the Deity deviated from those general laws which he has established, and according to which he sees it best to act.

I now proceed to the examination of the first and principal of the objections, (and indeed chiefly the foundation of the others) which Y. N. states against the divine government, as it respects the happiness of the present state. "In contemplating human society," says he, "the first consideration that offers itself is, that men like all other animals, increase in number or

multiply much faster, than their means of subsistence." He is however mistaken in supposing that no writers on this subject have attempted to answer this argument. The fact is admitted by Dr. Paley, in his "Natural Theology," and the observations which he makes on this part of the constitution of things I shall transcribe, as tending at least to abate the force of the objection. "The order of generation proceeds by something like a *geometrical* progression. The increase of provision under circumstances even the most advantageous, can only assume the form of an *arithmetic* series. Whence it follows that the population will always overtake the provision, will pass beyond the line of plenty and will continue to increase, till checked by the difficulty of procuring subsistence."—*Paley's Nat. Theol.* p. 548.

"In what concerns the human species, it may be a part of the scheme of Providence, that the earth should be inhabited by a *shifting* or perhaps a *circulating* population. In this economy, it is possible there may be the following advantages; when old countries are become exceedingly corrupt, simpler modes of life, purer morals and better institutions may rise up in new ones, whilst fresh soils reward the cultivator with more plentiful returns. Thus the different portions of the globe come into use in succession as the residence of man." —P. 520.

When a country possesses a greater population than the means of affording it provisions, *distress* must be the result to a *portion* of its inhabitants. The evils however arising from such a state of things will not, generally speaking, rush on them suddenly, but approach by gradual steps. As the difficulties increase of procuring a livelihood, many of the lower classes of society, especially mechanics and husbandmen, are induced to remove to countries less thickly inhabited, and which promise to reward their exertions with a more comfortable subsistence. Hereby the barren desert becomes a fruitful field, and the wilderness, before the haunt of beasts of prey, in due time is changed into a safe and commodious habitation for man; "joy and gladness," in the words of the prophet, "are found therein, thanksgiving, and the voice of melody.". Countless millions of human beings are hereby brought into existence, Y. N. thinks to be *miserable*, but more justly I trust it may be said, to partake of the bounties of Providence here, and to be trained up, by a course of moral discipline *begun* in *time* and *completed* in *eternity*, ". to glorify God and enjoy him for ever." This law of the divine government, then, by which population increases in a greater proportion than the means of subsistence, producing no doubt many *partial evils*, effects most extensive and general good. On a large scale comprehending the *whole* of this habitable globe, it is a law which evinces both the wisdom and goodness of the common Parent of mankind, by being favourable to the production of a *greater sum* of human happiness. Yet to Y. N. "it appears with so dreadful an aspect, that he says the *statement* of it is *horrible*."

Considering the misery which he supposes to be our lot after arriving at a certain age, he must surely view the following statement of his, as a *great blessing* to the *children* who thus meet with an early grave, however much it may be regretted by their *parents*. " It is calculated that not less than one fourth part of the human species perish, before they become moral agents, before four years of age." Granting this, there is good reason to conclude, that their sum of enjoyment exceeds their painful sensations, during their short scene of mortal existence; the balance therefore in respect of happiness is in their favour. That *some* of them (not " *many*" comparatively) " perish by diseases brought on by want," may be admitted as a melancholy fact, without its disproving the position just stated.

I now proceed with Y. N. to consider the condition of those who arrive at the period of youth and manhood. In his view, both the *single* and the *married* must necessarily be *miserable:* the former because they are *single* and have no " help meet for them ;" the latter, because the parties are often ill-sorted, or have great anxieties respecting their children, or their connexion is embittered by disease or dissolved by death. Alas ! for poor mortals, let them do as they will, their condition must be sad indeed.

Be it known however to my readers, that the present writer is a *bachelor* on the wrong side, as it is usually termed, of *fifty*, yet (let every one speak for himself) he could tell Y. N. that he has not experienced that *overwhelming misery*, which is the unavoidable lot it seems, of all those who are doomed to pass *singly* through life's varied scenes. As to the *generality* of those who are in the same pitiable situation with myself, I do not perceive such very gloomy and desponding countenances, as indicate their being weary of existence. With respect to married persons also, as far as my observation reaches, their cup of life has mingled ingredients of bitter and sweet, with so great a proportion of the latter however, as to make it upon the whole tolerably palatable.* Another objection to the present constitution of things, is the appointment of the separation of the parties, if happily coupled, by the unsparing hand of death. " Disease and death come," says Y. N. " and the survivor is doomed to wear out a wretched life in aggravated solitude. Instances of this kind are no doubt to be met with, which cannot but excite the sympathy of every one who has a heart to feel. As Y. N. looks around him and draws his inferences from

---

* The present writer has in the course of his life, known a considerable number of married persons in different ranks, chiefly in the middle and lower classes of society. The result of his observations is this, that in a *few instances* matrimony produces somewhat like a *heaven* upon earth.

" How blest the sacred tie that binds,
In union sweet according minds !
How swift the heav'nly course they run,
Whose hearts, whose faith, whose hopes are one !"

Mrs. Barbauld.

This on the other hand is balanced by the union of parties so ill-sorted, that as Dr. Watts says, in his celebrated lines on " Few Happy Matches," " As well may heav'nly consorts spring, From two old lutes with ne'er a string, Or none besides the bass." The great majority of marriages are, I believe neither the one nor the other; neither characterized by any *great degree* of felicity or of misery ; but in which, as might be expected from an institution of the benevolent Parent of mankind, *happiness preponderates.*

what he conceives to be real life, I shall adopt the same mode. As to the generality of widowers and widows then, judging of those *I do not know*, from the persons of this description I *do know*, however much affected at the painful separation, *time* and *reflection* alleviate their grief, and they are not such *wretched objects* as this gloomy painter draws them. Many of them indeed, not altogether relishing the "*solitude*" in which they are left, have no objection to repair their loss by *another union*, a proof by the way that they were not led by *experience* to entertain such formidable, terrific ideas of matrimony as your Correspondent Y. N.

I shall not enter into the argument to which he refers of Mr. Lindsey and others, that the *comparatively few* instances of *suicide*, furnish a proof of mankind in general not being unhappy. Some who are weary of their mortal existence are no doubt restrained from rushing on death for relief, from fear of the consequences hereafter, which " makes them rather bear those ills they have, than fly to others they know not of." I cannot however agree with Y. N. in thinking, that if self-murder was " not disreputable," and if a general conviction prevailed that this world ends all human feeling, hundreds of thousands would thus die." Happy for mankind the experiment is not likely to be made ; but even in this supposable case, the *love* of *life* is I conceive so *strong* and *ardent*, and there is such a natural dread of losing that existence and those active powers we possess, as would prevent those hundreds of thousands of whom he speaks, from effecting self-destruction. The *wisdom* which Y. N. applauds of those philosophers who said "the best thing possible was never to be born, and the next best to die the hour of one's birth," will be very differently appreciated, I presume, by most of my readers who believe in the infinite wisdom and goodness of our Creator, and the pure doctrines of the Christian revelation, teaching us that man is destined for an immortal life, for the enjoyment of which he is furnished with the means of preparing, in this state of trial and probation.

As the design of this paper is chiefly to obviate the leading objections of Y. N. to the divine government respecting the present constitution of things, I shall not enter on the statement of the many and forcible proofs both positive and presumptive of the prevalence of happiness over misery in this varied scene, introductory to a future and more perfect state of being. For that satisfaction on this point which the present writer has himself received, he takes leave earnestly to recommend to Y. N. the attentive perusal of the chapter, "on the Goodness of the Deity," in Dr. Paley's "Natural Theology," Mr. Lindsey "on the Divine Government," and more especially "Illustrations of the Divine Government," by T. Southwood Smith, a work which was judiciously reviewed in the Monthly Repository for August, and which may be justly ranked among the most masterly productions of the age, on this important subject.

Many useful reflections and much moral improvement may be derived, from the inquiry proposed by Y. N. Whether happiness or misery really preponderates, it becomes us as men and professing Christians, to learn, with the Apostle Paul, " in whatsoever state we are to be therewith *content*," as the appointment of a Being whose wisdom cannot err, whose providence is universal, and whose goodness is infinite and unchangeable. In forming a due estimate of human life, let us guard against mistaking the *exceptions* to the usual course of things, for the *general rule*, and deducing our inferences from the *former* instead of the *latter*. This it appears to me Y. N. has done, which has led him to his gloomy conclusions. It has pleased the Supreme Lord of the universe to act by general laws (excepting peculiar cases of *miraculous* operation) : and that this mode of government is the wisest and best of any conceivable plans, Dr. Priestley adduces many solid arguments to prove, in the first volume of his " Letters to a Philosophical Unbeliever." It is evident, however, that this constitution of things, must be attended with unavoidable *partial evils*. The same element of *fire* for instance which is of *incalculable utility* to the world, will sometimes consume the comfortable habitations of men and occasion great distress. Are we therefore justified from the latter accidental circumstance, in reasoning

While contemplating any part of the plan of the divine administration, let us make due allowance for the narrow limits of the human understanding. We shall not be then surprised to find some of the dispensations of Providence respecting both nations and individuals, to our view involved in clouds and darkness. Can a *finite* mind *comprehend infinity?* How *few links* do we see of that amazing chain of causes and effects, which is suspended from the throne of God, and extends from everlasting to everlasting? To censure therefore any of the proceedings of Heaven, because we do not immediately perceive the rectitude, wisdom and goodness of them, would be more unreasonable and presumptuous, than for an ignorant peasant, seeing only a single wheel or spring of an ingenious complicated machine, to pronounce this wheel or spring *useless*, though really so *connected* with *other parts*, that without it the whole piece of machinery would cease to move. The instructive pages of history, sacred and profane, present us with many events of direful aspect when viewed separately by themselves, which, under the disposals of the *propitious Power* that presides over the world, and is continually educing good from apparent evil, have been made to produce invaluable blessings to mankind. That this will be the actual result of those astonishing changes and revolutions (attended with atrocities and calamities deplored by every friend to humanity and liberty) which have for many years past agitated Europe, is as reasonable to conclude from the wisdom and goodness of "the Most High who ruleth in the kingdom of men, and giveth it to whomsoever he will," as it is consolatory to the pious and benevolent Christian. "The Lord

This is incumbent on us as children of the same gracious Parent, and therefore brethren of the same family of mankind, as members of the same community, and I may add professors of the religion of the gospel, the chief characteristic of which is *love*. The happiness of society is promoted by improvements made in the arts of civilized life, by the education of the rising generation among all ranks and conditions, by the diffusion of general knowledge, and more especially by the spread of just and worthy sentiments respecting God and religion. The estimate of human life, I doubt not, as to the preponderance of its sum of enjoyments over its evils, will be proportionally *more favourable*, as attention is paid to the important objects just mentioned. To a state of society greatly more *enlightened*, more improved in *moral excellence*, and consequently *happier*, than in any preceding period of the world; to a state of society distinguished by the prevalence of truth, peace and righteousness, inspired prophecy directs our views : and the many pious and benevolent institutions which do honour to this age and country (among which may be ranked those that are established for the promotion of free inquiry, of pure Christianity, and the practice of virtue as not of the least importance), are some of the *means* which the Supreme Disposer of all things will probably adopt, for bringing about this auspicious era.

SIR, *Bristol, September* 10, 1816.

IT was with much pleasure I read the article on Doctrinal or Controversial Preaching, in the Repository for last month, [p. 456,] the writer of which is entitled (I feel no hesitation in saying) to the most cordial thanks of all those who

wish well to the cause of rational
Christianity. I am the more dis-
·posed to make this observation, on
account of having often been pained
to see the free pews in our chapels
filled with strangers whose attendance
was doubtless with an intention to
hear what might be said in behalf of
the doctrines held by Unitarians, but
who must inevitably have gone away
with disappointment, perhaps with a
determination to come there no more,
having been disgusted rather than
informed by hearing (what is called)
a dry moral discourse. I do most sincerely hope that this subject will be
taken into serious consideration by
Unitarian ministers, particularly those
of our more opulent congregations.
If a doctrinal or controversial sermon
were to be preached regularly once a
fortnight, I think it would be calculated to do much good; for those who
felt an interest in the cause would
then know when to invite their
friends who are of a different opinion,
but not indisposed to inquiry. A lecture on theological subjects given on
a week day evening, is I think another
thing very much to be desired; for,
no doubt, there are many people who
would attend our meetings, at convenient opportunities, but cannot conscientiously absent themselves from
the service of their own respective
places of worship.   J. B.

On Controversial Divinity.

Sept. 7th, 1816.

" THE dispute about religion," says
Dr. Young, " and the practice
of it, seldom go together." This assertion must be taken with some grains
of allowance. It could be designed
only to guard us against the influence
of a contentious and controversial spirit,
to the neglect of real religion; and not
to discourage the sober investigation of
truth: for this eminent writer was
himself, saving perhaps in some articles
of his creed, one of the profoundest reasoners. The disputatious professor enters into the church or into company
to criticize, to judge and to condemn.
He can discern a minister's creed by the
turn of his prayers, by the naming of
his text,* or even by the lines of his

* " *That's an Arminian text*," said a sage
disciple once to his pew-mate as soon as the
minister had spoken it.

countenance; and in company he
often drags his associates into a contention about some favourite and perhaps
frivolous topic, or at best not fit to be
debated in a mixed assembly, where,
if the subject of religion be introduced,
it should be discussed only upon acknowledged principles. An old Puritan
thus describes such professors :

" They crowd about a little spark,
Contend and wrangle in the dark;
Never more bold than when most blind,
And they run fastest when the truth's
  behind."

Such a spirit is of hurtful tendency ;
it is the bane of that common love we
owe to all mankind, of peace and friendly
intercourse; it will wither our virtues
and reflect disgrace upon our profession : nevertheless, as just hinted, we
must sometimes dispute; for what
topic of religion or of morals hath not
been made a subject of controversy?
Only let us be careful to observe the
essential circumstances of time, place
and manner.

As in a mixed company, so in a
sermon delivered to a mixed congregation, we should not enter much into
disputed points, meaning here, not the
great outlines of natural and revealed
religion, which, though they have
been controverted, are supposed to be
acknowledged and partly understood
by the majority of Christian hearers,
but those points about which the sincere professors of the gospel differ.
The former will ever constitute an
essential part of all sound legitimate
scriptural preaching; the latter it is
plain should be treated of only in a
general way. It is impossible in a
single discourse to state all questions
relative to a disputed article or to answer all objections : there is a decorum,
a manner to be observed in a sermon,
never to be departed from. At the
same time that the faithful minister
should guard against every thing that
would nourish foolish and hurtful prejudices, every thing that has the appearance of trimming, compounding
or reconciling things in themselves
irreconcileable, he should avoid in
matters of speculation; for in morals
there must be no ceremony though
there should be method : in treating of
matters of speculation he should avoid
every thing irritating or calculated to
hurt the feelings of the weak, but
humble believer, who certainly had

better for the present be suffered to retain a simple error of the intellect, rather, than that by having his evil passions awakened, he should unhappily fall into some vice of the heart. The preacher in this case is in danger of alarming the prejudices of his hearers without convincing their understandings, and perhaps, to shorten his work, will unawares be led into railing instead of reasoning.

These remarks do not apply to religious conversations strictly so called, to printed sermons on particular occasions, or to lectures in the form of sermons professedly treating on particular subjects where the hearers are prepared for discussion, and which may all be eminently useful in their way, though even here the character of a sermon should be preserved, but chiefly to general preaching. "It is a kind of sacrilege," says Dr. Hartley, "to rob God's flock of the nourishment due to them from public preachings, and in its stead to run out upon questions that minister no profit to the hearers, at least to the greatest part. These things are much better communicated to the world by the press than to a mixed assembly by the pulpit."

It may not be amiss here to offer a few remarks upon the several names and denominations into which the Christian church is divided; and to which, to names and not to things our present reflections will be confined. It is indeed certain that as " the evil shall bow before the good, and the wicked at the gates of the righteous;" so, things as well as names will finally settle upon their proper bases. That which hath an unstable foundation must necessarily fall of itself; and were it not so, the decree as to all the corruptions of religion is final and irrevocable: " every plant which my heavenly Father hath not planted shall be rooted up." But names may become obsolete long before the things signified by them are fallen into decay; that is, the asperities and excrescences of sects and parties may wear off, and they may learn to view one another without aversion and disgust, and even with cordial amity and good will, though they should still retain many of their own peculiar notions. And this desirable event appears to be rapidly accomplishing every day. Some eminent Protestants have written to prove that the Pope is Anti-Christ, and in the

opinion of their own party they have written well : but we must not confine Anti-Christ to any particular denomination : wherever there is a desire of governing consciences or of lording it over God's heritage, there is Anti-Christ.*

But wherever these obnoxious principles are disowned, we must not judge our brother " because he followeth not with us." The charity of the great Founder of our religion and of the sacred writers, is extended to a degree of which a true bigot of any denomination, cleric or laick, established or un-established, can scarcely form an idea. Our Lord would not permit those strangers to be forbidden who attempted to cure diseases in his name; and St. Paul permitted those to preach the gospel who built nothing upon it but " wood, hay and stubble;" and allowed that though their works should be made manifest " by the spirit of judgment and the spirit of burning," the men themselves might be saved ; and he rejoiced that " Christ was preached," though from improper motives : and thus must we act if we would approve ourselves true Christians, though we should find it impossible entirely to coalesce with some particular communities.

If a Protestant of the denomination

what would be his sensations ?—the gorgeous temple, the holy water, the superb ornaments, the pompous processions, the change of postures and of vestments, the blaze of candles at noonday, the smoke of incense, the instrumental music, the chanting of the choristers, the prayers in an unknown tongue—would altogether serve in their general effect absolutely to distract him ! Or if perchance he could gain an interval of reflection, it would be to say within himself—is this the religion of Jesus Christ ? are these the disciples of the prophet of Nazareth, " the man of sorrows and acquainted with griefs?" of him who laid down " poverty of spirit" as the first stone in his spiritual building; of him whose " kingdom was not of this world ?" Perhaps he

---

* " Ignorance in doctrine, superstition in worship and persecution in temper, are full proofs of Anti-Christ."

Robinson on Claude.

might be told in the sermon, if perchance it should be preached by a L'abbé Pluche or a Fenelon, that all this pomp and pageantry was nothing, any further than as it served to promote internal sanctity and the religion of the heart: but this would not suffice; he would immediately reply—if it be nothing, then it is nothing worth, a needless expence upon the public, and much better omitted. And even in a church of more chaste and sober forms, the pealing organ, the frequent repetitions, the monotonous buz of a general response and the careless gabble of charity children, would tend rather to depress than to exalt his devotion. And on the other hand, bring an uninformed Romanist into a silent meeting, and, from a total ignorance of their peculiar principles, he would inquire—wherefore they were come together?

And yet, might not the Romanist and the Friend, together with some of the intermediate classes, converse together upon the outlines of natural religion and of Christian faith; and if accidentally cast into situations where their particular worship was not to be had, meet together on the Lord's day, depute one as the organ of the congregation to pray with or without a form, read some portions of Scripture, exhort either from a written table or from " the table of the heart," and praise the great Creator and Governor of the universe, through Jesus Christ? Nay, might not those among them who held the perpetuity of the ordinance of the Lord's Supper, unite in eating bread and drinking wine, in commemoration of their common Lord, together with some short and appropriate prayers and thanksgivings; and yet each retain for the present his own peculiar ideas as to the nature of this religious rite? Certainly all this may be done by sober and considerate persons in different parts of the world, not only without offence, but much to their mutual comfort and edification. But if upon any such occasions a Gardiner or a Bonner should unexpectedly enter, thunder out his anathema, tell those of his own community that a ceremonial worship was necessary to their religious improvement, that public prayer cannot be duly celebrated without the priest, nor the sacrament without the mass-book; and they were to believe him ;—

then indeed for the present there must be an end of the business! In such a case those who are left ought, in a religious view, to think and act for themselves. " The whole world," says Dr. Hartley, " will never be reformed but by those who are of a truly Catholic spirit."

And to promote this desirable and important end we are called upon as Christians, both in our private and public capacities. Nothing can be more obvious, if we believe Scripture, and, as it hath been well illustrated by many eminent writers, than that the world is carried on for the sake of the church, not this or that particular church, not the clergy as distinct from the laity, but the church of God, consisting, first, of " the household of faith," emphatically so called, that is, true Christians of every denomination, and secondly, of " the children of God who are scattered abroad, those other sheep who are not of the first fold, the sons and daughters whom God shall bring from afar, from the east and the west, the north and the south, to sit down with Abraham, Isaac and Jacob, in his kingdom." The Jewish nation also, which, as such, was the ancient and peculiar people of God, the only nation which has any right to plead favouritism, and that not on their own account—which was never entirely cast off, and which is to be finally restored, must be included in this general idea. It is no enthusiasm to say that in this sense " dominion is founded in grace," and that " the saints shall judge the world ;" but then this is a spiritual and not a civil dominion—the dominion of virtue over vice, of truth over error, of simple real religion over superstition, of a spirit of peace and charity over a spirit of bigotry and intolerance : " For the needy shall not always be forgotten, the expectation of the poor shall not perish for ever; nor shall the rod of the wicked for ever rest upon the lot of the righteous!" Providence sometimes brings about these events by gradual means, and sometimes He operates more sensibly. There is a period when the church is represented as crying out, " It is time for Thee, O Lord! to work, for they have made void thy law: Arise, O Lord! judge the earth, for thou shalt inherit all nations." In the 24th and 34th chapters of Isaiah we have a description of what

is called " the day of the Lord's vengeance, and the year of recompences
for the controversy of Zion," in language the most awfully sublime, when
" The indignation of the Lord shall be
upon all nations, and his fury upon
their armies; when the hosts of heaven
shall be dissolved, and the heavens
themselves rolled together as a scroll,
as a leaf falleth from the vine, and a
falling fig from the fig-tree: When
the earth shall reel to and fro like a
drunkard, and be removed like a cottage; and the transgression thereof
shall be heavy upon it, and it shall fall
and not rise again: When the moon
shall be confounded and the sun
ashamed, and the Lord of Hosts shall
reign in Mount Zion, and in Jerusalem
and before his Ancients, gloriously;"—
figurative expressions, no doubt, in a
great measure, which, nevertheless,
must have a precise and determinate
meaning, though we may possibly mistake in their application.

In the mean time, it behoves both
subjects and the rulers of churches and
kingdoms to " discern the signs of the
times;" the former, to attend chiefly
to personal and family reformation, to
" pray for the peace of Jerusalem,"
and for a spirit of wisdom and justice
in their governors; not to forestal the
Divine plans, never to disturb the state,
in order to purify the church; to wield
no sword in defence of the truth, but
" the sword of the spirit;" and, while
they " abide in their several callings,"
and perform their duty, to leave the
rest to time and Providence:—and the
latter, to revise obsolete and to change
obnoxious laws; not to obstruct reasonable and gradual reformation; never
to encourage the horrid and flagitious
principle of national enmities and an-
tipathies, (for a heathen could say
" *Homo sum, nihil humani a me alienum
puto*") ; and ever to act under the impression of this important maxim, that
that is likely to prove the most durable
government, which hath its foundation
in justice and equity, and in the good
opinion of the people.

AN OCCASIONAL READER.

P. S. The above was written before
An Occasional Reader had read the ingenious letter of *Homily* (p. 456—460).
There are only some slight shades of
difference between *Homily* and himself
as to controversial discourse and controversial preaching.

Newington Green,
Sir,   *October 8th,* 1816.

I RELY on your candour for the
insertion of the following remarks,
occasioned by the notice of *Philosophic
Etymology* in your last Number (p.
538—544). That notice is not more
severe but less candid and sufficient
than I expected. The writer of it has
remarked, indeed, that if the book
" should not have a fair and impartial
trial, the author will have principally
himself to blame. Mr. Gilchrist's peculiar manner has made it impossible
that his work should be tried dispassionately by many of those who are
qualified to sit in judgment upon it."

It is generally understood, I believe,
that judges ought to be peculiarly dispassionate: whether they could justify
themselves, in conducting an unfair
trial and pronouncing angrily an unjust
sentence by saying it was impossible to
be dispassionate, may admit of doubt.
It were unreasonable indeed to exact
extreme virtue from the gravest judges
or most learned doctors; and therefore
I " principally blame myself for not
having a fair and impartial trial." Had
I written as libellously of law and
lawyers, as of our learning and the
learned, of schools and schoolmen, it
is probable that my condign punishment would have been far more afflictive, and that ridicule and hisses
would have pursued me to Newgate.

I wish not to offer any remarks on
the notice of my work considered as a
review: the real merits or demerits of
the book are still before the judges:
your contributor has (prudently perhaps) left them to the sagacity of my
readers. The capital, I may say sole
offence, preferred in the indictment, or
set forth in the sentence pronounced
upon me, is, " arrogant contempt of
all who have gone before me or who
stand beside me." On this charge I
wish, both in respect for the public
and in justice to myself, to solicit a
patient and candid hearing.

I acknowledge that there is much
bitter contemptuousness in my writings. I acknowledge such contemptuousness to be very wrong and very
reprehensible, and promise that I shall
carefully weed it out of my publications
whenever (if ever) any of them shall
pass through my hands into a second
edition. Had I been fortunate enough
to study deeply the doctrines of a certain

masterly dissector of human nature and human society before commencing authorship, my compositions would have been untinctured with that rude, audacious disdain, which is one of their discriminative features. I ought not indeed to have vailed or cloaked my contemptuous feelings *a. la mode*, but I ought to have suppressed and subdued them as workings of that untaught vicious nature, in renouncing and mortifying which consists the moralist's victory over himself. The contempt which I have so plentifully displayed did not originate in but was sanctioned by an error of judgment, which error was only rendered more obstinate by such rebukes as those grounded on *Philosophic Etymology*. Commonplace criticism and stale satire are, to persons of original thinking, offensive for insipidness rather than sourness, and, instead of diminishing, increase the acidity of contemptuous feeling. I have however derived much profitable reflection and feeling from my present reprover; and I can sincerely assure him (though he despaired of me) that arrogance, contempt (especially if forced or affected), and angry vanity, &c. are become so odious in my sight, that I hope never to be guilty of them any more. Contemptuousness is one of the spurious offspring of pride; yet even pride ought to make elevated minds despise it: any person can look or speak scornfully, but every person cannot think clearly or reason powerfully.

Having frankly confessed my guilt, it cannot be unreasonable to remonstrate against the injustice of some of the charges brought against me. I am accused of " contempt of *all* who have gone before me." Others have charged me with extravagant admiration of some who have gone before me. Surely my antagonists ought not to blow cold and hot upon me thus with the same mouth of crimination. Will my worthy admonisher assert that I have shown contempt towards Shakspeare, Bacon, Hobbes, Wilkins, Tucker, Locke and Horne Tooke? It may be said that these did not stand in my way, and therefore I had no temptation to wish to thrust them aside or knock them down: but I beg to say that they were all great masters in the science of words and ideas, and are the best teachers in our language of *Philosophic Etymology* or *Rational Grammar*.

VOL. XI. 4 G

My Reviewer has intimated that I think it an act of condescension on my part to instruct my kind—insinuating that I vainly look down with disdain from some fancied eminence on all men. But I will not yield to him or any other in respect for common men and common-sense. I have found at least a considerable portion of the different classes of society philosophers in their *own way*; and I always respect *thinking* beings whether they think rightly or wrongly, with me or against me. I would rather converse a whole day with the plainest ploughman concerning the important science of husbandry, than a single hour with some learned doctors concerning grammar, etymology, rhetoric or logic. It is *more blessed to give than to receive* : I think it a privilege to communicate instruction. I have (as already acknowledged) expressed much contempt for some who have gone before me and some who stand beside me : but when it is considered that Johnson's Dictionary and Murray's Grammar, &c. are adopted as standards of the English language, will not those who have attended to the philosophy of language admit that there was much temptation in my way? And if I have attempted to undervalue some popular works as much as they are usually overvalued, it should be remembered, that if a rod or rule has been bent to one side, it must be as much bent to the other to bring it straight.

JAMES GILCHRIST.

SIR, *October* 11*th*, 1816.

HAVING presumed in a former Number [p. 386] to call the attention of your readers to the apprehended failure of the Proposal for a New Edition of Dr. Priestley's Theological Works, and to suggest a few imperfect hints with a view of promoting the design, I am happy to observe in your present Number [p. 521] that the observations then made have called forth an abler pen to advocate the same cause. Sensible of my own incompetence to render any important service to such a design, I did, however, indulge the expectation that an appeal (however imperfect) in its behalf, would not be altogether in vain : that expectation has not been disappointed, nor am I willing to abandon the hope that the projected plan may yet be placed " beyond the probability of failure."

The appeal to " the sons of respectable and wealthy laymen" so suitably made, and so forcibly urged, will not fail, it may humbly be presumed, to meet with immediate and deserved attention on their part: and I am sure your worthy Correspondent will forgive me for extending that appeal to " laymen of easy fortunes who have families to provide for, and whose benevolent hearts deeply commiserate the sad condition of the poor around them ;" and even to those who, " amid the daily toils for their subsistence, find time to ruminate on the grand truths of religion, and whose minds are often more enlightened on these subjects than many of those who are favoured with a higher place in the scale of society."

It is most probable the number of volumes printed in a year will not exceed three; upon which calculation the expense of taking in the Works (after the first subscription) will not exceed seven-pence halfpenny per week, a sum which few individuals or families desirous of possessing them, might not spare by a little attention to economy, which would be abundantly compensated by the acquisition of so great a treasure. Instances are not rare among the more popular sects, in which persons of very limited circumstances contrive to take in Commentaries, Histories, Magazines, &c. by such means, and thus set an example well worthy of imitation in the present instance.

I gladly take occasion in this place to express my warm concurrence with your worthy Correspondent in his eulogy on Dr. Priestley's excellencies, and " the effect that would arise from a perusal of his Works." The remarks in the quotation at the bottom of page 523, will not surprise any persons who have observed the air of superiority so frequently assumed by *orthodox* writers over their *heretical* opponents, and the disingenuous mode of crying down the reputation of Unitarians as men and as Christians, to prevent their works from being read—whether from a pious alarm at the danger that might accrue to their cause I shall not presume to determine.

Involved as the Christian world has been in error for ages, it is a subject for congratulation that a spirit of inquiry has gone forth, and the work of reformation is gradually advancing. Truth will eventually prevail, and scatter all the clouds of darkness. The labours of Priestley have contributed in no small degree to enlighten mankind: it remains only that those who know their value, and are disposed to encourage the proposed undertaking, should without delay signify their intention, and thus contribute to perpetuate those Works, which will be a lasting monument to the name of their author.

J. CORDELL.

Sir,   *Hackney, Sept.* 18, 1816.

I REGRET in common with other admirers of the Theological Works of Dr. Priestley, that so little encouragement has been given to the proposed re-publication of them by the very able and respectable Editor, who has announced his readiness to devote his best care to the work, if indemnified against the cost of publishing: at the same time I am not disposed to consider the want of numbers to the list of subscribers as a proof of indifference to the writings of Dr. Priestley, or as shewing that a re-publication is not wanted: many persons are in my situation, they have already several of the books and wish to have others (now out of print) but cannot afford to purchase the whole, and consequently do not subscribe to a complete edition; I wish therefore, through the medium of the Repository, to submit to the Editor the propriety of either receiving subscriptions for the work separately, or binding subscribers of two guineas each, to take such only of the books as they may want, and shall make choice of at the time of subscribing. If this plan be adopted, I have hope it will be found that one subscriber will take one half, and another the other half, and that by this means the required sum for defraying the charges of publishing will be obtained. Should this suggestion be acted upon, I think it would be useful to publish a list of the Works, with their respective prices affixed.   T. H.

Sir,   *Sept* 21, 1816.

A FEW individuals belonging to a country congregation are endeavouring to raise among themselves and their friends, the subscription price of a copy of Mr. Rutt's intended edition of Dr. Priestley's Works. Their plan is, to circulate the Work among themselves, in the first instance, and afterwards make a present of it to their minister. If a scheme of this sort were generally adopted by Unitarian congregations, they would have the perusal of the Work at a very trifling individual expense, do a real service to their ministers, who cannot, in general, afford to purchase large Works, and, also, effectually assist Mr. Rutt in the prosecution of his laudable undertaking.   X.

Sir, · *Palgrave, Oct.* 7, 1816.

THE Morning Herald Newspaper of October the 1st, contained the following article: "Married at Deene, near Wansford, Lincolnshire, yesterday se'nnight, Mr. William Giddings, aged 36, to Miss Hannah Spendilo, aged 16. When the pair first appeared at the altar, the clergyman asked the young woman whether she was a Christian. Her answer convinced him that she had not been baptized, and therefore he refused to perform the marriage ceremony: the couple thus left the church, but returned shortly afterwards with godfathers and godmothers, when the intended bride was christened and married."

Before I read this curious article, I was not aware that a clergyman could refuse to marry persons who had not been baptized, or, as it is vulgarly and erroneously called, christened: and I should be glad to learn from some of your Correspondents by what law, civil or canonical, this refusal is justified: for I cannot discover in the prayer book, where the marriage service is recorded, any directions on this head; neither does Blackstone mention the not being baptized as a disability against entering into the holy state. In regard to the provision in the *burial* service, while we may regret that any relic of superstition should be suffered to remain, of which nature this prohibition certainly partakes; still it is, comparatively speaking, of little consequence, for it concerns the deceased not at all whether consecrated or unconsecrated ground receives the mouldering body. But in respect of the marriage ceremony the case is very different: for what was the above pair to have done, had the lady from *principle* refused to be *baptized*? Were the two lovers driven to the cruel necessity of flying

from each other for ever? Or, if firm both in love and religious principles, rather than separate, or submit to a ceremony which one of them considered as improper, they had chosen to live together; is any one, the most squeamishly delicate, prepared to say that they ought to be shunned by society for persevering in an improper connexion, or that their issue could by any probable law of equity be subjected to the evils of illegitimacy? If this is the case, if these evils would ensue on a refusal to be *baptized*, it becomes a matter of necessity that the power of the clergyman should be curtailed, and furnishes an additional reason for Unitarians exerting themselves to get relieved from our present marriage service, to those which have already been suggested by some of your Correspondents in the early part of the present year. Unless I greatly mistake, an opinion is certainly gaining ground among the Unitarians that baptism was a ceremony intended only for converts, and that it does not relate to the children of Christian parents. I am not now discussing the propriety of this opinion, but though I have not a very large acquaintance, I could mention several families in which this opinion prevails. The children in these families are not christened or baptized—the parents considering that if they see the propriety of baptism when they arrive at years of discretion, they can submit to the ceremony and join the community of Baptists. But suppose these children *should* be of the same opinions as their parents, are they to be prohibited from enjoying the blessings of domestic harmony, unless they submit to a ceremony which with their views is nothing short of downright mummery?

The prohibition, if it really exists, must be founded on either a human or divine law. If it rest upon a human law, it is a flagrant persecution, infinitely worse than that of making the participating in the Lord's Supper a test for the occupation of an office; for if a man refuses to take the Sacrament, as it is commonly and absurdly stated, though he cannot accept of certain civil offices, he feels no inconvenience from not accepting them, except as far as he is deprived of being, as he might wish to be, publicly honoured and useful. He still enjoys private life quietly and respectably. But by making baptism a test of the fitness for marriage we go much farther, for the party must either submit, or for ever be denied the enjoyment of the "only bliss of paradise which has survived the fall," or be continually exposed to the taunts and scorn of society, for permitting affection to triumph over the injustice of the law. If it rests upon the divine law, surely it should for the benefit of the ignorant be pointed out; or how are the parties wishing to be married to confess the existing impediments to their marriage, which very early in the service they are charged to do? Moreover, does it rest with the clergyman whether he makes these inquiries or not? Because if so, it is making the law the creature of caprice. I ask this, knowing that unbaptized persons have been married without questions being asked. Now was the Lincolnshire clergyman righteous over much, or was the other clergyman to whom I allude negligent of his duty?

But what an apparently shameful prostitution of an ordinance of Christ was exhibited in Lincolnshire on the above occasion—I mean on the baptism of the lady. Baptism is, at least according to the Church service, a Christian ordinance: and if so should not be resorted to without due reflection and consideration. Yet it is scarcely to be supposed that the lady in this case could have duly considered the subject. If she had never thought about it, she was not a fit subject to submit to it, in an hour or two; if she had considered it, and approved it, why had she not previously been baptized? If she disapproved it, her religious principle was sacrificed for the sake of her spouse. But if in the above case, notwithstanding appearances, due consideration had been exercised, and every thing was as it ought to be, it is manifest, that the tendency of the anecdote is to make the public believe that a person *unbaptized* is *no Christian*, and that therefore baptism is a most important ordinance; *though it may be performed nevertheless, without previous thought*, in order to remove an obstruction to the performance of what the law positively enjoins on all as a necessary civil compact.　　J. F.

July 19, 1816.

SIR,

IN the *Curiosities of Literature*, 1791, is an article on *the Destruction of Books*, in which it is remarked that "the greater part of the books of Origen and the other Heretics, were continually burnt by the Orthodox party." On this passage some former possessor of my copy has written the following note.

"The illustrious *heretic* of our times has met with a similar treatment at Birmingham, in 1791, and was personally ill-used at Warwick Assizes in 1792."

In a passage of Dr. Priestley's Fast Sermon, for 1794, quoted in his Memoirs (12mo. p. 131,) there is a reference to some unkind treatment "at the Assizes at Warwick," I suppose when he sued the county for his loss of property at Birmingham.

I have a particular reason for wishing to ascertain what was the personal ill-usage to which the manuscript note refers, and shall thank any of your readers for information.

BREVIS.

———

July 19, 1816.

SIR,

I VERY lately met with the Life of Sir Michael Foster, by his nephew, the late Mr. Dodson, which was published in 1811, from a copy designed for Dr. Kippis's Biographia Britannica.

I know not that a general reader has any right to complain of such a Life as containing scarcely a page interesting to any but the learned *profession*, to whom the justly reverenced *dicta* of a great lawyer must be highly valuable. Yet I doubt whether the Life of a *dignitary* of the *long robe* ever exhibited a reputation more exclusively legal than that of Judge Foster, who appears never to have *recreated* himself, like Sir Edmund Coke, in his *Forest Laws*, by a ramble among *Dido's deer*.

But I am rambling from my purpose, which was to propose to animadversion a sentiment in the Biographer which follows his notice of the opinion maintained by Judge Foster in his famous *Argument* "that the right of impressing mariners for the public service is a prerogative inherent in the crown, grounded upon common law, and recognized by many acts of parliament."—P. 12.

On this passage Mr. Dodson remarks, "the question touching the legality of pressing mariners for the public service, is a point of the greatest importance; and wise and good men still entertain different sentiments on the subject." I cannot help regretting that so excellent a man as Mr. Dodson, whom I describe from personal knowledge, should have been content to treat so mildly this moral enormity. One who has been taught to consider himself as a free citizen of a free country, whatever be his outward condition, is yet dragged from his home as a criminal, without the pretence of any crime, because he once pursued an industrious life as a mariner, and instead of having acquired property is still dependant on his personal labour for his own, and probably, a family's support; for a *regulating officer* will scarcely venture to detain a man of property, should such an one be accidentally *kidnapped* by a *pressgang*. Such then is the man convicted only of poverty whose case a benevolent Christian, writing more like a *lawyer* than a *gospeller*, can treat as a question of mere legal uncertainty, on each side of which wisdom and virtue might be equally divided. Mr. Dodson had the honour to be a *Heretic*, and, in the contemplation of law, was liable to punishment. What would he have said to a commentator on penal statutes, who had coolly written that "the question touching the *prosecution of those who impugn the established creeds*, is a point of the greatest importance, and wise and good men still entertain different sentiments on the subject."

Every one has read Franklin's Notes on Judge Foster's *Argument*, and most I believe have admired the deserved satire they convey on the "idolaters of forms and precedents." But the unjust principle which supports the practice of *impressing*, and its frequent melancholy consequences, can scarcely be represented with more truth and propriety than in the following passage from a "Reply to Mr. Burke's Invective against Mr. Cooper and Mr. Watt, in the House of Commons, April 30, 1792," by Mr. Cooper, formerly of Manchester, distinguished as an acute metaphy-

sician, and now for many years a judge in the *United States.* In this *Reply*, the war is carried with no small success, into the enemy's country. Mr. Burke's *Invective* having been utterred in a debate on *Parliamentary reform*, Mr. Cooper shews, in various instances, "how little the interests of the poor are taken care of, and how necessary it is that the voice of the poor man should be heard with attention and respect in the House of Commons." He then adds, "A still more flagrant instance of cruelty and injustice towards the poor, is the practice of *impressing.* The labour of the poor man constitutes the whole of his wealth, and his domestic connexions almost the whole of his happiness. But on a sudden, under the dubious authority of a press warrant, he is cut off from his peaceful habitation and domestic society, and forcibly dragged on board the floating prison of a tender: he is compelled to labour in the dreadful service of murdering his fellow-creatures at the command of his superiors, and paid such scanty wages, not as he can earn or deserves, but as the niggardly system of government finance thinks fit to allow. His family meanwhile, who look up to him for comfort and subsistence, ignorant of his misfortune, are anxiously expecting his wonted return; perhaps their homely repast for the night depended on his earnings for the day; but his usual hour of return to his family is gone by, each passing footstep, each noise of distant similarity, is eagerly listened to in vain. Hope still draws out the lengthened evening, till a sleepless night of lamentation and despair succeeds the dreary melancholy hours of successive disappointment and fruitless expectation."

After reading this description, which must have been often realized, what a sound of unmeaning rant or rather of cruel mockery is the following burst of oratory by Lord Chatham on the equal liberty enjoyed in England: "Every Englishman's house is his castle. Not that it is surrounded by walls and battlements, it may be only a straw built shed. All the winds of heaven may whistle through it, every element of nature may enter it, but the king cannot, the king dare not."

IGNOTUS.

SIR,   *August 26, 1816.*

IN the Miscellaneous Works of Robert Robinson, edited by Flower, the following passage occurs, at page 79, Vol. 1. *Remarks on Deism.* "The learned and pious Dr. Bekker, one of the pastors of Amsterdam, renounced the popular opinion of the power of the devil, and published a book against it. He seemed to doubt also of the eternity of hell torments. He was reputed a Deist, and the consistory, the classes and the synods, proceeded against him, suspended him at first from the communion, and deposed him at last from the office of a minister."

Will some Correspondent of the Monthly Repository have the goodness to point out where a more particular account of Dr. Bekker, of his book, and of the proceedings instituted against him, may be met with? This will much oblige an Inquirer,

A. F.

P. S. Perhaps some of the readers of the Monthly Repository who have visited the Netherlands and Germany since the peace, may be able to give an account of Unitarianism in those countries. The Menonite Baptists, a large and increasing sect, are strictly Unitarians, with the addition of (what to British Unitarians would appear) an austere system of church discipline. An account of the present state of the Menonite Baptists could not fail to interest the readers of your Miscellany.

SIR,   *Clapton, August 28, 1816.*

I HAVE found unexpectedly the following letter, written by a friend whom I have just seen committed to his grave, waiting, I doubt not, *the resurrection of the just,* after having eminently *served his generation,* in the vigour of his life, and endured with Christian fortitude the sufferings which were allotted to its decline. I read the letter, as you will suppose, with those sensations, which can be well understood by all who had opportunities of appreciating the character of the late Mr. Vidler.

I am persuaded that I shall bring no discredit on my friend's memory, by requesting you to preserve his letter. Though scarcely more than a written message and little designed by him for the public eye, I cannot allow myself to conceal this truly honourable testi-mony to his continued desire of moral and intellectual improvement, and his just views of the serious purposes to which both should be conscientiously applied.

It may, perhaps, be regretted, with reference to his personal gratification, that Mr. Vidler, in earlier life, had not been introduced to those literary advantages which he could have so well improved. Yet I confess, that, for the sake of the cause, of which he was an able advocate, I feel no such regret. He would probably have been a profoundly learned divine, and in that character, deservedly esteemed, yet he might never have become the instructive and impressive preacher, such as I have often listened to him. Nor would he then have left to his contemporaries, and, as I trust, to other generations, that valuable bequest, an encouraging example of what may be attained by great good will to man's highest interests, actuating a vigorous mind to an unceasing occupation of common advantages. I remain, Sir, Your's,

J. T. RUTT.

" DEAR SIR,

" I very gratefully thank you for the offer of the use of any books which you have in your own library, or the Westminster Library to which, you say, you have access. You could not perform a more pleasant or useful service for me. If you have a catalogue of your own, or of the Westminster Collection, or both, that you would indulge me with, it would greatly assist me in my choice.— Meanwhile I will mention some :

" Hartley on Man.

" Bayle's Dictionary, English.

" Modern Universal History.

" Priestley's History of Vision.

" —————————Electricity.

" —————————Lectures on Oratory and Criticism.

" Belsham's Philosophy of the Human Mind.

" Robinson's Ecclesiastical Researches.

" Lardner's History of Heretics.

" Chandler's History of the Inquisition.

" A good Latin Grammar.

" Latin Dictionary.

" ——— Bible.

" And any other Latin books fit for a *young* student in that language. You will probably smile, but I really do not think myself too old to learn any thing that depends on mental application. You know I cannot afford to buy books : I have more leisure than I ever had in my life, and wish to use it so, as to give a good account of it, both to God and the congregation that I serve.

" Any part of the above list which could be procured would much oblige me; only let me have enough.

" I will return the books I now have next Sunday, by my youngest son.

" I am, Dear Sir,
" With unfeigned respect and gratitude,
" Your friend and servant,
" WILLIAM VIDLER.

" *West-Ham, August* 19, 1811.

" P. S. My son will take back any books which you may have gotten ready to go.

" *Mr. J. T. Rutt, Goswell Street.*"

GLEANINGS; OR, SELECTIONS AND REFLECTIONS MADE IN A COURSE OF GENERAL READING.

No. CCLXXVII.

Greatness in Death.

Though sinking under the accumulated pressure of advancing age, as well as of disease and infirmity, *Maria Theresa* (Empress of Germany) retained the possession of all her faculties nearly to the last moments of her life. Religion and resignation smoothed its close.—Only a short time before she breathed her last, having apparently fallen into a sort of insensibility and her eyes being closed, one of the ladies near her person, in reply to an inquiry made respecting the state of the Empress, answered that her Majesty seemed to be asleep. *No,* replied she, *I could sleep if I would indulge repose ; but I am sensible of the near approach of death, and I will not allow myself to be surprized by him in my sleep. I wish to meet my dissolution awake.*

Wraxall's Hist. Memoirs, I. 364, 5.

No. CCLXXVIII.

The King's View of the Sacrament.

Towards the end of the month of January, 1805, at a time when he (the present King Geo. III.) was much occupied in preparations for the Installation of the Knights of the *Garter,* destined to take place on the approaching twenty-third of April; and while conversing on the subject with some persons of high rank, at Windsor; one of them, a nobleman deservedly distinguished by his favour, said, " Sir, are not the new knights now meant to be installed, obliged to take the sacrament before the ceremony?" Nothing could assuredly have been further from his idea or intention, than to have asked the question in a manner capable of implying any levity or irreverence. Nevertheless, his Majesty

instantly changed countenance; and assuming a severe look, after a moment or two of pause, " No," replied he, " that religious institution is not to be mixed with our profane ceremonies. Even at the time of my coronation, I was very unwilling to take the sacrament. But, when they told me that it was indispensible and that I must receive it ; before I approached the communion table, I took off the bauble from my head. *The sacrament, my lord, is not to be profaned by our gothic institutions.*" The severity of the king's manner while he pronounced these words impressed all present, and suspended for a short time the conversation. *The Same,* 1. 384—386.

No. CCLXXIX.

Early Quakers Unitarians.—The Athenian Mercury.

Whether the early Quakers were Unitarians is a purely historical question : — Unitarianism is neither the better nor the worse for the determination of it : nor needs the opinion of the founders of Quakerism to influence the present Quakers. The old Quakers had simplicity and sense and a love of liberty, but none of these, any more than their religious principels, are hereditary.

Abundant facts may be produced to shew that the Quakers of a century ago were accounted and described as Unitarians. Some of these have been produced in our volumes ; we shall bring forward another proof.

In that most singular periodical work, *the Athenian Mercury,* published by J. Dunton, 1691, in folio, each Number containing a folio half sheet, there is, Vol. III. No. 23, the following question [The object of the work is to *resolve all the most nice and curious questions proposed by the ingenious*] : " Suppose a Jew, a Mahometan, a Church of England man, an Anabaptist, a Quaker and a Muggletonian, all living together in one house peaceably and according to their own principles :—may they not all expect happiness after this life?" The *Athenian Club,* who undertook to answer all questions, were they high as heaven or deep as hell, manifest their temper, by the first clause of their oracular response, viz. " It's pity the Querist did not put in an *Atheist* too to have made it up a *perfect number.*" They then proceed to say that the question is already answered by the Church of England! which anathematizes all who say in the affirmative. The Scriptures, too, they allege positively damn Jews, and Mahometans and also Muggletonians, who they add are known by nothing but "hating the Bible, some blasphemy and a great deal of nonsense." They then pronounce sentence on the *Quakers*, in form following.: "For the Quakers:—We are sure that many, or most of 'em have held very dangerous and detestable opinions. They generally speak contemptibly of the Bible, and will by no means allow it to be *God's word*: they have turned it into an odd sort of a jejune allegory, even the highest and most sacred truths therein contained, and have spoken not very honorably of our Saviour, and *almost generally deny the Trinity*, and many, if not all, embrace *the other Socinian dream* of *the soul's sleeping* till the resurrection. Besides, they use neither of the Sacraments, and if our most authentic accounts do not impose upon us, were at their first appearance in England, commonly acted by a *worse spirit* than what they pretend to. These 'tis hard to hope well of, nor can we see how with any manner of propriety they can be called Christians. But if there be any of 'em who have left their first principles, and are *degenerated into Christianity*, (we ask pardon for the harshness of the expression) and grown more religious, as well as more mannerly, there may be more hopes of 'em."

This judgment on the Quakers was evidently not prompted by passion merely, for if *Socinian* had been applied to them as a term of reproach because they were disliked on other accounts, it would also have been branded on the forehead of the "Anabaptists," whom no Church of England oracle ever spared; but there is some sort of candour in the determination concerning these once fearful heretics; e. g. "For the Anabaptist, it's certain both from Popish and Protestant writers, and even eye-witnesses themselves, that there never was a fiercer or more dangerous enemy to all order both sacred and humane, than he was at his first appearance in Germany: but we hope he's now grown better, and that our soil has a little mended his crab-stock. For we

must own according to their present writings, there are not many articles of common Christianity, if any, which our English Anabaptists disown, besides that of infant baptism, *wherein some great men of the Church of God have erred together with them.*" The Athenians may probably refer to Bp. Jere. Taylor, whose *Liberty of Prophesying* wears an "Anabaptist" face. Other parts of their work will scarcely allow us to suppose that in "great men of the Church of God," they include *John Milton*, who was tainted with the heresy of the "Anabaptists."

The Athenian Mercury is very amusing, as an exhibition of the inquiries, the doubts, the wit and the mirth of our great grandfathers, who in spite of their broad-brimmed hats, their doublets and hose, were much the sort of folks that we now are. The greatest difference between them and us consists in the bolder and more dignified spirit of civil and religious liberty that, through their exertions, we have acquired. We may smile at their *questions*, but they led to questions of more moment. A Correspondent in the Mercury gravely asks, What was the sex of Balaam's ass? and is solemnly answered by proofs from the history that it was a *she-ass*. Another inquires, how infants, and aged and deformed persons shall arise at the day of judgment? and the unhesitating answer is that all shall arise of the age of thirty or thirty three, our Saviour's age at his resurrection!

No. CCLXXX.
Alcoran.

It has long been a question agitated among the Mahometans, and with great heat, whether the Alcoran was created or increated? Those who said it was created, seemed to others to diminish and lessen its authority: but they defended themselves many ways; among which one is, that 'tis the express saying of God, *We have put the Alcoran*; now that which is put is created. Others took the opposite side of the question. They took the safest side who adhering to the words of the Alcoran, said, *that it was put, or sent down*, and were silent about its creation.

Reeland, of the Mahometan Religion, in *Four Treatises,* &c. 8vo. 1712. p. 24.

REVIEW.

" Still pleased to praise, yet not afraid to blame."—POPE.

ART. I.—*A Course of Lectures, containing a Description and Systematic Arrangement of the several Branches of Divinity :* accompanied with an Account both of the principal Authors, and of the Progress, which has been made, at different Periods, in Theological Learning. By Herbert Marsh, D. D. F. R. S. Margaret Professor of Divinity. Part IV. On the Interpretation of Prophecy. Cambridge, Printed, Sold there by Deightons, &c. and in London by Rivingtons. 1816. 8vo. pp. 86.

THE subject here discussed by the Margaret Professor, is so important, curious and difficult, and his reputation, as a theological scholar, so deservedly high, that we opened this pamphlet with more than common eagerness : an examination of it's contents, will shew in what degree our expectations have been gratified.

At the conclusion of the third part of his Lectures, he treated of typical interpretation, " with which," says he, " the interpretation of prophecy is so far connected, as types are *prophetic* of their antitypes."* In our review of that publication, we hinted our doubts with respect to the correctness of his definition of a *type,* and, at the same time, expressed a hope that the matter would " be more largely and satisfactorily considered in some of" Dr. Marsh's " succeeding Lectures."† It is resumed, accordingly, in No. XIX. the second paragraph of which begins with the following sentences :

" To constitute a type, something more is requisite, than a mere *resemblance* of that, which is called it's antitype. For one thing may *resemble* another, when the things themselves are totally *unconnected.* But it is the very essence of a type, to have a necessary connexion with it's antitype. It must have been *designed,* and designed from it's very beginning, to prefigure it's antitype ; or it partakes not of that character which belongs to a real type ; a character, which implies, not an accidental parity of circumstances, but a pre-ordained and inherent connexion between the things

themselves. Where *this* character is wanting, there is wanting that relation of type to antitype, which subsists between the things of the Old Testament, and the things of the New." (Pp. 1, 2).

The Margaret Professor's representation of " the very essence of a type," is perfectly agreeable to certain systems of theology : we are convinced however that it receives no countenance from the Scriptures. If our readers will look into their English Bibles, they will find only a single passage which speaks of *types :* this is 1 Cor. x. 11.; and even this is nothing more than the marginal reading in the larger copies—the word *examples* being preferred in the text and adopted by Newcome. On examining, too, the places in which the corresponding Greek substantive occurs, we can discover no support to the doctrine that a type is a *designed* resemblance.

Dr. M. indeed says *(ib.),*

" —— the only mode of distinguishing the cases, where this relation [of type to antitype] *actually* exists, from the cases where it is only *supposed* to exist, is to examine what things in the Old Testament have been represented by Christ and his apostles as *relating* to things in the New. For then we have *authority* for such relation : then we *know,* that one thing was designed to prefigure the other."

To *this authority* we implicitly subscribe : but we shall soon perceive that it does not warrant the conclusion at which the Lecturer arrives.

Before he considers (3) the *prophetic character* of a type, he ought to have indubitably that a type, such as he describes it, has an *existence* in the volume of Revelation. Here, we think, his reasoning and his illustrations fail :

" Whether a future event is indicated by *words,* or indicated by *other* tokens, the connexion of that event with the words in one case, or the tokens in the other, will be equally a fulfilling of prophecy."

True——if the connexion be in *both* instances *designed* ; which is exactly the point to be proved, instead of being assumed. On this proof the Professor enters in the course of his third paragraph. According to Dr. M.,

" We cannot have a more remarkable, or a more important example, than that of

---

* A Course of Lectures, &c. p. 117. (Part III).

† M. Repos. VIII. 677.

the paschal lamb, as applied to the death of Christ. For not only was the paschal lamb sacrificed for the sins of the Jews under circumstances *resembling* those, under which our Saviour was sacrificed for the sins of the world, but we have the authority of Scripture itself for the assertion, that the sacrifice of the paschal lamb was from the very beginning *designed* to indicate the sacrifice of Christ on the cross. When John the Baptist first saw our Saviour, he exclaimed, ' Behold the lamb of God, which taketh away the sins of the world.' St. Paul is still more particular : for he says, ' Christ, our *passover* is sacrificed for us :' and St. Peter declares, that we were redeemed ' with the precious blood of Christ, as of a *lamb* without blemish and without spot, who verily was *fore-ordained*, before the foundation of the world.' From a comparison of these passages we learn, not only that the two sacrifices *resembled* each other, but that the sacrifice of the paschal lamb was *originally intended* to designate the sacrifice of Christ. The former sacrifice therefore has all the qualifications, which are necessary to constitute a type." (3, 4).

Does this conclusion flow legitimately from the premises? The *resemblance* is granted : but proof is wanting of it's being a *designed* resemblance. Our Saviour, we know, has been denominated ' the lamb of God' and ' our passover :' this fact however is no evidence of the paschal lamb and supper being *typical* of him——with equal reason might it be alleged that, because he speaks of himself as ' the good shepherd,' his pastoral character was the antitype of David's. Such a principle of criticism would conduct us, in truth, to doctrines and inferences which scarcely any theologian, of any denomination, could endure. Nor can Dr. M. fairly lay stress on the word *fore-ordained*, in his quotation from the writings of the Apostle Peter. On consulting the original, our readers will be fully sensible that the antecedent is *Christ : he* it is " who was fore-ordained before the foundation of the world ;" a declaration to which we unreservedly and gratefully assent, but which is far from being identical with the proposition " that the sacrifice of the paschal lamb was *originally intended* to designate the sacrifice of Christ."

Our author endeavours to evince that there are " two very remarkable types of the Old Testament, the one applying to the Sacrament of baptism, the other to the Sacrament of the

Lord's supper" (13, 14). Let us begin with weighing his observation in regard to the latter, " the Lord's supper" (4) :

" Since the sacrament of the Lord's supper was instituted by Christ himself in remembrance of his death and passion, the ceremony, which was a type of the one, may be considered as a type also of the other."

In plainer language, the meaning of Dr. M. is, that of the Lord's supper the paschal supper *may be considered* as a type. His manner of expressing himself, should not be passed in silence. Instead of saying, *totidem verbis*, that it is actually a type, or that, on the principles of sound reasoning, we must infer it to be such, he simply remarks, that it *may be considered* as a type. No doubt, there is a large class of persons by whom 'it *may be* so *considered :* an unscriptural system of theology, combined with fervour of imagination, will behold *types* in almost every page of the Jewish records. It is highly probable that, under the influence of these causes, men will multiply resemblances of this description, and that they *may consider* every resemblance as typical. The point at issue between the Professor and us, is the ground on which *he* considers the paschal supper as typical of the Eucharist. Now this would seem to be the *supposed* relation of the sacrifice of the paschal lamb [as the type] to the sacrifice of Christ [as the antitype]. However, since no such relation is asserted, or even implied, in Scripture, it follows that the alleged relation of these two ceremonies to each other is also imaginary. The foundation being removed, the superstructure falls.

Equally unsuccessful is this Lecturer in his attempt to shew that " the sacrament of baptism was prefigured by an event of great importance in the history of the Jews." Though he labours the point at some length, he only convinces us that the proof of it is too weighty a task for even the abilities and learning of Dr. Marsh. Let us hear the Professor's statement (4) :

" St. Paul, in his first Epistle to the Corinthians (x. 1.), says, ' Brethren, I would not that ye should be ignorant, how that our fathers were under the cloud, and all passed through the sea, and were baptized unto Moses in the cloud, and in the sea ; and did all eat the same spiritual meat, and did all drink the same spiritual drink ;

for they drank of that same spiritual rock, that followed them, and that rock was Christ.' In this passage [adds Dr. M.] it is evident that St. Paul considered the being baptized unto Moses, as typical of being baptized unto Christ."

That the Margaret Professor chuses so to consider it, is sufficiently " evident." But there is no *evidence* whatever that the case was viewed by the Apostle in the same light. Let the reader determine, whether persons who had never heard of this theological fiction of types would put such a construction upon Paul's words: it is an interpretation which, we venture to pronounce, they will not bear. The passage has some obscurities: we may perhaps admit that it implies *comparison* and *resemblance*; concerning a type however it is profoundly silent.

The existence of proselyte baptism among the Jews, must not be assumed (5) as an indubitable fact; writers of eminent impartiality and erudition * having called it in question. Conceding, nevertheless, to Dr. M. that this was one of their customs, it is altogether irrelevant to remind us that they " appear to have *generally* considered the passage of their forefathers through the red sea, not as a mere insulated historical fact, but as something representative of admission to the divine favour, *by baptism.*" When we inquire into the doctrine of the Scriptures, on this or any other matter, the comments of the Jewish Rabbins can be of no authority: in truth, the language of Maimonides, as quoted by Whitby (in loc:), conveys no further idea than that of an imagined *resemblance* between the passage of the red sea and the rite of baptism: and this is the sum of Whitby's own commentary on the verse.

But if this text will not sustain Dr. Marsh's inference, still less support can he acquire from the words of Paul in the passages which he proceeds to cite.† It is a mere assumption that, when the Apostle speaks of baptism, any reference is intended to a memorable event in the Jewish history: his language and his argument require no such explanation.

So far then are we from " here"

having " another instance of type and antitype, ratified by the authority of a divine Apostle, in all their various relations," that, if we will only be content to make this sacred author his own interpreter, we shall be sensible of his being a total stranger to the comparatively modern doctrine " of type and antitype !"

We have no inclination to become parties in the controversy now carrying on within the pale of "the Church of England" on baptism and regeneration. The Margaret Professor takes occasion to communicate to his auditors and his readers his thoughts concerning it: " if," says he, " we detach regeneration from baptism, we not only fall into the absurdity of making the outward act a visible sign of *nothing to be signified*, but we destroy the sacrament of baptism *as* a sacrament altogether"—and, again, " they who wilfully and deliberately detach regeneration from baptism, impugn *essentially* the doctrine of our Established Church, inasmuch as they impugn it in one of our holy sacraments." Such then is the claim of the " Established Church"— to bestow *regeneration* by means of baptism :* we are less astonished at her preferring the claim than at the difference of judgment among her sons respecting the import of her articles. The disputants might be seasonably employed in ascertaining the sense of the term " regeneration" in the Scriptures. It is deserving of remark that words which are sufficiently current in systems of theology, rarely present themselves in the New Testament. This is true of the expression before us: we meet with it in only two passages,‡ in neither of which does it describe a personal and moral change, but an improvement in point of religious knowledge and privileges.

Dr. Marsh does not reason in a manner worthy of himself till he dismisses the subject of types and antitypes. When, apparently unwilling to relinquish it, he asks (16), " Who would deny that the sacrifice of the paschal lamb is *declared* in the New Testament to be a prefiguration of the death of Christ?" We reply, by ad-

---

* In particular, Lardner. Works. Vol. XI. 320.

† Rom. vi. 3. Gal. iii. 27. Acts xxii. 16. Tit. iii. 5.

* See Article xxvii. as quoted by Dr. M.

‡ Matt. xix. 28. Tit. iii. 5.

dressing to him another question, with which himself (ib:) has supplied us,

"Must not the *silence* of the New Testament, in the case of any *supposed* type, be an argument against the *existence* of that type?"

Systematical divines differ not a little among themselves in defining a type: let us compare for example, the statement of Doddridge with that of Dr. Marsh:

"One person, or event, or institution in the divine dispensations, of which an account is given us in the word of God, may be said to be TYPICAL of another and greater person, or event, afterwards' to appear, when there is a remarkable *resemblance* between the former and the latter; whether that resemblance be or be not known by the manifestation of the latter. This may be called the *theological* sense of the word, &c."*

A type then, agreeably to Dr. Doddridge's account of it, is not of the nature of a *prophecy*, but consists simply in *resemblance*. Certainly however the Margaret Professor's use of the word is *theological*; while the other is, with a single exception, correct and *Scriptural*. To the received notion of types no plausibility is given by the Epistle to the Hebrews, which, though it contains many comparisons of the Christian with the Jewish dispensation, holds forth no example whatever of a *designed* resemblance.

In the remainder of the nineteenth Lecture Dr. M. assigns two causes of "the variety observable in the expositions of Hebrew prophecy:" these are an inadequate knowledge of the original language and inattention to "the situation and circumstances of the writer, whose works it is proposed to explain." There is scarcely any age of the church in which such remarks as the following (18) could be justly styled unreasonable:

"—— though the difficulties attending the interpretation of the Hebrew prophets are confessedly great, those difficulties are not insurmountable. And if the interpretation of prophecy is . *really* subject to determinate rules, the conclusions, to which such rules must eventually lead, will be no less certain, when those difficulties are overcome, than if they had never existed. The sole difference consists in the labour, in the skill, and in

the time, which are wanted in the case, but not in the other. If it b jected therefore, that the sacred .o are ambiguous, because the explani of them are various, we may confid answer, that the fault is in the inte tation, and not in the text. It is no der that in the explanations of the He prophets we should discover inconsist when an office, for which so many q¡ cations are required, is undertake men, in whom those qualification wanting altogether."

The Margaret Professor enter his twentieth Lecture with a refe to those "general rules for the i pretation of the. Bible, which been fully explained in former tures,"† and which, he says, applicable, as well to the *pro* books, as to other parts of the sz volume." This introductory pos being illustrated and vindicated, proceeds "to the particular consi tion of the prophecies, which i to the Messiah;" since when we amine these, "we examine question of real interest in the su of prophecy at large."

As the result of "an inquiry that *connexion* which subsists betv the truth of our religion" and class of prophecies, Dr. M. give opinion in the following terms,

"There must be prophecies in the Testament, which strictly, literally, directly predict the coming of our Sav There must be something more than sages, which may be *accommodated* it is called) to his life and character.'

Here, we presume, all theolo scholars will agree with the Prof On a subject concerning which are less unanimous he offers it a decided judgment, that

"A prophecy which relates to Saviour in a mere *remote* or *my* sense, can hardly come within that scription of prophecy, by which preaching of Christ was made *manife*

Before we accompany our auth his next Lecture (No. XXI.) which he collects and explains passages which he conceives, ' dict the coming of Christ in plain, literal, and proper sense,' shall concisely notice a sentence senting itself in page 23. and pz a note in pp. 33, 34.

---

* Lectures, &c. Vol. II. (ed. 4.) 408.

† XIII—XVII.

. Speaking of the ability that our own reason gives us " to argue from the past to the future," he adds, by way of illustration,

" If, for instance, we compare the *present* situation of our church with it's situation at a former period, we must have our apprehensions, and perhaps our fore-bodings."

We think it unfortunate that Dr. M. loses sight, even for a moment, of the character and dignity of the Academical Professor, to re-echo the ill-founded complaint of ecclesiastical alarmists. The *situation* of " the church," is perfectly safe, provided her dignitaries are enlightened, tolerant and candid, and offer no violence to the spirit of the times, by urging claims which are alike discountenanced by the Scriptures and by the genius of our civil constitution.

It is with pleasure we make a quotation of a very different kind ; happy when *our* humble judgment on points 'of theology ‡ is confirmed by the sagacity and research of this learned Lecturer :

" —— even a late Prelate' of our own church,* has very incautiously subscribed to the Jewish doctrine, that *evil spirits* have the power of working miracles : a doctrine which tends to *destroy* the argument from miracles, since the performance of a miracle, if it does not *in itself* imply divine authority, cannot possibly do so by any accidental circumstances, whether of benevolence or of any other attribute, which may accompany the miracle." [Note pp. 33, 34.] .

The twenty-first Lecture principally consists of examples of literal prophecies relating to the Messiah ; in the selection of which the Professor follows Bishop Chandler. Though we do not *uniformly* agree with Dr. M. and his able precursor, in respect of the translation and application of these passages, yet we are in general instructed as well as gratified by their observations.

In the remaining Lecture (No. XXII.) an inquiry is made into the foundation of *secondary* senses ascribed to Hebrew prophecy. The difficulties attending this notion, are justly and strongly represented. And the Lecturer is particularly successful in shewing that the alleged double sense of

prophecy has nothing analogous to the double sense of allegory. From the whole of his investigation he concludes " that there is no system *whatever*, by which we can either establish the *existence* of secondary senses, or by which, on the *supposition* of their existence, we can discover their real *meaning*. We must be contented," he adds, " to resolve the question of secondary senses into a question of *authority*."

He allows " that there are some passages of the Old Testament, which really have a secondary sense :" In this class he places Jer. xxxi. 15; quoted in Matt. ii. 17, 18. Whether it should be ranked among them, depends however on the meaning of the formula ' then was fulfilled,' which not improbably, expresses *accommodation*, rather than the completion of a prophecy. In the whole range of theological literature nothing perhaps is more arduous than to ascertain the exact signification of this mode of speech and of some kindred expressions. Indeed, Dr. Marsh is far from having exhausted the topic of the double sense of prophecy; although he has said enough to make us suspect that this notion is untenable.

"The celebrated author of the Divine Legation," explained secondary senses in Hebrew prophecy on the supposition of their 'logical propriety and moral fitness :' he conceived that they were essential to the genius of the Jewish dispensation, in its reference to the Gospel. Dr. Marsh has admirably exposed the difficulties accompanying this hypothesis, and with reason pronounces them " insurmountable."

From the fourth part of his Lectures we have derived less pleasure and instruction than we expected. Besides the unsatisfactory manner in which he treats of *types* and *the double sense of prophecy*, we have to complain of some capital omissions in this pamphlet ; and particularly of two. A course of Lectures *on the interpretation of prophecy* ought in reason to contain remarks on the prophetic style and figures, together with an arrangement of the predictions of the Old and of the New Testament in distinct classes. We are willing to believe that the Professor means to deliver his sentiments on these matters to the University and to the public when he resumes his academical duties; though, to say the truth, he has given no intimation of this design.

---

‡ Mon. Repos. VI. 237.

* Horsley. See the last note.

With a few exceptions, his present set of Lectures are unworthy of his fame. His vigorous and inquisitive mind, seems to be fettered, in it's examinations, by spells which, in certain situations, it is almost impossible to resist. At the distance of somewhat more than half a century, theological scholars and authors in this country, did not cherish a panic fear of deviating in the smallest degree from current systems of divinity. Not so their successors in the chairs of our universities and in the pulpits of the established church. A favourable opportunity of revising the articles and liturgy, was suffered to be lost: and that church is doomed to be torn by internal controversies, to be "a house divided against itself." Her ministers are fiercely disputing with each other for the name of *orthodoxy*.

Such is the crisis at which Dr. Marsh has been elevated to the episcopal bench. He has merited his preferment, and will adorn it, by his learning, his talents and, we trust, his moderation. Intimately conversant with the whole circle of theological studies, he excels however in his knowledge of the principles and the history of Biblical Criticism: in this department of literature he has deservedly obtained the gratitude and applause of the public, and has virtually brought himself under an obligation to finish his Annotations on the *Introduction, &c.* of Michaelis. Henceforth, we may presume, he will have leisure for this employment. The Bishoprick of Landaff presents no very extensive field of service: and to *compleat* his original plan of placing the celebrated work of the Gottingen Professor within the reach of the English scholar, will add new lustre to the name of *Dr. Marsh!*

Art. II.—*The First Report of a Religious Tract Society in the West Riding of the County of York.* To which are added, The Rules—A Catalogue of the Tracts—A List of Donors and Subscribers—And the Proceedings of the First General Annual Meeting, June 6th, 1816. pp. 16. Halifax.

THIS comprehensive title is a table of contents to this interesting pamphlet; which though we are not aware of its having been published or having obtained more than a local circulation, appears to us to contain matter of such importance as to render it worthy of being more generally known. The Report gives an Account of the Proposal of a Tract Society at the Annual Meeting of Protestant Dissenting Ministers held at Leeds, in June, 1815, of the subsequent Establishment of the Society, and of its proceedings up to the date of the Report, June 6, 1816.

This West Riding Tract Society consists of *nine* Auxiliary or Local Tract Societies, and appears to have associated in the first year of its existence 37 Donors and 355 Annual Subscribers, producing in the aggregate the sum of £62. 9s. 9d. The number of Tracts purchased by the Society amounts to 2,143; of which in about six months (the period that the Society has been fully formed) 1,243 have been distributed through the Local Societies. The proportion of Donors and Subscribers in the respective Local Societies is as follows:

	Donors	Sub-scribers
York,	7	40
Leeds,		58
Wakefield,		137
Halifax,	17	53
Bradford,	2	20
Lidyate,	11	13
Newchurch (Rossendale)		16
Elland,		11
Chesterfield,		7
	37	355

It appears that in each of these Congregational or Local Societies, a Committee, Treasurer and Secretary are in office; that to them is committed the local business, the choice of Tracts and collection of the Donations and Subscriptions. That once a quarter (and on the same Lord's day evening in all the Associated Congregations) viz. on the second Sunday in June, September, December and March, the local business of the Auxiliary Societies is transacted, and in the following week, a list of the Tracts wanted, and the amount of the money collected, are transmitted to the General (or Central) Secretary and Treasurer. Thus in one week, once a quarter, the whole communication betwixt the *depôt* and the consumers is transacted. The *Subscriptions* are limited to *one penny* a week; *Donations* to any amount are received; one collector for every ten subscribers is appointed, and pays over the collection to the Local Treasurers, and the Local Treasurers to the General Treasurers. This is the principal machinery of the Society; and it appears sufficiently simple and efficient. The Rules are of two classes; the *first* containing the fundamental laws of the Society; the *second* containing regulations proposed to the adoption of the Local Auxiliary Associations. These Rules do not admit of abridgment, though perhaps they might be simplified. We shall conlude this article with giving a copy of them. We cannot however conclude without recommending the plan to the serious and dispassionate consideration of our readers; and especially of such as have the direction of our Tract Societies, and are desirous of spreading their ramifications, and of extending their benefits into the several neighbouring congregations with which a Tract Society may be surrounded.

The Report before us modestly says, "This Society has only been established about half a year: what has been done must be considered rather as an experiment towards the formation of a Tract Society than as the proceedings of a matured Institution.". The experiment is successfully begun, and we trust will be productive of extensive and beneficial results. The field of operation is wide and full of population. The number of Tracts distributed and sub-distributed by the Local Societies, will in a few years be considerable, and must produce a decided effect. We have already observed that the present number of Subscribers is 355. Supposing this number to be stationary (though the prospect of increase appears in the Report) and the Donations to be limited to the first year of the Establishment, yet from this number of members an annual sum of nearly £80 will arise; and if in not more than half a year upwards of twelve hundred Tracts have been put in circulation, the aggregate result in course of time must be numerically and morally very considerable.

It appears a part of the plan that a Report shall be read to the Subscribers at the "Annual Meeting of the Association of the Ministers usually denominated Presbyterian, in the West Riding of Yorkshire." This will give rise to pleasing and important discussion. The Catalogue and Rules will be thus revised and improved from year to year.

The Catalogue contains several important Works scarcely to be considered as *Tracts*, unless the example of Mr. Locke and the late Bishop Watson sanction this use of the term. It presents, however, a selection and union of such useful and well-known publications, as are calculated to increase piety to God, and practical godliness; and to give just views of the character, government, and revealed will of the God and Father of our Lord Jesus Christ.

We subjoin the Rules:

"Rule 1. That the following Congregations of Protestant Dissenters in Yorkshire, be united into a Society for the distribution of Religious Tracts: viz. The Congregations assembling in St. Saviour-gate, York; Mill-Hill, Leeds; Westgate, Wakefield; Chapel-lane, Bradford; Northgate, Halifax; Lidyate; and South-End, Elland; and such other Protestant Dissenting Congregations, as may be disposed to join this Union.

"Rule 2. That this Society be denominated, 'A Society of Protestant Dissenters in the West-Riding of Yorkshire, for Promoting, by the Distribution of Tracts, the Knowledge of the Christian Religion, and the Practice of Piety and Righteousness.'

"Rule 3. That the Annual Meeting of this Society be held on the day, and at the place, of the Annual Meeting of the Association of Ministers usually denominated Presbyterian, in the West-Riding of Yorkshire, immediately after the close of the morning's service; when a Report of the proceedings during the past year shall be read, and a Secretary, a Treasurer, and two Auditors of Accounts appointed for the year ensuing.

"Rule 4. That the Rev. Henry Turner be Secretary; Mr. Thomas Hollings, Treasurer; and Mr. C. H. Dawson, and Mr. George Stansfeld, Auditors, for the year ensuing.

"Rule 5. That the Subscription to this Society be limited to a penny a week, or 4s. 4d. a year; but that *Donations* will be thankfully received.

"Rule 6. That Tracts be allotted to the full amount of the Subscriptions, and to as large an amount of the Donations as the state of the Funds will admit.

"Rule 7. That the Depository of Tracts be at Bradford, under the care of the Secretary. That it be open during the whole of the week following the second Sunday in the months of June, September, December and March: and that all applications from Subscribers for Tracts be made at those times; and that the Secretary is not bound 'to give an immediate attention to applications made at any other time.

" Rule 8. That it be recommended to the Congregations above mentioned and to others which may be favourable to this Society, that, for the purpose of carrying its objects more completely into effect, the members of this Society in each Congregation form an union amongst themselves, and observe such local regulations as may appear suitable to their respective circumstances: and that where nothing of the kind is practicable, the individuals subscribing to the Society, be requested to communicate with the Depository through the medium of the nearest Congregation in which this plan is adopted.

" Rule 9. That a Catalogue of the Tracts placed in the Depository and the prices at which they are sold to Subscribers, be forthwith printed, and that a copy be sent to each Subscriber, in order that he may select such Tracts as he prefers, to the amount of his Subscription; and that this Catalogue be revised and receive additions at each Annual Meeting.

" Rule 10. In case the Local Societies neglect to claim Tracts to the amount of their contributions within three months after the Annual Meeting (notice of the amount of such claims having previously been given by the Society's Secretary to the Local Secretary, at least fourteen days before the expiration of that period,) the claim shall lapse to the Society."*

" *The following Regulations are* RECOMMENDED *for Adoption, as far as may be deemed expedient, in the Congregations forming the Union.*

" 1. That the members of this Society in each of the Congregations hold a Quarterly Meeting for the dispatch of business.†

* " Local Societies or Subscribers may transfer their claims, in favour of the Vestry Library or Sunday Schools, on signifying the same through the Local Secretary to the Society's Secretary."

† " It is recommended that at every Quarterly Meeting some one of the Society's Tracts be read: and likewise any Tracts which it may be the wish of any member to propose to the Society. And the Society's Secretary shall send a copy of each new Tract to the Secretary in each Congregation that he may circulate it amongst the members."

" Note. It is recommended to form Congregational or Vestry LIBRARIES in the respective Congregations; and also in

" 2. That the first Quarterly Meeting in each Congregation, be held on the Sunday evening next following the Annual Meeting, when a Committee shall be chosen, consisting of not less than five members, for attending to the concerns of the Society within the respective Congregations.

" 3. That the Committee appoint a Secretary to keep the Minutes of the proceedings of the Committee and of the Quarterly Meetings of the Members, and to correspond with the Society's Secretary.

" 4. That the Secretary in each Committee shall draw up an *account* of *the proceedings* of the year in each Congregation, and shall transmit the same to the Society's Secretary, not less than fourteen days *before the Annual Meeting;* inserting therein any facts or suggestions appearing to deserve the attention of the Society; and that the Society's Secretary shall embody these into a *general Report* to be read to the Annual Meeting.

" 5. That the Minister be, ex-officio, a member of the Committee.

" 6. That in each Congregation, for every *ten* members the Committee shall appoint a *Collector,* who shall collect their Subscriptions either weekly, monthly, or otherwise; but if otherwise than *weekly,* that the Subscriptions be paid in advice.

" 7. That conformably to this Regulation it shall be the duty of the Collectors to bring to the Quarterly Meeting in each Congregation a Statement of the Tracts required by their Subscribers, along with the Amount of Subscriptions; and that the Secretary shall unite these into one Statement, which he shall immediately transmit along with the money to the Depository at Bradford.

" 8. That the Quarterly Meetings in each Congregation have power to modify these Regulations in any way that may be deemed expedient, provided there be nothing contradictory to the fundamental Rules of the Society."

ART. III.—*An Essay on the Existence of a Supreme Creator, possessed. of Infinite Power, Wisdom and Goodness, &c. &c.*

[Concluded from p. 538.]

BEFORE he proceeds to the statement of the difficulties regarding the Wisdom and Goodness of the Deity, Dr. Brown treats briefly of the Spirituality and Unity of God. With regard to the Divine Unity his concep-

general to *lend* Tracts, rather than to *give* them; as a Tract lent is more likely to be read than one given."

tions are clear and just, such as must be suggested to every enlightened mind by the contemplation of the works of creation and the study of the testimony of Scripture: nor for any thing that appears in this work is there reason to believe that the creed of the worthy Principal is burthened with the contradictory notions which generally prevail on this subject. His language is plain, decisive and unqualified :

"There is only *one Being* to whom all the perfections already considered, and every other belonging to Deity can be ascribed. God is self-existent and infinite and the original cause of all. Those qualities and attributes exclude the supposition of plurality. Self-existence extends every where and admits no limitation. Infinity implies both unlimited essence and unlimited perfection, and this excludes the supposition of two or more beings of whom these can be predicated. The wisdom and power of each of such beings must be limited by the wisdom and power of the others; and therefore they cannot all be infinite or supreme beings. The notion of two or more first causes is absurd in itself, and involves contradictory notions. It supposes that there is *one* original to the others, and at the same time denies this supposition."—P. 245.

There are many appearances in nature, and many occurrences in human life, which seem absolutely inexplicable upon the principle, that there is seated at the helm of affairs, a Being of infinite wisdom and benevolence, who ordains and regulates all the trains of events that happen to all creatures. And those difficulties have excited the attention of reflective persons from very early ages. The knowledge of nature which philosophy has disclosed; the just way of conducting inquiries of this kind which is now pursued, and above all the clear light of revelation, guiding the effects of intelligence and piety; have removed much of the obscurity in which this interesting and important subject was involved : and in a work, to which was adjudged a prize, instituted on purpose to clear away this darkness, it was natural to expect at least a lucid and consistent statement of all that the ablest writers had advanced. Never were we more disappointed than in this expectation. The author is always in a mist; it is only now and then that he seems to have a rapid and indistinct glance of the only clue that can

conduct him through the labyrinth; and we are much deceived if the perplexities of a thinking mind will not be increased rather than diminished by the perusal of this Essay.

In repelling the objections against the Divine wisdom and goodness, Principal Brown proposes, p. 272, 1. To ascertain the proper notions of perfection and evil, and then to evince that the permission of this last, is not only not inconsistent with the former, but is in some measure necessary to its highest displays; that is, that the all-perfect nature of God required that a certain portion of evil both natural and moral should be permitted. 2. That many evils which are produced as evidences against the wisdom of Providence, are grossly exaggerated and for the most part exist only in the irregular imaginations of men. 3. That these evils to which the human race is exposed, could not be excluded from the wisest and best system of the world, but are so controlled and directed as to be productive of the greatest sum of good. And 4. That the present state of man is adapted to his present faculties and powers.

With regard to the nature of perfection, Dr. Brown says, p. 276 :

"We call every thing perfect which possesses all that is necessary to its nature, or has been brought to a higher degree of improvement than belongs to individuals of the same kind, but in an absolute sense nothing that is subject to any defect or privation, or is circumscribed by any limits, nothing but the Divine nature can be denominated perfect."

With regard to the nature of evil, he says:

"Evil has been divided into natural and moral, the one implying and caused by some derangement of the corporeal system, the other implying and caused by some disturbance of the mental frame, considered in a moral point of view. To these two, a third species of evil has been added by metaphysicians, and has obtained the name of *metaphysical evil*. It expresses the absence or privation of certain powers, faculties and capacities, and of the felicity which these are the means of obtaining."

And with regard to this last he adds—

"That the permission of metaphysical evil, or of a certain deficiency in created beings, can imply nothing repugnant to the

God, must have remained inert, and no creation have been produced. There is then in the very nature of created being, an absolute necessity of metaphysical evil or defect."—Pp. 276. 280. 281.

After these observations the author proceeds to state, that from this necessity of defect or of metaphysical evil in the very nature of every creature, we shall be gradually led to apprehend that the permission of the two other classes of evil, namely, moral and physical, is not inconsistent with the Divine perfections of wisdom and goodness; that it may be proper to consider first moral evil, because natural evil proceeds in a great measure from it; and that as moral evil has been defined the abuse of free agency, it becomes necessary to shew that men are free agents and to explain and illustrate the specific nature of free agency itself. P. 286.

In doing this the learned Principal defines liberty, " the power of perceiving, choosing and pursuing some object:" and adds—" But the term liberty when used to signify the power of executing volition, is employed in a lax and popular sense. Its more accurate meaning is that of volition and choice. Whoever wills to move or to act, is mentally as free as he who really moves or acts. His mind exercises its energy even when his body is chained." P. 290.

In thus making liberty consist in volition, the learned Principal differs somewhat from the libertarians who have gone before him. The liberty of a moral agent, Dr. Reid says, is " a power over the determinations of his own will." And Dr. Gregory affirms that man possesses " an independent, self-governing, self-determining power, which he may at his own discretion exert, by acting either according to

" All beings possessed of intelligence and reason *must* also enjoy freedom of will. Indeed to will and to act, imply to will and to act freely. To will and to act necessarily involves a downright contradiction, because necessity is applicable to what is passive and cannot be predicated of volition and action. From this it appears that the genuine notion of liberty consists in the power of acting, or abstaining from action, and of electing among various modes of action. A free agent cannot choose whether he shall have volition or not. For to free agency volition is necessary, and by this he to whom it belongs is disposed either to action or to rest. In a word wherever *will* exists there is freedom."

Dr. Brown defines necessity to be " that the contrary of which involves a contradiction, and can neither exist nor coalesce in one idea." p. 295. And this is the only necessity of which he speaks. But he adds, " Certainty of event is often confounded with necessity of existence, although these terms express very different notions." p. 295. " Those," he says, p. 297, " who maintain a constant series of independent causes and effects, by which the human will is influenced without any internal principle of motion and action, maintain an eternal series *originating no where*" !!

" Still it is urged," adds the Doctor, p. 298, "that the will is influenced by the last determination of the understanding, and is therefore constrained." Constrained certainly it is in every sense which the advocate of necessity attaches to the term. The last determination of the understanding is, let us suppose, that an object which it has contemplated is desirable; that no cir-

---

* Dr. Gregory's Philosophical Essays: Sec. 1. P. 3.

cumstance exists to counteract its impression; that its attainment will be productive of happiness, and that the means to attain it are within its reach. This perception and determination of the understanding places the mind in a certain condition, namely, in the state of desire and of determination to exert its power to gratify that desire. Now this peculiar condition of the mind is termed will, or volition, and the question is, whether it could probably be different from what it actually is. The state of the mind and all the circumstances remaining exactly the same, that is, an object appearing desirable and nothing occurring to counteract the impression, that the attainment of it will be productive of happiness, can it avoid desiring it? And perceiving the means by which it can obtain the gratification of its desire, can it avoid exerting them? If not, if the desirableness of an object must excite desire, and the consciousness that the means of attaining it are within reach must induce the determination to excite them; then it is most obvious that volition and action are necessary in the only sense which in this controversy is meant to be conveyed by this term: that is to say, volition and action could not possibly be otherwise than they are, the constitution of the mind and the circumstances in which it is placed remaining the same.

What has led to so much confusion on this subject, is the indistinct and false notion which has been annexed to the term *will.* Will is nothing but a modification of desire, and therefore cannot possibly be excited by the mind itself at its own pleasure. It is induced by objects which the mind perceives to be good or evil, pleasing or painful, or imagines to be so. The mind cannot will will; but objects appearing to it pleasurable excite the desire or will to possess them, or appearing painful, induce the desire or will to avoid them: and the question again recurs, can an object apprehended to be thus painful or pleasurable, fail to induce the corresponding desire or will and the consequent action?

The whole of this controversy turns, as has been well stated by Mr. Belsham on this simple question : "Can volition take place independently of motive? meaning by motive whatever moves or influences the mind in its choice; thus including both this bias of the mind

itself and the end in view : in a word, comprehending every circumstance immediately previous to the volition; and which in the least degree contributes to generate the choice. Can volition take place independently of motive as thus defined? The libertarian contends that in the same previous circumstances and with views and inclinations precisely the same, a *different* choice may be made. The necessarian denies this, and maintains that there can be no difference in the choice without a correspondent difference in the previous state of the mind; that is, in the judgment or inclination of the agent."[*] This is the simple question stated in plain and simple language; and had Dr. Brown taken the pains to understand it, he would not have written the many absurdities by which this part of his work is deformed. He would not, for example, have defined necessity to be "that the contrary of which involves a contradiction and can neither exist nor coalesce in one idea." For if to the term necessity some metaphysicians have affixed the notion expressed in this definition, Dr. Brown knew, or ought to have known, that the advocates for the doctrine of Philosophical Necessity expressly distinguish between this sense of the word and that which they annex to it. Dr. Brown takes upon himself to say, p. 269, that Dr. Priestley, together with Hobbes and Spinosa and Bayle and Voltaire and Hume, has acquired celebrity by attacking the doctrines of *a Divine Providence* and of *the freedom of the will.* Was the Reverend Principal really acquainted with the writings of Dr. Priestley? Dr. Priestley has acquired celebrity by attacking the doctrine of a Divine Providence! And this affirmation goes forth to the world with the authority of the Reverend Principal of Marischal College. To attempt to justify Dr. Priestley from the charge of attacking the doctrine of a Divine Providence were an insult to his memory and to the understanding of the reader; and with regard to his attacking the freedom of the human will, the most charitable opinion is that Dr. Brown was utterly ignorant of the writings of the man even on this subject whom he presumes thus deeply to censure.

----

[*] Belsham's Elements of the Philosophy of the Mind. P. 230.

"I would observe," says Dr. Priestley, in the very beginning of his Illustrations of the Doctrine of Philosophical Necessity, p. 2, "that I allow to men all the liberty or power that is *possible in itself*, and to which the ideas of mankind in general ever go, which is the *power of doing whatever they will or please*, both with respect to the operations of their minds and the motions of their bodies, uncontrolled by any foreign principle or cause. Thus every man is at liberty to turn his thoughts to whatever subject he pleases, to consider the reasons for or against any scheme or proposition, and to reflect upon them as long as he shall think proper, as well as to walk wherever he pleases, and to do whatever his hands and other limbs are capable of doing.—All the liberty or rather power that I say a man has not, is that of doing several things when all the previous circumstances (including the state of his mind, and his views of things,) are precisely the same. What I contend for is, that with the same state of mind, (the same strength of any particular passion, for example) and the same views of things, (as any particular object appearing equally desirable,) he would always, voluntarily, make the same choice and come to the same determination. For instance, if I make any particular choice to-day, I should have done the same yesterday, and shall do the same to-morrow, provided there be no change in the state of my mind respecting the object of the choice. In other words I maintain, that there is some *fixed law of nature respecting the will*, as well as the other powers of the mind, and every thing else in the constitution of nature; and consequently that it is never determined without some real or apparent cause, foreign to itself; that is, without some motive of choice, or that *motives influence in some definite and invariable manner*; so that every volition or choice is constantly regulated and determined by what precedes it. And this *constant determination of mind, according to the motives presented to it, is all that I mean by its necessary determination.*"

But the fact is, Dr. Brown is himself a believer in this very doctrine, as far as it is possible to judge of his belief on the subject.

"What," says he, pp. 298, 299, "do we signify by willing or choosing any thing but that of judging it preferable. The human will is always inclined to prefer good to evil, and among goods to prefer that which appears to afford the greatest sum of happiness, and among evils to avoid that which appears to bring the greatest sum of misery. This is its *constant* and *invariable determination*. But in order to enable it to make this election, the understanding must carefully scrutinize the respective natures of the objects presented, and decide on their tendencies to happiness or misery. When this decision, just or erroneous, is once made; election or reprobation immediately ensues. The determination of the will towards agreeable and blissful objects, and its aversion from those which are productive of pain and misery, are *uniform* and *invariable*."——"Modern opponents of liberty have directed their principal efforts to prove that human action, as influenced by motive, always follows a *certain* and *definitive* course. *This is readily granted.*"—P. 304,

And this being granted, all is granted for which Dr. Priestley, or any other advocate of the doctrine of Philosophical Necessity, who understood the subject, ever contended: but such is the looseness with which Dr. Brown allows himself to think and write, that he absolutely confounds with this which is his own opinion and the opinion of Dr. Priestley and of all other modern necessarians, the doctrine of *fate*, or as he terms it *absolute necessity*, *fatal necessity*, &c. (p. 304): a doctrine which no one as far as we know has pretended to maintain in modern times.

Having discussed in this clear and erudite manner the great question between the necessarians and the libertarians, Dr. Brown applies his doctrine of free agency to the removal of the difficulties which press on the Divine character and administration from the existence of natural and moral evil. He argues that moral evil is the result of free agency; that where the latter exists the permission of the former is unavoidable; that since it is consistent with the Divine wisdom and goodness to create free agents, the permission of moral evil cannot be inconsistent with those perfections, because the one infers the other. P. 316.

Should this reasoning be capable of removing from any mind the slightest difficulty which appeared to it to involve the Divine administration, we should despair of being able to benefit it by any thing which we could say; nor should we have much greater hope if it could derive any instruction or comfort from the following illustration of this argument:

" Who can impute to the Author of the admirable fabric and constitution of nature, that perversion which is most repugnant to his will, but which his wisdom and goodness suggested to him not to prevent? When a ship has been wrecked by the ignorance of the master, can we blame the ship builder who fitted it for all the purposes of navigation, and displayed admirable skill in its construction, because he did not render it incapable of perishing? Can we blame an architect who has planned a most convenient and elegant house, or the mason who has built it, when it has been destroyed by fire, because neither of them secured it against this calamity? Nor can we with more reason lay it to the charge of the great Author of human nature, that the noble faculties with which he has endowed it, and whose tendencies are to improvement and happiness, have been most unnaturally perverted and depraved."— Pp. 320, 321.

Dr. Brown asks, whether it were inconsistent with the infinite wisdom and goodness of God to create such an order of beings as men. We answer decidedly, on his scheme, *it was,* If there be one proposition clear and undeniable, it is that a Being of infinite wisdom and goodness must impart to every creature which he calls into existence a greater sum of happiness than misery, the whole of its existence being considered: if this be not the case he is not good, nor is it possible for any ingenuity or sophistry to prove him to be so. Nay Dr. Brown himself affirms that the goodness of the Deity must be " a constant and immutable disposition to communicate and extend the highest measure of happiness to all his creatures, and that this necessarily implies the communication of all possible happiness *to the whole and to every part of his sensible creation."* P. 223. How then is this consistent with his appointment from all eternity of the great majority of mankind to unutterable and unending torment? Why thus:

" It has been already shown that the permission of moral evil is inseparable from free agency. The natural and necessary consequences of corruption, proceeding from the abuse of freedom, must also be permitted. Every species, every degree and every extent of depravation however small or short is inconsistent with the Divine perfections and laws, and whatever those require must, in the order of things, in-

fallibly take place. If free agency, the chief source of happiness to man, and the foundation of all virtue and religion, required the permission of vice and its continuance during a state of trial, its misery TO WHATEVER EXTENT OR DURATION, when it has become habitual to the soul, follows as a *necessary consequence."* Vol. II. p. 203. " And no person can complain of the severity of the Divine threatenings, if he is fully warned of his danger, is furnished with every necessary aid for avoiding it, and as long as life continues has still space left for repentance." P. 207. " The only effectual encouragement to virtue, the only effectual restraint to vice, is the enactment of rewards sufficiently animating and of punishments sufficiently formidable. The greater those are in prospect the more powerful is the check and the more invigorating the encouragement. I grant indeed that the infliction of cruel human punishments in this life, while the course of probation is still unfinished, has rather a tendency to corrupt than to correct a people by inuring them to savage and barbarous spectacles. But the case is different, when all hopes of amendment are gone, and the period of probation is closed. Then every character is completely formed. Vice is rivetted on the soul. Its natural consequences are allowed to take place. It is necessary that its final result should be tremendous and irreversible."—P. 210.

And this is the final result of the moral administration of a Being of infinite power, wisdom and goodness, in regard to the great majority of mankind—of that Being " whose constant and immutable disposition it is to communicate and extend the highest measure of happiness to all his creatures—to communicate all possible happiness to the whole and to every part of his sensitive creation !"

Since endless punishment cannot benefit those who are saved and can of course be of no advantage to those upon whom it is inflicted, it had always been considered somewhat difficult to explain the *use* of it under the wise and benevolent government of the Deity. But Dr. Brown easily solves this difficulty, and intimates that it may be of great service to the people of the Moon or the inhabitants of Saturn.

" As we find that among men, prisons, public examples and places of punishment are useful for impressing vicious minds with terror ; so the *eternal* sufferings of the incorrigibly perverse and wicked of the human race, as they certainly convey an awful warning to those of our own species who are still in a state of trial, may also prove salutary to other classes and orders of rational creatures."—Vol. II. p. 211.

We do not deem it necessary to follow Dr. Brown through the remaining parts of his work. We shall only add in respect to those that the worthy Principal is a very orthodox and zealous believer in the comfortable doctrine of original sin. His ideas on this subject are at least clear and consistent, if not perfectly satisfactory.

"Whether, after the shock of sin was once given to man's nature, it could recover primitive innocence, is at least matter of great doubt, and is a point which I shall in the sequel endeavour to illustrate according to the measure of my abilities. It is certain, if I may be allowed to employ so distant an analogy, that among the inferior animals, whole breeds degenerate; and that all the individuals of a succeeding race are affected by the declension of the antecedent generation. Nay, we see in our own species, diseases both of body and mind daily transmitted. This may lead us in the mean time to conceive the *fact*, if not the *manner* of the transmission of *moral* corruption!"— Vol. II. p. 130.

Upon the whole, we never recollect to have read a book which so completely disappointed our expectations. For the honour of our age and country we are sorry that it should have been found necessary to award such a prize to such a production. Yet occasionally and for a paragraph or two there occur some faint approaches to just conception and to good writing. We shall conclude by extracting a passage which affords a favourable specimen of the author's style and manner. Had there been more of this kind, we should have read and commented on his work with much greater pleasure; had there been nothing of it, we should not have deemed it necessary to notice it.

"When we consider the deep ignorance in which so many of the human race are plunged, the errors which have been transmitted from generation to generation; the prejudices which adhere even to those whose improvement has not been entirely neglected; the defects of education both public and private; the false maxims which without dispute or inquiry are established in the world; the power of example, of habit and of temptation; the manner in which the desires and passions are imperceptibly excited and strengthened, so that they bid defiance to the controul of reason; the first motives to the most abominable deeds—motives in themselves sometimes laudable and often innocent: if we consider all this, we shall be led to acknowledge that the greater part of men sin more from imprudence and error, than from deliberate and desperate wickedness, and that even crimes which appear to us invested with the most detestable colours, may to Him who *looketh at the heart*, and knoweth all its springs and modifications, appear more deserving of compassion, than of interminable unmitigated punishment. These reflections have sometimes occurred to me on the recital of some of the most atrocious crimes by which our nature is degraded. Their motives can hardly be conceived by us who have so little knowledge of the internal state of the human frame. *The Lord seeth not as man seeth: for man looketh at the outward appearance, but the Lord looketh on the heart.* Though human judgments must be pronounced accord'n; to the evidence produced, yet that evidence cannot in many instances exhibit the *exact* moral complexion of the action which is tried. Men must therefore judge of the same action differently from Him who is Omniscient and to whom certain deeds, characterized by the blackest features of external guilt, may appear less criminal, than even some of those faults, which in human estimation, are hardly deserving censure."—Vol. II. p. 9.

S. S.

Art. IV.—*Twenty-one Short Forms of Morning and Evening Prayers, for the Use of Families.* By a Member of the British and Foreign Bible Society, and of the Society for Promoting Christian Knowledge. 12mo. pp. 144. Hunter. 1816.

THESE Forms are distinguished by their simplicity and conformity to the style of Scripture. They breathe also a fine moral spirit, and in this respect are superior to almost all the prayers that we have read. They remind us of the compositions of the late Rev. Theophilus Lindsey, and are evidently the production of a kindred mind; artless, gentle, placid, pure, benevolent and aspiring towards heaven.

The Forms are short, and might have been made shorter by the omission, at least in all but the first, of the Lord's Prayer.

This useful manual of devotion is introduced and concluded with serious and suitable exhortations and admonitions.

ART. V.—*Sermons on Select Subjects:* By John Hyatt. 8vo. pp. 369. Williams.

MR. JOHN HYATT is one of the ministers of the *Tabernacle*, the temple of modern "Evangelical" worship; and he has here favoured the public with ample specimens of that kind of preaching which, throughout all England, is drawing the multitude away from their parish churches, and forming them into "a peculiar people, zealous"—for a more rigid species of Calvinism than was taught by the mortal enemy of Servetus.

The "Evangelical" preachers will not, we apprehend, object to Mr. Hyatt's being considered as the representative, as from his station he is the chief, of their order. He is regarded, we are told, as one of the best preachers of the sect; and he appears to be a man of thought and to possess a vigorous imagination.

"Evangelical" preaching is, we need not say, preaching without book. The preacher believes himself, and is believed by others, to be under the influence of the Holy Ghost; a written discourse would *stint the spirit*, and, instead of the words of the Holy Ghost, the speaker, degenerated to a reader, would utter the words of man's wisdom.

Extempore speaking is winning from its familiarity, and, in Mr. John Hyatt's specimens, is rendered more attractive by certain tender appellations by which the auditory is addressed. *Poor sinners! Precious souls! my dear friends!* and other similar expressions of endearment go, we imagine, a great way in helping forward the effect of this strain of preaching.

Mr. John Hyatt and his brethren are pleased with themselves for lowering their discourses to the rude apprehensions of the lowest vulgar; not once thinking that it is possible, or feeling that it is desirable, to improve their taste and enlarge their understandings. Hence they deal out common-places with great self complacency, and the merest truisms with a pompousness which indicates self-admiration. Their words drop from them with a volubility which makes the multitude stare; for they preach against critics and would think it criminal to stay to sift and select

words and phrases and to consult purity and elegance of language.

These preachers think it necessary to prove nothing; every thing is taken for granted; but then there is a text for every thing,—though it is seldom deemed requisite to justify the application of the words of Scripture to the preacher's subject. It seems as if minister and people considered their creed as matter of absolute certainty, and regarded it as the end of preaching to deliver out the articles of their faith, and to express pity for, or to denounce judgments against, such as cannot understand or will not embrace them.

In point of composition, the sermons of Mr. John Hyatt's class of preachers are artless, to a degree that borders on childishness. A whole paragraph will often consist of a self-evident proposition, repeated in several forms, sometimes put in a broad simile, followed by a set of Scripture quotations, unconnected and unexplained, mingled with interjections, and the whole concluded by an anecdote, a dying experience, a stanza from Dr. Watts, or possibly a couplet from Dr. Young.

Perhaps, nothing has contributed more to the illusion which "Evangelical" or *Tabernacle* preaching brings over the mind than its abounding in Scriptural quotations, which seem to invest it with sanctity and solemnity, and to cover its meagreness and folly. In a great mass of citations, some must be appropriate; and we have observed, occasionally, in this volume, a happy use of the sublime and affecting language of Holy Writ. Great wrong, however, is done to the Bible, in the ordinary way of selecting texts for this class of sermons; passages are plainly taken more for sound than sense, and, whether moral, devotional, doctrinal, prophetic or historical, are forced to speak *Tabernacle* theology.

But the principal and most availing part of "Evangelical" preaching is its damnatory style, its denunciation and description of the torments of the damned in hell:——this is the heavy artillery of Calvinism, with which the least skilful engineer can beat down the proud heart and storm the stubborn conscience. A great part of the conversions recorded in the *Evangelical Magazine* have been effected by the sons of thunder; thundering, however, as Dr. South remarks, from hell and not from heaven. To thoroughly ignorant, vicious men, it is in the nature of things that such preaching should be interesting and affecting: we believe that it rarely produces striking effects on the minds of men of information and good moral habits.

But it is proper we should exhibit Mr. John Hyatt himself to our readers: we shall select a few passages from him which explain the style of *Tabernacle* preaching and illustrate some of our remarks.

In nothing is the good sense of a preacher more tried than in the announcement and developement of the plan of his discourse; his division, if he adopt one formally, should be natural, simple and distinct, and the several branches of his subject should be connected together and all appear important. The terms in which the plan of a sermon is laid down should be plain and precise. Ingenuity and eloquence should here be avoided; a painted, ornamented threshold would be a silly device even for the entrance to a palace.

We have not to blame Mr. John Hyatt for ingenuity or eloquence in this particular; he is, on the contrary, blunt and quaint. The first sermon, for instance, "On the Importance of Meditation," from Gen. xxiv. 63, *And Isaac went out to meditate in the field at the even-tide,* is thus divided :—

"Let us first notice the nature and importance of the *exercise* mentioned in the text; secondly, mention some suitable subjects for the *believer's* meditation; and thirdly, urge it upon Christians to *imitate Isaac in this exercise.*"—P. 4.

Sermon IV. on "The Death of the Righteous," from Numbers xxiii. 10, *Let me die the death of the righteous, and let my last end be like his,* is thus divided :—

"From these words we shall observe; I. *Death is the common lot of mankind,* both the righteous and the wicked must die. II. It is most desirable to die as the righteous die [*dies*], and that our end be like *his.* III. However desirable is [*be*] the death of the righteous, the wish for it is vain, without *a gracious change* produced in the mind by the Holy Ghost."—P. 80.

The following extract from Sermon II. on "Abundant Grace," is a favourable specimen of the preaching of the *Tabernacle* school :—

"Grace is one of the most comprehensive and interesting terms, with which *any of mankind* are acquainted. If its real importance was [*were*] understood and *experienced* by every one present, each countenance would brighten, each heart would leap with joy, and all would readily unite in expressing the sentiment of the truly excellent Doddridge—

'Grace! 'tis a charming sound,
    Harmonious to the ear.'

"There is infinitely more in this term, when its meaning is understood and its blessings are realized, to encourage the heart of man, than there is in all the terms by which the consequences of sin are expressed, to discourage. Grace is an effectual remedy for all the spiritual maladies of the soul. Sin has not produced an evil in the nature of man, which grace cannot effectually counteract, and finally remove. Hath sin blinded the understanding?—grace can enlighten it. Hath sin perverted the will?—grace can reduce it to subjection. Are the affections defiled?—grace can sanctify them. Is man impoverished?—grace can enrich him. Is he ignorant?—grace can instruct him. Is he guilty?—grace can pardon and justify. Is he an heir of hell?—grace can make him an heir of heaven. Nothing else has ever performed such wonders. The loudest note that is heard in *glory* sounds in praise of grace. It is an inexhaustible theme; its wonders will be

'Ever telling—yet untold.'"—Pp. 28, 29.

The conclusion of the same sermon is in the terrific style which we have adverted to :—

"Is there in this assembly an individual whose desperately wicked mind derives encouragement to sin from *the aboundings of grace?* Because God is able to make all grace abound towards the chief of sinners, are you resolved to try how far you can proceed in a course of ungodliness? *Abominable wretch!* how knowest thou but thy *base determination* is the effect of thy having been given up by the Almighty to hardness of heart? How knowest thou but God hath said concerning thee, 'Let him alone?' Should this be the case, O! how tremendous will be the end of thy mortal course! *Miserable wretch!* what wilt thou do when the heavens lower, and the tempest roars, whither in thine extremity wilt thou turn for shelter? Then, no voice of pity will address thine ear, *no place of refuge* will encourage thy flight, but, *without refuge and without hope,* thou wilt be *hurled* to the dismal abodes of everlasting *despair.*"—P. 50.

But this is feeble, compared with the following address to an " *ungodly sinner,*" [words which could not be *associated,* with propriety, under any system but Calvinism] in Sermon III., entitled, "The Christian's Desire of Heaven :"—

· " *Ungodly sinner,* if you die in your present state, when absent from the body you will be *present with the devil* and innumerable fallen spirits in the world of *endless misery.* Thoughtless sinner, did you see how near death is to you, and how *thin is the partition between death and hell,* how would you *tremble!*—how *terrible* to die in your sins, and sink into *everlasting darkness.* You may now indeed enjoy health and vigour ; and anticipating many years in this world, nothing that we can say concerning *death* and *eternal misery alarms* you ; but your *days* upon earth may be fewer than you expect *years;*—yes, to-morrow, or before to-morrow, *death's cold hand may press hard upon you, your countenance may be distorted,* your pulse irregular, and HORROR STARING FROM YOUR EYES, TERRIFY THOSE ABOUT YOU; sad state, unable to live, and most reluctant to die. Your friends may crowd around your bed and weep bitterly, but alas! they will not be able to afford you the least relief; your unwilling soul at length may be forced out of her ' earthly house,' then *with a dismal groan she will leave the world,* TO GROAN IN HELL FOR EVER."—Pp. 71, 72.

Enough of this outrageous rant! fit only for Bedlam or the Court of Inquisition. We gladly turn to the following amplification of a pleasing image of Scripture, occurring in Sermon VIII., entitled, "The Redeemer's Sympathy," from Isa. lxiii. 9 :—

" ' Ye have seen (said God to the children of Israel) how I bare you on eagles wings, and brought you unto myself.' ' The Lord's portion is his people, Jacob is the lot of his inheritance. He found him in a desert land, and in the waste howling wilderness; he led him about, he instructed him, he kept him as the apple of his eye. As an eagle stirreth up her nest, fluttereth over her young, spreadeth abroad her wings, taketh them, beareth them on her wings, so the Lord alone did lead him, and there was no strange God with him.' What a fine description of the 'tender care of Jehovah towards his people! The maternal eagle perceiving that her young ones are in danger from

an enemy, is anxious to preserve them; she flutters over her nest, thus exciting them to fly by her example ; but the nestlings are not sufficiently fledged for flight. What then will she do? will she forsake her helpless brood, and leave them all exposed to the merciless foe? No, finding that they cannot by their own strength avoid the danger which threatens them, she takes them upon her wide-spread wings and bears them away to some place of safety. Thus the Almighty secures his people from the cruel designs of all their potent and inveterate adversaries. O ye *persecuted and tempted saints,* fear not! While the eternal God can afford you support and protection, you shall not perish. He will ' bear you as on eagles wings' to the world of perfect and everlasting felictiy."—Pp. 203, 204.

In Sermon III., "The Christian's Desire of Heaven," is some appearance of argument in favour of an intermediate state of conscious existence between death and the resurrection; and this is almost the only passage we have observed in which there is any argument : the preacher has stated pretty strongly and tolerably well the scriptural proofs in favour of the popular scheme. He concludes with repeiling the interpretation put by the Materialists on our Lord's address to the penitent malefactor; and finishes with this burst of fanaticism and intolerance, which, we are happy to remark, is not countenanced by any similar passage in the volume :—

"——in this way is Scripture tortured and distorted, with a view to make human souls sleep. *One wonders that the wrath of God sleeps*— that it is not roused to resent such daring insolence in presumptuous man."—P. 59.

Apostrophe is a favourite figure with the preacher of the Tabernacle—there is something ludicrous in the following use of it, S. III. p. 73 :

" Precious Bible! I love thee, because from thee I have received direction in many difficulties, &c., &c. TABERNACLE, *I love thee,* because within thee I have often enjoyed the presence of my much-loved Saviour; here have I beheld his goings, &c."

The Sermons are fourteen in number, but it is observable that there is not one on a practical subject. This may be mentioned as another feature of modern "Evangelical" preaching; which is indeed explained to be *preaching up the* DOCTRINES *of grace.* "Holiness" is insisted on in several of these Discourses, as we suppose it is in most discourses bearing the *Tabernacle* stamp, the mint mark of orthodoxy; but we fear the common people would not understand by this term, "doing justly and loving mercy." It imports something done for them, rather than any thing which they are to do. We shall not, however, here borrow the language of the alarmists on the subject of the anti-moral teachers, partly because we believe that it is commonly unjust, and therefore mischievous, but principally because Mr. John Hyatt has not provoked censure by a single remark or expression, that we have met, in disparagement of good works and moral worth.

These Sermons considered as the official homilies of the *Tabernacle* or "Evangelical" party, present us with the idea of a sect not far advanced in knowledge and refinement; they can be relished only by persons of little inquiry and of mediocrity of talent.

ART. VI.—*An Open and Fearless Avowal of the Unitarian Doctrine Recommended and Enforced.* A Sermon preached at the Unitarian Chapel in Artillery Lane, London, on Wednesday, June 5, 1816, before the Friends and Supporters of the Unitarian Fund. By W. Broadbent, Minister of the Unitarian Chapel at Warrington. 12mo. pp. 36. Hunter and Eaton.

IT seems strange that amongst such as agree in the Unitarian doctrine as the truth of Divine revelation, there should be any division of opinion with regard to the duty of avowing it openly and promoting it to the furthest possible extent. Such division of opinion however exists, though it is lessening daily; and Mr. Broadbent's Sermon will, we trust, increase the number, already great, of those that think that to hinder *the truth* when it may be furthered, is a species of *unrighteousness.**

Mr. Broadbent argues the subject coolly and charitably, and we see not how the argument can be opposed by such as admit the truth of Christianity. If divine truth be revealed, it must be esteemed of supreme importance to the happiness of mankind, and neither piety nor benevolence can allow us to be indifferent to its success. The same principles that in former times made martyrs, will at all times form zealous proselytes.

* Rom. i. 18. See Wakefield's Translation and Note.

POETRY.

Inscription on a Tombstone in Cheshunt Church-Yard.

THIS STONE
IS ERECTED IN MEMORY OF
THE REV. JEREMIAH JOYCE,
Who was Born Feb. 24, 1763,
And Died June 21, 1816.

Ye who in solemn contemplation tread
These precincts, sacred to the silent dead,
Pause, and with rev'rence mark the spot,
  where rest
HIS cold remains, who erst, with dauntless breast,
Firm in his Country's and in Freedom's
  cause,
Brav'd the dread peril of perverted laws.
Though bold, yet gentle, his well cultured
  mind
Glowed with a generous love of human
  kind.

Whilst Friendship's joys expansive and
  sincere,
And bliss domestic crown'd each passing
  year,
Swift flew the bolt that sped him to the
  tomb:
But check the bursting tear that mourns
  his doom.
The task perform'd to humble mortals giv'n,
A sudden death's the easiest way to
  Heav'n.

From the Portugueze of Bocage.

When midst the busy world I found me
Eagerly I look'd around me
For a silent couch and a peaceful home;
But alas! I look'd in vain—where'er
I turned,—but tumult and toil were
  there—
So I smiled contempt and I sought the
  Tomb.   A.

From the Italian of Pellegrino Gaudenzi.

Brightest of spirits! proudly thron'd on
    high
  Midst the gold flames that flash from
    star and sun,
In the wide deserts of th' ethereal sky—
  Th' Incomprehensible,—Almighty One!
    Dart the pure radiance of Thy pre-
      sence down
On this benighted vale ;—to mortal eye
Display the splendours of Thy Majesty
    And open all the glories of Thy
    throne.

Ages of old Thee recognized,—tho' seen
  Dimly amidst Thy works :—and man
    upraised
    Temples and altars to thy shadowed
    name.
A GOD, a Father *all* thy works pro-
    claim
Who is, and shall be, and hath ever
    been,
  Tho' veil'd in darkness, and in silence
    praised !

                    A.

From the German of Herder.

————The influence of the good
Spreads like the widening shadows of the
  evening
Till life's last sun-beam dies.

                    A.

The Philosophy of Evil.

(From Mr. G. Dyer's Poetics.)

It was when dark November frown'd ;—
  Country and town alike were dreary ;
Nothing was smiling all around,
  Nought within cheary.

" Oh ! for some pure æthereal sphere,
  " To which no dregs of matter cling,
" Where flows serene th' all-perfect year.
  " From mind's pure spring."

It might not be—a Form I view—
  Stern was his front, and fierce his eye ;
His robe mix'd of November's hue,
  On crimson dye.

Clamour, and Rage, and trembling Fear,
  In grim wild state before him go ;
And in his hand he couch'd a spear,
  As towards some foe.

" Sing not to me," he cried, " of loves ;
  " Sigh not to me in Pity's strains ;
" Nor think to lure me to the groves,
  " To pipe with swains.

" Different my joys—I traverse earth,
  " I range thro' air, I pierce the sea ;
" And every creature by its birth,
  " Is bound to me.

" Each from me some strong instinct
    draws,
  " Which towards its kin engenders
    strife ;
" Birds, fishes, yielding to my laws,
  " Prey upon life.

" Have you not heard in distant wood,
  " How greedy beasts pursue their way ?
" By turns, each drinks some creature's
    blood,
  " By turns the prey.

" Have you not mark'd the busy world,
  " Where reason forms its wisest plan ?
" How man, by furious passions whirl'd,
  " Preys upon man ?

" 'Tis mine—I stir the active thought,
  " I rouse the passions, urge the deed ;
" And there I feast, where thousands
    fought,
  " And thousands bleed.

" 'Midst storms and fires I sit and sing,
  " Most pleas'd where least I see of
    form ;
" I sail upon the whirlwind's wing,
  " And guide the storm.

" When Ætna belches flame around,
  " I gaze and gaze with greedy eye,
" Where cities, late with plenty crown'd,
  " In ruins lie.

" Does ocean rave ? I look and think
  " Unruffled on the sounding shore,
" And rise with joy, as thousands sink,
  " To rise no more.

" Do earthquakes growl beneath the
    land ?
  " I wait expectant of the sight ;
" And grow, as earth's wide jaws ex-
    pand,
  " Wild with delight.

" Of life their babes when Hindoos spoil,
  " The pious deed I loud proclaim ;
" And of their widow's funeral pile,
  " I light the flame.

" 'Tis mine—all mine—I boast the
    deeds—
  " And call myself the friend of man—
" 'Tis mine—and see ! the work pro-
    ceeds—
  " 'Tis nature's plan.

" On man what crowding ills attend !
  " See how creation pants for room !
" Ah ! wretch—I haste, that wretch's
    friend,
  " To build his tomb."•

  • The Persian Magi held two principles, one the author of good, the other of
evil ; the latter was called Arimanes.
This personage is called in the Chaldaic
oracles by different names, Hecate, ἄζο-
στημα κακης ὑλης, Dæmon ; other bar-

OBITUARY.

Died, Sept. 9, at her house, in Sidmouth, Mrs. ELIZABETH CARSLAKE, the eldest sister of John Carslake, Esq. of the same place, whose death we recorded fourteen months ago [X. 522.] She had completed the 78th year of her age, and for some time past had been evidently in a declining state. She had a large circle of relatives and friends, and was deservedly esteemed by them. She was a steady Dissenter, but had not the smallest dislike to any who conscientiously differed from her: the liberty she claimed for herself in religious matters, she freely accorded to others. She was entitled to still higher praise than this: her faith was *practical*, as well as *liberal*, it led to *good works*. She was well aware that the mere calling of Christ Lord was

not sufficient to prove her his true disciple, and to fit her for that eternal life which he is appointed to bestow. This venerable and amiable woman supported through the whole of her long life, a blameless and lovely character. She was placed by Providence in very favourable circumstances, and she was neither insensible of the advantages she enjoyed, nor an unfaithful steward of them. Her friendship was not lightly given; but when once imparted, it was steady and durable, nothing but worthlessness of character could shake her attachment. Her virtues were all of the mild and unobtrusive kind; her mind was serious, but not at all gloomy. Her natural temper was good, and the views she entertained of the paternal character of the Almighty, and of the wisdom and goodness of all his dispensations, led her to acquiesce in all his appointments and satisfied her that every thing was tending to good. The great Christian doctrines of a resurrection from the dead, a future re-union with her beloved relatives and friends, and an intercourse with all the virtuous of mankind in the kingdom of their common Father, were frequently the subject of her thoughts and conversation. These doctrines gave her high delight, and no wonder that they should, they are full of consolation, and fitted to cheer and support in all the calamities and decays of mortality. Like her aged and good brother, she was eminently a child of peace, and nothing upon earth gave her so much satisfaction, as when she witnessed a just and peaceful temper in those about her. Her life being thus goodness, it was in the natural order of things that her end should be peace. " Mark the perfect man," says the Psalmist, " and behold the upright, for the end of that man is peace." This was fully verified in the subject of this account. Her last illness was not very long, nor was it very painful; she retained her senses to the last. About an hour and half before her death she swallowed a little milk, and then gradually, and tranquilly, resigned herself to the sleep of death. " Blessed are the dead who die in the Lord." B:

---

barous names, as it is there expressed, are given it by God. The Indian mythology paints it under different forms, more particularly as Seeva. By the northern nations it was called Surtur, who is described in the Edda as making war upon Odin. In the Funeral Song of Hacon, it appears as the wolf Fenris, chained, now, but who will break loose hereafter, and destroy the world. In the Greek and Roman poets, particularly Ovid and Claudian, it is conspicuous in the Battle of the Giants against Jupiter, and has thence passed into the poetry of Milton. Pindar, after describing the confinement of these Giants in Ætna, represesents them as belching out streams of fire. (Pyth. 1.) αϊπλατ8 πυρος αγνοταται παγαι. Mars is made by Homer a fierce malicious being, destructive to men and delighting in blood,

Αρες, Αρες, βροτολοιγε, μιαιφονες·
  IL. lib. v.

—In the sacred writings of the Jews, also, this principle appears, and is called *Na-kas*, a serpent, (Gen. iii. 1.) and on this the Christian doctrine is founded. It seems to be, and thus it is explained by many critics, the principle of evil, as personified in the philosophy of the East. And it is remarkable, that in Persia both the principles were personified under the symbol of two serpents contending for the MUNDANE EGG.

In the above poem no allusion is made to the origin of evil, it only admits its existence, and accords with that philosophy, which supposes it a necessary part of the present system, and that partial evil may be universal good.

Memoir of the late
Mr. RICHARD REYNOLDS.

IN our Obituary of last month, (p. 554) we briefly noticed the death of MR. RICHARD REYNOLDS, of *Bristol*. Various memoirs of that excellent man have already appeared; and it is hoped that the public will ere long be favoured with a minute and correct narrative of his useful life by one who knows how to appreciate his worth, and has been conversant with many of the more secret acts of Mr. Reynolds's benevolence. We should however regret that our readers should not be informed of some of the more prominent features of this pious and venerable Christian. A knowledge of his plans may induce the well disposed to go and do likewise.

Mr. Reynolds was a native of Bristol. His father was an opulent tradesman, and a minister among the Society of Friends. He was solicitous that habits of early industry should be implanted in his children. These were properly applied by his son, who at no advanced age became a proprietor and conductor of very extensive iron works in Shropshire. Perseverance and skill were accompanied by integrity; and the consequence was the great improvement of the concern and the accumulation of an ample fortune by Mr. Reynolds. This he used in a manner becoming the philanthropist and the Christian. He ascribed all his blessings to the Giver of all good, and considered himself only a steward of Divine bounty. He regarded his talents, whether of money or ability, as treasures for which he must hereafter give a strict account—hence his self denial was uniform, his circumspection great, and his generosity without partiality, either as to sect, party, or country. Piety was his ruling principle, and pride was a stranger to his actions. The good effect of his religious principle, was strikingly shown in the government he acquired over a temper naturally irritable. Benevolence is often the offspring of feeling: in Mr. Reynolds it was the consequence of faith, working by love. A discretion rarely to be found, was the companion of his zeal to do good. But a willingness to search out the case he knew not, was not its only feature: there was a penetration in his mode of proceeding that discovered the clearness of his judgment and the acuteness of his observations.

But his deeds were not done to obtain the praise of men: he sought the means of conferring a favour in private, and redoubling the obligation by not seeming to have bestowed one. A striking instance of this kind occurred when a lady applied to him in behalf of an orphan, whom he had liberally aided: "When he is old," the lady said, "I will teach him to name and thank his benefactor." "Stop," said the good man, "you mistake; we do not thank the clouds for rain; teach him to look higher, and thank Him, who giveth both the clouds and the rain." So great was Mr. Reynolds's modesty, that he seemed wounded if his praise were sounded, or if his deeds of kindness were brought before the public eye. Partly with a view of concealing the author, and partly to give a wider diffusion to his beneficence, he employed persons in different parts and men of all professions and religious persuasions, to relieve objects deserving of assistance, in the places in which they resided. One method was lending sums of money to the deserving, permitting them to repay the amount by instalments; if they were able to pay interest, it was received, if not, it was not demanded. The same money to be again and again applied to similar cases. Expectation was not awakened and then disappointed. But the advice accompanying the aid bestowed was frequently found of the highest utility. Mr. Reynolds gave to public charities with munificence; but to his own name only such sums were affixed as others might easily imitate, who were well disposed to the cause. "A Friend," or "A Friend by ditto," contributed what awakened admiration. To give instances would be endless: suffice it to refer to the records of the Committee for relieving the Germans—to those of the Spital-fields Weavers—of the Bible Societies—to those of the African Institution—and to those of the various charities in Bristol. Mr. Reynolds held it to be a duty that each one should as much as possible be his own executor—not only to avoid giving trouble to survivors, but also, because our talents are required to be faithfully used, whilst we ourselves are in the body. On this ground, during his life, he purchased an estate for £10,000, the interest of which is to be appropriated, at the discretion of the trustees whom he named, to the assistance of seven charities which he specified. With the same view, he gave a sum of money to the Corporation of Bristol, to augment a fund, of which that body has the application, for relieving blind persons, by granting £10 a year to each recipient. The charity which for a long time occupied his attention, is worthy of its advocate : it was to raise a sum of money to enable all the inhabitants in the almshouses of Bristol to receive at present equal to the intention of the founders of the several almshouses, or to grant 5s. per week to each of them. It is unnecessary to add, that his own contributions were suited to the magnitude of the design. To him the Samaritan Society owes its origin. Its object is to relieve those cases, which other charities could not assist. Many persons who have been patients in the Infirmary, many who are recovering from sickness, many who have been recalled from vicious habits, and have formed virtuous resolutions, often suffer greatly before they can gain employment, or pursue their former avocations with effect. Through want of temporary aid lasting difficulties frequently arise. To bestow this aid, and to lead the members of a society to do what their Saviour hath commanded, was the intention of the Institution, which bears the name its founder justly merited, *the Samaritan.*

Hence it will appear that although Mr. Reynolds was solicitous to avoid praise, he was not inactive, or merely following the suggestions of the well disposed. He was ever ready to excite others to fulfil the trust committed to their care. His manner of appeal in behalf of the distressed did not derive its only force from his own example. There was an appeal to the judgment and to the heart which could scarcely be resisted. On one occasion of this kind, it is said, that when addressing a gentleman whom he supposed to be rich, in order to stimulate his exertions, he remarked, " When gold *encircles* the heart it *contracts* to such a degree that no good can issue from it ; but when the pure gold of faith and love gets *into* the heart it expands it, and causes each drop of blood to flow through the channels of benevolence." In his life was witnessed the truth of the remark, " When the eye saw him it was glad, when the ear heard him it

rejoiced." But it must be left to a Clarkson to recount his services towards the abolition of the Slave Trade, and ameliorating the condition of the oppressed Negro : it must be left to an Allen to tell what he hath done for the education of the poor : it must be left to an Owen to enumerate his benefactions to the British and Foreign Bible Society : and to an Harrison, or some other member of the Society of Friends, to enumerate Mr. Reynolds's gifts to the various charitable institutions belonging to that respectable class of Christians. Mr. Reynolds continued a zealous and consistent member of the society in which he was born and educated. In him they have lost a burning and shining light of faith, hope, and charity—in him a firm and consistent supporter of one of their fundamental principles, that all wars are unjust, impolitic, and unchristian : in him they have lost one, who was ever calling them to use their utmost efforts to ameliorate the condition of the distressed, whether Indian, African, or Briton. Mr. Reynolds embraced with ardour the hope that our penal statutes would become less sanguinary—and that capital punishments would be removed from our code. When the citizens of his native place had determined upon building a new gaol, Mr. R. was peculiarly solicitous that the improvements upon the plans of a Howard, in Munich, America and other countries, might be concentered in Bristol. He wished for the moral and religious improvement of those who had violated the laws of their country ; and considered it incumbent to apply kindness, instruction and the motives of industry, to recal the offender to the paths of integrity. To trace the more public acts of this philanthropist would occupy the whole of the pages of a periodical publication : but to enumerate his private exertions to comfort the widow, to help the fatherless, to raise the desponding, to encourage the industrious and to reward the deserving, would require a volume, and even then the language of the queen of Sheba, when she had witnessed the wisdom of Solomon, might be employed, " Not half hath been told me." He now rests from his labours, but his works shall follow him.

The closing scenes of his life were in unison with his former conduct. In the spring of this year he began to decline. He was advised in August to try the waters of Cheltenham. This was done evidently to satisfy his friends. He did not expect to recover from the attack, but was perfectly resigned to what Divine mercy should ordain. He continued from the 7th of August to the 6th of September with little variation. During his illness he was exceedingly placid and kind to every one: his conduct and countenance indicating that all within was peace. A short time before his death, when an endeared female friend had been administering to him some religious consolation, he said, ' My faith and hope are, as they have long been, on the mercy of God, through Jesus Christ, who was the propitiation for my sins, and not for mine only, but for the sins of the whole world.' He closed his earthly career at Cheltenham, Sept. the 10th, in the 81st year of his age. His children, grand children, and many beloved friends were present when this great man in Israel fell.

Is it wonderful that the news of his death excited general regret in Bristol and its neighbourhood? Is it surprising that the melancholy event created a gloom from the peasant's cot to the extensive mansion? Is it singular that a chasm should be contemplated when he was removed who for many years had bestowed upwards of £10,000 per annum in relieving the distress of others? Was it not to be expected that men of all classes and of all opinions should unite to request to shew the last sad tribute of respect, by following to the grave the remains of one who had practised pure and undefiled religion, who had employed self-denial that he might bestow liberally on others, who refused the indulgences of affluence that he might lessen the miseries of his brethren; who ordered his household with economy that he might give to him that was in want—who had cherished a zeal for godliness free from bigotry, and in exercising the right of private judgment himself, had still an ardent affection for those from whom he differed? No contrasted view of Divine mercy dwelt in his soul; and whilst he considered himself a debtor to the Jew and to the Greek, to the bond and to the free, he embraced all men with affection who strove to preserve the unity of the faith in the

bonds of peace and righteousness of life.

Such was Richard Reynolds. His corpse was followed to the grave by deputations from the several charities in Bristol, to which he belonged. The Committee of the Bible Society took the precedence, and was in close train with the long string of weeping relatives. It was composed of aldermen, clergymen, and dissenting ministers of all denominations. The greatest decorum was observed, though the crowd of spectators surpassed calculation. In the Square in which the deceased had resided, the children of the several charity-schools to which he had been a generous patron, were arranged. The shops were shut in the streets through which the procession passed, and the toll of bells from several churches announced, that one was carried to the grave, who bore with him the affections of the living. On the Sunday following, funeral sermons were preached at most of the places of worship in Bristol and its neighbourhood. But the respect of survivors did not terminate with these marks of their regard. A public meeting was convened at the Guildhall, on October the 3d, at which the mayor presided, to consider of the most effectual method of supplying the great loss the city of Bristol had sustained, and of perpetuating the memory of Mr. Reynolds. On that occasion it was unanimously resolved to form a new society, called *Reynolds's Commemoration Society*, to keep up his subscriptions to the charities in Bristol to which he was a public contributor, and especially to cherish and strengthen the *Samaritan*, of which he was the founder. At the public meeting, various proofs were adduced of the distinguished excellence of the deceased, by the Rev. T. Biddulph, the Rev. W. Thorpe, the Rev. W. Day, the Rev. Mr. Simeon, of Cambridge, and the Rev. M. Maurice. At the same time, appropriate addresses were delivered by R. H. Davis, Esq. M.P. H. Davis, Esq. M. P. J. Butterworth, Esq. M.P. the Sheriffs of Bristol, Alderman Birch, Dr. Pole, Dr. Stock and Counsellor Smith, by whom the business was ably introduced and forcibly recommended.

May the mantle of Elijah fall on his descendants! May the chasm that has been made be filled up by the efforts of many! May the spirit of benevolence which actuated a Reynolds, dwell with those who are associated to supply his place! Then will it be for good to others as well as for himself, that he has rested from his labours. May the seed that he has sown hear a rich harvest of love and good works: and whilst his name is held in everlasting remembrance, may his bliss hereafter be augmented by an union with those who have here trod in his steps! May his admirers be his imitators, and their desire like him be to ascribe unto God the praise for every blessing they enjoy!

M. M.

INTELLIGENCE.

DOMESTIC.

RELIGIOUS.

Plan of a Fund by the Unitarian Church, Edinburgh, for obtaining a more commodious Place of Worship.

It is proposed to constitute a Fund, which shall have for its object the Erection of a small, neat, and commodious Church, in some respectable situation in this City, for conducting Divine Worship on Unitarian principles.

On the necessity for such a building, it is almost needless to enlarge. It must be obvious to every one, that the present place of worship labours under great disadvantages, as to situation, outward appearance, and internal accommodation, which operate to a considerable extent in deterring strangers from entering it, and detract very much from the comfort of the congregation. But it may be proper to observe, that although any resources which can at present be calculated upon, must be quite inadequate, we are not therefore to suppose the object in view undeserving of *present attention.* This very circumstance calls for immediate consideration of the subject; for it is only by an accumulation of our present small resources, that we can calculate upon the accomplishment of so desirable an object with any certainty. It is therefore further proposed, that the Fund should be established by Annual Subscriptions, and incidental Donations, to be lodged in a Bank for accumulation, until the purpose above mentioned shall be attained.

Let every one who would feel himself called upon to contribute to the Erection of a Church, were such an intention to be immediately carried into effect, determine the sum he would give, and divide it into five, six, or seven instalments, according as his own opinion of the time which may be required shall direct him: and, at the end of five, six, or seven years, it is not surely altogether vain to expect that this Society may find themselves in possession of a sum, which, though not, perhaps, quite adequate, will enable them to commence the operation, and to borrow a few hundred pounds, upon the security of the building, to enable them to complete it: which debt, in the course of a few years thereafter, will be easily paid off upon the same plan.

P. S. Subscriptions in favour of this object, will be received by T. S. Smith, M. D. Yeovil, Somersetshire; the Rev. John Evans, Islington; and the Rev. R. Aspland, Hackney Road.

A Course of Sunday Evening Lectures, which will be Delivered at the Unitarian Chapel, St. Thomas's Street, Southwark; Commencing Nov. 3rd, 1816.

Service to begin at Half past Six o'Clock precisely.

(FIRST COURSE.)

*Nov. 3.—Rev. R. Aspland.—*Reproach for the Name of Christ the Christian's Glory.

*Nov. 10.—Rev. W. J. Fox.—*The Rise and Prevalence of Christ's Deity traced and accounted for.

*Nov. 17.—Rev. J. Gilchrist.—*The Doctrine of Hereditary Depravity.

*Nov. 24.—Rev. W. J. Fox.—*The Sacrifice of Christ.

*Dec. 1.—Rev. T. Rees.—*Our Lord's Agony in the Garden.

*Dec. 8.—Rev. R. Aspland.—*The Faith which the New Testament represents as necessary to Salvation.

*Dec. 15.—Rev. J. Gilchrist.—*The Mediation of Christ.

*Dec. 22.—Rev. T. Rees.—*The Scriptural Idea of Christ's coming into the World.

*Dec. 29.—Rev. R. Aspland.—*Reflections on the Close of the Year.

The List of Preachers and Subjects for the remaining Portion of the Winter, will be delivered before the Conclusion of the present Course.

The Treasurer will attend in the Vestry every Evening after Service, to receive the Subscriptions of those who may be disposed to contribute to the Support of these Lectures.

A Course of Thursday Evening Lectures, which will be Delivered at the Meeting-House, in Worship Street, near Finsbury Square: Commencing Thursday November 7th, 1816.

Service to begin at Half-past Six o'Clock precisely.

(FIRST SERIES.)

Nov. 7th. Rev. W. J. Fox. The Practical Influence of a Belief in the Unity of God.

Nov. 14th. ————— Practical Importance of the Difference between Calvinism and Unitarianism.

Nov. 21st. ————— On Religious Feeling.

Nov. 28th. ————— The Final Happiness of all Men predicted in Scripture.

Dec. 5th. Rev. R. Aspland. The Loveliness of the Divine Character on the Unitarian Scheme.

Dec. 12th. Rev. T. Rees. The Titles and Offices of Christ consistent with his Humanity.

Dec. 19th. Rev. J. Gilchrist. The Doctrine of the Atonement.

Dec. 26th. Rev. R. Aspland. The Importance of the Birth of Christ on the Unitarian Scheme.

Before the expiration of the year, the Conductors of the Lecture design, with the Divine Blessing, to publish a List of Subjects for the remainder of the Course.

The Treasurer will attend in the Vestry every Evening after Service, to receive the Subscriptions of those who may be disposed to contribute to the Support of these Lectures.

———

Unitarian Fund Lectures, in the Presbyterian Meeting-House, Hanover-Street, Long Acre.

Lectures will be carried on in the above Place of Worship on the Sunday and Tuesday Evenings, during the Winter Season, 1816—17, to commence on Sunday Evening, Nov. 10.

Service to begin each Evening at Half-past Six o'Clock.

Sunday, Nov. 10.—Rev. R. Aspland.— The Unity of God the Plain, Invariable Testimony of Divine Revelation.

Tuesday, Nov. 12.—Rev. W. J. Fox.— Glorying in the Cross of Christ.

Sunday, Nov. 17. ————— Christianity Corrupted by False Philosophy.

Tuesday, Nov. 19. ————— Scripture Doctrine of the Holy Spirit.

Sunday, Nov. 24.—Rev. T. Rees.— God the Father the only Object of Religious Worship.

VOL. XI.

Tuesday, Nov. 26.—Rev. W. J. Fox.— Christ's Temptation.

N. B. Lists of the Preachers and Subjects for the First Course terminating with the year 1816, will be issued in a few days, and may be had at Worship Street and St. Thomas's, on the Evenings of Service at those Places.

———

Lancashire Presbyterian Quarterly Meeting.

SIR,

The last Quarterly Meeting of Ministers, generally denominated Presbyterian, was held at Chewbent, on the 2d instant. The Rev. Mr. Ashton conducted the devotional parts of the service, and the Rev. Mr. Brettell preached from Matt. vi. 9, a very useful and acceptable discourse on the paternal character of God. The extreme wetness of the day precluded the attendance of all distant friends, and must have considerably lessened the attendance at the chapel, which, nevertheless, was not inconsiderable. Between twenty and thirty persons dined together after the service, and spent the afternoon in a manner not unworthy of the occasion; and in the evening the greater part of the company retired to the hospitable mansion of a valuable member of the congregation, and a steady friend to the interests of religious truth and liberty. On some occasions, the attendance at the chapel has disappointed the expectation of the members of the Quarterly Meeting, but at Chewbent, the reporter can say with great truth, that they are always gratified with beholding a numerous and devout congregation of Christian worshippers. W. J.

Manchester, Oct. 14, 1816.

———

Mr. Saint on the Chapel at Southampton.

SIR,

I have long been expecting to see, through the medium of your valuable Miscellany, a statement of the sums raised by different congregations, in aid of the Unitarian cause at Southampton. From what I have heard within the last few weeks, I fear indisposition is the cause of the delay. I sincerely hope that Mr. B. Travers, or one of his friends, who are in possession of the documents, will for the satisfaction of those persons who have subscribed, lay an early statement before the public, through the medium of the Monthly Repository. I am the more earnest in this request, because I am myself in some small degree connected in the collections made in behalf of that interest, (though at the time I was so engaged, I was not fully aware of the tenure by which the Chapel was held,) which induced me to decline accepting the invitation given me by the people at Southampton to become their minister. If I could have

4 L

seen a prospect of the Society raising the *rent*, and other expences, I would have given my services gratis for twelve months with pleasure : but finding that even this was not in the power of the Society to perform, I thought it advisable to leave the affair in the hands of those who were its first projectors, and have accepted an invitation from the small Society of Unitarians in this place, where I hope to be the means under Providence, of raising this drooping Society to its former health and vigour.

However we may fail in the object of our wishes, or however unfortunate we may be in our speculations, it is a duty which we owe to our friends, and to ourselves, to lay a statement of all monies collected, and to express our thanks to those persons who have assisted us.

I sincerely hope, notwithstanding the situation of the Chapel at Southampton, arrangements will be made by our Unitarian friends in the South, to keep up Unitarian worship in that town. I trust that this Southampton speculation will not fail of answering some useful purpose, that of leading those who profess a rational religion, to exercise reason in building their places of public worship.

Your giving this a place in the next Number of your valuable Repository, will much oblige   Your Constant Reader,

                C. N. SAINT.

Alcester, Warwickshire, Oct. 14, 1816.

Oldbury Double Lecture.

On Tuesday September 10th, 1816, was the Anniversary of the Double Lecture, at Oldbury, in Shropshire. The Rev. John Kentish, of Birmingham, conducted the devotional service : the Rev. John Corrie, of Handsworth, and the Rev. Thomas Bowen, of Walsall, preached—the former on Matt. xiii. 24—30.—*The parable of the tares in the field* *—the latter on 2 Cor. iv. 13.—" We also believe, and therefore speak."

---

* May the reporter be excused if he here expresses his high admiration of the acuteness with which Archdeacon Blackburne has availed himself of this parable, in his Remarks on Johnson's Life of Milton.

The Doctor, speaking of Milton's Areopagitica, says, " From the danger of such unbounded liberty [of unlicensed printing,] and the danger of bounding it, have produced a problem in the science of government, which *human understanding* seems unable to solve."

Let us then have recourse to a *Divine understanding* for the solution of it. *Let both the tares and the wheat grow together till the harvest, lest, while ye gather up the tares, ye root up also the wheat with them.* Remarks, page 59.

Mr Corrie introduced his discourse with observing that the parable teaches a lesson of forbearance, of forbearance even to those who will hereafter receive from the all-seeing and unerring Judge, the just punishment their crimes have merited. And this forbearance, we should remember, may be shown not merely by the magistrate or his tribunal, but by every individual in the formation of his own opinions, and the guidance of his own conduct—in that kind, feeling and that proneness to support or to relieve, which attaches to those whose characters we respect and love, and which should never be withdrawn except in cases in which it is morally impossible to confound the innocent with the guilty.

This interpretation of the parable harmonizes with the whole tenor of the gospel, with all that is recorded of our Saviour's conduct and all that is preserved of his discourses. " And here," said Mr. Corrie, " I think we may justly feel surprised that any who have professed themselves to be the disciples of Christ should have preached or practised persecution.

Viewing the subject, moreover, as we do, in all the light that has been poured upon it by powerful and sagacious writers, we must be allowed to feel still more surprised that mankind should have been so slow to learn that the most perfect toleration in religion is not more the doctrine of the gospel than the dictate of the soundest human policy.

And our surprise is still augmented, when we consider what those offences have been which have provoked the rod of the persecutor, and could be expiated only by the severest punishment : for those offences have been differences of opinion in the interpretation of what is, in some respects, a most obscure volume, and upon subjects which it confessedly exceeds the most vigorous grasp of the human faculties perfectly to comprehend, and all the powers of human language adequately to express. Yet there is scarcely an exposition of those mysterious doctrines that might not have been written in the blood of some virtuous and learned martyr who has died in its defence.

The eloquent preacher then proceeded to recommend unlimited toleration in religion, on the following grounds :

I. From the nature of the subjects which have generally been made the occasions of persecution—the doctrines of the Trinity, of the atonement, and of original sin—doctrines confessed, on all hands, to be very abstruse and far removed from the apprehension of the mind.

II. From the nature of the evidence to which all must alike appeal in support of their opinions. Under this head, Mr. Corrie pointed out the difficulties attendant on a critical examination of the Scriptures.

III. From the doctrines which are usually the occasion of persecution having, as Mr. Corrie conceives, little or no connection either theoretically or in fact with the proper discharge of the duties of life or with the formation of the character. Granting, said he, that their doctrines are the doctrines of Scripture, will any one contend that they are held forth to our belief as matters of the first importance, that they are revealed as clearly as the great principles of Christian morality, or the awful declaration of the resurrection of the dead, and a future eternal state of retribution?

The principles which bear immediately on the conduct of mankind are the moral principles: and the sanction which gives all their peculiar efficacy to religious principles, is the doctrine of a future state. For, what moral principle can be more forcibly impressed upon the heart, on the Trinitarian, than on the Unitarian system?—To what height of Christian perfection can the one aspire, which the other may not humbly hope is attainable by him? On reading a treatise of Christian morality, who can decide from its contexts, what articles formed its author's creed? In sketching a picture of Christian perfection, where is the church in which we may not find a model? He surely has not read much of Christian history and has not seen much of Christian sects, who has not found among the votaries of the most discordant creeds, much of all that most adorns the Christian character: and who would not be filled with a holy transport, could he hope that in his final doom, his soul might be with some whom he could name, whose creed is much more ample or much more scanty than his own. If the Trinitarian errs, he errs with almost all the learning and almost all the virtue which have ever graced the Christian world:—if the Unitarian errs, his errors have been sanctified by the learning of a Lardner, by the saintly virtues of a Lindsey, by the talents of a Newton, a Locke, a Priestley.

Mr. Bowen's discourse breathed throughout a pleasing spirit of piety and kindness. He earnestly recommended the union of diligence in the investigation of Divine truth with manly courage and unwearied zeal in its defence.

Fourteen ministers were present, viz. Messrs. Guy, Kell, and Kentish, of Birmingham; Small, of Coseley; Scott, of Cradley; Bransby, of Dudley; James Yates, lately of Glasgow; Currie, of Handsworth; Fry, of Kidderminster; Lloyd, of Kingswood; Davis, of Oldbury; Bowen, of Walsall; Steward, of Wolverhampton; and Benjamin Carpenter, Jun. of Wymondley Academy.

The Rev. Robert Kell and the Rev. James Scott were appointed to preach on the next Anniversary.   J. H. B.

Irish Presbyterian Association.

SIR,

During a late visit to Cork, I was invited to attend a meeting of Christians held on the 16th of July, at Bandon. The object of the association was to form a friendly and religious union between the Presbyterian congregations of Cork and Bandon. It was the first meeting ever held in the South of Ireland, with such professed sentiments and prospects. I sincerely trust it will prove a foundation on which pure, rational religion will erect her standard for ages yet to come. The congregation was numerous and highly reputable. The public service was opened by the Rev. James Armstrong, of Dublin, in the most impressive manner, by reading and prayer; after which the Rev. William Hincks, of Cork, (colleague with the venerable Mr. Hort) preached from the words of Paul to the Corinthians, "To us there is but one God the Father, of whom are all things and we in him; and one Lord Jesus Christ, by whom are all things and we by him." The sermon was highly interesting throughout, and delivered in the spirit of Christian meekness united with firmness of principle. The chief design the preacher had in view, was to affirm and prove the *Unity of God* as satisfactorily declared in the Old and New Testaments; that Jesus Christ was a distinct being from the Father, deriving all his authority and powers from him; that all the blessings of the gospel proceeded from the *unpurchased grace* of God the Father; and that Jesus Christ was the messenger by and through whom the Divine mercy was made known to the children of mankind.

After establishing in a masterly manner the above important points, he insisted not only on the *believing*, but on the *propriety and utility of publicly declaring* our religious sentiments: herein his arguments are reasonable, strong and conclusive. He remarked, with great judgment, the more simple any religious system is, the easier will be its truths established and believed; while on the contrary, the more irrational and mysterious, the greater must be the difficulties to prove the Divine origin. Many other observations were made, exceedingly interesting and important; a spirit of Christian candour, moderation and charity is diffused throughout the discourse, towards those Christians who think differently, so that bigotry form no part.

After the close of the public service, several friends met together belonging to each congregation, and after dinner a string of resolutions were entered into with a view to promote the religious interests of each society, by the establishment of half yearly meetings to be alternately held at Cork and Bandon. Mr. Hincks was requested by the company present to print his sermon, to which he kindly consented.; and Mr. Armstrong was invited to preach the next sermon at Cork, to which he replied, that if circumstances suited his convenience, he would cheerfully comply with the wishes of his friends.

I cannot help congratulating the friends of rational religion on the commencement of so auspicious an event, when the power of ancient prejudices and blind superstition too much prevail.   .E. C.

Birmingham, Aug. 26, 1816.

MISCELLANEOUS..

Prosecution of a Methodist Preacher.

. At the General Quarter Sessions, holden at Wisbeach, on the 17th of July instant, a singular, and, happily, from the liberal temper of the times, a novel appeal came before the magistrates for their determination; in which Robert Newstead, a preacher, in the Methodist connexion, was appellant, and the Rev. Algernon Peyton, Rector of Doddington, and Thomas Orton, Esq. two of his Majesty's Justices for the Isle of Ely, were respondents. It appeared from the conviction, and the evidence adduced in support of it, that the offence with which Mr. Newstead stood charged was, the collecting together a congregation or assembly of persons and preaching to them, otherwise than according to the liturgy and practice of the Church of England, in a field which had not been licensed. This was Mr. Newstead's *crime:* it was for this, that the Reverend Rector of Doddington, caused his fellow-labourer in the work of reformation to be apprehended; and that he and his brother Magistrates convicted him in the *utmost* penalty which the Toleration Act imposes ! Against the legality of this conviction Mr. Newstead appealed. After several objections had been taken to the form of the conviction, by Mr. Newstead's Counsel, and which were over-ruled by the Court, Richard Vince, servant to Mr. Peyton, proved that he heard Mr. Newstead preach in a field at Doddington, on Sunday the 7th of April last; that he preached contrary to the Liturgy of the Church of England; and that there were more than twenty persons present. On his cross-examination, he admitted that he did not know what it was he preached, whether it were a prayer or a sermon; it was something, but he knew not what; and that he knew he preached contrary to the Liturgy of the Church of England *only* be-

cause he had not the Prayer-book in his hand ! J. Lane, another of Mr. Peyton's servants, corroborated the testimony of the last witness, but he would not swear that there were twenty persons present.—Mr. Bevill, Counsel for Mr. Newstead, submitted to the Court, that the prosecutors had not made out their case. The Toleration Act requires that the *place* where any congregation or assembly shall meet, at which there shall be present more than twenty persons, *besides the family and, servants* of the person in whose house such meeting shall be held, shall be certified and registered. In order, therefore, he contended, to render a religious meeting unlawful, according to the provision, of this act, there must be present twenty persons, of a *particular description*—of a *certain class,* twenty, *exclusive* of the family and servants of the owner or occupier of the place of meeting; but for aught the Court knew from the testimony of the witnesses,, (one of whom could *not* swear that there were twenty persons present,) the congregation might be chiefly composed of the family of the owner of the field. He further contended, that a *field* is not a place which required registration : the term "*place*" of meeting is used throughout the Act : and, in the 11th section, that term is explained, and defined to be,. a place with *doors,* bolts, bars, and locks. As therefore it did not appear, in evidence that there were twenty persons present of the particular class required by the Act, and as a *building,* and not a field, was contemplated by the legislature,, he contended that the conviction was unlawful, and must be quashed.—The magistrates, however, confirmed it; and hence Mr. Newstead became liable to the penalty of thirty pounds, or to three months' imprisonment. A case was demanded on the part of Mr. Newstead, for the opinion of the Court of King's Bench ; but the prosecutors having proposed to abandon the prosecution, and engaged not to enforce the penalties, the friends of Mr. Newstead withdrew their application, having obtained all they could desire. . The question of right, however, between the Rector and the preacher remains undecided. The writer of this article is assured, that Mr. Newstead, conscious of the purity of his intentions, and feeling the firmest conviction that no human authority had a *right* to interfere in matters purely religious, that penal laws cannot be thrust between man and his Maker, without a violation of the inalienable rights of conscience and of private judgment, was prepared to submit with cheerfulness to the consequences of his actions ; and that he envied not the Reverend Rector the possession of those feelings and motives, which could induce him to instigate and carry on this prosecution. No one can differ more widely in his religious sentiments than the writer from both Mr. Peyton and Mr. Newstead; but God forbid that he should use against them any weapons but those of reason and persuasion. He did hope that the temper of the times had shamed them out of Persecution and Intolerance; and he is reluctant even now to give up the hope that these monsters sleep never to wake again.—*Stamford News.*

: *Society for Converting the Jews.*

. Four Dutch Jew merchants and two other persons of the same persuasion in this country, named Solomons and Abrahams; attended at the Mansion House at the instance of another Dutchman, who stated that he belonged to the Society for the Conversion of the Jews: he stated his name to be Mechtz, that he had but recently arrived from Holland, and had become a Christian. On his arrival, he had introductions to several Jews, and among others Mr. Solomons, in the neighbourhood of Soho Square. This gentleman took him into a private room and lectured him on the impiety of his embracing the Christian faith, of which he (Mr. Solomons) spoke in the most blasphemous language. Some days afterwards, witness was invited to dine at a house in Duke's place, with some Dutch Jews: he went there, but instead of a good dinner, was assaulted by the persons present, and he at length escaped in the greatest terror of his life. This conduct he attributed to the fact of his having ceased to be a Jew. In opposition to this statement, Mr. Solomons represented, that the complainant had been in great distress in Holland, that several of the Jewish merchants clothed him, and sent him to England,

with recommendations to persons to further his interests. On his arrival, however, he went to the Society for the Conversion of the Jews, and tendered himself as disposed to abandon the religion in which he was educated. He was in consequence adopted a member of that Society, and received some assistance. Some days afterwards, he called on him, and told him he had something to inform him of, which he thought of importance to poor Jews: he then described the encouragement which the Society were disposed to give to any who were willing to become Christians,—to this he added the enumeration of the names of several persons who had pretended to become Christians, but who were Jews at heart, and who had got ample sums from the Society; he for one, he said, had taken the same course, and although he hated the Christian religion, should make the most of the Society. Understanding that it was the intention of some of his (Mr. Solomons') friends to do something for this man, he had felt it his duty to inform them of the principles he had avowed; he accordingly wrote him a letter, in consequence of which, when the complainant made his appearance, he was turned out of the house. The Lord Mayor said he had himself contributed to the Society alluded to, and very much feared his money had produced very little good; he had reason to believe that many designing persons had imposed upon the Society merely for fraudulent purposes. Whether the story now told was correct or not, he could not say; but at all events he could only recommend the injured party to prefer an indictment against the persons by whom he stated himself to have been so ill treated.

Public Ledger, August 19, 1816.

MONTHLY RETROSPECT of PUBLIC AFFAIRS;
OR,
The Christian's Survey of the Political World.

THE last month was distinguished by a remarkable occurrence in the Metropolis, the re-election of the Lord Mayor to the office which he has for the last year supported with so much honour to himself, and advantage to the city. Perhaps there never was an instance in which all parties concurred so completely with respect to the character of the person who was thus highly honoured; for though firm in his political principles, and those principles were in opposition to what had had the ascendancy for many years, yet in every instance all parties had reason to be satisfied with him; and for zeal, activity and integrity he has not been surpassed by

any who before him filled the magisterial chair. The Common Hall, alive to his merits, displayed by the shew of hands a very commanding majority in his favour; yet the Alderman who was next in rotation thought it right to demand a poll, and thus gave the opportunity to the friends of his Lordship to come forward, and prove by a very great majority how high he stood in the estimation of his fellow-citizens. By the constitution of the city, the members of the Common Hall present two candidates to the Court of Aldermen to elect one, and in this case though the latter did not feel exactly like the Common Hall, and the ideas of rotation might have an impression on their minds, yet his Lordship was returned by them as the new Lord Mayor elect, and was to the satisfaction of every one, who is gratified at the honours bestowed on real merit, and sensible of the benefits of his administration, invested with a second chain.

The idea of rotation, or that every Alderman should in his turn be Lord Mayor, is of weight with those who do not rightly consider the nature of election, and who are guided by precedent rather than reason. If rotation is allowed, then what need is there of a Common Hall to fix upon two candidates for the office? The two next to the chair might be presented to the Aldermen, and the first returned without any form of meeting. But this would be taking away from the freemen their right of choice; and as the Aldermen are not elected by the whole body, but each separately by his own ward, it would be giving to each ward the right of appointment in succession, to the highest office of the city. If, therefore, a ward from certain causes should elect an improper person in the opinion of the other wards, yet the right of setting him aside is destroyed by this pretended right of rotation.

Again, when a person has distinguished himself by every thing valuable in the character of a magistrate, as in the case of the present Lord Mayor, and the re-election of him might be highly advantageous to the city by the completion of the plans which he had formed in his first mayoralty, yet according to the strange notion of rotation, the city is to be deprived of the benefit of his services, because forsooth the next person conceived that it was his next turn to fill the office, and he must be forced upon the city, though perhaps the consequence would be the paralysing of all the efforts of his predecessor. In fact it is necessary to mention only these few circumstances to shew the absurdity of the notion of rotation, which may be a tolerably good rule not to be broken into, except on such occasions as presented themselves at the last election.

But the re-election of the Lord Mayor is of consequence in other respects, as it manifests the declining influence of those persons who had for many years exercised a very great sway in the metropolis. The person next in rotation was a very decided advocate for the line of politics maintained by that party, and every nerve was strained to promote his election. Yet with every degree of exertion on the one side, and on the other every thing being left to the spontaneous movements of the electors, the rotation candidate could not obtain nearly half as many votes as his Lordship. Indeed the principles of that party being

now thoroughly understood, and the advantages of adhering to it being very much diminished, its zealous advocates are becoming less active, and so many have suffered from its prevalence, that no new adherents are to be expected in the rising generation.

The above remarks on the pretensions of rotation may be applied to many other similar cases, where people are inclined to give up the use of their reason, and to be guided by mere precedent; to be slaves to paper documents instead of listening to the dictates of common sense; being servants of the letter, not of the spirit. This is no common case, but it is hoped that few of the readers of this survey are led away by such notions. They will examine for themselves, and act upon higher principles, reflecting that, even in the votes they may be called upon to give, there is a duty which they owe to themselves and their country, not to be frittered away by paltry considerations.

The account of several parts of the country has been melancholy from tumults, that have arisen from the depressed state of the manufactures, particularly those of iron. They have been quieted by the interference of the civil power, which prevents indeed the injuries that misguided men may do to themselves and their employers, but still their situation is a call upon the benevolence of others, which happily in this country will not be denied. To add to this distress a very extraordinary wet season has been highly injurious to the harvest, and the ports will soon be opened to our relief, which, from the Corn Bill, so injudiciously passed two years ago, have been shut. Thus, to add to our distresses, the bread has been made dearer, and with all the supplies to be expected from abroad, it is not likely that it should be lowered during the approaching winter. It is our duty to submit with resignation to this dispensation of Providence; and every one high or low, must endeavour to alleviate as much as possible the calamity.

Meetings have been held in several parts of the country, to take into consideration those distresses, and in most of them resolutions have been passed containing very severe animadversions on the state of the House of Commons, and the representation of the country. The facts, authorized in the House of Commons itself, and no where contradicted, of the imperfection in the representation, the corruption attending the election of representatives, and the places and pensions held by the members, are particularly dwelt upon; and as the abuses are now universally known and felt, it is to be hoped that the remedy of them will no longer be delayed. The House of Commons is indeed by no means what it is represented in theory. Three circumstances have principally led to. the change in the nature of that body.

The first is the innovation introduced in the reign of Henry the Eighth, of governing by sessions of parliament, instead of parliaments called for the business of the nation, and dissolved as soon as that business was performed. Before that time, two parliaments have been held in a year; after the innovation was made, a lengthened term was thought more convenient, and by that very improper bill now called the septennial act, parliaments are familiarly looked upon as for seven years duration, and the price of seats in the House is adjusted upon that principle.

The second circumstance is the allowance of placemen and pensioners to sit in the House : the consequence of which is, that in certain questions the votes of members may be determined by their situation, not by the propriety of the measure. This is an evil, intended to be guarded against by our ancestors ; and now, when a member takes a place under government, a new election must be made for his town, borough, county, but the placeman by being re-elected, returns to his seat, and thus it is in the power of the proprietor of a borough to frustrate the intentions of the bill, by which placemen were excluded.

The third circumstance is, that many boroughs have through course of time greatly. decayed, but the right of election remaining in them, they become the property of a few individuals. Thus London is represented by four members, but certain individuals in the country have twice that number placed in the House by their influence, and expected to vote according to the inclination of their principal.

Whilst these abuses prevail it is improper to say that the Commons in England are represented in parliament, or that the original institution is preserved ; and it is not to be wondered at that in the legal and constitutional meetings of the country such abuses are inveighed against. But though every friend of his country would gladly see these abuses destroyed, yet we must not be so sanguine in our expectations as to expect that the reform of parliament would be the panacea for all our evils. Indeed had the people been fairly represented in the House of Commons, no such measure as the late very injurious bill the Corn Bill could have passed, a measure as injurious to the land owners interest, which it was intended to protect, as it has been hurtful to the manufacturing and commercial interests, which it has nearly ruined. But still if the government of a country depends more on the people, the . more requisite it is,, that that people should.be well instructed and virtuous. Let the reformers then promote virtuous education and right principles, and then a House of Commons, the free objects of their choice, will be found capable of framing good laws for the public welfare.

France is exhibiting to the world a specimen of representative government. All the accounts, if they may be depended upon, manifest how little sensible that nation is of the value of such a government, how incapable they are of acting up to the principles of enlightened patriotism. If in our country there are men so desperately wicked as to use the name of government in the election of a member of parliament, still they have not the audacity to commit their crimes in the face of day. It is done privately and secretly. Their menaces or their bribes are conveyed with a certain degree of decorum, a tacit confession, that they are traitors to their country, in abusing their offices, and betraying even the government they pretend to support. But in France it is said, that the name of the king is publicly made use of, and persons are designated as being agreeable or disagreeable to him, who ought not in any way whatever to interfere in the choice of the people.

The result of the elections is said to be favourable to the ministers ; that is the Ultra-royalists will not have the ascendancy in their new that they had in the last parliament. This will be a happy thing for France, as that wretched country may have a chance for something like government, if it has got rid of the ignorant and prejudiced men, who would have restored all the iniquity of bigotry, by which the Bourbon administration, particularly under the reign of Louis XIV. had been distinguished. One circumstance is favourable to their country : these Ultra-royalists, who were the first to destroy the liberty of the press, now feel the effects of their own base measures, and begin to find out the benefits of its freedom. The police too, whose arbitrary sway they admired, whilst they themselves governed its secret springs, has been a great curb to them ; and in fact they are compelled now to acknowledge, that something must be done for the public as well as themselves. The debates therefore of the new legislative body will be interesting.

The King of Holland has opened his parliament at Brussels by a speech from the throne, in which he laments the increase in the price of provisions from the unfavourable weather that has prevailed on the Continent ; speaks. of measures to be introduced favouring industry, commerce and works of public utility, of some statement of expenditure and income, of changes of territory with Prussia, of the formation of a militia and a complete statement of expenditure and income to be laid before them. . This parliament promises to be engaged in acts beneficial to their country, though their tariff of duties lately published shews them to be as blind as their neighbours to the advantages of a free intercourse between nations, which unfortunately in all of them are cramped by financial considerations.

The King of Wirtemburg is still quarrelling with his subjects, who seem resolutely employed in placing such checks on his authority, as are not suited to the old system of the petty German Princes. It is probable however, that the congress for the whole empire may take up some of these questions, and prevent the petty sovereigns from being too despotic in their dominions. The movements of that congress will be very interesting, but it is not likely that it will engender any thing like the Holy Roman Empire, which has been happily for the country so completely destroyed. The Prussians are still looking anxiously for their new constitution. The Emperor of Russia is said to have promised to abstain from any interference in German politics. This monarch has made a tour through great part of his European dominions, and has every where, particularly at Moscow, been received with the enthusiasm which his virtues excite. Poland under his dominion will be much happier than with its former aristocrats,

who wished no one to enjoy liberty but themselves.

The Dey of Algiers is employed in repairing his broken walls, but he will be long before he provokes again a similar chastisement. The event has however produced a very extraordinary letter, if the papers have not been deceived, and palmed a fiction on the public, from Lord Exmouth to his pretended Holiness the Pope. Little would our ancestors have expected, that a peer of parliament should salute such a character with the title of Holy Father, and much less to request his prayers. This is one of the symptoms of the decay of the ancient Protestant spirit, and makes it more incumbent upon us to set our children upon their guard against the delusive influence of the times.

The American accounts are favourable to the successes of the old Spaniards over their opponents in the countries bordering on the Gulph of Mexico, but still the agitation remains and it will not easily be quelled. The King of Spain has published upon his marriage a general pardon, but with so many exceptions, that the patriots of that country are not likely to be benefited by it. They are so much behind the rest of the world in knowledge and information, that it is in vain to expect there a speedy overthrow to despotism, priestcraft and the inquisition.

NEW PUBLICATIONS IN THEOLOGY AND GENERAL LITERATURE.

Useful Knowledge; or, A Familiar and Explanatory Account of the Various Productions of Nature, Mineral, Vegetable and Animal, which are chiefly employed for the Use of Man. Illustrated with Figures. By the Rev. William Bingley, A. M. 3 vols. 12mo. 1*l.* 1s.

The Life of William Hutton, F. A. S. S. including a Particular Account of the Riots at Birmingham in 1791. To which is subjoined the History of his Family, written by Himself and published by his Daughter, Cath. Hutton. 8vo. portrait, 12s.

Baptism.

(See pp. 308 and 436.)

An Answer to the Question, Why are you a Strict Baptist? A Dialogue between Thomas and John. By William Hutton. 2s. 6d.

A Plea for Primitive Communion, occasioned by the Rev. R. Hall's recent Publication, by George Pritchard, of London. 1s. 6d.

The Decision of a General Congress convened to agree on "Terms of Communion," occasioned by the Rev. R. Hall's Pamphlet. By Christmas Evans, of Anglesey. 4d.

Ivimey's History of the English Baptists. 2 Vols. 8vo. 1*l.* 5s. boards.

A Candid Statement of the Reasons which induce the Baptists to differ in Opinion and Practice from so many of their Christian Brethren. By J. Ryland, D. D. 2s. 6d.

The System of the Baptists Exposed, in a Letter to a Friend. By one of their own Ministers. 3d.

CORRESPONDENCE.

We are sorry that we are not at liberty to report from Mr. Belsham any other answer to the inquiry of D. D. p. 471, than that the *Commentary upon the Epistles of Paul*, which is the subject of that inquiry, is not yet in a state of preparation for the press.

ERRATA.

XI. p. 479. col. 2, four lines from the bottom, dele the comma after "party."

—— 480. col. 2. line twelve from the top, place an inverted comma after *Scriptures.*

THE

𝕸𝖔𝖓𝖙𝖍𝖑𝖞 𝕽𝖊𝖕𝖔𝖘𝖎𝖙𝖔𝖗𝖞,

&c.

| No. CXXXI.] | NOVEMBER, 1816. | [Vol. XI. |

HISTORY AND BIOGRAPHY.

Estimate of the Philosophical Character of Hobbes. *

[From Dissertation I. by Dugald Stewart, prefixed to Supplement to Encyclopædia Britannica, Vol. I. p. 59—65.]

THE rapid advancement of intellectual cultivation in England, between the years 1588 and 1640 (a period of almost uninterrupted peace), has been remarked by Mr. Fox. "The general improvement," he observes, "in all arts of civil life, and above all, the astonishing progress of literature, are the most striking among the general features of that period; and are in themselves causes sufficient to produce effects of the utmost importance. A country whose language was enriched by the works of Hooker, Raleigh, and Bacon, could not but experience a sensible change in its manners, and in its style of thinking; and even to speak the same language in which Spencer and Shakespeare had written, seemed a sufficient plea to rescue the Commons of England from the appellation of *brutes*, with which Henry the Eighth had addressed them."—The remark is equally just and refined. It is by the mediation of an improving language, that the progress of the mind is chiefly continued from one generation to another; and that the acquirements of the enlightened few are insensibly imparted to the many. Whatever tends to diminish the ambiguities of speech, or to fix, with more logical precision, the import of general terms;—above all, whatever tends to embody, in popular forms of expression, the ideas and feelings of the wise and good, augments the natural powers of the human understanding, and enables the succeeding race to start from a higher ground than was occupied by their fathers. The remark applies with

peculiar force to the study of the mind itself; a study, where the chief source of error is the imperfection of words; and where every improvement on this great instrument of thought may be justly regarded in the light of a discovery.[†]

In the foregoing list of illustrious names, Mr. Fox has, with much propriety, connected those of Bacon and Raleigh; two men, who, notwithstanding the diversity of their professional pursuits, and the strong contrast of their characters, exhibit, nevertheless, in their capacity of authors, some striking features of resemblance. Both of them owed to the force of their own minds, their emancipation from the fetters of the schools; both were eminently distinguished above their contemporaries, by the originality and enlargement of their philosophical views; and both divide, with the venerable Hooker, the glory of exemplifying to their yet unpolished

† It is not so foreign as may at first be supposed to the object of this Discourse, to take notice here of the extraordinary demand for books on *Agriculture* under the government of James I. The fact is thus very strongly stated by Dr. Johnson, in his Introduction to the Harleian Miscellany. "It deserves to be remarked, because it is not generally known, that the treatises on husbandry and agriculture, which were published during the reign of King James, are so numerous, that it can scarcely be imagined by whom they were written, or to whom they were sold." Nothing can illustrate more strongly the effects of a pacific system of policy, in encouraging a general taste for reading, as well as an active spirit of national improvement. At all times, and in every country, the extensive sale of *books on agriculture*, may be regarded as one of the most pleasing symptoms of mental cultivation in the great body of a people.

* Born 1588, died 1679.

countrymen, the richness, variety, and grace, which might be lent to the English idiom, by the hand of a master.*

It is not improbable that Mr. Fox might have included the name of Hobbes in the same enumeration, had he not been prevented by an aversion to his slavish principles of government, and by his general disrelish for metaphysical theories. As a writer, Hobbes unquestionably ranks high among the older English classics; and is so peculiarly distinguished by the simplicity and ease of his manner that one would naturally have expected from Mr. Fox's characteristical taste, that he would have relished *his* style still more than that of Bacon†

---

* To prevent being misunderstood, it is necessary for me to add, that I do not speak of the *general style* of these old authors; but only of detached passages, which may be selected from all of them, as earnests or first fruits of a new and brighter era in English literature. It may be safely affirmed, that in *their* works, and in the prose compositions of Milton, rare to be found some of the finest sentences of which our language has yet to boast. To propose them *now* as models for imitation, would be quite absurd. Dr. Lowth certainly went much too far when he said, "That in *correctness*, *propriety* and *purity* of English style, Hooker hath hardly been surpassed, or even equalled, by any of his successors." *Preface to Lowth's English Grammar.*

† According to Dr. Burnet (no contemptible judge of style), Bacon was " the first that *writ* our language correctly." The same learned prelate pronounces Bacon to be " *still* our best author;" and *this*, at a time, when the works of Sprat, and many of the prose compositions of Cowley and of Dryden, were already in the hands of the public. It is difficult to conceive on what grounds Burnet proceeded, in hazarding so extraordinary an opinion. See the Preface to Burnet's Translation of More's *Utopia.*

It is still more difficult, on the other hand, to account for the following very bold decision of Mr. Hume. I transcribe it from an Essay first published in 1742; but the same passage is to be found in the last edition of his Works, corrected by himself. " The first polite prose we have, was *writ* by a man (Dr. Swift) who is still alive. As to Sprat, Locke, and even Temple, they knew too little of the rules of art to be esteemed elegant writers.

---

or of Raleigh.—It is with the *philosophical* merits, however, of Hobbes, that we are alone concerned at present; and, in this point of view, what a space is filled in the subsequent history of our domestic literature, by his own works, and by those of his innumerable opponents! Little else, indeed, but the systems which he published, and the controversies which they provoked, occurs, during the interval between Bacon and Locke, to mark the progress of English Philosophy, either in the study of the Mind, or in the kindred researches of Ethical and Political Science.

" The philosopher of Malmesbury," says Dr Warburton," was the terror of the last age, as Tindall and Collins are of this. The press sweat with controversy; and every young churchman militant would try his arms in thundering on Hobbes's steel cap."* Nor was the opposition to Hobbes confined to the clerical order, or to the controversialists of his own times. The most eminent moralists and politicians of the eighteenth century may be ranked in the number of his antagonists, and even at the present moment, scarcely does there appear a new publication on Ethics or Jurisprudence, where a refutation of Hobbism is not to be found.

The period when Hobbes began his literary career, as well as the principal incidents of his life, were, in a singular degree, favourable to a mind like his; impatient of the yoke of authority, and ambitious to attract attention, if not by solid and useful discoveries, at least by an ingenious defence of paradoxical tenets. After a residence of five years at Oxford, and a very extensive tour through France and Italy, he had the good

---

The prose of Bacon, Harrington, and Milton, is altogether stiff and pedantic, though their sense be excellent."

How insignificant are the petty grammatical improvements proposed by Swift, when compared with the inexhaustible riches imparted to the English tongue by the writers of the seventeenth century; and how inferior, in all the higher qualities and graces of style, are his prose compositions, to those of his immediate predecessors, Dryden, Pope, and Addison!

* *Divine Legation*, Pref. to Vol. II. p. 9.

fortune, upon his return to England, to be admitted into the intimacy and confidence of Lord Bacon; a circumstance which, we may presume, contributed not a little to encourage that bold spirit of inquiry, and that aversion to scholastic learning, which characterize his writings. Happy, if he had, at the same time, imbibed some portion of that love of truth and zeal for the advancement of knowledge, which seem to have been Bacon's ruling passions! But such was the obstinacy of his temper, and his overweening self-conceit, that, instead of co-operating with Bacon in the execution of his magnificent design, he resolved to rear, on a foundation exclusively his own, a complete structure both of moral and physical science; disdaining to avail himself even ot the materials collected by his predecessors, and treating the *experimentarian* philosophers as objects only of contempt and ridicule!

In the *political* writings of Hobbes, we may perceive the influence also of other motives. From his earliest years, he seems to have been decidedly hostile to all the forms of popular government; and it is said to have been with the design of impressing his countrymen with a just sense of the disorders incident to democratical establishments, that he published, in 1618, an English translation of Thucydides. In these opinions he was, more and more confirmed by the events he afterwards witnessed in England; the fatal consequences of which he early foresaw with so much alarm, that, in 1640, he withdrew from the approaching storm, to enjoy the society of his philosophical friends at Paris. It was here he wrote his book *De Cive*, a few copies of which were printed, and privately circulated in 1642. The same work was afterwards given to the public, with material corrections and improvements, in 1647, when the author's attachment to the royal cause being strengthened by his personal connexion with the exiled king, he thought it incumbent on him to stand forth avowedly as an advocate for those principles which he had long professed. The great object of this performance was to strengthen the hands of sovereigns against the rising spirit of democracy, by arming them with the weapons of a new philosophy.

The fundamental doctrines inculcated in the political works of Hobbes, are contained in the following propositions. All men are by nature equal; and, prior to government, they had all an equal right to enjoy the good things of this world. Man, too, is (according to Hobbes) by nature a solitary and purely selfish animal; the social union being entirely an interested league, suggested by prudential views of personal advantage. The necessary consequence is, that a state of nature must be a state of perpetual warfare, in which no individual has any other means of safety than his own strength or ingenuity; and in which there is no room for regular industry, because no secure enjoyment of its fruits. In confirmation of this view of the origin of society, Hobbes appeals to facts falling daily within the circle of our own experience. "Does not a man (he asks) when taking a journey, arm himself and seek to go well accompanied? When going to sleep, does he not lock his doors? Nay, even in his own house, does he not lock his chests? Does he not *there* as much accuse mankind by his actions, as I do by my words?"* An additional argument to the same purpose may, according to some later Hobbists, be derived from the instinctive aversion of infants for strangers; and from the apprehension which (it is alleged) every person feels, when he hears the tread of an unknown foot in the dark.

For the sake of peace and security, it is necessary that each individual should surrender a part of his natural right, and be contented with such a share of liberty as he is willing to allow to others; or, to use Hobbes's own language; "every man must divest himself of the right he has to all things by nature; the right of all men to all things being in effect no better than if no man had a right to any thing."† In consequence of this transference of natural rights to an individual, or to a body of individuals, the multitude become one person, under the name of a State or Republic, by which person the common will and power are exercised for the common defence. The ruling power

---

* *Of Man*, Part I. chap. xiii.

† *De Corpore Politico*, Part I. chap. i. § 10.

cannot be withdrawn from those to whom it has been committed; nor can they be punished for misgovernment. The interpretation of the laws is to be sought, not from the comments of philosophers, but from the authority of the ruler; otherwise society would every moment be in danger of resolving itself into the discordant elements of which it was at first composed. The will of the magistrate, therefore, is to be regarded as the ultimate standard of right and wrong, and his voice to be listened to by every citizen as the voice of conscience.

Not many years afterwards,[*] Hobbes pushed the argument for the absolute power of princes still further, in a work to which he gave the name of *Leviathan.* Under this appellation he means the *body politic*; insinuating, that man is an untameable beast of prey, and that government is the strong chain by which he is kept from mischief. The fundamental principles here maintained are the same as in the book *De Cive*; but as it inveighs more particularly against *ecclesiastical* tyranny, with the view of subjecting the consciences of men to the civil authority, it lost the author the favour of some powerful protectors he had hitherto enjoyed among the English divines who attended Charles II. in France; and he even found it convenient to quit that kingdom, and to return to England, where Cromwell (to whose government his political tenets were *now* as favourable as they were meant to be to the royal claims) suffered him to remain unmolested. The same circumstances operated to his disadvantage after the Restoration, and obliged the king, who always retained for him a very strong attachment, to confer his marks of favour on him with the utmost reserve and circumspection.

The details which I have entered into, with respect to the history of Hobbes's political writings, will be found, by those who may peruse them, to throw much light on the author's reasonings. Indeed, it is only by thus considering them in their connexion with the circumstances of the times, and the fortunes of the writer, that a just notion can be formed of their spirit and tendency.

[*] In 1651.

The ethical principles of Hobbes are so completely interwoven with his political system, that all which has been said of the one may be applied to the other. It is very remarkable, that Descartes should have thought so highly of the former, as to pronounce Hobbes to be " a much greater master of morality than of metaphysics;" a judgment which is of itself sufficient to mark the very low state of ethical science in France about the middle of the seventeenth century. Mr. Addison, on the other hand, gives a decided preference (among all the books written by Hobbes) to his *Treatise on Human Nature*; and to *his* opinion on this point I most implicitly subscribe; including, however, in the same commendation, some of his other philosophical Essays on similar topics. They are the only part of his works which it is possible now to read with any interest; and they every where evince in their author, even when he thinks most unsoundly himself, that power of setting his reader a thinking, which is one of the most unequivocal marks of original genius. They have plainly been studied with the utmost care both by Locke and Hume. To the former they have suggested some of his most important observations on the Association of Ideas, as well as much of the sophistry displayed in the first book of his Essay on the Origin of our Knowledge, and on the factitious nature of our moral principles; to the latter (among a variety of hints of less consequence), his theory concerning the nature of those established connexions among physical events, which it is the business of the natural philosopher to ascertain,[†] and the

[†] The same doctrine, concerning the proper object of natural philosophy (commonly ascribed to Mr. Hume, both by his followers and by his opponents), is to be found in various writers contemporary with Hobbes. It is stated with uncommon precision and clearness, in a book entitled *Scepsis Scientifica,* or Confessed Ignorance the way to Science; by Joseph Glanvill (printed in 1665). The whole work is strongly marked with the features of an acute, an original, and (in matters of science) a somewhat sceptical genius; and, when compared with the treatise on witchcraft, by the same author, adds another proof to those already mentioned, of the possible union of the highest intel-

substance of his argument against the scholastic doctrine of general conceptions. It is from the works of Hobbes, too, that our later Necessitarians have borrowed the most formidable of those weapons with which they have combated the doctrine of moral liberty; and from the same source has been derived the leading idea which runs through the philological materialism of Mr. Horne Tooke. It is probable, indeed, that this last author borrowed it, at second hand, from a hint in Locke's Essay; but it is repeatedly stated by Hobbes, in the most explicit and confident terms. Of this idea, (than which, in point of fact, nothing can be imagined more puerile and unsound,) Mr. Tooke's etymologies, when he applies them to the solution of metaphysical questions, are little more than an ingenious expansion, adapted and levelled to the comprehension of the multitude.

The speculations of Hobbes, however, concerning the theory of the understanding, do not seem to have been nearly so much attended to during his own life, as some of his other doctrines, which, having a more immediate reference to human affairs, were better adapted to the unsettled and revolutionary spirit of the times. It is by these doctrines, chiefly, that his name has since become so memorable in the annals of modern literature; and although they now derive their whole interest from the extraordinary combination they exhibit of acuteness and subtlety with a dead palsy in the powers of taste and of moral sensibility, yet they will be found, on an attentive examination, to have had a far more extensive influence on the subsequent history both of political and of ethical science, than any other publication of the same period.

lectual gifts with the most degrading intellectual weaknesses.

With respect to the *Scepsis Scientifica*, it deserves to be noticed, that the doctrine maintained in it concerning *physical* causes and effects does not occur in the form of a detached observation, of the value of which the author might not have been fully aware, but is the very basis of the general argument running through all his discussions.

A remarkable Example of God's Providence, visible during a Journey of Christopher Crellius. Copied (Amsterdam, 1774,) from MS. Papers of Samuel Crellius, and now Translated from a Dutch Copy. The Original Letter was written in Latin.

[Communicated to the Editor by Mr. Van der Kemp, of the United States of America.]

SAMUEL CRELLIUS wishes happiness to H. V. O.

I WILL, to gratify your desire, communicate to you in writing the remarkable event, which you listened to with pleasure. When my father, Christopher Crellius, with other Unitarians was driven from Poland in the year 1666, he became acquainted in London with a pious woman, who was instructed by John Biddle and was called Stuckey, the mother of Nathaniel Stuckey, a youth of bright hope, and mentioned by Sandius, in his Biblioth. Antitrin. page 172, but who, very prematurely, and if I am not mistaken, died in the sixteenth year of his age. This woman spoke to my father in this manner—" You, my dear Crellius! wander now as an exile, in poverty—a widower—burthened with four children; give me two of these, a son and a daughter, in England, and I will take care of their education." My father thanked her cordially, and promised to consider it: when returned to Silesia he consulted his friends on the subject, and departed with his eldest son and daughter in the year 1665 from Breslau, through Poland, towards Dantzic, to embark from there to Holland, and so to England. This voyage to Dantzic my father undertook with his own waggon and horses. His driver was the pious Paul Sagosky, from whom I heard an account of the event in Brandenburg, Prussia, in the year 1704, when he was far advanced in age.

It was afternoon, the sun declining to the west, when my father, only twelve Polish miles from Dantzic reached a tavern, in which he resolved to tarry that night, because he saw before him a large wood, which he could not pass through by day light, and he deemed it unadvisable to enter it towards night, uncertain if he should find another house, and, moreover, was not well acquainted with the road. They stopped then at the tavern, and brought the waggon into a large stable, and fastened the horses to the manger. The landlady, her husband being from home, received them with civility. She gave orders to take the baggage from the waggon and bring it into the inner room, where she invited my father with the children to the table. Meanwhile the driver, when he had fed the horses, explored the spacious stable, not forgetting to scrutinize with careful anxiety every corner, because the taverns in Poland, at such a distance from cities and villages as this was, are seldom a safe refuge for travellers, and there is always apprehension of robbers and murderers. In this search he discovered in one corner of the stable a large heap of straw, of which he moved a part with a stick, when he perceived that this straw covered a large hole which emitted an offensive smell, while the straw was tainted with blood. On this he directly returned to the inner room, mentioned to my father in secret what he had seen, and saying that he doubted not that the landlord was a robber and murderer. My father left the room directly, and, having verified the fact, ordered directly to bring the baggage again on the waggon, and harness the horses.

When the landlady observed these preparations, she shewed her surprise, and dissuaded my father to proceed on his journey through such a large wood in a cold night, with two young children, and engaged that she would endeavour to render his stay as comfortable as it was in her power; but he replied, that something very interesting had struck his mind, which rendered it impossible for him to remain there, and compelled him to proceed on. He thanked her for her civilities, went with his children into the waggon, and departed.

When they were arrived in the wood, they met the landlord driving home a load of wood, who accosted my father, "Sir," said he, "I beg of you, what moves you to enter this wood, so large and extensive, and cut in two or three cross roads, in the fall of the evening, at the approach of night; I doubt not, that you will lose the right road, and remain in the wood during night: you endanger your health and place that of these

young children in jeopardy; return, rather with me to my tavern, there you may refresh yourself and your horses, spend the night comfortably, and continue your journey early in the morning. My father answered, that he was obliged to proceed on his journey, however unpleasant it was. The landlord urged his entreaties with greater importunity, and approaching my father's waggon, and taking hold of it, he renewed to dissuade a further process with a lowered brow and a grim countenance, and insisted that they should, and must return; on which my father ordered the driver to lay his whip over the horses, to disengage himself from this dangerous man, in which he succeeded.

They then proceeded on. My father, sitting in the waggon, sent up his prayers in an audible voice to his God, as was his usual custom on his travels, and recommended himself and those dear to him in this perilous situation to his providential care, in which devotion he was accompanied by the driver and his two children. Meanwhile the sun was set, an increasing darkness prevailed, they lost the road, entered a deep swamp, in which soon the waggon stuck, the horses being too fatigued to draw it out again. My father and the driver jumped from the waggon in the mud, strengthened every nerve, and animated the horses with words, and the whip, but all in vain; the waggon could not be stirred one single inch. My father became apprehensive that he must pass the night in that dreary spot, and that he or his driver should be compelled to leave the wood next morning, and search for assistance in the nearest village, without even a prospect of success; meanwhile nothing was left him but silent ejaculations to his God.

After having covered his children as well as he could, and secured them against a rigorous cold night; he walked to a little distance from his waggon, and employed himself in sending up his prayers to his God, when he saw a man of small stature, in a grey or whitish coat, with a stick in his hand, approaching him. After mutual salutations, this man asked my father what he did there, and why he travelled in the night, and especially through such a wood? My ather explained then to him the whole, and begged him to assist him and his Iriver, to try once more if with his assistance they might draw the waggon and horses from the mire of that swamp, and bring them into the right road. I will try, said he, if I can effect something; upon which he approached the waggon, and placed his stick under the fore wheels, and appeared to lift these a little; the same he did to the back wheels, and then put his hand to the waggon, to draw it with my father and the driver, out of the mire. He called at the same instant to the horses, who, without any appearing difficulty, left the swamp and drew the waggon upon solid ground. After this the stranger conducted them into the right road, from which they had wandered, and told them to keep how that road, and neither deviate from it to the right or left, and when, said he, thou shalt arrive at the end of this wood, you will 'discover at some distance a light in one of the nearest houses of the village, which you must pass. In that house lives a pious man, who, although it is so late, will receive you civilly and give you lodgings for the night. My father cordially thanked this man for his assistance and instruction, and, while he had turned his face from him to put his hand in his pocket and offer him some money, he had disappeared. My father looking towards him again saw nobody; he looked all around him, and even searched awhile for him, but could not find him again: then he called with a loud voice, where art thou, my friend! return, I pray you, towards me, I have yet something to say to you; but he received no answer, neither saw his deliverer again. Surprised and astonished, he waited yet a long while, ascended his waggon, and thanked God for this favour. They arrived in safety through the wood, and saw the light in that house, of which the stranger had spoken. My father knocked softly at the window, upon which the master of the house opened it, and looked out to see who there was. My father asked if he could give him lodgings? He replied by asking how

they came so late, and why they proceeded on their journey after midnight, not far from daybreak? My father developed the reason in few words, and was then amicably received. When at table my father gave him a more circumstantial account, and asked him if he ever had seen or known such a man, as he who conducted him to the right road in the wood, and of whose countenance and clothes he gave him a description: he answered, that he knew not such a man, but that he knew very well that the tavern at the other side of the wood was no safe place for travellers. After awhile, he looked accidentally to one of the corners of the room, not far from the table, where he saw some books on a bench. Taking one of these and looking into it, he saw it was a book of a Polish Unitarian. This curiosity alarmed the master of the house; but as soon as my father perceived this, he said to him, keep good courage, friend! I shall not bring you into any difficulty for that book, neither inform against you for heresy; and to give you more confidence in this assurance, I must tell you that I too am an Unitarian. Then he told him his name, which by fame was known to his landlord, who now full of joy was delighted to receive such a guest in his house. My father adored the ways of God's Providence, in bringing him to this place. This man was a linen-weaver, who, when the Unitarians were banished from Poland, remained here for several years hidden through the favour of a nobleman, the lord of his village, and liberal-minded in religion. He would not permit my father to start next day, but persuaded him to tarry with him a few days more, and treated my father, with his children and the driver and horses, very hospitably.

There are more examples of a particular providence in regard to the Polish Unitarians, of which I lately told you some; and it would be a desirable thing, if all these had been directly recorded by those who could bear witness to them. Farewell.

Amsterdam, Aug. 1730.

MISCELLANEOUS COMMUNICATIONS.

Some Observations on the Sermons of Missionaries. Translated from the Spanish of P. Feyjoo, *a Monk and Public Writer to the King of Spain, in the last Century.*

[Translated and Communicated by a Lady, S. E. D.]

FRIEND AND SIR,

I RECEIVED your letter of the 4th of November, which I perused with singular pleasure, as in it you express an inclination to employ that portion of your time usefully, which being exempted from the duties of your profession is at your own disposal, and cannot be better employed than by continuing the sacred ministry of preaching in the neighbouring towns in the manner of a missionary. On this subject you tell me you not only hope for my approbation, but likewise that I would impart any particular observations which may occur to me on this topic, to render the employment more beneficial.

To this I answer, that in regard to my approbation there can be no doubt, when the thing proposed is such as demands from the most indifferent not merely acquiescence but applause. I assure you if I had been endowed with necessary talents for preaching, when the king granted me an exemption from the service of the cathedral, I should in some measure have devoted myself to this ministry, alternately with that of public writer, an occupation in which I was already engaged; and in all probability my health would have been benefited by some bodily exercise being mixed with the inevitably sedentary employment of writing: however I wanted the two indispensable qualifications for missionary labours, virtue and strength of lungs, or, in other words, neither soul nor body allowed my undertaking the office of a preacher. With respect to virtue even in an exemplary degree, I know I might have acquired it, my free will co-operating with the aid of divine grace; but weakness of chest was incurable, being constitutional, and a defect I have suffered from even in my earliest years.

As to the observations you desire me to make, what can I say that you have not already anticipated? But as I have for a long time remarked certain inconveniences which result from the discourses of particular preachers, owing to the vehemence of their zeal to correct vice, though otherwise discreet and learned men, I shall offer two reflections to your consideration on those inconveniences and their cause.

First, I have observed that in the sermons of missionaries, it frequently happens that the preacher becomes heated by exaggerating the mischief occasioned by some one particular vice to the souls of his auditors: I repeat, it is very common to magnify much beyond its real extent the prevalence of this vice amongst the inhabitants of the town where he preaches. This is highly reprehensible, and, far from conducing to reformation, tends to increase the general corruption. I will explain my position. The diseases of the soul are not less contagious than those of the body; they are even more so. It is only some particular species of bodily sicknesses that are infectious, but every malady of the soul (all moral vices) may be communicated. Two circumstances must concur to render a distemper contagious, a transmission of the breath of the sick person and a previous disposition to the disorder in the receiver. When an epidemic disease rages in any town, all the inhabitants are not affected, either because the morbid exhalations from the sufferers do not extend to all those in health, or because there is not a disposition in every constitution to imbibe that kind of contagion. Now for the application of this theory. The maladies of the soul transfuse or communicate their malignant influence by being known: while they are concealed they only injure the heart that engenders them, but when they are published, their noxious vapours form an atmosphere more or less extended according to the degree of publicity, sometimes reaching to a large town, sometimes to a whole province; and within this sphere their baleful influence is felt by every individual in the least disposed to inhale the poison: in short, on all whose ruling passion inclines them to the vice thus published.

But to explain the thing in simple and natural terms, throwing aside metaphors and allusions, I will make the moral mechanism (if I may be allowed the expression) of what passes in this matter appear clearly.

Men reciprocally inspire each other with decency: those especially who are eminently modest, possess great influence over others. The man who lives in the society of persons whom he believes to be virtuous, is checked by this consideration, and restrained from indulging any passion that may lead him to the commission of a particular fault; because he is aware his shame would be in proportion to the scarcity of bad examples to keep him in countenance. Let us suppose the case that by some means this man discovers the persons whom he thought virtuous are in reality vicious characters, that they have yielded to the temptations which assault him, what will be the consequence? He will more easily give way to his irregular propensities, not only through the direct incentive of bad example, but also by the removal of the restraint which the supposed virtue of his companions and neighbours had hitherto imposed on his mind. From hence it is plain how much harm may be produced by proclaiming the prevalence of any particular vice in a town or district. However, may not this abuse of the pulpit be a mere imagination of my own, raised for the sake of combating it? Would to God it existed only in my fancy! I have received but too certain information of its reality, and sometimes I have witnessed it myself. I once heard a preacher of no small eminence declaim in his discourse against a particular vice, which although frequently very mischievous, was not more prevalent in the town where he preached, than in any other place of equal size:—however, his mind inflamed with zeal represented the evil of such magnitude, that he exclaimed all the inhabitants were guilty without exception, raising his voice to its utmost pitch, and repeating *all, all,* that he might leave no doubt of the universality of the inculpation. Was not the effect on his congregation such as I have stated, answerable to the enthusiasm of the orator? In general, whatever multiplies delinquents in opinion, in reality multiplies crimes.

There exists another abuse very nearly allied to the former, which, by being more common, is, perhaps, still more pernicious:—many preachers in sermons they call moral (and all ought to be of this description), frequently introduce invectives against the sex, insisting on the fragility of women, not reflecting that this encourages vicious men in their criminal enterprises. To exaggerate the weakness of one party is to strengthen the audacity of the other, and augments the evil on both sides; since while the confidence of men is increased, women are furnished with an excuse for their failings. Would it not be more adviseable to reprove the aggressors, than inveigh against their victims? I have written elsewhere what I repeat here, *That whoever would render all women, or nearly all women chaste, must begin by reforming all men.*

The second remark I have to offer on missionary sermons, is, that they call on men to repent through dread of the Divine justice, but rarely or very slightly excite them to love God on account of his infinite goodness. I allow that God is not only supremely benevolent and merciful, but likewise rigorously terrible and just, but with this difference, he is good from the excellence of his nature, he is terrible on account of our wickedness. I likewise allow that the fear of God is holy; I allow there are circumstances in which it is proper to give particular weight to motives derived from terror; I allow God ought to be feared as well as loved: there is no doubt in all this;—but the question is, whether fear or love is the strongest incentive to obedience, and which of the two is most agreeable to our Creator. On this point I shall call in the great authority of St. Bernard to decide. "God," says he, Sermon 83, "exacts from his rational creature, that it should fear him as a master, honour him as a father, and love him as a husband. Now which of these three species of tribute is most pleasing to him? which most suitable, which most worthy? Without doubt it must be that of love." He pursues this subject through the whole discourse, extolling in the most beautiful language the great superiority of love over fear, both as to its pleasing God and being useful to ourselves.

The divine St. Francis de Sales goes

still further (Practice of the Love of God, Book II. Chap. 8): he says—" Love is the universal means of our salvation, which mingles with every thing, and without which nothing is salutary." This is to assert that love is the universal remedy for all the diseases of the soul; it is the liquid gold that the alchymist sought in vain to cure bodily infirmities. Christ, our Redeemer, when he came into the world, drew it from heaven to heal all those of a spiritual nature: before his coming, the prophets, who were the preachers under the ancient law, denounced threats and terrors; but when Jesus appeared, the tone of preaching changed, passing as we may say from the warlike Phrygian to the soft Ionian measure, wooing with the most affectionate sweetness of the lyre, those who were before intimidated by the martial sound of the trumpet. The Gospel no where resounds with the formidable titles of God strong and terrible, God of vengeance, Lord of hosts, or God of armies, which in the Old Testament made the nations tremble; on the contrary, in our Saviour's discourses, he very frequently calls God our Father. He is mentioned fifteen times in a sermon that is contained in the 5th, 6th and 7th chapters of St. Matthew, and always under this denomination, either simply your Father, or with the addition your heavenly Father, so that he calls on us to fulfil our duties not as servants through fear, but as sons through love.

St. Paul as well as Jesus represents God as the beneficent, the universal Father of mankind. He generally begins his Epistles, which are really so many missionary sermons, with this salutation full of benevolence and kindness—" *Gratia vobis, et pax a Deo Patre nostro et Domino Jesu Christo:*" nor does he omit this kind introduction even to the Galatians, who deserved the severest rebukes for their declared propensity to apostatize from Christianity to Judaism, which they had before abandoned.

Thus spake St. Paul because Christ had thus spoken. Christ was the promulgator of the law of grace and St. Paul a learned interpreter of that law; he who most deeply penetrated its spirit, as opposed to the spirit of the ancient law. In what does this difference consist? One is a law of servitude, the other a law of liberty. In the first God treated men as his servants, in the latter he regards them as children: in one he rules them by motives of fear, in the other by motives of love. This is precisely what the Apostle writes to the Romans (chap. 8.) intimating that those who embraced the Gospel should no longer be subject to the timid spirit of bondage, but should be governed by sentiments of love suitable to the children of adoption. (" *Non enim accepistis spiritum servitutis iterum in timore, sed accepistis spiritum adoptionis filiorum, in qua clamamus abba Pater.*")

Having now strongly inculcated the propriety of leading men to virtue by motives of love rather than those of fear, an opinion founded on the most venerable authority; it is easy to enforce it by considerations of the greater utility of this method, motives to obedience derived from love being more agreeable to the goodness of God, and more conformable to the nature of rational creatures. The submission of a servant which springs from fear, is very different homage from the willing tribute of affection: the servant obeys reluctantly, the son with delight; one follows his inclinations, the other struggles against difficulty; one is allured by the beauty of the object, the other cannot advance a single step without subduing himself; one finds road if not entirely smooth, at least with but few inequalities, the other in every passion encounters a fresh impediment.

You must clearly perceive by what I have said of fear, as opposed to love— I mean *servile dread*; for filial fear is not only compatible with love, but may be regarded as a disposition conducive to it. The dependence of a slave on his master differs widely from the dependence of a child on his father: the slave dreads the scourge, the child only fears to give offence. The Lord is terrible to the slave, but the father is venerable to the child; the slave suffers chastisement as an act of vengeance, the child receives it as intended for his good; the slave regards it as the effect of stern dominion, the child as means employed for his improvement in virtue.

I think I have sufficiently proved by what has been said, that a preacher ought to avail himself of motives drawn from love, preferably to those that spring from fear. But one excellence still remains to be mentioned, which gives infinite advantage to the former; it consists in this, that love ennobles every good work that proceeds from this generous sentiment, and renders it much more pleasing to God than any thing which is the offspring of fear, inasmuch as when love has attained that perfection, which we denote by the term *charity*, it becomes deserving of that ineffable felicity, the duration of which no time can limit, and that surpasses in greatness all the human mind can conceive. To this happiness neither obedience to the commandments of God, nor freedom from sin, can ever raise us, if we are merely influenced by fear: it is the reward of love alone.

But supposing eternal felicity were doubtful, would not the certainty that God loves us, oblige us in return to love him with all our powers? Men love each other, and run the risk of meeting with reciprocal affection. Examples of this are innumerable: we meet with them in every page of history. Here we read of a man who, at the expense of his fortune, relieves his friend from want, and is afterwards reduced to the same situation, without receiving the smallest assistance. In another place we find a veteran who, after shedding his blood in defence of his country, is repaid by total neglect. Again, a third person divests himself of his offices and employments to confer them on his friend, and raise his consequence on the ruins of his own.

Let us revert to what passes between the sexes in this matter, and gives rise to such endless complaints; though I must remark that if the affection be criminal, the ingratitude is well deserved: each party accuses the other of perfidy, and what is worse, the accusation being true on both sides, the warning is of use to neither. How differently does God behave towards us! That he loves all those who love him, is a proposition of eternal truth—a sentence he himself has pronounced by the mouth of Solomon, " *Ego diligentes me diligo*," (Prov. viii.) : and it is repeated in the Gospel of St. John, chap. xiv. What honour! what happiness! Among mortals, he who loves the best cannot be sure of a return, even when the claims of gratitude are superadded to the strongest titles; for how often does it happen, that the man who receives a favour turns his back on his benefactor, the subject abandons the prince, the prince the subject, the son forsakes his father or the father neglects his son.

[*To be concluded in the next No.*]

Notes for the Monthly Repository, by Mr. Fr. Adr. Vander Kemp.

Oldenbarneveld, S. of New York,
July 1, 1816.

Mon. Repos. V. 49..

I DO not hesitate in the least to declare that note in the Eclectic Review without any truth. I am persuaded I must have heard of the fact, if it were as it is asserted. Venema, who wrote against Crellius, and respected him, La Croze, who loved him, and was his constant correspondent, and bewailed his errors, as is evident from their correspondence, never suspected it. Till his death Crellius was a member and a patron of the collegiants at Amsterdam, who were generally Unitarians. He went to their place of meeting with his sister every Sabbath day, when they were the *only* remaining members, and she proposed to serve their God at home, which he declined, full in hope of a revival, and he lived till he did see the congregation again increased to seventy. This I have been often told by respectable members of that congregation, who at *that* time could not suspect that Crellius's religious opinions would stand in need of their evidence. I know all this is negative proof. I shall therefore copy you the opinion of Bockius, whose orthodoxy as a Trinitarian was, as far as I know, never doubted. He says, in the *Nova Litteraria*, Hamburg. 1747, p. 703, " there is a story that Crellius repented of his errors towards the close of his life, and gave clear proofs of unfeigned penitence." This Paul-Berger, Archdeacon of Harmspruck, thinks not improbable (see the same Work, 1748, p. 345,) because, while he was residing at Amsterdam, Crellius in the year 1731 informed him that in consequence of conferences with the celebrated Schaaf, his belief of some opinions had been shaken, so that he was in doubt concerning them.

But in the same Work for 1749,

pp. 92 and 480, we are assured that Crellius to the last moments of his life remained an Unitarian. This, also, his brother Paul has repeatedly declared to me. Stosch, in his History of the Eighteenth Century, which Jablonski has made the third volume of his Ecclesiastical History, page 424, says, " I remember that Crellius, when I visited him at Amsterdam, in 1742, and we conversed much on various doctrines of Christianity, declared to me with some warmth that he did not adopt the system of Socinus, but rather with his whole heart believed the doctrine of the satisfaction of Jesus Christ, in the sense in which it is taught by the Remonstrants, and that he was persuaded that through Jesus Christ all men would at some time be saved and delivered from the pains of hell." He added, " that he was certain that there were now to be found few or no Socinians, properly so called." In Strodman's *Europ. Litter.* tom. i. p. 280, Crellius himself thus writes, " I have at all times as well among the Unitarians as the Remonstrants, taught the expiatory sacrifice of Christ, and my instructions have not been contradicted." Fred. Sam. Bock. Hist. Antitrin. Lips. 1774. tom i. pt. i. pp. 167, 168.

Stosch, mentioned above by Bock, likewise says, " it seems to me to be asserted without good reason, that Crellius renounced his errors before his death." Stosch was a Trinitarian as well as Bock. His book is a college book, used in the Dutch Academies as a text book in ecclesiastical history.

I ought, perhaps, to notice, that Samuel Crellius, referred to in what precedes, is not to be confounded with his great uncle, the famous John Crellius, who was one of the Fratres Poloni.

His works are mentioned by Bockius.

Gen. Repos. and Rev. Vol. IV. pp. 387—389. Cambridge, 1813.

Mon. Repos. No. LIII. *Vol. V. April,*
1810.—*Stricture on J. Crellius by*
a French Writer, justified.

Ephes. v. vs. ult. Quia maritus punire etiam potest inobedientem et immorigeram. Omnis potestas præcipiendi (suo inquam nomine non alieno) potestatem etiam habet, aliquam saltem, puniendi.

Page 430. *Coloss.* iii. 19. Non pro hibetur autem ab Apostolo, nec cha ritati maritali in uxores adversatur moderata admodum et prudens, a emendationem salutemque uxorun comparata castigatio, sive verbis e perficiatur, quæ omnium est brevissima et maxime licita, sive factis aliquibus ad quod castigationis genus tarde ad modum et lente, et non nisi summe cum consilio accedendum est, nec ie leves ob causas, sed ob gravissima demum suscipiendum.

Ethicæ Christ. cap. xii. p. 429 *Jo. Crellii* Op. Bibl. Frat. Pol. tom iii.

———

Add. to p. 11, of Socinus's Life, by
J. Toulmin.—*Socinus visiting Grea*
Britain.

Przipcovii Op. in fol. p. 419. Eleu theropoli, 1692.

———

Sir,　　　*Wisbeach, Oct.* 14, 1816.

I BELIEVE it is very generall understood that field-preaching i illegal; and, until a recent prosecu tion under the Toleration Act, (se p. 624,) which rendered a new an more close examination of the subjec necessary, I had been accustomed t consider the law so established. Tha examination raised considerable doub in my mind; and although the magi trates in that case decided that field is a " place of meeting" withi the contemplation of the legislature and therefore requiring registratior I was very far from being satisfie with their decision, and subsequer consideration has convinced me it w: wrong.

The prosecution to which I hav alluded arose at Doddington, in th Isle of Ely, and was instituted by th Reverend *Algernon Peyton*, Rector that village, against Mr. *Robert Net stead*, a preacher in the Methodist co nexion, who early in the spring the present year thrust himself in th Rector's estimation, into his paris and preached in the open fields part of his flock. The Reverend Re tor deeming this a very serious ar unpardonable offence, in the plei tude of his zeal to put down sectaris and support mother-church, convict Mr. Newstead, with the assistance a brother magistrate, in the *full* nalty which the Toleration Act i poses. Mr. Newstead appealed to t last General Quarter Sessions, at W beach, where, as his friends had expected, the conviction was confirmed. It was the intention of Mr. Newstead's friends to remove the conviction into the Court of King's Bench; but the Rector perceiving their determination, and being very well disposed to get out of a business which was likely to become more troublesome to him than at first he seemed to apprehend, proposed that if they would desist from carrying the projected measure into effect, he would not enforce the payment of the fine, but would suffer the prosecution to rest. This proposition was acceded to; and such, Sir, is, and always hath been, either immediately or remotely, the certain effect of a persecuting or illiberal interference in religious matters: the Doddington prosecution, like all which have preceded it, hath terminated in the establishment and advantage of the party intended to have been suppressed; for a chapel hath been since erected in the parish, which is attended, I am informed, by a considerable number of the parishioners, to the extreme vexation of the orthodox spirit of the Rector.

It is important to Unitarians, and particularly so to Unitarian Missionaries, to ascertain how far this decision is correct; and it becomes the more important, since, if preaching abroad be illegal, I am extremely doubtful whether a prosecution might not be instituted under the statutes of Elizabeth and James I. which do not appear to be repealed, but merely suspended, by the act of William and Mary, as well as under the late Toleration Act.

At the time of the Revolution, Popish recusants were viewed with a very jealous eye; their principles were deemed subversive of the laws of civil society, and their attachment to the expelled family rendered them just objects of suspicion and alarm to the new dynasty. The Protestant recusants, as friends to liberty, were warm in their approbation of the change; and such was the opinion which the new government entertained of their loyalty, that, but for the danger which might have resulted to it in its then infant state, from the grant of unrestrained religious liberty, in consequence of the avowed hostility of the Papists, and the ease with which they might have availed themselves of that grant to effectuate their machinations, it is highly probable that no qualifications would have been required from Dissenting Protestants, nor any restrictions imposed upon them, save such as were common to Established Protestants. The meetings of the former might, in that event, have been of the most private kind; and under colour of Dissenting Protestant religious assemblies, the most seditious and dangerous meetings might have been held by the friends of the old dynasty, and these might have terminated in the subversion of the new order of things. Hence the necessity for registration, which renders the meeting public, and enables the agents of government to resort to it without difficulty, to ascertain the cast of its character. If then *publicity* be the sole object of registration, can it be necessary to register a field? Is not a meeting in a field necessarily *public?* Of that public nature, that no plans dangerous to the government can be there entered into, or even projected, without immediate detection? Publicity is certainly the only object of registration; and as a field is necessarily public, the registration of it cannot be requisite.

The words of the statutes are "place of meeting," which would certainly comprehend a field, if the object of the acts required that construction; but the object of these statutes appears to be answered by the nature of a field; and, moreover, this term, "place of meeting," is defined, in the eleventh section of the late act, to be a place with a *door* capable of being locked, bolted, or barred. A field cannot come within this description; it is necessarily excluded. A *building* may have a door, and it is a place of this kind only, where meetings may be secretly held, which was contemplated by the legislature at the time the Toleration Acts were passed.

Agreeably to this view of the subject, wherever the legislature have deemed the registration of a field necessary in order to effectuate the object of a law, the term has been used. Thus in Pitt's notorious acts of 1796 and 1799, for suppressing popular assemblies, the terms are "house, room, field, or other place;" and since the object of the Toleration Acts does not seem to require the registration of a field, this is a conclusive argument, in my opinion, in favour of the construction I have endeavoured to establish.

For these reasons, I submit, that in order to legalize field-preaching, it is unnecessary to register the field.

W. REDIN.

Letter to the late Rev. T. Lindsey, from Paris, 1801. Communicated by Mr. Rutt.

Sir,　　　*Clapton, Oct.* 12, 1816.

THE following letter was communicated to me by my excellent friend, to whom it was addressed, with liberty to copy it. Should you wish to preserve the letter as a record of some appearances and expectations, at the time when it was written, described by an intelligent person well situated for observation, it is at your service.

I was acquainted with the gentleman who wrote this letter, when he lived in England, which he left in 1791, and has since resided constantly at Paris. He is yet living there, or at least, was so, subsequent to the restoration, or rather the *imposition* of the Bourbons.　　　J. T. RUTT.

To the Rev. Theophilus Lindsey.
　　　　　Paris, 25th Dec. 1801.

" Dear Sir,

" I know not whether I ought to make any apologies for writing to you, but I have been in the habit of doing, or at least supposed to be doing so many strange things for these ten years past, that I seem to myself as privileged beyond the ordinary routine of society. My letter, however, will be of a very harmless nature, compared with others which I am accused of having written, and will commit neither of us, if it should fall into other hands than your own. The business is as follows.

" About two or three months since, a letter from a society in London, calling itself a missionary society, was sent me; the writers of which requested information on divers subjects, particularly with respect to the state of religion in France, and the best modes of propagating the pure Gospel of Jesus Christ. The society proposed at the same time the printing

and distributing ten thousand copies of the New Testament, with a prologomenon of about one hundred pages, containing proofs of the truth of the Sacred Writings. I collected from the style of the letter that the writers and the society they represented were of the Calvinistic persuasion, and I presume belonging to the class called in England Methodists.

As the inquiry appeared to me to come from good and somewhat intelligent men, I answered their letter at some length, I believe, in eight or ten sheets. I gave them an account of the present state of religion and irreligion in the republic of the different sects, both Catholic and Protestant, which at present divide it. I gave them a sketch of what had been done by the government for the restoration of worship, and what were likely to be the effects of its interposition. My letter in short was so couched as to apply to Christians of every denomination; and I was careful not to prevent by the explanation of my sentiments the good which I might in future do by furthering the views of the society, since their views appeared to me benevolent and praise worthy.

" An answer has been received to that letter, in which the society at large to whom my letter has been read, return me their thanks and request a continuance of the correspondence. Now as the continuance of this correspondence will necessarily draw me into further measures, for this is meant by the letter, I am very desirous of knowing what this society is, and with what propriety I can hold intercourse with it. The society knows nothing farther of my religious opinions than that I am a Dissenter. Of this I thought it right to inform them. It appears that they are also of this class. This is a point of contact which gives me some confidence. As Christians, Protestants and Dissenters, we are agreed, but I presume that in all other points we are very diversant. I have mentioned this plan of religious revolutionizing to some Italian prelates, and have taken measures for settling a correspondence with a Benedictine Monk of considerable abilities, who is at present in a convent at Rome. The society from a hint I gave them are anxious to make a proselyting excur-

·sion into the Cisalpine, and Ligurian Republics. · I think there would be a plentiful harvest, but the disposition in these countries to reform is much more liberal than they are aware of. My ecclesiastical acquaintance on that side, those who are believers, are in general Unitarians, which is a kind of proselytism the society would not perhaps wish to promote. I have conversed, also, with M. Gregoire, the late bishop of Blois, on the subject. He will support it so far as the general interests of Christianity are concerned : but though he has quitted his ecclesiastical functions, having been just named a senator, I do not hope that he will enter into all the projects of religious reform, though he will go pretty far.

"You know that we are on the eve of great religious changes in this country; what they will be I know not yet, for the opposition is great and various. I am about to publish a translation of *The Corruptions of Christianity,* and *Priestley's* Answer to *Volney,* or rather *Dupuis,* of which I have acquainted those gentlemen. I should like, also, to publish the *Comparison,* which the Dr. has had the attention to send me ; but I must wait for assistance. I am convinced these Works would be very seasonable at this moment: there are many yet who have not bowed the knee to Baal, and many also who want only a little assistance to put themselves in an erect posture.

"As our house is the general rendezvous of strangers, I have pretty good opportunities of knowing the progress of religious opinion on the Continent. I am assured that Unitarianism is making very rapid progress in Germany; and that there is scarcely a church, of which the pastor, if he be at all intelligent, is not a convert to this faith. With the state of the church of Geneva you are no doubt acquainted.

"I do not enter on any political topic, except to offer you my congratulations on the restoration of peace between the two countries. I say nothing respecting myself except to observe, that whatever my former friends in England (for I do not presume I have any now left,) think of my conduct, there are very few points, and those points of prudence, in which I do not feel the most perfect self approbation.—I have laboured, not against England, but for the establishment of rational liberty in

France without which it would have been lost in the [heart] of Europe. Happily for England, for France, and the world, our efforts have not been in vain. I beg my best respects to your respectful colleague, Dr. Disney, and to Mr. Hollis : I should also request you to present them to ———— but I am told I have entirely forfeited that gentleman's friendship: I have received that information, indeed, from a suspicious quarter ————, whose conduct in London has led me to break off all communication with him for some years past.—I shall be glad to be mistaken. To those who may still remember me I beg to be equally remembered, and remain,

"Dear Sir,
"Your affectionate & faithful Servant,
————————."

"*Rue Varennes,* 667."

———

Pullin's Row, Islington,
Sir, *Oct.* 11, 1816.

YOUR readers will, probably, be pleased with the following particulars of Sir John Dodderidge, ancestor of the pious and amiable Dr. Philip Dodderidge, and noticed by Job Orton at the commencement of his excellent Life of Dodderidge, in terms of high commendation. According to Orton, he died at Forsters, near Egham, Surrey, though he was buried at Exeter, in the cathedral, where a superb monument is erected to his memory. Such a truly estimable character is at once an ornament to human nature and a blessing to his country.

"Sir John Dodderidge, Knight, was born in this county (Devon) bred in Exeter College, Oxford, where he became so general a scholar that it is hard to say whether he was better artist, divine, civil or common lawyer, though he fixed on the last for his public profession, and became second justice of the king's bench. His soul consisted of two essentials, ability and integrity, holding the scale of justice with so steady an hand, that neither love nor lucre, fear nor flattery, could bow him on either side. It was vehemently suspected in his time, that some gave large sums of money to purchase places of judicature ; and Sir John is famous for the expression 'that as old and infirm as he was, he would go to Tyburn to see such a man hanged that should 'proffer money for a place of that nature ;' for certainly those who buy such offices by wholesale, must sell justice by retail, to make themselves savers. He was commonly called the sleeping judge, because he would sit on the bench with his eyes shut; which was only a posture of attention to sequester his sight from distracting objects, the better to listen to what was alleged and proved. Though he had three wives successively, out of the respectful families of Germin, Bamfield, and Culme, yet he left no issue behind him. He kept a hospital at Mount Radford, near Exeter, and dying 1628, the 13th of September (after he had been seventeen years a judge), in the 73d year of his age, was interred under a stately tomb, in our Lady's Chapel, in Exeter."———*Nicholls's Edition of Fuller's Worthies of England.*

. J. EVANS.

Sir,   *October* 10*th*, 1816.

IN the following passages amongst many others, the Article is found with the word λογος, used merely in the sense of Revelation, or the Gospel. Mark vii. 13, The Word of God, τον λογον τ8 Θε8. Luke iv. 32, His Word, ο λογος αυτου. Luke xi. 28, Blessed are they that hear the Word, τον λογον τ8 Θε8. John xv. 3, Now are ye clean through the Word, δια τον λογον. John xvii. 17, Thy Word, ο λογος ο σος. V. 20, Through their Word, δια του λογε αυτων. Acts vi. 2, The Word of God, τον λογον τ8 Θε8. Acts xii. 24, The Word of God grew, ο λογος τ8 Θε8. Acts xiii. 7, He desired to hear the Word of God, τον λογον τ8 Θε8. V. 44, To hear the Word, τον λογον. Acts xiv. 3, Testimony to the Word, τω λογω. Acts xix. 20, The Word of God increased, ο λογος.

In the following passages among others, the Article is omitted before the word Θεος, used to express the true God. Matt. vi. 24, Ye cannot serve God and Mammon. ου δυνασθε ΘΕΩ δουλευειν. John xx. 17, I ascend to my Father and your Father, to my God and your God, τον πατερα μου, και ΘΕΟΝ μ8, και ΘΕΟΝ υμων. Acts v. 29, It is proper to obey God rather than man, πειθαρχειν δει ΘΕΩ μαλλον η Ανθρωποις. 1 John, iv. 12,

No man hath seen God at any time, ΘΕΟΝ ουδεις πωποτε τεθεαται.

I humbly conceive that the Article is of less value than a legible and faithful hand-post to a bewildered traveller. The system that depends upon ο η το, must be truly desperate. In 2 Cor. iv. 4, the Devil is dignified with the Article. ο Θεος του αιωνος τ8τ8. The God of this world, or rather of this age, a period of abounding idolatry, vice and folly.

JER. POLYGLOT.

Sir,   *Oct.* 11, 1816.

THE following fact is taken from D'Israeli's "Calamities of Authors."

"It was in the 80th year of his age that the antiquary Stowe at length received a public acknowledgment of his services, which appear to us of a very extraordinary nature. He was so reduced in his circumstances that he petitioned James I: for a *licence to collect alms* for himself! ' as a recompense for his labour and travel of forty-five years, in setting forth the chronicles of England and eight years taken up in the survey of the cities of London and Westminster, towards his relief now in his old age; having left his former means of living, and only employing himself for the service and good of his country.' Letters patent under the great seal were granted. After no penurious commendation of Stowe's labours, he is permitted " to gather the benevolence of well-disposed people within this realm of England: to ask, gather, and take the alms of all our loving subjects.' These letters patent were to be published by the clergy from the pulpit; they produced so little that they were renewed for another twelve months; one entire parish in the city contributed seven shillings and sixpence! Such was the public remuneration of a man who had been useful to his nation, but not to himself!"

J. F.

Higham Hill, Nov. 11, 1816.

Sir,

TO some of your younger readers who may be disposed to inquire into the evidences of Christianity, the following remarks on Mr. Hume's objection to miracles, may not be useless. I have considered this celebrated objection, and I think impartially, at different times for more than thirty years, and I have never had but one opinion concerning it, which is, that it has *no force whatever.*

The objection, indeed, has been ably answered again and again, and by some more elaborately than it required. To meet the conceptions of the multitude it may indeed be desirable that error should be exposed in many words; but it is a maxim with me, that false reasoning always admits a short refutation, when it is once clearly discerned in what the fallacy consists.

Mr. Hume's objection amounts to this, that a miracle being a violation of the order of nature, can never be rendered credible by testimony, as the falsehood of testimony can in no case be deemed miraculous. It would perhaps have been more correct to define a miracle to be a deviation from the order of nature; but let this pass. It is to be observed that Mr. Hume does not object to the evidence which is produced in favour of the Christian miracles as being deficient in *quantity,* but denies *in toto* that this species of evidence can confirm a miracle. This makes it necessary to inquire a little into the force of this evidence. It will suit Mr. Hume's purpose that we should consider testimony in the gross, in which view of it, it must be confessed that it not unfrequently deceives. But testimony differs from testimony as much as error does from truth, and it *may* be so circumstanced and so accumulated in force that its falsehood will be deemed *impossible.* Let the actions and the fate of the late Emperor of France be for a moment called to mind. These are admitted by thousands, upon the evidence of testimony alone, and admitted with as *full conviction* as can be produced by mathematical or *ocular* demonstration. And will any one presume to say that this evidence may be false? Is it not to suppose a *violation of the order of nature* to suppose it false?[*] It has just been intimated

that testimony of a certain kind produces a conviction equal to what is produced by ocular demonstration. And whence does this arise? It is the spontaneous and necessary result of experience. That kind and degree of testimony which we have never known to deceive us, we rest assured cannot deceive us; and such is the confidence which we place in it, that the supposed improbability of the fact to which it bears witness, usually detracts nothing from the strength of the conviction which is effected by it. It is true enough that according to Mr. Hume's observation we cannot rationally admit any fact, till we conceive it to be more improbable that the evidence should be false than that the fact should be true. But in order to a just judgment, it is necessary that we consider on what ground we pronounce any fact to be antecedently improbable; and it is certain that when our notions of their improbability arise, as they often do, from a mere defect of knowledge, they instantly yield to certain testimony.

Such being the force of testimony and such the nature of the faith which we place in it, I ask what fact cannot be supported by testimony, the falsehood of which would be deemed *impossible,* except that which should itself appear to involve an *impossibility.* But the Christian miracles do not come under this predicament, nor does Mr. Hume's argument proceed upon such a supposition. What then is it which renders them incapable of being supported by testimony? Their *antecedent improbability.* And of this improbability how are we to judge? Were they not referred to a superior power; were they supposed to be effected by some hidden law of nature which was never in action before nor since; were it necessary to maintain that they took place without any assignable cause and to acknowledge that they produced no important effect, their antecedent improbability would certainly be great. But from what data are we to conclude that God would never interfere miraculously in

[*] How far the evidence which is produced in favour of the Christian miracles falls short of the strongest possible testimony, is a question with which I have nothing to do. Mr. Hume's is an abstract position, that no testimony can prove the reality of a miracle. When this has been

shewn to be false, it remains with every one to consider for himself whether the antecedent improbability of the Christian miracles appears to him to be surmounted by the testimony which is brought forward in their behalf.

the government of the world, or in other words would never *communicate to mankind such a revelation as the Christian ?* And this improbability is the *precise improbability* which, if Mr. Hume is to be believed, no testimony can overcome. But such an interposition is *contrary to experience.* It has been observed that this expression is not quite accurate; but waving this, I ask, may it not with equal truth be affirmed that the falsehood of testimony in certain circumstances is contrary to experience? But to *what* experience is the interposition in question contrary? To say that it is contrary to *universal* experience is to beg the question. When, therefore, it is said that such an interposition is contrary to experience, the meaning must be that it is contrary either to *our* experience or to *general* experience. To urge that it is contrary to *our* experience would be to lay it down as an axiom, that if God should ever interfere miraculously in the affairs of men, he must interfere also in our age and for our particular satisfaction. To press the objection that such an interposition is contrary to *general* experience, would subject the objector to a very perplexing question. What reason is there to suppose that if God should interfere miraculously in the administration of the world, such interpositions would be so frequent as to be matters of general experience? In the case of events which must take place, if they take place at all, by the operation of the laws of nature, general experience will reasonably influence our belief, and the want of similar instances will render us slow in admitting facts which seem to set the ordinary course of nature at defiance. But to bring a miraculous interposition of Providence, which is recorded to have taken place at a certain time and for a certain purpose, to the test of general experience, is palpably absurd, unless it could be proved that if miracles were ever wrought they must be wrought frequently, which is a proposition that no one would choose to defend. But to shew how little experience has to do with the credibility of a Divine revelation, let us suppose that God had never interposed miraculously in the government of the world to the present hour, and that the question were now put, whether he ever would so interpose. The only

rational reply would be, who can tell but he who sees the end from the beginning? Allowing the improbability of such an interposition from the want of past experience, would this improbability amount to any thing like a *proof* that the future would in this respect correspond to the past? And shall that become incredible, when attested, which it was by no means certain would not take place? In a word, that any thing short of the absolute *incredibility* of a fact *in itself considered* should render it incapable of being proved by testimony, is a paradox which it may require some ingenuity to defend, but which it is truly wonderful that any human being should be found seriously to believe. I affirm, then, without fear of refutation, that the evidence of testimony may be so circumstanced as to render a miracle wrought for a certain purpose, the object of rational belief. And I have no hesitation to affirm, also, that whoever would not believe such miracle upon the strongest possible testimony, would not believe it on the evidence of ocular demonstration. But in fact, a being so incredulous does not exist. I once, indeed, heard an unbeliever say, that he would not believe a miracle if he saw it. I approved his consistency, though I did not give credit to his declaration. Man, however reluctant, may be compelled to believe his eyes, and he may also be compelled to put faith in testimony in spite of all the refined and subtle reasonings in the world. In many cases, he cannot wait to calculate between the strength of the evidence and the improbability of the fact ; and in some cases, could he wait for ever, he would not know how to manage the calculation. And conscious of his infirmity he chooses in such cases rather to examine the validity of the testimony, of which he can judge with tolerable exactness, than to fatigue his faculties with endeavouring to balance the evidence which is laid before him against improbabilities, the force of which he cannot estimate. And in the case of Christianity, if he conceives himself to be an incompetent judge of the antecedent credibility of a Divine Revelation, his business is to inquire into the evidence with as much impartiality as he can, and to abide by the result of such inquiry. If any Christian has precisely calculated the preponderance of this evidence above the *à priori* improbability of the facts, I should be glad to be acquainted with the balance. And if any disciple of Mr. Hume will point out the measure in which the antecedent improbability of the facts preponderates above the strength of the testimony, added to the *improbability* of the prevalence of Christianity, had the miracles been false, he may call upon me to abjure the Christian faith.

One word more on the subject of miracles, and I have done. Though we could not judge *à priori* whether God would interfere miraculously in the government of the world, yet when such an interposition has taken place, its credibility may be heightened by the end which was proposed by it, and the consequences by which it has been followed. Thus the Christian dispensation, among other objects, was avowedly intended to overthrow the idolatry of the heathen world, and to establish the worship of the One living and true God. And this purpose it has most fully and gloriously accomplished. The miracles, then, recorded in the Christian Scriptures, are not events which have left no trace behind them, but are events of which the effects have been experienced from the season of their occurrence to the present hour, and which will continue to be experienced till time shall be no more.

It has, I think, been made to appear that Mr. Hume, while he threatens destruction to Christianity at a blow, has in fact effected nothing, and that the Christian does not set aside every principle of rational belief, when he acknowledges Jesus of Nazareth to have been a man approved of God by MIRACLES and signs which God did by him.

E. COGAN.

A Sermon for Preachers.

IT is without any design to give offence, and with a sincere wish to do good, that the writer would venture to point out a fault that he has observed in some preachers, and would earnestly desire to have it banished from among Unitarians. He means excessive egotism. That self-esteem is a powerful and universal passion of the human race he is well aware; and therefore clergymen as well as others may be expected to have their share of it. But it is obvious that in every transaction of life mankind feel it necessary to hide

this passion as much as possible from the view of others. For as every one is in some degree under its influence, it is certain that I cannot obtrude my own self-love upon the notice of others, without risking an abatement of that respect for me, which they might possibly feel while they were not sensible that my own vanity was an obstacle to my perceiving the preferable qualities which they suppose themselves to possess. Hence, he is sure to succeed the best in obtaining the approbation of other men, who is not niggardly in his commendations of their virtues whether real or imaginary, and who says but little of his own. This forgetfulness of ourselves is of more importance in proportion to the publicity of the station we are called to occupy. Not only because more eyes are upon us, and our frailties are placed in a glare of light which scarcely allows one of them to be invisible; but also because it is generally expected that such men should live for the public and not for themselves, that they are wholly devoted to the public good, and consecrated to their advantage. No man can forget himself always, and certainly ought not. But it must surely be thought that when a preacher cannot get through a single paragraph of his sermon without some such phrases as I shall next observe—I propose to shew—I affirm—In the course of *my* reading—In *my* opinion—In *my* former discourse—with perhaps twenty other similar forms of expression, his *own* views, and the operations of his *own* mind, have a disproportionate place in his thoughts. There are also gesticulations and accents, which can never be mistaken, as intimating the strong impression of self-importance under which a teacher delivers his instructions. Whatever may be the temporary effect of such things on young and inexperienced persons, they almost uniformly produce in the minds of men of maturer years and extensive knowledge of the world, a low opinion of the judgment of such instructors, and a sort of pity for the vanity so unguardedly betrayed.

It is not necessary for the sake of avoiding egotism, studiously and universally to discard the use of the first personal pronoun in the singular number, nor would this be always effectual, for by the perpetual substitution of the plural *we*, vanity is not a whit less conspicuous. Let our preachers have their thoughts absorbed in their subject, when they write and when they speak, and I am disposed to think they will make very few allusions either to the person who is teaching, or to the process by which he acquired the ideas he is communicating.   L.

Letter of Mr. Jefferson's (on Religion,) in Answer to one from a Quaker.
[From Niles's American Register.]
Copy of a Letter addressed by ——— *to Thomas Jefferson, dated 29th 8th Mo. 1813.*

ESTEEMED FRIEND THOMAS JEFFERSON,

I HAVE for years felt at times affection towards thee, with a wish for thy salvation: to wit, the attainment, while on this stage of time (in the natural body) of a suitable portion of *divine life,* for otherwise we know little more than the life of nature, and therein are in danger of becoming inferior to the beasts which perish, in consequence of declining the offers of divine life made to every rational being. But I have long had better hopes of *thee,* and have thought (particularly in our little quiet meeting yesterday) that thou hast been faithful (at least) over a few things, and wish thou mayest become ruler over more, and enter into the joy of our Lord, and into his rest; and it occurred in order thereto, that we should become Christians, for he that hath not the spirit of Christ, is none of his, and this knowledge and belief is, I think, strongly insisted on by divers of the Apostles, who had personally seen, and were eye-witnesses to his Majesty, particularly in the Mount, and others who had not that in view, which however, was insufficient to perfect them, and was to be taken away that they might be more effectually turned to that spirit which leadeth into all truth, whose power alone is able to reduce the spirits of nature to suitable silence and submission.   Thy Friend,

————.   ————.

Reply by Thomas Jefferson.
SIR,
I HAVE duly received your favour of August 29, and am sensible of the kind intentions from which it flows, and truly thankful for them, the more as they could only be the result of a favourable estimate of my public course—

as much devoted to study as a faithful transaction of the trust committed to me would permit. No subject has occupied more of my consideration than our relations with all the beings around us, our duties to them, and our future prospects. After hearing all which probably can be suggested concerning them, I have formed the best judgment I could as to the course they prescribe, and in the due observance of that course, I have no reflections which give me uneasiness. An eloquent preacher of your religious society, Richard Mott, in a discourse of much unction and pathos, is said to have exclaimed aloud to his congregation, that " he did not believe there was a Quaker, Presbyterian, Methodist, or Baptist in heaven." Having paused to give his congregation time to stare and to wonder, he added, that, " in heaven God knows no distinction, but considered all men as his children and brethren of the same family." I believe with the Quaker preacher, that he who observes these moral precepts, in which all religions concur, will never be questioned at the gates of heaven as to the dogmas in which all differ: that on entering there, all these are left behind us, and the Aristideses and Catos, the Penns and Tillotsons, Presbyterians and Papists, will find themselves united in all the principles which are in concert with the Supreme Mind. Of all the systems of morality, ancient or modern, which have come under my observation, none appears to me so pure as that of Jesus. He who follows this steadily, need not, I think, be uneasy, although he cannot comprehend the subtleties and mysteries erected on his doctrines by those who, calling themselves his special followers and favourites, would make him come into the world to lay snares for all understandings but *theirs.* Their metaphysical heads usurping the judgment-seat of God, denounce as his enemies all who cannot perceive the geometrical logic of Euclid, in the demonstrations of St. Athanasius, that three are one, or one three. In all essential points, you and I are of the same religion, and I am too old to go into the unessentials. Repeating, therefore, my thankfulness for the concern you have been so good as to express, I salute you with friendship and brotherly love.

T. JEFFERSON.
Monticello, Sept. 18, 1813.

Sir, *Bath, 9th Nov.* 1816.

YOUR Correspondent *Sigma* (p. 514) has made many good observations upon what is usually termed the doctrine of *Original Sin.* I wonder, however, that he has not noticed the 18th chap. of Ezekiel, in which that impious doctrine is so clearly and emphatically condemned. There the prophet, speaking in the name of the Lord, asks the people of Israel why they used this proverb, saying, the fathers have eaten sour grapes, and the childrens teeth are set on edge: and there they are also assured that they should no longer have any reason to make use of this proverb. For, behold all souls are mine; as the soul of the father, so also the soul of the son is mine: consequently the souls of all his descendants, as well as the soul of their first progenitor, are the offspring of God. It is added, The soul that sinneth, it shall die. Therefore no man nor men shall be condemned for the crimes of any of his ancestors, but every man for his own transgressions only. The just, or righteous man, shall surely live, saith the Lord God. On the other hand, if this just man beget a wicked and impenitent son, he shall surely die, his blood shall be upon him. If he, however, have a son, who seeth all his father's sins which he hath done, and doeth not such like, he shall not die for the iniquity of his father, but shall surely live. The soul that sinneth, it, that is, it alone, shall die. Then follows hope for the truly penitent and despair for every one who forsaketh righteousness and becomes iniquitous. In short, this chapter is a complete confutation of all the assertions which ever have been, or ever shall be introduced, in support of the doctrine of Original Sin.

In the next place, I wish your readers to consider what is the real meaning of praying or doing any thing in the name of Christ. There is a letter in the *Theological Repository,* which had the full approbation of Dr. Priestley: that letter clearly shewed, that doing any thing in the name of Christ, means acting as his disciples: we should therefore seriously consider, when we pray in his name, what we call down upon ourselves, if we be engaged in any iniquitous practices. As his disciples, we must depart from every known transgression, and cultivate every virtuous sentiment and holiness

of life. If we therefore pray in his name whilst we know ourselves to be the servants of sin, we pray for our condemnation. We should, therefore, be prepared with holy hearts, to desire always to walk in the ways of righteousness and truth, according to the clear declarations of the blessed Gospel, when we presume to pray in his name: otherwise we act more unadviseably than those who never pray at all, unless they humbly pray for pardon, acceptance, and to be wholly devoted to all piety and goodness.

Having still some room, I announce to you the opening of a very large Methodist chapel at Bath. On the front of this building is inscribed, *Deo Sacrum,* in capitals. I wish to be informed what they mean by *Deo.* Do they mean the One Father of all, or do they mean Jesus Christ, contrary to his own declaration? Or do they mean Trinity, according to the idolatrous doctrine of the Church of Rome, and of some other churches?

W. H.

Mr. Cornish's Communication of a curious Ecclesiastical Document, with his Reply and Remarks, and of Two Letters of the late Dr. Toulmin's.

Colyton, September 27th, 1816.

Sir,

THOUGH personally unknown to you, I am in habits of particular friendship with many of your correspondents and constant readers, several of whom have been very desirous that a letter addressed to me by four ministers, with my reply, might be inserted in the Monthly Repository.

The excellent Dr. Toulmin, who began his ministry at Colyton, was for fifty years my tried and faithful friend, and between him and the society here a mutual regard and attachment continued to the close of his valuable life. In all my personal and ministerial concerns he felt a warm interest. The attention paid to his memory by others, and particularly my good Brother Howe, in the Monthly Repository for January last, rendered any particular notice from me unnecessary. The letter and my reply were put into his hands, to procure his opinion as to the publication of them. His various engagements, attended with bodily indisposition, and his lamented death, prevented the correspondence, as I have no doubt, from being forwarded in due time to you.

Though often urged, I had given up the idea of bringing it forward now; but a judicious and amiable friend (Dr. Carpenter) lately urged the publication as a curious anecdote in private ecclesiastical history.

Some of my friends were for giving the names of the ministers; others with myself thought it better not to publish them. They themselves might hereafter see the impropriety of their conduct; and the feelings of many of their particular acquaintance, who highly disapproved this part of their conduct, urge the suppression. If without them you think fit to insert their proposal and my answer, both are at your service.

It will give satisfaction to many respected friends at a distance, should the letters appear, to be informed that not one of my little flock has deserted me. A place has been built and opened these two years: though small, it is only occasionally well filled; those regularly attending are few, and such as before went to some neighbouring places. Strangers who contributed on the representation given that the place would be thronged by those who could not find the way to heaven without this aid, have been deceived.

The enclosed letters from the guide of my youth, when I was a student at Hoxton, under those able tutors, Dr. Savage (the intimate acquaintance and successor in his congregation to the renowned Dr. Watts), Dr. Kippis and Dr. Rees, are at your service. They shew at what period, when he was about 30, Dr. Toulmin began to alter his views, always the result of previous diligent inquiry; and his not having brought off me from what is distinguished by the name of the high, very high Arian scheme, never withdrew from me his most affectionate regards or interrupted our ministerial connection.

Mr. Moffat, ever pious and progressively liberal, carried on his useful ministry at Nailsworth, and honourably concluded them at Malmesbury, several years since. Mr. Ward, whose valuable life Dr. Toulmin recorded in the Protestant Dissenters' Magazine, adopted modern Unitarian ideas, or at least inclined to them. Dr. Amory, and his friend (whom I had the honour also to call mine) the venerable Mr. Towgood, ever adhered to Dr. Clarke's ideas, as securing effectually the unity

and supremacy of the One God, and the honour and dignity of the One Lord Jesus Christ.

On my last visit to London, in 1800, that able supporter of the Dissenting cause, my friend and correspondent Mr. Palmer, of Hackney, informed me of an attempt made by some connected with the Hoxton Academy, which had given him such disgust, that he intended and I believe had withdrawn his subscription. A letter had been written to a member of the congregation at Kingston upon Thames, concerning the low state of the interest there, and proposing that they should dismiss their then minister, giving him a year's salary or so, and take one of their connection in his room. The indignation of the whole society was excited, an attachment to their minister increased, and some years afterwards, when by his removal and that of one of the most active members (with whom I am well acquainted) regular preaching was discontinued, none joined the independent place, which possibly most of them might have done, had it not been for the ungenerous proposal made by some of that party, which somewhat resembles that sent to

JOSEPH CORNISH.

P.S. Mr. William Morgan, in his Life of his Uncle, Dr. Price, thus writes: " I have often heard him say, that his attendants were now so few, as to make it impossible for him to be animated before such an assembly; nay that he thought every attempt at exertion or energy would be completely ridiculous." Pp. 30, 31.

But he writes in another place, p. 28, " Although grieved and dispirited, he never uttered a murmur of discontent. In time he became familiarized to those scenes which had at first so deeply depressed his spirits; and though always affected by them, he so far recovered himself as to divide his hours more equally between the study of philosophical and religious subjects, and to review the result of his labours in both through a less gloomy and discouraging medium."

The close of Dr. Price's ministry at Poor Jewry Lane, was the period to which Mr. Morgan refers. I was then a frequent hearer of that admirable preacher, and used to wonder that discourses delivered with so much animation and such commanding seriousness, did not attract a numerous audience.

Some who attended, I know, like myself, were warm admirers; and though he might feel discouraged, and full of modesty as he was, be insensible of the energy with which he spoke, his manner as well as his matter deeply affected all serious hearers.

. Had it been the Doctor's infirmity to be unable to attempt exertion, his example in this respect should by no means be imitated. Small congregations may be made less through want of exertion in their minister; the improvement of every individual present should be a point continually kept in view, and how few soever the number of hearers may be, the preacher is bound in duty to exert his best abilities.

Mr. Morgan might have drawn up a more interesting memoir, though what he has written is acceptable. Some account of Dr. Price's associates would have been pleasing. At Poor Jewry Lane his fellow-labourer was the accomplished Mr. Radcliffe. That he declined preaching for many years before his death was much to be regretted. He continued, however, a steady adherent to the cause which he had so ably served in the pulpit, yet the continuance of his services there might have proved of essential benefit. The truly respectable Mr. White, of the Old Jewry, was chosen afternoon preacher at Hackney, when Dr. Price became pastor; and the excellent Dr. Amory succeeded in the morning service at Newington Green, continuing his services at the Old Jewry the other part of the day; Mr. White being co-pastor there with him. Dr. Amory and Dr. Price were kindred souls. The best qualities which can adorn Christian ministers, and the most amiable dispositions as members of society, distinguished both. Never had a small or any congregation two preachers more worthy of their most serious and attentive regard. Dr. Amory, during his long residence at Taunton, was much esteemed by and frequently preached to the respectable Baptist Society there. He expressed to me the great pleasure he felt when Mr. Toulmin was fixed in it. Mr. Ward his successor was advancing in years, as were the principal supporters of the place where Dr. Amory had officiated: He rejoiced, therefore, in the thought, that those sentiments of religion which represented God " as

love," and which his uncle Grove and himself had long inculcated, would still continue to be held forth in his native town, and among the posterity of his beloved hearers.

Colyton, Devon, April 28, 1814.
To the Rev. Mr. Cornish.
REV. AND DEAR SIR,

WERE we to regard our own feelings only in making you this joint address, we should be disposed to preface it with a long apology for interfering in a point in which you are so deeply interested. Be assured, dear Sir, it is far from our intention to wound them in the slightest degree. A sense of duty to the great head of the Christian church, and a sincere regard for the spiritual eternal welfare of our fellow-creatures, are the principal motives which have prevailed upon us thus to address you.

We are given to understand that the Dissenting interest at Colyton has not been of late years in that flourishing state which doubtless you yourself wish. The attempt which has been lately made to gain the attention of the people to a concern for their spiritual good, seems to have been attended with a Divine blessing. The attendance is very considerable and would in all probability be much greater were there a suitable place of worship. A plan has been proposed and in part proceeded upon, for fitting up a more commodious house. The expence attending this object would be considerable, though no doubt it might be effected.

Having understood this to be the situation of things, it has occurred to us, that, as you are now advancing in years, and may not be so well able to make those exertions which are necessary to gather and keep together a congregation at all numerous, you might feel disposed to give up the meeting-house which you occupy into the hands of approved trustees, in order to accommodate those who are evidently willing to attend the ministry of the young men who have preached to them the word of life.

If this proposal were acceded to on your part, much expence would be saved in building, &c. and we should conceive it would be much more to your satisfaction to see the place where you have so long laboured and in which doubtless you feel an interest, filled with hearers anxious to learn the way to heaven, though that way might be pointed out with another finger than your own, · than to preach to a few individuals in your own meeting-house, while you knew that another in the same town was thronged.

To impart the greatest good to the greatest number of their fellow-creatures, is the high motive which has operated with those who are interested in the support of the infant cause at Colyton.

Private feelings as well as private interests must give way to the public good. We hope this sentiment will be adopted and acted on by all concerned, and trust you are so much interested in the general welfare of man; especially in the salvation of his soul, that whatever will contribute most effectually to this end, and depends on you, you will not withhold.

You will readily believe we can have no other interest to serve than that of the cause of God and truth, and to support and promote that we stand pledged. We beg leave therefore to make this friendly proposal for your consideration, trusting you will see how much public good may arise from acceding to it, as well as how probably you may expect therein the Divine approbation.

Your reply may be addressed if you please to either of the undersigned.

Wishing you health and prosperity under the Divine blessing, We are,

Rev. and Dear Sir,

Your's respectfully,

—————

To Mr. A. B. C. D.

Colyton, May 1814.

TO prevent my being troubled again with such a letter as came by post, signed by yourself and Messrs. B. C. D. is my only reason for sending any reply. Mr. —— may possibly blush hereafter at recollecting that his name appeared. Of Mr. —— I entertain less hope. At Mr. —— (if it be Mr. —— the elder and not his son) and yourself I am astonished. Those of my little flock to whom the letter has been shewn, feel most indignant. I am persuaded that four ministers could not be found in the kingdom amongst those disposed to exchange pulpits with me, who could have made so unjust (for you desire me of

myself and as my own personal act to give up the place where my hearers assemble), so unfeeling and insulting a proposal.

Could four such lost to every feeling becoming men and Christians have done it, to a minister of an approved character for more than forty years, and to whom the Almighty graciously continues decent abilities for public service; a large majority of their people and I believe many open-hearted laymen of your connection would have joined in saying, "Fie upon them, fie upon them."

I found the society at Colyton very small; for some years it increased; by deaths and removals it is again lessened. Should you and your friends think the cause of religion will be served by erecting a new place here, any real good done will rejoice the heart of your sincere well-wisher,

JOSEPH CORNISH.

P. S. I was much impressed in early life with a remark of good Mr. Lavington's, in his Charge to Mr. Stephens, at Axminster, 1772. "Should the number of your hearers lessen, do not be discouraged so as to grow remiss in your endeavours; remember Jesus Christ preached an excellent sermon to one woman."

—————

Extracts by Joseph Cornish.

Mr. Lavington being deservedly a favourite author with his party, I directed my correspondents to a passage, Vol. I. p. 320, of his Discourses addressed to a Minister.

"Suppose you have been unusually earnest for many sabbaths following, in exhorting sinners, and beseeching them by the mercies of God to be reconciled, you find yourself so assisted in your preparations, and so animated in the delivery of these discourses, that you are strongly persuaded of being remarkably successful; and every time you let down the net, you seem assured of inclosing a multitude of fishes: now, if after all you catch nothing; if you cannot perceive that one soul has been converted by all your prayers and preaching, and, in short, that for aught that appears, you have laboured in vain, and spent your strength for nought; do you not think it possible that pride may suggest 'what signifies my toiling, if God give not his blessing?' No man could exert himself more. But I might as well have sat still and done nothing. Let God · send some other messenger, whose labours he may think fit to bless: I see I am no longer worthy of being employed.'. No, my dear Sir, this must not be: this is not the proper language from a servant to his master; Christ has taught you better, and you must learn to say after him, ' Though Israel be not gathered, yet shall I be glorious in the eyes of the Lord, 'and my God shall be my strength.' "

A pious minister saying that he thought of not preaching on a particular day, because very few would attend: Oh! preach, said a pious friend, no one can tell what good may be done till the day of judgment.

The pious Dr. Stonehouse was so discouraged by his want of apparent success, though well attended, that in a letter to Mr. Orton, he observed, " that to preach was his duty, but he was become almost indifferent whether his audience consisted of eighteen hundred or only eighteen."

Taunton, Nov. 24, 1770.

My Dear Friend,

I WAS rather surprised at the contents of your's, though I must regard it as a proof of your integrity. It induced me to look into Mr. Boyse's Answer to Emlyn; and by what I saw from a slight inspection, his reasonings appear to me only calculated to puzzle a plain thing, and to cloud a matter with chicanery, which common sense would easily determine: and notwithstanding all he appeared to advance, on his principles I see not how our Master can be cleared from the suspicion of equivocation, in Matt. xiii. 32, and I suppose Mr. Emlyn's Reply has obviated his specious reasonings. But surely you do not test the controversy on one text. The point to me appears, What is the idea the Scriptures in their general strain and language afford us of the Divine Being. The most exact and precise definition of the One Supreme God, is a Being consisting of Father, Son and Holy Ghost, i. e. on the Trinitarian principles: but where is this idea and definition to be met with in the Scriptures? On the contrary, it appears that the word *God* occurs 1288 times, and there are several hundred texts wherein the Father is styled God absolutely by way of eminence, it being impossible by the construction itself, that it should have any other sense. As to the point of worship, all prayers, praises and glory are either directed to the One God and Father of all, or to his ultimate glory. Besides, no Trinitarians are, or indeed can be consistent in their debates on this matter; for they cannot fix on an uniform definition of the word, and are obliged to understand by it a distinct consciousness, which runs them into Tritheism, or some nominal relative distinction, which is Sabellianism. However, you will meet with more pertinent and forcible observations than I can suggest in the course of your reading on this article. Let me mention to you the Appeal to Common Sense, and the Review of the Trinitarian Controversy, both by the same worthy author, Mr. Hopkins. You should also peruse Lowman's three Tracts, and Dr. Lardner's Letter on the Logos: perhaps the Socinian notions of Christ's dignity are nearest to truth and Scripture. I can scarcely believe you will terminate your inquiries in the reception of Athanasianism. May the God of Truth guide and bless all your inquiries! J. TOULMIN.

Taunton, April 10, 1771.

My Dear Friend,

YOUR candour will excuse my delay; it was partly owing to the waiting for an opportunity of taking Mr. Ward's sentiments on the subject of your's. We both approve of the motives by which you are influenced, and of your rational zeal in the services of men's best interests. As to the propriety of your design with respect to Kingston, we are both such strangers to the circumstances of things there, that we can do no more than concur in every scheme (as far as our approbation at least) which promises to serve the cause of religion; and in this case would wholly rest on Dr. Amory's knowledge and judgment. Only we would refer it to you to consider whether a connection you propose with Mr. Moffat will be agreeable and have a favourable aspect. Will not your sentiments clash? Will not this appear in your prayers and sermons? Or will he consent to confine himself to a practical strain and Scripture language? Would he deem such a connection on his own account prudent or proper, as it probably would draw some suspicions of heresy on him? Have you consulted him on these points? Or would you choose to refer them to his consideration? I would farther observe that I have heard Mr. H—— mention an old gentleman, a Dissenting minister, (his name I cannot recollect) who resided at Kingston,[*] and opened a room in his own house to preach in on Lord's Day: and though his character and sermons were good, he had no great encouragement, as not above a dozen besides his own family ever attended. Indeed, I do not think that this should determine you to lay aside your scheme; for even to do good to so few, will not lose its pleasures or reward; and I should apprehend so small a sphere would be a good introduction to the world: for my own part I believe I shall like to exchange with you sometimes. If on consulting Dr. Amory, you pursue the scheme, you should apprize Mrs. Haddon of it, that she may licence her house; which she can do only at a Quarter's Session.

I imagined you would not long retain the Trinitarian sentiments: but your candour and impartiality, whatever opinions you embraced, gave you a claim to esteem with men, will delight on reflection, and if persevered in, will meet a noble recompence with the God of Truth! The prospect, my friend, is great and animating! *Edward's Book* I have never seen, and cannot say I have had much inclination to see it, as I thought it was intended to reason us out of our feelings, and to perplex with metaphysics what is plain and incontestable at the bar of *common sense*. Have you seen *Beattie on Truth?* if you have not, you have much improvement and entertainment to come. It carries conviction, confirms faith, and gives that lively and rational pleasure to which the sceptical mind must remain an unhappy stranger. I could wish you to purchase *Lardner's Letter on the Logos.* Dr. *Chandler* declared he could not answer Lowman. There is another book in that controversy which merits at-

tention; *The Scripture Doctrine of Jesus Christ,* published three years since. My sentiments are not fixed on the point: I have it in review: and my mind leads much to the Socinian scheme. May your's be directed *to truth,* and ever feel the power, the hopes and zeal of real goodness and piety. Accept our joint respects, and the best wishes of,

Dear Friend,

Your's very affectionately,

J. TOULMIN.

Harlow Mills, Nov. 9, 1816.

SIR,

IN answer to the inquiries of your Correspondent, A. F. in your last Number, (p. 594,) respecting Dr. Bekker, I have no doubt but he will find ample information by referring to almost any of the larger biographical Dictionaries, and more particularly the French—*Bayle, Moreri, Chauffepie,* &c. but being absent from my late residence near the metropolis, the only work of the kind I have now an opportunity of referring to in the library of a friend, is the *Dictionnaire Historique, Litteraire, et Critique,* a work in 6 vols. 8vo. and which, allowing for the prejudices of a Roman Catholic, appears to be written with fairness and impartiality. The following is a translation of the article respecting the above-mentioned divine.

" BEKKER (BALTHASAR,) a famous Dutch Theologian, born in Friesland, 1634, who, after having commenced his studies under his father, and pursued them in the Academies of Groningen and Franker, was employed in different churches, and died minister of that at Amsterdam, in 1698. He was suspended from his functions for a certain period on account of his work entitled, *Le Monde Enchanté,* 2 vols. 12mo. in which he denied the doctrine of possessions and of witchcraft by any compact with the devil, and affirmed 'that the evil spirit had no power over men.' The system of Bekker was refuted by various writers, but they could never persuade him to retract, nor could they prevent him from defending himself: he was therefore deprived of his functions by the ecclesiastical synod, although they continued his salary as minister. He was the author of various other works, *Recherches* *sur les Comètes*, in 8vo. *La Saine Theo- logie; Explicatio Propheticæ Danielis*, in 4to. &c."*

In the volume of Robinson's Works, quoted by your Correspondent, there is another allusion to Dr. Bekker, by which it appears that one of the charges brought against him, was that which I fear may be brought *against almost every thinking, serious divine, who is so unfortunate as to be a member of any of those Anti-Christ- ian communities, the handy-work of kingcraft, priestcraft and statecraft— *civil establishments of religion.* The Dutch synod condemned the Doctor, " because he had explained the Holy Scriptures so as to make them contrary to the *Catechism,* and particularly to the *articles of faith,* which he had himself subscribed."† Mr. Robinson, however, finishes the paragraph quoted by your Correspondent, by giving it as his opinion, that " although Dr. B. was reputed a Deist, he was a fast friend of revelation, and all his crime lay in expounding some literal pas- sages allegorically. Not the book, ut the received meaning of it he denied."‡

When I was in Holland about twenty-five years since, I turned over Dr. Bekker's Heretical Work alluded to, and which passed through several editions. Notwithstanding it abounds with singular opinions and fancies, it displays much learning, ingenuity and entertainment.

You will perceive by the account of the French Biographer, that although the synod first suspended, and after- wards deprived the learned but here- tical divine of his functions, they con- tinued him his salary. Should other ecclesiastical bodies take it into their heads to inquire into the heterodoxy of their members, should they act with similar liberality, and only de- prive them of their *employments,* it will not perhaps render the proceedings of those learned bodies very alarming to the generality of ecclesiastics.

B. FLOWER.

Sir, *Clapton, Nov. 9, 1816.*

YOUR Correspondent A. F. (p. 594) will find *Dr. Bekker* mentioned in several Works which preceded Mr.

* Dictionaire Historique, &c. Vol. II. p. 428.
† Robinson's Works, Vol. I. p. 84.
‡ Ibid. p. 78.

Robinson's *Remarks.* Mosheim, in his *Ecclesiastical History,* (C. xvii. S. 1, No. xxxv) from that neglect of dis- crimination, too common, and not al- ways undesigned, classes Bekker with *Spinosa,* and imputes to him a design of using " the principles of *Des Cartes,* to overturn some doctrines of Christ- ianity, and to pervert others."

A larger account of Bekker and his *World Bewitched,* published in 1691, will be found in Part II. S. 2, No. xxxv. of the same History. But the fullest satisfaction I can offer your Correspondent, is by quoting some passages, and especially the concluding paragraph, from the Article *Balthasar Bekker,* Biog. Dict. 1784.

He was born in 1634, " at Warth- nisen, in the province of *Groningen,* in whose university he was educated. In 1665, while minister at Oosterlingen, " he took his degree of Doctor of Di- vinity, at Francker, and the next year was chosen one of the ministers of that city." He had published " A Short Catechism for Children, and another for Persons of more advanced Age." The latter was censured as containing " strange expressions, unscriptural po- sitions, and dangerous opinions," for which " the author was prosecuted be- fore the ecclesiastical assemblies," and for four years endured " much trouble and vexation."

" In 1679 he was chosen minister at Amsterdam. The comet which ap- peared in 1680 and 1681 gave him an opportunity of publishing a small book, in Low Dutch, entitled, *Ondersoch over de Kometei,* that is, An Inquiry concern- ing Comets, wherein he endeavoured to shew that comets are not the presages or forerunners of any evil. This piece gained him great reputation, as did likewise his *Exposition on the Prophet Daniel,* wherein he gave many proofs of his learning and sound judgment. But the Work which rendered him most famous, is his *De Betover Wereld,* or *The World Bewitched.* He enters into an inquiry of the common opinion concerning spirits, their nature and power, authority and actions; as also what men can do by their power and assistance. He tells us in his preface, that it grieved him to see the great honours, powers, and miracles which are ascribed to the devil. ' It is come to that pass,' says he, ' that men think it piety and godliness to ascribe a great many wonders to the devil, and impiety and heresy if a man will not believe that the devil can do what a thousand persons say he does: It is now reckoned godliness, if a man who fears God, fear also the devil. If he be not afraid of the devil, he passes for an Atheist, who does not believe in God, because he cannot think that there are two Gods, the one good, the other bad. But these, I think, with much more reason may be called Ditheists. For my part, if on account of my opinion they will give me a new name, let them call me Monotheist, a believer of but one God.' This work raised a great clamour against Bekker. The consistory at Amsterdam, the classes and synods, proceeded against him, and after having suspended him from the holy communion, deposed him at last from the office of a minister. The magistrates of Amsterdam were so generous, however, as to pay him his salary as long as he lived. A very odd medal was struck in Holland, on his deposition: it represented a devil, cloathed like a minister, riding upon an ass, and holding a banner in his hand, as a proof of the victory which he gained in the synods. With the medal was published a small piece, in Dutch, to explain it, in which was an account of what had been done in the consistory classes and synods. Bekker died of a pleurisy, June 11, 1698."

In the *Nouveau Dictionnaire Historique,* Paris, 1772, is a short article of Bekker, whose design in the work for which he was persecuted is thus described : " *Le livre est fait pour prouver, qu'il n'y a jamais eu, ni possedé, ni sorcier, et que les diables ne se mêlent pas des affaires des hommes, et ne peuvent rien sur leur personnes.*"*

The article closes in the following terms, contrasting the disadvantageous form of Bekker with his agreeable character and accomplishments : " BEKKER *étoit horriblement laid; mais il avoit l'esprit assez juste. Ses mœurs etoient pures, et son ame ferme et incapable de plier.*"†

---

* That book is designed to prove that there never was really a *professed* sorcerer, and that devils have no influence in the concerns of men nor power over their persons.

† Bekker was shockingly deformed, but he possessed a correct understanding. His manners were pure, with a strength of mind incapable of unworthy compliance.

This contrast of the biographer reminds me of the following lines which I have somewhere read as written in compliment to *Pope :*

" What to thy outward form all-righteous
        heav'n
    Deny'd, to thy more perfect mind was
        giv'n ;
    So nicely pois'd great Nature's scale was
        see,
    So just thou uniform deformity."

The case of this persecuted theologian attracted the attention of Mr. Locke who during his exile in Holland, from 1682 to 1689, had probably met with Bekker at Amsterdam, in the society of Professor Limborch, to whom he thus writes from London, 14th November, 1691 :—

" *Quid tandem factum est cum doctor isto theologo qui tam mira docuit de angelis, in libro suo, de spirituum existentia? An non expertus est fratrum suorum pro religione, pro veritate, pro orthodoxi zelum? Mirum si impunè evadat!*"v. In the margin of the *Familiar Letter* (1708, p. 535), is printed *Balthasa Bekker.**

I recollect also to have once seen a respectful reference to Bekker and his opinion, in the preface to a French translation of Dr. Sykes's *Inquiry into the Meaning of Demoniacs,* &c. printed I think, at Leyden, in 1738.

But it would be unjust to the memory of this innovating theologian, not to shew how Dr. Bentley has avoided the fault of Dr. Mosheim, and even left Bekker in orthodox company. I refer to his *Remarks* on the *Discourse of Free-thinking,* in which he has been severe enough against *Collins,* and, occasionally, more severe than just. The latter, in the *Discourse* (pp. 28—30) had attributed the prevalence of a belief in diabolical agency to the influence of priests, and its decline to a freedom of thinking encouraged at the Revolution. Bentley, under the character of *Phileleutherus Lipsiensis,* or a Lover of Truth, at *Leipsic,* thus replies to his professed correspondent in England :

" What then has lessened, in E

---

* What has been done, at last, with the learned divine who has broached such strange opinions concerning angels in his book on the existence of spirits? Will not prove the zeal of his brethren for religion, for the truth, for orthodoxy? It will be strange indeed if he escape with impunity.

gland, your stories of sorceries? Not the *growing sect*, but the growth of philosophy and medicine. No thanks to Atheists, but to the Royal Society and College of Physicians; to the *Boyles* and *Newtons*, the *Sydenhams* and *Ratcliffs*. When the people saw the diseases they had imputed to witchcraft quite cured by a course of physic, they too were cured of their former error. They learned truth by the event, not by a false position, *à priori*, that there was neither witch, devil, nor God. And then as to the frauds and impostures in this way, they have most of them been detected by the clergy. The two strongest books I have read on this subject, were both written by *priests*, the one by Dr. *Bekker*, in Holland, and the other by a Doctor of your own, whose name I've forgot, that was afterwards Archbishop of York."——*Remarks*, 8th ed. 1742, pp. 48, 49.

It is obvious how little to Dr. Bentley's purpose, or rather how directly opposed to his conclusion, was the case of *Bekker*, who for ceasing to be a *priest*, or authoritative supporter of an established dogma, had been persecuted by all the *priests* of a consistory, and saved from want only by the kind consideration of the civil magistrates.

Can any of your readers say who was the *Doctor* whose name the pretended *Leipsic* theologian did not choose to recollect, and who had been Archbishop of York before 1713—the date of the *Remarks?* During that year Dr. Sharp died, who had filled the See of York ever since 1692. He was an intimate friend of Tillotson, and might be more disposed to rational innovation than many of his contemporaries.

R.

Sir, *Nov.* 2, 1810.

I WOULD fain draw the attention of your classic and learned readers to a subject of great logical importance. It has been long assumed as a kind of axiom by rhetoricians, that there are hardly two words in any language which have precisely the same idea; but with much deference to venerable opinions, I think the converse of the above position the true one, namely, that there is hardly any idea which may not in every language be expressed by several words, or different modes of speech. With the intention of invi-

ting some useful discussion on *synonimes*, I shall present you with a few quotations from Cicero. Let it not be supposed, however, that I wish to depreciate the merits of that great master of wisdom and rhetoric. Whoever does not admire, or rather adore every particle of his original, profound, eloquent, and truly classical compositions, is to be pitied for want of true taste, rather than convicted of bad judgment. Language has two offices—one to express meaning, another to produce harmony: the purposes of harmony require many insignificant particles, beautiful tautologies, and elegant expletives. My object is simply to point out a few of the beautiful tautologies or elegant expletives which abound in the incomparable compositions of the divine Tully. Such words as I consider tautological, I shall distinguish by *italics*; and let it be observed that though I am not satisfied with any thing I have yet seen on the doctrine of synonimes, and though I have thought a good deal on the subject, I am far from assuming any infallibility of opinion, or attempting to dogmatize, and ought to be considered (even if a heretic) as only provoking mild and fair discussion.

Sintque *pares* in amore et *æquales*.—amicitiarum sua cuique permanent *stabilis* et *certa* possessio.—Quin etiam necesse erit *cupere* et *optare* ut quam sæpissime peccet amicus—necesse erit *angi, dolere* invidere.—Sunt *firmi* et *stabiles* et *constantes* eligendi—quis natura desiderat *abundantiam* et *copiam*—sic habendum est nullam in amicitiis pestem esse majorem quam *adulationem, blanditiam, assentationem.*—Quibus nihil opis est in ipsis ad *bene beateque* vivendum, iis omnis gravis est ætas.—Nec vero corpori soli subveniendum est sed *menti* atque *animo* multo magis:—huic divino *muneri* ac *dono* nihil esse tam inimicum quam voluptatem.—quin nihil sit animus *admixtum* nihil *concretum* nihil *copulatum* nihil *coagmentatum* nihil duplex. Quod cum ita sit, certe nec *secerni* nec *dividi* nec *discerni* nec *distrahi* potest.—*Mens* enim et *ratio* et consilium, in senibus.

The above are a few quotations selected without much searching; and your classic readers know that if all similar words were marked in *italics*, the compositions of Cicero would appear richly gemmed with elegant tautologies. Some of the above synonimes are merely different spellings, or forms of the same word: *mens* is a contraction of *animens*, the same as *animus, anima*, contraction of πνευμα, πνευμων, &c. from πνεω, πνυη, a softened form of πλεω, flo, blow, which primarily signifies to *move*, whatever it be connected with; as air, water, &c. for fleo, flo, pluo, &c. are merely different spellings of the same word. Were it not that etymology is below the notice of an elegant rhetorician, we might wonder that Cicero should have gravely inquired whether *animus* was *anima* or *ignis*, and then left the matter in solemn doubt, by declaring that he was not like some, ashamed to confess wherein he was ignorant.

When *animus* is employed like *soul*, (from *halo*) metaphorically to denote mind or the rational part, thing, act or whatever it should be called, I cannot distinguish any meaning in it different from *ratio*, which seems to me like rate, reck, reckon, reason, &c. nothing but *rect* or *right*, with what is called a substantive termination. Hence *right reason* or *recta ratio* is merely right rightness, or straight straightness (compounded of ex or est, and rect or right); and wrong reason is crooked right, that is a plain contradiction.

Perhaps some will think that we are stretching what has been called metaphysical etymology too far; but unless we rectify the instrument of logic, that is *logos* or language, our opinions will on most subjects continue to be not rational or right, but crooked or wrong. ETYMOLOGUS.

Narrative of a celebrated Auto de Fé, in the City of Logrono.
[Continued from p. 577.]

THE principal band of wizards and witches discovered by the zeal and diligence of our holy inquisitors, was one accustomed to meet for the celebration of their "infernal rites" at Zugarramurdi, a village in the valley of Bantan, at the foot of the Pyrenean mountains. Fifty or sixty persons composed this assembly,—which was interrupted, and its members handed over to the "mercy" of our tribunal, in consequence of the following circumstances.

"A woman who had been an inhabitant of Zugarramurdi, went into France with her father, and was there persuaded by a witch (whose name the inquisitors could not discover) to accompany her to the Aquelane,* where she was told she would enjoy herself wonderfully. She consented,—went,—found the Devil† presiding there, and on her knees renounced her God;—but being required to renounce the Virgin also, she refused to proceed, though she did acknowledge the Devil as her lord and master. This excited the rage of her sister-witches, who marked her out as the object of their constant persecution. She continued, however, eighteen months in communion with them, but constantly fancying the Devil could not be the *God* he pretended. Her uneasiness of mind increased daily, and when Lent arrived she determined to go to confession, but not to own her witchcraft—she attended mass, and to her astonishment found that she could neither see the holy wafer when it was offered to her, nor the host when it was elevated; nothing but a black cloud appeared be-

* This is the provincial name for the place where witches assemble to celebrate their mysteries.

† He is thus described (*tr. verbatim*) in another part of the details of the auto, on the authority of the different witnesses. "He is seated on a throne, which sometimes appears of gold, and sometimes of ebony. He has a gloomy, careless, ugly countenance. He is quite black, and wears on his head a crown of thorns, three of which are larger than the rest, viz. one on each side, and one on his forehead, from whence a light proceeds brighter than that of the moon, but dimmer than that of the sun, with which he illumines the Aquelane. His eyes are large, round, widely opened, flaming and frightful. His beard is shaped like a goat's, and his appearance is altogether goat-like. He has fingers all of equal length on his hands and feet, and his nails are sharp as the talons of a bird of prey. His fingers are crooked and his feet are webbed like those of a goose. His voice is fearful, discordant, like the braying of a mule, but not quite so loud. His pronunciation is bad, and he often speaks unintelligibly. His tone is gloomy and harsh, but full of dignity and arrogance. He constantly looks in a melancholy humour, and seems unceasingly angry."

fore her (and it is acknowledged by all that on becoming witches they cease to see the Holy Sacrament). Her mind was tortured by this circumstance, and she was at the very door of death, when she determined to confess every thing, and she sent for a learned priest, who, though he cheered and consoled her, refused to grant absolution without consulting the Bishop of Bayonne, but from this time forward she could see the consecrated bread, and she left the diabolical sect to which she had been attached.

This woman afterwards returned to Zugarramurdi, and denounced the junta of witches which assembled there. Among these was Maria Yurreteguia (who afterwards became *the principal evidence under our commission against the accused*). She denied the charge at first with furious ravings, oaths and threats of vengeance; but the woman protesting that if publicly confronted with her she would prove her crimes, was led to her house and there convinced every one present of the truth of her accusations; for Yurreteguia fell down in an agony, making signs that something in her throat prevented her uttering the truth. On recovering, she heaved a deep sigh, and a pestiferous stench issued from her mouth. She then owned her guilt in its fullest extent, and that she had been a witch from her very childhood up. The Vicar of Zugarramurdi was sent for, to whom she confessed all she knew, prayed forgiveness for all the injuries done to her neighbours, and from this time she began to see the host which before she had never been able to distinguish.

The Devil feeling his critical situation, and the alarming evil which would result from this discovery, addressed the wizards at their next meeting, and it was determined to go to Yurreteguia's house and to bring her by force to the Aquelane. For this purpose they took the forms of divers animals, dogs, cats, pigs and goats, and hurried on (the Devil at their head) to her dwelling, having left the noviciates and inexpert young wizards behind them in the garden. The Devil then opened the doors and windows, and introduced all his followers. Their intended victim was

sitting in the kitchen, surrounded by her friends, whom she had collected together, anticipating this visit on account of its being the Aquelane night. The Devil and two or three others then hid themselves behind a bench, from whence they just shewed their head, and beckoned to the woman to come away with them. This was in vain, and they next lifted up their hands, and threatened her in every possible manner. She then called loudly on her friends for assistance, pointing to the place where the Devil was, but the Devil had blinded their eyes, and they could see nothing. She continued crying "leave me traitors, I have followed Satan too long already"—and then elevating her rosary, "*this* will I follow, *this* will protect me." On hearing which the Devil and the witches fled with a great noise, and to revenge themselves they tore up all the cabbages in the garden, destroyed all the trees in the orchard, and then went to a mill, rented by a relation of Yurreteguia, where they were joined by a legion of demons, who lifted up the mill from the pillars on which it was built, and carried it through the air to the top of the mountain, where they all danced round it, laughing and singing: the most aged of the witches, being as active as the rest, shouted "girls here, though old women at home;" and afterwards they carried back the mill to its place, after breaking the machinery and hurling the mill-stone into the water.

The Devil endeavoured to corrupt Maria, and to weaken the force of this evidence, but she persevered, and was rewarded by the tenderness shewn her, in consequence of her disposition to communicate *all* she knew. When the other criminals were being exhibited, she was allowed to put off the garments of degradation, and to return home—a striking instance of mercy from her judges, and of recompence for the frankness and firmness of her confessions!"

The next paper will give the report of the inquisitors on the discoveries they made of the proceedings of the Devil at Zugarramurdi and other places.

B.

GLEANINGS; OR, SELECTIONS AND
REFLECTIONS MADE IN A COURSE
OF GENERAL READING.

No. CCLXXXI.
Mahomet Mortal.

On the death of Mahomet (Hegira
11, March 28, A. D. 632), a great
confusion arose among his followers;
some of them deserting him, and many
believing he was not dead; among
whom was *Omar*, who drew his sword,
and swore that if any durst say he was
dead, he would cut him in pieces. But
Abubeker coming in, and knowing the
mistake, cry'd: " Do you worship Mahomet, or the God of Mahomet? If
you worship the God of Mahomet, he
is immortal and liveth for ever; but as
to Mahomet, he is certainly dead."
And then from several passages in the
Alcoran, he proved that he must die as
well as other men. And since that
time, no one among the Mahometans
ever expected that he should return to
them here on earth, till the general
resurrection of all mankind.

Life of Mahomet, pp. 76, 77, prefixed
  to *Four Treatises concerning the*
  Doctrine, &c. of Mahometans.—
  London. 8vo. 1712.

No. CCLXXXII.
Mahometan Assumption and Immaculate
Conception.

Phatima, the favourite daughter of
Mahomet, one of the only four women
whom he allowed to be perfect,* and
whom he gave in marriage to his cousin
Ali, is held in such veneration among
the Mussulmans, that she is reckoned
the most excellent woman of all ages;
and the people of Com believe that
God carried her into heaven, and that
there is nothing in the temple where
she was buried but a representation of
her. They believe likewise that she
is an immaculate and spotless virgin,
notwithstanding she was the mother
of several children. It is not therefore
the Church of Rome alone that honours the assumption of virgins, and
believes the immaculate conception
and perpetual virginity of a mother.
     The Same, p. 80.

---

* The other three were *Asiah*, the wife
of Pharoah, *Mary*, the mother of Christ,
and *Cadigha*, Mahomet's first wife, the
mother of Phatima.

No. CCLXXXIII.
Mahometan Prayers.

The observance of prayers is much
commended among the Mahometans,
and the richer or greater any one is,
the sooner he is reputed impious, pagan,
and infidel, if he neglect prayers, once
or oftener. Men of lesser note are
thrown out of their parishes by their
dervises or priests, if they go not to
public prayers in the temple; for they
say " prayers are the *pillar of religion*,
and whosoever forsakes the prayers,
overthrows religion." A *Turk* counts
it a great injury, and the greatest reproach upon him, if any one calls him
a man without prayers, viz. who does
not daily say his prayers. Moreover,
the Turkish preachers have a satirical
cant against those who don't pray
daily, by which they contemn them
and represent them as ridiculous.

Bobovius on Turkish Liturgy, with
  Notes by Hyde.

No. CCLXXXIV.
Composition of the Trinity.

Mahomet made way amongst Jews
and Christians by denouncing and opposing the corruption of the Trinity.
He represents the Trinity as formed
of God, Jesus Christ and the Virgin
Mary. Had he, like John the Baptist's disciples mentioned by Luke in
the Acts, not so much as heard whether there be any Holy Ghost? The
idolatry of Christians towards a woman
might be the reason of the ungallant
spirit of Islamism.

The Mahometan notion of the Trinity may be attributed to ignorance or
malice; yet one of the fathers, Cyril
of Alexandria, had called the *Mother*
of God, the *Complement* or *Supplement*
of the Holy Trinity.

See *Reflect. on Mahom.* in the *Four*
  Treatises, p. 174.

No. CCLXXXV.
Happy Apology for a Speech.

A Swedish gentleman was lately
present at the dinner of the Friends of
Foreigners in Distress, and a toast
being given complimentary to his
country, it was expected that he should
rise and address the company. He
arose after some hesitation and under
great embarrassment, from his not
thoroughly understanding the English
language, and not being in the habit
of public speaking, said, " I wish you
to consider me *a foreigner in distress*."

No. CCLXXXVI.
Sir Robert Howard.

Sir Robert Howard (says Toland, in his Life of Milton, Works, I. 43.), lately deceased, a gentleman of great generosity, a patron of letters and a hearty friend to the liberty of his country, being told that he was charged in a book with whipping the Protestant clergy on the back of the Heathen and Popish priests, he presently asked *What they had to do there?* He was a great admirer of Milton to his dying day, and being his particular acquaintance would tell many pleasant stories of him: as, that he himself having demanded of him once, *What made him side with the Republicans?* Milton answered, among other reasons, *Because their's was the most frugal government;*

for that the trappings of a monarchy might set up an ordinary commonwealth.
The work of Sir Robert Howard's alluded to was *The History of Religion. Written by a Person of Quality.* 8vo. 1694. He thought and probably conversed with the early English Unitarians. He was a great admirer of Archbishop Tillotson, and was accused, together with Tillotson, of Deism if not Atheism, by ' the accuser of the brethren,' Lesley. There is a letter of his in reply, in a well-written and amusing book, called *A Twofold Vindication of the late Archbishop of Canterbury and of the Author of the History of Religion.* 8vo. 1696. The writer of the second part of this work, a clergyman, was an Unitarian, though not a Socinian. See pp. 89, 101, 145.

BIBLICAL CRITICISM.

Nov. 1st, 1816.
Observations on the intended Sacrifice of Isaac by Abraham.

AS Isaac was the child of the old age (for such we should call it) of Abraham and Sarah; as, in the event of *his* death, there was no human prospect of his place being supplied; and as it was expressly promised that in the patriarch's seed all the families of the earth were to be blessed, we may with ease conceive how particularly dear such a son would be to his parents. What then would be the trial of their faith, of the faith of the father especially, were they summoned to surrender such a gift! This test of confidence, of duty and submission, they actually underwent.

" God," says the Apostle James (i. 13), " is not tempted with evil; neither *tempteth* he any man." Yet, in the sacred history, we read (Gen. xxii. 1) " God did *tempt* Abraham." For the removal of this seeming difficulty, I observe that the original expression, which our translators almost invariably render by the word *tempt*, does not always admit this sense. Sometimes, as in the clause now quoted from the book of Genesis, it means simply, to *try*, or make trial of, the faith and virtue of an individual; at other times, it has the signification commonly affixed to the verb *tempt*, and imports " to *seduce* into sin." Now as it cannot without injustice and im-

piety be affirmed of God that he seduces any being into wickedness, and as, so far, he " *tempteth* no man," it is equally true that he sees fit to *prove*, by various tests, the integrity and devout confidence of his servants.

In this manner, to this extent, and no further, did he *tempt* Abraham, when he said, * " Take now thy son, thine only son, Isaac, whom thou lovest, and get thee into the land of Moriah; and offer him there for a burnt-offering, upon one of the mountains which I will tell thee of." Nor was the patriarch disobedient to the celestial voice, whether it spake to him in vision, or otherwise. ——" Abraham stretched forth his hand, and took the knife, to slay his son." It was an eventful moment: with what contending emotions must his heart have struggled! But every painful feeling soon vanished before the joy and wonder of which he was conscious: for, at this critical period, the angel of the Lord called unto him out of heaven, and said, † " Lay not thine hand upon the lad, &c." As the consequence, the blessings of which Abraham had more than once received assurances were again promised to him, in terms yet stronger than before: and this test of his obedience, while it answered the end of illustrating and heightening the

---

* Gen. xxii. 2.
† Gen. xxii. 11—14.

excellence of his personal character, subserved the interests of even his remote descendants.

The intended sacrifice of Isaac, is never represented in the Scriptures as typical of the death of Christ. On a subject of this nature conjecture must not be opposed to facts: nor must imagination gain ascendancy over the understanding.

It has been asked, whether God did not require Abraham to commit an aggravated *murder*, to slay, with his own hands, a tenderly beloved child? Now that a voice from heaven called on the patriarch to make this sacrifice, is undeniable. Yet, before we pronounce it murder in intention, we should attend to the circumstances of the case, to the situation, the prerogative, the motives of the parties. The Sovereign Lord of life, may doubtless revoke this grant, when and how he pleases. In fact however it was not his design that human blood should be shed in the present instance. Consequently, no *murder* was authorized by the Divine *decree*, which ought to govern our interpretation of the language here employed. And though Abraham was on the point of sacrificing his son, no malignant feelings prompted him to the action. The crime of *murder*, which has different shades of guilt, essentially consists in " taking away life unlawfully." What, nevertheless, if, under circumstances so peculiar that they are not likely to befal any other individual, or to occur in any other age, a father's devout confidence and attachment be tried by the injunction himself to slay his child? If *murder* be estimated by the existence of the wicked mind and principle which dictates it, I maintain that the deed represented is not *murder*.

Some men, it is certain, are fond of appealing to precedents, real or supposed, in justification of their own views and conduct. Nor shall I shrink from granting the possibility that a particular description of persons may be disposed to seek in the example before us a defence of actions from which our nature shudders. Still, I cannot recollect a single case of this abuse of Abraham's history: and every thinking man will be sensible that it

could not be so perverted excepting by individuals whom either enthusiasm or vice has rendered absolutely insane. Thus, the only question which remains to be considered is, whether the patriarch had rational evidence of the command being addressed to him, by God? And that it proceeded from no inferior authority, is amply proved by previous and by subsequent events in the life of Abraham. He had already been favoured with many important communications from the Deity, and was able to distinguish between these, and the suggestions of his own mind. The substantial benefit of obeying these communications he had also experienced; and therefore he would not be less disposed to exercise a similar obedience at present. I add that he actually reaped the advantage of his readiness to make this costly sacrifice to the Divine Will. The remainder of his life, was eminently peaceful and happy: the faith thus tried was invigorated by the trial; and the men of that age and country, and distant generations, would receive important lessons from the event.

Abraham was specially educated by God, for purposes of infinite moment to all mankind. To form a just opinion of his history and character, we should go back, in our thoughts, to other times and regions than our own, to the infancy of the world, to a period when the sun of Divine Truth was far indeed from having reached it's perfect day. And if any person be still inclined to exclaim respecting the command of which I am treating, " It is a hard saying: who can bear it?" I may be permitted to illustrate this language by Solomon's,[*] on a memorable occasion: *he* ordered that a living child should be divided in two; not designing however that the order should be executed, because it was not fit to be executed—and yet, remarks the author[†] to whom I am indebted for the illustration, " the success of this method shewed the command to be very fit and expedient."

N.

---

* 1 Kings iii. 16.

† Grove, in a Sermon on this part of Abraham's History.

REVIEW.

ART. I.—*A Letter to the Unitarian Christians in South Wales, occasioned by the Animadversions of the Right Reverend the Lord Bishop of St. David's.* To which are annexed 1. Letters, before published in The Gentleman's Magazine, in Reply to his Lordship's Letters to the Unitarians. 2. A Brief Review of his Lordship's Treatise, entitled "The Bible, and Nothing but the Bible, the Religion of the Church of England." 3. An Estimate of his Lordship's Character and Qualifications as a Theological Polemic. By Thomas Belsham. 8vo. pp. 144. Hunter.

IT is said that some animals counteract their venom by the repetition of their own bite. Certainly, bigoted and angry polemics become in a little time perfectly harmless. Their power of hurting is derived from public opinion, which, however it may be misled for a moment, will not finally lend itself to prejudice and passion.

Bishop Burgess has found in Mr. Belsham a champion whom he cannot alarm by his vauntings, terrify by his menaces, or worry and vex and weaken by his continual attacks. Secure in his argument, steady to his point and conscious of his powers, Mr. Belsham enters the arena with firm and intrepid step, maintains the conflict according to the rules of honourable warfare, detects and foils his antagonist whenever he takes up unlawful weapons, and retires when the contest is fairly ended, cheerfully awaiting the decision of the intelligent and learned public, the only proper judges, but expecting, not presumptuously nor unreasonably, that to him the palm will be awarded.

Mr. Belsham explains in an *Advertisement* that he addresses the Unitarian Christians in South Wales, because they are a numerous and rapidly increasing body; because that district being the principal seat of Bishop Burgess's residence, it is there that his Lordship's works are most likely to be read and to make impression; and because he has been actually called upon by some persons of consideration among the Unitarians there to take notice of his Lordship's animadversions.

To the Advertisement is annexed the Letter which Mr. Belsham inserted in our last Volume [X. 746], on some passages in Dr. Estlin's late publication in reply to Bishop Burgess, reviewed in a recent Number (p. 544). The Resolutions of the South Wales Unitarian Book Society, at their last meeting, an account of which is given in this Volume of our Magazine (p. 427), shew that Dr. Estlin was mistaken in supposing that any disservice had been done to the Unitarian cause in the Principality by any of Mr. Belsham's writings. There are points on which the Unitarians amicably divide; but there can be but one opinion amongst them concerning the merits of Mr. Belsham as the defender of their great and good cause.

The question between Mr. Belsham and the Bishop of St. David's is a historical and learned one; but Mr. Belsham has we think made it intelligible to every English reader. Why, indeed, should not any controversy, excepting only such as are verbal and grammatical, which cannot be of the first importance, be intelligible to all men of understanding and general reading, or, in words which we flatter ourselves are of the same meaning as these last, to Unitarians in the humbler ranks?

In the Letter, Mr. Belsham makes a happy use of the philosophical argument for Unitarianism. He puts the following case with regard to the *silence* of the New Testament on the Deity of Christ:

"If Bishop Burgess had undertaken to write a history of Jesus Christ for the instruction of early and uninformed converts, would he, like Matthew, Mark, and Luke, have passed over his Divine nature in absolute silence, or with an incidental, distant, and ambiguous allusion to it? If this learned prelate had continued the history of the apostles' preaching and doctrine for thirty years after our Lord's Ascension, would he, is it possible that he could, have forborne to record a single instance in which the apostles taught, or the first disciples professed, the sublime doctrine of our Lord's divinity? Would the venerable Bishop of St. David's, when dictating a pastoral and paternal charge to his younger clergy,

the express design of which was to direct
them in what manner they were to act,
and upon what topics to insist in their
ministerial instructions, forget to mention, or at best, but obscurely hint at
those sublime mysteries, the belief and
profession of which are essential to salvation? I am confident that the learned
prelate, lukewarm and indifferent as his
feelings must be upon these subjects in
comparison with those of the early believers, would never have been guilty of so
important an omission. How then can
this omission be accounted for in the apostles of Christ and in the writers of the
New Testament!"—Pp. 10, 11.

He argues also very conclusively
upon the necessary effect of the revelation of the divinity of Christ upon the
minds of the apostles:

"Their whole souls would have been
absorbed in this unexpected and overwhelming discovery. Their imaginations
would have been wholly occupied with the
stupendous idea. Their minds could have
thought, and their tongues could have
spoken of nothing but the Divine glories
of their great Master, of the amazing
condescension of the Almighty Creator in
becoming incarnate, and in submitting to
be rocked in a cradle and suspended on a
cross. This wondrous theme would have
been the first and the last, the Alpha and
Omega, of their discourse, the unceasing
topic of their public harangues, and the
darling subject of their social conversation.
Their writings would have been filled with
it from beginning to end. Nor would it
have been possible for Matthew, Mark,
and Luke, for Paul, and Peter, and James,
to have left it to the Apostle John, many
years after their decease, to have disclosed this great mystery to the astonished
world."—Pp. 16, 17.

We are much pleased with the following hint to the Bible Society, by
which, if its judgment and honesty be
equal to its resources and zeal, it will
not fail to profit: the passage refers to
the notorious forgery of the text relating
to the Three Heavenly Witnesses, 1
John v. 7:

"This spurious text is wanting in the
Syriac manuscripts which have been found
among the native Christians in the Peninsula of India. It is said the Bible Society
are printing the New Testament in Syriac
for the use of these Christians. It is to
be hoped that they will not presume to
insert this exploded text into the printed
copies, and thus pollute and debase their
great and honourable work by a wilful
adulteration of the sacred text. See Dr.

Buchanan's interesting 'Account of the
State of Christianity in India.'"—Note,
p. 22.

It is fortunate for the cause of truth
that Bishop Burgess provoked a discussion concerning the merits of Dr.
Priestley's celebrated argument with
Dr. Horsley, in the *Gentleman's Magazine*; for by dragging Mr. Belsham
into a correspondence in that work, he
has forced a number of clerical and
other readers to understand a dispute
of which they would otherwise probably have gone down to their graves
in utter ignorance. Mr. Belsham has
proved that Dr. Horsley was completely vanquished by Dr. Priestley,
and in exhibiting this proof in his
usual able manner, he himself has
satisfactorily confuted the present Bishop of St. David's. The argument is
of so much consequence that we shall
extract Mr. Belsham's statement of it:

"Your attentive readers will recollect
that the Emperor Adrian razed the city
of Jerusalem to the ground; that nearly
upon the same site he built a new city,
which he called Ælia; which he colonized
with Gentiles, to which he granted many
privileges, and from which he excluded
all Jews under pain of death; also that a
Christian Church was formed in the new
city, of which Marcus, a Gentile, was
the first Bishop. Mosheim, in his Commentaries, states his opinion, that this
church consisted chiefly of believing Hebrews, who abandoned the rites of Moses
for the sake of being admitted to the privileges of the Ælian colony. In support
of this hypothesis, Mosheim appeals to
the testimony of Sulpitius and Epiphanius;
and to his judgment Bishop Horsley ac-
cedes. Dr. Priestley opposes Mosheim's
supposition. He makes light of that
learned writer's authorities; and with
Tillemont, Fleury, and the great body of
modern ecclesiastical writers, he maintains that all Jews, without exception,
were excluded from Ælia by Adrian's decree.

"Bishop Horsley pursues the argument
in the following words ('Tracts, p. 409) :—

"'To convict my adversary of shameful precipitance, absolves not me of the
imputation, that I have related, upon the
authority of Mosheim, what Mosheim related upon none. I will therefore briefly
state the principles which determine me
to abide by Mosheim's account of the
transactions in question. I take for
granted then these things :—

"'1. A Church of Hebrew Christians,
adhering to the observance of the Mosaic
law, subsisted for a time at Jerusalem,

and for some time at Pella, from the beginning of Christianity until the final dispersion of the Jews by Adrian.

" ' 2. Upon this event a Christian Church arose at Ælia.

" ' 3. The Church of Ælia, often, but improperly, called the Church of Jerusalem, (for Jerusalem was no more in its external form, that is, in its doctrine and its discipline,) was a Greek Church, and it was governed by Bishops of the uncircumcision. In this I and my adversary are agreed. The point in dispute between us is, of what members the church of Ælia was composed. He says, of converts of Gentile extraction. I say, of Hebrews : of the very same persons, in the greater part, who were members of the antient Hebrew Church, at the time when the Jews were subdued by Adrian. For again I take for granted,

" ' 4. That the observation of the Mosaic law in the primitive Church of Jerusalem was a matter of mere habit and national prejudice, not of conscience. Again, I take for granted,

" ' 5. That with good Christians, such as I believe the primitive church at Jerusalem to have been, motives of worldly interest, which would not overcome conscience, would overcome mere habit.

" ' 6. That the desire of partaking in the privileges of the Ælian colony, from which Jews were excluded, would accordingly be a motive that would prevail with the Hebrew Christians of Jerusalem, and other parts of Palestine, to divest themselves of the form of Judaism by laying aside their antient customs.

" ' It may seem,' adds Bishop Horsley, p. 419, ' that my six positions go no further than to account for the disuse of the Mosaic law among the Christians of Palestine, upon the supposition that the thing took place ; and that they amount not to a proof that a church of Hebrew Christians, not adhering to the rites of Judaism, actually existed at Ælia. To complete the proof, therefore, I might appeal to Epiphanius.——But I will rather derive the proof from a fact which I think still more convincing. I affirm then,

" ' 7. That a body of orthodox Christians of the Hebrews were actually existing in the world much later than in the time of Adrian.

" ' I will rest the credit of my seventh proposition upon the mention, which occurs in St. Jerome's Commentary upon Isaiah, of *Hebrews believing in Christ*, as distinct from the *Nazarenes*. These were orthodox believers,—and were not observers of the Mosaic law,—and actually existing somewhere in the world from the reign of Adrian to the days of St. Jerome, if they were not members of the church at Ælia, dwelling at Ælia. Dr. Priestley,

if he be so pleased, may seek their settlement—'

" ' For,' as Bishop Burgess pertinently adds, in confirmation of this most novel and satisfactory demonstration, ' where should we seek but at Jerusalem, the primitive seat of Hebrew Christianity ?'

" In his sixth disquisition (Tracts, p. 549), Bishop Horsley states,

" ' That the proof of his proposition rests in part only upon St. Jerome's evidence. The entire proof rests upon the seven positions. And St. Jerome's evidence goes *barely* to the proof of the last of those positions, the seventh ; namely, that a body of orthodox Christians of the Hebrews was actually existing in the world much later than the time of Adrian. St. Jerome's evidence is brought for the proof of this position *singly*, and this, proved by St. Jerome's evidence, in conjunction with six other principles previously laid down, *makes the whole evidence* of the main fact which I affirm, that a Church of orthodox Christians of the Hebrews existed at Ælia, from the final dispersion of the Jews by Adrian, to a much later period.'

" These are Bishop Horsley's own words. He expressly asserts that the seven positions make *the whole evidence* of the main fact—that of these positions, the six first ' go no further than to account for the disuse of the Mosaic law among the Christians in Palestine in Adrian's reign, *upon the supposition* that the thing took place ;' and that " St. Jerome's evidence goes *singly* and *barely* to the proof of the seventh position, namely, that a body of orthodox Christians of Hebrews was actually existing in the world much later than the time of Adrian ;' that is, in the days of Jerome, more than two hundred and fifty years after the reign of Adrian. But it is evident that this fact proves nothing as to the actual state of things in Adrian's time. This cypher, therefore, added to the other six, constitutes, by Bishop Horsley's own concession, the whole of his proof that the Church of Ælia, in the time of Adrian, consisted chiefly of orthodox Hebrew Christians, who had renounced the rites of Moses to obtain the privileges of the Ælian colony.

" Being thus in possession of the whole of the case, your intelligent readers will be enabled to form a correct judgment of the question at issue between Bishop Burgess and your present correspondent, and of the arguments alleged by each, which otherwise it would be impossible to understand."—Pp. 60—65.

There is much sprightliness and humour as well as sound argument and manly and Christian expostulation in the " Brief Review," following the

Letters, extracted from the Gentleman's Magazine. The Bishop's mode of argument would provoke a smile on the most woeful countenance.

"And last, though not the least remarkable, in p. 54, figures a goodly train of Trinitarian *physicians*. But I fear that the profane reader will hardly preserve a becoming gravity of countenance when he reads that such men as Dr. Young, and even Dr. Baillie, have condescended to suspend the labours and the duties of the profession for which they are so justly celebrated, and of which they constitute such distinguished ornaments, in order to extract from the neglected volumes of the dark ages a few venerable names to eke out the deficient catalogue of medical orthodoxy. Still, however, these learned gentlemen owe some obligation to the courtesy of his Lordship, that he did not impose upon them the much harder task of making out a list of orthodox physicians in modern times.—In a note, p. 150, the Bishop says, 'For the following additions of medical names I am indebted to Dr. Baillie and Dr. Young.' Then follow the *illustrious* names of Solenander, Schenkius, Plater, Sennert, Hildanus, and Bartholin. 'Wepfer also, a judicious Swiss physician, uses the expression *Deus ter. optimus Maximus*,' which affords great reason to hope that he also was of the *true* faith."—Pp. 86, 87.

Mr. Belsham has been censured for publishing the private letters of the Bishops of Elphin and Carlisle: we extract his vindication of himself, which we believe has proved satisfactory to almost the only person who was entitled to complain. The passage is particularly valuable for the character which it exhibits, by contrast, of the author of " The Considerations."

"In page 16, Mr. B. is upbraided in no courtly style, with violating private confidence in publishing the Bishop of Elphin's letter to Mr. Lindsey, which contained a draft for a hundred pounds for Dr. Priestley, and another letter from Dr. Edmund Law, Bishop of Carlisle, the Bishop of Elphin's father, which accompanied a present of the last edition of his celebrated Theory of Religion " *corrected and much enlarged*:' and 'purged,' as the learned prelate expresses it in his letter to his friend, 'of some antient prejudices relating to the pre-existence of Christ.' The present respectable Bishop of Chester likewise alleges the same charge of violated confidence, in publishing his father's and his brother's letters, without leave being requested of the surviving family. The same answer will apply to both. In the

mean time it may be remarked, that if Bishop Burgess had read and digested that last corrected and improved edition of Bishop Law's admirable work, he might have spared the sarcasm upon the venerable prelate's advanced age, as though it indicated decline of intellect. Nor would it disgrace the clergy of the present day, if they should condescend to take a lesson from the mild and candid Bishop of Carlisle as to the style and spirit with which theological controversy should be conducted. In Bishop Law the urbanity of the gentleman was combined with the accuracy of the scholar, the impartiality of an ardent lover of truth, the erudition of a theologian, the sound judgment of a logician, and the candour and piety of a Christian. Unfettered in his inquiries, and fixed in the principles which from conviction he had embraced, he defended those principles with firmness and dignity, and disclaimed all weapons but those of calm discussion and fair argument. He did not affect to bear down an adversary with hard words and bitter reproaches: he did not impute motives to his opponent which that opponent disavowed, nor charge him with consequences which he distinctly denied: he did not magnify inadvertencies into crimes, nor repeat charges again and again after they had been completely refuted. It was not his method to defame his opponents instead of answering their arguments, to misstate their sentiments in order to confute them more easily, and to invent calumnies for the sake of rousing the indignation of the public. Never did it enter into the heart of this venerable and pious prelate to deny the appellation of Christian, to those who, equally with himself, looked for the mercy of God through the Lord Jesus Christ unto eternal life, much less to brand them with the infamous epithets of miscreants, infidels, blasphemers, and *God-denying apostates*,[*] because they differed from him in some mysterious points, which neither he nor they pretended either to explain or to understand. And as to invoking the terrors of the law upon those who had the misfortune to differ from him in articles of faith, it is an idea from which the feelings of this truly Christian prelate would have recoiled with horror.

"Prepossessed with the conviction that nothing but what indicates an enlightened

***

[*] "The Bible, &c. p. 19.' His Lordship of St. David's seems to plume himself upon having discovered in the late learned work of Dr. Routh, that Unitarians, in very early times, were branded by their ignorant and malignant enemies with this odious epithet, and the charitable prelate is determined it shall not be lost."

and liberal mind could proceed from a descendant of Dr. Edmund Law, it was with equal surprise and regret that I read, in page 17 of Bishop Burgess's work, the following letter from his son, Dr. George Law, the present Bishop of Chester, to the Bishop of St. David's: dated Palace, Chester, Sept. 20, 1814.

" 'I have read Belsham's Memoirs of Lindsey, and have no hesitation in informing you that the Letters, concerning which you make inquiry, were published without the knowledge or assent of the family. Such permission, had it been requested, would certainly not have been granted. The publication of my brother's Letter was *an act of ingratitude*, as well as a *breach of confidence*: because he particularly requested in it, that ' his name might on no account be mentioned to any one.' With respect to the Letter of my father, I would observe, that at the time of writing it he was more than eighty years of age ! ! ! and his health was greatly declining. Surely, then, less stress ought to be laid on any change of opinion under such circumstances, and at such an advanced period of life. As *the Divinity of our Saviour appears to me to be the very corner-stone of Christianity, and as it may be inferred from, or proved in, almost every page of Scripture,* you may easily conceive how painful it must be to my feelings, to witness the advantage which is thus taken of this Letter of my revered father, and to think that his name may be handed down to future ages as an abettor of the doctrines of Socinus.'

"This Letter has much the appearance of being confidential: and, had I been the Bishop of Chester's friend, my regard for him would certainly have prevented the publication of it, had I not been expressly required to print it. As it is, one cannot but admire that a doctrine, which, to the pious and learned *parent*, after a critical and diligent examination of the Scriptures for more than half a century, appeared to be erroneous and anti-christian, should be regarded by the *son* as the *very corner-stone of Christianity*, and what *might be inferred from, or proved in, almost every page of Scripture.* As to the insinuation, surely much to be regretted, that 'little stress is to be laid upon any change of opinion at such an advanced period of life,' the observation would have been perfectly correct, had it related to a relapse of the learned prelate into the errors of his childhood; for that is the common retrograde movement of frail human nature. But, when the change alluded to appears to have been an advance upon preceding acquisitions in consequence of further and persevering inquiries, and when the work which he published at that time does not

contain the slightest indication of a debilitated intellect, we cannot but conclude, that, though his *outward man* was perishing, his *inward man* was in full vigour: and that at the age of fourscore the Bishop was as competent to judge of the validity of an argument, as others are in the prime, or in the meridian of life. And if it is right to boast of human authority in a case which must be decided by divine testimony alone, the Unitarians may justly pride themselves in the name and character of Dr. Edmund Law, Bishop of Carlisle.

"But the Bishop of Chester accuses Mr. B. of not having 'requested permission of the family' to publish the letters of the Bishops of Carlisle and Elphin. Most certainly it never entered into Mr. B.'s thoughts that it was at all necessary or expedient to request any such permission. Had the Letters contained any thing which could be considered as disreputable to their authors, Mr. B. would have suppressed them altogether.—Had they touched upon private affairs, Mr. B. would never have published the Letters without the consent of the Bishop's highly respectable and dignified family. But, when one of these communications only mentions an omission in a work which is in the hands of every biblical student, and the other only brings to light an act of generosity which deserves to be held up to the admiration of mankind, Mr. B. did not conceive that he was exceeding the limits of the most scrupulous delicacy in exhibiting such documents to the world.

"But the Bishop of Chester is pleased to say that 'it was an act of ingratitude, as well as a breach of confidence,' to publish his brother's Letter, because he particularly requested in it 'that his name might on no account be mentioned to any one.'

"But why did the Bishop of Elphin desire this? Let the excellent prelate speak for himself.—'My name,' says he, 'must on no account be mentioned to him, [Dr. Priestley,] or to any one else, *as it would involve me with some acquaintance here, and do me more mischief than you can imagine.*' But surely when the cause ceased, the restraint likewise ceased. And when the generous prelate was removed out of the reach of bigotry, malignity, and envy, there can be no just reason why his liberality should not be proclaimed for the instruction and imitation of mankind. The charge of ' ingratitude,' can hardly be serious. The lame, the blind, the paralytic, and the insane, who were healed by Christ, could not refrain from publishing the blessings they received, though expressly prohibited by their great benefactor. Nor do we find that their disobedience in this particular was severely rebuked by our Lord himself, or that they are charged with ingratitude by the historians of his miracles."—Pp. 88—95.

The following are the letters referred to, accompanied by Mr. Belsham's remarks.

" It is not out of disrespect to the family, but as an act of self-defence, that I here republish the letters of the Bishops of Carlisle and Elphin, the publication of which in the Memoirs of Mr. Lindsey has subjected the writer to such severe and unexpected animadversion.

" The first is from the late Bishop of Carlisle to the Rev. Theophilus Lindsey, and is dated Cambridge, September 23, 1783. Let the reader judge how far it indicates any symptom of imbecillity of intellect in the learned and venerable prelate.

" 'DEAR SIR,

" ' I received the favour of your Historical View, and read it with satisfaction. You appear to have cleared up all the passages of Scripture usually alleged in favour of the contrary opinion, and to have exhausted the subject. As a small return for the obligation I must desire your acceptance of a new Cumberland edition of my Theory, purged of some antient prejudices relative to præ-existence, &c. I have recommended to my executors to procure a publication of Dr. Bullock's two Discourses which clear up the doctrine of atonement, and which I think I communicated to you formerly. The Bishop of Clonfert was returned to Ireland before your letter reached us. He would have been delighted with seeing your account of his favourite author A. Tucker, whose work I have often said wanted methodizing and abridging to be of more general use. My compliments to your worthy coadjutor and to my old friend Dr. Jebb. That all the success and satisfaction may attend your labours to which they are so justly entitled, is the most hearty wish of Your sincere Friend and Servant, " 'E. C.' "

" The letter from Dr. John Law, Bishop, first of Clonfert and afterwards of Elphin, to Mr. Lindsey, appears in the Memoirs of that venerable man, p. 447, and is thus introduced by the author, who, in a note, is giving an account of a subscription which was set on foot to defray the expenses of Dr. Priestley's Church History, and Notes on the Scriptures. The reader will judge how far the author is chargeable with *ingratitude* and *breach of confidence.*

" And now that he is at rest beyond the reach of envy and of calumny, from which neither exalted station nor exalted merit could have protected him here, it may be permitted to mention that by far the most liberal subscriber to this object was the late Right Reverend Dr. John Law, Bishop of Elphin. His letter is addressed to Mr. Lindsey, who had sent him a copy of his last publication: it is dated Elphin, October 7, 1802.

" 'MY DEAR SIR,

" ' Want of health and indisposition have prevented me from thanking you for your letter and obliging present sooner. I have read your valuable work with as much attention as pains in the head and stomach, arising from a flying gout, would let me, and think it is calculated to do a great deal of good.

" ' Enclosed is a draft for one hundred pounds, which you will apply in aid of Dr. Priestley's publication in any way he chooses: but my name must on no account be mentioned to him, or to any one else, *as it would involve me with some acquaintance here, and do me more mischief than you can imagine, and which I am sure you would not wish.* Our religion hereabouts is evidenced chiefly in hating and abusing those who differ from us: and, excepting this zeal, we scarce shew that in other things we have any. You will be surprised at it: but neither popery nor methodism are losing any ground.

" ' Reprint my father's Life of Christ whenever you please, and believe me to be, with the sincerest esteem,

" ' Your very faithful and obedient Servant, J. ELPHIN.' "
—Note, pp. 95—97.

In the " Estimate of his Lordship's Character," Mr. Belsham uses the dissecting knife boldly but dexterously. This anatomical exhibition will be displeasing to the Bishop and his friends, but may be serviceable to them, or at least to theological science. Bishop Burgess appears to Mr. Belsham to possess great learning with little judgment:

" Having thus given his Lordship ample credit for his learning, his sincerity, and his zeal, truth constrains me to add that the learned prelate appears to labour under a marvellous debility of the discriminating and reasoning powers, and a great want of comprehension of mind. It was a maxim of my late revered friend Dr. Priestley, that the contemplation of great ideas creates and even constitutes greatness of mind. The reverse of this seems also to be true: that an habitual and close attention to minute objects creates and constitutes littleness of mind: it incapacitates the intellect for expansion of thought, and comprehension of views. The microscopic eye, which discerns the anatomical construction of a flea or a mite, cannot, like the Herschel telescope, penetrate the recesses of infinite space, or range over the structure of the heavens. It is difficult for the same person to be a minute verbal critic, and a liberal and comprehensive reasoner. A man of words is not often a man of ideas. And his Lordship, in the course of his studies, has so limited himself to the minutiæ of words, that it is not at all surprising that his ideas should be very indistinct, his reasonings proportionably confused, and his views uncommonly limited."—Pp. 117, 118.

A *Postscript* relates the history of the Horsleyan and Priestleyan controversy:

" As the controversy concerning the rival claims of Bishop Horsley and Dr. Priestley is now brought to a close, it may not be amiss to take a brief review of the manner and spirit in which the advocates for the learned prelate have conducted their defence.

" Bishop Horsley himself was the most wary and guarded of all controversial writers. He knew his own strength, and he chose his own ground. Declining absolutely to enter into the general question concerning the belief of the primitive church, he merely undertakes to prove the incompetency of Dr. Priestley as an ecclesiastical historian. And the facts upon which he principally relies are, those which he borrows from Mosheim, viz. the sudden dereliction of the rites of Moses by the Hebrew Christians in order to enjoy the privileges of the Roman colony at Ælia, and the wilful falsehood of Origen, whose testimony contradicts this representation. Had these facts been true, they must have been notorious; Dr. Priestley must have been struck dumb; and his credit as an ecclesiastical historian would have been lost for ever. But the facts being contested, Dr. Horsley soon discovered his mistake, and began his retreat, which, however, he conducts like a consummate general; first abandoning the posts which were occupied by Mosheim, and afterwards giving up the entrenchments which he had himself thrown up: disputing every inch of ground, every now and then facing about, taking advantage of every oversight of the enemy, and at last quitting the field with a firm countenance, without any formal concession, or explicit acknowledgment of defeat.

" The Reverend Heneage Horsley next advanced as the pious and zealous advocate of his father's disputed claims; and what he wanted in knowledge and argument, he abundantly made up in calumny and abuse. But he soon found that his un-

practised arm was not equal to the management of the bow of Ulysses, and he wisely withdrew from the field. I hope the Prince Regent has not been unmindful of the pathetic expostulation of so pious, loyal, and dutiful a subject.

" Of Bishop Burgess it is difficult to know what to say. This venerable prelate, esteeming it his duty at all events to advocate the claims of his learned predecessor, without giving himself leisure to study the controversy, and only assuming two principles, viz. that all which Bishop Horsley says must be *true*, and all which Dr. Priestley and Dr. Priestley's advocate affirm must be *false*, he rushes *ving-dong* into the field, dealing out his blows indiscriminately upon friend and foe, especially the former ; all the while shouting *Io Triumphe!* and, after contradicting Bishop Horsley in almost every particular, he fondly imagines that he has laid the Bishop's opponents prostrate at his feet. The hero of La Mancha himself could not be better satisfied, when the whole flock of sheep lay bleeding under his puissant arm. His Lordship, however, has every appearance of being quite in earnest; and yet, so strangely ignorant is he of the true bearing of the controversy, that in his very last Address to the Unitarians he actually states *that* as the principal question in discussion between Dr. Priestley and Bishop Horsley, which Bishop Horsley formally, explicitly, and repeatedly, declares that he has not, and that he will not meddle with.

" Last of all come my old friends *the wise men* of the British Critic, who in their journal for November last, professing to review ' the Claims of Dr. Priestley,' &c. after writing four or five pages in their usual temperate style, at length come to this honest acknowledgment. ' As infallibility is not the lot of man, Bishop Horsley, we fear, has suffered himself to be led into error. Deserting the footsteps of Bishop Bull, who marshalled his way with a steady and unerring light, for the conjectural wanderings of Dr. Mosheim, who, on many subjects of primitive antiquity, is not merely a *blind* but a *treacherous* guide, he made a false step at the outset, which, with all his ability, he was unable to reclaim.'

" By this memorable concession, thus reluctantly extorted from these champions of orthodoxy, the claims of Dr. Priestley are established—the whole fabric of the famous church at Ælia, *consisting chiefly of orthodox Hebrew believers*, who, to obtain the privileges of the Roman colony, had apostatized from the rites of their ancestors, is overturned from its foundation —the character of Origen is redeemed—.

the testimony of that learned father to the Unitarianism of the Hebrew Christians of his own time remains unimpeached—the probability of a similarity of faith in the primitive Jewish believers is confirmed—and the conclusion, that the Unitarian doctrine was that which Christ and his apostles taught, is manifest and undeniable. Since, therefore, the mighty Dagon of these lords of the Philistines has thus fallen prostrate before the Ark of Truth, these illustrious critics are at full liberty to impute whatever share they please of this happy result to ' the restless and meddling confidence of Mr. B.'

" But why need they attack the character of the venerable Mosheim, to whose learned and indefatigable labours every friend of truth and biblical literature acknowledges unspeakable obligations, notwithstanding the error into which he has fallen in the present instance? When will theological writers learn to conduct their inquiries with candour, and to disuss their differences of opinion with good temper and good manners!"—Pp. 128—132.

The able, learned and successful champion of the Unitarian cause thus concludes this interesting work :

" To Bishop Burgess, I now once more bid farewell. In these discussions, into which I have been involuntarily dragged, I trust that I have not been deficient in that respect which is due to his Lordship's acknowledged talents and learning, to his private virtues, and to his elevated rank and station in society, and that upon all occasions I have treated him with as much civility and deference as was consistent with a supreme regard to truth. If I have exposed the futility of his Lordship's arguments, and the great impropriety of his dictatorial and overbearing manner, it is no more than I intended. Against his person I bear no ill-will : I neither wish to offend, nor hope to convert the Bishop of St. David's. But I trust that I have succeeded in encouraging my Unitarian brethren not to be " frightened at a few hard words," and to their candour and the judgment of the public I commit these papers."—P. 127.

We congratulate the Unitarians on their possessing such an advocate, and if our voice could avail we would intreat Mr. Belsham to continue those contributions to the cause of sacred learning and intellectual freedom which are expected by his numerous friends and admirers, from the resources of his mind and the eminence of his station in the church of Christ. Referring to that station, we venture to address him

in lines which have at least t[
of exactly expressing our senti[

Ibi beatus dissidentes adspicis[
Vultu sereno, quique dente te pe[
Temnis malignum et obstrepentiu[
Macte hoc honore, perge sanctæ[
Adferre lumen spiritu plenus saci[
Supraque vulgum credere (haud [
Amice perge, salva dum sit unita[
Et dum recepta casta servetur fid[

ART. II.—*The History and A[*
      of Dissenting Churches, [
      [Continued from p. 549.[

MR. WILSON has great [
   bringing to light obs[
not uninteresting characters. [
these is *Thomas Beverley*, wh[
the close of the seventeenth [
was pastor of an Independent [
meeting in *Cutlers' Hall, Clo[*
He was a busy and adventur[
ter on prophecy ; and, unfo[
for his reputation, assigned da[
predictions.   Smitten with [
tion of the Protestant Hero, [
III. and of the Revolution [
he foretold in that year, tha[
ten years the papacy would p[
the millenium commence. [
pointed period arrived and t[
was yet in power and the k[
of the world as far as ev[
Christian truth and purity an[
Disappointed and mocked, [
retired from the world to inc[
speculations in private. Ou[
has enumerated thirty-two of [
lications, chiefly relating to h[
ary expectations. (II. 63—6[
The plan of the History ob[
Wilson to confine his biogr[
the most part, to the p[
churches ; but he has occ[
inserted notices of other disti[
individuals amongst the I[
The following note relates [
eminently learned and virtuou[

" JOHN EAMES, F.R.S. As t[
person never undertook the past[
and, therefore, will not come[
under our notice, a brief accou[
in this place, cannot prove una[
Mr. Eames was a native of Lo[
received his classical learning at [
Taylors' School. He afterward[
a course of academical studies w[
to the Christian ministry : yet[

* Adrianus Van Wena ad[
Hackmannum, Fil.

preached but one sermon, when he was so exceedingly agitated and confused, that he was scarcely able to proceed. There was, also, unhappily, a great defect in his organs of speech, and his pronunciation was exceedingly harsh, uncouth and disagreeable. These circumstances discouraged him from renewing the attempt, so that quitting the pulpit entirely, he devoted himself to the instruction of young men, whose education for the ministry among Protestant Dissenters, was patronized and assisted by the Independent fund. His department included the languages, mathematics, moral and natural philosophy. On the death of Dr. Ridgley, who filled the divinity chair, in the same seminary, he was prevailed upon to add to his course on those subjects lectures in divinity, and to teach the oriental languages, assisted in the other branches by a learned colleague, Mr. Joseph Densham. Mr. Eames was a man of extensive learning, and a universal scholar. Dr. Watts once said to a pupil of his, (Mr. Angus) 'Your tutor is the most learned man I ever knew.' He excelled particularly in classical literature, and in a profound knowledge of mathematics and natural philosophy. His scientific learning procured him the acquaintance and friendship of Sir Isaac Newton, to whom he was on some occasions singularly useful. Sir Isaac introduced him to the Royal Society, of which he became a member; and he was employed, in conjunction with another gentleman, to prepare and publish an abridgment of their transactions. With his great talents, Mr. Eames united a diffidence and bashfulness of temper, that very much concealed his merits. He was of a candid and liberal disposition, and a friend to free inquiry, which exposed him, as it is said, to much opposition and uneasiness from some narrow-minded persons. He was instrumental in training up many persons of learning and worth; and, among others, the eminent Archbishop Secker was some time under his care. His death took place June 29, 1744. 'What a change (said Dr. Watts, who dedicated to him his Treatise on Geography and Astronomy) did Mr. Eames experience! but a few hours between his lecturing to his pupils, and his learning the lectures of angels.'—*Monthly Mag. April*, 1803.

" Mr. RICHARD DENSHAM above-mentioned, was a pupil of Mr. Eames, whom he afterwards assisted in the academy. Such was his proficiency in the mathematics, and in classical as well as theological learning, that upon Mr. Eames's death, Dr. Jennings, who succeeded to the office of principal tutor, made it a condition of his accepting that situation, that Mr. Densham should be his co-adjutor. But this he declined. Mr. Densham preached occasionally for a

short time, but afterwards relinquished the ministry, and continued in various secular employments, till disabled by old age.— Among his pupils were, Mr. Collins, of Bath, who bequeathed him his library; Dr. Savage, Dr. Price, and the benevolent Mr. Howard; all of whom left him some token of respect. Howard, in particular, before his last journey, gave him an unlimited order to draw upon his banker for whatever money he might want; but such was Mr. Densham's integrity, that, although at that time possessed of no more than twelve or thirteen pounds a year, in the funds, he chose rather to sell out, and diminish the capital, than accept a discretionary offer, which he could not do conscientiously while he had any thing of his own remaining. The late Mr. Whitbread hearing of his disinterested conduct, begged his acceptance of an annuity of twenty pounds during life. This he accepted, but to shew his gratitude, left Mr. Whitbread eighty pounds in his will, by way of acknowledgment. It may be mentioned to the honour of the latter, that he relinquished the bequest to Mr. D.'s nearest relations. Mr. Densham died at his apartments in Kingsland Road, July 18, 1792, leaving behind him a pattern of integrity that has been but rarely equalled. He compiled Mr. Howard's first book on prisons, and was urged to draw up a life of that benevolent man, but his infirmities prevented.—*Gent. Mag. August*, 1792." —II. 73, 74.

Carter Lane, Doctors' Commons, is behind none of the churches in the value of its pastoral names. The three first are familiar and endeared to every well-informed Nonconformist, viz. *Matthew Sylvester, Richard Baxter* and *Edmund Calamy*. Dr. *Samuel Wright* enjoyed a respectability and popularity which after the lapse of more than half a century is scarcely forgotten. *Thomas Newman* (there were two persons, father and son, of the name of Newman, John and Samuel, about the same time at Salters' Hall,) is yet remembered with great respect. His assistant, the late Mr. *Edward Pickard*, preached his funeral sermon, to which, when it was published, there was subjoined a paper, written and subscribed with Mr. Newman's own hand, in which there is the following *good confession* :

" I make no doubt but some of my own sentiments in Christianity might be errors in judgment. I full well know I was fallible; but I can as truly say, that I was a sincere lover and searcher after truth; and upon the most impartial search into my own breast, I never could discern any degree of prejudice sufficient to bias my researches, or to prevent my embracing truth as it hath appeared to me. If I am really mistaken in any point, I can most truly say, that those my errors have been taken up amidst an impartial desire to know the truth as it is in Jesus : they were always ready to be given up upon conviction of their being errors; and that conviction I thankfully accepted at any hand. What I believed to be the truths of the gospel, I never dissembled upon all just and prudent occasions of declaring them, and as I found those I ministered to could bear them, how different soever they were from a public faith, synodical determinations, or (O monstrous absurdity!) from *religious sentiments established by law.* All such usurped, self-exposing power, I live, I die disclaiming."—" There is no truth about which I am more clear than this, that God will not condemn any man for *mere error.* I can no more think that any shall be punished for involuntary mistakes, than I can think that God is unjust. Though I am convinced that many of our sentiments will appear mere blunders in a future state, yet this does not in the least affect my hopes of future acceptance with God. I have no more fear of suffering for any sentiments that I have embraced, though they were deemed fundamental errors by men, than I have a doubt that God is righteous and merciful : nor dare I indulge any suspicion of that kind, any more than of cruelty and tyranny in the all-perfect God." —II. 151, 152.

This noble passage excites the historian's displeasure, who *denounces* the pernicious sentiment of the innocence of mental error, in a passage of nearly two pages in length. We submit to him, however, that all his assertions and quotations of Scripture are unavailing, unless he can prove that it is in every man's power to believe what he chooses. But, whatever may be thought of Mr. Wilson's argument, it will be allowed by all his readers that it was a work of supererogation to correct the sentiments of such a man as Mr. Newman.

Mr. Newman is still known as an author, by his Sermons (2 vols. 8vo.) on Happiness, and on the Progress of Vice, and his Essay on the Case of the Penitent Thief.[*]

---

[*] Any reader possessing this pamphlet would much oblige the Editor by the loan of it. The Editor takes this opportunity of making the same request with regard to Dr. Bullock's *Two Discourses on Atonement* mentioned in Bishop Law's Letter, extracted in the last Article, p. 668.

Mr. *Edward Pickard,* the assistant and successor of Mr. Newman, has left an imperishable monument of his generosity and piety in the Dissenters' Orphan School, in the City Road, which owes its existence to his public spirit, wisdom and activity. There is a brief memoir and a well-drawn character of this gentleman in Mr. Belsham's Memoirs of Mr. Lindsey, pp. 63—66. Mr. Pickard, according to the reluctant admission of our historian, was " in his views of *some doctrines,*" an Arian, but happily he was a High Arian, and still more happily, " he was wont to express himself in terms of strong disapprobation of the writings of Dr. Priestley and other Socinians" (II. 159). In balancing the account, however, our orthodox biographer should have recollected that Mr. Pickard preached and published Dr. Benson's Funeral Sermon, in which he praises the virtue and good sense and Scriptural labours of the deceased *heretic* as if he had forgotten that he was a " Socinian."

John Tailor, was for some time an assistant to Mr. Pickard : he was previously minister at Stow Market, where " he had been called a Tillotson, and went by the name of the Suffolk Orator," and where " he was the intimate acquaintance and cordial friend of Dr. Priestley, who, in his younger days, was settled at Needham, three miles from Stow Market" (II. 160).

The singular custom formerly prevailed at Carter-lane, of repeating the Apostles' Creed, every Sunday, after the reading of the Scriptures. Mr. Tayler, the successor of Mr. Pickard, who is still living in a venerable age and a truly Christian reputation, first discontinued the practice (II. 163). In early life, Mr. Tayler was the chaplain of Mrs. Elizabeth Abney, whose family name is associated so honourably with that of Watts.

In an account of the *Swedenborgians* (II. 170) it is stated that the proposition for abolishing the Slave Trade originated in that denomination.

Mr. Wilson attributes the existence of any *General Baptist Church* in London at the present day to the estate which Capt. Pierce Johns bequeathed in 1698 for the use of that branch of the Baptists. Six churches were originally supported on this foundation ;

there are now only five, one (Dunning's Alley) having become extinct: these we believe, are the churches under the pastoral care of Messrs. Evans, Gilchrist, Moon, Dan Taylor and Shenston. The question of the influence of endowments upon Dissenting congregations is difficult of decision; most readers will think, we believe, that our author has in this case pronounced an opinion (II. 175) for which he was not qualified.

A large space is properly allotted by Mr. Wilson to the biography of Dr. Daniel Williams, the great benefactor to the Dissenters, especially of the Presbyterian denomination. In one instance the biographer censures, where he ought, in our judgment, to have commended him. We extract the passage as far as it is historical:

"During the troubles of Ireland, at the latter end of the reign of King James the Second, he was driven from thence, after escaping some threatening dangers by the tyrannical and violent proceedings of a popish administration. He returned to England in 1687, and made London the place of his retreat. Here he was of great use upon a very critical and important occasion. Some of the court agents at that time, endeavoured to bring the Dissenters in the city, to address the king upon his dispensing with the penal laws. In a conference at one of their meetings, upon that occasion, in the presence of some of the agents, Mr. Williams declared, ' That it was with him past doubt, that the severities of the former reign upon the Protestant Dissenters, were rather, as they stood, in the way of arbitrary power, than for their religious dissent: so it were better for them to be reduced to their former hardships, than declare for measures destructive of the liberties of their country; and that for himself, before he would concur in an address which should be thought an approbation of the dispensing power, he should chuse to lay down his liberty at his Majesty's feet.' He is said to have pursued the argument with such clearness and strength, that the company present rejected the motion, and the emissaries went away disappointed. There was a meeting at the same time of a considerable number of the city clergy, waiting the issue of their deliberations; who were greatly animated and encouraged by this brisk resolution of the Dissenting ministers."—II. 199, 200.

Mr. Wilson says it was absurd, *infinitely* absurd in the Presbyterians to quarrel with their liberty, on account of the quarter from whence it came. We

see not the absurdity: we see on the contrary a wise and constitutional jealousy of the court. Had the dispensing power been admitted, what security would the Dissenters or any other class of the community have had for liberty, property or even life? The decision adopted by the Dissenters at the instance of Dr. Williams, is virtually justified by Mr. Fox, who shews (Hist. of James II. *passim*) that the liberty granted to Nonconformists was merely a pretext for granting liberty to Papists, and that that was ultimately designed to introduce and establish arbitrary power. As Dissenters, we should have blushed for our forefathers, if they had truckled to a mean and treacherous tyrant, and, for the sake of a momentary peace, a merely sectarian advantage, had bartered away the antient liberties of Englishmen.

" *New Broad Street, Petty France, Presbyterian*, Extinct," enjoyed the services of several respectable ministers, of whom Dr. Daniel Williams was the third in succession, and Mr. John Palmer the last.

" JOHN PALMER.—This gentleman was born in London, in the year 1729. His father carried on the business of an undertaker, in Southwark. Both his parents were serious persons, of the Calvinistical persuasion, and members of the Independent church in Collier's Rents, Southwark, under the pastoral care of the Rev. John Rogers. They devoted their son to the ministry, and after giving him a school education, placed him under the care of the learned Dr. David Jennings, under whom he pursued his theological studies. Upon the death of Mr. James Read, in 1755, Mr. Palmer was chosen assistant to Dr. Allen, at New Broad-street; and upon his removal to Worcester, in 1759, succeeded to the pastoral charge.

" Mr. Palmer's first publication, we believe, was ' A Sermon occasioned by the Death of King George II. preached at New Broad-street, Nov. 2, 1760, on 1 Chron. xxiv. 27, 28.' In 1766, he revised, corrected, and prepared for the press, a posthumous work of the Rev. John Alexander, of Birmingham, with whom he had been upon terms of peculiar intimacy. It was entitled, ' A Paraphrase upon the fifteenth Chapter of the first Epistle to the Corinthians; with Critical Notes and Observations, and a preliminary Dissertation. A Commentary, with Critical Remarks upon the sixth, seventh, and part of the eighth Chapters to the Romans: To which is added, a Sermon on Eccles. ix. 10, composed by the Author the day preceding his

Death. London. 1766. *Quarto.'* In 1769, Mr. Palmer published an Oration at the interment of the Rev. Timothy Laugher, of Hackney; which was annexed to Dr. Kippis's funeral discourse upon the same occasion. His next publication, we believe, was a small octavo volume, entitled, 'Prayers for the Use of Families, and Persons in Private.' This little work passed to a second edition, in 1785, and has been much esteemed by those who are called rational Dissenters. In 1779, he published, 'Free Thoughts on the Inconsistency of conforming to any Religious Test, as a Condition of Toleration, with the true Principles of Protestant Dissent.' It was in this year that he was called to lament the loss of an intimate friend in the Rev. Caleb Fleming, D. D. whose death he attempted to improve, in a sermon at New Broad-street, August the 1st, in that year. This discourse was afterwards printed, together with an oration at the Doctor's interment, in Bunhill-Fields, by Dr. Towers. The text of Mr. Palmer's sermon is, 2 Cor. i. 12. In the same year he published, in octavo, 'Observations in Defence of the Liberty of Man, as a Moral Agent; in Answer to Dr. Priestley's Illustrations of Philosophical Necessity.' This is a judicious and able piece upon the subject; and in the following year, he published a defence of it in 'An Appendix to the Observations;' occasioned by Dr. Priestley's letters to the author, in defence of the doctrine of Necessity. Mr. Palmer's last publication, which was printed in 1788, was, 'A Summary View of the Grounds of Christian Baptism; with a more particular Reference to the Baptism of Infants: containing Remarks argumentative and critical, in Explanation and Defence of the Rite.'

"Some years before the publication of the last piece, Mr. Palmer had desisted from any ministerial work. The lease of his meeting-house expiring about 1780, the congregation, which was in a very reduced state, did not judge proper to renew it, and the society dissolved. After this, Mr. Palmer wholly left off preaching, and retired to Islington, where he lived privately to the time of his death. He married a lady of considerable property, and during the latter years of his life, kept up but little connexion with the Dissenters. He was a man of considerable talents, and accounted a very sensible and rational preacher. His pulpit compositions were drawn up with much perspicuity, and delivered with great distinctness and propriety. He allowed himself great latitude in his religious sentiments, and was a determined enemy to any religious test whatsoever. In this particular, he differed from several of his brethren, who, notwithstanding, favoured the application to parliament for the abolition of subscription to the Thirty-nine Articles. Though he was bred up and educated in Calvinistical principles, yet he gradually relinquished them, and, at length, imbibed the Socinian scheme. He died at his house in Islington, June the 26th, 1790, aged 61 years. Mr. Palmer was for many years one of the trustees for Dr. Williams's charities."—II. 227—229.

There was another Dissenting minister of the same name, John Palmer, of Macclesfield, and afterwards of Birmingham, who was also an author and an Unitarian. He corresponded in the *Theological Repository* with Dr. Priestley, who has given an account of him in that work, VI. 217, 224.

In the history of "*Pinners' Hall, Independent, Extinct*," our author encounters the unwelcome names of *Dr. James Foster* and *Dr. Caleb Fleming*. He says of the former (II. 280) that "he rejected those doctrines which are purely matters of revelation," and without meaning it, *unsays* this slander again and again; and of the latter, (II. 286, 287) that most of the doctrines of revelation "afforded him subject of ridicule," that he "discovered enmity to those doctrines which are the peculiar glory of the gospel," and that "he set down for fools and enthusiasts all who were not Socinians." Dr. Foster's reputation and Christian character are so well established that it has long seemed unnecessary to protect him either against the spiritual *Bacchanals* who dance over the graves of heretics [M. Repos. II. 63, 64,] or the *Sicarii* who strive to wound the good name of men of creeds different from their own, when conscience or cowardice restrains them from more honest persecution; but Dr. Caleb Fleming is less known and therefore less respected and less secure from the attacks of bigotry. It is sufficient however for his vindication that his life was unblameable; that he made considerable temporal sacrifices for conscience sake; that he was incessantly employed in promoting, according to his own persuasions, the interests of truth and freedom; that by Dr. James Foster, whose assistant he had been, he was recommended to his congregation as his successor; that between his flock and himself there subsisted great harmony and friendship; that he enjoyed the esteem of the most respected of his brethren, one of whom, Mr. John Palmer, pronounced the highest eulogium upon him in his funeral sermon; and especially that he was for years the confidential friend of Dr. Lardner. The list of his publications is enough to prove both the impartiality and the activity of his mind. His theological system was of his own framing from the Scriptures. He was the zealous advocate of revealed religion, of Protestantism, of nonconformity, and of some doctrines which are accounted orthodox, such as the immortality of the soul, the sanctity of the Sabbath, and the liberty of the will. His Unitarianism only was against him. But for that, the present historian, who reports the opinion and feeling of a large body of theologians, would not have termed his "specimens of divinity" "wretched," or his interpretations of Scripture perverse; nor would he in a virtual comparison of him with "Mr. John Dove, a member of Mr. Pike's congregation," who was known by the name of "The Hebrew Tailor," have given the seeming preference to that learned artificer. Mr. Wilson has, however, made some amends to Dr. Fleming, by inserting in his work a handsome engraving of him, from a Portrait in Dr. Williams's library, and a full and tolerably correct list of his publications. The number in this list is sixty, and there are several in our possession not included.

A life of Dr. Fleming was looked for at the hands of the late Dr. Towers, who came into possession of his papers, including, according to Dr. Kippis (Life of Lardner, p. xcvi.), "a series of letters written to Dr. Fleming by Dr. Lardner, in which he freely disclosed his thoughts concerning men and things." Why will not the representative of Dr. Towers, who is so capable of doing justice to the characters of the friends of truth and freedom, gratify our wishes? If he had not considered this gentleman as the proper biographer of Dr. Fleming, the late Dr. Toulmin would have communicated a memoir of this decided, intrepid, zealous and laborious Unitarian teacher, to the Monthly Repository. Notices of him are scattered through this work [III. 485—487. IV. 151. VI. 44. VIII. 339. X. 283], which we refer to in the hope that they may excite suitable attention to a neglected character. It is right to add that should a complete memoir of Dr. Fleming be prepared for the press, the compiler will find Mr. Wilson's

account, with all its faults, of no small use.

In a *History of Dissenting Churches* we did not expect an account of a fanatical Deist who delivered lectures at Carpenters' Hall [II. 290, 292]. This was *Jacob Ilive*, a printer and letter-founder. He published several pamphlets, for one of which "Remarks on the Bishop of London's (Dr. Sherlock's) Discourses" he was imprisoned in Clerkenwell Bridewell two years. During his confinement he appears to have written "The Book of Jasher," which he procured to be privately printed, and which purported to be a translation from the original of Alcuin, a British monk. It is a small folio. Ilive died in the year 1763. There is an account of him in Gough's British Topography, I. 637.

The *Old Jewry* is rich in Dissenting biography, having been always celebrated for the number and respectability of its congregation and the eminence of its ministers. At the beginning of this article, the historian *notes down*, what from the specimens lately given the reader might not have observed, that "the words *Calvinist* and *Arian* he uses as terms neither of honour nor reproach, but for the sake of convenience" (II. 305).

We cannot even enumerate all the ministers that as pastors, assistants or lecturers have rendered the Old Jewry so distinguished a Dissenting station, but must content ourselves with a few notices and remarks.

Mr. Wilson relates a "very striking anecdote" (II. 322—326), of *John Rogers*, one of the Bartholomew confessors, and father of *Timothy Rogers*, minister at the Old Jewry. The anecdote is, in substance, that Mr. Rogers was on the point of being sent to jail for his Nonconformity, by Sir Richard Cradock, a persecuting Justice of the Peace, but was delivered by Sir Richard's grand-daughter, a headstrong girl of six or seven years of age, who took a liking to the Puritan preacher and threatened to drown herself if he were ill-used. Mr. Timothy Rogers once related this story at the house of a Mrs. Tooley, where he was dining in company with Mr. T. Bradbury; when the hostess revealed that she was the grand-daughter of Sir R. Cradock, and the person to whom the story referred. Her guests were anxious to learn her religious history, and she proceeded to narrate by what means she had been converted; these were the artifices of a religious apothecary who laid her under an involuntary obligation to read the New Testament, and a dream eventually realized in a Sermon from Mr. Shower at the Old Jewry.

The story is "striking" enough, and may also be true; but Mr. Wilson has omitted his authority for relating it. We read it in our boyish days in the *Spiritual Magazine,* the wrapper of which was rendered awful in our eyes by the head of *John Calvin,* in a wood-cut. It is in the Number for *March,* 1784, and is thus headed, with an appearance of authority, "The substance of a letter from Mr. Davidson, of Braintree, to Mr. Archibald Wallace, Merchant, in Edinburgh, dated 12th Oct. 1767."

A very interesting account is given, (II. 338—358,) of *Simon Browne,* whose peculiar malady has procured him a degree of fame which his talents and virtues, though great, would not alone have obtained. Dr. Hawkesworth has described the case with all his usual fascination of style in No. 88, of the *Adventurer.* Browne imagined that Almighty God had annihilated his thinking substance; yet whilst he was under this melancholy delusion he composed works which discovered remarkable strength and acuteness of mind. There are various accounts of the origin of his disorder. Dr. Percival suggests [Works, II. 80.] that it might be owing to his study of the Platonic writers, who represent the most perfect worship of the Deity as consisting in *self-annihilation.*

It is recorded to the honour of Simon Browne that he was one of the non-subscribing ministers at the Salters' Hall synod: He appeared before the public and encountered present reproach as their advocate. Mr. Wilson has furnished us with two admirable extracts from his pamphlet on that occasion:

"Upon the subject of subscribing he expresses himself thus: 'For my own part, I always took it, that subscriptions of all kinds, whether to liturgies or articles, had been a grievance to our fathers, as well as to us; though rather than be rendered utterly incapable of public usefulness, they and we have submitted to the hardship, and subscribed to some of the 39 articles.—But there are many that judge,

and, as I think, with very good reason, that it is an infringement of Christian liberty, to use compulsive methods, to oblige men to do even what they take not to be sinful, or to subscribe all that they believe: forasmuch as this is confining where God has left at liberty, and making necessary what he has left indifferent.'—'How happy had it been for the church and world, if this method of subscribing had never come into the mind of men, more than into the mind of God! If, as that holy man, Mr. Baxter, expresses it, the devil had never put on his gown, stept into the infallible chair and in a fit of reverend zeal, taken upon him to preserve and perfect the faith of the church! This was opening Pandora's box. Had not Satan turned orthodox, and tempted Christian ministers to make, and mend, and enlarge creeds, and prevent and cure heresy by subscription, to their own terms and forms, peace and truth had been much better preserved than they have been, or ever will be, till the engine of the devil, as that wise and good man called it, be overthrown.'"—II. 340, 341.

Browne's publications were numerous. He was one of the authors of "The Occasional Papers," and also one of Matthew Henry's Continuators; the part assigned to him was the first Epistle to the Corinthians.

The life of *Chandler* must occupy a large space in any history not merely of the Old Jewry but likewise of the Dissenters. His fame as a preacher has not yet died away; and his writings will be ever valued by the biblical student. He possessed extensive and correct learning, a penetrating and comprehensive intellect and a sound judgment. The memoir of him, which is here given, is creditable to Mr. Wilson's liberality. The following notice may be useful to future translators and commentators on the Scriptures:

"Dr. Chandler left in his interleaved bible, a large number of critical notes, chiefly in Latin. They are drawn up in the manner of Raphelius, Bos, Eisner, and other writers of the like kind. Those on the Old Testament are thinly scattered, excepting in a few particular places. But those on the New Testament are very copious and display a close study of the Holy Scriptures, and an extensive acquaintance with ancient authors. They were purchased for a small consideration by Dr. Amory, Mr. Farmer, Dr. Furneaux, Dr. Price, Dr. Savage, and Dr. Kippis, with an intention of committing them to the press, if any bookseller could be found who would be willing to run the risk of publication. But it was not judged that the taste of the age would afford sufficient encouragement for the prosecution of the design. Dr. Furneaux employed much labour upon the manuscript; having transcribed some of the notes, and examined the authorities on which they are founded. Dr. Kippis, the last surviving proprietor, deposited the work in Dr. Williams's Library, Redcross-street. It is in the quarto form, very fairly written, and the Hebrew in particular, remarkably correct and beautiful."—II. 381.

The article " Free-Thinkers" (II. 523) savours of bigotry. The people referred to denominate themselves " *Free-Thinking Christians.*" Whatever be thought of the name, whether it be considered impolitic, or quaint, or arrogant, or, in the present instance, misapplied, it is the appellation of the party, and as such ought to be adopted by their historian. " Free-thinkers" is, Mr. Wilson knows, synonimous, in common acceptation, with Sceptics or Unbelievers; and for that reason, probably, he uses the term, for he says, somewhat unintelligibly, " they meet to discuss *subjects, connected* indeed with theology, but *intended to undermine the doctrines of revelation*, and *erect a sceptical indifference* upon the ruins of the Christian faith." This is sitting in judgment upon men's motives, and pronouncing sentence upon them not according to their professions or actions, but according to the censor's suspicion or ill-nature. The " Free-thinking Christians" always declared themselves believers in Divine Revelation, and since Mr. Wilson wrote this part of the history, they have published a very valuable pamphlet on the Evidences of Christianity, (See Mon. Repos. X. 515.) Unfortunately for Mr. Wilson, he recollected that this little party met in a room contiguous to that in which another party still less, the Haldanites, were accustomed to meet, and called to mind some lines of De Foe's, and was unable to resist the temptation to laugh, though at the expence of charity: he assails the " Free-thinking Christians," with these couplets;

" Wherever God erects a House of Prayer,
The Devil always builds a chapel there ;
And 'twill be found, upon examination,
The latter has the largest congregation."

We are aware of the defence which the author would set up for his mode

of describing this and kindred parties; but we would remind him that nothing can absolve a Christian from the duties of truth and justice and candour; that any appearance of artifice or unfairness towards such as throw out large accusations against their fellow-Christians, only confirms them in their surmises and ill-will; and that, in reality, the fittest objects of fair-dealing and charity are those that know not how to contend without animosity or to differ without resentment.

ART. III.—*A Faithful Enquiry after the Antient and Original Doctrine of the Trinity, taught by Christ and his Apostles.* By Isaac Watts, D. D. 1745. 8vo. pp. 56. Eaton. 1816.

DR. WATTS's last sentiments have been frequently and fully discussed in our pages [VIII. 683, 714, 715—723, 768—770]; and it is we think quite clear that he died in the disbelief of the Trinity. The tract before us is a record by his own pen of his misgivings, doubts and inquiries. It was printed in 1745, but carefully suppressed. One copy at least escaped and fell into the hands of the Rev. Gabriel Watts, of Frome, who re-published it in the year 1802, with a Preface explaining the manner in which it came into his possession. The edition had been long out of print, and therefore the present Editor has, with the leave of the former Editor, issued a third impression.

Dr. Watts's *Solemn Address to the Trinity* is prefixed; a striking monument of the distracting tendency of the doctrine upon an intelligent and conscientious mind.

This little publication is better adapted than any other with which we are acquainted to dissolve that persuasion of infallibility which prevails amongst Trinitarians, and which renders them inaccessible to argument; and on this ground we earnestly recommend its distribution.

ART. IV.—*Heresies Considered, in Connexion with the Character of the Approved.* A Sermon, preached at the Opening of the Unitarian Chapel, in Thorne, on Friday, 28th of June, 1816. By Nathaniel Philipps, D. D. 8vo. pp. 40. Hunter.

HERESY was once a stinging term, but Unitarians have rendered it innoxious, as children are taught to make nettles, by bold and forcible handling. It is now retorted and will probably hereafter fix alone on those that make separation in the church by imposing unscriptural and unwarrantable terms of communion.

Dr. Philipps's text is 1 Cor. xi. 19. He first states the proper meaning and use of the term *Heresy*; 2ndly explains the reason and scope of the expression, " Heresies *must* be ;" and 3rdly shews the effect of Heresies upon virtuous and independent minds, and the ultimate good, which such corruptions and abuses, (though a great evil in themselves) by the firm and excellent example of those who expose and reject them, may be made the means of producing.

The following argument on the Unity of the Divine nature and person is well stated and is unanswerable.

" The general and popular creed, which maintains that God exists in three Persons, combining three intelligent minds, each of which is perfectly God, distinctly and alone, while yet the three united constitute but one Deity, appears to us to teach a palpable contradiction ; because an omnipresent spirit and a perfect mind cannot be divided—because a whole cannot be a part, nor a part equal to the whole. To divide is to destroy. Who can divide a thought ? or the intellectual principle which is the parent of that thought ? Various as are the powers of mind, the existence of mind is identified with its unity."—P. 24.

In an Appendix, Dr. Philipps relates the rise and progress of Unitarianism at Thorne ; which exhibits another of those cases, now becoming numerous, in which plain men with the help only of their Bibles discover the error of the popular creed and worship.

POETRY.

Translation of some Latin Lines of Jortin's.

SIR,

YOU are no doubt acquainted with the beautiful Latin lines of Jortin, in which a very striking contrast is drawn between the renovations of nature, and the hopeless dissolution of man. They are given in a note to Mr. John Kenrick's eloquent sermon, " On the Necessity of Revelation to teach the Doctrine of a Future Life." I here send you an attempt at a translation of those lines, which, if they meet your approbation, you are at liberty to insert them in your valuable Repository.

The radiant sun, bright regent of the day,
Pursues a fix'd, undeviating way ;
To night you trace his beaming chariot's
    wheels
Roll slowly down the purple western hills :
To morrow he shall climb the eastern
    sky,
And all the world his rising beams descry.
The silver moon, mild empress of the
    night,
Changes her form, and oft withdraws her
    light,
Yet beams again within the ev'ning sky,
And sheds a milder radiance from her
    eye :

The beauteous stars, when morning brings
    the day,
Fainter and fainter shine—then fade
    away :
But night draws out her beaming hosts
    once more,
Which shine as bright and splendid as
    before.
Earth's lowly children, herbs which drink
    the show'rs,
And all the fragile race of colour'd flow'rs
That give their beauty to the verdant
    vales,
And shed their fragrance on the summer
    gales ;
The cruel blasts of winter sweep away,
And wither all their blossoms in a day.
But spring returns—on every naked plain
The living verdure spreads its hues again,
At Zephyr's call the flow'rs resume their
    bloom,
And rise more fragrant from their wint'ry
    tomb.
But man ! the vaunted lord of all below,
On whom the Gods their choicest gifts bestow :
Vain man ! who boasts of reason's purest
    ray,
And seems in thought to tread the realms
    of day ;
Alas ! when his short spring of life is o'er,
Fades like the grass, and dies for evermore ;

No second spring revives his mould'ring
frame,
It mingles with the dust from which it
came.

Additional lines occasioned by the above.

Is such, my soul, thy melancholy fate?
Most wretched then is man's exalted state!
Rais'd 'bove the brutes his misery to know,
And pine in vain for happiness below.
O child of woe! thy wisdom is a curse,
Reflection makes thy sad condition worse.
The beast that wanders o'er the flow'ry
vale,
And thoughtless bites the grass or snuffs
the gale;
The bird that o'er the plains extends its
wings,
Or careless on the bush delighted sings;
The bee that wanders still from flow'r to
flow'r,
And joyful hums within the fragrant
bow'r,
Is happier far than man in all his bloom,
If death awaits him in the silent tomb:
That fate once known his happiness de-
stroys,
And threat'ning death blasts all his earthly
joys.
In vain the cheerful seasons round him
smile,
And playful wanton o'er the fields awhile;
In vain the spring on winged zephyr flies,
And paints the landscape with her verdant
dies;
In vain hot summer flings his golden
beams
On waving harvests and on glitt'ring
streams;
In vain the heav'ns with brightest colours
glow,
And on the earth's fair bosom sweetest
roses blow;
In vain the charms of nature court his
eye,
What are they all to him, if he must die?
Was man then made the lord of reason's
ray,
More wretched than the beasts to pine
away?
Was he created in the form of God,
To lose that form beneath the mould'ring
clod?
Were all the faculties bestow'd in vain,
Or but to aggravate his mortal pain?
This faith let sceptics preach, who will be-
lieve,
Yet prompting nature cannot sure deceive.
Who does not feel within his breast arise
Hopes that aspire and look beyond the
skies?
Where is the savage, in what realms of
night,
Though thickest clouds obscure his mental
sight,

Who to the sky where'er his footsteps
roam,
Does not look up as to his native home?
But lo! the sage of wisdom's words pos-
sess'd,
Confirms the hope in ev'ry human breast,
Whilst round his form the list'ning throng
attend,
And on his beaming face their eyelids
bend;
Inspir'd by heav'n he lifts his hand on high,
And promises the good a home within the
sky.
Oh! kind Instructor, still be thou my
guide,
May sophistry ne'er draw me from thy
side:
Support me when the vale of death I tread,
And mingle with the shadows of the dead.
Then 'midst the gloom bid nobler prospects
rise,
And burst with glory on my longing eyes;
Beyond the tomb reveal the glorious way,
That leads to realms of everlasting day.

J. B. M.

TRANSLATIONS.

From the Portugueze of Ferreira.

Pilgrim of untired spirit! who dost tread
Unerring, unappalled, life's wearying
road,
And seest the brightness of the throne
of GOD
Its smiles of invitation o'er thee shed:—
I wake, dear traveller! from my slothful
bed
To follow where thy holier feet have
trod,
Thro' paths that lead to heav'ns sublime
abode,
(Veil'd from my eyes till now)—The hours
are fled,
When sad and solitary,—woe-begone
Midst vain desires, and heart-consu-
ming cares,
I saw the stream of my existence
roll;
Now comfort beams upon th' awakened
one,
And, full of joy, my liberated soul,
Recalls (but to forget) life's wasted
years. A.

From the Portugueze.

Every promise of hope is gone—
Joy is interred in the grave beneath;
Life, unenvied lingers on—.
And there's nought but solitude in
death.

O this world is a world of woe,—
Shunned by peace and slighted by love;
And darkness reigns like a tyrant below;—
Say is there brightness or bliss above?
A.

INTELLIGENCE.

DOMESTIC.
Religious.

An Account of Mr. Wright's Mission in Wales. Extracted from his Journals.
[In a Letter to the Secretary of the Unitarian Fund.]

DEAR SIR,

HAVING never been in Wales before, the ground was to me entirely new. This occasioned some difficulty in the outset, as to the arrangement of my plans, and occasioned me much more travelling than would have been necessary, had I possessed as much information respecting the country, and the state of the Unitarian cause in it, at the commencement as I did at the close of the journey. The ground being new, I shall be the more particular in my account of what I did, the information I collected, and my views of what may be done in that interesting part of the kingdom. I spent seventy-four days in Wales, travelled about eight hundred miles, preached sixty-nine times, and in forty-three places; administered the Lord's supper twice, delivered an address at a public baptism, and had much theological conversation with friends in different places. The congregations were generally large, in many places crowded, and the hearers, with very few exceptions, always deeply attentive. I have the higher opinion of the Welsh people for having travelled among them, and of the success of Unitarianism in that part of the island, from what I saw and heard during my journey.

During part of this mission, viz. the first thirty-eight days in Wales, I was favoured with the company and assistance of Mr. Meek, one of the students in the Unitarian Academy, who preached seven times, administered baptism, and participated in many interesting conversations. Mr. Meek also preached several times as we were on our way to Wales.

I was happily disappointed in three things. 1. In the number of places where an English preacher can be understood by the hearers in general, and that in *most* places in South Wales there are many who can understand him. 2. In the number of people in most of the towns and even villages,

who are disposed to hear an Unitarian preacher. It is probable the novelty of a missionary from England of that description excited their attention the more. 3. At the progress Unitarianism has already made in Wales, which is far greater than I had anticipated.

Our brethren had kindly appointed Mr. B. Phillips to be our conductor from place to place; and as in many places there were some hearers who could not understand English, Mr. Phillips acted also as interpreter; on such occasions he repeated the substance of the sermon in Welsh, and I was told, did it with much accuracy: I am sure he did it with much energy, and apparent eloquence. It was gratifying to see a number of persons unacquainted with English, sit with the greatest composure through a long service, that they might afterwards hear the discourse repeated to them in a language they could understand. In most instances a large proportion of the bearers understood English, in many nearly all of them, and in a number the whole congregation.

According to the plan proposed, it was my intention to have gone from Wales to Cornwall; but, when I had been three weeks in Wales, I found it would be absolutely necessary, in order to the proper execution of my mission in that country, that I should devote my time to it until the season for daily travelling, during the present year, would be over: and that if I attempted to embrace both Cornwall and Wales in the present journey, I could not have sufficient time in either. This led me to alter my plan.

We entered the principality on the 22nd of July. After passing through Wrexham, where there are friends to the cause, having no introduction to any person or place, not having been able to gain any information respecting any Unitarians, or persons favourable to Unitarianism, in North Wales, and finding the English language very little understood there; we travelled across that part of the country with as much expedition as possible, directing our steps towards Cardiganshire, where we began our mission. In South Wales I learned that there are some persons, in more places than one in the Northern counties, who are in whole or in part Unitarians, but could gain no definite account of them. I shall be thankful to any person who can and will communicate to me any information respecting the state of inquiry and progress of religious opinions in North Wales; in particular if they will communicate the names and places of residence of any persons who are favourable to Unitarianism in that part of the principality. It appears to me that a correspondence with that part of the country is desirable, and might lead to some important results.

After the preceding introductory remarks, I proceed to state succinctly the particulars of this mission. It was extended to six counties.

I. CARDIGANSHIRE.

In this county Unitarianism has been openly professed, and plainly preached, for a number of years; and ceases to excite the degree of horror which attends its first introduction, and which can be removed only by a continued fearless avowal, and plain statement of its doctrine, accompanied by a truly Christian spirit and conduct. I was informed that reputed orthodoxy has here lost much of its asperity, and its professors are more mild and charitable than in other parts of the principality. The cause here owes much of its success to the labours and consistent conduct of Mr. David Jenkin Rees, of *Lloyd-Jack*, the oldest Unitarian in this part of the country, and of Mr. J. James, lately removed to Glamorganshire. These worthy men were several years joint ministers of the Unitarian churches in Cardiganshire. The following are the places where I preached in this county.

1. *Pant-y-Defaid.* The congregation in this place is well established in the Unitarian doctrine. I preached once, and Mr. J. Thomas, from Islington, afterwards delivered a sermon in Welsh. The audience were deeply attentive.

2. *Capel-y-Groes.* Here also the congregation are steady, well-informed Unitarians. I preached to them once, and Mr. B. Phillips interpreted to those who did not understand English.

3. *Lloyd-Jack*, a farm house. Unitarian worship is here conducted in a

large school-room. I preached to a numerous assembly of attentive hearers. Mr. Phillips gave an outline of the discourse in Welsh.

These congregations are supplied by the before-mentioned Mr. D. J. Rees and Mr. Thomas, from Carmarthenshire, who succeeds Mr. James.

4. *Lampeter*, a market town. Here I preached in a room at the inn, which was crowded with hearers.

5. *Llandyssil.* Here I preached in a school-room to a large company. Mr. Meek preached at *Lloyd-Jack*, to a pretty large and attentive audience; and Mr. Phillips gave an outline of the discourse in Welsh.

At some of the above places many strangers attended, persons of different religious denominations.

Among our friends in Cardiganshire, we found much intelligence, simplicity, Christian affection and rational zeal.

There are five congregations in this county who rank as Arians. They meet at the following places:

1. *Llwyn-rhyd-Owen.* 2. *Penrhyw.* 3. *Cilieu.* 4. *Alltblacca.* Of these four, Mr. *Davis*, and Mr. *William Rees*, are the ministers. I found Mr. Davis very infirm and unwell. Mr. Rees I had for a hearer at Panteg.

5. *Llechrhyd.* Of this Mr. *Griffiths* is the minister.

II. PEMBROKESHIRE.

Unitarianism has been but recently introduced in this county; one congregation only is yet formed, but there are persons favourable to the doctrine in several other places. As the English language is chiefly spoken in Pembrokeshire (indeed in a considerable part of it they know nothing of Welsh), I thought it right to pay a particular attention to this district, and to the infant church which has been lately formed at Templeton. After going forward into Carmarthenshire and Glamorganshire, I returned and spent eight more days in Pembrokeshire. The following are the places I visited.

1. *Templeton.* Here a decent house has been erected for the worship of the One and Only God, on the most economical plan possible, and one individual who is the chief support of the cause in the place, and who has a large family, is still £43 15s. 6d.

out of pocket, by the erection; which small debt it is highly desirable he should be repaid. The building of this meeting-house first introduced Unitarian preaching as a regular thing into Pembrokeshire, and it is said this circumstance so alarmed some of the reputed orthodox, that they offered up public prayer to Almighty God, to prevent such dangerous doctrine proceeding any further in that county. Mr. *B. Phillips* preaches one Sunday in the month at this place, and Mr. *David Johns* preaches at other times. I preached at Templeton nine times, and Mr. *Meek* twice; we had always good, sometimes crowded congregations, though the weather was mostly rainy, and many of the people had to come a considerable distance. Several new hearers attended regularly during our stay, and seemed to have their minds stirred up to serious inquiry after truth. I administered the Lord's Supper twice to the little society, Mr. Meek baptized one person, and I delivered an address on the occasion. It is of the more importance to encourage and promote the Unitarian cause at Templeton, as it is in the midst of a district where the English language only is spoken, and where Unitarianism was till lately unknown. I think, if proper encouragement be given, and steady exertions be continued, much good will be done at Templeton and the country around it: there are many openings for preaching, where occasional lectures might be delivered, and much attention and inquiry is already excited.

2. *Narbeth*, a market town, a short distance from Templeton. Here I preached to a multitude of people: I stood in a window at the inn, which answered the purpose of a pulpit; a number of people were in the room, and several hundreds abroad; indeed the market place, which was before the house, was pretty well filled. The audience was generally very attentive. I learned afterwards that the clergyman of the parish threatened the owner of the house for suffering us to meet there, but I believe some inquiry was excited. Some of the inhabitants came afterwards to Templeton to hear me.

3. *Saundersfoot*, a village on the sea side. I visited and preached twice at this place, in the house of a widow

woman: the last congregation was much the largest; both were very attentive. A week evening lecture might be delivered regularly at this place, and there is reason to think it would be productive of good.

4. *Jeffreston*, a small village among the collieries. I preached here to a small attentive audience. I should have visited this place again, but the state of the weather and roads rendered it impracticable to get there at the time.

5. *Carew*, a village. I preached here in a cottage, which was crowded with attentive hearers. There are two Unitarian families in this place. Here meetings might be occasionally held to good purpose.

6. *Pembroke*, a corporate town. The minister of the parish is also the mayor. He forbade the bellman to publish a meeting in the open air, and said he would not suffer such a meeting to be held. The minister of the Tabernacle lent us the use of it, and we had a large and attentive audience.

7. *Haverfordwest*. A friend of mine applied to a Dissenting minister in this town, to know whether I could have the use of his chapel: his letter in reply shewed that if I went in disguise, and said nothing about my peculiar sentiments, I might be admitted: he said, if I went merely in the character of a Dissenting minister I should be cordially welcomed; but considering the character in which I should appear, my visit would be turned to their disadvantage. I however went and [a] preached in a house which had been an inn. We had a large congregation. I found afterwards several persons were friendly to the cause. I was informed four clergymen heard me: one of them, the next morning, sent me the Bishop of St. David's paper, called " The Unitarian Catechised," and I ordered to be sent to him " The Unitarian Catechised, and Answering for Himself."

I visited *Milford*, but could procure no place; and from the number of rough sailors, and what appeared to be the general state of society there, did not think it prudent to preach in the open air: besides, there were two meetings in the town that evening: however I had some interesting conversation.

I also went to *Tenby*, hoping to

preach there, but no place could be procured, and I learned that the clergyman, who is also the mayor, would suffer no meetings to be held in the open air. He had, a short time before, prevented the bellman's publishing a preaching in the Methodist meeting-house.

In the parts of Pembrokeshire bordering on Cardiganshire, I understand there are a number of Unitarians; but learning that the Welsh language is chiefly spoken there, and those parts being more remote, I thought it best to employ my time in that part of the county where the English is chiefly spoken. I was told of two congregations near Cardigan. These are visited occasionally by Mr. B. Phillips, and supplied at other times by others.

III. CARMARTHENSHIRE.

Though in this county, some who raised expectation, and seemed disposed to inquire freely after truth, a few years since, have disappointed that expectation, and fallen back into the regions of mystery, the Unitarian cause is still advancing. Its most violent opposers have aided its progress, by even their bitter invectives against it; they have helped to draw the attention of the public to the subject. The seeds of Unitarianism are too widely scattered, and have taken too much hold to be rooted out. In this county I preached at the following places:

1. *Pantcg.* In this village there is a congregation of Unitarian Baptists. Mr. B. Evans is their minister. I preached among and had interesting conversation with some of them. Mr. Phillips gave the substance of the discourse in Welsh.

2. *Rhyd-y-Park.* Mr. David Phillips and Mr. J. Evans are the ministers in this place. The former is in years and infirm; but his conversation is very interesting. I preached to a good congregation.

3. *Felin-Court.* Here I preached at the house of the sister of my worthy friend Mr. Johns, of Manchester; the room was well filled with attentive hearers.

4. *St. Clears.* I visited and preached twice in this place, at the house of Mr. B. Phillips, to very attentive congregations. There is a small Unitarian Baptist society in the neighbourhood of this town, which is supplied by Mr.

Phillips, and Mr. D. Johns, of St. Clears. This Mr. Johns is said to be an excellent Welsh preacher; he is poor, and supports himself and family by the labour of his hands.

5. *Carmarthen.* The Unitarian cause in this town is highly important, and is in a promising state. The congregation at Carmarthen is respectable, and a number of its members zealous in the cause. I preached there five times, and Mr. Meek once. The congregations were always good, several of them crowded ones, and the hearers very attentive. A number of strangers, of different religious denominations, attended. I was glad to find Mr. Evans, late of Ilminster, who is now the minister at Carmarthen, much better in health. There is reason to hope his labours will be very useful in his present situation. On the whole, Carmarthen exhibits a good prospect of success to the Unitarian cause.

6. *Kidwelly.* The minister in this place, Mr. Abel, ranks as an Arian. He very readily granted me the use of his meeting-house. By some means the notice of my preaching did not arrive in time, yet a good company was called together in a few minutes, who were very attentive to the discourse I delivered.

7. *Llanelly.* I visited and preached at this place twice, in a room in an uninhabited house. Mr. Meek also preached here. We had many attentive hearers. The last audience would have been much larger, had it not been for a heavy rain which continued through the evening. I am told there are about twelve Unitarians in Llanelly and its vicinity. It is very desirable a regular congregation should be formed, and Unitarian worship conducted in this place.

8. *Llangyndeirn.* This is an Unitarian Baptist congregation, of which my late friend, Mr. William Thomas, was the minister. Since his death the place has been supplied by various ministers. The congregation is not at present in a good state. I preached here once, and Mr. Phillips gave the substance of the discourse in Welsh.

9. *Brechfa.* The meetings are held here in a private house; the people are Unitarian Baptists. Mr. B. Davies, a poor man, is their preacher. The room where the meeting was held was crowded with attentive hearers, who

had been waiting nearly two hours before we arrived, there being a mistake respecting the time when the service should be held. I preached, and Mr. Phillips repeated the discourse in Welsh.

10. *Llandilo.* Here I preached in a room at one of the inns, had a large and attentive company, and much conversation before and after the service. Mr. Phillips translated.

11. *Llandyfaen.* Here I had a better audience than might have been expected, the service being in the middle of the day. Mr. Phillips gave the substance of the sermon in Welsh. Mr. J. Griffiths, of *Llandybie,* an Unitarian Baptist, preaches to this and several other small congregations.

12. *Llandybie.* Here I preached at the house of Mr. Griffiths, just before mentioned, to a crowded congregation, and Mr. Phillips interpreted. I visited this place again; but the notice having miscarried, we could not have a public meeting.

On the whole, Carmarthenshire presents an extensive, and in many places an encouraging field for the propagation of Unitarianism.

Mr. Jones, one of the Academical Tutors at Carmarthen, who ranks as an Arian, has a congregation at *Capel-Zion.*

[*To be concluded in our next No.*]

Unitarian Baptist Chapel, York.

ON Saturday, November 2nd, the Trustees of the Independent Chapel in the city of York, gave possession of the same to the Trustees named by the Unitarian Baptists.

The following morning, the Chapel was opened for Unitarian worship by Mr. Torrance, who conducted the devotional part of the service. After which, Mr. Griswood, of Hull, preached an excellent sermon from 1 John v. 29. "Behold the Lamb of God, which taketh away the sin of the world," in which he took a view of the state into which man was brought by Adam's transgression, proving that the doctrine of Original Sin is unsupported by the Scriptures. He then shewed in what sense Christ took away the sin of the world; that it was not by becoming a *vicarious sacrifice,* but by his example and obedience to the will of God; that he brought life and immortality to light: closing his

discourse by an attempt to impress the minds of his auditory with the necessity of attending to Scripture as the only proper guide in matters of religious faith and practice. The congregation consisted of nearly 300 persons.

In the afternoon, Mr. Torrance preached a sermon to a very numerous and attentive congregation, on the Divine Unity, from 1 Pet. iv. 11. "If any man speak, let him speak as the oracles of God." He proved by a variety of arguments, that both nature and revelation declare God to be One. He also took a brief view of the doctrine of satisfaction, and shewed it to be contrary to every idea we have of the goodness of the Father and Friend of man. At six o'clock in the evening the chapel was crowded to excess; it is supposed there were near 500 persons present, to whom Mr. Griswood preached a sermon from Mark xvi. 16, in which he exhorted his hearers each for himself to form his religious creed by the Gospel, that is alone calculated to promote the love of God and the happiness of man. He also made some apposite remarks on the moral effects likely to be produced in the temper and conduct of those whose actions are regulated by it.

York.   R. D.

The following is a statement of the Accounts.

	£	s.	d.
Unitarian Baptists, York, -	63	18	6
Unitarian Fund, - - - -	20	0	0
Mr. Hall, York, - - - -	2	2	0
Rev. C. Wellbeloved, - - -	1	1	0
—— J. Kenrick, - - - -	0	10	6
—— W. Turner, - - - -	0	10	6
—— H. Turner, Bradford, -	1	0	0
Students at York College, -	2	13	6
J. Rawdon, Esq. York, - -	1	1	0
Mr. Robson, Newcastle, - -	1	0	0
Mrs. Cappe, - - - - -	0	10	6
Miss Hotham, York, - - -	0	10	6
Sundry Subscriptions, - -	1	7	6
	96	5	6
Paid for the Chapel, Writings, &c. - - - - - -	320	3	0
Debt upon the Chapel, - -	223	17	6

Manchester College, York.

THE Rev. William Lamport, of Lancaster, has offered a prize for an essay in answer to a work lately published, entitled, "An Enquiry into the Integrity of the Greek Vulgate, or received Text of the New Testament, &c. by the Rev. F. Nolan." The prize to consist of books of the value of five guineas. The candidates to be such Dissenting ministers as have received their theological education in Manchester College, York, and have left the College within the last seven years. The Essays to be sent in anonymously before the 1st of May, 1817, each distinguished by a descriptive motto; and the prize to be awarded by the Visitor at the next annual examination, to the author of the best Essay, on the decision of the Visitor and Tutors.

Manchester, Nov. 15, 1816.

Manchester College, York.

The following new subscriptions have been received on account of this Institution.

Rev. E. O. Jones, Duffield. -	1	1	0
Matthew Needham, Esq. Lenton, near Nottingham. - -	2	2	0
Mr. W. Falla, Newcastle, (Additional). - - - -	1	1	0
Rev. N. T. H. Heinekin, Gainsborough. - - - -	1	1	0
Rev. Benj. Mardon, Glasgow.	1	1	0
Rev. R. W. Wallace, Chesterfield. - - - - -	1	1	0
Rawdon Briggs, Jun. Esq. Halifax. - - - -	1	1	0
Barnabas Leman, Esq. Norwich. - - - - -	1	0	0
W. Henry, M. D. Manchester.	1	1	0
Rev. L. Pollock, Macclesfield.	1	1	0
Rev. J. Kenrick, Manchester College, York. - - -	2	2	0
Rev. W. Jevons, Altrincham.	2	2	0
Rev. T. C. Holland, Preston, (Additional). - - - -	0	10	6
	16	4	6

G. W. WOOD.
Manchester, Nov. 16, 1816.

Unitarian Fund Lecture, Hanover Street, Long-Acre,
To be carried on the Sunday and Tuesday Evenings in the Winter Season.

Service to begin each Evening at Half-past Six o'Clock precisely.

(FIRST SERIES. Concluded from p. 621.)
Sunday, Dec. 1.—*Rev. J. Gilchrist.*—
The First Principles of Christianity.
Tuesday, Dec. 3.—*Rev. R. Aspland.*—
"The Prince of this World." John xiv. 30, 31.

Sunday, Dec. 8.—*Rev. T. Rees.*—
Objections to the Doctrine of the Trinity.
Tuesday, Dec. 10.—*Rev. J. Gilchrist.*
—The True Grace of God.
Sunday, Dec. 15.—*Rev. R. Aspland.*—
The Sufficiency of Scripture.
Tuesday, Dec. 17.—*Rev. T. Rees.*—
Christ's Doctrine concerning Himself.
Sunday, Dec. 22.—*Rev. J. Gilchrist.*—
Hindrances to the Reception of Truth.
Tuesday, Dec. 24.—*Rev. R. Aspland.*—
Jesus " the Carpenter's Son."
Sunday, Dec. 29.—*Rev. T. Rees.*—The
Creation of all Things by Jesus Christ.
Tuesday, Dec. 31.—*Rev. J. Gilchrist.*
—Scripture Doctrine concerning the End of the World.
The Conductors of the Lecture design, with the Blessing of Providence, to publish the Subjects of the Second Course before the Expiration of the Year.

A Gentleman will attend in the Vestry every Evening to receive Subscriptions for defraying the Expenses of the Lectures.

FOREIGN.

Account of an Unitarian Church in America.

(In a Letter to the Rev. T. Belsham.)

Trenton Oneida, Co. New York,
DEAR SIR, *June* 24, 1816.

Notwithstanding the intervention of the Atlantic prevents personal acquaintance and intercourse, yet, since we believe with you that rational system of theology taught by Jesus of Nazareth, which though obliterated for ages by an anti-christian spirit, is now beaming again upon the human mind, to the unspeakable joy of the thousands whom it has redeemed from a gloomy state of worse than pagan errors, we are led by the spirit of a congenial faith to extend the hand of fellowship and to address you as our brother in Christ. And while we unite in fervent gratitude to Almighty God, who causes the Divine light of the Gospel again to shine in its original simplicity, we at the same time express to you our thankful acknowledgments for your apostolic exertions in this heavenly cause. We would here speak of the exultations of our hearts inspired by this unadulterated system of Divine truth: but are restrained by the consideration, that we address one who has been vindicated from the same Calvinistic and Trinitarian distractions that we have, and is well apprised of the heavenly transports which such a redemption never fails to produce. We join in the rapturous expression of St. Paul, on this occasion, " Thanks be to God for his unspeakable gift!"

The wonderful progress of primitive Christianity in England within a few years, and the rapidity with which it is now extending itself, seems the opening of a truly glorious reformation not less important to mankind than that of the sixteenth century. When we consider what this system of primitive faith is, compared with the prevalent orthodoxy, and reflect upon the mighty obstacles which it has had to encounter, and which still array against it, we behold this progress with astonishment. The Unitarian doctrine not being tinctured in any the least degree by mystery, fanaticism, superstition or implicit faith, which, in all ages, have beguiled the multitude, but a plain artless scheme of rational sentiment, without any of that pomp, that external display, that lofty pretension, which feeds the pride, amuses the curiosity and excites the veneration of the feeble-minded, this reformation bears upon its countenance a Divine stamp. It is a reform with which the passions and propensities of man have no concern. It is of a nature purely intellectual, in which preconceived notions, deeply imprinted by education and sanctioned by their adoption throughout Christendom, are nevertheless abandoned ; and abandoned solely on the ground of their being weighed in the balance of cool investigation, of sober judgment, of rational evidence, and found wanting—a reformation in which benefits of a worldly character instead of being acquired are lost, and most serious evils are incurred : from whom? from the self-styled orthodox! Wherefore? for becoming open and honest votaries of the rational decisions of the mind! The case, in its most prominent features, corresponds so exactly to that produced by the publication of Christianity in the beginning, it would be highly gratifying to us to see the parallel particularly drawn and presented to the public. A pamphlet of this character, ingeniously executed, could hardly fail to produce conviction in the common mind, as the argument would be an appeal to common sense, and the same by which Christianity itself is supported. It would at least convince its readers of the *honesty of Unitarian advocates :* of the *intelli-*

gence of the champions of this cause, the orthodox are already sufficiently assured.

In this country the light of genuine gospel truth has, we think, been too much concealed from the public eye, by its earliest converts. Its progress has been less, certainly far less, than it must have been, had they been guided by the intrepid spirit of Jesus and his apostles, rather than the mistaken notion of a temporising prudence. We do not mean to accuse : we only regret it as a misfortune that they failed to perceive in the example of their Master and his disciples the more excellent way. As a scheme of Divine Providence, however, we think we can perceive there is reason in it. We shall probably have less Arianism in this country than otherwise might have been. The change from Trinitarianism to the simple humanity of Christ is so great, that few have passed immediately from the one to the other.

Mankind abandon their gross errors by degrees, especially in case they have not before them a complete exhibition of the true doctrine with its various evidences. In this predicament were the early converts of our country. They were not more than half illuminated. The exhibition of the doctrine as they understood it, might have pointed us to a by-path, but could not have directed us into the highway to the temple of truth. The plain road is now trod by numbers; the temple itself is in full view of all, and the half-way resting-house of Arianism is demolished.

As things are, may we not look with some confidence to the period as not very distant, when the seed of Divine truth which is here and there sowing in this land of liberty and free inquiry, shall under the auspices of Heaven yield an abundant harvest? At present the labourers here are, indeed, comparatively few ; but the minds of these few are more enlightened, and they possess a more laudable zeal. It is also true that the prejudices of education wherever it exists (and it exists every where) is undoubtedly a powerful obstacle to the prevalence of truth. But you are witness that truth has often triumphed over it even when backed by civil establishments, the mortal foe to freedom of inquiry and ingenuous confession of the faith. The recent events at Boston and in its vicinity, together with the state of things at Harvard College, are such as not only to generate a hope, but to inspire with confidence, that the doctrine of Divine Unity has at length come to the birth, and is actually born in New England, under circumstances so propitious as to allow no longer of alarm or even anxiety about its destinies. It must of necessity prevail. In our new settlements, which are populating with an unexampled rapidity, surpassing the belief of any but eye-witnesses, and which are composed of enterprising spirits from the older establishments, who, of course, are more inquisitive and liberally-minded than the mass of the communities they have left behind, the primitive faith, supported as it is by reason and the plain letter of the Sacred Scriptures, needs only to be preached with fidelity in order to obtain converts. From the success which has attended the exertions in this town, and in the neighbouring regions where the Divine Unity has been occasionally preached, we feel an undoubting assurance, that, did our new settlements enjoy the regular ministration of the unadulterated gospel, Unitarian churches might be easily established in all its parts: and notwithstanding the scores of orthodox missionaries who swarm in every district, the truth would certainly and speedily triumph.

The church here has considerably increased in numbers of late, and daily additions are made to it of worthy and respectable citizens. Its members are not only-seriously convinced of the Unitarian doctrine, but are (its females not excepted) so well versed in the argument and bare so often put to silence their orthodox neighbours, that they are far from being held in contempt. Indeed our society is becoming more respectable in the eyes of the community around us: our congregation is increasing, and had we a decent and commodious house of worship, in all probability it would secure a permanent establishment to our society, and consequently to the cause of Unitarianism in this district. Numbers would flock to the standard, and the rising generation, even the children of the orthodox, would hear the plain truth of primitive Christianity and be liberated from their errors.

Under these impressions, some of our enlightened, worthy, and most respectable sisters of the church, formed a few months since an eloquent address to the friends of Christianity here, and put in circulation a subscription for the erection of a house of public worship in this village. This eloquent address roused the dormant spirit of the society, and, considering the embarrassments incident to new settlers, who have a forest to prostrate, their lands to pay for, and habitations to erect for their accommodation, the friends of Unitarian worship have exhibited a highly laudable zeal beyond what would have been imagined. Still, however, the sum raised is inadequate. Our friends in Philadelphia, although pressed with the expense of erecting a chapel for themselves in that city, have, nevertheless, manifested their zeal for the promotion of the common cause, by a contribution of fifty dollars. The disposition of our brethren in Boston is good, but their peculiar situation requires all their exertions at home.

Unwilling to abandon the highly important object, and knowing that you and your worthy brethren in England are earnest for the dissemination of primitive Christianity throughout the world, we feel a degree of freedom in stating our condition, and requesting such aid as your circumstances may warrant. Should a collection for this object be obtained, we wish it to be made " to the Reformed Christian Church in Trenton." Aware from the new societies which are continually forming in your own country, that you must probably have numerous applications of this nature, and fully persuaded that you are always inclined to aid to the extent of your ability, we shall rest satisfied, should we receive little or no assistance, that it cannot be imputed to your disposition.

We rejoice, that though we are yet weak, you are growing daily more strong; and notwithstanding our present low estate, in comparison with yours, we indulge the pleasing hope that our feeble, but well-intended exertions, will meet the approbation of Heaven, and that genuine gospel truth will extend itself here, with as high effect as it has done in Great Britain.

The distribution of books, which our worthy Mr. Vander Kemp has, from time to time, received from his friends in England, has greatly contributed to the dissemination of correct principles in this region.

Any aid which our brethren in

England may be disposed to furnish in this way for the promotion of Christian knowledge among us, will be thankfully received and gratefully acknowledged. The hope of establishing Unitarian societies in the adjoining towns, leads us to mention particularly the Rev. Mr. Aspland's Hymn Books for their use; also the *Welsh* Hymn Books, mentioned in the Monthly Repository, as the Welsh are very numerous in our neighbourhood.

And now, worthy and dear Sir, we commend you to Him, who rewards with a blissful immortality, the faithful in the cause of truth and virtue. May He preserve your valuable life to venerable old age, and render it as happy as it has been useful to mankind.

With the highest respect and the most affectionate regard, we subscribe,

Your Brethren in Christ,

JOHN SHERMAN,

ISAAC BLISS PEIRCE,

Pastor of the Reformed Christian Church.

The Rev. Thomas Belsham, Minister of the Chapel in Essex Street, London.

Articles of the American Reformed Church.

[Communicated by Mr. Vander Kemp, of Oldenbarneveld, New York, United States of America.]

The *Reformed Christian Church* was composed from a part of the United Protestant Religious Society—the remaining members continuing to associate with it in religious worship.

Articles of Association.

I. We acknowledge the Scriptures of the Old and New Testament to contain a revelation of God's will to mankind, and that they are in matters of religion the *only* standard of doctrines and rules of practice.

II. We acknowledge that no other confession or test of Christian fellowship, and standing in the visible church of God, ought to be established, than that which Christ and his Apostles made necessary, or on which they received believers in the Gospel. Matt. xvi. 15—17, " He said unto them, but whom say ye that I am? and Simon Peter answered and said, thou art Christ, the Son of the living God : and Jesus answered and said unto him, blessed art thou Simon Bar-jona, for flesh and blood hath not revealed it unto thee, but my Father which is in heaven." Acts viii. 36, 37, " And as they went on their way, they came to

a certain water; and the eunuch said, see, here is water, what doth hinder me to be baptized?" And Philip said, if thou believest with all thine heart thou mayest—and he answered and said, I believe that Jesus Christ is the Son of God." 1 John iv. 15, " Whosoever shall confess that Jesus is the Son of God, God dwelleth in him and he in God." 1 John v. 1, " Whosoever believeth that Jesus is the Christ, is born of God; and every one that loveth him that begat, loveth him also that is begotten by him."

III. *Liberty of conscience shall be preserved inviolate.* Every member shall be maintained in his right of free inquiry into the doctrine of Scripture, in publishing what he believes the Scriptures to contain, and in practising according to his understanding of his duty. This liberty shall not be abridged as to his understanding and practice respecting the ceremonies, ordinances, or positive institutions of Christianity.

IV. The government and discipline shall be according to the directions of our Lord, Matt. xviii. 15—17, " Moreover if thy brother shall trespass against thee, go and tell him his fault between thee and him alone; if he shall hear thee, thou hast gained thy brother; but if he will not hear thee, then take with thee one or two more, that in the mouth of two or three witnesses every word may be established; and if he shall neglect to hear them, tell it to the church; but if he neglect to hear the church, let him be unto thee as a heathen man and a publican." The executive authority of the church shall be rested in the minister, the elders and deacons; but if any one suppose that by the church there mentioned is intended the brotherhood generally, he shall have the liberty of referring his cause for adjudication to the body at large.

V. The officers of the church, elders and deacons, shall be chosen by ballot, and hold their office during the pleasure of the church, or that they choose to decline serving any longer.

VI. The mode of admission to the church shall be, that any person wishing to become a member, shall make known his desire to the consistory, the minister, elders and deacons, who shall, if the applicant be a person of good moral character, refer his case for decision to the church at large.

VII. The Lord's supper shall be celebrated four times a year, twice in *Oldenbarneveld*, and twice in *Holland's Patent*, on such particular days as shall be found convenient.

VIII. The name by which this church is designated shall be *The Reformed Christian Church*.

N.B. Our first pastor was Rev. *John Sherman*, the present, Rev. *Isaac Bliss Peirce*.

LITERARY.
Mr. Rutt on his Edition of Dr. Priestley's Theological Works.

SIR, *Clapton,* Nov. 19, 1816.

I BEG leave to acquaint those of your readers who may take any interest in the success of the project for collecting Dr. Priestley's Theological Works, that it is my present intention to send for your next Number a list, as correct as I can ascertain it, of the names of all those who have already become subscribers to the proposed edition. Thus the friends to the writings and memory of Dr. Priestley will have an opportunity of observing what support a design to do honour to both has yet received, and they will judge for themselves what further patronage such a project may require or deserve.

As it is, of course, very desirable that the list should be as full as possible, I am induced to request any persons who design to possess the edition, to send their subscriptions before the middle of December, that their names may be inserted. The amount, though but a single subscription, would be received by any Bank in the country to be paid to me in London, and if such subscriber would write to me at *Clapton, Middlesex*, mentioning the Bankers in London where the money might be received, the business would be easily settled and the receipt be sent as they should direct. I take the liberty of requesting those who have already subscribed, but whose subscriptions have not been received, to employ the same mode of remittance.

I cannot omit to acknowledge Mr. Cordell's renewed attentions, (p. 589c) and to thank two other Correspondents for their expressions of good-will. I should readily adopt the proposal of T. H. (p. 590.) if I could perceive it practicable on my plan of bringing together so many publications, of such various sizes, and connecting them by notes and a general Index. Those who have had occasion frequently to consult such a publication as Lardner's Works, can best appreciate the superior use of the writings of a voluminous author in a connected form. From such persons, especially, I very naturally expected, what I have received from several of them, a ready support of the present undertaking.

I remain, your's,
J. T. RUTT.

The Franklin Manuscripts.

We congratulate the public, that after a lapse of so many years, these valuable treasures are at length about to be laid open by the Doctor's grandson, William Temple Franklin, Esq. to whom they were bequeathed, no doubt, with the intention that the world should have the chance of being benefited by their publication. It was certainly so understood by the person in question, who, we know, shortly after the death of his great relative, hastened to London, employed an amanuensis for many months in copying, &c. and had so far prepared them for publication, that proposals were made by several of our principal booksellers for the purchase of them.

The terms asked for the copy-right were however so high, amounting to several thousand pounds, that a demur arose, and the negociation broke off. From this period to the present year nothing more was heard of the manuscripts, and it was asserted by various persons, both in this country and America, of whom some were intimate with the grandson, that the proprietor had found a bidder of a different description, in some emissary of government, whose object was to withhold the manuscripts from the world, not to benefit it by their publication, and that they had thus either passed into other hands, or the person to whom they had been bequeathed had received a remuneration for suppressing them. We are glad to find that this conclusion was erroneous, and that the interesting remains of this profound philosopher, sound politician, and excellent moralist, are to appear forthwith. They consist, we understand, first, of his life, written by himself, to a late period, and continued to the time of his death by his grandson; the whole of his correspondence, private and political, numerous literary and philosophical papers, hitherto unpublished, &c.

The first, and perhaps the most interesting portion which is to appear, is his correspondence; the second will be the genuine life; and the third the hitherto unpublished literary and philosophical papers, &c.

The correspondence is most impatiently expected; and this may well be the case, when it is considered that among the most intimate friends of this great man, were Dr. Priestley, Dr. Price, Burke, Fox, the Bishop of St. Asaph, Sir Joseph Banks, Brand Hollis, Granville Sharp, Buffon, David Hartley, Lord Shelburne, Lord Grantham, Baron Maseres, the Earl of Buchan, Beccaria, Baskerville, &c. &c. &c.

MONTHLY RETROSPECT of PUBLIC AFFAIRS;

OR,

The Christian's Survey of the Political World.

ANOTHER deliberative body has commenced its discussions, which are likely to be of considerable importance to Europe. The members of this body are of the higher ranks, and their object is to settle the affairs of Germany. The overthrow of the Germanic or holy Roman empire was followed by the confederation of the Rhine, in which Buonaparte held a rank similar to that so long possessed by the House of Austria. The changes that have taken place in consequence of the destruction of the system set up by Buonaparte, have rendered it necessary to take some steps for a new constitution in Germany. This is taken in hand chiefly by the great estates, that have parted out this fine country amongst themselves. They have sent their deputies to Frankfort, and their session resembles that of the antient diet. It was opened by the deputy from Austria, who presides on this occasion; and in his speech he expatiated in strong terms on the excellencies of the German nation, and promised on the part of his master not to exercise any farther interference in the debates, than what became him as chairman of so august an assembly. He was followed by the deputy from the King of Holland, whose speech was wholly panegyrical, and it now remains to see what will be the result of this meeting.

All that the above-mentioned speaker advanced on the excellence of the German character is very little if at all exaggerated; but this praise belongs to the people, not to the class which has so long domineered over them. Nothing could be more wretched than the antient state of Germany, in which three classes were

strongly marked: the noble, the learned, and the common people. The noble distinguished by pride and ignorance; the learned by indefatigable application; the people by unwearied industry and the heavy yoke of oppression. To the two latter classes the world is indebted for great improvements in literature, science, and for much mechanical ingenuity. The trade of the former class was war, and young and old improved their fortunes by commissions, in their own and neighbouring countries. One great benefit of the French revolution is, the lowering of the pride of the nobles; for not to them but to the people is Europe indebted for the final overthrow of the mighty monarch.

In consequence of the late struggle, the people of Germany are alive to their rights, and this will probably be seen in the course of the discussions. It is not to be expected, that the line of distinction between the nobles and the other classes will be completely withdrawn. The former will continue to pride themselves on the quarterings in their arms, and may disdain to mix their blood with that of the classes, whom they look upon as so much beneath them: but still they will be brought nearer to each other, and offices of state will be more widely diffused. The discussions also that will arise throughout Germany on the subject of the debates, will be beneficial; and it is not improbable that an effort will be made to introduce the representative system. We shall see more of this however in the issue. The debates will partake of the slowness of the German character, but something will be gained on the side of freedom.

The death of the King of Wirtemburg promises to put an end to the disputes in his domains. This kingdom, founded by Buonaparte, seems likely to be the first to enjoy the representative system. The new sovereign was friendly to the demands of the subjects, and he has a fine opportunity to begin his reign in a popular manner. It is probable also, that the power given to the Duke of Cambridge may be beneficial to the Hanoverian states. Prussia begins to feel some embarrassments from its new subjects of Saxony. This latter country was the best as Prussia was the worst governed of all the States of Germany, and the ideas of the new may be beneficial to the old subjects. Indeed, if it is true that a minister from one of the pulpits of Prussia, who had served against Buonaparte, inquired what have we been fighting for if we are not to have a constitution? we have reason to believe that the subjects may answer the question, and keep the sovereign to his promise.

The national assembly of France has met. The sessions was opened by the king with the usual formalities. He went in solemn procession to the temple of her who is profanely called the Mother of God; was addressed by the priests in language which Protestants deem profane; and after assisting at their rites, delivered an oration to his assembled states. His speech has been re-echoed by the usual addresses, and the chambers have been employed in verifying the powers of the deputies. Great questions are to come before them; but by all accounts the ultra-royalist party seems to be in a minority. This augurs well for the French people, and it will be curious to see the ultra-royalists taking up the cause of liberty. Their grand advocate has already published doctrines consonant to those held by the Whigs at our Revolution. The liberty of the press is loudly called for, and the espionage of the police held out to deserved contempt. But it does not seem likely that their ministers will part with this too grand engine of despotism. Not do the French seem to have acquired as yet just notions of the decorum that belongs to a deliberative body. The affairs of the church seem likely to form a prominent part in the debates; some agreement has been negotiated with the pope; and the clergy will aim at raising themselves a little by the

measure. It is in contemplation to let them receive testamentary gifts, but it is in vain to attempt to raise them to their former splendour. The age of delusion is gone by; and unless they come nearer to Christianity, which is not very likely, they will sink lower in public estimation. The Protestants, however, will be preserved from such proceedings as took place at Nismes; and, if they conduct themselves with prudence, will at least not suffer any infringement on their rights.

The affairs of the insurgents on the shores washed by the gulph of Mexico, appear to be unsuccessful, but how far this extends to the country properly called the kingdom of Mexico, is not ascertained. French officers are said to be expatriating themselves in great numbers for these regions, and we are yet to learn what has become of Humboldt and his expedition. In South America the cause of independence bears a more favourable aspect, and the shores of La Plata seem to be advancing fast towards a settled constitution.

At home, meetings continue to be held, some on the subject of parliamentary reform, others on the distresses of the times. Amongst the former, Cornwall holds a high pre-eminence; and that county in which the abuses of representation are the greatest, speaks the loudest for the correction of them. The late meetings have also had very beneficial effects. A general disposition prevails to alleviate as much as possible present distress; and let us hope that benevolence duly exerted will be crowned with success. In this as in every thing belonging to his office, the Lord Mayor co-operates with his usual energy. His entrance into office for the second time must not pass without a remark. The procession upon these occasions returned not as usual by water, but by land through Westminster; and wherever the state coach passed, the acclamations of the people, and the crowded windows manifested the delight of the two cities in the popularity so well earned by this exemplary magistrate. Some umbrage was taken at this procession by one of the ministers; but the publication of the correspondence between him and the Lord Mayor, tended only to raise the latter in public estimation.

The case of Lord Cochrane has again been brought before the public. He appeared before the judges to receive their sentence for breach of prison, to which crime they attacked a penalty of one hundred pounds, and of course imprisonment till the fine was paid. His Lordship not paying the fine was conveyed to prison, and his friends had a meeting to raise it by subscription. To this no objection can be made. The subscribers may gratify themselves in thus releasing his Lordship from confinement; but it is evident that the laws must be obeyed, and after a trial by jury and commitment on that trial, there cannot be a doubt that breach of prison is a crime. If in the imprisonment there has been any injury sustained by the person confined, he has his redress by law: but in this case as far as the crime and penalty are connected together, it will be generally thought that his Lordship can have no reason to complain of the severity of his last sentence.

The moral world has been shocked by a transaction rendered too notorious between two barristers. A violent altercation it seems took place between them, and one of the parties thought it requisite to demand satisfaction according to the false principles of honour, against which they ought to have been the first to set themselves in opposition. Some demur took place in accepting the challenge, and in the mean time the parties were prevented from putting their murderous intentions into execution, by being bound over by a magistrate to keep the peace. After a lapse of time, the party challenged became the challenger, and in a very scurrilous letter appointed Calais for the place of settling their differences within a time limited. Thither the parties resorted, and fired each his pistol at the other nearly instantaneously, and one of them only was wounded. They then returned to England, and the account of these disgusting proceedings was set forth in all the public papers. Whether the last challenger has received what is vulgarly called satisfaction, we do not know, for no explanation took place on the ground. He has returned unhurt, and all that has been gained by their attempts at murder, has been the proof, that each can stand to be shot at. The annals of duelling do not present an instance, in which such vulgar abuse and scurrilous language have been used. It remains to be seen what part the bar will take on this transaction; but surely it cannot be countenanced by a profession to which we look up for peculiar attention to the laws of our country. On the folly and wickedness of this mode of settling differences, it is not necessary for us to expatiate. The characters of the parties cannot be raised in our estimation by such a paltry expedient; and, if either of them had died, we should not have acquitted the other of the guilt of murder.

NEW PUBLICATIONS IN THEOLOGY AND GENERAL LITERATURE.

Heresies Considered in Connexion with the Character of the Approved: A Sermon preached at the Opening of the Unitarian Chapel, in Thorne, on Friday June 28, 1816. By Nathaniel Philipps, D.D. To which is added an Appendix, stating the Rise and Progress of Unitarianism in the above Place. 8vo. 1s. 6d.

The Jewish and Christian Dispensations compared with other Institutions. By the late William Craven, D.D. Master of St. John's College, Cambridge. 8vo. 8s.

Oppression and Persecution; or, a Narrative of a Variety of Singular Facts that have occurred in the Rise, Progress and Promulgation of the Royal Lancasterian System of Education. By the Founder of the Lancasterian System under Royal Patronage, Joseph Lancaster. 8vo. 1s. 6d.

Twenty-one Short Forms of Morning and Evening Prayers, for the Use of Families. By a Member of the British and Foreign Bible Society, and of the Society for Promoting Christian Knowledge. 8vo. 3s. 6d. boards.

The Substance of a Farewell Sermon: in a Letter addressed to the Members, Subscribers and Congregation of the Unitarian Meeting, Dorchester. By B. Treleaven, late Minister of that Chapel. 8vo. 1s.

A Faithful Enquiry after the Ancient and Original Doctrine of the Trinity, taught by Christ and his Apostles. By Isaac Watts, D.D. 1745. 8vo. 1s. 6d. [Reprinted from the edition of Mr. Gabriel Watts in 1802.]

ERRATUM.
XI. p. 565—572, for Mr. William Mathews, read Mr. William Matthews.

THE

𝔐𝔬𝔫𝔱𝔥𝔩𝔶 𝔕𝔢𝔭𝔬𝔰𝔦𝔱𝔬𝔯𝔶,

&c.

No. CXXXII.]   DECEMBER, 1816.   [Vol. XI.

HISTORY AND BIOGRAPHY.

Estimate of the Philosophical Character of the Antagonists of Hobbes.

[From Dissertation I. by Dugald Stewart, prefixed to Supplement to Encyclopædia Britannica, Vol I. p. 65—71.]

CUDWORTH[*] was one of the first who successfully combated this new philosophy. As Hobbes, in the frenzy of his political zeal, had been led to sacrifice wantonly all the principles of religion and morality to the establishment of his conclusions, his works not only gave offence to the friends of liberty, but excited a general alarm among all sound moralists. His doctrine, in particular, that there is no *natural* distinction between right and wrong, and that these are dependent on the arbitrary will of the civil magistrate, was so obviously subversive of all the commonly received ideas concerning the moral constitution of human nature, that it became indispensably necessary, either to expose the sophistry of the attempt, or to admit, with Hobbes, that man is a beast of prey, incapable of being governed by any motives but fear, and the desire of self-preservation.

Between some of these tenets of the courtly Hobbists, and those inculcated by the Cromwellian Antinomians, there was a very extraordinary and unfortunate coincidence; the latter insisting, that, in expectation of Christ's second coming, "the obligations of morality and natural law were suspended; and that the elect, guided by an internal principle, more perfect and divine, were superior to the *beggarly elements* of justice and humanity."[†] It was the object of Cudworth to vindicate, against the assaults of both parties, the immutability of moral distinctions.

---

[*] Born 1617, died 1688.

[†] Hume.——For a more particular account of the English Antinomians, See Mosheim, Vol. IV. p. 534, *et seq.*

In the prosecution of his very able argument on this subject, Cudworth displays a rich store of enlightened and choice erudition, penetrated throughout with a peculiar vein of sobered and subdued Platonism, from whence some German systems, which have attracted no small notice in our own times, will be found, when stripped of their deep neological disguise, to have borrowed their most valuable materials.[‡]

[‡] The mind (according to Cudworth) perceives, by occasion of outward objects, as much more than is represented to it by sense, as a learned man does in the best written book, than an illiterate person or brute. "To the eyes of both, the same characters will appear; but the learned man, in those characters, will see heaven, earth, sun, and stars; read profound theorems of philosophy or geometry; learn a great deal of new knowledge from them, and admire the wisdom of the composer; while, to the other, nothing appears but black strokes drawn on white paper. The reason of which is, that the mind of the one is furnished with certain previous inward anticipations, ideas, and instruction, that the other wants."—"In the room of this book of *human* composition, let us now substitute the book of Nature, written all over with the characters and impressions of *divine* wisdom and goodness, but legible only to an intellectual eye. To the sense both of man and brute, there appears nothing else in it, but, as in the other, so many inky scrawls; that is, nothing but figures and colours. But the mind, which hath a participation of the divine wisdom that made it, upon occasion of those sensible delineations, exerting its own inward activity, will have not only a wonderful scene, and large prospects of other thoughts laid open before it, and variety of knowledge, logical, mathematical, and moral displayed; but also clearly read the divine wisdom and goodness in every page of this great volume, as it were written in large and legible characters."

I do not pretend to be an adept in the

Another coincidence between the Hobbists and the Antinomians, may be remarked in their common zeal for the scheme of *necessity*; which both of them stated in such a way as to be equally inconsistent with the moral agency of man, and with the moral attributes of God.* The strongest of all presumptions against this scheme is afforded by the other tenets with which it is almost universally combined; and accordingly, it was very shrewdly observed by Cudworth, that *the licentious system* which flourished in his time, (under which title, I presume, he comprehended the immoral tenets of the fanatics, as well as of the

<hr>

philosophy of Kant; but I certainly think I pay it a very high compliment, when I suppose, that, in the *Critic of pure Reason*, the leading idea is somewhat analogous to what is so much better expressed in the foregoing passage. To Kant it was probably suggested by the following very acute and decisive remark of Leibnitz on Locke's Essay: " Nempe, nihil est in intellectu, quod non fuerit in sensu, *nisi ipse intellectus*."

In justice to Aristotle, it may be here observed, that, although the general strain of his language is strictly conformable to the scholastic maxim just quoted, he does not seem to have altogether overlooked the important exception to it pointed out by Leibnitz. Indeed, this exception or limitation is very nearly a translation of Aristotle's words. Και αυτος δε νους νοητος εστιν, ωσπερ τα νοητα. επι μεν γαρ των ανευ υλης, το αυτο εστι το νοουν και το νοουμενον. " And the mind itself is an object of knowledge, as well as other things which are intelligible. For, in immaterial beings, that which understands is the same with that which is understood." (De *Anima*, Lib iii. cap. v.) I quote this very curious, and, I suspect, very little known sentence, in order to vindicate Aristotle against the misrepresentations of some of his present idolaters, who, in their anxiety to secure to him all the credit of Locke's doctrine concerning the Origin of our Ideas, have overlooked the occasional traces which occur in his works, of that higher and sounder philosophy in which he had been educated.

* " The doctrines of fate or destiny were deemed by the Independents essential to all religion. In these rigid opinions, *the whole sectaries*, amidst all their other differences, unanimously concurred." Hume's *History*, chap. lvii.

Hobbists), " grew up from the doctrine of the fatal necessity of all actions and events, as from its proper root." The unsettled, and, at the same time, disputatious period during which Cudworth lived, afforded him peculiarly favourable opportunities of judging from experience, of the practical tendency of this metaphysical dogma; and the result of his observations deserves the serious attention of those who may be disposed to regard it in the light of a fair and harmless theme for the display of controversial subtility. To argue, in this manner, against a speculative principle from its palpable effects, is not always so illogical as some authors have supposed. " You repeat to me incessantly," says Rousseau to one of his correspondents, " that truth can never be injurious to the world. I myself believe so as firmly as you do; and it is for this very reason I am satisfied that your proposition is false."†

But the principal importance of Cudworth, as an ethical writer, arises from the influence of his argument concerning the immutability of right and wrong on the various theories of morals which appeared in the course of the eighteenth century. To this argument may, more particularly, be traced the origin of the celebrated question, Whether the principle of moral approbation is to be ultimately resolved into reason, or into sentiment?—a question, which has furnished the chief ground of difference between the systems of Cudworth and of Clarke, on the one hand; and those of Shaftesbury, Hutcheson, Hume, and Smith, on the other.

The *Intellectual System* of Cudworth, embraces a field much wider than his treatise of *Immutable Morality*. The latter is particularly directed against the ethical doctrines of Hobbes, and of the Antinomians; but the former aspires to tear up by the roots, all the principles, both physical and metaphysical, of the Epicurean philosophy. It is a work, certainly, which reflects much honour on the talents of the author, and still more on the boundless extent of his learn-

<hr>

† " Vous répétez sans cesse que la vérité ne peut jamais faire de mal aux hommes; je le crois, et c'est pour moi la preuve que ce que vous dites n'est pas la vérité."

ing; but it is so ill suited to the taste of the present age, that, since the time of Mr. Harris and Dr. Price, I scarcely recollect the slightest reference to it in the writings of our British metaphysicians. Of its faults (beside the general disposition of the author to discuss questions placed altogether beyond the reach of our faculties), the most prominent is the wild hypothesis of a *plastic nature*; or, in other words, " of a vital and spiritual, but unintelligent and necessary agent, created by the Deity for the execution of his purposes." Notwithstanding, however, these, and many other abatements of its merits, *the Intellectual System* will for ever remain a precious mine of information to those whose curiosity may lead them to study the spirit of the ancient theories; and to *it* we may justly apply what Leibnitz has somewhere said, with far less reason, of the works of the schoolmen, " Scholasticos agnosco abundare ineptiis; *sed aurum est in illo cœno.*"*

Before dismissing the doctrines of Hobbes, it may be worth while to remark, that all his leading principles are traced by Cudworth to the remains of the ancient sceptics, by some of whom, as well as by Hobbes, they seem to have been adopted from a wish to flatter the uncontrolled passions of sovereigns. Not that I am disposed to call in question the originality of Hobbes; for it appears, from the testimony of all his friends, that he had much less pleasure in reading than in thinking. " If I had read," he was accustomed to say, " as much as some others, I should have been as ignorant as they are." But similar political circumstances invariably reproduce similar philosophical theories; and it is one of the numerous disadvantages attending an inventive mind, not properly furnished with acquired information, to be continually liable to a waste of its powers on subjects previously exhausted.

The sudden tide of licentiousness, both in principles and in practice, which burst into this island at the moment of the Restoration, conspired

with the paradoxes of Hobbes, and with the no less dangerous errors recently propagated among the people by their religious instructors, to turn the thoughts of sober and speculative men towards ethical disquisitions. The established clergy assumed a higher tone than before in their sermons; sometimes employing them in combating that Epicurean and Machiavellian philosophy which was then fashionable at court, and which may be always suspected to form the secret creed of the enemies of civil and religious liberty;—on other occasions, to overwhelm, with the united force of argument and learning, the extravagancies by which the ignorant enthusiasts of the preceding period had exposed Christianity itself to the scoffs of their libertine opponents. Among the divines who appeared at this era, it is impossible to pass over in silence the name of BARROW, whose theological works (adorned throughout by classical erudition, and by a vigorous, though unpolished eloquence), exhibit, in every page, marks of the same inventive genius which, in mathematics, has secured to him a rank second alone to that of Newton. As a writer, he is equally distinguished by the redundancy of his matter, and by the pregnant brevity of his expression; but what more peculiarly characterizes his manner, is a certain air of powerful and of conscious facility in the execution of whatever he undertakes. Whether the subject be mathematical, metaphysical, or theological, he seems always to bring to it a mind which feels itself superior to the occasion; and which, in contending with the greatest difficulties, " puts forth but half its strength." He has somewhere spoken of his *Lectiones Mathematicæ* (which it may, in passing, be remarked, display *metaphysical* talents of the highest order); as extemporaneous effusions of his pen; and I have no doubt that the same epithet is still more literally applicable to his pulpit discourses. It is, indeed, only thus we can account for the variety and extent of his voluminous remains, when we recollect that the author died at the age of forty-six.[†]

* The *Intellectual System* was published in 1678. The *Treatise concerning Eternal and Immutable Morality* did not appear till a considerable number of years after the author's death.

† In a note annexed to an English translation of the Cardinal Maury's *Principles of Eloquence*, it is stated, upon the

To the extreme rapidity with which Barrow committed his thoughts to writing, I am inclined to ascribe the hasty and not altogether consistent opinions which he has hazarded on some important topics. I shall confine myself to a single example, which I select in preference to others, as it bears directly on the most interesting of all questions connected with the theory of morals. "If we scan," says he, "the particular nature, and search into the original causes of the several kinds of naughty dispositions in our souls, and of miscarriages in our lives, we shall find inordinate self-love to be a main ingredient, and a common source of them all; so that a divine of great name had some reason to affirm, —that *original sin* (or that innate distemper from which men generally become so very prone to evil, and averse to good); doth consist in self-love, disposing us to all kinds of irregularity and excess." In another passage, the same author expresses himself thus : "Reason dictateth and prescribeth to us, that we should have a sober regard to our true good and welfare; to our best interests and solid content; to that which (all things being rightly stated, considered and computed) will, in the final event, prove most beneficial and satisfactory to us: a self-love working in prosecution of such things, common sense cannot but allow and approve."

Of these two opposite and irreconcilable opinions, the latter is incomparably the least wide of the truth; and accordingly Mr. Locke, and his innumerable followers, both in England and on the Continent, have maintained, that virtue and an enlightened self-love are one and the same. I have quoted the two pas-

sages here, merely to
little attention that had
the era in question, to
by one of the most lea
found divines of his age
more remarkable, as h
where inculcate the pu
practical morality, and
gular acuteness and jus
the observation of hu
Whoever compares the
row, when he touches
of morals, with those
fifty years afterwards
in his *Discourses on I*
will be abundantly sa
this science, as well as
progress of the philo
during the intervening
inconsiderable.

The name of WILK
he too wrote with so
against the Epicureans
now remembered chi
quence of his treatises
universal language and c
With all the ingenu
them, they cannot be
accessions of much val
and the long period
during which no atte
made to turn them t
use, affords of itself no
tion against the solidit

A few years before
Hobbes, Dr. CUMBE
wards Bishop of Pete
lished a book, entitle
Naturæ, Disquisitio P
principal aim, of whic
firm and illustrate i
Hobbes, the conclusio
concerning *Natural La*
is executed with ability
juster views of the id
science, than any mod
had yet appeared; the
the strength of his arg
Grotius had done, on
tion of authorities, bu
ples of the human fi
mutual relations of th
The circumstance, he
chiefly entitles this pu
notice is, that it seem
the earliest on the sub
tracted, in any consi
the attention of En
From this time, the w
tius and of Puffendor
generally studied, and
their way into the U

---

authority of a manuscript of Dr. Doddridge, that *most* of Barrow's sermons were transcribed three times, and some much oftener. They seem to me to contain very strong intrinsic evidence of the incorrectness of this anecdote.—Mr. Abraham Hill, (in his *Account of the Life of Barrow*, addressed to Dr. Tillotson), contents himself with saying, that "*Some* of his sermons were written four or five times over;"—mentioning, at the same time, a circumstance which may account for this fact, in perfect consistency with what I have stated above,—that "Barrow was very ready to *lend* his sermons as often as desired."

Scotland, the impression produced by them was more peculiarly remarkable. They were every where adopted as the best manuals of ethical and of political instruction that could be put into the hands of students; and gradually contributed to form that memorable school, from whence so many philosophers and philosophical historians were afterwards to proceed.

Free Speech on the Subject of Reformation, in the House of Commons, in the Reign of Henry VIII. 1530.

[We extract the following very singular speech, with the necessary preface, from *Cobbett's Parliamentary History of England*, I. 501—506. It may be found also in less modern language, in *Collier's Eccles. Hist.* (folio) II. 45—47. Collier makes this comment upon it;—" This odd speech is not mentioned either by Hollingshead, Goodwin or Stow: neither does Lord Herbert tell us the person's name. All that I shall observe upon this Free-thinker is, that he gives too much liberty to private reason. His maxims are dangerous, and his scheme ill suited to the general capacity." Ed.]

MANY abuses which the laity received daily from the clergy were loudly complained of; and the king, being now willing that they should be strictly inquired into, referred the redress thereof to the Commons in this parliament. Complaints also being made in that House against exactions for probats of testimonies and mortuaries; for pluralities, non-residence, and against priests that were farmers of lands, tanners, wool-buyers, &c. the spirituality were much offended at these proceedings; and, when the bills for regulating these exorbitances were brought before the House of Lords, John Fisher, Bishop of Rochester, made a remarkable speech against them, of which the following is a copy, as it is printed in a small treatise on the life and death of that prelate, by Dr. Thomas Bailey.

' My Lords—Here are certain bills exhibited against the clergy, wherein there are complaints made against the viciousness, idleness, rapacity and cruelty of bishops, abbots, priests and their officials. But, my Lords, are all vicious, all idle, all ravenous and cruel priests or bishops? And for such as are such, are there not laws provided already against such? Is there any

abuse that we do not seek to rectify? Or can there be such a rectification as that there shall be no abuses? Or are not clergymen to rectify the abuses of the clergy? Or shall men find fault with other mens' manners while they forget their own; and punish where they have no authority to correct? If we be not executive in our laws, let each man suffer for his delinquency; or, if we have not power, aid us with your assistance, and we shall give you thanks. But, my Lords, I hear there is a motion made, that the small monasteries should be given up into the king's hands, which makes me fear that it is not so much the good as the goods of the church that is looked after. Truly, my Lords, how this may sound in your ears I cannot tell, but to me it appears no otherwise, than as if our holy mother the church were to become a bondmaid, and now brought into servility and thraldom; and by little and little to be quite banished out of those dwelling-places, which the piety and liberality of our forefathers, as most bountiful benefactors, have conferred upon her. Otherwise, to what tendeth these portentous and curious petitions from the Commons? To no other intent or purpose, but to bring the clergy in contempt with the laity, that they may seize their patrimony. But, my Lords, beware of yourselves and your country; beware of your holy mother the Catholic church; the people are subject to novelties, and Lutheranism spreads itself amongst us. Remember Germany and Bohemia, what miseries are befallen them already; and let our neighbours' houses that are now on fire teach us how to beware of our own disasters. Wherefore, my Lords, I will tell you plainly what I think; that, except ye resist manfully, by your authorities, this violent heap of mischiefs offered by the Commons, you shall see all obedience first drawn from the clergy, and secondly from yourselves; and if you search into the true causes of all these mischiefs which reign amongst them, you shall find that they all arise through want of faith.'

The same authority tells us, that this speech pleased or displeased several of the House of Lords, as they were diversely inclined to forward or flatter the King's designs. But none made a reply to it, but only the Duke of Norfolk, who said to the Bishop, " My

Lord of Rochester, many of these words might have been well spared; but I wist it is often seen that the greatest clerks are not always the wisest men." To which the Bishop replied, "My Lord, I do not remember any fools in my time that ever proved great clerks."

When the Commons heard of this speech, they conceived so great indignation against the Bishop, that they immediately sent their Speaker, Audley, attended with a number of the members, to complain of it to the King; and to let his Majesty know, "how grievously they thought themselves injured thereby, for charging them with lack of faith, as if they had been infidels or heretics," &c. To satisfy the Commons, the King sent for the Bishop of Rochester, and demanded of him why he spoke in such a manner? The prelate answered, "that being in parliament, he spake his mind freely in defence of the church, which he saw daily injured and oppressed by the common people, whose office it was, not to judge of her manners, much less to reform them. And therefore he said he thought himself in conscience bound to defend her in all that lay within his power." However, the King advised him "to use his words more temperately another time."

But the injury the Commons thought they had received, by this reflection, was not so easily digested; for, one of the members making use of the gospel doctrine so far, says Lord Herbert, as to take a reasonable liberty to judge of things; and being piqued at the Bishop for laying it all on "want of faith," stood up in that House and spoke to this effect:[*]

'MR. SPEAKER—If none else but the Bishop of Rochester or his adherents did hold this language, it would less trouble me. But since so many religious and different sects, now conspicuous in the whole world, do not only vindicate unto themselves the name of the true church, but labour betwixt invitations and threats for nothing more than to make us resign our faith to a simple obedience; I shall crave leave to propose, what I think fit in this case for us laick and secular persons to do. Not that I will make

my opinion any rule to others when any better expedient shall be offered, but that I would be glad we considered hereof, as the greatest affair that doth or may concern us. For if in all human actions it be hard to find that medium or even temper which may keep us from declining into extremes, it will be much more difficult in religious worship; both as the path is supposed narrower, and the precipices more dangerous on every side. And because each man is created by God a free citizen of the world, and obliged to nothing so much as the inquiry of those means by which he may attain his everlasting happiness, it will be fit to examine to whose tuition and conduct he commit himself. For as several teachers, not only differing in language, habit, and ceremony, or at least in some of these, but peremptory and opposite in their doctrines, present themselves, much circumspection must be used. Here then taking his prospect, he shall find these guides directing him to several ways, whereof the 1st yet extends no further than to the laws and religions of each man's native soil or diocese, without passing those bounds. The 2nd, reaching much further, branches itself into that diversity of religions and philosophies, that not only are, but have been extant in former times, until he be able to determine which is best. But in either of these, no little difficulties will occur. For, if each man ought to be secure of all that is taught at home, without inquiring further how can he answer his conscience? When looking abroad, the terrors of everlasting damnation shall be denounced on him, by the several hierarchies and visible churches of the world, if he believe any doctrine but theirs. And that, amongst these again, such able and understanding "persons may be found, as in all other affairs will equal his teachers. Will it be fit that he believe God hath inspired his own church and religion only, and deserted the rest; when yet mankind' is so much of one offspring, that it hath not only the same 'Pater communis' in God, but is come all from the same carnal ancestors? Shall each man, without more examination, believe his priests in what religion soever; and when he hath done, call their doctrine his faith? On the other side, if he must argue controversies

---

[*] Lord Herbert has not given us the name of this speaker. Hall says he was a gentleman of Gray's-inn.

before he can be satisfied, how much leisure must he obtain? How much wealth and substance must he consume? How many languages must he learn? And how many authors must he read? How many ages must he look into? How many faiths must he examine? How many expositions must he conster, and how many contradictions reconcile? How many countries must he wander into, and how many dangers must he run? Briefly, would not our life on these terms be a perpetual peregrination; while each man posted into the other's country to learn the way to heaven, without yet that he could say at last he had known or tried all? What remains then to be done? Must he take all that each priest, upon pretence of inspiration, would teach him, because it might be so; or, may he leave all because it might be otherwise? Certainly, to embrace all religions, according to their various and repugnant rites, tenets, traditions, and faiths, is impossible, when yet in one age it were not possible, after incredible pains and expences, to learn out and number them. On the other side, to reject all religions indifferently is as impious, there being no nation that in some kind or other doth not worship God; so that there will be a necessity to distinguish. Not yet that any man will be able, upon comparison, to discern which is the perfectest, among the many professed in the whole world; each of them being of that large extent, that no man's understanding will serve to comprehend it in its uttermost latitude and signification. But, at least, that every man might vindicate and sever in his particular religion, the more essential and demonstrative parts from the rest, without being moved so much at the threats and promises of any other religion that would make him obnoxious, as to depart from this way: there being no ordinary method so intelligible, ready, and compendious, for conducting each man to his desired end. Having thus therefore recollected himself, and together implored the assistance of that Supreme God whom all nations acknowledge, he must labour in the next place to find out what inward means his Providence hath delivered, to discern the true not only from the false, but even from the likely and possible; each of

them requiring a peculiar scrutiny and consideration. Neither shall he fly thus to particular reason, which may soon lead him to heresy; but after a due separation of the more doubtful and controverted parts, shall hold himself to common, authentic, and universal truths, and consequently inform himself, what in the several articles proposed to him is so taught, as it is first written in the heart, and together delivered in all the laws and religions he can hear of in the whole world: this certainly can never deceive him; since therein he shall find out how far the impressions of God's wisdom and goodness are extant in all mankind, and to what degrees his universal Providence hath dilated itself; while thus ascending to God by the same steps he descends to us, be cannot fail to encounter the divine majesty. Neither ought it to trouble him if he find these truths variously complicated with difficulties or errors; since, without insisting on more points than what are clearly agreed on every side, it will be his part to reduce them into method and order; which also is not hard, they being but few, and apt for connection: so that it will concern our several teachers to imitate us in this doctrine, before they come to any particular direction; lest otherwise they do like those who would persuade us to renounce day-light to study only by their candle. It will be worth the labour, assuredly, to inquire how far these universal notions will guide us, before we commit ourselves to any of their abstruse and scholastic mysteries, or supernatural and private revelations. Not yet but that they also may challenge a just place in our belief, when they are delivered upon warrantable testimony; but that they cannot be understood as so indifferent and infallible principles for the instruction of all mankind.— Thus, among many supposed inferior and questionable deities, worshipped in the four quarters of the world, we shall find one chief so taught us, as above others to be highly reverenced. —Among many rites, ceremonies, volumes, &c. delivered us as instruments or parts of his worship, he shall find virtue so eminent, as it alone concludes and sums up the rest. Insomuch as there is no sacrament which is not finally resolved into it; good life, charity, faith in and love of

God, being such necessary and essential parts of religion, that all the rest are finally closed and determined in them.—Among the many expiations, lustrations, and propitiations for our sins, taught in the several quarters of the world in sundry times, we shall find that none doth avail without hearty sorrow for our sins, and a true repentance towards God, whom we have offended.—And lastly, amidst the divers places and manners of reward and punishment, which former ages have delivered, we shall find God's justice and mercy not so limited, but that he can extend either of them even beyond death, and consequently recompence or chastise eternally. These, therefore, as universal and undoubted truths, should, in my opinion, be first received; they will at least keep us from impiety and Atheism, and together lay a foundation for God's service and the hope of a better life. Besides, it will reduce men's minds from uncertain and controverted points to a solid practice of virtue; or when we fall from it, to an unfeigned repentance and purpose through God's grace to amend our sinful life; without making pardon so easy, cheap, or mercenary, as some of them do. Lastly, it will dispose us to a general concord and peace; for when we are agreed concerning these eternal causes and means of our salvation, why should we so much differ for the rest? Since as these principles exclude nothing of faith or tradition, in what age or manner soever it intervened; each nation may be permitted the belief of any pious miracle that conduceth to God's glory; without that, on this occasion, we need to 'scandalize' or offend each other. The common truths in religion, formerly mentioned, being firmer bonds of unity, than that any thing emergent out of traditions, whether written or unwritten, should dissolve them. Let us therefore establish and fix these catholic and universal notions; they will not hinder us to believe whatsoever else is faithfully taught upon the authority of the church. So that whether the Eastern, Western, Northern, or Southern teachers, &c. and particularly whether my Lord of Rochester, Luther, Eccius, Zuinglius, Erasmus, Melancthon, &c. be in the right, we laicks may so build upon these catholic and infallible grounds of religion, as whatsoever superstructures of faith be raised, these foundations yet may support them.'

MISCELLANEOUS COMMUNICATIONS.

Remarks on Mr. Fox's Argument from Scripture for 'Universal Restoration.

SIR,

IT is highly gratifying to the friends of rational religion, that Unitarians discover so much anxiety to wipe away the reproach of inactivity and want of zeal with which they have been so long assailed by their opponents. And among the various efforts of their newly acquired zeal for the dissemination of their peculiar opinions, the institution of weekly lectures in different parts of the metropolis, is one of the most promising, and has I understand been already eminently successful. One of the pre-eminent advantages of the Unitarians over other religious parties, is the unfettered freedom which its ministers and members may and do exercise in the discussion of disputed subjects in theology. Perfectly united in the grand fundamental truth of their system, that "there is but one God, even the Father," they entertain various shades of difference on almost all the minor parts of Christian speculation, and that without breaking the union and co-operation that ought to exist among all Christian brethren. Perhaps no other sect has allowed, or is capable consistently with their principles of allowing, such freedom of private judgment and public avowal of individual opinion, among their members, without dissolving their social union. It is desirable that this peculiarity should be well understood by the members of other sects, especially by those who are hostile to our general opinions; otherwise they will be apt to impute to the body, sentiments that only belong to some of its members; and hence, no doubt some of our adversaries have derived (what they consider) a ground for triumph, in the discordance and inconsistency of our system. Let them know that we have no differences among us, that are inconsistent with the simplicity and integrity of Christian worship, or unfeigned subjection to the moral precepts of the gospel; and all differences of another description we hold it a duty and privilege to respect in our brethren. The weekly lectures I have alluded to, are adapted to bring these varieties of opinion into view; and as it is likely that each preacher will state on such occasions, the strongest grounds upon which he supposes his peculiar views to rest, they afford a fair opportunity of canvassing fully those subjects which may be considered as principally of Unitarian growth and culture. The result must be, the more speedy detection of the weakest parts of the system, and the stronger confirmation of its unquestionable truths. I am sure your valuable Miscellany will be always open to every proper attempt to promote these objects. Permit me then to offer a few thoughts on the lecture delivered by Mr. Fox, at Worship Street, on Thursday, Nov. 28th. The subject was, *The final happiness of all men predicted in the Scripture.*

The perspicuity and energy of the preacher's style, the unhesitating and copious appeals to the express declarations of Scripture, the brilliant eloquence, the correct and classical taste with which it was delivered, did great honour to Mr. F. and was eminently calculated by immediate impression to silence objections, and to satisfy the advocates for the opinion defended, that the whole was unanswerable. I suppose few persons who were present could be insensible that the dazzling lustre thrown upon the subject, rendered scepticism for the moment almost impossible. For myself I had several powerful incitements to faith, such as, my high esteem for the preacher, whom I am permitted to call my friend; a strong *wish* that the position expressed in the title of the lecture might be true; nay further, a persuasion that the doctrine of the final happiness of all men is a most rational conclusion, from the known character of the Deity, from the observed tendencies of Providence, and from many very plain declarations of Scripture: so that as an inferential doctrine I hold it as strongly, as perhaps a doctrine ought to be held,

which rests apparently only on that foundation. But with all this predisposition in favour of the subject, will you believe it, Mr. Editor, I remained unconvinced. For it must be observed, as Mr. F. very correctly told us, his business was not to prove the doctrine by reason, nor to trace its natural production from other known truths of Christianity, nor to shew how many preponderating arguments might be accumulated to make it *almost certain* to every one that the truth was on that side; but it was to shew that the *fact itself was predicted in the Scripture. Hoc est opus, hic labor.* This if I am not mistaken he failed to accomplish. Nor can it be thought any depreciation of his talents to say this. He did all that can be done, all that his various predecessors have done, and did it in my estimation in a better manner than any of them; but the proposition itself is too strong to be borne out by Scripture, and what in such a case can any man do? Of the texts adduced as predictions of *the ultimate deliverance of all men from sin and misery,* there appeared to me none but what were capable of a very different explication without any torture. It was certainly very injurious to alledge Matt. xxv. 46. No doubt *punishment* may be corrective as well as vindictive; and everlasting, very frequently means a limited duration: but I cannot think it would ever enter into the thoughts of a common reader of the Scripture that the expression, "shall go away into everlasting punishment," should mean a *prediction* of the final happiness of the wicked.

Romans viii. 19—23, seems as little to the purpose. Suffice it to say that "the world itself may be delivered from the bondage of corruption, being universally blessed with the liberty of God's children;" during a long period of paradisaical happiness in which the wicked who are dead, shall not be partakers. As for the phrase "ourselves also which have the *first fruits* of the spirit," it does not seem as Mr. F. supposes to refer to the body of true Christians in this life in contradistinction from the wicked, who he thinks will be the last fruits of redeeming grace; but it evidently points to the Apostles and primitive Christians who partook of those eminent gifts of the Holy Spirit which distinguished and sealed the commencement of Christianity. Yet highly favoured as they were, they looked forward to the resurrection of the dead as their final and best deliverance.

1 Corinthians xv. 24—28, Mr. F. thought so decisive of the question, as to render elucidation unnecessary, its language being scarcely explicable on any other principle. Upon a repeated perusal of this passage, I am constrained to say that it does not appear to teach any thing like the doctrine of final restoration. The whole of the Apostle's reasonings and predictions throughout the chapter relate to the *resurrection of the dead.* It is quite a gratuitous assumption, that "the end," in ver. 24, signifies something *beyond* the resurrection and judgment. Nor can it be granted, for the *end* of Christ's mediatorial government is when the last enemy death is destroyed, ver. 26, that is when all the dead are raised to die no more; then shall he deliver up the kingdom to the Father, and himself be subject like the rest of his brethren, to that arrangement which infinite wisdom may appoint to follow the present dispensation. The Scriptures seem uniformly to speak of the general judgment of mankind, as the *last* act of Christ's administration of the moral government of the world. And as the Christian Scriptures only speak of things belonging to the Christian dispensation, all beyond is left at present involved in impenetrable mystery.

Philippians ii. 10, 11, is another text quoted as a prediction of the glorious restoration of all men from sin and punishment, by their being brought to confess that Jesus Christ is Lord, &c. The whole passage in its connexion is a declaration of the glory conferred upon Jesus Christ in reward of his humility and obedience unto death. This reward as we learn from many other passages consists in his being invested with authority over all men, and made their final judge, to reward or punish every one according to their deeds. Every knee therefore will bow to him, and every tongue confess that he is Lord, in that day when even the wicked must answer for themselves at his righteous tribunal. This text therefore does not necessarily imply any thing beyond.

Some passages were mentioned as auxiliary evidences of the truth of the doctrine, though not insisted upon as predictions of the fact. Such as Ephes. i. 10, " That in the dispensation of the fulness of times, he might gather together in one all things in Christ, &c." But as it is well known that "the fulness of times" is a phrase used by Paul to signify the time of Christ's first coming into the world, (see Gal. iv. 4,) I do not see that any thing more is meant in the highly figurative passage in question, than that during the gospel dispensation the distinction of Jew and Gentile should be done away in religious matters, and Christ be the one head of one great body of believers, as is afterwards insisted on.

1 Timothy ii. 4, "Who will have all men to be saved, and to come unto the knowledge of the truth." I think Macknight has shewn, that the original word here translated "will," has the force of the verb *command,* as also in ver. 8, " I will (command) that men pray every where, &c." God in sending his gospel to the nations, "commandeth all men every where to repent," Acts xvii. 30, which is the same as commanding them "to be saved and come to the knowledge of the truth." It seems therefore unwarrantable to extend the signification of this passage to a future state of being. I do not know whether the next text was adduced by Mr. F. or not, for I only write from recollection—but I have heard it mentioned by others and therefore notice it here.

1 Timothy iv. 10, " The Saviour of all men, specially of those who believe." The Apostle is speaking, as the connexion shews, of the dangers and hardships he was exposed to in preaching the gospel; and he says he trusted in the protection of the living God who is the Saviour (or Preserver) of all men, but particularly so of sincere and active Christians who devote themselves to his glory. But what has this to do with the universal happiness of mankind?

If any other passages were produced they have escaped my memory; but upon a review of these, I would ask any impartial person, whether here is any thing like a prediction of that sublime and astonishing scene, the brilliancy of which overpowers the imagination of him who most confidently expects it, and fills the believer of it with rapture in contemplation of an whole universe filled with life, happiness and love? I am not one of those who think the news too good to be true. I have already expressed my belief that as a deduction from premises already admitted, concerning the Divine perfections and government, the doctrine is a highly rational one, and what every enlightened reasoner must feel *disposed* to receive. But I am afraid we go too far when we presume to ascribe this doctrine to Jesus Christ or his Apostles. They certainly predicted some events in terms sufficiently distinct and clear, such as the resurrection and a future judgment, e. g. "God hath appointed a day in which he will judge the world in righteousness by that man whom he hath ordained." "The trumpet shall sound and the dead shall be raised incorruptible." And it was just as easy for them to have said, *the wicked shall be severely punished for a while, but shall afterwards be brought to repentance and be saved,* if they had been appointed to reveal any thing upon this subject.

Finally, Sir, it appears that the New Testament is completely silent on this subject, which some of our brethren seem so anxious to make a part of Christian belief; and when we reflect on what has been the consequence in former ages, of admitting various additions to the primitive doctrine, merely because they seemed to be deducible from certain texts ill-understood, or to result from principles already established, or were supported by the authority of eminent names, Unitarians cannot be too careful how they enlarge their creed. A certain class of the orthodox consider their preachers inspired, and every thing uttered from the pulpit has the force of Divine truth; it is with them the word of God. But as Unitarian preachers make no such claim, it will be the indelible disgrace of their hearers, if they have no better reason for their belief, than that such are the opinions of their teachers.

I am, Sir,
Your's, &c.
R. L.

Sir. *Dec.* 3, 1816.

I AGREE with your excellent Correspondent, Mr. Cogan, in your last Number, (p. 644,) that Mr. Hume's argument against miracles is inconclusive, and that testimony may be of a nature to amount to absolute *certainty,* and of *certainty* there can be no degrees. Probability is a word by which we express nothing but our ignorance of causes; and, in fact, no event ever took place, agreeable to the laws of nature, that was or could be previously improbable. Such an event may have appeared to us improbable, from our ignorance of existing causes; but, certainly, whatever has taken place, to him who knew all the causes in action, was not in the slightest degree improbable. We are somewhat acquainted with the laws that govern human testimony, but we are in general wholly ignorant of the previous circumstances, which produce any given event, in all cases where testimony is wanted; for of our own transactions we want not testimony. It is then, perhaps, not correct to say, that a very slight testimony will overcome a greater previous improbability; for of any given fact, there was in the thing itself no previous improbability, and we are always conscious that what we call improbable, is only owing to our ignorance of causes, of which ignorance we are also conscious, as to almost every occurrence where testimony can be required. Still this argument which sets aside all previous improbability, supposes that the fact contemplated happened according to the operation of known general laws; and as all we see and observe may be explained, when the particulars are known, by these general laws, there will still attach to the mind a sense of improbability, when a fact is reported, in contradiction to the known operation of these general laws. For instance, Mr. Cogan, in spite of himself, would require stronger and more circumstantial testimony, to satisfy him that a man had risen from the dead, than that a man had died. How does this feeling arise, for it is evident that if this be the fact, testimony is sufficient to ascertain it? It arises, I presume, from such a fact being contrary to general experience, and to its being a violation of a known general law. Now this gives a certain degree of force to Hume's reasoning, and I think it must be admitted that it seems to shew that testimony should be here of the strongest kind.

I think it to be impossible for any man to read of the miracles of the second and third centuries of the Christian æra, without being more inclined to disbelieve the miracles than to believe the testimony. But why? From a lurking suspicion, of which the improbability of such miracles is the foundation. He begins to question the testimony, and to bring forward certain general reasons against its credibility, such as that it was then the interest of many that such miracles be believed, and that men's minds were then prepared to receive easy proof of miracles. But these are only _general_ and indeed very _flimsy_ reasons, by which to impeach the veracity, or observation, of multitudes of religious men, who were ready to suffer death for religion, and many of whom did suffer death. If we make thus free with human testimony at this distance of time, when the circumstances are to us most imperfectly known, where are we to stop? I fully agree with Mr. Cogan, that the degree of testimony is to determine the particular question concerning any miracles, and I am quite sure that testimony may be such as to establish any fact, be it miraculous or otherwise. As the human mind is constituted, _rarity_ passes for _improbability_, and one miraculous fact being established, the conceived improbability of others is diminished, until their frequent occurrence takes away all sense of improbability from the mind, and their proof becomes as easy as that of any other fact. In the abstract, therefore, there is nothing in Mr. Hume's argument, yet it is one which will ever carry with it an imposing air of reason. If these remarks procure us a few more lines from Mr. Cogan, your readers will be pleased.

A. B. C.

'SIR,'   _Bristol, Nov. 25, 1816._

YOUR valuable Miscellany frequently contains hints to ministers for their improvement in the mode of conducting their pulpit exercises. In your Repository of last month (p. 584), J. B. recommends it to Unitarian ministers to preach statedly once a fortnight upon a doctrinal or controversial subject—those who invite their friends to this _treat_, would not then be pained by their disappointment and _disgust_ at hearing in its stead a _dry_,

moral discourse. The epithet dry is so frequently applied to morality, that I wish to know what there is in it to justify or occasion its being so called. I think it must meet some morbid quality in the mind which receives it with _disgust_; to such a mind, how very dry and _disgusting_ must be our Saviour's Sermon on the Mount, as that is entirely composed of moral precepts. Were these precepts reduced to practice, it would so improve the mental taste and moral constitution, that what is now dry and disgusting would be received even with a zest—that happy union would then take place between faith and works which constitutes the religion of Christ.

That Unitarian ministers should occasionally preach doctrinal sermons, and defend their opinions against their opponents, is useful and necessary; but while so many preachers are depreciating morality (and the _relish_ with which this is received their crowded audiences declare), it behoves the former rather to increase than to abate their exertions in that important part of their Master's work, the enforcing the _precepts_ of the gospel. Who are they whom the Scriptures dignify by the appellation of his peculiar people? those who are zealous of good works.

I would recommend it to J. B. when he invites his friends to a controversial entertainment at a Unitarian chapel, to warn them of the possibility of their meeting with only moral fare, which though less palatable, may, if it does not meet a disposition to indigestion, afford solid and wholesome nourishment.

A.

SIR,   _Dec._ 3, 1816.

I WISH our friends at Edinburgh all possible success in their plan of raising a fund for a new chapel, and shall be happy to contribute my mite to so desirable an object. I think, however, they would do well, in the first instance, to imitate the conduct of their brethren at York, Thorne, &c.—see what they can raise among themselves, and then lay their case before the public.

There seems no mode of supporting the great cause of Unitarianism so free from objection, as that of giving encouragement to the building and rebuilding of chapels, where circumstances render such measures prudent. Let us therefore hope, that as chapels are called for, they will receive *prompt* as well as general support. The Unitarians are a wealthy body ; and if, on every such occasion, a small number only of those who are able would immediately subscribe, each, his guinea, a most important object would be easily obtained.

Your's respectfully,

A CONSTANT READER.

Some Observations on the Sermons of Missionaries. Translated from the Spanish of P. Feyjoo, a Monk and Public Writer to the King of Spain, in the last Century.

(Concluded from p. 639.)

I FIND I have imperceptibly assumed the style of the pulpit, no where more superfluous than in a letter addressed to a preacher : all I intended was simply to propose the subject, leaving to you, who are so well accustomed to the ministry, to chuse the means of persuasion. You may perhaps apprehend, that by not denouncing the threats of God's anger against sinners, your sermons will be but of little use. It is this fear that in reality induces so many zealous missionaries to insist so frequently on the torments and horrors of hell. I shall not deny the utility of these images if properly introduced : however, the sentiment of love to God has not only a superior value and dignity far excelling any incentive derived from fear, (as I before hinted), but it should also be considered that the impressions made by love on the soul are more lasting than those of fear. The reason is that love being sweet, gentle and pleasing, the heart finds itself at ease, and far from repelling, opens to receive and cherish it : fear on the contrary, is severe, violent and disagreeable, the heart therefore rejects it as much as possible. Love allures, fear oppresses ; love is enjoyed, fear is suffered ; love being always an act of the will, is likewise often the object of it, that is, the will loves with another act of reflected love : but fear is invariably an irksome guest wherever it gains admission, and is received much in the same manner as we grant a lodging to an enemy who forces us to open the door sword in hand ; we accordingly apply all our power to expel the invader, and frequently succeed.

The pernicious and horrible doctrines of various unbelievers, spring from this principle ; they either deny the existence of God, or strip the soul of its immortality. All the errors of these misguided men proceed from contemplating the Deity as an inexorable judge rather than a merciful Father ; and to shake off the dread inspired by this idea, they use every effort to delude themselves into the belief, either that there is no God to punish them, or that all they have to apprehend is some slight and temporary chastisement, for example, some worldly misfortune. But what do they gain by this persuasion ? they are exactly in the situation of a criminal, who, flying from justice, flings himself down a precipice, and to avoid a probable punishment, embraces certain death : they seek to avoid Divine justice by the most tremendous of all precipices, that of impiety : yet even those who deny the existence of God, when they would dethrone the awful Judge who will pronounce sentence on their iniquity, do not so much flatter themselves that they can fly from Divine justice, as that Divine justice will fly from them.

Other unbelievers who assert the soul to be mortal, think by this means to escape from God and eternal misery : one party seek to annihilate the Deity, the other to annihilate themselves, hoping their souls will perish when their bodies return to dust. Both schemes are impious, but the first is much more horrible and more palpably false : it is therefore probable that the supporters of this opinion have been fewer in number, because all nature proclaims the existence of its Maker in so loud a tone, that it seems impossible any intellectual deafness can be so great as to resist its impression.

The majority of infidels giving up this cause as desperate, have ranged themselves with the second party : freed alike from the hopes and fear of a future life, they feel at liberty to enjoy the present, and give a loose to all their disorderly passions. But there is as much inadvertence as impiety in this attempt to escape from God. If the terror of Divine justice impels them to shun it, (and I acknowledge they are right to fly from its punishments, what criminal but would do the same?) yes, let them fly from justice but not from God. How is this possible? To avoid justice they must fly from the judge. Every human tribunal has a limited jurisdiction ; the culprit may escape to another province, or he may retreat from one kingdom to another; but if God is omnipresent and omnipotent, whither can we flee from his vengeance? This is not what I mean when I allow we may fly from Divine justice; I am sensible it is impossible to escape from God: where then can we take refuge? where, but in Divine mercy? If in a certain sense this may be deemed escaping from God, it is to shelter ourselves from the terrors of our judge under the protection of our Father; to appeal from the God of terror to the God of pity, from the God of vengeance to the God of mercy.

I infer from all that has been said, that the principal or only end that the evangelical orator ought to have in view, is to instil the love of God into the hearts of his hearers. It may indeed be in general proper to attain this end by motives of fear. "*Timor Dei initium dilectionis ejus*," says the sacred text in Ecclesiasticus,—The fear of God is a preparatory disposition to love him. The greater number of commentators indeed explain this to mean filial fear; but it may with propriety be extended to servile fear also, when the latter conducts to love, as I have already endeavoured to shew.

Suppose now the first object of a missionary sermon should be to alarm the auditors by a description of the intenseness and eternal duration of future punishments; terror being once raised in every bosom, it ought to be intimated that the only way to escape this fearful and boundless abyss of misery and torment, is an humble application to Divine mercy to shield us from Divine justice. The better to impress the minds of the congregation, the preacher may represent on one hand the awful tribunal of offended Deity surrounded by the ministers of his avenging wrath, and on the other a throne of grace on which is seated a compassionate and forgiving God, who opens wide his arms to embrace all who will have recourse to his mercy—that benignant Being whom the greatest of the apostolic preachers defines as the Father of mercies and God of all consolation. Oh! what a spacious, what a beautiful field is here displayed to the preacher on which to exert his zeal and eloquence. The latter indeed is superfluous: let him but use the energetic phrases, the appropriate similes, or rather the animated images of Holy Scripture, especially the New

Testament; for in comparison of their power to affect the mind, the eloquence of Demosthenes or Cicero on other subjects is but unmeaning words.

In one place we meet with a shepherd so solicitous for the preservation of his flock, that he seeks the lost sheep over hills and mountains, climbing steeps and treading on thorns, and having found it, he places it on his shoulders to secure it from the attacks of the wild beasts. In another we behold a kind and tender father highly insulted and offended by his son, who, after having forsaken him and spent all his wealth in riot and dissipation, when forced by necessity he returns home, he is embraced and received by his forgiving parent with every demonstration of affection. Who is this Father but the Redeemer of the world, the Sovereign Lord of heaven and earth? who the strayed sheep, the prodigal son? but the man who abandons Jerusalem for Babylon, the deserter from the noble army of the just to the infamous squadron of the wicked: Notwithstanding he has outraged and offended his God, let but the sinner have recourse to his clemency; all he demands is an humble and contrite heart. Let him only confess, "Father I have sinned against heaven and before thee, and I am no more worthy to be called thy son," this alone is requisite to obtain forgiveness. The Saviour of the world has assured us of it by the pen of the Evangelist (Luke xv).

It is plain the mercy of God must be infinite towards sinners, since nothing less could make him receive the criminal with caresses, who had evinced his hatred by insult and disobedience. Do earthly monarchs thus admit to their favour a vassal who has not only been ungrateful but rebellious? No, their clemency is as limited as their existence is finite; the mercy of God is boundless, because his being is infinite.

By these and similar representations, the minds of the auditors may be elevated above the servile dread of punishment to confidence in the Divine mercy; and one step is alone wanting to lead them to that height of love we are desirous they should attain. The gradation is natural and easy; for man being convinced that God is supremely merciful and full of loving-kindness, therefore infinitely amiable; that his forbearance is so great that even after repeated provocations he is ready to forgive the returning penitent; that even whilst in the actual commission of sin he requires no satisfaction from the offender, nothing but what is necessary for his own sake to ensure his eternal felicity; how can he resist such powerful motives to love his God, and prostrate before him say from his heart, " Most merciful and heavenly Father, I have sinned against thee like a most vile and ungrateful creature, therefore I am not worthy to be called thy son, but to be treated as a vile and rebellious slave."

Thus the path is clearly marked out by which the missionary may lead men from servile to filial fear: and it likewise appears that both servile and filial fear verifies that sentence of Scripture, " *Timor Dei initium dilectionis ejus.*" The consciousness of deserving punishment shews us the necessity of imploring mercy; and as this attribute of the Supreme Being is perfectly amiable, the transition to love is natural and easy. It may indeed be proper, and it is frequently requisite, to impress the sinner with the hazard he incurs of eternal perdition and the dread of everlasting torment; but he ought not to be left under the dominion of terror, both because love is a more noble principle of action, more suited to human nature, and more efficacious to direct him in the road of virtue, and because unqualified terror overwhelms the soul and weakens our inclinations to obedience; for fear though it may restrain a man from the commission of sin, wants the sweetness that incites to good works: it may deter us from evil, but it will not render us virtuous. The business of the preacher is to recall sinners to God; but he who represents the Almighty armed with vengeance, is more likely to drive the criminal to despair than to reclaim him.

It is easy to perceive that a conversion effected by love will not only be sincere but permanent. God when considered as a master supremely merciful and benignant, is an attractive object, a magnet that with gentle force draws towards it the wills of men, and gives them an admirable disposition to persevere in their resolutions of not relapsing into sin; for before the heart can be torn from so lovely an object, it must suffer great violence from the repeated assaults of some most impetuous passion, or it must exert the strongest force

against itself. Experience confirms this opinion. The very reverend Father M. Fr. Bentio Angerich, in an account which he published of the life and virtues of our celebrated legate of Montserrate, Fr. Joseph de San Benito, chap. x. relates that this monk enjoyed throughout the principality of Catalonia the reputation of a most enlightened understanding, not only amongst the ignorant but amongst learned men, and was frequently consulted when any doubts were entertained in spiritual affairs. An apostolic minister belonging to the fraternity of Escernalbon, complained to him of the very little good his sermons effected, soliciting his advice and instructions how he might render them more useful; to this request the holy man made the following reply, (I quote the exact words of the writer) " that he should endeavour to inculcate the infinite mercy of God more than he had hitherto done, and that he would assuredly reap that harvest of souls he desired." The writer thus proceeds: " the event justified the advice; the missionary adopted the counsel of his brother, and returned after some years to Montserrate, having converted innumerable souls, and raising many to a steadfast and chearful hope that were before in imminent danger of despair, by reading to them the short compendious treatise in verse at the end of San Benito's works." The account concludes thus: " Fr. Joseph had a special grace by his discourses and writings to infuse hope into the heart and inspire it with confidence in the Divine mercy."

The proper and distinctive character of mind in this admirable ecclesiastic, was a profoundly rooted persuasion of the mercy and clemency of the Supreme Being. This formed the prominent feature of all his discourses and conversations: by inspiring others with the same sentiments, he accomplished the most extraordinary conversions of sinners who were reputed absolutely incorrigible. The method he pursued was to introduce his opinions casually by way of conversation, as M. Angerich was assured by the monks of his convent, who had witnessed many of the cases. The chapter ends thus: " This holy father was so intimately convinced of the necessity of impressing sinners with the hopes of pardon through the infinite mercy of God, that he used to say to a spiritual director, who frequently requested his opinion on particular cases, that he should always treat his penitents with mildness, and encourage them to confide in the mercy of their Creator. To those who confessed relapses into sin, the only remedy he ought to give them to relieve their misery, should be to advise them whenever they fell into the same fault to confess it anew, with a firm reliance on the mercy and forgiveness of their heavenly Father, not doubting but by so doing they would ultimately reform; which proved to be the fact: by degrees they became exemplary in their lives and manners."

For my own part I consider the conduct of this monk highly calculated to ensure the salvation of souls. To fear God is good, but to love him is still better; and what means can more effectually contribute to this end, than to impress men with the clearest idea possible of his unbounded mercy.

Goodness is the genuine object of love: the conceptions which we form of the infinite mercy of God raises in our minds the most lively and sensible of his infinite goodness. I have

incompatible with each other; that from servile fear we may rise to filial love. I have also proposed the method to be pursued in conducting the sinner from one to the other, adhering in this method to a proper and literal explication of the sentence, " *Timor Dei initium dilectionis ejus,*" comprehending in it even servile dread. But enough of missions. May heaven preserve you many years.

Ed.]

An Answer to the Question, What is Blasphemy?

[This paper has been in print before: we copy it from a printed sheet communicated by a Correspondent.

TO speak *blasphemously,* as far as I am able to understand that expression, can only signify, to speak dishonourably of God; to speak in derogation of his Divine nature and attributes. Now, since both reason and revelation teach us, that the only true God is IMMUTABLE, INCORPOREAL, and OMNIPRESENT, should any doctrine, on the contrary, assert that the Divine nature hath undergone a change, and assumed a corporeal form, which must be local, I think there can be no doubt but such

doctrine would be highly injurious to the Deity, and derogatory from his most essential attributes as well as most pernicious in its consequences to the salutary purposes of true religion. For this reason, when the Israelites, at Mount Horeb, meaning to worship the true God, erected the golden calf as a fit emblem of the object of their religious adoration, it will not I presume be denied, that they were guilty of *the most blasphemous idolatry*; and, when exulting in the restoration of that mode of religious worship, in behalf of which they had acquired an habitual prejudice in the land of Egypt, they loudly proclaimed that four-footed image to be a just representation of the Almighty Being whose miraculous interposition had so lately delivered them from their Egyptian bondage; whether we judge their conduct by the dictates of reason, or by the law of Moses, they were most certainly guilty of *speaking blasphemously against God.* Let us suppose then, for a moment, that the means of forming the molten image had failed them, but that they had asserted that the God *who brought them up out of the land of Egypt,* had theretofore taken the *bovine nature* upon him in the belly of a cow, been made an ox, and had appeared in Egypt, and, though then in heaven, still continued incarnate in the body of that animal; and, that even without the use of any visible symbol, they had instituted a form of divine worship, adapted to the name and properties of the fabulous God, Apis;—surely, in this case, both the worship and the language of the Israelites would have been, at least, equally *blasphemous* as in the other.

There may be some, perhaps, who will readily allow the charge of *blasphemy* in so monstrous and disgusting an instance, as is here supposed, but who do not think it equally, nor even in any degree, blasphemous against Almighty God, to teach, that, in another place and period, he became incarnate in the body of an animal of a more excellent nature and superior rank. But, certainly, whatsoever difference there may be in the nature of finite beings, when compared with each other, there is absolutely none at all when we consider them with respect to the infinite and eternal Creator of the universe; and consequently, both the *blasphemy* of the expression, and the impossibility of the fact, must be exactly the same, whether. we affirm the Almighty to be incarnate, by having been made one of the lowest, or one of the highest order of those creatures, which his own power and goodness hath called into existence.

If then it should be found, that the Emperor Constantine, and almost all those who have succeeded him in the possession of either the whole or any part of the civil power of Europe, have abused their temporal authority to the purpose of propagating, and enforcing upon their subjects, the doctrine of the incarnation of the infinite unchangeable Deity, with all the gross absurdities and impieties that necessarily flow from such a source, shall we not be forced to acknowledge, that they have indeed *opened their mouths in blasphemy against God, to blaspheme his name and his tabernacle?* Shall we not also both see and admire the singular propriety of the prophetic language, in fixing this charge of *blasphemy* upon the temporal rulers and not the ecclesiastics, when we consider, that these are of necessity under the dominion of the former; that the impiety or innocence of such a doctrine is a question of common sense, not of theological science; that even if any Scriptures could be procured wherein it was expressly warranted, the doctrine itself would afford much stronger reasons for rejecting such a Scripture, than the best authenticated Scripture could do for admitting so blasphemous a doctrine; and that nothing less than that powerful influence upon the strongest passions of the human mind, which must needs be the effect of the rigid pains and penalties on one hand, and the alluring rewards and emoluments on the other; annexed by the laws of the state to the rejection and admission of this particular tenet, could have induced mankind so far to abandon their own sense of right and wrong, to give up every rational and becoming idea of the eternal Deity, and to submit patiently, nay, to adhere with obstinacy, to so gross and impious a *delusion?*

But as things were long circumstanced in every state of Christendom, it was, in a very high degree, dangerous for any man to venture to see with his own eyes, and avow the most

obvious dictates of his understanding respecting this first and most important article of theology. For the legislative power having in consequence of this boldest and most unreasonable *petitio principii* that ever was heard of, proceeded to assert, that a particular created being, an earthly animal was the one true God and the proper object of Divine worship; if any reflecting conscientious Christian was led to question the truth and piety of that orthodox persuasion, he was immediately, with the most uncharitable and opprobrious language, accused of *denying* the *divinity* of the legal and only God; and the bigoted zeal of some, and the malicious rancour of others, recurred eagerly to the inhuman edicts and avenging arm of the civil magistrate to condemn and punish, as a *blasphemer*, the man who only meant to avoid the guilt of so heinous a sin, and no longer dared to join his voice in uttering *blasphemy* against the infinite majesty and incommunicable attributes of that awful Being, whom an inspired teacher of Christianity assures us, *no man ever hath seen nor can see.*[*]

Having mentioned the impossibility of the *Incarnation* of God, as well as the *blasphemy* of such a doctrine, lest I should appear to speak rashly, and to revile long established opinions without sufficient grounds, I beg you to consider, that the Deity is, in his very nature, omnipresent; that his becoming incarnate, in a particular body, evidently implies his being more immediately present with that body, than with any other: whereas, the very meaning of omnipresence is, that he is equally present, equally close connected, as far as such a being can properly be said to be connected, with all the bodies in the universe. You will be pleased to recollect, likewise, that God is *immutable*, another attribute absolutely inconsistent with his *Incarnation*. To evince this, let us only attend to the commonly received opinion of man, as a being compounded of two natures, the one spiritual, the other carnal. Allowing this idea to be just, and that, at the dissolution of this composition by death, man exists simply in a spiritual state, it is certain that the alteration made by death in the mode of

---

[*] 1 Tim. vi. 16.

his existence, is the greatest change such a compound being can undergo. It is evident, therefore, that were a purely spiritual being, such as the soul of man is usually presumed to be, when separated from the body, to become compounded with a carnal nature like our own, he would suffer a change exactly equivalent to that which man is said to suffer at his death. And since the difference between the nature of God and that of the most perfect created being, is infinitely great; to assert that he who has existed from all eternity in a spiritual, incorporeal, uncompounded state, hath at length adopted another mode of existence, and is become compounded with the material, animal body, is to assert, that the only unchangeable being in the universe hath undergone a change infinitely greater than any of his own mutable creatures can undergo.   B.

Dr. Benson on Socrates' Sacrifice of a Cock.

Sir,

ON reading Dr. Benson's Life of Christ, in a note, pp. 91, 92, I met with the following remarks on the conduct of Socrates just before his death, in ordering a cock to be sacrificed to Æsculapius, which, to say the least, appear to be ingenious and may not be generally known. On these accounts, I have thought that perhaps they might be worthy of a place in your useful Miscellany.

I am, your's, &c.

P.

SOCRATES, according to Plato in his Phædo, ordered a cock to be sacrificed to Æsculapius. Some think that was in ridicule. Others think it was without any regard to Æsculapius, whether serious or ridiculous. Perhaps the critics have not done justice to Socrates upon this article. It might possibly then be at Athens a well known custom to offer a cock to Æsculapius the God of medicine, upon a person's recovering from some threatening indisposition; and consequently to have offered a cock to Æsculapius, and to have been restored to health from a dangerous disease, were expressions of the same import, by putting the sign for the thing signified. Plato in the person of Phædo, informs us, that when Socrates had found the poison had in-

vaded his bowels, i. e. to say when he found himself upon the point of expiring (and they were the last words) that he spake to Crito: "I owe a cock to Æsculapius, which I desire you would pay. Do not neglect it." q. d. "I am just upon the point of being cured of all the disorder and pains attending this mortal frame, and of entering upon a better life, a state of perfect health and happiness; and I desire you would thus publicly signify my belief and persuasion to the whole city of Athens, in that way which they are all acquainted with, and will understand." Thus have I given the most favourable interpretation that I have met with to the last words of that truly great man, whose memory and character I esteem and reverence, though formerly that order from Socrates to his friend, when dying, to offer a cock to Æsculapius, used to appear to me ridiculous and a desire unbecoming so wise and good a man as Socrates.

Sir,   *Newington Green,*
                       Nov. 2, 1816.

THE following communication is intended to invite the assistance of your philological readers in searching into the meanings and origins of our words. Some of them are probably in possession of old English and Saxon books and manuscripts (or have access to them) which the writer of this has not been able to procure: and if they will occasionally send to the Repository curious or singular passages, accompanied by etymological criticism and comment, I shall deem it a privilege, to contribute a share, in the same manner, to the common stock of philological knowledge. It may perhaps be useful to etymological students, to inform them, that after much search, and being long convinced to the contrary, I am now of opinion, that nearly the whole (if not the whole) of our language may be traced to Rome and Greece. It is of the more importance that this be well considered, because the ingenious though paradoxical doctrines of Horne Tooke respecting a Northern origin, have given modern philologers a false scent. I cannot enter into *proof* of my opinion in this communication (for the *evidence* is commensurate with the wide extent of lexicography); but I think it demonstrable by every right principle and fair rule of *etymologizing*, that even the Gothic and Saxon are composed chiefly, at least, of Latin and Greek words.

The following translation of the twenty-third Psalm is from the Psalter of Richard Rolle, hermit of Hampole as given by the biographer and editor of Wickliff, from a MS. in the British Museum. Will any of your readers who can conveniently consult the MS. have the goodness to transmit a few extracts from it to the Monthly Repository?

"Our Lord gouverneth me and nothyng to me shal wante : stede of pasture thar he me sette. In the water of the hetyng forth he me brought: my soule he turnyde. He ladde me on the stretis of rygtwisnesse: for his name. For win gif I hadde goo in myddil of the shadewe of deeth: I shal not dreede yueles for thou art with me. Thi geerde and thi staf: thei have comfourted me. Thou hast greythid in my syght a bord: agens hem that angryn me. Thou fattide myn herred in oyle: and my chalys drunkenyng what is cleer. And thi mercy shal folewe me: in alle the dayes of my lyf. And that I wone in the hous of oure Lord in the lengthe of dayes."

What are commonly called pronouns, conjunctions, &c. with adjective and verbal affixes and prefixes, &c. have been already explained or attempted in Philosophic Etymology: I shall here attempt a few of the *radicals* of the above quotation.

Lord is a contraction, *hlaford*, (Saxon) the same as *calif* or *khalif* with the affix *ord*; the same word appears softened and contracted into caput, captain, chief, chieftain, &c. govern, guberno, super, huper or hyper, (Greek) sovereign, cover, over, &c. will be perceived to have the same origin. " Have ghe mynde of ghoure *sovereyns* that have spoken to ghou the word of God." Heb. xiii. 7. Wickliff's translation.

Stede is employed by our old writers where we would employ *place*; and it has still the same application in the compound word *instead* : stead, steady, study, studes, stand, seem to be essentially the same word : steading is in the North a building, and we have in English home-stead; stepfather, stepmother, &c. are properly as they are still spelt in Danish steadfather,

steadmother, that is a person in the stead, standing or place of father, mother, &c.

Sette, sit, sedo, sedeo, &c. are merely softened forms of *cado :* cadens sol and setting sun are identical : west is resolvable into ge-set, the quarter in which the sun sets; *hetyng* in the above translation is evidently a different form of *cadens*. A fundamental rule of etymologizing is, that the more easy forms of a word to the organs of speech are to be resolved into that form which is most difficult, not vice versa.

Stretis (paths in our translation) and stride, strut, striddle, tread, trudge, tramp, trip, stair, step, &c. seem all resolvable into grad-ior ; ced-o, cess-us, I also take to be a contraction of grad-ior, gress-us. A *mile* is in the Durham book, mile stræden, thousand steppan, that is a thousand strides or steps; answering to mille passus in Latin, or thousand paces. It would seem to some perhaps straining etymology to resolve pace, pass, foot, pes, ped-is pous, pod-is (Greek) ced-o, grad-ior, &c. into one common origin. I am not yet certain whether *street* as well as *stratum*, &c. have the same connection and origin ; I would only remark here (what is suggested by association of ideas) that both *walk* and *kick* are resolvable into *calc-o*, and that *heel* is a contraction of *calcaneum*.

To etymologize on every word of the foregoing quotation would make too long an article ; I shall therefore confine myself to a few words evidently connected with Latin, though common readers would not think so: *Mercy* is a striking instance of *contraction*, being resolvable into misericordia or miseresco : folewe (follow) is the same as fellow, and is resolvable into colligo (which is also collect, connect, &c.) Richard Rolle has spelt the word more nearly to the primitive form in his preface. " In the translacione I felogh the letter als meikle as I may, and thor I fyne no proper Ynglys I felogh the wit of the wordis. In the expowning I felogh holi doctors." Chaucer writes it felow. " At last ne drede ne might overcame thoe muses that thei ne werren fellowes and feloweden my waie."

Day, *dies*, &c. are evidently the same word, which properly signifies *light*, but my limits are too narrow here to go into its origin and many forms and applications. *Dawn* is a different spelling for *daying*; which is contracted into *dew*, which is properly an adjective put elliptically; for if the ellipsis be filled up, it is dew drops, or dawn drops, or wetness, &c.

Wone (which is still used in some parts of Scotland), is resolvable into maneo, as *dwell*, which we now employ instead of *wone*, is to be resolved into *colo*. The etymological student must have observed that the Latin guttural c or k frequently softens into c soft, ch, s, t, d, &c. when it passes into the modern dialects: car-us (cher French) becomes dear; colo becomes as well as dwell, till, &c.; *wont* (as in *wont* to resort) is *wone* with a usual affix.

Hous is merely a slight variety of casa, which primarily and properly means what covers or protects: thus *case*, casket, chest, cask, casque, &c. which have all probably originated in claus-us, a, um, close, or closed, &c. garda is employed for house in Codex Argentum: castle or castel, castrum, &c. are radically the same word. One of the most rational explanations in Johnson's Dictionary is that given to castle, namely " a house fortified."

JAMES GILCHRIST.

Sir,

IN the third volume of the Correspondence between the Countesses of Hartford and Pomfret, published in 1806, I met with the following singularity of a convent at Rome with scarcely any thing of conventual restraint, and this so long ago as in 1741, when papal power was something very different from what it is at present. Lady Pomfret thus describes to her friend " a convent called the *Sette Dolori*."

" They receive all their friends' visits, both men and women, in parlours without grates. They go abroad with their near relations; and they make no vow, but that of obedience to their superior. They are all people of quality and live in good esteem. Should the nuns wish to marry, they are under no obligation not to do so, though the incident has never yet happened." Lady P. " found here the fewest nuns she ever saw in such a place."

In the same volume is a Letter from Lady Hartford in London, describing the debut of a celebrated lady since " come to her grave in a full age." " I inclose you some verses by Mrs. Carter who gave them to me. She was here the other morning, and surprised me with her morose looks and conversation. The former resemble those of Hebe, the latter has a tendency to a little pedantry: however she has certainly real and extensive learning."

I am, your's,

SELECTOR.

Jewish Creed.

Sir,   *Norwich.*

PRESUMING that the creed of our Unitarian Jewish brethren may be admissible in an Unitarian Christian Miscellany, I have transcribed it from the Prayer-book in use amongst the descendants of Abraham.

1. I believe, with a firm and perfect faith, that God is the Creator of all things; that he doth guide and support all creatures; that he alone has made every thing; and that he still acts and will act during the whole eternity.

2. I believe, with a firm and perfect faith, that God is one, there is no Unity like his; he alone hath been, is, and shall be eternally, our God.

3. I believe, with a firm and perfect faith, that God is not corporeal, he cannot have any material proportion, and no corporeal essence can be compared with him.

4. I believe, with a firm and perfect faith, that God is the beginning and the end of all things.

5. I believe, with a firm and perfect faith, that God alone ought to be worshipped, and none but him ought to be adored.

6. I believe, with a firm and perfect faith, whatever hath been taught by the prophets is true.

7. I believe, with a firm and perfect faith, the doctrine and prophecy of Moses is true. He is the father and head of all the doctors that lived before or since, or shall live after him.

8. I believe, with a firm and perfect faith, the law that we have is the same as was given by Moses.

9. I believe, with a firm and perfect faith, that this law shall never be altered, and God will give no other.

10. I believe, with a firm and

perfect faith, that God knoweth all the thoughts and actions of men.

11. I believe, with a firm and perfect faith, that God will reward the works of all those who perform his commandments, and punish those who trangress his laws.

12. I believe, with a firm and perfect faith, that the Messiah is to come; although he tarrieth, I will wait and expect daily his coming.

13. I believe, with a firm and perfect faith, the resurrection of the dead shall happen when God shall think fit. Blessed and glorified eternally be the name of the Creator. Amen.

I hope some liberal-minded and learned son of Israel will favour us through the medium of your Repository, with a brief historical account of the compilation of this creed and the prayers in use amongst the worshippers of Jehovah in the Synagogue at this day.

It is I think more than probable that the writer of the Athanasian Creed had never been a Jew, for in such creeds as the above there is perspicuity and no tincture of illiberality. Notwithstanding all that the enemies of Athanasius have advanced against him, historical evidence acquits him of having written the creed which is passed on the world under his name. If the writer had drunk deep of the streams of Polytheism, and acquired a smattering of the learning of the schools, it is not difficult to account for the *singularity* of the composition. Some persons on the supposition that the author is unknown, have considered it as a *jeu d'esprit* to shew what consequences were fairly deducible from the doctrines of the Trinity. Not however to treat lightly what is considered by some Christians as solemnly religious, I apprehend there can be neither levity nor heresy in according with Archbishop Tillotson, who did not hesitate to say, " I wish we were well rid of it."

I remain,

Your's respectfully,

MELANCTHON.

Sir,

SEVERAL professors of medicine in Great Britain, have been known as writers on theology and metaphysics. Among these Dr. Hartley is justly distinguished, whose *Ob-*

servations on Man attracted so much attention out of his own country as to have been translated into French, not long after its first publication in 1749. I lately met with an account of an eminent French physician, who had also pursued his inquiries beyond his own profession.

This was Dr. Astruc, who died at Paris in 1766, aged 83. In " Letters concerning the Present State of the French Nation," 1769, p. 230, is a list of his numerous publications, nearly all medical except the following, of which perhaps some of your readers may be able to give an account. *Conjectures sur les mémoires originaux dont il paroit que Moyse s'est servé pour composer le livre de la Genese,* 12mo. 1753.

Conjectures concerning the original records from which Moses appears to have compiled the Book of Genesis.

Dissertation sur l'immatérialité, l'immortalité, et la liberté de l'ame, 12mo. 1756.

Dissertation on the immateriality, the immortality and the freedom of the soul.

Whatever opinions Dr. Astruc maintained, they do not appear to have brought into question his faith in revelation, though he could scarcely have held the common' notion of inspiration in connection with the first of these publications. In the *Nov. Dict. Histor.* Par. 1772, (I. 238,) both works are mentioned, and the author is immediately commended as displaying *l'ardeur et le zéle d'un medecin, ami de l'humanité et d'un philosophe Chretien.* The ardent zeal of a physician, the friend of humanity and of a philosophic Christian.

In the *Letters* which I have quoted, there is also a list of the numerous works of *Calmet.* Among them I observe *Dissertation sur les apparitions des esprits,* 12mo. 1746, and *Dissertation sur les vampires ou revenans de Hongrie.* 12mo. 2 vols. 1749. It would be a gratification to curiosity to know how a learned father of the Romish Church had treated those subjects at so late a period as the middle of the last century. From a note to one of Lord Byron's poems it appears that Hungary is famous for spectral credulity and especially for a belief in *vampires.*

OTIOSUS.

SIR,   *Clapton, Dec.* 1, 1816.

ALLOW me a few words more respecting Dr. Bekker, that his case may be left as correctly stated as possible in your present volume.

There are several general biographies under the same title of *Dictionaire Historique*, &c. published at different places.in France. That consulted by Mr. Flower, (p. 654,) for his account of Bekker, appears to describe " the ecclesiastical synod," by which he was " deprived of his functions," as having " continued his salary as minister." This lenity the *Dictionaire* which I quoted (p. 656,) as well as the *Biographical Dictionary*, expressly ascribes to " the *magistrates* of Amsterdam." The words are *les magistrats lui en conserverent la pension*, and I am sure no one will be more disposed than Mr. Flower to allow the importance of the distinction.

From a passage in a letter of *Locke* to *Limborch* subsequent to that I quoted, and which I then overlooked, it appears that he was not a little interested in the fate of *Bekker*. Mr. Locke thus inquires in his letter of 29 Feb. 1692.

Quid tandem devenit paradoxorum ille de angelis auctor scire cupio, si evasit mirum est, quanquam °eo res inclinare videbatur quo tempore scripsisti, favente etiam Amstelodamensium prædicatorum desidiâ, vix tamen veniam ei datam credo. Hujus modi orthodoxiæ propugnatores non solent errantibus ignoscere.†

There can be no doubt that among the ministers of Amsterdam Le Clerc and Limborch, at least, would have skreened *Bekker* if they had not the courage to share his lot; but these, as *remonstrants*, had little influence, if indeed they could belong to the *synod*, which is scarcely probable.

R.

P.S. In the note * p. 656, the second line should have been printed " there never was really a *possessed* or a sorcerer."

† I wish to know what is at last to become of the author of the paradoxes concerning angels. It will be wonderful if he escape, although things looked that way when you wrote; for however favourable to him may be the dilatory proceedings of the preachers at Amsterdam, he will scarcely be acquitted. These champions of orthodoxy are not accustomed thus to excuse the erroneous.

SIR,   *Chichester, Dec.* 9, 1816.

A LETTER appeared in the Repository for October, [p. 621], from Mr. C. Saint, calling on Mr. B. Travers, or some of his friends, for the publication of a statement of the sums collected for the Southampton Chapel. It is surprising that Mr. Saint's respect for the feelings of an afflicted family should not have led him to the more delicate mode of a private application. He well knows that Mr. Travers is incapacitated, by a heavy affliction, for making any reply to his inquiries. He, and every one acquainted with that gentleman, must also know that he was by no means cold or backward in expressing his gratitude to those who by exertions. or contributions seconded his own strenuous and well meant efforts to introduce Unitarianism at Southampton. Illness alone, frustrated his intention of making in the course of this year such exertions as would have freed the chapel from its incumbrances; after which it was his design to publish in the Repository, a complete statement with his acknowledgments to the donors. He had drawn up a list for this purpose, which will be forwarded for your insertion. Had Providence seen fit to preserve his health, and powers, it is not improbable that the ability and perseverance with which he was conducting the cause at Southampton would have been attended with a success that would have satisfied all the contributors and been the most eloquent thanks for their liberality.

W. J. FOX.

List of Collections and Subscriptions for the Chapel at Southampton, from a paper drawn up by Mr. Travers, dated July 15, 1816, and inscribed "To be inserted in the Repository."

BY B. TRAVERS.

	£	s.	d.
Southampton	120	10	0
London	138	13	0
Bridport	40	0	0
Portsmouth and Portsea	27	0	0
Bristol	24	3	6
Bath	23	2	0
St. Albans	20	0	0
Chichester	18	1	0
Poole	16	4	0
Taunton	13	0	0
Plymouth and Exeter	12	0	0
Isle of Wight	11	1	0
Carried up	463	14	6

Brought up	463	14	6
Sheffield	10	0	0
Birmingham	5	0	0
Sherborne	5	0	0
Romsey	4	0	0
Yeovil	4	1	0
Dorchester	4	0	0
Reresby	2	0	0
Crewkerne	3	0	0
Ilminster	1	1	0
Kidderminster	1	0	0
Ringwood	1	0	0
Beaminster	1	0	0
Wareham	1	0	0
Rochdale	1	0	0
Manchester	0	10	0

By C. N. Saint.

Southern Fund	6	0	0
Birmingham ⎱ Bewdley ⎰ Dudley	33	10	0
Coventry	6	5	0
Warwick	2	1	0
Shrewsbury	5	10	0
Chester	4	0	0
Liverpool	7	0	0
Gateacre	8	0	0
	579	12	6

Proposed Publication of an Account of the Rise, Progress and Present State of a Society of Unitarian Christians at Newchurch, in Rossendale.

Sir,

SOME of your readers may remember that in the brief account of an Unitarian church at Rossendale, in Lancashire, Mon. Repos. X. 313, I expressed a hope that the brevity and deficiences of that account would be supplied by an enlarged narrative from the pen of Mr. John Ashworth, the resident minister at Newchurch, and I engaged that such detailed narrative should somehow or other be laid before the Unitarian public. That hope has been realized, and that pledge I am about to redeem. Mr. Ashworth has drawn up a series of letters to a friend containing a particular account of the rise, progress and present state of the religious societies with which he is connected, and more especially of the manner and order in which the doctrines of reputed orthodoxy came into discussion and were relinquished by them ; and has stated minutely the arguments from Scripture and from common sense which led them to relinquish their former sentiments and

to settle down into their present convictions. These letters will form a pamphlet of considerable size, and may consist probably of about sixty thickly printed octavo pages. I am unable definitively to fix the price, but I hope it may be afforded for about ninepence to subscribers. Profit is not an object in its publication, but indemnity from loss is desirable. It is proposed therefore to publish very few more copies than are previously subscribed for. With this view I address myself more particularly to the secretaries and committee-members of our tract societies, and should be glad to receive orders from them for as many copies as their local exigencies may require, *on or before the first of February*, 1817 ; as on that day the pamphlet will be put to press, and the number of copies will be determined by the previous orders.

This pamphlet it is presumed will be peculiarly well adapted to promote the leading object of the tract societies, viz. to disseminate amongst the lower classes of society, and in a form level to the humblest capacity, plain statements of the Unitarian doctrine and Scriptural arguments in its support. Doubtless there are at this moment many knots of inquirers, many small bodies of Christians, connected or scarcely connected with other religious denominations, who are dissatisfied with their present profession, but who do not clearly see the way out of their doubts and difficulties. This pamphlet affords a clue to lead them out of the labyrinth, by detailing the doubts and difficulties in which others similarly circumstanced were involved, and the means by which they were led step by step to the light, truth and liberty which they at present enjoy.

I am, Sir,

Your's, &c.

JOHN THOMSON.

All orders may be sent, post paid, to Dr. Thomson, Halifax, on or before the 1st of February, 1817.

Sir, *Nov.* 15, 1816.

IN a late Number of your Repository, (p. 684) I observed an appeal from the Unitarian Baptists at York to the Unitarian public, soliciting donations in aid of purchasing a new chapel. I have been given to understand that by this church at

York, baptism is held as an essential pre-requisite to communion. If so, I think this ought fairly to have been stated. It is no part of my present object to inquire how far such a term of church communion is Scriptural or not. I believe it is rejected by a very great majority of the Unitarian body, and it is for the members of that body to determine how far they are called upon to assist in purchasing a place of meeting for a church, which whatever opinions it may hold in common with that body, maintains a principle which is one of exclusion to all Unitarians who have not submitted to adult baptism. I shall be glad to find that I have been misinformed in this particular; and if so, will send you a donation for the baptists at York.

I am, Sir,
A. F.

GLEANINGS; OR, SELECTIONS AND REFLECTIONS MADE IN A COURSE OF GENERAL READING.

No. CCLXXXVII.
Unitarian Martyr.

Francis 1. King of France, had a bastard son by Madame Cureau, of Orleans, who was brought up and sent to college by the name of Stephen Dolet. He published *Commentarii Linguæ Latinæ*, in two volumes folio, which were beautifully printed at Lyons in 1536. He also wrote *De Re Navali*, and a poem on his father's gests. Unfortunately he got acquainted at Lyons with the celebrated Serveto, became a zealous propagandist of his opinions, sent heretical books to Paris, incurred first an imprisonment, and after relapsing, the condemnation to be burnt alive. This horrible sentence was executed at Paris in 1546, and was the model and precursor of that which Calvin inflicted on Serveto at Geneva.

Calvin mentions Dolet in the same phrase with Agrippa and Serveto, of Villanova, as follows :—*Agrippam, Villanovanum, Doletum, et similes vulgo notum est tanquam Cyclopas quospiam evangelium semper fastuose sprevisse.* This is a singular figure of vituperative oratory, to represent the Unitarians as one-eyed and to call them Cyclops.

Monthly Mag.

No. CCLXXXVIII.
Matt. Henry's Continuators.

It is well known that Matt. Henry was taken away by death in the midst of his great work, the Commentary. He had proceeded no further than the Acts of the Apostles. The following is a list of his Continuators:

Rev. John Evans, Rom.
Simon Browne, 1 Cor.
Daniel Mayo, 2 Cor. and 1 and 2 Thess.
Joshua Bayes, Gal.
Samuel Rosewell, Ephes.
William Harris, Philipp. and Col.
Benjamin Andrew Atkinson, 1 and 2 Tim.
Jeremiah Smith, Tit. and Philem.
William Tong, Heb. and Rev.
Samuel Wright, James.
Zechariah Merrill, 1 Pet.
Joseph Hill, 2 Pet.
John Reynolds, 1, 2, and 3 John.
John Billingsley, Jude.

No. CCLXXXIX.
A Singular Orthodox Preacher.

Acosta the Spanish author, who was born about the year 1539 and died in 1600, published a celebrated work, highly praised by Dr. Robertson, *De Natura Novi Orbis.* In this work he acknowledges the cruelties of the Spaniards in their conquest of America; but represents them as the agents of heaven in the conversion of the natives, supported in their mission by various miraculous attestations. He says, however, that a curious orthodox preacher had preceded them: his words are, "That which is difficult in our law to believe, has been made easy among the Indians; because the DEVIL *had made them comprehend even the self-same things, which he had stolen from our Evangelical law,*—as, their manner of confession, *their adoration of three in one,* and such like; the which against the will of the enemy, have holpen for the easy receiving of the truth."

This extract is taken from the English Translation of the History, published at London, in 4to. in the year 1604.

BIBLICAL CRITICISM.

Mr. Jevans on the Levitical Sacrifices.

SIR,

I HOPE it was proved in my first letter on sin offerings, [Vol. X. p. 646], that the patriarchs offered such sacrifices to God, and that the real design of them was pointed out. I shall now endeavour to shew what is said on the same subject in the Levitical law.

I. It appears that a sin offering was offered to God, and atonement made with its blood for Aaron and his sons when they were consecrated, or set apart, to the priest's office. Levit. viii. 14—17. For the altar, Exod. xxix. 36. For the sanctuary and tabernacle, Levit. vii. For the Levites, Numb. viii. 11, 12, and 21. For Aaron and his sons, and all the people of Israel, when the whole congregation of Israel was at one and the same time, set apart for God, Levit. ix. 1—11. And for a woman who had been in childbed, Levit. xii. 8. For a leper, Levit. xiv. 20—24. For a Nazarite, Numb. vi. 13, 14.

II. Sin offerings were offered for all sins of ignorance, though sometimes there must have been a considerable degree of guilt attached to them. Levit. iv. 2. 23. 26. v. 1—15. Heb. ix. 22. Acts viii. 1—3. comp. 1 Tim. i. 13.

III. A sin offering was offered to God, and atonement made with its blood for certain wilful transgressions. It is said, Levit. vi. 1—7, And the Lord spake unto Moses, saying, if a soul sin, and commit a trespass against the Lord, and lie unto his neighbour in that which was delivered him to keep, or in fellowship, or in a thing taken away by violence, or hath deceived his neighbour; or have found that which was lost, and lieth concerning it, and sweareth falsely; in any of all these that a man doeth, sinning therein: then it shall be, because he hath sinned and is guilty, that he shall restore that which he took violently away, or the thing which he hath deceitfully gotten, or that which was delivered him to keep, or the lost thing which he found, or all that about which he hath sworn falsely; he shall even restore it in the principal, and shall add the fifth part more thereto, and give it unto him to whom it appertaineth, in the day of

his trespass offering. And he shall bring his trespass offering unto the Lord, a ram without blemish out of the flock, with thy estimation, for a trespass offering unto the priest: and the priest shall make an atonement for him before the Lord: and it shall be forgiven him, for any thing of all that he hath done in trespassing therein. Also Numb. v. 5—8.

From hence it appears that atonement was made for the wilful sins of lying, fraud, theft, dishonest traffic, attended with perjury; which are breaches of several of the laws contained in the decalogue.

Hallet says, " it is certain that there were sacrifices under the law appointed to make atonement for moral evil, and for moral guilt; particularly for lying, theft, fraud, extortion, perjury, as it is written, Lev. vi. 1, 2, &c."—Notes and Dis. Vol. II. p. 277, 278.

It is said, Levit. xix. 20—23, Whosoever lieth carnally with a woman that is a bondmaid betrothed to an husband, and not at all redeemed, nor freedom given her; she (LXX. *they*) shall be scourged: they shall not be put to death, because she was not free. And he shall bring his trespass offering unto the Lord, unto the door of the tabernacle of the congregation, even a ram for a trespass offering. And the priest shall make an atonement for him with the ram of the trespass offering before the Lord, for his sin which he hath done: and the sin which he hath done shall be forgiven him. Comp. Deut. xxii. 24.

Here is another wilful crime of no small magnitude, for which atonement was appointed to be made. It is also evident that some of these crimes would often be committed, and therefore atonement not unfrequently be made for them.

IV. All the males of the children of Israel, who were of a proper age, were required to appear before God at the city of Jerusalem every year, at the three great feasts; at other seasons they probably might go or not as they pleased. Exod. xxiii. 14—16. xiii. 17. xxxiv. 23. Deut. xvi. 6. At each of these feasts a sin offering was appointed to be offered to God for the sins of the congregation in general.

1. The feast of the passover and

the feast of unleavened bread were both kept on the first month. of the year; one began on the fourteenth and the other on the fifteenth day of the month. Levit. xxiii. 5, 6. Exod. xii. 1, &c. Numb. xxviii. 15, 22, And one goat for a sin offering, to make an atonement for you.

2. The feast of pentecost was kept fifty days after the passover. Exod. xxiii. 16. Levit. xxiii. 10—21. Numb. xxviii. 26—32. At ver. 30, it is said, and one kid of the goats to make an atonement for you.

3. The day of expiation and the feast of tabernacles were both as one, as they were only four days apart. Levit. xvi. 23. 26—34. Numb. xxix. 12, &c. Ezek. xlv. 19, 20. On this annual day of expiation, Aaron first made atonement with the blood of a bullock for himself and his family; and then with the blood of a goat for all the congregation of the children of Israel. Levit. xvi. 3. A bullock for a sin offering, &c. ver. 6. 9. 11—13. Then shall he kill the goat of the sin offering; that is for the people. These atonements were made by sprinkling the blood before the Lord in the most holy place, ver. 14, 15. In relation to which things, and his confessing their sins over the head of the scapegoat, it is said, ver. 21, and confess over him all the iniquities of the children of Israel, and all their transgressions in all their sins, ver. 30, to cleanse you, that ye may be clean from all your sins, before the Lord. Ver. 33, he shall make an atonement for the priest and all the people of the congregation, ver. 34, for *all their sins* once a year.

4. It also appears from Numb. xxviii. 11—15, that a sin offering was offered at the beginning of every month for the congregation.

By these various appointments, provision was made for the expiation of the generality of these sins which the children of Israel were exposed to; which are not declared, by the law, to be capital.

V. It appears that whenever any person committed a really wilful offence, which was not notoriously presumptuous, nor expressly declared by the law to be capital, that they did not put the person to death; but offered a sin offering to cleanse him from the guilt of it, which also appears to have been right, as their offerings on such occasions were accepted

of the Lord. See Numb. xvi. 46—48, where we are informed that Aaron made atonement by incense, to remove the anger of God for the murmuring of the people, and the plague was stayed. David also offered burnt offerings and peace offerings to God for his sin in numbering the people. 2 Sam. xxiv. 25. And on another occasion, when he thought that God might possibly be displeased with him, he said, let him accept an offering. 1 Sam. xxvi. 19. And when many of the Israelites had broken the law by marrying strange wives, they offered a ram for their trespass. Exod x. 19. 1 Esdras ix. 13—20. In 2 Maccab. iii. 32, 33, there is an account of a sacrifice offered for the health of a sick person, and atonement is said to have been made. They probably thought his affliction was the fruit of his sins. See also 2 Maccab. xii. 29—45. Ezek. xlv. 19, 20.

VI. It also appears that in some cases in which the offences were evidently wilful, not to say presumptuous, but either were not expressly declared by the law to be capital, or were attended with some circumstances which pleaded in favour of the criminals, that they did not immediately put them to death, but kept them in ward until they had consulted the oracle of God : so it was in the case of the youth who blasphemed God, Exod. xxxii. 30, and also of the man who gathered sticks on the Sabbath day, Numb. xv. 32—36.

So far were they from considering every breach of the law as capital—so enlarged were their views of making atonement for sin.

VII. It is however acknowledged that the law of Moses says, " but the soul that doeth aught presumptuously, &c. the same reproacheth the Lord ; and that soul shall be cut off from among his people." Numb. xv. 30. Deut. xvii. 12.

Human language is imperfect. Every presumptuous sin must be wilful ; but probably it will appear that every wilful offence is not, in the eye of the law, presumptuous.

1. This is in part evident from the many instances that have been adduced of atonement being made for wilful transgressions of the law.

2. To make a wilful offence presumptuous, there must, it seems, be some aggravating additional circumstance or circumstances attending it, such as a deliberate, determinate, in-

solent and daring opposition to the will of God. Esther. vii. 5.

The neglect of Moses in circumcising his son was a wilful offence, but probably not presumptuous, as Zipporah perhaps had opposed the doing of it. Exod. iv. 24, 25. So the captive Jews marrying strange wives at Babylon was a wilful offence, but probably not a presumptuous transgression, as there might be a scarcity of Jewish females there. Exod. x. 2.

But when Moses and Aaron commanded the Israelites to go up against the Canaanites, and they would not, but murmured, and talked of making a captain and returning to Egypt, and even proposed to stone them with stones, their offence was highly presumptuous. Numb. xiii. 17—35, and xiv. 1—10. Therefore they were very severely punished for it, ver. 23. And afterwards, when they saw their folly, and would go against their enemies, though neither Moses nor the ark of God was with them, their behaviour was especially criminal, and they were made to suffer for it, ver. 42 —45. Therefore Moses, many years after, said unto them, in reference to this circumstance, so I spake unto you, and ye would not hear, but rebelled against the commandment of the Lord, and went presumptuously up into the hill. Deut. i. 48. xviii. 20—22. Accordingly it is said in Deut. xvii. 12, and the man that will do presumptuously, and will not hearken unto the priest, &c. or unto the judge, even that man shall die.

The character of such persons is described by the prophet Jeremiah, chap. xviii. 12, who said to him, when he brought a message from God to them, there is no hope; we will walk after our own devices, and we will every one do after the imagination of his own evil heart.

3. The Hebrew words found in the above passages signify acting with a high hand, or doing a thing proudly, or arrogantly : as Numb. xv. 30, *excelsa manu*, Deut. xvii. 12, And the man that will do *presumptuously, superbia* So Deut. i. 43, and Exod. xxi. 14, and Ps. xix. 13, derived from *superbivit, superbè, arroganter egit.* See Buxtorf's Lex. And Nehemiah speaking of the very proud, haughty, daring conduct of Pharoah, uses the same term. See Nehem. ix. 10.

It therefore appears that every wilful offence is not, in the eye of the law, a presumptuous one, at least not that high presumption which is threatened with death. Therefore it still remains true that wilful sins are, in general, atoneable by the law of Moses, i. e. where the law has not expressly determined it otherwise.

VIII. No sin offering was appointed for idolatry, murder, blasphemy, adultery, witchcraft, lying with a beast, &c. or for any capital offence. See Exod. xxii. 18—20. Levit. xxiv. 11— 16. Numb. xxv. 3. Deut. xiii. 6. xxii. 22—24. 1 Kings xxi. 10. These are all presumptuous offences, and therefore no atonement was to be made for them. When therefore David was guilty of murder and adultery, he said to God, thou desirest not sacrifice, else would I give it thee. Ps. li. 16. And when Cain slew his brother Abel, no sacrifice was accepted, but he was banished from the presence of the Lord. Gen. iv. 11—16.

It may be proper to add here, that if a person knew himself to be ceremonially polluted; or guilty of a breach of the law, and nevertheless presented himself before God at the tabernacle or temple service, his crime was presumptuous, and he became liable to be cut off for it. Levit. xv. 31. Numb. xix. 13. Acts xxiv. 6, 18.

Sometimes atonement was made with money, Exod. xxx. 12—16, with prayer and incense; Numb. xvi. 46, 47. And if a guilty person was so poor that he could not procure two young pigeons for a sin offering, he was required to present the tenth part of an ephah of fine flour, part of which was burnt on the altar. Levit. v. 7—13. But the standing rule was to do it with blood.

If it should be said that atonement was made by the scapegoat without blood, Levit. xvi. it may be replied, that there were two goats provided for the business of that day, and that these two goats were considered so much as one, and the service one, that they cast lots which of them should be offered a sacrifice to God, and which should be the scapegoat. That one of them was put to death, and atonement made with his blood, for the very sins which were afterwards confessed by the high-priest, over the head of the scapegoat; and therefore the manner in which the scapegoat was disposed of probably was designed to teach the Israelites that their sins and uncleannesses were as certainly taken away from them by means of the atonement which was made before with the blood of the sacrificed goat, as if they had all been actually heaped upon the head of the scapegoat for him to carry away with him into the wilderness, from which he was never to return. We have a very similar ceremony in Levit. xiv. 4—7, which relates to the cleansing of a leper.

Upon the whole it appears that atonement was made for all the sins of the children of Israel except for presumptuous transgressions, which the law declared to be capital, and many of which offences it actually names.

If it had not been so, a far greater number of Israelites must have been put to death than we have any reason to believe were; or else there must have been a great body of out-casts from among them, a thing which we never hear or read of; for no guilty or polluted person was permitted to appear before God at the tabernacle or temple service, on pain of death.

IX. How far did the efficacy or the sin offering extend?

1. They cleansed the offerer from certain bodily pollutions. It is said in Levit. xii. 8, of a female who had been in child-bed, and the priest shall make atonement for her and she shall be clean. And of the leper, and the priest shall make atonement for him, and he shall be clean. Levit. xiv. 20. See also Levit. xv.

2. They procured the offerer the forgiveness of such real sins as they were offered up for, or for which atonement was made with their blood; for of such a person it is said, and the priest shall make atonement for him before the Lord, and it shall be forgiven for any thing of all that he hath done in trespassing therein. Levit. vi. 1—8. v. 1—14. xix. 20.

The primary sense of the Hebrew word which is translated atonement, signifies to cover over, as Noah's ark was covered, or smeared over with pitch, to preserve it from sinking in the flood of waters. Gen. vi. 14. So sin atoned is covered over, that is, forgiven. Ps. xxxii. 1, Blessed is the man whose iniquity is forgiven, whose sin is covered.

3. If it be said, but supposing the guilty offerer was not really penitent, would he nevertheless be forgiven? To this it may be replied, that no such supposition should be made.—The Almighty God commanded him to repent; he presented the appointed sacrifice to the priest at the door of the tabernacle, laid his hand in a solemn manner on the head of the victim, and confessed his sin; and on the annual day of expiation for sin, fasted, and humbled himself before the Lord for his iniquities; and therefore it was taken for granted that he was really so; and in many cases it would most certainly be so; the sin offering therefore became a medium of forgiveness to the offerer. Levit i. 4. xvi. 29. 2 Sam. xxiv. 22—25. Job i. 4, 5. xlii. 7—9.

What if a similar supposition was raised against the real penitence of a wicked heathen, who presented himself as a penitent believer in Jesus Christ, and who is promised, on his being baptized into Christ, that his past sins shall be forgiven?—There is no end of such *nice queries*, which ill accord with the spirit of revelation, and especially with the *liberal spirit* of the gospel. The language of Scripture is, *"it shall be forgiven him."*—That is enough, and ought to suffice us.

X. If it should be asked, but why was such a method of purifying the unclean, and pardoning the guilty, adopted? Perhaps some persons would consider it as a bold question, and say, who knoweth the mind of the Lord? His understanding is infinite, and his judgment a mighty deep. However, as the government of God is evidently formed to promote our moral improvement, it seems probable that it was adopted,

1. Because it is so well adapted to teach us the purity or holiness of God. As these sin offerings are said to cleanse and sanctify the tabernacle and temple, the utensils of them, and the priests, &c. (Exod. xxix. 33. 36, 37. viii. 34, Heb. ix. 22,) and as an unclean person was said to pollute it, and it was death for any person wilfully to commit this offence, (Numb. xix. 13, Levit. xii. 4, 5), therefore these things would necessarily suggest to the Israelites that God is indeed a most pure and holy Being. Thus ceremonial purity would lead their thoughts to moral purity, and shew them that they must be holy, for Jeho-

vah their God is holy. Levit. xix. 22,
xi. 43, 44.

2. It would lead them to consider
God as the righteous Governor of the
world, who notices the different actions of men, and treats them according to them. Human beings are very
apt to imagine that God takes little or
no notice of the nature of their actions,
or will ever call them to account for
them. See Leland's Reason. of Christ.
Vol. II. p. 290. 293. 304, 313. 367.
374, octavo ed. Dr. Priestley's Comp.
of the Hindoo Laws with the Law of
Moses, p. 54. 271. God himself says,
these things hast thou done, and I
kept silence; thou thoughtest that I was
altogether such an one as thyself: but
I will reprove thee, and set them in
order before thine eyes. Ps. l. 21. But
the business of sin offerings tended
very much to prevent or correct such
erroneous notions of the moral government of God. In close connection
with this, I would observe,

3. That it would excite them to
consider their past ways, and to repent
of what had been amiss in their behaviour. It should be carefully observed
that the victim for the sin offering
was provided by the offerer (Levit. v.
6, 7), which put him to some expence;
that he brought it to the priest at the
door of the tabernacle; that it is called
his sin; that solemnly laying his hand
upon the head of the victim he confessed his sin, and put it to death himself, or the priest for him; that some
of the blood was caught in a bason,
and sprinkled upon the side of the
altar (Levit. v. 9), that the offerer was
not permitted to eat any part of his
sin offering, though the priest did
(Levit. x. 16, &c.), that there was no
oil of incense used, as that would have
expressed joy; that the annual day of
expiation was a day of general humiliation for the people to afflict their
souls (Levit. xvi. 17), that then the
whole of the sin offering was burnt
without the camp, ver. 27, 28; that
the person who burnt it was defiled by
it, and the vessel broken or cleansed
which was used in the service (Levit.
xvi. 28), and that all their sins were
on that day confessed by the high
priest over the head of the scapegoat,
and the goat then sent away into the
wilderness, from whence he was never
to return; and that the high priest

and the person who led the scapegoat
into the wilderness were both defiled
by this service.

It is therefore very obvious that this
solemn service would lead them, and
was designed to lead them to consider
their past ways, and to excite them to
repent of their sins and reform their
lives. For in those sacrifices there is
a remembrance again made of sins
every year. Heb. x. 3.

4. It would encourage the penitent
to hope and believe that his sins were
forgiven. The language of this service was, there is forgiveness with God
that he may be feared. The law of
Moses expressly said, *and it shall be
forgiven him,* Levit. vi. 7, xvi. 30.
And those persons who lived in the
latter periods of the patriarchal and
Mosaic dispensations knew that many
persons had actually obtained forgiveness in this way. See Numb. xvi. 46,
47. xxv. 11. 1 Sam. xxvi. 19. 2 Sam.
xxiv. 21—25. Ezra x. 9. 1 Esdras ix.
13—20. 2 Maccab. iii. 32, 33. xii.
39—45.

To conclude; these things evidently
form a part of a religious dispensation,
not indeed calculated for innocent
creatures, or for mankind in their
highest possible state of improvement,
but admirably adapted to the character
and state of ignorant and sinful beings
who require the plainest and most
striking modes of moral and religious
instruction; and therefore they manifest the great wisdom and goodness of
God who appointed them. The fool-
ishness of God is wiser than men, and
the weakness of God is stronger
than men. 1 Cor. i. 25.

The moral philosophers whose mental feelings are hurt by such humble
modes of instruction, should recollect
in what plain and simple ways their
parents first instructed them. When
Solon the Grecian lawgiver was asked
whether he had given the Athenians
the best laws? he answered, the best
of those that they would have received. There is no giving a perfect
religion to imperfect creatures. All
things must be adapted to the relations
which they bear to those things or
persons for whose use or benefit they
are made. To act thus is the highest
wisdom.

I am, your's,
JOSEPH JEVANS.

REVIEW.

"Still pleased to praise, yet not afraid to blame."—Pope.

Art. I.—*The History and Antiquities of Dissenting Churches, &c.*
[Concluded from p. 677.]

MANY of the ejected ministers were men of solid and extensive learning. Some of them possessed very valuable libraries. That belonging to Dr. *Lazarus Seaman*, the first pastor of the Presbyterian Church, in Silver Street, now extinct, who died in 1695, was sold by auction after his death, and produced seven hundred pounds, a very considerable sum in that day. This is said to have been the first library that was sold by auction in England. A catalogue of it is preserved in the Museum of the Baptist Academy at Bristol, (III. 12.) Dr. *Thomas Jacomb*, the colleague of Dr. Seaman, at Silver Street, possessed "an incomparable library of the most valuable books, in every branch of learning." On his death, which took place in 1687, his books were brought to the hammer, and produced thirteen hundred pounds. (III. 19.) The celebrated Dr. *Thomas Manton*, who was pastor of a Presbyterian congregation, gathered by himself in Bridges Street, Covent Garden, and who died in 1677, "had a fine collection of books, which sold for a considerable sum after his death. Amongst them was the noble Paris edition of the Councils, in thirty volumes, folio, which the bookseller offered him for sixty pounds, or his Sermons on the 119th Psalm; but finding it too great an interruption to his other work, to transcribe these discourses, he chose rather to pay him the money." (III. 562.) A history of the libraries of the Bartholomew Confessors would illustrate their characters, and we apprehend furnish affecting proofs of the distress into which many of them were plunged.

Mr. Wilson passes a high and deserved encomium upon Dr. Toulmin's edition of Neal's History of the Puritans (III. 99, 100). This, as well as the former editions has now become scarce and sells at a very high price. A person, competent to the undertaking, might render great service to the Dissenters, and gain no small reputation, by a new edition, with such improvements as the great number of

recent publications on English history would enable him to make. Such a work would, we cannot doubt, be countenanced, if not taken in hand by the more respectable booksellers. Mr. Wilson has the requisite knowledge of the subject, and we are inclined to hope that we might rely upon his impartiality.

In the latter part of the history of the place of worship in Silver Street, which has been transformed into a Methodist chapel, Mr. Wilson makes some spirited remarks upon *Dissenting Pluralist ministers* (III. 124, 125). The poverty of the Dissenters alone prevents the instances of *ecclesiastical polygamy* being more common amongst them. Some recent events shew that, congregations would secure each a portion of the services of some of the more popular *evangelical* ministers, if they were wealthy enough to procure them by a suitable offer.

The Independent congregation at *Haberdashers' Hall* is said to have been formed by a church that met, in the days when lords were voted useless, and bishops a nuisance, first in the House of Peers and afterwards in Westminster Abbey. Several of Cromwell's lords and members of parliament, and two at least of the judges, that sat on Charles I. and condemned him to the block, were amongst its members (III. 148—150).

One of the earliest ministers here was *Theophilus Gale*, M. A. the author of "The Court of the Gentiles," who is amongst the greatest literary ornaments of the Nonconformists. He was born in 1628, and died in 1678, having lived long enough to establish a lasting reputation, but too short a period to execute all the works that he had planned and his friends expected for the promotion of sacred learning. Our author has drawn up a judicious and interesting account of this distinguished scholar (III. 161—168).

In the list of the pastors of this same congregation are the respected names also of *John* and *Thomas Rowe*, father and son: the latter is well known to have been the tutor of Dr. Watts. He had many other pupils who rose to eminence. His death was sudden and untimely, in the year 1705, and the 49th of his age. Amidst some common place reflections upon this occurrence, Mr. Wilson relieves the reader by relating that Mr. Grove published a sermon on the fear of death, in which the subject was treated in so masterly a manner, that a person of considerable rank in the learned world declared, that after reading it he could have laid down his head and died with as much satisfaction as he had ever done any thing in his life (III. 171).

We have an interesting account (III. 185—190), of the meeting-house in Monkwell Street, the first that was built after the fire of London, 1666, and probably the oldest in London. Here, however, the author has been betrayed by his prejudices into a very impertinent remark. He says, of this place, "at present the number of pews greatly exceeds that of the hearers, who are *so few that the ends of public worship seem scarcely answered by their meeting together.*"* Has Mr. Wilson then authority to determine the exact number of persons in a congregation that make public worship effectual? He may perhaps have heard of high sanction being given to the meeting together of "two or three" in the name of Christ. A sarcastic reader might ask whether he would have been better pleased if he had been obliged to record that Presbyterian congregations were much more numerous than they really are? In the present instance he is, we believe, mistaken in point of fact. The congregation at Monkwell Street is accustomed to take the lead, and to set an example that is scarcely ever equalled, in congregational collections, which is a presumption that the place is not quite deserted; and we are informed that the congregation has been of late years on the increase. That the actual number of members and hearers is matter of surprize when the talents and character of the present minister are taken into account, we readily acknowledge; and we will add that it is not creditable to the Presbyterian body that an unfriendly observer

should be able, with any semblance of justice, to taunt them with the paucity of attendants at their oldest place of worship, and on one of their most able and eloquent preachers.

Thomas Doolittle, M. A. one of the Bartholomew sufferers, was the first minister at Monkwell Street, the meeting-house being, indeed, of his own erection. In the "troublous times" in which he lived it was not likely that he should escape persecution: the following extract shews the dangers to which he was exposed and the temper of the age, both for good and for evil.

"A king's messnger, with a company of the trained bands, came at midnight to seize Mr. Doolittle in his house; but while they were breaking open the door, he got over the wall to a neighbour's house, and made his escape. He purposed to have preached the next morning, but was prevailed upon to forbear; and the minister who supplied his place, narrowly escaped being taken. For while in his sermon, a company of soldiers came into the meeting-house, and the officer who led them cried aloud to the minister, 'I command you in the king's name to come down.' The minister answered, 'I command you in the name of the King of kings, not to disturb his worship, but let me go on.' Upon which the officer bade his men fire. The minister, undaunted, clapt his hand upon his breast, and said, 'Shoot, if you please, you can only kill the body, and after that can do no more.' Upon which, the people being all in an uproar, and the assembly breaking up, the minister got away in the crowd, unobserved, and without hurt.* After this, Mr. Doolittle was absent from home for some weeks, and on Lord's-days, guards were set before the meeting-house, to prevent the worship of God being carried on there. At length the justices came, and had the pulpit pulled down, and the doors fastened, with the king's broad arrow set upon them. The place being convenient, was soon after used as a chapel for the Lord Mayor, without any allowance to the owner. Thus liberty and property were invaded by tyrants, and Christ's faithful servants, by the heat of persecution, driven into corners."—III. 193, 194.

We cannot refrain from quoting an extraordinary relation of a rhetorical

---

* The same reflection occurs with regard to two other *heretical* places, *Princes Street, Westminster* (IV. 58), and *St. Thomas's, Southwark* (IV. 295).

* "The minister above alluded to, was Mr. Thomas Sare, the ejected minister of Redford, in Gloucestershire, concerning whose history no particulars are preserved."

artifice practised by Mr. Doolittle for the sake of *winning a soul.*

"Being engaged in the usual service on a certain occasion, when he had finished his prayer, he looked around upon the congregation, and observed a young man just shut into one of the pews, who discovered much uneasiness in that situation, and seemed to wish to go out again. Mr. Doolittle feeling a peculiar desire to detain him, hit upon the following expedient. Turning towards one of the members of his church, who sat in the gallery, he asked him this question aloud, 'Brother, do you repent of your coming to Christ?' 'No, Sir, (he replied), I never was happy till then; I only repent that I did not come to him sooner.' Mr. Doolittle then turned towards the opposite gallery, and addressed himself to an aged member in the same manner. 'Brother, do you repent that you came to Christ?' 'No, Sir, (said he) I have known the Lord from my youth up.' He then looked down upon the young man, whose attention was fully engaged, and fixing his eyes upon him, said, 'Young man, are *you* willing to come to Christ?' This unexpected address from the pulpit, exciting the observation of all the people, so affected him, that he sat down and hid his face. The person who sat next him encouraged him to rise and answer the question. Mr. Doolittle repeated it, 'Young man are *you* willing to come to Christ?' With a tremulous voice, he replied, 'Yes, Sir.' 'But when, Sir?' added the minister, in a solemn and loud tone. He mildly answered, 'Now, Sir.' 'Then stay (said he) and hear the word of the Lord, which you will find in 2 Cor. vi. 2. *Behold now is the accepted time; behold now is the day of salvation.* By this sermon God touched the heart of the young man.' He came into the vestry, after service, dissolved in tears. That unwillingness to stay, which he had discovered, was occasioned by the strict injunction of his father, who threatened, that if ever he went to hear the fanatics, he would turn him out of doors. Having now heard, and unable to conceal the feelings of his mind, he was afraid to meet his father. Mr. Doolittle sat down, and wrote an affectionate letter to him, which had so good an effect, that both father and mother came to hear for themselves. The Lord graciously met with them both; and father, mother, and son, were together received with universal joy, into that church."—III. 198, 199.

There are some mistakes in the incidental account of the congregation at *Newington Green* (III. 215). Mr. (now Dr.) Lindsay did not resign his

office of afternoon preacher so early as 1803, nor till two years after that period; and the place was not "shut up" on his resignation. Mr. Barbauld was then morning preacher, and Mr. Thomas Rees was chosen for the afternoon. When Mr. Barbauld resigned, Mr. Rees undertook the morning service, and the afternoon service was dropped. On Mr. Rees's removal to St. Thomas's in the Borough, Mr. Gilchrist became morning preacher, and still continues to exercise that office along with the pastorship of the General Baptist afternoon congregation at Worship Street.

The history of "*Paul's Alley, Barbican,* General Baptist, extinct," includes memoirs of the three most eminent men whom the General Baptists have had in their denomination, viz. *John Gale, Joseph Burroughs,* and *Dr. James Foster.* The life of the last preacher was before given; those of Burroughs and of Gale here inserted are drawn up in a truly liberal spirit. In the list of the Works of Burroughs there is mentioned, "A Latin Discourse on the Holiness of Places, from Isaiah lxvi. 1—3; delivered at the annual meeting of the Dissenting Ministers at Dr. Williams's Library, Red Cross Street." Was it formerly the custom for the London Ministers to have annually a *concio ad clerum?* Why was it dropped? We can conceive that it would be of great use to revive the custom. The three Denominations might select in turn one of the ablest elders of the body to deliver a discourse on some one of the many points in which they have an equal interest. The true Dissenting principle would thus be kept alive; and the yearly meeting would be much more interesting and attractive than it now is, being convened for the sole purpose of passing resolutions which are matters of course, and which every one knows beforehand and expects.— Mr. Wilson has given a good engraving of Mr. Burroughs from a painting in the Red Cross Street Library. (III. 228 *et seq.*)

Paul's Alley was given up by the General Baptists in 1777, on the erection of the new meeting-house in Worship Street, and fell into the hands of the *Sandemanians,* of whose tenets and of whose leaders, *John Glas* and *Robert Sandeman,* there is a good account (III. 261 *et seq.*). The peculiar Sandemanian tenet is well expressed in the epitaph on the tomb-stone of Sandeman, who died at Daubury, in the United States of America, 1771, aged 53 years, viz. "That the *bare work* of Jesus Christ, without a deed or thought on the part of man, is sufficient to present the chief of sinners spotless before God." If any thing be necessary in explanation, it is only that the simple belief of this truth is saving faith. With this notion the Sandemanians unite many of the ceremonies and customs of the primitive church, and a most rigid and formidable discipline.

We have mention (III. 289), of *Mr. William Manning*, who in the beginning of the last century was minister of a nonconformist church at *Peasenhall*, in the county of Suffolk or Norfolk, and who was distinguished in his day for his zeal on what Mr. Wilson calls "the Socinian side of the question." He is said to have been instrumental in changing the views of Mr. Emlyn, whilst that celebrated Unitarian confessor was minister at Leostoff. Can any of our readers refer us to any further account of Mr. Manning?

The history of *William Jenkyn, M. A.* is a striking exemplification of the baseness and cruelty of the reign of Charles the Second. This gentleman had been always a royalist, and had nearly perished with Christopher Love in the undertaking, 1651, to bring in *Prince Charles.* The prince was at length brought in and the noted Bartholomew Act followed, by which Jenkyn with hundreds of others was thrown out of the church, and exposed at times to unrelenting persecution. He was cast into Newgate, September 2, 1684, for assembling with other friends to spend a day in prayer, and for refusing the Oxford oath of passive obedience and non-resistance. At this time he was in an ill state of health, and his physicians represented to the king that his life was in danger from close imprisonment: nothing could move Charles's iron heart; he replied sternly, "Jenkyn shall be a prisoner as long as he lives." The threat was fulfilled, and the confinement made more rigorous than ever; insomuch that he was not suffered to pray with his own daughter who went to ask his blessing. As was intended, he died in Newgate, where,

as he said a little before his death, a man might be as effectually murdered as at Tyburn. This event took place January 19, 1685. The martyr, as he is truly styled in the inscription on his tomb, was aged 72 years. His friends buried him with great honour in Bunhill Fields; his remains being attended thither by at least one hundred and fifty coaches. His daughter who was a high-spirited woman, gave mourning rings at her father's funeral, with this motto: *Mr. William Jenkyn, murdered in Newgate.* A nobleman having heard of his happy release said to the king, "*May it please your majesty, Jenkyn has got his liberty.*" Upon which Charles asked with eagerness, "*Aye! who gave it him?*" The nobleman replied, "*A greater than your majesty, the King of kings,*" with which the king seemed greatly struck, and remained silent (III. 328—335).

The "Non-Jurors" are introduced (III. 358 *et seq.*), with questionable propriety into a "History of Dissenting Churches." They would have esteemed it the lowest degradation to have taken shelter under the Toleration Act. The author shews them no mercy; but he may justly plead that they were on some occasions disposed to be merciless. We are more inclined than he to allow to some of them the praise of integrity and piety as well as of learning. We are indebted to them for some of the best devotional books in the English language. *Collier* was quite a Puritan in his morals; and few English primates have lived or died more irreproachably and exemplarily than the deprived Archbishop *Sancroft.* Some interesting anecdotes are told of his simplicity, frugality, meekness and charity in his village retirement of Scarding. On his death-bed he said to one of his chaplains who had conformed by taking the oaths to the revolution government, "You and I have gone different ways in these late affairs; but I trust heaven's gates are wide enough to receive us both. What I have done, I have done in the integrity of my heart—indeed in the great integrity of my heart."

After some of the preceding strictures we are bound in justice to commend Mr. Wilson's impartiality in his memoir of *Thomas Emlyn*, (III. 398 *et.seq.*), which is quite as full as the plan of the History admitted, and not accompanied by a single unbecoming reflection. He conjectures that Mr. Emlyn's small society of Unitarians assembled in a meeting-house in the Old Bailey. To this conjecture is opposed the testimony of a contemporary, Leslie, who says (Socin. Controv. 6 Dial. p. 40), that the place used by Mr. Emlyn was *Cutlers' Hall.* His words are, "The Socinians have now for a long time had an open meeting-house in Cutlers' Hall, in London, their preacher one Emlyn, formerly a Dissenting preacher in Dublin." Mr. Wilson brings the history of Cutlers' Hall no lower down than 1697, when it was quitted by Beverley the Prophet (II. 63 et seq.), after which it might be occupied by Mr. Emlyn's congregation. This supposition is countenanced by a passage in another of Leslie's works less known, which fixes the date of Mr. Emlyn's ministry in London. We refer to "A View of the Times, their Principles and Practices, in the Rehearsals, by Philalethes," in 6 vols. 12mo. The *Rehearsal* was a jacobite paper which appeared twice a week. In the conclusion of No. 279, published *Saturday, January* 17, 1707, (Vol. IV. 235, 2nd ed.), the writer says, "there is one Emlin who was a Presbyterian preacher in Dublin, but spewed out by them for his Socinianism, and (to their honour I speak it) they prosecuted him also at the law for it, and he was fined and imprisoned. But he found means to escape and came over hither, and *for these several years has kept a publick meeting-house in London, as he still does.* And one of his congregation (I was told his name) is gone over to the *Camisars,* but still keeps his Socinianism. And I have a book generally said to be written by this Emlin since he came over hither, which is reckoned a master-piece of Socinianism. And I know where he lodges, if any body has a mind to speak with him. In the Life of Mr. Thomas Firmin it is told to his honour that he had a design to have a Socinian church or meeting set up in London, and now we see it brought to pass by way of moderation." This furious author's zeal against Socinians must have made him eager to find out, and his wish to bring them into trouble must have disposed him to make public, their true place of assembly. We may conclude, therefore, in the

absence of better evidence, that Mr. Emlyn preached at Cutlers' Hall: it was on the south side of Cloak Lane, Upper Thames Street.

The account of the "United Brethren" or Moravians (III. 420—426), gives a just and pleasing picture of this once enthusiastic and now declining, but always amiable sect.

The article "Essex Street, Unitarians" (III. 479—491), is entitled to great praise. The anecdote of Mr. Lindsey contained in the following extract is quite new to us; the whole passage will shew Mr. Wilson's candour:

"The character and sentiments of Mr. Lindsey are so well known to most of our readers, that they require but little illustration from our pen. By the admirers of his theological system, the highest eulogium has been passed upon both, and its most strenuous opposers cannot, but subscribe to the general excellence of his character. He appears to have set out in life under strong impressions of the value and importance of the ministerial office, and his conduct as a parish priest, while he had the superintendance of a parish, was truly exemplary. That late excellent minister, Mr. David Simpson, of Macclesfield, as we find in his life, owed his first attention to sacred things, to the care of Mr. Lindsey. Soon after his entrance at St. John's College, he spent part of a vacation at the vicarage of Catterick. Before the visit closed, Mr. Lindsey took occasion to inquire of the young collegian concerning the nature of his studies, and the manner in which he employed his time. From the nature of the reply, he soon perceived that his young visitor had been altogether inattentive to the study of the Sacred Scriptures. After expressing his surprize, Mr. Lindsey, in a very emphatical and pointed address, urged him to turn his attention to his hitherto neglected Bible. His remarks and advice produced a very serious effect upon Mr. Simpson's mind, which was filled with conviction and remorse, and henceforward he became an altered man.[*] This simple anecdote will tell a thousand times stronger in favour of Mr. Lindsey's character, than the most laboured panegyric. If some of our readers should lament the change that afterwards took place in the theological opinions of so exemplary a person, and which went to the full extent of modern Socinianism, they will at the same time admire that noble disinterestedness, and integrity of conduct, which induced him to resign a situation,

[*] "Life of Simpson, *apud* Theol. Mag. for Nov. 1801."

not only of ease, but of affluence and honour, for the possible alternative of poverty and contempt. Men who have the courage and principle to make this sacrifice upon the altar of conscience, whatever may be their individual sentiments, deserve to be enrolled amongst those illustrious confessors, whose names impart dignity to the human character."—III. 486, 487.

We are a little surprised that the author did not furnish a more complete list of the publications of Dr. Disney. He has not mentioned the very valuable memoirs published by this gentleman of Sykes and Jortin. This is the more singular, as the Life of Sykes is quoted III. 385. There is a similar imperfection in the notice of Mr. Belsham's works. The author has been more careful in his catalogues of the publications of some of our "Orthodox" contemporaries. [See particularly the articles *George Burder*, III. 469—471, and *Robert Winter*, D. D. III. 544, 545].

The reader will be much amused with the lives of those "Orthodox" wits, *Daniel Burgess* and *Thomas Bradbury*, who were both pastors for many years of the respectable Independent congregation, *New Court, Carey Street*. Burgess once assigned, we suppose in the pulpit, a curious reason why the people of God, who descended from *Jacob*, were called *Israelites*; it was because God did not choose that his people should be called *Jacobites* (III. 498, *Note*). The following, with other anecdotes of Bradbury, are still related by his respectable descendants:

"The gloomy state of public affairs, in consequence of the intrigues that were carried on in favour of the Pretender, excited in all true Protestants the most dismal apprehensions for the safety of the nation; when to their unspeakable joy, the storm suddenly blew over by the death of the Queen, after a short illness, on Sunday, August the 1st, 1714. On that very morning, as we are informed, while Mr. Bradbury was walking along Smithfield, in a pensive condition, Bishop Burnet happened to pass through in his carriage; and observing his friend, called out to him by name, and inquired the cause of his great thoughtfulness. 'I am thinking,' replies Mr. Bradbury, 'whether I shall have the constancy and resolution of that noble company of martyrs, whose ashes are deposited in this place; for I most assuredly expect to see similar times of violence and

persecution, and that I shall be called to suffer in a like cause.' The Bishop, who was himself equally zealous in the Protestant cause, endeavoured to quiet his fears; told him that the Queen was very ill; that she was given over by her physicians, who expected every hour to be her last; and that he was then going to the court to inform himself as to the exact particulars. He moreover assured Mr. Bradbury that he would dispatch a messenger to him with the earliest intelligence of the Queen's death; and that if he should happen to be in the pulpit when the messenger arrived, he should be instructed to drop a handkerchief from the gallery, as a token of that event. It so happened that the Queen died while Mr. Bradbury was preaching, and the intelligence was communicated to him by the signal agreed upon.* It need hardly be mentioned what joy the news gave him; he, however, suppressed his feelings during the sermon; but in his last prayer returned thanks to God for the deliverance of these kingdoms from the evil counsels and designs of their enemies, and implored the Divine blessing upon his majesty, King George, and the house of Hanover.† He then gave out the 89th Psalm, from Patrick's collection, which was strikingly appropriate to the occasion. Mr. Bradbury ever afterwards gloried in being the first man who proclaimed King George the First.

"This bold and unexpected proclamation could not but greatly surprize Mr. Bradbury's congregation, and excite their alarm for his safety. Accordingly, when he came down from the pulpit, some of his friends expressed their apprehension on his account; he, however, soon convinced them that he was upon safe ground, by a relation of what had happened. The sentiments of joy which were diffused throughout the nation by the Queen's death, will be better conceived than expressed; and from what has been already related, it may be supposed that Mr. Bradbury partook largely in the public rejoicing. This, he was not backward to declare, both from the pulpit and from the press; and it is commonly reported that he preached soon after that event upon the following text: *Go, see now this cursed woman, and bury her; for she is a king's daughter.‡* Mr. Bradbury was one of the Dissenting ministers who carried up the congratulatory address to George I. upon his accession to the throne. As they were dressed in cloaks

* "The messenger employed upon this occasion, is said to have been his brother, Mr. John Bradbury, who followed the medical profession."

† "*Private Information*."

‡ "2 Kings, ix. 31."

according to the fashion of the court, upon that occasion, a certain nobleman* accosted him with, ' Pray, Sir, is this a funeral ?' —' Yes, my Lord,' replied Mr. Bradbury, ' it is the funeral of the schism bill, and the resurrection of liberty'."—III. 512, 514.

We are told (IV. 32), that on the lease of the meeting-house in Peter Street, Soho, expiring, the landlord refused from pure bigotry to allow the use of it any longer to the Dissenters : this scrupulous churchman was no other than Mr. Horne, a poulterer in Newport Market,† the father of the late celebrated John Horne Tooke, who inherited his father's high church principles, though they did not make him religious, and frequently spoke of the Dissenters with bitterness.

Princes Street,' Westminster, gives occasion to some of the richest pieces of biography in the work (IV. 57 —118). The author has done justice to the able Nonconformist historian, Calamy. As this eminent divine was engaged in controversy with the French prophets, his biographer properly traces the history of those extraordinary enthusiasts, whom he does not with Messrs. Bogue and Bennett survey with any feeling of doubt or wonder. [See Mon. Repos. IV. 634. Also III. 467.] With the memoir of Mr. Samuel Say, of whom and his papers there is a full account in our fourth and fifth volumes, we have a good portrait from a painting in the possession of the Rev. S. S. Toms, of Framlingham. In the biography of Dr. Kippis, which is well drawn up, there is a piece of advice to " Socinians," founded we apprehend upon a mistake. It is allowed that the Dr. " inclined to the distinguishing tenets of Socinus" (there was more than *inclination*), but it is added to his praise that he " disapproved of the conduct of the modern Socinians, in assuming to themselves the exclusive appellation of Unitarians." Did then Dr. Kippis wish that *Trinitarians* should be called

---

* " Said to have been Lord Bolingbroke."

† The humble calling of his father gave occasion to one of the earliest sallies of John Horne Tooke's wit. His classfellows at one of the public schools were one day boasting of their families. Horne was silent, but being pressed on the subject of his parentage escaped contempt by a well-timed pun : his father, he said, was *a Turkey merchant.*

Unitarians ? The extension of the term was never debated with regard to them, but in reference solely to the *Arians,* to whom the majority of the Unitarians of the present day are in the habit of applying it. Encouraged however by Dr. Kippis's example, Mr. Wilson proceeds seriously to advise the "Socinians" to drop a name which will always be withheld from them by intelligent "Anti-Socinians." This reminds us of the old practice of re-baptizing heretics. With submission, we venture to pronounce that the name Unitarian will not be always withheld from those that claim it by *Anti-Socinians,* whether " intelligent" or " unintelligent." A mass of books must be destroyed in order to eradicate the term, and amongst them Mr. Wilson's History, in the third volume of which the running title for twelve pages together is " Essex Street —*Unitarian.*"

We are indebted to Mr. Wilson for a better biographical account than we had before seen of *John Canne,* the Puritan annotator. He was a thorough reformer and upon the whole a very interesting character. There is a statement here of the charge against him [see Mon. Repos. X. 418, 547] of designing a Bible " without note or comment." Canne emigrated from England to Holland, with other Brownists, to avoid persecution. He settled at Amsterdam, and there followed the art of printing for a livelihood : his name appears as printer to a 4to. tract before us (which is referred to by Mr. Wilson) entitled " Man's Mortallitie, &c. by R. O. 1643."* His being accessary in any degree to the appearance of a work designed to explode the common notion of the human soul, is a proof of his being at least a friend to free inquiry.

Canne preached whilst he was in

---

* There is a large account of this book in Archdeacon Blackburne's Hist. View of the Controv. concerning an Intermediate State, ch. xv. It is there stated by mistake that the date of the first, Canne's, edition was 1644. The Archdeacon is also in error with regard to the date of the 2nd edition at London. He assigns the year 1655 ; but the year in a copy in our possession is 1674. This edition is (not as Blackburne says 24to. but) very small 8vo. The title is altered to *Man wholly Mortal,* &c.

England at *Deadman's Place*, South-wark, where he was succeeded about 1633 by "Cobler How," principally known by a sermon against a learned ministry, which has passed through several editions, some of which have the following lines in the title-page (IV. 138):

What How? How now? hath How such
　learning found,
To throw art's curious image to the
　ground;
Cambridge and Oxford may their glory
　now
Veil to a Cobler, if they know but How.

This lay-preacher was much persecuted, and dying under the sentence of excommunication, was buried in the highway, in a spot where many of his people afterwards directed their ashes to be laid.

A good story is related (IV. 155, 156), of *Richard Baxter*. Villiers, Duke of Buckingham, and Wilmot, Earl of Rochester, wits and debauchees of the court of Charles II. meeting the old nonconformist teacher as they were riding in the country, and wishing to have a little merriment at his expence, accosted him gravely, " Pray Mr. Baxter, which is the nearest road to hell?" The good man replied, it may be supposed to their surprise and confusion,

　　　"Rochester some say,
But Buckingham's the nearest way."

It is remarked (IV. 225), as a singular fact with regard to the Baptist church, *Carter Lane*, Tooley Street, that during the ninety-four years that it has existed, it has had but two pastors, Drs. Gill and Rippon, of whom the latter is still living, and, it may be added, actively performing his ministerial duties.

The introduction to the account of *St. Thomas's, Southwark* (IV. 294 *et seq.*), contains some reflections uncalled for by the subject. The decline of the congregation since the time of its having Calvinistic ministers is charged directly to its departure from "the old Protestant doctrines;" but how many declensions has the historian recorded in churches that have never swerved from the Assembly's Catechism? He has not accounted for these, nor was it his province; and his work would have been fully answerable to its title if he had contented himself with giving the history of

Presbyterian churches without speculating upon the causes of their decay.

He insinuates a charge against this congregation of "an approximation to the world." Can the reader guess the reason? it is because the people at St. Thomas's call their place of worship an "Unitarian chapel." The worldliness is not, we presume, in the former of these terms; but what new superstition would the writer introduce, by thus dividing the nonconformists into worldlings or saints, according as they denominate their houses of prayer chapels or meeting-houses?

This change, too, as well as the institution of Unitarian Lectures in the chapel, is attributed to the passing of the Trinity Bill; whereas both the Lectures and the inscription were, if we remember rightly, set up before that wise and just legislative measure had been adopted.

There is the error (p. 296 and 319) of *Thomas* for *John Kentish*; and Mr. Kentish is represented as having been afternoon preacher at St. Thomas's from the time of his removal from Plymouth, to his settlement at Birmingham, whereas he was for several years the afternoon preacher to the Gravel-Pit congregation, Hackney. The author is mistaken also with regard to Mr. *Edmund Butcher's* leaving Sidmouth and being "now (1814) at Bridgwater" (IV. 405). Mr. Butcher is and has been for many years the much-respected pastor of the Presbyterian congregation at Sidmouth.

We have an interesting memoir (IV. 408—410) of John Humphrey, one of the ejected ministers, who is said to have survived all his brethren, living to nearly his hundredth year. Calamy relates that when he was writing his account of the ejected ministers he sent to Humphrey for a list of his writings: "The good old gentleman," says he, "sent me word for answer, that he desired no more than to go to his grave with a sprig of rosemary." He complied, however, with the request, and communicated with the account of his publications some anecdotes of his life, which may be seen in Calamy.

We might extend our remarks, and multiply our extracts, but we have already exceeded the limits of our review and must desist.

Our opinion of this work has been

freely expressed in the course of our review; but we shall have misrepresented our own sentiments if the reader have not gathered that we regard it, with all its little defects, as the most valuable contribution that has been made of late years to the records of nonconformity. It is entitled to a place in all our congregational libraries. We wish the author had not so often indulged his religious partialities; but, as it is, we cordially thank him for his volumes, and if our voice could have any influence over him, we would earnestly intreat him to favour the public in some shape or other with the remainder of his historical collections.

A large *Appendix* is added to the IVth volume, on the present state of the Dissenting interest and other branches of ecclesiastical history, which contains many just thoughts and seasonable remonstrances, but which occupies room that we would rather have seen filled with memoirs of nonconformist churches.

There are twenty-six portraits, in the four volumes, of the following ministers: Timothy Cruso, William Harris, D. D. Samuel Wilton, D. D. Benjamin Grosvenor, D. D. Benjamin Robinson, William Kiffin, John Newman, Samuel Pike, Samuel Wright, D. D. John Evans, D. D. John Allen, M. D. Caleb Fleming, D. D. Timothy Rogers, M. A. Thomas Amory, D. D. Richard Steel, M. A. Hanserd Knollys, Joseph Burroughs, William King, Benjamin Avery, LL. D. Daniel Burgess, Samuel Say, Joshua Oldfield, D. D. Timothy Lamb, Thomas Cotton, Joshua Bayes, Joseph Hussey.

OBITUARY.

Died Tuesday November 26, the Rev. DAN TAYLOR, who had been pastor of the General Baptist congregation, Church Lane, White-Chapel, London, thirty one years, aged 78. Mr Taylor was active and respected in his profession. He was considered as the head of the new connexion of General Baptists, and for some years superintended their academy for ministers. He was several times appointed to the chair at the meetings of the Dissenting ministers at Dr. Williams's Library.

He was born in the neighbourhood of Halifax, in Yorkshire, December 17, 1738, and became a preacher about the year 1760. He married about 1763, and by his first wife had thirteen children, of whom six, namely one son and five daughters, survive him. He had been married five weeks to a fourth wife at the time of his death. He had been subject to faintings for some months, and was sometimes affected in the street, and obliged to' casual passengers for conveyance home. Thursday November 21, he had a severe epileptic attack, but recovered in a few hours, and preached twice on Sunday, November 24. Monday 25, he walked not less than seven or eight miles, but was excessively fatigued. Tuesday morning, November 26, at three o'clock, he was seized suddenly and very seriously; afterwards, however, he became tolerably cheerful, conversed much in his usual way, got up to dinner, smoked his pipe, and afterwards slept very calmly for two hours, got up again in the afternoon, conversed and smoked as before, walked a little at intervals till seven o'clock, when he died almost instantaneously, while sitting in his chair. He was cheerful, composed and peaceful to the last.

His remains were interred on Bunhill Fields, December 5: Mr. Kello, the Independent minister spoke at the grave. His funeral sermon was preached at his meeting-house on Sunday December 15, to a numerous auditory, by the Rev. Robert Smith, of Nottingham, from 2 Tim. jv. 6, 7, 8.

Mr. Taylor's opinions were, with the exception of baptism, nearly the same as those of the Wesleyan Methodists. He separated some years ago from the General Baptist assembly. Of late years he has been heard to express respect for some of the members of the old connexion to whom his zeal for a higher system of orthodoxy caused him to appear for a time hostile.

The following is the most complete list of his numerous publications which his family can furnish.

1. The Necessity of Searching the

Scriptures; with directions. A Sermon.

2. The Faithful and Wise Steward. A Sermon addressed to young ministers at an association.

3. The Mourning Parent comforted. The substance of two Sermons, occasioned by the death of two of the author's children.

4. The Scriptural Account of the way of Salvation; in two parts.

5. The Duty of Gospel Ministers, explained and enforced at an ordination.

6. An Humble Essay on Christian Baptism. The second edition, with two Letters to the Rev. Dr. Addington on the subjects and mode of Baptism.

7. Our Saviour's Commission, explained and improved. A Sermon on Matt. xxviii. 19, 20.

8. Scrutator's Query, respecting the extent of our Blessed Saviour's death.

9. Scrutator to Responsor; or an Introduction to a farther proof (if need be) that Jesus Christ laid down his Life for the Sins of all Mankind.

10. Scripture Directions and Encouragements for Feeble Christians.

11. Rules and Observations for the Enjoyment of Health and Long Life. Extracted from Dr. Cheyne.

12. Candidus Examined with Candour. On Free Communion.

13. A Practical Improvement of the Divinity and Atonement of Jesus, attempted in Verse.

14. Entertainment and Profit united. Easy Verses on the chief subjects of Christianity, for children and youth. Third edition.

15. The Stroke of Death, practically improved. A Funeral Sermon for Mrs. Susanna Birley, late wife of the Rev. George Birley, of St. Ives, Huntingdonshire. To which is prefixed the Speech delivered at her Interment, by the Rev. Robert Robinson, of Cambridge.

16. An Essay on the Right Use of Earthly Treasure, in Three Letters to a Friend.

17. Observations on the Rev. Andrew Fuller's Pamphlet, entitled "The Gospel of Christ worthy of all Acceptation." In Nine Letters to a Friend.

18. Observations on the Rev. Andrew Fuller's Reply to the above, or a Further Attempt to prove that the Universal Invitations of the Gospel are founded on the Universality of

Divine Love, and the death of Jesus Christ, as the propitiation for the sins of the whole world. In thirteen Letters to a Friend. Second edition.

19. The Friendly Conclusion with the Rev. Andrew Fuller, respecting the Extent of our Saviour's Death. In four Letters to a Friend.

20. The Cause of National Calamities, and the Certain Means of preventing or removing them. A Fast Day Sermon on 1 Sam. xii. 14, 15, Feb. 25. 1795.

21. The Eternity of Future Punishment, asserted and improved.

22. The Eternity of Future Punishment re-asserted, the Importance of the Doctrine stated, and the Truth of it vindicated, in a Reply to the Exceptions of the Rev. Mr. Winchester against it. In six Letters to the Rev. G—— B—— of C——.

23. The Interposition of Providence in the Recovery of his Majesty King George the Third, illustrated and improved. A Sermon.

24. A Dissertation on Singing in the Worship of God, interspersed with occasional Strictures on the Rev. Mr. Boyce's Tract, entitled, "Serious Thoughts on the Present Mode and Practice of Singing in the Public Worship of God."

25. A Second Dissertation on Singing in the Worship of God, in defence of the former.

26. The Consistent Christian, or Truth, Peace, Holiness, Unanimity, Stedfastness and Zeal recommended. The substance of five Sermons.

27. A Charge and Sermon, delivered at the Ordination of the Rev. John Deacon, on Wednesday, April 26, 1786, at Leicester; together with the Introductory Discourse, the Questions proposed to the Church and the Minister, the Answers returned, and Mr. Deacon's Profession of Faith. The Introductory Discourse and Charge by D. Taylor, of London; the Sermon by W. Thompson, of Boston.

28. A Charge and Sermon, together with a Confession of Faith, delivered at the Ordination of the Rev. George Birley, on Wednesday, October 18, 1786, at St. Ives, Huntingdonshire. The Charge by D. Taylor, of London, the Sermon by R. Robinson, of Cambridge.

29. Memoirs of the Life, Character and Ministry of the late Rev. William

Thompson, of Boston, in Lincolnshire. To which is prefixed a Discourse on 2 Cor. xiii. 11, occasioned by his death.

30. The Principal Parts of the Christian Religion respecting Faith and Practice. A new edition corrected and enlarged.

31. A Compendious View of the Nature and Importance of Christian Baptism. Fifth edition.

32. A Catechism; or Instructions for Children and Youth, in the Fundamental Doctrines of Christianity. Tenth edition.

33. A Good Minister of Jesus Christ. A Sermon occasioned by the death of the Rev. Samuel Stennett, D.D.

34. A Sermon occasoned by the Death of Mrs. Elizabeth Taylor (the author's first wife) who died October 22, 1793, with a short account of her Life and description of her Character.

35. The Nature and Importance of Preparatory Studies prior to entering on the Christian Ministry considered. A Sermon delivered at Loughborough before the Governors of the General Baptists' Academy, on Matt. xiii. 52.

36. An Essay on the Truth and Inspiration of the Holy Scriptures.

37. A Letter on the Duties of Church Members to each other.

38. A Letter to the Churches on the Universality of our Saviour's Death.

On Saturday, November 23, 1816, the Rev. BENJAMIN CARPENTER, of Old Swinford, near Stourbridge, after a pilgrimage of sixty-four years, entered on his eternal rest. It must be left to a future occasion and to some other pen, minutely to describe the excellencies of his mind and character, to do justice to his seriousness of temper, his zeal in what he conceived to be the cause of his Divine Master, and his constant, delicate, undissembled sympathy in the sorrows of the poor, the sick, the mourning and the destitute. The friend who offers this tribute to the memory of one whom, amidst important differences of opinion, he cordially esteemed and loved, had many opportunities of knowing that Mr. Carpenter possessed unfeigned candour of disposition. The seeming departure from this spirit, which his writings may have been thought occasionally to exhibit, arose from no unkindness of

feeling; for his affection was extended beyond that of most men, to the sincere and upright of every sect and communion. It was the great object of his ministerial labours to promote inward and practical piety—the religion of the heart and life. On the Lord's day preceding his dissolution, he twice preached with his usual solemnity and earnestness, on those remarkable words, Job ii. 10, "Shall we receive good at the hand of God, and shall we not receive evil?" in a train of reflections which may now console his deeply afflicted family and friends. On the following Wednesday, an apoplectic seizure deprived him of speech: but from that period, till the powers of nature were exhausted and he sunk into the arms of death, his countenance indicated the serene and holy confidence with which his heart was fixed on a better world—where the tender and endearing intercourses of love will be renewed, and the voice of thanksgiving and praise will alone be heard.

J. H. B.

On Sunday, Dec. 15, at his seat at Chevening, in Kent, CHARLES EARL STANHOPE, in the 64th year of his age; an enlightened, zealous, incorruptible and courageous champion of civil and religious liberty. [We hope to receive a more extended account of this patriotic nobleman.]

Died, on Sunday, November 10th, 1816, aged 41, MRS. BROOKS, the wife of the Rev. James Brooks, of

was interred

month, in the cemetery attached to the chapel at Hyde. On the following Sunday, in the afternoon, a funeral sermon was delivered to a numerous congregation, by Mr. Parker, of Stockport, from 1 Thess. iv. 13, 14.

Mrs. B. had not possessed perfect health for some years; she was, however, generally not only placid, but cheerful. A nervous fever was the disorder supposed to have been the immediate cause of her death;—and this in less than ten days, deprived her neighbours and acquaintance of a much respected friend, and her husband of an excellent wife. She was one who united an attention to domestic concerns with a relish for mental pursuits. Her disposition and manners were not of the obtrusive kind, so that the knowledge and taste which she possessed were, perhaps, not fully known to all her friends. Her partner is most deeply affected by the painful dispensation of Providence, which has taken away one who contributed much to his happiness. But he consoles himself with the idea, that as she was the humble follower of Jesus Christ, she will at length be raised by him to glory, honour and immortality;—and that virtuous friendship begun on earth shall be completed in heaven.

S. P.

Stockport, Dec. 10, 1816.

———

September 17, 1816, after an illness of nearly two years, JOHN FORDHAM, of *Kelshall*, Herts, who has left behind him to lament his loss, a disconsolate widow and four children. In him the community are deprived of a sincere and zealous friend of civil and religious liberty, the Dissenters of a thorough supporter of free and impartial inquiry, his acquaintance of an intelligent, friendly and lively companion, and the neighbourhood of a man remarkable for a frank, straightforward integrity. So prominent was this last rare moral quality, that one and the same observation was made by all ranks on hearing of his death, "Well, we have indeed then lost a truly honest man." Nor was he less distinguished for the constancy and sincerity of his friendship; what he was to day, you might rely upon finding him on the morrow. And so companionable was his nature, that he always instantly dismissed all private concerns upon the entrance of a friend, and to them in every sense of the word he was always at home.

His views of Christianity differed very materially from the popular creed; but he seldom made his own creed the subject of conversation. He appeared to have no desire to make converts to his own opinions. He thought all sects too zealous for creeds, and not sufficiently attentive to the spirit and example of the founder of their religion. He would say, "If Christianity is a dispensation of grace, it is not less a system of morals and motives: every disciple had talents distributed to him, and his appointed work to do." He read with great attention and discrimination the con-

tomed to remark, that controversy was necessary to a more correct knowledge of the Scriptures, the best antidote against bigotry, and no bad remedy to the errors of education; but he deprecated controversial preaching, which as he thought, usually leads to a misstatement of the creed of others, imputing to them conclusions which they disavow, and productive of irritation instead of peace and love.

Amongst his particular friends he was fond of promoting religious discussion, and his acquaintance will long remember the strength of argument as well as sweetness of temper he uniformly displayed. Against all intolerance he was accustomed to express a pointed abhorrence; free, unfettered inquiry he considered as the birthright of Christians, and the glory of the gospel; to substitute any creed whether oral or written in the place of the sacred volume, was an evident return to popery, but to anathematize, to excommunicate, was to beat our fellow servants, and to lord it over God's heritage. In conformity to this truly Christian and liberal way of thinking, almost the last act of his life was to provide a few friends with a place of worship, where the New Testament, not human creeds, Christian love, not uniformity of opinion, are the bonds of Christian union. His children are too young to know the extent of the loss they have sustained, but at some future time this imperfect sketch of his character may assist to impart some faint image of the virtues of the parent they have been so early deprived of.

E. F.

———

On Sunday morning, November 24, at Runwell-house, near Farnham, died, aged 80, MRS. ANN, relict of Mr. Thomas PIESLEY, and was interred the following Sunday in the General Baptists' burying ground, Mead Row, near Godalming, in the same vault with her husband. Mr. T. Moore performed the funeral service, and before a numerous assemblage of friends preached from a passage which she had chosen from the 31st Psalm, part of verse 5, "Into thine hand I commit my spirit." From this subject the preacher took occasion to show the character, present privileges, and future portion of the servant of God, and concluded with observing that the life and death of the genuine Christian was most happily exemplified in the deceased. She was a native of Ditchling, Sussex, where her father, Mr. Agate, was a preacher in the General Baptist connexion : she was of the same persuasion, and a worshipper of the one, living and true God, strict in the practice of moral virtue, and rich in the possession of Christian graces. Her sympathy and benevolence, her unruffled patience, her unaffected piety, the ease and simplicity of her manners, her stedfastness of faith, confidence of hope and serenity in death, reflect lasting credit on her religion, and endear her memory to her friends and acquaintance. That habitual peace of mind which she enjoyed was not disturbed at the prospect of dissolution : she desired it, but feeling neither rapture nor depression, she breathed her last with composure, fell asleep in Jesus, and rested from her labours.

T. M.

On Wednesday, December 11, at *Guildford*, THOMAS OSBOURN, aged 77, after a long season of weakness and bodily pain. He in early life enlisted in the service of the East India company, and served several years in the Peninsula, and after his return to England he followed the military profession, beloved and esteemed by those who knew him ; but at times he drank to excess, and then he was very profane. After his discharge he came to Guildford, where he went to hear Mr. Chamberland, the minister to the Particular Baptists: here he became convinced of the necessity of repentance and newness of life, and was admitted a member of this church, and was very conscientious and circumspect. Prior to this epoch, six or eight of the most enlightened and pious members of this church had been expelled for heresy, (viz. the unity and supremacy of the Father), which they had imbibed through the preaching and conversation of Mr. J. Marsom. Our deceased friend associated with one of these heretics, Mrs. S. Matthews, a devout and intelligent woman, who still attended at the chapel, and was on friendly terms with Mr. Wood, the successor to Mr. Chamberland ; she conversed with them freely on the doctrine of the divine unity. Our friend saw reason to consider, and then to believe this

article of the Christian faith ; and going to Godalming to hear Mr. Thomas Foster, one of the expelled members, and who had by his zealous exertions collected a small church, he became confirmed in this fundamental truth. Some of his brethren suspected, then questioned, and lastly accused him before the church of disbelieving Jesus Christ to be God. He confessed and contended that Jesus Christ was the Son of God. They replied, that is not enough—you must believe that he is God, you came into the church with this faith. He denied this ; it was not faith, I thought it was so, I assented to your creed (this was a written formulary of faith read over and assented to by incoming members). They proposed to suspend him from the Lord's supper which was to be celebrated the next Sunday. He objected, While I continue a member of the church, I am entitled to all the privileges of the church. They would not break bread with an heretic ; and they cast him out, not after the second admonition as the Apostle directs, but at this very time when he was first charged with this heresy. He retained his other religious tenets, as did Thomas Foster, with whose church he then united and regularly attended at the distance of nearly five miles. He was bold and unreserved in the avowal of his religious principles, and defended them with zeal and ability from the Scriptures against the attacks and insinuations of his opponents who were many and violent ; and although he never entirely relinquished all his former Calvinistic opinions, yet he became very moderate and candid, which will appear from a circumstance that I will relate, and which I myself witnessed. Mr. Foster had embraced the doctrine of universal restoration, and Thomas Osbourn after hearing him for the first time preach on the subject, when he came down from the pulpit took him by the hand and said, " Friend, where did you get this new old doctrine?" which he cordially received, and ever afterwards rejoiced therein. He read and studied the Holy Scriptures very diligently, and his conversation was fraught with passages from those lively oracles, and he used to express himself with uncommon feeling and thankfulness on the love of God in Christ Jesus. He died in peace, with a hope full of immortality.

INTELLIGENCE.

DOMESTIC.

RELIGIOUS.

An Account of Mr. Wright's Mission in Wales. Extracted from his Journals.
(Concluded from p. 684.)

IV. GLAMORGANSHIRE.

THIS is the most populous county in Wales, and the most important in a commercial point of view; and here Unitarianism appears to have made greater progress than in any other part of the principality. I preached at the following places.

1. *Gelligron.* Here I preached in a farm house, to an attentive audience; and Mr. Phillips gave the substance of the discourse in Welsh. Had also the pleasure of visiting the relations of our respected friend, Mr. T. Rees, whose aged grandmother, near her hundredth year, feels a lively interest in the success of the Unitarian cause.

2. *Swansea.* In this populous and increasing town there is a very respectable and improving congregation. Many of its members, some of them persons of superior rank in society, discover much zeal in the Unitarian cause. Mr. Aubrey's labours in Swansea appear to have been highly useful. The success of Unitarianism seems to have given considerable alarm to some of the reputed orthodox; what they have published, notwithstanding their illiberality, and the temper in which they have been replied to, can hardly fail to excite inquiry and promote the knowledge of the truth. I preached at Swansea four times, most of the congregations were pretty large; and had much pleasant conversation with the friends. Some of them are very active in pushing into circulation small Unitarian tracts.

3. *White Rock,* a place near Swansea, connected with the copper works. Here I preached in a large schoolroom, which is occupied as a place of worship by Christians of different parties. We had a crouded congregation, a number of genteel persons from Swansea and its vicinity attended. Mr. Phillips repeated the discourse in Welsh.

4. *Neath.* The congregation has been raised in this place by the exertions of Mr. D. Davis. They have erected a very neat and commodious chapel, in which they now meet. In defraying the expence of erecting this building, they have been assisted by subscriptions from several places: still a considerable debt remains; the discharge of which would be beneficial to the cause. The contributions of those friends who have not yet given any thing towards the Neath chapel would be thankfully received. I preached in this place four times; we had respectable, and some of them large congregations. The Unitarians at Neath are not without zeal in the cause. By steady and persevering exertions much good may be done in this town. Mr. Meek preached here twice.

5. *Gellionnen.* Here is a large and well built meeting-house, among the mountains, of which some Calvinists, who have no kind of claim to it, endeavoured lately to possess themselves, but were defeated in the attempt. This place was the scene of the useful labours of the late Mr. Josiah Rees. Mr. James is now the minister here, and at *Bridgend* and *Bettws*. I preached once, but it being in the middle of the day, and a busy time among the far-

mers, the congregation was small. I am informed it is very good on a Lord's day.

6. *Wick.* In this village there is an Unitarian Baptist congregation. I preached to a pretty large audience.

7. *Newton-Nottage.* Here also the congregation ranks as Unitarian Baptists. I preached to a crouded assembly. Mr. Phillips at both these places gave an outline of the sermon in Welsh. Mr. *Evan Lloyd* is the minister of both these churches.

8. *Bridgend.* Here is a good meeting-house, but the congregation has long been in a low state. Mr. James has lately undertaken to try what can be done to revive it: he preaches here one Sunday in the fortnight, and Mr. Evan Lloyd supplies the other Sunday. I preached here three times; the hearers were very attentive. In this congregation there is a respectable family who are relations of that truly excellent man the late Dr. Price.

9. *Bettws.* I preached here to a congregation which was said to be much larger than what usually attends.

10. *Cardiff.* There are Unitarians in this town, but some of them want courage and zeal. I preached in the Presbyterian meeting-house to a respectable congregation. Mr. Phillips gave an outline in Welsh.

11. *Caerphilly.* Here I preached in the Town-Hall, to a large assembly. There are several Unitarians in this place and its vicinity. In this town and at Cardiff it is much to be lamented that Unitarian worship is not regularly carried on.

A short distance from Caerphilly is a small congregation, said to be chiefly Antitrinitarian.

In going from Cardiff to Caerphilly I had the pleasure of visiting the relations of my highly respected friend Dr. Carpenter.

On the evening of the day when I preached at Caerphilly it was appointed for me to preach at *Craig-Fargod*, but the distance was so great, the road some part of it so bad and difficult to find, that we arrived too late! Here is an old Unitarian Baptist congregation. We conversed with some of the brethren.

12. *Merthyr-Tydvil.* This is a very populous town situated in the midst of the iron works. The Unitarians meet here in a large school-room, and seem to be pretty numerous, and to have zeal in the cause. I preached three times to crouded audiences, who were very attentive.

13. *Blaengwrach.* The meeting-house here is said to be one of the oldest in the principality, and stands on an hill in the midst of trees, some way from any habitation. I preached to an attentive audience. A Mr. Williams is the minister in this place.

14. *Aberdare.* I preached here twice, had very good congregations. Mr. Phillips repeated in Welsh the substance of the sermons. There seems to be a good Unitarian congregation in this place. Mr. T. Evans is the minister at Aberdare and Merthyr-Tydvil.

15. *Cymmar.* Here I preached to an attentive assembly. Mr. James gave the substance of the discourse in Welsh. I know not with what class of Christians the minister of this congregation ranks, but he appears to be a truly liberal man.

There is reason to think there are Unitarians in some parts of Glamorganshire who do not openly profess the doctrine, nor contribute to its promotion by uniting with its friends. Still the knowledge of the truth is making progress; and in a few years the name Unitarian instead of being thought reproachful, will be esteemed honourable. Our brethren in this county, especially in the eastern part of it, have many openings for their exertions in the great cause of divine truth.

Unitarian Chapel, Thorne, Yorkshire.

At a meeting of the Unitarian Society at Thorne, held in their new chapel after afternoon's service on the Lord's day, December 15, 1816, Francis Moat reported the particulars of his late excursion, and stated that he had left home with a debt of £208. 6s. 11d. upon the chapel, and that after an absence of six weeks he had succeeded in collecting £229 6s. 6d.; that his expenses had been £4 18s. 3d. only (owing to the kind hospitality with which he had been received), leaving a balance of £16. 1s. 4d. in the hands of the Treasurer.

It was resolved unanimously:

1. That the grateful and affectionate thanks of this Society are hereby given to the friends at Halifax, Rochdale, Manchester, Stockport, Bolton, Stand, Bury, Monton, Warrington, Gateacre,

Liverpool, Chowbent, Sheffield, and other places, for their kind reception of Francis Moat, and for the Christian liberality with which they entered into the object of his journey.

2. That the heartfelt thanks of this Society are hereby given to all our Christian brethren who have by contributions assisted in extinguishing the debt; and to the Committee of the Unitarian Fund for its grant of £20.

3. That it has been strongly recommended to us, and is very desirable, to increase the burial ground attached to the chapel (which at present consists of only 72 square yards); that 144 square yards of ground contiguous may be obtained, which with a plain substantial wall to enclose the whole burial ground is estimated at £55; towards which a balance of £16. 1s. 4d. remains on hand. That the assistance of our brethren who have not hitherto contributed is respectfully requested to enable us to effect this object; and that the proceeds be reported in the Monthly Repository.

4. That the expences of building the chapel amounted to £408 1 3

Expences of F. Moat's Journey 4 18 3

Balance in Treasurer's hands 16 1 4

£429 0 10

Subscriptions by Unitarians at Thorne and its neighbourhood £ 88 1 0

Subscriptions of friends as reported in M. Repos. 111 13 4

Received by Francis Moat during his late journey 229 6 6

£429 0 10

(Signed)
William Darby, Treasurer,
Charles James Fox Benson, Secretary.

Thorne, Dec. 16, 1816.

LITERARY.

Mr. Rutt on his Edition of Dr. Priestley's Theological Works.

SIR, *Clapton, Dec. 18, 1816.*

When, in your last number, I mentioned my design of publishing a list of the subscribers to the proposed edition of Dr. Priestley's Theological Works, I did not take into consideration how soon such a list must be furnished you, from the necessity of completing the ensuing number at the press much earlier than usual, on account of the Index.

I am also disposed to delay the publication of the List from some encouraging appearances of a desire to promote the subscription, which, I trust, may enable me very early in your next volume to announce the required number of 200 subscribers, as they now amount to 160, by the assistance of a subscription for ten copies from a gentleman who knew and respected Dr. Priestley, and is attached to his memory, but who will not allow me to mention him under any other description.

I remain, Sir, your's,
J. T. RUTT.

The Rev. Dr. Estlin, of Bristol, has issued Proposals for publishing by subscription, in two volumes octavo, price to subscribers 24s. Familiar Lectures on Moral Philosophy. Dedicated to the Gentlemen who have been his Pupils. To be published by R. Hunter, St. Paul's Church Yard.

MISCELLANEOUS.
Breach of the Sabbath.

It will scarcely be believed, but the fact is certain, that notwithstanding the severity of the weather, and the critical state of the crops in Scotland, two farmers were fined last week by the Sheriff of Kircudbright £10 each for carrying their corn on the preceding Sunday, in violation of the act of the Scottish Parliament for punishing the breach of the Sabbath. The defendants in justification pleaded the necessity of the case, but the plea was overruled by the Sheriff, and the fine was enforced! *M. Chron. Nov. 28.*

A private letter from Dublin states that the Rev. Mr. Maturin, the author of *Bertram*, is likely to be deprived by his bishop of a small living which he now has, in consequence of his having written that tragedy. It was considered a harsh and bigoted proceeding in the Church of Scotland, which is more strict than the Church of England, to have degraded Mr. Home, for having written the tragedy of Douglas. *Examiner, July 7.*

NEW PUBLICATIONS IN THEOLOGY
AND GENERAL LITERATURE.

Sermons, by John Disney, D. D. F. S. A. Vols. III. and IV. 8vo. 18s. boards.

Sermons, on Various Subjects. By the late Richard Price, D. D. F. R. S. 8vo. boards.

Evening Amusements; or, the Beauties of the Heavens Displayed; in which the Striking Appearances to be observed in Various Evenings during the year 1817 are described. By William Frend, M. A. 3s. boards.

Chrestomathia: being a Collection of Papers explanatory of the Design of an Institution proposed to be set on foot, under the Name of the Chrestomathic Day School, for the Extension of the New System of Instruction to the Higher Branches of Learning. By Jeremy Bentham, Esq. 8vo. Part I.

Lowman on the Hebrew Ritual. New Edit. 8vo. 10s. 6d.

Unitarianism a Scriptural Creed; occasioned by the Pamphlets of Mr. Law and Mr. Baxter, in defence of the Doctrine of the Trinity. By T. C. Holland, Minister of the Unitarian congregation at Preston. 8vo. 1s. 6d.

On Persecution. A Discourse delivered in the Protestant Dissenting Cha Lewin's Mead, Bristol, June 16, 1816 recommendation of a Subscription for Relief of the Protestant Sufferers Conscience-sake in the South of Fra By John Prior Estlin, LL. D. 1s. 6d.

Baptism.

(See p. 308. 436. 628.)

Considerations on the Doctrines of generation in the Sense in which term is used in the Church of Engl in her public Formularies. By the l Charles Daubeny, Archdeacon of Sar 2s. 6d.

An Apology for the Ministers of Church of England, who hold the I trine of Baptismal Regeneration, in Letter addressed to the Rev. Ge Stanley Faber, B. D. in consequence Misrepresentations of their Opinions tained in his Sermons on Regenerat By Christopher Bethell, M. A. Dear Chichester.

The Doctrine of Regeneration in Case of Infant Baptism, stated in R to the Dean of Chichester's Apology. G. S. Faber, B. D. 2s. 6d.

CORRESPONDENCE.

We hope to be able to present our Subscribers in the ensuing Number, the firs Vol. XII. with a Portrait of the late Rev. *William Vidler*, accompanied with a Mem

In this Number we insert the Resolutions of the *Unitarian Society at Thorn* the settlement of their accounts. The names of all the Subscribers are also sen for insertion, but we have not room for them ; indeed we feel considerable objectio this mode of filling up our pages, and recommend that in this and similar cas printed list be stitched up with our wrapper as an advertisement. This will answer the end and leave us room for communications of more permanent value.

The *Rossendale* account will be closed in the next Number.

Mr. Wilson's strictures on the Review of his *History of Dissenting Churches,* too late for insertion. We have returned it to the Publishers for him, and we the liberty of recommending him to withdraw it. It would, we fear, produce an e contrary to the design of the writer. We must, at least, require him to shorten it, a great part of it has no more reference to the Review of the History than to al any other theological article in any one of our Miscellaneous Volumes.

Various other communications are of necessity reserved for the next Volume.

ERRATA.

In the Account of Oldbury Double Lecture, p. 622. col. 2. l. 8. for *or* his bunal, read *on* his tribunal. l. 26. insert inverted commas at *persecution*. p. 633. for *their* doctrines read *these* doctrines. l. 28. for *contexts* read *contents*.

P. 600. col. 1. 12 lines from the bottom, for *unreasonable* read *unseasonable*.

INDE.

A

GENERAL INDEX

OF

SUBJECTS AND SIGNATURES.

Addenda to the General Index.

Errata in ditto.

P. 745, col. 1. dele the four first lines.
P. 746, col. 2. after last line insert,
" On moral improvement, 449. His answer to Y. N.'s objections to the Divine government, 580."

A

TABLE OF TEXTS

EXPLAINED OR ILLUSTRATED.

To the Binder:—Portrait of Dr. Toulmin to face the title.